The Handbook of
SOCIAL PSYCHOLOGY

SECOND EDITION

Edited by GARDNER LINDZEY and ELLIOT ARONSON
University of Texas

VOLUME TWO
RESEARCH METHODS

58391

ADDISON-WESLEY PUBLISHING COMPANY
Reading, Massachusetts
Menlo Park, California · London · Amsterdam · Don Mills, Ontario · Sydney

ISBN 0-201-04263-0
EFGHIJKL-HA-7987

Preface to the First Edition

The accelerating expansion of social psychology in the past two decades has led to an acute need for a source book more advanced than the ordinary textbook in the field but yet more focused than scattered periodical literature. Murchison's *Handbook of Social Psychology* (1935), the only previous attempt to meet this need, is out of date and out of print. It was this state of affairs that led us to assemble a book that would represent the major areas of social psychology at a level of difficulty appropriate for graduate students. In addition to serving the needs of graduate instruction, we anticipate that the volumes will be useful in advanced undergraduate courses and as a reference book for professional psychologists.

We first considered the possibility of preparing a *Handbook* three years ago. However, a final decision to proceed with the plan was not reached until the fall of 1951. During the interval we arranged an outline of topics that represented our convictions concerning the present state of social psychology. We then wrote to a large number of distinguished social psychologists asking them whether they felt our venture was likely to be professionally valuable and asking for criticisms of the outline we had prepared. The response to these letters was immensely gratifying—social psychologists as a group appear sufficiently altruistic to spend large amounts of time criticizing and commenting on a project of which they approve even though they may be unable to participate in it themselves. We also asked for specific recommendations of people who seemed best qualified to prepare the various chapters. After receiving answers we drastically revised our outline and proceeded to invite authors to prepare the various chapters. It was not until the spring of 1952 that we completed our list of contributors and even this list later underwent change. We first suggested (tongue in cheek) that the manuscripts be submitted by September 15, 1952. However, as we secretly expected, we were forced to change this due date to January 1, 1953. This "deadline" we tried hard to meet. But of course we failed and shifted our aspiration to June 15, 1953. Again we failed, although by now we were making substantial progress. By early in the fall of 1953 we had all the chapters excepting two, and the first volume was completed and in the hands of the publishers. The last two chapters were not received until early in 1954, when the second volume went to press.

Something should be said concerning the basis for the organization of the subject matter of these volumes. It became apparent early that there are many ways to subdivide social psychology but very little agreement concerning just which is best. Although we sought the advice of others, we found for almost every compelling suggestion an equally compelling countersuggestion. Thus, in the end, it was necessary to make many arbitrary decisions. So much for our knowledge that the *Handbook* could have been organized in many different ways. There is no single scheme that would satisfy all readers.

We early discovered that the subject matter was too voluminous to be contained in a single volume. Given this decision it seemed quite natural to present in one volume the chapters that dealt primarily with theoretical convictions or systematic positions, and also the methods and procedures commonly employed in social psychology. Likewise it seemed wise to present in one volume those chapters that focus upon the substantive findings and applications of social psychology. The decision to place the historical introduction, theory, and method chapters in the first volume reflects a bias in favor of investigation that begins with an awareness of the message of the past, an attempt at theoretical relevance, and finally with a full knowledge of the procedural or measurement alternatives. All of the content of the first volume is seen, at least by the editor, as a necessary preparation for good investigation. These are the things the social psychologist should know before he lifts a single empirical finger. The second volume, then, can be seen as a justification of the contents of the first volume. Here are the empirical fruits stemming from the theories and methods summarized in the first volume.

But does this ideal scheme mirror common practice? Are the major empirical advances summarized in the second volume in reality a legitimate by-product of theoretical conceptions and sophisticated method? In fairness to science in action (as opposed to science on the books) we are afraid the answer is No. Social psychology has made its advances largely on the shoulders of random empiricists and naive realists. Inability to distinguish between analytic and synthetic and a tendency toward reification of concepts has accompanied many of the most significant advances in this field. Who would say that those who view an attitude as a "construct" created by the investigator have made more of a contribution to this area of psychology than those who naively view attitudes as real and concrete entities? Thus we sorrowfully admit the organization we have imposed upon the *Handbook* may bear little relation to the path thus far trod in the development of social psychology. Nevertheless, it stands as a suggestion of the manner in which future development may well take place and as a reminder that the powerful weapon of systematic theory is now more nearly within the grasp of the wise psychologist than formerly. Where yesterday the theoretically oriented investigator and the random realist may have been on even terms, recent developments within the field may well have destroyed this equality. An approach efficient in the wilderness may be foolish in a more carefully mapped region. In summary, the precedence we give to theoretical positions reflects our conviction of the importance of theories as spurs to research, but may also represent a program for the future rather than a reflection of the past.

It must be conceded that not all areas of social psychology are covered in these volumes with equal thoroughness. Some gaps are due to the blind spots of the editor while others are the result of contributors failing to cover an area they originally agreed to cover and, in a few cases, to contributors who withdrew altogether. In spite of these shortcomings, the volumes in their present state provide the most comprehensive picture of social psychology that exists in one place today.

While deficiencies of the final product are my own responsibility, they exist in spite of a number of advisors who gave their time and energy generously throughout the venture. Of these collaborators none was nearly so important as Gordon Allport. In fairness he should be co-editor of the volume, as he contributed immeasurably both in matters of policy and in matters of detail. I owe a very special debt of gratitude to my wife Andrea for her tolerance, encouragement, and detailed assistance. Likewise of great importance is the contribution of Shirley H. Heinemann, who has been of constant help throughout the editorial process and in preparing the Index. Crucial to the success of this work were various additional colleagues who served as referees, reading individual chapters and suggesting changes and deletions. On this score I express my gratitude to Raymond Bauer, Anthony Davids, Edward E. Jones, Kaspar Naegele, David Schneider, and Walter Weiss. In addition, many of the contributors served as referees for chapters other than their own. I am indebted to E. G. Boring, S. S. Stevens, and Geraldine Stone for many helpful suggestions based on their experience in arranging the *Handbook of Experimental Psychology*. Mrs. Olga Crawford of Addison-Wesley played an indispensable role in final preparation of the manuscripts.

April 1954   G. L.

Preface to the Second Edition

In the fourteen years that have elapsed since the last edition of this *Handbook,* the field of social psychology has evolved at a rapid rate. The present volumes are intended to represent these changes as faithfully as possible and at a level appropriate for the beginning graduate student as well as the fully trained psychologist.

The reader familiar with the previous *Handbook* will realize that we have employed the same general outline in the present volumes. The many new chapters reflect the increased quantitative and methodological sophistication of social psychologists, the development of certain specialized areas of research, and the increased activity in a variety of applied areas. In some instances we have attempted to compensate for known deficiencies in the coverage of the previous edition.

One can never be certain of portraying adequately the changes in a large and diverse area of scholarship, but we can be certain that this *Handbook* is very different from its predecessor. It is substantially larger—instead of one million words, two volumes, and 30 chapters, there are now approximately two and one-half million words, five volumes, and 45 chapters. We are convinced that our decision to present this material in five volumes will increase its utility for those who have specialized interests linked to either teaching or research activities. But the difference goes beyond mere size. The list of contributors has a decidedly new flavor—of the 45 authors in the previous edition, only 22 have contributed to this volume. Viewed from another vantage, of the 68 authors contributing to the current volume, 46 are represented in the *Handbook* for the first time. Only one chapter is reprinted without a thorough revision, and this, an essay (Hebb and Thompson) presenting a point of view that seems little affected by recent research and formulation. There are 15 chapters that are completely new and, in addition, a number of the replacements bear little resemblance to the chapter of the same, or similar, title that appeared earlier.

Plans for the current revision were begun in January of 1963. By July of that year a tentative chapter outline had been prepared and distributed to an array of distinguished social scientists, including the previous contributors to the *Handbook*. We benefited materially from the advice of dozens of persons in regard to both the chapter outline and the nomination of potential authors; we are grateful for their efforts on behalf of the *Handbook*. By fall of 1963 we had succeeded in constructing a final outline and a list of contributors. Our initial letters of invitation asked that completed manuscripts be submitted by January 1, 1965. We managed to obtain the bulk of the chapters eighteen months and several deadlines later, and the first two volumes were sent to the publishers early in 1967. The final chapters were secured the following July, when the remaining volumes went to press.

In selecting contributors we made every effort, within the general constraints of technical competence and availability, to obtain scholars of diverse professional and institutional backgrounds. Thus, we take special pleasure in the fact that almost all areas of the country are well represented, that six of the contributors are affiliated with institutions outside the United States, and that the authors include political scientists, sociologists, and anthropologists as well as psychologists.

We consider it extremely fortunate that of the chapters listed in our working outline, all of those that we regarded as "key" or central chapters are included here. Indeed, there are only three chapters from that list that are not a part of the present volumes; this includes one (attitude change) that was deliberately incorporated within another chapter because such an arrangement seemed to offer a greater likelihood of satisfactory integration and coverage. It should be noted that this success is in marked contrast to the previous *Handbook,* where such essential areas as attitudes and social perception were omitted because of last-minute delinquencies. Although a few invited contributors did withdraw from the present *Handbook* after initially having agreed to prepare a chapter, in all cases we were fortunate in being able to find equally qualified replacements who were willing to take on this assignment on relatively short notice. To these individuals we owe a special debt of gratitude.

We wish to acknowledge the indispensable assistance of Judith Hilton, Shirley Cearley, and Leslie Segner in connection with the final preparation of the manuscript. Finally, we would like to express our gratitude to Mary Jane White-side for her tireless efforts in the final indexing of all volumes of the *Handbook*.

February 1968   G. L.
Austin, Texas   E. A.

Acknowledgments

The Editors wish to thank a number of publishers and copyright holders for permission to reproduce tables, figures, and excerpts from the following sources:

Academic Press, Inc.: D. T. Campbell, "Systematic Error on the Part of Human Links in Communication Systems," in *Information and Control*, Vol. 1 (1958).

American Anthropological Association: E. T. Hall, "A System for the Notation of Proxemic Behavior," in *American Anthropologist*, Vol. 65 (1963); R. Naroll and R. G. D'Andrade, "Two Further Solutions to Galton's Problem," in *American Anthropologist*, Vol. 65 (1963).

American Association of Public Opinion: B. Berelson and P. J. Salter, "Majority and Minority Americans: An Analysis of Magazine Fiction," in *Public Opinion Quarterly*, Vol. 10 (1946); M. L. DeFleur, "Occupational Roles as Portrayed on Television," in *Public Opinion Quarterly*, Vol. 28 (1964); P. Johns-Heine and H. H. Gerth, "Values in Mass Periodical Fiction, 1921–1940," in *Public Opinion Quarterly*, Vol. 13 (1949); D. B. Jones, "Quantitative Analysis of Motion Picture Content," in *Public Opinion Quarterly*, Vol. 6 (1942); W. C. Schutz, "On Categorizing Qualitative Data in Content Analysis," in *Public Opinion Quarterly*, Vol. 22 (1958).

American Educational Research Association: N. L. Gage (Ed.), *Handbook of Research on Teaching* (published by Rand McNally, 1963).

American Foundation of Mental Hygiene: E. F. Borgatta, "A New Systematic Interaction Observation System: Behavior Scores System (BSs System)," in *Journal of Psychological Studies*, Vol. 14 (1963).

American Museum of Natural History: A. F. McBride, "Meet Mister Porpoise," in *Natural History Magazine*, Vol. 45 (1940).

American Sociological Association: T. B. Lemann and R. L. Solomon, "Group Characteristics as Revealed in Sociometric Patterns and Personality Ratings," in *Sociometry,* Vol. 15 (1952).

Association for Education in Journalism: E. R. Cony, "Conflict-Cooperation of Five American Dailies," in *Journalism Quarterly,* Vol. 30 (1953); A. Geller, D. Kaplan, and H. D. Lasswell, "An Experimental Comparison of Four Ways of Coding Editorial Content," in *Journalism Quarterly,* Vol. 19 (1942); G. Gerbner, "Ideological Perspectives and Political Tendencies in News Reporting," in *Journalism Quarterly,* Vol. 41 (1964).

Basic Books, Inc.: P. E. Hammond (Ed.), *Sociologists at Work* (1964).

Bobbs-Merrill Company, Inc.: F. W. Young, *Initiation Ceremonies: A Cross-Cultural Study of Status Dramatization* (1965).

Cambridge University Press: G. U. Yule, *The Statistical Study of Literary Vocabulary* (1944).

Cornell University Press: S. M. Parrish (Ed.), *A Concordance to the Poems of Matthew Arnold* (1959).

F. A. Davis Co., Philadelphia: J. M. Tanner, *Growth at Adolescence* (published by Charles C. Thomas, 1962).

Duell, Sloan & Pearce, Inc.: P. F. Lazarsfeld and F. N. Stanton, *Radio Research 1942–1943* (1944).

W. H. Freeman and Company, for Scientific American, Inc.: S. S. Levine, "Stimulation in Infancy," in *Scientific American,* Vol. 202 (1960).

Harper & Row, Publishers, Inc.: R. G. Barker and H. F. Wright, *Midwest and Its Children* (published by Row, Peterson and Co., 1955).

Holt, Rinehart and Winston, Inc.: L. Festinger and D. Katz (Eds.), *Research Methods in the Behavioral Sciences* (1953).

Houghton Mifflin Company: C. R. Rogers, *Counseling and Psychotherapy* (1942).

The Journal Press, Provincetown, Mass.: E. F. Borgatta, "A Systematic Study of Interaction Process Scores, Peer and Self-Assessments, Personality and Other Variables," in *Genetic Psychology Monographs,* Vol. 65 (1962); M. Spiegelman, C. Terwilliger, and F. Fearing, "The Content of Comics: Goals and Means to Goals of Comic Strip Characters," in *Journal of Social Psychology,* Vol. 37 (1953).

Langley Porter Institute: P. Ekman, "Communication Through Nonverbal Behavior" (1965).

McGraw-Hill Book Co., Inc.: S. Koch (Ed.), *Psychology: A Study of a Science,* Vol. 6 (1963).

Macmillan Company: B. Berelson, *Content Analysis in Communication Research* (published by The Free Press, 1952); R. Merton and P. Lazarsfeld (Eds.), *Continuities in Social Research* (published by The Free Press, 1950).

The M.I.T. Press: H. D. Lasswell, N. Leites, *et al.* (Eds.), *The Language of Politics: Studies in Quantitative Semantics* (published by George Stewart, 1949); H. D. Lasswell, D. Lerner, and I. de S. Pool, *The Comparative Study of Symbols* (published by Stanford University Press, 1952); I. de S. Pool, *The "Prestige Papers": A Survey of Their Editorials* (published by Stanford University Press, 1952); I. de S. Pool, *Symbols of Democracy* (published by Stanford University Press, 1952); I. de S. Pool, *Symbols of Internationalism* (published by Stanford University Press, 1951).

Mount Sinai Hospital, New York, N.Y.: R. G. Barker, "Observation of Behavior: Ecological Approaches," in *Journal of the Mount Sinai Hospital,* Vol. 31 (1964).

Prentice-Hall, Inc.: C. P. Stone (Ed.), *Comparative Psychology* (3rd ed., 1951).

Princeton University Press: G. A. Almond, *The Appeals of Communism* (1954).

The Rand Corporation: A. L. George, *Propaganda Analysis* (published by Row, Peterson and Co., 1959).

The Regents of the University of California: S. W. Head, "Content Analysis of Television Drama Programs," in *Quarterly of Film, Radio and Television* (now *Film Quarterly*), Vol. 9 (1954).

Society for Applied Anthropology: E. D. Chapple, "Quantitative Analysis of Complex Organizational Systems," in *Human Organization,* Vol. 21 (1962).

Springer Publishing Co.: S. S. Tomkins, *Affect, Imagery, and Consciousness: The Positive Affects,* Vol. 1 (1962); S. S. Tomkins and C. E. Izard (Eds.), *Affect, Cognition, and Personality* (1965).

Stanford University Press: W. Schramm (Ed.), *One Day in the World's Press* (1959).

University of Chicago Press: D. Waples (Ed.), *Print, Radio, and Film in a Democracy* (1942).

University of Illinois Press: I. de S. Pool (Ed.), *Trends in Content Analysis* (1959).

University of Michigan, Institute for Social Research: D. J. McGranaham and I. Wayne, "German and American Traits Reflected in Popular Drama," in *Human Relations,* Vol. 1 (1948).

University of Minnesota Press: L. Festinger, H. W. Riecken, and S. Schachter, *When Prophecy Fails* (1956).

University of North Carolina Press: R. C. Sorenson and T. C. Sorenson, "Proposal for the Use of Content Analysis in Literary Infringement Cases," in *Social Forces,* Vol. 33 (1955).

D. Van Nostrand Company, Inc.: J. W. Atkinson (Ed.), *Motives in Fantasy, Action and Society* (1958).

Wenner-Gren Foundation for Anthropological Research: G. P. Murdock, "Comment on Naroll's 'On Ethnic Unit Classification'," in *Current Anthropology,* Vol. 5 (1964); R. Naroll, "On Ethnic Unit Classification," in *Current Anthropology,* Vol. 5 (1964).

John Wiley & Sons, Inc.: R. D. Mann, *Interpersonal Styles and Group Development* (1967); P. H. Mussen (Ed.), *Handbook of Research Methods in Child Development* (1960).

Williams & Wilkins Co., Baltimore: E. T. Hall, "Silent Assumptions in Social Communication," in *Disorders of Communication,* Vol. 42 (1964).

Contents

VOLUME TWO

RESEARCH METHODS

9. Experimentation in Social Psychology   1
   Elliot Aronson, University of Texas
   J. Merrill Carlsmith, Stanford University

10. Data Analysis, Including Statistics   80
    Frederick Mosteller, Harvard University
    John W. Tukey, Princeton University and Bell Telephone Laboratories

11. Attitude Measurement   204
    William A. Scott, University of Colorado

12. Simulation of Social Behavior   274
    Robert P. Abelson, Yale University

13. Systematic Observational Methods   357
    Karl E. Weick, University of Minnesota

14. Measurement of Social Choice and Interpersonal Attractiveness   452
    Gardner Lindzey, University of Texas
    Donn Byrne, University of Texas

15. Interviewing   526
    Charles F. Cannell, University of Michigan
    Robert L. Kahn, University of Michigan

16. Content Analysis   596
    Ole R. Holsti, University of British Columbia
    With the collaboration of Joanne K. Loomba and Robert C. North

17. Methods and Problems in Cross-Cultural Research   693
    John W. M. Whiting, Harvard University

18. The Social Significance of Animal Studies   729
    D. O. Hebb, McGill University
    W. R. Thompson, Queen's University

    Author Index   775

    Subject Index   795

VOLUME ONE

HISTORICAL INTRODUCTION

1. The Historical Background of Modern Social Psychology
   Gordon W. Allport

SYSTEMATIC POSITIONS

2 Stimulus-Response Theory in Contemporary Social Psychology
   Seymour M. Berger and William W. Lambert

3. Mathematical Models of Social Behavior
   Seymour Rosenberg

4. The Relevance of Freudian Psychology
   and Related Viewpoints for the Social Sciences
   Calvin S. Hall and Gardner Lindzey

5. Cognitive Theories in Social Psychology
   Robert B. Zajonc

6. Field Theory in Social Psychology
   Morton Deutsch

7. Role Theory
   Theodore R. Sarbin and Vernon L. Allen

8. Organizations
   Richard M. Cyert and Kenneth R. MacCrimmon

VOLUME THREE

THE INDIVIDUAL IN A SOCIAL CONTEXT

19. Psychophysiological Approaches in Social Psychology
    David Shapiro and Andrew Crider

20. Social Motivation
    Leonard Berkowitz

21. The Nature of Attitudes and Attitude Change
   William J. McGuire

22. Social and Cultural Factors in Perception
   Henri Tajfel

23. Person Perception
   Renato Tagiuri

24. Socialization
   Edward Zigler and Irvin L. Child

25. Personality and Social Interaction
   David Marlowe and Kenneth J. Gergen

26. Psycholinguistics
   George A. Miller and David McNeill

27. Laughter, Humor, and Play
   D. E. Berlyne

28. Esthetics
   Irvin L. Child

VOLUME FOUR

GROUP PSYCHOLOGY AND PHENOMENA OF INTERACTION

29. Group Problem Solving
   Harold H. Kelley and John W. Thibaut

30. Group Structure: Attraction, Coalitions, Communication, and Power
   Barry E. Collins and Bertram H. Raven

31. Leadership
   Cecil A. Gibb

32. Social Structure and Behavior
   Wilbert E. Moore

33. Cultural Psychology: Comparative Studies of Human Behavior
   George A. DeVos and Arthur E. Hippler

34. National Character: The Study of
   Modal Personality and Sociocultural Systems
   Alex Inkeles and Daniel J. Levinson

35. Collective Behavior: Crowds and Social Movements
   Stanley Milgram and Hans Toch

36. The Social Psychology of Infrahuman Animals
   J. P. Scott

VOLUME FIVE

APPLIED SOCIAL PSYCHOLOGY

37. Prejudice and Ethnic Relations
    John Harding, Harold Proshansky, Bernard Kutner, and Isidor Chein

38. Effects of the Mass Media of Communication
    Walter Weiss

39. Industrial Social Psychology
    Victor H. Vroom

40. Psychology and Economics
    Herbert A. Simon and Andrew C. Stedry

41. Political Behavior
    David O. Sears

42. A Social Psychology of Education
    J. W. Getzels

43. Social-Psychological Aspects of International Relations
    Amitai Etzioni

44. Psychology of Religion
    James E. Dittes

45. Social Psychology of Mental Health
    Howard E. Freeman and Jeanne M. Giovannoni

9

Experimentation in Social Psychology

ELLIOT ARONSON, *University of Texas*
J. MERRILL CARLSMITH, *Stanford University*

In preparing this chapter, we decided to aim our discussion primarily at the graduate student in social psychology who is interested in carrying out a laboratory experiment. Accordingly, we will be addressing the reader in much the same way that we address our own graduate students. We hope this approach does not prove to be unduly offensive to the professional; indeed, it is our fond hope that there may be something of value in these pages even for the battle-scarred veteran of dozens of experiments.

This chapter is not intended to provide an exhaustive description of experiments in social psychology. Virtually every chapter in this *Handbook* is studded with detailed accounts of experiments; these need not be repeated here. Neither is it our intention to devote much space to an encyclopedic discussion of experimental designs. Such analyses of designs in social psychology and in general psychology have been ably written by others and cannot be improved upon by us. Obviously, no chapter on experimentation can avoid these topics entirely—we *will* describe experiments and we *will* mention experimental design problems. The major focus of this chapter, however, will be on some of the more mundane and less explicit aspects of the experimental process in social psychology. We will devote much space to such concerns as the process of translating an abstract idea into a hypothesis, and the process of concretizing the hypothesis into a reasonable and workable set of experimental manipulations. We will discuss how an experimenter handles human subjects: what he says to them, how he says it, the conditions under which he must depart from a rigorous set of instructions, how to handle such occurrences, and how to minimize them. We will discuss these problems and a host of others, many of which are essential ingredients in the social-psychology experiment but are difficult to specify in research reports or in methodological discussions because of their relatively "artistic," intuitive, ephemeral nature. Thus, in reading a research report we find ourselves continually

1

asking "why." Why did the experimenter choose this experimental manipulation rather than one of at least ten alternatives that, at first glance, might seem at least as good? Indeed, what constitutes a "good" manipulation? If the experimenter employed deception we might wonder (1) whether deception was necessary and (2) how he arrived at *that* particular "cover" story. Was it insight, intuition, previous experience, a lucky guess, trial and error? We might wonder whether the experimenter could be certain that the subjects did not suspect what the real hypothesis was. Did he try to find out? How? At the close of the description of his "method" section, when the investigator confidently assures us that, in spite of his blatant mendacity and any psychological pain the subject might have incurred, the latter was not upset and left the laboratory in good spirits, we might wonder how he could be so sure. Exactly how did he check on this? Did he come right out and ask or did he probe more subtly and more sensitively? How *does* one probe sensitively?

Because concrete aspects of an experiment, such as design and sampling techniques, are relatively easy to articulate, they *are* articulated with great frequency. This creates the illusion that these are the sole ingredients of an experiment. Although this makes for a neat, crisp, easy-to-read report, it presents an overly glossy picture of the experimental process. As others have suggested (Beveridge, 1957; Festinger *et al.*, 1959), this is misleading to the fledgling experimenter. It implies either that experimentation is a simple, direct, cut-and-dried process where ideas spring automatically from clearly specified theories and experimental operations follow logically from hypotheses; or that there is one and only one somewhat magical process of conducting a given experiment and being a good experimenter is a matter of learning (or being handed, along with the Ph.D. diploma) this secret formula. These myths make it difficult if not impossible for the novice to master the art of experimentation.

This chapter, then, is a discussion of the experimental process in social psychology written from the point of view of the working social psychologist. In it we attempt not only to specify certain problems of design and technique, but also to make explicit some of the intuitive leaps that experimenters perform in the course of designing and conducting experiments.

In our discussion we will use many of our own experiments for illustrative purposes. This should not be construed as an indication that we feel our own experiments to be superior to others in the field, or even that our experiments best exemplify the points to be made. Rather, our own experiments are the only ones with which we are familiar in their embryonic stage, the only ones for which we are sure of the answers to the above questions. Moreover, as will become clear, our own work is used to illustrate blunders as well as successes. Just as being close to an experiment puts us in a better position to relate the "clever" reasoning behind some of the decisions, by the same token it allows us to observe, perhaps too clearly, the oversights, pitfalls, pratfalls, and weaknesses as well. Second-guessing another man's experiment is a difficult and precarious occupation. An alternative manipulation that the critic judges to be far better than the one employed may have been considered and rejected (for good reason) by the experimenter. We tried to avoid this problem by limiting most of our second-guessing to our own experiments.

There are almost as many ways of building and conducting an experiment as there are experimenters. As experimenters, we do not believe that all of these are equally effective or fruitful. Consequently, in discussing how experiments *do* get done, we will unavoidably be imposing our own recommendations as to how experiments *should* be done. We hope we have not stated these recommendations dogmatically, for ultimately, the question of how to conduct an experiment is, in itself, an empirical one.

One final note: We have said that the things we are trying to articulate are often inarticulable. By this we mean that there are few general rules which apply to all concrete situations. In this chapter we try to state examples of what we mean, but for specific situations the reader will be forced to reconstruct these examples almost from scratch. Ultimately, it is impossible to lay down a set of rules which will make someone a good experimenter. This would be akin to writing a handbook for the creative writer. One can teach certain fundamental rules of experimentation in much the same way that, in writing, basic laws of grammar and syntax can be taught. To push the analogy a little, perhaps fundamental rules of sampling and design are the syntax and grammar of experimentation. In this chapter we avoid these topics in an attempt to make the student aware that there is something else of importance to be learned, and to specify as best we can what this something might be. At the same time, we feel strongly that good experimentation cannot be taught through the printed page, but it can be learned—learned primarily through observing good experimenters and by doing experiments under their guidance. This chapter is intended primarily as a supplement to such guidance.

THE ADVANTAGES OF EXPERIMENTATION

There are many ways of gathering information about social-psychological phenomena; several of them are described in detail in other chapters in this *Handbook*. One can simply observe ongoing social behavior; one can ask questions about attitudes or behaviors; using the cross-cultural method, one can study correlations between social behaviors in different societies. The list of techniques and variations on these techniques is filled with interesting possibilities; such techniques have provided us with some of our richest and most fascinating data about social phenomena. We describe in this chapter another technique, the laboratory experiment.

The first and most obvious question must be, "Why bother doing a laboratory experiment?" Its disadvantages are several. It is often difficult to design. It is likely to be laboriously time-consuming. Typically, a single person must be seen for an hour or two by an experimenter and one or more assistants or confederates. Frequently the experimenter goes to elaborate lengths to set the stage, motivate the subject, and, on occasion, to deceive him. After expending all of this time and effort, the investigator may obtain only a single datum, perhaps something as simple as a "yes" or a "no" response. Furthermore, and this is perhaps the most frequent criticism, the experiment is usually far removed from the "real life" phenomena we are interested in. To the layman it might seem ludicrous for psychologists interested in the formation and change of basic attitudes and important values to study spinach eating, toy preference, the perception of lines, or the relative attractiveness of a group of people whose only contact may be through the passing of handwritten notes. Why, then, do we bother with these pallid and contrived imitations of human interaction when there exist rather sophisticated techniques for studying the real thing?

In attempting to answer this question, let us look first at one laboratory experiment in some detail, and compare some of the alternative approaches which might have been used to answer the same questions. For illustrative purposes we have chosen an experiment by Aronson and Mills (1959) which clearly depicts not only the advantages of the experimental approach, but embodies some of the problems as well. Aronson and Mills set out to test the hypothesis that an individual who undergoes a severe initiation in order to be admitted to a group will find that group more attractive than he would if he were admitted to the group with little or no initiation. To test this hypothesis they conducted the following experiment.

Sixty-three college women were recruited as volunteers to participate in a series of group discussions on the psychology of sex. This format was a ruse in order to provide a setting wherein subjects could be made to go through either mild or severe initiations in order to gain membership in a group.

Each subject was tested individually. When a subject arrived at the laboratory, ostensibly to meet with her group, the experimenter explained to her that he was interested in studying the "dynamics of the group discussion process," and that, accordingly, he had arranged these discussion groups for the purpose of investigating these dynamics, which included such phenomena as the flow of communications, who speaks to whom, and so forth. He explained that he had chosen as a topic "The Psychology of Sex" in order to attract many volunteers, and that this had proved to be a successful device since many college people were interested in this topic. He then went on to say that this topic presented one great disadvantage to him, namely, that many volunteers, because of shyness, found it more difficult to participate in such a discussion than they would if the topic had been a more neutral one. He explained that his study would be impaired if any group member failed to participate freely. He then asked the subject if she felt able to discuss this topic freely. The subjects invariably replied in the affirmative.

The above instructions were used to set the stage for the initiation. The subjects were randomly assigned to one of three experimental conditions: a severe-initiation condition, a mild-initiation condition, or a no-initiation condition. The subjects in the no-initiation condition were told, at this point, that they could now join a discussion group. It was not that easy for the subjects in the other two conditions, however. The experimenter told these subjects that he had to be absolutely certain that they could discuss sex frankly before admitting them to a group. Accordingly, he said that he had recently developed a test which he was now using as a "screening device" to eliminate those girls who would be unable to engage in such a discussion without excessive embarrassment. In the severe-initiation condition this embarrassment test consisted of having each subject read aloud (to the male experimenter) a list of 12 obscene words and two vivid descriptions of sexual activity from contemporary novels. In the mild-initiation condition the girls were merely required to read aloud words related to sex which were not obscene.

Each of the subjects was then allowed to "sit in" on a group discussion which they were told was being carried on by members of the group they had just joined. This group was described as one that had been meeting for several weeks; the subject was told that she would be replacing a group member who was leaving because of a scheduling conflict.

To provide all subjects with an identical stimulus, the experimenter had them listen to the same tape-recorded group discussion. At the same time, the investigators felt that it would be more involving for the subjects if they were made to believe that this was a live, ongoing group discussion. In order to accomplish this while justifying the lack of visual contact necessitated by the tape recording, the experimenter explained that people found that they could talk more freely if they were not being looked at; therefore, each subject was in a separate cubicle, talking through a microphone and listening in on headphones. Since this explanation was consistent with the other aspects of the cover story, all the subjects found it convincing.

It was important to discourage the subject from trying to "talk back" to the tape, since by doing so she would soon discover that no one was responding to her comments. In order to accomplish this, the experimenter explained that it would be better if she didn't try to participate in the first meeting since the other group members had done some reading for the meeting and the subject would, therefore, not be able to participate on an equal footing. He then disconnected her microphone.

At the close of the discussion, the experimenter returned and explained that after each session all members are asked to rate the worth of that particular discussion and the performance of the other participants. He then presented her with a list of rating scales. The results confirmed the hypothesis. The girls in the severe-initiation condition found the group much more attractive than did the girls in the mild-initiation or the no-initiation conditions.

This procedure certainly has some of the disadvantages mentioned earlier. Most striking is the fact that the experimenters constructed an elaborate scenario bearing little relation to the "real life" situations in which they were interested. The "group" which the subject found attractive was, in fact, nothing more than a few voices coming in over a set of earphones. The subject was not allowed to see her fellow group members nor was she allowed to interact with them verbally. This is certainly a far cry from group interaction as we know it outside the laboratory. In addition, reading a list of obscene words is probably far milder than an actual initiation outside the laboratory. Moreover, the use of deception raises ethical problems as well as more pragmatic ones such as whether or not the deception was successful.

This hypothesis could have been investigated more directly and perhaps more simply by employing some of the nonexperimental methods we have mentioned. For example, one might try to study it cross-culturally, using ratings of the severity of the initiation rites into manhood, and correlating these with some index of the extent to which adult males find their group attractive. A still more direct and perhaps simpler method would be to study existing fraternities. One might first observe whether or not initiations are required for membership. If initiations are required, one would rate them for severity. At a later time one could return and interview the members of the various fraternities, assessing the degree to which they liked each other or found their particular fraternity attractive. If it turned out that the men in fraternities requiring severe initiations liked their group better than did those in fraternities with no such requirement, this would seem to provide far greater support for the hypothesis, since the evidence would have been gathered in a real setting. Unquestionably, this procedure has certain obvious advantages. First, it is simpler than the laboratory experiment. There is no necessity for recruiting volunteers, tape-recording a discussion, or going through an elaborate set of instructions designed to deceive college women. In addition, it is the real thing. Rather than a collection of individuals who do not know one another listening to a tape recording of disembodied voices for a short period of time, the actual fraternity situation involves real people living together in real groups over a relatively long period of time, developing strong positive or negative feelings toward one another. This would virtually guarantee more reliable ratings since they would be based on a longer and more intense interaction among members. Moreover, there would be little question that the initiation we label as severe would, in fact, be a severe initiation. In the most extreme instances the initiation would most certainly reach a level of magnitude which is not easily equaled in the laboratory.

On the other hand, there are some difficulties with this approach. First, the stimulus object, that is, the members of the fraternity, vary a great deal in their inherent attractiveness. The severity of initiation, although hypothesized to be a cause of attractiveness, is certainly not the only cause. Obviously, people have many characteristics which others find more or less attractive. Some people are attractive because they are friendly, perceptive, intelligent, athletic, "nice," generous, handsome, witty, etc. Others are unattractive because they are dull, stupid, too loud, too quiet, too outgoing, too inhibited, etc. In such a complex stimulus situation, the severity of initiation, although important, might be only one drop in a large bucket. Thus, because there is great variation among the fraternity members in these and other attributes, it might be very difficult to demonstrate differences between severe-initiation fraternities and mild-initiation fraternities even if initiation were the most important single determinant of attractiveness.

One of the great advantages of the experiment is that, in the laboratory, the experimenter can often exert a great deal of control over possible random variation and thus ensure that the stimuli in his experimental conditions are similar. Thus, in the initiation experiment described above, the group whose attractiveness was to be judged was identical for all subjects. By doing this, Aronson and Mills succeeded in eliminating literally thousands of factors which may cause one group to be more attractive than another and, accordingly, increased markedly the possibility of being able to observe existing differences due to their experimental treatment. Thus, although some degree of realism was sacrificed, one of the great gains was the achievement of considerable control over possible random variation in all aspects of the situation.

This control, although highly desirable, is not in itself the major advantage of an experiment. There is one advantage which is far more important: the random assignment of experimental units to experimental conditions. Let us suppose that the random variation mentioned above was not great enough to obscure the relationship between severity of initiation and attractiveness. That is, suppose we conducted a study of existing fraternities and discovered that the members of severe-initiation fraternities found one another more attractive than members of mild-initiation fraternities. If this occurred, we must consider the possibility of other explanations.

The fundamental weakness of such a correlational study is its inability to specify causes and effects. We wish to assert as a conclusion to our study that severe initiations cause increased attractiveness of the group into which one is initiated. In our fraternity example there are a variety of other possible and, indeed, plausible explanations which involve different causal sequences. The simplest explanation for these results might involve a relationship which is the exact opposite of the one we have proposed. Rather than severe initiation causing high attractiveness, it may be that high attractiveness causes severe initiation. The more attractive groups may perceive that they are attractive and may attempt to maintain this pleasant situation. Since they perceive themselves as attractive, they may try to make it difficult for people to get into the group; perhaps out of a desire to prevent the group from becoming diluted, they try to discourage applicants by requiring a severe initiation. One could list many other reasons why the attractive groups might tend to have more severe initiations. The point is that any such reasons point to an explanation for our data which involves a causal sequence which is the exact opposite of the one we hypothesized. Since this study necessitates the investigation of a group that was in existence before we arrived on the scene, there is no clear way to determine from these data which of the two is correct.

Partial solutions for this and other problems involving the establishment of causal relationships nonexperimentally have been suggested (Campbell, 1957, 1963, in press; Campbell and Stanley, 1963; Selltiz *et al.*, 1960). Campbell and Stanley (1963) provide the most extensive discussion of the strengths and weaknesses of these various quasi-experimental designs. These will not be discussed here, save to say that they are useful when experimentation is impossible, because the best of these frequently provide a reasonable basis for inferring causality. Nevertheless, none of these methods provides definite proof of a causal sequence; in this respect they are inferior to the true experiment.

The above analysis is nothing more than an elaboration of the old phrase "correlation does not prove causation." Whenever we observe that a variable X (say severity of initiation) is correlated with variable Y (say attractiveness of a group), we cannot be sure whether X caused Y or whether Y caused X. In our laboratory experiment, of course, there is no ambiguity. The experimenter knows what caused X—he did. Consequently, when the experimenter observes that Y is correlated with X, he can be certain that Y cannot have caused X; X must have caused Y.

In some instances such ambiguity may not be too serious. Anyone who lacks faith in the development of a science through the exclusive use of correlational methods need only look to the history of astronomy. An understanding of the direction of causality is important, but if we could really be sure that there was a causal relation between X and Y, regardless of direction, there is no question that we would have made a great stride forward. A more distressing alternative is the possibility that neither X causes Y nor Y causes X; rather the observed correlation is simply produced by some third variable which affects both of them. A classic example of this problem is the observed correlation between the viscosity of asphalt and the incidence of polio in children. We would hardly conclude from this correlation that asphalt of low viscosity is the cause of polio. Nor do we conclude that polio causes asphalt to become softer. We know that a third variable, a warm temperature, causes the asphalt to become softer and also tends to increase children's exposure and/or susceptibility to the polio-causing virus. Thus, even though there might be a perfect correlation between the viscosity of asphalt and the incidence of polio, the two phenomena are not causally related to each other. Returning again to our fraternity example, it may well be that some constellation of personality traits produces people who are very attractive but who, at the same time, are rather sadistic—the kind of people who like to administer severe initiations. If such were the case, we would certainly find that those fraternities which had severe initiations also had members who liked the group a great deal, but in fact there would be no direct causal connection between these two variables.

Again the laboratory experiment circumvents this pitfall. In the experiment, it is extremely unlikely that there is some adventitious third variable which is correlated with the two variables under consideration. The reason for this is apparent when we look at the defining characteristic of the experiment. In the experiment the experimenter has control over what treatment a subject receives and he determines that treatment by the principle of randomization—by the simple device of assigning subjects to conditions in a random manner. The statistical niceties and elaborations of randomization have been ably discussed by others; here we merely wish to note that if the treatment a subject receives is truly determined at random, it is virtually impossible for a third variable to be associated with that treatment; consequently, such a third variable could not affect the dependent variable. In the real-life fraternity example, the demon which is of constant concern to the investigator is the possibility that the independent variable, severity of initiation, has not been randomly assigned to the various fraternities. Insofar as some unknown third variable affects how severely a given fraternity initiates its new members, that third variable might also affect how attractive the group will be to its new members.

A common example of this is the existence of possible differences in the subjects' initial motivation. For example, it is reasonable to assume that some people will join *any* fraternity while others are motivated to join a specific fraternity, perhaps because they have reason to feel that they will be happier with the members of that group. If a specific fraternity has a reputation for requiring severe initiations prior to admission, those people who have a strong desire to join that particular fraternity would be willing to go through the initiation in order to join. On the other hand, those people who simply want to belong to a fraternity —any fraternity—would be much more likely to choose a fraternity that requires little or no initiation. After all, if it makes no difference to a person which fraternity he joins, why would he bother to go through a severe initiation in order to get into a particular fraternity? Consequently, a fraternity that requires little or no initiation will attract many people who initially have no great desire to be in that specific fraternity as well as some people who do have a great desire to be in that specific fraternity. On the other hand, a fraternity that requires a severe initiation will be joined primarily by those people who have a strong desire to be in that specific fraternity, strong enough to allow them to endure the initiation. Therefore, any relationship between attractiveness and severity of initiation may be strictly a function of a disproportionate number of highly motivated people joining the severe-initiation fraternity. This problem is averted by the experiment. Thus, not only does random assignment guarantee that no other variable is causing one group to administer a more severe initiation than another, it also prevents the possibility that systematic motivational differences among the potential joiners will cause the observed relationship.

Finally, in the laboratory experiment, one has the opportunity to vary the treatment in a systematic manner, thus allowing for the isolation and precise specification of the important differences. If one were to study fraternities with different initiations, the likelihood would be that the different initiations would differ both quantitatively and qualitatively on a large number of dimensions. Suppose that the fraternity requiring a severe initiation asked its pledges to do a large number of unpleasant jobs, wear funny clothes, submit to severe physical punishment, expose themselves to danger, and eat insects. In order to be sure which aspect of this complex treatment was causing the increased attractiveness, it would be ideal to have another fraternity which asked pledges to do all of these things *except* submit to severe physical punishment. This ideal second fraternity would ask pledges to submit to mild physical punishment. Such a fraternity would probably not exist, but if we were experimentally creating initiation, we could produce the appropriate initiation, identical in all respects except the severity of physical punishment.

In sum, the major advantage of the laboratory experiment is its ability to provide us with unambiguous evidence about causation. Second, it gives us better control over extraneous variables. Finally, it allows us to explore the dimensions and parameters of a complex variable.

SOME PROBLEMS WITH EXPERIMENTS IN SOCIAL PSYCHOLOGY

Our discussion of the advantages of the experiment presents a rosy picture of the information to be gained and the pitfalls to be avoided by use of the experiment. However, the description ignores some very serious difficulties with the use of the experimental method in an area as complex as social psychology. Consider first the question of control. There are severe limitations on the kinds of control that can be achieved in social-psychological experimentation. Some of these limitations may be overcome by new approaches, others may be inherent in the nature of the field.

One of the major limitations on control which concerns us is the extent to which unmeasured individual differences may obscure the results of an experiment. The ideal of an experiment is to take two identical units (corn plants, rocks, rats, children, or fraternities) and to apply different experimental treatments to them. It is a philosophical truism that no two units are ever precisely identical, but the experimenter strives to make them as close to identical as possible. One can approximate this ideal much more satisfactorily in most sciences, and even in most of psychology, than is possible in social psychology. Our subjects differ from each other genetically, in learned personality characteristics, in values and attitudes, in abilities, and in immediate past experiences. Any and all of these differences may have a large impact on the way in which subjects respond to our experimental treatments.

The experimenter who studies the behavior of infrahumans can minimize these difficulties by using a single known genetic strain and by keeping his experimental units in a similar stimulus-controlled environment. The experimenter who studies human learning can reduce these problems by using each subject in all of his experimental conditions, that is, by using each subject as his own control. Such solutions are, at present, not often possible in the social-psychological experiment. Social psychologists have precious little knowledge of or control over the genetic strain or the preexperimental experiences of their subjects. Moreover, in social psychology, most experimental treatments are not of the type which can be presented to a subject one after the other. Once a girl has been asked to read a list of obscene words and then listens to a group discussion, it is very difficult to ask her to read a list of mild words and again listen to a group discussion. Having told a subject that *Pravda* estimates that atomic-powered submarines are presently feasible, it is difficult to estimate the effect on the same subject of the same communication subsequently attributed to J. Robert Oppenheimer.

What about control over the stimulus situation? We argued that one great advantage of studying the effects of initiation under laboratory conditions was that subjects could be exposed to identical discussion groups. In that situation the control was quite good since the group discussion was tape-recorded and all subjects were exposed to the same recorded discussion. Often, of course, since we are studying social situations, the crucial event will involve an interaction between the subject and other individuals. If this is the case, the stimulus may vary greatly from one subject to the next. Furthermore, we typically present the subject with a stimulus situation which is familiar, one that is similar to other situations he may have encountered outside the laboratory. Consequently, this is certain to interact with individual differences among the subjects; there is bound to be more variation in how this situation is perceived by different subjects than would be the case if we could use unfamiliar stimuli like nonsense syllables. For example, if one experimental condition calls for having a confederate reject the subject, this experience of rejection might be responded to in very different ways by different subjects. A subject who had recently been rejected by his girl friend might be more shaken by the experimental situation than one who was more secure in his social relationships.

Such sources of variability in our data are accentuated by the relatively narrow limitations imposed on the kinds of experimental treatment a social psychologist can use. Ethical considerations, restrictions of time, the mere fact that the subject usually knows he is in an experiment—all these factors combine to limit the impact the experimenter can have on the subject. Typically, we see a subject for only an hour or two. In that short period of time we attempt to expose him to a complex social stimulus. The range of possible stimuli to which we expose him is sharply restricted by ethical considerations; there are many interesting questions which we cannot study simply because they involve doing things to people which we are not willing to do. As a consequence, the treatment used is a compromise between the experimenter's desire to maximize the effectiveness of the experiment and his genuine concern with the welfare of his subjects. For example, consider the Aronson and Mills (1959) experiment. There are many possible ways to provide a severe initiation which would be preferable to the technique employed. The initiation actually used by Aronson and Mills was rather pallid in comparison with initiations used by primitive societies and even some college fraternities. Because the experimenter is limited in the amount of impact he can have on the subject, differences between subjects loom large relative to the experimental treatment and, consequently, tend to have a noticeable effect. If, as God sees it, a severe initiation is indeed one of the determinants of group attraction, we suspect that no matter who the subject was, what his personality was like, or what his recent experiences had been, a painful and permanent circumcision would have had certain effects on how he would feel about the group into which he had been initiated. But reading a short list of obscene words is such a comparatively mild initiation that it may not be enough to overcome existing individual differences in the values, attitudes, and experiences of the subjects.

In an experiment on animal learning, it is usually fairly easy to have impact on the animal, to force him, if you will, to take the situation seriously. For a pigeon at 75 percent of free-feeding body weight, the learning of a food-producing response is important. It can certainly be argued that it is possible to set up a social-psychological experiment where the subject is as concerned about his performance as our hypothetical pigeon. In order to do this, however, the situation must be a very realistic one for the subject; and this realism always tends to lead to great difficulty in understanding precisely what the experimental treatment consists of. Social experiences which are realistic and meaningful tend to be complex, and any two such experiences (treatments) tend to differ on a large number of dimensions. For this reason, as we increase realism in an attempt to have greater impact on the subject, we frequently sacrifice control.

We see this as the basic dilemma of the experimental social psychologist. On the one hand we want maximal control over the independent variable. We want as few extraneous differences as possible between our treatments. We want to specify as precisely as possible the exact nature of the treatment we have administered and its exact effect on the subject. This leads us to try to develop manipulations which are highly specifiable, in which the differences between treatments are extraordinarily simple and clear, in which all manipulations are standardized —in short, to an approximation of something like a verbal learning experiment. On the other hand, if the experiment is controlled to the point of being sterile, it may fail to involve the subject, have little impact on him, and therefore may not affect his behavior to any great extent.

As an example of this dilemma, let us consider a typical experiment on attitude change. The standard design for such an experiment might be to have two identical communications, one attributed to a source of high credibility, the other to a source of low credibility. For maximal control, the ideal would be to have the communication written out in both cases and be absolutely identical except for the attribution of source. A good example of this kind of control is evidenced in the work of Hovland and his associates at Yale (for example, Hovland and Weiss, 1951). Frequently experiments done in this manner show extremely weak effects, often too weak to be statistically significant. In other cases, although statistical significance is achieved, the actual magnitude of the differences between conditions is not great. It is a reasonable conjecture that these weak effects are due to the fact that the impact of such a manipulation is very small. It is generally dull and uninvolving for a subject to be asked to read a printed communication on an issue of little direct consequence to him. To show a strong effect, it would be much more desirable to have the communicator present, delivering a dramatic speech articulately and with great passion, perhaps even interacting and arguing with the members of the audience. An example of such a technique brilliantly used can be seen in some of H. A. Murray's (1963) studies on stressful interpersonal disputations in which each subject's philosophy of life was attacked by a talented lawyer. It is reasonably clear from Murray's report that impact was achieved. But at what price in control? In these studies it is difficult to be certain exactly what was going on. The point we are trying to make is not that one method is uniformly better than the other, but that the two goals of a social-psychological experiment, impact and control, are in constant tension; as one becomes reasonably great, the other tends to be sacrificed.

Often a good compromise can be worked out. In the communication example mentioned above, one might achieve the best of both worlds by using a film or video tape of a dramatic and articulate communicator. If we made it clear that he had great credibility in one condition and low credibility in the other, there would be a high degree of control. Moreover, such a film should have a great deal of impact on the subjects—perhaps not so much as a live, interacting communicator, but almost certainly more than would be achieved by a printed page. Control has been achieved, since we are certain that subjects in each condition have received identical stimuli and we can exactly reproduce our experimental conditions.

This kind of general solution may appear to be completely satisfactory, but the problem of control versus impact extends even deeper. Attaining impact may result not only in a diminution of experimental control, but it may also lead to an increase in the number of possible conceptual constructs associated with the independent variable. We shall call this "multiple meaning," because, quite literally, certain manipulations contain a multitude of possible interpretations. The problem of multiple meaning is one of the most perplexing and pervasive problems in social-psychological experimentation primarily because the manipulations which make most sense to the subjects and produce the most impact tend to involve a complex bundle of stimuli, and consequently these operations can be interpreted in more than one way. It is a sobering experience to go through any issue of a social-psychological journal from cover to cover, noting down alternative explanations for each of the experiments. It is a rare article that does not suggest at least one possible interpretation which differs from the one proposed by the investigator. It is even more sobering to try to redesign the experiment in a manner which is free of alternative interpretations. In some cases the most plausible alternative explanations can be eliminated by a slight change in the design or manipulations, but these are rare.

In examining a completed experiment, one, in effect, asks the following question: What is the defining difference between our two (or ten) experimental conditions? What is happening in Condition A that makes the subjects behave differently (on some dependent variable) from the people in Condition B? It is usually possible to list several differences. But this is not what the investigator originally had in mind. The investigator wanted to *conceptualize* some variable which he felt was theoretically important and which apparently caused the observed difference in the subject's behavior. We shall refer to this as the *conceptual variable*. The difficulty occurs because in building the experiment we do not deal directly with conceptual variables; we must deal with imperfect translations of conceptual variables. In psychology, one frequently used conceptual variable is hunger. A frequently used experimental translation of hunger is percentage of free-feeding body weight. When we say that in an experiment one pigeon was at 75 percent of free-feeding body weight while the other was at 100 percent, we also say that the reason for observed behavioral differences is *hunger*. How do we make this leap? There are several differences between birds at 75 percent of free-feeding body weight and birds at 100 percent. How can we be certain that differences in their performance are attributable to hunger rather than physical strength or "jumpiness"? To return to the Aronson and Mills (1959) experiment, what is the distinction between the different experimental conditions? Is it, as the investigators assert, that the subjects in the severe-initiation condition have undergone a greater expenditure of unpleasant effort than the subjects in the other conditions? Could it not have been the result of having passed a demanding test? Or was it that reading obscene words may have had a sexually arousing function? One can list a great many differences among the experimental conditions. Thus, although the Aronson-Mills experiment had a great deal of control over the manipulation of experimental conditions and the presentation of the stimulus to be judged, the interpretation of the results is open to question because the investigators' experimental translation of the conceptual variable (unpleasant effort) contained multiple meaning.

Let us restate the problem in general terms. In any given experiment, the experimental treatments differ in many ways. We wish to isolate some conceptual variable which "explains" or "is the reason for" our observed differences. Actually, in the design (or planning stage) of experiments, the problem usually arises in the reverse order. We have a conceptual variable (for example, unpleasant effort) whose effects we wish to study. There are many ways to translate this abstract conceptual variable into a concrete experimental operation. If we have our subjects read a list of obscene words, how can we be sure that this operation is, in fact, an empirical realization of our conceptual variable? Or, conversely, how can we abstract a conceptual variable from our procedure?

This problem is hardly unique to social-psychological research. However, it does tend to be more acute in this area because our manipulations are often (but not necessarily) extremely complex, partly for the sake of producing sufficient impact on the subject. There is a sense in which the complex social situation used by Aronson and Mills has many more possible interpretations than does the use of a pigeon at 75 percent of free-feeding body weight. But this is not the whole story, for even simpler variables may possess multiple meaning. Thus, if instead of using obscene words, Aronson and Mills had asked their subjects to perform some exhausting physical task, this *by itself* would not have made the results much clearer. For, although this translation would have eliminated sexual arousal as an alternative explanation, it would have opened a Pandora's box of alternative explanations having to do with physical fatigue (for example, perhaps fatigue makes a person more acquiescent; or perhaps fatigue reduction is a pleasant feeling which happens to be contiguous with the stimulus to be judged). If electric shock were used, it opens the door for a myriad of interpretations based on fear and fear reduction.

Thus there is no cheap solution to the problem. This is largely due to the fact that in social psychology there exist relatively few standard methods of manipulating any given conceptual variable. This is less true in some other areas of psychology. How can we be certain that 75 percent of free-feeding body weight is an empirical realization of hunger rather than of physical strength? The major reason is that there are a great number of experiments which have been performed in a manner that increases our confidence in this particular translation. Essentially, there are two properties which we demand of a series of experiments before we are convinced that we understand what the conceptual variable should be. First, we ask for a number of empirical techniques which differ in as many ways as possible, having in common only this basic conceptual variable. If all these techniques yield the same result, then we become more and more convinced that the underlying variable which all techniques have in common is, in fact, the variable which is producing the results. Miller (1957) lists one example dealing with hunger in which this was done. Several different procedures which might be thought to influence hunger were manipulated in different experiments. These procedures included a bilateral lesion in the region of the ventromedial nuclei of the hypothalamus, injection of enriched milk directly into the stomach, injection of isotonic saline directly into the stomach, and normal intake of milk via the mouth. Interestingly enough, the different effects observed led to changes in the conception of hunger as a variable.

Similarly, if we want to be certain that degree of unpleasant effort is, in fact, the key variable in the Aronson-Mills experiment, then the experiment should be repeated using a number of different methods of arousing a degree of unpleasant effort. These methods should be as different as possible from one another, in order to eliminate overlap between conceivable alternative explanations. That is, if we suspect that in the original experiment sexual arousal might have been the variable which was mediating our observed differences, it is important that the second technique does not involve sexual arousal. Perhaps the initiation might consist of some exhausting physical exercise. If both these techniques produce similar results, then we have ruled out sexual arousal as well as a large number of related interpretations. But both these experiments might have in common the feeling of a job well done. Therefore, a third experiment should be done using still a different method, a method which eliminates this explanation. This technique of "purification" can go on indefinitely and as the number of such systematic replications becomes larger and more diverse, we gain additional confidence that we understand the conceptual variable which underlies all of them.

The technique, as described above, is concerned with replications across experiments. The same principle may also be applied within a single experiment. For example, instead of attributing a particular communication to Oppenheimer, we might attribute it to several different sources of high credibility (each for several subjects). If all these sources produce similar effects, then we gain confidence that this effect is due to credibility rather than to some attribute peculiar to Oppenheimer. Paradoxically, this suggests that control, in the sense of having *all* stimuli identical for every subject, may not be desirable. We will discuss this in greater detail in our section on the independent variable.

The second procedure is to show that a particular empirical realization of our independent variable produces a large number of different outcomes, all of which are theoretically tied to the independent variable. Again, we may point to Miller's (1957) examples. In one study he compared volume of food consumed, stomach contractions, rate of bar pressing to obtain food, and amount of quinine tolerated in the food. Some of the similar results obtained here with the various different measures of hunger lend support to a notion of a single unitary variable. Similarly, if it can be shown that asking a subject to read a list of obscene words not only makes her like the group she joins as a result, but also enhances the attractiveness of any outcome which is gained as a result of reading the words, we are more convinced that it is effort which is important in this experiment. We might ask for effects which are even further removed, but still theoretically follow from our notions of unpleasant effort. For example, if exerting unpleasant effort to attain an ambiguous goal should lead to seeking social support for the behavior, our confidence would be increased by an experiment which showed that subjects who had read a list of obscene words were more likely to seek social support for the behavior.

These solutions are not entirely new; similar solutions have been discussed at length by Brunswik (1956), by Campbell (1957), and by Campbell and Stanley (1963), but they have not been used consistently in social-psychological experimentation; in fact, they are rarely seen. Far more frequent are single, isolated studies which stand in the literature as the only evidence for some process, with no evidence that the leap from the conceptual variable to its supposed empirical realization was justified.

Why is this technique so rarely used? The most general answer is that it is often difficult to carry out. In many situations it is difficult to modify the particular operational definition of the independent variable without changing the entire experimental setting. The independent variable must not only be conceptually sound, it must make sense to the subject. Thus a replication of the Aronson-Mills (1959) study might necessitate a major change in the context of the experiment. If the subjects were asked to perform 30 push-ups (instead of reading obscene words), one could hardly maintain the format of a group discussion on the psychology of sex without straining the credulity of the subjects. Even the most naive of subjects would have second thoughts about doing push-ups as a screening device for a discussion on sex. Thus, one must often redo the entire experiment, changing not only the particular operations used in setting up the independent variable, but also the general setting, the experimental instructions, the stimulus to be rated, and the measurement of the dependent variable.

This means that we can seldom perform the systematic replication we were aiming for at first; we are forced into the awkward position of letting a large number of factors vary simultaneously. If this hypothetical second experiment does not produce similar results, what can we conclude? Which of the many changes was the crucial one? Should we conclude that the independent variable was not "really" degree of effort? This would be unjustified, for it is possible that something unique exists in this second situation which is obscuring the relationship. If such a conceptual replication does produce similar results, of course, the gain would be that much greater. We would have good evidence that neither the particular method of manipulating the independent variable nor the particular method of measuring the dependent variable, nor the specific stimuli, nor the particular context of the experiment was causing the result. Noteworthy in this regard is a conceptual replication of the initiation experiment by Gerard and Mathewson (1966). Their experiment was constructed so as to differ from the Aronson-Mills study in many respects. For example, Gerard and Mathewson used electric shocks instead of the reading of obscene words; the test was introduced as a measure of emotionality rather than an embarrassment test; the tape recording was that of a group discussion of cheating rather than one of sex; the measure of the attractiveness of the group differed slightly. Their results confirmed the Aronson-Mills (1959) interpretation: people who underwent painful electric shocks in order to become members of a dull group found that group to be more attractive than did people who underwent mild shocks.

As useful as it is, the Gerard-Mathewson experiment is only one link in a chain of replications necessary to attain complete confidence in a conceptual variable. Because it is usually necessary to reconstruct a procedure several different times in order to perform a series of systematic replications, the task becomes extremely time-consuming. The experimenter is often forced to make a decision whether to allocate several months or even years to pinning down a single conceptual variable or to move on to a new area which has begun to capture his interest. Quite frequently, an experimenter will attempt a compromise which will enable him to move into a novel experimental situation but which still has a bearing on the interpretation of previous data. This procedure is by no means a satisfactory solution to the underlying problems, since it does not move us directly toward the development of standard operational definitions of conceptual variables. Nevertheless, if several such studies all point in the same direction, it can increase our confidence in a given interpretation.

To get a better idea of whether some conceptual variable is producing the observed results, one can sometimes measure the intervening processes involved. For example, in the Aronson-Mills experiment, the conceptual variable of degree of unpleasant effort implies that the subject felt very uncomfortable when reading the words; one alternative explanation implies that she felt sexually aroused. To the extent that we can obtain some direct indication of which of these two processes was going on, we gain confidence in a given interpretation. One method may involve physiological indicators. For example, if a physiological indicator like the galvanic skin response (GSR) could distinguish positive from negative emotional states, this could be used to help clarify the interpretation of results like those obtained by Aronson and Mills; that is, if a physiological indicator showed negative affect during the recitation of the obscene words, we would gain confidence in their interpretation. Unfortunately, physiological indicators of the processes that interest social psychologists are rare. Furthermore, most physiological indicators reflect emotional arousal without differentiating the quality of this emotion; this has led to some ambiguity (for example, see Burdick and Burnes, 1958). Nevertheless, we may hope that techniques currently being developed will make such procedures more feasible. Recent work by Hess (1965) indicating that pupillary dilation and constriction reflect positive or negative feelings toward an object may be a step in this direction. (For a review of this area, see Chapter 19 in Vol. 3 of this *Handbook.*)

In the absence of more direct measures of an ongoing process, subjective reports might be used; for example, after an investigator attempts to manipulate anger he might simply ask the subject if he feels angry. Subjective reports, however, are of limited value and must be used with caution, since they themselves present serious problems of interpretation. The major problem is that frequently the subject may be either unable or unwilling to report an ongoing process. For example, in one experiment (Aronson and Carlsmith, 1963) children were threatened with very mild punishment for playing with a desirable toy. In this experiment the conceptual variable implied that the child was experiencing dissonance between refraining from playing with the toy and his awareness that the threatened punishment was not severe. But the investigators did not wish to assert or imply that the child was consciously aware of this process or that he could have reported it if asked. The difficulty involved in methods using subjective reports emerges even more clearly in an experiment by Latané and Darley (1966) in which subjects were placed in a room and smoke began pouring in. When the subjects were alone, they tended to escape immediately. When placed in the room with two calm confederates, the subjects remained in the smoky room for as long as six minutes. When questioned afterwards, almost all the subjects reported that they were not paying attention to the other people in the room. It is likely that they *were* paying attention.

Another problem with subjective reports is the ever present possibility that simply asking a subject to report on some process may actually accelerate that process. If this occurs, it is possible that, by the time the subject replies, he has completed the process and no evidence of it is left. For example, even if the child in the Aronson-Carlsmith experiment were able to report his feelings accurately, it is likely that, as the experimenters forced him to think about whether this conflict was present, they would likewise be forcing him to resolve this conflict; he could do this by deciding that he didn't like the forbidden toy anyway. Therefore, there would be no need to play with it, and hence no conflict. Indeed, this end result was the predicted outcome in the experiment.

Finally, in many experiments that employ deception, asking a subject to report on such an internal process is very likely to make that subject aware of the purpose of the experiment. For example, consider Asch's (1951) experiment on perceptual judgment. Suppose that in the course of the experiment, each time a subject was in conflict with his peers, Asch had asked him how he felt. It is likely that the subject might have begun to suspect the true purpose of the experiment. Moreover, even if the question does not give away the purpose of the experiment, the answer may be worthless because the context of the question might make it perfectly clear to the subject what answer the experimenter expects —or conversely, the answer it would be best to avoid giving. For example, in the Aronson-Mills experiment, since the subject was told that the reading of the obscene words was designed to eliminate people who showed excessive embarrassment, she was aware that the experimenter expected her to be a little embarrassed. Many subjects tend to be very cooperative; thus, if they are sure what you want to hear, they will frequently say it. Conversely, subjects may have purposely claimed *not* to be embarrassed in order to ensure gaining membership in the group.

These comments are not meant to imply that subjective, introspective reports are of no value. Often they are very valuable in helping to frame hypotheses for experiments. The old saw, "If you want to know what's going on, why not simply ask the subject," is not entirely without merit. A subject's introspective report frequently provides clues as to what kinds of variables to manipulate and what kinds of questions to ask in *subsequent* experiments. But, because of the many problems mentioned above, it is risky to take an introspective report as conclusive evidence. Rather, during pretesting or at the close of each experimental session, subjective reports should be systematically collected, for they can frequently provide interesting clues which may lead to a modification of the experiment or to follow-up experiments. Let us repeat, however, that they are often of little value and should not be relied upon too heavily. Moreover, if they are collected in the course of the experimental session, they might distort the subject's response on any subsequent dependent variable. For example, if a subject in the Asch experiment had become suspicious after he had been asked for his subjective report, he might subsequently have shown great independence of judgment; whereas, if the question had not been asked, he might have conformed throughout all the sessions.

Still a different technique for increasing confidence in the empirical realization of a conceptual variable involves carrying out a modified version of the experiment in question. These modifications should be aimed at producing a different kind of data, but data which will be consistent with a specific conceptual interpretation. In this case the results may refine the meaning of the variable without adding to our knowledge about its effects. For example, in the study by Aronson and Carlsmith it would have been possible to carry out another experiment using mild threats and severe threats, but increasing the degree of temptation in order to induce some subjects to transgress in spite of the threats. Evidence that more subjects transgressed when the threat was mild would increase our certainty that the difference between the two conditions *did* involve strength of threat. Obviously, this must be a separate experiment since one cannot collect data concerning the effects of threat on attitudes if more than a few subjects ignore the threat.

On a different level, it should be noted that occasionally some of the problems of interpretation may be solved by employing a more sophisticated design. That is, the conceptual variable can be illuminated by including additional conditions which are operationally (but not conceptually) similar to the conceptual variable.

Such a procedure reduces the need for exhaustive systematic replications. For example, in the Aronson-Carlsmith experiment, as mentioned above, the experimenters' conceptual variable implied the existence of a negative drive state (dissonance) following the subject's decision not to play with a desired toy (when left alone with it) in the face of a mild threat. According to the theory, this should lead to a derogation of the toy under mild threat but not under severe threat. Although Aronson and Carlsmith found the predicted result, they did not test for the existence of this negative drive state. As suggested above, this procedure is probably impossible at the present stage of the development of our science. Nevertheless, some germane indirect evidence could have been provided by the employment of a more sophisticated research design. Such a design was used in a subsequent experiment by Freedman (1965). Essentially, Freedman replicated Aronson and Carlsmith's results using a different dependent variable. In addition, he employed two conditions in which the child was not allowed to decide to forego playing with the forbidden toy. In his experimental conditions (like Aronson and Carlsmith's), Freedman issued either a mild or a severe threat of punishment for playing with the toy, then left the room, allowing the children to decide not to break the sanction and, therefore (supposedly), to experience dissonance in the mild-threat condition. In these conditions, like Aronson and Carlsmith, he found great differences between the mild-threat and severe-threat treatments. In addition, Freedman ran two control conditions in which he issued either a mild or a severe threat for playing with the toy, but remained in the room where he could watch the child. This made it impossible for the child to *decide* not to play with the toy; since the experimenter was standing right there looking at him, he knew he could not play with the toy and, consequently, would not experience dissonance. Since there was no dissonance, one would expect no difference between the severe and mild conditions. The results were consistent with this reasoning: these conditions were not different from each other and both were very similar to the results in the severe-threat condition when the experimenter did leave the room. Thus, of the four conditions, the only one where dissonance was expected was the only condition that produced the predicted effect. Although this procedure does not prove the existence of dissonance and, therefore, does not conclusively demonstrate the empirical realization of the conceptual variable, it does increase our confidence in the interpretation of the original experiment.

SUCCESSFUL AND UNSUCCESSFUL REPLICATIONS

When a replication by a different experimenter succeeds in producing an effect similar to that found by the original experimenter, we gain some confidence not only in the reproducibility of the finding, but also in its generality. This is true because even though the second experimenter may have been trying to keep things as similar as possible, in practice there are certain to be some deviations from the original study. At least the experimenter is different; frequently the subject population is different as well. In addition, because social-psychological variables tend to be complex and lack standardization, there are probably minor (perhaps even major) changes in the instructions, tone of voice, emphasis, etc. Thus, replication by a different experimenter indicates that the original finding is a sturdy one, that it is not dependent on specific extraneous factors. This increases our confidence that our conceptual variable was responsible for the outcome.

However, when an attempted replication fails, one must interpret this failure with caution because it is difficult to draw firm inferences. The most we can say is that there was something about the original experiment which was not accurately specified and which seems to have had an important effect on the results. One obvious but frequently overlooked problem about failures to replicate is that negative results are easily produced by incompetence. If an effect cannot be obtained, it may be that the effect does not exist or it may be that the experimenter is not skillful enough to obtain it. Hence, there is a fundamental assymetry between positive and negative results. If proper techniques have been employed to preclude bias, positive results carry their own proof of competence; negative results must be supplemented.

Frequently, a failure to replicate is attributed to some intentional change in the procedure. For the reasons just listed, it is imperative to have a design which includes a successful "exact" replication. Suppose, for example, that Jones, a hypothetical psychologist at the University of Illinois, produces a specific experimental result using Illinois undergraduates as subjects. Suppose further that Smith, at Yale University, feels that these results were not a function of the conceptual variable proposed by Jones, but rather, were a function of some artifact in the procedure. Smith then repeats Jones's procedure in all respects save one—he changes the operations slightly in order to eliminate this artifact. He fails to replicate and concludes that this demonstrates that Jones's results were artifactual. This is only one of many possible conclusions. Smith's failure to replicate has several possible causes and is therefore uninterpretable. It may be a function of a change in experimenter, or a different subject population (Yale students may be different on many dimensions from Illinois students), or countless minor variations in the procedure such as tone of voice, etc. Most of this ambiguity could be eliminated by a balanced design which includes an "exact" replication of the conditions run by the original experimenter. That is, suppose Smith's design had included a repeat of Jones's conditions with the suspected artifact left in, and his results approximated those of Jones's experiment. If, as part of the design, he changed the experiment slightly and produced no differences, or differences in the opposite direction, one could then be sure that this result was *not* merely a function of incidental differences like the experimenter, the subject population, etc. The different results must be a function of the change in the procedure. If he failed even to replicate Jones's basic experiment, we would have to conclude that there was some important factor in the variables used in the original experiment, that it was limited to a particular population, that Jones had unconsciously biased his data, that Smith had unconsciously biased his data in a negative direction, that Smith is simply incompetent, etc. To sum up, an unbalanced replication design is not worthless, but is often misleadingly overinterpreted when replication is not achieved.

EXPERIMENTAL REALISM VERSUS MUNDANE REALISM

In this chapter we have used the term *realism* or *realistic experiment,* and used it rather loosely. There has been a great deal of confusion concerning this concept and we feel that this is largely due to the fact that "realism" has more than one meaning. We would like to distinguish broadly between two senses in which an experiment can be said to be realistic. In one sense, an experiment is realistic if the situation is realistic to the subject, if it involves him, if he is forced to take it seriously, if it has impact on him. This kind of realism we will call *experimental realism.* The term "realism" can also be used to refer to the extent to which events occurring in a laboratory setting are likely to occur in the "real world." We will call this type of realism *mundane realism.* The mere fact that an event is similar to events that occur in the real world does not endow it with importance. Many events that occur in the real world are boring and uninvolving. Thus it is possible to put a subject to sleep if an experimental event is high on mundane realism but remains low on experimental realism.

Mundane realism and experimental realism are not polar concepts; a particular technique may be high on both mundane realism and experimental realism, low on both, or high on one and low on the other. Perhaps the difference between experimental and mundane realism can be clarified by citing a couple of examples where a high degree of experimental realism is achieved, but little mundane realism. Let us first consider Asch's (1951) experiment on perceptual judgment. Here the subjects were asked to judge the length of lines and confronted with unanimous judgments by a group of peers which contradicted their own perceptions. For most subjects this experiment seems to have contained a good deal of experimental realism. Whether subjects yielded to group pressure or stood firm, the vast majority underwent a rather painful experience which caused them to squirm, sweat, and exhibit other signs of tension and anxiety. They were involved, upset, and deeply concerned about this evidence which was being presented to them. We may assume that they were reacting to a situation which was as "real" for them as any of their ordinary experiences. But the experiment was hardly realistic in the mundane sense. Recall that the subjects were judging a very clear physical event. In everyday life it is rare to find oneself in a situation where the direct and unambiguous evidence of one's senses is contradicted by the unanimous judgments of one's peers. Although the judging of lines is perhaps not important or realistic in the mundane sense, one cannot deny the impact of having one's sensory input contradicted by a unanimous majority.

Another example is the general procedure employed by Milgram (1963) in a series of studies of obedience. In these experiments, Milgram asked subjects to give a series of electric shocks to a person, ostensibly as part of a learning experiment. Unknown to the subject, no shocks were actually dispensed. After each "incorrect" trial the subject was asked to increase the intensity of the shocks by pressing one of a continuous series of levers labeled from "Slight Shock" at one end to "Danger: Severe Shock" near the other end. The majority of the subjects continued to increase the shock level to the maximum in spite of the fact that the "recipient" (actually a confederate) who was closeted in the next room indicated that he was in severe pain, pounded on the door, and finally fell silent. Since the confederate's silence constituted an incorrect response on the "learning" task, the subjects were asked to increase the intensity. The majority obeyed. Milgram provided a vivid description of the effects this procedure had on the typical subject who complied with the experimenter's requests. His behavior included sweating, stuttering, profuse trembling, uncontrollable nervous laughter, and, in general, an extreme loss of composure. There is no doubt that a high degree of experimental realism had been achieved. We suspect that few of these subjects easily forgot the experience they had under the "contrived," "artificial" conditions of the laboratory. And yet there is no doubt that similar experiences do not happen to most people in the real world.

On the other hand, consider an experiment by Walster, Aronson, and Abrahams (1966) which, while high on mundane realism, was low indeed on experimental realism. In this experiment, subjects read a newspaper article about the prosecution of criminal suspects in Portugal. In this article, various statements were attributed either to a prosecuting attorney or to a convicted criminal. The article was imbedded in a real newspaper and, hence, the subjects were doing something that they frequently do; they were reading facts in a newspaper. Thus the experiment had a great deal of mundane realism. But nothing was happening to the subject. Very few American college students are seriously affected by the reading of a rather pallid article about a remote situation in a foreign country. The procedure does not have a high degree of experimental realism.

Murray's (1963) procedure would appear to be high on both. Recall that in this study a subject's general philosophy was attacked by a skillful confederate. There is no doubt that this procedure had a good deal of impact on the subject (experimental realism). At the same time, it *is* the kind of situation which can and *does* occur in dormitory bull sessions (mundane realism).

It is frequently argued (by students as well as some professionals) that experiments in social psychology are artificial and therefore worthless. The argument runs that the mere fact that a subject enters a laboratory lends a nonworld atmosphere to the proceedings which renders the data invalid. There may be some merit to this argument, but we feel that in large part it stems from a confusion between experimental and mundane realism. There are some experiments which are so deficient in experimental realism that they do not even capture the subject's attention, let alone influence his behavior. It is the major objective of a laboratory experiment to have the greatest possible impact on a subject within the limits of ethical considerations and requirements of control. In effect, the experimental situation and operations must hit the subject squarely between the eyes; that is, they must have experimental realism. It is difficult to argue that the Asch experiment, the Milgram experiment, or the Aronson-Mills experiment had no impact on the subjects.

In certain situations, increasing mundane realism will also increase impact to some extent. But if an experimental procedure already has a good deal of impact, it is unnecessary to make it occur in a real-world setting. On the other hand, occasionally the requirements of an experiment are such that adding mundane realism is the only way that impact can be achieved. For example, the experienced experimental social psychologist knows that in the laboratory it is difficult either to convince subjects to believe that someone is angry at them or to get subjects to express aggressive behavior. That is, most subjects believe that such behavior is inappropriate within the confines of an experimental situation. Consequently, if one is performing an experiment in which the manipulation or expression of hostility is essential, it may be helpful to use an approach that has mundane realism. A recent experiment by Abelson and Miller (1967) provides an excellent example of the creative employment of mundane realism. Under the guise of conducting a "man on the street" interview, the experimenter approached a person who was sitting on a park bench and got him to express his views on an issue. He then queried a man sitting on the same bench, actually an accomplice, who proceeded to express opposite views, and in so doing mercilessly mocked the views of the subject. The experimenter then queried the subject again, who, as predicted, tended to take a more extreme position as a function of having been insulted.

There is little doubt that the realistic setting of this experiment added impact that would have been lacking in a more artificial setting. But this is probably due to the fact that this kind of procedure lacks experimental realism in the laboratory. If a laboratory experiment has experimental realism, and if other aspects of the experiment are well controlled so that the intrusion of such factors as "acquiescence," "experimental demands," and/or "evaluation apprehension" are minimized, we contend that there is no need for an experiment to strive for mundane realism.

Before we elaborate our position further, it would be fruitful to discuss an interesting distinction made by Campbell (1957), the distinction between the internal validity and external validity of an experimental effect. According to Campbell, an experimental result has *internal validity* if the experimental stimulus has some significant effect within the experimental situation. *External validity* refers to the generalizability of the effect—to what populations and settings it is applicable. Internal validity is increased by having a well-controlled, well-designed experiment. It is also increased by selecting procedures and operations which have a great deal of experimental realism for the subject. Internal validity may suffer (although not necessarily) if the subject sees through the experiment, if he does not take it seriously, or if he responds "like a subject" rather than like a person. External validity may be maximized by increasing the heterogeneity of the sample and the experimental situations, by purifying the empirical realization of the conceptual variable actually involved, and/or by using a multiplicity of response measures. Like internal validity, external validity can also be improved by increasing the experimental realism of the situation; if subjects are aware of the true hypothesis and are "cooperating," then any results obtained are only generalizable to "cooperative experimental subjects."

According to Campbell, the optimal design for an experiment in a social setting is one that maximizes both internal and external validity. But of the two, internal validity is, of course, the more important, for if an experimental effect does *not* occur it makes no sense to worry about its generality. The ways of assuring internal validity in a laboratory experiment are clear and have been discussed throughout this chapter. On the other hand, it is not easy to decide the extent to which a laboratory finding has external validity. Although one can gain confidence in the external validity of an experiment if one follows the procedures outlined above, there are several sources of difficulty in attempting to generalize. Most of these focus on the problem of defining what variables are involved in that especially complex situation which obtains in the world outside the laboratory. Although a laboratory experiment may be an exact analog of some process which occurs in the outside world, we still cannot be sure that the same variables will operate in a new situation. One cannot guarantee generalizability simply by providing an experiment with a certain amount of mundane realism. This does not increase our confidence in our ability to generalize from the results, for in the final analysis the question is an empirical one.

In our opinion, concern over the artificiality of an experiment is not idle concern; it is simply misplaced. In part, it is a reflection of the fact that in social psychology we lack confidence in our operational variables because they have not been purified through systematic replication. In any given experiment, the investigator chooses a procedure which he intuitively feels is an empirical realization of his conceptual variable. All experimental procedures are "contrived" in the sense that they are invented. Indeed, it can be said that the art of experimentation rests primarily on the skill of the investigator to judge the procedure which is the most accurate realization of his conceptual variable and has the greatest impact and the most credibility for the subject. At the same time, this introduces the disquieting possibility that the experimenter may be unwittingly selecting a particular example of his conceptual variable, not because it seems to capture the flavor of his conceptualization, but because he has a hunch that it will work—and that this hunch is based in part on specific extraneous factors. For example, if we look only at Milgram's first study (1963) on the antecedents of obedience, we may hesitate to generalize his results very far—say, to the behavior of the German people in the 1930's and 1940's. But this is not because Milgram's experiment was artificial and lacked mundane realism; rather, it is because, on the basis of that experiment alone, we are not convinced that the effect would have been so strong under slightly different circumstances. For example, we may feel that the scientific setting of the original experiment may have increased the tendency to obey. Subsequently, Milgram has performed a series of well-executed, systematic replications (1965) which have gradually increased our knowledge of the extent to which his initial finding can be generalized. Our confidence in the generality of the finding would be increased still further if the same conceptual variable (obedience) were operationalized in the context of scenarios which were even more different from the situation in the original experiment.

This is not to say that mundane realism has no value. As previously mentioned, under certain circumstances, moving outside of the laboratory increases the experimental realism of a situation. Moreover, although mundane realism does not increase our confidence in the external validity of any given data, it may increase our confidence in the applicability of the data in a given setting. For example, consider an experiment by Taylor, Berry, and Block (1958) in which it was shown that brainstorming is an ineffective technique of problem solving. The applicability of these findings to industrial settings has been questioned primarily because the investigators studied college students rather than industrial employees. Subsequently, Dunnette, Campbell, and Jaastad (1963) replicated these results on industrial employees in an industrial setting. Because of this change, it seems reasonable to conclude that the latter results are more applicable to industrial situations. On the other hand, it should be obvious that these findings, taken by themselves, have no greater external validity than those of Taylor, Berry, and Block; we could generalize to a greater extent if either experiment had used a heterogeneous sample, a wide variety of problems, a wide variety of settings, or a wide variety of response measures.

EXPERIMENTAL REALISM AND THE DECEPTION EXPERIMENT

In the previous section we argued that experimental realism is essential in social-psychological research. One way of attaining experimental realism is through the use of deception. A plausible cover story not only masks the experimenter's intention, it can also provide a setting which has great impact on the subject. It is an apparent paradox that experimental *realism* can be achieved through *falsehood,* but it is nevertheless the case. The use of deception by an experimenter presents many ethical problems which cannot be taken lightly. These will be discussed in a later section. Here we might only note that on occasion, in an attempt to avoid the problems posed by deception, experimenters have tried other techniques of involving subjects in an experimental situation. One such technique is the role-playing or "as-if" experiment in which the subject is asked to behave as if he were a particular person in a particular situation (for example, Jordan, 1953; Rosenberg and Abelson, 1960).

In the experiment by Rosenberg and Abelson, each subject was asked to play the role of owner of a department store. He was then presented with various attitudes that, as a store-owner, he was supposed to have. These attitudes were purposely arranged so that they bore different kinds of imbalanced relationships to one another. For example, all subjects were told that they should set a positive value on keeping sales high; one group was then told that they should feel negatively toward modern art and positively toward Fenwick, the manager of their rug department. (Other groups were fed different attitudes about Fenwick and modern art.) All subjects were then given beliefs to the effect that (1) displays of modern art reduce sales, (2) Fenwick plans to display modern art in the rug department, and (3) Fenwick, while manager, has increased the volume of sales. As predicted, the results indicated that people choose the simplest paths toward resolving unbalanced cognitive structures.

This experiment has the great virtue of not requiring deception. It is also rather high on mundane realism in the sense that similar things might actually happen to people, whether or not they own department stores. Indeed, it has been argued (Brown, 1962) that this procedure is actually a better technique for carrying out experiments than the more elaborately staged experiment of the kind we have been discussing (for example, the Asch, Milgram, and Aronson-Mills experiments). As Brown (1962, p. 74) said, "We believe that a role-playing subject will behave in a way that corresponds more closely to the life situation than a hoodwinked subject will." We cannot agree. There are some very serious difficulties with the role-playing approach; these are similar to the problems arising from introspective reports which we discussed earlier. When we ask a subject to predict how he would behave in a given situation, he may well be unable to do so in a veridical fashion. For example, without having had the experience, few of us would be able to predict how we would behave in a military situation with shells exploding all about and with wave upon wave of enemy soldiers sweeping down upon us. It is difficult to imagine the selection of marine officers on the basis of a "brave" response to this question in a hypothetical role-playing situation. A role-playing situation lacks experimental realism; it has little impact on a subject for the simple reason that nothing is happening to him. Our guess is that we would make a better assessment of a person's bravery under fire by placing him in a simulated situation under fire, with dummy ammunition. In all probability we could assess his bravery still better if we informed him that the dummy ammunition were live, even though he would now be a "hoodwinked" subject. Indeed, a moment's reflection should make it quite obvious that the more thoroughly and more successfully he has been "hoodwinked," the more reliable will be our assessment of his future behavior under fire.

Moreover, even if the person were able to predict accurately how he would behave in some hypothetical situation, he is all too likely to tell the experimenter what he thinks is a reasonable response. This might stem from fear that the experimenter might think him queer if he does not respond in an apparently conventional way. Or it might stem from a desire to be of aid to the experimenter. Thus he is apt to tell the experimenter what he thinks most people would do, knowing that he himself would not behave in that way. For example, suppose we ask a subject to role-play a situation where he is seeking a date, and we tell him to predict for us how he would respond when faced with a choice between a moderately attractive girl and a very stunning girl. Suppose that in a real situation, out of shyness or a low level of aspiration, he would choose the moderately attractive girl. Furthermore, suppose that he can predict this accurately. Still, he might feel that *most* people would choose the very stunning girl, and in order to appear normal or in order to help us out, he might tell us that he would choose the very stunning girl. Thus, when there exists in the folk culture a theory that most people do X, the subject might respond "X," *knowing* that he does not do X, because he feels that it is an accurate description of human behavior—and he wants to provide us with an accurate description of human behavior. Several investigators have suggested that subjects are very sensitive to the experimenter and concerned about the latter's opinion (Riecken, 1962; Rosenberg, 1965). Others have shown that they tend to be cooperative and "help" the experimenter whenever possible (Orne, 1962). It should be clear that the problem is a particularly sticky one when, as in the case of the Rosenberg-Abelson (1960) experiment, the actual hypothesis involves a course of action that the subject might regard as one that would make sense for most people. Thus, in this kind of study, we are always faced with the possibility that our data are nothing more than the opinions of a random sample of people about how most people would behave in a given situation.

To repeat, although the role-playing experiment does possess a certain degree of mundane realism, it is totally lacking in experimental realism. We can conceive of a continuum of experimental realism ranging from the low end, where the subject is merely role-playing, attempting to predict how he *would* respond if he *were* in some situation, up to the high end, where the subject is totally unaware that he is in a laboratory experiment and instead is faced with a social situation to which he must respond as best he can. Let us illustrate this continuum by giving some examples of how the Asch experiment might have been run in different ways.

At the low end of the continuum one could describe the Asch situation to a subject and ask him to predict how he would behave. Our guess is that fewer people would conform in this situation than in the experiment as Asch ran it. A slightly more realistic technique might be to show him the lines and simply provide him with false information about how all previous subjects had responded. If he believed the experimenter, this might cause him some concern, but there is not a great deal of immediate pressure for him to conform. More realistic yet would be the technique used by Deutsch and Gerard (1955) and by Crutchfield (1955), where the subject sees the ostensible responses of the other observers on a panel in front of him. Asch's own technique is still more realistic. Here the subject is faced by a number of confederates, all of whom state their judgment while the subject watches them. Perhaps even more realistic would be a situation in which the subject was not in a laboratory and was unaware that an experiment was going on, but was faced with the same type of contradiction of his senses as in Asch's experiment. Here mundane realism would increase the experimental realism of the situation.

There may be situations in which a role-playing type of design would be useful, for example, a situation in which individuals are unlikely to report falsely or unable to decipher the desires of the experimenter. But, by and large, the more experimental realism a procedure has, the more accurate and meaningful are the data. To the extent that a subject can stand back and make impersonal intellectual guesses about what his behavior might or should be, the data are a less accurate statement of what he would do.

ETHICAL PROBLEMS

On the preceding pages we discussed the use of deception as a technique of experimentation, as well as other procedures which might cause the subject some discomfort. These methods raise serious ethical considerations. Ethics in the context of social-psychological research presents a complex problem stemming from the tension that exists between two sets of related values which are held in our society: a belief in the value of free scientific inquiry and a belief in the dignity of man and his right to privacy. In this chapter, we will not dwell on the historical antecedents of these values or on the philosophical intricacies of the ethical dilemma posed by the conflict of these values. It suffices to say that the dilemma is a real one that cannot be shrugged off either by making pious statements about the inviolable dignity of man or by glibly pledging allegiance to the cause of science. It is a problem that every social psychologist must face up to, not just once, but each time he constructs and conducts an experiment, because it is impossible to delineate a specific set of rules and regulations governing all experiments. In each instance the researcher must decide on a course of action after giving careful consideration to the importance of the experiment and the extent of the potential injury to the dignity of the participants.

Our aim in this section is largely descriptive. We will attempt to describe the nature of the ethical problem faced by the social psychologist and how he attempts to resolve this problem in a manner which is consistent with the value he places on scientific inquiry and which does a minimum of violence to the value he places on human dignity.

The scientist must concern himself with the health and welfare of his subjects. Thus, at the outset, we feel that it is necessary to assert that, wherever possible, the experimenter should attempt to avoid the use of deception or any measures which cause discomfort to the subject. If there is a reasonable way of building a specific experiment which avoids these problems, the experimenter is obliged to find it. We agree with other commentators (for example, Kelman, 1967) in deploring the fact that many novice experimenters assume that extreme measures are inevitable without first attempting an alternative solution to the problem of operationalizing an experiment in social psychology. Such solutions may be difficult to find, but, nonetheless, the experimenter has an obligation to try to find them.

On the other hand, many questions in social psychology can be answered only by designing experiments which cause subjects some psychological discomfort, such as anxiety, embarrassment, annoyance, insecurity, etc. One simply cannot investigate the effects of anxiety except in situations where people are being caused anxiety. And for the greatest clarity of inference, the experimenter must be able to schedule that anxiety. Moreover, it is sometimes impossible to answer particular questions without concealing the true nature of the experiment by the use of deceptive devices; some questions invite bias due to the defensiveness or cooperativeness of subjects; as will be discussed shortly, deception is a practical technique for avoiding this kind of bias. For example, one cannot imagine an experimenter studying the effects of group pressure on conformity (as in the Asch experiment) by announcing his intentions in advance. What specific problems are posed by the employment of these techniques? If deception is used, the experimenter is not only misleading his subjects, he is also invading their privacy by extracting data under false pretenses. This usually involves an outright lie; that is, the experimenter presents the subject with a "cover story" which is largely untrue. But deception occurs in more subtle forms as well. Thus, any projective technique is a deceptive device unless the subject is forewarned of the true purpose of the instrument. This is, of course, true whether the experimenter introduces the instrument (say, the TAT) under a different name (say, as a test of creativity) or does not describe it at all. A simple interview often contains an even more subtle element of deceptiveness. As Shils (1959) has pointed out, interviewers frequently gain the confidence of the respondent by simulating agreement with his attitudes or by behaving in a pseudo-friendly manner, thus seducing him into "voluntarily" revealing himself under false pretenses.

The social-psychological experiment frequently involves less subtle forms of deception. Often the deception is innocuous, being designed either to ascertain the subject's reaction to a particular untrue event, or merely to keep the subject from guessing the true purpose of the experiment. An example of innocuous deception is the typical communication-persuasion study (for example, Hovland and Weiss, 1951), in which the experimenter deceives the subject by falsely attributing a statement to a given source. So far as the subject is concerned, it is usually of little consequence whether or not a particular source did or did not make a particular statement. Nevertheless, deception, even when innocuous, presents an ethical problem simply because a lie has been told.

Often the deception is *not* innocuous but results in some anguish, upset, or discomfort on the part of the subject. For example, in the experiment by Asch (1951), subjects were led to believe that their own perceptions were seriously at variance with those of their peers. In this experiment the subject is put into a state of conflict: he must decide whether to go along with the judgment of the others or to stand alone. Either way, he is apt to experience some misgivings, discomfort, and upset. If he resists, he feels that he might suffer scorn or ridicule from the others. If he yields, he may feel that he is a gutless and wishy-washy person. This feeling might be intensified rather than relieved when, at the close of the session, the experimenter confesses that the entire situation had been rigged. Indeed, far from relieving discomfort, the experimenter may be adding insult to injury. The yielder may leave the experimental situation with reduced self-respect. He may realize, perhaps for the first time, that he is a conformist who lacks the courage to stand up for his beliefs. Although in this instance such increased self-awareness provides him with a valuable educational experience, it is nevertheless an experience which is much more than the subject bargained for when he volunteered for an experiment on visual perception. Experimenters have no special right to expose people to unpleasant facts about themselves in the name of education.

The word "bargain" was not chosen loosely, for it is this concept which is at the heart of the ethical dilemma faced by experimental social psychologists. Whether deception is innocuous or not, if a subject has not agreed in advance to allow the experimenter to manipulate and observe a specific aspect of his behavior, his privacy is being invaded. This is no less true if he volunteers for an experiment which might appear to be more unpleasant than the real one. For example, in Schachter's experiments on affiliation (1959), the subjects volunteered for an experiment in which they were told they would receive some painful electric shocks. This did not happen; instead, the experimenter observed the effect of fear on their affiliative behavior. The subjects almost certainly sighed in relief when they were told that it was not necessary for them to undergo the shock. Nevertheless, they had not been forewarned that the experimenter was going to observe the effect of fear on their choice to be in the presence of another person.

It should be mentioned that the problem of the subject's potential loss of dignity is not the exclusive province of those who run deception experiments. Unless the experimenter is careful, even the most innocent-looking procedure can cause a subject to feel uneasy and diminished. Because the experimenter-subject relationship is, by nature, one of unequal status, it is relatively easy for an experimenter, wittingly or unwittingly, to make a subject feel small and powerless. For this reason it is virtually impossible to determine the actual discomfort caused to a subject simply by studying the "method" section of a published report. In the hands of a sensitive, careful, and considerate experimenter, a procedure which may appear harmful can produce little if any discomfort. Similarly, in the hands of an insensitive person or one who has high dominance needs, the most innocent-looking procedure may cause the subject a great deal of discomfort.

Whether employing deception or not, the experimenter is obliged to go to great lengths to protect the welfare of his subjects. One important aspect of this is the postexperimental session. Typically, in a deception experiment, the experimenter will spend more time with the subject after the experimental session than in the experimental session itself. Much of this time is spent in describing the true nature of the experiment and the reasons for the deception.

But it is not that simple. Debriefing a subject is not simply a matter of exposing him to the truth. There is nothing magically curative about the truth; indeed, as suggested earlier, if harshly presented, the truth can be more harmful than no explanation at all. There are vast differences in how this is accomplished, and it is precisely these differences that are of crucial importance in determining whether or not a subject is uncomfortable when he leaves the experimental room. There are undoubtedly many effective techniques for debriefing the subject. Some of these are discussed later in this chapter. Here we will elaborate on those aspects of the debriefing session designed to minimize the discomfort caused by the employment of deception. Perhaps the one essential aspect of the process is that the experimenter communicate his own sincerity as a scientist seeking the truth and his own discomfort about the fact that he found it necessary to resort to deception in order to uncover the truth. No amount of postexperimental gentleness is as effective in relieving a subject's discomfort as an honest accounting of the experimenter's *own* discomfort in the situation. Although no one enjoys being deceived, much of the displeasure stems from a feeling that the deceiver may be feeling smug about it. The experimenter must frankly explain that deception was necessary and that he personally regrets it because he does not enjoy lying to people. He must make it perfectly clear to the subject that he could find no other way to test his predictions in a satisfactory manner. He must also provide the subject with an account of the experiment, why he thinks it is important, etc., in order to allow the subject to decide whether or not it was worthwhile. Obviously, it would be presumptuous for the experimenter to make light of the subject's discomfort or to suggest that everyone would agree that the scientific ends justify the means. The experimenter has no right to assume that his commitment to science is shared by the subject. Although a careful and thorough debriefing procedure is costly in terms of time and effort, it is well worth the price; it is our experience that a goodly number of subjects gain understanding of the complexity of experimentation and actually become enthusiastic about the research process in general, and the experiment in particular, as a direct result of the debriefing process. It also has the advantage of serving an educational-didactic purpose, which results in some "payment" to the subject for his services.

The above discussion is terribly vague; indeed, it is impossible to give concrete recommendations for actions based on the experimenter's expression of sincerity. As we have said, the experimenter should not embark on an experiment if he has not previously considered less extreme or less deceptive alternative procedures and judged them to be unsuitable. If he has proceeded in a conscientious manner, he should have no difficulty communicating this to the subject. Likewise, if he has a firm belief in the importance of his research, this should be easily communicable. If he lacks this belief, he has no business in the laboratory.

Let us attempt to be a bit more concrete by elaborating on the debriefing process. Debriefing, in itself, can cause a subject considerable embarrassment. Most people do not enjoy learning that they have acted in a gullible manner. Thus, even if the subject is convinced that the experimenter has not enjoyed deceiving him, he may feel foolish simply because he has been taken in. The experimenter can reduce this somewhat by explaining that he spent a great deal of time and effort constructing a situation which would be convincing. By so doing he assures the subject that being taken in does not in any way reflect on his gullibility, but rather it reflects on the credibility of the cover story. If the experiment is a viable one, then virtually all subjects will have believed the cover story. The experimenter should convey this fact to the subject in order to prevent him from feeling extraordinarily gullible.

Similarly, suppose the operations are such that they induce the subject to behave in a "negative" manner, for example, to conform in the Asch experiment. Clearly, if the experiment is designed to produce this kind of behavior, and if it is a good experiment, then most subjects will be manifesting this behavior at least some of the time. The experimenter should point this out to the subject and stress the fact that he is not extreme in this dimension; rather, the experimental operations must have been extremely powerful, since they induced this kind of behavior from most of the people who served as subjects.

In a later section of this chapter we recommend that the experimenter explain the true purpose of the experiment in a gradual fashion. Going even further, we would recommend that, where possible, the experimenter lead the subject to discover the truth about the experiment for himself. This technique has many scientific advantages which will be discussed in detail later in this chapter. It also has the great virtue of removing some of the possible negative consequences of debriefing. Specifically, when the subject gradually discovers the truth for himself, he is, in effect, showing the experimenter that he is not extremely gullible.

In experiments in social psychology, the subject can remain anonymous, except to the experimenter. That is, social psychologists tend to be interested in "human" behavior rather than in the behavior of any specific individual. Consequently, where the experimenter has invaded a subject's privacy by collecting unvolunteered data, it is only the experimenter who will ever be aware that a specific person behaved in a particular manner. Moreover, the experimenter has absolutely no interest in linking the person to the behavior. At the close of the session, the subject's data are transferred to a coded, unnamed data sheet. The very impersonality of this process is a great advantage ethically, because it eliminates some of the negative consequences of an invasion of privacy. At the close of the session the experimenter should advise the subject of his anonymity.

How can we be sure that the subject no longer feels uncomfortable? We can never be entirely sure. It is conceivable that, in order to be a "good sport" to help the experimenter save face, some subjects may pretend to be in good spirits while remaining in inner turmoil. The experimenter should not allow himself to be too easily satisfied by such pretenses. Rather, he should convince the subject that it is desirable for the latter to express any misgivings he might feel about the experiment. The best way of eliciting an honest expression of upset (if one exists) is to solicit the subject's aid in helping to improve the experiment. The rationale for this as well as a specific procedure will be discussed in a subsequent section.

Many experimental procedures are inherently disquieting whether or not deception is used. An experiment might require subjects to submit to painful electric shocks, perform monotonous tasks, undergo embarrassment, act aggressively toward another person, tell lies, resolve a moral dilemma, eat grasshoppers, etc. When deception is not involved, the problem is less intense because the subject can be told of these procedures in advance, and is free not to participate. Of course, it may be extremely difficult for him to refuse to participate, and thus the ethical problem is not completely removed, but ultimately he has much more choice than in a deception experiment. Whether or not deception is employed, an additional question arises: How much discomfort can an experimenter inflict on a subject in the name of science? We cannot answer this question definitively. The reasons for this should be clear. First, one cannot easily quantify psychological discomfort caused by an experimental procedure. As discussed previously, in most cases the amount of psychological discomfort is as much a function of the incidental demeanor of the experimenter as of the actual procedure involved. Also, the amount of discomfort should be weighed against the worth of the experiment. Few experimenters would cause even a small amount of discomfort to a subject "just for the hell of it," that is, without a clear idea of what they were after in the experiment. On the other hand, most experimenters might be willing to burden their subjects with some discomfort if the experiment were an important one and if there were no other way of performing it. But in practice, it is almost as difficult to arrive at an objective judgment of the ultimate importance of an experiment as it is to judge the extent of the subject's discomfort. Most experimenters feel that their own experiments are very important; however, their readers may not agree. A good rule of thumb should place the degree of discomfort at the mildest possible level which is consistent with the hypothesis; although this is far from ideal scientifically, it is a reasonable and necessary compromise. Similarly, the degree of discomfort an experimenter is willing to allow should also be a function of the number of precautions he takes. A given degree of discomfort may be within reasonable bounds if the experimenter has guarded against serious consequences. In this regard, the reader is referred to a recent controversy regarding Milgram's research (Baumrind, 1964; Milgram, 1964).

An additional consideration is the timing of the debriefing. Many experimenters find it efficacious to wait until after all the subjects have completed their participation before informing each subject of the true nature of the experiment. This is usually accomplished *en masse* through the use of a dittoed explanation. This procedure has certain economic and methodological advantages; namely, it saves time and it makes it impossible for a subject to reveal the true nature of the experiment to a future subject. There may be some experimental circumstances in which it can be usefully employed. However, we would *not* recommend this kind of shortcut debriefing where the deception or its revelation might be painful to the subject. Moreover, even if no discomfort has been caused, other aspects of an experiment may make it wise to debrief the subject immediately after the session. For example, in a typical opinion-change study, the subject may have changed his opinion because, in the experiment, a particular point of view was falsely attributed to a prestigious person. It would be undesirable for the experimenter to allow this changed opinion to affect the subject's behavior outside the laboratory. Clearly, the sooner the subject is debriefed, the better.

In addition, in many experimental situations students serve as subjects, and as mentioned previously, one of their reasons for volunteering (and one of our rationales for using them) is the educational value of the experience. If the experimenter personally provides the subject with a clear and detailed explanation of the experiment as soon as it ends, the subject receives maximum educational benefit from the experience.

It is conceivable that under some circumstances the experimenter may feel that the debriefing process should not be complete. For example, the experiment may be so complex that it is difficult and unnecessary to convey a complete picture of it to the subject. Under these circumstances the experimenter might present only those aspects of the experiment which are easily explainable and which are most relevant to the subject. It would be a mistake, however, to hold back aspects of the deception, especially if there is any possibility of the subject's discovering them on his own. This could result in a legitimate feeling of having been cheated.

No matter how skillfully an experimenter may explain the experiment and reestablish rapport with the subject, the fact remains that he has deceived the subject, and no amount of restoration can erase the fact that he *has* behaved dishonestly. Most experimental social psychologists are willing to assume this ethical burden, feeling that, if using deception experiments is the only feasible way to uncover an interesting fact, then the truths so uncovered are worth the lies told in the process so long as no harm befalls the subject. The experimenter can also take some comfort in the knowledge that in most cases, although the subject was not aware of the true purpose of the experiment, he at least knew that he was in an experiment. As such, he is aware of the fact that his relationship to the experimenter is that of a subject. Indeed, the two principals are, in effect, parties to an experimenter-subject contract. The occasional use of deception can be considered one of the implicit clauses in this contract. A significant minority of subjects, while not aware that there is deception in a given experiment and certainly not cognizant of what that deception might be, nevertheless have an inkling that things often are not what they seem in psychological experiments. Thus most of us, in debriefing subjects, will hear an occasional person saying "Yes, I had a feeling that there might be something more involved in the experiment, but I didn't know what it might be." In short, they are not shocked or even surprised that they were deceived. They *do* seem to accept this as part of an implicit bargain. Many experimenters find it desirable to make this implicit clause explicit by saying that some aspects of the experiment cannot be explained in advance and may be slightly different from what they appear to be.

An example may help illuminate this point. Consider a medical experiment testing the effectiveness of several tranquilizing drugs. Suppose that a volunteer is placed in the placebo condition. Obviously, the experimenter has not told him in advance that he was given a placebo rather than a tranquilizer. This is part of the experimental contract. The subject may feel foolish if he subsequently manifests behaviors associated with the taking of the test drug, but the deception in the experiment is not, in and of itself, a violation of the contract between the experimenter and the subject. However, if a patient comes to a physician complaining of hypertension and is given a pill and told it is a tranquilizer, he has a right to expect it to be a tranquilizer. He has entered into a therapeutic contract, not an experimental contract. It would be a serious violation of the therapeutic contract for a physician to decide to use this patient as an experimental subject by giving him a placebo and labeling it a tranquilizer.

In a social-psychological experiment, the same general rules apply. Suppose a subject volunteers for an experiment on group problem solving and the experimenter assigns a routine task to a male and a female subject. In the course of their performance of that task, the experimenter leaves the room and the female subject, who is very attractive, begins to flirt with the male subject. Suppose further that the female is really a confederate of the experimenter and the purpose of the experiment is to observe the subject's response to flirtation. Admittedly, such a situation is highly deceptive and constitutes an invasion of privacy. But this is tempered by the fact that the subject has come to that room willingly in order to participate in a psychological experiment. Compare this with a situation in which the confederate approaches the subject outside a classroom, in the dining hall, or in his dormitory, and engages in the same kind of flirtatious behavior. As soon as he makes a pass, the young lady explains that it was all an experiment and hands him a 25-item questionnaire. The latter situation has certain naturalistic advantages, but many experimental social psychologists might prefer to avoid it on the grounds that the "subject" has not entered into a contractual relationship. This procedure is more extreme than either a naturalistic observation study, in which a person's privacy is being invaded but his behavior is *not* being affected, or a laboratory deception experiment, in which the subject has agreed to be studied but has *not* agreed to reveal the specific aspects of himself that he is revealing. Rather, his behavior is being affected without his knowledge or permission regarding participation in any experiment. This is not to say that experiments should not be conducted in natural or field settings. We are merely suggesting that the experimenter should exercise a great deal of caution when he is outside the laboratory.

In sum, what we have been emphasizing in this section is that social-psychological experimentation often places the researcher in an ethical dilemma. The researcher must resolve this dilemma in a manner which avoids the extremes of (1) giving up the idea of experimentation in this area and (2) ignoring the rights of his experimental subjects. The experimenter should always keep the welfare of his subjects in mind, even if it involves compromising the impact of his experimental procedures. Most important, the experimenter, as he goes about his business, should never lose sight of the obligations he owes to his subjects, and should be constantly on the alert for alternative techniques.

PLANNING AND CONDUCTING AN EXPERIMENT

In this section we will attempt to present concrete suggestions for conducting an experiment. In general, there are five stages to the experimental process: (1) getting an idea and stating it in a researchable way; (2) setting the stage for the experiment; (3) constructing the independent variable; (4) deciding on a technique for measuring the dependent variable; (5) the postexperimental interview or debriefing session.

We shall not dwell on the problem of where ideas come from, save to say that few fields have the wide and diverse sources for ideas that exist in social psychology. First, of course, ideas come from the usual sources—from theories and from previous research. But in addition, since we all live in a social environment, ideas for experiments fairly leap at a person from countless aspects of his everyday life; indeed, every time we see, read about, or hear about some aspect of human interaction, we are tempted to explore it further. Ideas come while riding a bus, watching a ball game, scolding one's children, teaching class, reading *Time* magazine, or watching a movie. In one experiment (Walster, Walster, Abrahams, and Brown, 1966) the investigators hypothesized that forming a strong opinion of someone leads to an overcompensating reaction when one encounters irrefutable evidence to the contrary. In introducing their experiment, the investigators stated that they derived this hypothesis from several personal experiences (pp. 71–72). Similarly, Aronson, Willerman, and Floyd (1966) conducted an experiment in which they demonstrated that a blunder will *enhance* the attractiveness of a highly competent person. They developed this hypothesis after stumbling upon a statement in a national magazine to the effect that President Kennedy's popularity had increased immediately after the Bay of Pigs fiasco.

Where the idea comes from is not terribly important. Indeed, ideas—even interesting ones—are cheap in social psychology. The important and difficult feat involves translating a conceptual notion into a tight, workable, credible, meaningful set of experimental operations. All too often exciting ideas lose a great deal in translation. It is to this problem that we now turn.

SETTING THE STAGE

After getting an idea, the experimenter must determine how to bring it into the laboratory. Since there are very few standard operational procedures in experimental social psychology, this process often requires a great deal of imagination and ingenuity. The experimenter must create a set of procedures which captures the meaning of his conceptualization and which is workable. This not only demands the invention of a procedure for manipulating the independent variable and a method of measuring the effect this has on the subject's behavior; it also necessitates the concoction of a context—a setting within which the basic manipulations and measurements make sense and have impact, and which integrates all the necessary aspects of the experiment. In a deception experiment, the setting must include a false rationale for the research as well as a context which makes the experimental operations reasonable in terms of this rationale or "cover story."

Providing a cover story is necessary lest the subject attempt to decipher the reasons for the experiment. A good cover story is one which accounts for all the necessary aspects of the experiment in a plausible manner so as to prevent the subject from speculating about what the experimenter really has in mind. It also should capture the subject's attention so that he remains awake and responsive to the experimental manipulations. This is not meant facetiously; if a cover story strikes the subject as being a trivial or silly experiment, he may simply tune out. If the subject is not attending to the independent variable, it is guaranteed to have little impact on him.

The setting may be a relatively simple one or it may involve an elaborate scenario, depending on the demands of the situation. Obviously, the experimenter should set the stage as simply as possible. If a simple setting succeeds in providing a plausible cover story and in capturing the subject's attention, there is no need for greater elaboration. But frequently a more elaborate setting is necessary. For example, suppose one wants to make a subject fearful. One might achieve this simply by telling him that he will receive a strong electric shock. But one is much more confident of arousing strong fear if one has set the stage with a trifle more embellishment. This can be done by providing a medical atmosphere, inventing a medical rationale for the experiment, having the experimenter appear in a white laboratory coat, and allowing the subject to view some formidable electrical apparatus, as in Schachter's (1959) experiments. One might go even further by providing the subject with a mild sample shock, implying that the actual shocks will be much greater.

It is perhaps already clear that what we have called "setting the stage" not only leads into the independent variable, but is often part of it. That is, in the above example, the electrical paraphernalia, the medical cover story, the white coat, and the electric shock constitute the experimental manipulation as well as the setting. Indeed, in a well-built experiment it is often difficult to determine where the one leaves off and the other begins. Similarly, if the stage has been properly set, the measurement of the dependent variable follows naturally from the setting. The behavior asked for by the cover story may be, in fact, the actual dependent variable. For example, in the Asch (1951) experiment, the subject was told that the experiment was about his judgments of the lines. At the same time, his stated judgments of the lines were the crucial data; they were the dependent variable of the actual experiment. Similarly, in Milgram's (1963) study the dependent variable was the point at which the subject ceased administering the electric shocks, the same electric shocks which were an integral part of the cover experiment. This technique is not always possible, however. More often, the dependent variable is not the behavior asked for by the cover story, but some other behavior. For example, in Festinger and Carlsmith's (1959) experiment on forced compliance, the crucial datum was an evaluation of a boring task that the subject had performed. These data were not collected until after the cover experiment was completed, and they were collected not by the experimenter but by a totally different person for an apparently nonexperimental purpose. Similarly, in Schachter's (1951) experiment on deviation and rejection, the attractiveness of various group members was the dependent variable; the data were collected after the group had met and were not an integral part of the cover experiment. A similar technique was used in the experiment by Aronson and Mills (1959), where subjects were asked, seemingly as an afterthought, to evaluate the group they had joined. Although the data collection cannot always be integral to the cover story, it is important that it not appear tacked on; it must make sense in terms of the general setting. For example, in Schachter's (1951) experiment, the attractiveness of the group members was measured by the poshness of the committee assignments that the members awarded to each of their fellows and by the nature of their selections when asked to reconstitute the group for a future meeting.

Let us conclude this section by taking another look at the Aronson-Mills (1959) experiment (previously described on pp. 4–5). Here we shall indicate how each aspect of the setting enhanced the impact and/or plausibility of the independent and dependent variables and contributed to the control of the experiment. The major problem presented by the hypothesis was that of justifying an initiation for admission to a group. This was solved by (1) the format of a sex discussion and (2) the cover story that the experimenters were interested in studying the dynamics of the discussion process. Combining these two aspects of the setting, (3) one could then mention the fact that shyness about sex distorts the discussion process so that (4) it is necessary to eliminate those people who are shy about sexual matters by (5) presenting the subject with an embarrassment test.

All aspects of the setting led directly to the manipulation of the independent variable in a manner that made good sense to the subjects, thereby allaying any suspicions. Moreover, this setting allowed the experimenter to use a tape-recorded group discussion (for the sake of control) while at the same time maintaining the fiction that it was an ongoing group discussion (for the sake of impact). The experimenter simply informed the subjects that some participants *still* found it difficult to talk about sex freely because the presence of others staring at them made them self-conscious; therefore, to make it easier on the participants, they were placed in separate cubicles and communicated through microphones and earphones.

This fiction of an already formed group was made to serve a dual function. It also allowed the experimenter to explain to the subject that the members had been recruited before the initiation was made a requirement for admission. This procedure eliminated a possible confounding variable: namely, that subjects might like the group better in the severe-initiation condition because of the feeling that they had gone through a common harrowing experience.

Finally, because of the manner in which the stage had been set, the dependent variable, the evaluation of the group, seemed a very reasonable request. In many experimental contexts, obtaining a rating of attractiveness is difficult because it often arouses suspicions. In this context, however, it was not jarring to the subject to be told that each member stated her opinion of each discussion session, and therefore it did not surprise the subject when she was asked for her frank evaluation of the proceedings of the meeting. Ultimately, the success of a setting in integrating the various aspects of the experiment is an empirical question: Do the subjects find it plausible? In the Aronson-Mills experiment only one of 64 subjects expressed any suspicions.

The testing of some hypotheses is more difficult than others because of their very nature. But none is impossible; with sufficient patience and ingenuity a reasonable context can be constructed to integrate the independent and dependent variables regardless of the problems inherent in the hypothesis.

CONSTRUCTING THE INDEPENDENT VARIABLE

How does an experimenter actually go about choosing and constructing some independent variable? Unfortunately, there are few standard, agreed-upon techniques. In this area, few experimental manipulations are identical; rather, the researcher must construct an experiment to fit his situation, borrowing only ideas and innovations from previous work. This is the case because, for the most part, social-psychological experiments depend so heavily on the special nature of the subculture in which they are presented that even those relatively standard procedures which do exist must be modified drastically so that they make sense in terms of the particular population the experimenter is working with. Thus it is useless to outline specific techniques for varying cohesiveness, self-esteem, effort, commitment, conformity, aggression, guilt, or whatever. These may be gleaned from specific reports and used where appropriate. What we hope to be able to do in this section is to provide some general guidelines, some rules of thumb, some intuitions, and some recommendations which may serve to direct an experimenter toward a sensible and effective manipulation of his independent variable.

The first and perhaps most important guideline grows out of our earlier discussion of the advantages of the experiment over the correlational study. If we are to carry out an experiment, we must determine by the principle of randomization exactly which treatment each subject gets. Such a statement may seem obvious, but in practice there is a seemingly infinite number of paths to failure. The most common potential pitfall occurs when the independent variable of concern is something which we feel is already inside the person, and so we do not try to manipulate it directly; instead, we measure it and then look at its effects. For example, if we are concerned with differences in performance of subjects with high and low self concepts, we might give some scale which measures self-esteem and compare "highs" and "lows" on the performance we are interested in. This, of course, is nothing more than a correlational study, even though it may be performed in the laboratory with a high degree of control over the subsequent measures. As a correlational study, of course, it suffers from all the indigenous weaknesses already described.

This can be avoided. In many cases it is possible to effect a temporary systematic change even in relatively important aspects of a person's personality characteristics through the judicious employment of an experimental manipulation. Typically, one can influence personality characteristics only for a short period of time and only in one small area; but that may be enough for the purposes of the hypothesis involved. Aronson and Carlsmith (1962) did attempt to vary a person's self concept experimentally by taking one small area of that self concept—social sensitivity—and giving the subject a series of tests followed by false feedback about his ability in that area. By so doing, they succeeded in convincing one group of subjects that they had a high degree of social sensitivity and another group that they were low on this dimension. The resulting differences between subjects were probably not so large as those which would have been observed had Aronson and Carlsmith selected subjects who scored high and low on a test of the relevant ability. But the great advantage of their procedure was that the treatments were under the direct control of the experimenter. We are not suggesting that existing individual differences are unimportant. Their investigation is important as an end in itself. Moreover, when used in conjunction with a good experimental technique, evidence concerning individual differences can add a good deal to the precision of the experiment. For example, a measure of "chronic" self-esteem of subjects *before* their self concept was changed experimentally would provide useful information. But a measure of "chronic" self-esteem by itself is of limited use because of ambiguities which we have already discussed.

Nonrandom assignment of subjects to experimental conditions is not confined to the use of personality measures in lieu of experimental treatments. It usually takes place in more subtle ways. One of the most common occurs when the experimenter is forced to perform an "internal analysis" in order to make sense out of his data. In this case, the experimenter has tried to assign subjects randomly, but when he looks at the effects of his independent variable, he finds that it was not powerful enough to make a discernible difference between his conditions. But suppose he has had the insight to provide an independent test of the effectiveness of his experimental treatment. This "check on the manipulation" is useful in that it provides the experimenter with important information. For example, if the experimenter tried to lower a subject's anxiety, he might want to measure anxiety afterward in order to determine the success of his procedure. If the procedure is unsuccessful, one would not expect it to produce a discernible effect on the dependent variable. If an experiment fails, experimenters occasionally analyze the data separately, depending on whether or not the procedure was successful; that is, they separate subjects into two conditions on the basis of their response to this manipulation check. This is an internal analysis. As an example, Schachter (1959) attempted to vary the extent of anxiety experienced by his subjects through varying the description of the task the subjects were to engage in. However, in some of these studies, when subjects reported their anxiety levels, it appeared that many who had been given the treatment designed to produce low anxiety were actually more anxious than some who were given the high-anxiety treatment. When one looks at the results of an internal analysis of these data, anxiety does seem to be related to the dependent variable. Again, these data can be useful and provocative, but since the effect was not due to the manipulated variable, no causal statement can be made. Although many of the "highly anxious" subjects were made anxious by the "high-anxiety" manipulation, many were highly anxious on their own (so to speak). Since people who become anxious easily may be different kinds of animals from those who do not, we are dealing with a personality variable. This means that we are no longer dealing with random assignment.

Another situation in which the treatments are assigned nonrandomly occurs when the subject assigns himself to the experimental conditions. That is, in certain experimental situations the subject, in effect, is given his choice of which of two procedures to engage in. The experimenter then compares the subsequent behavior of subjects who choose one alternative with those who choose the other. For example, in one experiment, Wallace and Sadalla (1966) placed subjects in a room with a complex machine and had a confederate tempt them to press a conspicuous button on the front of it. When a subject pressed the button, the machine exploded. Unfortunately, whether or not a particular subject opted to press the button was determined by the subject himself. Since there may be important differences between those who choose to press and those who do not, the experimenters have relinquished control of the situation to the subject and are left with a nonexperimental study.

The problem of free choice is a particularly sticky one because, if the hypothesis involves the effects of choice, it is of obvious importance to give the subject a perception of clear choice. Yet this perception must remain nothing more than a perception, for as soon as the subject takes advantage of it we are beset with the problems of nonrandom assignment.

One solution to this problem is to pilot-test until a level of a variable is found which is just sufficient to inhibit subjects from actually choosing the "wrong" behavior. For example, in the experiment by Aronson and Carlsmith (1963) in which children were given either a mild or a severe threat to prevent them from playing with a desirable toy, it was important to make the mild threat strong enough to ensure compliance. On the other hand, it could not be too strong, for the experimental hypothesis hinged upon the child's not having a terribly good reason for declining to play with the toy. The situation had to be one where the child was making a choice whether to play or not to play and was bothered by the lack of a good reason to avoid playing with the toy. It is sometimes possible to find such a level by elaborate pretesting.

In some experimental situations a different solution can be effected through the use of instructions which give a strong perception of choice, although little choice is actually present. For example, one might present some of the relevant negative information about a choice after the person has committed himself to the decision under circumstances where the decision is irrevocable and the implication is strong that any reasonably intelligent person would have been aware of these aspects of the chosen alternative and that, indeed, few subjects chose this alternative.

Assuming that one is able to get subjects randomly assigned to conditions, how does one go about manipulating an independent variable? As we see it, there are three major problems to concern the experimenter when he tries to construct an experimental variable. First, what specific event should he use to correspond with his theoretical variable? (This problem has been discussed at length, from a theoretical point of view, in a previous section; below, we offer a few suggestions which are somewhat more concrete.) Second, how is he to present this variable so as to have maximum impact on the subject, and how does he know that he has had the impact he wanted? Third, if the results are such that they could be affected by "cooperative" subjects, how is the experimenter to prevent the subject from realizing the effect this variable is supposed to have on his behavior?

The basic decision for the experimenter to make is whether his independent variable will be produced by some set of instructions to the subject, or whether it will be some event which happens to the subject. In practice these two techniques are not always completely separable; the two usually blend into each other, at least slightly. Most "event" experiments contain some verbal instructions to the subject, at least as a means of setting the stage. In other experiments, some of the instructions consist of descriptions of things which might happen to the subject. Nevertheless, it is possible to separate the two conceptually. A good example of the manipulation of an independent variable primarily through the use of instructions is to be found in the well-known "group cohesiveness" experiments conducted by Festinger and his colleagues (for example, Back, 1951; Festinger and Thibaut, 1951; Schachter, 1951). In these experiments the cohesiveness of a group was usually varied simply by informing the subject that the group members were specially selected so that they would like one another (high cohesiveness) or that, try as he might, the experimenter was unable to accomplish this feat (low cohesiveness). A different approach is to use a group-cohesiveness manipulation in which the confederates actually perform attractive acts. Similarly, in an experiment by Cohen (1959), effort was varied merely by informing subjects that a communication they were about to read would be difficult (or easy) to understand. This can be contrasted with an "event" manipulation of effort such as delayed auditory feedback (Zimbardo, 1965), the reciting of obscene words (Aronson and Mills, 1959), or electric shock (Gerard and Mathewson, 1966). Again, these "event" manipulations were preceded by an important set of verbal instructions.

Theoretically, the difference between the two techniques is intimately tied up with our earlier discussion of "control versus impact." Typically, when things happen to a subject, we have much less control over them (and their interpretation) than when we read a list of statements or instructions to him. On the other hand, it is almost always the case that events which happen to a subject during the course of an experiment will have a far greater impact on him than a mere set of instructions. For example, being told that a group has similar values or that you will find a group to be attractive is almost certain to have less impact on people than the existence of real people doing "attractive" things. However, how can we be sure that subjects will interpret these behaviors as "attractive"?

In spite of the problem posed by the difficulty of interpretation, we would favor the use of an event rather than a set of instructions. As discussed previously, the meaning of an event can often be ascertained through the process of purification, whereby different events with overlapping meanings can be used to test the same hypothesis in different experiments. In addition, it is often possible to increase the likelihood that an event will be interpreted by the subject in the same way that the experimenter interprets it. In some experimental situations this can be accomplished through the skillful combination of events and instructions. An example is a recent experiment (Landy and Aronson, in press) in which the investigators wished to test the hypothesis that if subjects were positively evaluated by a "discerning" confederate, they would like the confederate better than if he were nondiscerning; whereas, if they were negatively evaluated by a discerning confederate, they would *dislike* him more than if he were nondiscerning. How does one vary the subject's perception of the confederate's ability to discern? One could do it by instruction; that is, one could simply say to the subject, "Say, by the way, this fellow has a great deal of discernment—I thought you might be interested." But for reasons to be discussed in the next paragraph, the investigators felt it would be best to allow the subject to discover this on his own. They therefore had the confederate perform a task in the presence of the subject; the task was such that, by varying the confederate's behavior, the subject might easily regard the confederate as discerning or nondiscerning. The word "might" is a problem. The subject *might* interpret this behavior in a multitude of ways. In order to be certain that the subject would consider this behavior as being relevant to discernment and nothing else, the investigators (1) asked the subject to observe the confederate's behavior on a task (in the context of an experiment on social judgment); (2) told the subject that "degree of discernment" was an aspect of the confederate's behavior which was particularly interesting to the experimenter; (3) asked the subject to rate the confederate's discernment; (4) informed the subject exactly how the confederate's behavior might reflect high or low discernment; (5) had the confederate behave either one way or the other; (6) had (in the form of the subject's actual rating) a handy and meaningful check on the manipulation. It can readily be seen that this technique is a compromise. It may lack the impact of obscene words or electric shock, but it certainly has more potential impact than a set of verbal instructions, while at the same time it capitalizes on the easy interpretability of these instructions.

The advantages of events over instructions are even clearer when we consider the third problem, that of the subject's becoming aware of our hypothesis and allowing this awareness to influence his behavior. For many if not most experiments in social psychology, the ideal manipulation of an independent variable is an event that happens to the subject which he does not connect with the experiment at all. This is the best way to guarantee that he has no hypotheses of concern to the experimenter. It is also frequently the best way to guarantee that the manipulation has an impact on the subject. A subject told that a particular communication was written by T. S. Eliot (Aronson, Turner, and Carlsmith, 1963) may yawn and ignore this fact, or, still more important, may have the detachment necessary to sit back, relax, and begin to develop hypotheses that the experimenter is concerned with the effect of high-prestige communicators. For this reason, this manipulation was a relatively weak one. But consider a subject suddenly faced with the fact that a person, to whom he has been administering electric shocks, is now kicking, screaming, and asking to be let out of his room (Milgram, 1963); or consider a subject who discovers that suddenly the equipment in the experiment has short-circuited and he is in danger of being electrocuted (Ax, 1953). Or consider a subject who, to his dismay, discovers that a group of normal-looking people *all* judge the length of a line differently from him. These subjects are unlikely to yawn or to start playing the intellectual game of "being a subject." In a very real sense they are too busy to play such games; they have problems of their own (like what to do about this poor fellow who's screaming in the next room).

One can list several classes of techniques which have been used successfully to present the independent variable as an event unrelated to the experiment, and which accordingly have a maximum impact on the subject and are not perceived as something to hypothesize about. Many experiments have actually used a combination of several of these techniques. Perhaps the most effective, but one of the more difficult to set up, is the "accident." The Ax (1953) experiment mentioned above is one of the best examples of this. In this experiment, while the subject was connected to an electrical recording apparatus, it "accidentally" gave him an electric shock. The experimental assistant behaved as if the situation was out of control; he depressed a lever causing sparks to fly from the apparatus and exclaimed in confusion that there appeared to be a dangerous short circuit in the system. Another example comes from the experiment by Wallace and Sadalla (1966). Recall that in this experiment the subject was tempted (by a confederate) to touch a large button projecting from some apparatus. When he touched it, it exploded and the apparatus was apparently destroyed. Festinger and Carlsmith (1959) used a similar technique when they told the subject that due to an accident, the regular confederate had not shown up, and the subject was asked to play the role of the confederate. Indeed, this general procedure has been used so frequently and so effectively that it might be said that part of being a good experimental social psychologist involves learning to say "whoops" convincingly.

A variation on this procedure is to have a confederate who introduces the manipulation of the independent variable. This procedure is easier, but more likely to arouse suspicion. For example, in an experiment by Aronson and Linder (1965), the subject heard herself being evaluated by the confederate in the context of a verbal-reinforcement experiment. Since this was described to the subject as a standard part of the procedure, it struck a few subjects as odd that such volatile material would be used to measure the effects of reinforcement on verbal behavior. The ideal is to have it appear that this manipulation is an event which happens only once (namely, to this particular subject), not that it is or even could be something which happens regularly. For example, Schachter and Singer (1962) attempted to manipulate euphoria by having a confederate who waltzed around the room shooting rubber bands, playing with hula hoops, and practicing hook shots into the wastebasket with wadded paper. Presumably, this behavior was interpreted by the subject as an accidental or a unique event unrelated to the experiment. Similarly, Brehm and Cole (1966) attempted to produce feelings of "reactance" in the subject by having a confederate place the subject in the position of feeling obligated. They accomplished this by having the confederate buy himself a Coke from the vending machine and "thoughtfully" bring one back for the subject. This unique event, although it appeared to be unrelated to the experiment, succeeded in making the subject somewhat uncomfortable in his feelings toward the confederate.

A third method of having the independent variable perceived as independent of the experiment is to use the whole experiment as the independent variable, measuring the dependent variable at some later time. This is rather difficult, in practice, since a subject may look at some of the events as intended to manipulate him; but if the procedure is carried out well, he is unlikely to perceive the whole experience as a manipulation. For example, Carlsmith and Gross (in press) performed an experiment aimed at investigating the effects of hurting someone on subsequent compliance. In their experiment they induced their subjects to shock a confederate. The entire procedure was presented as a learning experiment, with subjects acting as teachers. After the subjects performed their chore, the experiment was explained and terminated. At a later time, the confederate made a request for compliance. The subjects responded to this request completely without awareness that it was part of the experiment.

A fourth general technique, and one of the best when it is feasible, is to have no aura of an "experiment" at all. The independent variable is introduced in such a way that it appears to the subject to be unrelated to any experiment. A good example is the experiment by Abelson and Miller (1967) in which a confederate ridiculed the subject's opinion as part of a man-on-the-street interview. Since the subject was approached by the "interviewer" while sitting on a park bench minding his own business, he was completely unaware of the fact that an experiment was being conducted. In another vein, Milgram (1966) has been using a technique in which he distributes stamped addressed envelopes where they can be found by subjects. The question is, does the subject drop the envelope in the mailbox? In these studies the address on the envelope constitutes the independent variable. Clearly, the subject either mails or does not mail the envelope without any awareness that he is participating in an experiment.

The question of how to present the independent variable so as to have maximum impact on the subject and, at the same time, to be sure that it has the correct impact is one that cannot be answered with a list of techniques. Yet some important general guidelines can be established. We feel that at the heart of the question is one crucial yet frequently misunderstood point: it is extremely important for all subjects to be brought to the identical point by the manipulation of the independent variable. This does not necessarily mean that all subjects be exposed to the identical version of the independent variable. What it *does* mean is that the experimenter use his skill and wisdom to see to it that all subjects understand the instructions at pretty much the same level. To achieve this goal, the experimenter should allow himself considerable latitude in delivering his instructions. This is a tricky suggestion, and one that many investigators might take issue with. Our point is this: in their zeal for standardization, many experimenters are prone to have all instructions to the subject tape-recorded or printed, trying to ensure that all subjects are exposed to identical stimuli. Such a goal is admirable, but in practice it ignores the fact that people are different, and that the same instructions do not mean the same thing to all subjects. More prosaically, yet more importantly, subjects differ greatly in their ability to understand instructions. For example, one of the most common mistakes the novice experimenter makes is to present his instructions too briefly; consequently, a large percentage of the subjects fail to understand some of the important aspects of the instructions. To ensure that all subjects understand what is going on in an experiment (especially one as complicated as most social-psychological experiments), a good deal of redundancy must be present.

More important than simple redundancy, however, is ensuring that each subject fully understands all the instructions and events that occur in the experiment. This can be done only by a combination of clear instructions, questions, pauses, and probes in which the experimenter repeats or paraphrases key parts of the instructions until he satisfies himself that the subject is completely clear about all of them. The point seems obvious, but it has been our experience that many experiments have failed precisely because the instructions were never made clear and redundant enough to get through to all the subjects.

An example from a recent study may point up the difficulties. In an experimental investigation of compliance (Carlsmith and Gross, in press) there were three participants: a teacher (the true subject or a confederate), a learner (a confederate), and a witness (the true subject or a confederate). In order to keep one confederate (the learner) blind as to what condition the subject was in, it was important that he not know whether the true subject was the teacher or the witness. However, it was also important that the subject know what role the two confederates were in. Accordingly, the three participants were separated by partitions so they could not see each other; the true subject was brought into the experimental room alone and the whole experiment was explained to him, with heavy emphasis on which person (sitting where) would play which role. Despite strong attempts to make the instructions redundant, 12 of the first 15 subjects missed enough of the instructions so that they did not know which confederate was in which role. It was only by chance that postexperimental probing revealed this ignorance, which would have vitiated the entire experiment. By having the confederates wear very different clothes, by having the true subject introduced to one but not the other before the experiment began, and by making the description "overly" redundant, it was finally possible to get that key fact of the experiment into the subjects' heads.

There should be little argument over the merits of making sure that the subject understands the experiment by using simple and redundant instructions. What we are suggesting goes beyond this, however. First, although instructions should be clear and repetitious, it is unwise to make them too repetitious, lest the brighter subjects become bored or annoyed. Moreover, regardless of how clear or repetitious a set of instructions is, there are bound to be some subjects who miss the point. Thus the same instructions may simultaneously escape some subjects and annoy others by being too simple. How can one avoid this? A good experimenter can and should be able to judge whether or not a particular subject is comprehending the instructions. We recommend that the experimenter modify his instructions accordingly. If, in the course of delivering his instructions, redundant as they may be, the experimenter sees a vacant or uncomprehending look on a given subject's countenance, he should increase his efforts to get through to that subject, even at the expense of departing from a standard set of instructions. Again, we anticipate that many experimenters will disagree with us, suggesting that standardization is the hallmark of an experiment. We feel that way too, but exactly what is it that should be standardized? What the experimenter says or what the subject understands and feels? Of course, by allowing the experimenter to depart from a standardized script, one increases the possibility of introducing systematic bias. But if proper techniques are employed to eliminate bias, this ceases to be a problem. (Some of these techniques are discussed elsewhere in this chapter.) In addition, the experimenter should keep a record of exactly what was said to each subject, in the interests of replicability.

It is possible to carry this still further, to a point beyond the presentation of instructions and into procedures which might entail the presentation of dramatically different stimuli to different subjects. This is shaky ground indeed, and here the authors of this chapter are not themselves in agreement (E. A. taking a more conservative position than J. M. C.). In any event, let us present a polarizing example. Suppose we want to study the effects of sexual arousal on liking. Our independent variable consists of getting all subjects sexually aroused. Should we present each subject with the same written material which we hope will get him sexually aroused, or should we use different written material with different subjects, trying to find that kind of material which will arouse each subject? "Stimulus standardization" argues for the first, but although that is desirable when feasible, it may be much more important to see to it that all subjects are in the state which we hope the independent variable will produce, even if different amounts or even kinds of events are required to get them there.

Consider the analogous situation in animal research. If we want to study the effects of anxiety on some performance and we decide to arouse anxiety by administering an appropriate drug, we do not administer the same amount to each subject. Typically, the variation comes about because we correct for some individual-difference factor, such as the animal's weight. Thus, although we administer different dosages to each animal, we are, in fact, administering a "standard" amount per kilogram of body weight. But at other times we may determine the amount we give by some aspect of the animal's performance; for example, we might administer enough dosage to cause the animal's bar-pressing rate to drop off by 50 percent.

Some of the resistance to a flexible administration of the independent variable in social psychology stems from the fact that, at the present state of development of our techniques, we lack procedures for deciding how much of a given variable is needed for a given subject to bring him to some standardized level. Occasionally we can find such a procedure. For example, in order to determine sexual arousal, we might attach a subject to a phalloplethismograph and continue to present material until a given response is observed. More typically, however, we must rely on what cues the subject can give us as to whether our manipulations have succeeded in arousing the independent variable we hoped for. These cues may be subtle behavioral responses or they may be gross verbal reports.

The great difficulty with all this, of course, is that we cannot always specify exactly what we did. But often we can. To return again to our sexual-arousal example, we might have a standard series of literary selections which we present one at a time until the subject is aroused. When this is not possible, it would be desirable to have several experimenters carry out the same experiment. If the results are similar across experimenters, then we can be confident in our ability to specify what it is they were all doing, or at least that we can communicate it (since we were able to communicate it to each of them). In fact, we can be more certain that we varied, say, aggression, if we have six experimenters who each act "aggressive" in their own way, and all of them produce similar results, than if we have just one experimenter behaving in a completely standardized way.

Obviously it is desirable to be able to specify in exact detail just what was done with a subject. And as techniques become better and we become more and more certain how to manipulate variables, it may be possible to develop increasingly specific and standardized methods. But until that time arrives, and so long as we interact with the subject, variability in the way an experimenter interacts with different subjects is inevitable. We are *not* recommending that experimenters go out of their way to present variable instructions. Our recommendation is that we recognize that variability exists in the subject's understanding of the instructions, and that on occasion, we might consciously increase stimulus variability in order that there be less variability in what is actually going on in the subject's head.

How can we be sure that we have the right realization of our theoretical independent variable? How do we know that this particular complex bundle of stimuli which we present to the subject really is arousing what we think or hope it is? We have discussed some of the answers to this question at an abstract theoretical level; here we will attempt to present some practical advice on how one might determine it. The most general technique for finding out just what an independent-variable manipulation is doing is to run some pretests. During the pretesting, one can conduct long, probing interviews with the subject after the experiment or better yet, after the manipulation of the independent variable. Often the subject is capable of providing valuable hints as to where the weaknesses in the manipulation occurred, and as to parts of it which caused competing reactions to the one the experimenter wanted to effect. If deception is used, the subject is the best source of information concerning the effectiveness and credibility of the cover story. Such interviews can, of course, be continued during the time the experiment is actually being run, but it is usually during pretesting that the most valuable information is obtained. As implied above, it is often important to run pretest subjects for whom the independent variable is manipulated and who are then immediately interviewed. For if one also attempts to collect data on the dependent variable, it may be that the subject would no longer be able to describe how he had been affected by the independent variable. For example, in a dissonance study, the subject might well report that the manipulation of the independent variable had aroused no dissonance or discomfort whatever, if he had succeeded in reducing all of that dissonance via his responses to the dependent variable. Thus, in the study by Festinger and Carlsmith (1959), subjects might well report at the end of the experiment that they felt that $1.00 was a perfectly sufficient reward for the behavior, if they had already changed their attitudes so as to reduce most of the dissonance which had been created. However, if they were interviewed immediately after agreeing to perform the task, they might be better able to describe whether the variable had caused the appropriate effect. This problem is the major difficulty with introspective reports as a technique; too often subjects are unable or unwilling to explain just what the effects of some manipulation have been. Following an experiment, it is not at all uncommon to have a subject deny any feelings of the kind the experimenter hoped to arouse, while at the same time his actual behavior implies strongly that he had experienced precisely those feelings. By obtaining introspective reports immediately after the manipulation of the independent variable (in a pretest), one increases the likelihood of obtaining useful information; however, it is still not certain that subjects will be able to describe their feelings adequately.

A more difficult but far better technique of checking whether the independent variable is having the desired effect is to run a number of pretest subjects, collecting data on whether some other behavior corresponds with the independent variable in an appropriate way. We have already discussed this technique, but will elaborate on it here. Let us look again at the experiment by Aronson and Carlsmith (1963) in which children were asked not to play with an attractive toy. In one condition the admonition was in the form of a mild threat; in the other it was in the form of a severe threat. Although intuitively the two threats seemed to differ along a dimension of severity, it would have been desirable to pin this down by providing independent evidence of this difference. One way of doing this would be simply to ask the children how severe the threat was, but this was neither feasible nor valuable in the context of that experiment. As was previously mentioned, a better technique would be to run other subjects in a pretest in which the toys were made more desirable, so that a number of the children would in fact disobey the admonition. In the experiment as run, the threat was severe enough that, with the toys actually used, no child deviated. If the toys were made more desirable and if more children disobeyed the admonition under the mild threat than under the severe threat, we could be confident that the experimenters had manipulated severity of threat. This can best be done as a separate experiment; however, such a procedure is frequently tedious and is therefore not so common as it should be. It is sometimes possible to collect such data in the experiment proper. Typically, however, such checks are merely questionnaires given to the subject. For example, in an experiment designed to produce anxiety, one might ask a subject whether or not he felt anxious during the experiment. Although such questionnaires may sometimes be useful, they rarely provide a complete solution to the problem, for reasons discussed earlier. Certainly the best solution is to observe some other behavior which we expect to covary directly with our theoretical variable and see whether it does, as when a GSR is used to monitor anxiety throughout the course of the experiment (see, for example, Zimbardo *et al.*, 1966).

Finally, pretesting can provide an additional check on our independent variable by allowing us to find the precise intensity of the manipulation which will enable us to study its effects. For example, if one were conducting a study of obedience, it would be desirable for about half the subjects to obey and half to disobey, so that one could see differences between different experimental treatments. Fairly elaborate pretesting may sometimes be necessary to set levels of the independent variable which are neither so high that virtually all subjects obey nor so low that virtually no one obeys.

The number of independent variables

How many phenomena should one vary in a single experiment? There are no pat answers to this question. It is often desirable to manipulate more than one independent variable because certain events emerge only in interaction with others. Moreover, we become much more certain that our results are *not* merely an artifact of a specific operational definition if we can demonstrate interactions. For example, Aronson, Willerman, and Floyd (1966) predicted that a clumsy blunder would enhance the attractiveness of a highly competent person because (they reasoned) it would make him appear more human and, hence, more approachable. In their experiment, a person who had demonstrated that he was very bright committed a clumsy and embarrassing blunder, spilling a cup of coffee all over himself. As predicted, this increased his attractiveness—he was rated more attractive than the same competent person who did *not* spill coffee. But these results could simply be a function of the fact that coffee-spilling is not really so much a clumsy act as it is a charming act. That is, we may like people who spill coffee because coffee-spilling, in and of itself, is an endearing, attractive thing to do. But in this experiment, the authors also varied the competence of the stimulus person. In addition to a highly competent person, they exposed the subject to an incompetent person who either spilled or did not spill coffee. They found, as predicted, that the incompetent coffee-spiller was *less* attractive than the incompetent nonspiller. Thus, the experiment demonstrated that coffee-spilling, in and of itself, is no virtue; it only enhances the attractiveness of particular kinds of people, not all people.

We can see, then, that in certain situations, investigating combinations of variables adds essential clarity to an experimental finding. One could also vary several points along one or more continua. For example, one could build an experiment which contained three or four levels of competence and three or four levels of blundering. One could also add new dimensions. For example, we might want to measure the authoritarianism, competence, or masculinity of the subjects, vary the sex of the stimulus person, or introduce high or low cohesiveness, in order to determine how these variables interact with the competence-blunder relationship. Why not?

Why not, indeed? Theoretically, there is no limit to the number of factors one might vary. But in practice it is essential to realize that the more tests, measures, instructions, and events one hurls at the poor subject, the more confused, bored, irritated, or resentful he is apt to become. We cannot state specific rules for how complex an experiment should be. Our own rule of thumb is that it should be only as complex as is necessary for the important relationships to emerge in a clear manner. The "why not" approach to psychological research is frequently self-defeating. Simply because Professor Doe happens to have a measure of self-actualization lying around is no justification for plugging it heedlessly into every experiment being done under Doe's supervision. Such procedures often accomplish nothing but a blunting of the impact of the major variables in a procedure.

The advantages of a live experimenter

In an attempt to avoid bias and gain a kind of control over the stimuli presented to the subjects, many experimenters have turned, indiscriminately, to the use of canned operations in the form of tape recordings or printed instructions. It should be perfectly clear that there are many situations in which the use of these techniques is justified and even essential. On the other hand, we should not lose sight of the fact that a live experimenter is not simply a bias-producing machine; he is frequently a necessary ingredient in the experimental process. We have already discussed the important role an experimenter can play in making certain that all subjects understand the instructions. In addition, the live experimenter can frequently succeed in keeping the subject interested and attentive and, more important, in "selling" a cover story—to a degree that cannot possibly be matched by canned instructions, no matter how thoroughly they may have been prepared and produced. Often, when we read an experimental procedure of a deception experiment as reported in a journal article, we are struck by the simplicity and transparency of the subterfuge and are amazed that it was successful. But the success of a cover story in disguising the true purpose of the experiment cannot be judged solely by looking at the words spoken by the experimenter. The manner of delivery makes a crucial difference. This is enhanced by the physical presence of the experimenter who, through the earnestness of his demeanor and by the simple device of maintaining eye contact with the subject, can frequently succeed in convincing him that the "experimental problem" described in the cover story is not only a legitimate object of scientific inquiry, but even an interesting and exciting area of investigation.

Moreover, just as the live experimenter can detect the fact that the subject is not understanding a set of instructions, he might also detect when a subject begins to appear incredulous and may *deviate slightly from his prepared script* in order to allay the doubts that may be creeping into the mind of an occasional subject. Just as some subjects are, by nature or experience, brighter or more wide-awake than others, some subjects are more suspicious than others. For this reason, it would be absurd for the experimenter to avoid attempting to allay these suspicions in the name of the false god, stimulus control. Again, what we are advocating is *not* the abandonment of control, but rather the achievement of a richer kind of control through attempting to have subjects in approximately the same state of mind when the major independent variable hits them. Let us reemphasize the fact that the live experimenter often presents possibilities of bias in experiments. We are well aware of this. But there are many ways of avoiding bias which do not sacrifice the advantages of the "personal touch" of the breathing experimenter who, in our opinion, has not been and should not become another victim of automation. The problem of bias and techniques for avoiding it will be discussed shortly.

Parenthetically, it should be pointed out that "facing up" to a subject has other advantages as well. One of the more important is that, in attempting to convey a set of instructions to a subject, the experimenter may come to realize that these instructions are not viable; there is nothing quite like a yawn in the face to convince the experimenter that his instructions are dull and unmotivating. Similarly, if deception is used, there is nothing like the pitying look of an incredulous subject to convince us that we had best go back to the drawing board. As mentioned above, a talented experimenter can occasionally "sell" a rather incredible cover story. At the same time, there are some experimental situations which are inherently so transparent that a very sophisticated and elaborate cover story is required. In dealing with our own research assistants, we have found that we can waste a great deal of time and energy trying to convince a novice experimenter that his cover story is inadequate. A pilot trial on one subject is far more convincing.

Thus the live, two-way exchange between subject and experimenter is a great instructional device. Few things are as unnerving (and, therefore, as educational) as being stuck for an hour with a subject who makes it clear that he doesn't believe a word you're saying and couldn't care less. To avoid such experiences, we build better, more impactful experiments. A good experiment never bores a subject unless boredom is the conceptual variable.

Who's running this experiment, anyway?

We have placed great emphasis on the experimenter's role as a flexible interactor with the subject. Our suggestion has been that, in the course of presenting his instructions to the subject, the experimenter should be certain that he is communicating—that the subject understands the instructions. This inevitably involves asking the subject if he understands or if he has any questions. There is a danger inherent in this strategy, that of relinquishing guidance of the procedure. If given the opportunity, a verbal subject may attempt to wrest control of the session away from an unwary experimenter. For example, if the experimenter asks him if he understands, the subject may take the floor and begin to ask questions which are irrelevant to the experiment, discuss previous experiments he has been in, or ask questions pertinent to aspects of the procedure yet to come. If this occurs, the experimenter stands in danger of either invalidating the data by engaging in a long, friendly chat with the subject, or offending and angering the subject by cutting him off too short. Thus, while we advocate a flexible procedure, this flexibility should operate within a limited range of behavior. We wish to stress the fact that in most experiments a wide variation in the rapport between the experimenter and the subject is detrimental to the experiment. At best it can increase error variance; at worst it could conceivably interact with experimental treatments in a manner which would make significant results meaningless.

A good general rule in such a situation is for the experimenter to answer only those questions which clarify those aspects of the procedure already covered, never to allow a subject to ramble on and never to allow a subject to force him to reorganize the sequence of instructions, merely because he has asked a question pertaining to material that would have been covered five minutes further along in the procedure. This can often be avoided during the time that the experimenter spends setting the stage by a short introduction to the procedure in which the experimenter explains the importance of control and uniformity in experimental situations and asks the subject to ask questions only when he does not understand something. He should also state that he would be happy to chat with the subject after the experiment. Most subjects can understand this and are not offended. In spite of this preface, occasionally a subject will deviate. If this occurs, the best way to field irrelevant chatter or anticipatory questions in the course of the experiment is to repeat, politely but firmly, that it is necessary to achieve a high degree of experimental uniformity and that, consequently, (1) it would be preferable to shelve this discussion until after the experiment or (2) the question raised will be answered in a few minutes.

THE DEPENDENT VARIABLE

The problems of measuring a dependent variable are conceptually parallel to the problems we listed for manipulating the independent variable: (1) First, what specific thing (attitude, behavior, physiological response, or whatever) does the experimenter want to assess which will correspond most directly to his theoretical variable? (2) Second, paralleling the problem of impact in the independent variable, how does the experimenter make sure that the subject is taking the measurement seriously? (3) Finally, how can the experimenter prevent the subject from "cooperating" by consciously behaving in a manner which he feels will be most useful rather than in a manner which honestly reflects his response to the independent variable?

The decision facing the experimenter is whether he should use a behavioral measure or a pencil-and-paper measure. Actually, it is not that simple, for it is possible to conceive of a continuum ranging from behaviors of great importance and consequence for the subject down to the most trivial paper-and-pencil measures about which the subject couldn't care less. At one extreme the experimenter could measure the extent to which the subject actually performs a great deal of tedious labor for a fellow student (as a reflection of, say, his liking for that student, which has been experimentally influenced). At the other extreme one could get him to circle a number on a scale entitled "How much did you like that other fellow who participated in the experiment?" Close to the behavioral end of the continuum would be a measure of the subject's commitment to perform a particular piece of behavior, without actually performing it. We call this a "behavioroid" measure. An example of a behavioroid measure is supplied by Aronson and Cope (1968), who assessed the degree of the subjects' liking for the experimenter by having the departmental secretary ask them to volunteer to make telephone calls (to prospective subjects) on behalf of the experimenter. This could be easily scaled, the number of phone calls the subject agreed to make constituting the degree of his liking for the experimenter. The subject did not actually make the phone calls, for the experiment was terminated immediately after he volunteered.

Similarly, Marlowe, Frager, and Nuttall (1965) wanted to determine the extent to which a subject became *more* committed to his liberal beliefs as a function of having lost a money-making opportunity because of these beliefs. The major dependent variable was a statement by the subject as to whether or not he was willing to spend a great deal of time escorting some visiting Negroes around campus. As in the Aronson-Cope experiment, the procedure did not actually require the subjects to perform the behavior, only to commit themselves to do so. Note that although the data in both of these studies are merely verbal statements, they are far different from a simple statement like "I like the experimenter" or "I think Negroes are grand." The crucial difference between a simple questionnaire and a behavioroid measure is degree of commitment. Most subjects who volunteer to make phone calls or to escort Negroes do so with the firm intention of following through. It is much easier and, therefore, much less meaningful to check an attitude questionnaire.

On our continuum, somewhere in between a behavioroid measure and an attitude questionnaire is the interview. The great advantage of an interview over a questionnaire is that the interviewer, merely by his presence, can succeed in inducing the subject to pay heed, and therefore stands a better chance of getting a serious, honest response. A frequent dilemma in this field is between impact and concealment. In order to conceal the hypothesis from the subject, the experimenter is tempted to administer the dependent variable in a casual manner, almost as an afterthought. A common device is the "Oh, by the way" technique. "Oh, by the way," the experimenter might say, "the psychology department is interested in how subjects feel about experiments." He then rummages around and finds a dog-eared questionnaire lying around, hands it to the subject, and leaves the room. By thus deemphasizing his own interest in the questionnaire, the experimenter stands a good chance of masking its essential importance. The problem is that unless he is careful, he may succeed too well; the subject may treat the questionnaire as casually as the experimenter appeared to treat it, and may accordingly check off his responses almost at random. The interview is an improvement over the questionnaire, and when used judiciously, can be more powerful than a questionnaire without arousing suspicion. In this regard, Aronson and Linder (1965) reported an experiment which failed when the dependent variable was measured by a questionnaire but succeeded when the subjects were interviewed by a person who was, of course, unaware of the subjects' experimental treatment.

As implied above, the questionnaire and the interview are often valuable. Moreover, behavioral measures are not always perfect. A specific segment of behavior can be multiply determined; thus, behavioral measures and questionnaire measures, even though they may appear parallel, occasionally tap different things. For example, suppose in an experiment a confederate (posing as a fellow subject) either praises the subject, implying that he is brilliant, or insults the subject, implying that he is stupid. Suppose our dependent variable is how much the subject likes the confederate. We could measure this by handing the subject a rating scale and asking him to rate his liking for the confederate, from +5 to −5. Or, on a more behavioral level, we could observe the extent to which the subject makes an effort to join a group to which the confederate belongs. This latter behavior would seem to be a reflection of liking, but unfortunately it could be reflecting other things instead. For example, it might be that the subject wants to join the group in the "insult" condition in order to prove to the confederate that he is *not* stupid. Or it may be that he wants an opportunity to see the insulting person again so that he can return the insult. Neither of these behaviors necessarily reflects "liking," and consequently, they may produce results different from those produced by the questionnaire measure.

At the same time, it should be clear to the reader that the greater the degree of commitment demanded of the subject by the dependent variable, the more confidence we can have in our experiment. For example, we would have a great deal of confidence that an experiment *really* involves antecedents of aggression if the experimenter reports that an experimental treatment induced more subjects to punch him in the nose (or even to volunteer to "meet him outside") than a control condition. We would have far less confidence if the experimental treatment resulted in a higher rating of perceived feelings of aggression as measured by a questionnaire. In terms of the three goals mentioned above: (1) a punch in the nose is probably a much closer approximation to the conceptual notion of aggression than "+3, I feel somewhat angry"; (2) a punch in the nose is a good indication that the subject is taking the situation seriously; (3) since a questionnaire, by its very nature, asks a question, there is clearly greater likelihood that the subject will try to determine what he *should* answer in terms of his feelings concerning the experimenter's hypothesis. A piece of behavior, especially when not asked for (like the punch in the nose), is far less likely to reflect cooperation.

These points seem fairly obvious, but it is nevertheless uncommon for social psychologists to use behavioral or behavioroid data. Instead, they rely very heavily on the questionnaire or rating scale. Occasionally it is impossible to get anything more. But all too often it appears that the questionnaire is chosen because it is simpler to concoct and easier to administer. With more effort and ingenuity, many studies could be designed to include behavioral data. Often the change is a very simple one; for example, in Freedman's (1965) improvement on Aronson and Carlsmith's (1963) experiment, instead of asking children to rate the attractiveness of a bunch of toys, he merely observed the amount of time the children actually played with the toys.

Again, questionnaire data can be very useful, and because of the multiply determined nature of many behaviors, questionnaire data are often essential. When we must use questionnaires, we should use them in the most powerful manner possible. They key problem involves inducing the subject to respond in a serious fashion to the questionnaire. There is nothing more likely to produce error variance than a subject racing through pages of questions, checking without giving much thought, unconcerned about the exact nature or the wording of the question. We have already discussed the structured interview as a way of minimizing this possibility. In an interview, the precise meaning of the question can be emphasized, the subject can be exhorted repeatedly to think carefully before answering, and the experimenter can repeat sections of the questions which are unclear. This procedure requires more time than a questionnaire, but it is time well spent. The interview is usually shunned because of the fears of introducing bias, but if the experimenter has been properly blinded as to the condition the subject is in, or if the interviewer is someone other than the experimenter who is blind as to condition, it can be worked effectively (see Aronson and Linder, 1965; Aronson, Willerman, and Floyd, 1966; Festinger and Carlsmith, 1959).

A still better technique of forcing the subject to take the questions more seriously is to enlist his aid as an experimenter. We will discuss some of the other advantages of this technique in the next section, which is devoted to the problem of overcoming bias. This technique is especially adapted to studies of person perception, where the subject might be told that he is an experimenter, while the dependent variable is his perception of the other subject (or confederate). The Aronson and Linder (1965) study, described in greater detail in the next section, is an example of just this procedure.

There are several more mundane problems to be considered when one tries to make concrete decisions about what the dependent variable should be. One constantly recurring question is the extent to which one should constrain the behavior of the subject. This takes several forms. First, should one attempt to block most possible alternative behaviors so as to maximize the likelihood of observing changes in the specific variable of interest? For example, in a dissonance study, should the experimenter attempt to rule out all possible methods of reducing dissonance except the one the experimenter has decided to study? Clearly this will maximize the likelihood of observing differences in the behavior studied. This is a perfectly sound and reasonable technique. Indeed, this is part of our definition of experimental control. But one does this only when one asks a certain kind of question, namely: "Is there dissonance in this situation, and does it get reduced?" If this is the kind of question he is asking, the experimenter should attempt to construct his experiment so that he is ready and able to measure the effects of his independent variable as powerfully as possible. For example, in a typical dissonance study in the area of communication and persuasion, if a person hears a very credible communicator state a position which he does not agree with, he experiences dissonance. There are four major ways to reduce dissonance: (1) by changing his own opinion; (2) by trying to get the communicator to change; (3) by seeking social support; (4) by derogating the communicator. One *can* easily devise an experiment which makes it difficult for the subject to utilize all but the first of these techniques. The experimenter then stands a good chance of validating his hypothesis because he has sealed most of the leaks, as it were; most of the dissonance that is aroused will be channeled in the direction of attitude change—and that's where the experimenter has piled his measuring instruments.

But the investigator may have a different question in mind. He may want to find out how people typically reduce dissonance. If this is the question, the above technique may obscure what the subject *really* is likely to do in a situation of this sort, and present the experimenter with an artificial relationship.

The same concern arises when one tries to decide whether to use open-ended questions or rigidly constrained measures. The more quantitative measure may increase the likelihood of observing differences between experimental treatments, but it also may obscure what the behavior of the subject would normally be like. Any experimenter who has seen many subjects close at hand has experienced the feeling that a given subject is "really" showing lots of interesting effects, but that the measures are too constrained to be sensitive to them.

The best answer to both of these concerns is to run a reasonably large number of pilot subjects with the dependent variable as unconstrained as possible. Thus, in pilot research it may be most effective to present the subject with the independent variable and then essentially ask him to say or do what he wants. By this means we may get some ideas as to exactly what behaviors we can look at which are likely to reflect the processes we believe are taking place. As one observes what the subjects do and say in response to the manipulations, it becomes possible to select dependent measures which may assess accurately the responses of the subjects, and to rule out certain alternative behaviors so as to maximize the likelihood of change on an important variable. Once the pilot stage of an experiment is over, however, there are many advantages to rigidly defined, quantitative measurement of the dependent variable.

Disguising the measure

For reasons which should be obvious by this time, it is frequently important to disguise the fact that a particular collection of data is actually the measurement of the dependent variable. This presents problems very similar to those involved in attempting to disguise the independent variable. Again, we can identify several general classes of solutions. The problems here are very similar to those discussed in the next section on guarding against demand characteristics, and will be elaborated in that section.

Assessment of the dependent variable can be done in a setting totally removed from the remainder of the experiment. This is perhaps the most common solution. An excellent example of this technique is the Marlowe, Frager, and Nuttall (1965) study referred to earlier. In this case, the experimenter who asked the subject whether he would be willing to escort Negroes around campus was described as a professor who was in charge of a visiting program and who had nothing to do with the experiment. Similarly, Carlsmith, Collins, and Helmreich (1966) had the dependent variable assessed by a Madison Avenue consumer research analyst. Another common procedure here is to pretend that the dependent variable is being collected for some other and unrelated study.

Festinger and Carlsmith (1959) presented the dependent variable as some information being collected for a study being carried out by other members of the psychology department. Let us repeat the caution that we issued earlier: if, as part of this "different context" technique, the experimenter finds it necessary to pretend to be uninterested in the data, he may succeed in making the subject uninterested. Our recommendation is merely that the experimenter be aware of this possibility and attempt to walk the fine line between appearing too interested and too disinterested. If he is too interested, the subject will become suspicious; if he is too disinterested, the subject may respond in a random or jocular fashion.

Second, as stated previously, we may assess behaviors which are, in and of themselves, of some significance to the subject. In this case we are less concerned about his perception that we are interested in them. A subject may check a different point on a liking scale to go along with the experimenter, but we feel he is less likely to choose a roommate for the entire year for the same reasons.

Third, we may observe some behavior of interest where the subject does not know we are observing him. Bennett (1955) used as her dependent variable the presence or absence of the subject at the experiment for which he had volunteered. Presumably none of the subjects was aware that the experimenter was simply interested in whether or not they showed up. Lefkowitz, Blake, and Mouton (1955), in a field experiment, used such measures as whether or not people jaywalked or disobeyed signs.

In attitude-change experiments, the most typical solution is to embed the key items in a large questionnaire which is given to the subject. One may have some qualms about the extent to which this always disguises the measurement from the subject, yet it has been used effectively in some instances.

An alternative technique involves actually *telling* the subject that you are interested in a particular measure, but disguising the reasons for your interest. That is, instead of implying that it is the dependent variable, one may describe it as a covariate which must be measured because of its possible confounding effects. Thus, Aronson (1961) was interested in the changes in attractiveness of colors as a result of effort expended to get them. He told the subjects that he wanted them to rate how attractive the colors were because he suspected that the attractiveness of the colors might have affected how hard they had worked.

One can dispense with the need for disguising the dependent variable by using experimental organisms who are, by nature, unsuspicious. For example, Aronson and Carlsmith (1963) were able to use a very simple and transparent method of collecting the dependent variable only because the subjects in that experiment were four-year-old children. These children were not suspicious of anything that was going on; they saw nothing peculiar about someone asking them to rate a number of toys on two occasions within a span of 20 minutes. The same procedure would not have been so effective with college sophomores as subjects.

There is a family of techniques for measuring a dependent variable which is parallel to the "whoops" procedure for manipulating an independent variable. The most common member of this family involves claiming that the pretest data had been lost, so that a second set of measures must be collected. A complicated variation on this theme was employed by Aronson and Carlsmith (1962). Here, the experimenter timed the subject's performance on four successive tests; he then pretended to neglect to time the final administration of the test. After much pacing, breast-beating, and rumination, he asked the subject to retake the test so that the experimenter could time his performance. But the crucial purpose of this procedure was to provide the subject with an opportunity to change his answers. The number of answers changed was the dependent measure, and was presumed to reflect the amount of discontent with the original score. As we pointed out in our discussion of the independent variable, this kind of procedure has the advantage of appearing to be an event which happens only once—to this particular subject—and thus is unlikely to be perceived as a situation which is of interest to the experimenter.

Another procedure which has the advantage of appearing to the subject as being a once-only phenomenon, or at least as unrelated to the interest of the experimenter, is to have a confederate collect the data. Thus, Carlsmith and Gross (in press) had a confederate act as the learner in an experiment where the independent variable consisted of what the subject (as teacher) did to the learner. After the experiment was ostensibly concluded, the confederate made a request of the subject; the subject's response constituted the dependent variable.

The final technique we outline here is in many ways the best when it can be used. This involves taking physiological measures, which hopefully are not under the subject's conscious control. As mentioned previously, the major difficulty has been that there are few physiological measures which reflect the kinds of dependent variables that social psychologists are interested in. Recent research, however (Gerard, 1961, 1964; Hess, 1965), suggests that such techniques may be practicable and may indeed be a common and important dependent variable in a few years (see Chapter 19 in Vol. 3 of this *Handbook*).

Reactivity

One of the major problems in measuring the dependent variable has been labeled "reactivity" and discussed at some length by Campbell and Stanley (1963). This concept refers to the observation that at many times the mere measurement of the dependent variable reacts with the independent variable or other events in the laboratory so that effects are found that would not be seen otherwise. For example, suppose a person views a movie designed to reduce prejudice. The person may be completely unaffected by this movie *until* someone hands him a questionnaire which clearly deals with prejudice. As a result of seeing this questionnaire, the subject may realize for the first time that the movie was about prejudice. The questionnaire may induce him to reflect on the movie and this combination of events may influence him. In effect, the dependent variable has served as a kind of independent variable. Note that this is conceptually different from the problems of demand characteristics to be discussed later. We are not postulating that the subject changes his prejudiced attitudes because the experimenter wants him to, but only that no change would have taken place without the intrusion of a very obvious measurement of a dependent variable; this cued changes which otherwise would not have appeared. Many of the techniques listed above may reduce this problem. Along these lines we refer the reader to the excellent recent book by Webb *et al.* (1966) which surveys a number of possible techniques which have been used to prevent or minimize the occurrence of reactivity.

ON THE AVOIDANCE OF BIAS

The possibility of systematic bias in experimentation has been well documented. This problem has plagued scientists in all fields for a good many years, but it has only been in recent years that social psychologists have rediscovered bias and have attempted to demonstrate its existence in a systematic fashion.

Basically, there are two types of bias which may intrude into social-psychological experiments: bias due to the demand characteristics of the experimental situation itself (McDavid, 1965; Orne, 1962; Riecken, 1962; Rosenberg, 1965; Silverman, 1965) and bias due to the unintentional influence of the experimenter (for example, Rosenthal, 1966). These are different but related problems. The possibility of either type of bias raises important questions concerning the validity of many experiments. Social-psychological experiments in particular would appear to be more susceptible to bias because of the latitude experimenters frequently allow themselves in order to establish rapport with their subjects and because of the sensitivity of human adult subjects to subtle cues. In this section we will describe these types of bias and outline some methods for dealing with them—either for eliminating them altogether or, at least, minimizing the extent of their effects.

Bias due to demand characteristics

Bias due to the demand characteristics of the experimental situation is closely related to the placebo problem in medical research. The subject knows that he is in an experimental situation and is aware of the fact that he is being observed carefully and that certain behaviors are expected from him. Thus, he is not responding to the experimental operations *per se,* but is responding to his interpretation of what behaviors these experimental operations are supposed to elicit from him. As Riecken (1962) has pointed out, the experimenter-subject relationship is one of unequal power and unequal knowledge. There is a one-sided distribution of information in which the experimenter conceals what is a "right answer" as well as his criteria for judging the subject's responses. Even if the subject is told specifically that there are no right or wrong responses, he knows that there are answers that will enhance or diminish his value as a person in the experimenter's eyes. From the point of view of the subject, the experiment may be seen as a game or a contest in which the subject tries to discover the true purpose of the experiment. This is done either to make a good impression on the experimenter (Riecken, 1962; Rosenberg, 1965) or out of a desire to "help" the experimenter by seeing to it that his hypothesis is verified by the subject's performance. In either case, many subjects are actively searching for a hypothesis about what is going on in the experiment, or more specifically, the subjects are searching for the experimenter's hypothesis. Unless the experimenter takes special precautions to conceal the true purpose of the experiment, it is relatively easy for a bright, discerning subject to discover it.

As suggested above, once the subject discovers the hypothesis, he may respond in a manner consistent with it, tailoring his responses to fit the theory, in an attempt either to cooperate with the experimenter or to be considered normal in his behavior. On the other hand, an occasional subject may attempt to express aggression against the experimenter or try to outwit him by behaving in a manner opposite to the experimenter's prediction. Although there is little direct evidence for either of these behaviors in social-psychological experiments, there is a great deal of evidence which indicates that subjects attempt to put themselves in the best possible light. For example, a subject may try to respond in a manner which is socially desirable during clinical interviews (see Masling, 1960). Moreover, there is a host of experimental results pertaining to the docility and cooperativeness of subjects in experimental situations. Orne (1962), attempting to find a set of operations which would lead the subject to refuse to cooperate, found that this was virtually impossible. He designed a set of tasks which were psychologically noxious, meaningless, and boring and found that subjects would perform these tasks for several hours, with few errors, little decrement in speed, and relatively little sign of overt hostility. In one situation, after subjects had performed a very dull task, the experimenter instructed them to tear up each of their answer sheets into 32 pieces and go on to the next sheet of paper and continue working. Orne repeated this procedure for several hours; none of the subjects showed any evidence of discontinuing the activity. Similar evidence for the docility of subjects in experimental settings can be found in experiments by Pepitone (1958) and by Milgram (1963), among others. If the subject extends this docility and cooperativeness to include specific behaviors which are consistent with the experimenter's hypothesis, the results of any such experiments are meaningless.

There are several possible solutions to this problem. Perhaps the best one is to follow the medical placebo model; that is, one should try to devise manipulations that appear essentially identical to subjects in all conditions, just as placebo pills look identical to the actual pills in a medical situation. In this case any attempts that the subject might make to discover the experimenter's hypothesis cannot possibly have a systematic effect on the results of the experiment. Such attempts on the part of the subject will simply increase error variance. Unfortunately, in most social-psychological experiments this solution is difficult to apply.

A more common attempt to solve this problem is the full-blown deception experiment in which the subject is provided with a plausible hypothesis about the experiment which is unrelated or orthogonal to the true hypothesis. If a subject attempts to modify his behavior so as to support or refute this incorrect hypothesis, the results of the experimental test of the true hypothesis will not be affected in a systematic way. It is important to realize that providing the subject with a false, but credible, hypothesis is a much better procedure than providing him with no hypothesis at all. For if there are loose ends to an experimental pro- cedure the subject will attempt to tie these up by devising his own hypothesis, which may be identical to or very similar to the experimenter's true hypothesis. If the experimenter can tie the loose ends together for the subject by providing him with a plausible hypothesis which is unrelated to the true hypothesis, he may succeed in satisfying the subject's curiosity and may thereby eliminate this source of bias. Indeed, this is the primary advantage of the use of deception in experi- ments. This procedure is really an attempt to provide a cognitive analogy to the placebo; all subjects receive identical explanations of what is being done, just as all subjects receive identical pills in the placebo procedure.

It should be noted that in practice the suspicious subject may not take the false hypothesis at face value. Rather, the false hypothesis may offer the subject a new basis for speculating about the true purpose of the experiment. Thus, regardless of what the experimenter tells him, the subject may form his own hypotheses and make some responses on the basis of these hypotheses. Hopefully, these responses are not the ones which the experimenter is interested in. Rather, the experimenter, in a sense, brings his measures of a dependent variable in through the back door, while the subject is not thinking about them. As an illustration, consider Schachter's (1959) experiments linking anxiety to the desire to affiliate with other people. Most of the subjects may have accepted Schachter's cover story to the effect that he was interested only in learning about physiological reactions to shock. But, since the experimenter seemed to be going out of his way to frighten his subjects, some of the more suspicious ones might have developed hypotheses somewhat different from the cover story. For example, they might have guessed that the experimenter was trying to raise their anxiety level in order to see what effects this might have on their responses to shock. At the same time, it is doubtful that any of the subjects would have made the con- nection between the fact that the experimenter was raising anxiety and the "incidental question" about whether they would prefer to wait alone or together with other people. Thus, it is almost immaterial whether or not the subject actually accepts the false hypothesis offered by the experimenter, so long as it prevents him from deciphering the true experimental hypothesis.

The most serious difficulty with this solution is, of course, that there is no foolproof way of being absolutely certain that the subject's hypothesis is really independent of the experimenter's hypothesis. Furthermore, even though the subject's hypothesis may be different from that of the experimenter, it may still have some effect on the response that the experimenter is interested in. Take, for example, a typical attitude-change experiment like that of Hovland and Weiss (1951), in which a given communication is attributed either to J. Robert Oppen- heimer or to *Pravda*. The subject may form the following hypothesis: "The experimenter is trying to see whether or not he can change my opinion of Oppenheimer by showing me some improbable statement that Oppenheimer made. O.K. I'll go along. I'll indicate that I do not like Oppenheimer as well as I formerly did." This new dislike for Oppenheimer as a result of the subject's attempt to cooperate may, in turn, diminish the effectiveness of the communication, even though the subject had no direct hypothesis that the study dealt with the effect of source credibility on attitude change. In much the same way, the subject's incorrect hypothesis could conceivably lead to behaviors which might *enhance* the effect for the wrong reasons.

Of course, at the close of the experiment the experimenter should probe into the actual hypothesis that the subject may have developed during the course of the experiment. It is possible, however, that even the most sensitive probing might not reveal the reasons behind the subject's behavior and thus would not provide a guarantee that the results were not artifactual. Moreover, if the experimenter discovers at the close of the experiment that many of the subjects did behave in an artifactual way, he has discovered nothing more than that his results are meaningless. Thus, although postexperimental probing is very useful, no amount of this probing, no matter how effective, can take the place of a more reliable solution to this problem.

As mentioned earlier, a better solution involves having the measurement of the dependent variable take place in quite a different context from the manipulation of the independent variable. This can usually be brought about by convincing the subject that he is actually taking part in two experiments being run during the same block of time. For example, Rosenberg (1965) had subjects write essays opposed to their own point of view in the education department and subsequently, in the guise of a totally different experiment, their attitudes on this issue were tapped in the psychology department. A more elaborate separation of the independent variable from the dependent variable was carried out in an experiment by Carlsmith, Collins, and Helmreich (1966). In this experiment, subjects were paid varying amounts of money to perform a very dull task. The dependent variable was measured in a context which was completely non-experimental. Under the guise of doing consumer research, a different experimenter asked the subjects to give their opinions of various pop records. The "consumer researcher" convinced them that their general mood had a marked effect on their opinions of the records and that it was essential for him to find out what kind of mood they were in. In the course of finding this out, he asked them what kinds of things they had done during the day and how they enjoyed them. Since all the subjects had recently completed the "dull task" experiment, it was both easy and reasonable for the experimenter to get a reading of how much they enjoyed the task. Also, since the context of the consumer research study was far removed from that of the original experiment psychologically, it was virtually impossible for any of the subjects to realize that the two procedures were connected.

There are alternative techniques for preventing a subject from guessing the true hypothesis. One that has proved highly successful involves convincing the subject that he is not a subject; this can be done by enlisting his aid as an "experimenter." For example, Aronson and Linder (1965) were interested in studying the effects of increases and decreases in person *A*'s esteem for person *B* on person *B*'s liking for person *A*. In essence, the subject was allowed to overhear another person evaluate him on several occasions. This was the independent variable. He was then asked to evaluate that other person. This kind of situation is a difficult one to study because the basic rudiments of the experiment are transparent. If the experiment were presented in a straightforward manner, virtually all subjects would realize that the two events were connected, at least in the experimenter's mind. In order to camouflage their purpose, Aronson and Linder enlisted the aid of the subject to help them run an experiment on instrumental verbal reinforcement. In this context, the essential rudiments of the experiment were presented in a manner which made it difficult for the subjects to suspect that they were actually the subjects in a rather simple experiment on interpersonal attractiveness.

The problem of the cooperative subject may be circumvented in still another manner simply by removing the experiment from the context of the laboratory. If subjects are unaware of the fact that they are in an experiment, it is obvious that they will be unlikely to form hypotheses as to what the situation is "really" about. The experiment by Abelson and Miller (1967), described earlier in this chapter, provides an excellent example of this kind of technique. On the other hand, it should be noted that this kind of naturalistic or field experiment is not a panacea; one need only recall the Hawthorne effect (Roethlisberger and Dickson, 1939) to realize that, even in a natural setting, the docility and cooperativeness of subjects can be a serious impediment to research. The great advantage of the Abelson-Miller experiment is that their subjects did not know they were being studied, whereas in the Hawthorne study, although it took place "in the real world," subjects were fully aware that they were being observed and investigated.

Another possible solution to this problem involves the avoidance of such response measures as the checking of an attitude scale. The reader will recall that one reason why we prefer dependent-variable measures which reflect behavioral commitment over attitude measures is that the responses on the latter are easily influenced by either the subject's desire to help the experimenter, on the one hand, or by his inattention or cantankerousness, on the other. It is relatively easy for a subject to check +5 rather than +1 on an attitude scale if he feels that this will help (or hurt) the experimenter or if he feels that it will create a good impression. This is less likely to occur if we investigate behaviors which are of interest for their own sake and which are not so easily influenced by the demands of the situation. For example, suppose we are interested in increasing the attractiveness of the person for the subject. We could measure the subject's liking for this person by getting him to fill out a series of rating scales. We could also get some indication of his liking for the person by getting him to select this person as a roommate for an entire college semester. Since this latter behavior involves much more of a commitment on the part of the subject, it is less likely that this behavior would be influenced by the subject's desire to please the experimenter. All things being equal, the greater the commitment involved in the dependent variable, the less likely it is to be due to cooperation or evaluation apprehension on the part of the subjects. At any rate, there is no reason why this cannot be checked empirically. That is, as a control condition, the experimenter may simply imply that he would like it if the subject would perform a particular behavior. If it were to turn out that this behavior could not be produced simply because the experimenter wanted it to be produced, then the experimental operations could be interpreted as the cause of the behavior. At this point, little is known about the correlation between stated opinions and a serious commitment to behavior as functions of the same experimental manipulation. For this reason it should be reemphasized that this is not meant to provide a blanket endorsement for behavioral measures over verbal measures. As stated previously, in certain situations a verbal measure might present a much closer approximation of the subject's feelings than a behavioral measure.

We might add here that there are certain kinds of designs and procedures which, because of their inherent characteristics, tend to increase or decrease the possibility of bias due to acquiescence or cooperativeness on the part of the subjects. The before-after design is one that frequently telegraphs the hypothesis to the subject. Thus, for example, if a subject is asked to state his attitude on an issue and then asked to read a communication regarding that issue and is subsequently asked to restate his attitude on that issue, it should become obvious to him that the manipulation is expected to have some effect on his attitude. Inherently, there is less possible bias in an after-only design.

Moreover, this kind of bias is sometimes minimized by a hypothesis which is not intuitively obvious. There has been a great deal of discussion recently about the advantages of "nonobvious" predictions. We are not at all certain that nonobvious predictions are more valuable than obvious ones. We do suspect that such experiments can minimize the possibility of bias by making it more difficult for subjects to decipher the true hypothesis. If this is to be claimed as a defense against demand, however, it is necessary to run a control condition where subjects are asked to guess the hypothesis and the direction of the results predicted by the experimenter. Most experimenters feel that their predictions are nonobvious; it is important to find out whether their subjects concur.

Bias due to the unintentional influence of the experimenter

Recent experiments have served to remind us of something we have known for some time—that the experimenter is not simply a passive runner of subjects, but can actually influence the results. Experimenters differ regarding sex, skill, technique, and personality, all of which can interact with the experimental operations. McGuigan (1963), for example, used nine experimenters in testing the effectiveness of four methods of learning with comparable groups of subjects. Some of the experimenters found no difference among the four methods; others found significant differences, but the order of effectiveness varied, depending on the experimenter. Recently, Rosenthal (1965) has shown that male experimenters behave in a more friendly manner than female experimenters. These results indicate that the experimenter is a variable, but not necessarily a problem.

More disconcerting are the many examples from other sciences (*cf.* Wilson, 1952) which show how experimenters can bias data in extraordinarily subtle ways to support their hypotheses. In recent years, Rosenthal and his associates have presented systematic data about how this can happen in psychology (Rosenthal, 1963, 1966; Rosenthal and Fode, 1963a, 1963b; Rosenthal and Lawson, 1964; Rosenthal, Persinger, Vikan-Kline, and Fode, 1963a, 1963b; Rosenthal, Persinger, Vikan-Kline, and Mulry, 1963). The basic paradigm of Rosenthal's studies has involved inducing contradictory hypotheses in equivalent samples of experimenters. As it turns out, the experimenters obtained data from their subjects which lean significantly in the direction of this "false" hypothesis. In one experiment, for example, Rosenthal and Fode (1963b) devised a person-perception task in which they utilized 20 photographs of humans that were previously judged to be neutral with respect to reflecting success or failure. The subject's task was to rate each photo along a success-failure continuum. Several experimenters ran the study expecting high ratings; several expected low ratings. Those expecting subjects to rate the pictures high got significantly higher ratings than those expecting low ratings. Indeed, there was no overlap among the distributions! More disconcerting than the data themselves is the fact that any cues given by the experimenter would have had to be extremely subtle—they were not readily apparent from sound films taken of similar experimental sessions.

Even more dramatic results were obtained in experiments involving learning in rats (Rosenthal and Fode, 1963a; Rosenthal and Lawson, 1964). In these experiments each experimenter was randomly assigned a rat after being told that the animal had been specially bred for brightness or dullness. Lo and behold, when the results were tabulated, it was found that the so-called bright rats learned more quickly than the so-called dull rats.

The consistency of Rosenthal's data, as well as the wide variety of experimental situations that he has employed, argue against treating this problem lightly. The problem of experimenter bias is a serious one and should be taken into account by anyone planning an experiment. But much of the response to Rosenthal's data has been perhaps too extreme and too pessimistic. Our major reason for this belief is that virtually all of Rosenthal's findings have occurred in contexts which are essentially different from the usual laboratory experiment, and that the difference is one that *invites* bias. In Rosenthal's paradigm, each experimenter runs only one of the experimental conditions. For example, in the learning experiment, an experimenter ran either a "bright" or "dull" rat. This does not occur in an actual experiment; here the same experimenter usually runs subjects in all conditions. It may be that it is easier for an experimenter to bias a subject's behavior, without being aware of it, if he is running only one condition; if he is running both conditions, he may be more likely to notice systematic differences in his behavior toward subjects.

If our argument is meaningful, it would suggest that in the average experiment bias may not be so prevalent as one might infer it to be from a reading of the bulk of Rosenthal's experimental evidence. However, Rosenthal has demonstrated recently that bias can exist (albeit less dramatically) even when the experimenter runs all conditions (Rosenthal, 1966).

Prevalent or not, it is important to devise techniques for eliminating this kind of bias. One technique that has been suggested involves keeping the experimenter (research assistant) unaware of the hypothesis. We find this an unfortunate solution for two reasons. First, it probably would not be effective. In a recent experiment (Rosenthal, Persinger, Vikan-Kline, and Mulry, 1963) it was shown that the research director could covertly communicate his own expectancies to his assistants even when he did not directly communicate the hypothesis to them. In short, assistants trained by each experimenter generated appropriately biased data even though they were not told the hypothesis. This has led these authors to recommend the elimination of personal contact between the experimenter and his assistants while they are being trained for a particular experiment. We suspect that this technique is likewise doomed to failure. One characteristic of the good researcher is that he is a hypothesis-forming organism. Indeed, this is one characteristic of all intelligent humans. Thus, if not told the hypothesis, the research assistant, like a subject, attempts to discover one. Since most research assistants are more sophisticated than most subjects, it is more likely that the assistant will arrive at the correct solution. Moreover, either keeping the assistant in the dark or eliminating contact with his supervisor would reduce the value of the educational benefits derived from running subjects. Most experimenters are graduate students and full participation in an experiment is the most effective way of learning experimentation. Any technique involving the experimenter's ignorance of the hypothesis or a reduction of contact with his supervisor would be doing him a disservice.

A more reasonable solution involves allowing the experimenter to know the true hypothesis but somehow keeping him ignorant of the specific experimental condition that each subject is in. Thus, in the Rosenthal-Fode experiments this might involve revealing the hypothesis but not informing the experimenter which of the rats was bright and which was dull. In theory, this is a simple and complete solution to the problem and should be employed whenever possible. It can be done easily, in the above example, by placing all the animals together and using a complex coding system, or one that is invisible to the naked eye. The major drawback with this technique, of course, is that in social psychology it is not always possible to design an experiment in which the experimenter does not know the condition the subject is in. The placebo, whose contents are unknowable on inspection, is not a frequent type of manipulation. However, with some thought and ingenuity, it is certainly true that many more experiments can be run blind than is presently the case. To continue our analogy between the placebo and a solution to demand characteristics, we are saying that the "double-blind" experiment is the ideal solution to experimenter bias.

A partial solution to the implementation of the "blind" technique would involve the experimenter's carrying out the entire experimental procedure in ignorance, up to the crucial difference in manipulations. That is, in most studies, the experimenter need not know what condition the subject is in until he performs the crucial manipulation. When the choice point is reached, a randomizing device can be used, and the remainder of the experiment is, of course, not carried out in ignorance. For example, in the Aronson-Mills (1959) study, it would have been easy to delay assignment of subject to condition until the point of initiation; by reaching into his pocket and randomly pulling out one of three slips of paper, the experimenter could determine whether the subject would recite the obscene words, the mild words, or no words at all. Thus, all the pre-manipulation instructions would be unbiased. This is only a partial solution because the experimenter loses his ignorance midway through the experiment. However, if the experimenter left the room immediately after the recitation and assigned a different experimenter (ignorant of the subject's experimental condition) to collect the data, this solution would approach completeness. The use of multiple experimenters, each ignorant of some part of the experiment, offers a solution which is frequently viable. See, for example, Aronson and Cope (1968) and Sigall and Aronson (1967).

Another technique for implementing the blind experiment is through the use of taped instructions. After greeting the subject and explaining the general nature of the experiment, the investigator can randomly decide on the experimental condition and conduct the rest of the experiment from another room via a set of standardized tapes. We have found that the use of tapes can be easily justified to the subject simply by telling him the truth, that is, that you are using tapes for greater control and standardization. As previously discussed, the use of tape recordings is not an ideal device because it does reduce the impact of the manipulation and it sacrifices several important aspects of the live experimenter. But it can effectively preclude experimenter bias and should therefore be utilized when other techniques are not feasible. Closed-circuit television provides a more powerful impact, and the experimenter can still be blind as to the condition the subject is in.

An interesting and effective variation on the blind technique can be performed by running subjects in all the experimental conditions simultaneously (for example, Aronson, Turner, and Carlsmith, 1963; Cottrell, 1965). Cottrell manipulated whether a person developed an expectancy of high performance or of low performance on a task, as well as whether this expectancy was confirmed or disconfirmed. He recited the general instructions to subjects in all the conditions simultaneously, manipulating the conditions by randomly assigning written scores to each subject. This technique makes it almost impossible for the experimenter to bias the results in a systematic manner.

Where complete ignorance of the experimental conditions is not feasible, partial ignorance may be sufficient. Consider a design in which the manipulations are crossed, such as the factorial. It is frequently possible to have the experimenter ignorant about one of the dimensions of the subject's condition, although he may be aware of the other. For example, in a typical attitude-change experiment in which fear arousal and adequacy of fear-reducing behaviors are crossed factorially, the experimenter may know what the level of fear arousal is (since, for example, he shows a movie to the subject), but if the possible avenues of fear-reducing behavior are presented in a written communication, there is no need for the experimenter to know which communication the subject receives. Now if, as in many social-psychological experiments, the hypothesis concerns the inter-action between these two variables, and no main effects are expected, this is an effective blinding of the experimenter. For knowledge of one experimental variation without knowledge of the other is not sufficient to predict where the subject should fall on the dependent variable. Even if one is concerned with more than just the interaction, ignorance of one variable precludes bias on all main effects and interactions involving that variable. Again, the use of two or more experimenters can be effective. One experimenter can know the condition a subject is in only on one variable; the other experimenter knows the condition only on the second variable.

In sum, the possibility of systematic bias is forever present in social-psychological research. However, this is no cause for despair. It is a rare experiment which, with some ingenuity, cannot be built in such a way as to allow the experimenter to be kept ignorant of at least one crucial aspect of the subject's condition.

THE POSTEXPERIMENTAL INTERVIEW

The experiment does not end when the data have been collected. The experimenter will want to interview the subject in order to determine his reaction to the procedure. The experimenter should invite the subject to comment freely on how the experiment struck him, why he responded as he did, etc. This is an important means of determining whether or not the procedures were interpreted by the subject in the manner which the experimenter intended. Moreover, if any deception has been employed, the experimenter must attempt to determine the extent to which the deception worked. If the subject *did* entertain some suspicion, the experimenter must probe systematically and make some judgment as to whether the suspicion was specific enough and accurate enough to render the results invalid.

Whether or not deception was used, the experimenter should provide the subject with a full explanation of the experiment and should make certain that the subject has a complete understanding of it before leaving the laboratory. If an experiment involved some disquieting events, the experimenter should explain why these were essential. If any deception was involved, it is almost always best if the subject is informed of the deception and why it was necessary.

It is impossible to overstate the importance of the postexperimental interview. Accordingly, it should never be performed in a glib or cavalier manner. This aspect of the experiment is as much an art as is each of the preceding phases, and the art of debriefing should be an important part of research training. The two major purposes of the interview are intertwined. That is, if we assume for the moment that the experiment involved deception, (1) the experimenter must probe gently in order to determine the precise qualitative and quantitative nature of the subject's suspicions (if any), and (2) as mentioned in our section on ethical problems, it is important that the experimenter explain the deception in a considerate and gradual manner. In practice, these two aims are mutually consistent and can be simultaneously realized by the same general procedure.

Why the need for gradualness? Why not simply ask a subject if he suspected that he was the victim of a hoax? Subjects may not be responsive to an abrupt procedure for a variety of reasons. First, if a person *did* see through the experiment, he might be reluctant to admit it out of a misplaced desire to be helpful to the experimenter. Second, most people are reluctant to admit that they can be easily fooled. Consequently, if the subject is told that he was fooled, he is apt to imply that he suspected it all along, in order to save face. Thus, such an abrupt procedure might falsely inflate the number of suspicious subjects and might, consequently, lead the experimenter to abandon a perfectly viable procedure. Moreover, as mentioned previously, abruptly telling the subject that he has been deceived is a harsh technique which could add unnecessarily to his discomfort and could make him justifiably angry.

The best way to begin a postexperimental interview is by asking the subject if he has any questions. If he hasn't any, the experimenter should ask if the entire experiment was perfectly clear to him—the purpose of the experiment as well as each aspect of the procedure. He should then be told that people react to things in different ways and it would be helpful if he would comment on how the experiment struck him, why he responded as he did, how he felt at the time, etc. Then he should be asked specifically whether there was any aspect of the procedure that he found odd, confusing, or disturbing.

At this point, if the subject has had any suspicions, he is almost certain to have revealed them. Moreover, the experimenter should have discovered whether the subject had misunderstood the instructions or whether he responded erroneously. If no suspicions have been voiced, the experimenter should continue: "Do you think there may have been more to the experiment than meets the eye?" This question is virtually a giveaway. Even if the subject had not previously suspected anything, he will probably begin to suspect that the experimenter was concealing something. In our experience, many subjects will take this opportunity to say that they did feel that the experiment, as described, appeared too simple (or something of that order). This is desirable; for, as mentioned previously, whether the subject was *really* suspicious or not, the question allows him to indicate that he is not completely naive; this enables him to appear less gullible than he otherwise might. The experimenter should immediately ask the subject to explain what might have been involved in addition to what he has been told. He should then ask him how this suspicion might have affected his behavior. From the subject's answers to this question, the experimenter can make a judgment as to how close a subject's suspicions were to the actual purpose of the experiment and, consequently, whether or not his data are admissible. Obviously, the criteria for inclusion should be rigid and should be set down before the experiment begins, and the decision should be made without knowledge of the subject's responses on the dependent variable.

The experimenter should then continue with the debriefing process by saying something like this: "You are on the right track, we *were* interested in some problems that we didn't discuss with you in advance. One of our major concerns in this study is . . . ." The experimenter should continue by describing the problem he is studying, specifying why he thinks it is important, and explaining clearly exactly how he deceived the subject and why the deception was necessary. He should make absolutely certain that the subject fully understands these things before he terminates the experimental session. (A more detailed description of this procedure and the reasons for proceeding with caution and thoroughness can be found on pp. 29–36.)

It is a good idea to enlist the subject's aid in improving the experiment. That is, just before dismissing the subject, the experimenter might explain that he is forever searching for ways of improving his experimental procedure to make it more powerful, more credible, and more pleasant for the subject. He should state that he would be most appreciative if the subject would point out any weaknesses in this regard. This is the best way we know of finding out any of the negative aspects of the experiment. As many investigators (for example, Orne, 1962) have pointed out, experimental subjects tend to be cooperative. This usually prevents them from admitting that the procedure caused them unnecessary anguish, that the procedure did not have any meaning for them, or that it did not mean what the experimenter thought it should mean. By specifically appealing to the subject to help improve the experiment, the investigator can turn this cooperativeness to the advantage of the research. If this is done, the subject will be only too pleased to criticize the experiment. This often leads to improvement and is an indispensable aid to the experimenter, especially in the pilot stages of the research. In addition, this procedure often allows the subject sufficient latitude to admit that he was (or still is) upset by the procedure or the deception; if this should occur, the experimenter knows that he must go further in his efforts to undo any damage done by the experimental procedure.

Finally, the experimenter must attempt to convince the subject not to reveal anything about the experiment. This is a serious problem because even a few sophisticated subjects can invalidate an experiment. Moreover, it is sobering to reflect on the fact that it is almost impossible to screen sophisticated subjects in advance. It is not easy to swear a subject to secrecy; he may have friends who might subsequently volunteer for the experiment and who are almost certain to press him for information. It should be noted that the experimenter should attempt to minimize intersubject communication in constructing the experiment. In addition, he should attempt to forestall it after the session by graphically describing the colossal waste of time and effort which would result from experimenting on people who have foreknowledge about the procedure or hypothesis of the experiment. He should also explain the damage that can be done to the scientific enterprise by including data from such subjects. He should discuss the fact that such information usually spreads rapidly, so that telling only one person might result in several subjects whose performance is either unusable or misleading. If the experimenter has been sincere and honest in his dealings with the subject during the postexperimental debriefing session, he can be reasonably confident that few subjects will break faith. To check on this, Aronson (1966) enlisted the aid of three undergraduates who each approached three acquaintances who had recently participated in one of his experiments. The confederates explained that they had signed up for that experiment, had noticed the friend's name on the sign-up sheet, and wondered what the experiment was all about. The experimenter had previously assured these confederates that their friends would remain anonymous. The results were encouraging. In spite of considerable urging, begging, and cajoling on the part of the confederates, none of the former subjects revealed the true purpose of the experiment; two of them went as far as providing the confederates with a replay of the cover story, but nothing else.

What if the subject has been forewarned before he enters the experimental room? That is, suppose a subject does find out about the experiment from a friend who has participated previously. He probably will not reveal this to the experimenter before the experiment for fear of being disqualified from earning credit, points, money, love, or whatever incentive may have enticed him into the laboratory. Moreover, if not prodded, it is unlikely that he will confess this after the experiment, out of reluctance to implicate his friend, who, after all, broke his promise to the experimenter. Yet, if the experimenter is unable to elicit this information, his results may be extremely misleading and his statement that no subjects were suspicious or sophisticated may be gravely in error.

How can we be sure? Once again, the experimenter must attempt to utilize the cooperativeness of the subject as well as the good will which he (hopefully) has built up during the postexperimental interview. First, as described above, the experimenter should carefully and vividly explain the disastrous problems presented to science and to himself personally if he unwittingly were to report erroneous data. He should then explain to the subject that, although he cautions subjects not to discuss the experiment, occasionally a former subject will accidentally slip. He should then appeal to the subject to help him out by mentioning *now* if he heard even a little about the experiment. He should, of course, assure the subject that he is uninterested in learning how or from whom. In the face of such a plea, very few non-naive subjects would remain silent. We cannot over-emphasize the importance of this kind of procedure as a safeguard against the artifactual confirmation of an erroneous hypothesis due to the misplaced cooperativeness of the subject. If the subject is indeed cooperative, he will probably cooperate with the experimenter in this regard also, and will respond to a direct plea from the experimenter.

If at first you don't succeed

What does the experimenter do when his experiment does not work? Does he conclude that his hypothesis was incorrect? It is not that simple. As implied throughout this chapter, there are literally dozens of reasons for the failure of a given experiment to confirm a hypothesis, only one of which is that the hypothesis is wrong. In an area like social psychology, with few standardized procedures for manipulating the independent variable, where ethics and good taste confine us to weak empirical operations, and where our measuring instruments are rather insensitive, it seems almost miraculous that *any* "true" hypotheses are confirmed experimentally. Consequently, it would be somewhat arrogant of the experimenter to conclude, after one failure, that the hypothesis was incorrect—arrogant in the sense that such a conclusion implies that the experimental operations were perfect. Moreover, the running of an experiment, even a successful one, is almost always instructive. An experimenter can usually see weaknesses in his experiment; by making a few changes he can frequently strengthen his procedure and increase the probability of confirming a true hypothesis. Consequently, following an unsuccessful experiment, the investigator can and *should* pick up the pieces, return to the workroom, and attempt to improve his procedure.

But how many times should he do this? It should be clear that, by testing the same hypothesis on several occasions, the experimenter begins capitalizing on chance factors. We would not have much confidence in a finding (significant at the .05 level) if we knew that the experimenter had failed on 19 previous occasions to verify the same hypothesis. Clearly, 19 failures are unnecessary to make us question the real (as opposed to statistical) significance of a given positive finding—any number will do (see McNemar, 1960).

An experimenter can decrease the probability of failure if he pretests each aspect of his procedure, strengthening his independent variable, shoring up his dependent variable, setting the stage in a more interesting and more impactful manner, etc. For example, one might run the experiment only up to the point where the independent variable had been induced, terminate the procedure, and attempt to determine how successful that induction had been—not by observing effects on the dependent variable but by direct checks on the manipulation. Thus, when he finally does run the experiment itself, the experimenter is fairly well convinced that his procedures are as good as he can make them. This renders failure more meaningful and, hence, more conclusive. This is not to say that one should *never* rework an unsuccessful experiment. But pretesting can trim this to a minimum.

One cannot overemphasize the importance of pretesting. As we have indicated throughout this chapter, a great deal of time and effort can ultimately be saved if the experimenter carefully hones his manipulations and measures before beginning the experiment proper. But there is a danger inherent in elaborate pretesting also—the danger of "piddling." There is a world of difference between the careful scientist who wishes to make sure of his instruments before plunging into his experiment, and the anxious novice who can spend an incredible amount of time piddling with a series of pretests as a means of avoiding the ultimate test (and the possibility of failure) presented by the experiment itself. Unfortunately, what is a "world of difference" conceptually becomes a "fine line" behaviorally; it is frequently difficult to be certain where reasonable caution leaves off and piddling begins.

This kind of piddling behavior is not uncommon with novice experimenters and not difficult to understand. As a reading of this chapter should indicate, experimentation in social psychology presents a multitude of formidable problems. However, we must hasten to add that it is the challenge presented by these problems that makes this area such an exciting one to work in. In this chapter we hope that we have been able to describe a sample of the difficulties encountered when one experiments in this field. But we will have failed miserably if we have not also conveyed the excitement inherent in overcoming these difficulties. Although it is generally considered unbecoming for scientists to talk this way, we feel that we must close this chapter with a statement regarding what to us is one of the most important aspects of experimentation in social psychology: It's fun.

REFERENCES

Abelson, R. P., and J. C. Miller (1967). Negative persuasion via personal insult. *J. exp. soc. Psychol., 3,* 321–333.

Aronson, E. (1961). The effect of effort on the attractiveness of rewarded and unrewarded stimuli. *J. abnorm. soc. Psychol., 63,* 375–380.

———— (1966). Avoidance of inter-subject communication. *Psychol. Reports, 19,* 238.

Aronson, E., and J. M. Carlsmith (1962). Performance expectancy as a determinant of actual performance. *J. abnorm. soc. Psychol., 65,* 178–182.

———— (1963). Effect of the severity of threat on the devaluation of forbidden behavior. *J. abnorm. soc. Psychol., 66,* 584–588.

Aronson, E., and V. M. Cope (1968). My enemy's enemy is my friend. *J. Pers. soc. Psychol., 8,* 8–12.

Aronson, E., and D. Linder (1965). Gain and loss of esteem as determinants of interpersonal attractiveness. *J. exp. soc. Psychol., 1,* 156–171.

Aronson, E., and J. Mills (1959). The effect of severity of initiation on liking for a group. *J. abnorm. soc. Psychol., 59,* 177–181.

Aronson, E., Judith Turner, and J. M. Carlsmith (1963). Communicator credibility and communication discrepancy as determinants of opinion change. *J. abnorm. soc. Psychol., 67,* 31–36.

Aronson, E., B. Willerman, and Joanne Floyd (1966). The effect of a pratfall on increasing interpersonal attractiveness. *Psychon. Sci., 4,* 227–228.

Asch, S. (1951). Effects of group pressure upon the modification and distortion of judgment. In H. Guetzkow (Ed.), *Groups, leadership, and men.* Pittsburgh: Carnegie Press. Pp. 177–190.

Ax, A. F. (1953). The physiological differentiation between fear and anger in humans. *Psychosom. Med., 15,* 433–442.

Back, K. W. (1951). Influence through social communication. *J. abnorm. soc. Psychol., 46,* 9–23.

Baumrind, Diana (1964). Some thoughts on ethics of research: after reading Milgram's "Behavioral study of obedience." *Amer. Psychologist, 19,* 421–423.

Bennett, Edith (Pelz) (1955). Discussion, decision, commitment, and consensus in 'group decision.' *Hum. Relat., 8,* 251–274.

Beveridge, W. I. B. (1957). *The art of scientific investigation*. New York: Vintage.

Brehm, J. W., and Ann H. Cole (1966). Effect of a favor which reduces freedom. *J. Pers. soc. Psychol., 3,* 420–426.

Brown, R. (1962). Models of attitude change. In R. Brown, E. Galanter, E. H. Hess, and G. Mandler (Eds.), *New directions in psychology*. New York: Holt, Rinehart, and Winston.

Brunswik, E. (1956). *Perception and the representative design of psychological experiments* (2nd ed.). Berkeley: Univ. of California Press.

Burdick, H. A., and A. J. Burnes (1958). A test of 'strain toward symmetry' theories. *J. abnorm. soc. Psychol., 57,* 367–370.

Campbell, D. T. (1957). Factors relevant to validity of experiments in social settings. *Psychol. Bull., 54,* 297–312.

———— (1963). From description to experimentation: interpreting trends as quasi-experiments. In C. W. Harris (Ed.), *Problems in measuring change*. Madison: Univ. of Wisconsin Press. Pp. 212–242.

———— (in press). Quasi-experimental design. In D. L. Sills (Ed.), *International encyclopedia of the social sciences*. New York: Crowell-Collier and Macmillan.

Campbell, D. T., and J. C. Stanley (1963). Experimental and quasi-experimental designs for research. In N. L. Gage (Ed.), *Handbook of research on teaching*. Chicago: Rand-McNally. Pp. 171–246.

Carlsmith, J. M., B. E. Collins, and R. L. Helmreich (1966). Studies in forced compliance: I. The effect of pressure for compliance on attitude change produced by face-to-face role playing and anonymous essay writing. *J. Pers. soc. Psychol., 4,* 1–3.

Carlsmith, J. M., and A. Gross (in press). The effect of guilt on compliance. *J. Pers. soc. Psychol.*

Cohen, A. R. (1959). Communication discrepancy and attitude change. *J. Pers., 27,* 386–396.

Cottrell, N. B. (1965). Performance expectancy as a determinant of actual performance: a replication with a new design. *J. Pers. soc. Psychol., 2,* 685–691.

Crutchfield, R. S. (1955). Conformity and character. *Amer. Psychologist, 10,* 191–198.

Deutsch, M., and H. B. Gerard (1955). A study of normative and informational social influences upon individual judgment. *J. abnorm. soc. Psychol., 51,* 629–636.

Dunnette, M. D., J. Campbell, and Kay Jaastad (1963). The effect of group participation on brainstorming effectiveness for two industrial samples. *J. appl. Psychol., 47,* 30–37.

Festinger, L., and J. M. Carlsmith (1959). Cognitive consequences of forced compliance. *J. abnorm. soc. Psychol., 58,* 203–210.

Festinger, L., W. R. Garner, D. O. Hebb, H. F. Hunt, D. H. Lawrence, C. E. Osgood, B. F. Skinner, D. W. Taylor, and M. Wertheimer (1959). Education for research in psychology. *Amer. Psychologist, 14,* 167–179.

Festinger, L., and J. Thibaut (1951). Interpersonal communication in small groups. *J. abnorm. soc. Psychol., 46,* 92–99.

Freedman, J. L. (1965). Long-term behavioral effects of cognitive dissonance. *J. exp. soc. Psychol., 1,* 145–155.

Gerard, H. B. (1961). Disagreement with others, their credibility, and experienced stress. *J. abnorm. soc. Psychol., 62,* 559–564.

——— (1964). Physiological measurement in social psychological research. In P. Leiderman and D. Shapiro (Eds.), *Psychobiological approaches to social behavior.* Stanford: Stanford Univ. Press. Pp. 43–58.

Gerard, H. B., and G. C. Mathewson (1966). The effects of severity of initiation on liking for a group: a replication. *J. exp. soc. Psychol., 2,* 278–287.

Hess, E. H. (1965). Attitude and pupil size. *Sci. Amer., 212,* No. 4, 46–54.

Hovland, C. W., and W. Weiss (1951). The influence of source credibility on communication effectiveness. *Publ. Opin. Quart., 15,* 635–650.

Jordan, N. (1953). Behavioral forces that are a function of attitudes and of cognitive organization. *Hum. Relat., 6,* 273–287.

Kelman, H. C. (1967). Human use of human subjects: the problem of deception in social psychological experiments. *Psychol. Bull., 67,* 1–11.

Landy, D., and E. Aronson (in press). Liking for an evaluator as a function of his discernment. *J. Pers. soc. Psychol.*

Latané, B., and J. M. Darley (1966). Bystander intervention in emergency situations: II. Defining the situation. Paper read at American Psychological Association, New York, September, 1966.

Lefkowitz, M., R. R. Blake, and Jane S. Mouton (1955). Status factors in pedestrian violation of traffic signals. *J. abnorm. soc. Psychol., 51,* 704–705.

McDavid, J. W. (1965). Approval-seeking motivation and the volunteer subject. *J. Pers. soc. Psychol., 2,* 115–117.

McGuigan, F. J. (1963). The experimenter: a neglected stimulus object. *Psychol. Bull., 60,* 421–428.

McNemar, Q. (1960). At random: sense and nonsense. *Amer. Psychologist, 15,* 295–300.

Marlowe, D., R. Frager, and R. L. Nuttall (1965). Commitment to action taking as a consequence of cognitive dissonance. *J. Pers. soc. Psychol., 2,* 864–868.

Masling, J. (1960). The influence of situational and interpersonal variables in projective testing. *Psychol. Bull., 57,* 65–85.

Milgram, S. (1963). Behavioral study of obedience. *J. abnorm. soc. Psychol., 67,* 371–378.

——— (1964). Issues in the study of obedience: a reply to Baumrind. *Amer. Psychologist, 19,* 848–852.

——— (1965). Some conditions of obedience and disobedience to authority. *Hum. Relat., 18,* 57–76.

——— (1966). Four studies using the lost letter technique. Address given at American Psychological Association, New York, September, 1966.

Miller, N. E. (1957). Experiments on motivation. *Science, 126,* 1271–1278.

Murray, H. A. (1963). Studies of stressful interpersonal disputations. *Amer. Psychologist, 18,* 28–36.

Orne, M. (1962). On the social psychology of the psychological experiment. *Amer. Psychologist, 17,* 776–783.

Pepitone, A. (1958). Attributions of causality, social attitudes, and cognitive matching processes. In R. Tagiuri and L. Petrullo (Eds.), *Person perception and interpersonal behavior.* Stanford: Stanford Univ. Press. Pp. 258–276.

Riecken, H. W. (1962). A program for research on experiments in social psychology. In N. F. Washburne (Ed.), *Decision, values and groups.* Vol. 2. New York: Pergamon Press. Pp. 25–41.

Roethlisberger, F. J., and W. J. Dickson (1939). *Management and the worker.* Cambridge: Harvard Univ. Press.

Rosenberg, M. J. (1965). When dissonance fails: on eliminating evaluation apprehension from attitude measurement. *J. Pers. soc. Psychol., 1,* 28–42.

Rosenberg, M. J., and R. P. Abelson (1960). An analysis of cognitive balancing. In M. J. Rosenberg, C. I. Hovland, W. J. McGuire, R. P. Abelson, and J. W. Brehm (Eds.), *Attitude organization and change: an analysis of consistency among attitude components.* New Haven: Yale Univ. Press. Pp. 112–163.

Rosenthal, R. (1963). On the social psychology of the psychological experiment: the experimenter's hypothesis as unintended determinant of the experimental results. *Amer. Scientist, 51,* 268–283.

———— (1965). Covert communications and tacit understandings in the psychological experiment. Paper read at American Psychological Association, Chicago, September, 1965.

———— (1966). *Experimenter effects in behavioral research.* New York: Appleton-Century-Crofts.

Rosenthal, R., and K. L. Fode (1963a). The effect of experimenter bias on the performance of the albino rat. *Behav. Sci., 8,* 183–189.

———— (1963b). Psychology of the scientist: V. Three experiments in experimenter bias. *Psychol. Reports, 12,* 491–511.

Rosenthal, R., and R. Lawson (1964). A longitudinal study of the effects of experimenter bias on the operant learning of laboratory rats. *J. psychiat. Res., 2,* 61–72.

Rosenthal, R., G. W. Persinger, Linda Vikan-Kline, and K. L. Fode (1963a). The effect of early data returns on data subsequently obtained by outcome-biased experimenters. *Sociometry, 26,* 487–498.

———— (1963b). The effect of experimenter outcome-bias and subject set on awareness in verbal conditioning experiments. *J. verb. Learn. verb. Behav., 2,* 275–283.

Rosenthal, R., G. W. Persinger, Linda Vikan-Kline, and R. C. Mulry (1963). The role of the research assistant in the mediation of experimenter bias. *J. Pers., 31,* 313–335.

Schachter, S. (1951). Deviation, rejection, and communication. *J. abnorm. soc. Psychol., 46,* 190–207.

———— (1959). *The psychology of affiliation: experimental studies of the sources of gregariousness.* Stanford: Stanford Univ. Press.

Schachter, S., and J. E. Singer (1962). Cognitive, social and physiological determinants of emotional state. *Psychol. Rev., 69,* 379–399.

Selltiz, Claire, Marie Jahoda, M. Deutsch, and S. W. Cook (1960). *Research methods in social relations.* New York: Holt-Dryden.

Shils, E. A. (1959). Social inquiry and the autonomy of the individual. In D. Lerner (Ed.), *The human meaning of the social sciences.* New York: Meridian. Pp. 114–157.

Sigall, H., and E. Aronson (1967). Opinion change and the gain-loss model of interpersonal attraction. *J. exp. soc. Psychol., 3,* 178–188.

Silverman, I. (1965). Motives underlying the behavior of the subject in the psychological experiment. Paper read at American Psychological Association, Chicago, September, 1965.

Taylor, D. W., P. C. Berry, and C. H. Block (1958). Does group participation when using brainstorming facilitate or inhibit creative thinking? *Admin. Sci. Quart., 3,* 23–47.

Wallace, J., and E. Sadalla (1966). Behavioral consequences of transgression: I. The effects of social recognition. *J. exp. Res. Pers., 1,* 187–194.

Walster, Elaine, E. Aronson, and Darcy Abrahams (1966). On increasing the persuasiveness of a low prestige communicator. *J. exp. soc. Psychol., 2,* 325–342.

Walster, Elaine, B. Walster, Darcy Abrahams, and Zita Brown (1966). The effect on liking of underrating or overrating another. *J. exp. soc. Psychol., 2,* 70–84.

Webb, E. J., D. T. Campbell, D. Schwartz, and L. Sechrest (1966). *Unobtrusive measures: nonreactive research in the social sciences.* Chicago: Rand McNally.

Wilson, E. B. (1952). *An introduction to scientific research.* New York: McGraw-Hill.

Zimbardo, P. G. (1965). The effect of effort and improvisation on self-persuasion produced by role playing. *J. exp. soc. Psychol., 1,* 103–120.

Zimbardo, P. G., A. R. Cohen, M. Weisenberg, L. Dworkin, and I. Firestone (1966). Control of pain motivation by cognitive dissonance. *Science, 151,* 217–219.

10

Data Analysis, Including Statistics

FREDERICK MOSTELLER, Harvard University

JOHN W. TUKEY, Princeton University and Bell Telephone Laboratories

A. APPROACHING DATA ANALYSIS

Introduction

A1. *The staircase and the shortcut to inference*

A2. *Student's true contribution*

A3. *Distributions and their troubles*

A4. *A classical example: Wilson and Hilferty's analysis of Peirce's data*

A5. *Kinds of nonnormality and robustness*

A6. *The role of vague concepts*

A7. *More vague concepts*

A8. *Indication, determination, or inference*

Every student of the art of data analysis repeatedly needs to build upon his previous statistical knowledge and to reform that foundation through fresh insights and emphases. This account of data analysis assumes that all of its readers are familiar with elementary statistical concepts and techniques; a few starred sections and paragraphs assume that some readers already have moderately advanced knowledge of both statistics and data analysis. The article analogous to this one in the previous edition of this *Handbook* (Mosteller and Bush, 1954) was written after a period of innovation among techniques designed to handle nonnormality. Those whose concern is learning more about such techniques now have a choice among many books, though they may still find that article helpful. As we look at the recent past, however, we see greater gains in philosophy, insight, and unity than in new techniques for the simpler problems, so that the present account

---

A section of acknowledgments appears at the close of the text ahead of the references.

emphasizes attitude and understanding, with considerable attention to techniques that make more difficult problems quite approachable.

Applications of mathematics are always complicated by the obligation to be true to the subject matter treated as well as to the mathematics. The structure of the art of data analysis makes its exposition especially difficult because it does not branch neatly like a tree, nor does it seem susceptible to an orderly progressive treatment. Consequently, we repeatedly deal with new insights and old fundamentals. Our purpose is to develop ideas profitable to both practitioners and critics of the analysis of data.

Many mathematical and philosophical discussions begin with a general theory, from which are derived general principles; from these, in turn, specific procedures are produced and finally exemplified. In discussing data analysis, we find the following somewhat opposite order more practical.

a) First, what to do. (What treatment to apply to the data of a given sort of problem, arithmetically or graphically.)

b) Then, why choose that treatment. (What reasons are there for choosing this treatment, from among so many, to meet this sort of problem? Usually the explanation must be made in terms of specific mathematical models.)

c) Next, what to include in the why. (What can be said about types of models, and classes of reasons, that have proved useful in carrying out this choice, and which types and classes, by contrast, have proved misleading.)

d) Last, how to structure our thinking about the overall process of data analysis. (What general theories produce the reasons of (c) as deductions rather than as inductions from experience.)

Great overturns at the (d) level have had little effect on what is done in practice, in comparison with the effects of less imposing changes at the (b) level.

In this introductory section (Section A, divided into Sections A1 to A8), we strike a number of the themes that run throughout the account: the staircase of primary, secondary, tertiary, . . . statistics and Student's shortcut to inference; the distributional properties of observations and measurements; the need for vague concepts in the evaluation of more definite concepts and criteria; the distinction between indication, determination, and inference. Each theme recurs.

The main thrust of the later sections is toward a flexible, realistic data analysis that tries to let the data speak freely through techniques that meet realistic assumptions. Sections B, C, D, and E follow a sequence from basic statistics without statistical inference, which we call indication, through the realistic assessment of variability.

The character of the two closing sections is different; they deal with approaches and techniques that are, so far as we know, only applicable under restrictive hypotheses. Section F introduces the reader to Bayesian ideas. Section G treats many of the uses of binomial probability paper, an effective tool for examining counted data when the individual observations can be treated as independent.

A1. THE STAIRCASE AND THE SHORTCUT TO INFERENCE

Before Student's time, every analysis of data that considered "what might have been" resembled a long staircase from the near foreground to the misty heights. One began by calculating a primary statistic, a number that indicated quite directly what the data seemed to say about the point at issue. The primary statistic might, for instance, have been a sample mean. Then one faced the question of "How much different might its value have been?" and calculated a secondary statistic, a number that indicated quite directly how variable (or perhaps how stable and invariable) the primary statistic seemed to be. The secondary statistic might have been an estimate of the standard deviation of such a sample mean. After this step, one again needed to face the question of "How much different?", this time for the secondary statistic, which again and again turned out to be less stable (of itself) than the primary statistic whose stability it indicated. In principle, one should have gone on to a tertiary statistic, which indicated the variability or stability of the secondary statistic, then to a quaternary statistic, . . . , and so on up and up a staircase which, since the tertiary was a poorer indicator than the secondary, and the quaternary was even worse, could only be pictured as becoming mistier and mistier. In practice, workers usually stopped with primary and secondary statistics.

Student (1908) broke new ground by asking essentially "What if I have n observations randomly drawn from a normal distribution about whose average and variance I wish to assume nothing?". Let $\bar{y}$ be the sample mean, μ the population mean, y_i a measurement, n the sample size. We shall think of $\bar{y}$ and y_i as random variables for the moment, rather than as the numerical values realized in an investigation. Student's name identifies the *ratio:*

$$t = \frac{\text{sample mean} - \text{distribution mean}}{\sqrt{(\text{sample estimate of distribution variance})/n}}$$

$$= \frac{\bar{y} - \mu}{\sqrt{\dfrac{s^2}{n}}} = \frac{\bar{y} - \mu}{\sqrt{\left(\dfrac{\Sigma(y_i - \bar{y})^2}{n-1}\right)\Big/ n}}$$

$$= \frac{\text{sample mean} - \text{distribution mean}}{\sqrt{\text{sample estimate of variance of numerator}}}$$

$$= \frac{\bar{y} - \mu}{s_{\bar{y}}} = \frac{\bar{y} - \mu}{\sqrt{\dfrac{\Sigma(y_i - \bar{y})^2}{(n-1)n}}},$$

whose distribution, on normal theory, was found to depend only upon n. Student calculated some numerical aspects of the distribution of t. Then, after applying empirical sampling to 3000 measurements of finger lengths and 3000 heights which had been collected as an aid in identifying criminals, he succeeded in correctly guessing the mathematical form of the distribution of t. R. A. Fisher (1925) verified Student's guess 17 years later.

This approach cut off the misty staircase after the third step—indeed, almost after the second step. For, in order to tell us about the population mean, the data were asked to provide only

a1) the sample mean—a primary statistic,

a2) the sample estimate of variance—a secondary statistic,

a3) the sample size—a tertiary statistic, one that was easy to obtain and remarkably stable, at least so long as one compared this sample with other possible samples of the same size.

All else was provided by the assumption of exact normality.

Note that, while the sample mean, sample variance, and sample size are primary, secondary, and tertiary statistics for this purpose, they may play other roles in other circumstances.

Given the normality assumption, these three numbers, and any contemplated value μ_C for the distribution mean, we can calculate

$$t = \frac{\text{sample mean} - \text{contemplated value}}{\sqrt{\text{sample estimate of variance of numerator}}} = \frac{\bar{y} - \mu_C}{s_{\bar{y}}} .$$

The contemplated value could be any number, and could be changed many times for a single set of data. It might be zero if we were studying group differences and thought, either seriously or as a straw man, to find none. It might be 500, if we were comparing a group of students, perhaps the Freshman Class of some college, with the standard offered by a national average on a test standardized as the Educational Testing Service often does (mean 500, standard deviation 100). It might take on, in turn, all possible values, as when we seek a confidence interval.

Each time we insert a contemplated value in the formula for t, we take the first step in making a significance test. When the contemplated value exactly equals the population mean from which the y_i are drawn, the distribution of t is the one given by the usual tables. When the contemplated value is far from the true population mean, t is likely to yield a number large in absolute value. These ideas, applied to this and other key statistics, made a bit more precise with tables of critical values, and extended by the concept of operating characteristics or power of tests (see, for example, Mosteller and Bush, 1954), provide the whole machinery of significance testing and almost all the machinery used in practice to set confidence intervals.

By the 1930's and through the 1940's, people were learning to short-cut the staircase without making such strong assumptions. They introduced "non-parametric" or "distribution-free" procedures, thus eliminating dependence on the normal distribution for making "5%" really 5%, yet another stage in a continuing revolution.

A2. STUDENT'S TRUE CONTRIBUTION

In the half-century following its introduction, Student's t has been used extremely often in practice, as have many and diverse techniques that have evolved out of the same chain of development. Its impact on the usage of words and on the development of statistical theory have been equally striking.

TABLE A2–1

STANDARD CONFIDENCE POINTS FOR STUDENT'S t

f = degrees of freedom	$1/40 =$ 2.5%	$1/6 =$ $16\frac{2}{3}$%	$1/2 =$ 50%	$5/6 =$ $83\frac{1}{3}$%	$39/40 =$ 97.5%	$24/f$ (for interpolating)
1	−12.71	−1.73	0.00	1.73	12.71	
2	−4.30	−1.26	0.00	1.26	4.30	
3	−3.18	−1.15	0.00	1.15	3.18	
4	−2.78	−1.10	0.00	1.10	2.78	
5	−2.57	−1.07	0.00	1.07	2.57	
6	−2.45	−1.05	0.00	1.05	2.45	4
8	−2.31	−1.03	0.00	1.03	2.31	3
12	−2.18	−1.01	0.00	1.01	2.18	2
24	−2.06	−.99	0.00	.99	2.06	1
∞	−1.96	−.97	0.00	.97	1.96	0

Note 1: 2.5% and 97.5% points combine to give two-sided 95% confidence limits or a two-sided 5% significance test.

Note 2: Interpolation in the reciprocal of the degrees of freedom gives good accuracy. For example, for 48 degrees of freedom $24/f = 0.5$. Consequently the corresponding 97.5% point is halfway between 2.06 and 1.96 or 2.01.

Note 3: When we expect to use a t in a symmetrical two-sided way, it is often convenient to think of the distribution of $|t|$, the absolute value of t. We write $|t|_{.95}$ for the two-sided 95% point of $|t|$, which is given above in the column headed $39/40$. We write $|t|_{2/3}$ for the two-sided $2/3$ point, which is given above in the column headed $5/6$. We use similar notations for any two-sided % points of t.

The value of Student's work was not that it led to great changes in the numbers obtained in the analysis of data, because in the main it did not. To see this look at Table A2–1 where we show some % points that would be used to set two-sided $95\% = 19/20 = 38/40$ confidence limits (and also those needed for two-sided $2/3 = 66\frac{2}{3}$% confidence limits, a less usual level selected for reasons we explain later). One measure of the effect of Student's t is the ratio of the length of confidence interval obtained by using it to the length obtained when the standard normal distribution, which is equivalent to t for infinite degrees of freedom, is used. Long before Student came along, many people calculated the same ratio used today (except for a slight change in the definition of the sample standard deviation as discussed below), namely,

$$\frac{\text{sample mean} - \text{contemplated value}}{\text{sample standard deviation}/\sqrt{n}}.$$

Not having Student's table, all they then knew how to do was to refer this ratio to a table of the standard normal distribution and to use varying amounts of verbal caution in interpreting the result.

How great was the change? We find from Table A2–1 that, for example, if 95% confidence limits are set using the standard normal distribution, the multiplier of the standard error $s_{\bar{y}}$ is 1.96; while using a t distribution with 12 degrees of freedom, the multiplier is 2.18. Since $2.18/1.96 \approx 1.11$, the use of the t distribution adds only 11% to the length of the 95% confidence interval when we have 12 degrees of freedom. (*We use the symbol* "$\approx$" *to stand for* "*is approximately equal to*" *or* "*approximates*" *or similar phrases implying approximation rather than strict equality.*) (If a slightly different definition of $s_{\bar{y}}$ were used, again with the standard normal distribution, namely $\sqrt{\Sigma(y_i - \bar{y})^2/n^2}$, the ratio would rise to 1.15.) For levels of confidence less extreme, the effect is less marked. For example, for two-sided 2/3 confidence, we can go as low as 5 degrees of freedom before the ratio of lengths of confidence intervals based on t to that based on the normal is as much as 1.1 ($\approx 1.07/0.97$).

We are not trying to sweep under the rug the gigantic ratio of $6.5 \approx 12.7/1.96$ associated with 95% confidence and 1 degree of freedom. But most investigators use more degrees of freedom; indeed, an important impact of the t table has been to encourage investigators to get more degrees of freedom so as to avoid such terrible ratios as the 6.5, 2.2, and 1.6 offered at 95% by 1, 2, and 3 degrees of freedom, respectively. Note that for 2/3 confidence the corresponding ratios are only 1.8, 1.3, and 1.2.

The value of Student's work lay not in a great numerical change, but in:

b1) recognition that one could, if appropriate assumptions held, make allowance for the "uncertainties" of small samples, not only in Student's original problem but in others as well.

b2) provision of a numerical assessment of how small the necessary numerical adjustments of confidence points were in Student's problem, and as we have just seen, how they depended on the extremeness of the probabilities involved.

b3) presentation of tables that could be used—in setting confidence limits, in making significance tests—to assess the uncertainty associated with even very small samples.

Besides its values, Student's contribution had its drawbacks, notably:

b4) it made neglect of the proviso "if appropriate assumptions held" too easy;

b5) it overemphasized the "exactness" of Student's solution for his idealized problem; and

TABLE A2–2

STANDARD CONFIDENCE POINTS FOR BURRAU'S MODIFICATION OF STUDENT'S t

$$\sqrt{\frac{f-2}{f}} \cdot t = \frac{\bar{y} - \mu}{\sqrt{\Sigma(y_i - \bar{y})^2/n(n-3)}} \qquad \text{where} \quad f = n - 1$$

f = degrees of freedom	$1/40 =$ 2.5%	$1/6 =$ $16\frac{2}{3}$%	$1/2 =$ 50%	$5/6 =$ $83\frac{1}{3}$%	$39/40 =$ 97.5%	$24/f$ (for interpolating)
3	−1.84	−0.66	0.00	0.66	1.84	
4	−1.96	−0.78	0.00	0.78	1.96	
5	−1.99	−0.83	0.00	0.83	1.99	
6	−2.00	−0.86	0.00	0.86	2.00	4
8	−2.00	−0.89	0.00	0.89	2.00	3
12	−1.99	−0.92	0.00	0.92	1.99	2
24	−1.98	−0.95	0.00	0.95	1.98	1
∞	−1.96	−0.97	0.00	0.97	1.96	0

Note 1: The variance of t is infinite for 2 or fewer degrees of freedom, so that Burrau's formula is inapplicable for $f = 1$ and 2.

Note 2: 2.5% and 97.5% points combine to give two-sided 95% confidence limits or a two-sided 5% significance test.

b6) it helped to divert the attention of theoretical statisticians to the development of "exact" ways of treating other problems;

b7) it failed to attack "problems of multiplicity": the difficulties and temptations associated with the application of large numbers of tests to the same data.

The great importance given to exactness of treatment is even more surprising when we consider how much of the small differences between the critical values of the normal approximation and Student's t disappears (see Table A2–2), especially at and near the much-used two-sided 5% point, when, as suggested by Burrau (1943), we multiply t by the constant required to bring its variance to 1. (Regardless of its practical pros and cons, Burrau's modification frees our insight from the possibly misleading effects of the quite nonconstant variance of t.)

The time has long since come to pay attention to the advantages of Student's work and to recognize its drawbacks for what they are, skimping neither in comparison to the other.

A3. DISTRIBUTIONS AND THEIR TROUBLES

Student himself always remembered that observations and measurements were never distributed in magic bell-shaped curves, even when they were chemical determinations of commercial importance made under his own supervision (Student, 1927). The history of statistics and data analysis is a messy mixture of healthy skepticism and naive optimism about the exact shapes of the distribu-

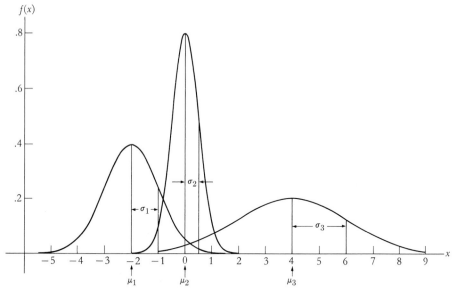

Fig. A3–1. A collection of three normal or Gaussian probability density functions with differing means and differing standard deviations: $\mu_1 = -2$, $\sigma_1 = 1$; $\mu_2 = 0$, $\sigma_2 = 0.5$; $\mu_3 = 4$, $\sigma_3 = 2$.

tions of observations. Such optimism has often been inflated by the wonderful properties of a single family of distributions, the "normal" distributions whose probability densities are given by

$$f(x) = \frac{1}{\sqrt{2\pi}\sigma} e^{-\frac{1}{2}(x-\mu)^2/\sigma^2} \qquad \text{for} \quad -\infty < x < \infty,$$

where μ and σ are the population mean and standard deviation, respectively, e is the base of the natural logarithms 2.7182818 . . . , and π is our old friend 3.1415926 . . . . Figure A3–1 portrays three instances of normal distributions with differing combinations of μ and σ.

We use the adjectives "normal" and "Gaussian" interchangeably for distributions that fit this formula *exactly*. Neither term is wholly satisfactory. Some misinterpret the word "normal" to mean "the ordinarily occurring", but so far as we know distributions that exactly fit this formula never occur in practice—not for individual observations, not for sample means, not for other derived quantities—though we have both theory and evidence that many empirical distributions do approximate this shape, sometimes quite usefully, but sometimes only apparently rather than meaningfully. (The characteristics that matter most are often those that are concealed, not revealed, by conventional histograms.)

The connection of the distributions of derived statistics, such as sample means and Student's t, to the underlying distribution of individual values is often subtle, as we shall illustrate shortly. Since distributions of the derived statistics usually determine the adequacy of our statements of uncertainty, significance, and confidence, the particular aspects of approximation that matter in practice differ from situation to situation and are often not easily checked by examining a single sample, or even the whole body of data before us, which may consist of hundreds of observations.

The term "Gaussian" is fairly widely known, mainly among physical scientists, but is strange to most behavioral scientists. Its use runs into problems of scientific priority (in France, for example, one must say "Laplacean").

We say of the three distributions in Fig. A3–1 that they all have the same "shape". Let us discuss the concept of shape.

Suppose that we have many observations, so that the histogram representing actual counts closely approximates the underlying distribution. Suppose that this histogram has been plotted on graph paper, but that someone has forgotten to put numbers along the axes. What can we learn from what we have? What have we lost? Without numbers on the vertical axis, we cannot tell how large the sample was. Since our interest centers on the distribution, not the sample, and the sample was large, we may be able to forget this. Without numbers on the horizontal axis, we cannot tell near what value the observations fell, or how widespread or concentrated they were; we can tell nothing about location or about scale, to use technical terms. These are important things to have lost. What remains?

By giving up location and scale, by classing together all distributions that differ only by a linear transformation, we have given up only 2 numbers; accordingly much remains: all, indeed, that is usually meant by the word *shape*. Distributions, even distributions belonging to the same mathematical family, can differ widely in shape. The family of beta functions, for instance, though still a very special case, includes distributions of many shapes, as Fig. F6–1 illustrates.

Given the histogram, we can locate the central 2/3rds of all cases and find the number of spaces along the graph paper required to cover them. We can do the same for the central 19/20ths, and compare the two lengths. If this ratio is almost exactly 2 to 1, we have confirmed one characteristic of a normal distribution. If it is appreciably larger than 2 to 1, we have evidence that the two-sided 5% points of our distribution are more widespread than we would have expected on the basis of how the central part of the distribution is spread out and how normal distributions behave. If the sample is large enough, this is already clear evidence that the population is not normal. (Other indications can be more revealing in small or moderate-sized samples, as we illustrate in the next section.)

We can look at such ratios further and further into the tails. If, when we do this, either for the whole population, or for sufficiently large samples, these ratios eventually tend to be too large for normal distributions, we know that we are dealing with tails that are *more straggling* than those of a normal distribution. This statement has nothing to do with the overall spread of a distribution. Rather it concerns the spread of the extreme tails in comparison with the spread of the central body of the distribution.

A glance at Table A2–1 shows that the distributions of Student's t appear more straggling than the Gaussian, except, of course, for the case with ∞ degrees of freedom, which has exactly the Gaussian shape. The ratio just mentioned (length of middle 19/20ths to length of middle 2/3rds), which is about 2.02 for the Gaussian, is 2.16 for 12 degrees of freedom, 2.4 for 5, 3.4 for 2, and a whopping 7.3 for 1 degree of freedom. If you know that 2/3 of a Gaussian distribution lies in a certain interval, and you consider an interval 7 times as long but with the same center, you know that all but an extremely tiny part (1 in a hundred billion) of that Gaussian distribution lies in the larger interval. If you know that 2/3 of a "Student's t with one degree of freedom" distribution lies in a certain interval, and you consider an interval 7 times as long but with the same center, we have just seen that more than $5\% = 1/20$ of the distribution can fall outside the longer interval. When tails straggle a lot, the center of a distribution can fool the eye about the behavior of the tails. Real distributions often straggle a lot compared to a normal distribution.

A4. A CLASSICAL EXAMPLE:
WILSON AND HILFERTY'S ANALYSIS OF PEIRCE'S DATA

An example investigating unusually extensive data for normality of shape of distribution may be illuminating.

In an empirical study intended to test the appropriateness of the normal distribution, C. S. Peirce (1870) analyzed the times elapsed between a sharp tone stimulus and the response by an observer, who made about 500 responses each day for 24 days. Though Peirce seems to have concluded that the normal shape of this distribution was on the whole verified, when Wilson and Hilferty (1929) reanalyzed Peirce's published material sixty years later, they came to very different conclusions.

They calculated many different statistics from Peirce's data, treating each day's measurements separately. We select a few of the 23 statistics Wilson and Hilferty reported and display them in Table A4–1. Column (2) gives an estimate of the distance from the 25% (Q_1) to the 75% point (Q_3) of that day's distribution (based on the corresponding % points of the distribution of that day's sample), divided by a suitable multiple of the s computed from the very same observations. For a normal distribution these numbers should vary around 1.00, roughly symmetrically. In Peirce's data, however, all 24 numbers are less than 1.00, many substantially. Column (6) shows that too many measurements deviate from their mean by more than 3.1 sample standard deviations ($3.1s$) in each direction. For a normal distribution, 1 observation in 500 on the average would be more than $3.1s$ from $\bar{x}$, half in either direction, whereas Peirce's data average 5.6 per 500. Similarly, measures of skewness and kurtosis are consistently positive instead of varying around zero, as they should for a normal distribution. Furthermore, according to column (3) too many measurements are near the mean for normally distributed data, again, by comparison with s. Thus Peirce's data clearly do not follow the normal or Gaussian "law".

Some would try to ascribe this to the choice of reaction *time,* properly asserting that, in 1968, an informed worker would not suppose that such times were

TABLE A4–1

DAILY STATISTICS FROM WILSON AND HILFERTY'S ANALYSIS OF C. S. PEIRCE'S DATA

	(1)	(2)	(3)		(4)	(5)	(6)		
			No. within 0.25s of $\bar{x}$				Errors $> 3.1s$		
Day	$\bar{x} \pm s_{\bar{x}}$ (milliseconds)	$\dfrac{Q_3 - Q_1}{2(0.6745s)}$	Observed	Expected	Skewness	Kurtosis $\hat{\beta}_2 - 3$	Negative	Positive	Total
1	475.6 ± 4.2	0.932	110	98	1.18	3.1	1	3	4
2	241.5 ± 2.1	0.842	113	97	0.43	0.9	1	0	1
3	203.1 ± 2.0	0.905	113	97	1.09	3.6	0	7	7
4	205.6 ± 1.8	0.730	134	99	1.82	9.7	1	7	8
5	148.5 ± 1.6	0.912	110	97	0.39	1.3	0	4	4
6	175.6 ± 1.8	0.744	119	97	1.48	6.4	0	6	6
7	186.9 ± 2.2	0.753	132	98	2.96	24.9	0	6	6
8	194.1 ± 1.4	0.840	120	97	0.48	4.1	2	6	8
9	195.8 ± 1.6	0.756	132	98	1.71	13.8	2	4	6
10	215.5 ± 1.3	0.850	120	99	0.84	8.8	2	1	3
11	216.6 ± 1.7	0.782	135	99	1.69	9.8	1	5	6
12	235.6 ± 1.7	0.759	103	78	0.63	4.7	3	5	8
13	244.5 ± 1.2	0.922	101	97	−0.22	2.6	6	1	7
14	236.7 ± 1.8	0.529	192	99	5.74	63.6	2	3	5
15	236.0 ± 1.4	0.662	162	98	1.68	27.9	4	4	8
16	233.2 ± 1.7	0.612	162	98	6.39	90.6	4	2	6
17	265.5 ± 1.7	0.792	123	100	0.21	4.3	3	5	8
18	253.0 ± 1.1	0.959	114	98	0.27	1.8	0	4	4
19	258.7 ± 1.8	0.502	187	99	10.94	143.9	1	3	4
20	255.4 ± 2.0	0.521	179	98	7.71	91.4	0	3	3
21	245.0 ± 1.2	0.790	120	99	0.23	8.2	3	4	7
22	255.6 ± 1.4	0.688	142	99	5.27	68.1	2	4	6
23	251.4 ± 1.6	0.610	158	98	2.73	31.1	0	3	3
24	243.4 ± 1.1	0.730	113	98	−0.02	5.4	3	3	6
Averages							1.7	3.9	5.6

likely to be normally distributed, and arguing that perhaps the logarithm of the reaction times might well be nearly normally distributed. A glance at the table shows that this approach cannot succeed. Indeed, the number of negative errors beyond 3.1s is already 3 times that for a normal distribution, and a logarithmic transformation would *increase* this number.

The important deviations from normality in Peirce's data are not matters of discreteness, nor are they matters of gross differences in shape. Columns (2) and (3) agree generally with each other both as to typical value and in day-to-day changes. As Winsor's "principle" predicts for the distributions that arise in practice, the distributions of these very large samples are, except for discreteness, reasonably "normal in the middle". However, the normal distribution that would fit the center of the observed distribution would have a spread only about 3/4 of that of the distribution fitted to the observed value of the standard deviation.

The median value in column (2), omitting day 1, is 0.756, which corresponds to a variance due to the "normal body" of the distribution of about $(.756)^2 \approx 0.57$ of that observed. Thus more than 40% ($\approx 100\% - 57\%$) of the observed variance comes from the fact that the tails straggle more than for a normal distribution. Again we see that Peirce's observations are glaringly far from being normally distributed.

A5. KINDS OF NONNORMALITY AND ROBUSTNESS

When a distribution does not have the Gaussian shape, its failure to be Gaussian may arise from:

a1) *discreteness and irregularity:* (i) Ordinarily the value of an actual observation or measurement can never be just any number from minus infinity to plus infinity—its possible values will be limited; often, in particular, to multiples of some least count. (For example, children and marriages come in whole numbers, prices on many stock markets come in 1/8's, and many machine shop measurements are in thousandths of an inch.) (ii) Beyond this, both real and theoretical distributions are subject to further irregularities, such

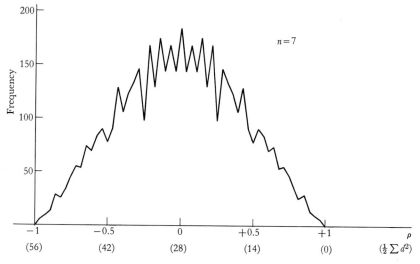

Fig. A5-1. Distribution of rank correlation coefficient for $n = 7$. To obtain probabilities, ordinates should be divided by 7!. Probabilities are zero unless half the sum of squares of differences $\frac{1}{2}\Sigma d^2$ is an integer. Example: given the two matched rankings $\frac{1234567}{3214567}$, the sum of squares $\Sigma d^2 = 2^2 + 0^2 + 2^2 = 8$ and $\frac{1}{2}\Sigma d^2 = 4$. (After Kendall, Kendall, and Smith, 1938.)

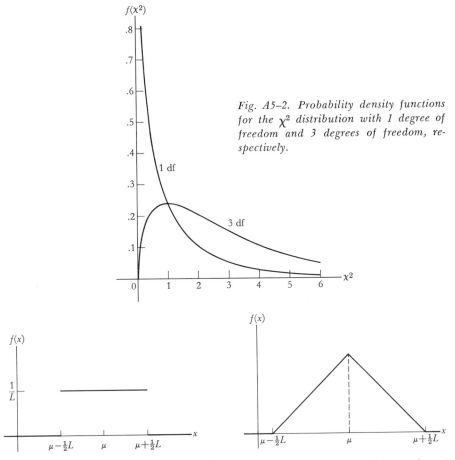

Fig. A5–2. *Probability density functions for the χ^2 distribution with 1 degree of freedom and 3 degrees of freedom, respectively.*

Fig. A5–3. *Probability density function for rectangular distribution with range* L *and mean* μ.

Fig. A5–4. *Probability density function of a triangular distribution.*

as those caused by observers' digit preferences and those that appear even in theoretical distributions, such as the sampling distribution of the rank correlation coefficient in the null situation (when the variables being correlated are actually independent) (see Fig. A5–1). To help guide the eye, the successive ordinates of this discrete distribution have been connected by straight lines.

a2) *gross differences in shape:* Among these we include those differences, such as the gross skewness of χ^2 (or F) with few degrees of freedom, that can be reliably detected in samples of, say, 50 to 100. The abrupt ends of a rectangular distribution, which spreads its probability evenly over a fixed range, are barely this gross. Figure A5–2 represents the density of χ^2 distributions with 1 and 3 degrees of freedom; Fig. A5–3 represents the density of a rectangular distribution; Fig. A5–4 represents the density of a symmetrical triangular distribution, which incidentally represents the distribution of the sum of two independent and rectangularly distributed (uniform) random variables, each with range $L/2$, whose means sum to μ.

a3) *minor differences in central shape:* difficult to separate from either of the first two and rarely of importance on their own.

a4) *behavior in the tails:* hard to detect, yet often important because a few straggling values scattered far from the bulk of the measurements can, for example, alter a sample mean drastically, and a sample s^2 catastrophically.

In the usual measurement situations, behavior in the tails is both the most vital and the least securely tied down of all. It is not well tied down because changes in tail size by large and important factors need involve only a few percent of all observations, and are therefore both difficult to detect by sampling and easy for transient causes to produce. It is vital because the extreme tails of the distribution of individual values are likely to influence large portions of the distributions of many derived quantities.

Consider the situation where, perhaps because of human actions, there is one chance in a thousand of a huge deviation (an observation strikingly far from some central value like a mean or median). In samples of size 100, there will be one such huge deviation per 10 samples, or about 100 huge deviations per 1000 samples. Thus 10% of all sample means will be affected. This can be enough to distort 5% points seriously. If these "wild shots" are extreme enough, they will clearly perturb sample means seriously. Student's t, on the other hand, is a function of the observations that behaves in quite a different way than a sample mean does. The effect of one observation differing very greatly, both from the mean of the other observations and from the contemplated value, is to make the value of t fall close to $+1$ or -1. When working at 95%, this is going to cause little distortion of % risk, thus "failing safe", but can make many instances that would otherwise be "significant" come out "not significant". Our real need is accurate answers, not just safe statements. Often the use of other significance tests will avoid such ill effects from outliers and bring us closer to describing the real state of affairs.

Much needs to be done to modify our statistical procedures to make them not only tolerant of nonnormal tails, but highly effective in their presence. The next edition of this *Handbook* may offer improvements, since much work is in progress.

Both of these desirable properties are kinds of *robustness,* kinds of lack of susceptibility to the effects of nonnormality. The first property, tolerance of nonnormal tails, has been called *robustness of validity,* and is exemplified by confidence intervals for μ which have a 95% chance of covering μ, whatever population may have been sampled. We get this sort of robustness exactly, for example, when a confidence interval for the population median is based on the sign test, Section G–6, Example 5. The second property, high effectiveness in the face of nonnormal tails, is called *robustness of efficiency,* and is exemplified by confidence intervals for μ which tend to be almost as narrow, for any roughly normal distribution (that is, any one "approximately normal in the middle") as the best that could be done if the true shape of the distribution were known to a close approximation. We now know, for example, that a variety of procedures (see Tukey and McLaughlin, 1963) for setting approximate confidence limits on the basis of the central 90% or 95% of the observations in the sample have both robustness of efficiency and robustness of validity so long as we require only approximate validity and efficiency and confine our attention to distributions approximately normal in the middle.

You will find that most analytical studies of the effects of "nonnormality" consider only what happens when behavior in the tails of the distribution agrees with the results of naive extrapolation from the behavior of the body of the distribution. In the real world things are usually different, since many causes that could have contributed to each of the values that we had observed, like *gross* human error, act only infrequently. As a result, real tails rarely match the body of the distribution, and are likely, when very large samples begin to reveal their true behavior, to appear poorly pasted on.

Both sorts of tail misbehavior can be of considerable importance. The difference between grossly nonnormal distributions and distributions "normal in the middle" but with straggling tails is not mainly in the consequences, which are rather similar. Rather it is that gross nonnormality is likely to be detected, or even brought forcibly to one's notice, but straggling tails tend to escape both notice and careful examination.

One way to give specific examples of distributions with straggling tails is to consider mixtures of normal distributions. For example, we might consider a distribution formed from observations drawn from two normal distributions having identical means, but unequal standard deviations. Almost all of the measurements would come from the normal distribution with the smaller standard deviation, but a small fraction, say 1%, comes from a distribution with 3 times the standard deviation of the first. Such mixed distributions are sometimes called *contaminated distributions.* This one would be called 1% contaminated at scale 3.

We shall also need the notion of relative *efficiency.* Roughly speaking, when two estimates of the same quantity have unequal variances, the ratio of the smaller variance to the larger is called the efficiency of the estimate with the larger variance. To be more careful in our definition, the distributions of the two statistics should have roughly similar shapes, and their variances should approximate constant multiples of $1/n$. Under these conditions, the efficiency satisfactorily gives the ratio of the sample sizes required for two statistics to do the same job. As an example, for large samples from normal distributions, the sample median has variance approximately $(\pi/2)\sigma^2/n$, and the sample mean has variance σ^2/n. We say that the median has efficiency $2/\pi \approx 0.64$. Or, a sample of size 100 using the sample median estimates the population mean about as well as a sample of 64 does using the sample mean.

Consider an extreme case, where we compare a normal distribution with a distribution 1% contaminated at scale 3. This represents a lengthening of tails of the basic normal by so little as to require thousands of observations for reliable detection. Yet the effect on the distributions of derived quantities can be very serious. In large samples, we can compare two estimates of spread: (i) that based on the standard deviation, *s*, where squares of deviations are summed, and (ii) that based on the mean deviation, where absolute values of deviations are summed $(\Sigma \, | \, y_i - \bar{y} \, | \, /n)$. For the relative efficiencies we find (Tukey, 1960)

for normality:	mean deviation	88% as good as *s*
for 1% contamination:	mean deviation	144% as good as *s*

Clearly quite small differences in shape of distribution can greatly affect the efficiency and therefore the comparative palatability of different procedures.

A6. THE ROLE OF VAGUE CONCEPTS

Effective data analysis requires us to consider *vague concepts,* concepts that can be made definite in many ways. To help understand many definite concepts, we need to go back to more primitive and less definite concepts and then work our way forward. Let us take a simple example. Most beginning students of statistics know that the standard deviation of a distribution is one of the useful things to estimate. The concept of standard deviation is hard enough to grasp and use; students have not, as a rule, had much time to consider why and when to use it. Let us discuss these questions.

One approach from the vague toward the particular begins with the crude and qualitative idea that some distributions are more widely spread out, others are more tightly packed, and with the insight that it might be well to measure this by some numerical measure of *spread.* This leads us to the sequence of ideas:

a1) Spreads differ.

a2) A numerical measure may be useful.

a3) One numerical measure is the standard deviation.

a4) How do we judge whether this is a good choice?

Notice that we have so far been discussing the problem only for a complete distribution or population, and that no questions of sampling or estimation have yet been considered. We are still interested in what questions we want answered, not yet with how to get their approximate answers.

The usual answers to (a4) that are both acceptable and favorable to the standard deviation include the following:

b1) The definition of a standard deviation (of a complete distribution) is relatively clear and widely applicable.

b2) So long as one is concerned with simple or weighted sample means, or with many of the other conventional linear combinations of observations (such as

5 + 2x + 3y, where *x* and *y* are observations), the standard deviation (or its square, the variance) is a peculiarly useful measure because there are convenient relationships between the variance of the defined statistic and the variance of the underlying distribution that do not depend upon distributional shape. For example, with *x* and *y* as observations, *a* and *b* as constants, σ_x, σ_y, and σ_{ax+by} the standard deviations of the indicated quantities, and ρ the correlation coefficient between *x* and *y*, we have the relation:

$$\sigma^2_{ax+by} = a^2\sigma^2_x + 2ab\rho\sigma_x\sigma_y + b^2\sigma^2_y.$$

b3) Certain algebraically convenient relations hold "on the average" between sample and population for the variance (and hence for its square root, the standard deviation); for example, the expected or average value of s^2 is σ^2, where s^2 is the sample variance, $s^2 = \Sigma(y_i - \bar{y})^2/(n-1)$, and σ^2 is the population variance.

b4) If one can confine his attention to distributions of given shape (all normal, all rectangular, all symmetric triangular, etc.), then any two measures of spread are connected by multiplication by fixed constants, and so it doesn't really matter which population measures of spread you choose. (Recall from Section A3 that many larger families of closely related distributions, for example, all beta distributions, do not have a single shape.) Consequently, why not choose the standard deviation?

On the other hand,

c1) Some distributions have infinite standard deviations; indeed, we have seen the examples of the *t* distribution with 1 and 2 degrees of freedom in the first footnote to Table A2–2. When such a distribution is just twice as widely spread as another, their standard deviations do not tell us this, though a variety of other measures of spread, including the interquartile range, do.

c2) Means are a poor way to summarize samples from distributions with infinite standard deviations, so that (b2) is irrelevant when working with such distributions.

c3) Even though the population variance is infinite, all the sample variances are finite, so that (b3) buys us little or nothing in such cases.

c4) If, for a distribution with finite variance, we change shape enough to make the variance infinite, the relation of the standard deviation to other measures of spread that remain finite changes drastically.

c5) An imperceptible probability of sufficiently deviant values can make the variance infinite.

c6) Consequently the difference, in most practice, between distributions with infinite variances and distributions with finite variances and long straggling tails cannot be great, so that (b4) buys us little or nothing in practice.

We do not wish to conclude from these arguments that the standard deviation is a poor choice. In many situations, it is still an ideal choice as a description of a population—and in some it is far from ideal.

We do wish to conclude:

d1) that the standard deviation is *a choice*.

d2) that, in order to understand that it is a choice and to decide whether it is a good choice, we need the vaguer idea of *measures of spread*.

We shall repeatedly need vague concepts like spread to help us understand and appraise the usefulness of definite concepts like standard deviation, range, and interquartile range. Sometimes the specific concepts come first, and the vague concept is sought out to help in dealing with them. More often, however, the vague concept comes first and guides us in identifying corresponding specific concepts.

A7. MORE VAGUE CONCEPTS

The student of elementary statistics may have learned to classify some experimental results as "significant" and others as "not significant". And he may have learned that observed sample means, as well as many other expressions calculated from the sample, can generate "confidence intervals" for population means. These are specific ways of realizing another vague concept: "expressing amounts of uncertainty".

Here, the sequence of ideas is:

a1) Observed numerical summaries, such as sample means, from small or medium-sized samples do not coincide with what would have been found "by the same methods" from either extremely large samples or complete populations.

a2) We do not know the difference between sample summary value and population summary value in any one instance (if we did, we would make the adjustment), but we may be able to assess about how large it might reasonably be.

a3) The plausible size thus assessed will be different in different circumstances; obviously some sample summary values are subject to greater uncertainties than others.

a4) Thus there is a place for ways of assessing and expressing amounts of uncertainty.

Different specific ways of "expressing amounts of uncertainty" are in daily use. One whole class of choices, often closely related to one another, is provided by confidence intervals. (To give a 90% confidence interval is not the same as to give a 99% confidence interval, but in simple problems, the information conveyed by the one is usually roughly translatable into that given by the other.) Besides confidence intervals, there are not only significance tests but a number of other ways of expressing extent of uncertainty.

We cannot be effective in thinking about these ways comparatively, to say nothing of their use in practice, without some attention to a more primitive vague notion: assessing the uncertainty of a numerical summary.

We have introduced above, perhaps without your notice, an approximation to another important, but vague concept. The term "numerical summary" was

illustrated by the example of a sample mean. It was hoped that the usual meanings of "numerical" and "summary" would be enough to seem to give it meaning
for the moment. A still more general notion covers any of those things that
have been drawn from a body of data to exhibit at least one aspect of what that
body can suggest. This may be a numerical summary—or a graphical summary.

We are going to call any such summary an *indication*, and we shall insist on
its meeting only two of the statistician's obligations:

b1) It must differ from an anecdote by allowing each of the observations to contribute to it.

b2) It must be expressed in such a way that at least some of those who are interested in the subject can think about its interpretation.

These conditions are important, but should not be interpreted too stringently.
The mean of a sample of 15 is an indication, but so is the median of that sample,
since each observation contributes to the median in the sense that, in the absence
of ties at the median, if that one observation had been sufficiently different, the
median would have been different. Each observation had its effect, even though
small changes in a single observation (each of which would have an effect on the
mean, smaller than on the individual value, but still present) need not change the
median in the slightest.

Both mean and median belong to a special class of indications one might call
typical values. In particular, for nicely behaved data where the observations
follow a crudely bell-shaped distribution, both mean and median usually indicate, roughly, where the center or body of that distribution falls. (If the tails are
straggling and unsymmetrical enough, the mean may fail to do this.)

Measures of spread, measures of association, all the results of most of the
standard procedures of statistical analysis are indications, as are interesting bumps
on curves, greater wiggliness of a graph on its left-hand side than on its right, or
apparent segregation of a scatter diagram into clumps.

Statistics courses tend not to emphasize indication; instead, they concentrate
upon how to express the uncertainties of particular kinds of indications. In im-
pressing the student with the importance of assessing uncertainties when one can
(and can afford the effort), it is perhaps inevitable that they may give the impression that indications whose uncertainties have not been assessed are worthless.
This is, of course, just not so. We need to assess uncertainties vigorously and often,
but we also need to look at indications of unassessed uncertainty, especially
where assessment is impossible or uneconomic.

A8. INDICATION, DETERMINATION, OR INFERENCE

Since Student's revolution, many kinds of formal inference have been developed;
today we have our choice of three levels of statistical analysis. We can be concerned with any or all of the following:

a) pure indication, in which, for example, we attend only to primary statistics,
such as means and percentages, with no attempt to assess uncertainties;

b) determination, or augmented measurement, where both primary and secondary statistics are to be calculated and considered, for example, a mean and an estimate of its standard deviation (and where, though nothing is said about inference, the secondary statistics are most often only interesting as tools for appraising uncertainty);

c) formal inference, where some relatively precise specification or description of a manageable mathematical model allows us, at least apparently, to tie up our uncertainties in a neat package, for example, through confidence limits, significance tests, fiducial inference, posterior distributions, or likelihood functions.

In some specific situations, course (c) is not open to us, perhaps for some of the following reasons:

d1) the data do not allow some of the important causes of variation to show their effects,

d2) the causes show themselves in a distinctly nonrandom way,

d3) no formal inference procedure is available because none has been developed, or those that have been worked out all employ such stringent assumptions as to make their use unwise or misleading (or even perhaps because the computational effort required would be impractically great).

Sometimes, indeed, we may appear to lack, as in (d2) for instance, even any reasonable way to compute secondary statistics. Then we are likely to appear forced to resort to pure indication.

When our concern is with indication alone, there is an important distinction between indications that point toward something definite and those that point usefully but not toward anything, as when a graph causes its viewers to say "Look, there's a kink in the curve!". Indications of the former kind are also called estimates. Their indicators are also estimators. We discuss estimates and estimators further in Section B4.

This distinction between estimators and nonestimators is closely similar to, but definitely not the same as, the distinction between quantitative indicators and qualitative indicators. A large value of chi square, for example, often indicates that some hypothesis fits poorly, yet the value of chi square itself points toward no number that has a real meaning for the underlying situation.

B. INDICATION AND INDICATORS

Introduction
B1. *The value of indication*
B2. *Examples of stopping with indication*
B3. *Concealed inference*
B4. *Choice of indicators*
B5. *An example of choice of indicator*
B6. *Indications of quality: cross-validation*

Indication is elementary, important, and neglected.

In beginning to remedy this neglect, we have to show indication as valuable and often the best that can be done. We have to illustrate how indicators may be reasonably chosen; how indication can require care, as illustrated by cross-validation; and how graphs are of great value, almost entirely because of their function as indicators.

B1. THE VALUE OF INDICATION

One hallmark of the statistically conscious investigator is his firm belief that however the survey, experiment, or observational program actually turned out, it could have turned out somewhat differently. Holding such a belief and taking appropriate actions make effective use of data possible. We need not always ask explicitly "About how much differently?", but we should be aware of such questions. Most of us find uncertainty uncomfortable; the history of data analysis can be read as a succession of searches for certainty about uncertainty. Each of us who deals with the analysis and interpretation of data must learn to cope with uncertainty in a way that meets his own needs.

A caricature of one recipe might read: apply a significance test to each result, believe the result implicitly if the conventional level of significance is reached, believe the null hypothesis otherwise. Such a complete flight from reality and its uncertainties is fortunately rare, but periodically considering its extremism may help us keep our balance.

To the researcher the primary value of data lies in what they *indicate,* what they appear to show. Such an appearance may be quite correct and exact, may be a matter of chance, and probably is a mixture. In some fields, when it is only a matter of counting noses or counting punched cards, assessing the indications tends to be overlooked or regarded as an unimportant detail, though demographic and population studies offer good exceptions.

Nose-counting and reporting counts form only one extreme of indication. At the other, the most essential parts of our most complicated schemes of analyzing data—complex analyses of variance, multiple regression analyses, factor analyses, latent structure analyses—have as their main function the assessment of indication.

The word indication is a vague concept intended to include, at one extreme, all of the classical descriptive statistics (for example: mean, median, mode, quantile, standard deviation, correlation), but also, at another extreme, to include any hints and suggestions obtained from data by an understandable process, suggestions that might prove informative to a reasonable man. Examples are appearances of similarity (all the curves look S-shaped or ogival) or general behavior (the frequencies seem to be falling off roughly exponentially, or, again, although the means of the groups vary widely, the standard deviations are all close to those usually found in these experiments). Indication includes not only isolated numbers (differences, slopes, and other indices), but also inequalities and trends (the female appears to be more deadly than the male, blood pressure appears to rise with age), and appearances of graphs and diagrams (these scatter diagrams appear doughnut-shaped).

What indication is *not* is inference or treatment of uncertainty; indication does not include confidence limits, significance tests, posterior and fiducial distributions, or even standard errors.

The treatment of variation or uncertainty looms large and that of indication small in most discussions of data analysis. This imbalance arises naturally: important considerations in assessing indications are often specific to a particular problem and therefore difficult to generalize about; since the study of variation is often neglected by the beginner in his eagerness to find regularities and simple appearances, he needs his attention brought to problems of uncertainty; and for many, it is psychologically satisfactory to seek certainty. These are some of the many reasons that have combined to generate a bulky literature about measuring and allowing for variation, and to make most introductory statistics texts give their main attention to what is done once the indication is found. Naturally, we all desire an adequate assessment both of the indications and their uncertainties, but we shouldn't refuse good cake only because we can't have frosting too.

B2. EXAMPLES OF STOPPING WITH INDICATION

Often, the analyst of data stops his calculations with pure indication. (His thoughts may still go on and give him judgmental impressions of the uncertainties involved.) Let us illustrate a few such circumstances. Suppose, for example, that in a haphazardly assembled remedial-reading class of 23 taught by a single teacher using one special method, the reading of 5 students substantially improved and that of 18 was substantially unchanged. The indication is that the treatment of the students improves perhaps 1/4 of the students. This figure is fraught with uncertainties about which the data give us little aid. All the same, if other teachers and methods are getting improvement for 85% of the students, we ignore at our peril the indication that this method is not as good as general practice.

If we sought to assess the uncertainties of our 5/23, what could we do with such problems as:

a1) From what population was this class something like a random sample?

a2) Is that population something like those from which the samples taught by other methods were drawn?

a3) How much do the teacher's personality and his tendencies to deviate from the assigned method matter?

In this example, a good assessment of uncertainty seems most unlikely. We have an indication, nevertheless, which can be the basis for action.

Matters need not be so simple as this example of indication suggests. To get data to yield a sensible indication may require subtle and complex analysis chosen with sophistication. As an example, let us simplify a problem that was much discussed in scientific quarters in the early 1960's. Consider choosing the adjustments required to take equitable and defendable account of background characteristics in a comparison of Negroes and whites on a standard intelligence test. (To illustrate difficulties of indication, we need not raise either the hard issue of proper measures of intelligence or the biological problem of purity of strains.) Age, family size, socioeconomic status, population density, years of schooling, kind of schooling, strength of home life and its orientation toward things of the mind might provide a basis for handling this question. We still have the tough question of how these data shall be used. Obviously multiple-control methods are required, and we may be delighted to stop with indication. The techniques of indication often go far beyond the descriptive statistics found in first courses in quantitative methods.

Problems of multiplicity. Another kind of problem arises when we want to distinguish two groups of individuals by a difference in variability for at least one of a large number, say 100, of measured characteristics, having one measurement on each characteristic for each individual. We can, if we are careful, compare the variances on any one aspect of the two populations in a way that is reasonably reliable at, say, 95% confidence. Even if the null hypothesis of equal variability were true, the average number of tests individually significant at 5% is just the product of 5% and the number of tests, namely $(.05)(100) = 5$.

By the same token, the average number of tests individually significant at 0.05% (1/20 of 1%) is $(.0005)(100) = 0.05$, which can be interpreted to mean that one or more such will occur in about 5% of such situations (a situation means a repetition of the whole: here 100 tests each at a 0.05% level). This means that if the apparently most-extreme variance ratio is to be significant at the 5% level *in its role as the largest of 100,* it must be *individually* significant at about 0.05%!

Such an extreme value must fall in a region where the exact but unknown shape of the underlying distribution may have large effects on the probability of our test ratio, whether $(s_1^2/\sigma_1^2)/(s_2^2/\sigma_2^2)$ or something more robust, falling beyond a given value. No sort of statistical procedure yet dreamed of can deal with this difficulty. The only way to obtain adequate control of such uncertainty may be to make a repeat study confined to those few characteristics which appeared in the first study to differ a lot from one group to another. In the interim, even though the data may have given the relevant sources of variation full opportunity to reveal themselves, it may be quite unwise to do anything beyond indication.

An example further along, but in a somewhat more familiar direction, arises when we are searching for interesting indications that may serve as hints in approaching further data. The intent here is not one of attaining a conclusion, nor of making measurements for record, but only of hunting out interesting indications. Suppose that we have looked at many aspects, say 1000 to 10,000, instead of only 100, and have selected from this exploration a list of aspects whose values appear interesting. Now the dangers of implicit belief in very extreme % points are even greater. Here we must stop our calculations with indications and be careful to think of our results only as hints as to what to study next, rather than as established results.

A seemingly slight modification arises when exploration and hint-searching has been carried out on a portion, say one-third, of the total data, with the intention of coming up with approximately a given number of hints, say 10 or 20, which are to be tried out, either for measurement unaffected by selection or as subjects for conclusions, on the remaining two-thirds of the total data. Here, at the transition from exploration of the first third to confirmation by the other two thirds, we need nothing but indication; our problem is to pick the best-looking hints for immediate trial. (Compare this process with cross-validation discussed in Section B6 below.)

[Indeed, on the closely analogous problem of selecting the "best" of many new strains of a crop, it is often wise to make the first selections in circumstances where one knows that observed differences will almost certainly not be provably real (Yates, 1950). Some find this paradoxical. Breeders can measure accurately if they raise many specimens of a very few strains with, of course, little chance that an especially good strain has been included. Or they can raise many strains and measure them relatively inaccurately because they have few individuals of each strain. Following the latter procedure increases the chance of raising a good strain, but, because of poorer measurement, decreases the chance of detecting it. Attaining a desirable balance produces the paradox.]

Some of the important reasons for stopping with indications are:

a) The form of the data (its structure) masks the important sources of variability.

b) We have no good way to deal with what may be substantial differences in variability of this sort of indication, differences that experience suggests may occur but to an extent not detectable in a single set of data. Usually this difficulty arises from the multiplicity of variables or aspects being examined.

c) Preliminary exploration of data of high multiplicity has led to selection of a few indications for later confirmation.

Consider, as a final example, comparing short and long forms of a projective test in order to study the effect of form length on reliability of scoring. Each form has 32 different ways of scoring a single protocol. Suppose that, as would be the case for the Rorschach test, the scores are available on a split-half basis, so that the calculation of reliability coefficients is quite feasible. To reduce the effects of sampling upon the final comparison, the investigator gives the short and long forms to the same people at the same time, perhaps by having the short form part of the long form. He finds it easy: to calculate 32 reliability coefficients for the short form, and their average; to do the same with the reliability coefficients for the long form; and to look at the difference (or perhaps the ratio) of these average reliability coefficients. This indication is, he hopes, reasonably responsive to the original question of the comparative reliability of long and short forms.

What if he seeks to pass from indication to inference? His statistical advisor is apt to tell him that each of his 64 basic scores is correlated, to unknown and probably differing extents, with each of the others. Here are $\frac{1}{2}(63)(64) = 2016$ correlation coefficients to consider. And each correlation coefficient between basic scores requires conversion, not a trivial task, to a correlation coefficient between the corresponding split-half reliabilities. When this is done, the variances and covariances of the reliabilities can be found, then those of the two average reliabilities, and finally the variance of their difference. If large-sample theory is adequate, as it may be if he happens to have 10,000 protocols, the uncertainty of the difference can now be assessed. After thinking about the effort involved, what would you do?

Under the conditions described, indication would be the end of the road for most investigators. (We shall introduce below, in Section E, a new technique that makes inference feasible even in problems this gory.)

Sometimes results that individually might reasonably have arisen from purely chance variation are worthy of report because they strengthen one another. Sometimes we have parallel results based on independent bodies of data, all contained in a single study where the assessment of mutual support is easy. Or there may be parallel results on overlapping or interrelated data, as where 7 questions have all been answered by the same respondents, where the results agree in direction but the amount of mutual support is hazy. Or it may be that one result in today's study is likely to be paralleled in due course by other results in other studies.

In all these situations, it can be quite wasteful to suppress results because they are not individually significant or because their joint significance cannot be satisfactorily appraised.

B3. CONCEALED INFERENCE

When we study data for the answers to a specific question, we sometimes find the evidence so strong as to obviously resolve the question. When matters are so clear-cut, quite informal inference is usually adequate, both in analysis and in communication.

If the data are only obviously strong, the reader or listener is often asked to look at the indications, and "see" the situation. The investigator typically says "No statistics is necessary to see that . . . ", meaning "simple ultraconservative statistical methods are overwhelming". Back of such statements lies some notion of statistical analysis that is not being displayed. As examples: "85 successes out of 100 cases could scarcely be compatible with a probability of success of 0.1" or "the standard deviation of the difference is obviously over 100, but even if it were as small as 50, a difference in sample means of 10 could scarcely be strong evidence in favor of either method". Although such discussions are common, considerable sophistication or experience may be required to be able to dispense with formal inference, and many of us have been brought up short by a neophyte's saying that he does not find himself convinced, sometimes because the obvious has required a rather lengthy demonstration.

If the data are much stronger than this, only the indications are given, and nothing at all is said to the reader or listener.

Such instances are not instances of stopping with indication, as we use this term. They are merely cases of inference where there has been no need for any of the formalities of inference. Informal inference, perhaps expressed by "obviously", or by "looking at . . . , we see that", or by absence of any remark at all, is the only sort of inference felt necessary. Yet, even if no word be written or spoken, it is inference.

When we speak of stopping with indication, we do not intend to include these pleasant cases of informal inference. Rather we refer, in the main, to cases of indication, without even the barest sort of appraisal of the indicator's stability, variability, or reliability to provide a basis for informal or formal inference.

B4. CHOICE OF INDICATORS

The analyst often chooses which indicator to use. He compares the responsiveness of the different indicators to the specific question he has reached. He is likely to compare their ease of calculation. He frequently asks whether the results of one will, in his circumstances, be more, or less, stable than those of another.

Making such judgments takes more than looking things up in the proper book. Wholly inferior indicators are indeed subject to the struggle for existence and tend to die out. But as we saw at the close of Section A3, a difference in distributional shape so small as to be difficult to detect in samples of substantial size (like a few thousand) can alter the balance between two indicators drastically. In the example cited, the indicators happened to be estimators. One under ideal conditions did only nine-tenths as well as the other; under more realistic conditions it did almost half-again better.

Such difficulties and delicacies must be faced even, perhaps especially, if the indicator selected is to be used for pure indication alone.

Before discussing choices among estimating indicators—among estimators—we need to clarify the meaning of the verb "estimate". When does an indicator estimate something? What does it estimate?

One naive answer is: An estimate estimates a parameter. Historically, the word "parameter" has meant two quite different things:

a) The numerical value of a particular symbol in a particular way of specifying a family of distributions, as when the family of normal distributions is parametrized either by μ and σ^2 or by μ and σ.

b) A numerical characteristic of a distribution, as when any numerical population is partially characterized by its median.

To restrict "estimation" to estimating a particular coefficient in a distribution would lose much of the usefulness of this vague concept. The idea of estimation should be as general as possible. Thus, while it is usually helpful to know about the comparative performance of two estimators when the individual fluctuations in the data follow distributions of Gaussian shape, it can be misleading not to also know how they behave for other shapes.

Accordingly, even if the analyst knows just what he wants to estimate, a contingency not as frequent as is commonly thought, he needs to be guided, in choosing an estimate, by all that is known—or felt—to be true under a variety of alternate circumstances.

An estimator is a function of the observations, a specific way of putting them together. It may be specified by an arithmetic formula, like $\bar{y} = \Sigma x_i/n$, or by words alone, as in directions for finding a sample median by ordering and counting. We distinguish between the estimator and its value, an estimate, obtained from a specific set of data. The variance estimator, $s^2 = \Sigma(x_i - \bar{x})^2/(n - 1)$, yields the estimate 7 from the three observations 2, 3, 7. We say s^2 is an estimator for σ^2, and we call σ^2 the estimand. In the numerical example, 7 estimates σ^2.

Sometimes the estimator comes first, and we then ask what it points to. We speak of the estimator's target as an *estimand* (as something to be estimated) rather than as just a parameter. Our problem is to match estimands to estimators. When can we do this? How precisely? Are there general circumstances when we can expect a match?

These questions have not had the research attention they deserve. Although we might wish that it did not, the question of sample size plays a central role. In actual investigations, we use our estimator on a sample of a particular size. Yet today's approaches to the choice of matching estimands depend on what we would do with larger samples, a somewhat unsatisfactory state of affairs.

As a device to aid discussion of this question at this time, we divide the estimators we use for a particular sample size into three classes:

c1) those we would use for all larger samples,

c2) those we would use for much larger, but not arbitrarily large, samples,

c3) those we would not care to use for much larger samples.

Class (c3) is hard to deal with in the present framework. It may never provide us with satisfying matches between estimator and estimand.

Class (c2) occurs frequently in actual practice. The sample range is often an example. Within our framework, we can often get practical answers by forgetting that we would not use this estimator for arbitrarily large samples, by pretending that we have class (c1).

Class (c1), then, unrealistic though it may be, is the class we now act as if we have. Even in this Utopia we cannot lay down simple rules that will pick an estimand to go with our estimator. All that we can do is to list some alternative circumstances where we are likely to be satisfied with the match between estimator and estimand. These include:

d1) If the average value of the estimate (the result of averaging over all samples of a given size) has the same value for all sample sizes, this value is a good candidate for the matching estimand, as is the case for s^2 and σ^2, so long as σ^2 is finite. If, in addition, the distributions of the estimate condense around this estimand as the sample size grows, most would find the match more gratifying. Exceptions arise, for example, because the average value of the estimator is not at all typical of its distribution, as when considering s^2 for a distribution with infinite σ^2.

d2) If the average values depend on sample size, but converge to a limit as the sample size increases, as is the case for s when σ is finite, much the same can be said. Most are more pleased when the dependence on sample size is slight, as in the s, σ example for normal distributions for $n \geq 10$, say.

d3) In a similar vein to (d1) and (d2), if the median of the distribution of sample estimates is the same for all sample sizes, or if its value converges to a limit as the sample size grows, this common or limiting value is likely to be a satisfactorily matching estimand. For, especially in large samples, the median of an estimate distribution rarely fails to be reasonably typical of that distribution.

d4) The limit, as sample size grows, of any reasonable typical value (see Section A7), other than the mean or median, of the distribution of estimates for a fixed sample size is also likely to be a satisfactorily matching estimand.

These rules are not neat and detailed, but they do identify some matching estimands that many would regard as satisfactory. Our own diffident and tentative attitude toward this problem stems partly from the limited studies on which these remarks have been based, and partly from dissatisfaction with having the acceptability of estimands depend on properties of collections of sample sizes not present in the scientist's investigation. Let us hope for further progress on these questions.

B5. AN EXAMPLE OF CHOICE OF INDICATOR

Suppose that one can make repeated observations of some quantity, observations which behave rather like a sample from a population with long, straggling tails. Having collected these observations, the observer wishes to summarize them in a way which indicates their location with as much precision as can be simply obtained. He considers the arithmetic mean of all the observations, but he finds that the long straggling tails impart so much variance that this indicator is unduly imprecise. He next considers using the sample median, for he knows that it recovers about $2/3$rds (actually $2/\pi$ths in large samples as we noted in Section A5) of the information about location in a sample from a normal distribution and is likely to do even better than this in samples from distributions with more straggling tails.

The stability of the sample median depends on the height of the density near the population median. Figure B5–1 represents a density for which the median is a poor choice for measuring location. As long as his straggling-tailed distribution has a reasonable density in the middle, our observer prefers the median to the mean, but even then can he perhaps do still better? Some may think the median unduly variable; it is not likely to be a very good candidate for use of the jackknife (Section E) which he may want to use; it may miss enough information to matter.

An alternative to the median is the trimmed mean. The sample is trimmed of its possibly straggling tails by setting aside some fraction of the measurements from each tail of the sample. Specifically, let us suppose that he decides to set aside the lowest 10% and the highest 10% of the observations, and to take the arithmetic mean of the remaining 80%.

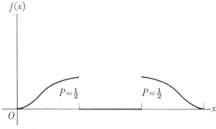

Fig. B5–1. Example of a density for which the sample median would be an extremely poor choice for measuring location. If the area under each part is close to 1/2, then from sample to sample, the median will flop back and forth between the left half and right half, producing substantial variability.

How well would he do for a normal distribution? Had he only kept the median, we know that he would have had an efficiency of about 2/3 (more precisely $2/\pi \approx 63.7\%$). By using the trimmed mean he gains a fraction of the remaining 1/3 of the information about μ contained in the sample. For symmetrical trimming this fractional gain obviously runs from 0% (for 50% trimmed from each tail, leaving only the sample median) to 100% (for 0% trimmed). Investigations we do not give here show that the gain is somewhat faster than linear, and so we will be conservative if we assign an efficiency for the proportion α trimmed from each tail of

$$\frac{2}{\pi} + (1 - 2\alpha)\left(1 - \frac{2}{\pi}\right) \approx \frac{2}{3} + (1 - 2\alpha)\frac{1}{3},$$

which gives in our example,

$$\frac{2}{3} + 0.8\left(\frac{1}{3}\right) \approx .93 = 93\%$$

of the information about location. In samples from distributions whose tails straggle moderately more than those of Gaussian distributions, trimmed means do even better than this. Trimmed means can be safely jackknifed, a technique described in Section E.

Our observer has chosen an indication. It indicates "location", for if we add a constant to all the observations, the trimmed mean changes by the same amount and in the same direction. Has there so far been a definite distributional model? No, except for the existence of a parent distribution. Or has a definite parameter to be estimated been explicitly identified? Again, no, though a class is implied by the specific choice, namely, the typical values of means from samples of this size trimmed 10% on each tail.

In our trimmed-mean example, as the sample grows larger and larger, the central 80% of the sample will more and more nearly match the central 80% of the population. This makes the natural choice of parameter the mean of the central 80% of the population.

We have reached our answer and expressed it understandably. The more mathematically inclined may like to see the result expressed more formally. Let θ be the parameter being estimated, the estimand; let F be the cumulative. Then

$$\theta = \int_{-\infty}^{\infty} y\psi(F(y)) \cdot dF(y),$$

where

$$\psi(u) = \begin{cases} 1.25 = 1/0.8 & \text{for} \quad 0.1 < u < 0.9, \\ 0 & \text{elsewhere.} \end{cases}$$

We gain even more from thinking about the finite-sample formulation:

$$\text{ave } \{10\% \text{ trimmed mean}\} = \int_{-\infty}^{\infty} y\psi_n(F(y)) \cdot dF(y),$$

where, writing $[n/10]$ for the number of observations (approximately 10% of n) set aside from each tail:

$$\psi_n(u) \begin{cases} \text{vanishes like} \quad u^{[n/10]} \quad \text{or} \quad (1-u)^{[n/10]} \\ \qquad \text{near} \quad 0 \quad \text{and} \quad 1, \quad \text{and} \\ \text{is mainly concentrated over} \\ \qquad \text{and near the interval} \quad (0.1, \ 0.9). \end{cases}$$

This formulation can be used to tell how large a sample is needed to reduce suitably the contributions to this average value from the extreme tails of the distribution.

We now understand what the estimand is, and a bit about when trouble from quite straggling tails is likely—*provided we are dealing with a sample of independent observations.*

B6. INDICATIONS OF QUALITY: CROSS-VALIDATION

Even though they are not always used for prediction, the results provided by some statistical techniques can be loosely described as "predictive" or "forecasting". A multiple regression of one variable upon a number of others, for example, may set forth what is hoped to be a standard property that holds for other data.

Users have often been disappointed by procedures, such as multiple regression equations, that "forecast" quite well for the data on which they were built. When tried on fresh data, the predictive power of these procedures fell dismally.

Let us discuss this situation in terms of a single example, multiple regression, while understanding that our insights and conclusions apply to many other techniques as well. In dealing with multiple regression, when we speak of a "procedure", we mean, for example, a specific regression equation:

$$z = 3.4x + 2.5y - 5.4.$$

When we speak of the "form", we mean, for example, choosing which variables from among many shall enter the regression and deciding individually for each variable whether we use the original measure, its logarithm, square root, or other transformation. We also have to choose how the variables shall be grouped and combined—sums, products, ratios, or how? In this discussion, then, a "procedure" consists of a "form" and numerical values for its coefficients.

When we use data to determine some procedure, we want to be able to answer the question: How well may I expect the chosen procedure to behave in use? Even when the specific variables to be used in a multiple regression have been picked in advance, so that the form is determined, the coefficients are chosen from infinitely many combinations of possibilities to make the results of substituting in the formula fit the data as closely as possible. Testing the procedure on the data that gave it birth is almost certain to overestimate performance, for the optimizing process that chose it from among many possible procedures will have made the greatest use possible of any and all idiosyncrasies of those particular data. Sometimes we say that "Optimization capitalizes on chance!". As a result, the procedure will likely work better for these data than for almost any other data that will arise in practice. The apparent degree of fit will almost never be representative.

No one knows how to appraise a procedure safely except by using different bodies of data from those that determined it. In other words, appraisal requires some form of cross-validation. We recognize two levels of cross-validation, simple and double, the simple being more widely recognized. They are:

a1) *Simple cross-validation*. Test the procedure on data different from those used to choose its numerical coefficients.

a2) *Double cross-validation*. Test the procedure on data different both from those used to guide the choice of its form and from those used to choose its numerical coefficients.

The second level of cross-validation, which by analogy with the physician's "double blind" study, we have called "double cross-validation", is to be had only by going to fresh data. These fresh data are best gathered after optimizing. When fresh gathering is not feasible, good results can come from going to a body of data that has been kept in a locked safe where it has rested untouched and unscanned during all the choices and optimizations (as in the studies of Macdonald and Ward, 1963, and Miller, 1962). For the full validating effect, the data placed in the safe must differ from those used to choose the procedure in ways that adequately represent the sources of variation anticipated in practice. For example, they may need to involve distinct school systems, distinct investigators, or distinct years of observation. Despite the high merit of double cross-validation, we cannot always afford it.

Whether we are content with, or stuck with, simple cross-validation, today the computer offers us new freedom and power. In the classical approach to simple cross-validation, the available body of data was divided into two (sometimes more) pieces of similar size. One was used for optimization, the other for testing. Some energetic workers would then interchange the two pieces and repeat, thus gaining more information from the same data. Although they learned more by this process, a subtle miasma of suspicion arose from the unknown correlation between the two estimates of quality.

Such suspicions show again how insistence on inference as *the* goal tends to distort attitudes toward indication. Unknown correlations among the component estimates do, indeed, destroy the possibility of using degree of mutual agreement to assess *stability* of the combined result precisely. On the other hand, whenever each estimate by itself is sound, a weighted combination of two or more, however much or little correlated, is both equally sound and more precise than the individual values.

The man who has halved his data and cross-validated in both directions has used *all* of his data to assess the quality of what is to be had by optimizing upon a body of data *half* as big as his total collection. If he has so much data that halving or doubling has little effect on the quality of the optimized procedure, well and good. He can do little more than he has done. Few are so fortunate.

When routine computation was expensive, even *doing* the cross-validation in both directions seemed an effort. Today, we can face much more. Suppose that we divide the data into ten parts of similar size. Then we can combine any nine parts, optimize the procedure for this nine-tenths, and validate on the remaining tenth. Once we have done this ten times, separating a different tenth each time, we have used *all* the data to assess the quality of what is to be had by optimizing upon a body of data *nine-tenths* the size of the total collection. This often comes appreciably closer to answering the most usual question: Approximately what performance may I expect from the result of optimizing upon *all* of my data?

With a computer, the ten calculations are often little more effort than the conventional one or two because we have only to repeat the same pattern of computation, with little more programming and debugging time.

Often we can profitably go much further. Suppose that we set aside one individual case, optimize for what is left, then test on the set-aside case. Repeating this for every case squeezes the data almost dry. If we have to go through the full optimization calculation every time, the extra computation may be hard to face. Occasionally, one can easily calculate, either exactly or to an adequate approximation, what the effect of dropping a specific and very small part of the data will be on the optimized result. This adjusted optimized result can then be compared with the values for the omitted individual. That is, we make one optimization for all the data, followed by one repetition per case of a much simpler calculation, a calculation of the effect of dropping each individual, followed by one test of that individual. When practical, this approach is attractive.

One drawback of all kinds of single cross-validation is that the test sample is all too often much more like the optimization sample than is typical of the population of individuals or situations to which we wish our indication to refer. Accordingly, single cross-validation is all too often weaker, by an unknown amount, than it appears to be.

The possibility of cross-validation is one of the main advantages of most automatic schemes of optimization. Approximate, cut-and-try, judgment-guided selection of procedures can often come very close in quality of result or even be superior to those that formally optimize, but because one cannot fully specify how the results were chosen, one cannot be sure that they are being tested on "independent" data. On the other hand, at the simple cross-validation level, every procedure generated by automatic optimization is easily tagged with the body of data used to determine the numerical values of its coefficients.

The difficulty with determination by subjective judgment recurs at the level of double cross-validation. When we choose the form of a procedure, the full body of data that was used may not be clear to anyone. Often the choice leans, sometimes very usefully, on a lifetime of experience, fact, and folklore, as well as the convenience of the specific analysis. The experienced investigator will find himself especially hard-pressed to behave "double blind" because the form he has chosen may have been picked with the idiosyncrasies of the next few sets of data to be gathered already in mind. Satisfactory cross-validation on these next few sets will verify the investigator's foresight and satisfy him about its use on that sort of data, but can over-assure him about the cross-validation for future uses that he may not have considered. Obviously we are not discussing an issue of "bad" versus "good". The investigator wants to be sure to consider as far as he can the whole range of his uses, so that he can expect different performance under different circumstances.

C. COMPUTERS AND GRAPHS

Introduction
C1. *Data analysis and the computer*
C2. *Graphs as indicators*
C3. *Graphs in determination and inference*
C4. *Barycentric coordinates*
C5. *The computer as a source of graphs*
C6. *Residuals and computers*

The computer age is widely advertised. To underestimate the impact of the computer on data analysis would risk considerable losses. Equally to expect the wrong things from this collision would lead to the neglect of important auxiliary tools.

The typewriter has not eliminated the pen; the desk calculator did not eliminate the slide rule, the tablet of graph paper, or the back-of-the-envelope computation; the electronic computer will not eliminate them either. Rather, as we come to use the electronic computer to its full, we will use the simple tools more often, not less.

Both computers and graphs are discussed in this section. Some numerical uses of the computer are illustrated in Section E. Here, after indicating what computers can do for data analysis, we emphasize the role of graphs in indication, mention their role in inference, and illustrate the use of barycentric coordinates.

Today the computer-microfilm plotter team can give us graphical output much more complicated than simple graphs. Whether or not we have a microfilm plotter, the computer can help us learn from residuals.

C1. DATA ANALYSIS AND THE COMPUTER

The byway of data analysis has almost become a highway; the plans for the interstate freeway are being drawn. The major improvements offered data analysts by a great era of mathematical statistics have been largely absorbed; we are learning rapidly which of the classical assumptions of niceness about data can and cannot be lived with in the real world. We are only beginning to use the electronic computer, which for a long time has offered us great opportunities. Now we can make more complicated, longer analyses than before. Less often than we might, we gain new methodological understandings both by analytical computation and by experimental sampling. At last, we begin to seize the opportunity to get greater knowledge by trying, on a given body of data, a larger fraction of the many analyses that look promising.

None of us has yet adjusted his practices in analyzing data to take adequate advantage of the power and cheapness of the electronic computer. We still suffer, in varying degrees, from cultural lag. We tend to behave as we used to when the actual conduct of computation was the expensive item. As the computer has come more and more of age, matters have changed—changed further and faster than we have realized. As a consequence we can use the computer at all stages of our work, beginning with the editing of the data. Today the key costs are likely to be those of getting the data into the machine, including editing, and those of programming, including debugging.

Ideally, we should use the computer the way one uses paper and pencil: in short spurts, each use teaching us—numerically, algebraically, or graphically—a bit of what the next use should be. As we develop the easy back-and-forth interaction between man and computer today being promised by time-sharing systems and remote consoles, we shall move much closer to this ideal.

Even then, data analysis will continue to be distinguished from most uses of computers because so much of its output reappears later as input (Tukey, 1965), and because its total volume of output, whether printed or displayed on cathode-ray screens, is so large.

C2. GRAPHS AS INDICATORS

The statistician has always learned a substantial amount from graphs. Not only do graphs show what the analyst thought he wanted to look for, but often they show the unsuspected as well.

Every graph is at least an indication, by contrast with some common instances of numbers obtained as intermediate steps in calculation, for no one will draw a straight or curved line, or even plot a point, unless someone could look at such a result and say "aha". It is this "aha" quality of the graph, its ability to show us the unexpected, that is the graph's transcendent virtue.

Given only the data, not the question, we have no one right way to make a graph. Certain "standards" for graphical presentation combine good advice about scales, widths of lines, and the like, with cautions that lead to strict conventions. Although these strictures are probably needed for communication with general audiences, they can greatly reduce the usefulness of graphs as a way of teaching the educated mind. Warnings against logarithmic scales, against scales that do not start at zero, and the like, have their place, yet this place is not in graphs addressed to psychologists, whether readers or investigators examining their own data.

Given pairs (x_j, y_j) and a fitted straight line, two kinds of plots have broad usefulness. To show "Look, the fit is really pretty good!", we plot y against x, showing the points and the fitted line. To inquire "What sort of deviations from linearity are suggested?", we plot

$$\text{residual} = y_{\text{observed}} - y_{\text{fitted}}$$

against x, whereby the fitted line becomes the x-axis. This choice between two major alternatives is an example of a general principle: fitting the graph to the question, not to the data.

C3. GRAPHS IN DETERMINATION AND INFERENCE

While most cases of graphs are for indication, graphs are used for inference in a variety of situations:

a) Control charts, of both Shewhart and cusum forms, are prominent in applications to industrial production.

b) Binomial probability paper (see Section G) has many applications to the analysis of counted data.

c) Several kinds of nonparametric significance tests and confidence procedures can be applied graphically. (See Section G6 for one instance.)

C4. BARYCENTRIC COORDINATES (A barycenter is a center of gravity.)

When fixed numbers of instances divide into two classes of interest—men-women, rich-poor, or quick-dead—keeping track of the number in one class loses no information about the other. (When totals vary, binomial probability paper—see Section G—is often helpful.) Similarly, when percentages tell the story, whether percent of cases, percent of income spent on necessities, percent of waking time spent on leisure activities, or percent of calories derived from meat, keeping track of one percentage loses no information about the other.

In these problems of two classes, we could plot the counts in the two classes simultaneously, though we usually do not. For example, in a postmortem of a baseball pennant race a team might plot its won-lost record in the 18 games it played against each of its 9 opponents as in Fig. C4–1, though the points would probably be labeled with the opponent's name. Such a plot displays both components symmetrically, and illustrates a use of barycentric coordinates. The

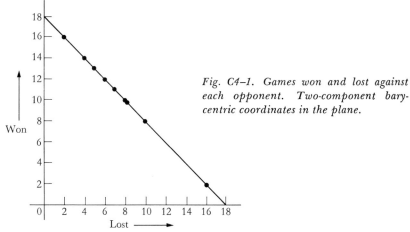

Fig. C4–1. Games won and lost against each opponent. Two-component barycentric coordinates in the plane.

expression barycenter means center of gravity, where the centers referred to are the plotted points. If we put a weight of 16 on the "won" end (0, 18) of the bar and a weight of 2 on the "lost" end (18, 0), then the center of gravity of these weights falls at (2, 16), which is the leftmost won-lost point. Each plotted point in its turn is a center of gravity.

In two-category problems, we rarely plot in this way because it is more convenient to plot on a one-dimensional figure as in Fig. C4–2. In either representation the team that won 16 from our heroes stands out as the villain, and attending to games won omits no information because the games lost are measured from the other end. It does not seem that things can be so easy with three components instead of two.

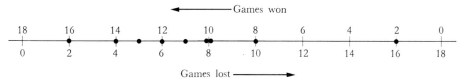

Fig. C4–2. Points in Fig. C4–1 replotted. Two-component barycentric coordinates on a line.

The problem of dealing graphically with the relative amounts of more than two kinds of behavior is a widespread one. Chemists have faced this for at least a century in a way suited for dealing with distributions among three things and even of some use when one must deal with more than three.

As an example, consider an ordinary social choice investigation where each individual in a group of size $n + 1$ "chooses", "rejects", or "omits" each of the others, but not himself. Then the numbers of choices c, rejections r, and omissions x *received* by any individual can be regarded as a number triple (c, r, x). But $c + r + x = n$, where $n + 1$ is the number of people rating, since a person is not allowed to rate himself. For each individual, the triple of numbers could be plotted in a three-dimensional space with coordinates c, r, and x. Since the total

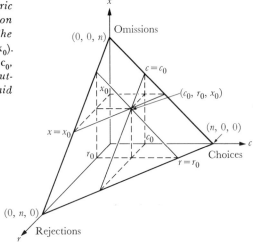

Fig. C4–3. Three-component barycentric coordinates in space; first octant portion of plane for which $c + r + x = n$. *The sample point has coordinates* (c_0, r_0, x_0). *Through that point pass the planes* $c = c_0$, $r = r_0$, $x = x_0$ *which rule the heavily outlined triangular plane segment that is laid flat in Fig. C4–4.*

number of ratings is fixed at n, analytical geometry tells us that the possible points are restricted to the slanting plane displayed in Fig. C4–3. More specifically, analytic geometry promises that any equation of the form $c + r + x = n$ defines a plane that crosses each axis at the distance n from the origin (0, 0, 0). Such a linear restriction (confinement of points to a plane) is a way of losing what, in statistics (by analogy with mechanics), is called a degree of freedom. Originally we had a three-dimensional space with three degrees of freedom, but the restraint cuts us down to a two-dimensional space, or two degrees of freedom. Indeed, since each coordinate is positive or zero, the points are restricted to the heavily outlined triangle in the first octant. We can take this triangle out of its original position and lay it down flat. The result together with a grid is shown in Fig. C4–4. The figure shows the point for the person with 15 choices, 3 rejections, and 62 omissions; it also shows the point with coordinates (12, 12, 56). Triangular coordinate paper, sometimes called *isometric,* is readily available in stationery stores that cater to scientific needs.

We have written our numerical grid so that the numbers are turned to line up with the grid lines they are supposed to label. Every little mnemonic helps because most of us are not used to examining this kind of plot.

Lemann and Solomon (1952) used barycentric coordinates for plotting sociometric ratings made by 21 girls living in a dormitory. Each girl was required to choose 3 and reject 3 other girls. Choice or rejection of self was not allowed. Lemann and Solomon had each girl make her choices and rejections on the basis of four criteria (as roommate, as a double-date companion, to take home for a weekend, to be friendly with after graduation). Each girl made $4(20) = 80$ ratings: 12 choices, 12 rejections, and 56 omissions. Consequently the total number of choices was $21(12) = 252$, and the average number of choices received was $252/21 = 12$. Similarly, the average number of rejections received was 12 and the average number of omissions received was 56. Therefore, the point (12, 12, 56) plotted in Fig. C4–4 represents the average set of ratings received by girls.

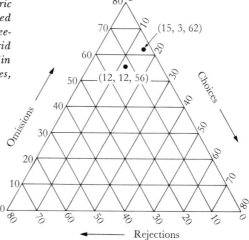

Fig. C4–4. Three-component barycentric coordinates in the plane: heavily outlined triangle of Fig. C4–3 removed from three-dimensional space and laid flat, with grid added. The values for coordinates (in parentheses) are in the order: (choices, rejections, omissions).

Table C4–5 shows the triples of choices, rejections, and omissions received by each girl in one of the dormitories studied. These triples are plotted in Fig. C4–6, each dot representing the result received by an individual.

Had the 80 ratings been independent, we could have used ordinary binomial theory to find that the lower and upper 1% level for choices received would be 5 and 20, with mean of 12 ($= 20 \times 4 \times 3/20$), and the same results hold for rejections. For omissions, the corresponding limits are 46 and 65, with mean 56. The limits for choices and rejections are plotted on the chart.

Lemann and Solomon divided their group into high status—significantly many choices and no more than average rejections; low status—significantly many

TABLE C4–5

TRIPLES OF CHOICES, REJECTIONS, AND OMISSIONS
RECEIVED BY EACH GIRL IN ONE DORMITORY

Girl No.	Choices	Rejections	Omissions	Girl No.	Choices	Rejections	Omissions
1	26	2	52	12	4	31	45
2	2	6	72	13	31	0	49
3	5	26	49	14	11	7	62
4	0	30	50	15	12	32	36
5	19	0	61	16	11	1	68
6	21	4	55	17	22	19	39
7	12	8	60	18	4	12	64
8	13	2	65	19	5	23	52
9	2	8	70	20	8	30	42
10	16	6	58	21	15	3	62
11	12	2	66				

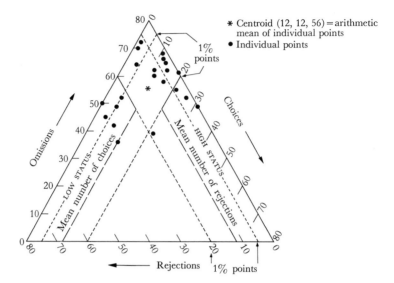

Fig. C4–6. Plot of (choices, rejections, omissions) for each of 21 girls in a dormitory. (After Lemann and Solomon, 1952.)

rejections with no more than average choices; and the remainder; and used these categories for further analysis.

Because Lemann and Solomon controlled the number of girls chosen and rejected (3 by each rater on each variable), the arithmetic mean of the 21 triples, shown by a ✳ in Fig. C4–6, was forced to fall at the prechosen point (12, 12, 56), as we noted above. So long as the cluster of 21 points is reasonably symmetrical, all of its points must fall reasonably near (12, 12, 56), a fact that accounts for much of the cluster's falling near the top of the triangle.

Particularly if we copy the 21 points of Fig. C4–6 by tracing them onto a piece of unruled paper, we can see a tendency of the cluster to leave a gap along a WNW–ESE direction (more or less joining (50, 0, 30) with (0, 20, 60)). There are too few cases to make this indication much more than a hint, albeit an interesting one. Because the plot treated all three categories alike, we can give more credence to such a hint than we could if we had used any one of the two-coordinate plots.

Thus the special triangular graph paper can be used to look for patterns, to separate into groups, and to look for variability, but especially to make numbers visual that might otherwise be hard to understand. If, instead, one merely plots two of the three coordinates on ordinary graph paper, the symmetry of the three coordinates is lost, and, for many viewers, almost all attention goes to the two coordinates plotted.

One can, of course, convert counts to fractions and always use a scale from 0 to 1, or use percentages. The basis of a triple of coordinates need not be counts —all that matters is that the total is constant—the basis could be measurements of some kind: for example, fractions of conversation time made up of fact, opinion, and other.

While we shall not treat it here, the reader might appreciate another example of an extended application of barycentric coordinates to a social science problem in a still more statistical vein by Strodtbeck, in Kluckhohn and Strodtbeck (1961). Among other things, Strodtbeck relates his graphs to the exact null distribution of a ranking statistic designed to compare three quantities in a comparative study of values in several cultures.

C5. THE COMPUTER AS A SOURCE OF GRAPHS

By 1965 computers had become better at drawing graphs and pictures. A few examples will suggest some of the possibilities.

One of the problems in space studies is the difficulty the human has of trying to visualize where satellites are at given times. This task is even more difficult if one wants to visualize which face of an object is pointed in a particular direction, what with the motion of the object around the earth, and its own movements about its center. In 1964, it was desired to study the tumbling of a satellite that would be so set in orbit that once it had stabilized itself, it would always have one face toward the earth.

A computer was programmed not only to show how the satellite would move, but also to draw successive pictures in perspective to help one visualize the motions. Figure C5–1 (Zajac, personal communication) shows the orbit of the box-shaped satellite and the point of perspective from which it was viewed.

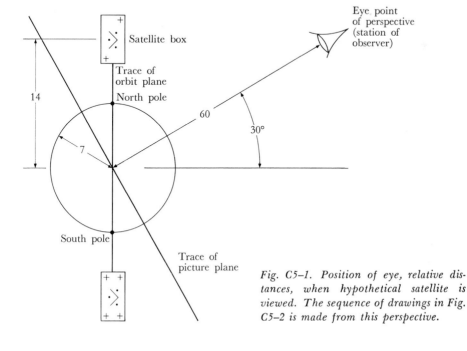

Fig. C5–1. *Position of eye, relative distances, when hypothetical satellite is viewed. The sequence of drawings in Fig. C5–2 is made from this perspective.*

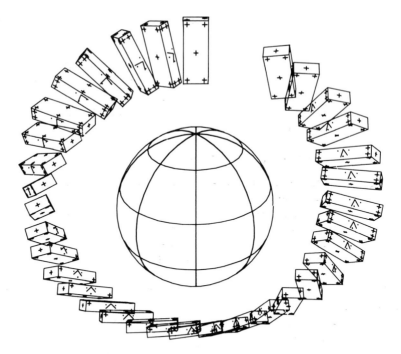

Fig. C5–2. Samples from the motion picture of the tenth orbit of the satellite.

Figure C5–2 (Zajac, 1964) shows one such sequence. (Actually, the computer made a motion picture and this figure shows samples from the part showing the tenth orbit.) The sides of the boxlike satellite are marked to aid the eye in following both its tumbling motion and the orientations of parts of its internal stabilizing mechanism.

To turn to a real satellite, at various points in its orbit, the first Telstar® 1 communication satellite collected data on the number of high-energy protons per square centimeter per second. Figure C5–3 (Zajac, 1964), also made by a computer, shows the points at which the Telstar satellite took readings over a 15-day period. While the job of plotting the 3 or 4 thousand points is not one that would have overwhelmed the old-timer, the idea of plotting them in many different ways, including stratification by amount of radiation observed, and replotting in many different sets of coordinates, each of which required a substantial calculation for each point before it could be plotted, clearly gets beyond even the most able and willing hand worker. Other figures thus produced from the observations showed sketches of the Van Allen belt as viewed by the Telstar satellite.

These examples show a little of the variety of the pictorial and graphical work computers and plotters are producing when programmed by skilled workers.

In 1967, the number of large computers fitted with oscilloscope-photography devices adequate for producing graphs is still small, but growing. A variety of commercial devices are available at a range of prices, and a few universities have built their own.

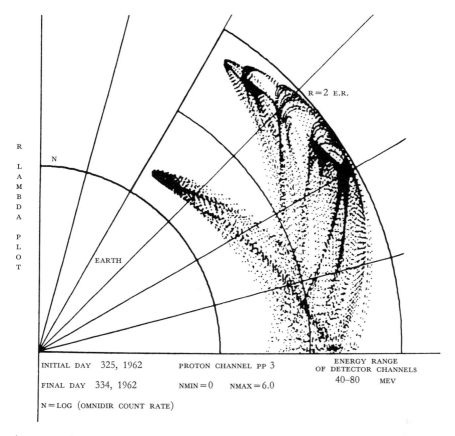

R
L
A
M
B
D
A

P
L
O
T

N

EARTH

R = 2 E.R.

INITIAL DAY   325, 1962   PROTON CHANNEL PP 3

FINAL DAY   334, 1962   NMIN = 0   NMAX = 6.0

N = LOG (OMNIDIR COUNT RATE)

ENERGY RANGE
OF DETECTOR CHANNELS
40–80   MEV

Fig. C5–3. Places where, during a 10-day period, the first Telstar® 1 communication satellite took readings of high-energy protons. Some points are "folded" up from the southern half of the plot.

C6. RESIDUALS AND COMPUTERS

Long before Gauss produced the theory of least squares, scientists learned many useful and helpful things by examining residuals. We can examine the explicit residuals that arise when we fit a curve or surface to data. We can examine the implicit residuals that are defined when we subject a two-way table to analysis of variance or, when the responses are counts, to a contingency table's chi-square test of independence.

In both cases, we are likely to gain insight into unexpected appearances; in both we may use a variety of different graphical presentations. (For some of these, see Anscombe and Tukey, 1963.)

In simple problems, we can graph our residuals by hand; on balance, the results are well worth the effort. In more complex problems the effort of hand graphing residuals is great enough to make the use of a computer desirable. Even if your computer lacks the graphical output that you would like, its printer can make quite useful graphs, usually 132 type bars wide and as many lines long as you wish.

Once your observations are being analyzed by computer, try calculating residuals of several kinds and try displaying them in a variety of graphs. Ordinarily such work is most rewarding.

Turning to a more complex example, notice that factor analysis has been almost entirely a matter of indication, although some work on inference suggests interesting consequences (Tucker, 1958). But no one seems to have begun, with the computer's aid, to find, analyze, *and* graphically display residuals that illustrate how one individual's behavior on one test, or on one factor, deviates from what the fitted factor structure makes most plausible. What new graphical indications are offered here?

D. HUNTING OUT THE REAL UNCERTAINTY

Introduction
D1. *How $\sigma/\sqrt{n}$ can mislead*
D2. *A further example of the need for direct assessment of variability*
D3. *Choosing an error term*
D4. *More detailed choices of error terms*
D5. *Making direct assessment possible*
D6. *Difficulties with direct assessment*
D7. *Supplementary uncertainty and its combination with internal uncertainty*

To go beyond indication, we need to assess the uncertainty of our indications. Although precision of assessment has value, reality of assessment is more basic, because we can be easily misled by variables not represented or recognized in a study.

We assign contributions to uncertainty to two sources: those that might be judged from the data at hand—internal uncertainty; and those that come from causes whose effects are not revealed by the data—supplementary uncertainty. Thus internal and supplementary uncertainty are two vague concepts intended to aid our understanding of uncertainty, variation, and stability. Failure to attend to both sources can lead to serious underestimates of uncertainty and consequent overoptimism about the stability of the indication. To avoid these traps, we need to choose a satisfactory error term from the data, and we need to allow for sources of variation that are present but not made visible by the data-gathering process.

Good design in observational programs and experiments can reduce the impact of all kinds of variation upon the uncertainty of our results. Design can be especially valuable in helping to make sure that major sources of variation are introduced into the investigation. It is often wise to "broaden the base" of a narrowly focused investigation so that the internal uncertainty can properly represent the real variation and the supplementary uncertainty can be reduced.

Once a good design has been executed, we want to get a sound estimate of internal uncertainty from the data at hand. Beyond this, we still need to assess the likely magnitude of effects that cannot be examined in the data. Some sources might be: systematic errors of measurement (example: tendency to omit young children from a census); mismatch between sampled and target population (example: in public opinion polling, the sampled population is not the voting population, and even if it were, the population of opinions prior to the official balloting need not be the population of opinions held in the voting booth); halo effect, where in repeated measurement of the same object the observer tends to agree too closely with his first measurement.

We begin our discussion of internal uncertainty by illustrating how the classical formula

$$\sigma_{\bar{y}} = \frac{\sigma}{\sqrt{n}}$$

may serve us poorly. Next, we notice that real or conceptual randomness of some accessible subdivision is, in practice, the basis for the assessment of internal uncertainty. Different levels of grouping offer a basis for the direct assessment of variability, and we offer some guidelines for choosing the appropriate level. After discussing an example, we suggest some major difficulties with direct assessment and point to some solutions.

Turning to supplementary uncertainty, we stress its importance, consider its appraisal, and discuss its combination with internal uncertainty.

D1. HOW $\sigma/\sqrt{n}$ CAN MISLEAD

Both nonmathematical and mathematical introductory treatments of statistics take pains to emphasize that the standard deviation of the sample mean is $\sigma/\sqrt{n}$, where σ is the population standard deviation and n is the sample size. This idea is most important, and it is part of the basis for the theory of sampling, but it leans, as an introduction must, on an oversimplified view of what is going on. Later on, the analysis of variance may introduce the idea of diverse sources of variation, but we should emphasize early and often the need to allow the data themselves to speak quite directly for their own variation. Peirce's study of reaction time (see Section A4) again provides an example with both substantive and methodological interest.

From Table A4–1 we draw the following values:

Day:	(1)	2	3	4	5	6 to 24
Observed mean:	(475.6)	241.5	203.1	205.6	148.5	175.6 to 265.5
$s/\sqrt{n}$:	(4.2)	2.1	2.0	1.8	1.6	1.1 to 2.2

Setting aside the first day's results, which are obviously discrepant, we observe that $s/\sqrt{n}$ varies from 1.1 to 2.2. If the values of $s/\sqrt{n}$ measured the standard deviations of the observed means, the variance of a difference from one day to the next would be between $(1.1)^2 + (1.1)^2 = 2.42$ for the smallest variability and

$(2.2)^2 + (2.2)^2 = 9.68$ for the largest. These limits correspond to standard deviations of the difference between means for pairs of days of $\sqrt{2.42} \approx 1.6$ and $\sqrt{9.68} \approx 3.1$. If these standard deviations based upon $\sigma/\sqrt{n}$ were appropriate, then the magnitude of most day-to-day differences would have to be less than two standard deviations, or less than 3.2 to 6.2, and that of almost all differences would have to be less than three standard deviations, or less than 4.8 to 9.3. The actual differences (see Table A4–1): -38, $+2$, -57, $+27$, $+11$, $+7$, $+2$, $+20$, $+1$, $+19$, $+9$, -8, -1, -3, $+32$, -12, $+6$, -3, -10, $+11$, -4, -8 impolitely pay little attention to such limitations.

In the language of analysis of variance, Peirce's data show considerable day-to-day variation. In the language of Walter Shewhart, such data are "out of control"—the within-day variation does not properly predict the between-days variation. Nor is it just a matter of the observer "settling down" in the beginning. Even after the 20th day he still wobbles.

The wavering in these data exemplifies the history of the "personal equation" problem of astronomy. The hope had been that each observer's systematic errors could be first stabilized and then adjusted for, thus improving accuracy. Unfortunately, attempts in this direction have failed repeatedly, as these data suggest they might. Thus the observer's daily idiosyncrasies need to have account taken of them, at least by assigning additional day-to-day variation. (What about hour-to-hour? Or week-to-week? We can only guess here, since these particular data are tabulated by whole days and do not stretch over many weeks.) The big change from first to all later days is also a common feature of many kinds of data, whose reduction in the main experiment by pilot work and training is often most important.

Wilson and Hilferty (1929, p. 125) made it clear that Peirce's data illustrate "the principle that we must have a plurality of samples if we wish to estimate the variability of some statistical quantity, and that reliance on such formula as $\sigma/\sqrt{n}$ is not scientifically satisfactory in practice, even for estimating unreliability of means".

Even in dealing with so simple a statistic as the arithmetic mean it is often vital to use as direct an assessment of its internal uncertainty as possible. Obtaining a valid measure of uncertainty is not just a matter of looking up a formula.

D2. A FURTHER EXAMPLE OF THE NEED FOR DIRECT ASSESSMENT OF VARIABILITY

Let us turn from a measurement problem to one of counting, where the binomial distribution suggests itself. We tend to think automatically of the binomial variation of counts, with standard deviation for the observed fraction $\sigma = \sqrt{pq/n}$, where n is the number in the sample and p is the proportion of successes in the population. Again, the idea of this microcosmic standard deviation is important for many purposes, yet it may underestimate actual variation considerably. Let us turn to mass production for an example involving mixing individual differences with the behavior of machines.

If among thousands of manufactured piece parts the observed fraction of defective piece parts is p, and 1000 pieces are produced by one operator on one machine in one shift, it is risky business to suppose that his long-run average proportion of defectives will be between $p - 3\sqrt{pq/1000}$ and $p + 3\sqrt{pq/1000}$. The fraction defective is likely to depend on many things: the day of the week (Mondays being notorious), the man, the machine, the shift, the supervisor, the inspector, and other plant matters we should not detail here. Appreciating this bramble of sources of variability led Walter Shewhart to devise methods of quality control with limits $p \pm 3\sqrt{pq/n}$ as an ideal to be nearly achieved only after the most strenuous and sophisticated engineering efforts. What mass production with all its control and measuring ability cannot attain, social science cannot expect formulas to give. Belief in such formulas may produce fancied security and sad surprises.

Nothing can substitute for relatively direct assessment of variability. In direct assessment, we base differences on large observational groups, differences more nearly representative of the many sources of variation that we must face. In the manufacturing example, we might look at numbers of defectives for several combinations of operators, shifts, machines, and days to get a notion of the variability actual manufacturing produces. (As we discuss in Section D7, we cannot ordinarily expect the data to tell us about all sources of variation.) In complicated investigations, the many sources of variability oblige us to assess variability directly.

Even if such a multiplicity of sources did not exist, the lack of an appropriate mathematical formula connecting micro-differences to macro-variability would often drive us to direct assessment. Even when one makes drastic oversimplifications (perhaps assuming independence, absence of many known sources of variability, and Gaussian distributions), the corresponding mathematical formula may never have been derived, may require an impractical effort to derive or locate, and may be misleading if found. The need for diverse and complex analyses also forces us to direct assessment.

D3. CHOOSING AN ERROR TERM

A large body of data offers considerable freedom for measuring its internal uncertainty. In a factor analytic study, for instance, we may have had all ninth grade students in a city school system as subjects. There is a natural hierarchy:

a) *student*   b) *class*   c) *school*   d) *city*.

We could, if we chose, regard those students who were, in the year in question, in the ninth grade in a particular school as a random sample of those who "might" have been there, considering, for instance, the socioeconomic, ethnic, and criminological background of the area from which this school draws its pupils. If we did this for each school in a city and regarded both the set of schools and the city as fixed, we would have an adequately specific model to support an assessment of internal uncertainty. Here we would turn to pupil-to-pupil differences within class as the basis of our measures of stability.

To the extent that our concern is with exactly these schools in this one city, such an assessment may be quite satisfactory. Alternatively, to the extent that broader, more encompassing, assessments are impossible (as when only one school in the city has ninth grade pupils), such an assessment may be the best that we can do.

If our concern is with the general nature of a broad urban milieu, in which no particular distribution of, say, socioeconomic and ethnic backgrounds has a distinguished role, then we will do better—in the sense of giving ourselves more useful information—by focusing our attention on school-to-school differences as a basis for assessing internal uncertainties. To do this means, in practice, to act as if the *schools* studied were a random sample from a larger population of schools.

By so doing, we bring into the assessment at least part of the neighborhood-to-neighborhood differences of our broad urban milieu. If there are regional differences, and "our" city belongs to a distinctive region, we will not have adequately represented neighborhood-to-neighborhood differences across regions in our assessment of instability. If, on the other hand, socioeconomic class is the dominant influence, and the fractions of socioeconomic classes for entire cities are nearly constant from city to city, then we may have overrepresented neighborhood-to-neighborhood variation. Our assessment may have imperfections of several kinds, but with data from only one city, it may be the best that can be done.

While it is easy to write down formulas based on other kinds of assumptions, assessment of variability in practice seems to be universally based upon treating suitable units—students, classes, schools, cities, or the tests that enter the battery to be factored—as if they were a random sample. Recognizing this is important, both for making certain general techniques of assessing variability broadly applicable (see Section E) and in making it clear that the practical choice is usually between "treat it as random" and "forget it, sweep it under the rug".

We have been discussing, in a very pragmatic vein, what the analysis-of-variance oriented worker usually calls "the choice of error term".

One might argue that it would be well to restrict the calculation of an indication of instability "as if so-and-so were random" to those cases where so-and-so was indeed random. The writers believe this position often leads to artificially lowered estimates of instability because of the exclusion of sources of variability which were sampled, though perhaps not very randomly or completely. Consequently, we encourage treating effects as randomly sampled in many circumstances where the randomness is at best dubious.

It would be a disservice to close by leaving the impression that the most all-encompassing assessment of internal uncertainty is always the best. Our purposes may make a less encompassing assessment more relevant. If we have studied the *only* three large cities in some state, for instance, then so far as decisions about policies that that state will apply uniformly to all its cities, city-to-city differences are irrelevant. (For a nationally oriented survey, conducted in Boston, New Orleans, and Seattle, the opposite might be likely.)

Then too, in many instances, large-scale differences involve so few comparisons as to make any assessment that includes these differences quite unstable. If a study is made in exactly two cities, for instance, it may be best to give assessments of internal uncertainty for the results of each city separately, and for the results for the two cities combined, allowing only for "sampling" *within* the cities, but stating pointedly that further allowance for city-to-city variation must be made.

By following this plan, different readers can combine both informed judgment and the observed city-to-city differences differently so as to assess an appropriate city-to-city contribution to uncertainty. There need not be any one "right" answer. Different purposes may well demand different assessments of instability.

D4. MORE DETAILED CHOICES OF ERROR TERMS

Given a number of groups (cities, years, etc.) the differences between which are to provide an error term, and given a result assessed separately for each, we are likely to proceed by using Student's t to get limits on the effects of internally expressed variability.

Often, we have little choice as to the number of groups to use, but sometimes we are freer to choose. If our principles for the selection of an error term leave us with 100 groups, all equivalent, we could consider assigning these 100 randomly into 20 supergroups of five each or randomly into five supergroups of 20 each. Making fewer supergroups saves computational effort; what will it cost elsewhere?

TABLE D4–1

TWO-SIDED 5% LEVELS FOR THE t TABLE, $|t_k|_{.95}$

df	$|t|_{.95}$	df	$|t|_{.95}$
1	12.71	6	2.45
2	4.30	7	2.36
3	3.18	8	2.31
4	2.78	9	2.26
5	2.57	10	2.23
		∞	1.96

How many groups should one take? Generally speaking, the more the better, but usually economic and data pressures force one to take few. A look at Table D4–1 showing the two-sided 5% levels for the t table is enlightening. Note that when we get to three degrees of freedom we are already about 89% on the way to an infinite number of degrees of freedom for the 5% point as measured in the t scale. And by 10 df we are only about 10% worse off on this scale than at ∞ df. (Actually the loss in variance terms, which may be more relevant, nearly corresponds to the square of the ratio of t-table entries.) Consequently, numbers of groups from 4 to 10 are quite practical. Subject to calculational difficulties, larger numbers are preferable. We often use 10 as a rule of thumb.

If groups of the right sort were always evident in the data, and if it were always easy to calculate results based on each group alone, and always efficient to use such results, the discussion of internal uncertainty could end here.

D5. MAKING DIRECT ASSESSMENT POSSIBLE

When the choice of independent groups of data is not automatic, it is often helpful to deliberately construct equivalent subsamples. For example, in making a sample survey from a list, we might draw several systematic subsamples (each consisting of every mth individual), having starting points randomly chosen from the first m on the list. To estimate the population mean μ, we first compute the mean $\bar{y}_i$ for each separate subsample. The means of each of these k subsamples are then treated as single independent measurements. Their mean $\bar{\bar{y}} = \Sigma \bar{y}_i / k$ estimates the population mean, μ. The estimated variance of $\bar{\bar{y}}$, $s_{\bar{\bar{y}}}^2 = \Sigma (\bar{y}_i - \bar{\bar{y}})^2 / k(k-1)$, makes it easy to compute confidence limits for μ:

$$\bar{\bar{y}} \pm \mid t_{k-1} \mid s_{\bar{\bar{y}}}, \tag{a}$$

where $\mid t_{k-1} \mid$ comes from the Student t table with $k - 1$ degrees of freedom for whatever two-sided confidence level has been chosen. In the limits given by expression (a) we have used a direct assessment of the variability of the $\bar{y}_i$.

Do not suppose that $s_{\bar{\bar{y}}}$ is equivalent to the $s/\sqrt{n}$ deprecated in the Peirce example (Section D1). True, we are still using the notion of variance to measure variability, but the appraisal of that variability in $s_{\bar{\bar{y}}}$ comes from differences between good-sized chunks, while that in the Peirce $s/\sqrt{n}$ comes from differences between single measurements.

In the same vein, several small stratified samples could be drawn, each a replicate sample drawn from the whole population by a method that specified a certain sort of stratification. Here, to estimate the population mean, a different $\bar{y}_i$, a weighted estimate for the population mean, might be constructed for each of the stratified samples. Then one would compute confidence limits on the population mean μ based on these $\bar{y}_i$, just as for the limits given by expression (a) above. One advantage of the use of such equivalent subsamples (they are often called "interpenetrating") is the ease with which they can be used to allow for the variation represented, for example, by different interviewers and supervisors, whose services can be assigned to different samples.

Exactly similar techniques apply to many statistics. For an example dealing with estimated slopes (regression coefficients, here linear combinations of observed y's with coefficients depending on the x's), let us consider part of an experiment by Johnson and Tsao (1944; Johnson, 1949).

Johnson-Tsao experiment. The subject holds a ring pulled upwards by one of seven initial weights (100, 150, 200, 250, 300, 350, or 400 grams). By means of liquid and valves the pull is increased at one of four rates (100, 200, 300, or 400 grams per minute). The subject announces "now" when he notices the increased heaviness. The difference limen (that is, the just noticeable change) is taken as the change in pull up to the instant the subject reports. Preliminary practice runs accustom the subject to the apparatus and procedure. Johnson and Tsao used 8 subjects, 4 sighted and 4 blind, 4 male and 4 female. Each subject executed the experiment twice. The experimenters randomized the order of procedure for 5 replications of each of the 28 ($= 4 \times 7$) measurements (for each of 8 observers at each session).

As a graphical examination of variability as a function of level will show, the logarithms of the observations seem more suitable for the analysis than do the raw observations. The data suggest that for a fixed rate of change the difference limens may not depend much upon the initial weights. Let us look further at this.

For the four sighted subjects and the rate 300 gm/min, let us compute the slopes of the regression lines of the common logarithms of the difference limens upon the coded initial weights (1 corresponds to 100 grams, 7 to 400 grams). Table D5–1 shows the raw and logarithmic difference limens. The slopes for the

TABLE D5–1

JOHNSON-TSAO EXPERIMENT

Coded weight	(1) Male	(2) Male	(3) Female	(4) Female
Original data: sighted subjects, 300 gm/min				
	Grams added before subject says "now"			
1	15.8	35.0	27.2	12.2
2	18.6	39.3	41.1	9.6
3	12.2	47.8	32.2	11.7
4	12.8	38.2	21.3	12.4
5	16.5	57.7	33.7	11.9
6	15.8	39.7	28.2	12.8
7	17.0	44.8	29.6	10.5
Transformed data log_{10}:				
x \ y	$y = log_{10}$ grams added before subject responds			
1	1.20	1.54	1.43	1.09
2	1.27	1.59	1.61	0.98
3	1.09	1.68	1.51	1.07
4	1.11	1.58	1.33	1.09
5	1.22	1.76	1.53	1.08
6	1.20	1.60	1.45	1.11
7	1.23	1.65	1.47	1.02
$\Sigma x = 28$	$\Sigma y = 8.32$	11.40	10.33	7.44
Σxy	33.36	46.03	41.14	29.82
$\Sigma x^2 = 140$	$(\Sigma x)^2 = 784$		$n = 7$	

four subjects, measured in $\log_{10}$ units per 50 gm change in initial weight, are: .0029, .0154, −.0064, .0021. The average slope is $\bar{b} = .0035$, and $s_{\bar{b}} = .0045$. Consequently, entering a t table with three degrees of freedom, we find the 95% confidence limits for the slope to be .0178 and −.0108.

For the whole change from 100 grams to 400 grams we would multiply these numbers by 6 $(= 7 - 1)$ to get, for example, $6\bar{b} = .0210$, 95% interval from −.065 to +.107. This corresponds to an estimated change in the raw limen by only about 5% (a factor of antilog$_{10}$ .0210 $= 1.05$) with a 95% confidence interval from −14% to +28% (a factor between 0.86 to 1.28). In view of the variation in the data from other sources, there are many purposes for which the variation owing to initial weights is not only not significantly different from zero, but clearly not very important.

Notice that the results here obtained by direct assessment of internal uncertainty are exactly those which would have followed from a straightforward complete analysis of variance, in which "slope × subjects" was used as the error term for "slope". Aside from the systematic attitudes it produces, perhaps the greatest single virtue of the analysis of variance is its provision of direct assessments of internal uncertainty.

We can carry out simple direct assessment of internal uncertainty for results that depend on the data in more complex ways than as linear combinations with fixed weights. In some problems such an approach is quite satisfactory, in others the difficulties about to be discussed are serious.

D6. DIFFICULTIES WITH DIRECT ASSESSMENT

Besides the question of supplementary variability treated in the next section, the major difficulties with direct assessment of variability, as just described, are these:

a) it may not be feasible to calculate meaningful results from such small amounts of data as properly chosen groups would provide, or

b) although the results would be meaningful, they would be so severely biased as to make their use unwise.

None of these difficulties arises in the examples of the last section, because the results there considered were all linear combinations of the observations with fixed weights. Thus, had we analyzed the same Johnson-Tsao data without separating the four subjects, our first act would have been to form arithmetic means over subjects, and our resulting regression coefficient would have been the arithmetic mean of those for the four individuals. Similar results hold for the particular types of interpenetrating subsampling described in Section D5. So long as we have linearity with fixed weights, everything is simple.

In Section E, we explain how to handle the more complex cases where difficulties (a) and (b) arise.

Beyond this sort of difficulty, the most prominent problem arises in the presence of two or more separately isolated measures of variability, all of which should contribute to a proper error term. Suppose that we have conducted a study of student reaction to world news in each of 20 schools, widely spread across the country, in each of 10 years. School-to-school differences, embodying regional differences as they do, are surely likely to be substantial and certainly reflect an important kind of variability. Year-to-year changes in the impact of world news cannot be neglected.

Happily, the effects of both of these major sources of uncertainty can be assessed within the data; we would not like to have had to assess either one purely as a matter of judgment. We must face the question of how to use two error terms at the same time.

It does not suffice to say that we have 200 groups, each made up of one school for one year, and that we need only use the variation among results for these groups to assess the variability of overall results. If everything were linear with fixed weights, and $\sigma^2_{schools}$ and σ^2_{years} represented the variances of school means (over years) and year means (over schools), the contribution of these variances to group-to-group differences among the 200 groups would be proportional to

$$20(10 - 1)\sigma^2_{years} + 10(20 - 1)\sigma^2_{schools}$$

—almost in equal proportions. But their contribution to the variance of the average for the 200 groups would be proportional to

$$\frac{1}{10}\,\sigma^2_{years} + \frac{1}{20}\,\sigma^2_{schools}$$

—in a ratio of 2 to 1. We need separate estimates of these two contributions. (The imbalance between the treatment of either of these σ^2 and a mean square for either true interaction or cell variation is much greater when schools and years are not separated.) We need a multiple-way analysis of variance or its equivalent; one in which estimates that involve $\sigma^2_{schools}$ and σ^2_{years} more or less separately can be recombined to yield an appropriate estimate of internal uncertainty.

D7. SUPPLEMENTARY UNCERTAINTY AND ITS COMBINATION WITH INTERNAL UNCERTAINTY

We want to be ready to make allowance for the effects of systematic error and of sources of variability excluded from our assessment of internal uncertainty. If our observations are confined to one city, city-to-city variation is not revealed in our data and cannot contribute to any assessment of internal uncertainty. (If only two cities are involved, we have already seen that it may be wise to leave city-to-city variation to judgment and include its effects in supplementary uncertainty.) Similar statements can apply to years, regions, and many other aspects of our data.

Besides the variations that might have been evident from more extensive data, some deviations are intrinsic to the way that the data were gathered. The instruments used, whether paper-and-pencil tests, questionnaires, or mercury-in-glass thermometers, are subject to imperfections of calibration and responsiveness to other variables than the one they seek to measure.

As a homely example, consider the market research analyst who plans to ask his respondents to perform an extra task beyond the initial questioning. In the pilot work, he finds that the interviewers report no difficulty about persuading the respondents to do the extra task. Indeed, of the respondents thus far approached only 2 of 50 have failed to respond to either the questionnaire or the task. How shall he suppose matters are going to work out in the actual survey? He can be helped if he knows, for example, that in his sort of survey, easy questionnaires alone lead to 15% nonresponse even with several callbacks. From his 96% indication, he is reduced at once to 85%. Next, he must consider a further discount for the extra task, but how much may depend heavily upon the enticements offered for the respondent's cooperation. At any rate, he should probably not be surprised by at least a further 15% loss.

(If the response rate is important to the analyst, he may design his pilot study with randomly chosen respondents and superimpose different incentives to discover what response rates they yield.)

Such sources of supplementary uncertainty should not be neglected. The fact that they have to be assessed by judgment, sometimes tempered by data from other sources, is no excuse for pretending they do not exist. Nor is the evidence that they are usually underestimated (even by physicists assessing their most fundamental constants; see DuMond and Cohen, 1958) any reason not to try to do as well with them as considered judgment permits.

How are we to do all this? As something wholly separate from our assessment of internal uncertainty? Or as something to be combined with the latter? The writers would like to be able to combine assessments of supplementary uncertainties and systematic errors with those of the internal uncertainties. In the end, all are matters of judgment. The investigator may find it worthwhile to communicate the internal uncertainty as well as the combined uncertainty; when the combining is something that only others can do, it may be better merely to communicate the separate components.

How is combination done in practice?

It is easy to expand an estimated standard deviation to an estimated root-mean-square error. One squares the standard deviation and adds on the square of the bias, and then takes the square root. Sometimes one can reduce an actual sample size to an effective sample size.

We can relatively easily combine supplementary uncertainties with results expressed as statements of confidence intervals. Suppose that we wish to add a "cookie cutter" type of uncertainty, such as "anything between -4% and $+1\%$ could be present". If our confidence interval already runs from 62% to 70%, we have only to move our cutting points outward to 58% and 71%. Similarly, if we want to make a significance test, we may wish to move the null hypothesis first one way and then the other, by a corresponding amount. If we wish to add a "distributional" type of uncertainty, such as "the systematic error tends to follow a normal distribution with average -1% and a standard deviation 3%", we will have to paste this onto our model and adjust the results somewhat more subtly. If the confidence interval is already based on a standard error of 2%, as in our

62% to 70% example, we could add the variances $2^2 + 3^2 = 13$, and get a pooled estimate of 3.6. The new center is $68\% - 1\% = 67\%$. Our final "confidence limits adjusted for supplementary uncertainty" would be about $67\% \pm 7.2\%$ or an interval from 59.8% to 74.2%.

If the supplementary uncertainty to be assessed by judgment is appreciable compared to the variability to be expected in repetitions of the overall study, then precisely what our internal "probability statements" are about is no longer important. Here, it is essential to describe *both* combined *and* internal uncertainty. Readers and hearers are entitled to see what their own judgments would lead to. When we wish to communicate an overall uncertainty, we ought to do so, and our use of probability statements should be kept flexible enough to enable us to do so.

However such details are to be handled, responsible researchers, and their statistical advisors, have a continuing and serious obligation to plan to assess supplementary uncertainties every time they assess an internal uncertainty. The results may come out in terms of "words of warning", rather than in terms of numbers. Words are often an acceptable minimum, but all of us should try to do better wherever we can. We owe supplementary and overall assessments of uncertainty to our readers, and to the researchers that come after us, even when we have made a direct assessment of internal uncertainty.

Although good methods of assessing supplementary uncertainties seem deeply bound to the subject matter of the analysis, extensive discussions by subject-matter experts may help statisticians find further methods of broad applicability. The area needs development.

In closing, let us emphasize that, for very different reasons, both the tightly controlled laboratory study and the large study that has had to have play in its methods to be done at all have special need for the appraisal of supplementary uncertainty.

E. A METHOD OF DIRECT ASSESSMENT

Introduction
E1. *The jackknife*
★ *Appendix to* E1. *Combinations and reexpressions*
E2. *Examples with individuals*
E3. *Jackknife using groups: ratio estimation for a sample survey*
E4. *A more complex example*
E5. *Cross-validation in the example*
E6. *Two simultaneous uses of "leave-out-one"*
E7. *Dispersion of the μ's*
E8. *Further discussion of the example*

The classical method of assessing variability directly evaluates the same statistic on several small groups of data. Their smallness often creates awkward problems which we can circumvent through the use of a method called the jackknife.

E1. THE JACKKNIFE

For statistics more complicated than weighted averages, we are likely to find difficulties in assessing stability, even when we have moderately large amounts of data. Thus for example, in fitting a multiple regression on k independent variables, one needs at least $k + 1$ data points, and not many people would be pleased to work with so few. Consequently, if a substantial body of data is needed in each group, the number of possible groups of data available for direct appraisal of variability by the standard method described in Section D5 may be severely restricted. Second, many statistics based on small samples give biased estimates; typically the leading term in the bias is proportional to $1/n$, where n is the sample size. Consequently, the mean of results based on several subsamples is likely to be more biased than is a single result based on all the data, at least to the extent that the individual samples are small. A method with wide application, intended to ameliorate these problems, is the jackknife.

The name "jackknife" is intended to suggest the broad usefulness of a technique as a substitute for specialized tools that may not be available, just as the Boy Scout's trusty tool serves so variedly. The jackknife offers ways to set sensible confidence limits in complex situations. The basic idea is to assess the effect of each of the groups into which the data have been divided, not by the result for that group alone, which we used in Section D5, but rather through the effect upon the body of data that results from omitting that group.

An illustration will speed understanding. For a simple mean of five numbers, any single value can be easily expressed as the weighted difference of two means, the mean of all five values and the mean of the four other than the selected value. Thus, for example, for the values 3, 5, 7, 10, 15, we can represent 7 by

$$5\left(\frac{3 + 5 + 7 + 10 + 15}{5}\right) - 4\left(\frac{3 + 5 + 10 + 15}{4}\right) = 7.$$

This result is not only trivial to prove, but appears to have trivial consequences. For means of equally weighted numbers, the consequences are indeed trivial. But when we deal with more complex statistics, the analogous computation does not give us the same result as we get by applying "the same" calculation to the individual pieces. Instead, it gives us something much more useful. In particular, as we see, such complex statistics might be regression equations rather than mere numbers.

The two bases of the jackknife are that we make the desired calculation for all the data, and then, after dividing the data into groups, we make the calculation for each of the slightly reduced bodies of data obtained by leaving out just one of the groups.

Let, then, $y_{(j)}$ be the result of making the complex calculation on the portion of the sample that omits the jth subgroup, that is, on a pool of $k - 1$ subgroups. Let y_{all} be the corresponding result for the entire sample, and define *pseudovalues* by

$$y_{*j} = ky_{\text{all}} - (k - 1)y_{(j)}, \qquad j = 1, 2, \ldots, k. \tag{1}$$

These pseudo-values now play the role originally played in Section D5 by the results of making the computation for each group separately. Note that, as in the example with five numbers, when the calculation reduces to forming a mean using equal weights, we have $y_{*j} = y_j$, where y_j is the result for the jth piece alone. Accordingly, for simple means, the use of the jackknife technique reduces to the technique of Section D5, as we would hope.

The final accuracy required for the y_{*j} is just about what would be needed for the y_j. Because of the multiplications by k and by $k - 1$, which may be large, one usually needs to compute y_{all} and the $y_{(j)}$ to more decimals than would be needed if they were to be used directly. Accordingly, the y_{*j} are particularly sensitive to computational errors or rounding changes in y_{all} and $y_{(j)}$, though their sensitivity to data variability is ordinarily if anything a little less than that of the y_j they replace.

The key idea is that, in a wide variety of problems, the pseudo-values can be used to set approximate confidence limits, using Student's t, as if they were the results of applying some complex calculation to each of k independent pieces of data. The words "as if" are vital here; Student's t performs well in many circumstances where the y_{*j} deviate substantially from independence.

The jackknifed value y_*, which is our best single result, and an estimate s_*^2 of its variance are thus given by:

$$y_* = \frac{1}{k}(y_{*1} + \cdots + y_{*k}),$$

$$s^2 = \frac{\Sigma y_{*j}^2 - \frac{1}{k}(\Sigma y_{*j})^2}{k - 1},$$

$$s_*^2 = s^2/k.$$

[When the $y_{(j)}$ are rounded, or otherwise quantized, after or during calculation, Tukey (unpublished manuscript) has suggested the conservative practice of increasing s_*^2 by $k^2\tau^2$, where τ^2 may often be taken as the variance of a uniform distribution over the rounding or quantizing interval. Thus if we rounded $y_{(j)}$ to 3 decimals, the corresponding displacement would have a uniform distribution over a range of 0.001, that is, from $x - 0.0005$ to $x + 0.0005$, where x is the rounded value. Applying the usual formula $L^2/12$ for the variance of a rectangular distribution of length L, we would have $\tau^2 = (.001)^2/12 = 0.00000008$. Unless k is large, or s_*^2 is very small, we need pay little attention to the $k^2\tau^2$ term for so small a τ^2. It costs little to compare $k^2\tau^2$ with s_*^2.]

Adjusting degrees of freedom

Difficulties with the jackknife seem to arise most frequently from two causes:

a) excessively straggling tails,

b) discreteness of the values produced.

About (a) no one has found anything to do in any circumstances or for any method of analysis.

We can do something about (b). Let us look at a natural and very extreme case. Suppose that we jackknife the median of a sample of even size, say $k = 2m$. If we delete any observation in the upper half of these $2m$ values, the median of what is left will be the mth value, counting up from the lowest. If we delete any observation in the lower half, the median will be the $(m + 1)$st value in the original sample.

Accordingly the $y_{(j)}$ have but 2 different values, taking on each m times, and the same holds for the pseudo-values. The stability of s_*^2 is not greater than that corresponding to a squared difference between 2 values. This would lead us to use only 1 degree of freedom for t's involving such an s.

Can we obtain a more stable s_*? By jackknifing in groups, as discussed in Section E3, we can arrange to have more than 2 different pseudo-values appear. This can be very valuable, since the only advantage to using individuals in ordinary situations is to preserve degrees of freedom. But even then it seems unlikely that we should use the full number of degrees of freedom.

Clearly a rule of thumb for reducing degrees of freedom is needed. The following simple rule should be helpful:

c) Count the number of different numbers appearing as pseudo-values, subtract one, and use the result as degrees of freedom.

This rule is only to be used when the sameness of the pseudo-values arises from the definition of the computation, as in the case of a median or a range, and not when it arises from the nature of the basic observations or the conduct of our arithmetic. Specifically:

c1) If slight changes in the basic observations—as when values by their nature either 0 or 1 are made -0.001, $+0.002$, 0.997, or 1.004—would make two pseudo-values different, they should *not* be considered "the same" in applying rule (c). Example: % of successes in binomial observations.

c2) If carrying more decimals in the computation would have made two pseudo-values different, they should *not* be considered "the same" in applying rule (c).

★ APPENDIX TO E1. *Combinations and reexpressions*

The results of data analysis are not always single numbers. When we deal with several numerical results, say y, z, v, and w, we can use a single choice of k pieces and go through the jackknife computation separately for each result. Having matched sets of pseudo-values $(y_{*j}, z_{*j}, v_{*j}, w_{*j})$ for each j, we can easily find a set of k illustrative values for any combination or function of these results, forming, for example,

$$\frac{y_{*j} + z_{*j}}{v_{*j} + w_{*j}}$$

to tell us something about the estimand corresponding to

$$\frac{y+z}{v+w}.$$

Similarly, we consider the log y_{*j} as telling us about the estimand corresponding to log y. This procedure extends to combinations that depend on an auxiliary variable or variables, as in

$$ye^{-zt}$$

or in

$$y \cdot x_1 + z \cdot x_2 + v \cdot x_3 + w \cdot x_4,$$

for we can consider such illustrative functions as

$$y_{*j}e^{-z_{*j}t}$$

and

$$y_{*j} \cdot x_1 + z_{*j} \cdot x_2 + v_{*j} \cdot x_3 + w_{*j} \cdot x_4.$$

In thinking about such questions of combination and transformation, we need to bear in mind that the order in which we do things will generally matter. Thus, for example, we will almost always have

$$(\log y)_{*j} \neq \log (y_{*j})$$

although the values of these two expressions are likely to be rather similar. We must, by definition, have

$$(\log y)_{(j)} = \log (y_{(j)}).$$

This identity, however, does not help, because

$$(\log y)_{*j} = k \cdot (\log y)_{\text{all}} - (k-1)(\log y)_{(j)}$$
$$= k \cdot \log (y_{\text{all}}) - (k-1)\log (y_{(j)})$$
$$= k \cdot \log (y_{\text{all}}) - (k-1)\log \left(\frac{k \cdot y_{\text{all}} - y_{*j}}{k-1}\right),$$

which need not equal log (y_{*j}). When, for example, $k=2$, $y_{\text{all}} = 4$, and $y_{*j} = 3$, the displayed expression becomes $2 \log 4 - \log 5 = \log 3.2$, which is not the same as log 3. Two corollaries are worth noting:

a1) There may be some advantage in jackknifing one expression of a given result rather than another (as when we jackknife log y or y^2 instead of y).

a2) If we deal with a *linear* combination of results, as in $y - 3z + 2v$, or in $y + zt + vt^2 + wt^3$ where t is an auxiliary variable, or in $y \cdot x_1 + z \cdot x_2 + v \cdot x_3 + w \cdot x_4$ where x_1, x_2, x_3, and x_4 are auxiliary variables (regression variables), the order of operation will *not* matter, so that jackknifing y, z, v, w separately, using the same pieces, is enough to deal with all combinations. Consequently when considering many possible sets of x's, jackknifing the coefficients is economical.

We know little about which choices of expression tend to polish up the behavior of the jackknife. What evidence we have suggests that:

b1) It is very desirable to *avoid* situations where the sampling distribution of the quantity jackknifed has an abrupt terminus or where the possible values of its estimand are restricted to an interval or half-line. For example, if one jackknifes estimates of probabilities, he might find a few final results negative or greater than 1. One possible approach would jackknife the logit, $\log [p/(1 - p)]$, and then form the antilogit of the final result. This would keep the numbers in bounds.

b2) It is desirable to *avoid* sampling distributions with one or more straggling tails.

b3) It is probably desirable to *avoid* markedly unsymmetrical sampling distributions.

In summary, we can use the jackknifing of several numerical results to tell us about any combination of these results. Our conclusions will usually differ somewhat from those reached by jackknifing that combination directly. This offers us choices that can sometimes allow us to improve our conclusions. If we deal with linear combinations, as for example in the relation of multiple regression equations to the coefficients that appear in them, these differences disappear.

E2. EXAMPLES WITH INDIVIDUALS

We plan four examples. The first is a toy to get ideas in mind and deals with inference about the standard deviation from a skewed and straggling-tailed distribution. The second example is rather clean and simple, the problem it treats is nonstandard, and theory for treating it is not generally available. On the other hand, it is not a problem where the jackknife does its best work, but without it . . . ? The third deals with a small survey example where it is convenient to use groups, each consisting of several units. The fourth treats a complicated multiple-response problem in some detail. It offers more than one illustration of the power of the method in a problem where indication would otherwise have been the most we would have hoped to seek.

Example (first of 4). *Confidence limits on a standard deviation.* A sample from a distribution produced the 11 values 0.1, 0.1, 0.1, 0.4, 0.5, 1.0, 1.1, 1.3, 1.9, 1.9, 4.7. There is no reason to suppose the distribution normal and some reason to suppose it is not. Set confidence limits on the standard deviation σ.

First solution. Since the data are few, let us use each measurement as a group of size 1. Call the measurements $x_1, x_2, \ldots, x_{11}$. Since each group is of size 1, we could not compute a sample standard deviation for a group. We compute standard deviations first for all the measurements together—that is, for all the groups together:

$$y_{\text{all}} = \sqrt{\Sigma(x_i - \bar{x})^2/10},$$

TABLE E2–1

JACKKNIFE FOR A SAMPLE STANDARD DEVIATION, FIRST SOLUTION

y_{all} = sample standard deviation = *1.34347*

j	x_j	Standard deviations omitting x_j $y_{(j)}$	$y_{*j} =$ $11y_{\text{all}} - 10y_{(j)}$
1	.1	*1.36382*	1.1400
2	.1	*1.36382*	1.1400
3	.1	*1.36382*	1.1400
4	.4	*1.38888*	.8894
5	.5	*1.39539*	.8243
6	1.0	*1.41457*	.6325
7	1.1	*1.41578*	.6204
8	1.3	*1.41563*	.6219
9	1.9	*1.39427*	.8355
10	1.9	*1.39427*	.8355
11	4.7	*.70742*	7.7040
	13.1		$y_* = 1.4894$

$s_* = 0.6244$

Two-sided confidence limits on σ:

$2/3$: $1.4894 \pm \mid t_{10} \mid _{\frac{2}{3}} s_* = 1.4894 \pm 1.02(.6244)$

  or the interval from 0.85 to 2.13.

95%: $1.4894 \pm \mid t_{10} \mid _{.95} s_* = 1.4894 \pm 2.23(.6244)$

  or the interval from 0.10 to 2.88.

shown at the head of column 3 of Table E2–1. Then, leaving the jth measurement out, that is, leaving the jth group out, we compute

$$y_{(j)} = \sqrt{\Sigma(x_i - \bar{x}_{(j)})^2/9},$$

where $\bar{x}_{(j)}$ is the mean of the 10 x's that exclude the jth, and the summation in $y_{(j)}$ omits $(x_j - \bar{x}_{(j)})^2$. We compute this for each of the 11 measurements (groups). These values are also shown in the third column of Table E2–1. From these we then compute pseudo-values

$$y_{*j} = 11y_{\text{all}} - 10y_{(j)},$$

shown in the fourth column of the table.

  Our estimate of σ is y_*, the average of these pseudo-values, which turns out to be about 1.49. The details are shown in Table E2–1 together with the $2/3$

confidence interval for σ: from 0.85 to 2.13, and the 95% confidence interval: from 0.10 to 2.88. Since we happen secretly to know that these data came from an exponential distribution with mean and standard deviation both unity, we need not be displeased with these limits.

Second solution. We are not compelled to jackknife s itself, as we just did. We might, for example, jackknife log s instead. Thinking about this possibility, we are encouraged to do just this, because the sampling distribution of log s is known to be better behaved than that for s. Specifically the distribution of the logarithm is usually more nearly symmetrical and has less straggling tails than the sampling distribution of s. The logarithm might be more biased. But unbiasedness is not of major importance, particularly in view of the bias-reducing feature of the jackknife.

The details and results are shown in Table E2–2. We have introduced Y's for the logged values of the y's from Table E2–1. The 2/3 confidence interval for σ now runs from 0.94 to 3.29, while the 95% interval runs from 0.44 to 6.93.

TABLE E2–2

JACKKNIFING OF $\log_{10} s$
FOR THE DATA TREATED IN TABLE E2–1

$Y_{\text{all}} = \log_{10} y_{\text{all}} = .12823$		
j	$Y_{(j)} =$ $\log_{10} y_{(j)}$	$Y_{*j} =$ $11 \log_{10} y_{\text{all}} - 10 \log_{10} y_{(j)}$
1	.13476	.06293
2	.13476	.06293
3	.13476	.06293
4	.14266	−.01607
5	.14470	−.03647
6	.15062	−.09567
7	.15100	−.09947
8	.15095	−.09897
9	.14435	−.03297
10	.14435	−.03297
11	−.15032	2.91373
		$Y_* = .24454 = $ mean

$s_*^2 = .071605,$ $s_* = .2676$

2/3 limits for $\log_{10} \sigma$: .2445 ± 1.02(.2676) or
the interval from −.028 to .517

95% limits for $\log_{10} \sigma$: .2445 ± 2.23(.2676) or
the interval from −.352 to .841

2/3 confidence interval for σ: from .94 to 3.29
95% confidence interval for σ: from .44 to 6.93

Unsatisfactory solutions. By way of contrast, let us display some solutions which treat the data as if they came from a normal distribution. The overall s^2 is 1.805; a chi-square table gives the following % points for 10 degrees of freedom: 2.5%, 3.25; 1/6, 5.78; 1/2, 9.34; 5/6, 14.15; 97.5%, 20.48. Accordingly the usual symmetric 95% confidence limits for σ^2 are

$$\frac{1.805}{20.48/10} = 0.88 \quad \text{and} \quad \frac{1.805}{3.25/10} = 5.55,$$

while the 2/3 limits are, similarly, 1.28 and 3.12. The corresponding confidence intervals for σ run from 0.94 to 2.36 and from 1.13 to 1.77. These limits may be optimistically short.

Similarly, using the range $w = 4.7 - 0.1 = 4.6$ and % points for w/σ in normal samples of 11, namely: 2.5%, 1.78; 1/6, 2.41; 1/2, 3.12; 5/6, 3.93; 97.5%, 4.86; we find intervals for σ from 0.95 to 2.58 at 95% and from 1.17 to 1.91 at 2/3 confidence.

Comments. The four sets of solutions compare as follows:

Source	2/3 limits	95% limits
jackknifing s	$0.85 \leq \sigma \leq 2.13$	$0.10 \leq \sigma \leq 2.88$
jackknifing $\log s$	$0.94 \leq \sigma \leq 3.29$	$0.44 \leq \sigma \leq 6.93$
s^2/σ^2	$1.13 \leq \sigma \leq 1.77$	$0.94 \leq \sigma \leq 2.36$
w/σ	$1.17 \leq \sigma \leq 1.91$	$0.95 \leq \sigma \leq 2.58$

The comparison between the two sets of jackknife limits shows fair similarity for the 2/3 limits and considerable difference for the 95% limits. A moment's reflection on the fact that the lower limit for σ based on jackknifing $\log s$ cannot be negative, while that based on jackknifing s can, offers one reason for preferring to jackknife $\log s$. Nevertheless, jackknifing s itself did nicely in this example. What information is available from experimental sampling (Havell, Robson, and Tukey, unpublished) about the closeness of true confidence to nominal confidence supports a preference for the use of $\log s$.

For the exponential distribution that we actually sampled, Var $s \approx 2(\sigma^2/n)$. Whereas for the normal distribution Var $s \approx \frac{1}{2}(\sigma^2/n)$. The ratio of these quantities measures the relative variabilities of sample standard deviations drawn from the different distributions. Consequently, the variability in variance terms for the kind of sample we are dealing with is four times that given by normal theory. We might expect then a factor of roughly $\sqrt{4} = 2$ in the lengths of the confidence intervals. Consequently, normal theory directly applied cannot possibly give nearly valid confidence limits, and we must discard the last two solutions as unsatisfactory.

Example (second of 4). *Estimating the 10% point of a pool of populations.* Each individual in a universe has associated with it a population of measurements. For each of a sample of 11 individuals, a group of 5 measurements is taken. Table E2–3 shows the measurements (hypothetical) arranged from greatest to least for

TABLE E2–3

MEASUREMENTS FOR 11 INDIVIDUALS

| | | *Individual* | | | |
1	2	3	4	5	6
6.880	4.660	6.950	4.756	4.411	4.257
5.172	4.522	3.948	3.792	4.357	3.572
3.598	3.403	3.062	2.458	3.571	1.809
3.034	3.211	2.906	.412	2.983	1.801
.628	.070	.482	−.458	1.825	1.480

| | | *Individual* | | |
7	8	9	10	11
2.642	12.541	8.404	3.262	3.286
2.276	4.081	5.137	2.874	2.858
2.007	3.853	3.172	2.120	2.787
1.922	.364	1.432	1.456	2.752
1.588	−2.945	−1.415	.780	2.047

each individual. Estimate the upper 10% point of the total population of measurements.

Solution. A variety of ways could be used to estimate the 10% point. One method pools the groups, estimates that the space between a pair of measurements contains $1/(n + 1)$ of the total distribution, and interpolates to 10%. For example, 5 measurements divide a population into 6 parts, each of which contains, on the average, 1/6 of the probability. With only 5 measurements, though, the upper 10% point is hard to estimate, because the estimate falls naturally into the block

TABLE E2–4

LARGEST 8 MEASUREMENTS
RANKED AND IDENTIFIED

Rank	Size	Individual
1st	12.541	8
2nd	8.404	9
3rd	6.950	3
4th	6.880	1
5th	5.172	1
6th	5.137	9
7th	4.756	4
8th	4.660	2

TABLE E2–5

JACKKNIFE QUANTITIES

y_{all}	5.151	Pseudo-values		
$y_{(1)}$	4.746	$y_{*1} =$	9.201 = 11(5.151) − 10(4.746)	
$y_{(2)}$	5.168	$y_{*2} =$	4.981	
$y_{(3)}$	5.099	$y_{*3} =$	5.671	
$y_{(4)}$	5.168	$y_{*4} =$	4.981	
$y_{(5)}$	5.168	$y_{*5} =$	4.981	
$y_{(6)}$	5.168	$y_{*6} =$	4.981	
$y_{(7)}$	5.168	$y_{*7} =$	4.981	
$y_{(8)}$	5.099	$y_{*8} =$	5.671	
$y_{(9)}$	4.746	$y_{*9} =$	9.201	
$y_{(10)}$	5.168	$y_{*10} =$	4.981	
$y_{(11)}$	5.168	$y_{*11} =$	4.981	
Total	55.866	Total = 64.611		
Total/11	5.0787	Total/11 =	5.874 = y_*	

Check: $y_* = 11(5.151) - 10(5.0787) = 5.874$
$s^2 = 2.78024$

$s_*^2 = 2.78024/11 = .25275$

$s_* = .503$

$y_* \pm |t_2|_{.95}s_* = 5.874 \pm 4.30(.503)$ or 95% confidence interval from 3.71 to 8.04

above the largest observation, which is often infinitely long. Here is another example where the pooling inherent in combining all pieces but one helps.

Our numerical work can be simplified by collecting, as in Table E2–4, a few of the largest observations. First, let us estimate the 10% point for the full sample of 55 points. Fifty-five points yield 56 blocks, and we want to include $56/10 = 5.6$ blocks counting from the top. In Table E2–4, we want y_{all} to be 0.6 of the way from the 5th to the 6th measurement. Thus $5.172 - 5.137 = 0.035$, $0.6 \times 0.035 = 0.021$, $5.172 - 0.021 = 5.151 = y_{\text{all}}$.

When the first individual is omitted we have to compute a $y_{(1)}$ based on 50 points or 51 blocks. We thus want to count down $51/10 = 5.1$ blocks. Omitting individual 1 eliminates two measurements, 6.880 and 5.172, from Table E2–4, because both measurements come from his group. We interpolate between the 5th and 6th remaining measurements, finding $4.756 - 4.660 = 0.096$, $0.1(0.096) = 0.0096 \approx 0.010$, and $y_{(1)} = 4.756 - 0.010 = 4.746$.

Table E2–5 shows the resulting $y_{(j)}$, y_{*j}, y_*, s_*, and the 95% confidence limits, where 2 degrees of freedom have been used since only 3 different values arise. Note that the estimate $y_* = 5.874$ is considerably larger than that obtained directly from $y_{\text{all}} = 5.151$. In this particular problem we secretly know that the 10% point is 5.773, because the populations associated with individuals were constructed to be normal with $\mu = 2$, 3, or 4 with probability 1/3 and independently $\sigma = 1$, 2, 3 with probability 1/3. Thus we had nine different equally likely normal populations. We chose one at random with replacement for each of the 11 individuals.

This example is one for which the jackknife is not especially well suited, for it deals rather repeatedly with single order statistics. The repetitions of the value 4.981 in Table E2–5 are symptomatic of the difficulty. Generally speaking, the variations of maxima and minima and of ranges depend heavily on the exact shape of the underlying distribution. Accordingly, it is probable that robustness of validity cannot be had for any confidence procedure concerning their values. Even in such circumstances, the jackknife is often as good a procedure as we have available. An approximate idea of uncertainty is better than none.

E3. JACKKNIFE USING GROUPS: RATIO ESTIMATION FOR A SAMPLE SURVEY

In practice, we usually divide our data less completely, working with and comparing groups made up of more than one individual or case.

Example (third of 4). *Ratio estimate.* In expounding the use of ratio estimates, Cochran (1953, p. 113; 1963, p. 156) gives 1920 and 1930 sizes (number of inhabitants) for each city in a random sample of 49 drawn from a population of 196 large U.S. cities. Table E3–1 repeats his values, and totals them, first by 7's and then overall. For computation on such an example by paper, pencil, and book of tables, it is worth noting that, so far, no extra work is involved, since these short additions are so much easier to check than the adding for all 49 cases would be.

The formula for the ratio estimate of the 1930 population total is

$$\frac{(1930 \text{ sample total})}{(1920 \text{ sample total})} \times (1920 \text{ population total}),$$

so that the logarithm of the estimated 1930 population total is given by log (1930 sample total) − log (1920 sample total) + log (1920 population total). Consequently, we find it natural to work with, and jackknife,

$$z = \log (1930 \text{ sample total}) - \log (1920 \text{ sample total}),$$

since this choice minimizes the number of multiplications and divisions.

Further computation is shown in Table E3–2, where in the "all" column the numbers 5054 and 6262 come directly from the previous table, and in the "$i = 1$" column the numbers $4303 = 5054 - 751$ and $5347 = 6262 - 915$ are the results of omitting the first seven cities, and so on for the other columns. Five-place logarithms have obviously given more than sufficient precision, so that the pseudo-values of z are conveniently rounded to 3 decimals. To be able to continue easily with hand calculation, an arbitrary central value of 0.100 was subtracted from

TABLE E3–1

POPULATION OF 49 LARGE CITIES IN 1920 (*x*) AND 1930 (*y*) IN THOUSANDS OF PEOPLE
(PARENTHESES EMPHASIZE NUMBERS THAT ARE OMITTED IN JACKKNIFING)

	1st 7		2nd 7		3rd 7		4th 7	
	x	*y*	*x*	*y*	*x*	*y*	*x*	*y*
	76	80	120	115	60	57	44	58
	138	143	61	69	46	65	77	89
	67	67	387	459	2	50	64	63
	29	50	93	104	507	634	64	77
	381	464	172	183	179	260	56	142
	23	48	78	106	121	113	40	60
	37	63	66	86	50	64	40	64
Subtotal 751		915	977	1122	965	1243	385	553

	5th 7		6th 7		7th 7		Summary	
	x	*y*	*x*	*y*	*x*	*y*	*x*	*y*
	38	52	71	79	36	46	(751)	(915)
	136	139	256	288	161	232	(977)	(1122)
	116	130	43	61	74	93	(965)	(1243)
	46	53	25	57	45	53	(385)	(553)
	243	291	94	85	36	54	(696)	(881)
	87	105	43	50	50	58	(830)	(937)
	30	111	298	317	48	75	(450)	(611)
Subtotal 696		881	830	937	450	611 *Total* 5054		6262

each z_{*i} and the result multiplied by 1000. These working values are used for the calculation of numerical values for

$$95\% \text{ limits} = \text{mean} \pm \text{allowance.}$$

Table E3–3 gives all the remaining details. The resulting point estimate is 28,300, about 100 lower than the unjackknifed estimate. (Since the correct 1930 total is 29,351, the automatic bias adjustment, which is effective only on the average, did not help in this instance.) The limits on this estimate are ordinarily somewhat wider than we would get if we had used each city as a separate group, since $| t_6 |_{.95} = 2.447$, $| t_{47} |_{.95} = 2.012$. The standard error found here was $\pm .0125$ in logarithmic units, which converts to about ± 830 in total (antilog $.0125 \approx 1.0292$, $0.0292 \times 28,300 \approx 830$). The agreement of this value, on only 6 degrees of freedom, with Cochran's value of 604 (1953, p. 119; 1963, p. 163) is fair.

In Section B3 we promised a way for the investigator who was comparing two forms of a projective test to do better than indication. Let us see what he should do. His experiment must involve a number of subjects; his desire is to generalize to a large class of similar subjects. He needs only to divide his subjects into a

TABLE E3-2

DETAILS OF JACKKNIFING THE RATIO ESTIMATE BASED ON TABLE E3-1

	all	$i=1$	$i=2$	$i=3$	$i=4$	$i=5$	$i=6$	$i=7$
$x_{(i)}$ (1920 sample)	5054	4303	4077	4089	4669	4358	4224	4604
$\log x_{(i)}$	3.70364	3.63377	3.61034	3.61162	3.66922	3.63929	3.62572	3.66314
$y_{(i)}$ (1930 sample)	6262	5347	5140	5019	5709	5381	5325	5651
$\log y_{(i)}$	3.79671	3.72811	3.71096	3.70062	3.75656	3.73086	3.72632	3.75213
$z_{(i)}=\log\,[y_{(i)}/x_{(i)}]$	.09307	.09434	.10062	.08900	.08734	.09157	.10060	.08899
$z_{*i}=7z_{all}-6z_{(i)}$	—	.08545	.04777	.11749	.12745	.10207	.04789	.11755
rounded z_{*i}	—	.085	.048	.117	.127	.102	.048	.118
1000 (rounded $z_{*i}-0.100$)	—	−15	−52	17	27	2	−52	18

Sum $= -55$; $-55/7 = -7.9 =$ mean $= z_*$ (in working units)
Sum sq. $= 6979$; $6979 - (-55)^2/7 = 6547 =$ sum sq. deviations

$$\frac{6547}{6\times 7} \approx 156 = s_*^2$$

$\sqrt{156} \approx 12.5 = s_*$ (in working units)

$|t_6|_{.95} = 2.447,\quad (12.5)(2.447) = 30.6 =$ allowance (in working units)

TABLE E3–3

FINAL COMPUTATIONS FOR THE RATIO ESTIMATE

Base data: 1920 total $= 22{,}919$, log (1920 total) $= 4.360$
log total $=$ log (1920 total) $+$ log ratio

| Quantity considered | | Results found | |
In words	In formulas	Good estimate	95% confidence intervals
working units	$1000\,(z_* - 0.100)$	about -7.9	-38.5 to $+22.7$
log ratio	z_*	about 0.092	0.062 to 0.123
log total	log (1920 total) $+ z_*$	about 4.452	4.422 to 4.483
total	antilog (log total)	about $28{,}300$	$26{,}000$ to $30{,}400$

suitable number of groups, and jackknife his whole calculation, obtaining a jackknifed estimate, and jackknifed confidence limits for the difference of the averaged reliability coefficients according to the two scorings. While a moderate amount of computation is involved, he need only make a routine application of the jackknife.

The ability to work with groups as well as individuals is a crucial advantage of the jackknife, not only as a way of keeping computation to a reasonable volume, but more importantly, as a way of insuring the use of an appropriately large error term. In particular, the way the sample was drawn controls the proper assessment of stability of any survey result. If the units were drawn in clusters, the correct error term involves cluster-to-cluster variation, and we must be sure that each piece is made up of one or more whole clusters. If the units were stratified and stratum sizes were known, stratum-to-stratum variation must be excluded from the error term, a condition that can sometimes be insured by the choice of pieces (and always by the choice of basic computation).

E4. A MORE COMPLEX EXAMPLE

We now turn to an example of jackknifing where we can offer no other bearable approach. The similarity between the "leave-one-out" form of cross-validation discussed at the end of Section B6 and the jackknife has, without doubt, occurred to the reader. The example we discuss next involves both the cross-validation issue and the complex stability issue. Thus there should be no surprise that we are going to use both a "leave-one-out" (that is, jackknife) assessment of stability and "leave-one-out" cross-validation. Indeed, as we shall see when we come to further discussion, there are questions about this example where it is natural to apply "leave-one-out" techniques not merely "two deep" but "three deep".

Example (fourth of 4). *Discrimination.* This example deals with an authorship problem. Alexander Hamilton and James Madison wrote during the same period about similar political matters, and their personal histories were also similar. One way of trying to discriminate between their writing is based upon the rates with which they used high-frequency words. Much more extensive and effective studies of this problem have been made (Mosteller and Wallace, 1964) than we are about to make. But since social scientists frequently find themselves involved in problems with the same basic difficulty—many variables, few data—we set out here, in a way that clearly reveals the jackknife methodology of assessing variability, a new small study of this problem.

We shall try to discriminate between some writings by Hamilton and some by Madison on the basis of the five words they used most frequently. Then we shall see how well the method works. An advantage of choosing the five most frequent words, from the point of view of the example, is that their choice is not based upon any prior estimate of whether these words are good or poor at separating these authors' writings, an advantage for simplification, though not necessarily for discrimination. The decision to use 5 words is arbitrary: we wanted an example complicated enough to imitate reality, but modest enough in size that neither we nor the reader need make a career of it. Another advantage is that, because one more occurrence, or one fewer, changes these rates so slightly, the rates of use of such high-frequency words should behave smoothly, making all standard techniques for measurement data effective.

We chose 11 papers known to have been written by each author, mainly from among the *Federalist* papers. These particular 22 papers were chosen because among the 100 or so papers we had available, their lengths were nearest to 2500 words, running from about 2200 to about 2800. For some purposes, it would have been better to have chosen randomly. For convenience in applying the jackknife, each Hamilton paper was randomly paired with a Madison paper. Perhaps we could have paired them more meaningfully by order of publication, but we did not. The number $k = 11$ was chosen partly because it is one more than the round number 10, and we frequently need to multiply or divide by $k - 1$. Also 10 is only about twice as big as 5, the number of variables chosen for analysis, and one of our purposes is to illustrate the variability that may occur in a study of several weakly discriminating variables when we have only a modest set of data available for establishing the technique of making distinctions. In our discussion, we work only with papers whose authorship is known, though the method of approach illustrated should produce a means of distinguishing unknown papers as well.

The standard device which seems most reasonable here is the linear discriminant function. When we have two classes of individuals measured on variables $x_1, x_2, \ldots, x_k$, the linear discriminant function is a linear function

$$\hat{y} = A(b_1 x_1 + b_2 x_2 + \cdots + b_n x_n) + B.$$

The coefficients b_i for the x's are chosen to separate the observed sample values of the two classes of individuals as widely as they can, considering the internal variation within the two classes. The numbers A and B are merely scale factors chosen for convenience, either of the investigator or of computation.

When convenient, as it is here, we may regard each Hamilton paper as having a y-value of 1, and each Madison paper as having a y-value of 0. The corresponding discriminant function is just the linear function obtained by fitting a multiple regression equation with the values of the dependent variable y to be forecast assigned 0 or 1 according as Madison or Hamilton is the author. As a consequence, the free coefficients A and B are automatically so chosen that the value $\hat{y}$

TABLE E4–1

RATES PER THOUSAND FOR THE 5 WORDS FOR EACH OF THE HAMILTON AND MADISON PAPERS USED (SUMS OF SQUARES AND THE CROSS-PRODUCTS FOR EACH AUTHOR ARE ALSO GIVEN)

Paper No.	Word i / Group j	*and* 1	*in* 2	*of* 3	*the* 4	*to* 5	Total
		Hamilton					
60	1	16.1	35.3	63.9	98.3	38.4	252.0
69	2	32.2	24.5	78.2	110.0	31.4	276.3
36	3	24.3	23.5	64.7	90.8	42.3	245.6
73	4	18.0	27.2	59.6	86.8	35.9	227.5
26	5	20.6	26.9	61.4	83.6	39.5	232.0
7	6	21.8	17.4	73.1	90.4	35.6	238.3
112	7	27.9	23.1	61.9	85.4	41.3	239.6
11	8	28.5	26.1	71.3	74.5	33.3	233.7
35	9	28.9	20.9	56.9	82.7	44.9	234.3
34	10	21.3	25.0	60.4	82.2	47.7	236.6
66	11	18.5	30.7	72.7	109.3	36.6	267.8
	Sum	258.1	280.6	724.1	994.0	426.9	
		Madison					
40	1	31.6	19.9	54.8	93.8	38.6	238.7
37	2	37.3	23.3	56.8	84.2	31.0	232.6
133	3	21.2	17.5	58.2	97.6	39.9	234.4
14	4	27.9	19.1	55.8	93.1	33.5	229.4
122	5	40.7	9.3	59.0	71.5	33.6	214.1
39	6	24.4	27.9	60.0	115.3	34.8	262.4
46	7	27.7	17.7	61.1	115.3	32.7	254.5
44	8	28.1	22.3	57.0	110.9	29.7	248.0
47	9	30.6	23.6	68.3	118.6	23.2	264.3
42	10	33.9	21.8	64.9	93.7	33.6	247.9
132	11	23.3	31.4	34.8	94.3	49.6	233.4
	Sum	326.7	233.8	630.7	1088.3	380.2	

(Continued)

TABLE E4–1 (Continued)

Hamilton: Sums of squares and of cross-products of deviations

	1	2	3	4	5
1	275.985				
2	−139.756	226.069			
3	95.181	−12.473	471.102		
4	−67.655	181.644	455.111	1267.465	
5	−31.396	−34.801	−260.843	−227.696	244.069

Madison: Sums of squares and of cross-products of deviations

1	351.920				
2	−173.050	334.287			
3	169.590	−212.312	719.265		
4	−514.910	381.708	364.715	2146.385	
5	−173.710	109.502	−479.175	−315.635	442.865

Pooled sums of squares and of cross-products of deviations

	1	2	3	4	5
1	627.905				
2	−312.806	560.356			
3	264.771	−224.785	1190.367		
4	−582.565	563.352	819.826	3413.850	
5	−205.106	74.701	−740.018	−543.331	686.934

Hamilton sum minus Madison sum

−68.6	46.8	93.4	−94.3	46.7

forecast by the discriminant function averages 1 for those Hamilton papers in the subset for which a particular discriminant function is constructed, while the average of $\hat{y}$ for the corresponding Madison papers is 0. We shall—arbitrarily, but naturally—decide that a discriminant score of over 0.5 is a Hamilton indicator, one of less than 0.5 a Madison indicator. This decision simplifies our work by making it unnecessary for us to estimate the optimum point of division for the scores.

Table E4–1 shows the rates per thousand words for the five high-frequency words *and* (x_1), *in* (x_2), *of* (x_3), *the* (x_4), and *to* (x_5) in each of the 22 papers. The numbers assigned to the papers are those assigned in Mosteller and Wallace (1964, pp. 269–270). Table E4–1 also shows the sums of squares and cross-products of deviations of these quantities for Hamilton and Madison. Let us first study the variability of the discriminant function in terms of the variability of its individual coefficients. Table E4–2 shows, in its top portion, the coefficients for the five variables and the constant term—first when all 22 papers are used for the fitting

TABLE E4–2

ORIGINAL DISCRIMINANT FUNCTION D_{all}, AND THE 11 DISCRIMINANTS, $D_{(j)}$, CONSTRUCTED BY OMITTING EACH PAIR OF HAMILTON AND MADISON PAPERS IN TURN: FROM THESE ARE CONSTRUCTED THE 11 PSEUDO-DISCRIMINANTS D_{*j} AND THEIR AVERAGE D_*, WHICH ARE ALSO GIVEN

| | Coefficient of: | | | | | Constant |
	x_1	x_2	x_3	x_4	x_5	term
D_{all}	−0.01902	0.02851	0.05264	−0.01642	0.04056	−2.83668
$D_{(1)}$	−0.01904	0.03032	0.05295	−0.01660	0.04120	−2.89257
$D_{(2)}$	−0.02747	0.02559	0.04532	−0.01964	0.03163	−1.47660
$D_{(3)}$	−0.02884	0.01467	0.04928	−0.01479	0.03962	−2.14043
$D_{(4)}$	−0.00716	0.02874	0.05631	−0.01248	0.05243	−4.21632
$D_{(5)}$	−0.01790	0.02789	0.05348	−0.01642	0.04172	−2.94733
$D_{(6)}$	−0.01695	0.03151	0.05182	−0.01455	0.04145	−3.10996
$D_{(7)}$	−0.02053	0.03063	0.05166	−0.01757	0.03681	−2.55988
$D_{(8)}$	−0.01648	0.03338	0.05660	−0.01979	0.04184	−2.99265
$D_{(9)}$	−0.02350	0.02910	0.05002	−0.01670	0.03074	−2.20700
$D_{(10)}$	−0.01093	0.03047	0.05406	−0.01559	0.04523	−3.40123
$D_{(11)}$	−0.01983	0.02953	0.05521	−0.01616	0.04188	−3.06431

| | Coefficient of: | | | | | Constant |
	x_1	x_2	x_3	x_4	x_5	term
D_{*1}	−0.01886	0.01041	0.04956	−0.01463	0.03422	−2.27783
D_{*2}	0.06548	0.05770	0.12584	0.01582	0.12988	−16.43747
D_{*3}	0.07914	0.16695	0.08621	−0.03268	0.04996	−9.79921
D_{*4}	−0.13765	0.02623	0.01591	−0.05584	−0.07806	10.95966
D_{*5}	−0.03020	0.03477	0.04425	−0.01639	0.02902	−1.73025
D_{*6}	−0.03967	−0.00149	0.06081	−0.03513	0.03166	−0.10390
D_{*7}	−0.00389	0.00736	0.06242	−0.00490	0.07810	−5.60468
D_{*8}	−0.04443	−0.02015	0.01308	0.01731	0.02776	−1.27696
D_{*9}	0.02582	0.02262	0.07885	−0.01364	0.13878	−9.13354
D_{*10}	−0.09988	0.00897	0.03843	−0.02470	−0.00606	2.80880
D_{*11}	−0.01090	0.01831	0.02697	−0.01905	0.02736	−0.56044
D_*	−0.01955	0.03015	0.05476	−0.01671	0.04205	−3.01416

and then when each group, here each matched pair, of Hamilton and Madison papers is omitted, one at a time, and the fitting executed for the other 20. Here the whole discriminant function is jackknifed column by column—that is, coefficient by coefficient—computing

11(coefficient for all) − 10(coefficient with jth pair omitted).

For example, the pseudo-coefficient for x_3 when we omit the fourth pair is given as (more decimals retained, both here and in the actual computation, than in Table E4–2):

$$11(0.0526442) - 10(0.0563169) = 0.015917.$$

This result appears in the second portion of Table E4–2 as the fourth value in the third column. Entries have been truncated to 5 decimals. These 11 new discriminant functions, together with the 12th formed by averaging them, are the pseudo-discriminants and the jackknifed discriminant, respectively. Note that whole functions are being jackknifed, not just values of functions, not just coefficients in functions, something we can do because the coefficients appear linearly in the values.

Let us look at D_*, the jackknifed discriminant function, and the standard errors of its coefficients.

$$D_* = -3.0141 - 0.0195x_1 + 0.0301x_2 + 0.0547x_3 - 0.0167x_4 + 0.0420x_5$$

Standard errors (jackknifed s_{b_i})	0.0193	0.0149	0.0105	0.00645	0.0181
Critical ratio $\lvert b_i \rvert / s_{b_i}$	1.0	2.0	5.2	2.6	2.3

These results suggest that the only coefficient seriously different from zero might be the third, which multiplies the frequency for *of*, a suggestion we shall not follow up here.

TABLE E4–3

VALUE OF DISCRIMINANTS D_{all} AND D_*
WHEN APPLIED TO EACH OF THE 22 PAPERS

Group of papers	D_{all}		D_*	
	H	M	H	M
1	1.170	0.039	1.206	0.024
2	0.833	−0.017	0.859	−0.033
3	1.001	0.338	1.023	0.333
4	0.764	−0.055	0.777	−0.075
5	1.000	−0.051	1.020	−0.080
6	1.052	0.171	1.073	0.172
7	0.822	−0.209	0.836	−0.227
8	1.246	−0.351	1.275	−0.374
9	0.668	−0.157	0.673	−0.167
10	1.235	0.380	1.263	0.381
11	1.203	−0.089	1.243	−0.107
Average	0.999	0.000	1.023	−0.014

When we apply the discriminants D_{all} and D_* to the 22 Hamilton and Madison papers used to construct these functions, we get the results shown in Table E4–3, which have been, arbitrarily, truncated to three decimals. First we note that the results for D_{all} and D_* are very similar. Second, when we use the value 0.5 as a cutoff, so that higher discriminant function scores are regarded as Hamilton forecasts and lower ones as Madison forecasts, we note that all 22 papers are correctly classified by both D_{all} and D_*.

Surprisingly good? Hard to be sure, since we used these same papers to select this discriminant. Cross-validation is needed.

E5. CROSS-VALIDATION IN THE EXAMPLE

So far the jackknife has provided us with an honest estimate of the variability of the coefficients. Let us try next to get an honest estimate of the ability of the final discriminant to sort out Hamilton and Madison writings. This is a new and major task.

To do just this, without any assessment of stability, we would have to cross-validate. With 11 pairs and 5 variables, we clearly dare not divide the data in halves. But, as suggested in Section B6, we could set aside each pair in turn and apply the discriminant based on the remaining 10 pairs to the set-aside pair. To do this, we need exactly the discriminants we have just calculated for a different purpose. When we apply each $D_{(i)}$ to the rates for the corresponding papers by Hamilton and by Madison, H_i and M_i, we find the values set out in Table E5–1. There is now one misclassification, paper M_3, whose value of 0.510 just barely assigns it to Hamilton.

Actually, the behavior of these discriminants, involving 5 coefficients fitted to 10 pairs of observations, is surprisingly good. The indicated separation of Hamilton and Madison subgroup means amounts to $.975 - .015 = .960$. This is a surprisingly large value, but one whose stability we have, as yet, no way to estimate. (If 22 papers have been divided into 11 and 11 *at random*, the average indicated separation of such means would be zero because the signs of the differences would tend to be $+$ and $-$ at random.)

The spread of each group around its observed mean is not small; the sample standard deviation falls between 0.28 and 0.31 for both Hamilton and Madison. This time, not only do we fail to have an indication of the stability of the result, but we are not at all sure that it is not misleading. For instance, all the data enter both into the value of $D_{(3)}$ at H_3 and the value of $D_{(7)}$ at H_7. Accordingly we have no assurance that these values are not correlated in some way that makes the average square of their difference substantially different from the sum of the corresponding variances.

By taking the mean squared deviations of the Hamilton papers about 1, and those of Madison about 0 (instead of about the observed means), we may obtain indications that, at the price of combining assessment of spread and shrinkage, are not exposed to this difficulty, since they are *sums* of terms each of which

TABLE E5–1

RESULTS OF APPLYING DISCRIMINANT FUNCTIONS $D_{(i)}$ OF TABLE E4-3 TO THE OMITTED PAPERS, THUS CROSS-VALIDATING THE DISCRIMINANTS

	$D_{(i)}$ applied to		Shift* from D_{all}	
i	H_i	M_i	H_i	M_i
1	1.205	−.044	+.035	−.005
2	.642	−.004	−.191	−.013
3	1.025	.510†	+.024	−.172
4	.592	−.130	−.172	+.075
5	.993	−.034	−.007	−.017
6	1.018	.230	−.034	−.059
7	.792	−.253	−.030	+.044
8	1.363	−.438	+.117	+.087
9	.567	−.091	−.101	−.066
10	1.269	.459	+.034	−.079
11	1.256	−.124	+.053	+.035
Average .975		+.015	−.024	−.015

* + means better discrimination; − means worse
† This paper misclassified

involves only a single value. (In this example, the numerical values are almost the same.) These measures are thus legitimate indications, but they still lack any measure of stability.

By omitting one pair at a time, then, we have had our choice:

a1) estimated stability for overall discriminant function (no estimate of quality of performance), as studied in Section E4.

a2) estimated performance by cross-validation (no estimate of stability for this estimate), as studied in the present section.

E6. TWO SIMULTANEOUS USES OF "LEAVE-OUT-ONE"

If both quality of performance and stability are to be estimated, we must combine cross-validation and jackknifing. This means dropping out one pair for each purpose. Accordingly we must find discriminant functions based upon sets of $9 = 11 - 2$ pairs of papers. We denote, indifferently, the discriminant obtained when both pair *i* and pair *j* are omitted by

$$D_{(i)}(j) = D_{(i)(j)} = D_{(j)}(i).$$

What we are going to do, from either point of view (that of the jackknifing or that of the cross-validation), is to set one pair aside and redo the whole analysis with the remaining 10 (instead of 11) pairs of papers.

With pair i set aside for cross-validation, the jackknife leads to pseudo-discriminants

$$D_{*j}(i) = 10D_{\text{all}}(i) - 9D_{(j)}(i) = 10D_{(i)} - 9D_{(i)(j)}.$$

For each i there are ten $D_{*j}(i)$, and one $D_{*}(i)$ which is the average of the $D_{*j}(i)$. No one of these discriminant functions used papers H_i and M_i in its formation. Therefore, when we apply the discriminants to H_i and M_i, we get $2 \times (10 + 1) = 22$ honest cross-validations.

Table E6–1 gives the results, cut to three decimals. (Two decimals would serve most purposes.) Look first at group 1 in Table E6–1. The first entry 1.250 is gotten from $D_{*2}(1)$ applied to H_1. Note that all Hamilton values exceed 0.5, though the 10th, gotten from $D_{*11}(1)$, had a close call at 0.535. Note that one Madison value crosses 0.5—we label this a mistake by the pseudo-discriminants. For these two papers, then, the error rate by the pseudo-discriminants is 5%. For all papers the error rate by pseudo-discriminants is about 16%.

For each paper, we would like to know how firmly a decision in favor of Hamilton or Madison is made. Let us conceive of an infinite number of pairs of Hamilton and Madison papers, all different from pair i, on which a discriminant function $D_{*}(i)$ might be based, and regard the 10 pairs actually used as a sample from this infinite population. The results of applying the infinite-population $D_{*}(i)$ to H_i and M_i would be $\mu_{\text{H}i}$ and $\mu_{\text{M}i}$, the true values for these papers. These are the values toward which our jackknifed answers are aimed. The jackknifed values for these papers, say $\bar{y}_{\text{H}i}$ and $\bar{y}_{\text{M}i}$ for the ith pair, combined with the variability of these jackknifed values, assessed from the individual pseudo-values by way of s_{*}^2, can be used to set confidence limits on the $\mu_{\text{H}i}$ and $\mu_{\text{M}i}$ at any chosen level. Insofar as these limits do not include 0.5, we have clear evidence, at that level, for Hamilton or for Madison. Naturally, then, we want to know how many standard errors each $\bar{y}_{\text{H}i}$ or $\bar{y}_{\text{M}i}$ is from the cutoff 0.5.

In Table E6–2, which includes values of s_{*}^2 we summarize the results for the 22 papers.

Note that 8 of Hamilton's papers and 8 of Madison's are beyond two standard errors from the cutoff, 1 Madison is at 1.7, while the other 5 have only relatively narrow margins.

We now have cross-validated estimates, combined with an assessment of their stability. Our results, though much more useful, are still far from perfect. We have assessed stability, climbing to the second step of the staircase, but, since we have not assessed the stability of this stability, we have not reached the third step. It it not surprising, in view of the small number of papers considered, that we have also failed to gain any appreciable information about the shape of the distribution of the $\mu_{\text{H}i}$ (or of the $\mu_{\text{M}i}$).

TABLE E6–1

RESULTS OF THE APPLICATIONS OF PSEUDO-DISCRIMINANT FUNCTIONS $D_{*j}(i)$ TO THE TWO PAPERS OF GROUP i, AND THE AVERAGE VALUE OF THE RESULT FOR EACH PAPER, WHICH ARE THE VALUES OF THE JACKKNIFED DISCRIMINANT FUNCTION $D_{*(i)}$, FOR THE PAPERS H_i AND M_i NOT ENTERING INTO THEIR CONSTRUCTION

j	Group 1		Group 2		Group 3		Group 4		Group 5		Group 6	
	H	M	H	M	H	M	H	M	H	M	H	M
1	—	—	0.492	−0.124	1.705	−0.388	−0.439	−0.716	0.582	−0.558	1.263	−0.701
2	1.250	0.167	—	—	0.855	0.409	−0.309	−1.170	0.811	−0.852	−0.703	0.062
3	1.723	−0.431	2.062	1.234	—	—	0.788	−0.127	2.329	−0.003	2.026	0.138
4	2.598	−0.354	−0.535	0.180	0.976	0.882	—	—	0.823	−0.019	1.127	0.206
5	1.446	−0.008	0.577	−0.213	0.958	0.429	1.283	0.133	—	—	1.021	−0.004
6	0.785	−0.126	0.146	−0.234	0.773	−0.036	0.925	−0.007	1.107	0.778	—	—
7	1.058	0.428	1.463	−0.044	1.358	0.635	0.435	−0.030	1.018	0.498	1.329	0.418
8	0.738	0.395	0.213	−0.465	0.852	1.077	0.937	0.500	0.544	−0.479	0.761	0.904
9	1.014	0.588	1.612	0.253	1.794	0.936	0.156	−0.301	1.197	0.938	1.314	0.039
10	1.383	−0.657	−0.957	−1.049	0.486	0.499	1.143	−0.211	1.036	−1.343	1.119	−0.084
11	0.535	0.102	0.976	−0.174	0.789	0.447	0.559	0.076	0.841	0.493	1.394	−0.348
Average	1.253	0.010	0.605	−0.063	1.055	0.494	0.548	−0.185	1.029	−0.054	1.065	0.203
$s^2 = 10s_*^2$	0.353	0.164	0.903	0.338	0.180	0.188	0.347	0.218	0.253	0.558	0.492	0.141

TABLE E6–1 (Continued)

j	Group 7 H	Group 7 M	Group 8 H	Group 8 M	Group 9 H	Group 9 M	Group 10 H	Group 10 M	Group 11 H	Group 11 M
1	1.301	0.222	1.402	−0.656	0.828	0.844	1.532	0.653	2.646	−2.106
2	0.886	−1.769	2.487	−1.165	0.402	−0.190	0.795	0.789	1.342	−0.467
3	0.681	−0.448	2.593	0.111	0.151	0.227	1.429	0.085	1.462	0.160
4	0.793	−0.215	1.167	−0.327	0.680	−0.086	1.261	0.222	1.206	0.091
5	0.810	−0.562	1.604	−0.742	0.711	−0.791	1.385	0.303	0.904	−2.121
6	0.661	−0.130	0.732	0.082	1.164	−0.157	1.548	0.671	1.464	0.372
7	—	—	0.969	−0.429	0.167	0.832	0.790	0.156	1.064	1.676
8	0.322	1.312	—	—	0.567	−0.151	2.284	0.785	1.270	1.836
9	1.634	−0.324	1.598	−0.636	—	—	1.020	0.318	1.117	−0.993
10	0.243	−0.519	0.798	−0.571	0.034	−0.468	—	—	0.862	−0.991
11	0.752	−0.225	0.696	−0.108	1.092	−0.651	0.943	0.401	—	—
Average	0.808	−0.265	1.405	−0.444	0.580	−0.059	1.299	0.438	1.334	−0.254
$s^2 = 10s_*^2$	0.170	0.578	0.469	0.158	0.152	0.309	0.203	0.070	0.255	1.870

TABLE E6–2

DEPARTURES OF OBSERVED MEANS FROM 0.5, USING s_*

	H			M		
Group	$\bar{y}_{Hi} - 0.5$	s_*	$(\bar{y}_{Hi} - 0.5)/s_*$	$0.5 - \bar{y}_{Mi}$	s_*	$(0.5 - \bar{y}_{Mi})/s_*$
1	.753	.188	4.0	.490	.128	3.8
2	.105	.300	0.3	.563	.184	3.0
3	.555	.134	4.1	.006	.137	0.0
4	.048	.186	0.3	.685	.148	4.6
5	.529	.159	3.3	.554	.236	2.3
6	.565	.222	2.5	.297	.119	2.5
7	.308	.130	2.4	.765	.240	3.2
8	.905	.217	4.2	.944	.126	7.5
9	.080	.123	0.6	.559	.176	3.2
10	.799	.142	5.6	.062	.084	0.7
11	.834	.160	5.2	.754	.432	1.7

E7. DISPERSION OF THE μ's

But we can learn a little more. If we had an infinite supply of papers to fix the discriminants, dropping one pair would not change the discriminants, or their coefficients. Accordingly, the μ_{Hi} must average 1, and the μ_{Mi} must average 0, since these constraints apply to the discriminant values before one pair is dropped. Thus, on the basis of quantities like

$$\Sigma(\bar{y}_{Hi} - 1)^2 = 1.011,$$

we could construct rough variance-component estimates of the standard deviation of the distribution (over i) of μ_{Hi}, the value that would be associated with Hamilton paper i if we had infinite material for constructing the discriminant function.

On the average, over papers and discriminants, $(\bar{y}_{Hi} - 1)^2$ will equal $\sigma_\mu^2 + \sigma^2$, where σ_μ^2 is the variance of the μ_{Hi}, and σ^2 the variability of assessing any single paper with a discriminant function based on only a finite number of pairs of other papers. We estimate σ^2 by s_*^2. We estimate the population average value of $(\bar{y}_{Hi} - 1)^2$ directly, pooling the results for the two authors, and then estimate σ_μ^2 by subtraction.

We find the average sum of squares of deviations (from 1 or 0, respectively, for Madison and Hamilton) to be $\frac{1}{2}(1.011 + 0.865) = 0.938$. To estimate the population average value of $(\bar{y}_{Hi} - 1)^2$ we divide by 11 (instead of the 10 that would have been appropriate if we had fitted a mean) finding 0.0853, thus confirming the possibly biased prediction (in Section E5) of about 0.30 for the standard deviations.

For the 22 values of s_*^2 we get a total of 0.8364 and an average of 0.0380 which estimates σ^2. Subtracting gives $0.0853 - 0.0380 = 0.0473$ as the estimate of σ_μ^2. Consequently we estimate σ_μ to be about 0.22. For both Madison and

Hamilton, the mean μ appears to be a shade more than two standard deviations from the cutoff of 0.5. Thus on Gaussian theory and for many other distributions, roughly 2.5% of each author's papers would be incorrectly assigned if we had only these 5 words on which to base the discrimination but infinite material to determine the discriminant function used. (Our estimate of σ_μ is far from precise, being worth perhaps a dozen degrees of freedom.)

There is now some interest in comparing the mean differences and standard deviations associated with different sorts of discriminants and the Hamilton and Madison subgroups. We have found these estimates:

	Separation of group means	Standard deviation of distribution	Ratio
Discriminant based on 10 other pairs:	.96	.29	3.3
Discriminant based on ∞ other pairs:	1.00	.22	4.5

where again we are dealing with indications of unknown stability. The improvement from basing the discriminant on many more pairs of papers appears to be rather less than one might have supposed, although the indicated gain is substantial.

Taken separately and as a whole, these results give us a picture of the strength and weakness of the proposed discriminant function when it is put into practice.

A few years ago the whole idea of an analysis this elaborate would have been regarded as wild—now it seems almost tame. At last we have some chance for honest estimates of variation bred entirely by the data. Being able to carry it out required a high-speed computer and double use of "leave-one-out" procedures, one a jackknife, one a cross-validation.

Again let us emphasize that the whole effort here is designed to illustrate the jackknife in a complicated problem with modest amounts of data, rather than to illustrate the full nature of the *Federalist* problem with its crucial problems of word selection.

E8. FURTHER DISCUSSION OF THE EXAMPLE

The question of the stability of the estimate of σ_μ might be worth investigating. We have here a number calculated by a definite procedure; we seek to assess its stability. We could jackknife again. We could drop out one more pair, calculate $11 \times 10 \times 9/6 = 165$ discriminant functions, one for each set of 8 pairs of papers, and work back to 11 more jackknifed estimates of σ_μ. Combining these in another grand jackknife, with the one we already have, gives us what we sought: an estimate of σ_μ, *and* an estimate of the stability of this estimate. What other technique offers even a crude approximation to an assessment of the stability of an estimate of σ_μ?

As still a further step, consider the man who has read the sentence (toward the end of Section E4) suggesting that one rate, that for *of,* is doing all the work, and who asks: what evidence do these data give about the superiority or inferiority of the 5-variable discriminant function to the use of *of* alone?

To answer such a question thoroughly requires double cross-validation (see Section B6), rather than single. We ought to study the question's answer on other data than those which suggested it.

But if this cannot be done, and we must peer into the same 22 papers again, there is no difficulty in attaining a single cross-validation with assessed stability. We have only to turn to each set of 9 pairs and determine two discriminant functions, one based upon all 5 words (already done), one based upon *of* alone (very easy). Turning to each omitted pair in turn we can calculate, for each paper,

a1) the behavior of the first discriminant,

a2) the behavior of the second discriminant,

a3) the difference in behavior, an indicator of which is better.

The jackknifing can then proceed on quantities of type (a3), producing, for each paper, both an estimate of improvement, and an assessment of the stability of this estimate. If our original question is really about how the two discriminants would compare if each could be based on a very large population of papers, this would give a relevant and useful answer.

Further references on the jackknife are Quenouille (1956), Tukey (1958), Durbin (1959), Mickey (1959), Kendall and Stuart (1961), Brillinger (1964), Miller (1964), Robson and Whitlock (1964), and Jones (1965).

F. BAYESIAN IDEAS

Introduction
F1. *Empirical priors*
F2. *Evidence as odds-changing*
★F3. *Bayes's theorem*
F4. *Gentle priors, an illustration*
F5. *Prior information for normal distributions*
F6. *Binomial data distributions and beta prior distributions*
F7. *Poisson data distributions and gamma prior distributions*
F8. *There could be much more*
F9. *A careful look at confidence statements*
F10. *Bayesian statements compared with confidence statements*

The battle of Bayes has raged for more than two centuries, sometimes violently, sometimes almost placidly. The Reverend Thomas Bayes did not publish his theorem during his lifetime; his friends published it after his death (see Bayes, 1763). Some attribute Bayes's failure to publish to his uneasiness about the truth of the result; others do not. Such a combination of doubt and vigor has been a notable characteristic of Bayesian ideas from that day to this.

We cannot here do justice to the literature on Bayesian ideas. As for other types of inference, there are several brands and schools. We have not tried to represent any particular one. The main thrust of our entire article is in the direction of data analysis in a modified classical tradition. In 1967, experience with published Bayesian analyses of data is still extremely limited, and the research literature about Bayesian methods mushrooms daily. Definitive views must wait.

A thoughtful, profusely illustrated, and sometimes mathematical discussion of Bayesian inference for psychological research by Edwards, Lindman, and Savage (1963) considers many of the standard difficulties and puzzles in the classical approach to inference and provides a fine set of references. Similarly, Savage *et al.* (1962) (with prepared contributions by M. S. Bartlett, G. A. Barnard, D. R. Cox, E. S. Pearson, and C. A. B. Smith together with discussion) offers a more verbal, but less psychologist-oriented, exposition of the Bayesian approach. For a large-scale application of the Bayesian approach to a problem of disputed authorship, including comparisons with classical methods, see Mosteller and Wallace (1963, 1964). The theoretical, as opposed to the applied, literature of data analysis already abounds with new research on Bayesian ideas. Books have appeared on both applied (Schlaifer, 1959) and theoretical (Raiffa and Schlaifer, 1961) decision making. Lindley (1965) offers an *Introduction to Probability and Statistics from a Bayesian Viewpoint*. From these varied sources and from their references, one can see how matters stood in 1965.

Without intending to push Bayesian ideas either very hard or very far, we do wish to discuss Bayesian approaches to data analysis in enough detail to make clear their purpose and relation to classical ideas. Even, perhaps especially, those who do not accept them need to understand what Bayesian ideas are about.

Bayesian inference built on a frequency-based prior distribution, correctly related to the real world, is an ideal most of us would like to find and use. Correctness might be available to a satisfactory approximation if a well-understood physical theory, supported by practical experience, provided the prior. Failing such a theory, extensive empirical data might provide a frequency-based prior. In either of these circumstances, the posterior probabilities obtained from Bayesian inference would, to a satisfactory approximation, have an objectively demonstrable relative-frequency interpretation.

Such relative-frequency interpretations are often not available, so that the meaning of a prior has often to be restricted to its other interpretation, that of expressing initial degree of belief. In such a situation, priors express in a suitable quantitative form, such as a cumulative distribution or a probability density function, what the thoughtful investigator believes about the state of the world; for example, what he believes about the atomic weight of gold, or about something for which a frequency interpretation is available. To be quite correct, we must say that his prior cannot be about some "true" atomic weight of gold, but rather that it must be about possible alternative distributions for gold's measured atomic weight. Though this refinement is repeatedly important, the greater stimulation of the looser language makes us often write as though the prior referred to ideal parameter values, rather than to parameter values defined by specific method of measurement.

In Bayesian data analysis, this prior information, whether objective or subjective, is then combined with the information provided by the data to produce a posterior distribution, that is, a distribution of beliefs posterior to the data. Thus the posterior distribution combines prior beliefs with data information.

The problem of reaching some consensus on the appropriate prior for such a situation has exercised many people. When it is agreed that very little information is available about a question relative to the amount to be available after a set of measurements is taken, then, while different individuals may use different priors, all these priors will have to be "gentle" in order to reflect this agreed-upon weakness. As a consequence, the various posteriors will be nearly identical, one with another. The notion of a "gentle" prior thus often keeps arguments about the distinctively Bayesian details of a Bayesian treatment of a specific problem from affecting the conclusions reached. Details in the choice of data distributions, on the other hand, may have substantial effects, just as in any system of inference. (There may remain arguments about philosophy and propriety in the choice of priors, but, since the conclusion is not appreciably affected, the practical importance of these arguments seems limited.) Finally, since every prior refers to alternative data distributions, rather than to bare parameters, the notion of "gentleness" must reside, not in the prior alone, but in that prior in combination with the alternative data distributions it governs.

Before either man or his instruments went to the moon, concern was expressed about the depth of a possible layer of dust on it. Whatever one's beliefs about the depth, they would count little compared to a few results obtained on the moon by machines designed to measure the depth of the dust. This example generally illustrates the notion of a gentle prior.

While in many situations one could readily agree that he knows little compared to the information that is about to be acquired, there are others where much is known in advance.

When considerable advance information is available, classical methods of inference have not ordinarily incorporated such information into the analysis except perhaps qualitatively or verbally, though it is usually incorporated into the design of the investigation. Bayesian methods by necessity handle such prior information smoothly, at least in principle—"by necessity" because Bayesian inference seems not to exist without some prior.

We cannot say that advance information *always* needs to be included in the analysis—or that it *never* needs to be included. We can say that the Bayesian approach makes it possible to do this.

In the next version of this *Handbook*, someone should be much better able to appraise the use of Bayesian inference in data analysis. In the present version, we must develop elementary ideas and discuss idealized or imaginary applications, remembering that today the issues about Bayes's theorem concern the extent of its useful applicability, not its mathematical truth or whether a particular problem can be given a Bayesian form.

F1. EMPIRICAL PRIORS

The simplest and least controversial examples of Bayesian inference arise when the prior distribution is solidly founded upon past observations or other data. Since the basic formulas and arithmetic are the same as for any other Bayesian treatment, such examples make a happy and helpful introduction to Bayesian analysis.

The general idea behind Bayes's theorem is that it provides a routine way of adjusting one's uncertainty when new information is received. Let θ be a parameter whose value concerns us. Suppose that, prior to the acquisition of data, we find it appropriate to treat θ as if it were a random variable with a prior distribution whose probability element is $f(\theta)\,d\theta$. We suppose also that, whenever the actual value of θ is θ_0, the distribution of the random variable X has the density $g(x \mid \theta_0)$—the distribution of the data. Once the data actually appear, we adjust the distribution of θ to a new distribution, called the posterior distribution, in which the probability element for θ is proportional to $g(x \mid \theta)f(\theta)\,d\theta$, where x is the observed value of X.

The easiest examples arise when both θ and X are discrete, because then the idea of a posterior probability and the closely related idea of conditional probability are both elementary and familiar. Suppose that we have extensive data indicating how, in 1964 in 3 Kansas counties, boys with both parents living preferred to talk with one or the other of their parents about school matters and about girls, namely, according to Table F1–1. Consider a random boy drawn from the population producing this table. The unconditional or prior probability that he prefers to discuss "girls" with his father is 0.5. If you have the extra datum that he prefers to discuss "school matters" with his mother, then you can quote the conditional or posterior probability that he prefers to discuss girls with father as $.2/.6 \approx 0.33$. The new datum narrows the relevant population and thus may appropriately change a probability.

Notice that, in this example, θ is the sex of the parent with which a particular boy prefers to discuss "girls", so that there is a whole population of θ's, one for the name of each boy. This frequently occurs when well-based empirical priors are at issue.

TABLE F1–1

TRUE PREFERENCES OF BOYS FOR DISCUSSION OF SUBJECT WITH PARENT

Girl questions		*School matters* Prefer to discuss with:		
		Father	Mother	
Prefer to discuss with:	Father	0.3	0.2	0.5
	Mother	0.1	0.4	0.5
		0.4	0.6	1.0

TABLE F1–2

APPARENT PREFERENCES WHEN REPORTING ERROR
FOR PREFERENCES "SCHOOL MATTERS" IS ADDED TO THE DATA OF TABLE F1–1

		School matters		
		Says prefers to discuss with:		
Girl questions		Father	Mother	
Does prefer to discuss with:	Father	0.31	0.19	0.50
	Mother	0.17	0.33	0.50
		0.48	0.52	1.00

So far x has been supposed to be "measured without error" in the sense that any one boy "does" or "does not" prefer to talk about "school matters" with his mother. Accordingly the result of our observation is to replace the original population of boys by a subpopulation. This is not usual: in many instances, the effect of knowing the observation is far less drastic.

Let us now make the example more complicated by supposing that, if a boy who really prefers to talk about "school matters" with his mother is asked about his preference, he will say "mother" 80% of the time and "father" 20%, without regard to his true preference for talking about "girls", and that if he really prefers to talk about school matters with his father, he will say "father" 90% of the time and "mother" 10% of the time. Pretend that Table F1–1 gives the true preferences. Then reports on talking about school matters conditional on reported preference for talking about girls will be distributed somewhat differently than they were unconditionally.

The table that tells us about $g(x \mid \theta)f(\theta)$ for a single asking now is Table F1–2. For example, the upper left-hand corner cell is found from two sources as follows. First, of the 0.3 who actually prefer to discuss both "girls" and "school matters" with father, 90% report they prefer father for "school matters", or a contribution of $0.3 \times 0.9 = 0.27$. Second, of the 0.2 who actually prefer mother for "school matters" and father for "girls", 20% report father for "school matters", or a contribution of $0.2 \times 0.2 = 0.04$. Finally $0.27 + 0.04 = 0.31$, as shown in the upper left-hand corner of Table F1–2. Similarly the 0.17 of the lower left-hand cell comes from $0.1 \times 0.9 + 0.4 \times 0.2 = 0.17$.

Now the observation: "When asked once he said he prefers to discuss 'school matters' with mother" alters the probability that he really prefers to discuss "girls" with father from 0.50 to $0.19/0.52 \approx 0.37$. This time the change is not a simple subdivision of a population. Each boy has a chance of giving the observed answer. Some are more likely to do this than others. Such incomplete differences are responsible for changing 0.5 to 0.37, their incompleteness being reflected by the failure of 0.37 to reach the 0.33 of the earlier version.

As a further example, consider a large state university which has extensive records on the joint distribution of combined entrance-examination scores x and Freshman-year standing y. Suppose that, when expressed on suitable scales, these are found to be rather closely bivariate normal with both average values close to 50 ($\mu_x = \mu_y = 50$), both variances close to 100 ($\sigma_x^2 = \sigma_y^2 = 100$), and covariance 85 ($\rho\sigma_x\sigma_y = 85$, where ρ is the correlation coefficient). Given a random Freshman, all we can predict about his Freshman-year grades is to wave our hands toward a normal distribution with average 50 and standard deviation 10. If we know one item more, that his combined entrance-examination score fell at $x = 70$, we would wave our hands toward a different normal distribution, one with an average of

$$\mu_{\text{forecast}} = \mu_y + \frac{\rho\sigma_x\sigma_y}{\sigma_x^2}(x - \mu_x) = 50 + \frac{85}{100}(70 - 50) = 67$$

$$= \mu_y + \rho(x - \mu_x)\sigma_y/\sigma_x,$$

and a variance of

$$\sigma^2_{\text{forecast}} = (1 - \rho^2)\sigma_y^2 = (1 - 0.85^2)100 = 27.75$$

(corresponding to a standard deviation of about 5.25). Our estimate of the chance that this Freshman would be eligible for a special curriculum requiring at least 60 in scaled Freshman-year standing would rise from about 16% to almost 91% (as this cutting point changes its interpretation from $\mu_y + \sigma_y$ to $\mu_{\text{forecast}} - 1.33\sigma_{\text{forecast}}$).

Here

> θ = Freshman-year standing (not yet determined) for one student,
> x = combined entrance-examination score for that student.

Except for the details of mathematical manipulation, the fact that we treat both x and θ as continuous variables has not made any essential changes in the problem. Again the population of θ's is large, one for each student.

F2. EVIDENCE AS ODDS-CHANGING

Sometimes, instead of presenting probabilities, it is convenient to present odds. If the probability of an event is $3/5$, the odds in its favor are 3 to 2 or 1.5 to 1, or more briefly 1.5 when we express odds as odds to 1. More generally, odds of m to n mean a probability of $m/(m + n)$. If the probability of an event is p, then the odds in its favor are p to $1 - p$ or $p/(1 - p)$ to 1.

Suppose, to begin an example, that we knew on the basis of extensive data that Alexander Hamilton used the word *upon* about 3 times per 1000 words, that James Madison used it about 0.2 times per 1000, and that for each author the distribution of counts is approximately Poisson. Then the two frequency distributions for the numbers of *upon*'s in 1000-word passages would be approximately as given in the table:

upon's/1000 words:	0	1	2	3	4	5	6	
Hamilton $f(x \mid 3)$:	.050	.149	.224	.224	.168	.101	.050	...
Madison $f(x \mid 0.2)$:	.819	.164	.016	.001	...			

If, when you are given 1000 words of connected text with assurance that it was written either by Hamilton or by Madison, you find it contains x *upon*'s, then you can compute approximate posterior odds for Hamilton's authorship of the piece as follows. Let $P(H)$ be your initial (prior) probability, in the sense of degree of belief, that Hamilton wrote the passage, $P(M)$ your initial probability for Madison, with, of course, $P(H) + P(M) = 1$. Further, let $f(x \mid 3)$ stand for the Poisson probability of x *upon*'s when Hamilton writes with his rate of 3 per thousand, and $f(x \mid 0.2)$ the corresponding probability for Madison as shown in the table above. Then the probability that Hamilton wrote a 1000-word passage *and* also used x *upon*'s is $P(H)f(x \mid 3)$; similarly the probability for Madison is $P(M)f(x \mid 0.2)$. The ratio of these probabilities can be written:

$$\text{Odds (H vs. M)} = \left[\frac{P(H)}{P(M)}\right]\left[\frac{f(x \mid 3)}{f(x \mid 0.2)}\right]$$

$$= \text{(initial odds) (likelihood ratio)}.$$

Note that $P(H)/P(M)$ is the initial odds given by the initial degrees of belief or prior probabilities for Hamilton's and Madison's authorship, and that the ratio $f(x \mid 3)/f(x \mid 0.2)$ is called the likelihood ratio. (The example as stated has been simplified in two important ways for presentation here: first, though nearly Poisson for most words, the actual distributions are even closer to a suitable negative binomial; and second, the average numbers of *upon*'s per 1000 words are not firmly known, contrary to our supposition. See Mosteller and Wallace, 1963, 1964.)

Suppose that you had read the new passage as a judge of these authors' writings without knowledge of the difference in *upon* frequencies between writers and had rated it as Hamilton 3 to 1 (initial odds, $P(H)/P(M)$). If, on later examination, you found 2 *upon*'s in the paper, then you would be entitled to multiply your initial odds of 3 by the likelihood ratio of about $14 = 0.224/0.016$ to get the posterior odds of about 42 to 1 in favor of Hamilton. Though individual investigators would differ in their initial odds, all who were willing to think of initial odds could reflect finding 2 *upon*'s by multiplying their initial odds by 14. An investigator with initial odds of only 1 to 14 for Hamilton would be brought up to 50–50 by this *upon* evidence, if he accepted it. For many of us, initial odds near 1 are quite satisfactory in such a problem. The 14 to 1 likelihood ratio is likely to be a useful summary of the evidence offered by the number of *upon*'s, especially in such a simple situation.

In this example, $\theta =$ Hamilton's or Madison's authorship of the 1000-word paper. The random variable X is the number of *upon*'s. $P(H)$ and $P(M)$ give the prior for θ. This example, by assuming rate parameters exactly known, avoids direct concern with the more complex prior that would otherwise have to be used for the rate parameters of the authors. Hence, it does not tangle directly with the issues arising from uncertainty in the choice of that prior, which might have to be a joint distribution of two variables (rate for Hamilton, rate for Madison). Accordingly, we are still in an area of relatively complete agreement.

Both Bayes's theorem and likelihood ratios are long-time tools of the classical approach to inference. Bayes's theorem is used in the inner workings of the mathematics of classical inference. Likelihood ratios appear quite openly there, especially in tests of significance. The Neyman-Pearson lemma tells us, for example, that in making tests between two Poisson rates μ_1 and μ_2 the likelihood ratio $f(x \mid \mu_1)/f(x \mid \mu_2)$ leads to the most powerful tests for a given significance level. (Interestingly enough, this important result only holds when the parameter value has exactly two alternatives, and no correspondingly strong result about likelihood ratios is available in the absence of such a restriction. The support for use of likelihood ratio tests with less restricted parameters then depends largely on analogy with this result and on special investigations. Both classical and Bayesian inference have more trouble when the parameters are not restricted to very few values.) In our present context, interest in the likelihood ratio is guided by our interest in exposing Bayesian ideas, but that does not confine its use to Bayesian territory. Indeed, we could have written a large part of this section without using ideas or words that are distinctly Bayesian.

★F3. BAYES'S THEOREM

In Section F2, we gave an illustration of an application of Bayes's theorem in the form of odds. The present section gives some of the standard forms of Bayes's theorem.

Let the events $A_1, A_2, \ldots, A_k$ be mutually exclusive and exhaustive, and let B be another event; then one form of Bayes's theorem is

$$P(A_i \mid B) = \frac{P(A_i)P(B \mid A_i)}{\sum_{i=1}^{k} P(A_i)P(B \mid A_i)}.$$

In our example of Hamilton and Madison's writing, A_1 could correspond to Hamilton's writing the passage, and A_2 to Madison's, $k = 2$. The event B could be the occurrence of the particular number of *upon*'s in the passage—for example, 2. This form arises naturally from a $2 \times k$ contingency table:

	A_1	A_2	$\cdots$	A_k	Total
B	$P(A_1 \text{ and } B)$	$P(A_2 \text{ and } B)$	$\cdots$	$P(A_k \text{ and } B)$	$\Sigma P(A_i \text{ and } B)$
not $B = \bar{B}$	$P(A_1 \text{ and } \bar{B})$	$P(A_2 \text{ and } \bar{B})$	$\cdots$	$P(A_k \text{ and } \bar{B})$	$\Sigma P(A_i \text{ and } \bar{B})$

The conditional probability of A_i given B is

$$P(A_i \mid B) = \frac{P(A_i \text{ and } B)}{\Sigma P(A_i \text{ and } B)} = \frac{P(A_i)P(B \mid A_i)}{\Sigma P(A_i)P(B \mid A_i)}.$$

Frequently, the parameter θ corresponding to the set of events A_i is continuous, rather than discrete. Then $P(A_i)$ is replaced by the probability element $f(\theta) \, d\theta$. And corresponding to $P(B \mid A_i)$, when X is discrete, we have the conditional probability $g(x \mid \theta)$ that the random variable X takes the value x, given that the parameter has taken the value θ. Then one form of Bayes's theorem gives the posterior probability element for θ

$$h(\theta \mid x) \, d\theta = k \, f(\theta)g(x \mid \theta) \, d\theta / \int f(\theta)g(x \mid \theta) \, d\theta,$$

where the integration is over the possible values of θ, and k is a constant, guaranteeing total probability one, that can be found from the integral or otherwise as may be convenient.

If X follows a continuous distribution, the formula just given still applies, with $g(x \mid \theta)$ interpreted as the conditional probability density function of X, given θ.

As a brief illustration for this second form, consider the uniform data distribution with density

$$g(x \mid \theta) = 1/\theta, \qquad 0 < x \le \theta.$$

Suppose that θ has a prior quadratic density

$$f(\theta) = 3\theta^2, \qquad 0 < \theta \le 1.$$

Then the posterior distribution, after observing that $X = x$, has the density

$$h(\theta \mid x) = k \, f(\theta)g(x \mid \theta) = 3k\theta, \qquad \theta \ge x, \ 0 < \theta \le 1,$$

where

$$1 = \int_x^1 3k\theta \, d\theta = 3k(1 - x^2)/2,$$

and so

$$k = 2/3(1 - x^2).$$

Thus

$$h(\theta \mid x) = 2\theta/(1 - x^2), \qquad 0 < x \le \theta \le 1.$$

Numerical example. Find the posterior mean of θ when $x = \frac{1}{2}$ in the example just discussed.

Solution.

$$\text{Posterior mean} = \mu = \int_x^1 \theta \cdot 2\theta \, d\theta / (1 - x^2) = \frac{2(1 - x^3)}{3(1 - x^2)},$$

and for $x = \frac{1}{2}$, we get

$$\mu = 7/9.$$

F4. GENTLE PRIORS, AN ILLUSTRATION

To set the stage for later work, we carry out an example where normal data distributions are naturally given a gentle prior distribution. Our main purpose is to use the technique of Bayesian inference in a familiar setting.

Example. A lantern slide projects a bar of light on the wall at the front of a 50-feet-long room familiar to you, the subject. From your seat in the middle of the room, you are asked to estimate the bar's length. Later you are going to measure the length, μ, of this bar of light as precisely as you can with a steel tape.

Sometimes people say that they know nothing about the length before they use the tape, but they are being too strict with themselves. They know, for example, that it isn't a mile long. You would know something about it because you could tell that it is more than an inch long and less than 10 feet long. Indeed, the more you think about it, the more you are pretty sure it is between 2 and 3 feet long. Suppose that the distribution in Fig. F4–1 represents, more or less, your beliefs about the length. We shall call this distribution your *prior distribution* on the length of the bar of light. This is a *belief prior*, not an *empirical prior*. It represents your belief before taking more exact measurements.

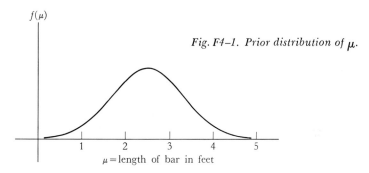

$f(\mu)$

Fig. F4–1. Prior distribution of μ.

μ = length of bar in feet

When we measure the length of the bar of light with a steel tape, the answer varies from one measurement to the next, partly because the light does not cut off sharply at each end of the bar and partly because of inaccurate reading of the tape. Inaccuracies in the tape itself are likely to be slight enough that we can neglect them. We can think of a distribution of repeated tape measurements of the length of the bar of light. Suppose that they are approximately normally distributed about an average value that we shall regard as the precise value for this method of measuring. (Different methods of measuring probably have different precise values—at least they seem to behave this way in most areas of science. Here, as often happens, we have fixed on one method and taken it to define our precise value. Though precise values are often called true values, the old term "precise" is less misleading.) Our prior distribution really applies to data distributions, but in situations like the present one, we can fib a little and say that they apply to our precise values. Suppose the standard deviation of our measurements is 0.25 inch.

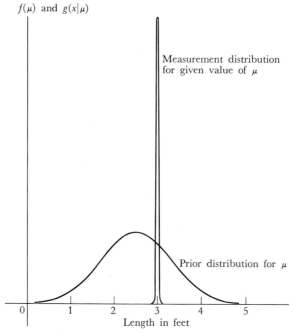

$f(\mu)$ and $g(x|\mu)$

Measurement distribution
for given value of μ

Prior distribution for μ

0   1   2   3   4   5

Length in feet

Fig. F4–2. Comparison of gentle prior and tight measurement distribution. If drawn to scale, the tall thin data distribution would be about 48 times as tall as the short fat normal prior, instead of about 4 times as tall, as schematically drawn here.

Such a small standard deviation (0.25 inch) means that a very large part of the distribution of the measurements for *this* bar of light is confined to a 1-inch long segment (within 2σ of μ, the mean and the precise value). These ideas are illustrated in Fig. F4–2, where the vertical scale is not stretched enough to picture properly the spiky quality of the distribution $g(x \mid \mu)$ of the measurement given the precise length μ.

Note that within the 1-inch range your prior distribution is quite flat, as it would be for other nearby 1-inch ranges. Just notice how flat the prior is for every 1-inch range near the center of the normal distribution. Remember that one unit on the horizontal axis of Fig. F4–2 corresponds to one foot, not one inch.

For a completely flat prior and a normal measurement specification with fixed σ, we are led by a limiting argument to a distribution of our beliefs concerning the precise value μ, after the measurement is taken, that is just the mirror image of the distribution of the measurement itself. In our example, since the normal distribution is symmetric, the posterior distribution of μ is normal with average x (the observed measurement) and standard deviation 0.25 inch. Had there been n independent measurements, the average would be $\bar{x}$ and σ_μ would be $0.25/\sqrt{n}$ inches.

One way to get a close approximation to a flat prior is to use a normal prior with a large variance. Later on, in Section F5, we shall see that, if the initial

TABLE F4–3

COMPARISON OF POSTERIOR MEAN AND STANDARD DEVIATION FOR PRIORS OF DIFFER-
ENT LOCATION AND GENTLENESS FOR EACH OF THREE DIFFERENT MEASUREMENTS x
FROM A DATA DISTRIBUTION WITH STANDARD DEVIATION $\sigma = 0.25$ INCH (′ AND ″
STAND FOR FOOT AND INCH, RESPECTIVELY)

μ_0	σ_0	x = 1′ μ_1	σ_1	2′ μ_1	σ_1	3′ μ_1	σ_1
1′0″	6″	1′0″	0.24978″	2′ −0.021″	0.24978″	3′ −0.042″	0.24978″
2′0″	6″	1′ +0.021″	0.24978″	2′0″	0.24978″	3′ −0.021″	0.24978″
3′0″	6″	1′ +0.042″	0.24978″	2′ +0.021″	0.24978″	3′0″	0.24978″
1′0″	12″	1′0″	0.24995″	2′ −0.005″	0.24995″	3′ −0.010″	0.24995″
2′0″	12″	1′ +0.005″	0.24995″	2′0″	0.24995″	3′ −0.005″	0.24995″
3′0″	12″	1′ +0.010″	0.24995″	2′ +0.005″	0.24995″	3′0″	0.24995″
1′0″	24″	1′0″	0.24999″	2′ −0.001″	0.24999″	3′ −0.003″	0.24999″
2′0″	24″	1′ +0.001″	0.24999″	2′0″	0.24999″	3′ −0.001″	0.24999″
3′0″	24″	1′ +0.003″	0.24999″	2′ +0.001″	0.24999″	3′0″	0.24999″
1′0″	∞	1′0″	0.25″	2′0″	0.25″	3′0″	0.25″
2′0″	∞	1′0″	0.25″	2′0″	0.25″	3′0″	0.25″
3′0″	∞	1′0″	0.25″	2′0″	0.25″	3′0″	0.25″

variance of a normal prior, σ_0^2 is large compared to the measurement variance, σ^2, then the posterior mean, μ_1, approximates x and the posterior variance,
σ_1^2, approximates σ^2. See formulas (d1) and (d2) of that section. To illustrate
what happens, we give the results for these formulas for a number of values of
σ_0, μ_0, and x in Table F4–3. Its main feature is that the gentler priors make a
smaller adjustment on x to get μ_1, the posterior mean. The table shows how slight
the adjustment can be for a really gentle prior.

F5. PRIOR INFORMATION FOR NORMAL DISTRIBUTIONS

The next three sections present a few specific examples of the formulas applied in
simple cases of Bayesian inference. Each starts by assuming a family of distributions for that data and a mathematically convenient prior distribution for the
parameter of the family. From these assumptions and the data, we produce a
posterior distribution for the parameter. We deal here with mathematical facts,
setting most issues of interpretation aside.

In each instance we have been motivated by a particular data specification
(family of distributions). Mathematical investigations have shown that, in the
examples that follow, particular combinations of data specification and prior
distribution for the parameter of the data specification itself are mathematically

convenient. Nothing says that these convenient combinations are appropriate to any particular real life problem.

Let us turn first to the normal distribution. Its many mathematical conveniences endear it to us all. No wonder we hate to leave it.

Let us consider the parameter μ whose value is to be determined (it corresponds to θ in our previous sections). Suppose that a prior distribution for μ is normal with mean μ_0 and standard deviation σ_0. The subscript 0 is intended to suggest that this is the initial condition. The probability element for the prior then has the form

$$p(\mu \mid \mu_0, \sigma_0) \, d\mu = \frac{1}{\sqrt{2\pi}\sigma_0} \, e^{-\frac{1}{2}(\mu-\mu_0)^2/\sigma_0^2} \, d\mu. \tag{a}$$

Furthermore, suppose for any precise value of μ, the distribution of the datum is normal with mean μ and standard deviation σ. Its probability element is thus

$$g(x \mid \mu, \sigma) \, dx = \frac{1}{\sqrt{2\pi}\sigma} \, e^{-\frac{1}{2}(x-\mu)^2/\sigma^2} \, dx. \tag{b}$$

Then Bayes's theorem says that if the observation x occurs, the posterior distribution of μ is normal with mean μ_1 and standard deviation σ_1 and has probability element:

$$f_1(\mu \mid x; \mu_0, \sigma_0, \sigma) \, d\mu = \frac{1}{\sqrt{2\pi}\sigma_1} \, e^{-\frac{1}{2}(\mu-\mu_1)^2/\sigma_1^2} \, d\mu, \tag{c}$$

where

$$\mu_1 = \frac{\dfrac{1}{\sigma_0^2}\mu_0 + \dfrac{1}{\sigma^2}x}{\dfrac{1}{\sigma_0^2} + \dfrac{1}{\sigma^2}} \tag{d1}$$

and

$$\frac{1}{\sigma_1^2} = \frac{1}{\sigma_0^2} + \frac{1}{\sigma^2}. \tag{d2}$$

Since reciprocals of variances play such a large role here, it is convenient to call them *precisions* and customary to use the letter h for them. With that notation we can rewrite:

$$\mu_1 = \frac{h_0\mu_0 + hx}{h_0 + h}, \tag{e1}$$

$$h_1 = h_0 + h. \tag{e2}$$

In this new notation it is especially easy to see that formulas (d1), (d2) and (e1), (e2) can be related to our usual way of putting together measurements from normal distributions. Think of μ_0 as a measurement from a normal with variance σ_0^2 that is, precision h_0, and think of x as a measurement from a normal with variance σ^2, that is, precision h. When we pool such measurements, we ordinarily weight them inversely as their variances as in (d1) or directly as their precisions as in (e1). Similarly, the variance of μ_1 is seen from (e1) to be

$$\sigma_1^2 = \frac{h_0^2 \sigma_0^2 + h^2 \sigma^2}{(h_0 + h)^2} = \frac{h_0 + h}{(h_0 + h)^2} = \frac{1}{h_0 + h},$$

which agrees with (d2) and (e2).

Thus for a normal prior with a normal data distribution, the posterior is normal with mean the weighted sum of the prior mean and the observed datum, weights being proportional to the precision expressed by the h's, *that is, inversely proportional to the variances. The precision of the posterior is the sum of the precisions for the prior and the observation.*

The posterior distribution of μ is equivalent to the distribution of a sample mean based on both the actual observations and enough advance observations with mean μ_0 for this advance mean to have variance σ_0^2. (Take fractional observations in your stride.) Thus the prior can be thought of as almost like bringing in a few extra measurements.

Example. Men in a club have long-run pistol shooting scores approximately normally distributed with mean and variance $\mu_0 = 50$, $\sigma_0^2 = 25$, and the variance of an individual's scores about his own mean μ is $\sigma^2 = 20$. An individual is known to have scored $x = 40$ on one target session. Estimate the posterior distribution for his long-run score μ.

Solution. Applying formulas (e1) and (e2) for $h_0 = 0.04$, $h = 0.05$, the posterior mean is

$$\mu_1 = \frac{0.04(50) + 0.05(40)}{0.04 + 0.05} \approx 44.4, \tag{f1}$$

and posterior precision is

$$h_1 = 0.04 + 0.05 = 0.09, \tag{f2}$$

so that

$$\sigma_1^2 = 1/0.09 \approx 11.11, \qquad \sigma_1 \approx 3.33. \tag{f3}$$

Now the posterior probability is 2/3 that the individual's long-run score is in the interval 44.4 ± 3.3, which runs from 41.1 to 47.7. Before getting the data, we were 2/3 sure μ was in the interval from 45 to 55. In the light of the assumed family of data distributions, the single measurement x, together with the prior information, has both shifted and shortened the interval considerably.

F6. BINOMIAL DATA DISTRIBUTIONS AND BETA PRIOR DISTRIBUTIONS

Consider n independent binomial trials, each with probability p of "success". Then the likelihood of the sample is the probability of getting the particular results in their particular order. For example, if x successes and $n - x$ failures occur, the likelihood is $p^x(1-p)^{n-x}$. If a further sample of m trials produces y successes, the likelihood of the whole sample in the order it occurred is

$$p^x(1-p)^{n-x} \times p^y(1-p)^{m-y} = p^{x+y}(1-p)^{n+m-(x+y)}. \tag{a}$$

The right-hand side shows the result as the likelihood of getting $x+y$ successes in one sample of $n+m$.

The neat way that further binomial data, with the same value of p, can be added to the likelihood shown in (a) is most attractive. It suggests further that a prior distribution of p would also fit smoothly into the likelihood if it too had such a form, the variable being p, rather than x. It is customary to write the probability element for this special convenient prior distribution of p as

$$f(p)\,dp = cp^{a-1}(1-p)^{b-1}\,dp, \qquad a>0, b>0, 0 \le p \le 1, \tag{b1}$$

where c is the constant that makes the total area under $f(p)$ equal to unity.

The expression (b1) is called a beta density function. When written in full it reads

$$f(p)\,dp = \frac{(a+b-1)!}{(a-1)!(b-1)!}\,p^{a-1}(1-p)^{b-1}\,dp \tag{b2}$$

$$= \frac{\Gamma(a+b)}{\Gamma(a)\,\Gamma(b)}\,p^{a-1}(1-p)^{b-1}\,dp, \tag{b3}$$

where the complete gamma function $\Gamma(t)$,

$$\Gamma(t) = \int_0^\infty x^{t-1}e^{-x}\,dx = (t-1)!,$$

offers a definition for the values of factorials of numbers that are not integers.

The forms of $f(p)$ given in (b2) and (b3) offer neat expressions for a family of probability distributions confined to $0 \le p \le 1$, and they could well have been selected for such a purpose without regard to a binomial distribution.

If we have a beta prior distribution for p, say (b1), and a binomial observation of x successes in n trials each with probability of success p, with likelihood $p^x(1-p)^{n-x}$, then the posterior density of p is proportional to the product

$$p^{a-1}(1-p)^{b-1} \times p^x(1-p)^{n-x} = p^{a+x-1}(1-p)^{b+n-x-1}. \tag{c}$$

As we have seen in (b2) this is a beta density, and the coefficient required to make the total probability unity is

$$\frac{(a+b+n-1)!}{(a+x-1)!(b+n-x-1)!}.$$

As suggested, these results are not confined to integer values of a and b, and the algebraic identities which underlie the results apply in general. As a result, for all a and b with $a>0$, $b>0$:

If p has a beta prior with parameters a and b, and x is binomial from n trials with probability p, then p has a beta posterior with parameters a + x and b + n − x.

If we are going to work with beta distributions, we need a reasonable insight into what shapes correspond to different combinations of parameters. Accordingly Fig. F6–1 shows 31 of the 36 beta densities which have their values of a and b selected from the special set 0.5, 1, 2, 4, 8, and 28. To avoid confusion from overlap of curves, we have not included $(2, 28)$, $(4, 28)$, $(8, 28)$, $(28, 2)$, or $(28, 8)$.

In Fig. F6–1 the horizontal axis in each small figure is p, running from 0 to 1, and the ordinate, which we have called β in the figure to refer to the beta density, is just $f(p)$ as computed from equation (b2) or (b3).

As we go on to discuss the various shapes, we shall write "(a, b)" to refer to the beta distribution with parameters a and b, just as has been done in the figure.

For a and b small, the beta distributions may be J-shaped $(0.5, 1)$, $(1, 0.5)$, U-shaped $(0.5, 0.5)$, flat $(1, 1)$, or triangular $(2, 1)$, $(1, 2)$.

If $a = 1$ but b is greater than 2, the curve is J-shaped; see $(1, 4)$, $(1, 8)$, $(1, 28)$.

When a and b are both greater than one, the curves are somewhat bell-shaped and have a mode at $\dfrac{a-1}{a+b-2}$. Note that this is just the exponent of p divided by the sum of the exponents of p and $1 - p$.

When $a = b$, the distributions are symmetric about $p = 1/2$ $(0.5, 0.5)$, . . . , $(28, 28)$, and tighten around $1/2$ as $a + b$ grows larger. For large $a = b$, the distribution is approximately normal with mean $1/2$ and variance $1/(8a + 4)$.

If $a \neq b$, interchanging the values of a and b "mirror images" the distribution; see, for example, $(8, 1)$ and $(1, 8)$.

If $a + b$ gets larger, but $\dfrac{a}{a+b}$ remains the same, the distribution tightens around the value $\dfrac{a}{a+b}$: compare $(1, 4)$ with $(2, 8)$, and also look down the diagonal from the upper left-hand corner. As $a + b$ increases, the distributions tend to the Gaussian but more slowly than when $\dfrac{a}{a+b} = \dfrac{1}{2}$.

If $a + b$ is the same, but $\dfrac{a}{a+b}$ moves close to zero or one, the distribution becomes "crowded" against one end or the other and hence has a higher peak than a distribution with $\dfrac{a}{a+b} = \dfrac{1}{2}$; compare $(8, 1)$ with $(4, 4)$ for an approximate idea.

($\star$When a is fixed and b is very large, the distribution is approximately a gamma distribution with parameters a and $1/b$, and hence its shape is approximately that of a chi-square distribution with $2a$ degrees of freedom.)

For any a and b, the mean of p is $\dfrac{a}{a+b}$ and its variance is

$$\frac{\dfrac{a}{a+b} \cdot \dfrac{b}{a+b}}{(a+b+1)}.$$

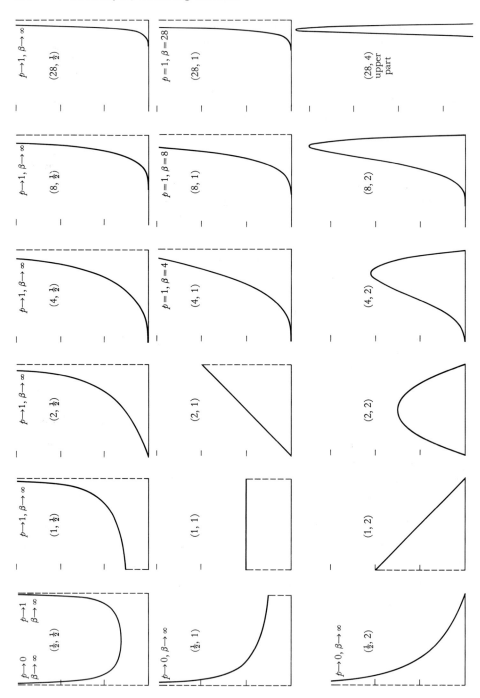

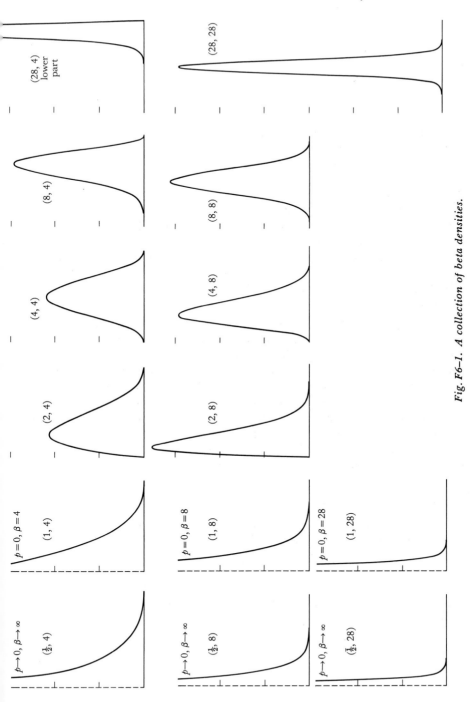

Fig. F6-1. A collection of beta densities.

Similarly the posterior mean and variance for p, after x successes in n binomial trials, are

$$\mu_{post} = \frac{a + x}{a + b + n}, \qquad \sigma^2_{post} = \frac{\mu_{post}(1 - \mu_{post})}{a + b + n + 1},$$

where, as must always be the case, we recover the prior distribution and its parameters when we set $n = 0$ (when x must also be 0).

The larger $a + b + n + 1$, the smaller the variance of the distribution of p and the more the distribution clusters near its mode. Thus $a + b + n + 1$ might be thought of as a kind of "information" which is represented as clustering measured in terms of number of measurements. This idea should not be pushed all the way, for the prior would have "no information" in the sense of "no clustering" when $a + b + 1 = 0$. Now $a + b + 1 > 1$ is a mathematical requirement on the system, which shows that all beta priors must be somewhat clustered, as we knew already since they are confined to the interval $[0, 1]$. When a and b are both near 0, the prior states that p is very likely near 0 or near 1 and unlikely to be in the middle range. In the limit, when $a = b$ and both tend to zero, each small neighborhood of $p = 0$ or of $p = 1$ has probability $1/2$, while intermediate values of p have probability 0.

Example. Suppose that you are willing to use a flat prior, which means $a = b = 1$, and have observed $x = 3$ successes and $n - x = 7$ failures in 10 trials. Then your posterior mean for p would be $(a + x)/(a + b + n) = 4/12$. The more usual estimate would have been $x/n = 3/10$. The relation between the two estimates is this: the Bayesian estimate of the mean with a flat (rectangular, uniform) prior acts as if, at least from the point of view of the usual estimator, there already were 2 observations on hand, one a success and one a failure. In Fig. F6–1 we have moved from $(1, 1)$ as prior to $(4, 8)$ as posterior. More generally, the Bayesian estimate of the mean based on the beta prior (a, b) acts as if there already were $a + b$ observations on hand, a successes, b failures.

F7. POISSON DATA DISTRIBUTIONS AND GAMMA PRIOR DISTRIBUTIONS

The Poisson distribution for counted data, for a mean count μ, gives as the probability for a count of x

$$P(x \mid \mu) = e^{-\mu}\mu^x/x!, \qquad x = 0, 1, 2, \ldots .$$

We want a prior distribution for μ that meshes well with the Poisson family. A good choice is the general gamma distribution whose density is

$$g_0(\mu \mid a, b) = \frac{\mu^{a-1}e^{-\mu/b}}{b^a(a - 1)!}, \qquad b > 0, a > 0, \mu \geq 0.$$

The posterior distribution of μ is now given by

$$g_1(\mu \mid x; a, b) = \frac{(1 + 1/b)^{x+a}}{\Gamma(x + a)} \mu^{x+a-1} e^{-\mu(1+1/b)}.$$

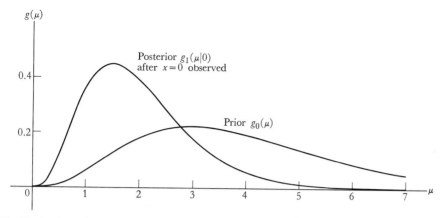

Fig. F7–1. *Posterior distribution of Poisson word rate μ derived from gamma prior and observation* x = 0.

This result means that *if μ has a gamma prior with parameters a and b, and if x is a Poisson observation with mean μ, the posterior distribution of μ is a gamma distribution with parameters a + x and b/(b + 1).*

The corresponding moments are

	mean	variance	"degrees of freedom"
prior	ab	ab^2	$2a$
posterior	$(a + x)b/(b + 1)$	$(a + x)b^2/(b + 1)^2$	$2(a + x)$

where the "degrees of freedom" column refers to the chi-square distribution with the same shape as the gamma distribution considered and is found from "degrees of freedom" = 2(mean)^2/variance.

Example. Suppose that, from writer to writer, the rate of use per thousand words, μ, of a certain word is gamma distributed with parameters $a = 4$ and $b = 1$. In particular, then, both the mean rate and its variance are 4. Suppose that each person's actual uses are Poisson distributed and that, in a specific 1000-word passage, a specific woman uses the word 0 times. The posterior distribution for her rate of use will then have parameters 4 and 1/2, corresponding to mean 2 and variance 1. Figure F7–1 shows both the prior and the posterior. What is not obvious from the figure is that, in this instance, both prior and posterior have the same shape, that of a chi-square distribution with 8 degrees of freedom. (To increase degrees of freedom in passing from prior to posterior in this situation requires observing more than zero usages.)

F8. THERE COULD BE MUCH MORE

In closing our discussion of Bayes techniques at this point, we owe the reader a clear notice that this discussion has hardly been begun. We have treated the two cases—empirical priors and gentle priors—where there is the least opposition to the use of priors. We have discussed the formulas involved in the mathematically simplest cases and have pointed out how the especially convenient priors involved can be interpreted in some of their properties as equivalent to assuming a certain number of additional observations. We have discussed the likelihood ratio, but have passed lightly over the touchy subject of initial odds. On all these things, both authors, and most other statisticians, can be in reasonable agreement.

We have not entered on the many controversial questions which include: Does rational behavior imply acting as if one had a prior for all states of nature? If one's purpose is communication, does any essentially Bayes statement, that is, one appreciably different from those that would have been made by a non-Bayesian, serve that purpose? (Ardent Bayesians and ardent non-Bayesians may not even find a common language to discuss this question.) What is to be done, either in statements or in social interaction, when two Bayesians have quite different and quite "firm" priors? And so on and on.

Our purpose has been to illustrate the mechanism in the simplest, and least controversial, situations. We have not tackled the major issues, which may change with time (see, for example, Mosteller and Wallace, 1964, pp. 266–267).

F9. A CAREFUL LOOK AT CONFIDENCE STATEMENTS

Now that we have exposited a few examples of Bayesian inference, with their consequent degree-of-belief intervals, it is time to turn again to confidence procedures and see what changes in ideas an additional approach can suggest.

The textbook statement about confidence intervals usually goes to some trouble to explain that the confidence coefficient, which we illustrate here with 0.95, does not apply to the inference being made on this specific occasion of the application. Instead, what is emphasized is that the 0.95 applies to a process that is to be repeated again and again. After each sample a statement is made. "The value of the parameter is in the interval computed from this sample." This statement is either true or false. In the long run 95% of the statements set in this manner are true. But the 95% does not necessarily apply to the specific occasion.

Just what 95% is it that does not automatically apply to this occasion? It is the 95% that is verifiable by a frequency count in which someone finds out after each experiment whether the single statement expressing the conclusion from that particular experiment was true or false, and then computes the fraction of correct statements.

Many people, of course, act *as if* the 0.95 did apply on the specific occasion. In a sense, such action is a judgment that the instance before us appears typical of a group of similar-appearing instances. If such a group of instances is large and unselected and the family of data distributions applies to each instance, we could expect that about 95% of all the corresponding statements would be verified. To the extent that "typicality" and "absence of selection" are rightly supposed, the 0.95 can now be validated by frequencies in the same and only sense that "the probability of heads the next time I flip this particular coin is 0.50" can be.

Whether or not these strong suppositions are rightly made, the nonmathematical implications of 95% confidence limits call for action at least resembling that corresponding to a 95% degree of belief that the parameter does fall in the interval. When there is no extra information about the parameter, and when typicality and absence of selection do not seem to need challenge, there seems to be nothing wrong with attaching such a degree of belief to the confidence interval; in fact, it is hard to see why there should be serious concern. We must emphasize, however, that

a1) this degree of belief is not confirmable by frequencies for the isolated instance, only for the large class of similar instances;

a2) either failure of typicality, or presence of selection, may (but need not) make such confirmation inapplicable to the specific instance.

Thus ordinary confidence limits can be given a degree-of-belief meaning, and when considered too specifically, may lose their property of being, in principle, verifiable from frequencies.

What confidence intervals mean, and how the confidence coefficient applies to the sample in hand, are questions that pass many individuals by, either because they have not thought about it before, or because they may think that the issue is a tempest in a teapot. Often it is but a microtempest, but not always. Let us illustrate with an extreme example. We emphasize that our sole purpose is clarification. We are not proposing this example as a criticism of confidence intervals, only as an illustration of the issue.

After drawing a sample from a continuous population, let us set confidence limits on the population mean as follows: Draw a 2-digit random number from a random number table. If the number is 01, 02, 03, 04, or 05, state that the true mean is exactly at the sample mean. This procedure gives a confidence interval of length zero, and ensures, with probability one, that the interval does not contain the true value. If the random number is 06, 07, . . . , 99, or 00, state only that the true mean is somewhere on the whole real line—anywhere between $-\infty$ and $+\infty$. In these latter statements, we are certain that the true mean is contained in the confidence interval.

In this pathological example, we have produced a set of confidence intervals that have the 95% confidence property. In 95% of the occasions the interval contains the true value and in 5% it does not. Nevertheless, each time we set the limits we know that the 95% is not the correct degree of belief for the particular interval we have obtained; more precisely, every instance belongs to a recognizable subclass of samples, within which 95% is not correct. Indeed, we are absolutely sure, in a recognizable 95% of the intervals, that the true value is within the limits, and equally sure, in a recognizable 5%, that the limits do not contain the true value. Clearly, on the bare face of matters, no one instance can possibly be thought to be typical. The 95% of this example is a blatant mixture of 100% and 0%.

Recall that we use this example to illustrate the notion that, as usually formulated, the 95% of a 95% confidence interval need not apply to a specific sample or to a recognizable class of samples—it may only apply in the long run. This is something that some textbooks have tried to warn us about, but the idea may not be easy to grasp without an extreme example.

We do not wish to leave the impression that we are against all mixing of probabilities. Not at all; we think moderate mixing offers valuable extra flexibility in the construction of confidence limits. For example, 4/5ths 96% with 1/5th 91% would provide 95% on the average, and might be present in a procedure that was a well-chosen compromise toward several objectives. We are merely clarifying an issue involved in applying a confidence coefficient to a particular occasion, or restricted class of occasions, such as "those with data very like the data we now have".

F10. BAYESIAN STATEMENTS COMPARED WITH CONFIDENCE STATEMENTS

Once we have a posterior distribution derived from Bayesian procedures, we can compute probability limits for the parameter. How nearly frequency-oriented these probabilities will be depends upon what went into the inference. For example, if we used a gentle prior and a normal data distribution with known standard deviation, as in our example of the bar of light (Section F4), and had n independent observations, we could readily set 95% *probability limits* on the true mean as follows:

$$\bar{x} + (1.96)0.25/\sqrt{n},$$

where $\bar{x}$ is the sample mean and n is the sample size. It happens that these two numbers are also the upper and lower 95% *confidence limits* for the precise length μ.

In the Bayesian context, these are the limits within which the probability is 0.95 that the precise value lies. Whether that probability has a frequency meaning or a purely degree-of-belief meaning depends on the surrounding circumstances.

The close match between gentle-prior Bayesian and conventional confidence procedures that we find in this example does not hold in general. Since many different confidence procedures are compatible with one distribution, they cannot all agree with a single Bayesian procedure. So long as we are working with really gentle priors (at least in problems where we can agree on the definition of gentleness), the near uniqueness of the Bayesian solution is one of the attractive features of the Bayesian approach. Another is that the gentle prior expresses modest knowledge relative to that about to be acquired in the experiment—modest knowledge that each person is willing to admit everyone has. Even though different choices of such priors would not match one another, their common gentleness produces results that should satisfy each user.

The diversity of confidence procedures based on the original measurements has an important balancing merit, for among them are likely to be some that are robust against such troubles as wide variations in the shape of the underlying distribution of the observations. As of this writing, no one has seen how to introduce this kind of robustness into a Bayesian procedure.

When neither the mean μ nor the variance σ^2 of a Gaussian distribution is known, but the joint prior distribution of μ and σ^2 is very gentle compared to the precision in the data, the posterior distribution of $\sqrt{n}(\mu - \bar{x})/s$ is the t distribution with $n - 1$ degrees of freedom. Thus if we wanted 95% belief limits for μ, they would be given by

$$\bar{x} \pm (s/\sqrt{n}) \cdot \left| t_{n-1} \right|_{.95}$$

where $\left| t_{n-1} \right|_{.95}$ is the two-sided 95% point of the t distribution with $n - 1$ degrees of freedom. Again, this result matches numerically a standard confidence limit result when σ is unknown, but the interpretation is different. The two-sample difference-of-means problem, including the case of unequal and unknown variances for the two populations (associated with the names of Behrens-Fisher and Aspin-Welch) can also be handled smoothly by the gentle-prior approach to Bayesian inference, though the result is less acceptable to many. We omit all details, since we are only trying to give a flavor, not presenting a text on Bayesian inference.

A common error in the reporting of the results of significance tests and confidence intervals is to interpret them in a Bayesian manner. The report may be, for example, when the null hypothesis is that of zero difference and a one-sided test is used, that "there is only one chance in twenty that the null hypothesis is true". Nothing in the usual significance-test approach allows this sort of report to be made, although it is the sort of report that, when accompanied by a careful interpretation emphasizing both the prior and the extent of selection, a Bayesian might be able to contribute to some kinds of problems. Similarly, when a 95% confidence interval is constructed, the report may be that the probability is .95 that the value of the parameter is in the specific interval. Again a Bayesian might, under suitable circumstances, word his report in this way, but as we saw by example in Section F9, the standard confidence-interval procedure need offer no basis for such statements.

G. BINOMIAL PROBABILITY PAPER

Introduction
G1. *Plotting*
G2. *Measurements of deviations*
G3. *Crab addition and chi square*
★G4. *Refinements in plotting*
G5. *Individual counts*
G6. *The sign test*
G7. *Paired counts and a theoretical proportion*
G8. *Homogeneity of paired counts*
G9. *Transformations of paired counts*

In analyzing data which have been counted rather than measured, the psychologist, biologist, opinion pollster, market analyst, geologist, physicist, or statistician frequently uses as a model the binomial distribution, its limiting case the Poisson distribution, or some of their generalizations. For many purposes, graphical accuracy is sufficient. The speed of graphical processes, and more especially the advantages of visual presentation in pointing out facts or clues which might otherwise be overlooked, make graphical analysis valuable. A special type of graph paper has been designed for such analysis (Mosteller and Tukey, 1946, 1949). It is available from the Codex Book Company, 74 Broadway, Norwood, Massachusetts, No. 31,298 on thin paper, No. 32,298 on thick paper.

Binomial Probability Paper is graduated with a square-root scale on both axes: 1[1]20[2]100[5]400[10]600 horizontally and 1[1]20[2]100[5]300 vertically. (The notation $A[a]B[b]C$ means: "from A to B by intervals of size a and thence from B to C by intervals of size b".) It serves to treat classification into two categories directly, and into more categories indirectly. Full and direct treatment of uncertainty for data with three categories would require three-dimensional graphing or a new kind of paper. If only indication is needed for three-category data, the barycentric coordinates of Section C4, above, provide a direct graphical treatment.

The account which follows, including the examples, draws heavily on Mosteller and Tukey (1949), with the permission of the Editor of the *Journal of the American Statistical Association.*

G1. PLOTTING

The classical example of the binomial distribution is the distribution of the number of heads in n independent throws of a coin, true (50–50), or biased (for example, 40–60 or 57–43). Two assumptions require emphasis here: (i) the throws are independent and thus do not influence one another, (ii) the probability of a head on each throw is the same. If we replace "head" and "tail" by "success" and "failure", or by "defective" and "nondefective", or by "drinker" and "abstainer", or the names identifying the two appropriate categories, these two requirements are the natural and sufficient conditions that the observed numbers in the categories be distributed binomially.

We must distinguish (i) the true relative probability of two categories, which we often refer to as the *split,* and (ii) the observed numbers in the two categories, which we often refer to as the *paired count.* In describing a split we do not bother with normalization (that is, with making the sum add to 1 like probabilities or to 100 like percentages)—the split of a "true" coin is equivalently stated to be 50–50 or 1–1 or 127–127. In describing a paired count we always give the actual numbers counted.

A *split* is plotted as a straight line through the origin: a line that passes through all the points whose coordinates represent it. To illustrate, in Fig. G1–1 the lowest line corresponds to the 80–20 split. In addition to going through (80, 20) this line goes through the points (8, 2), (16, 4), (20, 5), (120, 30), and so on —the corresponding splits are all the same. The 77–23 split is also called the 23% line. That is, we use the percent plotted vertically to name the line.

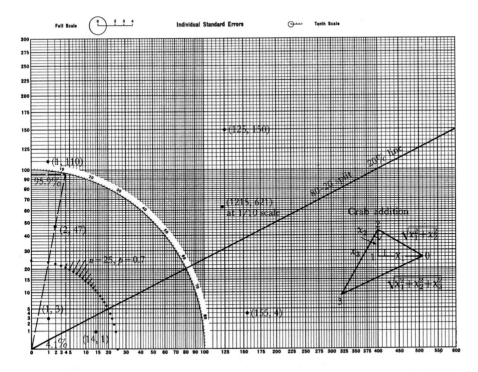

Fig. G1–1. *Illustrating plotting of splits, paired counts, percentages, tenth scale, distribution along a quarter-circle, crab addition.*

Unless extra accuracy is desired (and then see Mosteller and Tukey, 1949, p. 176 and elsewhere), plot a paired count as a point, using the horizontal and vertical scales. The pairs $(1, 3)$, $(14, 1)$, $(155, 4)$, $(1, 110)$, $(125, 150)$ are plotted in Fig. G1–1.

For a given value of n, the possible paired counts $(x, n - x)$ are plotted at points spread around a quarter circle. Figure G1–1 illustrates this for $n = 25$. The possible points are dotted. They fall along a circle of radius $\sqrt{n}$ because for a point representing the paired count $(x, n - x)$ the coordinate distances measured from the origin are $\sqrt{x}$ and $\sqrt{n - x}$. The plotted point (see Fig. G1–2) is at $(\sqrt{x}, \sqrt{n - x})$, and its distance from $(0, 0)$ is

$$d = \sqrt{(\sqrt{x})^2 + (\sqrt{n - x})^2} = \sqrt{x + n - x} = \sqrt{n}.$$

The labeling of the scales with the square roots of distances from the origin takes this into account, so that the printed quarter circle strikes the axes at positions marked n.

When n is not small, for a fixed proportion p, most of the distribution falls along a short arc of the quarter circle. A short arc of a circle is almost a straight line. To see this, look, for example, at the 10-degree arc between 40° and 50° on

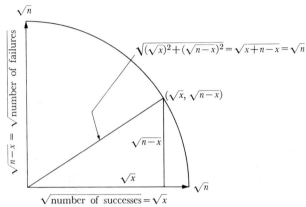

Fig. G1–2. Pythagorean theorem applied to binomial probability paper: x = number of successes, n − x = number of failures, n = x + (n − x) = number of binomial trials. For fixed number of trials, the outcome ($\sqrt{x}$, $\sqrt{n-x}$) falls on a circle of radius $\sqrt{n}$. (The numbers printed on the scales of binomial probability paper correspond to counts rather than to square roots of counts, so that the square rooting is done by the scale.)

the printed quarter circle or at any other 10° arc (Fig. G1–1). Approximately, then, the distribution runs along a short line segment perpendicular to the split and tangent to the circle of radius $\sqrt{n}$. See plot for $n = 25$, $p = 0.7$, in Fig. G1–1. To illustrate this distribution, we have gone so far in Fig. G1–1 as to erect ordinates for the points along the quarter circle for $n = 25$, ordinates whose lengths are proportional to the binomial probabilities when the probability of the event whose number of occurrences is plotted on the vertical axis is $p = 0.7$. These ordinates, which would not ordinarily have been put in, come from tables of individual probabilities of the binomial distribution. (Most binomial tables of individual probabilities would be suitable for this problem. Mosteller, Rourke, and Thomas, 1961, pp. 435–452, give both individual probabilities and cumulatives to 3 decimals for $n \leq 25$ and $p = 0.01$, 0.05, 0.1[0.1]0.9, 0.95, 0.99. These tables are unusual in that they cover $p > 0.5$ directly rather than relying on the application of identities to obtain these values from entries for $p < 0.5$. This offers a saving in effort, especially when one is working with cumulatives.)

Percentages

1. To convert a split into a theoretical percentage, read the rectangular coordinates of its intersection with the printed quarter circle (paying no attention to the angular scale). In Fig. G1–1, the 80–20 split intersects the printed quarter circle at the point (80, 20).

2. To convert a paired count into an observed percentage, draw the split from the origin through the paired count and read the rectangular coordinates of the point where the split crosses the printed quarter circle. (It is convenient to consider this an auxiliary line and draw it dashed.) Thus (2, 47) corresponds to percentages of 4.1 and 95.9 (Fig. G1–1).

G2. MEASUREMENTS OF DEVIATIONS

We ordinarily measure distances from paired counts to splits. The distance is the length of the perpendicular dropped from the paired count to the split (see Example 1, Fig. G2–1, for an illustration). These distances can be compared with the scale at the top left of the paper, which shows the sizes of small integer multiples of a standard deviation. One of the features of the double square-root transformation used in binomial probability paper is that it transforms binomial data so that perpendicular distance from a point representing a paired count to a split representing population probability is approximately normally distributed with a constant variance independent of sample size. (The *angle* can be read on the scale of the quarter circle; see Section G9.) The constant variance feature explains why we are not concerned with $\sqrt{npq}$ and a changing variance. The basic idea came from R. A. Fisher.

A ruler with a millimeter scale can be most helpful, especially because on the paper one standard deviation is 5 mm (more precisely 5.08 mm if the paper has neither shrunk nor stretched). Distances in millimeters can be compared with the % points of the unit normal distribution by referring to Table G2–2.

The figures presented in the text are reduced and so their millimeter measurements will not check; the measurements refer to distances on the standard graph paper.

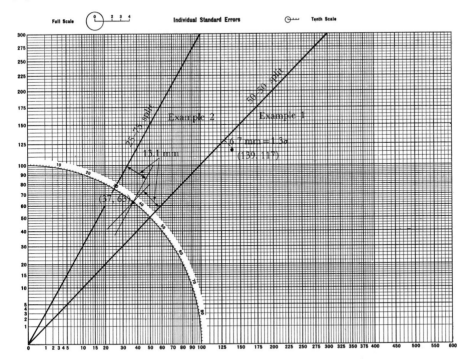

Fig. G2–1. Illustrating a binomial test of significance (Example 1); size of sample required to be able to distinguish two percentages (Example 2).

TABLE G2–2

MILLIMETER TABLE FOR UNIT NORMAL DEVIATE

Significance level		Unit normal deviate	
one-sided	two-sided	millimeters*	multiples of σ
50%	100%	0.0	.00
40%	80%	1.3	.25
30%	60%	2.7	.52
20%	40%	4.3	.84
16.2%	32.5%	5.0	.98
10%	20%	6.5	1.28
5%	10%	8.4	1.64
2.5%	5%	10.0	1.96
1%	2%	11.8	2.33
0.5%	1%	13.1	2.58
0.1%	0.2%	15.7	3.09
Conversion relation		5.080	1.000

* Entries correspond to separate scale on graph paper marked "Full Scale".

A 5-cent piece (USA nickel) has diameter almost exactly 4 standard deviations at full scale on binomial probability paper. This is a convenience for quick measurement. Even more convenient for constructions is the 1-cent piece (USA penny), because its diameter is just enough smaller than 4 standard deviations to make room for the thickness of the pencil point. Consequently, a penciled circle made by following the rim of a penny is just about 4 standard deviations in diameter. Thus a man with a penny can get along without a compass in many constructions on binomial probability paper.

G3. CRAB ADDITION AND CHI SQUARE

In order to sum the squares of deviations to form a chi square, we may proceed either by measuring, squaring and adding, or by crab addition, using the theorem of Pythagoras. Crab addition is easily done by using a piece of tracing paper. Figure G1–1 shows in the lower right-hand corner the sort of figure that will appear on the tracing paper when one follows these directions:

a1) Mark a small circle as the origin (0) on the tracing paper and center this circle over the theoretical line at the point of intersection with the perpendicular dropped from the first sample point.

a2) Mark point (1) on the tracing paper over the sample point—the distance on the tracing paper between the origin and point (1), which we may call χ_1, is the square root of the contribution of the first sample point to χ^2.

TABLE G3–1

MILLIMETER TABLE FOR CHI SQUARE

Degrees of freedom	Undoubled millimeters*			Multiples of σ^2		
	At an upper significance level of:					
	(50%)	5%	1%	(50%)	5%	1%
1	(3.4)	10.0	13.1	(.5)	3.8	6.6
2	(6.0)	12.4	15.4	(1.4)	6.0	9.2
3	(7.8)	14.2	17.1	(2.4)	7.8	11.3
4	(9.3)	15.6	18.5	(3.4)	9.5	13.3
5	(10.6)	16.9	19.7	(4.4)	11.1	15.1
6	(11.8)	18.0	20.8	(5.3)	12.6	16.8
10	(15.5)	21.8	24.4	(9.3)	18.3	21.2
15	(19.3)	25.4	28.1	(14.3)	25.0	30.6
30	(27.5)	33.6	36.2	(29.3)	43.8	50.9

* Doubled distances can be converted into multiples of σ^2 by using coordinate scales on graph paper.

a3) Put both the origin (0) and the point (1) on the tracing paper over the theoretical line, with the point (1) over the base of the perpendicular from the second sample point to the theoretical line, and plot a point (2) on the tracing paper immediately over the second sample point. The distance from point (1) to point (2) is χ_2, the square root of the contribution of the second sample point to χ^2, and the distance from the origin (0) to point (2) is $\sqrt{\chi_1^2 + \chi_2^2}$.

a4) Continue in this manner until all deviations have made their contributions.

After the crab-sum distance has been obtained from the individual deviation segments, we can convert it into an assessment of significance in either of two ways:

b) Double its length (by geometric construction), refer the doubled length to one of the coordinate scales of the graph paper (starting from the lower left-hand corner), and refer the number thus obtained to a conventional chi-square table.

c) Measure the length in millimeters, and refer to the millimeter portion of Table G3–1.

★G4. REFINEMENTS IN PLOTTING

Except for a glance at the headings, this section might be skipped on a first reading.

Plotting small counts as triangles

When dealing with small counts, greater precision can be had, if desired, by plotting each count as a triangle, rather than as a single point, the two additional vertices being obtained by increasing, in turn, each count by unity. For example, (6, 8) would yield (7, 8) and (6, 9). Distances can then be measured to any one of the three vertices or to the middle of the hypotenuse, whichever is more appropriate in a specific use. Details may be found in Mosteller and Tukey (1949). (See also the close of Section G9.)

Larger counts

Paired counts up to (600, 300) can be plotted directly. If there are more observations, but less than (6000, 3000), the paired count may be plotted at 1/10 scale; thus (1215, 621) would be plotted as (121.5, 62.1) as in Fig. G1–1. Then

1) the left-hand upper scale called "Full Scale" should be replaced by the right-hand upper scale called "Tenth Scale" in converting distances into multiples of the standard deviation;

2) distances in millimeters should be multiplied by 3.16 before using the millimeter tables, G2–2 and G3–1.

Very large counts

If significance tests are to be used for still larger samples, graphical accuracy is insufficient, and arithmetical methods are advised. A word to the wise is in order. Almost never does it make sense to use binomial significance tests on such data— for the inevitable small deviations from the mathematical model of independence and constant split will have piled up to such an extent that the binomial variability is deeply buried and unnoticeable by comparison with other variability. See Section D2. Graphical examination of such large samples, after dividing by a factor larger than 10, is often very worthwhile as indication, because it brings the results more vividly to the eye.

Very unsymmetrical counts

Occasionally the user may have data involving large counts of one kind and small counts of the other, where the total count may not be fixed. Such cases may be treated by choosing a suitable divisor, and using the divisor only for the category with the large counts. If this is done, the distance from paired count to split should be measured at right angles to the contracted axis (the axis of the paper corresponding to the count that is divided) and *not* at right angles to the split. For good accuracy, each small count should be less than 5% of the corresponding total count. (The quarter circle will no longer be useful.)

Poisson subcase

The Poisson distribution yields the subcase of the case discussed above where the total number is arbitrarily large and *fixed*. Binomial probability paper may still be used without difficulty, by plotting the various observations on any chosen, fixed vertical line, thus using an unknown horizontal divisor (or vice versa).

G5. INDIVIDUAL COUNTS

Given a sample, sorted into two categories, the numbers in the categories form a paired count, which is plotted as a point. If a probability or a population proportion, p, is assigned for the second category, then this is plotted as the q-p split, where $q = 1 - p$. The approximate significance level corresponds to the distance from the split to the point and may be obtained from Table G2–2.

Comparing an observed proportion with a theoretical proportion

Example 1 (see Fig. G2–1). Fisher and Mather (1936) have described a genetical experiment in which the individuals in 32 litters, each composed of 8 mice, were observed for the characteristic of straight versus wavy hair. Under the conditions of the experiment, the simplest Mendelian theory predicts that half the mice would have straight hair. It was observed that $n_1 = 139$ had straight hair, $n - n_1 = 117$ had wavy hair. Could such a discrepancy from the 128–128 split have arisen by chance?

The observed paired count $(139, 117)$ is plotted. The theoretical proportion is plotted as the 128–128 split (the 50% line). The distance is about 6.7 mm $= 1.3\sigma$. Since deviations from simple Mendelian genetics might reasonably occur in either direction, the two-sided significance level is appropriate, and from Table G2–2 this is found to be about 20%. Thus this test would not lead us to judge the simplest form of Mendelian genetics unlikely to apply.

Since the two-sided 5% distance is 10 millimeters and the two-sided $33\frac{1}{3}\%$ distance is 5 millimeters, which are worth remembering, Table G2–2 would not have been needed in routine testing, since beyond $33\frac{1}{3}\%$ and short of the 5% point would usually have been report enough.

Since binomial probability paper allows us to judge the approximate significance of a paired count, it must also let us plan binomial experiments to have desired properties.

Sample size necessary to resolve two given percentages

When designing a test to discriminate between two theoretical percentages, the experimenter often wishes to ensure that *any* result will give significant evidence *against at least one of the two theories*. The procedure is best described by an example.

Example 2 (see Fig. G2–1). A geneticist wishes to test whether a certain character appears in one-half or one-quarter of the progeny of a certain mating. He requires significance at the (two-sided) 1% level against at least one of these hypotheses and wishes to know the smallest sample size which will guarantee this. He draws the 50–50 and 25–75 splits and then parallel lines at a distance of 13.1 mm (2.58σ), which corresponds to the two-sided 1% level. These parallel lines intersect at $(37, 63)$. Thus a sample of $37 + 63 = 100$ individuals is about the right size.

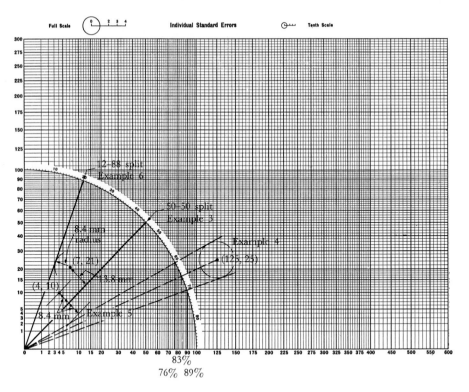

Fig. G6–1. Illustrating the sign test (Example 3); confidence limits for a percentage (Example 4); confidence limits on the median of a continuous population (Example 5); operating characteristic (power) of the sign test (Example 6).

G6. THE SIGN TEST

The classical sign test compares two materials or treatments, in terms of paired observations, where the observations in each pair are comparable except for the materials or treatments being tested. The sign test is a special case of the comparison of theoretical and observed proportions, where the theoretical proportion is always 50%. It has been thoroughly discussed by Dixon and Mood (1946).

Example 3 (see Fig. G6–1). Dixon and Mood cite the yields of two lines, A and B, of hybrid corn where 6, 8, 2, 4, 3, 3, and 2 pairs of plots were available from 7 experiments. In 7 out of 28 pairs line A yielded higher than line B. The distance of the $(7, 21)$ paired count from the 50–50 split is about 13.8 mm, so that the paired count is at the 1% level of significance.

Extension of the sign test

As presented above, the sign test applies to the hypothesis of equality in paired experiments. It can be easily extended, by constructing dummy observations, to cover (i) the hypothesis of a constant additive difference, (ii) the hypothesis of a constant percentage difference, or (iii) the hypothesis of a certain population median. Suppose that 7 experiments have produced the following numbers:

Set:	1	2	3	4	5	6	7
Condition *A:*	57	53	59	56	51	57	54
Condition *B:*	26	31	24	28	31	29	25

There is clearly little need to test for equality.

i) A test of the hypothesis that condition *A* runs 30 units above condition *B* may be made by adding 30 to each observation under condition *B*, which yields 2 positive and 5 negative differences so that the paired count is (2, 5). We learn that "*A* 30 units above *B*" is plausible, although "*A* 19 units above *B*" is not.

ii) A test of the hypothesis that condition *A* gives numbers double those of condition *B* may be made by doubling the condition *B* numbers, which yields 3 positive, 1 zero, and 3 negative differences [the corresponding paired count is (3, 3) because in significance testing it is well to set ties aside rather than halve them!]. We learn that "*A* twice *B*" is also plausible.

iii) A test of the hypothesis that the median number in condition *A* is 57 may be made by replacing the results in condition *B* by an imaginary experiment always giving 57, which yields 1 positive, 2 zero, and 4 negative differences [the corresponding paired count is (1, 4)!]. We learn that "median *A* = 57" is also plausible.

Confidence limits for population proportions

If we have a sample divided into two categories, we may wish to set confidence limits on the percentage of the population in each category. This is accomplished by plotting the paired count which was observed and then constructing two splits whose distances from this point correspond to the two-sided level of confidence required. Thus if 95% confidence is required, distances of 10 mm are used. The coordinates of the intersections of the two splits with the quarter circle give the confidence limits for percentages.

Example 4 (see Fig. G6–1). A random sample of 150 farms from a certain region yields the information that 125 of the farmers plant corn on the farms they work. Set 95% confidence limits on the % of farms in this region planting corn.

Plot (125, 25). Draw arcs of a circle of radius 10 mm centered at the point, and draw the tangent splits and the split through (125, 25). Find the intersection of the split through (125, 25) with the printed circle, and from that intersection, drop a perpendicular to the horizontal axis. There read the estimate of the percentage of corn-planted farms as between 83% and 84%. To get 95% confidence limits, find the intersections of the tangent lines with the printed quarter circle, drop perpendiculars from the intersections to the horizontal axis and read the limits as 76% and 89%.

Critique of Example 4. If the sample is truly random, the method is sound. If stratified sampling is correctly done, these confidence limits will be unnecessarily large, since stratified sampling usually reduces variability below that obtained from random sampling. The increase in efficiency by stratification is often small enough for these limits to be a satisfactory choice. On the other hand, in cluster sampling, where the variability is usually greater than binomial, the limits are likely to be too narrow, possibly seriously.

Confidence limits for the population median

By combining the ideas of the sign test and the last example, we may obtain confidence limits for the population median. If x_0 is the population median, and is used to divide samples into paired counts, then certain extreme paired counts will occur with probability at most $1 - \alpha$, where α is the desired confidence. By determining these unlikely paired counts, and expressing them in terms of the observations, it is possible to set confidence limits for the population median. While strict confidence levels require taking blocks of paired counts with at most a certain probability, interpolation can usually be carried out with safety.

Example 5 (see Fig. G6–1). The differences between reaction times of individuals in an experimental group from those of subjects matched to them in a control group were 6, 5, 3, 2, 1, −1, −2, −3, −5, −12, −13, −13, −15, −28, when expressed on a logarithmic scale (actually in terms of 100 times the log to the base 10). Within what limits do we have 90% confidence that the median of the population lies?

Drawing the 50–50 split, and the parallel lines at ±8.4 mm (for 90%), we find that points (10, 4) and (4, 10), where $4 + 10 = 10 + 4 = 14$ (the number of cases), are crossed by these parallel lines. A (4, 10) split would put us somewhere between 2 and 1 and a (10, 4) split somewhere between −12 and −13. Let us say halfway for each. We interpolate 1/2 of the way from 1 to 2 (these are the fourth and fifth values from the top) and 1/2 of the way from −13 to −12 (these are the fourth and fifth values from the bottom) to obtain approximate 90% confidence limits of $-12\frac{1}{2}$ and $1\frac{1}{2}$ for the median of the population of differences from which the 14 observed differences were a random sample. (For further discussion see Moses, 1965 or 1953.)

Critique of Example 5. The interpolation is based on the fact that the use of 1.001 (say) for a cutting point would give the paired count (4, 10), as would any cut up to 1.999, while 2.001 would give (3, 11). One way to take account of the grouping and rounding process is to widen these interpolated values by 1/2 the grouping interval. Thus if the difference were rounded from more decimals to the nearest tenth, and were actually 6.0, 5.0, 3.0, . . . , −28.0, then we should use $-12\frac{1}{2} - \frac{1}{20} = -12.55$ and $1\frac{1}{2} + \frac{1}{20} = 1.55$. If, as might more plausibly have been the case, they had been rounded to integers, we should use $-12\frac{1}{2} - \frac{1}{2} = -13$ and $1\frac{1}{2} + \frac{1}{2} = 2$.

The operating characteristic of the sign test

We often want to know how well the sign test will discriminate.

Example 6 (see Fig. G6–1). In Example 3 we considered 28 pairs of observations and decided to treat (7, 21) as significant. It is natural to inquire what population percentage of pairs favorable to line *B* is needed to insure significance at this level 95% of the time. We must then find a split so that the point (7, 21) is 8.4 mm = 1.65σ away. This leads to the 12–88 split, and so the sign test with 28 pairs discriminates very well between 50%, where the lines of corn are equally matched, and 88% (or 12%).

G7. PAIRED COUNTS AND A THEORETICAL PROPORTION

A set of several paired counts may give evidence against a fixed theoretical proportion in two ways. If the observed proportions are too variable, they indicate lack of homogeneity, implying that the samples came from populations with different proportions. If the average observed proportion deviates too much from the theoretical, it indicates a change (or error) in level, and thus it indicates that the theoretical proportion does not apply.

It is common to test a homogeneous set of paired counts for agreement with a preassigned population proportion by adding them together, and then testing the sum (as in Example 1 in Section G5). Tests of homogeneity alone are the subject of the next section. Many delicate testing procedures involve first a test of homogeneity and then a test of level. Combined tests are mainly used to make quick and easy tests.

Example 7 (see Fig. G7–1). A production process has been producing an average of 15% defective pieces over a long period. After the introduction of a new batch of raw material, successive shifts produced the following four paired counts of nondefectives and defectives:

$$(155, 20), \qquad (164, 41), \qquad (106, 12), \qquad (41, 10).$$

Is it reasonable to think that the production process is producing the same proportion of defectives as before? We plot the points and the 15% line. Since no distance from the line is as great as $2\sigma = 10$ mm, and since the points are about equally spread about the line, there seems to be no reason to suppose the new batch of raw material has made a change in the percentage defective.

If some points are found outside 2σ, the resulting paired count (of points inside 2σ versus points outside 2σ) would be compared with the 19–1 split by the method of Example 1.

An alternative procedure is to combine the distances from the theoretical line by crab addition (Section G3) and consider this a chi square with as many degrees of freedom as there are paired counts.

Example 8 (see Fig. G7–1). Taking the same data as in Example 7, the crab sum of the deviations is a length, which when doubled may be read on the marginal scale

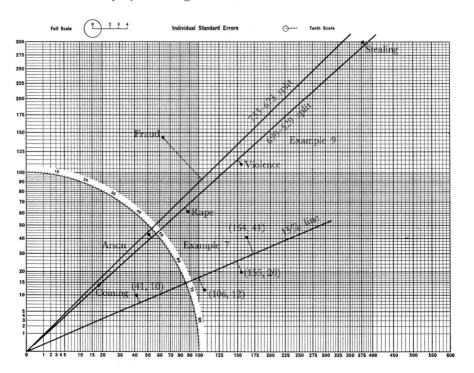

Fig. G7–1. Plotting several paired counts: to compare with a given level (Example 7); to study homegeneity (Example 9).

as $\chi^2 = 9.0$. That value falls between the upper 10% and upper 5% points for 4 degrees of freedom.

G8. HOMOGENEITY OF PAIRED COUNTS

Usually we have no theoretical proportion; we are only given 5 or 50 or 500 paired counts which we wish to test for homogeneity, to test if it is reasonable that they have arisen from sampling a population with the same percentages in the two categories. The problem is the same, however many paired counts we have, but the practical solution can be different. In every case we plot the individual paired counts and draw the best fitting split, either by eye or through the sum of paired counts.

We shall discuss three methods here, namely:

1) graphical chi square,
2) range,
3) counts in $\pm 1\sigma$ and $\pm 2\sigma$ strips.

Each of these has advantages and disadvantages, and, as best we know, they compare as shown in Table G8–1.

TABLE G8-1

THREE METHODS OF TESTING FOR HOMOGENEITY OF PAIRED COUNTS

| Method | Number of samples | | Advantages | Disadvantages |
	Feasible	Recommended		
χ^2	2 to ∞	2 to 8 or 15	efficiency	labor
range	2 to ?	2 to 20	ease and speed	limited efficiency
counts	15 to ∞	15 or 20 to ∞	80% efficiency; relative simplicity	

The range is only recommended for 20 paired counts or less. Its use for larger k would involve the delicate details of the normal distribution and provide lower efficiency than the counting method.

To apply the χ^2 test, plot the paired counts and the split through their sum, and combine the distances by crab addition as explained in Section G3.

Example 9 (see Fig. G7–1). The following classic data by C. Goring—quoted by K. Pearson in 1909 and by M. G. Kendall (1943)—compare the number of drinkers and abstainers among criminals according to crimes committed. The first number in each pair is the number of drinkers:

Arson	(50, 43)	Stealing	(379, 300)
Rape	(88, 62)	Coining	(18, 14)
Violence	(155, 110)	Fraud	(63, 144)
		Totals	(753, 673)

The graphical display shows very clearly that (1) the observations are discrepant, (2) the crime of fraud is the only one for which the proportion of drinkers is really different. Graphical chi-square computation gives 30.2 on 5 degrees of freedom—highly significant. When criminals convicted for fraud are removed from consideration the remaining five groups are each less than one standard deviation away from the new fitted line (the 690–529 split).

Critique of Example 9. If the classification of "drinker" were sufficiently objective, and if the sample of convicted criminals represents a random sample of criminals, then the analysis seems sound. It cannot, of course, throw any appreciable light on the connection between drinking and crime in general, bearing only on the question "excluding fraud, do drinkers tend to be convicted of some types of crime and abstainers of others?".

A quicker method of analysis, and one well suited for drawing lines by eye, is to compute the range of the sample, that is, the sum of the greatest distances to the right and left of the line. Then the range can be compared with Table G2–2 to discover whether the samples deviate enough among themselves to provide evidence that the observations did not arise from random sampling from a single proportion in the population.

Fuller treatments

For those who are fortunate enough to be able to read Japanese, M. Masuyama (1951) has prepared a well-illustrated paperback book giving the theory and many kinds of applications of (a modified and improved) binomial probability paper.

A more extensive discussion than the present one, including many more illustrations and other kinds of applications, appears in Mosteller and Tukey (1949). (The procedure given there for the four-fold table is slightly conservative.)

G9. TRANSFORMATIONS OF PAIRED COUNTS

Binomial probability paper is also convenient for expressing paired counts in either % or angles, providing accuracy enough for many purposes.

The angular transformation

The analysis of variance of counted data is frequently facilitated (Bartlett, 1947, and references cited therein) by making the angular transformation. If the data involve small numbers, the accuracy of graphical transformation will suffice. The observation is plotted, a line through the origin produced to the quarter circle, and the corresponding angle read off.

TABLE G9–1

ANALYSIS OF KAPPAUF-SMITH EXPERIMENT

	Errors in 60 trials			*Corresponding angles*		
Observer	Size I	Size II	Size III	Size I	Size II	Size III
B_O	7	4	4	20.2	15.0	15.0
B	15	6	3	30.2	18.6	13.1
K	10	7	5	24.1	20.2	16.9
R	28	20	16	43.2	35.6	31.2
S	11	8	9	25.2	21.6	23.0
T	25	17	15	40.0	32.2	30.2

Source	df	Sum of squares	Mean square
Observers	5	991.64	198
Sizes	2	257.15	129
Interaction	10	73.16	7.3
Binomial	–	–	$\frac{821}{60} = 13.7*$

* Asymptotic variance of an angle obtained from binomially distributed data $\frac{1}{4n}$ (radians)$^2 = \frac{821}{n}$ (degrees)^2.

Example 10. W. E. Kappauf and W. N. Smith (personal communication) tested the performance of six observers in reading three sizes of dials. Sixty readings were made by each observer on each size. The errors, angles, and analysis of variance are shown in Table G9–1. (The reader will find it easy to check on the computation of the angles on his own piece of graph paper. Plot number of errors horizontally, nonerrors vertically. Read the angle in degrees from the printed quarter circle by drawing the split through the plotted point.)

The usual test for significance of the effect of size would be $F = 129/7.3 = 17.7$ on 2 and 10 degrees of freedom, which is highly significant.

Critique of Example 10. A possibly more conservative test would be $F = 129/13.7 = 9.4$ on 2 and ∞ degrees of freedom, which is still very highly significant. Although 7.3 on 10 df is not significantly less than 13.7, there is reason to believe, in this particular case, that the error mean square in a large-scale repetition of this experiment might well be less than 13.7. For the analysis above assumes the errors distributed binomially, and the probable differences in difficulty of the various dials attempted might reduce this variance.

Currently, the best angular transformation for variance stabilization for the binomial comes from Freeman and Tukey (1950). Now that a table (Mosteller and Youtz, 1961) of

$$\theta = \frac{1}{2}\left[\arcsin\sqrt{\frac{x}{n+1}} + \arcsin\sqrt{\frac{x+1}{n+1}}\right],$$

where x is the number of successes and n is the sample size, is available for all x and n with $n \le 50$, the thought of using this transformation is more inviting. When θ is measured in degrees, its variance is about $821/(n + \frac{1}{2})$ squared degrees. This transformation corresponds to computing the simply defined angle for $(x + 1, n - x)$ and for $(x, (n - x) + 1)$ and averaging the results, a process that leads (as noted in Section G4) to thinking of an observed paired count $(x, n - x)$ as plotting into the three points corresponding to $(x, n - x)$, $(x + 1, n - x)$, $(x, (n - x) + 1)$. (See Mosteller and Tukey, 1949, for further details.)

ACKNOWLEDGMENTS

The preparation of this article was facilitated by Grant GS–341 to Harvard University from the National Science Foundation and by Contract DA–31-124-ARO(D–215) between Princeton University and the Army Research Office (Durham). Reproduction is permitted for any purpose of the United States Government.

We appreciate the cooperation of the editors and publishers in allowing us to follow British practice in the use of a logical relation of quotation marks to punctuation that is not part of the quotation.

For her work in connection with the calculations, figures, and coordination of the manuscript, we are indebted to Cleo Youtz. Steven Fosburg programmed most of the extensive calculations of Section E. David B. Peizer contributed to the development of Section F.

Among our colleagues, Robert P. Abelson, John Gilbert, Richard Link, and David L. Wallace have given us their criticisms.

Students in a course in the Department of Social Relations, Harvard University, helped us by pointing out ways to improve the organization and exposition: Peter M. Allaman, Robert A. Boakes, William R. Bowerman, Richard F. Cromer, Lawrence R. Ephron, Harriet A. Feinberg, James M. Freeman, Roxane Harvey, Dean Richard Hoge, Momoyo Ise, Susan Marie Jenny, A. M. Kotimsky, John Kramer, John Paul Laszlo, David A. Martin, Colin Martindale, Lenore F. Monello, Nicholas C. Mullins, John A. Newmeyer, Peter S. Panchy, Judith D. Porter, Michael Potegal, L. P. Richardson, Edwenna M. Rosser, Anita Gail Rui, Geraldine Schreier, Michael H. Schwartz, Mark Alan Sherman, George J. Smiltens, Kent Warren Smith, Jeffrey R. Travers, Richard H. Weller, J. B. Williamson.

Similarly, graduate students in the Department of Statistics, Harvard University, gave us their suggestions: Yvonne M. Bishop, Samprit Chatterjee, Jonas H. Ellenberg, William Fairley, Stephen Fienberg, Steven Fosburg, Ivor S. Francis, Chien-Pai Han, Gudmund Iversen, Robert M. Kleyle, Thomas Lehrer, Richard J. Light, Barry H. Margolin, Mikiso Mizuki, Joel Owen, Paul Switzer, Rhett Tsao, and Mary C. Vioni; and from the Department of Mathematics, Princeton University: W. Morven Gentleman.

For work in preparing a frequently revised manuscript, we thank: Marianne Blackwell, Jane Bryan, Elizabeth L. LaJeunesse, William S. Mosteller, Marguerite O'Leary, Patricia Scott, Emily Sorenson, Frances Suda, Rebecca C. Werkman, and Cleo Youtz.

REFERENCES

Anscombe, F. J., and J. W. Tukey (1963). The examination and analysis of residuals. *Technometrics, 5,* 141–160.

Bartlett, M. S. (1947). The use of transformations. *Biometrics, 3,* 39–52.

Bayes, T. (1763). An essay towards solving a problem in the doctrine of chances. *Philos. Trans. Roy. Soc., 53,* 370–418. Also reprinted in *Biometrika, 45* (1958), 296–315.

Brillinger, D. R. (1964). The asymptotic behavior of Tukey's general method of setting approximate confidence limits (the jackknife) when applied to maximum likelihood estimates. *Rev. Int. Statist. Inst., 32,* 202–206.

Burrau, Ø. (1943). Middelfejlen som Usikkerhedsmaal. *Mat. Tidskr. B.,* 1943, 9–16. (See *Mathematical tables and other aids to computation, 2,* 1946, 74–75.)

Cochran, W. G. (1953). *Sampling techniques.* New York: Wiley. (2nd ed., 1963.)

Dixon, W. J., and A. M. Mood (1946). The statistical sign test. *J. Amer. Statist. Assoc., 41,* 557–566.

DuMond, J. W. M., and E. R. Cohen (1958). Fundamental constants of atomic physics. In E. U. Condon and H. Odishaw (Eds.), *Handbook of physics.* New York: McGraw-Hill (LC: 57–6387). Pp. 7-143 to 7-173.

Durbin, J. (1959). A note on the application of Quenouille's method of bias reduction to the estimation of ratios. *Biometrika, 46,* 477–480.

Edwards, W., H. Lindman, and L. J. Savage (1963). Bayesian statistical inference for psychological research. *Psychol. Rev., 70,* 193–242.

Fisher, R. A. (1925). Applications of "Student's" distribution. *Metron, 5*(3), 90–104. (References to this paper often use the date 1926, as Fisher did in his bibliography in *Statistical methods for research workers;* the journal gives 1926.)

Fisher, R. A., and K. Mather (1936). A linkage test with mice. *Ann. Eugenics, 7,* 265–280.

Freeman, M. F., and J. W. Tukey (1950). Transformations related to the angular and the square root. *Ann. math. Statist., 21,* 607–611.

Havell, F. W., D. S. Robson, and J. W. Tukey (unpublished). Sampling experiments investigating the robustness of jackknife-derived confidence interval estimates of variance.

Johnson, P. O. (1949). *Statistical methods in research.* New York: Prentice-Hall. P. 299.

Johnson, P. O., and F. Tsao (1944). Factorial design in the determination of differential limen values. *Psychometrika, 9,* 107–144.

Jones, H. L. (1965). The jackknife method. In *Proc. IBM Scientific Computing Symposium on Statistics,* October 21–23, 1963. White Plains, New York: IBM Data Processing Division. Pp. 185–201.

Kendall, M. G. (1943). *The advanced theory of statistics.* Vol. 1. London: J. B. Lippincott. P. 356.

Kendall, M. G., Sheila F. H. Kendall, and B. B. Smith (1938). The distribution of Spearman's coefficient of rank correlation in a universe in which all rankings occur an equal number of times. *Biometrika, 30,* 251–273.

Kendall, M. G., and A. Stuart (1961). *The advanced theory of statistics.* Vol. 2: Inference and relationship. London: Charles Griffin & Company. Pp. 5–7.

Kluckhohn, Florence R., and F. L. Strodtbeck (1961). *Variations in value orientations.* Evanston, Ill.: Row, Peterson. Pp. 124–129, 151–173, 264–283, 379–400.

Lemann, T. B., and R. L. Solomon (1952). Group characteristics as revealed in sociometric patterns and personality ratings. *Sociometry, 15,* 7–90.

Lindley, D. V. (1965). *Introduction to probability and statistics from a Bayesian viewpoint.* Part 1: Probability. Part 2: Inference. Cambridge, Eng.: Cambridge Univ. Press.

Macdonald, N. J., and F. Ward (1963). The prediction of geomagnetic disturbance indices: 1. The elimination of internally predictable variations. *J. geophys. Res., 68,* 3351–3373.

Masuyama, M. (1951). *How to use an improved binomial probability paper.* Japanese Standards Association, Bureau of Patents (Sannen-cho, Chiuoda-ku), Tokyo.

Mickey, M. R. (1959). Some finite population unbiased ratio and regression estimators. *J. Amer. Statist. Assoc., 54,* 594–612.

Miller, Robert G. (1962). Statistical prediction by discriminant analysis. *Meteorol. Monogr., 4* (25), 1–54.

Miller, Rupert G., Jr. (1964). A trustworthy jackknife. *Ann. math. Statist., 35,* 1594–1605.

Moses, L. (1953). Non-parametric methods. In Helen M. Walker and J. Lev, *Statistical inference*. New York: Henry Holt. Pp. 426–450.

——— (1965). Confidence limits from rank tests. *Technometrics, 7,* 257–260 (Query 10).

Mosteller, F., and R. R. Bush (1954). Selected quantitative techniques. In G. Lindzey (Ed.), *Handbook of social psychology*. Cambridge: Addison-Wesley. Pp. 289–334.

Mosteller, F., R. E. K. Rourke, and G. B. Thomas, Jr. (1961). *Probability with statistical applications*. Reading, Mass.: Addison-Wesley.

Mosteller, F., and J. W. Tukey, designers (1946). *Binomial probability paper*. Norwood, Mass.: Codex Book Company.

——— (1949). The uses and usefulness of binomial probability paper. *J. Amer. Statist. Assoc., 44,* 174–212.

Mosteller, F., and D. L. Wallace (1963). Inference in an authorship problem. *J. Amer. Statist. Assoc., 58,* 275–309.

——— (1964). *Inference and disputed authorship: The Federalist*. Reading, Mass.: Addison-Wesley.

Mosteller, F., and Cleo Youtz (1961). Tables of the Freeman-Tukey transformations for the binomial and Poisson distributions. *Biometrika, 48,* 433–440.

Peirce, C. S. (1873). Theory of errors of observations. *Report of Superintendent of U.S. Coast Survey* (for the year ending Nov. 1, 1870). Washington, D.C.: Government Printing Office. Appendix No. 21, pp. 200–224 and Plate No. 27.

Quenouille, M. H. (1956). Notes on bias in estimation. *Biometrika, 43,* 353–360.

Raiffa, H., and R. Schlaifer (1961). *Applied statistical decision theory*. Graduate School of Business Administration, Harvard University.

Robson, D. S., and J. H. Whitlock (1964). Estimation of a truncation point. *Biometrika, 51,* 33–39.

Savage, L. J., *et al.* (1962). *The foundations of statistical inference*. London: Methuen. New York: Wiley.

Schlaifer, R. (1959). *Probability and statistics for business decisions*. New York: McGraw-Hill.

"Student" (W. S. Gosset) (1908). The probable error of a mean. *Biometrika, 6,* 1–25. Also in *"Student's" collected papers* (edited by E. S. Pearson and J. Wishart), issued by the Biometrika Office, University College, London, 1942. Paper 2. Pp. 11–34.

——— (1927). Errors of routine analysis. *Biometrika, 19,* 151–164. Also in *"Student's" collected papers* (edited by E. S. Pearson and J. Wishart), issued by the Biometrika Office, University College, London, 1942. Paper 14. Pp. 135–149.

Tucker, L. R. (1958). An inter-battery method of factor analysis. *Psychometrika, 23,* 111–136.

Tukey, J. W. (1958). Bias and confidence in not-quite large samples. Abstract in *Ann. math. Statist., 58,* 614.

——— (1960). A survey of sampling from contaminated distributions. In I. Olkin, S. G. Ghurye, W. Hoeffding, W. G. Madow, and H. B. Mann (Eds.), *Contributions to probability and statistics*. Essays in honor of Harold Hotelling. Stanford: Stanford Univ. Press. Pp. 448–485.

—— (1965). The technical tools of statistics. *Amer. Statistician, 19*(2), 23–28.

—— (unpublished). Data analysis and behavioral science. Princeton University and Bell Telephone Laboratories.

Tukey, J. W., and D. H. McLaughlin (1963). Less vulnerable confidence and significance procedures for location based on a single sample: Trimming/Winsorization 1. *Sankhyā, Series A, 25,* 331–352.

Wilson, E. B., and Margaret M. Hilferty (1929). Note on C. S. Peirce's experimental discussion of the law of errors. *Proc. Nat. Acad. Sci., 15*(2), 120–125.

Yates, F. (1950). Recent applications of biometrical methods in genetics: 1. Experimental techniques in plant improvement. *Biometrics, 6,* 200–207. (Especially pp. 204–205.)

Zajac, E. E. (1964). Programmed pictorial display. In *Proc. 1964 Symposium on Digital Computing,* January 30–31, 1964. Holmdel Laboratory, Bell Telephone Laboratories, Inc. Pp. 33–44.

11

Attitude Measurement

WILLIAM A. SCOTT, *University of Colorado*

The elaboration of theoretical constructs in psychology entails an obligation to measure them or to specify behavioral manifestations which can be measured. Otherwise the theoretical exercise yields only a proliferation in terminology, instead of the promise of empirical advance. The construct *attitude* falls, by historical accident, within the domain of social psychology. It might more reasonably have been elaborated within general personality theory, for an attitude is always formulated as a property of an individual personality—somewhat less enduring, perhaps, than *temperament,* somewhat more enduring than a *motive* or a *mood.* Though the major determinants of attitudes are commonly conceived in terms of social influences, such as norms and roles, this does not distinguish them sharply from other personality constructs, at least not in the view of most social psychologists. A comprehensive psychology would assign a prominent place to social processes in the development of attitudes, no more—and no less— than in the development of other characteristics of individual personality.

DEFINITION

As a hypothetical construct, an attitude is defined by the properties assigned to it in theoretical formulations. It is common practice to treat those properties in categorical terms as when, for instance, an attitude is defined as "a state of readiness for motive arousal" (Newcomb, Turner, and Converse, 1965, p. 40) or as "an enduring organization of motivational, emotional, perceptual, and cognitive processes with respect to some aspect of the individual's world" (Krech and Crutchfield, 1948, p. 152). According to such categorical definitions, if the

Preparation of this chapter was aided in part by Grant No. MH–07998 from the National Institutes of Health. I am indebted to Bert Green, Jane Loevinger, David Saunders, and M. Brewster Smith for their helpful comments on an earlier draft.

motivational component (for instance) were absent, the psychological event would not be called an attitude.

Within such a framework, an attitude may be regarded as a subclass of the construct *motive,* since it embodies both an affective component and an action tendency. It may be distinguished from other subclasses of motives by the presence of a cognitive (and perhaps also an evaluative) component. A subclass of attitudes may be designated *values,* which, according to some formulations (for example, Jacob and Flink, 1962; Kluckhohn, 1951; Scott, 1965), include the belief that the focal object is desirable or undesirable, independently of the person's own appraisal of it. *Opinion* usually refers to one kind of verbal manifestation of an attitude—the expressing of an evaluative appraisal or prediction concerning the object (Hovland, Janis, and Kelley, 1953; Scott and Withey, 1958).

Attitudes are commonly distinguished from *cognitions* or *beliefs* by the presence of *affect* in the person who entertains the concept (which corresponds, in some languages, to *valence* in the phenomenal object). Attitudes are commonly distinguished from *abilities, capacities,* or *intelligence* not only by the presence of an affective component but also by the conventional assumption that the mere presence of the relevant object is enough to trigger the prepared response, which does not require additional motivation. A person who "knows how" to add will not necessarily do so in the presence of numbers, but the person who "likes" to add may be expected to do so when given the opportunity.

It is customary to distinguish an attitude from a *habit* primarily on the basis of the person's awareness of his propensity or on the availability of channels other than overt action through which to express it. The "habit" of driving on the right side of the road may or may not be verbalized by the habituated person, but he nearly always expresses it in practice. The "preference" for right-hand driving (an attitude) presumably reflects a conscious state that can be expressed verbally, even though the person may not be following his preference at the moment. This distinction between attitude and habit was obliterated in Doob's (1947) behavioristic formulation—a fact which illustrates, in a way, the conventional nature of all such categorical distinctions.

Just what other constructs an attitude is to be distinguished from, or assimilated to, depends on (1) convention within the discipline—which is remarkably loose on this matter, (2) the user's own theoretical purposes—which may vary from one investigator to another, and (3) the outcome of empirical investigations designed to establish the distinctions and similarities (see D. T. Campbell, 1963). These determinants of the definition can be expected to develop and change over the years; hence it is unrealistic to expect a single, final definition of "attitude" to emerge within the foreseeable future.

Instead of pursuing a categorical definition that merits some claim to enduring consensus, one may treat all the defining properties as dimensions which can be conceptualized and measured in varying degrees. Just where, on any of the dimensions, an attitude is to be distinguished from some other concept thus becomes a matter of convenience. Variable properties suggested by recent theoretical formulations include the following.

1. *Direction.* Attitudes are generally conceived as embodying a favorable or unfavorable component representing, on the one hand, *positive* feelings, appraisals, and tendencies to approach or support the object and, on the other hand, *negative* feelings, appraisals, and tendencies to avoid or harm the object (see, for example, Hartley and Hartley, 1952). Though among the most widely accepted properties, direction is a rather complex concept, including such diverse manifestations as hate, suspicion, withdrawal, and attack, or their "opposites," love, trust, and aid. Perhaps these can all be subsumed under the general construct, "increase or decrease of psychological distance from the object," but it is still necessary to establish the functional equivalence of the diverse reactions by something more than verbal classification.

The "directional" property raises, but does not automatically answer, the question as to how *neutral* attitudes are to be conceived. Are they midway between positive and negative attitudes? Should they be subdivided into *indifferent* and *ambivalent* attitudes? (We exclude the possibility that they are not attitudes at all, which would be conceivable from the standpoint of a categorical definition.) The conception of favorable and unfavorable as "opposites" implies that persons will not be found with attitudes simultaneously at both ends of the dimension. Yet an alternative formulation might treat degree of favorableness and degree of unfavorableness as conceptually distinct (though no doubt empirically correlated) components, on which persons may take, simultaneously, a variety of position combinations. In other words, it is only by convention that the direction of an attitude is conceptualized as a single bipolar attribute.

2. *Magnitude.* The magnitude or extremity of an attitude refers to its "degree" of favorableness or unfavorableness (Hartley and Hartley, 1952). A more explicit designation of this property would be *affective magnitude,* in recognition of the fact that other properties may be conceived in terms of magnitude also. But the abbreviated term will be used here throughout, with the expectation that it will not be misunderstood. It is toward measuring this property that most efforts at attitude assessment have been directed; magnitude is readily confused with (or often not distinguished from) intensity.

3. *Intensity.* This property refers to the "strength of feeling" associated with an attitude (Cantril, 1946; Hartley and Hartley, 1952). It seems to be empirically correlated with extremity (Suchman, 1950b). Whether or not one regards this as a tautology depends on one's ability to conceptualize the two attributes in ways that are sufficiently distinct to generate distinguishable sets of measures.

4. *Ambivalence.* This property follows from (1) the conception of "direction" in bipolar terms and (2) the empirical observation that both favorable and unfavorable components may be present in the attitude composite. The greater, and the more equal, these "opposite" tendencies, the higher is the degree of ambivalence (Scott, 1966a).

5. *Salience.* This is the "prominence" of an attitude, or the readiness with which a person expresses it (Hartley and Hartley, 1952; Stern, 1938). It is closely re-

lated to (and perhaps undistinguishable from) the property of *centrality* (Krech and Crutchfield, 1948), which is the "importance" of the focal object to the person.

6. *Affective salience.* The degree of contribution to the attitude constellation of each of the major components (affective, cognitive, conative) may itself be conceived as a property. The term *affective salience* (Scott, 1966a) has been used to refer to the degree to which the person's view of the object is dominated by evaluative or affect-laden content.

7. *Cognitive complexity.* This refers to elaboration of the cognitive component of an attitude—the "richness" of the ideational content, or the number of ideas the person has about the object. Other terms for this property are *differentiation* (French, 1947; Lewin, 1936; Zajonc, 1960) and *multiplexity* (Krech, Crutchfield, and Ballachey, 1962). The degree of complexity may depend, in part, on the scope of the focal object; for example, the collective object "people" may be more complex than "George," simply because "people" includes "George." One may wish to count as contributing to complexity only those ideas which are distinct, rather than redundant with one another; for example, if "personable" and "nice" are synonymous ideas for a particular individual, it is debatable whether their combined use by him in referring to an object represents a more complex attitude than the use of either alone (see Scott, 1962, 1963a).

8. *Overtness.* The prominence of the conative (action) component may be designated as the degree of *overtness* of the attitude (*cf.* "action tendency" in Krech, Crutchfield, and Ballachey, 1962, p. 140). This conceptualization implies that the overt enactment of an attitude is at least partly attributable to characteristics of the person. Situational characteristics undoubtedly play a part as well, and to the degree that they do, the contribution of overtness (as an intraindividual characteristic) will be correspondingly reduced.

9. *Embeddedness.* It has been said that an attitude may exist in relative isolation from other cognitive elements (for example, beliefs, values, other attitudes) or may be connected to such elements through associations, classifications, rationalizations, and so forth (see French, 1947; Krech and Crutchfield, 1948; Scott, 1959). The degree of isolation versus connectedness is referred to here by the term "embeddedness." This may readily be confused with *cognitive complexity* (see above); which term is more apt in any given instance may depend on the scope of the object conceived. The object "mother" may be embedded in a network of associations with distinct concepts (woman, protectiveness, Junior League, and so forth) or, alternatively, such a constellation of ideas may constitute the person's very definition of "mother," in which case it may be preferable to consider the attitudinal object complex, rather than embedded.

10. *Flexibility.* The ease with which an attitude may be modified by a variety of pressures has often been referred to as *flexibility* (or its opposite, *rigidity*). Perhaps most frequently this property has been conceptualized as a pervasive trait of the person rather than as referring to a single attitude, as in the present usage. Moreover, there is usually some implication that the pressures to change are

veridical, that is, that they faithfully reflect characteristics of the focal object (see Scott, 1966b).

11. *Consciousness.* Some writers (for example, French, 1947; Hovland, Janis, and Kelley, 1953) admit the possibility of "unconscious" attitudes, apparently referring to behavior tendencies without direct phenomenological counterparts, that is, attitudes in which the cognitive and affective components are missing (or are not verbalizable by the person). A logical extension of this notion is to conceive a dimension of "degree of consciousness" in the definition of an attitude, admitting a range of availability to awareness. Such a conception encounters problems of operationalization, in that it is difficult to establish criteria for detecting an attitude which is largely "unconscious." If this could be achieved, there would probably remain a question as to the appropriateness of the designation *attitude,* as against, say, *motive* or *habit.*

All the above properties, and many more, refer to characteristics of concepts (ideas) which have been used to define or describe attitudes. Here they are conceived as variable properties which may describe any concept in differing degrees. Whether it is appropriate or useful to conceptualize attitudes so elaborately is an issue we may bypass for the moment. The critical point to be noted is that, if one is to "measure attitudes" as they are conceptualized in the literature, one needs to find ways of operationalizing, and converting to numbers, such diverse and vague properties as these. In actual practice, most of them have not been operationalized satisfactorily, let alone scaled. By far the greatest attention has been devoted to the measurement of magnitude (or intensity), so the ensuing description of measurement procedures will focus exclusively on this property. Comparable measuring procedures could, in principle, be applied to most of the other properties as well.

CONTRIBUTIONS TO ATTITUDE MEASUREMENT

Most attitude measurement, as currently practiced by psychologists, goes on without much attention to formal models of measurement. Yet the various current procedures are in some sense derived from conceptions about measurement that were developed earlier, in a formal or informal way.

Perhaps the most influential, and certainly the best developed, source is psychometric theory, or the *theory of mental tests* (for example, Gulliksen, 1950). Though currently under fire for its evident inadequacies (*cf.,* for example, Dunnette, 1963; Ghiselli, 1963; Loevinger, 1957), it at least has the virtue of explicitness, which renders its inadequacies obvious. A systematically developed alternative has yet to take its place in applied assessment.

Much of scaling theory (for example, Edwards, 1957b; Guilford, 1954; Thurstone, 1959; Thurstone and Chave, 1929; Torgerson, 1958) has roots in psychophysics. A principal concern within this tradition has been with the development of "subjective sensory scales" that correspond to "objectively" definable dimensions of physical stimuli. By contrast, psychometrics is for the most part concerned with traits that have no obvious physical counterparts; nevertheless some simple psychophysical techniques are often used to construct "objective" dimensions based on consensus among judges.

Elaborations and variants on psychometric theory stem from factor analysis (see Cartwright, 1964; Cattell, 1961) and from the recent concern with "moderator variables" (Ghiselli, 1956, 1960; Saunders, 1956). Alternative models of measurement have been proposed, such as Guttman's (1944, 1950) model of ordinal scaling, Guttman's (1953, 1960) image theory, Lazarsfeld's (1950, 1960) latent structure model, and Coombs's (1953, 1964) theory of data. But aside from Guttman's ordinal scaling procedures, none of these models has found wide application to attitude assessment. This may be due, in part, to the belief that the rather laborious procedures for data collection and analysis associated with them are unlikely, under present circumstances, to yield commensurate gains in precision and validity. If this belief is justified, it does not necessarily impugn the models. Quite possibly the fault lies in our imprecise conception of *attitude* or in the laxness of our requirements for validity. If these were more stringent, it is possible that alternative models could be demonstrated superior to classical psychometric theory.

Other influences on attitude-measuring procedures have come from clinical theory and practice. Though not precisely formulated, such notions as *ego defense* and *projection* have led numerous investigators to use techniques intended to assess attitudes without the subject's knowing that this is being done.

The theories and techniques of attitude measurement today are by no means integrated or similarly followed by all psychologists. Therefore, any discussion of them is necessarily inadequate in at least one of two ways: insofar as it is comprehensive, it must be fragmentary and inconsistent; insofar as it is systematic it must neglect a large portion of current practice. The following presentation will display both kinds of inadequacy. Perhaps more coherent systematizations will be possible in the future; and perhaps actual practice will come more and more to reflect the best tentative systematizations of the time.

Measuring direction and magnitude

Of the many properties that have been theoretically attributed to attitudes, most researchers have been concerned with measuring only two: direction and magnitude. Moreover, systematic theories of psychological measurement have generally focused on the second of these two. For the sake of clarity, we shall proceed as if these were the only properties of concern in attitude measurement. However, most of the considerations to be raised here will apply in some way to the measurement of other properties as well—indeed, to the measurement of most psychological variables, attitudinal or not. Therefore, the reader is urged to consider the problems and procedures as they might apply to salience, ambivalence, and other properties enumerated above.

The procedures of attitude assessment may be conveniently separated into three stages: administering, scoring, and interpreting. Though what is done in any one stage depends intimately on what is done in the others, the separation has *prima facie* meaning in that administration deals mainly with the subject's task, scoring is primarily a matter of how the investigator treats the obtained data, and interpretation depends largely on knowledge of results other than those obtained from the persons whose attitudes are currently being assessed.

ADMINISTRATION: TYPES OF MEASURING INSTRUMENTS

Since an attitude is a hypothetical construct, it cannot be directly measured, but must be inferred from subjects' responses. Instruments for measuring attitudes are commonly classified according to the types of responses subjects make. Occasionally, one may rely on naturally emitted responses, but these would be quite undependable under normal circumstances, so it is almost universal practice to present some standardized stimulus calculated to elicit responses which manifest the attitude, without at the same time altering it (or creating it).

Verbal responses are most commonly used, either because they can be easily elicited or because researchers conceive of attitudes in such a way that verbal behavior constitutes the most relevant manifestation. In the typical *open-question* procedure, the subject is presented with a question that invites him to express his attitude (or opinion, belief, feeling) about the focal object. Examples would be: "How do you like the way the President is doing his job these days?" "What do you think is wrong with this country?" "Do you think the sales tax is a good thing?" Besides mentioning the focal object (which may be as simple as "sales tax" or as complex as "this country") and indicating some dimension or dimensions of appraisal (such as "how do you like?" or "what's wrong with?"), the instrument is supposed to suggest no particular response. If it does, it may be criticized as a *leading question*. One should note, however, that even suggesting a dimension of appraisal tends to restrict the subject's responses to a limited number that are most likely to suit the researcher's purpose. The legitimacy of restriction depends on the inferences to be drawn from the response. "What's wrong with this country?" may be an inappropriate leading question if the reply will be used to assess the respondent's overall direction of attitude. But if this has already been ascertained in a less restrictive fashion, then the question is not objectionable for eliciting cognitive elaboration of the attitude.

Advantages typically claimed for the open-question method are that (1) it does not suggest particular answers, which might be uncritically accepted by acquiescent respondents, (2) it permits the researcher to find out whether or not the respondent has *any* attitude toward the object in question, (3) it aids the discovery of a variety of attitudes that might not have been anticipated *a priori*, and (4) it enhances rapport by allowing the respondent to talk about the topic in a way that is natural and interesting to him.

Disadvantages of the open-question procedure are that (1) it is time-consuming for the interviewer, who must record the subject's answers verbatim, (2) it is time-consuming for the coder, who must content-analyze the response according to meaningful dimensions, (3) respondents tend to ramble, so that interviewing time is not used efficiently, (4) in their replies many respondents fail to touch the dimension that the researcher is interested in, so their responses are uncodable, and (5) any particular attitude is assessed from just a small number of questions (due to time limitations in the interview), and hence cannot be so reliably measured as from the multiple-question approach possible with closed questions.

A *closed question* is one in which the subject is confronted, not only with the focal object and the dimension of appraisal, but also with a set of categories from which to choose his reply. The presented categories are typically of the "yes-no," "agree-disagree" variety, though more refined gradations of these dimensions and more complex sets of alternatives are possible with reasonably literate subjects. The advantages and disadvantages of this mode of assessment are the reverse of those listed for open questions. Provided that response categories have been appropriately developed from a pilot study with open questions, the strongest advantage of closed questions is that they force respondents' replies onto the dimension of interest to the researcher, thereby limiting the proportion of uncodable answers. Very likely the strongest disadvantage lies in their threat to rapport; many respondents find long lists of closed questions tedious and even insulting.

Though this is by no means a necessary conjuncture, it typically happens that open questions are used as *single items* (that is, any particular attitude is assessed from responses to one question), while closed questions are more often presented in *multiple-item* sets, so that the subject expresses his attitude in different ways. Multiple-item assessment may be preferred for a variety of reasons: that single items are subject to too much random response error, that any single item necessarily reflects attributes other than the one in which the investigator is interested, that a composite score constructed from multiple items yields a better representation of the intended attitude, that any inference from a measure to a construct requires multiple measures. These arguments are all quite compelling (see below) and lead to one of the clearest recommendations in the entire area of attitude assessment, namely, that any single attitude should be appraised in a sufficient number of different ways to ensure convergence on the intended construct and to obtain a reasonably reliable score for each subject or group of subjects of interest. There is no reason why this practice cannot be followed for open, as well as closed, questions. The only real limitations are set by the subject's tolerance for repetition and by the researcher's desire to assess many attitudes, rather than just a few, in a single instrument.

Given an option for multiple items of the closed-question variety, there are any number of things the subject may be asked to do with them (see Coombs, 1953, 1964). These vary in complexity, from a simple "yes-no" response to each item separately, through a rank-ordering of an entire set according to some designated attribute, to a judgment for every possible triad of items as to which two are closest together and which two are farthest apart on a particular dimension. In general, the more complex the subject's task, (1) the more information can be obtained from his replies and (2) the narrower becomes the range of persons and circumstances for which the technique is applicable. For purposes of measuring attitude magnitude most researchers have not ventured beyond the fairly simple response formats to be described here.

METHOD OF SINGLE STIMULI

The respondent is faced, one at a time, with a series of items which he is invited, in effect, to accept or reject. An example would be: "Do you think that war is inevitable?" Degrees of acceptance or rejection can be discriminated by such questions as: "How likely do you think it is that we are in for another world war—very likely, somewhat likely, quite unlikely, or almost impossible?" Though considerations of rapport and continuity make it desirable to include a related set of items together in the instrument, this practice has the possible disadvantage of inducing spurious consistency among responses. An alternative procedure sometimes employed is to present items from several different attitude domains in mixed-up order, so that questions relevant to any particular domain are scattered throughout the instrument.

METHOD OF FORCED CHOICE BETWEEN PAIRS

Instead of accepting or rejecting each item individually, the subject may be asked, in effect, which member of a pair is more acceptable to him. For example: "Which would you rather do, read a good book or spend an enjoyable evening with friends?" "Which do you think is the more serious crime, treason against your country or sexual perversion?" In general, the aim of the forced-choice technique is to increase the discriminating power of an item by obtaining approximately equal proportions of acceptances and rejections. If presented alone, either of the alternatives might be either uniformly accepted or uniformly rejected, thus contributing nothing to the assessment of individual differences. When paired with another item of equal popularity, its chances for acceptance are more moderate (that is, increased or decreased toward the 0.50 probability range).

The method of forced choice between pairs thus salvages many items which would otherwise be discarded for lack of discrimination. It may also be useful for assessing very weak attitudes which would not be admitted by the person with single-stimulus items. However, the method has at least two attendant disadvantages: (1) The choices are quite frequently unrealistic ones, which may antagonize some people and elicit responses that are highly unstable. (2) If the same two attributes are consistently pitted against each other in the choices, this procedure necessarily generates a perfect negative correlation between them; hence, their status as "opposites" is established by definition rather than by empirical demonstration. Even if a single critical attribute is pitted against alternatives representing a number of different attributes, the resulting contamination by extraneous variables reduces the internal consistency of the multiple-item set.

METHOD OF MULTIPLE CHOICE

A logical extension of this kind of forced choice is a procedure in which the subject is presented with a set of stimuli and asked to distinguish two or more degrees of acceptability among them. The set of stimuli may be constructed in at least two ways, depending on the purpose of assessment. If the aim is to elicit an ordering of equally popular (or unpopular) alternatives, then one stimulus representing the critical attribute is paired with a noncritical stimulus of equal popularity. The number of such pairs included in the set may vary and the instructions to subjects concerning the number to be picked will be adapted accordingly. For instance, one might wish to assess anti-Semitism with a triad such as:

A. A large city typically contains people of diverse ethnic backgrounds and different political beliefs.

B. It is desirable to have some communists in a large city.

C. It is not desirable to have many Jews in a large city.

Only alternative *C* reflects the intended attribute. It is paired in popularity with *B*. The subject's task is to choose the two statements which he finds most nearly acceptable.

Another set might consist of two popular and two unpopular statements, from which the subject is to choose the one with which he agrees most and the one with which he disagrees most. For example:

A. Jews have contributed a great deal to all aspects of society.

B. A society thrives on diversity of viewpoints.

C. This country would be better off without the Jews.

D. All candidates for political office should be members of some established church.

It is intended that *A* and *C* measure the critical attribute, that *A* and *B* are equally popular, and that *C* and *D* are also paired for popularity. A major purpose of such enlarged stimulus sets is to make the forced choice more palatable to respondents, while at the same time eliciting unpopular replies.

Quite a different aim is embodied in sets of stimuli which are graded *a priori* along a single dimension. It is assumed that any subject will find one or more of the alternatives acceptable; hence, no limit need be placed on the number of choices. For example:

Which of the following proposals about the United Nations do you agree with? (Check as many as applicable.)

A. The United Nations should be disbanded.

B. The United States should withdraw from the United Nations.

C. *We should continue to belong to the U.N., but not participate in, or rely on, its procedures.*

D. *We should continue to participate in U.N. procedures very much as we have been doing.*

E. *We should try to find ways of strengthening the U.N. so that it becomes more effective.*

F. *We should be prepared to give up some of our national sovereignty in order to make the U.N. stronger.*

G. *The United Nations should be made into a government of the world, with power to control the armed forces of all member nations.*

H. *There should be only one world government, and separate national governments should be disbanded.*

If the magnitudes of the items can be established (see pp. 224–230), then it is possible to interpret the subject's choice as indicating his own "position" on the scale of magnitude; that is, it may be assumed that he accepts those items closest to his own position. If a subject accepts more than one item, his own scale position is taken as the average of those chosen.

INDIRECT MEASURES

The vast majority of attitude tests are constructed to take advantage of the subject's self-awareness and readiness to communicate this verbally. It is assumed, in effect, that the meaning he attributes to the stimulus item and the meaning he intends to convey by his reply are roughly similar, respectively, to the meanings intended and inferred by the investigator. This is not to say that the intended and inferred meanings are identical; a sufficiently searching inquiry would undoubtedly detect misunderstandings even with the best of communications. Nor is it to say that the subject knows and communicates his "true" attitude with fidelity; the investigator's construct of the subject's attitude may be only approximated by the latter's construct of his own attitude, if indeed he has one. Rather, it is assumed that the investigator's operationalization of the attitude, embodied in the test items, is understood similarly by both himself and the subject and that the latter replies in such a way that the researcher understands him in fair congruence with his own intent. For example, the reply "no" to the question, "Would you want your daughter to marry a Negro?" may not be intended by the subject to manifest an anti-Negro attitude, even though the experimenter interprets it in this way. But both subject and experimenter may reasonably assume that the other interprets this reply to mean that the subject would not want his daughter to marry a Negro. Now the experimenter may additionally interpret this response as a categorical rejection of the hypothetical event under all circumstances, whereas the subject intends it only as an expression of preference, other things being equal. Thus, the meanings intended and inferred are not, in detail, identical; the construct inferred by the experimenter departs from the subject's own construct about himself. Yet, in this interchange, there is an intent on both sides to communicate veridically with shared meanings.

There are some circumstances in which the researcher may feel that he cannot assume a common intent and readiness to communicate with shared verbal symbols. This may be attributed to the subject's incapacity for understanding the symbols in the intended way, but more commonly it is attributed to his unwillingness to convey his own introspections, once he has understood how the experimenter intends to interpret them. Thus, the subject's introspections and understandings are deemed likely to impede, rather than aid, the experimenter's appraisal of his attitude. There is very little evidence about the conditions under which this reversal of assumptions may be justified, or about how one can find out, for any particular subject, whether to assume that shared symbols facilitate or impede assessment of attitudes. Perhaps the contrast is overdrawn; it may be better to assume that in some ways shared symbols facilitate and in other ways they impede this procedure. Still one would wish to know, for a given subject, which direction of effect is likely to predominate, and how best to overcome the impedance.

One approach to overcoming impedance is rapport building, attempting to convince the respondent that he ought to reply veridically with shared symbols. Techniques applied in this direction include the use of interviewers (or test administrators) whom the respondent is likely to trust, the promise of anonymity, repeated assurances that a variety of replies (including, presumably, the respondent's own reply) are common and acceptable, and appeals to conscientiousness that are relevant to the subject's evident interests. Another approach to overcoming impedance is instruction, an attempt to convey in the interview or questionnaire the meanings of the symbols as intended by the researcher. (This approach assumes that the chief source of impedance is not intent to deceive but a failure to understand the symbols in the experimenter's terms.)

An entirely different approach is for the experimenter himself to forsake the common symbol system and present stimulus items that will be understood by the subject in a way different from the experimenter's intent. A disguised measure of attitudes is one in which the task presented to the subject conveys one meaning to him, while the experimenter's interpretation of his response is based on a different meaning system. Techniques for disguised appraisal (see Campbell, 1950; Cook and Selltiz, 1964) include:

1. The presentation of pictured objects to which the subject reacts with a statement of preference and the experimenter interprets the reply as indicating the subject's attitude toward a particular class to which the object may be assigned. For example, Horowitz (1936) had children rank pictures of Negro and white children for acceptability and inferred degree of anti-Negro prejudice from their replies. In such a task, the subject's and the experimenter's meanings may be quite close (if the subject's replies are based on the particular class distinction made by the experimenter, and if the significance of the subject's discriminations is the same as that imputed by the experimenter), or they may be very different

(for example, if the subject is responding on the basis of familiarity and the experimenter interprets the category preference as implying readiness to injure the nonpreferred object).

2. The presentation of pictures in which the subject's task is defined to him as one of interpreting or telling a story about them (a cognitive or imaginative meaning), and the experimenter interprets the reply as conveying an attitude toward the person or situation portrayed (see Proshansky, 1943; Scott, 1956).

3. The presentation of informational questions together with answers that can be scored according to their degree of favorableness toward the object. Two answers "wrong" in opposite directions may be provided, as in the *error-choice* technique (Hammond, 1948; Weschler, 1950); or correct answers included among the distractors may sometimes favor and sometimes disfavor the object (Campbell and Damarin, 1961; Rankin and Campbell, 1955).

4. Other disguised techniques (see Cook and Selltiz, 1964) include memorization of favorable and unfavorable material about an object, completion of syllogisms with favorable and unfavorable conclusions, and judging characteristics of test items, such as their degree of favorableness toward the object or their plausibility (Waly and Cook, 1965). The subject's task in these as well as in the error-choice method is defined as a cognitive one, but the investigator interprets his response in attitudinal terms. Actually, it is a rare study in which such techniques are used as a primary means of diagnosing attitudes; rather, the investigators have generally been interested only in demonstrating that performance on such tasks was a function of attitudes which were assessed in other ways (for example, by self-report or by group membership).

The strategy of such disguised techniques requires that the subject interpret his response as reflecting a characteristic different from the one the experimenter is prepared to infer. In order for the subject to adopt the desired interpretation, this would normally require that performance on the task actually depend substantially on some nonattitudinal determinant, such as information, logical reasoning, or capacity for making discriminations. To the extent that this is so, the attitudinal component must be correspondingly reduced.

PHYSIOLOGICAL MEASURES

Another possible approach to attitude measurement suggested by Cook and Selltiz (1964) entails a short-circuiting of the subject's introspection and verbal communication altogether. One may obtain measures of autonomic arousal, such as heartbeat, galvanic skin response, pupil dilation, and so forth, while the subject is viewing, or thinking about, or interacting with, the object (see Rankin and Campbell, 1955; Westie and DeFleur, 1959). In spite of recent optimistic reports from Hess (1965), it is unlikely that such autonomic responses can be used to represent any property of attitudes other than intensity (see Loewenfeld, 1958; Woodmansee, 1965); if one is concerned with the other properties enumerated earlier, one will probably find physiological measures of these kinds unprofitable. But it is quite possible that some combination of autonomic responses would yield a measure of intensity more valid than direct verbal reports for certain attitudes of certain persons. Since this technique would be quite cumbersome to administer, one would probably want to use it in conjunction with some preliminary diagnostic device (see pp. 231–232) to ascertain whether or not the autonomic measures will be necessary and useful.

OVERT BEHAVIOR

Many researchers would maintain that the ultimate criterion for any alleged measure of an attitude is the person's behavior in regard to the focal object. From this perspective, it follows that the most appropriate measure of an attitude is provided by a sample of the behavior which is to be predicted. One is still confronted, however, with the pragmatic necessity of confining one's sample of assessed behaviors to those which can conceivably be elicited and, more restrictively, to those which can be elicited conveniently. Cook and Selltiz (1964) describe three kinds of readily elicited behaviors: role playing, sociometric choices, and realistically contrived decisions which the person believes will affect him.

In role playing, the subject is asked to make believe he is relating to the critical object under defined circumstances. His way of dealing with it may be coded into categories representing certain properties (usually direction or magnitude) of an inferred underlying attitude.

The sociometric method (see Chapter 14) is most easily applied to person objects, but it could also be extended to other objects, such as nations and institutions. It requires the person to choose from a list those objects with which he would most like to relate in a specified context. (Alternatively, all objects on the list may be rated.) The responses elicited by such instruments are scarcely more overt than those required by the usual self-report inventories. However, if the subject believes that his choices will have consequences for himself (as recommended by Moreno, 1934), he may take them more seriously than the typical introspective question.

Among the realistic decision situations discussed by Cook and Selltiz (1964) is one developed by DeFleur and Westie (1958), in which white respondents were asked whether they would be willing to pose with a Negro for photographs which the researcher would subsequently publish. Comparably meaningful decisions could be contrived for a variety of attitudinal objects. The purpose of the realism and fabrication concerning consequences for the subject is to make him consider his reply very carefully and be sure that he means it. Rarely is there a deliberate attempt to conceal from the subject the attitudinal implications of his response, although this too might be accomplished by appropriate contrivances.

SCORING RESPONSES

Responses elicited in the test administration phase—verbal, physiological, or overt—must be converted into scores by means of some scale representing that property of the attitude which is of interest. The property of direction is typically represented on a two- or three-point scale, whose categories are defined as *favorable, unfavorable,* and (perhaps) *neutral.* The property of magnitude may be represented dichotomously (by the categories *present* and *absent*), or with a more finely articulated verbal scale (such as *very favorable, moderately favorable, slightly favorable,* and *not favorable*), or with a set of numbers that are intended to represent finer gradations.

JUDGMENTAL SCORING

Depending on the kind of stimuli presented and the kind of response elicited, the translation from response to scale will be made in different ways. Responses to open questions or overt behavior elicited by role playing, for example, are typically scored judgmentally. The researcher chooses to distinguish two or more categories of magnitude into which all responses are classified. Usually the direction and magnitude scales are combined; for example, the category set *very favorable–favorable–neutral–unfavorable–very unfavorable* represents two directions, each with three degrees of magnitude (if we count the middle category as the lowest value for both directions).

The fineness of discriminations (that is, the number of categories) will depend on the coder's judgmental acuity, the variability among the responses coded, and the purpose to which the scale is to be put (for example, to predict a dichotomous or a multichotomous criterion). The central tendency and variability of judgments are presumably subject to anchor effects, so that classification of one response depends somewhat on the sample of other responses with which it is considered. Ideally, the researcher will first peruse a representative sample of responses to which the category set is to be applied, then code these and try the set out on another representative sample. Tentatively satisfied with his own judgments, he will next train a coworker to perform the same discriminations and the two will independently code still another representative sample of responses and check their agreement. Their level of agreement will depend on the similarity of their conceptions of the attribute, on the equivalence of their judgmental acuities, and on the variability of responses in the sample.

SUMMATIVE SCALES

We shall use the term *summative* to designate a scale that is scored by adding the response scores on its component items. Variations on the summative scoring procedure appear throughout psychological testing. In the Likert (1932) technique of attitude assessment, subjects respond to a series of items in single-stimulus form, indicating their degree of agreement or disagreement, usually on a five-point rating scale which might be represented by the whole numbers from -2 to $+2$. The direction and magnitude of the attitude is computed as the sum of item scores; this sum may therefore range, maximally, between $-2k$ and $+2k$ (where k is the number of items).

Under classical psychometric procedures (see Gulliksen, 1950) subjects respond to a series of items in single-stimulus form, indicating whether or not they possess the attribute (for example, intelligence or arithmetic ability) that is presumably required in order to "pass" all items. The magnitude of the attribute is represented by a score (between zero and k) which shows the number of items passed.

In the method of forced choice between pairs, subjects are confronted with successive pairs of statements, one of which always represents a particular attribute that is of focal interest, and the other of which may represent either another single attribute (assumed "opposite" to the focal one) or else a variety of different attributes which are not, in themselves, of focal interest. The magnitude of each subject's focal attribute is represented as the number of pairs in which he picks the critical alternative. The scale thus ranges, maximally, between zero and k (the number of pairs).

In the method of controlled marginals (Willis, 1960, 1961) the subject responds to a series of single-stimulus items, indicating in each case his extent of agreement or disagreement, as in the Likert technique. The distribution of responses to each item is subsequently dichotomized as close to the median as possible, and the item is scored zero (lower half of the distribution) or 1 (upper half). The magnitude of the attribute is represented as the sum of (dichotomous) item scores; thus the scale will range, maximally, between zero and k.

In any of these procedures, adding the item scores together implies that each item is a linear (or at least monotonic) function of the same attribute. (Such an item has been called *monotone* by Coombs, 1953.) The relation of any item to the (presumably) common attribute is ordinarily established by correlational procedures. A simple method is to correlate each item score with the total scale score. Since the latter includes the former as a component, it will be artificially inflated. This contamination may be eliminated by means of a correction formula developed by Peters and Van Voorhis (1940):

$$r_{i(T-i)} = \frac{r_{iT}\sigma_T - \sigma_i}{\sqrt{\sigma_T^2 + \sigma_i^2 - 2r_{iT}\sigma_i\sigma_T}},$$

where r_{iT} is the correlation between item and uncorrected total, σ_T is the standard deviation of total test scores, and σ_i is the standard deviation of the scores obtained on the item.

Items which show a sufficiently high correlation with the total score are retained in the scale, and items which do not are rejected. A new scale is then constructed, comprising only the remaining items.

While quite rapid as a method for item selection, this procedure will yield deceptive results if the initial scale is made up of two or three different kinds of items (that is, independent clusters) constituting roughly equal portions of the total. Each item may then correlate with the total score, even though it would correlate much better with its own independent cluster, considered alone, and would thus better be included in that subscale only. If the scale consists of two subclusters of items which are negatively correlated with each other, item-total correlations are likely to be near zero and the subscales will not be detected.

If one has reason to suspect that all items in the scale may not measure a single attribute, it is better to correlate each of them with every other item. Inspection of the correlation matrix may reveal some items which are responsible for substantial numbers of negative correlations and other items which form highly intercorrelated subsets that are relatively independent of one another. Such an inspectional analysis may thus lead to the conception of two or three distinct attitudes instead of the one from which the items were developed. Even if the analysis leads only to discarding a few bad items, this will require comparing them with the remaining items to see if a reconceptualization is in order. If the discards consist entirely of items with low variance, the original conception may stand. But if the differences between retained and rejected items are attributable instead to item content or wording, then the investigator will need to redefine the attribute represented by the remaining items, being careful to distinguish it from whatever the rejected items seem to represent. Ideally, he will then proceed to write new items which fit the revised conception, administer them together with the remaining items to a new sample of subjects, and intercorrelate as before, to test the adequacy of the new definition. (Loevinger, Gleser, and DuBois, 1953, proposed an analytic method, subsequently adapted by Loevinger, 1962, which enables quite mechanical decisions on item clusters via computer. The phase of reconceptualization and writing of new items remains highly judgmental.)

This cyclic process of writing items, intercorrelating responses, and reconceptualizing the construct may continue for quite some time before a satisfactory cluster of mutually intercorrelated items results. A common reason for slow convergence is the researcher's stubborn clinging to a preconception of what constitutes the relevant attitudinal domain. He may, for instance, insist on trying to measure an overall "attitude toward Negroes" in a population whose conceptions of the object are so role-specific that it would be necessary to distinguish "attitude toward working with Negroes" from "attitude toward letting one's children play with Negro children," etc. If, in fact, such item clusters are empirically independent, nothing is gained by pooling them into a total score of "overall attitude," for the total score (except at its extremes) yields no information from which to predict any particular external criterion. If, for purely theoretical (rather than pragmatic) purposes, several subclusters of items are to be subsumed under a single comprehensive term, it is first necessary to establish their functional equivalence. The fact that they all refer to the same object is insufficient for this purpose, for the object may have quite different meanings depending on the context within which the person views it. If this is the case, then the notion of "overall attitude" toward the object is not useful.

FACTOR SCORING

Instead of accepting the apparent meaning of mutually correlated items as defining the attribute, some researchers prefer to search for genotypes that underlie superficial similarities and diversities. One approach to this search for genotypes is via the several techniques of factor extraction and rotation (Harman, 1960).

It is believed by many practitioners that "factors" resulting from such analyses represent the psychologically primary genotypes better than do the simple clusters of intercorrelated items.

A factor score may be developed in either of two ways. The simpler method is to add, for each subject, his score on those items which load the factor above a certain arbitrary value (such as 0.30). Alternatively, one may build a weighted factor score, multiplying each item score by the loading of that item on the factor, and adding these products over all items. Either of these scoring methods typically results in the inclusion of several items in more than one factor score. This produces spuriously intercorrelated factor scores and makes it difficult to conceptualize a factor from the manifest content of the items included in it. Indeed, if an item loads substantially on two different factors, this may result from the fact that some subjects respond on the basis of one factor and other subjects respond on the basis of the other factor. For any given subject, therefore, it is hard to tell in which factor score the item should be included. Some practitioners regard such a consideration as sufficient ground for eliminating any multiple-factor items from an attitude scale.

CUMULATIVE SCALING

Another method of scoring multiple items of the single-stimulus form is proposed within the scaling theory developed by Guttman (1944, 1950). It is based on the assumption that a set of items which measure a single, unidimensional trait can be ordered along a continuum of "difficulty" or magnitude, representing the amount of the trait required for a person to accept the item. (See pp. 246–248 for an elaboration of this assumption.) For items of this "cumulative" type, acceptance of one implies that the person possesses enough of the attribute to accept all items of lesser magnitude.* In practice, item magnitude is measured as the complement of item popularity. If p is the proportion of subjects who accept an item, then $q \ (= 1 - p)$ represents its order of magnitude. Examples of cumulative items for two different traits are:

Trait: *arithmetic ability*

Least difficult: *A. What is 2 + 3?*

                 B. What is 25 + 38?

                 C. What is 14 + (38 − 17)?

                 D. What is 12 ÷ (7 + 4 − 5)?

Most difficult: *E. What is 43 (19 + 84) ÷ 17 (312 − 176)?*

---

* Other writers (for example, Loevinger, 1957) use the term *cumulative* in the same sense as *summative* was defined above, to refer to scales scored by adding items together. The present terminology seems more descriptive. A *cumulative* scale is one whose items can be ordered in magnitude, representing cumulative amounts of the common trait. Items in a *summative* scale may be ordered in popularity, but this is not interpreted as representing differential magnitude; in scoring, all dichotomous items are treated as if they required the same amount of the attribute for acceptance.

Trait: *favorableness of attitude toward fluoridation* (manifested by acceptance of item)

Least difficult: *A. It is all right for people to drink fluoridated water if they wish.*

B. If people want fluorine in their water but can't afford it, it is all right for the city to pay for it.

C. The city should publicize the availability of free fluorine for those who want it.

D. The city should add fluorine to the water so that all people get it automatically.

Most difficult: *E. The city government should require that all citizens drink some fluoridated water each day.*

The method of scoring responses to such cumulative scales is based on the derivation that, if the items are ordered in magnitude along a single dimension, only the following answer patterns will appear:

Accept no item. (score 0)
Accept item *A* only. (score 1)
Accept items *A* and *B* only. (score 2)
Accept items *A*, *B*, and *C* only. (score 3)
Accept items *A*, *B*, *C*, and *D* only. (score 4)
Accept all items. (score 5)

Any other response pattern (for example, accept *B* only) is taken to imply either that the subject is not responding according to the intended dimension or that he made an error of response.

The investigator's first task in analyzing cumulative scales is to ascertain the degree to which the initial set of items represents a single dimension; this is inferred from the degree to which subjects respond with the admissible answer patterns (known as *scale types*). It is assumed, tentatively, that any nonscale pattern reflects one or more response errors. The number of response errors counted is the minimal number of changes required to convert a nonscale response pattern into a scale type. For instance, the pattern, accept *C* only, could be made scalar with a minimum of one change: to reject *C*. The pattern, accept *D* and *E* only, could be made scalar with a minimum of two changes: reject *D* and *E*. The pattern, accept *B* only, requires one change: either accept *A* or reject *B*.

The total number of response errors (*e*) made by a sample of subjects is divided by the total number of all responses they make (*nk*, where *n* is the number of subjects and *k* is the number of items). This ratio is subtracted from unity to yield the *coefficient of reproducibility*, *R*:

$$R = 1 - \frac{e}{nk}.$$

The value of *R* may be used as a measure of the degree to which the set of items is scalable, that is, represents a unidimensional attribute. An arbitrary value of

0.90 is sometimes taken as the minimal boundary of the acceptance region. However, the value of R depends largely on the magnitudes of the items in the scale. With five items all having popularities of 0.90, the *minimum* value of R (if we assume that no item is scored in the wrong direction) is 0.92; if the popularities of the items were all 0.50, then R could be as low as 0.19. Thus the value obtained for R is best interpreted in relation to its minimum value, given the popularities of items in the scale. This may be represented by the *coefficient of scalability* (Menzel, 1953), the *index of consistency* (Green, 1956), or the *error ratio* (Borgatta, 1955). Loevinger's (1947, 1948) index of test homogeneity, H_t, is also preferable to R as a measure of unidimensionality, since it varies between 0 and 1, regardless of the distribution of item popularities.

Generally, the reproducibility or scalability of a set can be increased by eliminating certain items which account for a disproportionate number of errors. This may be done visually if analyses are performed on a *scalogram board* (Suchman, 1950a), or analytically with a computer program (Gordon, 1963; Werner, 1966). However, the number of errors contributed by an item is a function of its popularity, moderately popular items contributing the most. Two equally popular items will either contribute a substantial number of errors or be mutually redundant. In either case, one of them will not improve discrimination among subjects, since it appears at the same point of magnitude on the dimension as the other. Such an item may be eliminated in the course of scale analysis, or it may be dichotomized at a different point (to change its level of magnitude), or it may be combined with one or more other items to produce a single artificial "item" (see Stouffer *et al.*, 1952).

Once a scalable item set has been selected from preliminary analyses, it should be administered to a new sample of subjects and the results replicated before it is treated as a unidimensional scale. (This step is often short-circuited, and scoring is performed on the same subjects whose responses were used to establish the scale. Such a procedure takes undue advantage of chance, inflating the apparent scalability of the item set and yielding scores that may be misleading because they include items that would not scale in a cross-validation.) Scoring of subjects then proceeds according to the principle of minimal errors on the assumption that the order of magnitude of the items is established by their relative popularities. A subject's responses are changed minimally to obtain a scalar type; his scale score is then taken to be the number of accepted items in that type. For example:

$$A^+ \; B^+ \; C^- \; D^- \; E^+$$

is changed to

$$A^+ \; B^+ \; C^- \; D^- \; E^-$$

and the subject is scored 2. Or

$$A^+ \; B^+ \; C^- \; D^+ \; E^-$$

may be changed to

$$A^+ \; B^+ \; C^- \; D^- \; E^-,$$

in which case the subject is scored 2; or to

$$A^+ \ B^+ \ C^+ \ D^+ \ E^-,$$

in which case he is scored 4.

Though cumulative scales, like summative scales, are composed of monotone items (that is, item scores are positively correlated with scale scores), the additional property of item magnitude is taken into account by the scoring procedure just described. Clearly, this procedure is cumbersome, arbitrary, and difficult to specify analytically so that a computer program can be written for it. Some researchers, instead, score cumulative scales as if they were simple summative scales, just by counting the number of items accepted, regardless of their magnitudes (Ford, 1950; Green, 1956). Though logically inconsistent with the theory of the scale, this simpler procedure has been found to yield scores that are substantially correlated with the minimal-errors procedure (Green, 1954). This result suggests that the magnitude model embodied in cumulative scales (see pp. 246–250) is perhaps superfluous.

There are other reasons besides analytical complexity for rejecting the cumulative scaling procedure. Whether items are retained or discarded depends more on variations in item popularities than on degree of intercorrelation or functional equivalence. The ideal model of scalogram analysis assumes unidimensional items, which probably do not exist (since this implies that responses depend on a single attribute only, which is contrary to most psychological conceptions). The kinds of items retained are typically those which are widely spread in popularity (this minimizes the number of errors). Given the usual contribution to item responses of "random" and item-specific variance, a wide distribution of item magnitudes will not contribute maximally to the detection of intersubject differences in the focal attribute (see pp. 258–259). Therefore, the cumulative scaling procedure is mentioned here only because it has been widely used; it is not recommended for attitude measurement.

CONSENSUAL LOCATION SCALING

The scoring procedure employed with Thurstone scales (Edwards, 1957b; Green, 1954; Thurstone, 1959; Thurstone and Chave, 1929) is also based on the assumption that the items measuring an attribute can be ordered according to a dimension of magnitude (that is, varying amounts of the same attribute are required for acceptance). However, the items in this case are noncumulative; acceptance of one does not imply acceptance of all those of lesser magnitude. They are also nonmonotone (hence nonsummative), in that item scores do not correlate with each other or with the common attribute. Rather, each item represents a level of magnitude distinct from that of other items. Examples of nonmonotone items relating to a single attitude dimension might be:

Trait: *favorableness of attitude toward fluoridation*

Least favorable: *A. The use of fluorine in drinking water should be prohibited.*

B. *People should be allowed to use fluorine in their water by a doctor's prescription only.*

C. *People should have the right to use or not use fluoridated water as they wish.*

D. *City water should be fluoridated, but people should be permitted to use nonfluoridated sources if they wish.*

Most favorable: E. *The city should require that all citizens drink some fluoridated water each day.*

A comparison of the above scale with that presented on page 222 illustrates the intended difference between monotone and nonmonotone items. The former have to be written so that acceptance of a high-magnitude (or low-popularity) item does not preclude acceptance of a low-magnitude item. The latter have to be written so that acceptance of any item tends to preclude acceptance of all others. These aims are very difficult to accomplish for many attributes. It is almost impossible to write sensible nonmonotone items for an ability dimension. Monotone items at the extreme low (or negative) end of an attitudinal dimension are difficult to write in a direct way, so the usual practice is to write reverse-worded items, the rejection of which is taken to manifest the intended attitude. The extreme items in a consensual location scale generally turn out to be monotone (as items *A* and *E* in the present example), and could equally well be used in a cumulative scale, provided one of them is reverse-scored.

Whereas the magnitude of a cumulative item is taken to be the complement of its popularity, this is not appropriate for nonmonotone items, whose acceptance rates are unrelated to item magnitude. Instead, the magnitude scale is established by judges before the instrument is ever administered to subjects. The task set for judges is different from that which will ultimately be required of subjects (that is, the acceptance or rejection of each item for themselves). Judges are asked to react to the items, not in relation to themselves, but in relation to the dimension specified. This may be done in various ways, for example, by paired comparisons or by variations on the method of single stimuli (Edwards, 1957b; Guilford, 1954). For example, in the *method of successive intervals*, judges are required to sort a preliminary sample of items into a number of piles according to the magnitude of the attribute they represent. (With noncumulative items, direction and magnitude can both be represented in the same scale, so the piles usually range from extremely favorable to extremely unfavorable, instead of from weak to strong.) In the *method of paired comparisons* every item is presented in a pair with every other item, and the judges' task is to state which member of each pair represents more of the attribute.

Items which elicit fair consensus among judges are retained in the scale, and numbers representing magnitude are assigned to them on the basis of assumptions contained in Thurstone's Laws of Comparative Judgment (Thurstone, 1959; Thurstone and Chave, 1929). Case V of these Laws contains enough strong assumptions to make it attractive to practitioners: for instance, that the difference in magnitude between any two items, A and B, can be represented by the standard normal deviate which divides the area under a normal curve in proportion to the ratio between the frequency of judgments that $A > B$ and the frequency of judgments that $B > A$. Some pairs of items are so far apart on the scale that there is no disagreement among judges as to their relative magnitudes; the distance between such items cannot be ascertained directly, for the standard normal deviate would be indeterminate. Only those pairs of items close enough together on the scale to elicit some disagreement as to their relative magnitudes can be used to establish the distance function. (In standard practice, only pairs for which there is at least $2\frac{1}{2}$ percent disagreement are considered, under the assumption that the standard normal deviate is unreliably estimated for percentages smaller than that.)

It is ordinarily the case, with a large initial item pool, that the distance between any pair of items can be measured in several indirect ways. For instance, the distance between items A and B can be measured indirectly as the difference between their respective distances from C, or from D, and so on. The number of such indirect measurements that can be taken depends on the density of items in the region of the scale near the AB pair. Items so far away from one of these that little interjudge disagreement as to relative magnitude occurs cannot be used to obtain indirect measures. The mean of all direct and indirect measures available from the set of judgments is taken as the best estimate of the distance between adjacent items. Table 1 illustrates, with hypothetical data, the procedure for assigning magnitudes to items on the basis of paired comparison judgments.

First, it is advisable to arrange the items in order of their magnitude (this can be ascertained, approximately, by inspecting the pattern of judgments), numbering them from 1 (representing greatest amount of the attribute) to k (total number of items). This will tend to make the values in the third column greater than 0.50 and those in the fourth column greater than 0.00. The third column indicates the proportion of times that item A was judged to represent more of the attribute than item B. Since the judgment "equal" is not permitted, the complements of these figures indicate the proportion of times item B was judged to represent more of the attribute than item A. The fourth column shows the z-scores corresponding to the p-values of the third column. These may be read from an ordinary table of areas under the normal curve, by subtracting 0.50 from the values in the third column, and determining the z-value which includes that proportion of the area to the right of the mean (0.00). If any p-value in the third column is less than 0.50, it should be subtracted from 0.50, and the z-score which is read from the normal curve table should be entered as negative.

The z-scores in the fourth column represent, according to the Laws of Comparative Judgment (Case V), estimates of the psychological distances between the respective pairs of items: z-scores larger than 2.00 (absolute value) are omitted, because they are quite unreliable; that is, they would change markedly with a trivial change in p. The best estimate of the scale distance between items A and B is determined as the mean of all z-differences in which both items are involved. For instance, z_{12} can be estimated from $z_{13} - z_{23}$ ($= 0.67 - 0.39$) and from $z_{14} - z_{24}$ ($= 1.13 - 0.81$). (It cannot be estimated, in the present illustration, from $z_{15} - z_{25}$

TABLE 1

CONSENSUAL JUDGMENT SCALING BY THE METHOD
OF PAIRED COMPARISONS (ADAPTED FROM GREEN, 1954)

A	B	$p_{A>B}$	z	Indirect z-scores for adjacent pairs	Mean
1	2	0.55	0.13	$0.00 - (-0.13)$; $0.13 - 0.00$; $0.67 - 0.39$; $1.13 - 0.81$	0.22
1	3	0.75	0.67		
1	4	0.87	1.13		
1	5	0.98			
1	6	1.00			
2	3	0.65	0.39	$-0.13 - (-0.67)$; $0.00 - (-0.39)$; $0.39 - 0.00$; $0.81 - 0.67$; $1.65 - 1.34$	0.35
2	4	0.79	0.81		
2	5	0.95	1.65		
2	6	1.00			
3	4	0.75	0.67	$-0.67 - (-1.13)$; $-0.39 - (-0.81)$; $0.00 - (-0.67)$; $0.67 - 0.00$; $1.34 - 0.99$	0.51
3	5	0.91	1.34		
3	6	0.99			
4	5	0.84	0.99	$-0.81 - (-1.65)$; $-0.67 - (-1.34)$; $0.00 - (-0.99)$; $0.99 - 0.00$; $1.41 - 0.77$	0.83
4	6	0.92	1.41		
5	6	0.78	0.77	$-0.99 - (-1.41)$; $0.00 - (-0.77)$; $0.77 - 0.00$	0.65

Item:		6	5	4	3	2	1
Scale value:		0.00	0.65	1.48	1.99	2.34	2.56

or from $z_{16} - z_{26}$, because some of these z-values are indeterminate or unreliable.) In addition, it is assumed that if item 1 had been paired with itself the p-value would have been 0.50 and the corresponding z would be 0.00. This assumption provides two more estimates of the z-distance between items 1 and 2, that is, $z_{11} - z_{21}$ $[0.00 - (-0.13)]$ and $z_{12} - z_{22}$ $(0.13 - 0.00)$—which is equivalent to including twice the direct estimate of the z_{12}-distance (0.13). All of these estimates are averaged to yield the mean z-distance indicated in the right-hand column, and the same is done for each of the other adjacent pairs (mean z_{23}, mean z_{34}, mean z_{45}, and mean z_{56}).

The mean values in the right-hand column thus represent the best estimates of the distances between the successive stimuli on the psychological continuum. Since the origin of this continuum is arbitrary, it is customary to assign the value 0.00 to the lowest-valued item and add the estimated intervals (mean z-values) successively to yield the subsequent item values. These are indicated at the bottom of Table 1.

The conception underlying this scaling procedure is sound but, unfortunately, the gain in precision of estimated scale values does not justify the labor involved. A much simpler procedure will yield equivalent results in nearly all practical cases. This procedure is to assign scale values directly from the table of p-values as the mean proportion of times that each item is judged greater than every other item on the stimulus dimension. Table 2 illustrates this simplified procedure. Entries below the diagonal are identical to those contained in Table 1; entries above the diagonal are their complements. The mean column percentage for any item (if one ignores the assumed diagonal p of 0.50, which is never actually assessed) may be taken as its scale value. In the present example, scale values assigned in this simplified way correlate 0.998 with the scale values arrived at in Table 1 by the traditional method. The reason for this close correspondence is that the relation between p and z is very nearly linear (product-moment correlation = 0.98) within the range of values customarily considered (that is, between $p = 0.03$ and $p = 0.97$).

TABLE 2

SIMPLIFIED SCALING FROM PAIRED COMPARISON DATA
(TABLE ENTRIES REPRESENT $p_{A>B}$)

		A					
		1	2	3	4	5	6
B	1		0.45	0.25	0.13	0.02	0.00
	2	0.55		0.35	0.21	0.05	0.00
	3	0.75	0.65		0.25	0.09	0.01
	4	0.87	0.79	0.75		0.16	0.08
	5	0.98	0.95	0.91	0.84		0.22
	6	1.00	1.00	0.99	0.92	0.78	
Mean:		0.83	0.77	0.65	0.47	0.22	0.06

Since, with a large number of items, the method of paired comparisons is extremely tedious, it is customary to resort to some quicker method of obtaining judgments, such as the *method of successive intervals* (Edwards, 1957b). With this method judges are required to sort every item into one of several piles (usually an odd number, such as 9), indicating the degree to which it represents the critical attribute. There are some rather elaborate methods for analyzing these ratings, consistent with Thurstone's Laws of Comparative Judgment (see Edwards, 1957b; Green, 1954; Guilford, 1954), but these are largely a waste of time, for the scale values obtained thereby correlate very highly (about 0.98) with the values that would be obtained simply by using the mean rating which judges give to each item.

Once the scale locations of items have been established, they are administered to subjects, with instructions to indicate agreement or disagreement with each item. A subject's location on the attitude scale is then taken as the average (mean or median) of the items he accepts.

The method of scoring assumes that the items have determinate scale positions and that these are the same for subjects as for judges. This assumption, however, raises two questions: First, one may ask what degree of consensus among judges is required in order to establish the location of a test item. No precise criteria for this are provided in the model; rather, the discarding of items with "too wide" a spread over the categories is largely a matter of experience and subjective judgment (see Green, 1954). Ideally, the model requires that differences in judged location of a particular item are "random" and do not depend on systematic characteristics of the judges. This assumption has been challenged by Hovland and Sherif (1952), who showed that judges with extremely favorable attitudes toward Negroes distorted the locations of moderate items toward the unfavorable end of the scale. Scott (1963b) found judgments concerning the "social desirability" of test items positively correlated with subjects' own self-ratings on those items, and about as variable. In another study (Scott, 1965) members of college fraternities tended to rate their colleagues by contrast with their own judged positions when rating "objective" attributes (studiousness and contribution to house activities), but they tended to rate by assimilation to their own judged positions when rating more "subjective" attributes (liking for the colleague and ability to get along with others). Altogether, there is substantial theoretical and empirical reason to suspect the assumption that ratings of a stimulus vary randomly about the "true" stimulus location. Since it eliminates interjudge differences in means and variances of ratings, the method of paired comparisons substantially reduces the effect of the judges' own positions; hence, there is less distortion from this source with the method of paired comparisons than with the method of successive intervals (see Green, 1954). However, this is an artificial accomplishment if one considers judges' means and variances as essential components of the judged stimulus locations.

The second problem in inferring subjects' scale positions from the items they select stems from the fact that the task of the subjects is different from that of the judges. The subjects have to indicate agreement or disagreement with the items, while the judges have rated the items on a specified dimension. Though the items may be discriminable along the particular attitudinal dimension of interest in the study, this may not be the principal dimension that determines subjects' responses of acceptance or rejection. One way to ascertain the degree to which the intended dimension exclusively affects subjects' responses is to compute the average standard deviation within subjects over the scale positions of items which each accepts. A small mean standard deviation together with a wide range of mean subject locations would constitute fairly convincing evidence for the assumption of unidimensionality. However, in order to avoid distortion caused by adjacency effects, the items should be presented in some "random" order other than their intended scale order.

Several studies (for example, Edwards and Kenney, 1946; Likert, 1932) have found the method of summative scaling to yield scores that are very highly correlated with those based on consensual location scaling. This implies that the sheer number of monotone items accepted, regardless of their difficulty, provides as good a measure of magnitude as a method which goes to great pains to establish magnitude in a theoretically coherent manner. Since the amount of labor entailed in developing a location scale, and in scoring subjects' responses to it, is somewhat more than that required for summative scaling, this result also argues, pragmatically, for use of the latter technique whenever monotone items are easily written. This will generally be the case for verbal instruments (including indirect measures) of the closed-question variety. But if attitudes are to be assessed from overt behavior, it will often be difficult to restrict the subject's actions to a set of dichotomous choices that can be interpreted as monotonic functions of a single underlying attitude continuum. Many naturally emitted behaviors may not be monotone in form, and may not imply the correlated occurrence of other symptomatic behaviors. To the extent that nonmonotone manifestations are used for attitude measurement, some judgmental procedure will generally be required in order to establish a magnitude scale.

CRITERION-ORIENTED SCALES

A great deal of applied psychometric work proceeds within a criterion-oriented framework, in which items are selected according to the degree to which they correlate with some external variable. Typically the external variable is defined by membership or nonmembership in a criterion group. For example, hospitalized psychotics may constitute one group and college students the comparison group; or juveniles incarcerated for criminal offenses may be compared with high school students who have no court records. In attempting to develop a scale to measure the presumed underlying attribute (for example, psychosis or social deviancy), the investigator administers a large number of test items to both groups, then compares the mean group responses on each item. Those items which significantly discriminate the two groups are retained in a tentative scale, which is then cross-validated on a new sample from the two populations to be distinguished.

Such an approach is quite different from the other psychometric procedures discussed here, in that its objective is to develop, not a unidimensional scale, but rather a scale which will reliably discriminate the criterion groups. If successful, it can be quite useful for the particular circumstance in which it was developed, provided there is no easier way to detect a psychotic or a juvenile delinquent. But one is usually at a loss to identify the attribute which the scale measures. It is probably more appropriate not to try to name the attribute at all, but simply to identify the scale as a "predictor of X-criterion." The various items included in such a scale need have no functional unity whatsoever, but merely correlate with the criterion as a cultural happenstance. (For example, hospitalized psychotics are likely to be of lower socioeconomic status than normal persons and to have poorer physical health; hence, these characteristics could conceivably enter a criterion-oriented scale, even though they do not help define the psychotic syndrome.)

Given the usual conception of an attitude as a functionally unitary (if not unidimensional) trait, the criterion-oriented method of scale *development* would seem quite inappropriate for measuring attitudes. (This does not preclude *validation* of an attitude scale, once established, against a variety of specific criteria, including "known groups" of subjects; see p. 253.)

CONFIGURAL SCORING

All of the scoring procedures discussed so far have at least one critical assumption in common: namely, that a given test item has a comparable meaning for all respondents, or, operationally, that a given response should be scored identically for all respondents. Any item to which this assumption does not apply for a large proportion of subjects will generally be eliminated in the course of scale development, for it will fail to correlate with the total scale, fail to yield a cumulative pattern of responses, or fail to elicit consensual judgments as to its location on a magnitude dimension. Though the assumption has not been seriously questioned by most practitioners of attitude measurement, it has been challenged by researchers in the wider field of mental testing (for example, Coombs, 1953; Loevinger, 1957) and by psychologists concerned with the application of ability tests to industrial settings (for example, Dunnette, 1963; Ghiselli, 1963).

Configural scoring, pattern scoring, and the use of moderator variables (Ghiselli, 1963; McQuitty, 1959; Saunders, 1956) represent attempts to take account of subject-item interactions, which reflect variability in the meanings of items depending on characteristics of the subject. If the subject characteristics responsible for the interactions can be assessed in the test itself by means of one set of items, then a subject's score on these can be used to determine the appropriate method of scoring another set of items from which the focal attribute is to be assessed. This is the *moderator-variable* approach to treating subject-item interactions. So far, it has been used primarily in a dichotomous fashion, yielding, from the moderator variable, only two groups of subjects for whom different sets of items are used to measure the principal variable (for example, Ghiselli, 1956, 1960, 1963; Kogan and Wallach, 1964). Saunders (1956) has refined the method to incorporate the moderator variable as a continuous function for weighting the principal measure. Both of these procedures assume that the items which compose the moderator variable (or basis for distinguishing groups) are themselves noninteractive; that is, that they should be scored the same for all subjects. Finding such items may prove to be less economical than the straightforward development of noninteractive items to measure the principal variable, which would obviate the need for a moderator variable.

The *configural* approach to test scoring (Lee, 1961; McQuitty, 1959, 1961) represents another way of allowing for variable item meaning depending on the subject. It is assumed that the diagnostic significance of any single response depends on the pattern of other responses with which it appears. If the researcher's theory of how the attribute is manifested is sufficiently explicit, he can specify in advance which combinations of item responses can be taken as indicators of the attribute; these combinations can then be treated as composite items, possibly to be pooled in an additive or interactive fashion to yield total scores of varying magnitude. In the absence of such an explicit theory, the appropriate combinations must be arrived at empirically by relating a large number of different combinations to some external criterion. Such an empirical search procedure will be exceedingly laborious, even with computers, and it may not be possible to establish a satisfactory criterion for this purpose. In any case, whatever combination of responses is taken as a scorable manifestation of the attribute, this combination must be considered as having a common meaning for all persons who manifest it. If this is not the case, then higher-order interactions are involved and an infinite regress ensues.

All of which is to say that, in scoring responses to multiple-item attitude inventories, the researcher has a choice of treating each item individually as a unit or treating certain clusters as units of the total score. Whatever the size or complexity of the scoring unit, it must be scored similarly for all individuals; otherwise the requirement of interindividual comparability cannot be met. At the present stage of the science, most attitude researchers are content to work with single responses as the components of their scale scores—though many psychological theories invite configural or moderator scoring procedures, and available technology would readily permit these, provided the interactions could be precisely specified. The present contribution of this approach has been somewhat discouragingly appraised by Loevinger (1959) and D. Campbell (1963), who conclude that empirical studies to date do not reveal any consistent superiority of configural over simple additive methods of scoring. Loevinger's comment about projective tests may well apply more broadly: "Interaction effects are significant, often more so than main effects, but the capture of scorable interactions remains an unrealized program" (Loevinger, 1959, p. 306).

GROUP SCALES AND INDIVIDUAL SCALES

The aim of the scaling procedures described above is to yield a set of items or item clusters that can be scored identically for all persons in a particular population of interest. It can readily be shown, for almost any such scale established from group data, that some individuals within the group do not interpret certain items in the standard way. The interactions implicit in configural scoring imply the inadequacy of a group-derived summative scale. Numerous subjects, when confronted with the standard order of items in a cumulative scale, established from group-defined popularities, would see slightly different orders of magnitude. In addition, the judged scale values of items in a consensual location scale depend to some extent on the attitudinal position of the person doing the judging.

Such widespread evidence regarding the nonstandard character of attitude scales can impel investigation in at least two directions. One is toward the development of techniques for establishing individual scales: for instance, determining item orders or item magnitudes for each subject separately and not attempting to compare individuals whose scales do not correspond. This is essentially the approach taken by Coombs (1964), and the classical methods of psychophysics (Ekman and Sjöberg, 1965; Guilford, 1954; Torgerson, 1958) can readily be applied to the establishment of individual scales.

The other direction of investigation aims toward the development of group scales which apply to as many members of the target population as possible, so that when these scales are used for interindividual comparisons, the results will seldom be misleading. This goal is approached, generally, by analyses that result in the retention of items with fairly standard meanings and the rejection of items that are (among other things) diversely interpreted. After such item-culling, one typically retains a set whose content departs substantially from the conception on which the initial set was based. Such a result requires a redefinition of the original attitude concept. The new definition should be restricted, for example, to those meanings that are shared by members of the population on which the scale was developed. It will omit idiosyncratic meanings with reference to which these persons cannot be compared.

Certainly such a restriction limits considerably the significance of both the scale and the refined concept. It leaves undefined and unmeasured the numerous individualistic ways of expressing an attitude which may, for some purpose, constitute the focus of concern. But failure to recognize the limitations of his scale leaves the researcher talking about an attitude that he has not yet measured. He implies the existence of individual differences that are uninterpretable in terms of his measuring instrument. Of course, failure to demonstrate the initially intended domain may be attributable to inappropriate scaling techniques, rather than to a faulty initial concept. But if so, then what is needed is some other, logically defensible, procedure for scale development which will assure the functional equivalence of all those manifestations which the researcher attributes to a single underlying attitude. Perhaps one future direction of development will be toward devising methods of scale construction which represent in a more general fashion current notions of functional equivalence.

EXTRANEOUS DETERMINANTS OF RESPONSES

Attitude scales are constructed, administered, and scored with the aim of yielding measures that can be interpreted to represent some property of the attitude which the investigator has set out to assess. Interpretation does not, however, follow directly from the kind of task set for the subject and the way in which his responses are combined into a scale score. It also depends substantially on additional information about the test which has been obtained from prior investigations. Relevant information serves, broadly, a validating function, in that it helps one ascertain what the test does and does not measure, what it does and does not predict. The topics treated in the remainder of this chapter are all related, in one way or another, to the problem of interpreting a subject's score on an attitude scale. Before confronting the question of validity directly, however, it is appropriate to consider certain sources of invalidity commonly encountered.

One would like to interpret responses to attitude inventories as if they reflected the particular variable of concern. Yet most psychological theories agree that any response, including an answer to a question, is multiply determined. Thus, in order to make valid inferences about the attitude in question, the investigator needs to find ways of excluding or discounting the influence of extraneous response determinants.

The determinants of responses (including question-answering, picture interpretation, and autonomic processes) can be classified roughly into three categories: characteristics of the person, of the measuring instrument, and of the circumstances in which assessment occurs. Since attitudes are conceptualized as relatively enduring properties of the person, any response determinant which arises primarily from the measuring instrument or from the circumstances of assessment can be considered extraneous. Just what intrapersonal response determinants are extraneous and what are germane depends on the psychological properties from which the particular attitude is to be distinguished. If the investigator intends to measure attitude X, then every other theoretically distinct psychological property, including attitudes W, Y, Z, etc., can be considered extraneous. Given the ambiguity and diversity of current conceptualizations, the separation of theoretically distinct from theoretically equivalent properties will not be obvious in all cases. Measurement technology can make a contribution toward theoretical clarification by ascertaining which constructs can be empirically distinguished, and which cannot, at a given stage of technological development.

The distinction between subject, instrument, and situational determinants of test responses is overdrawn, since all three have to contribute in some way to the occurrence of any response. A more careful analysis would consider interactions among the three classes, as well as their main effects; interactions would undoubtedly contribute substantially to the determination of test responses. Nevertheless, for the sake of simplicity, and for lack of systematic evidence concerning interactions, we will treat each class independently, though recognizing that the extent to which it influences responses to attitude inventories will depend on variables from the other classes.

SUBJECT CHARACTERISTICS

Subject variables have traditionally been classified into two categories, random and systematic. Random components include "response errors" and miscellaneous subject characteristics which are differentially elicited by irrelevant features of the test items. Though most psychologists would not seriously conceive such determinants as truly random, they may conveniently be treated this way to the extent that they are uncorrelated from one response to another. (Even "random" responses may yield correlated systematic effects in tests with items that have response distributions all skewed in the same direction.) Systematic components are those which tend to affect all responses in a similar way, and hence tend to bias the total scores constructed from those responses. Two kinds of systematic response biases have received particular attention in the literature on personality (including attitude) measurement: the tendency to "fake good" or reply in a "socially desirable" manner, and the tendency to "acquiesce" or accept all statements presented. The latter has been conceived by many as a general subject characteristic, but recent evidence (see Rorer, 1965) suggests that it is more properly classified as an instrument factor not consistently manifest in nontest behavior. Emphasis on these two sources of bias probably results from the development of techniques that are presumed to overcome them, rather than from the belief that they are the sole contributors to systematic error. In fact, a variety of psychological traits such as verbosity, flamboyance, uncertainty, imaginativeness, intelligence, and so forth may bias test scores, if the component items are constructed and scored in such a way as to reflect them as well as the intended attitude.

In addition to such general traits that may bias test scores, numerous specific attitudes, beliefs, or opinions may be called forth by the test stimuli, which usually contain references to objects other than that which is the focus of assessment. The statement, "Negroes commit more crimes than whites," may elicit attitudes toward crime and toward whites, as well as toward Negroes. Though every attempt may be made to vary such irrelevant objects over the several items in a test, so that their contributions may be treated as "random," this can be done (even approximately) only if the researcher has identified the irrelevant object appropriately. The general attitude of misanthropy may be called forth by any item that is intended to refer to a specific ethnic group. The general attitude of xenophobia may be called forth by any item intended to refer to a specific nation. If the researcher intends to distinguish the specific attitude from the more general, then the latter must be considered as an irrelevant determinant for the present purpose. Thus, the designation of what is germane and what is irrelevant is, first of all, a matter of theoretical definition.

Social desirability

Most definitions of attitude refer to an enduring characteristic of the person that is independent of his desire to make a particular momentary impression on the person to whom he is speaking. If such a conception be cogent, then it clearly excludes the tendencies of subjects to "fake good," to place themselves in a "desirable" light, to avoid unpleasant consequences of a "truthful" reply. The identification of a faking component of attitude test scores implies that some subjects may give different responses to the test as administered than they would to the same test presented under circumstances that facilitated "honest" replies. This implication has rarely been investigated directly, but demonstrations of differences between "public" and "private" attitudes (for example, Schanck, 1932; Gorden, 1952) have suggested strongly that such discrepancies would emerge for some attitudes if they were similarly measured under the two conditions. Cook and Selltiz (1964), for example, suggest that most persons, when responding to a test that has "respectable" auspices, will try to give answers that place them in a favorable light—"well adjusted, unprejudiced, rational, open minded, and democratic" (p. 39).

Concern for this kind of response bias usually implies at least two assumptions about the respondent: (1) that he is motivated to present an untrue (that is, overly favorable) picture of himself, and (2) that he knows what responses will be favorably regarded.

Other modes of self-presentation

Though not so much studied as the social-desirability tendency, other modes of self-presentation may be expected to influence test responses in a consistent fashion. A desire to appear cooperative may confound many types of test scores in the direction of fuller replies and fewer "don't know" responses or refusals to answer. A wish to appear thoughtful may appear in the shape of many qualifications, mention of noncentral considerations, and "depends" responses. If a person regards himself as self-determined, endowed with free will, and responsible for his actions, he may feel compelled to predict his future behavior with inordinate precision. In a way, such modes of self-presentation are attempts to appear "desirable," but they do not imply intentional faking, and they depend on the person's own private conception of what constitutes a "desirable" response. Whereas the social-desirability tendency is regarded as similarly manifested in all persons, these other modes of self-presentation may be quite different from one person to another.

INSTRUMENT-SPECIFIC DETERMINANTS

The distinction between subject factors and instrument factors is a hard one to draw; different investigators would specify different boundaries, and some would assert that all response tendencies depend on the interaction between subject and instrument. The singling out of self-presentation styles as subject factors implies that they would be similarly manifested in most testing situations commonly used today, and that they represent enduring personality characteristics which transcend any particular method of testing. The designation of an instrument factor implies that the irrelevant response tendency appears only in a limited class of instruments, and is mainly attributable to those instruments (actually, to an interaction between subject and instrument), rather than to a general disposition of subjects that would be manifested in nontest performance. What is seen as an instrument factor thus depends on the range of instrument types one uses to assess the attitude and on the degree to which one's conception of the attitude is tied to a particular class of assessment procedures. Cattell (1961), for instance, designates as *refraction factors* certain subject traits which appear only with a particular method of assessment; other investigators might not regard these as subject traits, but rather as instances of subject-instrument interaction.

Verbosity. Assessment procedures which depend on the coding of extremity or intensity from free responses are likely to be confounded by verbosity. This is patently true for scoring systems which depend on the number of manifestations of the attribute that are contained in the reply (see van Zandt and Himelstein, 1961, for evidence pertaining to motive assessment from imaginative stories). It may also hold, to some extent, for judgmental scales of extremity, since extremity is often inferred from the degree of elaboration contained in replies to open questions. Verbal *flamboyance,* likewise, may induce inferences concerning intensity or extremity of the attitude, even though it may represent a style of expression more than a feeling tone associated with the specific attitude.

Carelessness. Carelessness of replies may affect scores on almost any instrument, but the nature of the effect will depend on the type of instrument. Carelessness may be manifested in unduly brief replies to open questions or projective stimuli, and in hasty reading of closed questions, resulting in mischecks or random responses or position habits. It is likely that carelessness is substantially attributable to the particular conditions of rapport which surround the test taking.

Acquiescence. An acquiescence set (Cronbach, 1950) or style (Rorer, 1965) may be manifested in a test consisting of closed questions with two answer categories, one representing acceptance of the statement ("yes," "agree," "true," etc.) and the other representing rejection. Some investigators (for example, Couch and Keniston, 1960; Jackson and Messick, 1958, 1961; Messick, 1962) regard acquiescence as a stable subject trait, but this is probably not an appropriate designation in view of the fact that the tendency to accept items is not consistently correlated from one type of test content to another and does not correlate well with nontest behaviors (Edwards, 1963; Rorer, 1965; Schutz and Foster, 1963; Stricker, 1963). However, if statements are ambiguously phrased, there is often some tendency for items scored in the same direction (that is, positively or negatively worded for the trait) to intercorrelate higher than items scored in opposite directions (Miklich, 1965; Peabody, 1966). Thus, if all items are worded so that acceptance of them manifests the attitude of interest, one can reasonably suspect a content-specific (or test-specific) confounding of acquiescence with test scores.

Extremity. A set to check extreme answers may be elicited by a closed-question instrument with answer categories that distinguish "strongly agree" (or other equivalent wording) from "moderately agree" and "neutral." It may also appear as a tendency to check the extremes of a numerical scale (say, the numbers 1 or 7 on a seven-point scale, rather than the neutral point 4). One cannot be certain about the degree to which an extremity set will be similarly manifested in different tests (see Forehand, 1962; Schutz and Foster, 1963), but within a single instrument it may confound scores in which an extreme response is always taken to indicate more (or less) of the attitude than a moderate response.

Other instrument factors. Though the four instrument factors described above may be among the most frequently encountered in attitude testing, these by no means exhaust the potential sources of irrelevant test variance. Almost any response format is apt to elicit a characteristic response style in some subjects. Campbell and Sorenson (1963) report a small but significant response set associated with the order of response alternatives in Clark's (1961) Minnesota Vocational Interest Inventory. Mullins (1963) found some subjects showing a preference for the alternative "correct answer not given" when this was provided on mental-test items. Physiological measures of attitudes, such as GSR and pupillary dilation, elicit their own characteristic contaminating influences (Cook and Selltiz, 1964; Woodmansee, 1965).

We prefer the designation *methods factors* or *instrument factors* to *response set* or *response style* as a way of referring to determinants of test responses that are instrument-specific and extraneous to the particular trait of interest. The notion of "set" or "style" implies some relatively enduring characteristic of the subject that is manifested in nontest behavior; there is little evidence for such stylistic generality at the present time. Of course, any subject trait is likely to be better measured by certain kinds of instruments, and by certain kinds of items, than by others. The typical process of test development consists in finding those items which best measure the intended trait. Response styles such as acquiescence and extremity might be regarded as reflecting subject characteristics, even if they are not manifested similarly in all items or all instruments. But a conventional strategy of test development would entail item analyses for these traits comparable to the analyses typically undertaken to purify a measure of any other personality trait. To the extent that a particular test item elicits an acquiescence tendency, it cannot be expected to reflect faithfully the subject's attitude toward Negroes (if we assume that these traits are conceived as distinct). The reverse is equally true. Thus, adequate item analyses should normally yield instruments which are maximally saturated with the trait of focal concern and minimally influenced by some other trait. If the particular items chosen happen to depend substantially on two different traits, then scores on the scale will represent either a confounding or a compromise that is difficult to interpret.

For most programs of attitude-test construction, such "response styles" may be appropriately treated as methods factors, which are to be suppressed rather than accentuated in construction and scoring of the instruments.

MINIMIZING EXTRANEOUS DETERMINANTS

There are at least four basic ways of attempting to overcome potential contaminating determinants of test responses: (1) modify the conditions of administration, (2) modify the instrument, (3) detect and discard subjects whose responses are largely affected by irrelevant factors, and (4) correct the scores of all subjects in proportion to the amount of their known contamination. None of these approaches can be depended on to provide a certain solution; they are frequently used in combination; and the use of one method for circumventing extraneous determinants may introduce other contaminating variables that were not previously present.

CONDITIONS OF ADMINISTRATION

Some pains are usually taken in administering interviews or questionnaires to establish adequate rapport with subjects. This typically consists in a motivational appeal to convince the respondent of the importance of his participation, an assurance that his replies will be kept confidential, and repeated insistence that his own frank opinions are wanted, rather than some seemingly desirable reply. It is hoped thereby to reduce the contributions of at least two potentially contaminating variables, carelessness and faking. Certain techniques for doing this may be suggested as standard practice. For example, if alternative replies to controversial questions are presented or implied, the instructions can be phrased something like: "Some people say . . . and others say. . . . What do you think?" Also, the subject may be told that the questionnaire is still in a preliminary form, and that his comments concerning its clarity and personal relevance will be welcomed.

Though such rapport-building techniques are an essential part of the data-collection process, their successful implementation depends primarily on human relations skills and familiarity with the respondent's culture; detailed guides to these are almost impossible to provide. Therefore, many investigators prefer to seek more mechanical methods of controlling extraneous variables that do not depend so heavily on *ad hoc* procedures and unspecifiable skills.

INSTRUMENT CONSTRUCTION

A more straightforward technique, applicable to all subjects alike, is to construct the instrument in the first place so as to minimize certain irrelevant determinants. Random subject variables are typically overcome by lengthening the instrument. The classical procedure of taking repeated measurements to increase reliability is seldom applicable, because memory of previous replies, boredom, and even hostility may introduce additional contaminating influences. The usual practice with verbal, pictorial, or other symbolic stimuli is to include many items relating to the same attitudinal object but phrased differently or set in different contexts. This satisfies another desideratum of test construction by providing a better sample of the attitude domain than a single question would. It is not a panacea, however, for it will not overcome sources of systematic errors (those repeated from one question to another, such as the very format of the instrument); and indefinite lengthening, aside from inducing respondent fatigue and precluding other questionnaire content, may actually alter the very trait that is being measured, by heightening the subject's concern for consistency.

The contribution of acquiescence response set in "accept-reject" items is typically counterbalanced by using equal numbers of pro (direct-worded) and con (reverse-worded) statements, acceptance of the latter implying absence of the critical attribute. This would appear to be an appropriate technique, provided sensible reversed items can be written. Two checks on the adequacy of item reversals may be recommended. The first is to ascertain that the variances of direct and reversed items are the same, on the average, so that they will contribute equally to the total test variance. The second check is to intercorrelate all items to see that they are positively related (when scored for content). In some cultures the acquiescence tendency may be strong enough to overcome content, resulting in zero or negative correlations between the two kinds of items (scored appropriately for content). Should this be the case, then some other method must be found for establishing the functional equivalence of the two sets of items, perhaps by showing that they correlate similarly with some other defining measure that is not itself subject to acquiescence contamination.

TABLE 3

BALANCING ITEMS FOR EXTREMITY RESPONSE SET

| Item | Direction of wording | | *Response* | | |
			"Agree"	"Don't know"	"Disagree"
A	+	Score:	2	1	0
		p:	50%	50%	0%
B	−	Score:	0	1	2
		p:	50%	50%	0%
C	+	Score:	2	1	0
		p:	0%	50%	50%
D	−	Score:	0	1	2
		p:	0%	50%	50%
E	+	Score:	2	1	0
		p:	33%	33%	33%
F	−	Score:	0	1	2
		p:	33%	33%	33%

The set to give extreme (or neutral) replies is invited by any kind of rating scale which presents more than two ordered response categories to the subject. It is theoretically possible to counterbalance the effect of extremity so that it will not confound the content variable of interest. This may be accomplished if pairs of oppositely worded (that is, direct-scored and reverse-scored) items have the same response distributions. Table 3 shows six hypothetical items measuring a common attribute and eliciting response distributions as indicated: Items *A* and *B* have no "disagree" responses, but equal proportions of "agree" and "don't know." Since item *A* is direct-worded, an "agree" response is scored 2, and "don't know" is scored 1. Since item *B* is reverse-worded, an "agree" response is scored 0. Items *A* and *B* are counterbalanced for extremity, because an extreme response to both would yield the same total score as a neutral response to both. Likewise, items *C* and *D* are counterbalanced for extremity response set, and so are items *E* and *F*, since the expected sums of scores for consistently neutral and consistently extreme responders are identical. However, the remaining pairs of oppositely worded items (*AD*, *AF*, *BC*, *BE*, *CF*, and *DE*) are not counterbalanced for extremity response set, because in every case the subject who replied "don't know" to both would obtain a different (expected) total score than the subject who gave extreme answers. As a set, these six items are counterbalanced for both acquiescence and extremity. But it is very difficult to construct such balanced sets that will remain balanced from one sample of subjects to the next, because the distributions of item responses may change substantially. For this reason, many testers (for example, Loevinger, 1962) recommend avoiding the use of multiple (ordered) response categories altogether.

The forced-choice technique has been widely used for reducing the irrelevant effects of a "social desirability" set (see Edwards, 1957a). Subjects are confronted with pairs (or larger sets) of items that have been equated for "desirability" or popularity, and required to choose the member of each pair which comes closer to representing their own opinion. If the two items appear equally desirable from the subject's standpoint, it is reasoned, his choice will be determined solely by their contents. The problem lies in determining that the items are indeed seen as equally desirable by all subjects, for the procedure of equating items on the basis of group mean ratings does not assure this (see Saltz, Reece, and Ager, 1962).

Surprisingly little research has been done to demonstrate that the forced-choice technique actually does reduce the tendency of the subject to present himself in a favorable light or, more importantly, that it increases the validity of the instrument beyond that provided by a single-stimulus form. The evidence from studies of personnel ratings is somewhat conflicting (see Cozan, 1959; Zavala, 1965) and of unknown relevance to self-appraisal attitude scales. Gordon (1951) found a forced-choice form of personality test a better predictor of sociometric nominations than a single-stimulus form; Scott (1963b) found a single-stimulus form of the Edwards (1953) Personal Preference Schedule superior to the standard (forced-choice) form in predicting self-reported behaviors; Bergs and Martin's (1961) study yielded inconclusive results in the measurement of manifest anxiety. The only comparison of the two formats in attitude assessment known to this writer is the study by Bartlett, Quay, and Wrightsman (1960), from which the authors drew a dubious conclusion concerning their relative validities.

Another strategy of instrument construction that is aimed at eliminating the faking tendency is the use of "disguised techniques." These may consist of projective tests, stimulus judgments, loaded-information tests, and the like, designed to circumvent the subject's awareness of the focal attribute (see Campbell, 1950; Cook and Selltiz, 1964). One rationale for their use is the belief that, though subjects may distort their true attitudes when questioned directly, they are not able to do this when they don't know the purpose of assessment. Another, quite different, rationale is that direct report provides an insufficiently representative measure of the postulated attitude, and that manifestations in overt behavior and in cognitive and imaginative processes provide equally valid and necessary indicators. Evaluation of the former rationale requires empirical evidence that is rarely collected. Evaluation of the latter rationale depends more on how one conceives attitudes to be manifested most directly. Most writers would probably agree that attitudes are expressed in a variety of ways; but which of these should be considered measures (that is, operational definitions) and which should be treated as correlates (or consequences) is a moot point.

From the present perspective, attitudes are most directly manifested through verbal self-reports under conditions of optimum rapport; the attempt to measure them indirectly is likely to encounter more confounding variables than it circumvents, for example, situational influences, experience with the tasks, attitudes toward the tasks, etc. Regardless of one's opinion on this controversial issue, it is safe to say that not enough evidence has been amassed concerning the conditions under which, and the subjects for whom, either the direct or the indirect approach to assessment may be more appropriate. Given the relative difficulty of constructing and administering indirect instruments, it would seem desirable to ascertain first whether or not more convenient direct methods are sufficiently valid for the purpose.

Considering that any type of instrument is likely to elicit its own instrument-specific confounding factors which will be very difficult to overcome, some investigators (for example, Campbell and Fiske, 1959; Cattell, 1961; Cook and Selltiz, 1964) have advocated a broader strategy of assessment. This strategy is to develop many different measures of the attitude, using a variety of procedures which do not share the same method-specific sources of variance. The idea is akin to that conventionally applied in test construction under the classical psychometric model: to randomize extraneous sources of variance, so that a composite score constructed from the entire battery will reflect the common content more than it will reflect irrelevant methods factors.

A complementary approach, suggested by Cartwright (1964) and by Cattell and Tsujioka (1964), is to stratify or counterbalance tests and test items according to their irrelevant sources of variance. The procedure here would be an extension of that used to control for acquiescence set by including equal numbers of direct- and reverse-worded items in the same test. What is also required is to identify other irrelevant contaminants of test scores by factor analysis, then to build composite batteries of tests loaded similarly on the critical (trait) factor, and loaded in counterbalanced fashion on all of the other specifically identified factors which are to be excluded from the total test score.

At their present stage of development, these last two approaches, randomizing and counterbalancing of methods factors over instruments, are largely programmatic. Their applications to the assessment of specific attitudes have yet to be worked out in detail.

DETECTION OF CONTAMINATED SCORES

Even if one despairs of constructing any instrument impervious to systematic distortion, one may still wish to minimize such contributions at the scoring or analysis stage of the investigation. Two approaches to post-administration correction have been used: one involves the discarding of subjects whose scores seem grossly contaminated; the other introduces a correction for every score in proportion to its assumed degree of contamination. Both approaches require an explicit measure of the confounding attribute that is independent of the basic attitude measure. Two confounding attributes for which explicit measures have been developed are the tendency to "fake good" and the tendency to give careless responses (see Campbell and Trockman, 1963; Filbeck and Callis, 1961; Hathaway and McKinley, 1945; Kuder, 1956; Norman, 1963).

Measures of carelessness have typically been constructed with items that are normally very popular or very unpopular, under the assumption that any person who gives a large number of deviant responses is not taking the test seriously. It may be noted that a similar response tendency may be interpreted alternatively as manifesting either essential deviance (Berg, 1961) or a tendency to appear "socially undesirable" (Edwards, 1957a). Campbell and Trockman's (1963) verification scale for the Minnesota Vocational Interest Inventory (Clark, 1961), for example, included items whose probabilities of acceptance ranged between 5 percent and 9 percent. A subject who accepted 13 or more of 58 such items would be identified as "careless," according to one standard. This cutoff point was established by comparing the verification scale scores of persons who took the test as intended with the scores of persons who filled out the answer sheet blindly; it eliminated 97 percent of the "blind" respondents and only 9 percent of the "careful" respondents.

Measures of the tendency to "fake good" have been developed by at least two different methods. One is to write items with dichotomous answer categories, one of which is presumed to be factually true of all subjects, but undesirable, while the other is presumed to be desirable for all subjects, but contrary to fact. Crowne and Marlowe's (1960) social desirability scale, for example, includes the item, "I'm always willing to admit it when I make a mistake." The other procedure is to select items that show marked shifts in popularity when subjects take the test under instructions to present themselves in a favorable light (see Gough, 1957; Norman, 1963). The validity of both kinds of scale is normally established by demonstrating that subjects score higher on them when given instructions to fake than when given standard instructions that encourage a veridical self-report.

Three critical observations may be made concerning such detection scales. First, the establishment of cutoff points for discarding subjects is necessarily somewhat arbitrary, implying a sharp distinction between subjects who are, and those who are not, affected by the irrelevant trait. Second, the scales imply that all subjects are likely to manifest the irrelevant attribute in the same way, that careless persons tend to select unpopular alternatives and fakers tend to distort their replies in the same directions on the particular items used in the scale.

Finally, the procedures for validating the detection scales are not necessarily relevant to the interpretations to be placed on scores in the usual testing situation. Role-playing instructions (for example, "fake good") do not necessarily create the same set as that present in persons who possess the trait naturally; hence, responses associated with role-playing may bear little resemblance to those employed by fakers or careless respondents in the natural situation. Even if it could be demonstrated that an appropriately induced attribute *can* elevate scores on the detection scales, this does not validate the obverse inference that all such elevated scores in the normal testing situation necessarily manifest *that* particular attribute. Though selection of unpopular alternatives *may* be increased by careless responding, it does not follow that careless responding is even an important source of such responses under circumstances in which the test is usually administered; hence, the inference from the detection scales might be quite erroneous. A more appropriate way to validate a detection scale would be to demonstrate that subjects rejected on this basis yield less valid measures of the critical attitude than do subjects who are retained. The problem would still remain that the attitude scale could be considered applicable only to those persons who survived the detection scale. This group would not be definable in advance of testing, and it might be substantially smaller than the total population of concern to the investigator.

CORRECTING SCORES FOR CONTAMINATION

A logical extension of the above procedure is to use the detection scale, or some other diagnostic scale, to correct raw scores on the attitude measure according to the amount of systematic error that can be attributed to the contaminating variable. The *K*-scale of the Minnesota Multiphasic Personality Inventory (Meehl and Hathaway, 1946) is often used this way as a correction for some of the scales intended to diagnose psychopathology. Since the latter consist of self-report items for which the desirable direction of response is generally obvious, it is believed that defensive subjects may not admit to the symptoms and hence obtain lower scores than they should on the diagnostic scales. A subject's score on the *K*-scale is intended to measure his degree of defensiveness (or tendency to place himself in a favorable light), and is used as a basis for incremental corrections in certain of the diagnostic scales. The proportional increments which maximize validities of the diagnostic scales have been determined empirically in one population of subjects (McKinley, Hathaway, and Meehl, 1948) and these optimal increments are often used as standard correction factors.

However, other researchers (reviewed by Heilbrun, 1964) have reported no improvement in prediction from use of the *K*-scale, and Heilbrun (1963) has found quite a different set of optimal correction factors in a different population, some of these optima actually involving no change in the raw scores. It seems that a generally applicable scale to correct for faking has yet to be developed. In fact, it is doubtful if any useful correction scale can be developed so long as the validities of the scales to be corrected are low to begin with. Norman (1963, p. 234) recommends that

... as long as the primary predictor is accounting for less than half the criterion variance— a situation universally true in personality assessment today and likely to persist for some time—one is well advised to attack the unexplained criterion variance rather than attempt to suppress invalid test variance. Statistically, a suppressor scale has to be a very effective suppressor—better than any currently available or likely to be constructed soon—to effect any appreciable improvement over an only moderately valid primary predictor.

A somewhat different approach to eliminating the effect of an irrelevant variable via the scoring procedure is suggested by Messick (1961). He modifies a formula proposed by Helmstadter (1957) to make it applicable to personality tests, which have no *a priori* "correct answers." Essentially, the method requires separate scoring of items which are positively confounded, and items which are negatively confounded, by the irrelevant variable. Applied to the elimination of acquiescence, the corrected score is an average of the score obtained on positively worded items and the score obtained on negatively worded items, with the scale of measurement transformed so that corrected scores range between +1 and −1. The content score, independent of acquiescence, is defined as

$$C = \frac{R_A}{N_A} + \frac{R_B}{N_B} - 1,$$

where N_A is the number of items for which an "accept" response is scored for positive content, N_B is the number of items for which a "reject" response is scored for positive content, R_A is the number of A-type items accepted by the subject, and R_B is the number of B-type items rejected by the subject.

The formula assumes that content and acquiescence are independent, that is, that the negatively worded items and the positively worded items represent the content equally well. It is also necessary to have either an equal or a substantial number of both kinds of item, since a proportion based on a small number of items will not provide a reliable indicator of the content variable. It is probably more efficient to construct the test in the first place so that positively and negatively worded items are represented equally (see pp. 239–240); then simple raw scores can be used.

Another approach to eliminating the confounding effect of a variety of methods factors is to include in the assessment some content-free measure of each suspected contaminant (such as verbosity, extremity, etc.). Though "content-free" measures would be ideal, in practice one can at best elicit responses over a range of content different from the focal attribute to be measured. The correlations between focal-content scores and each of the measured methods factors could be calculated, and a corrected content score computed from a regression equation which systematically eliminates each of the contaminating variables. Besides being laborious, such a procedure assumes no interaction between content and method, for example, that a given subject will tend to be as verbose on the attitude test as he is on the "content-free" measure of verbosity. Since such an assumption is tenuous at best (see Miklich, 1965; Schutz and Foster, 1963), it is necessary to apply the final criterion of adequacy to this or any other procedure for correcting raw test scores: namely, whether or not the corrected scores provide more valid measures than the uncorrected scores.

ADEQUACY OF ATTITUDE MEASURES

Thus far we have considered various procedures for measuring attitudes and for reducing the likelihood that the measure reflects characteristics other than the one intended. In passing, we have noted briefly some difficulties with each of the procedures and indicated that none of them is without shortcomings. The very judgment of adequacy or inadequacy and the guiding of steps toward improvement require explicit, preferably quantitative, criteria; the criteria chosen depend, in turn, on assumptions about the nature of psychological measurement.

MODELS OF MEASUREMENT

Most contemporary methods of attitude measurement are based on the notion of a quantitative continuum along which people may be arrayed, depending on the magnitude of the attitude which they possess. One alternative conception, generally out of fashion these days, is that of discrete classes, or types, to which people may be assigned, depending on *what* attitude they possess. Perhaps the basic reason for unpopularity of the type model is that it results either in exclusion of a large portion of the subject population from the set of types or in a proliferation of types to the point where the set becomes inelegant and intellectually unmanageable.

Another alternative to the quantitative continuum model is to reject completely the notion of enduring, pervasive personal attributes, in favor of a person-stimulus transactionalism. While such a perspective may be empirically demanded, it has yet to inspire an explicit model of measurement and, in any case, it would find present conceptions of attitudes uncongenial.

Scaling models

The magnitude model probably owes more to analogs of physical dimensions, especially length, than to psychological theories about how an attitude is manifested. Two general approaches to the measurement of magnitude are represented in attitude-scaling procedures. One of these, embodied in cumulative and consensual location scales, assumes that the magnitude of an attribute in a person is reflected in the kind of stimulus item that he finds acceptable. Stimulus items are assumed to be quantifiable according to the amount of the attribute which they require for acceptance; accepting an item of a particular magnitude implies *that* magnitude of the attribute within the subject. Comparably, one may assume that emitted behaviors toward an attitudinal object may be arrayed along a dimension representing degree of favorableness or unfavorableness, and the person's location on the scale may be inferred from the magnitude of the behaviors which he emits.

Ideally, the measurement model may be represented as in Fig. 1, where items (or emitted responses) are arrayed along the magnitude dimension. Selection of any of these items implies that the subject may be located at about the same position on the continuum as the item.

Empirically, the precise locating of subjects is limited by the impossibility of writing items (or defining behaviors) which represent the intended attribute only and which have a precise location on the dimension which is the same for all persons. Incidental contents of the items (presumably differing from subject to subject and from item to item) and fluctuations in the item position, across

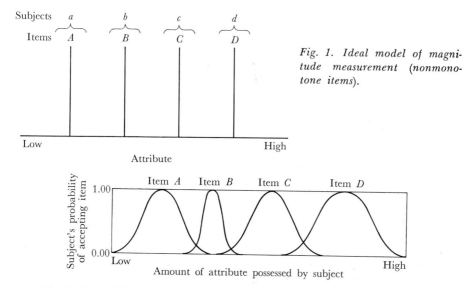

Fig. 1. Ideal model of magnitude measurement (nonmonotone items).

Fig. 2. Probabilistic model of magnitude measurement (nonmonotone items).

or within subjects, invariably occur; these are regarded as random perturbations which blur the precise item location. Therefore, the subject's likelihood of accepting an item is treated as a probabilistic, rather than a deterministic, function of the magnitude of the critical attribute which he possesses. One probabilistic measurement model may be portrayed as in Fig. 2, which shows each item located at some point representing its mean value for all subjects in a given population. The probability of accepting the item (or emitting the behavior) is assumed to depend on the nearness of the subject's location to the item on the attribute dimension. The closer he is, the more likely he is to accept the item.

The function describing the probability of item acceptance for varying subject positions is known as the *item operating characteristic*. Figure 2 shows normal, or in general, *nonmonotone*, item operating characteristics, under the assumption that this is a consensual location scale, in which the stimuli are acceptable within a small range of subject location, but not outside that range.

If items are written so as to be cumulative (or summative) in form, then a *monotone* item operating characteristic obtains. The more of the attribute a subject possesses, the more likely he is to accept any item on the scale. The probability of accepting a more popular item is always greater than the probability of accepting a less popular item on the same dimension. This operating characteristic is generally represented as a sigmoid function, the integral of a normal curve, under the assumption that departures from a one-to-one correspondence between item location and the location of subjects who accept it are due to random perturbations. (See Fig. 3.)

If the relation between item position and subject acceptance were deterministic, then it would be necessary to elicit only one response from any subject

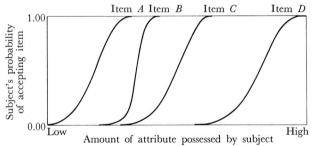

Fig. 3. Probabilistic model for monotone items.

to determine his position. With nonmonotone items, one would merely ask him, "Which item do you find most acceptable?" With monotone items, one would ask, "Which item represents the most extreme action you would approve in regard to the object?" Treating the item-subject relationship in probabilistic terms, however, requires that the subject respond to all items, so that his own location can be estimated as the average of the items accepted (consensual location scales) or according to the minimal-errors principle (cumulative scales).

Additive response model

Fundamental to both the cumulative and the consensual location scaling models is the assumption that stimuli can be arrayed along a continuum corresponding to the attribute continuum to be appraised in subjects. The notion of item magnitude forms an essential part of the models. Item magnitude is assessed from consensual judgments or from item popularities. Without some such measure of item magnitude, the appraisal of attribute magnitude in subjects is meaningless.

Quite a different approach is taken in classical psychometric theory (see Gulliksen, 1950). Here, the magnitude of a psychological attribute is represented simply by the number of manifestations on a test instrument, that is, the number of items accepted, without regard to their popularities. Popularity is not interpreted as a reflection of item magnitude, and the notion of "item magnitude" has no meaning. Instead, the additive scoring procedure is based on the assumption that each item constitutes an imperfect measure of the critical attribute, imperfect in that responses to it are determined not only by the common single attribute but also by various irrelevant influences which are uncorrelated from one item to another. Uncorrelated determinants may be treated as random error; thus the components of each item score may be formulated as

$$X = t + e,$$

where X is the obtained score on the item (usually 0 or 1), t is the "true-score" component, representing the common attribute, and e is the "error" component, representing irrelevant contributions, treated as random.

The model is again akin to certain measurement models in physics, wherein an empirical measure is assumed to reflect the intended property, primarily, but also "errors of measurement," secondarily. To the extent that errors of measurement are large, it is necessary to pool the results of many different measures, averaging them to arrive at the best estimate of the "true" magnitude. Since the sum of several measures is a linear function of their mean, the psychometric procedure of adding scores over items is exactly equivalent to the practice of averaging measures of a physical quantity. The total score on a test thus comprises a "true" attribute component and a composite error component:

$$\Sigma X_i = \Sigma t_i + \Sigma e_i.$$

The true-score component is assumed to be similar from one item to another, while the errors are uncorrelated among the several items. As more items are added to the test, the proportion of total-score variance attributable to intersubject differences in the attribute increases much more rapidly than the proportion of variance attributable to random components. With a long enough test, the relative magnitude of the latter can be considered trivial, and the raw score is deemed to provide quite an accurate measure of the true score (the amount of the trait present).

The relative magnitudes of true and error components are, of course, not known, but it is assumed that the shared variance between any two items is attributable to their common true component; hence, the magnitude of the coefficient of correlation between them provides one index of their common trait variance. When dichotomous items are used, however, differences in item popularities will depress the correlation between them. So the tetrachoric correlation is often computed as a corrected estimate of their common trait variance. Even so, psychometric theory is very lenient concerning the magnitude of inter-item correlation required in order to justify the pooling of item scores into a total score. In principle, no matter how small the average inter-item correlation, pooling is permitted, and the error component is overcome simply by adding more items. This practice is justified by the assumption that all nontrait variance in any item is random, and therefore cannot systematically distort total (summated) scores, however large it may be.

The assumptions of psychometric theory are probably not met in most circumstances of attitude measurement. First of all, the common variance between any two items is contributed not only by the particular trait which is of interest, but also by various extraneous factors which they share in common, and which are therefore not random. Common extraneous factors include both instrument factors and irrelevant traits. Therefore, the total test score reflects not just the magnitude of the focal attribute, but some composite of this plus other shared sources of inter-item covariance. This limitation is, of course, not unique to the psychometric model, but applies equally to all other measurement procedures considered here. Scale scores include everything systematically measured by the scale, including those things not intended to be measured.

However, the irrelevant sources of common variance may differ from one pair of items to another, or from one cluster of items to another. Such a circumstance would generate a matrix of inter-item correlations varying widely in size.

If the average intercorrelation among items were small, there could be a substantial number of negative correlations in the matrix, indicating that certain pairs of items tended to measure opposite things. Under such a circumstance, pooling them all into a single composite score would seem illogical, unless their functional equivalence could be established in some other way. If the negative or zero intercorrelations can be attributed to known extraneous factors that have been systematically counterbalanced within the test, adding uncorrelated items makes sense; otherwise, it would be more appropriate to identify subsets of substantially intercorrelated items, construct separate scales from these, and redefine the initial construct so as to recognize the empirically obtained distinctions.

Dimensionality

Common to the above models is the aim of distributing subjects along a dimension representing the magnitude of the attribute that the scale is supposed to measure. This implies that the scale is undimensional in the sense that, except for random error, all items measure the intended attribute only. Such an assumption is patently unrealistic if one takes seriously the widely held psychological principle that any response is multiply determined. At best, it is possible to construct a set of items each of which reflects the intended trait more than it reflects any other trait. Usually one is satisfied with a more modest achievement, with the irrelevant determinants differing from one item to the next so that a composite score represents, for most subjects, the intended trait predominantly. This is the practical meaning of unidimensionality in nearly all applications to attitude testing.

If one or more of the test items elicits substantially, in some subjects, an attribute different from (or in addition to) the common focal property, this circumstance will result in nonscalar types (in Guttman scaling), in widely distributed item choices (in Thurstone scaling), or in factorial complexity of an inter-item correlation matrix. Such common outcomes as these may induce quite different behaviors in researchers. One may become fascinated with the "dimensional properties" of the test and attempt a multidimensional scaling of its items, by procedures which result from elaborations of the above models of measurement. This research strategy tends to forsake (at least temporarily) the aim of measuring attributes of people. Another investigator might attempt to use such a dimensional analysis of items to locate subjects in the same hyperspace. Or, alternatively, he might use it to construct items that are balanced on the attributes considered irrelevant in order that the composite score reflect the focal dimension unconfounded by irrelevant dimensions.

Others would tend to avoid multidimensional items, because responses to them are so difficult to interpret; they would rather attempt to select and expand subsets of items each of which represents predominantly one of the distinguishable dimensions. Given that such unidimensional subsets can be constructed, the problem of interpreting them poses a semantic option. One investigator might identify the several dimensions by distinct concepts, while another would prefer to subsume them all as "independent aspects" of a more generic concept, usually the one from which the original item set was derived. The latter option is inconsistent with the dimensional model, and must be justified either on *a priori* grounds or by some different empirical procedure for establishing the functional equivalence of two "independent aspects."

The dilemma of multidimensionality stems from the acceptance of a measurement model which equates *dimension,* in the geometrical sense, with psychological notions of *attribute magnitude.* There seems to be, at present, no cogent alternative model which would circumvent this difficulty.

MEASURES OF TEST ADEQUACY

Given the conception of an attitude as a relatively enduring property of the person (rather than a transient reaction to a specific stimulus), which varies in degree along several dimensions embodied in its theoretical definition, an adequate measure of one of its properties would have the following characteristics:

1. *It would reflect the intended property veridically.*

2. *It would be unaffected by irrelevant characteristics either within the subject or within the testing situation.*

3. *It would not modify the property in the course of measuring it.*

4. *It would make sufficiently fine distinctions among persons to represent gradations along the dimension as conceived.*

5. *It would yield results substantially equivalent to those produced by another adequate instrument measuring the same property.*

6. *It would yield equivalent scores on a retest administered within a time period in which the property can be assumed to remain constant.*

7. *It would be relatively easy to construct, administer, score, and interpret.*

Ideally, one would like to have precise, quantitative indices for each of these criteria, in order to compare available instruments and to guide the construction of improved instruments. Quantitative indices for some of the criteria have been developed, but their applicability rests on certain assumptions about the psychological and measurement processes involved. In the absence of consensus concerning these assumptions, universally appropriate indices cannot be specified. The quantitative measures to be enumerated here are therefore subject to acceptance or rejection depending on how the investigator views the attribute to be assessed.

Validity

To say that an instrument measures the intended property may mean different things. One classical meaning, still employed by some investigators, is that scores on the instrument predict a unique external criterion, for instance, that scores on a scale of attitude toward fluoridation will predict how a person is going to vote on the issue in a city election. Given such a meaning, one possible index of validity is the product-moment correlation between the attitude scale and an objective measure of the criterion. This widely used index is deficient, however, in that it fails to specify the scale translation between the predictor and the criterion. A regression equation will do this, but it assumes a continuous function, which is meaningless for many criteria. A more generally appropriate procedure is to divide the attitude scale into segments that correspond exactly to the classes in the criterion that are to be distinguished (for example, favorable vote, unfavorable vote, no vote), then to compute an intraclass correlation (see p. 256) between the two variables, with their categories scored in corresponding fashion. This measure will represent the degree to which the predicted classification matches the obtained classification. (If the relation between the two variables is known to be nonlinear, the categories on the attitude scale must be reordered before they are combined to correspond with the criterion categories.)

This meaning of validity seems appropriate to certain very specific attitudes which are defined in such a way as to make a single criterion uniquely or pre-eminently relevant. Attitudes that are conceived primarily as intentions to behave are probably of this sort—for instance, voting preferences or statements about action policies, where veridicality of self-report or ability of the subject to predict his own behavior is the only question at issue. Evidence concerning criterion validities for such circumstances is rather fragmentary, and varies all the way from extremely poor correspondence (LaPiere, 1934) to quite good prediction (Campbell *et al.*, 1960). The former instance is the well-known case in which restaurant and hotel managers' stated policies regarding the admission of Chinese guests did not correspond to their actual practices on at least one occasion. The latter instance represents the relationship $(r = 0.80)$ between attitudes toward election issues and reported vote—not quite a *criterion* in the present sense—among early deciders. Neither of these two extremes necessarily represents typical experience with criterion prediction from attitude measures, and a more systematic review of representative results would be required to warrant reasonable guesses concerning the determinants of this kind of predictive validity. A major limitation on the veridicality of self-report is undoubtedly a tendency among researchers to require, and a tendency among respondents to provide, predictions or generalizations about behaviors which they are in no position to report. The question, "Would you allow your son to marry a shikse?" has no clearly valid answer, in the present sense, except "I don't know."

Instances in which the notion of single-criterion validity is applicable are exceedingly rare in attitude research, for an attitude is usually defined in less precise terms, as relevant to a variety of behaviors—behaviors which themselves are subject to many influences besides the particular attitude. This circumstance requires a multiple-criterion approach if the concept of validity is to be retained. One seeks partial correspondences between attitude scores and a variety of theoretically relevant variables; such variables do not serve to "define" the attitude in an exhaustive sense, but merely to provide other instances of its manifestation which can be accepted with greater confidence than the attitude scale itself. In this sense, they serve as "criteria," but their status in this regard may be an impermanent one; once a measuring instrument has gained wide acceptance (as, for example, in the case of the Doppler effect or the Stanford-Binet intelligence test), it takes on criterial properties stronger than the variables against which it was once validated.

Given an uncertain status of the measuring instrument, it may be validated against multiple criteria, provided the investigator has sufficient confidence in his measures of the latter, and in the theory which defines their relevance, so that negative results can be confidently attributed to invalidity of the questionable instrument. The product-moment correlation is ordinarily adequate for representing the degree of relationship, since no precise predictions from instrument to criterion are implied.*

One technique that is often used is the "known-groups" method of validation, in which the instrument is administered to two groups of subjects, one of which can be confidently assumed to possess the attribute to a greater degree than the other. It is misleading, however, to infer the extent of validity from the significance level of the resulting t ratio or from the magnitude of the point-biserial correlation coefficient. These indices are substantially affected by the sizes of the groups and by the way in which the samples are selected. Very large mean differences and point-biserial correlations can be obtained for instruments that have little predictive value, simply by an opportunistic selection of the "known groups" and by equating their sizes. If either of these indices is to be used (and the point-biserial correlation is to be preferred), they should be based on a representative sample of the population to which the instrument will be applied (see Dawes, 1962; Meehl and Rosen, 1955; Milholland, 1964). This procedure will yield "known groups" proportionate to their actual population sizes, hence will require a very large sample if the group membership is small. The correlation should be computed from the entire sample if it is to reflect accurately the instrument's diagnostic validity in the intended population.

Correlation between instruments

The procedures for establishing multiple validities via correlation with theoretically relevant variables are sometimes referred to as methods of *construct validation* (American Psychological Association, 1954; Campbell, 1960; Cronbach and Meehl, 1955; Loevinger, 1959), because they serve to substantiate an interpretation

---

* Throughout this discussion, we are ignoring the distinction between interval- and ordinal-scale statistics which is made by some investigators, because "validity" is an inference rather than a number, and because sampling distributions of statistics are independent of "scale type" in the usual sense (see Lord, 1953a). Though it would be uncommon to predict a curvilinear relationship from current conceptions of attitudes and their measures, such a function could be described by an equation and an appropriate goodness-of-fit index. If the criterion is measured as a multiple-category nominal scale, it is best to order the categories according to a reasonable linear prediction or to make a series of comparisons between pairs of groups; for this procedure a point-biserial correlation will be adequate.

of test scores in accordance with the psychological construct from which the test was developed. This approach to validation is gradually replacing the earlier single-criterion approach. It implies a much more ambitious program of research which is only in part made feasible by the developing computer technology. (See pp. 263–264.) Before a researcher proceeds very far into systematic construct validation he may want to collect preliminary evidence that the proposed instrument is actually measuring the intended attribute. One common way of doing this (which is called *convergent validation* by some investigators) is to compare scores obtained from two separate instruments aimed at the same construct.

An absence of correlation between two such instruments is ordinarily taken as discouraging evidence, but a positive correlation must be interpreted rather critically. It may reflect similarities between the two instruments (methods factors) or test-taking styles and irrelevant subject properties besides those implied by the focal construct. Therefore, it is prudent to intercorrelate quite different instrument types, if their correspondence is to be attributed primarily to common content. Unfortunately, there is no certain way of determining how different two instrument types are, or of establishing appropriate bounds of diversity. The program of attitude measurement proposed by Cook and Selltiz (1964) approaches the widest conceivable limits of diversity; other investigators might prefer to stay within narrower bounds in order to avoid encroaching on distinct constructs. At present one must depend largely on informal guides of theory, intuition, and experience to select those instruments which represent the same content but differ in potentially confounding factors. The multitrait-multimethod mode of analysis (see pp. 260–262) provides some assistance in detecting instrument artifacts.

Homogeneity

All models of measurement which assume monotone item operating characteristics (including the cumulative scaling model and classical psychometric theory) imply that items within a scale will be mutually intercorrelated. The average level of inter-item correlation can be represented by the *homogeneity ratio* (Scott, 1960), defined as

$$HR = \frac{\sigma_t^2 - \Sigma\sigma_i^2}{(\Sigma\sigma_i)^2 - \Sigma\sigma_i^2},$$

where σ_t^2 is the variance over subjects in total scale scores, σ_i^2 is the variance over subjects in scores for each item, $\Sigma\sigma_i^2$ is the sum of these item variances over all items, and $\Sigma\sigma_i$ is the sum of item standard deviations over all items.

This formula, similar to that of Loevinger (1947), is based on the observation that, as the homogeneity of a scale increases, the variance among total scale scores increases. The homogeneity ratio represents the degree to which the actual total-score variance exceeds the variance that would be obtained with uncorrelated items ($\Sigma\sigma_i^2$), in ratio to the maximum difference that would be found if all items were perfectly correlated; HR is also equal to a weighted average inter-item correlation, in which the correlation between every pair of items is weighted by the geometric mean of their variances.

A negative homogeneity ratio would imply that the several manifestations of the attribute included in the scale tended to be mutually exclusive. Under such a circumstance, the additive model for assessing magnitude would not apply, and it would make little sense to add item scores into a total score. A homogeneity ratio of 0.00 would represent an average inter-item correlation of zero, which also suggests that a single scale score should not be established by addition of items. The maximum value of +1.00 could be reached only if all items were perfectly correlated, that is, yielded identical distributions of subjects. This would mean that the items were mutually redundant and any one of them would represent the attribute as well as the total scale score. Though such an outcome might be a desirable objective for physical measurement, it is rarely pursued in psychological assessment, since it could probably be attained only by asking the same question repeatedly and relying on subjects' memories to ensure identical answers, thus confounding irrelevant variables with the focal attitude.

In a way, the magnitude of the homogeneity ratio represents the degree to which the researcher has defined the attribute with sufficient precision to construct redundant measures of it. Such precisely defined attributes may be of little interest because they are too instrument-specific and unlikely to be manifested outside the particular test. Thus some compromise is generally sought between a representative sample of items which assess the attitude in various ways, and a homogeneous sample of items which assess it identically. A high homogeneity ratio may be acceptable if the investigator is satisfied with the representativeness of item content and can be sure that it reflects the intended attribute rather than some irrelevant factor. A very low homogeneity ratio should be treated as a signal that some of the items may be poorly (even negatively) correlated with the others; hence, a detailed inter-item correlational analysis may be in order, to discard from the scale those items which do not reflect the common attribute.

Experience with attitude-test items indicates that they typically generate widely varying intercorrelations. Sometimes these are attributable to known sources of irrelevant variance (such as acquiescence) which were purposely built into the test in order to balance this factor out in the total test score. However, there may appear item clusters which were not expected *a priori,* and which may not even be explainable *post hoc;* one simply has to conclude that the items did not measure the same single attribute, as intended, and try another set of items or a more specific definition of the attribute, in the hope that more interpretable results will emerge from another sample.

Even if inter-item correlations did not vary widely (as is usually the case), but instead maintained a fairly constant low value, this would still pose a problem to interpretation of the scale. It would be difficult to judge their common component by simply perusing the set of items, and therefore difficult to write new items which represented the same domain. Until the investigator can write new items which intercorrelate with the previously established scale, he cannot pretend to have understood what the scale measures; also, pragmatically, he probably cannot construct a test of sufficient length to meet minimum standards of reliability.

Reliability

Since it is impossible to arrive at a single index of validity for most psychological tests, many psychometricians would prefer to concentrate on maximizing reliability instead. This objective stems from the assumption that the most valid measure of a trait must be an instrument that has been specifically designed to measure it, rather than some external criterion which is necessarily a function of many variables. The best measure, from this perspective, is one which yields precise scores—a scale on which any subject can be exactly located and his position distinguished clearly from those of other subjects.

The precision with which subjects' locations are determined may, in principle, be established by repeated measurements. To the extent that identical scores are obtained on both occasions, subjects' locations are precise and the instrument is reliable. The degree of similarity between two scores can be established only in relative terms, however, and it is customary to use the intersubject variability of scores as a standard of comparison for test-retest discrepancies. The coefficient of reliability may be expressed by the intraclass correlation coefficient:

$$\rho = 1 - \frac{\Sigma(X_1 - X_2)^2}{2n\sigma_c^2},$$

where X_1 is the score obtained by a particular subject on the first test, X_2 is the score obtained by the same subject on the retest, n is the number of subjects, and σ_c^2 is the variance of the test and retest scores combined.

If one assumes that the means and standard deviations of the initial test and retest scores are equal (as they should be if the two tests measure the same, unchanged attribute), this formula becomes the familiar product-moment correlation coefficient. However, the intraclass correlation makes the point more explicitly: that reliability depends on precision of measurement (a small discrepancy between test and retest scores), and that the degree of precision is appraised relative to the variability among all scores. A given average discrepancy will yield a high coefficient of reliability if intersubject variability is large, and a low coefficient of reliability if intersubject variability is small. Thus, the reliability of a test is not a constant property, but depends on the population to which it is applied.

Ideally, a high coefficient of reliability may be interpreted to indicate that the measuring instrument locates subjects precisely on the attribute dimension, in relation to all other subjects tested. However, if the test score consists of a composite of item scores, such an interpretation requires additional assumptions: namely, that the several items represent a single common attribute, and that they represent it equally well. This implies that all test items are equally correlated with the total score.

The straightforward way of assessing instrument reliability—administering the same test to the same subjects on repeated occasions—is normally precluded in psychological testing, because subjects' memories for previous responses might confound the correlation between test and retest scores. Instead, reliability is ordinarily determined from a single test, by considering it a composite of tests all measuring the same attribute. If any random subset of items is assumed to be equivalent to any other random subset of the same length, then the total test reliability, that is, the degree to which it would correlate with an equivalent test, may be estimated from the formula known as Kuder and Richardson's (1937) Formula 20 or Cronbach's (1951) coefficient alpha:

$$\alpha = \frac{k}{k-1} \frac{\sigma_t^2 - \Sigma\sigma_i^2}{\sigma_t^2},$$

where k is the number of items in the test, σ_t^2 is the variance over subjects in total test scores, σ_i^2 is the variance over subjects in scores on each item, and $\Sigma\sigma_i^2$ is the sum of item variances over all items.

If the test has been constructed so as to counterbalance certain extraneous determinants, or to represent them in different sets of items, then random subsets of items will not provide equivalent measures, and the above formula will underestimate the degree to which a parallel (that is, similarly stratified) test would correlate with the present one.

The magnitude of α depends on (1) the homogeneity of the test (average inter-item correlation) and (2) the length of the test (k). A test of fairly high homogeneity can be made as reliable as one may wish simply by adding items that measure the same trait equally well. However, a very high homogeneity implies that intersubject discrimination is accomplished by separating scores into two extreme groups, and that very little discrimination is made in the middle range of the scale (because few subjects fall there).

If a test has low homogeneity, reliable discrimination among subjects on a single dimension may be impossible to accomplish. If all items have uniformly low (though positive) intercorrelations, it will be necessary to increase the test to an unreasonable length, which may induce subject fatigue or carelessness and thereby change the attribute being measured. If low homogeneity reflects widely varying (including negative) inter-item correlations, then it is likely that more than one attribute is being measured by the test, and the total score does not locate subjects precisely on any single dimension.

Just as in the case of homogeneity, measures of test reliability reflect covariance among items with respect to all characteristics that they have in common, including irrelevant methods variance. Therefore, in constructing and scoring the test it is desirable to minimize known sources of irrelevant variance. If this is done, for instance, by balancing items for acquiescence or "social desirability" or extremity, the composite will necessarily be less homogeneous than when these factors are confounded with the "true trait score." The matrix of inter-item correlations will show clusters of items that are similar with respect to irrelevant features. This consideration makes it clear that the reliability coefficient, the homogeneity ratio, and the inter-item correlation matrix must be interpreted in the light of known sources of contamination and the controls that have been introduced to overcome them.

Distribution of test scores

One generally wants to discriminate among subjects in some way other than simply assigning them to two extreme groups. If a single, dichotomous criterion is to be predicted, an optimal distribution of test scores is one that divides subjects fairly clearly into two groups of the same size as the criterion groups. This may be accomplished with items whose popularities (p_i) are all set equal to a value less extreme than the proportion (P) of the criterion group to which they correspond. The optimum p_i depends both on P and on the test homogeneity. The more homogeneous the test, the closer will p_i be to P. (See Lord, 1952, 1953b, 1955.)

It is more frequently the case that no single criterion is of predominant interest in attitude-scale construction; one wishes instead to discriminate among subjects equally throughout the entire range of test scores. For this purpose a rectangular distribution of scores is to be preferred. In principle, the score distribution for a given population of subjects can be controlled by the test constructor to the extent that he can manipulate its two principal determinants, inter-item correlations and item popularities (see Humphreys, 1956). If all items are of equal popularity and uncorrelated, summative scores will tend to be normally distributed. As the average intercorrelation among equally popular items increases, the distribution will flatten out, then become bimodal, and eventually become two points, for perfectly correlated dichotomous items. A bimodal distribution can be made more rectangular, or a rectangular distribution more normal, by constructing items of varying popularities while keeping their average intercorrelation constant.

If one assumes a set of dichotomous items, all with popularities of 0.50, their summated scores will be distributed approximately rectangularly if the average inter-item correlation is about 0.33. Smaller intercorrelations will yield a more normal distribution. Actually 0.33 is an unusually high value for psychological tests; most of these are likely to have average inter-item correlations of 0.20 or less. Thus the total score distribution will be substantially on the normal side of rectangular even without varying item difficulties. This means that, in most practical circumstances with an unspecified criterion, the researcher would be well advised to keep all item popularities as close to 0.50 as possible, in order to yield maximal discrimination among subjects throughout the range of scores.

The degree of intersubject differentiation provided by the total scores is one way of representing the precision of a test. One possible index of differentiation is $1/\Sigma P_i^2$, where P_i is the proportion of subjects who obtain any particular score, and the summation is performed across all score categories. Another possible index is 2^H, where H is a measure of nominal-scale dispersion (see Attneave, 1959; Scott and Wertheimer, 1962), defined as:

$$H = \log_2 n - \frac{1}{n} \Sigma n_i \log_2 n_i,$$

where n is the total number of subjects tested, n_i is the number of subjects who obtain any particular score, and the summation is taken over all score categories.

Either of these indices may be interpreted as the number of "items-worth of discrimination" made by the test, that is, as the minimum number of items with optimum popularity and optimum intercorrelation that would be required to discriminate as well as the present test. They will be large to the extent that (1) the number of test items is large, (2) the items are all of 0.50 popularity, (3) the items are all intercorrelated 0.33, and (4) the sample size is large enough to yield fairly stable values of n_i (which probably means at least five times the number of items). So long as the average inter-item correlation is 0.33 or smaller, item popularities of 0.50 will yield the best discrimination. To the extent that the average inter-item correlation exceeds 0.33, discrimination will be maximized by a wider distribution of item popularities around 0.50. Conditions 2 and 3 depend on a particular population of subjects; if this is changed, item difficulties and inter-item correlations may change too, thus altering the discriminating power of the test.

Insensitivity to extraneous variables

In order to ascertain that an attitude scale measures the intended construct only, it is necessary to show that it yields scores different from measures of other variables from which the focal construct is to be distinguished. Appraisal of a test according to this criterion would theoretically require two prior steps: designation of specific characteristics deemed irrelevant and the construction of measures for them. In practice, these steps are difficult to accomplish in a completely satisfactory fashion.

Sometimes one can specify in advance certain characteristics that should be completely uncorrelated with the attitude. These may include known instrument factors, such as acquiescence, extremity, verbosity, social desirability, and so forth. But the distinctiveness of a particular attitude from certain other psychological constructs may be only partial; one might expect attitudes toward ethnic groups, for example, to be correlated with the subject's general level of hostility. Some psychologists would even be reluctant to exclude acquiescence from the definition of authoritarianism (see Gage and Chatterjee, 1960; Gage, Leavitt, and Stone, 1957; Leavitt, Hax, and Roche, 1955; Rokeach, 1963) or social desirability from the definition of mental health (see Heilbrun, 1964), even though others would regard these as irrelevant instrument factors. The fact that definitions of attitudes are not entirely consensual, and are not usually independent of other constructs, implies that their measures will not be completely distinguishable from certain other measures. Relative distinguishability, then, must replace absolute distinguishability as a realistic criterion for attitude scales.

Even if one can explicitly specify certain irrelevant characteristics from which an attitude is to be distinguished, it may not be easy to construct measures of them. A reliable measure of some response set, such as acquiescence or extremity, may be harder to construct than a reliable measure of the focal attitude (see Couch and Keniston, 1960; Messick, 1962). Given this difficulty, one of two expedients is usually chosen. First, the investigator may simply pick certain measures that are commonly used and well understood in the culture (for example, education level, intelligence, age), representing variables from which he wishes to distinguish his construct. Alternatively, he may develop a new instrument that is similar to his critical measure in all respects except for the particular attribute which he wishes to distinguish. For example, if extremity of attitude toward the Soviet Union were to be distinguished from extremity of attitudes toward all other objects, one might write a parallel item for each item in the first attitude scale, including the name of some other object, making sure that the item made sense and that, together, the parallel items sampled the domain of "other objects." If extremity of attitude toward the Soviet Union were to be distinguished from extremity of attitude toward all other nations, then the parallel items would refer only to other nations.

Given two tests, similar in form and content except for the critical attribute which is to be distinguished, one may intercorrelate their scores and compare the obtained correlation with the reliability of the critical test. To the extent that the latter exceeds the former, the critical attribute may be considered distinguishable from the extraneous variables built into both tests. This interpretation requires, however, that the irrelevant subject characteristics remain constant from one test to the other; one way of encouraging this is to intermix items from both tests so that order effects do not confound the test differences.

The comparison between test reliabilities and intertest correlations is one method of *discriminant validation* proposed within Campbell and Fiske's (1959) multitrait-multimethod model of analysis. The kind of question to which this comparison is relevant concerns the degree to which any single test measures the intended attribute in a differential way. If one considers the attribute as best measured, not by a single test, but by a composite of several different instrument types, then a second kind of comparison within the multitrait-multimethod matrix becomes relevant. This is between the average intercorrelation among tests aimed at the same attribute and their average correlation with tests aimed at different attributes.

Table 4 illustrates the comparisons with a reduced matrix from Scott (1963b). The traits represented are five "needs" included in the Edwards (1953) Personal Preference Schedule (EPPS): *A,* order; *B,* dominance; *C,* nurturance; *D,* change; and *E,* aggression. Each of these needs was measured by three instruments: (1) the standard forced-choice form of the EPPS, (2) a single-stimulus form of the same test, and (3) the subject's report of his own need-relevant behavior.* Reliability estimates (Cronbach's alpha) are shown in parentheses along the diagonal. The adjacent triangles show intercorrelations among the three instruments measuring each need (*monotrait* correlations). The remainder of the matrix reports correlations between pairs of measures aimed at different needs (*heterotrait* correlations).

---

* These data were collected for another purpose, and are not entirely appropriate to the model, since methods (1) and (2) are not independent and the forced-choice method of assessment (method 1) generates spurious negative intercorrelations among the traits. However, these were the only easily available results which provided complete reliability estimates, so they are included here for the sake of hypothetical illustration.

TABLE 4

MULTITRAIT–MULTIMETHOD MATRIX (DATA SELECTED FROM SCOTT, 1963b)

$n = 50$; $r_{05} = 0.23$ (ONE-TAIL), 0.28 (TWO-TAIL)

Trait:	A			B			C			D			E		
Measure:	1	2	3	1	2	3	1	2	3	1	2	3	1	2	3
A 1	(71)														
2	63	(80)													
3	31	55	(71)												
B 1	−04	−06	−09	(83)											
2	−34	−18	−06	67	(85)										
3	−06	−11	18	36	47	(65)									
C 1	−32	−08	−13	−48	−07	−26	(78)								
2	−26	09	18	−20	08	06	55	(60)							
3	02	04	10	08	−03	14	12	21	(50)						
D 1	−18	−11	18	−08	−07	09	−14	20	−16	(81)					
2	−28	−08	32	−02	06	03	−09	33	01	74	(80)				
3	−18	−16	02	−04	14	20	−02	07	23	25	31	(55)			
E 1	−16	−43	−22	33	13	08	−48	−47	−02	14	01	01	(81)		
2	−45	−37	−14	47	52	28	−21	−19	05	−10	06	−07	56	(68)	
3	−04	−25	−16	15	15	21	−02	−08	27	−21	−20	04	32	37	(31)
Mean *r*, monotrait:															
	0.47	0.59	0.43	0.52	0.57	0.42	0.34	0.38	0.17	0.50	0.53	0.28	0.44	0.47	0.35
Mean |*r*|, heterotrait:															
	0.19	0.16	0.15	0.17	0.15	0.14	0.19	0.18	0.10	0.14	0.12	0.10	0.20	0.24	0.15

In all cases the instrument reliabilities exceed their respective heterotrait correlations, and in all cases but one (need E, measure 3), they exceed their monotrait correlations, indicating distinctiveness of the instruments. (This may be attributed, in part, to adjacency factors, since in this study all measures 1 were administered together, followed by all measures 2, then by all measures 3.)

The monotrait correlations may be compared with the heterotrait correlations in various ways to determine whether the several traits are mutually distinguishable. In all cases the mean correlations within traits are higher than the mean absolute value of correlations across traits. A more detailed analysis shows, however, that the correlation between $C1$ and $C3$ (0.12) is exceeded in absolute value by seven heterotrait correlations in which measure $C1$ is involved and by four heterotrait correlations in which measure $C3$ is involved. Therefore, $C1$ and $C3$ are evidently not measuring a common trait that is distinguishable from certain other traits represented in the battery. (This conclusion stands even when the correlations are corrected for attenuation, to take account of the poor reliability of $C3$.) Similarly, four of $E1$'s heterotrait correlations are higher than its correlation with $E3$ (0.32), so the distinctive commonality of these two measures is also suspect. A comparable analysis indicates that traits B and D are quite distinctively measured by these three instrument types, since their monotrait correlations are higher in absolute value than nearly all of their correlations with different traits.

Though no standard indices of discriminant validity are yet available, it is possible to make some judgments, based on informal appraisals such as these, concerning the adequacy of the measures. If two instruments aimed at different traits intercorrelate almost as highly as their respective reliabilities, this may be attributed to the inclusion in one of them of items which belong in the other, indicating that the concepts from which the respective sets of items were developed had not been sufficiently distinguished. One useful step toward improvement in this respect is to intercorrelate all items from the two scales together, and discard those which fail to relate with items in their own scale better than they do with items in the other scale. Such a discriminant purification will usually require some redefinition of the respective constructs so as to represent the remaining items rather than the initial sets.

If two instruments aimed at different traits correlate about as highly as either of them does with some other instrument aimed at the same trait, then the remedial steps to be taken will depend on the kind of heterotrait correlation involved. If the two heterotrait instruments appear to have common irrelevant variance (for example, if both of them have the same response format, or if both of them invite similar distortions in self-report), then one might try to overcome these by the procedures discussed earlier (pp. 239–241). This attempt is likely to be only partially successful, for such irrelevant sources of variance have often been found to be more potent than trait variance in contributing to test scores. An alternative strategy is to widen the range of testing procedures employed, so that a composite score from the battery will not be predominantly affected by any single kind of irrelevant variance.

If the two highly correlated instruments appear to share neither trait variance nor irrelevant variance, then it is quite likely that the two traits were not adequately distinguished when their items were constructed. Clarification may be aided by intercorrelating all items from both tests together and discarding those which overlap both clusters. Alternatively, the tests may be reconstructed in such a way as to increase their correlations with adequate measures of the same traits. If one finds that two or more monotrait tests do show adequate convergent and discriminant validity, then individual items from the third (inadequate) test might be correlated with total scores on the first two, with the aim of determining what kind of item best measures whatever the two highly correlated monotrait tests have in common. If more items of this type can be written, then the monotrait correlations of the third test may be increased sufficiently to exceed its heterotrait-heteromethod correlations.

Correlation with external variables

Though two tests aimed at the same construct will ordinarily yield comparable results, it is possible that irrelevant confounding characteristics, working in different directions, may offset the common content to produce essentially zero correlation between them. Though a test is designed to measure a particular attribute, it may correlate so highly with some other, presumably distinct, measure that one does not know how to interpret the scores. Under either of these circumstances, the comparability or distinctiveness of the measures may not be appropriately represented by a single correlation coefficient, but must be investigated further by numerous theoretically relevant external correlations. While the notion of single-criterion "validity" is rarely appropriate, there is a sense in which the meaning of a test score depends on the kinds of predictions that can be made from it. Such predictions will ordinarily be established via correlations with certain external variables implicit in the conceptual definition of the attribute. This is the strategy of *construct validation*.

If, for example, a set of *favorable* statements about Negroes yields a homogeneous scale, and another set of *unfavorable* statements about Negroes yields an equally homogeneous scale, but the two scales do not correlate with each other, it is reasonable to infer that the effect of acquiescence was strong enough to overcome the content commonality. An alternative interpretation, however, is that the scales represent independent attitudes rather than reflections of the same dimension. In order to establish the former interpretation, it is necessary to show that scores on both scales predict the same theoretically relevant external variables, which are not themselves confounded by acquiescence. Only after such functional equivalence has been established can one feel completely comfortable in combining the two scales into a single measure of "attitude toward Negroes."

To illustrate a different interpretative problem, suppose that two measures of "satisfaction with self" correlate as highly with a measure of "tendency to give socially desirable answers" as they do with each other (see, for example, Crowne, Stephens, and Kelly, 1961). How are the test scores to be interpreted? In order to investigate this question, it is necessary to designate a set of external variables (including, perhaps, results of experimental manipulations) whose correlation with the scale follows logically from the "self-satisfaction" interpretation and a different set of external variables whose correlation with the scale would be predicted from the "social desirability" interpretation. An empirical study of the correlations between the scale and both sets of external variables may help one decide which interpretation of the scale is more appropriate. If different predictions cannot be made from the two constructs, there is little point in quibbling over the verbal label. If the empirical results do not permit a clear choice of interpretation, then it would seem appropriate to redefine the concepts and their associated measures, so that the proposed terminological distinctions correspond with the obtained empirical distinctions.

The functional equivalence of two tests, demonstrated by the similarity of their correlations with the same set of external variables, is a relevant consideration in construct validation, regardless of the magnitude of the correlation between them. A multitrait-multimethod matrix provides one way of checking such a functional equivalence. In the reduced matrix of Table 4 there are only twelve external variables (three measures for each of four traits) on which any pair of monotrait measures may be compared; hence, the inferences from this example cannot be regarded as conclusive. For illustrative purposes, one may nevertheless note that measures $B1$, $B2$, and $B3$ correlate similarly with the twelve external measures, the correlations over these correlations being 0.62 for $B1$ and $B2$, 0.71 for $B1$ and $B3$, and 0.66 for $B2$ and $B3$ ($p < 0.05$ with a one-tail test). Measures of the other four traits show less uniform functional equivalence: $A2$ and $A3$, $C1$ and $C2$, $D1$ and $D2$, $E1$ and $E2$, $E2$ and $E3$ all show significant degrees of correspondence between their correlations with external variables, but the remaining monotrait pairs do not. Considering these comparisons, together with those discussed above in connection with discriminant validity, one would wish to see some improvement in instruments $A1$, $C3$, $D3$, and $E3$ before claiming that the five traits had been properly measured.

If two tests aimed at the same trait do not correlate similarly with external variables, a number of alternatives might be explored. First, it is possible that an inappropriate set of external variables has been selected. One should try to include those which are of central theoretical relevance to the construct and omit those which are not. Second, it may be that the trait has been poorly conceptualized, so that the wrong external variables are being investigated. An empirical search for corresponding and noncorresponding correlations may aid in reconceptualization. Finally, it may be the case that the shared variance in the two tests is due to some extraneous factor (for example, common methods variance) which is not represented in the external measures. If one has sufficient confidence in his designation of relevant external variables, he might attempt to purify each test by selecting items which correlate appropriately with the external measures. Such a procedure is likely to be laborious, and perhaps even unprofitable, because it requires simultaneous consideration of several relevant variables, each of which must itself be adequately measured. A systematic procedure for this strategy of test development has yet to be applied to the measurement of attitudes.

Relations among the criteria

The foregoing discussion of criteria for appraising attitude scales has included precise indices for some, but only rather vague procedural descriptions for others. One may expect further development and widespread adoption of precise criteria as investigators come to specify more clearly just what is wanted in a measure of attitudes. This will depend, in turn, upon clearer conceptions of the properties of *attitude* to be measured and of the uses to which the measures are to be put. Since one can envisage multiple uses, it is unlikely that all of the criteria can be met in any single instrument. An exclusive focus on homogeneity or reliability may be expected to impair the validity of an instrument for some purposes. An optimal distribution of test scores for one population of subjects will not be optimal for another. Maximum validity with respect to a particular external criterion will not necessarily permit a clear inference concerning just what property the test is measuring. Thus, the direction of effort in test development, and the measure of success, must ultimately depend on theoretical and pragmatic considerations extrinsic to psychometric methods.

Conversely, the very conception of what is theoretically or pragmatically required may be refined by the development of precise indices for appraising the adequacy of measuring instruments. Conceptual clarification and precise measurement are mutually facilitative processes which are appropriately conducted in endless alternation. It seems doubtful that our presently vague formulations of *attitude* will survive many more generations of diligent attempts at measurement. Moreover, one may expect that the kinds of measures attempted in the future will reflect increasing sophistication of thought concerning just what properties we wish to describe.

SUMMARY

The construct *attitude* has become so complex that one can no longer talk clearly about "measuring an attitude." Rather, one must restrict discussion to procedures for measuring a particular property of an attitude as conceptually defined. Whether this degree of theoretical complexity in the construct should be tolerated is a matter of some concern. One might hope that future conceptualizations will distinguish different constructs for many of the properties now subsumed under the single term. Most effort at measurement to date has been directed toward assessing the properties of direction and affective magnitude (or extremity). The models on which these measures are based derive from physical analogies which do not necessarily reflect contemporary conceptions of the psychological properties represented.

Unfortunately, most psychological theories are not well enough developed to support any precise alternative models of measurement. Most researchers operate under the assumption that a precise though faulty model is preferable to an imprecise model which does not permit refined distinctions among people. Classical psychometric theory and certain varieties of scaling theory (notably Thurstone's and Guttman's) have been most widely applied in recent attempts at precise attitude measurement. Though not enough is known about the relative adequacies of these procedures, psychometric theory is the most elaborately developed and its methods for instrument construction and analysis are somewhat easier. It is possible that extensions of psychometric theory and method, particularly in the elaboration of factorial components and moderator variables, will improve the usefulness of this model for attitude assessment.

Though most attitude scales are composed of items that depend on subjects' introspections and self-reports, this is not an inherent limitation of the measurement models, for any of them can incorporate various types of emitted or elicited responses, from physiological indicants to complex overt acts. The adequacy of these kinds of testing procedures should be appraised by the same kinds of criteria that are applied to verbal measures.

It has been assumed here that the basic principles and procedures of measurement applied to attitude assessment are no different from those which may be applied to most other psychological processes. Only the designation of relevant responses to be incorporated in the measuring instrument will depend on the particular psychological property with which one is concerned. If this assumption is valid, then the development of any theory or technique of psychological measurement, regardless of the trait or process to which it refers, will make a contribution to attitude measurement.

REFERENCES

American Psychological Association (1954). Technical recommendations for psychological tests and diagnostic techniques. *Psychol. Bull., Suppl., 51,* No. 2, part 2 (38 pp.).

Attneave, F. (1959). *Applications of information theory to psychology.* New York: Holt.

Bartlett, C. J., L. C. Quay, and L. S. J. Wrightsman (1960). A comparison of two methods of attitude measurement: Likert-type and forced choice. *Educ. psychol. Measmt., 20,* 699–704.

Berg, I. A. (1961). Measuring deviant behavior by means of deviant response sets. In I. A. Berg and B. M. Bass (Eds.), *Conformity and deviation.* New York: Harper.

Bergs, L. P., and B. Martin (1961). The effect of instructional time interval and social desirability on the validity of a forced-choice anxiety scale. *J. consult. Psychol., 25,* 528–532.

Borgatta, E. F. (1955). An error ratio for scalogram analysis. *Publ. Opin. Quart., 19,* 96–100.

Campbell, A., P. E. Converse, W. E. Miller, and D. E. Stokes (1960). *The American voter.* New York: Wiley.

Campbell, D. (1963). Another attempt at configural scoring. *Educ. psychol. Measmt., 23,* 721–727.

Campbell, D. P., and W. W. Sorenson (1963). Response set in interest inventory triads. *Educ. psychol. Measmt., 23,* 145–152.

Campbell, D. P., and R. W. Trockman (1963). A verification scale for the Minnesota Vocational Interest Inventory. *J. appl. Psychol., 47,* 276–279.

Campbell, D. T. (1950). The indirect assessment of social attitudes. *Psychol. Bull., 47,* 15–38.

——— (1960). Recommendations for APA test standards regarding construct, trait, or discriminant validity. *Amer. Psychologist, 15,* 546–553.

——— (1963). Social attitudes and other acquired behavioral dispositions. In S. Koch (Ed.), *Psychology: a study of a science.* Vol. 6: Investigations of man as socius. New York: McGraw-Hill.

Campbell, D. T., and F. T. Damarin (1961). Measuring leadership attitudes through an information test. *J. soc. Psychol., 55,* 159–176.

Campbell, D. T., and D. W. Fiske (1959). Convergent and discriminant validation by the multitrait-multimethod matrix. *Psychol. Bull., 56,* 81–105.

Cantril, H. (1946). The intensity of an attitude. *J. abnorm. soc. Psychol., 41,* 129–135.

Cartwright, D. S. (1964). Base matrix methodology. Paper presented at meeting of Society for Multivariate Experimental Psychology, Princeton, N.J.

Cattell, R. B. (1961). Theory of situational, instrument, second order, and refraction factors in personality structure research. *Psychol. Bull., 58,* 160–174.

Cattell, R. B., and B. Tsujioka (1964). The importance of factor-trueness and validity, versus homogeneity and orthogonality, in test scales. *Educ. psychol. Measmt., 24,* 3–30.

Clark, K. E. (1961). *Vocational interests of nonprofessional men.* Minneapolis: Univ. of Minnesota Press.

Cook, S. W., and Claire Selltiz (1964). A multiple-indicator approach to attitude measurement. *Psychol. Bull., 62,* 36–55.

Coombs, C. H. (1953). Theory and methods of social measurement. In L. Festinger and D. Katz (Eds.), *Research methods in the behavioral sciences.* New York: Dryden.

——— (1964). *A theory of data.* New York: Wiley.

Couch, A., and K. Keniston (1960). Yeasayers and naysayers: agreeing response set as a personality variable. *J. abnorm. soc. Psychol., 60,* 151–174.

Cozan, L. W. (1959). Forced-choice: better than other rating methods? *Personnel, 36,* 80–83.

Cronbach, L. J. (1950). Further evidence on response sets and test design. *Educ. psychol. Measmt., 10,* 3–31.

——— (1951). Coefficient alpha and the internal structure of tests. *Psychometrika, 16,* 297–334.

Cronbach, L. J., and P. E. Meehl (1955). Construct validity in psychological tests. *Psychol. Bull., 52,* 177–193.

Crowne, D. P., and D. Marlowe (1960). A new scale of social desirability independent of psychopathology. *J. consult. Psychol., 24,* 349–354.

Crowne, D. P., M. W. Stephens, and R. Kelly (1961). The validity and equivalence of tests of self-acceptance. *J. Psychol., 51,* 101–112.

Dawes, R. M. (1962). A note on base rates and psychometric efficiency. *J. consult. Psychol., 26,* 422–424.

DeFleur, M. L., and F. R. Westie (1958). Verbal attitudes and overt acts: an experiment on the salience of attitudes. *Amer. sociol. Rev., 23,* 667–673.

Doob, L. W. (1947). The behavior of attitudes. *Psychol. Rev., 54,* 135–156.

Dunnette, M. D. (1963). A modified model for test validation and selection research. *J. appl. Psychol., 47,* 317–323.

Edwards, A. L. (1953). *Edwards Personal Preference Schedule.* New York: Psychological Corporation.

———— (1957a). *The social desirability variable in personality assessment and research.* New York: Dryden.

———— (1957b). *Techniques of attitude scale construction.* New York: Appleton-Century-Crofts.

———— (1963). A factor analysis of experimental social desirability and response set scales. *J. appl. Psychol., 47,* 308–316.

Edwards, A. L., and K. C. Kenney (1946). A comparison of the Thurstone and Likert techniques of attitude scale construction. *J. appl. Psychol., 30,* 72–83.

Ekman, G., and L. Sjöberg (1965). Scaling. *Annu. Rev. Psychol., 16,* 451–474.

Filbeck, R. W., and R. Callis (1961). A verification scale for the Strong Vocational Interest Blank, Men's Form. *J. appl. Psychol., 45,* 318–324.

Ford, R. N. (1950). A rapid scoring procedure for scaling attitude questions. *Publ. Opin. Quart., 14,* 507–532.

Forehand, G. A. (1962). Relationships among response sets and cognitive behaviors. *Educ. psychol. Measmt., 22,* 287–302.

French, Vera (1947, 1948). The structure of sentiments. *J. Pers., 15,* 247–282; *16,* 78–100, 209–244.

Gage, N. L., and B. B. Chatterjee (1960). The psychological meaning of acquiescence set: further evidence. *J. abnorm. soc. Psychol., 60,* 280–283.

Gage, N. L., G. S. Leavitt, and G. C. Stone (1957). The psychological meaning of acquiescence set for authoritarianism. *J. abnorm. soc. Psychol., 55,* 98–103.

Ghiselli, E. E. (1956). Differentiation of individuals in terms of their predictability. *J. appl. Psychol., 40,* 374–377.

———— (1960). Differentiation of tests in terms of the accuracy with which they predict for a given individual. *Educ. psychol. Measmt., 20,* 675–684.

———— (1963). Moderating effects and differential reliability and validity. *J. appl. Psychol., 47,* 81–86.

Gorden, R. L. (1952). Interaction between attitude and the definition of the situation in the expression of opinion. *Amer. sociol. Rev., 17,* 50–58.

Gordon, C. (1963). A note on computer programs for Guttman scaling. *Sociometry, 26,* 129.

Gordon, L. V. (1951). Validities of the forced-choice and the questionnaire methods of personality measurement. *J. appl. Psychol., 35,* 407–412.

Gough, H. G. (1957). *California Psychological Inventory Manual.* Palo Alto, Calif.: Consulting Psychologists Press.

Green, B. F. (1954). Attitude measurement. In G. Lindzey (Ed.), *Handbook of social psychology.* Vol. 1. Cambridge, Mass.: Addison-Wesley.

———— (1956). A method of scalogram analysis using summary statistics. *Psychometrika, 21,* 79–88.

Guilford, J. P. (1954). *Psychometric methods* (2nd ed.). New York: McGraw-Hill.

Gulliksen, H. (1950). *Theory of mental tests.* New York: Wiley.

Guttman, L. (1944). A basis for scaling qualitative data. *Amer. sociol. Rev., 9,* 139–150.

———— (1950). The basis for scalogram analysis. In S. A. Stouffer *et al., Measurement and prediction.* Princeton, N.J.: Princeton Univ. Press.

———— (1953). Image theory for the structure of quantitative variables. *Psychometrika, 18,* 277–296.

———— (1960). The matrices of linear least-squares image analysis. *Brit. J. statist. Psychol., 13,* 109–118.

Hammond, K. R. (1948). Measuring attitudes by error-choice: an indirect method. *J. abnorm. soc. Psychol., 43,* 38–48.

Harman, H. H. (1960). *Modern factor analysis.* Chicago: Univ. of Chicago Press.

Hartley, E. L., and Ruth E. Hartley (1952). *Fundamentals of social psychology.* New York: Knopf.

Hathaway, S. R., and J. C. McKinley (1945). *Manual for the MMPI.* New York: Psychological Corporation.

Heilbrun, A. B., Jr. (1963). Revision of the MMPI *K* correction procedure for improved detection of maladjustment in a normal population. *J. consult. Psychol., 27,* 161–165.

———— (1964). Social-learning theory, social desirability, and the MMPI. *Psychol. Bull., 61,* 377–387.

Helmstadter, G. C. (1957). Procedures for obtaining separate set and content components of a test score. *Psychometrika, 22,* 381–393.

Hess, E. (1965). Attitude and pupil size. *Scientific American, 212,* 46–54.

Horowitz, E. L. (1936). The development of attitudes toward Negroes. *Arch. Psychol.,* No. 194.

Hovland, C. I., I. L. Janis, and H. H. Kelley (1953). *Communication and persuasion.* New Haven: Yale Univ. Press.

Hovland, C. I., and M. Sherif (1952). Judgmental phenomena and scales of attitude measurement: item displacement in Thurstone scales. *J. abnorm. soc. Psychol., 47,* 822–832.

Humphreys, L. G. (1956). The normal curve and the attenuation paradox in test theory. *Psychol. Bull., 53,* 472–476.

Jackson, D. N., and S. Messick (1958). Content and style in personality assessment. *Psychol. Bull., 55,* 243–252.

———— (1961). Acquiescence and desirability as response determinants on the MMPI. *Educ. psychol. Measmt., 21,* 771–790.

Jacob, P. E., and J. J. Flink (1962). Values and their function in decision-making. *Amer. behav. Scientist, Suppl., 5,* No. 9 (38 pp.).

Kluckhohn, C. (1951). Values and value orientations in the theory of action. In T. Parsons and E. A. Shils (Eds.), *Toward a general theory of action.* Cambridge: Harvard Univ. Press.

Kogan, N., and M. A. Wallach (1964). *Risk taking: a study in cognition and personality.* New York: Holt, Rinehart, and Winston.

Krech, D., and R. S. Crutchfield (1948). *Theory and problems in social psychology.* New York: McGraw-Hill.

Krech, D., R. S. Crutchfield, and E. L. Ballachey (1962). *Individual in society.* New York: McGraw-Hill.

Kuder, G. F. (1956). *Manual for the Kuder Preference Record, Form C.* Chicago: Science Research Associates.

Kuder, G. F., and M. W. Richardson (1937). The theory of the estimation of test reliability. *Psychometrika, 2,* 151–160.

LaPiere, R. T. (1934). Attitudes vs. actions. *Soc. Forces, 13,* 230–237.

Lazarsfeld, P. F. (1950). The logic and mathematical foundation of latent structure analysis. In S. A. Stouffer *et al., Measurement and prediction.* Princeton, N.J.: Princeton Univ. Press.

———— (1960). Latent structure analysis and test theory. In H. Gulliksen and S. Messick (Eds.), *Psychological scaling: theory and applications.* New York: Wiley.

Leavitt, H. J., H. Hax, and J. H. Roche (1955). 'Authoritarianism' and agreement with things authoritative. *J. Psychol., 40,* 215–221.

Lee, M. C. (1961). Interactions, configurations, and nonadditive models. *Educ. psychol. Measmt., 21,* 797–805.

Lewin, K. (1936). *Principles of topological psychology.* New York: McGraw-Hill.

Likert, R. (1932). A technique for the measurement of attitudes. *Arch. Psychol.,* No. 140.

Loevinger, Jane (1947). A systematic approach to the construction and evaluation of tests of ability. *Psychol. Monogr., 61,* No. 4 (whole No. 285).

———— (1948). The technic of homogeneous tests compared with some aspects of scale analysis and factor analysis. *Psychol. Bull., 45,* 507–529.

———— (1957). Objective tests as instruments of psychological theory. *Psychol. Reports, 3,* 635–694.

———— (1959). Theory and techniques of assessment. *Annu. Rev. Psychol., 10,* 287–316.

———— (1962). Measuring personality patterns of women. *Genet. Psychol. Monogr., 65,* 53–136.

Loevinger, Jane, Goldine C. Gleser, and P. H. DuBois (1953). Maximizing the discriminatory power of a multiple-score test. *Psychometrika, 18,* 309–317.

Loewenfeld, Irene E. (1958). Mechanisms of reflex dilatation of the pupil: historical review and experimental analysis. *Documenta Ophthalmologica, 12,* 185–448.

Lord, F. M. (1952). A theory of test scores. *Psychometrika Monogr.,* No. 7.

—— (1953a). On the statistical treatment of football numbers. *Amer. Psychologist, 8,* 750–751.

—— (1953b). Optimum level of item difficulty. Research Memorandum 53–3. Princeton, N.J.: Educational Testing Service. (Ditto)

—— (1955). Some perspectives on the 'attenuation paradox in test theory.' *Psychol. Bull., 52,* 505–510.

McKinley, J. C., S. R. Hathaway, and P. E. Meehl (1948). The MMPI: VI. The *K* scale. *J. consult. Psychol., 12,* 20–31.

McQuitty, L. (1959). Differential validity in some pattern analytic methods. In B. M. Bass and I. A. Berg (Eds.), *Objective approaches to personality assessment.* Princeton, N.J.: Van Nostrand.

—— (1961). Item selection for configural scoring. *Educ. psychol. Measmt., 21,* 925–928.

Meehl, P. E., and S. R. Hathaway (1946). The *K* factor as a suppressor variable in the Minnesota Multiphasic Personality Inventory. *J. appl. Psychol., 30,* 525–564.

Meehl, P. E., and A. Rosen (1955). Antecedent probability and the efficiency of psychometric signs, patterns, or cutting scores. *Psychol. Bull., 52,* 194–216.

Menzel, H. (1953). A new coefficient for scalogram analysis. *Publ. Opin. Quart., 17,* 268–280.

Messick, S. (1961). Separate set and content scores for personality and attitude scales. *Educ. psychol. Measmt., 21,* 915–923.

—— (1962). Response style and content measures from personality inventories. *Educ. psychol. Measmt., 22,* 41–56.

Miklich, D. R. (1965). Item characteristics and agreement-disagreement response set. Unpublished doctor's dissertation, University of Colorado.

Milholland, J. E. (1964). Theory and techniques of assessment. *Annu. Rev. Psychol., 15,* 311–346.

Moreno, J. L. (1934). Who shall survive? *Nerv. ment. Dis. Monogr.,* No. 58. (Rev. ed. Beacon, N.Y.: Beacon House, 1943.)

Mullins, C. J. (1963). Self-confidence as a response set. *J. appl. Psychol., 47,* 156–157.

Newcomb, T. M., R. H. Turner, and P. E. Converse (1965). *Social psychology.* New York: Holt, Rinehart, and Winston.

Norman, W. T. (1963). Personality measurement, faking and detection. An assessment method for use in personnel selection. *J. appl. Psychol., 47,* 225–241.

Peabody, D. (1966). Authoritarianism scales and response bias. *Psychol. Bull., 65,* 11–23.

Peters, C. C., and W. R. Van Voorhis (1940). *Statistical procedures and their mathematical bases.* New York: McGraw-Hill.

Proshansky, H. (1943). A projective method for the study of attitudes. *J. abnorm. soc. Psychol., 38,* 393–395.

Rankin, R. E., and D. T. Campbell (1955). Galvanic skin response to Negro and white experimenters. *J. abnorm. soc. Psychol., 51,* 30–33.

Rokeach, M. (1963). The double agreement phenomenon: three hypotheses. *Psychol. Rev., 70,* 304–309.

Rorer, L. G. (1965). The great response-style myth. *Psychol. Bull., 63,* 129–156.

Saltz, E., M. Reece, and J. Ager (1962). Studies of forced-choice methodology: individual differences in social desirability. *Educ. psychol. Measmt., 22,* 365–370.

Saunders, D. R. (1956). Moderator variables in prediction. *Educ. psychol. Measmt., 16,* 209–222.

Schanck, R. L. (1932). A study of a community and its groups and institutions conceived of as behaviors of individuals. *Psychol. Monogr., 43,* No. 2 (whole No. 195).

Schutz, R. E., and R. J. Foster (1963). A factor analytic study of acquiescent and extreme response set. *Educ. psychol. Measmt., 23,* 435–447.

Scott, W. A. (1956). The avoidance of threatening material in imaginative behavior. *J. abnorm. soc. Psychol., 52,* 338–346.

——— (1959). Cognitive consistency, response reinforcement, and attitude change. *Sociometry, 22,* 219–229.

——— (1960). Measures of test homogeneity. *Educ. psychol. Measmt., 20,* 751–757.

——— (1962). Cognitive complexity and cognitive flexibility. *Sociometry, 25,* 405–414.

——— (1963a). Cognitive complexity and cognitive balance. *Sociometry, 26,* 66–74.

——— (1963b). Social desirability and individual conceptions of the desirable. *J. abnorm. soc. Psychol., 67,* 574–585.

——— (1965). *Values and organizations: a study of fraternities and sororities.* Chicago: Rand McNally.

——— (1966a). Measures of cognitive structure. *Multivariate behav. Res., 1,* 391–395.

——— (1966b). Flexibility, rigidity, and adaptation: toward a clarification of concepts. In O. J. Harvey (Ed.), *Flexibility, adaptability, and creativity: nature and developmental determinants.* New York: Springer.

Scott, W. A., and M. Wertheimer (1962). *Introduction to psychological research.* New York: Wiley.

Scott, W. A., and S. B. Withey (1958). *The United States and the United Nations: the public view.* New York: Manhattan Publishing Company.

Stern, W. (1938). *General psychology from the personalistic standpoint.* New York: Macmillan.

Stouffer, S. A., E. F. Borgatta, D. G. Hays, and A. F. Henry (1952). A technique for improving cumulative scales. *Publ. Opin. Quart., 16,* 273–291.

Stricker, L. J. (1963). Acquiescence and social desirability response styles, item characteristics, and conformity. *Psychol. Reports, 12,* 319–341.

Suchman, E. A. (1950a). The scalogram board technique. In S. A. Stouffer *et al., Measurement and prediction.* Princeton, N.J.: Princeton Univ. Press.

—— (1950b). The intensity component in attitude and opinion research. In S. A. Stouffer *et al., Measurement and prediction.* Princeton, N.J.: Princeton Univ. Press.

Thurstone, L. L. (1959). *The measurement of values.* Chicago: Univ. of Chicago Press.

Thurstone, L. L., and E. J. Chave (1929). *The measurement of attitude.* Chicago: Univ. of Chicago Press.

Torgerson, W. S. (1958). *Theory and methods of scaling.* New York: Wiley.

van Zandt, B. R., and P. Himelstein (1961). The role of verbal fluency on a projective measure of motivation. *Educ. psychol. Measmt., 21,* 873–878.

Waly, Patricia, and S. W. Cook (1965). Effect of attitude on judgments of plausibility. *J. Pers. soc. Psychol., 2,* 745–749.

Werner, R. A. (1966). FORTRAN program for Guttman and other scalogram analyses. Syracuse, N.Y.: Maxwell School of Citizenship and Public Affairs. (Mimeo)

Weschler, I. R. (1950). An investigation of attitudes toward labor and management by means of the error-choice method. *J. soc. Psychol., 32,* 51–67.

Westie, F. R., and M. L. DeFleur (1959). Autonomic responses and their relationship to race attitudes. *J. abnorm. soc. Psychol., 58,* 340–347.

Willis, R. H. (1960). Manipulation of item marginal frequencies by means of multiple-response items. *Psychol. Rev., 67,* 32–50.

—— (1961). An empirical test of the method of controlled marginals. *Educ. psychol. Measmt., 21,* 39–52.

Woodmansee, J. J. (1965). An evaluation of pupil response as a measure of attitude toward Negroes. Unpublished doctor's dissertation, University of Colorado.

Zajonc, R. B. (1960). The process of cognitive tuning in communication. *J. abnorm. soc. Psychol., 61,* 159–164.

Zavala, A. (1965). Development of the forced-choice rating scale technique. *Psychol. Bull., 63,* 117–124.

12

Simulation of Social Behavior

ROBERT P. ABELSON, Yale University

The advent of simulation techniques to the social sciences has been so widely heralded yet so sudden that many practitioners and students of a variety of disciplines are clamoring to use these techniques without any clear grasp of their essentials. In part this is a training problem; there are only a few universities and research centers where "simulations" of one sort or another are solidly established features of the technical environment. But in larger measure this is a problem of communication; writings on simulation have often been overdramatized, oversimplified, or both, and the general reader cannot easily develop a feeling for the texture and detail of these new methodologies. This state of affairs is not necessarily the fault of those who write about the subject. It is difficult, as E. G. Boring is wont to point out, to maintain enough distance from the *Zeitgeist* to review its meaning and implications objectively.

The present chapter is no exception; it will not be entirely free of a certain subjectivity. By choice, the review of the literature will be rather selective; much that is of dubious relevance will be omitted, while other tangential materials will be included if suited to the purposes at hand. Wherever particular technical details seem doomed to obsolescence because of the rapid rate of new developments in the field, an attempt will be made to direct the reader toward the most promising new developments. Wherever there are glaring deficiencies in the present state of the art, these will be frankly discussed. Throughout, the guiding intention will be to bring the simulation field into better focus for social psychologists.

Many individuals deserve thanks for constructive criticisms of early drafts, written while the author was a Fellow of the Center for Advanced Study in the Behavioral Sciences, 1965–1966. Among them are Willa Abelson, Hayward Alker, Donald Campbell, Kenneth Colby, Edward Feigenbaum, Bert F. Green, Harold Guetzkow, Jeanne Gullahorn, John Gullahorn, Edward S. Johnson, John Loehlin, Allen Newell, Forrest R. Pitts, Walter Reitman, Philip J. Stone, John W. Tukey, and Joseph Weizenbaum. Mention in no way necessarily implies their endorsement of opinions expressed in this chapter.

PROSPECTUS

Our first task will be to sort out the variety of meanings of the term *simulation*. One of the major sources of terminological confusion is the role of electronic computers. In various contexts, simulation refers to the construction of models of behavior which can be exercised or "run" on a computer so that certain aspects of the computer's symbolic behavior imitate or simulate real-world behavior. In other contexts, the term simulation has been used without implicating computers in any direct way. And in still further applications of so-called simulation techniques, the computer plays a variety of supporting if not essential roles.

In this chapter we will place almost exclusive emphasis on simulation techniques in which the computer is implicated directly. Such methods embody a striking innovation in social-scientific practice, and thus warrant the most thorough treatment. We will devote a very detailed section to an exposition of the techniques necessary to use computers in simulation, including sufficient anecdotal and interpretive comment to convey a realistic impression of this unusual and initially mysterious area.

In the two sections following we continue this detailed treatment by reviewing several applications of computer simulation in psychology. One section will cover applications to the study of cognitive processes, and the other, to the study of social behavior. The former is important for an understanding of the latter, since cognitive-process simulations are historically prior, and are more highly developed than social-behavior simulations. In these application sections we will emphasize those simulation projects with the greatest presumed long-range relevance to social psychology, albeit many of these projects are incomplete at the time of writing. There will be extended discussions of the difficult problems involved, covering questions of parsimony, qualitative versus statistical validation, communication of models, and suggestions for future developments.

No separate section will be devoted to other types of simulation of social behavior, such as "gaming" and internation simulation. The specific techniques involved are briefly discussed below, where appropriate references are given.

TYPES OF SIMULATION

The Oxford English Dictionary gives as the common meaning of *simulate*, "To assume falsely the appearance or signs of (anything); to feign, pretend, counterfeit, imitate . . . ." In similar vein, *simulation* is defined as "the action or practice of simulating, with intent to deceive . . . ." These everyday definitions are a potential embarrassment to the field under discussion and a source of amusement to critics.

However, in the sense employed in this chapter, simulation is the *exercise of a flexible imitation of processes and outcomes for the purpose of clarifying or explaining the underlying mechanisms involved.* The feat of imitation *per se* is not the important feature of simulations, but rather that successful imitation may publicly reveal the essence of the object being simulated. The possibility of deceiving the naive observer is reduced to the minor role of a potential criterion by which to judge the successfulness of the imitation. (There are other, perhaps better, criteria for making this judgment. This question is discussed in detail in later sections.)

There is one further aspect of the informally understood technical definition of simulation which helps distinguish it from other somewhat similar activities, namely, the presence of a large difference in the apparent natures of the system to be imitated and the system which imitates it. Such a difference, for which we here coin the term *simulation gap*, is exemplified by the apparently obvious difference between a computer and a human being. Reactions to the possibility of bridging such differences can range from bold optimism to tenacious negativism. The latter category includes denials of the legitimacy of drawing any isomorphisms whatever across the simulation gap, such as in some humanists' discussions of computer simulation of thinking (Barzun, 1965; Bunge, 1957; Jefferson, 1949; to mention a few).

A listing of the sorts of entities which can lie on opposite sides of the simulation gap provides a means for distinguishing among the major classes of simulations relevant to social psychology. Such a listing is given in Table 1. It does not exhaust the possible terminological distinctions in the simulation area, nor can it provide an absolutely clean separation between certain types which frequently shade into one another. Nevertheless, it provides reasonably illuminating distinctions in an admittedly confusing domain. (Alternative discussions of these distinctions appear in several sources, for example, Cohen and Cyert, 1965; Dawson, 1962; Fattu, 1965.)

In the first type of simulation, the investigator sets himself the goal of representing some aspect of an individual or group process by a set of symbolic instructions which can be carried out on a computer. Among the relatively well-known realizations of this type is Newell, Shaw, and Simon's (1959) General Problem Solver (GPS), which simulates the cognitive activity of individuals attempting to solve problems, given certain logical ground rules. Other examples are Feigenbaum's (1961) simulation of verbal learning behavior, and Simon and Kotovsky's (1963) serial-pattern learner. Although the intent of these (and other) computer simulations is to imitate individuals, it is important to realize that only very limited aspects of behavior are encompassed. A successful computer simulation of a human chess player, for example, might generate games that seemed quite "human," but the computer would certainly not be constructed and instructed in such a way as to locomote through parks on Sundays trying to find an opponent, nor would it brag about its clever moves, ask to retract blunders, and so forth. Silly misunderstandings about this matter have been compounded not only by science fiction writers but by authorities in the computer field who argue that *in principle* computers can be programmed to imitate all the capabilities of the human mind (Minsky, 1963a; Turing, 1950; von Neumann, quoted by Jaynes, 1963; and many others). *In practice*, however, it turns out to be so difficult to simulate given isolated aspects of human behavior that no serious work on the integration of disparate aspects has yet been attempted. In this respect, the simulation field is comparable to most other theoretical efforts in scientific

TABLE 1

TYPES OF SIMULATION AND RELATED ACTIVITIES

Descriptive term	Simulator	Simulated	Remarks
1. Computer simulation	Computer	Single individuals or groups of individuals	Usually of cognitive or social processes. Sometimes distinguished from Types 2(b) and 3 by the term *all-computer*.
2. System simulation	a) Computer b) Groups of individuals aided by computers	Abstract "systems" such as schematized organizations or communication networks	a) Sometimes hard to distinguish from Type 1. b) Sometimes referred to as *man-machine* simulation.
3. Internation simulation	Sets of groups of individuals	Sets of decision makers representing nations	*All-man* simulation, occasionally shaded toward Type 2(b). Situations usually include a great variety of variables.
4. Gaming	a) Groups of individuals b) Two protagonists	Groups of idealized individuals or roles	Usually involves hypothetical well-structured quantitative decision situations, with explicit goals. Thus, somewhat distinct from all-man simulation. In (b), the variables are sharply limited.
5. Artificial intelligence	Computer	Idealized intelligences	Not intended as imitative of real individuals. Thus distinct from simulation.

psychology. Much of the objection to the simulation concept, though not often expressed explicitly in this way, is fundamentally a reluctance to accept the scientific necessity of dividing the total study of organisms into small problem units.

We have said that the intent of computer simulations is to imitate real individuals, but this specification leaves ambiguous what is meant by *individuals.* In this regard, several subtypes of simulation can be identified. Sometimes the immediate simulation target is a *particular single individual,* as for example in Feldman's (1963) simulation of a subject making a long series of binary-choice predictions, or Colby and Gilbert's (1964) simulation of a neurotic belief system. At the other extreme of the dimension of specificity-generality is the case where the simulation target is an *unspecified prototypic individual,* or perhaps an *average individual performance,* as in Feigenbaum and Simon's (1961, 1963) applications of Feigenbaum's EPAM (Elementary Perception and Memory) simulation. The eventual target of both of these subtypes is a *variety of single individuals,* but the difficult problem of individual differences stands in the way of such an achievement.

A comparable distinction can be drawn on the level of the group. Sometimes one or more particular groups of individuals will provide empirical background for a simulation (*cf.* Rainio, 1965), but there also exist several simulations aimed at prototypic characterization of small-group behaviors (*cf.* McWhinney, 1964); other examples are discussed in detail in a later section. Even at the level of very large collectivities such as electorates, there is considerable variation along this dimension of simulation style. Pool, Abelson, and Popkin (1964, 1965), for example, set out literally to prognosticate the behavior of the U.S. electorate, whereas McPhee and Ferguson's (1962) simulation of "political immunization" is intended to reflect certain aspects of electorates in general or in the abstract. These variations in simulation target are crucial in terms of the available means for assessing the adequacy of simulations, a matter which will be of continuing concern throughout this chapter.

The next type indicated in Table 1 may also involve the use of computers as simulators, but the targets are of such a different nature as to justify the use of another phrase, *system simulation.* By a *system* is meant an integrated entity made up of interacting parts which differ sharply in their structure and function. In the context of simulation, a surplus aspect of the mystique surrounding the term *system* is that it refers to entities which one can design or manipulate, rather than to natural objects such as individuals or informal groups. Actual individuals are frequently used in system simulations as simulators of human reactions in certain roles within the system. (This is done when the important features of one or more roles are too difficult to simulate entirely by computer. The computer, however, may still be used to imitate other roles or to coordinate and display information flowing through the system. In this case the total model of the system is a mixture of automated and human components; hence the term *man-machine simulation.*)

System simulation is most often used in the service of optimizing *system design,* that is, arranging the system in such a way that peak performance or efficiency is achieved. There exist a large number of engineering, industrial, and military applications of these techniques (*cf.* Boyd and Krasnow, 1963; Chapman *et al.,* 1959; Forrester, 1961; Hawthorne, 1964; Naylor *et al.,* 1966; Shubik, 1960; Sweetland and Haythorn, 1961).

Most of these applications are not relevant to this chapter. Suppose, for example, that a particular position in a proposed air-defense network is found through simulation to be often overloaded and potentially a bottleneck. It may then be urgent for the individual or individuals occupying that position in the system to receive extra technical aids in carrying out their roles, or for the system to be redesigned entirely. Such insights may be extremely helpful to the designers of a particular system, but they are seldom of use for social psychologists. Furthermore, even when a system simulation purports to embody certain general interpersonal or intraorganizational processes, it is often difficult to crack the systems oyster to locate the psychological pearls. The interested reader is invited to sample some of this literature for himself (Borko, 1962; Lackner, 1965; Malcolm, 1958; Rome and Rome, 1961, 1962), but it will not be pursued further here.

The third major type of simulation uses people in a laboratory setting to simulate people in the real world. There is commonly a large simulation gap here too, even though computers are not involved, because the real-world people being simulated are usually members of elite groups placed in very special circumstances. In the most dramatic example, a number of groups of individuals are placed in a laboratory setting in which each group is instructed to imagine that it represents the foreign policy arm of the government of some nation. Simulated international situations involving trade, treaties, alliances, threats, wars, etc., are then played out by these laboratory groups (Guetzkow *et al.,* 1963). [International situations have also been represented in computer simulations (Abt, 1964; Benson, 1962).]

There is usually no intention in this type of simulation that particular individual decision-makers or even particular real nations be imitated. Instead, the emphasis is upon rather stylized situational questions suggestive of present international configurations, for example, the effects on international stability of the spread of nuclear capabilities (Brody, 1963). A great variety of theoretical questions may be investigated, using a large number of independent and dependent variables. In this light, internation simulation is not a new technique, but a very ambitious extrapolation of the usual techniques of the social-psychological experiment. There are hazards in generalizing even the simplest behaviors of small laboratory groups, and these hazards clearly increase when laboratory subjects are required to play unfamiliar elite institutional roles. However, if generalization to international situations be insisted upon, internation simulations no doubt provide a better base than simpler experiments. In addition, there is the heuristic possibility that new policy alternatives may be suggested in the laboratory. Internation simulation has earned both skeptics (Cohen, 1962; Etzioni, Chapter 43 in Vol. 5 of this *Handbook*) and enthusiasts (Hays, 1965; Rosenau, 1965). Sympathetic but balanced reviews have been provided by Verba (1964) and Hermann (1967).

Various other possibilities exist for this kind of simulation or *laboratory sociology.* Zelditch and Evan (1962), for example, have among other things used student subjects as laboratory occupants of stylized bureaucratic roles; Barber (1966) has brought real budget committees into the laboratory and given them budgets to trim, so that in effect they were simulating themselves. Many of these possibilities are interesting, but beyond the scope of this chapter.

All three types of simulation outlined above have as their goal an increased understanding *by the investigator* of the objects being simulated. Thus far we have not raised the possibility that in a simulation attempt involving human simulators, the *participants themselves* may gain a better appreciation of the class of situations being simulated. This possibility is central to the set of techniques referred to as *gaming*.

There are a great many types of laboratory "games," for example, "business games" (Cohen *et al.*, 1964; Dill and Doppelt, 1965), "war games" (Giffin, 1965), a legislative game (Coleman, 1964c), and even a "high school student life" game (Coleman, 1965). In these games laboratory subjects are presented with well-structured situations and asked to respond so as to maximize certain outcomes (usually quantitative) on behalf of the team, organization, or person they represent.

An educational feature of most if not all of these games is that a subject's involvement in the play of the game often leads him to behave in self-surprising ways, thus presumably increasing his later empathy for occupants of the assumed role. As for the scientific purpose of the experimental game technique, it may often be comparable to the general purpose of *all-man* simulation: namely, to formulate and test psychological generalizations about the persons and situations being simulated. However, the distinguishing characteristic of "games" is that the experimenter explicitly instructs the subject in the criterion of task success (for example, "Earn as many dollars as you can"), and the repertoire of responses available to the subject is usually severely limited. The range of relevant performance variables for the subjects is thus made much more circumscribed than in other all-man simulations.

In one subclass of games of especial social-psychological interest, there is a very sharp and narrow focus on important variables not heretofore often studied in the laboratory. A great deal of work has recently been done on the psychology of bargaining, threat, and cajolery, and the balance of cooperative and competitive tendencies that emerge in so-called *mixed-motive* games (Christie and Geis, 1968; Deutsch and Krauss, 1960; Kelley, 1965; Pilisuk *et al.*, 1965; Rapoport and Chammah, 1965; Shure, Meeker, and Hansford, 1965). Whether or not one takes seriously the metaphoric extension of these games to international politics, the social situations represented are nevertheless compelling and worthy of study.

One further aspect of gaming deserves mention. Sometimes a mathematical solution specifying rationally optimal play of the game is available. Often it is found, however, that subjects do not play according to this normatively "best" procedure. The obvious question then arises: "Under what circumstances do subjects not behave 'rationally'?" Generally speaking, there are two attitudes that are taken in approaching this question. In one, the *normative* approach, it is presumed that subjects typically would or should play optimally, and that exceptions are to be understood in terms of special difficulties, for example, insufficient experience with the game. The other, the *descriptive* approach, takes the psychological definition of the game to be typically distinct from the mathematical description. Actual play of the game is studied in its own right, irrespective of mathematically optimal play. Psychologists tend to favor the descriptive approach and economists, the normative.

For our present purposes this distinction is important because it helps to separate simulation from other activities. As normally understood by psychologists, *simulation is descriptive, not normative.* (A special exception will be noted in a later section.) Terminological confusion is apt to arise when computers are used in the field of "artificial intelligence," that is, the design of nonhuman intelligences. Computers can sometimes be programmed so as to respond with apparent "intelligence" to tasks of moderate complexity. A case in point is a computer checkers player with learning capacity of such power that it is capable of defeating leading human players (Samuel, 1963). This artificial checkers player can be said to imitate some of the functions ordinarily associated with what is meant by "intelligence." Thus one might be led to refer to this feat as "computer simulation" (of a checkers player). But note that the performance of the computer need not correspond to human performance. It need only be intelligent in some idealized sense, that is, normatively good (indeed, perhaps incredibly good), not descriptively accurate. Mathematicians and computer specialists are wont to blur the normative-versus-descriptive distinction by including artificial intelligence under the rubric of simulation (or perhaps even by assigning descriptive simulation a minor role within the domain of artificial intelligence). Many sophisticated observers such as Newell and Simon (1963b), Armer (1963), and Shepard (1964) have argued that the distinction between descriptive simulation and artificial intelligence should not be too rigidly drawn lest good ideas in each field be lost to the other. Nevertheless, the present author recommends that the distinction be taken rather seriously. If one does not know whether the simulation target is real or idealized, one does not know how to assess the simulation. And without assessment, the simulation enterprise lacks self-discipline. In all but the deftest of hands, an imitation of a target which could be either a frail human or an artificial mechanism is liable to end up instead resembling a frail mechanism or an artificial human. Thus in Table 1 we have reserved the separate term *artificial intelligence* as distinct from computer simulation.

The typology we have presented cannot be expected to provide a completely reliable guide to the various types and subtypes of simulation. Verbal designations have generally been rather loose, and sometimes simulations serve mixed or multiple purposes anyway. Regardless of terminology, it is always useful to ask in any given case what is being simulated by what, and to what end.

THE METHODOLOGY OF COMPUTER SIMULATION

It has been but twenty years since stored-program electronic computers were invented, ten years since they became available to universities, and five since they reached the stage of development and accessibility necessary to make large-scale computer simulation feasible. The earliest uses of computers were entirely of a numerical character, and it is only since 1954 that the vast possibilities of computers as general nonquantitative logical machines have been envisaged, and only since 1958 that such visions have found their way into the psychological literature. Furthermore, the translation of vision into reality has proved extremely time-consuming, and it is little wonder that the number of applications of computer simulation to psychology has as yet been relatively small and the necessary technology ill-diffused. In this section we shall try to provide enough material to help the reader become conversant with the major considerations in the construction of computer simulations. For broader coverage of other uses of computers in psychology, Green's (1963) excellent text should be consulted, and Uttal's (1967).

MISLEADING IDEAS ABOUT COMPUTERS

The naive animistic view of computers promoted in the popular press is a considerable barrier to a balanced understanding of these machines. Most pernicious is the magical idea that when there is a problem to be solved, one should "feed it to the computer," which will effortlessly provide an answer. Little or no distinction is made between numerical and nonnumerical problems, and there is a great tendency to regard the computer as responsible in a personal way for its successes or its stupidities.

It is not the computer which displays wisdom or shallowness, but the person who provides the program of instructions for the computer. Although this seems an obvious point, the popular tendency to deify computers has progressed so far that the role of the program of instructions itself has become grossly underplayed and misunderstood. Even many social scientists who have used computers for purposes of statistical analysis, and who ought to know better, often act as though a particular statistical program represented *the* program for their particular analysis.

Factor analysis provides a prototypic example. There are many variants of factor analysis, and several options the user might exercise (for example, specifying a criterion for the number of factors to be retained). Without thorough knowledge of the principles involved in the analysis and careful attention to the "program write-up" specifying how to use the computer program, the user can easily obtain results from the computer other than those which he really wants.

These remarks about statistical analysis by computer apply in even greater degree to *simulation* by computer. There is no such thing as a computer simulation of social interaction which is the mere mechanical result of pressing the computer start button. The number of possible ways of specifying the relevant variables and processes for a simulation of social processes is enormous. When one is exposed to the existence of a computer simulation of some complex cognitive or social process, the naive natural reaction is often an awed, "What will computers be doing next!" but the really relevant response should be to forget the computer and ask, "What is this simulation really about, what are its details, and how well does it work?"

The purpose of this introduction has been to underscore the importance of *content* rather than mystique in the construction and understanding of computer simulations.

THE NECESSARY STEPS

As emphasized above, the most crucial step in the construction of a computer simulation is the formulation of detailed ideas about the process being simulated. The steps to follow are somewhat less creative and more technical, though no less demanding. The whole sequence of steps may be outlined as follows, allowing for a good deal of liberty in the presence and order of the subsidiary steps:

1. *Choice of problem to be studied.*
2. *Formulation of a detailed psychological model of the processes involved.*
3. *Determination of whether simulation is a suitable strategy for developing and testing the model.*
4. *Transformation of the psychological model into an organized sequence of major steps for computer execution.*
5. *Investigation of the particular computers available.*
6. *Choice of a suitable "programming language" for conveying the sequence of instructions to the computer and a suitable representation of the data in the computer.*
7. *Writing the computer program.*
8. *"Hand simulation" of the program.*
9. *"Debugging" the program.*
10. *Revision of the model.*
11. *Running the model on full-scale data.*

The above prospectus is a long and arduous one. The various steps are heavily interdependent, and it often proves necessary to repeat some of them or to go back to earlier steps in order to make further progress. We shall now discuss each of the steps in turn as though the progression from one to the next were orderly and smooth, but the reader should keep in mind that the actual construction of a computer simulation never proceeds precisely according to the textbook.

Choice of problem

It goes without saying that an investigator should choose his problem area by virtue of interest and experience, not because he is intrigued with simulation and wants to find any old problem to use it on. However, if the investigator's problem area happens to involve what might be called a *middle-level* problem, that is, a problem too complex to be handled by traditional methods but not so global as to defy analysis, then computer simulation may be appropriate. Very circumscribed problems, for example, whether or not learning occurs under certain social reinforcement conditions, or whether there is more attitude change in one communication situation than another, do not require the complicated machinery of simulation. At the other extreme, diffuse high-level speculations concerning social issues and forces, for example, the questions of how mass movements are born and under what circumstances they survive, do not readily lend themselves to simulation because of the involvement of too many variables too dimly comprehended. Between these extremes lie many phenomena of social interaction and influence which can profitably be approached by *theoretical synthesis* of elementary propositions. As has been explained by Newell and Simon (1961), McPhee (1963), Coleman (1964a), and others, the power and novelty of computer simulation technique lies in its ability to synthesize.

From these general statements we now turn to a much more specific consideration of the many factors determining the aptness of the simulation approach to a chosen problem.

Formulation of a psychological model

There are no hard and fast general rules for the construction of psychological models, since so much depends on the nature of the problem and previous knowledge in the area. Nevertheless a few special desiderata may be specified for the sort of models that lend themselves to simulation.

First, what is being modeled must be a dynamic process, not a static structural representation. Something has to *happen over time*. While cross-sectional characterizations of individuals and social groups may sometimes be of great theoretical interest (for example, in psychological portrayals of national character, delinquent subgroups, authoritarian personalities, etc.), such characterizations are not dynamic *models* in the present sense of the term.

Second, there must exist *well-specified independent and dependent* variables. The theory or model must specify some sequence of responses emitted by an individual or group under identifiable circumstances. Furthermore, the relationships among the variables must be clearly and sharply spelled out by the theory; the "happenings" of the model must be chained together in some way.

These first two points may be amplified by consideration of a list of six features possessed by any well-specified dynamic model:

1. *Units:* a set of elements or entities defining the units of concern to the investigator, the units which embody or "carry" the processes of interest. These units will often be individuals, but sometimes the units will be at a finer level of analysis (for example, "beliefs") and sometimes at a broader level (for example, "groups"). It is also possible for units at more than one level to be included in the same model. A somewhat different kind of unit arises in some simulations of cognitive processes, for example, the "position" in a chess game.

2. *Properties:* a set of variables (and constants) which attach to each unit and define its state at a given moment. These would include the dependent variables affected by the processes of the model, the mediating variables governing the effects on other variables, and the parameters or qualitative specifications defining the type and mode of behavior of the units. When the units are individuals, the properties may include sociometric information, opinions, intentions, demo-

graphic characteristics, and many other possibilities. Most models confine attention to a rather restricted set of relevant properties.

3. *Inputs:* a set of stimuli or task variables putting the postulated psychological processes into relevant motion and possibly also intervening during the later course of these processes.

4. *Processes:* a set of specifications of what is supposed to "happen," that is, of which properties of which units are to change as what function of the inputs and the properties of the other units.

5. *Phasing:* the organization of the sequence in which the processes are to occur. In some models, this sequence is constant, but in other models the sequence is contingent upon the outcomes of ongoing processes.

6. *Consequences:* one or more final properties of key units or aggregations of units; the crucial events, performances, outcomes, or states of affairs about which the model is capable of making predictions.

The application of this general list of six features of dynamic models to the specific case of computer simulation models is drawn as follows. The *units* and *properties* are stored in computer memory, the *inputs* are presented to the computer from punched cards or magnetic tape, the *processes* are actuated within the computer as "subroutines" under the *phasing* specified by the "executive routine" or "program," and the *consequences* are output by the computer in card, tape, or printed form.

In judging whether or not a model is "well specified" in the sense of enabling a computer simulation, then, one must identify the above six features. Sometimes one or two of them cause great theoretical difficulty. The investigator may be quite uncertain at the outset about selecting appropriate inputs, formulating the phasing appropriately, or deciding on the most important consequences. (Indeed, sometimes published accounts of completed simulations are quite vague on one or more of these points.) However, if the model as conceptualized by the investigator does not even come close to the above outline of features, then he ought not even consider simulation as a possible strategy.

A final, rather different desideratum for a well-specified model is that it represent a *closed system.* There must be no undefined circumstances in the theoretical specification. The model cannot include disclaimers expressed in phrases such as ". . . other things being equal . . . ." "Other things" must be either included explicitly or excluded completely. Models of cognitive processes, for example, may or may not include some provision for variations in the intellectual ability of the individual, models of social processes may or may not include individual personality variables, and so on. Most often the model builder chooses the strategy of exclusion of complicated other variables for reasons of simplicity. A certain narrowness of theoretical conception may sometimes result as the necessary price of precision. There are two ways to mitigate undue narrowness. One is the classical scientific strategy: start with a simple model, intending later to incorporate additional variables as necessary. (Such an intention can be formalized at the outset via initial provision for dummy variables and empty processes.) The other is to admit probabilistic events into the model; that is, to summarize ignorance about "other variables" by selectively allowing some degree of randomness to enter the sequence of happenings.

Much of the above discussion is incidentally also applicable to models which can be subjected to mathematical analysis rather than to computer simulation. Of the two techniques, simulation has much greater flexibility in the representations it permits.

Is simulation a suitable strategy?

Some psychological models, though formulated in precise, dynamic, closed terms, are not especially suited for simulation. A frequent reason *not* to simulate the operation of a psychological model is that no new consequences of the model can be discovered by so doing. The theoretical connection between independent and dependent variables may be so direct and immediate that it is uninteresting to produce an imitation of the process (though it may still be of great interest to try to validate the model empirically). Models involving chains of monotonic functional relations, for example, are of this nature. The model: "As X increases, Y increases; as Y increases, Z increases" is qualitatively self-contained and does not require simulation.

As an illustration of the above remarks consider the following hypothetical model for the development of differential morale in communication network: (1) the higher the centrality (suitably defined) of an individual in a communication network, the more often he will receive communications soliciting his advice on the task; (2) the more often an individual is asked for task advice, the greater his favorable opinion of participation in the task.

If there were to be a simulation of this deliberately simpleminded model, each symbolic individual in a simulated communication network would be provided with a number of "messages" to be sent at intervals to other symbolic individuals, and a certain proportion of these "messages" would be categorized as advice-seeking. Every time a symbolic individual received such a message, the setting of his "satisfaction" variable would be increased a small amount, and these "satisfactions" could be reported at the conclusion of a given time interval. The entire symbolic process could be run on a computer for any desired number of different communication nets and assumed rates of transmission of messages, etc., but it is difficult to imagine why anyone would want to do so, inasmuch as the nature of the simulated results would be completely known in advance.

The simulation of a model is most worthwhile when the simulation is *capable of producing consequences unanticipated by the investigator.* Potential surprise can come about in at least three different ways: (1) the model embodies a sufficient *competition of forces* under a complex enough variety of circumstances that the direction of effect(s) on the dependent variable(s) is fairly often in doubt; (2) the model is *quantitatively very precise,* yet because of mathematical complexity or massive extent of quantitative data to be used in the model, the investigator is uncertain about the output quantities or functions; (3) the entities of the model are not quantitative variables, but *qualitative products* created or chosen from a set so large that the response system possesses an uncertain, emergent quality.

In our simpleminded illustrative model of morale in communication networks, a competition of forces might be introduced in many ways. For example, it might be assumed that satisfaction tends to decrease if the number of non-advice-seeking messages increases beyond some optimum load, and further, that any response to an advice-seeking message tends to increase the rate at which other messages are received. The competition between the positive effects of being consulted and the negative effects of overinvolvement in the task would produce an interesting situation in which it would not be at all obvious which positions in a communication network would optimize satisfaction. The answers might well depend critically on the particular choice of the exact functions relating each variable to the others, for example, the decrease in satisfaction as a function of the degree of message overload and the existing level of satisfaction.

Precise quantitative specification is of course always required in order to run a simulation model, but if the propositions of the model were originally intended to be only qualitatively expressive, one might hope that the precise choice of quantitative functions would not be terribly critical in determining the qualitative behavior of the total model. Depending on the specific model, this hope might or might not be borne out. (A strongly pessimistic and probably exaggerated view has been forcefully stated by Chapanis, 1961.) In any case, the point here is that even when a model is interesting enough to warrant simulation, *the theorist usually has to go much farther in specifying details than he may originally have intended.* If the additional assumptions he must make (for example, about exact quantitative functions) seem gratuitous because of insufficient knowledge in the area, at least two constructive, although tedious, strategies may be contemplated: (1) exploring a large set of reasonable assumptions in the course of simulation runs to see which assumptions, if any, are critical in what degree; (2) gathering data relevant to those propositions about which there is considerable quantitative ambiguity.

A rather different situation arises when the theorist is quite willing, indeed eager, to specify particular mathematical functions as operative in his model. This is usually for the sake of simplicity and elegance. The theorist may want to see whether some simple mathematical principle can account neatly for a great quantity of data, or alternatively, may desire to work out the consequences of interesting assumptions whether or not they are fully satisfactory empirically. (The latter strategy may give rise to what Coleman, 1964b, calls "sometimes true theories.")

In these cases, the question of whether simulation is a suitable strategy devolves on the feasibility of working out the consequences of the models by mathematical methods alone. Ordinarily when simulation and mathematical analysis are *both* feasible, the latter is preferred because its results tend to be more complete, compact, and general. It quite often happens, however, that available mathematical methods are insufficiently powerful to provide closed solutions or even good approximate solutions for moderately complicated models. Then simulation may be appropriate.

Still other suitability conditions pertain in those cases in which the response variables are cognitive constructions such as conversational English sentences, plans for proving theorems, rationalizations for protecting a belief system, etc. There has been a burst of recent interest in such models of constructive cognitive process, due largely to the breakthrough such models provide in the available styles of theory construction. A generation of social scientists long suffering from the insufficiency of the traditional S-R paradigm is delighted to welcome a kind of model-building which makes something "happen" inside the O of the more complete S-O-R paradigm. The design of computer programs which put words together more or less sensibly or which play intellectual games or otherwise act in a lively, animated, "intelligent" way is indeed an important and fascinating enterprise. However, investigators must beware the snare of simulations which achieve entertainment value through simple gimmickry lacking theoretical substance. (It is relatively easy, for example, to provide elaborate prefabricated verbal strings which the computer dutifully outputs under simple program commands.)

That we have urged very careful consideration of the theoretical model and of alternative methodological strategies before embarking on a computer simulation does not mean that simulation is to be regarded as an inferior strategy or a counsel of desperation. On the contrary, simulation offers substantial and unique advantages: (1) the theoretical model may have a number of gaps in it which are far more readily perceived in the course of constructing a simulation; (2) a simulation often leads to a synthesis of propositions which would otherwise stand as disparate verbal or mathematical statements, thus permitting the generation of predictions which could otherwise not be generated; (3) once constructed, a computer simulation constitutes a kind of "experimental animal" which can be manipulated in a vast number of exploratory ways; (4) computer simulation in principle permits bridges to be built between islands of theoretical analysis that otherwise might remain unrelated, namely, the psychology of individuals and the behavior of large groups.

The investigator will wish to be sure, before embarking on a simulation, that one or more unique advantages such as those above are likely to accrue to him.

Organizing the sequence of steps: flow charts

If computer simulation is adjudged a suitable strategy, then the model must be translated from its initial verbal or mathematical form into terms which will enable it to be "run" on the computer. A set of detailed instructions, the *computer program*, must be developed. Before tackling this sometimes formidable task, however, it is useful to organize the job schematically into its natural units.

The processes of a model can almost always be conceptualized hierarchically, that is, as detailed "microprocesses" that operate within larger "macroprocesses." Often a model contains a rather small number, say two to four, of macroprocesses, and the first step in bringing the model under conceptual control is to name, characterize, and interconnect them. As a specific illustration, consider McPhee and Smith's (1962) simulation model of voting behavior. There are three macroprocesses: the *stimulation* process, in which voters are exposed to campaign materials; the *discussion* process, in which voters confront one another and compare positions toward the candidates; and the *learning* process, in which the impressions made on voters during stimulation and discussion are assumed to cause semipermanent readjustments in their party loyalties. These three processes are taken by the model to occur in the order represented in Fig. 1(a).

This diagram is a rudimentary *flow chart*. It specifies the phasing of the macroprocesses. Even with only three processes involved, the choice of how to connect them is not entirely trivial. The learning process might be invoked after the stimulation process as well as after discussion, as is indeed the case in the

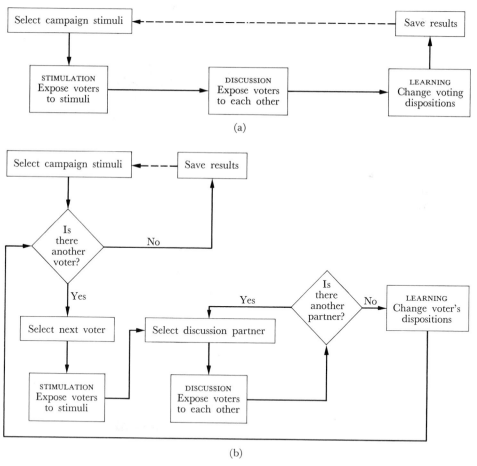

Fig. 1. Three macroprocesses. (a) A rudimentary flow chart. (b) The flow chart including minor technical detail. (Modified from McPhee, 1963, with simplifications.)

related model developed by Abelson and Bernstein (1963). This sort of choice will depend in part on the purposes of the particular model, in part on taste and intuition. The choice of phasing at the "macro" level can be changed very readily if desired, provided that the processes are each constructed as separate well-defined entities. "Modular" construction of a simulation model is a virtually indispensable convenience. This convenience does not stem primarily from the facility of putting pretty flow charts on paper. (Many skilled programmers effectively carry flow charts in their heads without writing them down explicitly.) Rather it is because, when the programming steps for each macroprocess are scattered widely without any separation into larger programming blocks, the resulting program is much more difficult to comprehend and tedious to change.

Note that in Fig. 1(a) the implication is that all individuals are *simultaneously* subjected to each macroprocess. While this may be the conceptual intent of the model, in actual practice it is not (at present) possible for computers to undertake "parallel processing." Instead, an artifice is used which achieves the effect of simultaneity by appropriate "serial processing." Each individual in turn is subjected to the macroprocess. Though the individuals are not literally processed at the same "time," it should be clear that elapsed time during a computer simulation is not proportional to real time anyway.

The serial requirement for computer operation is one of the things (others will be discussed later) that make it necessary for the model builder to attend to certain mechanics above and beyond those intrinsic to his model. In constructing the more detailed flow chart which will guide the actual writing of the computer instructions, the model builder is forced to include these extrinsic features. Figure 1(b), corresponding to Fig. 1(a), shows how this might be done for our particular example with three macroprocesses (omitting certain complications in the original model).

The figure is self-explanatory except for the diamond-shaped boxes. On flow charts, the diamond shape is more or less conventionally used to indicate *branches,* or places in the flow where what happens next depends on the outcome of a *test.* In this particular case, the test is a trivial but necessary one. If the computer has been instructed to continue repeating a set of steps always on the "next" unit (here, the next individual), it will attempt to continue forever unless supplied with a *stop rule.* The only way it can "know when to stop" is by applying a test which in effect asks, "Am I done?" following each pass or *cycle* through the set of steps. In this case, the test fails so long as another unit has yet to be processed, but succeeds or *exits* when the index number of the unit just processed is equal to an input number specifying how many units (individuals) there are altogether.

Most programming languages embody simple procedures enabling the programmer to specify stop rules with an absolute minimum of effort. The reader should therefore not feel intimidated by this and later "nuisance features" of the transformation of models into computer-simulable form.

The construction of a diagram such as Fig. 1(b), however essential, is only the bare beginning of the task. Within each macroprocess, the various microprocesses must be formulated and phased. It is at this lower level that the construction of flow charts becomes more intricate and sometimes agonizing. Difficulties arise because one discovers that verbally formulated process models are usually quite ambiguous on the fine details of individual events, and all sorts of unexpected nuances seem to appear out of nowhere.

A simple example may give some of the flavor of these difficulties. Suppose that a social-influence model specifies two microprocesses within a two-person discussion process: (1) a persuasion process by which the opinions of one individual may come to be accepted by the other individual; (2) the creation of "selective avoidance," such that individuals will tend to avoid discussion with those who disagree with them. The investigator may feel that he has a good formulation of the functional relationships necessary to specify these two processes precisely. Then he suddenly uncovers a dilemma: suppose that an individual in *initial* disagreement with another individual succumbs to persuasion and moves toward final agreement; should it then be assumed that he will tend toward future avoidance of the other because he initially disagreed with him or toward future approach because he now agrees with him? The investigator must make some choice as to when the effect of present discussion on the probability of future discussion is to take hold: at the beginning of the present discussion or at the end. These two possibilities are sketched in Fig. 2.

This kind of dilemma often tends to arise during the transformation of models into computer-simulable form because variables which for convenience one would like to regard as fixed at given moments in time are most likely to be rapidly in flux at such very moments. The mathematics of the differential calculus is not usually helpful either. The typical problem in many models is not

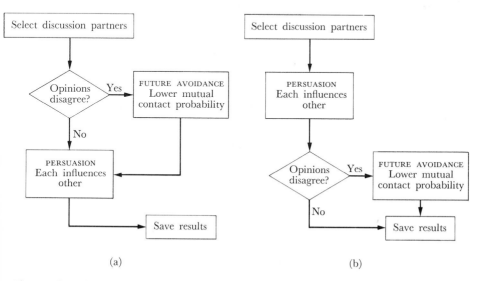

(a)   (b)

Fig. 2. Flow charts for the effect of social disagreement on future social contact. (a) First version. (b) Second version.

that several variables are all *continuously* changing, but that there are brief "flurries of events" or episodes of rapid change of several variables interspersed between slower adjustive changes.

Problems of specifying the phasing of microprocesses arise both in simulations of social processes and simulations of cognitive processes. Flow charts of typical complexity may be found, for example, in Gullahorn and Gullahorn (1963), Abelson (1963), Colby (1964), Rainio (1965), and Pool and Kessler (1965).

One virtue for the investigator in struggling with these flow-charting problems is that he may be forced into closer scrutiny of his own theory. To take the simple example above involving selective avoidance, consider the two choices sketched in Fig. 2. If the effects on the probability of future discussion are assumed to take hold at the *beginning* of the present discussion, as in Fig. 2(a), this is psychologically quite different from such effects taking hold at the *end*, as in Fig. 2(b). One might say that the former is a reinforcement principle, with initial disagreement a punishing state; the latter is a cognitive expectancy principle, with the individual expecting to find the next discussion as he left the last one. One might identify further theoretical subtleties beyond this simple distinction, but the point is made: once the investigator starts thinking about process timing, he must think more deeply about the psychology of the processes.

Availability of computers

At a rather early point in the construction of a computer simulation, the investigator ought to consider the properties of the computers available at his research installation. Almost all installations nowadays have some sort of computer present or nearby, but the range of machines going under the name "computer" is quite large. Plans for computer simulations must unfortunately often be sharply tailored because of one limitation or another of available computer facilities. A common problem is that the memory capacity of the local machine may be less than that necessary to store all desired properties of all the units in the simulation.

The other side of the coin is that the available computer facility may offer unusual features which make it easier to carry out the simulation than had been anticipated. This uncommon but happy possibility may arise more frequently in the future with technological advances such as *time sharing,* by which many users at remote typewriters can have simultaneous access to a powerful central computer (*cf.* Gibson, 1966; Greenberger, 1965).

The investigator should find out about the following features of the computer facilities available to him: (1) memory capacity; (2) computing speed; (3) available programming languages; (4) conditions of user access.

The memory capacity of computers is reckoned in units of "words," where the capacity of each word is a certain number of "bits" or elementary binary possibilities. Ordinarily one might plan a simulation so that each "datum" (for example, property of a unit) would occupy a single computer word, and on this basis one could estimate whether the problem would fit into the memory of the available computer. "Small" computers have *core memory* capacities of from two to eight thousand words, "standard-sized" computers thirty-two thousand, and "large" computers sixty thousand and up. In estimating whether memory capacity is adequate, allowance must be made for the consumption by the computer program of one word of space per instruction, and also for "systems programs" which are often maintained permanently in core memory by individual computer installations. Generally speaking, however, it is overextensive data rather than overextensive programs that cause capacity troubles.

When the simulation seems too big to fit in core memory, there are two recourses (other than the obvious one of trimming down the specifications of the model). Most computers have additional *auxiliary memories* that communicate with core memory at a sacrifice in computing speed and programming convenience. Unfortunately, the sacrifice is sometimes very great, and the task of making efficient use of auxiliary memory has taxed the patience of many programmers. The other recourse, known as "data packing," consists of the storage of more than one datum in each computer word. Typically a word contains 36 bits, that is, enough entries to accommodate 36 dichotomous variables, or four integers with a range from 1 to 500 or six alphabetic symbols, etc. Some machines have longer 48-bit words, others shorter words down to as little as 12 bits. In any case, the "packing" principle is the same, and may be illustrated by the following example. In Abelson and Bernstein's (1963) simulation model of community controversies, it was desired to store 300 properties for each of 400 individuals. At a word per property, this would occupy 120,000 words, well beyond the 32,768 available in the core of the intended machine. Upon consideration of the properties themselves, however, it turned out that most of them could be stored within fractions of a word. The first property, say, is the index number of the individual, varying between 1 and 400. Since the use of 9 bits would admit $2^9 = 512$ different possibilities, the index number can be stored within 9 bits. The next property is, say, the sex of the individual, and one bit accommodates the two possibilities. Age, categorized into four brackets, consumes two bits. Continuing in this way, the investigator codes all the constants and variables of the model into a small number of bits, in such a way that a total of 1080 bits are needed to accommodate the 300 quantities per individual. On the IBM 7090 used for this simulation, the word size was 36 bits; thus 1080 bits consumed 30 words, and the data on 400 individuals therefore occupied only 12,000 words instead of 120,000 as previously estimated. The organization of the data in this way, be it noted, required extra effort in writing the computer program, made the program somewhat awkward to change, and caused the simulation to run somewhat more slowly because the data often had to be "unpacked" and "repacked" during processing. However, this alternative was in this case superior to the use of auxiliary memory storage. Data packing is quite often a helpful recourse, but unfortunately some computer programming languages do not allow the possibility of data packing (see below). Eventually the problems of memory limitation will no doubt be solved technologically, but investigators with large simulations at small computer installations will continue to struggle for some years.

So far as computer speed is concerned, different computers vary widely. The standard unit of speed is the "cycle time" in millionths of a second (microseconds), but this characterization is not immediately useful to an investigator, since he seldom has any reasonable idea of how many elementary machine "cycles" will be consumed in a simulation run. Relative assessment among machines is fairly clear-cut, however. By "modern" standards (as of 1968), a "standard" machine has a cycle time of 1 to 10 microseconds. By contrast, older machines such as the once-popular IBM 650 have cycle times of a few *milli*seconds (thousandths of a second), which is a thousand times slower. Computers potentially emerging will offer another tenfold to hundredfold increase in speed (*cf.* Fernbach, 1965). Of course, it is entirely possible for a "slow" machine to be more than adequate for certain simulations, while other simulations are not feasible even on a "fast" machine. The investigator should try to make a rough comparison between his simulation problem and other simulation problems that have been run on his local machine or something comparable. If, as a rough guess, the time to run one simulation is of the order of a few minutes or less, then he can proceed without anxiety, planning to glean a more exact estimate from trial runs. If, however, the initial rough guess is a half an hour or more for a single run, then the investigator may well be in trouble if he has a limited budget and an expensive computer, since a great many simulation runs are usually needed. In this situation the investigator must simplify the simulation, find a faster computer, get a bigger research grant, or pray mightily that the original time estimate was in error.

The availability of various computer programming languages is as variable from one computer installation to the next as are the specific machines. The difficult choice of a particular language in which to write a simulation program must perforce be made in the context of what is actually available at the installation. Often there are problems of compatibility between a particular machine and a particular language. The present trend at leading computer installations is to maintain "package" capabilities via complicated systems that accept many languages. This is a helpful development. Nevertheless, particularly when little-used systems are newly imported by a computing center, there are often great gaps in local understanding of obscure programming details. Kenneth Colby, working on a simulation of neurotic belief systems (Colby and Gilbert, 1964), reports the following incident epitomizing the difficulties. His computing center had just installed a new version of the ALGOL programming language. A great deal of attention had been paid to the algebraic features of the language, since virtually all users were concerned with numerical applications. But nobody had paid much attention to the details of processing alphabetic materials. When Colby's output of English sentences came out mysteriously garbled the first time he tried the system, he consulted one local expert after another. Each one claimed competence only with numerical problems and referred Colby to someone else. Finally he was sent to see *the* local systems expert on the new version of ALGOL. This man listened at great length, furrowed his brow, and then with a sudden burst of earnest enthusiasm said, "You know, there's a fellow on campus who has worked a lot with this alphabetic stuff. You ought to go see him. His name is—er, um, yes—Colby!" The moral of such experiences is clear: the nominal inclusion of new programming languages in an installation's package should be greeted with great skepticism until there has been sufficient experience with them to guarantee trouble-free operation.

Less drastic considerations are involved in questions of user access to computer time. Of course the investigator will want to find out when and how he can submit his materials to the local computer, and what kind of technical help is available. An important variable is the "turn-around time," the average time that ready materials must spend waiting in line before they are run on the computer. When there are a great many users of a single "slow" machine, or when the user requires special system facilities not regularly in operation, the turn-around time may be as much as twenty-four hours; that is, an investigator could run his simulation program only once a day. Such a laggard pace would prove especially annoying during the phase of early simulation development, when it takes a great many computer runs to correct many tiny errors. With a turn-around time of an hour or two, the investigator can usually quickly try to iron out the "bugs" in the previous run, resubmit his materials to the machine operators, and soon see the consequences of the changes made.

The ideal situation of *immediate* access to the computer at any time is rare, although the recent development of time sharing is beginning to make this possible for a few fortunate users. Albeit subject to the frustrations inherent in the use of any new and complex technology, the advantages of direct, so-called *on-line* access to the computer via typewritten input are at least twofold: first, it makes the process of "debugging" easier because any number of hypothesized causes of error can be immediately explored without spending several hours per possible cause; second, the general exploratory attitude engendered by immediate feedback encourages the investigator to try out creative variations in his simulation model. In communicating with the computer, the difference between on-line access and once-a-day processing is like the difference between a telephone call and an exchange of cramped post cards (Weizenbaum, 1965). Indeed, if the simulation is itself concerned with conversation as a social process, then there is no feasible alternative to on-line access. Barring such access, most investigators will probably have to settle at best for short turn-around times.

Choice of a programming language and a data representation

Computer programming languages differ from each other in many ways, and the relative strengths and weaknesses have been much debated. In this section we shall not attempt to provide any final arbitration, but merely set forth some of the elementary properties and proposed advantages of the most common languages. New languages are continually being devised and some conceivably promising languages will perforce be neglected because of their unfamiliarity to the writer.

For every computer there is a basic "machine code" in which instructions may be written at the most elementary level of detail. In the machine code are embodied the basic processes of which all digital computers are capable: the four arithmetic processes, flexible information storage facility, and the ability to make tests of equality and to proceed conditionally upon the outcome of these tests. Information stored in computer memory is located, as noted, in "words," and each "word" has a particular numerical location or "address." If a set of instructions is written directly in machine code, the programmer soon discovers that he is involved in a bookkeeping chore: he must remember what numerical address has been set aside for each datum. This is the kind of chore for which computers are better suited than people, however. Therefore an early innovation in programming provided for *symbolic addresses*. The programmer, instead of referring to addresses numerically, can write instructions such as: enter THIS, multiply by THAT, and store in RESULT. The symbols THIS, THAT, RESULT, and so on can be translated into numerical addresses within the computer in a preliminary pass of the instructions through an *assembler*, that is, a separate program with the sole function of assigning numerical addresses consistently to alphabetic labels.

Many other maneuvers are available for freeing the programmer from the responsibility for nuisance details. It is commonly desirable in computations to repeat certain sequences of arithmetic steps many times with a simple change in some index or parameter. The programmer writing instructions for such repetitive *loops* often finds it onerous to write the branching instruction ensuring the proper set of repetitions without fear of an error. He would prefer to accompany the sequence of steps with a footnote, as it were, saying, "Do this N times, each time incrementing such-and-such parameter by so-and-so." Indeed, it is now easy to write such types of covering instructions for loops. Equally important, it is possible to write instructions for arithmetic operations entirely in the form of algebraic equations rather than the blow-by-blow put-and-take of elementary arithmetic steps. Both of these advances, among others, are made possible by the existence of "higher-level" programming languages, that is, languages more abstract than machine code yet readily translatable into machine code by the computer itself. This translation step is usually carried out in a preliminary phase by means of a translation program called a *compiler*.

To say that a programming language exists is to say two things: that there is a set of conventions which the programmer must follow in writing instructions; and that there exists a compiler that translates instructions obeying the conventions into the appropriate corresponding instructions in machine code. In theory, anyone with a thorough knowledge of a machine code can devise a new programming language by inventing congenial conventions and writing a compiler. In practice, however, this task is usually quite formidable, mainly because the invention of conventions creates all sorts of problems of what limitations to impose and how to maintain consistency between conventions. And so far as the user-at-large is concerned, a coherent explanation of all the conventions is necessary in order for a language written by someone else to be useful to him. Several programming languages have in fact remained the private property of rarefied groups of experts because such public "documentation" has been lacking.

Among the well-documented languages the most widely diffused is FOR-TRAN (*cf.* Organick, 1963), developed and vigorously promoted by the IBM Corporation for use with their computers. Almost all computer installations nowadays accept some type of FORTRAN, but it is important to note that there are differences between several successively evolving versions. A popular early version, FORTRAN II, imposed rather rigid constraints on some statement forms. The competitive languages, ALGOL-60 (McCracken, 1962) and MAD (Arden, 1963; Galler, 1962) both permit more flexible and elegant statements than FORTRAN II. This "elegance gap" has been narrowed by the appearance of FORTRAN IV (Golden, 1965). Recently, IBM has also developed an entirely new language (McCracken, 1964), now called PL/I (or simply PL), which may in due time become the leader in frequency of use.

While between FORTRAN IV, ALGOL-60, and MAD there are various technical differences which may excite the cognoscenti, so far as the amateur programmer is concerned they can be regarded as essentially equivalently power-ful. Writing programs in any of the three languages offers very great economy of effort (several hundred percent) over machine code. An even greater boon to the programmer is the relative ease with which programs can be *rewritten* in the compiler languages. As against these advantages, there is the slight relative dis-advantage that a program written directly in machine code will usually consume 10 to 30 percent less computer running time than the compiled counterpart. The reason for this is that compilers which translate from programming language to machine code are of necessity rather heavy-handed systems lacking sensitivity to potential shortcuts in the final machine-code rendition.

The conventions of these algebraic compilers require that the data on which the program is to operate be stored in *arrays* of prearranged maximum size. Arrays accommodate sets of values for "subscripted variables"; when there is one subscript, the array is a *vector,* when two subscripts, a *matrix,* and when three (or more) subscripts, a *three-* (or more) *dimensional array.* Arrays of various dimen-sionalities are of course very familiar in social science, ranging from the cross tabulations of the survey analyst to the factorial designs of the experimental social psychologist. The relevant data for a simulation, however, may or may not fall naturally into the form of arrays. A number of possibilities may be illustrated with the common case of sociometric network information. Suppose that some qualitative relationship X (liking, knowing, communicating, etc.) either obtains or does not obtain for every ordered pair (I, J) of individuals in a group. One way of representing the pertinent relationships is in matrix form: the doubly sub-scripted variable $X(I, J)$ takes on the value of 1 if individual I relates appropri-ately to individual J, and the value 0 if not. The sociometric matrix for N individuals then consists of $N \times N$ entries, each either 0 or 1. If N were 1000, then 1,000,000 entries would be necessary. If the relative density of 1's in the matrix were small relative to the number of 0's, however, then evidently there would be a much more economical way of storing the information. With each individual, I, could be associated the index numbers, J, of only those individuals with whom he stood in relevant relationship. If the number of such sociometric targets were constant for all individuals (as, for example, in the situation of sociometric choice whereby each person chooses a fixed number, M, of friends), then this more efficient storage method would consist of an array of dimensions $N \times M$ rather than $N \times N$. Formally speaking, one might denote $X(I, K) = J$ if the Kth choice of individual I were individual J. If M were, say, 5, then the choices of 1000 individuals could be represented by 5000 rather than 1,000,000 entries. (Each entry would occupy more bits than before, but the representation would still be much more compact than the full matrix.) This method of storing sociometric information for computer simulation has been used by McPhee and Smith (1962) and Coleman (1961), among others.

Now consider a complication. Suppose that the number of target individuals is variable from one chooser to another, averaging 5 each but ranging (for example) between 0 and 25. What should be the dimensions of the array of index numbers associating targets with choosers? Evidently one could set aside for each chooser space for the maximum number of choices, 25, thus wasting 80% of the available space by saving room for unmade choices. Alternatively, one could close up the wasted space, but then would have to provide a table of the number of choices $M(I)$ made by each I so that it would be possible to distinguish in memory where one individual's choices end and another's begin. Neither of these alternatives is especially convenient, although both are certainly conceivable under the general rubric of storage-by-arrays. Introduce one more complication, however, and the maintenance of fixed data arrays becomes untenable. Suppose that N is large, and that both the number and identity of chosen individuals is variable *over time*. This could occur in simulations for which sociometric choice is a dependent variable affected by various processes of the model. Proper memory allocation in this situation runs into the dilemma that the maximum number of choices per individual is not known in advance. The only alternative to the grossly inefficient expedient of storing the whole $N \times N$ matrix of (variable) 0's and 1's is some kind of "dynamic storage allocation" which allows changing *lists* (of individuals) to be associated with the individuals. The internal "bookkeeping" for this achievement requires the novel programming concepts embodied in *list-processing languages*.

Whereas a block of consecutive addresses is set aside in memory (by the compiler) to house an array, a list, on the other hand, may occupy any set of nonconsecutive addresses. The items on the list are "joined together" (that is, successively locatable) by virtue of a specification alongside each item of the address of the item to follow. When an item is to be added to the end of a list, the address of an empty word is found on an *available space* list, the new item is entered in that word, and a "pointer" to the new word is established alongside the last previous item. When an item is to be removed from the end of a list, the word containing the item is "erased" (set to zero), its address is placed on the available space list, and the previous pointer to that word is removed. These maneuvers are built internally into the functioning of list-processing languages and need not ordinarily concern the programmer directly, though he must understand the concepts involved.

The early work of Newell, Shaw, and Simon (1957) was instrumental in the development of list-processing languages. They wished to simulate the cognitive processes of individuals attempting to prove theorems in logic. Since strategies of proof were posited to involve selective exploration of flexible networks of possibilities, and since the logic problem content itself involved flexible "strings" of symbols, the necessity for some kind of list-processing programming capability was apparent. These workers developed several versions of a programming language they called IPL, and applied it subsequently to the simulation of a chess player (Newell, Shaw, and Simon, 1963), and to general strategies in problem-solving (Newell, Shaw, and Simon, 1959). The present version of their language, IPL-V (Newell *et al.*, 1964), has been very widely used in computer simulation and closely related artificial-intelligence activities (Abelson and Carroll, 1965; Feigenbaum, 1963; Green *et al.*, 1961; Gullahorn and Gullahorn, 1964; Hunt, Marin, and Stone, 1966; Lindsay, 1963). While there are certain disadvantages in IPL-V, its inventors have been extremely conscientious in disseminating it and in training social scientists in its use. Several rival languages have tended not to be used because of a lack of vigorous documentation and promotion. These include FLPL (Gelernter, Hansen, and Gerberich, 1960), historically important because it was devised contemporaneously with IPL, and used by Gelernter and Rochester (1958) in their early work on intelligent problem-solving by machine; LISP (McCarthy, 1963), an extremely compact and very elegant "expert's" language which is rather too difficult for amateur programmers, though a newer version, LISP-II, may be easier enough to become popular; and SNOBOL (Farber, Griswold, and Polonsky, 1964), a neat and flexible language very handy for the manipulation of textual materials and for list structures as well, provided its latent potential comes to be realized by more users. SNOBOL's very early precursor, COMIT (Yngve, 1962), is more useful for content analysis schemes like the "General Inquirer" (Stone *et al.*, 1966) than for simulation. Evolutionary trends in the design of list languages have been discussed in general terms by Raphael (1966). In addition, there are a large number of languages called "simulation languages" which will not be discussed here since they are almost exclusively concerned with applied, "systems" simulations, rather than the more theoretical process-oriented simulations under consideration. It is conceivable that some of these languages have something to offer social scientists, but to the writer's knowledge this possibility has not been adequately explored. The interested reader may consult a comparative review of five of these languages (SIMSCRIPT, CSL, GPSS, SIMPAC, and DYNAMO) by Krasnow and Merikallio (1964).

There have been at least two recent attempts to combine in one language the ability to manipulate arrays algebraically and lists qualitatively. These are DYSTAL (Sakoda, 1965) and SLIP (Weizenbaum, 1963). The conventions of the latter are rather more flexible than those of the former, and we shall therefore choose SLIP to discuss in contrast with IPL-V. A more extensive comparison of SLIP, IPL-V, LISP, and COMIT has been given by Bobrow and Raphael (1964).

In order to make our comparison, we must first describe the features of IPL-V. The strength of IPL-V is its ability to deal with *list structures,* that is, lists of symbols such that some symbols may refer to other lists of symbols, etc. By convention, *all* pieces of data in the language are referred to by "name" rather than directly. A set of individuals, for example, would be designated by a list of symbols such as C2, C7, C11, etc., each referring to a particular individual. Similarly, numbers must even be given names, and a column of numbers would be represented by a list of arbitrary symbols, each denoting a particular number. (Somewhere in memory, of course, a data table must appear which specifies which name denotes which number.)

To enable the processing of lists of symbols, IPL embodies a set of "subroutines" specified by the letter J followed by a particular number: for example, J2, "test if two symbols are equal"; J64, "add a given symbol to the end of a given list"; and so on. These "J-routines" are prepackaged into the deck or tape holding the IPL system at a given computer installation. To find out which of these routines are available, the user must consult the IPL manual and also check at his installation, since not all J-routines are available at all installations.

In addition to the J-routines, IPL provides simple coding conventions for moving symbols in and out of central working storage, for working systematically down a list, and so on. By interlarding the prepackaged subroutines with other programming statements, the programmer can write his own subroutines for performing the processes appropriate to his own problem. These subroutines can in turn be composed into larger routines, and so on, the whole program being constructed on the modular principle which typifies neat programming technique. In a simulation, the smaller modules usually correspond to microprocesses and the largest modules to macroprocesses.

In order to "fire" any subroutine, the relevant symbols must first be brought into what is called the "communication cell"; for example, J2, "test if two symbols are equal," "expects" to find in the communication cell the two symbols in question. If by mistake the programmer has neglected to supply the appropriate instructions for this, then the subroutine will either produce an inappropriate result or will fail completely, stopping the running of the program. It is a disadvantage of IPL that much of the programming burden is concerned with such "housekeeping" chores: ensuring that symbols are present when called for and are "cleaned up" or removed when no longer needed.

Several other criticisms of IPL-V can be made: (1) numerical processing is rather clumsy in IPL, and standard subroutines for such functions as square root and logarithm are not available; (2) the necessity of indirect symbolic referencing precludes the direct use of IPL for text-processing manipulations, such as syntactic analysis of sentences; (3) running time is usually longer for programs written in IPL because IPL instructions are "interpreted" by the computer during program execution, a slower process than preliminary compilation; (4) data packing is not permitted by IPL, and thus big data structures may create space problems; (5) because so much "housekeeping" is involved, IPL code is virtually unreadable without accompanying comments; (6) everything must be put in the form of lists, thus foreclosing even the occasional advantageous use of arrays.

No one of these disadvantages by itself is debilitating, some of them are being lessened in modified new IPL systems, and often there are ways to mitigate the problems involved. It is possible, for example, though inconvenient, to graft machine-code statements into IPL programs, thus facilitating numerical and text processing. Green *et al.* (1961) in fact used this device for their "Question Answering" program. Questions in simple natural English were first converted by a machine-coded dictionary look-up process into IPL symbols, and then an IPL program "answered" the questions.

Against the above listing of several small annoyances, IPL can claim the following advantages: (1) within the context of list processing proper, the power of IPL is formidable—with one minor possible exception to be noted below, no significant capability has been omitted from the language; (2) the relatively large body of experience with, and documentation of, the language gives relatively more assurance of trouble-free operation than is the case with newer languages; (3) IPL systems are available at more computing installations than any rival list languages.

The properties of SLIP stand in some contrast to those of IPL. The name SLIP derives from "Symmetric List Processor," a reference to the fact that in SLIP lists are treated "symmetrically"; that is, one can refer as easily to the "previous item" on a list as to the "next item." This is because two "pointers" are associated with every entry on a list instead of one. While this feature has some esthetic appeal, it is of limited practical import, since the inability to "back up" on a list is not very often a serious limitation for the list programmer. The real advantage of SLIP lies in the fact that SLIP subroutines have been written directly in one of the algebraic compiler languages. (There are at least two versions of SLIP, an early one written in FORTRAN, and a more recent one in MAD.) This is of great utility, since it permits SLIP statements for dealing with lists to be interwoven with FORTRAN (or MAD) statements for processing arrays. In one stroke, this solves at least three of the problems associated with IPL: it makes numerical processing easy, it permits text processing, and it allows the memory to be arranged partly in lists and partly in arrays as desired. Relative to IPL, furthermore, there is less "housekeeping" in SLIP; the code is more compact and (if the programmer does not get overly fancy) easier to read. As for the factor of speed, SLIP is discriminably faster than IPL, partly because compiled languages are faster than "interpretive" languages, and partly because it is quicker to treat arrays as such rather than as pseudo-lists. However, in view of its system of double pointers, SLIP is not especially economical of space and may even be rather wasteful relative to IPL. Also on the debit side for present versions of SLIP is a slight blind spot in its input conventions, such that it is inconvenient, though not impossible, to input lists whose entries are the names of other lists.

Altogether, the theoretical advantages of SLIP are considerable. Unfortunately, the availability of the language is limited. What diffusion it has had has been through informal contact with the inventor rather than by formal institutional arrangement. Such a diffusion method is not ideal, and at the time of this writing it is hazardous to predict the ultimate popular success of SLIP.

To sum up the rather confusing problem of choosing a programming language and a data representation for computer simulation, we offer the following advice (to be evaluated, of course, within the context of the situation at the user's computer installation):

1. *If it is at all possible to represent the data entirely in the form of arrays, do so and use one of the available algebraic compiler languages. They are widespread, powerful, and fast.*

2. *If the data demand accommodation as a pure list structure, if there is some IPL tradition at the local installation, and if none of the disadvantages of IPL are deemed serious, use IPL.*

3. *If the data can be conceptualized as part lists and part arrays, and if SLIP is readily available, use SLIP.*

4. *In cases of serious doubt about the appropriateness of the above-mentioned languages and some rationale for anticipating particular language improvements, carefully investigate other possibilities such as SNOBOL-IV, or agitate and/or wait for the development of a better language.*

Writing the computer program

There are four choices available to the investigator with ample research support: he may write a simulation program himself, hire an interested student with an amateur knowledge of programming, hire a professional programmer, or collaborate with one or more colleagues with programming skill.

The arguments in favor of the do-it-yourself alternative are very compelling. By writing the program oneself, one can maintain direct control over the fine details of its operation; when someone else does it, one might never be quite sure of what is going on, especially if the program is complicated. Fortunately, the art of programming is not so forbidding as it may seem to the novice. Programming courses and practice opportunities are widely available, and, unlike the situation that obtains in learning mathematics, no prior training is prerequisite to the achievement of a more or less adequate skill level within a few weeks or months. Furthermore, many people find programming fun.

Against the real advantages and the noble feelings that accompany doing one's own programming is the obvious drawback that programming can be extremely time-consuming. Investigators with already extensive research commitments will often prefer to hire a programmer than to abandon a promising simulation project. However, such a step ought only be taken *if the investigator is able himself to carry the planning through the stage of very detailed flow charting and can maintain continual close contact with the programmer's work.* In addition, it is extremely helpful if the investigator has had the experience of writing at least one previous program himself, so that he fully understands the problems and possibilities involved.

The above statements are more than idle preachments. If there were a magazine titled "True Confessions of Computer Simulators," it would contain many stories of the following type: "The student reported that he was making great progress with the program for my simulation. But then one day he (a) got sick, (b) stopped coming around, (c) graduated. After weeks of cajoling, I was able to obtain the most advanced version of his program from his roommate. I wanted to make some changes in it, but I didn't understand it well enough. Worse yet, it didn't even run properly. I hired another student programmer to straighten it out, but after two months he told me he couldn't understand what the other fellow had done. I cried all night."

To a large extent these problems are mitigated with good professional programmers, but such talent is astonishingly expensive. Well-funded investigators may find the luxury of professional programming occasionally very worthwhile indeed, but this recourse is not usually feasible. The other alternative, collaborative "team" effort, in which one member specializes in the details of the programming, has much to recommend it. The pioneering simulation work in psychology by A. Newell, J. C. Shaw, and H. A. Simon was of course collaborative, though it is important to note that all three men participated in varying degrees in the programming efforts, avoiding the pitfalls of overspecialization. The opposite pitfall, programming "by committee," is also to be shunned. Programming responsibility cannot be too widely shared.

Hand simulation of the program

It is almost always necessary to undertake "hand simulation" of a program to obtain outcomes against which to check the initial runs of the computerized version. This use of "hand simulation" is a standard one, consistent with the obvious checking devices used for trying out numerical computer programs. What is somewhat less obvious is that, in running slowly through a simulation step by step on a number of simple trial problems, one stands a fair chance of uncovering unanticipated shortcomings in the conception of the program. For this reason, hand simulation is a useful pedagogic device in teaching simulation.

While there exist isolated published examples in which simulations have been carried out entirely by hand (Clarkson and Tuggle, 1966; Simon and Simon, 1962), it would be going much too far to maintain that, if a simulation is well formulated, the computer can be dispensed with entirely. Such a statement may help to counter misunderstandings which assign the computer a magical role, but the differences in speed and accuracy between computer "runs" and pencil-and-paper "runs" of simulations are so huge that the computer is almost always indispensable.

Thus hand simulation should be thought of as accompanying, not replacing, machine simulation. There is often a strong temptation toward premature publication of interesting simulations which have never actually been run on a computer, but only casually by hand (if that). The danger in such publications is that they refer to particular simulations as though they were truly scientific objects, whereas, without the discipline of actually running the simulations, authors are prone to wishful manipulations: they tend to speak of how a contemplated simulation might come out rather than how a real simulation did come out, and often the reader cannot tell which is which. The present writer (Abelson, 1963) is among many who in their enthusiasm for computer simulation have occasionally committed this transgression.

"Debugging" the program

No programmer, not even the best professional, expects to write errorless code. Rather, he realistically assumes that there will be anywhere from one to ten errors per hundred lines of code, depending on the complexity of the problem and the sensitivity of the programming language, and he tries to maximize the efficiency of procedures for locating errors. The usual experience with new programs is that at the outset they do not run at all—a crucial systems card has been left out of the deck, or an early instruction has incorrect syntax, or the data are improperly identified. After a few frustrating false starts, the program begins to turn out plausible but not totally satisfactory output. "Bugs" are constantly found and eliminated. Then comes a euphoric stage when everything seems to run perfectly, to be spoiled only occasionally by previously unsuspected errors. For complicated simulations it often takes many months before the branches of the program are sufficiently explored that the programmer can be reasonably assured no errors lie hidden in some dark concatenation of circumstances.

Some types of "bugs" are relatively easy to find, for example, gross errors in the initial card-punching of the program, whereas others are extremely difficult, for example, those resulting from tacitly misunderstood minor programming conventions. Among the most commonly employed error-catching procedures are the following:

1. Careful reading of the "program listing" obtained by printing the punched program cards. (Punching errors are very common.)

2. Obedient attention to all *error messages* printed out by the computer during compilation (or interpretation). All programming systems embody checks for conformity to the programming conventions. When a specific convention is violated, an appropriate error message is keyed. Though occasionally some humorist at a computer installation will set up a knavish message such as "NO MACHINE LIKE ME SHOULD EVER WORK FOR AN IDIOT LIKE YOU," the more standard sorts of messages are "UNDEFINED VARIABLE," "INCORRECT FUNCTION STATEMENT," "NOT ENOUGH INPUTS FOR PROCESS," and the like. Usually the error will be found fairly easily from the printed clue. Sometimes, however, the programmer will be mystified. Novices will often be tempted to assume that the machine suffered an aberration, but this temptation should be resisted. The machine, like the proverbial customer, is theoretically "always right."

3. Tests of program operation in *small segments rather than all at once,* making it much easier to localize errors.

4. Use of a program *trace* during the running of questionable segments of the program. This is a feature, available to almost all programming languages, whereby the actions of the program can be printed out step by step through particular sequences. A related device called a *snapshot* prints contents of key cells before and after execution of certain routines. These features, especially the trace, must be used selectively; otherwise, the programmer will find himself overwhelmed with print-out.

5. Use of *memory dumps,* the static analog of program traces. A memory dump prints out on command the contents of specified blocks of words of memory. It might be called upon by the programmer if he suspects that one or more entries within a large group of variable quantities have somehow gone astray.

6. Invention of test problems to check specific hypotheses about causes of error. Like Hercule Poirot baiting a trap so that the murderer will reveal himself, the inventive programmer must often create unusual conditions so that one bug out of many alternatives can be positively identified.

If there is any single rule covering the whole art of debugging, it is this: when a program does not run properly, don't just make some idle change and try again; rather, explore the logic of the particular kind of failure and make changes relevant by that logic before trying again.

The outside observer of the debugging process is apt to underestimate the difficulties involved, and not understand why it should take so long for a program which is "almost running" to come to the stage where it is "really running." Those in the trade, recognizing the extraordinary patience required, have an informal unit for measuring time delay until completion of debugging. John von Neumann, one of the great geniuses of the early computer days, once satirically suggested a constant with the following property. The programmer is asked when his project will be complete, and he estimates some number of days, weeks, or months. This same estimate is taken to apply equally well when the programmer is again asked at any later date whatsoever. Thus no project is ever finished, but the perceived distance to the goal is a subjective constant expressing the problem's complexity. By the standards of this humorous scale, the von Neumann constant for debugging a big simulation program might typically range between two and six months (and the honest and actual time to do the job something like two or three times the von Neumann constant).

Revision of the model

It is inevitable that in running a simulation model for error-checking purposes, even with only skeletal data, various previously unrealized features of the model will become apparent. The theorist will find himself sorely tempted to tinker with his model, and indeed, there is no reason why he should not. One of the most frequently cited benefits of simulation is that it spurs and sharpens theory development (Gullahorn and Gullahorn, 1965b; Hunt, 1963; Reitman, 1959, 1963; Uhr, 1963). The investigator should beware, however, of becoming permanently "hooked" on potential theory improvement through continual program changes. At some point he must hold to a given model and proceed to full-scale simulation runs with real data.

Given the fact that a reasonable degree of program change is often desirable, it behooves the programmer to write the original program so as to facilitate change. At least two strategems are helpful in this regard. One is to write the program in small segments each of which can operate independently of the status of the others; the other is to make all "specifications" as general as is feasible. The first device has already been referred to in our discussion of microprocesses, but the second requires further explanation. By "specifications" are meant quantitatively variable determiners of the program's behavior, for example, the parameters of functions or the values of the probabilities that certain processes will occur. It is relatively easy to write a program so that all parameters, process probabilities, and assorted numerical constants are specified generally. One simply substitutes an appropriate general symbol for any occurrence of a specific number: thus, for example, the program statement for "apply such-and-such process with probability 0.5" would be replaced by "apply such-and-such process with probability P." Quantities such as P would be supplied as input by the programmer prior to each simulation run, and therefore changing them would be as easy as keeping them the same. This device seems fairly obvious, though it is by no means always scrupulously observed in practice. What is not so readily apparent, however, is that in most simulations a number of quantitative specifications are implicit rather than explicit: "If the process gives rise to a negative outcome, change such-and-such and repeat the process once"; "Try rationalization first, then denial, then differentiation"; "Generate all plausible moves by the opponent before analyzing any one of them"; and so on. Hidden in varying degrees of subtlety in statements such as these are specific quantitative assumptions about how many occurrences of certain processes are to take place, and in what order. Even a decision to omit a certain process at a certain juncture is in effect a quantitative decision taking on the value zero. If the programmer is aware of the "arbitrary" nature of these assumptions, he can in principle make the specifications more general: "If so-and-so, repeat the process K times"; "Apply the operations $0_1, 0_2, 0_3, \ldots$ in the order given by the permutation (π)"; and so on. Such ideas will not always occur to the programmer, and even if they do, they may not be easy to effect. For example, in simulations involving explorations of "trees" of alternatives (for example, with a chess player considering possible move sequences), differing program possibilities are not simply a matter of differing permutations of exploratory steps. Entirely new program organization (Newell, 1962) may be necessary.

There are many aspects of this "specification problem" which are of profound significance, largely beyond the scope of this chapter. In the present context, we may let the matter rest with the following summary bit of advice.

Wherever there are "degrees of freedom" clearly available to the programmer in his choice of programming options, he should try to write the program so as not to foreclose them; as many options as feasible should be put into the input specifications or made readily accessible through easily altered subroutines.

The utilization of data

There are at least three senses in which data may enter into computer simulations: as stimulants for models, as inputs for simulation runs, and as validation criteria. These uses have tended to receive very different emphases in different types of computer simulation, and discussion is deferred to the appropriate contexts. It is fair to say in general, however, that insufficient attention has been paid to data problems. For a simulation of even moderate complexity, it is such a considerable achievement to get a "dry run" version working that investigators often do not pitch their levels of aspiration much beyond that point. That a model may work well on simple illustrative data carried through a few representative steps, however, does not at all guarantee that it will behave properly when run full-scale with a large body of data.

An example from the writer's own simulation work demonstrates the point. As part of a larger project on the simulation of belief systems (Abelson and Carroll, 1965) a macroprocess called the "Credibility Test" was programmed. This program is rather long (1500 instructions in IPL) and represents a simulation project by itself. The program is supposed to simulate the processes by which an individual with a rigid belief system assesses the credibility of a relevant but unfamiliar assertion. Given an assertion as input, the simulation produces as output a statement of whether the simulated individual does or does not believe the assertion, and why. With simple mock data for its "beliefs" the simulation performed admirably within the range of knowledge for which its memory had been prepared. To the assertion "John loves spinach," it replied, "False. Obviously boys hate vegetables." But when the model was supplied with an extensive real belief system (a paraphrasing of right-wing foreign policy ideology), it failed to find relevant responses to several seemingly clear-cut input assertions. This, it developed, was largely because the memory structure was made so large that the initially postulated search mechanisms were insufficiently powerful to find all the relevant memory associations. A few programming changes to force the system to search more deeply in its memory were made, but these had the effect of making the system much slower. In fact, it often took ten minutes on a fast computer for the system to respond, whereas a human counterpart might have taken three seconds in comparable circumstances. Even though it was not the aim of this simulation to achieve a completely literal imitation, such a huge difference in the unexpected direction between computer and human speed of response raised the severe possibility that the modified simulation model was fundamentally on the wrong track. Meanwhile, another method of increasing the power of the system would have been to store more beliefs in its memory initially. But this method (which, incidentally, would have created great nuisance problems with machine storage capacity) raised another fundamental problem: to what extent do individuals "store" beliefs with which they potentially agree and to what extent do they "compute" them from other beliefs? We were led thus into various new questions at a gross structural level, having started with an interest solely in the functional problem of how the presence of one belief influences the response to another potential belief. The model thus never got to the stage of a full-scale empirical validation before it had to go "back to the drawing boards."

Many investigators are understandably covetous of fascinating prototypic simulation models in new areas and are not eager to expose them to the possibility of "data shock." However, if methodology in this area is to progress beyond demonstrations of feasibility to full scientific status, the investigator must face the prospect of reiterative development of simulations; that is, returning to a very early stage on the ladder of model development in order to climb back up again with a hopefully improved version. Such reiteration is of course characteristic of all scientific theory development. The computer provides no special protection from the necessary effort involved.

COMPUTER SIMULATION OF COGNITIVE PROCESSES

The first computer simulations in psychology were those of Newell, Shaw, and Simon (1957, 1959), concerned with human strategies of problem-solving. These simulations embodied a new kind of theorizing about cognitive processes. While the simulations themselves have evoked but limited reaction from the psychological community, the style of theorizing has had an enormous impact. The basic theoretical idea is that "thinking" has the functional properties of "running a computer program," despite any number of differences in the physical construction of brains and computers (*cf.* von Neumann, 1958). The roots of this "information-processing theory" of thought (Hovland, 1960; Newell, Shaw, and Simon, 1958; Simon and Newell, 1964) perhaps antedate the existence of digital computers. [Certain of the pertinent ideas have been traced by DeGroot (1965), among others, back to the Wurzburgers, notably Otto Selz.] Yet it took the concrete demonstration of the possibility of intelligent humanoid performance by machines to give the current version of the theory its great force. The work of Newell, Shaw, and Simon was pivotally different from other early efforts in coaxing "intelligent" performances out of machines because these investigators were genuinely concerned with psychological theory as well as with "artificial intelligence."

The breadth of influence of the Thought-is-a-Program theory may be judged from the variety of contexts in which computer simulations of cognitive processes have been proposed: game-playing (Newell, Shaw, and Simon, 1963), planning (Miller, Galanter, and Pribram, 1960), decision-making (Clarkson, 1962), rote learning (Feigenbaum, 1961), simple hypothesis testing (Feldman, 1962), concept formation (Hunt, 1962; Hunt and Hovland, 1961; Hunt, Marin, and Stone, 1966), clinical diagnosis (Kleinmuntz, 1963), defending social attitudes (Abelson, 1963), expressing neurotic beliefs (Colby, 1963), responding to social stimuli (Gullahorn and Gullahorn, 1963), and several others. (Many of the above examples are included in Feigenbaum and Feldman, 1963.) An ambitious attempt to formulate a fairly complete information-processing model of thinking has been undertaken by Reitman (1965) and others (Reitman, Grove, and Shoup, 1964). Some Soviet psychologists apparently have aspirations in this direction as well (Amosov *et al.,* 1965).

Computer programming concepts have also been used metaphorically to suggest reconstructions of cognitive processes which might explain certain response data: for example, Miller's (1965a) analysis of the difficulty of understanding "left-branching" grammatical constructions in terms of housekeeping difficulties when using recursive subroutines. Going somewhat farther afield, one finds the information-processing metaphor turning up in discussions of motivation (Taylor, 1960), personality (Reitman, 1963), and the central nervous system (Broadbent, 1965).

Perhaps the greatest indication of the powerful impact of information-processing theory is the degree to which it has strengthened the hand of critics of simple associationism. George Miller's (1965b) stinging critique of behavioristic accounts of language learning exemplifies this new trend. In the field of cognitive psychology, at least, the information-processing theorists appear at present to be gaining the upper hand (Green, 1966; Taylor, 1963), although there is still much room for debate (Kleinmuntz, 1966). Paradoxically, although many humanists tend to regard the computer as a symbol of mechanized dehumanization, the computer models of thinking in fact advance a conception of man as a purposive intelligence with a great deal of autonomy. The theoretical tradition in which information-processing models fall is clearly much more Tolmanian or Lewinian than Hullian or Skinnerian, although a Wertheimer would no doubt still complain that "insight" is insufficiently represented.

A few cognitive simulations are of direct relevance to the social psychologist because they impinge on some of his domains: beliefs and attitudes, for example. In the main, however, the existing body of cognitive simulations serves as a background against which to view the simulations of groups of individuals to be taken up in a later section.

EXAMPLES

The General Problem Solver

Although the computer-programming metaphor for human cognitive activity is easy to use glibly in verbal discourse, it is quite another matter to show in detail how particular cognitive performances may be simulated by particular computer programs. One of the pioneering attempts at such detailed specification is Newell, Shaw, and Simon's (1959) "General Problem Solver," abbreviated GPS.

The phenomenon which GPS is designed to capture in detail is the evidently selective, coherent, goal-directed nature of the problem-solving activity of sophisticated problem solvers. A great many puzzles, problems, and games are such that no fixed sequence of operations, or *algorithm,* exists which is guaranteed to provide the solution within a reasonable length of time. Lacking an algorithm, an experienced problem solver will resort to "heuristics"—a variety of cogent strategies and devices which offer reasonable promise, though no guarantee, of reaching the solution. Protocols of smart subjects "thinking out loud" while solving problems abound with evidence of strategic sequences of steps (*cf.* Newell and Simon, 1963a). The most interesting such sequences to simulate are those with the greatest generality of occurrence in different problem contexts. This is attempted with GPS, which uses a very powerful heuristic dubbed "means-ends analysis." A typical problem content used by Newell, Simon, and Shaw is the transformation via a set of rules from one given symbolic-logic expression to another, but the intent of GPS is to be general, and other problems have also been used (Newell and Simon, 1963a, 1963b).

The strategy of means-ends analysis consists in breaking the total problem down systematically into interlocking smaller problems. With symbolic-logic expressions, for example, this proceeds as follows. The major problem *goal* is to transform logical expression A into logical expression B. The program first compares the two expressions to identify differences between them, and then establishes the *subgoal* of reducing the set of differences. This subgoal is attacked by means of a search for a rule Q which when applied to A or something similar will produce a new expression less different from B than was A originally. As soon as such a rule is tentatively found, the further subgoal of actually applying this rule is established. But perhaps expression A is not exactly in the appropriate symbolic form to permit the application of Q, and this leads to the still deeper subgoal of reducing the difference between A as it stands and the form A' required by Q. Thence some other rule, say R, will become a candidate for application to A (to produce A' to which Q can be applied to produce something closer to B) —and so on, through what may become an elaborate network of subgoals. As Newell and Simon (1963a, p. 286) describe it, "These methods form a recursive system that generates a tree of subgoals in attempting to attain a given goal. For every difficulty that is encountered a new subgoal is created to overcome this difficulty."

The complete GPS program, written in IPL-V, is considerably more complicated than our condensation of the already condensed published descriptions might suggest. There were many problems of definition and phasing in developing the program and, to judge from the various publications describing GPS, its nature is continually changing so as to include other heuristics. It has been applied systematically only to small fragments of the protocols of individuals working on a few problems. Nevertheless, the sequences of problem-solving steps generated by the program seem often to be reflected in rather fine detail in the human protocols. As a prototypic if not totally literal model of certain very general and important features of human problem-solving, GPS may informally be considered successful. (The question of what sorts of tests might be required in order to consider a simulation theory to have been formally "validated" is an important matter to which we shall return in a later section.)

The Ideology Machine

Simulations of problem-solving and game-playing, albeit interesting in their own right, are rather remote from the areas of concern to social psychologists. An obvious area of extension of the information-processing concept of cognition, however, is to the areas of beliefs and attitudes. In view of the recent development of several cognitive theories concerning attitude structure and change, the computer simulation of attitude change processes would appear to be a timely venture. The present author has in fact been attempting such a simulation since noting (Abelson, 1963) that problem-solving simulations have always neglected "hot" affective and motivational factors which might tend to distort the "cold" reckoning induced by a straightforward problem orientation.

In a recent description of this simulation attempt (Abelson and Carroll, 1965), most of the emphasis is placed on cognitive mechanisms which abet *resistance to attitude change*. This emphasis derives from the authors' interest in the commonly observed phenomenon that strongly held belief systems are readily defended against persuasive intrusion. Many of the pertinent mechanisms have been extensively discussed in the social-psychological literature, but there has been no other attempt to formulate the details of these mechanisms in the depth required for computer simulation, except for the work of Colby on neurotic belief systems (Colby, 1963; Colby and Gilbert, 1964). The present brief review will confine attention to the discussion of a single defensive mechanism, denial.

Because of the emphasis in the Abelson and Carroll simulation on stable, resistant social or political belief structures rather than transient constellations of opinions, it seems appropriate to refer to the simulation as the "Ideology Machine." The Ideology Machine must be provided with an initial belief structure representing the important beliefs of the simulated individual in some circumscribed content area. This "initialization" requirement, incidentally, creates extra difficulties for the simulation of belief systems beyond those encountered by GPS and other problem-solving programs. This is because individuals to be simulated can differ from one another not only in their cognitive processes, but also in the particular cognitive content on which the processes operate. This content may be determined by the investigator in any of three ways (none without attendant difficulties): by interviewing the subject, by implanting elaborate experimental content, or by paraphrasing the public statements of the subject. The characteristics of these various alternatives are further discussed by Abelson and Carroll (1965). In one present implementation of the Ideology Machine, the belief content is that of a well-known political figure and the initialization is by paraphrasing of public statements.

The belief content is organized both "horizontally" and "vertically." The vertical organization consists of nested conceptual categories, with more abstract cognitive elements at the "top" and more concrete cognitive elements at the "bottom." The abstract element "countries," for example, might include the three instance classes, "Communist bloc countries," "Western bloc countries," and "neutrals," each of which might include further subcategories, moving down eventually to the level of individual countries. Cognitive elements representing potential *actions* can also be organized in this hierarchical way. For example, "interfere with countries," as a general action concept, might include "interfere economically with countries," "interfere militarily with countries," and so on, introducing different adverbial qualifiers; and also include "interfere with Communist bloc countries," "interfere with neutrals," and so on, using different instances of the original predicate object. The horizontal organization of the belief structure consists of simple stored "sentences" connecting actors with actions, for example, "Communist bloc countries interfere economically with neutrals," or whatever the appropriate subjective content might happen to be for the particular individual. A reasonably large number of such sentences (in one present implementation, about 500) characterizes the core beliefs of the simulated individual in the given content area. A further aspect of the stored belief structure is that *evaluations* are assigned to the important elements. The simulated individual considers certain actors or actions to be good or bad, and the system must store and use these evaluations.

The Ideology Machine is activated by the input of any simple sentence constructed from a dictionary list of elements stored in the belief system. This sentence is called the "input assertion." The system seeks to respond either by accepting or rejecting the input assertion, giving its reasons for so doing.

With this brief background, the mechanism of *denial* can now be sketched. Denial consists of a motivated search for evidence supporting the negation of the input assertion. Such a search is triggered when the input assertion embodies an evaluatively inconsistent state of affairs such as a "good" actor performing "bad" actions. The contrary assertion in this case would be that the good actor does not perform such bad actions. The plausibility of the desired contrary assertion is tested by a major subroutine called the "Credibility Test." The test consists of an extensive search up and down the vertical hierarchy for supportive evidence. The assertion that actors of class A do not perform actions of type B would be supported by one or more previously stored beliefs such as: actors of class A do not perform the type of actions exemplified by type B or do not perform a specific action of type B; a specific actor of class A does not perform actions of type B; etc. Successful search permits the Ideology Machine to deny the input assertion by producing the reasons in favor of the opposite view.

The search operation as now programmed in the simulation is apparently not very efficient, and the Ideology Machine stands in need of considerable further improvement before it is fully satisfactory as a simulation. Nevertheless, a start has been made in an interesting direction.

Other examples

Certain other simulations of cognitive processes will be briefly summarized here. Related recent summaries have been given by Reitman (1965), Green (1963), Gullahorn and Gullahorn (1965a), Jones (1963), Fattu (1965), Feigenbaum and Feldman (1963), Clarkson and Simon (1960), Newell and Simon (1963b), and

Simon and Newell (1965). Among the most relevant bibliographies are those assembled by Simmons and Simmons (1962), Minsky (1963b), and Sass and Wilkinson (1965).

Colby (1963, 1964, 1965, 1967) has over the past several years gradually developed an increasingly complex simulation of a neurotic belief system. In the system is initially stored a large set of beliefs about self and significant others. The organization of this memory is by arrays rather than lists, though otherwise there is a great deal of similarity to the Ideology Machine. Initialization has been by paraphrasing the beliefs of a particular psychiatric patient.

The program (written in a version of ALGOL) is activated with a given belief either input arbitrarily or generated by the system from previous ruminations. Various other relevant beliefs are then recruited by the system to form a "pool" of beliefs. The simulated patient then tries to express all the beliefs in the pool, but some of them arouse so much conflict that they must be distorted or "transformed" before they can be expressed.

For example, the belief "self rejects father" conflicts with "self ought not reject father" and is transformed by "deflection" to "self rejects Harry," which is then expressed. A whole series of well-defined transforms are included in the simulation, as well as a number of nonverbal indices such as anxiety, arousal, etc., which both regulate and are regulated by the ongoing verbal expression. The system is capable of a continuous flow of processing, each topic of concern leading to others. If the original belief content contains crucial self-defeating contradictions, the system engages in a futile and "neurotic" kind of shadowboxing with its own distortions. Here again, as with the simulations previously discussed, the computer program generates plausible general output in a prototypic case, though it lacks some of the richness of detail of the real human counterpart.

One of the interesting outgrowths of Colby's work (and the closely related work of Weizenbaum, 1966) is that the computer has also been programmed to elicit an interview from a "patient" (Colby, Watt, and Gilbert, 1966). This program (known informally as the "Mad Doctor") may be regarded as a simulation of the remarks of a nondirective therapist, although it is still in too early a stage of development to be considered a good simulation. A sample interview might run as follows:

> *Doctor:* Tell me what is troubling you.
> *Patient:* I feel very alone in the world.
> *Doctor:* Why do you feel very alone in the world?
> *Patient:* I can't find any friends.
> *Doctor:* Have you tried?
> *Patient:* Of course I've tried. Otherwise why would I come to you?
> *Doctor:* Why do you ask?

And so on. Many of the responses of the "doctor" are conversationally plausible, but some (like the last) are irrelevant or ridiculous. The simplest version of the doctor program operates via "key words." Whenever the patient says *"I can't . . . ,"* for example, the doctor says, "Have you tried?" Whenever the patient says,

"I feel . . . ," the doctor might say, "How long have you felt . . . ?" repeating word for word whatever comes after the key words. An extensive set of different key-word phrases can be provided to the program in an input list called the *script*. One obvious deficiency of such a simple program is that it loses track of what is being discussed, since it responds only to the previous response. This particular problem is curable by various devices for building up a "conversation tree" which will keep track of the branching points in conversational flow. Joseph Weizenbaum, who has independently developed conversational simulations (Weizenbaum, 1966), has been working on improvement of these devices.

In addition to their entertainment value (McGovern, 1960) and certain specialized pedagogic uses (Bitzer, 1965; Swets and Feurzeig, 1965), computer programs which "talk back" have stimulated a whole range of theoretical possibilities (sufficient, indeed, to have inspired at least one graduate seminar devoted entirely to brainstorming the uses of Weizenbaum's program). One of the most intriguing possibilities is that such programs may be helpful in eliciting elaborate cognitive structures from subjects. The "Mad Doctor," in the conversation exemplified above, does not in any sense "understand" what the patient is saying, but it is interesting to consider the possibility that some of the information given by the patient could in fact be retained and gradually "understood" as more and more new information was received (Colby and Enea, 1967). The initialization of belief systems for simulation would certainly be greatly facilitated by "automated interviewing." However, the conceptual problems in programming such a system are extremely formidable. The few computer programs for "understanding" natural language which have been devised (Bobrow, 1964; Green *et al.,* 1961; Lindsay, 1963; Quillian, 1967; Raphael, 1964; Simmons, 1965) operate within very highly constrained linguistic environments oriented toward narrow problem contents. The broad "General Inquirer" system for the content analysis of text (Dunphy, Stone, and Smith, 1965; Stone *et al.,* 1962; Stone *et al.,* 1966) is by contrast able to tabulate a greater variety of words but is weak in syntactic capability. It seems unlikely that programs which comprehend completely unconstrained natural English will be developed in the near future. Nevertheless we may look forward to many partial successes in the simulation of psychological processes involved in conversation and in comprehension (*cf.* Paige and Simon, 1966; Reitman, 1965, Chapter 9).

In areas of cognitive functioning somewhat less exotic than those we have been considering, one of the most important simulations is Feigenbaum's (1963) model of elementary perception and memorization (EPAM). This model attempts to account for a variety of classical experimental results in the learning and forgetting of nonsense-syllable lists, paired associates, etc. Simulation is not of any particular individual, but rather of an idealized prototypic experimental subject. The key construct in this model is that of a *discrimination net,* a sequence of progressively finer and finer tests for critical stimulus features. This net is designed to create new discriminative tests as it needs them, but the sequence of stimulus presentations and a variety of other factors can give rise to faulty or insufficient discrimination and thus to certain predictable types of learning errors (Simon and Feigenbaum, 1964). The model gives rather a good account of several well-known experimental findings such as the serial position effect (Feigenbaum and Simon, 1962). Whether the particular type of memory organization postulated by EPAM will be a useful description in realms involving complex meaningful material remains to be seen.

EVALUATION

Computer simulations of cognitive processes have had a great impact on psychological theorizing about memory, language, and thought. This influence has undoubtedly been greater at the level of general discourse than at the level of the particulars of given simulations. As has been noted, particular simulations have often been tentative and fragmentary. Nevertheless, discourse in the currency of information-processing theory would be of limited value without what Reitman (1965) calls the "silver backing" of the actual running programs. Doubts about what a theory "really means" can always be resolved by running the program on the computer.

How far it will be possible to go in simulating the full richness of human cognitive processes is unclear. Existing programs tend to be rather too rigidly bound to special purposes and not at all susceptible to open-ended phenomena such as the discovery of the solution to problem *B* while working on problem *A*. In a provocative analysis of the thought processes of master chess players, DeGroot (1965) identifies a ubiquitous strategy he calls "progressive deepening" in which there is continual reinvestigation of the same line of play with attendant transformation of the definition of the crucial problems in the game. Although this kind of possibility is being explored (Baylor and Simon, 1966; Newell and Simon, 1965), existing computer-simulation chess programs (*cf.* Newell, Shaw, and Simon, 1963) do not behave in this way. Neither do other present problem-solving programs nor the belief-system simulations we have discussed.

Whether the obstacles to writing more flexible programs are in any sense fundamental is moot. The sophisticated critical discussion of program limitations by Neisser (1963) has been rebutted by equally sophisticated but much more optimistic assessments by Reitman (1964) and others. All simulation and artificial-intelligence experts seem to agree, however, that the boundaries of the possible have nowhere near been reached, and that much further progress can be expected.

Of the several problems which bedevil such progress in simulation, the two most perplexing are the validation problem and the communication problem. It is to these that we now turn.

The validation problem

Almost all cognitive simulations to date have been informally evaluated rather than subjected to formal validation procedures. The most informal evaluation of all occurs when the investigator simply states that simulation runs produced plausible results. Somewhat less loose is the case in which the investigator presents sample output of the computer alongside sample responses from the human counterpart. This is the method used by Newell and Simon (1963a) in some of their published presentations of GPS. The parallel between human problem-solving protocols and computer program "protocols" (that is, traces of the steps undertaken by the program in pursuit of a solution) may sometimes be quite striking. Nevertheless, as a validation method this mode of presentation of results leaves something to be desired. Even if case material is scrupulously chosen so as not to conceal instances of poor fit, there is still a serious "degrees of freedom" problem (Frijda, 1967, p. 65). If a simulation is repeatedly redesigned to fit a given body of protocol materials, doubt may arise whether the resulting simulation is of general relevance or merely a forced imitation of idiosyncrasies in fragmentary data. As noted in a previous section, if all the sequencing and other hidden options available to the programmer are made explicit, the number of free "parameters" may become quite large. While it would be most unfair to speak of simulations as though they were snakes with 99 bends that could always be contorted to fit 101 points, still one would feel much more comfortable if validation tests were carried out on data completely independent of simulation design. One would like, in other words, some form of *cross validation* of simulation models on new data.

Let us consider the case in which the simulation target is a specific single person. A given body of protocol materials is used in the design of the simulation. The simulation program is then run for validation purposes and the output is "compared" with a new body of protocol materials either deliberately set aside from the outset or newly generated. But what sorts of "comparison" procedures are appropriate? Contemporary discussions admit three possibilities:

1. *Tabulation of response matches between person and program.*
2. *Global statistical comparison of the internal sequential properties of person output and program output.*
3. *An objective global judgment procedure known as "Turing's Test."*

The technique of tabulating response matches has been discussed by Feldman (1962). One of the problems is that there are no guidelines for the goodness of a match. Is it satisfactory if the program generates 81 percent of the particular responses made by the actual subject? It is impossible to say, unless there is some statistical process accounting for an anticipatable range of random nonmatches. (One nice possibility along this line has been suggested by Hunt, Marin, and Stone, 1966: one or more other subjects performing the same task can be compared with the target subject, response by response.) But a worse sort of difficulty for response-match validation is that the process being simulated may be so sequentially sensitive that small effects have great future ramifications. Thus a single nonmatching response by the program may lead inexorably to a long series of further nonmatches that the investigator justifiably feels should not count against the program.

Addressing himself to this difficulty posed by sequential dependencies, Reitman (1965) has suggested that validation should not be carried out match by match, but rather in terms of the comparability of the internal contingencies exhibited by both program and person. To illustrate simply, suppose that responses can be classified into two types, "zigs" and "zags." A 2×2 contingency table is drawn up for the person's protocol, specifying the frequencies with which zigs and zags are respectively followed by zigs and by zags. The same is done for the program output, and the frequencies in these two 2×2 tables are compared. It may well be that even though the program sometimes zigs when the person zags, the frequencies of comparable sequential patterns (zig-zag, zig-zig, and so on) are much the same for person and for program over a long series of responses. This simple comparison procedure could be augmented by further contingency comparisons such as those for (1) longer sequential patterns, (2) other response classifications, and (3) dependencies on initial conditions. If a variety of contingency tables turned out statistically comparable for person versus program, the program would be adjudged a good fit. Although there has not been much accumulated experience with this type of validation procedure, it seems reasonably promising.

The most famous suggested validation procedure was devised by the late A. M. Turing in a paper addressed to the question, "Can machines think?" (Turing, 1950; reprinted in Feigenbaum and Feldman, 1963). Turing's test is based on a situation which he called the Imitation Game, a situation of beautiful apparent simplicity.

There is some ambiguity in Turing's article about the intended conditions for his Imitation Game, but the usual interpretation runs approximately as follows: A human subject is concealed in one room, a computer in a second, and each is set to work on the same task. A judge seated in a third room has access to typewritten outputs from the two rooms. His job is to guess accurately which output belongs to the computer and which to the subject. If over many trials his guesses are correct no more than half the time, then the computer has successfully simulated the subject performing the particular task.

The task that Turing had in mind for the computer to perform was the extremely ambitious one of giving plausible replies to a judge instructed to pose difficult or trick requests intended to defeat the simulation (for example, "Write a sonnet for me"). Meanwhile, the concealed subject is encouraged to reply in as revealing a fashion as possible. To be successful, therefore, the computer must be programmed to respond in a deceitful and disarmingly human fashion ("Sorry, I never was much good at poetry").

The cunning gamesmanship pitting the judge against the computer program was of great interest to Turing, but is totally irrelevant to our present concern with Turing's Test as a validating procedure for computer simulations of limited task performances. In the discussion to follow, we exclude from consideration cases in which the judge can attempt to improve his guesses by strategic conversational probes. Instead, we assume that the judge is limited to the inspection of outputs over which he has no influence. (In the case of the "Mad Doctor" or other conversational simulations, this can be achieved by appropriately designed assignment of conversing and judging roles to different people.)

Even with chicanery excluded from the Imitation Game, there is still an annoying difficulty in using the judge's guesses as evidence for or against the verisimilitude of a simulation. Judges confronted with the task of distinguishing the subject from the computer will naturally seek out tiny clues, many of them quite misleading. Edward S. Johnson has reported to the writer a concept-learning simulation (Johnson, 1967) for which judges' guesses were worse than chance because the subject's output style happened to seem "mechanical." One would not regard this as a triumph of deception for the computer. There were many much more relevant subject-versus-program differences in the task performance, but the judges either did not attend to these differences or did not know how to use them. For unusual tasks, most judges have insufficient information (possibly even no information) about the way humans perform, to say nothing about the way computers perform. In view of the problem of irrelevant bases of judgment, therefore, this simple test can only be used with sophisticated, well-instructed judges. Even at that, the "Simple Turing Test" has not been popular, perhaps because there seems to be no easy way to use the failure of the test to improve an imperfect simulation.

Evidently Turing was aware of potential problems associated with the Simple Test. A careful reading of his original paper discloses that his intended version of the Imitation Game (Turing, 1950, p. 434) is probably not the version always attributed to him. We consider it worthwhile to revive some of his original suggestions and, adding and subtracting various embellishments, to refer to the resulting procedure as the "Extended Turing Test."

As before, there is a computer program intended as an imitation of a subject carrying out a set of tasks. But there is also another target person whom we may designate the anchor. *The anchor differs from the subject with respect to some simple dimension,* for example, sex, age, or skill. In a series of baseline runs of the Game, the subject works in one room and the anchor in the second. The judge, using typewritten output, must guess the correct identities of subject and anchor; for example, which is the man and which is the woman. Over a series of runs, the judge will guess correctly some percentage of the time. For illustrative purposes, suppose that this *base percentage* is 70 percent. At some point in the procedure, a computer program is substituted for the subject while the anchor continues as before. The judge must again guess the correct identities of (for example) the "man" and the "woman." Turing does not make clear whether the judge is ever told anything at all about the entrance of a computer into the game. The best procedure is undoubtedly *not* to inform him, and to interlace subject-versus-anchor runs with computer-versus-anchor runs. So far as the judge knows, he must on every run look for cues relevant to the announced dimension of difference between subject and anchor. The crucial datum is the percentage of correct identifications of the anchor when pitted against the computer-simulated "subject." Denote this percentage the *test percentage*. The simulation is judged successful if both base and test percentages reliably exceed 50 percent and *the test percentage is not statistically different from the base percentage.* Such a success (or failure) would, however, only partially validate (or invalidate) the simulation. *This validation test is relative to the dimension of difference between subject and anchor.* For illustrative purposes, suppose that in a problem-solving task situation with a man as subject and a woman as anchor, the base percentage were 70 percent and the test percentage 90 percent. That is, the computer's task protocols are more easily distinguished from the woman's protocols than the man's protocols are from the woman's. In view of the fact that the judge is told nothing about computers, only to distinguish the man's work from the woman's, such a result indicates that the computer behaves in a manner which is "too male." This would come about if the computer protocols contained an overabundance of some stereotypically male attribute, such as an analytic rather than intuitive approach to the problem task. On the other hand, if the test percentage were 55 percent, then this indicates that the computer program is "not male enough." In either case, a particular kind of change in the simulation is indicated. Finally, supposing the test percentage to have been 67 percent, or 72 percent, or anything within a statistically acceptable range around 70 percent, then the simulation is judged acceptable with respect to its maleness. The investigator might then wish to proceed to another validation test using a different anchor dimension, perhaps intelligence, or experience with problem-solving, etc. Our version of an Extended Turing Test is definitely meant to require the use of several anchor dimensions (and also anchors at different positions along continuous dimensions such as intelligence) before the simulation can be considered validated.

Note that this advocated test implies the philosophical position that *simulation validation necessarily involves some particularization of the simulation target.* The investigator does not simulate simply "a problem solver" or "a chess player" or "an ideologue." Rather, he simulates a "reasonably clever young adult male problem solver without previous experience at the particular task," or a "well-informed but closed-minded defender of an unpopular belief system." Unfortunately, many existing simulations consist of sets of diverse mechanisms which each capture something of psychological importance but collectively cannot be said to characterize any particular individual or type of individual. While such "meta-simulations" may be of great value as compelling abstractions, they preclude the employment of the Extended Turing Test or indeed of any formal type of validation. The Extended Turing Test as outlined is admittedly quite elaborate, and the astute reader will have noted that even further refinements are called for. The test had best be run with several judges, targets, and anchors. It might be useful to run the Simple and Extended Tests concurrently. The details can be filled out by any of a number of standard research designs. The matter will not be further pursued here, except to note that the judges need not literally sit in a room awaiting typewritten output, as Turing's original description would have it. Output protocols can be reproduced and shown to any number of judges. Our essential point is that designers of simulation models should exercise greater ingenuity in making empirical tests of their models possible, and not begrudge the effort to carry them out.

A type of validation procedure not involving the use of extended response protocols is the standard experimental strategy of developing new predictions which are then subjected to experimental test. Somewhat surprisingly, this time-honored procedure has hardly been used at all in connection with simulation models of cognitive processes. Simon and Feigenbaum (1964) have compared many of the performance properties of their EPAM model with human performances reported in the experimental literature, but independent experiments based on the model have been slow in making an appearance. One very minor aspect of the Abelson and Carroll (1965) simulation served as the basis for a prediction later verified experimentally by Gilson and Abelson (1965). Meanwhile there has been an encouraging tendency toward the generation of experimental predictions in a few simulations of concept learning (Hunt and Hovland, 1961; Hunt, Marin, and Stone, 1966; Simon and Kotovsky, 1963). The major independent variable in these predictions has been *task difficulty*. One hopes that there will be increasing mutual interplay in the future between simulation models and laboratory studies.

The communication problem

The details of simulation models are notoriously difficult to communicate. At a very general descriptive level such as has been used throughout this chapter, it is feasible to explain purpose and process, but when one comes down to the level of the coding of microprocesses, problems arise. Journal editors are less than eager to fill crowded journal space with copies of computer programs. Even were journals to be permissive in this regard, the interested reader would still not be much helped. It requires great effort and imagination to understand someone else's simulation program, even with an intimate knowledge of the programming language. Simulations of the sort considered in this chapter almost always involve microprocesses which do not have standardized programming recipes, as common mathematical processes do. The programmer will usually develop idiosyncratic private notations and methods in coping with various programming problems. Like the indispensable secretary who alone knows where to locate carbon paper, good corned beef sandwiches, and last year's correspondence, only the programmer will know what specialized information is kept in the memory location labeled RECALL or why process Z must occur before process Q.

There are three ways to try to increase public access to specialized information:

1. *Standardize procedures so that there is less scope for private specialization in the first place.*

2. *Arrange for informal communication of the specialized information to one or more other persons.*

3. *Require extensive written documentation of all specialized information.*

As already noted, the field of computer simulation of cognitive processes is in such an early stage of diversified development that one cannot expect much in the way of standardized procedures. However, there has been some progress in the other two approaches to the communication problem. The Social Science Research Council in 1965 financed a number of travel grants for scholars to visit sites at which simulation programs were being run. It is likely that some arrangements for direct informal teaching of program details will resume. (One "far-out" possibility which may become more realistic with the increased establishment of distant teletype connections to central computers is that simulation programs can be made accessible to many geographically remote investigators simultaneously. Instructions in their use could conceivably be conveyed by clever use of teletype facilities.) Reliable formal documentation of important simulation programs is, of course, always desirable. One factor which inhibits investigators from writing documentations, however, is their likely obsolescence. After a great deal of effort has been spent writing out every last detail, the simulation may be changed sufficiently to render the document useless.

There is acute present awareness of the communication problem (*cf.* Reitman, 1965, pp. 25–27). There has been some high-level discussion of the problems involved in finding appropriate journal outlets for simulation descriptions and documentations. With time and the accumulation of experience, some mitigation of these problems is reasonably likely.

SIMULATION OF SOCIAL PROCESSES

In passing from the simulation of cognitive processes to the simulation of social processes, we find that some totally new considerations come into play. There seems to be no direct analog at the social group level to the Thought-is-a-Program theory at the individual cognitive level. With any theory that might try to establish an isomorphism between ongoing group process and an ongoing computer program (a kind of interpersonal information-processing theory of shared social events), there is an obvious intuitive difficulty. Computer programs are organized sequentially under the control of the main program or "executive." But one does not know where to locate executive control of the social "organism," since social groups contain multiple centers of autonomy. Thus the apparent simulation gap between machine and group is greater than that between machine and individual.

We may roughly distinguish two lines of approach toward bridging the gap, the *aggregative* and the *systemic*.

In the aggregative approach, which comes most naturally to psychologists, the social group is conceived as a collection of individuals each pursuing his own goals. To be sure, the several individuals may interact in the pursuit of common or conflicting goals, but the locus of explanation of group phenomena is considered to reside within the individuals. The corresponding method for constructing simulations is to concentrate on the social behaviors of single individuals. If all goes well, these can later be aggregated into a simulation model for the behavior of a "group" or two or more individuals. The executive control problem is solved by having several executives, one per individual, take turns generating responses. The simulation targets of programs using this general style of approach include Loehlin's (1963, 1965, in press) abstract social "creatures," Gullahorn and Gullahorn's (1963, 1964) office workers, Pool and Kessler's (1965) elite decision makers, and Coe's (1964) generalized social actors.

If the number of individuals in the simulation becomes very large, then it becomes less and less feasible to provide each individual with rich psychological processes. The simulation becomes time-consuming and unwieldy, and there are problems in phasing the activities of the many individuals. Thus there is an inevitable tendency to trivialize or omit autonomous processes within individuals in favor of universal processes or forces acting between individuals or on the group as a whole. This is the "systemic" approach. The executive control problem is solved by placing program control in a detached external monitor which causes things to happen to a passive system. Examples of simulations using this approach include: Pool, Abelson, and Popkin (1964, 1965) on the behavior of the national electorate; Abelson and Bernstein (1963) on community controversies; McPhee (1963) and others (McPhee and Smith, 1962; McPhee and Ferguson, 1962) on large general electorates; Hägerstrand (1965a, 1966) and Pitts (1962, 1963) on the diffusion of innovations; Coleman (1965) and Levin (1962) on reference group phenomena; and Gilbert and Hammel (1966) on the implications of marriage rules for tribal population stability. Systemic simulations need not necessarily involve large groups of individuals. Another way in which individuality can be deemphasized in favor of an abstract formal conception of a social collectivity is through mathematical models. When such models cannot be solved analytically, they are often subjected to simulation, as with Coleman's (1965) model of coalition formation in the triad, or Rainio's (1965, 1966) stochastic models of social interaction. Also included in the category of systemic simulations, but outside the scope of this chapter, are economic simulations (Holland with Gillespie, 1963; Orcutt *et al.*, 1961; see also Orcutt, 1960, and Shubik, 1960) and a number of simulations oriented toward applications in business or service organizations (Balderston and Hoggatt, 1962; Bernstein, 1962; Bonini, 1963; Fetter, 1965; Sprowls, 1962; and several others).

In another type of general approach, favored by organization theorists, social organizations are viewed as having goals, plans, information, etc., at their disposal, much as individuals do. This category would include: Rufus Browning's unpublished model of a public agency submitting budget requests to a legislature; and the simulation of competitive situations involving business firms (*cf.* Cohen and Cyert, 1965; Cyert, Feigenbaum, and March, 1959; Cyert and March, 1963).

Because simulations of social processes comprise such a wide spectrum of types, with targets ranging from two-person groups to huge electorates, it is not easy to characterize the set of them *in toto*. In principle it is possible for a simulation jointly to involve detailed models of individual social behaviors and aggregative statistical treatment of very large groups. But in practice such simulations are very difficult to construct, and almost all social simulations constructed to date emphasize either the qualitative details of several interacting organisms or statistical characterizations of social systems. In both cases, new validational problems arise which were not present with cognitive simulations of single individuals.

EXAMPLES

Qualitative models of elementary social behavior

One way of building up models of social performance from individualistic considerations is to start with a rather constrained class of social situations for which a fairly elementary model of individual behavior may prove adequate. A common source of ingredients for elementary models lies in reinforcement theories of social learning. The most ambitious attempt to apply reinforcement principles in a social simulation is the Homunculus model of Gullahorn and Gullahorn (1963), using George Homans' propositions concerning the rewards of social exchange. The delimited social scenario of interest has one individual soliciting help from another in completing some task assignment. The model is evidently intended by the authors to apply to a broader range of contexts, and in a later paper (Gullahorn and Gullahorn, 1964) there is some hint of an increase in scope of application.

Though the responses of the Homunculus model are based primarily on the reinforcement history of the individual, the model, programmed in IPL-V, is very much in the style of most information-processing models of thought. List search operations are heavily emphasized. The simulated individual must be able to recognize and contrast different social stimuli, contemplate the "psychic cost" of different responses, and calculate on the basis of past events the probability and momentary incentive value of each of several types of rewards which may accrue to each contemplated response. Responses are chosen when they provide a sufficient excess of expected reward over expected psychic cost.

The simulation can be set into motion with receipt by one social actor of the activity emitted by another. The receiver decides upon and emits an activity of his own, which then serves as a stimulus for the other. This cycle presumably may continue indefinitely, although the Gullahorns (1964) state that it is extremely difficult to make program provision for the bewildering variety of possible qualitative activity sequences that can occur.

The problem will be illustrated here with a deliberately extravagant example. Suppose the simulation begins with an office worker named George soliciting help from a colleague, Ted. Ted decides that he is too busy, but rather than incur social punishment from George by flat refusal of the request, Ted refers George to another colleague, Harry. George has in the past not been rewarded when requesting help from Harry, let us say, and therefore refuses Ted's suggestion. George has not received satisfaction from his request, and therefore decides not to seek help anymore. Meanwhile Ted, having incurred a social loss because his suggestion was not rewarded with George's approval, decides that he should entreat Harry to help George. Harry agrees as a favor to Ted, but when George pridefully refuses, Harry asks Ted for an explanation. . . . And so on. The intricacies of such social situational "scripts" seem to carry the model beyond the emission of fixed activities by each actor in the face of fixed activities received. In the above example, one seems forced to invent new activities as one goes along, such as "asks for an explanation of the fact that the conditions assumed at the time a favor was granted do not hold." For the simulation to proceed, this conceivable activity must have been anticipated, and the simulated recipient of this activity must have been provided with a history of previous appropriate responses ("What did I do the last time so-and-so asked me for an explanation of the fact that the assumptions I made when he granted me a favor were false, and to what extent did he reward this previous response?").

Keeping track of a sprouting "situation tree" is a difficult problem somewhat comparable to the "conversation tree" problem mentioned in a previous section. It is an interesting area for further development, but has not been pursued with Homunculus. Instead, the investigators decided to proceed by grouping activities into broad conceptual classes. Using the twelve categories of the Bales system, each simulated actor was supplied with the capability of responding with any category to any category emitted by any of the other simulated actors. While this scheme avoids the open-endedness of the "activity sequence" scheme, it still taxes practical storage limits unless the number of actors is sharply limited. Using three actors and a "referee" in the program to compute whose turn it was to interact with whom, the Gullahorns (1964) undertook a series of simulation runs with this reformulated Homunculus.

At least one qualitative result was worthy of note. In the majority of cases, simulated social triads devolved into a friendly pair and an isolate. This simulated "coalition formation" was the result of snowballing mutually reinforcing episodes of friendly interaction, starting more or less fortuitously but tending gradually to push the third individual out of the focus of social attention. Interestingly, this same phenomenon had been observed by Kirk and Coleman in a completely independent simulation using similar but simpler reinforcement postulates. Coleman (1964a, 1965) discussed this result in detail, pointing out that although the simulation of course does not prove that coalition formation in the triad is the result of early mutual reinforcement when three people simultaneously compete for each other's attention, it at least demonstrates that more complicated mechanisms need not necessarily be invoked to account for this classical phenomenon.

The difficulties encountered by the Homunculus model are instructive. Starting with the goal of simulating behavior in a particular social situation, the investigators discovered that by giving the simulated actors too many qualitative choices they were overwhelming their model with conceptual possibilities. Limitation and stylization of choices solved this problem, but at the same time gave the simulation a more abstract, less situationally defined character than the investigators may originally have intended.

An alternative style of model construction involves the synthesis of simulated individuals from deliberately abstract features not specialized to any particular human social situation. One asks, "Supposing individuals to be constructed with such-and-such 'personality' processes and predispositions, what sorts of social behavior patterns can occur when these individuals interact?" This was the strategy adopted by Loehlin (1963) in his design of a hypothetical social creature he nicknamed Aldous. His hope was to generate interaction patterns of considerable nuance from very simple principles of individual motivation and learning, and he was not particularly concerned with the verisimilitude of Aldous as a person rather than as an unspecified social creature.

Aldous is equipped with three "emotions": joy, anger, and fear; and three social responses: approach, attack, and withdrawal. The strength and nature of the response emitted in any situation is a function of the momentary relative balance among the three emotions. The consequences of any given type of response depend on the environmental situation, and these consequences in turn cause emotional readjustment to the situation. When Aldous' "environment" consists of another Aldous, then schematic social consequences may fairly readily be specified. Loehlin (1965, in press), in his "interpersonal" experiments with Aldous, defined three such consequences: injury, satisfaction, and frustration. Injury results from an uncountered attack from the other creature, and causes subsequent increases in fear and/or anger; satisfaction results from successful approach, attack, or escape behavior, and causes increased positive and/or decreased negative emotional reaction, depending on the situation; frustration results from an incongruent reply to an approach response, or interference with an attack or escape, and can cause a variety of emotional changes, again depending on the situation. "Situation" is defined by Loehlin as *a sequence of two actions,* for example, a timid approach by Self followed by a mild attack by Other, a strong attack by Self followed by quick withdrawal by Other, etc. Loehlin considered but rejected the alternative definitions of "situation" as simply the action of Other, or as a sequence of three actions. The sequence-of-two-actions definition provides some degree of contextual continuity to a long string of actions and reactions while still preserving simplicity. (In the Homunculus model with the twelve Bales response categories, it was apparently not feasible or attractive always to specify context according to the 144 pairs, and the Gullahorns were content to define the social situation mainly according to the preceding response by Other. Whether this is a severe limitation on the simulation is not clear.)

Loehlin proceeded to run a number of different social "experiments" with paired Aldouses. One result suggestive of the flavor of the outcomes is the "lovers' quarrel" phenomenon. Two creatures, initially supplied with emotional profiles in which the positive emotion greatly dominated, were run through a long series of interactions. Uniformly positive response sequences resulted, until one critical trial when a mild attack fortuitously occurred. (Chance effects are included in the system.) The social relationship precipitously deteriorated, reaching the point where mutual attacks occurred fully as often as mutual positive interactions. Loehlin explains this effect in terms of the insufficient prior experience of the creatures in coping with mild attacks.

The flavor of this result is characteristic of existing qualitative social models. Intuitive plausibility may be present, but empirical anchorage is lacking. It is difficult to know what range of applicability the models are supposed to have, since no data-gathering operations have been specified as natural accompaniments to the simulations. Thus these qualitative social models might be regarded as simple *demonstration models:* they display what outcomes are possible given certain assumptions and omitting others. The degree of importance to be attached to demonstration models seems to vary with the temperament of the observer. There is a natural tendency in the self-consciously empirical discipline of social psychology to downgrade unanchored abstractions, yet these sorts of efforts undoubtedly have their place, particularly as spurs to the better articulation of theories.

Parenthetically, we note that Gullahorn and Gullahorn (1965a) were apparently sensitive to the charge of nonempiricism and recently endeavored to generate an empirical test of some of the features of Homunculus. In this attempt they invented so many special rules to cover a single narrow empirical situation that in the opinion of the present author the resulting model was not useful either as an extension of Homunculus or as an independent general model. However, the goal of this effort is laudable, and further attempts should be made. There is no fundamental barrier to the construction of qualitative social simulations which, in addition to their demonstrational features, also have suggestive connections to experimental or observational procedures.

Quantitative models of elementary social behavior

One way of bringing models into closer contact with data is to focus on limited and readily quantified features of social interaction. At some sacrifice in richness, though hopefully not in relevance, the investigator may try to gain tractability and testability for his models via simple equations carrying a very small number of dependent variables (perhaps no more than one or two) through time. This is the strategy of *mathematical modeling.* In the present context we do not propose to penetrate deeply into this extensive topic, but only to identify its boundaries with computer simulation. For detailed reviews of mathematical models in social psychology, the reader is referred to Rapoport (1963), Coleman (1964a, 1964b), Abelson (1967), and especially to Chapter 3 in Vol. 1 of this *Handbook.* A provocative confrontation of computer simulation and mathematical models of simple human concept formation has been provided by Gregg and Simon (1967).

In discussing the difference between computer simulation models and mathematical models there is some danger of semantic confusion. All computer simulation models are "mathematical" in the sense of dealing logically with closed systems of well-specified quantities and relationships. Conversely, mathematical models are sometimes (though by no means always) subjected to "simulation" by computer. As typically used, however, these two approaches identify contrasting poles of a particular dimension. The mathematical-models approach typically postulates very few mechanisms, makes very few assumptions, and keeps its equations simple. The computer-simulation approach very often involves a great many mechanisms and assumptions, and can invoke complex qualitative specifications and equations. This dimension of difference can perhaps best be characterized in terms of the *number of degrees of freedom* available to the model (though there are difficulties, as already noted, in defining this concept for complex simulations).

The two approaches tend sometimes to "meet in the middle." This often occurs when a moderately difficult mathematical model becomes completely unmanageable with an increase in the number of equations. Alternatively, the designer of a computer simulation may wish to avoid the considerable difficulties attendant upon qualitative complexity, and thence formulate his simulation with a rather small set of equations in the manner of the typical mathematical model. In either case, the resulting product is a quantitative model which is not approached analytically, but instead is run on the computer in order to investigate its behavior.

A clear case in point is Rainio's (1965) "stochastic theory of social contacts." One realization of this theory involves a (small) finite group of individuals engaging in pairwise social interaction. These interactions are determined probabilistically, with only one pair allowed to interact at a time. Each member of the pair states one of two possible opinions on some issue; thus each interaction results either in social agreement or disagreement. The heart of Rainio's model lies in its assumptions about the further consequences of these outcomes. Social agreement between two individuals is assumed to increase the probability of future mutual interaction and also the probabilities of separate future expression of the "reinforced" opinion. Both increases are quantitatively mediated by stochastic learning operators of the simple form well known in mathematical learning theory:

$$\Delta p = \alpha(1 - p),$$

where α is an appropriate "learning constant" (possibly different for opinion learning and social-contact learning). Conversely, social disagreement is assumed to decrease the probability of future mutual interaction and of the respective expression of the "punished" opinions. Simple stochastic operators again mediate these changes.

The model is conceptually simple and straightforward, but there is an inexorable proliferation of parameters. With a group as small as 12 individuals there can be as many as 48 different learning parameters and at least that many additional parameters to specify the initial state of the system. With a system as extensive as this, simulation becomes necessary in order to trace its behavior, since mathematics alone can probably not carry the analysis much beyond the statement of a few theorems in limiting cases (*cf.* Abelson, 1963). However, even a simulation cannot be fruitful unless the many free parameters are in some way "tied down." Rainio (1966) attempted to do this in at least three distinct ways: by estimation from independent empirical sources, by observation of the initial state of the group being simulated, and by consideration of special cases in which individual differences were ignored. The relative emphasis on these three strategies differed in the two different simulation tests to which Rainio subjected his model.

In a modest preliminary test, the investigator used three sociograms secured at about six-week intervals on a single group of twelve young schoolgirls. He used the initial set of sociometric choices to establish initial contact probabilities, assuming that the probability of contacts would be markedly higher in the direction of friendship choices. The initial probabilities of expression of the critical opinion were all assumed to be 0.5. The choice of stochastic learning parameters was guided by the results of earlier laboratory studies (Rainio, 1962) in which the author had observed changes in opinion expression and social contact over short time intervals. He had noted the following general tendencies: the strengthening effect of social agreement on opinion is greater than the strengthening effect of social agreement on social-contact tendency; the weakening effect of social disagreement on opinion is quite small; and social disagreement weakens social-contact tendency about as much as social agreement strengthens it. These three relative tendencies together with a specification of the average absolute level of effect enabled a reasonable guess of the average learning parameters. Denoting reward parameters by α and punishment parameters by β, effects on opinion by A and on contact by C, Rainio obtained the four guessed parameters $\alpha_A = 0.2$, $\alpha_C = 0.1$, $\beta_A = 0$, $\beta_C = 0.1$. He also made an attempt to introduce individual differences in parameters by means of observed variations on a suggestibility test, though he was not inclined to place much confidence in this attempt. At any rate, all free parameters were finally assigned specific numerical values, and a simulation of sociometric changes in this particular group of twelve girls was attempted.

The computer program embodying the processes of the stochastic model was run ten times and the numerical results averaged. (Multiple runs were made necessary because of the probabilistic nature of the model.) The social-contact probabilities of the model were converted back into the dichotomous variable of presence or absence of friendship choice, and thence the choice pattern of each social pair was classified as either "mutual," "one-way," or "indifferent." Cross-classifying these three patterns for initial versus final choices, a single overall chi-square test of goodness-of-fit of the simulation was carried out on the 3×3 table, with the (average) simulation providing the "expected" frequencies and the empirical sociograms the "observed" frequencies. This test did not reject the model.

The data used were admittedly fragmentary and the statistical test insensitive. Thus the adequate fit cannot be regarded as corroboration of the model, merely an indication that it was not grossly out of contact with reality in one particular case.

In a second and more elaborate test, Rainio fixed the parameters in a different way. Initial contact probabilities were assumed all equal (a not unreasonable initial situation for a group of strangers), and the four learning parameters were set so as to display individual differences averaging to the four values previously assumed. Since all individuals were initially treated symmetrically in their social connections, it did not matter which particular individuals were assigned which parameter values. Only the form of the multivariate distribution of parameters was relevant, and the author borrowed a form estimated from earlier laboratory studies.

Thus having fixed the parameters, Rainio ran the simulation forward for a group of 29 simulated individuals through a total of 1200 social contacts. Sociograms were printed out following every 300 contacts, and these were compared with actual sociograms on school groups of comparable size. On superficial visual inspection, the simulated sociograms resembled actual ones, but closer examination showed a tendency to overrepresent strictly mutual choices at the expense of friendship cliques of sizes three and four.

Rainio attributed this deviation to the unrealism of the assumption of independent pairwise social contacts. The model was subsequently modified to introduce a bias toward social contacts with friends of one's friends, and simulations using the revised model resulted in somewhat better fits to actual sociograms. We shall not give the statistical details here, other than to note that the few tests performed did not exhaust the possible ways to search for potential errors in the model.

For the model to be taken in a literal sense, of course, it is necessary to assume that but one opinion issue influences and is influenced by social contact. Realistically it is much more likely in the typical case that several cross-cutting issues, interests, and values mediate sociometric structure in the classroom, as Rainio himself pointed out in discussing possible extensions of his model. Indeed, his very estimates of the smallness of the parameters for change of social contact (about 0.1) are consistent with the common intuition that friendship is a matter of multiple determination, not easily changed by agreement or disagreement on a single opinion. One might imagine an exception to be possible if a striking issue were to command the focus of attention of a social group for an extended period of time. Suppose, for example, that the issue in question were not a matter of abstract opinion but of whether to engage in some visible and controversial behavior.

James Coleman has studied this situation in high school classes, using smoking as one critical behavior. In a brief review of several of his unpublished simulation studies (Coleman, 1965) the author refers to a simulation similar in purview to Rainio's simulations. Potentially, social contact might influence smoking behavior and behavioral concordance might influence future social contact. From an analysis of his survey data over time, however, Coleman concluded that the effects of friendship on smoking behavior far exceed the effects of smoking behavior on friendship. Coleman went on to simulate the effects of friendship on smoking behavior, fixing the free parameters of his model (a simpler one than Rainio's) with estimates from his previous survey data. The simulation was projected forward in time well beyond the last point for which survey data were available. The idea was not to validate the model, but to demonstrate what consequences would eventually follow by assuming the model to hold. Coleman claims the simulation demonstrates that the impact of friendship networks on smoking increases the overall number of smokers above the level one would expect simply on the basis of increasing adoptions of the habit with age.

It is difficult to evaluate this claim on the basis of the scanty published description. This simulation is noteworthy chiefly because it illustrates again the strategy of "borrowing" available empirical information in order to estimate free parameters, and because it uses simulation for a novel purpose as a synthetic generator of future empirical consequences. More will be said about the predictive or projective use of simulation in the next section.

Still a different purpose of elementary quantitative simulations may be identified. A simulation can be used, not as a purported imitation of reality, but as a generator of simplified baseline outcomes against which to judge reality, somewhat in the fashion of null hypotheses in statistical analysis. One deliberately omits interesting psychological forces from the model, relying instead on contentless random processes, in order to reveal the degree to which various empirical situations require something more than simpleminded explanations. Examples of this "null simulation" approach may be found in Roby and Budrose (1965) and McWhinney (1964), both of whom were interested in stylized small-group problem-solving situations.

A potentially powerful computer-simulation approach would be to use both null and full-blown simulation models of the same phenomenon, or even more generally, a wide range of models ranging from the most trivial to the most rich. It is very difficult to gain perspective on a model such as Rainio's without knowing how well alternative models would fit the same data. One of the major constraints on the breadth of simulation studies has heretofore been the limited availability of fast computers, particularly for European investigators, but this bottleneck will rapidly be broken. Hopefully we may look forward to broader and more comprehensive computer-simulation studies in the future.

Models of large-scale social and political processes

The models hitherto discussed have used small social groups as their simulation targets. A number of other simulation efforts have focused on large social aggregates. The dependent variable in these models is usually some behavior that is aggregatively observable, as for example in vote tabulations. As with the small-group simulations, one of the major processes of concern is the effect of social communication on the adoption of the particular behavior.

Much work has been done on the diffusion of innovations via local social influence. Several sociologists have carefully gathered data on various examples of innovation diffusion, for example, of new farming practices. Psychologists seem neither to have been much aware of nor deeply interested in this extensive body of diffusion data, perhaps because it is field rather than laboratory data, perhaps because the diffusion process seems to depend largely on the psychologically "uninteresting" factor of propinquity. Nevertheless the diffusion area is a very fertile one for the construction of models which can be simultaneously precise and realistic.

Torsten Hägerstrand (1965a) has been influential in promoting the possibility of computer-simulation models of innovation diffusion. In a recent statement (Hägerstrand, 1965b) of some of his previously unpublished work, he gives the example of the spread during the years 1929–1932 of acceptance of a subsidy offered to farmers by the Swedish government. The geographic locations of the adopters of the offer were a matter of official record, enabling a precise quantitative treatment of the spread of adoption.

In the simulation model, the following substantive assumptions were made: (1) information is spread only by telling at pairwise meetings; (2) the item is adopted at once when heard of; (3) during a flexible unit of time denoted the "generation interval," every adopter tells exactly one other person, adopter or nonadopter; (4) the probability of contact between teller and receiver varies inversely with an empirically determined function of the distance between them. In running this general model for a particular rural region subdivided into 125 small (5 × 5 km) grid cells, account was taken of the differential population of farms in the different cells, and also of the natural barriers to social communication such as lakes and forests. Telephone communication was frequently used by these farmers, but geographical obstacles nevertheless "deadened" such communication, apparently because the social contacts necessary to motivate telephone calls did not form across such obstacles. The social-distance function needed in realizing assumption 4 was estimated from independent data on the frequency of migration over various distances.

The model was set in motion by taking the actual grid locations of the set of earliest adopters of the government subsidy and running the postulated processes forward in time. The simulated geographical distribution of adoption at later points in time was compared with the actual distribution of adoption. The simulation model, being probabilistic, of course generates somewhat different results every time it is run, and Hägerstrand was by limitation of computing facilities able to replicate the simulation only a few times. However, he conducted a number of sensitive examinations of the goodness-of-fit data and was able to suggest that results of repeated simulations resembled each other slightly more than any of them resembled the actuality. Nevertheless the empirical fit was strikingly good in view of the extreme simplicity of the model.

Hägerstrand comments that for the type of innovation considered in this example there was high incentive and little or no psychological resistance to adoption. Thus assumption 2, "the item is adopted at once when heard of," is not at all absurd in this case. A revised assumption would be necessary to model the spread of innovations calling forth greater resistance. Different degrees of resistance would give rise to different spatial patterns of diffusion (the lower the resistance, the more polycentric the pattern). This raises the interesting possibility that a good comparative psychological analysis of different types of innovations could be validated with diffusion data, aided by simulation techniques. Preliminary work on a variety of generalized diffusion models has appeared in the emerging field of quantitative geography (*cf.* Hägerstrand, 1966; Morrill, 1963, 1965; Pitts, 1962, 1963).

It has been recognized (Pitts, 1963) that peculiar statistical problems arise in the comparison of simulated spatial distributions with actual spatial distributions. The presence of a two-dimensional geographical grid superficially suggests the use of a chi-square comparison between observed and "expected" frequencies. However, frequencies in adjacent cells are strongly dependent on one another by the very nature of probabilistic diffusion. The development of a satisfactory statistical technique in this context is a tantalizing but probably quite difficult problem.

The case in which competing ideas are simultaneously diffused through a population, creating controversy, is an attractive one for study. The simple innovation models do not readily generalize to this case, however. Analysis of the psychology of controversy suggests that more is involved than repeated tellings with or without resistance. The phenomenon of sudden development of interest in the controversial issue (and thus a higher rate of tellings) takes on theoretical significance. The social network itself may change to accord with the loyalties developed by the controversy. These are but two of a number of emergent phenomena more applicable to controversy than to simple diffusion. Abelson and Bernstein (1963) have argued that a very elaborate model is necessary to give an adequate account of the spread of competing opinions in a local controversy. These investigators wrote a simulation program which includes a great variety of social-psychological factors, as well as a number of variables representing differential exposure to the mass communication media (also unlike the Häger-strand model, which omits consideration of the media).

The Abelson-Bernstein simulation model has occasioned serious stylistic objections. Boudon (1965), for example, feels that it is a poor strategy to "renounce parsimony," as indeed Abelson and Bernstein have done by considering so many effects at once. The relative merits of their strategy will be much easier to assess when the data from Abelson's large-scale survey studies of fluoridation and school segregation controversies have been completely processed. (Extensive computer runs intended to test the validity of the simulation model were in process at the time of writing of this chapter.)

Less complicated from the social-psychological viewpoint than emergent controversy over new issues is the ritualized phenomenon of the American political campaign. McPhee (1961, 1963) has devised what he calls a "campaign simulator," a computer program which simulates the effects of both social influence and mass communication on the vote intentions of a group of individuals. The program was intended for the analysis of trends in electorates either over a time span of decades covering many elections (McPhee and Ferguson, 1962; McPhee and Smith, 1962) or over a span of a few months within a single election (McPhee, 1963). The former application involves quite an abstract and speculative examination of broad national political trends. Therefore we focus here on the short-term version, which seems closer to the interests of social psychologists.

Survey data are gathered on several hundred individuals sampled from the electorate of interest. The initial situation is then carried forward in time, taking into account the strength of the appeals made by the opposing candidates in relation to existing party loyalties. "Strength of appeal" is conceptualized as a probability distribution of the intensities of campaign stimuli favorable to the particular candidate. Different candidates are characterized by different average intensities within different subgroups of the electorate (for example, Kennedy with a very strong average appeal to Catholics). Individuals with weak loyalties to a party require strong appeals to maintain their voting preference, whereas those with strong loyalties require only weak appeals. Appeals stronger than necessary, however, serve to increase the individual's interest level, which in turn increases his participation in social discussions of the campaign (see below). Party loyalties in the model are also subject to probability distributions within different subgroups, and the process of exposure of the electorate to the mass media consists of a succession of random events, one for each simulated individual. The average outcomes are constrained by the initial choices of parameters, but individual events can vary considerably.

The most interesting of McPhee's theoretical assumptions concerns the effects of social influence. Following the mass media stimulation process (see Fig. 1a), each simulated individual is brought into contact with another sociometrically relevant individual for a potential discussion. If the interest levels of the potential discussants are sufficiently high, a "discussion" is held, consisting simply of a mutual disclosure of voting preferences. If the two individuals agree, their preferences are strengthened by being converted into firm voting decisions. If they disagree, however, their preferences are not necessarily weakened. Instead, social disagreement triggers a reapplication of the mass media stimulation process. Each individual is forced to resample the campaign stimuli, as it were, and thereby derive another impression of the candidates which may or may not coincide with his original one. The assumption that social disagreement exerts an *indirect* influence on opinion offers a constructive alternative to models which somewhat reluctantly assume a direct influence. In Rainio's model, for example, a direct weakening effect is postulated, although the parameter governing this effect is later given the value zero.

Unfortunately it is not possible to tell from McPhee's (1963) empirical test of his model what contribution for better or worse is made by this particular assumption. The test, carried out during the 1960 Wisconsin primary contest involving Kennedy, Humphrey, and Nixon yielded generally reasonable precinct-by-precinct results as well as the apt global prediction that cross-registration defections from Nixon would leave the relative standing of Kennedy and Humphrey unaffected. McPhee, a political sociologist, was satisfied with his model as broadly consistent with a range of campaign effects and did not pursue the strategy consistently urged in the present chapter for theoretical social-psychological purposes: namely, that several different models be run on the same data to assess their relative validity.

Another campaign simulation was also carried out in 1960: a simulation of the behavior of the national electorate in the final Presidential race (Pool and Abelson, 1961; Pool, Abelson, and Popkin, 1964). This project employed a rather different simulation strategy from the types heretofore discussed. At the national level, it is not feasible to represent directly in a simulation the process of social discussion between individuals. Too great a heterogeneity of types of individuals exists, and the unit of analysis shifts from the individual voter to the voting bloc or type. One may then assume certain summary impacts of particular campaign issues on particular blocs and carry out a predictive analysis by aggregating these effects over all voter types. This type of analysis has been referred to as "prognostic simulation" (Abelson, 1962) to distinguish it from the more usual "process simulation." A prognostic simulation, even though it be conceptually very simple by virtue of eliminating all the details of complicated stochastic processes, may nevertheless require the use of a computer because the quantity of data involved is so enormous as to be otherwise indigestible.

This was indeed the case with the Pool, Abelson, and Popkin simulation. The opinions of some 100,000 survey respondents served as the basis for the characterization of the political orientations of 480 voter types arising from cross classifications of occupation, race, religion, sex, region, and party. The relative prevalence of these various types was laboriously estimated from a combination of census and survey data. The sensitivity of individual voter types to appeals based on "issues" such as Kennedy's Catholicism was estimated via careful interpretations of the survey data. Prognoses of total gain and loss for each candidate were generated by assuming simplified campaigns consisting of only one or two issues.

The method rather successfully prognosticated state-by-state election returns by assuming that Kennedy's Catholicism was the dominant theme of the campaign. Simulation runs omitting or minimizing this factor were markedly less successful. Reasonably precise quantitative estimates of the effects of the "Catholic issue" in fact became available through a series of goodness-of-fit tests. These estimates were extremely valuable because they brought precision into an area which had been rife with rather loose speculation.

The Pool-Abelson-Popkin method cannot be applied mechanically to any given election, however. In a simulation of the 1964 Presidential election, considerable tinkering with assumptions about the joint impacts of several issues was necessary before a moderately successful prognosis was achieved (Pool, Abelson, and Popkin, 1965). The two successes were due largely to Professor Pool's good judgment in the choice of appropriate assumptions rather than to any magic inherent in the use of computer simulation. This simple point has been obscured in popular treatments of this use of computers in politics, even by sympathetic writers (*cf.* Morgan, 1961). Rosenthal (1965) has reviewed the details of these election simulations and suggested a number of new applications, for example, to foreign electorates. It is probable that this line of simulation work will continue and expand.

There have been other large-scale simulation enterprises oriented toward practical affairs. For example, Orcutt *et al.* (1961), interested fundamentally in the economic behavior of families, found it useful to simulate a population of individuals undergoing stochastic changes in family life cycle: births, marriages, divorces, and deaths were projected ahead in time, using baseline figures available from census tabulations. Various other computer-aided analyses and syntheses of census figures are discussed in a monograph edited by Beshers (1965). An interesting anthropological use of demographic variables in a computer simulation was recently described by Gilbert and Hammel (1966). They established hypothetical constellations of families living in small villages with prohibitions against various types of cousin marriages. By simulating many generations of mate selection and production of new offspring, the investigators were able to assess the implications of various marriage rules for population survival. A version of the simulation in which mate selection could cross village boundaries permitted deductions about the dependence of migration rates on marriage rules.

We shall not pursue these sorts of examples further, since their theoretical implications are apparently remote from social psychology. It is conceivable, however, that many computer-simulation approaches to large-scale phenomena in economics, sociology, anthropology, demography, urban planning, etc., will eventually require the inclusion of social-psychological insights, if any such are available. Computer simulation, in other words, may offer methodological scope to social psychologists interested in interdisciplinary research or in public affairs. It is too early to tell what particular shape such developments may take, although a general trend toward discipline bridging is clearly one of the consequences strongly implicit in the development of computer-simulation techniques.

PROBLEMS AND PROSPECTS

The validation problem

Evidently the set of appropriate validation procedures is not the same for social-group simulations as for individual simulations. In a previous section, four validation methods were considered: response matching; sequential dependency tests; Turing Tests (these three methods all based on individual protocols, real and simulated); and experimental tests of simulation predictions. The last-named method is certainly applicable to groups, limited only by the degree to which worthwhile predictions are available and feasible to test.

However, the methods based on response protocols are questionable at best in their potential application to social groups. *Response matching* is dubious because detailed sequences of occurrences in groups are usually "underdetermined"; that is, even though general outcomes might be orderly, event-by-event predictions are extremely chancy. Gullahorn and Gullahorn (1964) pointedly avoided the problems involved in tracing the sequential specifics of "situation trees," and others with brave intentions in this direction (for example, Hare, 1961) have apparently never followed them up. *Sequential dependency tests* are conceivable, although the problems of organizing the data become much more formidable than in the individual case. Generalizing from our previous discussion in which the two hypothetical responses "zig" and "zag" were to be tabulated (contingent upon prior response), we now note that for a group of N members, as many as $2N$ different responses must be distinguished. Thus with three group members, $A, B,$ and $C,$ the six events are "A zigs," "A zags," "B zigs," etc. A cross tabulation of sequential event dependencies thence requires a 6×6 contingency table, necessitating a large data base for stability of individual entries. With a group as "large" as 12 individuals (as in one of Rainio's studies), this method gets completely out of hand. Finally, *Turing Tests,* though possible, are awkward. Judges would be required to distinguish between the outputs of two groups: in the Simple Test, one group would be real and the other simulated; in the Extended Test, both groups would be real, differing along an "anchor dimension," but a simulated group would be substituted on critical trials for one of the real groups. To the writer's knowledge, neither procedure has yet been attempted. The judgment task is seemingly more obscure than in the individual case. At the very outset of the Simple Test, there would be the difficulty of making credible to a judge the notion of a machine producing outputs representing a whole group of individuals. Presupposing this feat, there would remain the usual problems associated with the Simple Test. As for the Extended Test, the specification of anchor dimensions and the elaboration of precise research designs would be extremely taxing for the investigator.

In compensation for the partial or complete vitiation of these three validation methods in simulation of social groups, there arises a whole new class of methods characterized by the analysis of *distributions of properties over individual units.* Each simulated individual or unit carries one or more variable properties through time, and at any time point a cross-sectional distribution of any summary property of the simulated group may be compared with an appropriate empirical counterpart.

Some imagination may be required in the specification of summary properties, as well as in the definition of units over which to summarize. The summary properties need not be identical to the dependent variables carried automatically throughout the simulation; instead, they may be computed specially for comparison purposes. For example, one might keep track of the number of social interactions of various kinds engaged in by each individual, or of the average change in some dependent variable per interaction, etc. As for the summary units, they need not be individuals. For Rainio (1966), some statistical summaries were, as we have noted, by social pairs. For Hägerstrand (1965b), summarization was by small geographical cells, for McPhee (1963) by voting precincts, and for Pool, Abelson, and Popkin (1964) by states. Several other possibilities exist. At any rate there are usually many ways to generate apt statistical distributions from social simulations if the number of individuals involved is sufficiently large. In the next section we present a modest preliminary attempt to characterize some of the unique problems associated with the statistical analysis of social simulations.

Statistical analysis of social simulations

Statistical techniques are presently underdeveloped and underapplied in simulations of social behavior. In part this has been due to preoccupation with the primary task of getting the simulations running, in part because slow computational facilities have in some cases made the cost of repeated simulations prohibitive. However, there has also been general innocence of the necessity for careful statistical treatment of simulation results and/or ignorance of what specific techniques might be applicable. We outline in this section a few useful conceptual distinctions and formulas apparently novel to one area of social simulation. Psychologists interested in simulation should also pay heed to the existence of prior statistical work in the context of applied simulations (*cf.* Tocher, 1963), though the emphasis there is quite different from the one we will develop.

A common design paradigm for social simulations could be named *panel simulation,* representing an extension of the "panel design" made familiar by survey research analysts. A group of individuals, the "panel," is surveyed and later resurveyed. The initial settings for the simulation model are constructed from responses on the initial survey, the simulation is run forward in time toward some terminal state, and the outcomes are checked against responses on the final survey. This paradigm, taken in a broad sense, covers a wide range of possibilities. By "survey" we do not necessarily mean a set of interviews, but any orderly field technique for eliciting quantifiable data from a group of individuals. Thus included are Rainio's (1966) sociometric measures and Hägerstrand's (1965b) government records, as well as the sample surveys employed in the field test of Abelson and Bernstein's (1963) model. In all these cases, measures and remeasures are taken on the same individuals. These individuals may or may not form a compact social entity, and the term "panel" should not be understood to imply that the relevant individuals are assembled together in one place for purposes of the survey measures.

Figure 3 illustrates the conceptual scheme for a panel simulation. First of all, we assume that the panel of individuals represents a sample from a popula-

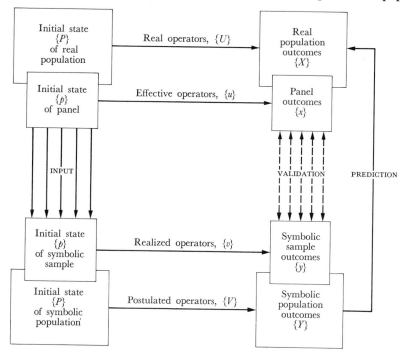

Fig. 3. The general scheme for panel simulation.

tion of individuals to whom the simulation is meant to be relevant. Even if it is operationally the case that the panel is selected in a body (a school class, a geographical district, etc.) rather than randomly sampled, it is usually still appropriate to conceptualize a (possibly infinite) population of (possibly hypothetical) individuals who might have been selected instead. The panel serves to construct a symbolic sample which will be run through the simulation, and this symbolic sample stands in the same relation to a hypothetical symbolic population as the panel stands to the real-world population. More specifically, we may view the situation as follows.

A simulation model ordinarily recognizes several (perhaps very many) different categories or classes of individuals who are to be treated differently in being carried forward in the simulation. These classes are recognized on the basis of single initial-state variables (for example, social-learning parameters, socioeconomic variables, media-exposure habits) or combinations of initial-state variables. The entire real population may be characterized according to the true proportions P_i of individuals occupying each respective class i. Because any given sample will not perfectly reflect these true proportions, we must consider a set of random variables, p_i, representing the obtained proportions of individuals in the respective classes. (We explicitly restrict ourselves here to the case in which every individual in the panel is assigned a single symbolic counterpart.) Now the simulation model may or may not recognize the appropriate classes, and the survey data may or may not reliably sort individuals into the intended classes, but we proceed with the analysis in terms of the classes of the model (rather than idealized true classes) precisely because we wish to discover and cure such deficiencies as may exist in the simulation model.

The assumptions of the model will imply particular qualitative and quantitative outcome dispositions for the individuals in each class, depending on the initial configuration of symbolic individuals and sometimes also on an ensemble of exogenous events or stimuli (for example, mass media exposures). For convenience let us focus the analysis on a single quantitative group outcome variable, denoted y for the symbolic sample and x for the panel of real individuals. The degree of correspondence between y and x is crucial for the simulation effort, for if the correspondence is poor then the model cannot be said to be a valid description. (We will not here consider the bothersome possibility of poor apparent correspondence attributable to unreliable measurement of x in the panel.)

Because social-simulation models generally include probabilistic or "Monte Carlo" features, we must be prepared to deal with statistical variations in y and x above and beyond such variations as can be attributed to sampling fluctuations in the p_i. Figure 3 sets forth a terminology for discussing such variations. The postulates of the model operate to produce a certain distribution of outcomes for members of each class. If one ran an infinite population of symbolic individuals, these postulated distributions would in fact be realized exactly. But since only a limited sample of individuals is available, then in any single computer run only a fragmentary selection from the distribution is realized. We denote the true mean simulation outcome for individuals in class i as V_i, and the corresponding obtained mean simulation outcome v_i. The true mean outcome for the entire symbolic population we denote by Y, as distinct from the obtained mean outcome y. By definition,

$$Y = \sum_i P_i V_i , \tag{1}$$

$$y = \sum_i p_i v_i . \tag{2}$$

In view of the strategy of including probabilistic effects in the simulation model, it seems reasonable to assume that the real world being imitated is also intrinsically probabilistic. Indeed, processes such as exposure to items in the mass media, interaction with particular conversational partners at particular times, etc., can hardly be imagined as free from chance factors. We speak, then, of the effective mean outcome u_i for panel members of each class as a random variable with hypothetical value U_i. The hypothetical aggregate mean value for the real population we denote by X, as distinct from the obtained panel mean x. Again by definition,

$$X = \sum_i P_i U_i , \tag{3}$$

$$x = \sum_i p_i u_i . \tag{4}$$

Neither the hypothetical mean X for the real population nor the mean Y for the symbolic population is subject to statistical variation. Thus the only sense in which they may fail to correspond is in terms of the fixed difference D between them. If one were seriously interested in prediction of a real population outcome from simulation of a sample (as, for example, in voting simulations), the ideal case would be one in which Y could be estimated with little or no error and thence applied as the predictor of X with little or no constant error D. In the more typical cases of social simulations, however, one is not interested in literal prediction, but rather in validation of the model for theoretical purposes. Validation comparisons would ordinarily be made between the panel mean x and the simulation sample mean y, rather than between population quantities. But the comparison $(x - y)$ involves two sources of "error": the constant error of prediction plus the variable error statistically present in x and y. We wish to derive some simple statistical properties of x, y, and $x - y$ in terms of the sampling deviations of the observed p_i from the true P_i, and the fluctuations of the obtained sets of means u_i and v_i around their true sets of values U_i and V_i. A few clarifying remarks are in order first.

For purposes of our analysis, the classes i recognized by the simulation model need not necessarily be amenable to explicit listing by the investigator. Some distinctions between individuals might conceivably be implied by the assumptions of the model in such a hidden way that the investigator could be unaware of them. But let us suppose that all classes are explicitly recognized. The question may be asked, why are the mean effects V_i not known in advance, since the assumptions of the simulation model are necessarily perfectly explicit? Why is it necessary to invoke the random variables v_i? The answer lies in the typical complexity of simulation models. Indeed, if it were possible to derive the V_i explicitly from the model, then mathematical modeling would be the appropriate technique rather than simulation. For certain simple cases or for certain classes of individuals it might sometimes be possible to derive some of the V_i mathematically, but in general we shall assume that the simulation must be run in order to know what the model implies—that is, that it is not possible to dispense with the random variables v_i.

Imagine repeated simulation runs for an arbitrary individual in class i. There will be some probability distribution of outcomes for this single individual, but the question immediately arises whether this distribution is dependent on sampling variations in the p_i. Many processes in social simulations involve, as we have seen, influences of one individual on another. Generally speaking, these "social couplings" such as friendship or conversational pairings cause increased homogeneity of outcomes between social partners. If, through sampling error, too many members of a particular class are initially present, the outcomes for other individuals socially coupled with them will tend over time to move toward the outcome appropriate to this overrepresented class. Social coupling, then, causes outcome distributions to be dependent on initial sampling variations. By contrast we may conceive of models without such dependency. An *uncoupled model* is one for which the outcome distribution over repeated simulation runs for any given individual is independent of the other individuals present in the simulation. This kind of model is rare. [All the models covered in detail in this section except the Pool, Abelson, and Popkin (1964) election simulation are *coupled models.*] Nevertheless, for simplicity we proceed here only with the analysis of the uncoupled case. Coupling introduces analytic complications which, while not insuperable, are clearly beyond the scope of this chapter. Furthermore, if the implications of the uncoupled case are clearly understood, the coupled case will be easier to attack later.

The mean of the outcome distribution for an individual in class i we have already denoted as V_i, and now we denote the standard deviation of this distribution as σ_i. Before exploring the correspondence between symbolic and panel outcomes, we first consider the properties of symbolic outcomes from a very simple simulation "design": N individuals are each run through the simulation K times. The resulting outcomes can be analyzed by an ordinary analysis of variance into a between-individuals mean square $(MS)_b$ with $N-1$ degrees of freedom and a within-individual mean square $(MS)_w$ with $N(K-1)$ degrees of freedom. (In the uncoupled case, no additional information is gained by separating out a "replications" mean square with $K-1$ df.) For the purpose of seeing what statistical information these mean squares provide, we define two theoretical quantities, the *realization variance* R_y and the *sampling variance* S_y:

$$R_y = \sum_i P_i \sigma_i^2, \tag{5}$$

$$S_y = \sum_i P_i (V_i - Y)^2. \tag{6}$$

The subscript y indicates that we are dealing with symbolic outcomes. Corresponding quantities for panel outcomes are defined below. The first quantity above is a weighted average variance of individual outcomes around their true means. The second quantity represents the variance of true class means around the true overall symbolic mean. The following formulas for the expected values of the mean squares are readily derived:

$$E[(MS)_b] = R_y + KS_y , \tag{7}$$

$$E[(MS)_w] = R_y . \tag{8}$$

From this it follows that the two fundamental quantities R_y and S_y can be estimated separately from the two obtained mean squares (by replacing the expected values above by the obtained values and solving for R and S). The theoretical importance of these quantities becomes apparent when we consider the operation of averaging the mean outcomes (y) of several simulation runs to obtain a more stable estimate $\bar{y}$ of the true mean Y. It can be shown that the expected value of $\bar{y}$ is

$$E(\bar{y}) = Y , \tag{9}$$

with variance

$$\text{Var} (\bar{y}) = [(R_y/K) + S_y]/N. \tag{10}$$

Increases in the sample size N will proportionately decrease the variance of the average outcome $\bar{y}$, as one expects. But increases in the number of replications cut down only on the realization variance R_y, leaving the sampling contribution S_y unaffected. In any case, with knowledge of the sizes of R_y and S_y, one can specify what size sample and how many replications are necessary to achieve any desired stability of $\bar{y}$.

Analogous definitions and formulas can be applied to the distributions of panel outcomes. Here U_i is the true mean outcome for real individuals which the simulation model would assign to class i. Defining δ_i^2 as the variance of panel outcomes for class i members, we have the analog definitions for realization variance and sample variance:

$$R_x = \sum_i P_i \delta_i^2 , \tag{11}$$

$$S_x = \sum_i P_i (U_i - X)^2 . \tag{12}$$

Now we discover, however, that the analog breaks down because *the panel cannot be repeatedly "run" the way a simulation can.* History cannot be exactly reset. Barring a special interpretation of a panel replication (discussed below), all we can do is assess the single outcome value for each individual in the panel. Denoting such individual values by x_j and the obtained mean by x, the between-individuals mean square is $(MS)_B = \Sigma_j (x_j - x)^2/(N - 1)$. Assuming the analog of an uncoupled model, namely an "uncoupled panel," we can show the expected value of $(MS)_B$ to be

$$E[(MS)_B] = R_x + S_x. \tag{13}$$

There exists no guaranteed statistical procedure for separate estimation of these two sources of variation. As we shall see, this is a bothersome difficulty.

Returning finally to a consideration of the correspondence between X and Y, we define the "noncorrespondence error" Q by

$$Q = \sum_i P_i(U_i - V_i)^2. \tag{14}$$

When one thinks of "validating" a theoretical social simulation, one should usually not aim to prove the model correct so much as to find out where and by how much it is deficient, in order to improve it. From this point of view the variable error Q is much more fundamental than the constant error $D = X - Y$. Sizable contributions to Q occur via big differences between the U_i and V_i, which can occur because the model recognizes the wrong classes or because the assumed processes within some or all classes carry the outcomes far from the real values. By contrast, the constant error D is much less sensitive to the details of the model. *If one uses constant error as a sole criterion, a simulation model can sometimes appear correct when in fact it is badly in error.* This point can be made more specific as follows.

In the panel simulation design, suppose that each of N individuals is simulated K times, and the average outcome compared with the obtained outcome for the counterpart individual in the panel. In this manner a set of N differences $d_j = x_j - \bar{y}_j$ is generated. Denote the mean of these differences by $\bar{d}$. Since $E(\bar{d}) = D = X - Y$, the natural test of the null hypothesis of zero constant error is a t test of $\bar{d}$ against a predicted value of zero, or, what is equivalent, an F test with 1 and $N - 1$ df, using $N\bar{d}^2$ as the numerator mean square and the between-individuals quantity $\Sigma_j(d_j - \bar{d})^2/(N - 1)$ as the denominator mean square. It can readily be shown that these quantities have the following expected values:

$$E[(MS)_{num}] = (R_y/K) + R_x + Q + ND^2, \tag{15}$$

$$E[(MS)_{den}] = (R_y/K) + R_x + Q. \tag{16}$$

From the appearance of Q in both expressions it follows that, with fixed D^2, the F test becomes less and less sensitive with increasing Q. In other words, the worse the model (in the sense of variable error), the more likely it is to accept the null hypothesis of perfect fit (in the sense of constant error). For this paradox to hold, of course, it is necessary that the model builder have the "luck" of designing the model so that errors in compensating directions allow D to remain small while Q is large.

Instead of being satisfied with a significance test of D, one should ideally like to estimate the size of Q with a formula such as (16). The first term, R_y, can be estimated from (8), but as we have noted, R_x cannot ordinarily be estimated separately from S_x. A variety of approximating devices might be tried to surmount this difficulty, for example, separating the panel into approximately matched halves which are then treated as replications. The most favorable case is undoubtedly that in which the entire panel can be run again at a later time under circumstances which approximate the original empirical situation. Then an analysis of between-individuals variance versus within-individual variance analogous to formulas (7) and (8) would be possible, and would yield an estimate of R_x. This case arises when the behavior being simulated is habitual, steady-state behavior such as repeated consumer purchasing, rather than a one-shot response to a novel or infrequent condition such as a Presidential election or an innovation diffusion. The philosophical dilemma here is suggestive of the problem that would be involved in assessing the reliability of a test with a single item. [It may be noted in passing that formulas (7) and (8) are intimately related to reliability analysis, with simulation replications taking the role of parallel "items."]

However this dilemma is to be approached, it would probably not literally invoke the formulas we have presented, since most social simulations involve the additional complication of coupling. We will not pursue the matter further in the present treatment, other than to note that coupling would give each sample a "life of its own," and multiple samples for simulation and panel testing would become statistically necessary. If reasons of economy preclude the use of many independent samples, applying the techniques introduced under the name "jackknifing" by Mosteller and Tukey (Chapter 10, in Vol. 2 of this *Handbook*) to the *running* of the simulation might prove useful. In spite of the difficulty of the problem, it is to be hoped that an appropriate statistical technology will soon evolve for the analysis of coupled cases of the panel simulation design, and that further attention will be given to the problem of estimating the noncorrespondence error, Q.

Being right for the wrong reasons

The preceding section makes salient a persistent problem in the philosophy of simulation. If a simulation could be "right for the wrong reasons," that is, fit the data by virtue of compensating errors, then in what sense can a good fit be regarded as support for the theory underlying the simulation model? Can one ever "prove" a simulation theory by displaying good imitations of particular outcomes?

This philosophical problem has sometimes been raised in the context of cognitive simulation, but apart from haggling over the bases for distinction between "machines" and "minds" (*cf.* Lucas, 1963), the issue is not a sharp one in the cognitive context. Most cognitive simulations are so rich in qualitative detail that it is very easy for them to fail, particularly when the most frail validating technique, response matching, is used. Because it is so hard to obtain good data fits, anything which comes close is impressive, and any cognitive model yielding an apparently perfect fit to a wide range of data would indeed deserve serious theoretical recognition.

With social simulations, however, the issue is probably more cogent. If the outcome variables of the model are few while the number of parameters to be juggled is great, there can always be the lingering suspicion that a good fit was too easy to achieve and thus not strongly supportive of the model. One remedy is to show, if possible, that the fit was not so easy by changing the model in various ways and demonstrating consistent lack of fit. Another remedy is to design the simulation so as to generate as large a number of outcome variables as possible. That the analysis of the preceding section was confined to a single outcome variable is not meant to imply that such a limitation is desirable. The more outcomes that can be validated, the merrier—and the more convincing the underlying theory. In this light, the philosophical context surrounding simulation is not fundamentally different from that of any other type of scientific theorizing. No theory can ever be "proved," only rendered more plausible by virtue of accounting well for more phenomena.

Future prospects

It is difficult to conjecture which of many possible directions of activity in the computer simulation of social behavior will prove to have the greatest vitality. Thus far the various examples are utterly diverse, and no single style of approach has dominated the scene. It is possible that a particularly dramatic new example will gain favor and set the fashion for a large number of other efforts. Such an example would very likely center on some new methodological development, much as Newell, Shaw, and Simon's pioneering work in the cognitive area was organized around the invention of the list-processing techniques of IPL. Present list-processing languages have played only a minor role in the social area (the variety of types of languages used in this area being great), but an imaginative way of describing the qualitative features of social interaction could conceivably give rise to a powerful new genre of list-like programming techniques. In order for any new technique to have impact, of course, it would be necessary for a good deal of care and effort to be devoted to documentation, communication, and training.

It is also quite possible that the mixture of styles of work in the social area will continue as at present, without any concentration of new emphasis. One factor which makes continuing diversity likely is the temperamental polarity between those who like to see simulation models patterned on the familiar parsimonious style of mathematical models and those who view simulation as a radically new tool which for the first time permits models to be as complex as the presumed complexities of the real world. The present writer leans somewhat toward the latter, "orchestrational" view of simulation, without gainsaying the possibility that very simple models can be quite elegantly pleasing when they work. The relative success or failure of the Abelson and Bernstein (1963) model may influence the degree of optimism accorded the construction of very complicated models. In that article it was wryly suggested that the phrase "Occam's Razor" as a metaphoric expression of the tool of parsimony might require modernization as "Occam's Lawnmower." In any case, the meaning and relevance for social simulation of the traditional scientific concept of parsimony will continue to be debated.

As part of a continuing diversity of interests in the area, it is to be anticipated that simulation methods will be extended to the investigation of a greater variety of social phenomena. We have already mentioned the possibility that simulation techniques (of the unparsimonious variety) will more and more come to be applied to broad social issues. Meanwhile, the growth of experimental social psychology in the last decade has brought forth a large number of social paradigms in the laboratory, some of them eminently suitable for simulation efforts.

Without intending to overstress it, we may suggest one particular example as typical of the kind of laboratory study apt to prove congenial to the computer simulator. Kelley *et al.* (1965) have designed a laboratory situation intended to capture the formal social characteristics of a panic episode. A group of individuals is instructed to "escape from danger" within a given time limit by each exercising an exit prerogative without mutual interference. Individual escape is effected by commandeering a master channel uninterruptedly by button for a number of seconds, but simultaneous attempts cancel the success of any. The individuals in the group are not allowed to talk with each other, although they receive information about the state of use of the master channel and the responses of individual members. This situation has been run under several conditions, varying the number of individuals in the group, the escape time and total time, the rewards and punishments for success and failure, etc. Group performance was recorded over trials in terms of the time at which the last individual in the group completed his escape.

The reason this type of laboratory social task is ideal for computer simulation is that group performance would appear to be compounded in a straightforward way from the simple behaviors of individuals. In the Kelley *et al.* situation, individual behavior might be characterized (as a function of the independent variables) by the rate of attempts to commandeer the escape channel and the probability of release of the channel under various conditions of prior occupancy or subsequent interference. Of course, different individuals might easily have very different characteristics, so that distributions of parameters would also have to be contemplated. The resulting model would very probably be much too difficult to analyze by standard mathematical methods, but would hopefully, after careful development, be tractable as a computer simulation. Laboratory data with many available independent variables and a precisely quantified dependent time variable would be easy to accumulate. If the simulation model did not fit, nevertheless the types of deviations of the data from the model would provide very useful information about the nature of individual performances in this situation. Finally, it is readily conceivable that for a task of this kind a portfolio of simulation models of varying complexity could be assembled, in the expectation that one or another would be the most appropriate under varying settings of the study (different task instructions, different subject populations, qualitative variations of punishment, etc.).

We must emphasize that this example is merely prototypic. There may be those who would judge the group panic situation uninteresting, artificial, or whatnot. The point is that there are many laboratory social situations which under appropriate scrutiny will prove ripe for simulation efforts.

The focus of future social simulations can be expected to settle not only on selected laboratory situations, but also on selected broad theoretical variables general to many contexts. Of all the variables that might be singled out for attention the two that have been most pivotal for computer simulation (indeed, if not for social psychology itself) are social interaction and opinion or attitude. The mutual effects of these variables on each other, as we have seen, have formed the basis for a number of existing simulations. It is obvious that future social simulations will depend heavily on the dynamic coupling between interaction and opinion, and it is to be hoped that the theoretical disparities between different conceptions of this coupling will be further illuminated. It is doubtful that a single dynamic law relates these two variables in all situations; rather, it would seem that the nature of this relationship is to some extent contingent upon the social context in which interactions occur and opinions are expressed. Simulation promises to play an important part in further theoretical ramification of this relationship by virtue of its synthesizing capability: the gross social group consequences of a network of individual behaviors can be projected forward in time, and the predictive and explanatory power of individual assumptions thus subjected to very sensitive test.

In spite of its robust future prospects, a skeptical attitude toward computer simulation may readily be advanced and defended. Some critics feel that the technique is too fraught with effortful confusion or at any rate lies outside the mainstream of appropriate methodology; others are more open-minded, but find that the present state of the art does not seem to justify the supercolossal advance press notices which computer technology has enjoyed. Certainly much of the existing work in social (and even cognitive) simulation is highly tentative and flawed. We have tried in this chapter to be frank about the frustrations and difficulties inherent in the technique, not to supply aid and comfort to the critics, but to adjust expectations to realities. The potentialities of the technique are indeed exciting, but it will take much more time to realize them than had been anticipated. Miracles are not to be expected; progress is.

REFERENCES

Abelson, R. P. (1962). The use of surveys in simulations. *Publ. Opin. Quart., 26,* 485–486.

——— (1963). Computer simulation of 'hot' cognition. In S. Tomkins and S. Messick (Eds.), *Computer simulation of personality.* New York: Wiley.

——— (1964). Mathematical models of the distribution of attitudes under controversy. In N. Frederiksen and H. Gulliksen (Eds.), *Contributions to mathematical psychology.* New York: Holt, Rinehart, and Winston.

—— (1967). Mathematical models in social psychology. In L. Berkowitz (Ed.), *Advances in experimental social psychology*. Vol. 3. New York: Academic Press.

Abelson, R. P., and A. Bernstein (1963). A computer simulation model of community referendum controversies. *Publ. Opin. Quart., 27, 93–122.*

Abelson, R. P., and J. D. Carroll (1965). Computer simulation of individual belief systems. *Amer. behav. Scientist, 8, 24–30.*

Abt, C. (1964). War gaming. *Int. Sci. Technol., 32, 29–37.*

Amosov, N. M., E. T. Golovan, S. Y. Zaslavsky, and V. S. Starinets (1965). O vozmozhnom podkhodye k modyelirovaniyu psikhicheskoy sfyeri chelovyeka [A possible approach to the simulation of psychic functions]. *Voprosi Psikhologii, 2, 49–56.*

Arden, B. W. (1963). *An introduction to digital computing.* Reading, Mass.: Addison-Wesley.

Armer, P. (1963). Attitudes toward intelligent machines. In E. A. Feigenbaum and J. Feldman (Eds.), *Computers and thought.* New York: McGraw-Hill.

Balderston, F. E., and A. C. Hoggatt (1962). *Simulation of market processes.* Berkeley: Univ. of California, Institute of Business and Economic Research.

Barber, J. D. (1966). *Power in committees: an experiment in the governmental process.* Chicago: Rand McNally.

Barzun, J. (1965). Man and the machine. In G. W. Peirson (Ed.), *Computers for the humanities?* Conference Report. New Haven: Yale University.

Baylor, G. W., and H. A. Simon (1966). A chess mating combinations program. *Amer. Fed. Information Processing Societies Conf. Proc., 28, 431–448.*

Benson, O. (1962). Simulation of international relations and diplomacy. In H. Borko (Ed.), *Computer applications in the behavioral sciences.* Englewood Cliffs, N.J.: Prentice-Hall.

Bernstein, A. (1962). Simulation and operations research. *Publ. Opin. Quart., 26, 482–483.*

Beshers, J. M., Ed. (1965). *Computer methods in the analysis of large-scale social systems.* Cambridge, Mass: Joint Center for Urban Studies.

Bitzer, D. L. (1965). PLATO: an electronic teaching device. In N. Fattu and S. Elam (Eds.), *Simulation models for education.* Bloomington, Ind.: Phi Delta Kappa, Inc.

Bobrow, D. G. (1964). A question-answering system for high school algebra word problems. *Amer. Fed. Information Processing Societies Conf. Proc., 26, 591–614.*

Bobrow, D. G., and B. Raphael (1964). A comparison of list processing computer languages. *Comm. Assoc. Computing Machinery, 7, 231–240.*

Bonini, C. P. (1963). *Simulation of information and decision systems in the firm.* Englewood Cliffs, N.J.: Prentice-Hall.

Borko, H., Ed. (1962). *Computer applications in the behavioral sciences.* Englewood Cliffs, N.J.: Prentice-Hall.

Boudon, R. (1965). Réflexions sur la logique des modèles simulés. *Europ. J. Sociol., 6, 3–20.*

Boyd, D. F., and H. S. Krasnow (1963). Economic evaluation of management information systems. *IBM Systems J., 2, 2–23.*

Broadbent, D. E. (1965). Information processing in the nervous system. *Science, 150,* 457–462.

Brody, R. A. (1963). Some systemic effects of the spread of nuclear weapons technology: a study through simulation of a multi-nuclear future. *J. Confl. Resol., 7,* 663–753.

Bunge, M. (1957). Do computers think? (II). *Brit. J. Philos. Sci., 7,* 212–219.

Chapanis, A. (1961). Men, machines, and models. *Amer. Psychologist, 16,* 113–131.

Chapman, R. L., J. L. Kennedy, A. Newell, and W. C. Biel (1959). The systems research laboratory's air defense experiments. *Management Sci., 5,* 250–269.

Christie, R., and F. L. Geis (1968). Machiavellian game playing. In R. Christie and F. L. Geis (Eds.), *Studies in Machiavellianism.* New York: Academic Press.

Clarkson, G. P. (1962). *Portfolio selection: a simulation of trust investment.* Englewood Cliffs, N.J.: Prentice-Hall.

Clarkson, G. P., and H. A. Simon (1960). Simulation of individual and group behavior. *Amer. econ. Rev., 50,* 920–932.

Clarkson, G. P., and F. Tuggle (1966). Toward a theory of group-decision behavior. *Behav. Sci., 11,* 33–42.

Coe, R. M. (1964). Conflict, interference and aggression: computer simulation of a social process. *Behav. Sci., 9,* 186–197.

Cohen, B. C. (1962). Political gaming in the classroom. *J. Politics, 24,* 367–381.

Cohen, K. J., and R. M. Cyert (1965). Simulation of organizational behavior. In J. G. March (Ed.), *Handbook of organizations.* Chicago: Rand McNally.

Cohen, K. J., W. R. Dill, A. A. Kuehn, and P. R. Winters (1964). *The Carnegie Tech Management Game: an experiment in business education.* Homewood, Ill.: Irwin.

Colby, K. M. (1963). Computer simulation of a neurotic process. In S. Tomkins and S. Messick (Eds.), *Computer simulation of personality.* New York: Wiley.

——— (1964). Experimental treatment of neurotic computer programs. *Arch. gen. Psychiat., 10,* 220–227.

——— (1965). Computer simulation of neurotic processes. In R. W. Stacy and B. D. Waxman (Eds.), *Computers in biomedical research.* New York: Academic Press.

——— (1967). Computer simulation of change in personal belief systems. *Behav. Sci., 12,* 248–253.

Colby, K. M., and H. Enea (1967). Heuristic methods for computer understanding of natural language in context-restricted on-line dialogues. *Math. Biosciences, 1,* 1–25.

Colby, K. M., and J. P. Gilbert (1964). Programming a computer model of neurosis. *J. math. Psychol., 1,* 405–417.

Colby, K. M., J. Watt, and J. P. Gilbert (1966). A computer method of psychotherapy. *J. nerv. ment. Dis., 142,* 148–152.

Coleman, J. S. (1961). Analysis of social structures and simulation of social processes with electronic computers. *Educ. psychol. Measmt., 21,* 203–218.

——— (1964a). Mathematical models and computer simulation. In R. E. L. Faris (Ed.), *Handbook of modern sociology.* Chicago: Rand McNally.

—— (1964b). Introduction to mathematical sociology. London: Free Press.

—— (1964c). Collective decisions. *Soc. Inquiry, 34,* 166–181.

—— (1965). The use of electronic computers in the study of social organizations. *Europ. J. Sociol., 6,* 89–107.

Cyert, R. M., E. A. Feigenbaum, and J. G. March (1959). Models in a behavioral theory of the firm. *Behav. Sci., 4,* 81–95.

Cyert, R. M., and J. G. March (1963). *A behavioral theory of the firm.* Englewood Cliffs, N.J.: Prentice-Hall.

Dawson, R. E. (1962). Simulation in the social sciences. In H. Guetzkow (Ed.), *Simulation in social science: readings.* Englewood Cliffs, N.J.: Prentice-Hall.

DeGroot, A. D. (1965). *Thought and choice in chess.* The Hague: Mouton.

Deutsch, M., and R. M. Krauss (1960). The effect of threat upon interpersonal bargaining. *J. abnorm. soc. Psychol., 61,* 181–189.

Dill, W. R., and N. Doppelt (1965). The acquisition of experience in a complex management game. In N. Fattu and S. Elam (Eds.), *Simulation models for education.* Bloomington, Ind.: Phi Delta Kappa, Inc.

Dunphy, D. C., P. J. Stone, and M. S. Smith (1965). The General Inquirer: further developments in a computer system for content analysis of verbal data in the social sciences. *Behav. Sci., 10,* 468–480.

Farber, D. J., R. E. Griswold, and I. P. Polonsky (1964). SNOBOL: a string manipulation language. *J. Assoc. Computing Machinery, 11,* 21–30.

Fattu, N. A. (1965). An introduction to simulation. In N. Fattu and S. Elam (Eds.), *Simulation models for education.* Bloomington, Ind.: Phi Delta Kappa, Inc.

Feigenbaum, E. A. (1961). The simulation of verbal learning behavior. *Proc. Western Joint Computer Conf., 19,* 121–132.

—— (1963). The simulation of verbal learning behavior. In E. Feigenbaum and J. Feldman (Eds.), *Computers and thought.* New York: McGraw-Hill.

Feigenbaum, E. A., and J. Feldman, Eds. (1963). *Computers and thought.* New York: McGraw-Hill.

Feigenbaum, E. A., and H. A. Simon (1961). Comment: the distinctiveness of stimuli. *Psychol. Rev., 68,* 285–288.

—— (1962). A theory of the serial position effect. *Brit. J. Psychol., 53,* 307–320.

—— (1963). Performance of a reading task by an elementary perceiving and memorizing program. *Behav. Sci., 8,* 72–76.

Feldman, J. (1962). Computer simulation of cognitive processes. In H. Borko (Ed.), *Computer applications in the behavioral sciences.* Englewood Cliffs, N.J.: Prentice-Hall.

—— (1963). Simulation of behavior in the binary choice experiment. In E. Feigenbaum and J. Feldman (Eds.), *Computers and thought.* New York: McGraw-Hill.

Fernbach, S. (1965). Computers in the U.S.A.—today and tomorrow. *Proc. Int. Fed. Information Processing Societies Conf., 1,* 77–85.

Fetter, R. (1965). Simulation of the activity in a maternity suite. In G. W. Peirson (Ed.), *Computers for the humanities?* Conference Report. New Haven: Yale University.

Fey, W. R. (1962). An industrial dynamics case study. *Indust. Management Rev., 4,* 79–99.

Forrester, J. (1961). *Industrial dynamics.* New York: Wiley.

Frijda, N. H. (1967). Problems of computer simulation. *Behav. Sci., 12,* 59–67.

Galler, B. F. (1962). *The language of computers.* New York: McGraw-Hill.

Gelernter, H., J. R. Hansen, and C. L. Gerberich (1960). A FORTRAN-compiled list-processing language. *J. Assoc. Computing Machinery, 7,* 87–101.

Gelernter, H., and N. Rochester (1958). Intelligent behavior in problem-solving machines. *IBM J. Res. Develpmt., 2,* 336–345.

Gibson, C. T. (1966). Time-sharing with IBM System/360: Model 67. *Amer. Fed. Information Processing Societies Conf. Proc., 28,* 61–78.

Giffin, S. F. (1965). *The crisis game.* Garden City, N.Y.: Doubleday.

Gilbert, J. P., and E. A. Hammel (1966). Computer simulation and analysis of problems in kinship and social structure. *Amer. Anthropologist, 68,* 71–93.

Gilson, C., and R. P. Abelson (1965). The subjective use of inductive evidence. *J. Pers. and soc. Psychol., 2,* 301–310.

Golden, J. T. (1965). *FORTRAN IV—Programming and computing.* Englewood Cliffs, N.J.: Prentice-Hall.

Green, B. F. (1963). *Digital computers in research: an introduction for behavioral scientists.* New York: McGraw-Hill.

——— (1966). Current trends in problem solving. In B. Kleinmuntz (Ed.), *Problem-solving: theory, practice and research.* New York: Wiley.

Green, B. F., Alice Wolf, Carol Chomsky, and K. Laughery (1961). Baseball: an automatic question-answerer. *Proc. Western Joint Computer Conf., 19,* 219–224.

Greenberger, M. (1965). The two sides of time-sharing. *Datamation, 11* (11), 33–36.

Gregg, L. W., and H. A. Simon (1967). Process models and stochastic theories of simple concept formation. *J. math. Psychol., 4,* 246–276.

Guetzkow, H. (1962). *Simulation in social science: readings.* Englewood Cliffs, N.J.: Prentice-Hall.

Guetzkow, H., C. Alger, R. Brody, R. Noel, and R. Snyder (1963). *Simulation in international relations: developments for research and teaching.* Englewood Cliffs, N.J.: Prentice-Hall.

Gullahorn, J., and Jeanne E. Gullahorn (1963). A computer model of elementary social behavior. *Behav. Sci., 8,* 354–362.

——— (1964). Computer simulation of human interaction in small groups. *Amer. Fed. Information Processing Societies Conf. Proc., 25,* 103–113.

——— (1965a). Some computer applications in social science. *Amer. sociol. Rev., 30,* 353–365.

——— (1965b). The computer as a tool for theory development. In D. Hymes (Ed.), *Uses of computers in anthropology.* The Hague: Mouton.

Hägerstrand, T. (1965a). Quantitative techniques for analysis of the spread of information and technology. In C. A. Anderson and M. J. Bowman (Eds.), *Education and economic development*. Chicago: Aldine.

—— (1965b). A Monte Carlo approach to diffusion. *Europ. J. Sociol., 6*, 43–67.

—— (1966). On Monte Carlo simulation of diffusion. In W. L. Garrison (Ed.), *Quantitative geography*. Evanston, Ill.: Northwestern Studies in Geography.

Hare, A. P. (1961). Computer simulation of interaction in small groups. *Behav. Sci., 6*, 261–265.

Hawthorne, G. B., Jr. (1964). Digital simulation and modeling. *Datamation, 10* (10), 25–29.

Hays, D. G. (1965). Simulation: an introduction for anthropologists. In D. Hymes (Ed.), *Uses of computers in anthropology*. The Hague: Mouton.

Hermann, C. F. (1967). Validation problems in games and simulations with special reference to models of international politics. *Behav. Sci., 12*, 216–231.

Holland, E., with R. W. Gillespie (1963). *Experiments on a simulated underdeveloped economy*. Cambridge: M.I.T. Press.

Hovland, C. I. (1960). Computer simulation of thinking. *Amer. Psychologist, 15*, 687–693.

Hunt, E. B. (1962). *Concept learning: an information processing problem*. New York: Wiley.

—— (1963). Simulation and analytic models of memory. *J. verb. Learn. verb. Behav., 2*, 49–59.

Hunt, E. B., and C. I. Hovland (1961). Programming a model of human concept formation. *Proc. Western Joint Computer Conf., 19*, 145–155.

Hunt, E. B., J. Marin, and P. J. Stone (1966). *Experiments in induction*. New York: Academic Press.

Jaynes, E. T. (1963). Missing links in computer intelligence. *Science, 140*, 216.

Jefferson, G. (1949). The mind of mechanical man. *Brit. med. J., 1*, 1105–1121.

Johnson, E. S. (1967). The computer as experimenter. *Behav. Sci., 12*, 484–489.

Jones, L. V. (1963). Beyond Babbage. *Psychometrika, 28*, 315–332.

Kelley, H. H. (1965). Experimental studies of threats in interpersonal negotiations. *J. Confl. Resol., 9*, 79–105.

Kelley, H. H., J. C. Condry, Jr., A. E. Dahlke, and A. H. Hill (1965). Collective behavior in a simulated panic situation. *J. exp. soc. Psychol., 1*, 20–54.

Kleinmuntz, B. (1963). A portrait of the computer as a young clinician. *Behav. Sci., 8*, 154–156.

——, Ed. (1966). *Problem-solving: theory, practice and research*. New York: Wiley.

Krasnow, H. S., and R. A. Merikallio (1964). The past, present, and future of general simulation languages. *Management Sci., 11*, 236–267.

Lackner, M. R. (1965). Toward a general simulation capability. In N. Fattu and S. Elam (Eds.), *Simulation models for education*. Bloomington, Ind.: Phi Delta Kappa, Inc.

Levin, M. L. (1962). Simulation of social processes. *Publ. Opin. Quart., 26*, 483–484.

Lindsay, R. (1963). Inferential memory as the basis of machines which understand natural language. In E. Feigenbaum and J. Feldman (Eds.), *Computers and thought.* New York: McGraw-Hill.

Loehlin, J. C. (1963). A computer program that simulates personality. In S. Tomkins and S. Messick (Eds.), *Computer simulation of personality.* New York: Wiley.

——— (1965). 'Interpersonal' experiments with a computer model of personality. *J. Pers. soc. Psychol., 2,* 580–584.

——— (in press). *Computer models of personality.* New York: Random House.

Lucas, J. (1963). Minds, machines and Gödel. In K. M. Sayre and F. J. Crosson (Eds.), *The modeling of mind.* Notre Dame, Ind.: Univ. of Notre Dame Press.

McCarthy, J., Ed. (1963). *LISP 1.5 programmers manual.* Cambridge: M.I.T. Press.

McCracken, D. F. (1962). *A guide to ALGOL programming.* New York: Wiley.

——— (1964). IBM's new programming language. *Datamation, 10* (7), 31–36.

McGovern, P. J. (1960). Computer conversation compared with human conversation. *Computers and Automation, 9,* 6–11.

McPhee, W. N. (1961). Note on a campaign simulator. *Publ. Opin. Quart., 25,* 184–193.

——— (1963). *Formal theories of mass behavior.* London: Free Press.

McPhee, W. N., and J. Ferguson (1962). Political immunization. In W. N. McPhee and W. A. Glaser (Eds.), *Public opinion and congressional elections.* New York: Free Press.

McPhee, W. N., and R. B. Smith (1962). A model for analyzing voting systems. In W. N. McPhee and W. A. Glaser (Eds.), *Public opinion and congressional elections.* New York: Free Press.

McWhinney, W. H. (1964). Simulating the communication network experiments. *Behav. Sci., 9,* 80–84.

Malcolm, D. G., Ed. (1958). *Report of system simulation symposium.* Baltimore: Waverly Press.

Miller, G. A. (1965a). Computers, communication, and cognition. *Advancement of Science, 21,* 417–430.

——— (1965b). Some preliminaries to psycholinguistics. *Amer. Psychologist, 20,* 15–20.

Miller, G. A., E. Galanter, and K. H. Pribram (1960). *Plans and the structures of behavior.* New York: Holt.

Minsky, M. (1963a). Steps toward artificial intelligence. In E. A. Feigenbaum and J. Feldman (Eds.), *Computers and thought.* New York: McGraw-Hill.

——— (1963b). A selected descriptor-indexed bibliography to the literature on artificial intelligence. In E. A. Feigenbaum and J. Feldman (Eds.), *Computers and thought.* New York: McGraw-Hill.

Morgan, T. B. (1961). The people-machine. *Harper's Magazine,* January, 1961.

Morrill, R. L. (1963). The development of spatial distributions of towns in Sweden: an historical-predictive approach. *Ann. Assoc. Amer. Geographers, 53,* 1–14.

——— (1965). The Negro ghetto: problems and alternatives. *Geograph. Rev., 55,* 339–361.

Naylor, T. H., J. L. Balintfy, D. S. Burdick, and K. Chu (1966). *Computer simulation techniques*. New York: Wiley.

Neisser, U. (1963). The imitation of man by machine. *Science, 139,* 193.

Newell, A. (1962). Some problems of basic organization in problem-solving programs. In M. C. Yovits, G. T. Jacobi, and G. D. Goldstein (Eds.), *Self-organizing systems*. Washington, D.C.: Spartan Books.

Newell, A., J. C. Shaw, and H. A. Simon (1957). Empirical explorations of the logic theory machine: a case study in heuristics. *Proc. Western Joint Computer Conf., 11,* 218–230.

―――― (1958). Elements of a theory of problem solving. *Psychol. Rev., 65,* 151–166.

―――― (1959). Report on a general problem-solving program. *Proc. Int. Conf. on Information Processing*. Paris: UNESCO.

―――― (1963). Chess-playing programs and the problem of complexity. In E. A. Feigenbaum and J. Feldman (Eds.), *Computers and thought*. New York: McGraw-Hill.

Newell, A., and H. A. Simon (1961). Computer simulation of human thinking. *Science, 134,* 2011–2017.

―――― (1963a). GPS, a program that simulates human thought. In E. A. Feigenbaum and J. Feldman (Eds.), *Computers and thought*. New York: McGraw-Hill.

―――― (1963b). Computers in psychology. In R. D. Luce, R. R. Bush, and E. Galanter (Eds.), *Handbook of mathematical psychology*. New York: Wiley.

―――― (1965). An example of human chess play in the light of chess playing programs. In N. Wiener and J. P. Schade (Eds.), *Progress in biocybernetics*. Vol. 2. Amsterdam: Elsevier.

Newell, A., F. Tonge, E. Feigenbaum, B. Green, and G. Mealy (1964). *Information processing language—V manual* (2nd ed.). Englewood Cliffs, N.J.: Prentice-Hall.

Orcutt, G. H. (1960). Simulation of economic systems. *Amer. econ. Rev., 50,* 893–907.

Orcutt, G. H., M. Greenberger, J. Korbel, and A. H. Rivlin (1961). *Microanalysis of socioeconomic systems: a simulation study*. New York: Harper.

Organick, E. I. (1963). *A FORTRAN primer*. Reading, Mass.: Addison-Wesley.

Paige, J. M., and H. A. Simon (1966). Cognitive processes in solving algebra word problems. In B. Kleinmuntz (Ed.), *Problem-solving: theory, practice and research*. New York: Wiley.

Pilisuk, M., P. Potter, A. Rapoport, and J. A. Winter (1965). War hawks and peace doves: alternate resolutions of experimental conflicts. *J. Confl. Resol., 9,* 491–508.

Pitts, F. R. (1962). Chorology revisited—computerwise. *Professional Geographer, 14,* 1–5.

―――― (1963). Problems in computer simulation of diffusion. *Papers and Proc. Regional Sci. Assoc., 11,* 111–119.

Pool, I., and R. P. Abelson (1961). The Simulmatics project. *Publ. Opin. Quart., 25,* 167–183.

Pool, I., R. P. Abelson, and S. Popkin (1964). *Candidates, issues, and strategies: a computer simulation of the 1960 Presidential election*. Cambridge: M.I.T. Press.

——— (1965). A postscript on the 1964 election. *Amer. behav. Scientist, 8,* 39–44.

Pool, I., and A. Kessler (1965). The Kaiser, the Tsar, and the computer: information processing in a crisis. *Amer. behav. Scientist, 8,* 31–38.

Quillian, M. R. (1967). Word concepts: a theory and simulation of some basic semantic capabilities. *Behav. Sci., 12,* 410–430.

Rainio, K. (1962). A stochastic theory of social contacts: a laboratory study and application to sociometry. *Transactions of the Westermarck Society,* Vol. 8. Copenhagen: Munksgaard.

——— (1965). Social interaction as a stochastic learning process. *Europ. J. Sociol., 6,* 68–88.

——— (1966). A study on sociometric group structure. In J. Berger, M. Zelditch, Jr., and B. Anderson (Eds.), *Sociological theories in progress.* Vol. 1. Boston: Houghton Mifflin.

Raphael, B. (1964). A computer program which 'understands.' *Amer. Fed. Information Processing Societies Conf. Proc., 26,* 577–590.

——— (1966). The structure of programming languages. *Comm. Assoc. Computing Machinery, 9,* 67–71.

Rapoport, A. (1963). Mathematical models of social interaction. In R. D. Luce, R. R. Bush, and E. Galanter (Eds.), *Handbook of mathematical psychology.* Vol. 2. New York: Wiley.

Rapoport, A., and A. Chammah (1965). *Prisoner's dilemma.* Ann Arbor: Univ. of Michigan Press.

Reitman, W. R. (1959). Heuristic programs, computer simulation, and higher mental process. *Behav. Sci., 4,* 330–335.

——— (1963). Personality as a problem-solving coalition. In S. Tomkins and S. Messick (Eds.), *Computer simulation of personality.* New York: Wiley.

——— (1964). Information processing models in psychology. *Science, 144,* 1192.

——— (1965). *Cognition and thought: an information processing approach.* New York: Wiley.

Reitman, W. R., R. B. Grove, and R. G. Shoup (1964). Argus: an information processing model of thinking. *Behav. Sci., 9,* 270–281.

Roby, T., and C. R. Budrose (1965). Pattern recognition in groups: laboratory and simulation studies. *J. Pers. soc. Psychol., 2,* 648–653.

Rome, S., and Beatrice Rome (1961). The Leviathan technique for large-group analysis. *Behav. Sci., 6,* 148–152.

——— (1962). Computer simulation toward a theory of large organization. In H. Borko (Ed.), *Computer applications in the behavioral sciences.* Englewood Cliffs, N.J.: Prentice-Hall.

Rosenau, J. N. (1965). Review of H. Guetzkow *et al.,* "Simulation in International Relations." *J. Politics, 27,* 201–203.

Rosenthal, H. (1965). Election simulation. *Europ. J. Sociol., 6,* 21–42.

Sakoda, J. M. (1965). *DYSTAL manual.* Providence, R.I.: Brown Univ. Sociology Computer Laboratory.

Samuel, A. L. (1963). Some studies in machine learning using the game of checkers. In E. A. Feigenbaum and J. Feldman (Eds.), *Computers and thought*. New York: McGraw-Hill.

Sass, M., and W. D. Wilkinson, Eds. (1965). *Computer augmentation of human reasoning*. Washington, D.C.: Spartan Books.

Shepard, R. N. (1964). Review of E. A. Feigenbaum and J. Feldman (Eds.), "Computers and Thought." *Behav. Sci., 9,* 57–65.

Shubik, M. (1960). Simulation of the industry and the firm. *Amer. econ. Rev., 50,* 907–919.

Shure, G. H., R. J. Meeker, and E. A. Hansford (1965). The effectiveness of pacifist strategies in bargaining games. *J. Confl. Resol., 9,* 106–117.

Simmons, P. L., and R. F. Simmons (1962). The simulation of cognitive processes: II. An annotated bibliography. *IRE Trans. on Electronic Computers, EC-11,* 535–552.

Simmons, R. F. (1965). Answering English questions by computer: a survey. *Comm. Assoc. Computing Machinery, 8,* 53–70.

Simon, H. A., and E. A. Feigenbaum (1964). An information-processing theory of some effects of similarity, familiarization, and meaningfulness in verbal learning. *J. verb. Learn. verb. Behav., 3,* 385–396.

Simon, H. A., and K. Kotovsky (1963). Human acquisition of concepts for sequential patterns. *Psychol. Rev., 70,* 534–546.

Simon, H. A., and A. Newell (1964). Information processing in computer and man. *Amer. Scientist, 52,* 281–300.

—— (1965). Heuristic problem solving by computer. In M. Sass and W. D. Wilkinson (Eds.), *Computer augmentation of human reasoning*. Washington, D.C.: Spartan Books.

Simon, H. A., and P. A. Simon (1962). Trial and error search in solving difficult problems: evidence from the game of chess. *Behav. Sci., 7,* 425–429.

Sprowls, R. C. (1962). Business simulation. In H. Borko (Ed.), *Computer applications in the behavioral sciences*. Englewood Cliffs, N.J.: Prentice-Hall.

Stone, P. J., R. F. Bales, Z. Namenwirth, and D. M. Ogilvie (1962). The General Inquirer: a computer system for content analysis and retrieval based on the sentence as a unit of information. *Behav. Sci., 7,* 484–498.

Stone, P. J., D. C. Dunphy, M. S. Smith, and D. M. Ogilvie (1966). *The General Inquirer: a computer approach to content analysis*. Cambridge: M.I.T. Press.

Sweetland, A., and W. W. Haythorn (1961). An analysis of the decision-making functions of a simulated air defense direction center. *Behav. Sci., 6,* 105–116.

Swets, J. A., and W. Feurzeig (1965). Computer-aided instruction. *Science, 150,* 572–576.

Taylor, D. W. (1960). Towards an information processing theory of motivation. In M. R. Jones (Ed.), *Nebraska symposium on motivation, 1960*. Lincoln: Univ. of Nebraska Press.

—— (1963). Thinking. In M. Marx, *Theories in contemporary psychology*. New York: Macmillan.

Tocher, K. D. (1963). *The art of simulation*. Princeton: Van Nostrand.

Turing, A. M. (1950). Computing machinery and intelligence. *Mind, 59,* 433–460.

Uhr, L. (1963). The development of perception and language: simulated models. In S. Tomkins and S. Messick (Eds.), *Computer simulation of personality*. New York: Wiley.

Uttal, W. R. (1967). *Real-time computers: technique and applications in the psychological sciences*. New York: Harper and Row.

Verba, S. (1964). Simulation, reality, and theory in international relations. *World Politics, 16,* 490–519.

von Neumann, J. (1958). *The computer and the brain*. New Haven: Yale Univ. Press.

Weizenbaum, J. (1963). SLIP. *Comm. Assoc. Computing Machinery, 6,* 524–544.

———— (1965). Conversation with a computer. In G. W. Peirson (Ed.), *Computers for the humanities?* Conference Report. New Haven: Yale University.

———— (1966). ELIZA—a computer program for the study of natural language communication between man and machine. *Comm. Assoc. Computing Machinery, 9,* 36–45.

Yngve, V. H., Ed. (1962). *Introduction to COMIT programming*. Cambridge: M.I.T. Press.

Zelditch, M., Jr., and W. M. Evan (1962). Simulated bureaucracies: a methodological analysis. In H. Guetzkow (Ed.), *Simulation in social science: readings*. Englewood Cliffs, N.J.: Prentice-Hall.

13

Systematic Observational Methods

KARL E. WEICK, University of Minnesota

Very few laboratory studies produce data such as these (Dawe, 1934; abstracted by Wright, 1960):

[During four months of observation on a school playground,] . . . two hundred quarrels were observed at the rate of three to four per hour among the 40 children. These quarrels were "amazingly short" indeed. Their average duration was twenty-four seconds, with only 13 lasting more than a minute. The time per quarrel was nearly twice as great outdoors as indoors. Quarrels stopped by teachers were not appreciably shorter than those settled by the children! The boys quarreled more often than the girls. Quarrels involving boys alone or girls were the more frequent, but these intrasex quarrels ended with some form of compromise about three times as often as intersex quarrels! So! Retaliative acts increased with age although the number of quarrels declined with age. Such motor activity as pushing or striking was absent in only three of the 200 quarrels! Truly argumentative quarrels increased with age, as Piaget (1952), for example, would assuredly have expected. Yielding to force was the commonest outcome. Quick and cheerful recoveries outnumbered resentful aftermaths about three to one.

Not only do these data suggest something about the duration, frequency, form, and process of quarrels, but they also hint at antecedents of quarrels and even at relationships that test existing propositions. Aside from the value of these data, there is the question of just what methodology they represent. While there would be general agreement that this is not a laboratory study, and that it is an instance of naturalistic observation, there would probably be wide disagreement about what features of these data best describe their methodological uniqueness.

The author would like to acknowledge the valuable criticisms of an earlier draft of this chapter that were contributed by Robert Bales, Paul Ekman, Stanley Feldstein, Wallace Friesen, William Hargreaves, and Robert Rosenthal. A special word of appreciation is due Marvin Dunnette and Donald King for their significant contributions throughout this revision. The support of the National Science Foundation through Grant GS-955 was instrumental in the completion of this project and is gratefully acknowledged.

THE PROBLEM OF DEFINING OBSERVATIONAL METHODS

The problem of designating what is meant by a "systematic observational method" is sizable because the term is so inclusive. Taken literally, the phrase means planned, methodical watching that involves constraints to improve accuracy. Thus observational methods consist of nothing more nor less than an extension to "the scientific area of a general skill which most humans have to some degree" (Heyns and Lippitt, 1954, p. 371). Any technique that serves to improve the skill of observation qualifies as an observational method. Traditionally, two major techniques have received the most attention, construction of category and rating scales and observer training (see Heyns and Lippitt, 1954; Heyns and Zander, 1953; Lambert, 1960; Medley and Mitzel, 1963; Wright, 1960).

However, when the term "observational method" has been used more informally, its meaning has been extended considerably beyond these two techniques. Some important distinctions are preserved by these extensions. For example, observational methods are often contrasted with experimental methods. It is useful to compare and differentiate between the two methodologies, but only if it is recognized that these differences are matters of degree and that at times observational methods may be indistinguishable from experimental methods.

Observational studies involve fewer controls than do experiments. Those controls that do exist pertain more to the observer and to the means he uses to record data, than to the setting, task, or subject population. Behavior that is the object of observation tends to be naturally instigated and to have multiple antecedents, whereas fewer antecedents systematically influence experimental outcomes. Behaviors that are recorded in observation tend to be molar, whereas those in experimentation are more molecular. In most observational work, fewer subjects are watched for longer periods of time in more varied circumstances than is true of experiments. Training in an observational study is directed more toward calibrating and sensitizing the experimenter to the flow of events, whereas most training activities in experiments serve to sharpen the judgment of the subject. Since the typical observational study involves multiple tasks, behavior is more diffuse and variable, there are more things to watch, and, therefore, more measures may be used and it may be more difficult to secure agreement on what occurs. Observational studies, almost by definition, are more concerned with public, visible, external events, and less so with covert or private events. This means not only that a limited number of processes are studied with observational methods (for example, dominance), but also that explanations involving noncognitive variables are more common.

Aside from the comparison between observation and experiment, the term "observational methods" is often used to refer to hypothesis-free inquiry, looking at events in natural surroundings, nonintervention by the researcher, unselective recording, and avoidance of manipulations in the independent variable. Technically, these extensions of the term do not refer directly to questions of method— the "how" of inquiry—but rather to issues of when, where, and why observations may occur. The surplus meaning that has become attached to the term "observational methods" has been valuable because it highlights important issues that are associated with the methods, but the additional meanings have also been dysfunctional because investigators sometimes treat them as if they were prescriptive. If an observer decides to watch a natural event, then he may feel pressures to avoid hypotheses and interventions, and to be unselective in his recording. When these additional properties of observational methods are treated as prescriptive, observers unwittingly reduce the quality of their studies because they overlook important sources of clarity. It is proposed that hypothesis testing, partial contrivance of events, intervention, counting rather than rating, and selective recording can be just as much a part of observational methodology as their opposites *because they improve the observer's skill and understanding.*

The central argument of this chapter is that the traditional view of observation is built on the model of the passive observer, an unobtrusive bystander in natural surroundings who obtains records or data with minimal intervention. The adoption of this model has meant that observers have spent more time worrying about issues of categorizing and training than about issues of the setting for observation or response measures. As a result, studies involving observational methods have often been inconclusive because records are incomplete, response measures are ambiguous, and settings are needlessly complex. Concern with categories and unconcern with the content of events has meant that excessive demands are made on category systems and on the observer. Both must cope with the fact that complex events are being observed and that intricate judgments of these events are required. Needless to say, measuring instruments are fallible and when these instruments must cope with complex events, these fallibilities become even more apparent. Thus it is not surprising that, despite the care that has been applied to categories and training, the conclusions that emerge from observational studies are often equivocal.

The present chapter maintains that passivity is *not* indigenous to observational methodology. Greater control and precision can occur in observational research if fewer demands are placed on the observer and on his category systems. The principal means by which these demands can be reduced are careful choice and modification of the setting and use of more explicit behavioral measures that make fewer inferential demands on the observer. Settings are more robust and resistant to change than observers have realized. Modifications can be made without a sacrifice of naturalness. If modifications are made, the observer can clear away distractions to observation and he can also prod relevant phenomena into greater prominence. Most behaviors of interest for observation are sufficiently stable and habituated that they appear with regularity even in the face of minor changes in the setting. It is argued that observers should exploit rather than ignore this fact.

Observations can also be clarified if the observer is more thorough and imaginative in his choice of behavioral measures. Many discriminable and significant responses are available to the naked eye which observers have not "seen." As an alternative to observing molar behaviors and summarizing these behaviors in ratings or categories, it is proposed that observers might also wish to count molecular behaviors which are valid indicators of psychological processes. This latter approach makes fewer demands on inference and therefore can lead to greater precision. Furthermore, if the more explicit response measures in fact do reflect important underlying processes, then validity is not sacrificed for precision.

The present approach does not minimize the importance of categories or training. If anything, these concerns are more central than in other surveys. What we propose is that if attention is also directed to issues of the setting for observation and to response measures, then there is less likelihood that a study will succeed or fail solely because of the sensitivity and precision of the codes that are employed. Additional sensitivity and precision can be added to a study if the observer attends to aspects of observational methodology that have often been overlooked. The body of folklore that has emerged around observational methodology has acted as an unintentional constraint on the ways in which this method is implemented. It is the purpose of this chapter to examine existing observational techniques and to suggest ways in which they can be made into a more potent methodology.

A DEFINITION OF OBSERVATIONAL METHODS

The following definition of the observational method is proposed because it retains important properties that are commonly associated with this term and because it is consistent with the point of view that is developed in this chapter. An observational method is defined as *the selection, provocation, recording, and encoding of that set of behaviors and settings concerning organisms "in situ" which is consistent with empirical aims.*

The first impression one may gain from this definition is that it really doesn't exclude very much. If it were not for the phrase *in situ* the definition could apply equally well to studies in the field and in the laboratory. Even then, the phrase *in situ* does not distinguish clearly among experimental and nonexperimental studies, as is evident in Aronson and Carlsmith's discussion of experimental and mundane realism (see Chapter 9 of this *Handbook*). While it is true that familiarity is heightened if the subject is watched in surroundings that are familiar to him, it is also true that experimenters can build settings that resemble familiar surroundings or, even if they do not, they can create realistic problems which subjects must take seriously (Weick, 1965). Rather than try to make definitive exclusions, the present definition attempts to capture important properties of observational methodology especially as these properties pertain to naturalistic settings. It is clear that the notion of a naturalistic setting is not precise, and it is also clear that the inclusion in this definition of the word "provocation" brings observational methodology quite close to experimental methodology. Given the focus of this chapter on ways to increase the precision and validity of observations, it should not be surprising that a closer tie with experimental methodology emerges. At the same time, this tie is not made at the expense of important benefits that are obtained when phenomena are examined in non-experimental settings. The distinctions in the definition are distinctions of degree. While "provocation" is viewed as a part of observational methodology, the provocations are of lesser magnitude than those commonly observed in experiments (see pp. 376–380, where this point is developed more fully). Similarly, when it is noted that observations occur *in situ,* it is assumed that the settings are more familiar to the subject than is common within laboratory experiments. Unless it is recognized that observational methodology is characterized on many of the same dimensions as experimental methodology and that it differs from experimentation only in degree, then pseudo-issues become confounded into an analysis of this methodology and important resources within this methodology remain untapped.

While the preceding gives a general idea of why this definition has been formulated, a more explicit view of its properties emerges if the words themselves are examined closely.

Selection: The word "selection" is included in this definition to underscore the fact that observers *do* make choices before, during, and after observations are made. It is not true that observation is free of editing or focusing. Editing occurs whether the observer intends it or not. If the several choice points in observational research are made explicit, then the observer is in a better position to see where his investigation can be improved and he can be more deliberate in his decisions. Observers tend to underestimate considerably the amount of discretion which they have.

Provocation: It has already been suggested that observers can make subtle changes in natural settings which increase clarity but do not destroy the setting. The rationale and methods for provocation will be discussed shortly. For the moment it is sufficient to note that settings and behaviors are robust and that interventions do not necessarily affect the ways in which they unfold. As was pointed out, it is "provocation" which tends, more than any other term, to blur the distinction between experimental and naturalistic methodology. We contend that such blurring is beneficial.

Recording: This word retains the distinction that a considerable portion of observational research consists of making extensive records of events which at some later time are subject to analysis. Films, diaries, and specimen records are perhaps the clearest examples of records. It is important that the term "selective" be joined to the word "recording" simply to point out that even the most extensive record involves some editing. The distinction between recording and encoding is also important because observers are often tempted to treat records as data, and to bypass simplification and transformation of the record. It is seldom true that a record itself suggests a clear simplified portrait of an event. For example, a film record of a psychotherapy session does not guarantee that the session will be understood. Reduction of data is crucial.

Encoding: Encoding involves the simplification of records through ratings, categories, or frequency counts. Encoding may occur at the time the event occurs or it can occur at some later time when a record of the event is available. Both types of coding are included in the present definition.

"That set": This somewhat ambiguous phrase is intended to emphasize the fact that most observational research uses more than one behavioral measure, and that these multiple measures are often obtained in several settings. Composite measures often serve to correct the flaws of individual measures and to provide a more complete picture of the natural event. The notion of set is also intended to imply that different groupings of behaviors and settings can produce different results. For example, one set of choices might be valuable to reduce the number of competing explanations for an observed outcome, a different set might permit the testing of an explicit hypothesis, and a different set might provide information about the ecology of the behavior.

Behaviors and settings: It was noted earlier that deliberateness in the choice of behaviors and settings can help the observer to reduce some of the demands that are made on his categories and judgments. Relevant phenomena typically crop up in several places and they can be detected from a variety of behaviors. The observer who chooses among these outcroppings in terms of criteria of precision and validity can effect sizable improvements in his outcomes.

Organisms: An earlier version of this definition used the term "persons" in place of "organisms," a usage that is clearly too narrow given the extensive and high-quality literature which involves observations of animal behavior (for example, Baerends, 1954; Calhoun, 1950; Christian, Flyger, and Davis, 1960; Dilger, 1962; Errington, 1961). While the present chapter is concerned primarily with human social interaction, it is important to note that some of the best and most precise applications of observational methodology are found in the animal literature.

"In situ": This phrase is perhaps more elusive than any other phrase or word in the definition. It is intended to preserve the distinction that observational methodology is typically used to watch persons in situations where they spend most of their time or in situations that at least are familiar to them. The implication is that if an investigator wishes to study a particular phenomenon (for example, jealousy, helping, conformity) he looks for those settings in everyday life where these phenomena occur or where it is plausible that they might occur if slight modifications were made. It should be emphasized that some of the examples used in this chapter will place considerable strain on the concept of naturalistic observation simply because the situations are contrived (for example, observations of mother-child interaction in laboratory nursery schools). These examples are included partly because they give relatively pure instances of situational modifications that can be made on a modest scale in natural settings, and also because they do contain several properties that resemble natural settings.

Empirical aims: This phrase was chosen intentionally to preserve the distinction that observational studies can be directed at hypothesis testing, hypothesis formulation, or description. Observational methodology can serve any of these purposes. A study can be adapted to any of these ends by making a different set of choices concerning recording methods.

OCCASIONS FOR OBSERVATION

There are several reasons why persons might wish to use observational methods, some of these being reasons of inherent strengths in these methods, others being weaknesses found in other methods. The purpose of this section is to review some occasions when observation seems advisable.

Observational methods, especially unstructured observation, are often valued because they provide a particular type of data, data with a wide range of detail and immediacy, and with "whole" events preserved (Riley, 1963, pp. 997–998). As was noted earlier, observation is valuable in the preliminary stages of an investigation to give some idea of relevant parameters (Butler, Rice, and Wagstaff, 1963, p. 5).

Observation methods are often useful to offset limitations that subjects have. Gellert (1955) suggested that it is necessary to use observation in studies of children because it is difficult for children to introspect and to remain attentive to lengthy adult tasks. Overinvolvement in an activity frequently makes it difficult for a subject to report what he is doing. When involved, the person "cannot be aware of dimensions of the event that would be apparent to a detached observer" (Richardson, Dohrenwend, and Klein, 1965, p. 9). Unawareness of events may also occur because the activities are habitual or because the activities are culturally patterned. In the latter case, the member of a culture "is likely to believe his customs are universal and, hence, neither novel nor interesting to the investigator" (Richardson, Dohrenwend, and Klein, 1965, p. 10).

Heyns and Lippitt (1954, p. 372) noted three more occasions where subjects are an inadequate source of data: when the desired score is not an individual score (for example, rate of interaction); when the phenomenon is fleeting and may not be noticed by the subjects; and when the subject's report might be distorted by defensive processes.

Observation is frequently necessary because persons do not have the language to describe their actions. Riesman and Watson (1964), for example, used observation to study sociability because persons were inarticulate about their social experiences. "People had no language for discussing sociable encounters, no vocabulary for describing parties except to say that they were 'good' or 'bad,' no way of answering the question 'what do you do for fun?'" (Riesman and Watson, 1964, p. 313). That people often find it difficult to describe social actions is interesting, because it is often argued that a narrative written in "lay language" is a sensitive observational tool to capture the nuances of complex events. It appears that there are important exceptions to this assumption.

Instead of being inadequate as reporters, persons may be unwilling to serve as informants, in which case observation may be more acceptable. Again in the studies of sociable interaction, Riesman and Watson reported that at one stage in their investigations they experimented with a "post-party reaction sheet." Needless to say, they found that the partygoers were unwilling respondents. "This technique proved extraordinarily annoying to participants: they had come to a point of satiation and/or fatigue *before* announcing their decision to leave, and the request that they pause at the door to recapture and reflect on their experience at the party was resented" (p. 300).

The fallibilities of retrospective data are often reason enough for an investigator to attempt an observational study. Back *et al.* (1950) reported that attempts to trace the course of a rumor by means of an interview were unsuccessful because the persons could not even recall the rumor unless it had been dramatic, and even if they could recall the content of the rumor, they could not remember who told it to them or to whom they told it. That there are numerous opportunities for distortion in retrospective data is demonstrated dramatically by Barker (1964). He suggested that the following chain of events, even though it is an extreme case, is often approximated (p. 279):

    I. An untrained observer
        1) makes casual observation, and
        2) retains its traces in his memory for x years when he
        3) tells it to an
    II. interviewer, who
        4) write it in his notes, and later
        5) dictates it to a
    III. recording machine which
        6) transmits it to a
    IV. typist, who
        7) prepares a typescript for an
    V. editor, who
        8) edits the record and returns it to the
    VI. typist, who
        9) prepares a second typescript and gives it to a
    VII. coder, who
        10) codes the content of the record and passes it to a
  VIII. puncher, who
        11) punches the code onto cards and gives them to a
    IX. sorter, who
        12) prepares the distributions and delivers the data to the
    X. investigator, for
        13) final analysis and interpretation.

Retrospective data, especially interviews, may tempt the investigator to make unwarranted generalizations about a population. This danger is discussed by Webb *et al.* (1966, p. 176):

When one is working within a single society, there is always the question of whether the differential verbal skills of various subcultures will mislead the investigator. It is possible, if groups vary in articulateness, to overgeneralize the behavior or attitudes of the group or individuals with the greater verbal fluency.

Observation of behavior as well as adequate sampling procedures can serve to offset the temptation to overgeneralize.

Many substantive problems require observational methodology. Riley (1963, p. 996) suggested that even though dispositions to act socially may best be assessed by questionnaire, observational methods are required to assess the "acting out" of these dispositions. Frequently, a phenomenon is not of theoretical interest unless it occurs in a specific natural setting (Baumrind, 1964, p. 7). Intimate relationships between the person and setting are often best preserved in observational studies. As Purcell and Brady (1965) commented, "opportunities for studying the contextual background of various behaviors are greatly improved by the observer's ability to 'see' the 'environment' in operation with the subject" (p. 4). Phenomena that are multidimensional and complex may be altered by experimental controls and, therefore, are best studied by observation under natural conditions. Sherif and Sherif (1964), in their recent field studies of delinquent groups, stated that observation was necessary because they needed to observe groups of the individual's own choosing, goal objects and status distinction in these reference groups, and, in general, "individual behavior *and* group *and* setting in their relationship" (p. 44). Laboratory groups were unsuited to these aims.

Baumrind (1964, pp. 7–8) suggested that observational methods provide the chance to validate data by control. Success in changing a phenomenon is a good indication of understanding. Since observational data are usually recorded in molar units and thus are directly transferable to practical situations, the observer can institute changes with a minimal amount of inference required. If the change makes a difference, the validity of the earlier observations is demonstrated.

A final set of circumstances in which observation may be necessary occurs when the variables are too "dangerous" to create in the laboratory, when excessive and distasteful demands must be made of the subjects, when it is impossible to debrief a subject after an experimental manipulation, or when laboratory inductions are excessively mild and, therefore, unrepresentative of everyday life. Lambert (1963) commented on the constraints that often haunt laboratory studies. Most of the sanctions that researchers can manipulate consist of cognitive feedback which is weak and "unrepresentative of the buffetings of real life." He suggested that psychologists will be able to experiment with more severe sanctions only when their status increases. In the meantime (pp. 226–227),

... researchers can only fall back upon animal studies or become more clever in being present with measurement devices when more powerful sanctions are being legitimately used. Fraternities still turn some hopefuls down, employers fire workers for various reasons, students are asked to leave college, and people are continually dying and friends are grieving for them. Fortunately, the more positive and happy aspects of these things also occur, and if social psychologists can learn to be there in an acceptable way, more representative measurements will be taken.

It is possible that many of the "safe" topics have already been studied in the laboratory and that observational methods will need to be applied to a greater proportion of the remaining topics. This should be true at least until there is greater public acceptance of manipulation and deceit in laboratory experiments and until laboratory technology is improved so that vivid, accurate replicas of significant events can be created under controlled conditions.

THE SETTING FOR OBSERVATION

One of the paradoxes of observation is that naturalistic settings are valued as sites for data collection, yet observers are surprisingly careless when they choose a setting. Any setting in which the relevant phenomenon occurs seemingly qualifies as a place for observation; hence, settings are viewed as equivalent and interchangeable. One of two additional assumptions often accompanies the belief in equivalence of settings. Sometimes it is presumed that the setting imposes minimal constraints on behavior and, therefore, can safely be ignored. Or the opposite view may predominate, namely, that properties of a setting maximally coerce behavior and therefore must not be altered if meaningful data are to be collected. Tampering of any kind presumably destroys the structure and sometimes the content of a natural event. Regardless of which assumption is made, the observer is apt to treat the choice of setting as a minor phase of his investigation.

The central argument of this section is that greater deliberateness in the choice and arrangement of an observational setting can lead to sizable improvements in the precision and validity of observational studies. Any setting has properties that detract from clear observation, but these distractions are more prominent in some situations than in others. Furthermore, some properties of naturalistic settings can be eliminated or modified, and new properties can be added without necessarily destroying the naturalness that is valued. In short, naturalistic settings do not require passivity from the observer. Settings afford significant opportunities to clarify observational data. Settings are also more flexible and permit more latitude for manipulation, intervention, and rearrangement than has often been realized.

There are several reasons why an investigator might want to select carefully and modify a natural setting. Many events occur infrequently and often the observer must simply wait until something relevant happens (Argyris, 1958, p. 510). Wright (1960, p. 100) suggested that there may be a negative relationship between the significance of behavioral events and the rate of their occurrence. An excellent example of the problems caused by rare events is a study by Gump and Kounin (1959). They spent six weeks in a summer camp with six full-time observers studying the "ripple effect," the influence of control techniques on persons who watch someone else being disciplined. During the six weeks, the effect was observed only 139 times or about once for every 18 pages of material that was recorded. The authors suggested that few effects were observed because the leaders did not single out the campers who were being disciplined, the campers did not hear or ignored many disciplinary efforts, and many punishments that were noticed did not have any effects.

Careful selection and modification may also help the observer to be more certain that "the materials under study were in fact equivalent or equal before they were modified by the critical responses" (Webb *et al.,* 1966, p. 43). Comparisons in observational studies often suffer because settings differ widely before events occur. Alternative explanations in terms of differential prior history threaten both the internal and external validity (Campbell, 1957) of observational studies.

Careful choice of setting also permits the observer to increase the range of behavioral variation, influence the magnitude of an outcome, evoke a novel response, amplify an incipient response, conceal the fact of observation, or assess the generality of an outcome. The important point is that each of these aims can be furthered by choice and modification of a setting *without* regard to the behaviors that will be recorded or the means that will be used to record them. Behaviors and codes afford *additional* means to clarify, but they can be supplemented by careful arrangement of the properties of a setting.

It may seem that modification of a natural setting defeats the purpose of observational studies, namely, to study persons in habitats that are familiar to them. Clearly, massive interventions do render the familiar unfamiliar and make participants aware that they are being watched and that their actions are for the benefit of the investigators and not themselves. This is not the type of intervention we are advocating. *Subtle* modifications are the key. Perhaps the phrase that best captures what we have in mind is *tempered naturalness.* The trappings of the natural event are preserved, it unfolds in a conventional manner, but some of its peripheral properties are qualified to accomplish the aims mentioned earlier. The most common means to accomplish such qualification is to put boundaries around some portion of the ongoing events. This means essentially that participants are exposed to an input that has a beginning and an end, an input that fits into the setting in the sense that it is plausible and expected, an input that is nonreactive and does not arouse suspicion, and an input that permits greater precision in measurement. The input that is referred to is essentially modeled after a laboratory task that has been altered sufficiently in appearance that it fits into the setting for observation. It is the task that elicits the behavior which the observer records. A directed setting consistent with this model can be created either when an intact task is plausibly "dropped into" the behavior stream (for example, visitors to a health exposition see films about lung cancer that vary in vividness and their subsequent actions are watched; Leventhal and Niles, 1964) or when the stream of activities is altered so that it contains the essential properties of a task (for example, the beliefs of a woman in a shopping center are mildly or strongly attacked by a communique which she reads during a feigned "man on the street" radio interview; Miller and Levy, 1967).

Subtlety in modifications, however, is a question of degree and it can plausibly be argued that subtlety is no guarantee that naturalness is preserved. Several points seem relevant to this objection. In the first place, it is clear that settings do constrain behavior and that these constraints are sizable (for example, Barker, 1960). Furthermore, it is clear that these constraints are quite resistant to disruption. Settings are adaptable and they accommodate modifications by spreading their effects among the several properties that were not changed. The net result is that slight modifications are absorbed with little apparent change in the event (Lewin, 1951, pp. 165–166).

Perhaps the most significant force that counteracts the disruptive effect of modifications is the fact that persons are operating in settings that are familiar. They are apt to be preoccupied with everyday events, and any slight changes in this routine are apt to be assimilated and to attract little attention. The modifications made by the observer may seem slightly out of the ordinary, but these discrepancies are likely to be swamped and forgotten because most of what the participants are doing is familiar. This state of affairs is quite in contrast to what occurs in the laboratory. Because of the unfamiliarity of the experimenter-subject relationship and the uniqueness of the demands that are made, the participant's attention is focused on the data-collection process. There are no routine or familiar activities to distract him or to make him less self-conscious. Even when deception is involved, the subject still is in a highly unfamiliar situation, and whatever happens tends to be organized around the fact that he is an object of study. In contrast, when the subject is in familiar surroundings doing familiar things, he is likely to organize his explanation of slightly unusual demands around the fact that they are part of his daily routine. When this occurs, the modifications made to clarify observation are minimally disruptive of natural events.

The investigator who is still doubtful that naturalness has been preserved has an obvious solution, namely, measurement. If the setting and associated behaviors are measured before and after the modifications are made by such means as a specimen record (Barker and Wright, 1955), then it is possible to learn how the modification has changed the situation. Even if some modification is detected, this does not mean that intervention should be avoided. Instead, the investigator now has a clearer idea of the actual changes that have occurred and he can judge whether or not the alterations will influence the outcome of hypothesis testing.

As a final point, it should be noted that objections to interventions are often confused with two other issues, psychological ecology and observer interference. Some observational studies (for example, Barker and Wright, 1955) are patterned after natural-history field studies and are intended to describe the structure, dynamics, and content of everyday behavior as it occurs in natural surroundings. In essence, data collection is free of hypotheses. Whatever happens, wherever it happens, constitutes the relevant information. Clearly, if the purpose of an investigation is to record what happens in natural settings, interventions are dangerous. They are not a part of everyday activities and, when interposed, destroy the very datum that the observer hopes to record. But the point is that not all observational studies are directed to questions of ecology. Attention is usually focused on a more selected range of problems, and portions of the setting that are not relevant to these problems can be altered with minimal effects on outcomes.

It should be noted that the confusion between issues of intervention and ecology is sometimes heightened because observers try to accomplish too much or are vague about what they want to accomplish. Observational studies are often initiated to test hypotheses, but then they become partially redefined as investigations of behavior in natural habitats. The observer attempts to gather both ecological data and data relevant to hypotheses, but his qualified interventions can easily disturb the "behavioral stream" for ecological purposes and also leave conditions unclear for hypothesis testing. Unfortunately neither aim is realized.

The second issue that is often confused with the question of intervention is that of observer interference. Observers are perceptible as well as perceptive. They are usually present in any observational situation. Whether this presence alters the course of natural events is the concern of every person who uses observational methodology. As important as this problem is—the next portion of this section will be devoted solely to it—it is only one source of disruption, it is localized, and its effects can be assessed or discounted. Interventions to clarify data collection usually do not involve the observer, and the issue of the effects of his presence should be considered apart from the question of situational alterations. Tempered naturalness is achieved by intentional modifications, not unintentional ones.

THE OBSERVER AS ARTIFACT

The observer is typically a fixture in any observational setting and his impact on events must be determined if observational studies are to have any value. There is little argument that the observer, in the process of watching an event, affects its course (Bachrach, 1962, p. 33). The real issues are how extensive the impact is, which settings and processes are most vulnerable to its effects, and whether interference can be detected. Several persons such as Sherif and Sherif (1964, p. 110) contend that even if an observer's presence is accepted and taken for granted, this is not enough:

People may lose their initial awareness of a piece of equipment or even of a live observer busily recording their words and deeds. But does reduction of initial self-awareness mean that they are behaving without regard to the very significant fact that they are being studied? It does not.

Similar unrest about how persons respond when being watched is found in the literature of laboratory experimentation, especially the concepts of evaluation apprehension (Rosenberg, 1965), deutero-problem (Riecken, 1962), demand characteristics (Orne, 1962), and experimenter bias (Rosenthal, 1964). While information is scant about whether persons behave differently when being watched, most investigators who study persons in *familiar* habitats argue that subjects soon forget that they are being watched or, if they do not, the observer will notice their concern. Schoggen (1964a, p. 56) has summarized this more moderate position:

One cannot completely set aside on a moment's notice the attitudes and patterns of social behavior which have been developed and practiced for years in favor of other, unnatural forms of behavior fancied to be more acceptable. Particularly this is true in dealing with children who are likely to react with blank, incredulous stares to parent behavior that deviates markedly from the usual pattern.

Instances of interference

There are times when observers do interfere with processes. It is important to localize these sources of interference so that they can be dealt with in a more direct manner. Observers are often conspicuous because they play an unusual role, that of nonparticipant. Inactivity in some situations makes the observer stand out (Barker and Wright, 1955, p. 212). Goode and Hatt (1952) noted that "we have no standard set of relationships or role patterns for the nonmember who is always present but never participating" (p. 122). Empirical support for the assumption that nonparticipants are disruptive is found in Smith's (1957) finding that a group member who is silent generally creates hostility and uncertainty among the more vocal members. It is possible that data collected by a non-participant observer with an inadequate rationale for his presence would show greater anger, hostility, and aggression among participants than is usually the case. It is important to note the kind of reaction that nonparticipation provokes. The usual assumption is that persons will be guarded, nonargumentative, and on their "best behavior" if they are sensitive about being observed. Any indication of anger is interpreted as evidence that the observer has not influenced behavior (for example, Bishop, 1951, p. 16). The preceding line of analysis suggests that just the opposite may be true. Angry remarks may signal discomfort at being observed rather than comfort.

Problems of interference are often intensified by the social structure of observational settings. Frequently, small groups of two (husband-wife, mother-child) or three (father-mother-son) are observed. Research with triads (for example, Gamson, 1964) suggests that three-person groups are unstable and tend to split apart. Two persons often combine their resources to control a third person and the outcome of an event. Vidich (1956) studied the interaction between husbands and wives whose task was to come to a verbal agreement on several issues about which they differed. Even though the discussion was supposed to involve only the couple, each participant frequently tried to elicit support from the experimenter. "The spouses viewed the interviewer not only as a public, but also as an audience whose support and sympathy were available for solicitation" (p. 237). Even though Vidich actually had two interviewers, a male and a female, and thus technically did not have a triad, it appears that the participants lumped the two observers into one category, that of outsider. It should be noted that Vidich probably added to his problems when, at the end of his standard instructions, he remarked, "We'll be here to answer any questions you may have" (p. 235). While the frequency with which persons turn to the observer for help is an interesting datum in itself, it is difficult to interpret under the present conditions.

Interference is a problem not just when three people gather, or when the roles of majority-minority are salient. Observers often have a marked effect on behavior when participants have reason to suspect the motives of observers. Goodrich (1959, p. 231) reported that when observations are made in treatment centers, observers can heighten paranoia, serve as objects for displacement, or deprive people of privacy with predictable effects on behavior. Paranoia is certainly not eased by a stranger's clipboard. That observation is still possible when there is a potential for suspicion is shown by Rokeach's (1964) study of three mental patients all claiming to be Christ. Even though the study took place in a mental hospital, Rokeach had an adequate explanation (p. 4) for his presence, namely, to conduct periodic quasi-therapy meetings.

Sometimes it is necessary to interfere in ongoing events in order to maintain rapport. Spiro (1958) reported that, while he was observing the behavior of children in a Kibbutz, frequent conflicts between scientific and humane values occurred when nurses momentarily left the children who were being observed. When aggression broke out, there was a conflict about whether to protect the victim or gather data (p. 466). If the investigators failed to stop a fight and the nurses learned of this, the nurses were more uncooperative when the observers needed their help.

These few examples suggest some forms that interference may take, but they also imply that the problem is localized and that, even when it occurs, there are steps that the observer can take to reduce its effect.

Assessment of interference

Recently, attempts have been made to assess systematically the magnitude of the interference problem. In this section we summarize some of these attempts.

The interference problem has been studied most extensively in the psycho-therapy setting (Bellak and Smith, 1956; Carmichael, 1956; Haggard, Hiken, and Isaacs, 1965; Harper and Hudson, 1952; Kogan, 1950; Roberts and Renzaglia, 1965; Sternberg, Chapman, and Shakow, 1958; Watson and Kanter, 1956). It is commonplace for therapy sessions to be recorded or filmed, yet there have been growing doubts about whether the sessions that are observed are representative. If the patient knows that he is being observed by someone other than the therapist, his willingness to confide in the therapist may be reduced and the therapy process altered markedly. Similarly, the therapist may also have reservations about being studied by his colleagues and these concerns may change his behavior.

An example of a tightly controlled investigation of interference is a study by Roberts and Renzaglia (1965) of the effect of tape recording in client-centered counseling. Eight counseling trainees each discussed adjustment problems for at least three sessions with two different clients. Each counselor conducted one of his three sessions under each of the following conditions: tape recorder visible and running during the hour (TR); microphone only present (MO); and not recorded (NR), a condition in which the client and counselor were told the session would not be recorded, but in which it actually was recorded.

Extensive analysis of comments by patients and therapists showed that the quantity of talk and the ratio of client-counselor talk did not differ significantly. Recording, however, did have some effects. Clients made significantly more positive statements about themselves when the recorder was visible than in either the MO or NR condition. More negative self references occurred in the NR condition than in the other two, but the smallest number of negative comments was in the MO and not the TR condition. Counselors also made significantly more interpretive comments under TR than under MO and NR.

Although the preceding results were obtained with inexperienced counselors, they do suggest that observation alters some processes but not others. These findings suggest the necessity of caution in interpreting other studies that involve recording.

Interference has also been assessed in nontherapy settings (for example, Barker and Wright, 1955, pp. 441–444; Purcell and Brady, 1965, p. 61; Soskin and John, 1963). The typical finding is that interference is not extensive, and when it occurs, its effects are usually localized in the period when observation begins. Barker and Wright's observers had perhaps the greatest potential for interference, since they followed subjects as they went about their everyday activities and tried to maintain "the role of a friendly, nonevaluating, nondirective, and nonparticipating person who is interested in what people do" (p. 211). Thus, the potential for interaction between the subject and observer was high. Extensive information about the kinds of interaction that materialized is presented. In 20 percent of the interactions for the Midwest children, the observer was involved either as an associate or a member. Roughly 82 percent of these interactions were initiated by the child, although there was considerable variability (62–93 percent). About half these interactions (54 percent) were cyclical, that is, involved an action-reaction-reply. There was a significant positive relationship ($r = 0.57$) between age and amount of interaction with the observer. Younger children were more prone to ignore the observer than were older children. When children interacted with the observer their modes of action were mainly nurturance and appeal, whereas most of the responses by the observer consisted of nurturance, compliance, or resistance. In almost all cases the frequency of interactions between the observer and subject were significantly lower than the interactions which the subject had with other adults.

While these data suggest that some alterations did occur, they also pinpoint the type of alteration and suggest qualifications that can be made in interpreting the data. Furthermore, it is important to realize that an interaction between the observer and subject is an important behavior in its own right. "It is . . . behavior which shows as well as any other how a given person in a particular setting of a particular community reacts to a definable situation" (Barker and Wright, 1955, p. 212).

A rather different situation where interference is a distinct possibility involves attaching radio transmitters to subjects so that every spontaneous comment they make is recorded. Purcell and Brady (1965) outfitted adolescents in a treatment center with transmitters for one hour every day, and Soskin and John (1963) had a married couple wear a transmitter the entire time they were on a two-week vacation. When the protocols in both studies were scored for the incidence of comments about observation, it was found that references dropped almost to zero after the first day of recording. While it is possible that an unseen observer in the form of a transmitter is less of a threat than a visible observer, it could also be argued that the sensitivity of the unseen observer—he hears whispered comments and comments muttered when someone else is talking—heightens the threat.

Solutions to interference problems

There are several ways to deal with the interference problem, one of which is *concealment*. In attempts to disguise the fact that observation is taking place, observers have hidden under beds in college dormitories (Henle and Hubble, 1938), eavesdropped on conversations in theater lobbies (Carlson, Cook, and Stomberg, 1936) and along streets (Watson, Breed, and Posman, 1948), and posed as radio interviewers (Miller and Levy, 1967).

Two prominent investigations in which observers did not reveal their intent are those of Festinger, Riecken, and Schachter (1956) and Sherif and Sherif (1964). While concealment controls one type of interference—concern about being watched—it may create another type of interference—diverting a natural event. Whether diversion occurs depends on the pretext persons use to join and remain in the group. Festinger, Riecken, and Schachter (1956) wanted to join a secret group preparing for the end of the world, but an innocuous pretext was not sufficient to gain entry. When rebuffed in their initial effort to join, it was necessary for these investigators to have a "psychic experience" before they were acceptable to the other members. The use of a "psychic experience" as a pretext for entry was crucial in this study because it probably affected the solidarity of the group and its subsequent behavior. Festinger, Riecken, and Schachter described the problem this way (p. 240):

There is little doubt that the addition of four new people to a fairly small group within ten days had an effect on the state of conviction among the existing members, especially since the four seem to have appeared when public apathy to the belief systems was great. . . . Most important of all, perhaps, is that the four observers could not be traced through any mutual friends or acquaintances to existing group members and thus the most common and expected channel of recruitment was evidently not responsible for their appearance.

Sherif and Sherif's (1964) observers were to become accepted into adolescent gangs in such a way that they were seen as helpful but not as rivals and *not* as actual members. They were to participate in everything except illegal activities, but were not to threaten the leader or at any time reveal that they were making observations (pp. 335–337). Special care was taken to ensure that the observer recorded in detail any instances of resistance, suspicion, secrecy, and deliberate misleading, so that interference could be detected if it occurred.

Aside from the problem that concealment may divert events, there is the additional problem of the ethics of concealed observation (for example, Amrine and Sanford, 1956; Burchard, 1957). Although the issue is exceedingly complex and cannot be dealt with here, it is valuable to reflect on two different views concerning this problem. Barker and Wright (1955) argued that concealment is never justified unless the behavior is open to public inspection. Concealment "is dubious, to say the least, if the behavior to be observed is not public and therefore open to scrutiny by all. It is clear that people living in a community have the right to say when and by whom their privacy is to be invaded. They differ in this respect from subjects who have consented to be guinea pigs behind one-way vision screens in psychological laboratories" (p. 211). While the phrase "open to scrutiny by all" is ambiguous in terms of just how many and what kinds of persons are included, the implication of this point of view is that none of the concealment studies reviewed above was justified. In each case members were participating in events that were not for public consumption, there were groups of persons whom participants definitely would not want to have learn about their activities (for example, nonbelievers, policemen), and participants admitted the observer to quasi-membership only when he met very specific requirements.

Concealment can sometimes be justified if the basis on which the observer joins the activity is not misrepresented, even though he may have additional interests. Riesman and Watson (1964) confronted the issue of ethics when they observed interaction at parties. They defend their concealment of observation in this way (p. 267):

Many people come to social gatherings with more than one objective: they do not announce everything they have in mind . . . the important thing is not the presence or absence of these other objectives but the question of whether the manifest role—that of friend and partner in sociability—is misrepresented. It is exploitation if the guise of friendship is assumed for an unfriendly purpose: but if the friendly interaction is entered into in good faith, with other objectives being *in addition to* and not *instead of,* we see no serious violation of ethical standards.

The essence of this argument is that if participants have multiple aims and if the observer's pretext for entry is genuine, then concealment is justifiable. From this perspective the studies involving the secret cult were less justified than the study of gangs when the observer joined and participated as a resource in addition to being an observer.

The issue of ethics is by no means encompassed by these two representative views. It remains a crucial issue which reflects increasing public concern about invasions of privacy. Rationales for concealment do exist, but they become apparent only after careful and honest deliberation.

As an alternative to concealment, some observers handle interference problems by *partial concealment.* The investigator does not conceal the fact that he is making observations but he does conceal who or what is being observed. This strategy is seen most frequently in studies of mother-child interaction. The investigator implies that only the child is being observed when, in fact, the mother's behavior is also being observed (Bishop, 1951, p. 3).

Many investigators try to minimize interference by *nonconcealment.* The observer indicates his purpose to subjects in advance and then tries to remain inconspicuous while recording their actions. Riesman and Watson (1964, p. 261) proposed that this is one of the differences in method between sociologists and psychologists: sociologists tend to be honest before data are collected, psychologists after they are collected. Our earlier description (p. 372) of the role adopted by Barker and Wright's observers exemplifies nonconcealment. Observers made their aims explicit, they were known by the participants, and they came to be accepted as interested bystanders. If nonconcealment is only partially attempted (that is, the observer is evasive about his aims) then interference may increase because participants continue to be uncertain of the observer's intent and they tend to pay closer attention to him. An excellent illustration of the problems that arise when an observer tries both to conceal and to be honest is provided by Blau (1964, p. 27).

There are several other ways to cope with interference. One way is to record behaviors that are not under conscious control of the subject. Even if the subject is concerned about being watched, these indices should not be affected. Mahl (1964, p. 469), for example, noted that voice frequencies of 500 cps and below furnish information about emotion and also seem to be less affected when the subject makes an obvious attempt to control them. Problems of interference also tend to be reduced with children (Wright, 1960, p. 76). Children "are simply too busy living their lives to be bothered with an observer who merely stands and watches" (Schoggen, 1964a, p. 55). However, adults as well as children can become engrossed in events, and when this occurs problems of interference are lessened. Straus (1964) proposed the "absorbing situation" strategy as means to counteract distraction. This strategy is characterized as follows: "the experiment or performance being observed must be sufficiently engrossing and demanding of attention that the actors will, at least temporarily, forget about the presence of an observer" (p. 372).

Occasionally it is possible to arrange the sequence of data collection so that the most disruptive measures are administered after most of the actions have occurred. Sherif and Sherif (1964, p. 358) did not interview group members until the very end of the study, since interviews make the observer-group relationship more visible.

Webb *et al.* (1966) suggested three relatively untapped sources of data that are not subject to interference. These include erosion measures, trace measures, and archives. Erosion measures are concerned with selective wear of natural objects. The rate at which floor materials must be replaced may be an indication of usage, movements, or attractiveness of some objects. If children are provided with shoes whose soles are of a standard composition, a measure of activity may derive from the rate at which the sole wears down (p. 43). Trace measures consist of articles that are deposited by subjects. Examples would be the number of cigarette butts in airport ashtrays before and after a major crash, the variety of fingerprints on a book or display case, or the frequencies at which pushbutton radios are tuned as a clue to where a car has been (p. 39). Archives are permanent records that can be adapted for hypothesis testing. Examples of archives include tombstones, *Who's Who*, Congressional Record, marriage records, voting records, and volume and kind of letters mailed by congressmen. While each of these measures is subject to error (erosion and trace are vulnerable to response sets, while archives may be inaccurate), they do provide more substantial solutions to the interference problem than has been recognized.

A final means to handle interference is the use of *lay* observers, persons who are legitimately on the scene when events occur. Hargreaves (1965) and Bunney and Hamburg (1963) used nurses to provide ongoing records of the behavior of psychiatric patients, and Back *et al.* (1950) used workers in an industrial firm to trace the course of planted rumors.

THE USE OF DIRECTED SETTINGS

The purpose of this section is to describe ways in which natural settings can be modified to provide more explicit answers to empirical questions. Our concern is with the activity of "provocation" cited in the earlier definition of observation and with the "tempering" of natural events. The types of direction to be discussed follow the model of a bounded event (see p. 367) which is nonreactive (it does not increase the salience of the research question), and in which the essential trappings of the natural event are preserved. So far it has been argued that the alteration of natural settings can improve the quality of observational studies, that alterations do not disrupt natural events, and that the observer is a minor influence in most settings. It remains to be demonstrated how subtle alterations are actually made.

This section describes representative studies in which the setting has been modified so that the observer can (1) embed a measure, (2) evoke a behavior, or (3) amplify an incipient response. In each study the natural setting is preserved but slight alterations are made to give the investigator more direct access to the phenomena he is studying.

Embedding a measure

An observational setting is often used to enclose and provide a plausible context for a laboratory task. Embedding, however, does not include just the use of existing tasks. Ongoing events often contain their own bounded tasks that share many properties with laboratory tasks. One of the better examples of this latter type of embedding is provided by naturalistic studies involving games (for example, Gump and Sutton-Smith, 1955; Harvey, 1953; Whyte, 1955). Games are surprisingly appropriate to test numerous hypotheses and they are a common part of everyday activity.

Sherif and Sherif (1956, pp. 312–316) sought to determine whether the members of competing groups would magnify the accomplishments of their own groups and depreciate the accomplishments of the other group. Summer campers in two groups were given the task of picking up as many beans as possible in a one-minute period. After the beans were collected they were sealed into individual sacks. The subjects then went to a hall where they saw, projected on a screen for five seconds, the number of beans supposedly gathered by each person. Campers were to estimate how many beans were in each picture (always 35). Differences in the amount of over- and underestimation were striking and were consistent with the hypothesis.

Games are not the only means by which a measure may be embedded. Barch, Trumbo, and Nangle (1957) studied conformity by observing whether drivers, making turns at an intersection, imitated the turn-signaling behavior of the preceding driver. Webb *et al.* (1966, pp. 163–164) suggested that driving behavior is an excellent setting in which to study persuasion. It is proposed that the content of traffic signs be varied systematically (for example, high fear appeal versus low fear appeal) and that driving behavior after the driver passes the sign be observed by radar or a helicopter. Allport and Vernon (1933, p. 52) suggested an engagingly simple means to embed a measurement of intensity or forcefulness. Subjects were asked to write a brief description of some frustrating event, and they wrote on a piece of paper which was actually a stack of papers interlaced with sheets of carbon paper. The measure of intensity was the number of sheets of paper through which the writing penetrated.

It seems clear that it is possible to embed explicit measures in a flow of events without disturbing natural processes. The preceding examples suggest some ways in which this can be accomplished.

Evoking a behavior

Careful choice and/or modification of a situation can enable observers to evoke behaviors that are of interest. Holmberg (1954) provided an excellent example of this tactic. On a field trip in South America, he encountered the Siriono Indians in Eastern Bolivia, a tribe that had very little contact with outsiders. After two months Holmberg introduced four items that were foreign to the Indians: six knives, six machetes, a small flock of chickens, and a shotgun. Numerous behaviors were evoked, many of which were unexpected. The machetes, for example, led to a rise of ingroup hostility. The machetes enabled the natives to extract more honey from trees so that they could make more beer with which they could have longer parties at which they could release more verbal and physical aggression (p. 108).

Questionnaires are a common device to evoke behavior in observational studies. Sometimes the participants (typically a family or married couple) fill out questionnaires in private, differences in opinion are revealed to them, and they are then requested to come to some agreement about these differences (for example, Strodtbeck, 1951; Scott, 1962). In other variations of this procedure the couple merely answer the questions as they go along without an initial census being taken (for example, Drechsler and Shapiro, 1961; Vidich, 1956).

Scarcity of props is a common means to evoke behavior. Gump, Schoggen, and Redl (1957) noted that, among campers, starting a fire is a rare activity; therefore, fire starting is apt to evoke more conflict than does getting water, an activity that is usually available to everyone. They summarized the issue of props in this way: "When props and performances are so organized that the valued actions are delayed or in short supply, an activity setting is likely to produce competitiveness" (p. 43).

A final means to evoke behavior without arousing suspicion is to use accomplices. Jung (1959) had persons pose as consumers and give a standard set of responses to see if they could persuade a car salesman to lower list prices. Garfinkel (1963) studied disconfirmed expectations by having students walk into a store and treat a customer as if he were a sales clerk. Lefkowitz, Blake, and Mouton (1955) studied conformity by having persons dressed in various clothes violate a traffic signal and recording the number of persons who followed the violator. Brock (1965) had experimenters pose as salesmen in a paint store and try to influence the purchases of consumers as a function of varying degrees of similarity between the consumer and salesmen. In each of these studies, the natural setting was preserved, the accomplices were plausible fixtures in these settings, and the desired behaviors appeared with greater frequency because of the programmed inputs of the accomplices.

Amplifying an incipient response

The distinction between modifications that evoke a behavior and modifications that amplify a response is undoubtedly difficult to make. The distinction has been preserved, however, because it seems possible that conditions which evoke may differ from conditions which increase prominence. To evoke a response, the investigator often adds new properties to a situation (for example, novel stimuli, accomplices). To amplify a response, the investigator usually intensifies or reduces properties that are already present in the setting. A behavior may need to be amplified either because it is buried amidst other behaviors or because it is held in check by situational constraints. If the behavior is buried, the investigator may try to increase the constraints on the competing behaviors, but if the behavior is constrained he may want to relax the constraints. The investigator will resort to amplification when he has reason to believe that the relevant behavior is already present but is not highly visible. The strategy of evocation will be adopted when there is reason to believe that the behavior is not present but can plausibly be aroused in and be appropriate to a given setting. Thus amplification means an alteration that increases the intensity and detail of a response that is too weak to be scored or to have an effect.

Chapple's (1953) stress interview is an example of an alteration that amplifies. Presumably, in any interview situation the interviewee has inclinations toward persistence, dominance, submissiveness, adaptability, and initiative, even though these responses are not highly visible. To increase the intensity of these responses the interviewer, after 10 minutes of nondirective discussion, attempts to induce stress by essentially remaining silent during the next 15 minutes. The only time he talks is when the interviewee remains silent for 15 seconds and then all he does is spend 5 seconds asking a question (p. 24). Following the silence period there are 5 minutes of normal discussion and then 15 minutes of stress induced by 12 interruptions each lasting about 5 seconds.

Perhaps most surprising and of especial relevance to the present discussion is the fact that these rather marked changes in interviewer behavior are difficult to detect. Matarazzo and Saslow (1961, p. 287) reported that experienced people who listen to the sessions cannot detect the changes and that virtually no interviewee believes that the interviewer's behavior is contrived. Since the standardized interviewer behavior occurs infrequently, this method of data collection is both precise and natural. The interviewer is permitted to discuss whatever topics the interviewee raises, so long as procedural rules are followed. Undoubtedly it is this freedom regarding content that leads participants to conclude that the interview is not contrived.

Studies of mother-child interaction frequently use minor situation changes to amplify incipient responses (for example, Bing, 1963; Sears, 1965). Baumrind's (1967) study of child-rearing antecedents of self-reliance, self-control, and mood involved two quite different means of amplification. First, to produce significant examples of parental control, nurturance, communication, and maturity demands, interaction between parents and children was observed in the home from the period just before dinner until the child's bedtime. This time was chosen because it is a period of maximum interaction and stress (for example, Blood, 1958; Raush, 1959).

The second means of amplification in the Baumrind study occurred in the laboratory. The mothers and children who had been observed at home came to the laboratory to participate in a teaching period and a play period, both of which were observed and coded. During the *teaching period* the mother was to teach the child up to 5 different concepts with the Cuisenaire Rods, but was allowed only 15 minutes to do this. Furthermore, the mother was told that since there were only 15 minutes for the task, the child should not play with any toys in the room, a rule that was difficult to enforce since the child's chair faced the attractive toys. The *play period* lasted 25 minutes and again the situation contained items such as water, attractive magazines, edible foods, art supplies, and a mouse in a cage which were intended to amplify the desired responses.

Barker (1960) has developed one of the more valuable sets of propositions and data (Barker and Gump, 1964) relevant to the issue of amplification. His argument is that any setting contains both obligations and opportunities for participants. The strength of these obligations and opportunities varies as a function of the number of people in the setting. For each setting there is presumed to be an optimal number of persons. If a setting contains fewer persons than the optimum, then the strength of these opportunities and obligations increases. This means that the remaining persons are pressured more intensively in a greater variety of directions. Their tasks become more varied, more difficult, and more important, with the result that fatigue and interfering skills lower the level of maximum performance. Each person does more things, but he does them less well. Because each remaining person is crucial for the maintenance of the setting, persons become more tolerant and less evaluative of each other. In addition, each remaining person feels more responsibility for the outcome and more insecurity because there are fewer "reserves" if he fails to perform his task;

and there are more instances of success and failure. Furthermore, persons in an undermanned setting are evaluated more in terms of what they can do than how attractive or personable they are.

The implications of undermanning for amplification are clear. When inadequate personnel must maintain a setting, they focus more intently on task performance; shifts from one activity to another should be more distinct because the same person must perform different, potentially incompatible actions; shifts in activity should be more frequent because more has to be done; involvement in activities should remain high because dawdling will leave several tasks unperformed; crucial tasks in the setting should be more apparent to participants; actions within the setting should be less obscured by evaluative overtones; and the content of discussions among participants should focus more directly on task performance. In short, participants in an undermanned setting should be more sensitive to its properties and should engage in crucial activities with greater intensity and perseverance than participants in an adequately manned setting.

The chief problems with undermanning are that it is difficult to know what the optimal population of a setting is and, even if this is known, it is difficult to gain a precise view of a phenomenon, since a reduction in size has multiple effects. However, as more is learned about size, these multiple effects can be taken into account more accurately and will produce less confounding of variables. Effort directed toward resolving these issues seems warranted because undermanning is an especially plausible means of modifying natural events. It is commonplace for persons to be absent when an event occurs, and if the event is valued and must occur anyway, the remaining persons will be pressured to preserve the crucial properties of the event.

BEHAVIORS FOR OBSERVATION

Another paradox of observation is that investigators who watch people *in situ* often record only what they hear. Furthermore, they typically "hear" only manifest content. Observational studies have been unduly narrow in the variety of behaviors that are recorded. As a consequence, reliability has suffered, findings are contradicted when other behavioral measures are used, competing explanations are extensive, generality is suspect, and descriptions are ambiguous. If an observer wants to increase precision in his behavioral measures without sacrificing naturalness, he should choose dependent variables that are plausible response measures within the setting, discriminable from other behaviors, easy to observe and score, compatible with other measures, defensible in terms of psychometric canons, sensitive to variations in the independent variables, and valid indicators of psychological processes. Most of these requirements are bypassed in the interest of finding a behavior that is visible. The predominance of prominence as the criterion for choice of behavior in observational research is understandable, given the complexity and multiplicity of responses in most naturalistic settings. However, it is not inevitable that observers must forego other desirable properties of response measures in the interest of visibility. It is argued here that the recording of more varied behaviors and their use as supplementary measures of complex processes can preserve visibility and naturalness, but can also improve other less desirable features of response measures common to observation. The purpose of this section is to detail some of the behaviors that are available for observation. Four general classes of behavior will be surveyed: nonverbal, spatial, extralinguistic, and linguistic. Several varieties of each type of behavior are noted. However, the intent in these discussions is to sample and to point to alternatives that are available. No claim is made that the sample is comprehensive or even representative. Those behaviors that are discussed here have been chosen because they can be detected and recorded in naturalistic settings, because they can be scored with only a small amount of training (this purposely excludes most of the linguistic methods which are described in Chapter 26, in Vol. 3 of this *Handbook*), and because they seem to be related to processes that are of interest to social psychologists.

NONVERBAL BEHAVIOR

Nonverbal behavior, which is defined as "the body movements of the organism . . . [and] . . . consists of motor expressions . . . [which] . . . may originate in various parts of the body" (Ekman, 1957, p. 141), has been perhaps the most active area of recent research that is of importance to observational methodology. Investigators such as Berger (1958), Birdwhistell (1952, 1959, 1961, 1962a, 1962b, in press), Deutsch (1963), Dittmann (1962), Ekman (1965a, 1965b, 1965c, 1965d), Haggard and Isaacs (1966), Hayes (1957), Krout (1935, 1954a, 1954b), Rosenfeld (1965), and Scheflen (1963, 1964, 1966) have shown that body movements are valid indices of psychological processes. Technological advances in the recording and description of bodily movements have also been made and these are represented in the work of Diersen, Lorenc, and Spitaleri (1961), Ellis and Pryer (1959), Jones and Hanson (1961), Jones and Narva (1955), Jones, O'Connell, and Hanson (1958), Lyle (1953), and Sainsbury (1954, 1955). While the apparatus used in these latter studies is often too cumbersome to use in the field, there are suggestions of recording procedures that might be modified for use in the field.

Observers who are accustomed to analyzing speech behavior in naturalistic settings may regard nonverbal actions as a redundant source of information. This point of view neglects the fact that humans spend a very small portion of their interactional time vocalizing (Birdwhistell, "Communication as a Multi-Channel System," in press). It seems that the emphasis in our society on vocal performance, and the large amount of information that is stored in vocalized written words, has tempted investigators to conclude that man is essentially a vocalizing animal and, therefore, his words should be closely attended. Needless to say, it is tautological to state that, because humans use language, language is the most important means of communication. Evidence concerning nonverbal behavior and its relation to verbal acts shows convincingly (Ekman, 1965b, p. 441) that

. . . the classes of information provided by nonverbal behavior can serve to repeat, contradict, or substitute for a verbal message, as well as accent certain words, maintain the communicative flow, reflect changes in the relationship in association with particular verbal messages and indicate a person's feelings about his verbal statement.

Although nonverbal behavior holds promise for observational research because of its visibility, naturalness, and discriminability, it can also be too subtle to record unless the observer has been trained to be sensitive to it. That persons are often unaware of the rich nonverbal language is not surprising, since much of it occurs unconsciously (Scheflen, 1965, p. 34). Jecker *et al.* (1964) found that teachers who were untrained in the analysis of nonverbal behavior could not predict, from filmed facial cues, whether a student had comprehended a lesson in algebra. Prediction improved significantly when verbal cues were added to the film. These results are not especially surprising. Jecker *et al.* directed their observers to use nonverbal cues to detect cognitive rather than affective information. However, it is possible that observers were actually using affective reactions (for example, interest, boredom, pride) to judge comprehension and, therefore, their task was somewhat misleading. They did not focus consistently on the relevant stimuli. Furthermore, the intensity of nonverbal reactions is apt to be reduced in an instructional setting where a motion picture camera is prominent. Finally, the judges themselves, because they are ideationally oriented, may be relatively insensitive to nonverbal cues (Taft, 1955). Despite these drawbacks, Jecker, Maccoby, and Breitrose (1965) were able, with only eight hours of training, to improve significantly the ability of teachers to detect comprehension from nonverbal cues. Ekman (1965d) has demonstrated that untrained observers can judge both personality and affect from nonverbal behavior depicted in rapid still or motion picture film records. It seems clear that general unawareness of nonverbal activities is not a serious drawback to their use as significant data in observational studies.

Three classes of nonverbal behavior relevant to observational methodology are reviewed in the following section: facial expressions; exchanged glances; and body movement, including gestures.

Facial expressions

Tomkins (1962) described the face as the "primary site of affect" and suggested the following in partial support of this view (pp. 207, 210–212):

The head and face not only precede the other parts of the body in development, but continue to dominate other parts of the body by virtue of the relative density of receptor-effector units in the face. . . . The centrality of the face in affective experience may also be seen in the relationship between the hand and the face. The hand acts as if the face is the site of feeling. . . . It is our argument that human beings slap, hide, stimulate, support, caress, inhibit, or reassure their faces with their hands because they correctly localize the face as the primary site of their concern.

Facial features have been found to distinguish between feelings of pleasantness and unpleasantness (Ekman, 1965b), to show changes in stress during childbirth (Leventhal and Sharp, 1965), to differentiate between students who comprehend what a teacher says and those who do not (Jecker, Maccoby, and Breitrose, 1965), to reflect changes in conflict during psychotherapy (Haggard and Isaacs, 1966), to distinguish between degrees of attentiveness and tension (Ponder and Kennedy, 1927), and to permit more accurate predictions of emotion than do vocalizations (Levitt, 1964). In addition, there appears to be support for the conclusion that the upper half of the face provides reliable cues for discriminating negative emotions, whereas the lower half of the face provides more cues for discriminating positive emotions (for example, Coleman, 1949; Hanawalt, 1944; Leventhal and Sharp, 1965). Finally, Ekman's (1965c) data suggest that head and facial cues communicate information about the type of affect the person is experiencing, whereas body position gives information about the level of arousal or intensity of the emotion; exceptions are that the hands can provide information akin to that provided by the face, and head movements can provide information akin to that provided by the body.

Even so slight a facial action as an eyeblink, which after all *can* be scored in natural settings, can be a source of valuable information. Ponder and Kennedy (1927), in an engaging series of laboratory and field studies, examined several parameters of blinking. They found that blinking typically is best described by a J-curve with the most common interblink interval ranging between 0.5 and 2 seconds. This interval, however, is very sensitive to changes in the person and the environment. As the subject's attention shifts, so also does the blink rate. Ponder and Kennedy noted that "excitement of any sort is usually accompanied by a marked reduction in the length of the interblink periods, provided, so far as we have been able to find, that the excitement is not associated with any sufficient outlet" (p. 103). For example, it was found that witnesses in jury trials blinked more rapidly when they were cross-examined than when they gave their initial testimony. Men in library reading rooms blinked less frequently (one blink every 11.2 seconds) than did women (one blink every 6.7 seconds), presumably because the attention of women was less directed toward reading. On streetcars, however, women were less attentive than men to surrounding events and, therefore, had longer interblink intervals. Ponder and Kennedy concluded that blinking is not reflexive, that it decreases in rate when the "mind is blank" or when mental activity is "internally directed" (for example, in solving a mathematics problem), and that "a state of mental tension which has no internal or external outlet, as impotent rage, anxiety necessarily accompanied by inactivity, or excitement which cannot be shown and expressed by physical movements, is accompanied by a rapid blinking rate" (p. 108).

A significant innovation in the study of faces is represented in the work of Haggard and Isaacs (1966) on micromomentary expressions (MME). An MME is a change in facial expression that is literally quicker than the eye. Such changes are detectable only when motion picture films of faces, made at the

TABLE 1

SYMBOLS USED TO SCORE FACIAL EXPRESSIONS (FROM LEVENTHAL AND SHARP, 1965)

Symbol	Meaning
	Forehead
	Comfort
——	1. Smooth (permanent thin wrinkles may or may not be present)
≋	2. Horizontal creases or folds (wrinkled) extend across forehead
	Discomfort
— ≋ —	3. Horizontal creases or folds in middle, smooth on either side
○ ⊞ 0	4. Horizontal depression, grated effect, or vertical depression
	Brow
	Comfort
— —	1. Brows horizontal, no ridge or depression between or over either brow
— ⌒	2. One brow raised
⌄⌄⌄ ⌄⌄⌄	3. Slight fluttering (up and down) of one or both brows
⌒ ⌒	4. Both brows raised
	Minor discomfort
⌣ ⌣	5. Depressions over one or both eyebrows
⋰⋱ ⋰⋱	6. Fluttering of brows leading to occasional V formation
	Major discomfort
\ /	7. Medial approximation of brows with clear V formation
\ₛ /ₛ	8. V formation between brows and depression over one or both brows
	Eyelids
	Comfort (normal state)
≡ ≡	1. Lids motionless except for normal blinks, no creases in upper lid if eye closed
	Discomfort
≋ ≋	2. Fluttering (up and down movement) of upper lids
⨯ ⨯	3. Creases in upper lids occur without movement
⨯⨯ ξ ≈≈	4. Both (2) and (3) occur simultaneously
≡ ≡	5. Eyes closed with exaggerated creases of upper lids and creases surrounding eye
≡ ≡	6. Opening and closing occurs at high rates

normal speed of 24 frames per second, are slowed to 1/6 of their normal speed (4 fps). When films are slowed and observers record changes in facial muscles, up to $2\frac{1}{2}$ times *more* expression changes are detected than when the film runs at the normal speed. A smile may change to a grimace and back to a smile within 1/8 second. The range of expression changes at normal film speed during filmed therapy sessions was from 5–27, whereas a range of 38–91 expression changes was observed at slow speed. Although work with MME's is sufficiently new that correlates of these changes are unclear, Haggard and Isaacs noted these properties of MME's: they occur in "bursts"; they occur during periods of general expressiveness and discussions of affective content; they are associated with denial statements or verbal blocking; and they recur with certain manifest content such as statements of cathexis.

Examples of category systems to encode facial expressions are found in Jecker, Maccoby, and Breitrose (1965, p. 241) and in Leventhal and Sharp (1965, p. 300). The system used by Leventhal and Sharp is reproduced in Table 1 to exemplify their categories and also to point out the value of "visual" reminders for the observer who must remain attentive both to the subtle distinctions in the category and to the object of observation. It is valuable to note the observational schedule used by Leventhal and Sharp, because it indicates the care that must be taken to get accurate records of fleeting facial cues. Women in labor were observed for 20 minutes every 2 hours. During the 20-minute period the observer spent 5 minutes each recording activity of the (1) forehead and brow, (2) eyes, eyelids, and eyeballs, (3) mouth, and (4) nose. During each 5-minute period that she observed a portion of the face, the observer watched for 5 seconds, recorded for 10 seconds, watched for 5, recorded for 10, and so on. It was found that the forehead, brow, and eyelid were sensitive indices of stress, whereas the mouth, nose, and other movements of the eyes were not.

In conclusion, it seems clear that facial changes are visible, that they relate to important psychological processes, and that they can be recorded with little distraction to the subject *if* there is a plausible reason why someone would be looking at the subject anyway (for example, spectator in a courtroom, passenger on a streetcar, therapist).

Exchanged glances

If an observer can position himself so that he can tell when two people look directly into each other's eyes, he may be able to obtain valuable indices of comfort and discomfort. A series of studies by Exline and his associates (Exline, 1963; Exline, Gray, and Schuette, 1965; Exline and Winters, 1965) presents important evidence that the exchange of mutual glances may be a sign of affective relationships among persons. When highly affiliative people are placed in situations where competitive and nonaffiliative behavior is required, mutual glances decline (Exline, 1963). On the assumption that visual avoidance helps persons to conceal affective information, Exline, Gray, and Schuette (1965) demonstrated that subjects exchange glances less with an interviewer who asks embarrassing questions than with one who asks innocuous questions. Subjects who were soundly criticized by an interviewer after first talking with him about leisure-time interests decreased their eye contact significantly more than did persons who were praised (Exline and Winters, 1965). Finally, subjects whose written stories were judged by two evaluators and who privately chose which evaluator they liked best halfway through the experiment exchanged more glances with the preferred evaluator and fewer with the unchosen partner (Exline and Winters, 1965). However, this was true more for females than males, and was also more evident when females were talking than when they were listening.

There are several aspects of these studies which suggest that care should be exercised in using this measure. One-way mirrors in the laboratory enable observers to be in an ideal position to score exchanged glances (Exline, 1963, p. 8), and in some instances, scoring is aided further because one member of the dyad is a stooge and stares steadily at the other person (Exline, Gray, and Schuette, 1965). To set up ideal conditions for field observation of exchanged glances may require rather sizable changes of natural settings. As noted earlier, there are marked sex differences in the use of exchanged glances. Women exchange more glances with members of their own sex than men do, and this is true whether they are talking or listening. The variance in eye-contact measures can be considerable (Friedman, 1964, pp. 119–120). Exline and Winters (1965) reported that 5 of their 14 males spent only 15 of 300 seconds looking at the male interviewer (p. 343). There is also the suggestion that situations may have different norms for eye contact. In a three-man group discussion with peers, only 5 percent of the time was spent in mutual glances (Exline, 1963), whereas about 47 percent of the time was spent in mutual glances in interview situations (Exline, Gray, and Schuette, 1965; Exline and Winters, 1965).

Despite these problems, the measure seems to be a promising one. Friedman, Kurland, and Rosenthal (1965) have found that one of the most potent predictors of experimenter effects (different experimenters obtaining different data from comparable subjects) is the number of exchanged glances during the instruction period. It appears that an exchange of glance generates a "positive feeling tone" which generalizes to ratings made by the subjects (Friedman, 1964, p. 35). Furthermore, Exline *et al.* (1961) found that highly Machiavellian subjects who cheated and were implicated maintained more eye contact with their accuser while denying the act than did persons with less Machiavellian dispositions.

Body movements

Significant nonverbal behaviors are not confined to the head and face. They occur with great frequency in other bodily areas, especially the hands. Several recent advances have been made in the conceptualization and description of bodily movements; the purpose of this section is to review some of these advances. Spiegel and Machotka (1965) suggested that "body movements are made for the purpose of performing some action, expressing some feeling, or making a gesture which has ritual, conventional or natural meaning" (p. 4). The fact that body movements are made for the purposes of both performance and expression is crucial for observation. Allport (1961) has clarified this distinction in his comparison of coping and expressive behavior (p. 463). Coping involves task activity and is the "what" of behavior. Expressive behavior is concerned with the "how" of behavior, the manner in which adaptive acts are performed. Allport makes the important point that as the coping component in behavior increases, the expressive component declines. If an observer watches persons who are performing a structured task, it is unlikely that he will see many expressive acts, and even if he does, they will assume a limited number of forms. This point, incidentally, underscores the close relationship between a choice of setting and a choice of behavior.

Nontask behaviors can be observed more readily when the subject has some latitude in what he is doing. For example, suppose an observer wanted to test the hypothesis that properties of gait (for example, regularity, speed, pressure, length of stride, elasticity, definiteness of direction, variability) are affected significantly by the amount of ambiguity in a situation. If he chose to observe differences in gait in an office setting where workers are moving from one desk to another in order to transact familiar or unfamiliar business, he might find fewer variations in the dependent measures than if he observed the movements of travelers in familiar and unfamiliar railroad stations, if he watched persons entering hospitals to admit a person or take home someone who is discharged, or if he observed faculty members entering a party at which they were recruiting or being recruited. Although these latter examples all involve some task, the task is not so prominent and this lesser prominence allows more variation to occur. As an aside, it should be noted that, even though expressive behaviors are commonly assumed to be more sensitive to personality characteristics than to situational variables, much of the recent work with these behaviors shows that this restriction is unnecessary. Changes in posture clearly distinguish among situations (for example, Werner and Wapner, 1953) as well as among persons (for example, Mahl, Danet, and Norton, 1959).

Sets of categories to encode body movements have been developed by Birdwhistell (1952), Ekman (1965a), R. Katz (1964), Krout (1954b, pp. 96–99), and Spiegel and Machotka (1965). The categories of foot, head, and hand movements developed by Ekman (1965a) to analyze the actions of mental patients at various stages of hospitalization are representative. The hand acts, of which Ekman has distinguished more than 100, appear to be especially sensitive to changes in the patient. The following interpretation of the hand acts of a newly admitted patient illustrates the kind of information encoded by Ekman (p. 36):

At admission the patient's hand acts convey a nervous agitation (Clothing Play, $N = 5$ and Chair Arm Rub, $N = 37$), immersed in a context of seeking contact and reassurance from herself (Chair Arm Rubs, $N = 37$); she wishes to support or lean on herself (Hand to Temple, $N = 4$, and Hand to Side of Face, $N = 2$), wishes to get rid of things which bother her (Hand Cover Mouth, $N = 1$), has intense feelings of frustrated helplessness (Hand Shrug Rotation, $N = 14$), feelings of angry frustration (Hand Wave Bang, $N = 5$), and becomes ashamed of her anguish and anger (Hand Eye Cover, $N = 4$).

While these interpretations may appear to be simply *post hoc* analyses, it is important to note that most of these interpretations are supported by independent studies in which certain acts (for example, Hand Wave Bang, Hand Shrug Rotation) were left in or edited from films of the patient and comparisons were made of ways in which judgments of the patient changed as a function of the kind of gestures observed by the rater. For example, when the films contained "bangs" and "shrugs," the patient was rated as significantly more argumentative, demanding, irritable, opinionated, stern, impatient, and resentful than when these acts were not present. That these gestures convey rather specific information is indicated by the fact that adjectives such as anxious, confused, nervous, worrying, deliberate, tense, awkward, and dissatisfied did not distinguish among the films.

Attempts to conceptualize body movements have been infrequent, but one of the more interesting efforts is represented in the work of Scheflen (1963, 1964, 1965, 1966). He argued that kinesic activities serve mainly to regulate and pace interpersonal relationships, especially interpersonal distance. Kinesic movements provide data about the other participants and about the state of the relationship. Of especial interest are postural actions of inclusion versus noninclusion, and congruence versus noncongruence. Inclusion-noninclusion refers to the use of bodies and extremities to define group membership. For example, "if they are located in a line, the members at each end turn inward and extend an arm or leg across the open space as if to limit access in or out of the group. This effect we call 'bookending' " (1964, p. 326). If relationships become too inclusive or close, it is common to find that persons turn away from one another, cross their legs, put their hands over the side of their face, or lean backwards. Congruence refers to whether persons who interact with one another in a face-to-face relationship hold their bodies in the same position. Congruence can assume two forms, direct (for example, each person has his head tilted to his own right) or mirror-imaged (for example, one person has his head tilted to the right and the other to the left, but to a third observer both heads look tilted in the same direction). It is assumed that persons maintain postural congruence with those whom they like and maintain incongruence with those whom they dislike. In addition, an incongruent posture may be a means to establish status distinctions (1964, p. 329).

It seems clear that bodily movements other than those directly associated with task accomplishment can be an important source of data in observational studies. Although these movements are sometimes difficult to detect and assume a variety of forms, they also tend to be patterned and repeated. This means that observers who have had some practice can detect movements quickly.

SPATIAL BEHAVIOR

People are active. They mill, move towards, move away from, linger, wander, dart, maintain closeness, maintain distance, or show any one of a number of attempts to structure the space around them. The frequency and range of these movements, as well as their outcomes (for example, cliques), are easily observed yet seldom recorded. One reason may be that they are so obvious. Whyte (1959, p. 48) said of the method of recording spatial relations and movement:

the method is on the lowest level of abstraction and deals with what are commonly thought of as "superficial" aspects of behavior . . . [For someone who wants to study what persons think and feel] the process of writing down names and charting spatial arrangements of people seems a mechanical operation of no real interest.

There is a growing body of literature which demonstrates that spatial behavior is a significant datum. Hall (1963a) has described the field of proxemics as the study of "man's need to lay claim to and organize territory, as well as to maintain a pattern of discrete distances from one's fellows" (p. 422). A set of concepts about the meaning of distances between persons has been developed (Hall, 1964), as well as an explicit and meaningful system of notation to record proxemic behavior in the field (1963b). Recently, Hall (1966) has developed a more comprehensive view of the field of proxemics in an engaging book which reviews the extensive literature concerning the use of space by animals, the physiology of overcrowding and spatial perception, cross-cultural comparisons of spatial relationships, and architectural implications of research on space. From this review there emerges the clear implication that space is structured with surprising regularity and that, when spatial boundaries are violated, significant changes in behavior occur. Other discussions of spatial behavior include those by Esser *et al.* (1965), Hare and Bales (1963), Hazard (1962), Little (1965), Rosenfeld (1965), Sommer (1959, 1961, 1962), Sommer and Ross (1958), Strauss (1952), Thomas (1929), Werner and Wapner (1953), and Winick and Holt (1961).

Hall's (1964) discussion of distances between persons exemplifies the use of data concerning spatial relations. Distance is treated both as a dependent variable (the more positive the relationship, the closer people will stand) and as an independent variable (as distance varies, so does the information that is learned about another). Hall distinguished among four distances, each of which has a near phase and a far phase: intimate (full contact to 18 inches), casual-personal (18 to 48 inches), social-consultative (4 feet to 12 feet), and public (12 feet to maximum carrying distance of the voice).

The basis on which these particular boundaries were chosen is intriguing as well as plausible (p. 45):

The perception of distance and closeness apparently is the result of an interplay of the distant and immediate receptor systems (visual, auditory, olfactory), the systems in the skin that record touch and heat flow and those in the muscles that feed back information concerning where a part of the body is at any given time. *The transition from one group of receptors to another is the boundary point between distance sets.*

Thus, as persons move closer to or farther from someone else, variables such as these change: clarity of facial detail, possibility of touch, loudness of voice, area of sharp vision, prominence of heat and odor cues, ability to see eyes and mouth in one glance, area covered by peripheral vision (person only or person-in-setting), amount of sensory input, and visual distortion of facial features. At each of the boundary points, several of these cues change, as do the conclusions that persons draw. Thus, accurate descriptions of distance give information about the cues that people exchange and about the quality and content of the relationship. Distance sets may also suggest the presence of incongruities, as when formal conversation is uttered at the intimate distance of 30 inches.

A slightly different approach to the study of spatial behavior is to observe ways in which organisms lay claim to and defend space (see Lyman and Scott, 1967). Even though the phenomenon of territoriality has been demonstrated repeatedly in studies of animal behavior (Carpenter, 1958), few attempts have been made to observe a similar phenomenon in humans. Esser *et al.* (1965) have recently begun to study the ways in which mental patients use territory. They drew a grid on the floor of a research ward and, every half-hour, recorded for each patient the square on which he was standing, his postural position, and the direction in which he was facing. Each patient was observed 330 times. If the patient was seen in a specific area for at least 1/3 of these observations, and if he spent more than 75 percent of this time on a specific square, he was said to possess territory. When the use of territory was correlated with dominance in the ward, it was found that the most dominant third of the patients were free-ranging and did not establish territory, that the middle third established territory, but in areas where they would have maximum contact with other patients and staff, and the lower third in dominance established clearly defined territory in a secluded spot. It was also found that most persons who had a defined territory were most aggressive toward other patients when this territory was violated.

A final example of spatial behavior is conversational clustering. If a person wants to talk to another person, he has to move within conversational distance of this person, and if he does not wish to have his comments overheard, he must move even closer. These movements are visible and a record of who talks to whom can be a surprisingly rich source of data, as is shown in Alger's (1966) observation of interaction among delegates in the Administrative and Budgetary Committee of the United Nations General Assembly. This committee has 110 member nations whose delegates are seated in alphabetical order around two large horseshoes. Alger observed 69 of the 70 meetings of this committee during the fall of 1962 from the front row of the press section (located 10 feet from the outside ring of the horseshoe). During these 137 hours of observation he recorded the length of public speeches, number of persons in attendance, participants in private conversations, length of private conversations, and the name of the initiator of the private conversation. In all, 3475 private interactions were recorded.

Although Alger reported numerous findings of interest, perhaps the most important is the fact that records of private interaction gave a different view of committee actions than did records of participation in public debate (for example, number of speeches, resolution sponsorship, attendance at meetings). Although the number of speeches correlated 0.70 with the number of private interactions, there were several delegations whose interaction rate was strikingly out of line with the number of speeches they gave. Furthermore, it was found that there was a consistently higher correlation between number of interactions and number of men in delegation, amount of U.N. support, and GNP of nation (a measure of power) than there was between number of public speeches and these same measures. Thus, interaction records are not redundant with records of public speaking activity, and they provide a different view of what occurs in the committee.

EXTRALINGUISTIC BEHAVIOR

When a person says something, the words or linguistic content actually constitute a relatively small portion of the verbal behavior which the alert observer can record. These noncontent behaviors are significant indices of psychological processes; consequently, the observer should consider them carefully when choosing the behaviors to record. Required reading for the observer who is considering the use of extralinguistic measures should be the definitive review of this area by Mahl and Schulze (1964). Application of extralinguistic and linguistic measures is well illustrated in the analysis of Pittenger, Hockett, and Danehy (1960) of five minutes of a single patient-therapist interview.

An initial word of caution is necessary. Extralinguistic behavior varies in subtle ways and generally requires sensitive apparatus or a well-trained observer if it is to be recorded accurately. In some naturalistic settings it will probably be impossible to secure some extralinguistic measures because of noise, simultaneous speech, whispering, etc. Despite these limitations, extralinguistic measures are discussed here because it may be possible for innovative observers to adapt the coding systems or the technology used in this area to suit the somewhat more demanding requirements of the field. Most of these measures seem to be of sufficient promise that effort devoted to field adaptation will not be wasted. Furthermore, many of these measures can be scored from tape recordings which observers can often obtain readily.

While there are numerous ways to classify linguistic methods (for example, Osgood, 1963; Trager, 1958), the distinctions suggested by Mahl (1957) seem adequate to convey an idea of the various indices that are available. He suggested that there are four dimensions: *vocal* (for example, pitch, loudness, timbre), *temporal* (for example, rate of speaking, duration of utterance, rhythm), *interaction* (for example, tendencies to interrupt, dominate, inhibit), and *verbal-stylistic* (for example, vocabulary and pronunciation peculiarities, dialect, characteristic expressions). Of these, the present discussion will dwell briefly on vocal quality and slightly more on temporal dimensions and continuity. Again, these dimensions, with the possible exception of quality, have been chosen because they relate to psychological processes and because they can be detected and recorded on location.

Vocal dimensions

Vocal characteristics such as pitch, loudness, and timbre have generally been neglected in psychological research, but they seem to be potentially sensitive indicators of underlying processes. Allport (1961, pp. 482–483) remarked:

untrained voices vary widely in pitch, timbre, and mannerism. Voice, therefore, especially if it is untrained, is a highly expressive instrument. *Speech,* by contrast, is concerned largely with coping. . . . Our speech is composed of conventional words, words put together according to rules of syntax, and directed toward purposive communication.

Since the development of the voice spectrometer (Hargreaves and Starkweather, 1963), it has been possible to record variations in vocal behavior with greater accuracy. This instrument encodes the power spectrum of the voice and provides a continuous record of the prominence in the voice of the fundamental pitch as well as higher overtones. In addition, recent modifications of the system permit the encoding of loudness variability. The type of information provided by the spectrometer is suggested by the following description of vocal behavior found in several depressed patients. They "showed a depressed voice, reduced in loudness and often lacking in high overtones, giving their voice a dull, lifeless quality with diminished inflection" (Hargreaves, Starkweather, and Blacker, 1965, p. 220).

The potential significance of pitch measures lies in the fact that they may be accurate indices of emotional states, especially pitches below 500 cps (Soskin, 1953; Soskin and Kauffman, 1954, 1961; Soskin, Kauffman, and Katz, 1955). Mahl (1959, 1964) suggested that the general pitch level at which one speaks is unimportant in the English language, persons receive little explicit training in it, therefore, it may be more sensitive to drive states. Soskin and Kauffman (1961) found that, even when semantic content was filtered out of speech, judges could infer beyond chance level the emotional state of the speaker, especially when the remaining vocal cues were between 100 and 550 cps.

Temporal dimensions

Persons make demands on time as well as on space. These time demands are accessible as well as patterned and, therefore, they provide valuable data *in situ*.

The use of time patterns to provide a structural analysis of talk has been extensive and it is difficult even to suggest the several uses that have been made of these measures. As a result of Chapple's (1939) initial discussion of the importance of timing in interaction, his subsequent development of the interaction chronograph (1949) and the stress interview to assess interaction characteristics (1953), and the application of these methods to the assessment of personality (Chapple *et al.,* 1960) and social systems (1962), investigators have been concerned with such temporal variables as duration (for example, Hargreaves, 1960), speech rate (for example, Goldman-Eisler, 1958), hesitations (for example, Maclay and Osgood, 1959), silence (for example, Matarazzo, Hess, and Saslow, 1962), synchronization (for example, Matarazzo and Saslow, 1961), and latency (for example, Krause, 1961). Advances have also been made in instrumenting the analysis of time scores (for example, Cassota, Jaffe, Feldstein, and Moses, 1964; Kasl and Mahl, 1956; Starkweather, 1960; Verzeano and Finesinger, 1949; Wiens, Matarazzo, and Saslow, 1965).

Two of the major systems, the Interaction Recorder (Wiens, Matarazzo, and Saslow, 1965) and the Automatic Vocal Transaction Analyzer (Cassota, Jaffe, Feldstein, and Moses, 1964) are alike in that they produce records of the amount of time that is spent by each participant in talk and silence, but they differ in the need for a human observer to mediate between the occurrence of the vocal behavior and the recording of the behavior. The Interaction Recorder requires an observer to press a switch when a person is talking and to release it when he quits. These tabulations are recorded on a paper tape which is then fed directly into a computer for immediate analysis. Because an observer must judge when a person has finished a remark and is not just hesitating or blocked, some inference is required. The AVTA system, however, is noninferential. It does not require the presence of an observer. In the AVTA system the voice of each participant in a dialogue is confined to one channel of a twin-track audio tape. AVTA samples simultaneously, at a rate of 200 times per minute, the presence and absence of each participant's speech, and records the sound-silence sequences directly on IBM punch cards such that each punched column represents a 300-msec interval during which speech was detected, while each unpunched column represents a 300-msec interval of silence. The AVTA system also records intensity fluctuations in the conversations. Commercial devices such as the Sequential Time Interval Measurement System manufactured by Iconix Inc. can also be adapted to the instrumentation of time recording. The STIMS apparatus accepts events such as key presses that are extended over time and records the time of each press on digital magnetic tape.

Because of the variety of time measures used, as well as the complex analyses that have been applied to several of them, it is difficult to find summaries that cover more than selected problems. However, there are several important reviews that fit the latter classification. The most extensive research that deals directly with the concepts proposed by Chapple has been the program conducted by Matarazzo, Saslow, and their associates. A lucid summary of the findings of this program is found in Matarazzo, Wiens, and Saslow (1965), and earlier papers present detailed descriptions of the methodology (Matarazzo, Saslow, and Matarazzo, 1956; Saslow and Matarazzo, 1959) as well as important comparative data on normals and deviants (Matarazzo and Saslow, 1961). While the extensive work of Goldman-Eisler has not been summarized in any one paper, her discussion of ways to discriminate the occurrence of various mental processes from subtle changes in speech behavior is both stimulating and representative (1958). Soskin and John's (1963) study of the spontaneous speech behavior of a married couple used several time measures and affords an opportunity to examine the relationship between measures of content and measures of duration (also discussed by Goldman-Eisler, 1961; Matarazzo, Weitman, and Saslow, 1963).

Among the gross time measures that have been used are "filled time," latency, and duration. "Filled time," or the available time that is used for talking measures speech density (Matarazzo, Wiens, and Saslow, 1965, p. 206) or demand for talking (Soskin and John, 1963, p. 251). This measure distinguishes among therapist styles, situations, and small and large groups. Matarazzo, Wiens, and Saslow (1965) distinguish two types of latency: reaction time and initiative time. Reaction time is the interval between the time that one person stops talking and the other one starts. Initiative time is measured as the time that lapses when one person stops talking, the other person says nothing, and the first person resumes. Duration of single utterances has been shown repeatedly to be a mirror-imaged J-curve (for example, Hargreaves, 1960). Soskin and John (1963, p. 261) reported that the average unit length of spontaneous speech increases as the size of the group increases. Kanfer (1960) reported a significant decline in words per minute uttered by female psychiatric patients when they talked about relations with the opposite sex instead of their present illness. However, duration did not distinguish among content topics for normals (Kanfer, 1959). Matarazzo, Wiens, and Saslow (1965) found that the mean length of an interviewee utterance is 26.54 seconds but that there is considerable variability around this value ($SD = 23.81$). When two persons talk, a distinct lengthening or shortening of one person's remarks affects the production of the other person (Matarazzo, Hess, and Saslow, 1962). This holds true in situations as different as a patient-therapist dyad (Matarazzo, Weitman, Saslow, and Wiens, 1963) and a ground communicator talking to an astronaut (Matarazzo *et al.,* 1964). The influenceability of verbal output suggests the importance of establishing baselines and also of using caution when comparing output across groups.

The various interaction patterns that can be distinguished in a dyad simply by using time measures are shown in Fig. 1. It can be seen that scoring consists of noting the beginning, endings, and durations of behavior. Even though temporal patterns can be analyzed in several ways (for example, number of times interviewee acted, average duration of each action plus/minus duration of the following inaction), Matarazzo, Saslow, and Hare (1958) found that if the interaction variables were factor-analyzed, the average duration of an interviewee's silence and the average duration of the interviewee's utterances accounted for most of the variance in interaction behavior.

Continuity

The continuity of speech is often disrupted by hesitations, interruptions, and errors, and these disruptions may signal underlying stress, as when students give public speeches (Levin *et al.,* 1960) or talk about personal problems rather than factual issues (Feldstein, Brenner, and Jaffe, 1963). Although disturbances of continuity have not been so extensively examined as have temporal variables, those data that have been obtained are suggestive.

Interruptions occur often enough and are sufficiently visible to qualify as potential measures in observational research. Mishler and Waxler (1966) have recorded the number of interruptions that occur when members of families of schizophrenics interact. It is assumed that schizophrenia may be prompted by

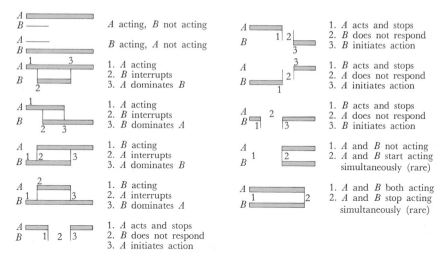

Fig. 1. Twelve temporal patternings of dyadic interaction. (From Chapple, 1962.)

fragmented, disjointed communication that has little continuity or meaning. Mishler and Waxler recorded both attempted interruptions and successful interruptions (the interrupted person stops before he has completed his idea). The data suggest that families of acute schizophrenic patients have the fewest interruptions and families of normal children have the most interruptions, with chronic patient families falling in between. Also, each of the members within these families tends to follow the family's "norm." No family type is consistently more successful in interrupting than any other. Thus the discontinuity indicated by higher rates of interruptions is associated with normal families, contrary to theoretical predictions.

Perhaps the best-known measure of disruptions in continuity is the Speech Disturbance Ratio or the "non-ah Ratio" proposed by Mahl (1956). This measure consists of seven speech-disturbance categories—sentence change, repetition, stutter, omission, sentence incompletion, tongue slips, intruding incoherent sound—that are summed and divided by the number of words spoken by the subject. The speech-disturbance ratio is assumed to be a valuable indicator of psychological states because disturbances are frequent (one occurs every 4.6 seconds or every 16 words), individual differences are apparent, and disturbances escape awareness (Mahl, 1959). Data concerning the incidence of these disturbances in several populations have been published (Kasl and Mahl, 1965, p. 426) as well as an example of the coding of an actual transcript (Mahl, 1956, p. 3). Mahl proposed that the speech-disturbance measure might be a useful measure of anxiety on the grounds that (1) speech is a fairly coordinated behavior liable to disruption by anxiety and (2) anxiety is more likely to affect the nonlexical than the lexical properties of speech. A series of clinical and experimental studies has strongly suggested that the measure does indicate differences in both situational and dispositional anxiety (Kasl and Mahl, 1965; Mahl, 1956, 1959, 1961; Zimbardo, Mahl, and Barnard, 1963). In two studies, there was little relationship between the frequency of speech disturbances and the kind of concurrent, emotional verbal content (Mahl, 1957; Schulze, Mahl, and Murray, 1960). The measure is referred to as the "non-ah" ratio whenever the tabulation of disturbances excludes a count of words such as "ah," "eh," "uhm," "uh," and so on. These words were found to have little relation to anxiety, but instead were found to indicate either that a speaker is deliberating and planning a sentence without sacrificing fluency or he is informing a listener that a message is forthcoming and no interruptions should occur (Mahl, 1958). Thus, there are more "ah's" expressed in phone conversation than in face-to-face conversation because there are fewer cues about communication intent in the former situation.

A provocative study of the vocal patterning of emotional expressions by Feldstein (1964) suggests that speech disturbances may distinguish among the affects of hate, anger, depression, sadness, joy, fear, nervousness, and neutral as in conversation. Data were collected by having 15 actors and 15 actresses read onto tape a standard passage to express each of the eight emotions. The readings could be repeated until the performers were satisfied with the outcome. The greatest number of disturbances was found in expressions of nervousness, next most in fear, and the fewest disturbances were found in the expression of hate and anger. Conversational expression had about the same number of disturbances as did depression and sadness.

Many of the preceding measures of continuity are commonly regarded as measures suitable for content analysis. They have been included in the present discussion because they can be scored in the field, and also because they appear to reflect variables that are often examined in observational studies. The measures, however, are by no means perfected.

LINGUISTIC BEHAVIOR

The behavior most frequently "observed" when people are studied *in situ* is talking. Even though some category systems encode structural characteristics of talk such as time, it is more common for manifest content to be recorded. This section describes four category systems to encode content.

While there have been several systems of categories developed within the past few years to encode social interaction (for example, Argyris, 1965; Baumrind, 1964; Dyck, 1963; Flanders, 1960; Gellert, 1961; Hoffman and Maier, 1964; E. W. Katz, 1964; Longabaugh, 1963; Medley and Smith, 1964; Mills, 1964; Perkins, 1964; Purcell and Brady, 1965; Schoggen, 1963; Watson and Potter, 1962), many of these are confined to specific problems and do not have general relevance. The four systems to be noted below can be applied to a variety of social interactions and they are topic-free.

The first method to be discussed, *Interaction Process Analysis* (IPA) (Bales, 1950), is the best-known category system and has recently been incorporated into a more general diagnostic system (Bales, in press) which promises to contribute substantially to the usefulness of the method. The next system to be summarized is the *Interaction Process Scores* (IPS) system (Borgatta, 1961, 1962, 1963b), which is a proposed refinement and expansion of IPA. The method of *Member-Leader Analysis* (Mann, 1967) is of interest because it was derived from analysis of long-term, self-analytic groups that were less centered on a single task than groups studied with IPA and IPS. The *Behavior Scores System* (Borgatta, 1963a) is of interest because of its grounding in the factor-analytic structure of peer assessments.

Interaction Process Analysis

The diagnostic system recently developed to supplement IPA is based on factor-analytic studies of peer assessments, content analysis of value statements, personality tests, and observations of interaction. A certain three-factor space has turned up repeatedly in studies of these areas by various investigators. Bales has called this space a Social-Psychological Evaluative space. He hypothesized that the evaluations persons make of other persons and their acts involve three dimensions: one of power, one of affection, and one of conformity to group norms which call for contribution to group tasks. These dimensions are orthogonal and represent an evaluative space. The following spatial metaphor is suggested as an aid to memory and visualization: an increase in power of the person may be thought of as upward movement, a decrease as downward; an increase in liking of the person, or affectionate feeling for him, may be thought of as a movement to the right (called positive), and the opposite, an increase in dislike of him, may be thought of as a movement to the left (called negative). Finally, an increase in his contribution to group tasks may be thought of as movement forward, and the opposite, interference with group tasks, may be thought of as movement backward.

Tendencies of a person to rate high or low on each of the 12 interaction categories in Bales's original system may be translated into their implication for the way other persons are likely to locate him in the evaluative space. For example, if a person is low on initiating opinion, low on receiving disagreement, and low on receiving antagonism, he most resembles persons described as downward (compliant), positive (likable), and backward (nonachieving) (Bales, in press, Appendix 1). The directions can be used to characterize evaluations made of persons with differing roles and status positions in the group (pp. 17–21) and to characterize the general direction of movement of the group as a whole, considered as a system. For example, it is proposed that one common pattern of phase movement in the attempt to reach a group decision unfolds in this way: Initially the group starts out on the positive side of the space with pleasantries; then it moves downward as the members concentrate on exchange of information in preparation for the decision-making task, from there moving forward and upward as they concentrate on opinion and analysis, and so on upward and negative as disagreements predominate over agreements. If agreement is reached, the group average tends to move on toward the upward-backward direction as joking sets in, and from there it moves downward-backward as laughing increases and the tension subsides, from whence it moves on toward the positive side approximately back to the starting point, in preparation for another cycle. It is clear that a more graphic view of process may emerge from tracing its changes in direction of movement within the social-psychological evaluative space.

Interaction Process Scores

Even though IPA has had surprising longevity and value, it is not without limitations. A common objection (for example, Longabaugh, 1963, p. 324) is that the categories blur too many distinctions and lump too many modalities into a single category. Borgatta (1962) subdivided and reorganized the system to meet some of these objections. He had two specific aims. One was to permit greater discrimination of intensity. Therefore, some of the crucial categories in the original system were split into two categories, one for a minimum response and one for an active response. The second change was to differentiate categories in which the obscuring of differences was most noticeable, for example, IPA 5 "gives opinion."

The revised IPS categories are listed below (Borgatta, 1962, p. 279). The numbers in parentheses indicate the major relationships to definitions in the original IPA system (Bales, 1950, pp. 177–195).

01 Common social acknowledgments (1a)
02 Shows solidarity through raising the status of others (1b)
03 Shows tension release, laughs (2)
04 Acknowledges, understands, recognizes (3a)
05 Shows agreement, concurrence, compliance (3b)
06 Gives a procedural suggestion (4a)
07 Suggests a solution (4b)
08 Gives opinion, evaluation, analysis, expresses feelings or wish (5a)
09 Self-analysis and self-questioning behavior (5b)
10 Reference to the external situation as redirected aggression (5c)
11 Gives orientation, information, passes communication (6a)
12 Draws attention, repeats, clarifies (6b)
13 Asks for opinion, evaluation, analysis, expression of feelings (8)
14 Disagrees, maintains a contrary position (10)
15 Shows tension, asks for help by virtue of personal inadequacy (11a)
16 Shows tension increase (11b)
17 Shows antagonism, hostility, is demanding (12a)
18 Ego defensiveness (12b)

In summary, it can be seen that of the original twelve IPA categories two were dropped (7, 9), three were retained (2, 8, 10), and seven were subdivided (1, 3, 4, 5, 6, 11, 12). Furthermore, certain "hard to categorize" behaviors were given more subtle distinctions in IPS. Joking, which could be categorized into categories 1, 2, or 12 of IPA, is now given a more decisive categorization into 1, 10, or 17. A statement such as "What do you suggest?" would be categorized as IPA 9, but inflections can make this statement have several meanings and these are preserved because the statement could be 1, 6, 7, or 15 in the IPS system.

Thus, the revisions permit more sensitive coding, the additions are consistent with the accumulating research on peer ratings, and they distinguish among tasks (Borgatta, 1963b) and among different role-playing assignments (Borgatta, 1961).

Member-Leader Analysis

The intent of this system developed by Mann (1967) is to give a more complete picture of individual dynamics by assessing the development of feelings toward the leader. Only acts expressing feelings relevant to the member-leader relationship are scored. When scoring an act, the coder asks essentially this question: "If this act is expressive of or, more conservatively, congruent with the member's feelings toward the leader, what is the best estimate of what those feelings might be?" The feelings themselves are categorized into one or more of three main areas: *impulse* or "the state of the member's aggressive and libidinal ties with the leader" (8 subcategories); *authority relations* or feelings of power and dependency (3 subcategories); and *ego state* or feelings toward self in the context of relationship to the leader (5 subcategories). The scoring unit consists of any set of sentences within which one feeling can be discerned.

The categories include the following:

Impulse area

1. *Moving against—expressing dislike, mistrust, or anger; attacking; rejecting, ridiculing, insulting.*
2. *Resisting—disagreeing, arguing, blocking or parrying the leader's suggestions or interpretations.*
3. *Withdrawing—ignoring the leader, leaving the room, or engaging in "out of field" behavior, expressing boredom, lack of involvement, or indifference.*
4. *Guilt inducing—blaming, complaining, accusing, feeling misunderstood or abused, shaming.*

   Affection:
5. *Making reparation—forgiving, apologizing, denying hostility.*
6. *Identifying—playing the leader's role in relation to another group member.*
7. *Accepting—agreeing, yielding, conforming.*
8. *Moving toward—expressing liking, trust, or warmth.*

Authority relations area

9. *Showing dependency—expressing a need for approval, direction, structure.*
10. *Showing independence—relating to the leader as a peer, stating one's own standards and/or judging one's own behavior by them.*
11. *Showing counterdependence—asserting a lack of need for direction.*

Ego state area

Anxiety (categories 12 and 13):

12. *Expressing anxiety—showing embarrassment, tension, or uncertainty, feeling criticized, judged, or threatened.*
13. *Denying anxiety—denying feeling tense, worried, or concerned about leader.*
14. *Showing self-esteem—feeling satisfied with self, capable of being open and honest.*

Depression:

15. *Expressing depression—feeling guilty, sad, helpless, powerless.*
16. *Denying depression—resisting an implied criticism, bragging and asserting own potency.*

These categories are encoded from either tapes or typescripts and effectively trace group development.

Behavior System Scores

This system of categories (Borgatta, 1963a) is based on the assumption that peer assessments are a means of societal control as well as the origin of self-appraisals. When these assessments are factor-analyzed, the two most prominent factors are assertiveness (talking, activity, visibility) and sociability (being likable, pleasant, friendly). The scoring categories in the BSs focus on definitions that maximize the content in areas corresponding to the peer assessments (p. 28).

A schematic representation of the six points which constitute categories and their relation to the two factors is shown in Fig. 2. The entire spectrum is not filled because the intermediate points "appear to be more easily described through judgments of larger segments of behavior than of individual acts" (p. 28). Within the system, subscores are used to indicate whether an act may be group-oriented

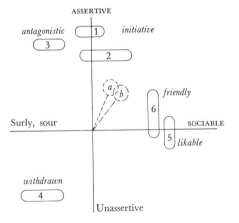

Fig. 2. Schematic diagram of reference points for Behavior Scores System. Major two-factor space is emphasized. The location of with- drawn *in the lower left quadrant was not confirmed empirically. (From Borgatta, 1963a.)*

(task-determining acts or group-maintaining acts), and whether the action includes excessive emotionality (tension displayed, unpredictable behavior). When a sequence is scored, a who-to-whom reference precedes each score.

The six major categories are as follows (p. 32):

Assertive actions

1. *Neutral assertions or communications (continuation, explanation, etc.)*
2. *Assertions or dominant acts (draws attention, asserts, initiates conversation, etc.)*
3. *Antagonistic acts (rejects other, rejects other's position implying rejection of other, is self-assertive or ego-defensive, etc.)*

Withdrawal

4. *Withdrawal acts (leaves field, fails to respond when the situation demands, etc.)*

Supportive actions

5. *Supportive acts (acknowledges, responds, etc.)*
6. *Assertive supportive acts (status raising, implies initiative beyond mere responsiveness, etc.)*

The potential advantage of this system is that it has few scores, yet these scores have high relevance to interaction. Furthermore, "it is proposed that every action of individuals that occurs as a noticeable or visible action can arbitrarily be classified according to the system" (p. 28). A manual for training coders to use the BSs system has been developed by Borgatta and Crowther (1965).

THE OBSERVATIONAL RECORD

Even if the observer chooses settings and behaviors with care, and improves precision through subtle interventions in the setting, his investigation will be on shaky grounds if he does not pay attention to issues associated with the recording of behavior. A concern with behaviors and settings does not supplant a concern with records, because behaviors can be recorded imprecisely, especially if several response measures are obtained at one time. Although this section has been labeled observational records, the issue of data reduction through categories will also be discussed. The reason for this joint inclusion is that processes of recording and coding often occur simultaneously. Furthermore, when these activities are separated and categorization occurs after a record is made, the conclusions that are drawn are vulnerable if they are based on an inadequate record. Thus, in many studies, problems of recording take precedence over categorization problems.

The collection and categorization of records is overlaid by an important issue, namely, whether or not the measurements that are made presuppose a conceptual definition. Byrne (1964, pp. 56–57) discussed the issue by comparing the inductive and deductive approaches, and Straus (1964) phrased a similar distinction in terms of the rational and empirical approaches. Observational methodology can be adapted consistently to either strategy; and both strategies, if employed thoroughly and rigorously, should lead to the same result. The rational approach is employed when the investigator begins with a conceptual definition, then specifies the components of the definition; after this he selects indicators, constructs an index, and then standardizes and validates the resulting instrument (Straus, 1964, p. 341). This approach sometimes falters because investigators halt their inquiry before they get to the validation phase. But an even more crucial problem is that, if the investigator fails to demonstrate validity, it may be difficult for him to decide whether this failure is due to the definition, components, indicators, or index.

As an alternative strategy, the investigator can employ an empirical approach whereby he first selects his indicators and indexes, and postpones conceptual definitions until he is assured that some stable phenomenon is being measured. The observer asks questions about what he is measuring only after he is comfortable that something stable is being measured precisely. This approach reduces the risks that a measure will prove invalid, but it is more likely that the investigator will bog down when he tries to explain his findings. Even if an explanation emerges, it is always possible that the phenomenon will turn out to be conceptually uninteresting.

There are several reasons for noting the distinction between the rational and empirical approaches. Observers who devote their efforts largely to collecting records are typically guided by the empirical approach. Conceptual definitions appear late in their inquiry, and while this approach increases the investigator's chances that he is looking at something stable, there is a greater risk that he will not know what that something is. This risk is partly offset by the fact that most observational records are rich in detail, and this often helps the investigator induce an explanation from his findings. Similar rich content is not always available when induction occurs in the laboratory.

The rational approach is implemented when categories are applied at the time the record is made. As suggested before, the rational approach may be risky because it is difficult to know in advance whether conceptual guidelines are imprecise and whether the translation from concepts to measures has been accurate. If a study proves to be inconclusive, it is difficult to know why. Furthermore, since the event is recorded only in the fallible categories, it is difficult for the observer to use a revised set of categories to encode the same record. Instead, he must obtain a second one. While this suggests that the empirical approach may be preferable in observational methodology, especially since it provides valuable assistance at a crucial step (the construction of a conceptual definition), the ideal solution is to use both strategies. In the ideal sequence, the observer would start with the empirical approach, obtain extensive records of natural events, induce some concepts from the records (probably after they had undergone a crude transformation), and then collect a second set of records which are more specific and pointed more directly at the induced concept. This ideal chain of events can often only be approximated, but the observer should be aware that, when approximation occurs, there are certain ambiguities in the interpretation of his study that must be tolerated.

GENERAL ISSUES IN RECORDING

Regardless of whether the observer decides to record and then categorize, or does both activities simultaneously, there are several general issues that he must resolve. Four of the most important issues are discussed in this section. First, the venerable problem of reliability will be noted. Depending on the type of record that is used, questions of reliability assume greater or lesser importance. Next, unique problems associated with the observation of interaction will be discussed. It is suggested that interaction is difficult to describe but that appropriate recording units can be constructed to surmount these difficulties. Two additional problems will be cited, problems dealing with the unintentional editing of records, and problems dealing with the use of multiple measures. It is suggested that both editing and multiple measures can strengthen observational methodology, but only if the observer is aware of problems associated with each and takes explicit steps to deal with them.

Reliability

Traditionally, much discussion of observational methods has centered on questions of reliability because of the large number of judgmental measures that are used. A general rule of thumb concerning reliability of categories is summarized by Gellert (1955): "the fewer the categories, the more precise their definition, and the less inference required in making classifications, the greater will be the reliability of the data" (p. 194). Questions of reliability, however, are not confined to judgmental techniques. They are also crucial when the observer attempts to gain precision through selection of and intervention into a setting and when he records more specific responses. The intimate linkage between reliability and a choice of settings and behavior is noted by Campbell (1961): "The greater the direct accessibility of the stimuli to sense receptors, the greater the intersubjective verifiability of the observation. The weaker or the more intangible, indirect, or abstract the stimulus attribute, the more the observations are subject to distortion" (p. 340). Support for Campbell's conjecture is provided by Gurman and Bass (1961, p. 370) and Bunney and Hamburg (1963).

Making a phenomenon visible, however, is no assurance that acceptable reliability will occur. Medley and Mitzel (1963, pp. 253–254), for example, suggested that there are three types of reliability, and it seems clear that the same set of behaviors and setting would yield different reliabilities depending on the type of index that is computed. The types include coefficient of observer agreement (different observers observing at the same time), stability coefficient (the same observer observing at different times), and the reliability coefficient (different observers observing at different times). The most common reliability measure in observational studies is observer agreement, and Kaplan (1964, pp. 127–128) argued that intersubjectivity is preferable to replicability as a criterion, especially when rare events are involved. Byrne (1964, p. 49), however, cautioned that high interscorer correlations may be unreliable because it is possible for scorers to disagree on many items and yet have equal total scores, and it is possible for one scorer consistently to give higher scores than the other, a difference that could not be detected in a correlation coefficient. Medley and Mitzel (1963, p. 268) contended that if compromises must be made, it is better to increase the number of observations than to increase the number of observers. The rationale for this argument is that the instability of behavior creates more problems of reliability than do observer errors.

Dunnette (1966) has also argued for the treatment of reliability as a multidimensional concept. He suggested that the meaning of the term reliability is imprecise and proposed that the terms "stability" and "precision" (interobserver agreement) be substituted. The argument is made that there are several sources of error when observations are made, and that the type of reliability which is necessary to estimate or to offset each of these various errors is different. He cited four sources of error that can occur in observations. The first, *inadequate sampling of content,* occurs when different observers sample only some elements of a complex behavior and these samples consist of different elements. The error of *chance response tendencies* stems from imprecise category definitions or inadequate understanding of the category by the observer. When these sources of imprecision are present, observers often fall back on informal intuitive definitions that are more variable. Two types of change over time also hinder reliability: subtle *changes in the environment* from observation period to observation period, and *changes in the person* being observed. The latter source of error is especially tricky. If a person is viewed at two different times, he may behave differently the second time because some real change has occurred in him or simply because he is more accustomed to having an observer watching his actions. In either case, the correlations between the two observations will be low.

Given these several sources of error, it should be apparent that it is desirable to assess reliability in several ways to ensure that the investigator has a substantial phenomenon in hand. In the ideal observational study, four comparisons would be made. First, the ratings of two persons observing the same event would be correlated, a measure that would rule out the errors of change in the person and the environment. Next, the ratings of the same observer watching a similar event at two different times would be compared (this would rule out error of content sampling). Then the agreement of two observers observing an event at two different times would be correlated. This measure is vulnerable to all four sources of error and would be expected to yield the lowest reliability of the four comparisons. Finally, the observations of a single observer watching a single event would be compared in a manner similar to odd-even item correlations in a test. This is a check on internal consistency or the extent to which the observer agrees with himself. If the category system is explicit and well defined, this measure of reliability would be expected to yield the highest correlation. Admittedly, it is possible only to approximate this ideal, but if the investigator must assign priorities to these four comparisons he should try hardest to secure satisfactory interobserver agreement of a single event, because unless this is achieved there is no assurance that any distinct phenomenon is being preserved in the record. Probably the lowest priority would be assigned to the reliability of two observers who record events at two different times. This measure assumes the lowest priority, because in many studies real changes are predicted and the investigator may wish to detect these changes as well as have stable measures.

Even though reliability is often discussed in connection with observational methods, ambivalence often surrounds these discussions. This ambivalence stems not from doubts concerning the importance of reliability, but rather from questions about when the investigator should become concerned with issues of reliability. The argument that a preoccupation with reliability can be dysfunctional at some stages in observational research is found in several places (Gellert, 1955, p. 192; Heyns and Lippitt, 1954, p. 371; Lambert, 1960, p. 884; Wright, 1960, p. 107). Heyns and Lippitt noted that excessive attention to reliability in the early days of observational research often meant that the final set of categories had little predictive efficiency or theoretical basis. They observed that recent studies differ from this emphasis in that "the theory underlying the research, rather than reliability considerations, has come to dictate what is to be observed. The movement has been away from exhaustive recording of all the behavior which occurs toward the selection of particular aspects of behavior in order to answer specific questions" (p. 371). Bott (1933, p. 184), commenting on the observational method in child study, argued that observers should worry about validity first, and reliability second:

if significance can be demonstrated with observations which have only a modicum of reliability, it is safe to conclude that a more rigorous control of procedure will only heighten the significance of what has already been demonstrated to have meaning in relation to the whole of the child's behavior.

There are at least two reasons to question part of Bott's logic. First, it is possible that if an investigator pays little attention to reliability he will miss valid observations. Records that have only moderate reliability often fail to produce significant differences. Insignificant differences often lead the investigator to discard or revise his hypothesis or to look at a different phenomenon. The point is that a real difference may exist, but it may be missed and the inquiry may be terminated prematurely if an imprecise instrument is used to record the phenomenon.

A second question can be raised concerning the presumed relationship between reliability and validity. While it is true that low reliability places an upper bound on validity, it is not necessarily true that validity will increase as reliability increases. The typical rule concerning the relationship between reliability and validity is that "the validity coefficient cannot exceed the square root of the reliability coefficient" (Cronbach, 1960, p. 129). Translated into practice, this means that "a little reliability can go a long way" (Straus, 1964, p. 360). Dunnette (1966), however, argued that the relationship between validity and reliability is more complex than this simple formula would suggest. He contended that with many problems it may be desirable to select measures that possess high reliability as assessed by one method, but low reliability as assessed by other methods. For example, if the determinants of a phenomenon change substantially over time, then the observer might wish to select a measure that has high precision each time it is administered, but which is also sensitive to changes over time. Increased sensitivity is purchased at the cost of low stability of the measure. This low stability, however, is not a reason to discard it. The measure is, after all, doing what it is supposed to do, namely, track a dynamic phenomenon.

There are no easy answers concerning reliability. Clearly, reliability need not impede versatility in observation. If demands for inference and judgment are reduced in the ways suggested in this chapter, then the problems of reliability also tend to be reduced. Nevertheless, the observer will at some time have to grapple with this issue. Byrne (1964, p. 57) has summarized in succinct form the nature of the choice that faces investigators:

The primary advantage of giving measurement a secondary position is that the initial theories and subsequent experimental findings provide guidelines which indicate what it is that is worth measuring. The primary advantage of giving precedence to measurement is that one's experimental results are not based on the shifting sands of error variance.

Observing social interaction

When social psychologists observe, they usually watch two or more people. Several unique problems in the recording and encoding of behavior arise from attempts to describe interaction.

Social interaction is said to occur (Dyck, 1963, p. 80)

. . . when an action by one person is in some way responded to by another person, when each person is aware of the other and of the action in question, and when the action responded to is directed to or is about the person who is responding.

One of the more surprising aspects of interaction is that, even though it pervades most of what persons do, it is difficult to describe. Narrative reports of interaction written in lay language are especially likely to show some of these difficulties. The problem is essentially that persons do not have the words to describe interdependent actions. Typically, the observer describes a single person and what he does vis-à-vis another person—that is, dominates, loves, fears, frightens. The nature of the interpersonal relationship, however, is not retained by such a description. As a result, "efforts to deal with [describe] such a system . . . tend to degenerate into an oscillating series of assertions about the participants: A behaves in such-and-such a manner towards B; then B does so-and-so to A; then A thus to B; and so on" (Pittenger, Hockett, and Danehy, 1960, p. 224). Inadequate as such a portrayal of interaction may be, this may be all the observer can accomplish since he must record what he sees. Higher-order explanations can be constructed, but they are difficult to translate into observable differences. The simple recording of actions and reactions is not without problems, and at times it can be misleading. Persons may appear to be interacting, as in the case of the social monologue or noncontingent interaction, when in actuality their acts are intrapersonal.

Attempts to depict social interactions are exemplified by the concepts of the axis (Watson and Potter, 1962) and social contact (Dyck, 1963). Although these concepts are not necessarily units of observation, they do suggest ways in which the observer might delimit social behavior for closer analysis. An *axis* occurs when "two or more persons for the duration of the episode, join together to create a single system" (Watson and Potter, 1962, p. 248).

A *social contact* is a unit of social interaction which contains "(1) one subject, (2) one agent, (3) one *raison d'être,* and (4) one continuous topic" (Dyck, 1963, p. 81). The important notion is the *raison d'être,* which constitutes the originating ground for interaction. Twelve different grounds are distinguished.

These two concepts illustrate general views of interaction that are adaptable to observation. Most concepts of interaction can be translated into specific observational units, the two most prominent units being the interact and the double interact. An *interact* consists of an initiating act and an outcome. Baumrind's (1967) use of the "sequence" as the unit of analysis illustrates an interact. A control sequence, for example, "consists of two or more causally related acts containing a single message and involving the same two family members as participants in an interchange initiated by one of them and ending with the other's compliance or noncompliance" (p. 64). "Sequences" vary considerably in their duration, lasting until some outcome occurs. More typically, an interact consists of an action and the immediate reaction.

A *double interact* consists of an instigation-reaction-subsequent act. The interchange unit used by Medley and Smith (1964) illustrates a double interact. The teacher asks a question, receives an answer, and then evaluates the answer. This is scored as one unit. The principal advantage of the double interact is that it reduces ambiguity. Intentions are often clarified when a double interact is recorded. If person A shows distress, person B offers sympathy, and then person A becomes composed, the original coding gains some support even though this support is tenuous. If sympathy fails to promote composure, then either A is not distressed or he finds the sympathy sufficiently enjoyable that he would like to elicit more of it.

Barker and Wright (1955, p. 328) encoded both interacts and double interacts (cycle) from specimen records with some interesting results (pp. 418–421). They found that age correlated -0.28 with percentage of cyclical interactions ($p < 0.05$). As persons become older, double interacts decrease and interacts increase in frequency. When children interact with adults or adults interact among themselves, there is a tendency for this action to consist largely of a simple action and reaction. Cycles are rare.

While the observation of social interaction imposes some unique problems of description, these problems can be solved, as is suggested by the category systems used by Argyris (1965), Barker and Barker (1963), and Watson and Potter (1962). It seems clear that the observer who wishes to observe interaction must look closely at his descriptive labels and at his units to be certain that he is, in fact, recording interaction and not merely the individual actions of persons who happen to be in the presence of one another.

The observer as editor

No recording system in current use provides an exact reproduction of an event, yet the fact that editing occurs is not always realized. Failure to acknowledge that events are never recorded in their entirety has led some investigators to claim more for their data than is warranted. It is argued here that editing is a fact of life and, because this is true, observers should try to make their editing systematic.

Regardless of whether behavior is recorded in a limited set of categories or in a narrative, the record involves simplification and "the final picture is not an exact reproduction of the original situation, but is a representation equivalent in selected features" (Back, 1962, p. 61). Frequently, the record is edited unintentionally because of implicit expectations about the outcomes of the study (Rosenthal, 1964), language structure, or undetected cultural influences. The impact of expectations on observation is noted by Kaplan (1964, p. 133): "An observation is *made;* it is the product of an active choice, not of a passive exposure. Observing is goal-directed behavior. . . . Data are always *data for* some hypothesis or other." That the language of observation edits content has been noted frequently (for example, Baumrind, 1964, p. 3; Yarrow and Raush, 1962, p. 11). Pittenger, Hockett, and Danehy (1960) observed that "the currently available terms for describing what people do with one another seem uniformly to carry overtones of hostility" (p. 224). Interaction is described by such words as blow-by-blow, transaction, gambit, ploy, strategy, tactics, or arsenal. Finally, editing may reflect undetected influences of culture. Selltiz *et al.* (1959, p. 213) commented that a common error in the observation of aggression is that acts that appear aggressive to middle-class boys are often seen as playful by lower-class boys.

Perhaps the most important point about editing is that it can be *beneficial.* Instead of being a disadvantage, it can be a strength of observational methodology. Barker (1964, p. 281) compared the observer with a camera or unidirectional microphone and noted that the latter instruments record too much. They make it harder to separate what is relevant because they provide so many distractions:

Behavior always occurs with reference to only a portion of the multiplicity of things and events surrounding the person. This behavior-and-context forms a pattern, a figure, against the nonrelevant background, and it can be seen and described by an observer.

Back (1962) argued that a selective record is consistent with the aim of science to simplify and abstract (p. 61). He noted, further, that natural events are often disorderly and confused and that "under conditions of noise in the signals themselves accurate transmission is not desirable" (p. 63).

Occasionally the issue of editing gets confused with the issue of intervention during data collection. Barker's (1965) recent distinction between the psychologist as transducer and as operator sometimes obscures the difference between editing and intervention. As transducer, "the psychologist is a docile receiver, coder, and transmitter of information about the input, interior conditions and output of psychological units" (p. 1). As an operator, the psychologist "is coupled into the psychological unit as an operative part of it, regulating input, and/or influencing interior conditions and/or constraining output. . . . He sends messages via the unit to himself as receiver and transducer" (p. 3). Even though data are different when interventions are mild (*T*-data) rather than intense (*O*-data), *both* kinds of intervention necessarily involve editing. Docility is no guarantee that the record is unedited.

Both selective and nonselective records can incorporate and systematize the fact of editing. Categories can be constructed so as to hasten, retard, or divert editing behavior. They can impose structure on editing. Time sampling (Arrington, 1943; Wright, 1960) can also be used to systematize editing. While it may be true that time sampling can be dangerous because it "does not honor natural behavior units" (Wright, 1960, p. 100), it is also true that several spaced periods of observation can give a more representative view of an event, and that the temporal properties of events vary sizably. While sampling may lead to a fragmented view of the event, the fragmentation at least takes a distinguishable form and the observer knows definitely what he has omitted and retained. Informal editing which remains undetected does not provide this kind of check on interpretation.

Multiple measures

Natural events are complex and the measures applied to them are often fallible. These facts argue in favor of a multimethod approach (for example, Campbell and Fiske, 1959; Cook and Selltiz, 1964) to observational research. Multiple measures are important not only to give independent and converging indications of validity, but also because the errors inherent in each imperfect measure tend to cancel when these measures are used for multiple confirmation. As Webb *et al.* (1966) noted, "if a proposition can survive the onslaught of a series of imperfect measures, with all their irrelevant error, confidence should be placed in it" (p. 3). The use of multiple measures, however, does not always ensure validity, for it is also true that as measures are added, error variance is also added.

One of the more common ways to get multiple measures is to look at a single event in terms of several behaviors. Hargreaves and Starkweather (1965), for example, assessed the improvement in depressed patients by analyzing the vocal and content characteristics of their interview remarks. The vocal characteristics that were measured included speaking rate, utterance length, latency, loudness, pitch, sighing, throat clearing, and total number of words that were dysphoric adjectives and adverbs, negative forms (for example, "no," "never"), nonactive verbs, self reference, group reference, somatic references, and references employing clinging, demanding, and complaining. It was found that timing, loudness, pitch, and number of words distinguished between interviews rated as "depressed" and "recovered" for three patients whose principal symptom was motor retardation. Changes in the content of speech for these patients was relatively minor. By contrast, a patient whose principal symptoms were tension and agitation showed no consistent changes in the voice measures, but dramatic changes in speech content.

Additional examples of a single event viewed in several ways include the extensive work on the relationship between vocal and gestural responses during psychotherapy (for example, Ekman, 1965d; Scheflen, 1963, 1964) and the relationship between content and temporal properties of talk (Phillips *et al.* 1961; Soskin and John, 1963). Visual and auditory records are sometimes supplemented by physiological measures, as in Murray's studies of stressful interactions (Murray, 1963). A person who had spent some time writing an extended and thoughtful philosophy of his own life presented it to another person (a lawyer) for comment whose criticism of it became "far more vehement, sweeping and personally abusive than . . . [the person was] led to expect" (p. 29). The subject's reactions to this event were recorded in several ways. These included a cardiotachometric tracing of heart and respiration rates, a sound film portraying physical expression and words that were exchanged, and a series of typed protocols of everything that the person said when he relived the experience at several intervals. Purcell and Brady (1965, p. 193) suggested that studies of spontaneous talk can also be adapted to physiological measures. They proposed, for example, that if the subject were outfitted with telemetric equipment, criteria for heart rate could be established such that when the rate exceeded a set level, an audible signal would be recorded automatically on the record of verbal output.

Instead of watching a single event and recording several varieties of behavior that appear in it, observers often use several different types of measuring instruments to record what occurs. This approach is probably closer to the "spirit" of the multimethod approach than is the recording of several different behavioral measures with the same type of instrument. Haeberle (1959) reported a study of aggression and dependency among emotionally disturbed preschool children who were placed in structured play situations (for example, they had to knock over a tower of cans to get a toy). Three kinds of observational records were made. One observer used only precoded categories developed from pilot studies, two observers took detailed notes on the actions and words of the child, and the experimenter who actually administered the task wrote impressions of her interaction after each session. It was concluded that the measures supplemented one another, but also that the division of labor was somewhat lopsided. The observer with precoded categories was overburdened and his tallies of acts were insensitive, and the experimenter was so preoccupied with procedures that she could not remember her own reactions. Additional examples of multiple measure are found in Loomis and Meyer (1959) and Baumrind (1967).

Somewhat related to the issue of multiple measures is the use of composite scores in which several scores on individual items are summated to provide a summary score. The justification for summated scores is essentially that single items, even though individually discriminative, may be tapping different aspects of behavior variance; hence, when summed, the total will show considerably greater discrimination than any one alone. The increase in discrimination, however, may be spurious because there are several problems involved in the use of composite measures. Perhaps the most crucial source of error is that summation assumes that each item is of equal importance in the total score, an assumption that may be unwarranted. Furthermore, the assumption of equal importance glosses over the fact that an item affects the total score in an amount proportional to its variance. Weighting of items is often arbitrary and offers no insurance that assumptions of equal importance will be offset. Straus (1964, p. 353) noted two additional problems with summation. First, validity may suffer if the total score contains items that are unrelated to the criterion variable or that are negatively related to it. Second, summated scores at best have only the properties of an ordinal scale, and this can produce problems of interpretation when the investigator wants to measure absolute differences or the amount of change.

Although issues concerned with composite measures are complex and can only be sampled in the present discussion, there is an additional assumption that is of considerable importance to observation. When an investigator uses summated ratings, he can make two different assumptions about the phenomenon being studied, and these assumptions have very different implications for the kinds of items he will use. The investigator may assume that he is observing a heterogeneous phenomenon and that he is summing in order to get a more complete picture of the event. If this assumption is made, then he will wish to construct diverse items to encompass a larger portion of the phenomenon. However, if he assumes that a homogeneous phenomenon is being observed, then he is summing in order to construct a more stable picture of the event. A homogeneous phenomenon places more constraints on the investigator to construct items that overlap and that do not have diverse content.

Formidable as the problems of composite scores are, they can be solved and the astute investigator who is alert to these problems can employ composite measures to improve discrimination without necessarily adding to the ambiguity of his measures.

Multiple indices are accessible in observational research, and they appear to be a valuable tool for investigators adopting this methodology. Not only are multiple indices valuable because they test hypotheses in several ways, but they take account of the facts that events have many manifestations, measures have limits, and redundancy aids the observation of relationships. Since different methods may produce different outcomes, an investigator can be more assured of the stability of a relationship if he has sampled more of the event. As indices increase, so also do the opportunities for *apparent* as well as actual contradiction. Apparent contradiction is emphasized because seeming contradictions produced by multiple indices can provide the occasion for the development of new concepts that accommodate the differences.

RECORDS OF EVENTS

If an observer obtains a record of a natural event in which detail is preserved, he not only has a permanent picture of what occurred, but he has an important prod to induction, as well as sufficient flexibility to impose several different systems of categories. As noted earlier, this flexibility is an important safeguard to some of the dangers inherent in the rational approach.

Traditionally, observers have used tape recordings and detailed narratives as their principal sources of records. Different records tend to have different strengths, and the purpose of this section is to survey additional sources of records. While there are several criteria that might be used to choose a method of recording, among the more important ones are that the method permit the observer to systematize or assess the amount of editing that occurs, that the method reduce the demands on the attention of the observer, and that the record be in a form which can be transformed into data. The records discussed below differ not only in their inclusiveness concerning complex events, but also in the adequacy with which they meet these criteria.

Motion picture films

Motion picture films have recently gained considerable stature as a means to collect records (for example, Carmichael, 1956; Ekman, 1965a; Friedman, Kurland, and Rosenthal, 1965; Haggard and Isaacs, 1966; Haworth, 1956; R. Katz, 1964; Kounin, Friesen, and Norton, 1966; Jecker *et al.*, 1964; Scheflen, 1963, 1964, 1966; Sternberg, Chapman, and Shakow, 1958; Stoller and Lesser, 1963; Worth, 1964, 1965). The interest in filming is understandable because motion picture records have several advantages. Michaelis (1955) noted that films have permanency, there is no limit to the size and complexity of the event that can be recorded, their range of time and velocity is greater than the human eye—if actions occur too slowly the film maker can use time-lapse photos (for example, Lewis, 1951); if events occur too rapidly the film maker can resort to slow motion (for example, Landis and Hunt, 1937)—films permit time sampling, film emulsions are more sensitive than the eye, and cameras can be concealed. Films also have the advantage that they provide a means whereby independent records can be made to improve validity and provide reliability checks. If two cameras are used to film an event, or if one camera films an event from two angles or with lenses of two different focal lengths, this is the equivalent of two independent observers watching from two different angles (Michaelis, 1955, p. 172).

Film records, however, also have disadvantages, and at times these drawbacks can be sizable. For example, the choice of camera angle is subjective and at the discretion of the film maker, film output is not immediately available because of time delays for processing, films and film equipment are expensive, and the analysis of film records is time consuming and complicated because of the variety of information that is available. In addition, lighting can afford problems. Maccoby *et al.* (1964) found that lighting affected the visibility of gestures. With low-key light, movements of facial muscles could be observed but gross bodily movements were difficult to detect. If back lighting was used to improve the visibility of body movements, observations of facial expressions suffered. Unless a camera is equipped with a zoom lens, the film maker is confined to recording only those data that come into the field of the lens. He cannot, without moving the camera, get close-ups of the subject. As with tape recordings, the sound tracks of films often contain an excessive amount of background noise that can make voices unintelligible. Microphone placement is crucial. At times it is not as easy to conceal a camera as it would appear. Maccoby *et al.* (1964, p. 61) experimented with a hidden camera mounted outside the window of a classroom. The camera was not detected, but it was also not very useful because distance could not be varied and the camera could not be moved. Friedman, Kurland, and Rosenthal (1965) filmed experimenter-subject dyads with a concealed camera fitted with a zoom lens. The camera was in a booth that had a small opening for the lens. In front of this opening was a fake glass-enclosed bookcase that contained books and empty picture frames to camouflage the opening. Concealment is less of a problem with television cameras because the camera is smaller, it makes less noise, and an operator does not have to be in the room while the camera is on. Kounin, Friesen, and Norton (1966) made videotapes covering the entire morning or afternoon activities in 80 classrooms, each of which had in it one or more emotionally disturbed children. Two cameras were used for recording, one to record the largest area of the room possible, the other to focus on the teacher, emotionally disturbed child, or whomever the project director chose.

Even though investigators have adopted motion picture techniques with considerable enthusiasm, they have not always realized that there are subtle conventions of film making which, if violated, can make a sizable difference in the conclusions that are drawn from films. Stated most bluntly, "the film can and does lie" (Michaelis, 1955, p. 168). For example, there are marked differences in the angle that can be encompassed by the eye and camera lens. The human eye subtends an angle of approximately 120 degrees, but a typical 50-mm camera lens covers only 25 degrees, and a telephoto lens (135 mm) subtends an angle of less than 5 degrees. Thus, much that meets the eye does not meet the lens. Lenses, especially telephoto lenses, also foreshorten perspective. This means that if an investigator filmed a group of persons who were standing quite far apart, on film they would appear to be packed closely together.

Perhaps the most prominent reason that films can lie is that persons are accustomed to conventions of film making that are used in feature films. If research films neglect these conventions, people may draw conclusions that are quite different from what actually occurred. Several examples of conventions can be cited. If a cameraman were filming a dancer and he moved his camera the length of the dancer's body, different impressions might result depending on the direction in which the camera was moved. "The tilt from head to toe tends to imply 'looking the man over,' again imitating the natural eye movement, and may thus give rise to a derogatory opinion of the dancer. A tilt in the opposite direction, from toe to head, would give the contrary impression, one of awe and admiration" (Michaelis, 1955, p. 177). If a camera is held low and pointed up at the subject he assumes excessive importance, but if the camera is held high, the person appears insignificant. If a film contains a series of sequences, each lasting for a very brief time, there is the illusion of excitement, speed, and disturbance, whereas a scene of long duration tends to convey the illusion of tranquillity. It should be noted that a single scene which lasts more than 30 seconds also produces inattention (Michaelis, 1955, p. 172). The pattern of camera movements that is most consistent with normal eye movements consists of several changes in camera position and in the area covered. When persons watch events, their eyes move constantly and fixations are brief. If these typical eye movements are not retained in the construction and editing of a film, then persons who rate the films may actually be encoding events that never occurred.

It should be noted that film conventions have not been crucial in much of the recording done so far, because most of it consists of records of two or more persons who are seated and talking. The camera remains at a fixed position. The problems of conventions become more crucial when observers take their cameras into the field to record complex events. But even films made in the laboratory with stationary people may be encoded inaccurately because coders are influenced by expectations developed from observation of feature films, and because the stimulus materials in the research films violate the typical manner in which a scene is scanned.

There are several motion picture techniques that can be of value in observational studies. Instant comparisons of the same person in two different settings or at two different times can be made by the split-frame technique. A mask is placed over half of the film so that, when the subject is photographed, only one half of the film is exposed. When the person is filmed a second time, the mask is placed over the exposed film and pictures are made on the portion that was previously unexposed. The result is that the two pictures of the subject taken at different times appear side by side on the screen. Quantification of movements is facilitated if a grid is placed behind the person who is being filmed or if it is superimposed directly over the film. Infrared filming in darkened settings is used infrequently but has several advantages for observation. Haworth (1956) filmed the reactions of children who were watching a puppet show in a darkened theater. She found that the films contained significantly more indications of movements than did the records of observers made during the show, and that the films confirmed suspected activities (for example, masturbation).

Memo-motion or time-lapse photography, in which the camera operates at speeds such as 1 fps instead of the usual 24 fps, produces films with a jerky "Keystone cop" quality, but films which are invaluable to detect patterns of movement. Wiener (private communication) used memo-motion techniques to study the problems that elderly persons have when they try to cross busy traffic intersections in St. Petersburg, Florida. Traffic signals seldom permit a person to move slowly across an intersection; Wiener used films of pedestrian behavior to determine how elderly persons cope with this problem. The principal advantages of memo-motion techniques are that they reduce the costs of film (gross details are preserved at about 6 percent of the normal cost of film), they permit time sampling, and they facilitate analysis. This latter point is especially crucial. Projection equipment especially adapted to memo-motion films permits the observer to study one frame at a time for as long as he wishes. Since each frame covers a rather sizable period of time, changes in position are easily detected as the coder moves from frame to frame, and the intervening movements are easy to deduce. Because of the set rate at which the film is exposed, accurate time records of an event are available without elaborate timing equipment being placed in view of the lens. Memo-motion techniques obviously are not adapted to the study of subtle and extremely rapid changes in gestures, such as those observed by Haggard and Isaacs (1966; see pp. 383–385 of this chapter), but they are unusually well adapted to problems of recording gross bodily movements or changes in spatial behavior.

Perhaps the most significant problem with motion picture records is analysis. Film records are sufficiently complex that it can be difficult to transform them into explicit data. An exemplary classification is the SCAN (System for the Classification and Analysis of Nonverbal Behavior) system developed by Ekman and Friesen (1965). This detailed procedure "is built upon the use of a human operator whose inspection is aided by magnification, slowed motion, repeat-viewing and retrieval systems, but whose decisions are based on visual recognition of readily observable similarities" (p. 31). Only the briefest outline of this intricate procedure can be indicated here. Three steps are involved: location, descriptive tagging, and classification into acts. In the location phase, the coder views an entire film and notes the frames at which a movement in a specific body region (for example, feet) begins and ends. In the descriptive-tagging phase, all movements within one bodily area are collected and each movement is described with up to 15 different descriptive items (for example, foot involved, location of feet, location of legs, direction of movement, torso change). In the classification phase, the coder sorts through the bodily movements again, this time looking for groups of identical descriptive tags. If for example, he finds that approximately ten of the movements in the foot region were tagged with the descriptive label "tapping", then he views these ten instances of tapping, compares them with a prototype film in which a pure instance of tapping occurs, and if all of the instances of tapping resemble the prototype, he designates this as an act and assigns it a code number. When these steps are completed, the investigator has a "listing of acts within each body area, with each act located in time, with descriptors attached to each act, and with the frequency of occurrence noted for each act within the interview" (p. 11). Once the coder has sorted the acts into groups that are characterized by similar tags, he can then proceed with data analysis and begin to answer such questions as what acts tend to follow what acts, what verbal content coincides with what acts, what functions do the acts perform, how do acts change over time, which acts tend to be associated with which clinical syndromes, etc.? Laborious as this procedure may appear, it is clear that once the data are in this form the investigator can ask more significant questions about the meaning of acts and expect to receive more definitive answers.

As a final indication of the flexibility permitted by motion picture films, the biodocumentary technique (developed by Worth, 1964, 1965, 1966) should be mentioned. A biodocumentary film is a subjective film made by a naive film maker "to show how he feels about himself and his world." A biodocumentary film "bears the same relation to a documentary film that . . . an autobiography has to a biography" (Worth, 1964, p. 3). Thus, if an investigator wanted to learn about the Navaho Indians he could go to the reservation and make a film *or* he could have a Navaho make the film. The latter type of film would give some indication of what the Navaho regarded as important or unimportant about his life and what he wanted to hide from others. While the interpretation of a bio-documentary film encounters many of the same problems commonly associated with the analysis of phenomenal reports, comparisons of a documentary and a biodocumentary made of the same event might yield valuable information. While it may stretch the definition of observational methods to include such usage of film in the present discussion, it seems clear that a biodocumentary might be a promising means to offset some of the limitations of films due to editing, to provide a check on the validity of conclusions made by a detached observer, to offset whatever preconceptions an observer might bring to an event, and to act as a check on significant events that might be overlooked.

The extensive discussion of films presented here is not meant to imply that this form of record is more important than other records. Instead, this topic has been sampled heavily because references to the use of films reside in the experience of persons who have worked extensively with this type of record, and because this type of record has received increasing attention as a result of improvements in motion picture technology, increased dissatisfaction with other forms of records, and increased interest in body movements as a datum.

Specimen records

A specimen record is perhaps the best-known nonselective record used in observational research. It is defined as "a sequential, unselective, plain, narrative description of behavior with some of its conditions" (Wright, 1960, p. 86). The following excerpt is taken from a specimen record describing the actions of Ben, a six-year-old boy with cerebral palsy (Barker, 1964, p. 272):

1:33   Olivia walked in from the occupational therapy room and made a few gay, happy, cheerful remarks about the fact that Ben was going to be six very soon.

Ben looked up at her but made no other response.

Then Tom said somewhat seriously, "Well, any little boy who's going to be six is going to have to learn to crawl."

With this Olivia and Tom walked to the far end of the room a distance of nine or ten feet, which was established as the goal for Ben's crawling.

Specimen records are assumed to have several advantages: face validity, permanence (see Barker *et al.*, 1961, for an example of a specimen record archive), theoretically neutral data, extensive detail, isomorphism with behavior, behavior recorded *in situ*, breadth due to lay language, and continuity. Furthermore, specimen records can be quantified (Wright, 1960, p. 89) and they can be collected by unsophisticated observers (Heyns and Lippitt, 1954, p. 389).

Perhaps the two greatest drawbacks of specimen records are that rapid, complex interaction is difficult to record and lay language may be less rich and less well-suited to description than is imagined. Language meanings are influenced by past experience and observers vary greatly in the demands they impose on themselves for precision in description and in the words they have available to write such descriptions.

An excellent example of research involving specimen records is Schoggen's (1964a) study of differences in interactions received by children with and without physical disabilities. Seven children with visible motor impairments were matched on sex, age, learning ability, family status, and structure with seven nondisabled children. Observers watched each of the 14 children up to 6 times at home and 6 times at school. Each observation lasted 20–30 minutes. To facilitate recording, each observer dictated a preliminary version of his comments on-the-spot into a microphone housed in a face mask (Schoggen, 1964b). The observer spoke into the mask with a normal voice, yet his remarks were not heard, even by persons sitting very close to him. After the observer had made crude notes on location, he then constructed a much more detailed description from these verbal notes and the detailed version was then made into a transcript. Transcripts were coded into environmental force units and instances of deference and control were compared.

Sign analysis

Category systems usually sample only one part of natural events, but it is the object of a sign system to sample numerous portions of a natural event without any assumption concerning the importance or relevance of a dimension. In a sense, sign analysis is concerned with the demography of events. Described more formally, the approach of sign analysis "is to list beforehand a number of specific acts or incidents of behavior which may or may not occur during a period of observation. The record will show which of these incidents occurred during a period of observation and, in some cases, how frequently each occurred" (Medley and Mitzel, 1963, pp. 298–299).

An example of this procedure is a recording form for classroom observation labeled OScAR-R (Observational Schedule and Record-Reading), designed by Medley and Smith (1964). The form is a 5 × 8 card, on one side of which are printed categories for static events (those analogous to a still photograph) and on the other side are categories of dynamic events (record of verbal behavior). The categories on both sides involve simple, nonevaluative discriminations. Each card contains a record of a ten-minute period.

When recording starts, the observer spends three minutes checking the static categories. He records the equipment being used (for example, slide projector) and the group structure (for example, small groups of 6), and indicates which group the teacher is with. Most of the static recording consists of checking which of 18 categories of materials are being used and which of 20 activities are being enacted. The static recording consists of a series of sequential discriminations. For example, if the observer notes that a book is being used, he then distinguishes whether the book is homemade or published, and if homemade, whether it is pupil-produced or teacher-produced. Activities of both teacher and student are recorded. For example, once it is decided that a teacher's activity is interactive rather than noninteractive, it can then be discriminated as either miscellaneous or oral, and if oral, as either "asks questions," "answers questions," or "drills."

Only one check is entered in a cell, no matter how many times a behavior may be observed.

After three minutes pass, the card is turned over and the observer categorizes each verbal statement made by the teacher and each interchange between pupil and teacher that occurs during the next six minutes (the final minute is used to record general comments). For example, if a teacher's comment is identified as a statement ("does not care for a pupil response"), it is then determined whether the statement is procedural, motivational, or problem-centered, and if problem-centered, whether it is problem-structuring-meaning (for example, "why is that quotation important"), problem-structuring-form (for example, "what is the first word on page 3"), or exposition (for example, story telling). Interchanges are scored only when there is a teacher question, pupil response, and teacher reply.

It is important to note some characteristics of this approach. The visit is divided into small time periods, and often an event is recorded only the first time it occurs. It is assumed that "the number of times a sign occurs over a few hours correlates highly with the number of short time-units in which it occurs at least once" (Medley and Mitzel, 1963, p. 302). Because of the large number of happenings that must be scanned, item content is crucial. There must be no ambiguity about the item because the observer has no time to recall unusual definitions. Each item has three characteristics: present tense, positive occurrence, and singular number (p. 302). Thus an item such as "teacher failed to recognize pupils' significant contributions" is changed to read "teacher ignores pupil's contribution." The suggestion that tense affects judgment is important, not just for items in this system, but for all items. An item which is phrased in the past tense suggests that behavior should be marked after the event, and this tends to draw attention away from the specific occurrence.

As a final point, it should be noted that sign analysis probably works best when events are *infrequent*. Since frequent events lead to tallies in every period, an undifferentiated picture of the event will result. However, this problem can easily be solved by appropriate choice of the length of a time period. Although sign analysis has been used primarily to record classroom interaction, it does seem to be a suitable means to gather records in a wider range of settings.

Field formats

Comprehensiveness as well as nonselectivity can often be promoted if the observer uses a format that ensures that he systematically attends to various aspects of a natural event. Formats of this kind are represented in work by Guest (1955), Hall (1963), and Melbin (1954).

Guest (1955, p. 22) developed several subcategories for each of six components of an event: topic, plan, activity (how it was done), contact, interaction (initiation of contact), time. Melbin (1954) used a somewhat similar format to aid participant observation in a department store. He coded on a 3 × 5 card (1) who talked with whom, (2) about what (for example, money, errors, exchanged goods), (3) when, (4) where (a grid was imposed on the floor layout and the appropriate column and row were noted on card), (5) under what conditions (for example, slack, medium, busy), (6) for how long.

Recording of proxemic behavior is facilitated by the system of notation developed by Hall (1963b). (See Fig. 3.) The system uses three types of notation: pictographic symbol, mnemonic symbol, and number code. The following

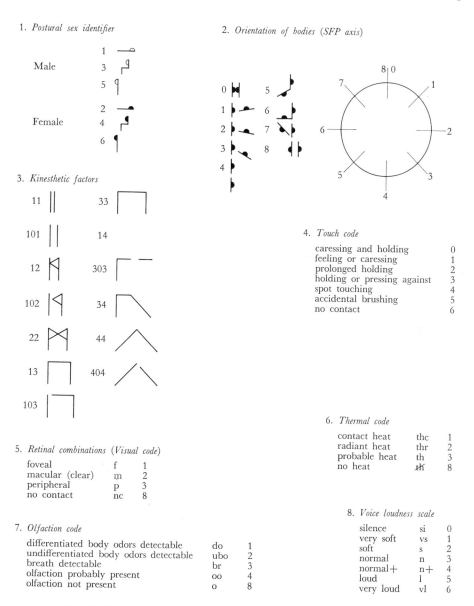

1. *Postural sex identifier*

2. *Orientation of bodies (SFP axis)*

3. *Kinesthetic factors*

4. *Touch code*

caressing and holding	0
feeling or caressing	1
prolonged holding	2
holding or pressing against	3
spot touching	4
accidental brushing	5
no contact	6

5. *Retinal combinations (Visual code)*

foveal	f	1
macular (clear)	m	2
peripheral	p	3
no contact	nc	8

6. *Thermal code*

contact heat	thc	1
radiant heat	thr	2
probable heat	th	3
no heat	th	8

7. *Olfaction code*

differentiated body odors detectable	do	1
undifferentiated body odors detectable	ubo	2
breath detectable	br	3
olfaction probably present	oo	4
olfaction not present	o	8

8. *Voice loudness scale*

silence	si	0
very soft	vs	1
soft	s	2
normal	n	3
normal+	n+	4
loud	l	5
very loud	vl	6

Fig. 3. Notation system for proxemic behavior. (From Hall, 1963b.)

example illustrates how the system is used (Hall, 1963b, p. 1021):

1. *two men standing (postural code 55);*
2. *facing each other directly (orientation code 0);*
3. *close enough that hands can reach almost any part of the trunk (kinesthetic code 101);*
4. *touch does not play any part (touch code 0);*
5. *man speaking looking at, but not in the eye, partner only viewing speaker peripherally (visual code 23);*
6. *close enough that radiant heat would have been detected (thermal code 2);*
7. *body odor but not breath detectable (olfaction code 2);*
8. *voice very soft (loudness code 1).*

Impressionistic analysis

It is generally easier to make a nonselective record of familiar events than of unfamiliar events. Words that accurately describe the unfamiliar are hard to find. One means to handle this problem is to use the observer's voice as a datum. As noted earlier, vocal cues are sensitive to changes in affect as well as cognition. Therefore, it is possible that a dictated record of behavior, made while the behavior occurs, may carry additional information in the vocalizations of the observer, especially if the observer is encouraged to describe the event without any limitations.

Such an approach was used by Loomis and Meyer (1959) to describe the actions of nonverbal, disturbed children. Since these children use mainly a private, unspoken language, it is difficult to learn about them. Loomis and Meyer had two observers watch the nonverbal child during 30 minutes of play and describe instantaneously and vocally everything that occurred, much as in a sports broadcast. The description included "his appearance, posture, motility, gestures, play or nonplay, vocalizations, emotional display, and the interweaving of all of these into his total behavior" (p. 576).

The freedom of the observer to use his voice to portray the subtle, changing, or confusing feeling states of the child took several forms. Unstructured rhetoric was encouraged. A more graphic picture of what occurred was often conveyed when the observer made up a new word or phrase instead of using standard descriptive terms. Observers were also encouraged to imitate gestures of the child that they were unable to describe. Imitation often suggested to the observer more graphic words to describe the gesture. An incidental but important effect of continual vocal reaction is that it unburdens the observer immediately of whatever surprise, disgust, disbelief, or puzzlement, he feels about a particular act and, therefore, enables him to experience less conflict about reporting subsequent acts. Bunney and Hamburg (1963) found that descriptions of affective states suffered when the actor provoked strong feelings in the observer. Immediate vocalization does not blunt the impact of an affect storm, but it does keep the reactions from spilling over into adjacent events.

As a supplement to sensitive vocalization, the observer continually made and tested short-run predictions to aid in the search for patterns of actions. The predictions were spontaneous and were phrased in terms of events in the situation. A simple prediction is illustrated in this observer's remarks: "He's grabbed the block and started to tap with it—No, he hasn't! He stopped just short of hitting the shelf, and put the block down oh-so-gently" (p. 578).

As a final aid to description and discovery of a pattern, observers were encouraged to "form and utilize 'trial identifications' with 'difficult-to-identify-with' children" (p. 580). It was assumed that, even though the actions of the child were bizarre, they might resonate with something experienced by the observer.

It is clear that the methodological problems involved in observing disturbed children are unique and that resourcefulness is mandatory. At the same time this method makes important points about nonselective observation in general. Self-observation or introspection may be neglected too often in the development of observational records. Many of the methods surveyed in this section attempt to preserve the observer's initial impressions, but at times they do this in ways that are self-defeating. Observation of affect is always a problem, but an observer may be helped in his description by noting the reaction he has to an actor. Finally, there is the important point, as was clear with Schoggen's (1964b) use of the Stenomask, that the spontaneous, detailed vocal descriptions of events as they occur convey different information than do tapes, films, or written notes.

CATEGORY SYSTEMS AS SELECTIVE RECORDS

Eventually, most observations are summarized in categories. Thus, issues concerned with the construction of category systems are of vital importance to observational methods. Surprisingly, even though categories have been used extensively, the mechanics of categories are seldom discussed (see Peak, 1953, for an important exception). Heyns and Lippitt (1954) described categorization as an observer task, and contrasted this with the task of assigning a numerical index to behavior (rating scale). More recently, Medley and Mitzel (1963) have discussed categories as a form of item and have distinguished between category items and sign items. A category-system approach (Medley and Mitzel, 1963, p. 298) is to

. . . limit the observation to one segment or aspect of . . . behavior, and construct a finite set of categories into one and only one of which every unit observed can be classified. The record obtained purports to show, for each period of observation, the total number of units of behavior which occurred and the number classifiable in each category.

Categories are exhaustive of the type of behavior that is recorded, they are derived from theory, they are recorded rapidly with little observer strain (the observer records an act and then forgets it) (Gellert, 1955, p. 182), and they focus on selected behaviors. Category systems differ in such ways as literal objectivity, psychological specificity, theoretical integration (Wright, 1960, p. 125), exhaustiveness, amount of inference required, scope, discreteness of units, size of unit, frame of reference for observation, and training required of coders (Heyns and Lippitt, 1954, p. 374).

Since categories are selective, they have sometimes been criticized because they violate the continuity and complexity of behavior (Gellert, 1955, p. 184). Campbell (1961, p. 346) suggested that it is impossible to decide *a priori* whether or not this fragmentation is consequential. Much of the debate concerning the values and drawbacks of categories is confused with the issue of when the categories are applied. Categorizing can occur when the behavior takes place or sometime later. If behavior is categorized as it occurs, there are such disadvantages as fewer reliability checks, more time pressure and therefore more errors, omission of descriptive detail, fewer chances to rework the data later, and a more fragmented impression of the event (Riesman and Watson, 1964, p. 248). As prominent as these limitations are, they may be offset by the fact that an observer who watches an event unfold is often in the best position to make accurate judgments about the behavior (Baumrind, 1964, p. 10; Yarrow and Raush, 1962, p. 54). Precoding usually benefits from the tendency of persons to omit superfluous details. Postcategorization seldom benefits from intelligent editing because too little context is preserved for the coder to judge which details are minor. The chief advantage of postcategorization is that a greater variety of categories can be applied in a more leisurely fashion by more coders. Furthermore, postcategorization may itself suggest new categories. Needless to say, postcategorization is only as good as the record on which it is based. Whether precoding is interchangeable with postcategorization depends largely on the variety of cues that are required to label behavior accurately. Postcategorization is often done from typescripts (for example, Mann, 1967; Mills, 1964), with the result that facial expressions, postural changes, and so on, are not available as cues. If such data would not change the categorization, even if they were known, then the systems are interchangeable.

In the remainder of this discussion about categories, we shall touch briefly on several topics. Under the general heading of category construction, the issues of explicitness, use of context, assumed equivalence, time units, and exhaustiveness will be discussed. Next, category content will be discussed and the material will center on the question of whether acts should be categorized according to their intent or their effect.

Category construction

Perhaps the most important requirement of any category is that it be *explicit*. By this we mean that the category should be specified "in terms of the behavior to be observed, the situation in which the behaviors occur, and the event which precedes or follows the behavior in question" (Beller, 1959, p. 569). Medley and Mitzel (1963, p. 301) added to these three criteria the stipulation that the language in which the behavioral cues are described should be understandable to anyone who is similar in sophistication to the original observers. An example of a category description that is consistent with these criteria is category 16, *shows tension increase,* in the Interaction Process Scores observational system (Borgatta, 1962, p. 278):

In this category are scored the periods of tenseness that grow largely out of impasses or bankruptcy of conversation. Most of the scores that fall into this category are the awkward pauses, which are usually punctuated by clearing of throats, looking around by one person or another, etc. For the whole group, however, it is sometimes noted that the level of participation grows more tense because of the general personal involvement of the group.

Category systems vary greatly in the amount of contextual information that the observer needs to assign a behavior to a category. The general rule is that context should be used as sparingly as possible, and the immediate situation should be the sole basis for categorization. Failure to follow this rule affects both reliability and validity. Reliability suffers because coders take varying amounts of prior context into account when they categorize a behavior, and this may change its meaning considerably. Purcell and Brady (1965, pp. 28–29) discussed the problems that occur when a response is used to confirm an earlier rating. For example, an act of gratitude may seem to confirm a prior rating of "being helpful." This presumption is dangerous because interpersonal responses are not invariably linked to behavioral stimuli. A person may express gratitude *regardless* of what occurs, or he may respond to helpfulness in ways other than showing gratitude.

Thus, category systems should permit immediate judgments and discourage the use of context. Time sampling may serve this purpose. Wright and Proctor (1961) used a sampling unit in which they watched for 15 seconds, recorded for 15 seconds, watched for 15 seconds, etc. This lessens the problems of context in at least three ways. The observer has time to think; he cannot see the consequences of the period he has watched, and therefore cannot use them in his judgment; and the event appears more discontinuous because his view of it is often interrupted. This latter point should increase the observer's tendency to treat each observation as an independent unit. Another way to handle context is to record units that can be coded immediately. Dittman and Wynne (1961, p. 201) remarked that this is one advantage of linguistic units such as phonemes.

Typically, every time a behavior is placed in a category there is the assumption that it is *equivalent* to every other behavior placed in that category. The intensity and significance of selected events is lost. Borgatta (1962, p. 369) made this observation about Bales's (1950) category of "shows solidarity" to indicate the difficulty of the equivalence assumption:

the cumulation of responses in an interaction category may have consequences in the perception of both objective and participatory observers that are quite different in meaning or much broader in meaning than the category that is being scored. The person who is rated as high in showing solidarity may be the one who is responsive primarily at the strategic and important moment for the group rather than most often.

There are several ways in which categories can be made to serve as more sensitive indicators of events. A single act may be assigned to several categories. Mann (1967) incorporated multiple scoring into his system, the only restriction being that only one entry could occur in each of the five subareas. Purcell and Brady (1965) observed for two minutes, and then summarized what happened during that time by distributing 11 points among three or fewer of the Leary (1957) categories. Thus, if the subject spent most of the two-minute period boasting of his athletic prowess, but occasionally was slightly uneasy and halting about his claims, 8 points might be assigned to category 2 (teach, brag) and 3 points to category 10 (embarrassment, uneasiness). The distribution of 11 points was based on judgments of quantity and intensity, with no attempt made to disentangle the two. It was assumed that this usage presents a reasonably accurate picture of the behavior.

Category systems often specify certain *time intervals* as the recording unit. Flanders (1960) scored the dominant pattern of a three-second interval in one of 10 categories, Moustakas, Siegel, and Schalock (1956) made entries in one or more categories every five seconds, and Kounin, Friesen, and Norton (1966) every 10 seconds. Time intervals as short as this decrease the likelihood that multiple codes will be necessary and, therefore, reliability is heightened. Errors tend to be low because observers readily adopt a rhythm and habitually watch for the prescribed interval of time with surprisingly little variance.

As time intervals between scoring increase in length, observers become more variable in their activities. Ekman (1957, p. 147) noted that, when observers were to mark five categories per minute, there was considerable variance in how long the observer looked before he marked a category. Some categories received more attention than others. To control for this variance in attention, Ekman used five mimeographed cards on each of which was one category with approximately five responses per category. The alternatives were also drawn in pictorial form to reduce demands for inference. With these procedures, the observer's task became more regular and better paced. Only if he worked steadily through the pack of five cards, and looked at the events for a set amount of time, could the observer be assured of completing the record in one minute.

Systems of categories vary in *number* and *exhaustiveness*. In number, categories vary all the way from a simple present-absent discrimination (for example, Medley and Smith, 1964) to discrimination among 82 categories (for example, Moustakas, Siegel, and Schalock, 1956). Many of the systems with large numbers of categories are actually more orderly than they appear; that is, the variables are subdivided into major and minor classes. Furthermore, if decision trees are constructed for some of the more extensive systems, it will be clear that only three to five binary choices are required to assign a behavior to a category.

Large numbers of categories do not necessarily mean that a system is exhaustive, nor do they ensure that the system is reliable or valid. With large numbers of categories, finer distinctions often exist and agreements on placement of specific items can be more difficult (Gellert, 1955, p. 184). Medley and Mitzel (1963, p. 300) recommended that no more than 10 categories should be used, but indicated that it is safer to err in the direction of having too many (they can be combined later) than too few.

A final issue related to exhaustiveness concerns the distribution of information. When a system is not exhaustive, a portion of the information falls into a residual or undifferentiated category. A system where a significant number of responses fall into a residual category may be as difficult to interpret as a system in which most observations fall into only one or two categories.

Category content

Although numerous references to and examples of principles for writing items have been scattered throughout this chapter, one important issue in category content has not yet been discussed. This concerns whether the content of the category should consist of statements about the presumed intention of the behavior or statements about the observed effect of the behavior. Discussion of this issue will constitute most of this section.

Most records in observation involve inferences. An act is identified by inferring the intent of the actor (for example, Schoggen, 1963, p. 66), the effects of an act regardless of intention (for example, Bales, 1950), the function of the act for a relationship (for example, Longabaugh, 1963), or the cultural meaning of the act (for example, Glad and Glad, 1963, p. 34). The two most common inferences involve intent and effect and these will be discussed shortly. First, the general issue of inferences deserves comment.

Noninferential observation is exceedingly rare (Kaplan, 1964, p. 131); consequently, most investigators make special efforts to have their observers be explicit about the inferences they make. Sherif and Sherif (1964, p. 334) and Barker and Wright (1955, p. 217) required their observers to set apart in brackets or paragraphs their inferences about the data. Glad and Glad (1963, p. 54) specified a position on their recording form where observer judgments were to be recorded. This position was "for characterizations of the behavior which are not visibly [sic] present in the behavior itself. Cultural value judgments, inferences, interpretations and all 'as if', 'might be', 'I wonder whether', 'some people might think that', kinds of observations about the subject's behavior would have their origin at this point" (p. 54).

Often, inferences are not quite so easy to detect as the preceding would suggest. They are embedded in category labels, lay language, and habitual ways of viewing events. This is not to say that inferences should be eliminated, only that their logic be explicated. The legitimacy and importance of inferences in observational records has been noted on several occasions (for example, Barker and Wright, 1955; Longabaugh, 1963). Lambert (1960, p. 889) suggested that inferences in observational research have fewer errors than might be expected because the observer, since he is detached, has more information, and because he has to state his inferences and how he arrived at them.

Several suggestions have been made about ways to clarify inferences. Heyns and Zander (1953, p. 391) suggested that high-level inferences are more accurate if they are made by sophisticated observers. Lambert (1960, p. 377) observed that the question of inference is largely a question of information processing. If an observer can receive and retain little information, he feels more pressure to fill in gaps and to make inferences. However, with a long attention span, the observer can see the outcome of an event and inference is unnecessary. Mann (1967) required coders to specify which of four levels of inference they had used to decide what feelings a member had toward a leader. These levels ranged from least inferential—"acts which make direct reference to the leader and in which the member either expresses the feelings as his own or attempts to differentiate himself from some other agent"—to most inferential—"acts which express feelings towards the leader or some symbolic equivalent for the leader by attributing feelings to another agent." Heyns and Lippitt (1954, p. 374) suggested an especially apt criterion for the clarification of inferences. They suggested that, in most analyses, inferences are made at one time or another. If the theory is sufficiently explicit, there is no reason why the observer should not make the inferences at the time the act occurs, rather than later. When inferences are postponed until some future time, an unnecessary extra step is added. Not many systems are explicit enough to permit inferences on location, but it is a reasonable and demanding criterion to strive for.

Whenever persons observe actions, they tend to impute purposes to the actor (Dickman, 1963, p. 36; Heider, 1944; Shor, 1957). In many observational systems, acts are differentiated according to the inferred *intent* of the actor. Barker and Wright (1955, p. 331), for example, described seven "action modes" which are categories to infer the goals of an actor from his actions. E. W. Katz (1964) has made perhaps the most extensive analysis of intent in her system of Intentional Content Analysis. Although this system of 56 categories (for example, "to avoid unpleasantness with," "to relate equally to," "not to improve relationship with") was originally designed to encode the content of short stories, it appears relevant to analysis of observational records, especially narratives such as specimen records. Not only does the system include an extensive list of intentions with several exemplars of each intention, but it also provides for the description of role relationships (1964, p. 34) and for the use of pairs of opposed intentions (1964, p. 33) in a format similar to that used for the semantic differential. Katz (1964, p. 19) compared the Action Modes proposed by Barker and Wright with the intentions she had categorized, and found that only 18 of her 56 categories covered similar material.

Observational records based on codings of intent have the advantage that they tend to be focused. Baumrind (1964) noted that the human observer "is capable of discounting acts and statements which are produced by a fleeting mood or set in favor of more permanent essential components of human interaction, and this capability can increase either the truth or error component of his judgment" (p. 5).

The chief problem with intent is specifying the bases for inferences. Intents are often more difficult to judge than environmental effects. Suggestions for increasing the clarity of judgments of intent have been made by Lambert (1960), and by Katz (1964) in her discussion of ways to translate literal connectors into intention. Barker and Wright (1955, pp. 238–239) summarized seven excellent behavioral indices to infer intent:

1. Action persists in the absence of instigating conditions. . . .
2. Change in position toward a part of the environment is renewed after digression or delay. . . .
3. "Preparatory adjustments" appropriate to imminent situational change, toward which the observed action contributes, accompany the action. . . .
4. Sustained locomotion is abruptly discontinued after an *end,* provisionally identified by the observer, has been reached. . . .
5. Action between observable beginning and end points shows continuity. . . .
6. Action between beginning and end points follows the shortest available path. . . .
7. Variance in behavior is concordant with variance in the position of an environmental object.

Acts are often encoded in terms of their environmental *effects* rather than the intent of the actor (for example, Harris, 1964, pp. 28–30; Leary, 1957). Medley and Mitzel (1962) argued that the recording of effects is often more precise and valid than the recording of intent. "Behavior identical in every respect except the teacher's purpose should have identical effects on the pupils, since the pupils are unaware of the purpose of the teacher so long as it is not manifested externally" (p. 9). Lambert (1963, p. 238) observed that a considerable number of the articles published by social psychologists focus on "the *effects* of the acts of another person or a subject." Borgatta's (1963) Behavior Scores System of observation derives from research on peer assessment, a clear example of environmental effects. The rationale for the system is consistent with the symbolic interactionist's position that "the identity of the individual is viewed as how he sees himself in the responses of others" (Borgatta, 1963, p. 26). Environmental effects are also consistent with an important principle in psychology, namely, that behavior is controlled by its consequences (reinforcement). Lambert (1960, p. 886) suggested that descriptions of effects also have the valued properties that they do not require a detailed statement of movements, they are close to usual language codes, and they are visible and serve as feedback. Finally, attention to environmental effects ensures that the observer will remain focused on the person-environmental unit.

As do records of intent, records of effect have certain ambiguities. Environmental effects rely very heavily on contiguous events, and Baumrind (1967) has argued that this diverts attention from delayed responses. Many actions consist of unsuccessful attempts to influence another person, and a record of environmental effects may omit these attempts. Since effects must often be inferred, it is especially important that observers be sensitive to those they are watching. Lambert (1960, p. 887) cited the example of a young child who hits a much bigger child and the bigger child laughs. The act is one of aggression, but the effect is humor. The rationale for describing this as an aggressive act lies in reference to the conventional "language of action" (p. 888) for persons of that age.

CALIBRATING THE OBSERVER

Observational methods are more vulnerable to the fallibilities of human perceivers than almost any other method. The consequences of this fact for methodology can be sizable. Miller (1962, p. 156) noted of humans that

> ... our perceptual equipment is designed to make many measurements simultaneously but to do a fairly crude job on each one. ... If a compromise is necessary, it seems far wiser to make rough decisions about everything than to make very acute distinctions as to a few aspects while ignoring completely the information provided by others. We do have some ability to trade breadth for accuracy.

Given this view, it is not surprising to learn that "the progress of psychology as a science goes hand in hand with the course of its rejection of 'facts' that come from everyday forms of observation and experience" (Hyman, 1964, p. 330).

The relevance to observational methods of human perceptual errors is probably greater than many have presumed. Fewer aids intervene between the observer and the event when records are made *in situ* than is the case in the laboratory. Observers are more on their own—this is one reason why we have argued for greater selectivity and structure in observation. Because investigators who use observational methods are subject to many of the same biases as persons in everyday life, a sizable portion of the research in general psychology carries implications for this methodology. Of relevance are studies of such topics as vigilance (for example, Frankmann and Adams, 1962), person perception (Cline, 1964), information processing (Miller, 1956), primacy-recency (Anderson, 1965), etc. Obviously it is impossible to sample even a few of the implications of these areas.

Instead, the purpose of this section is to detail briefly some of the more prominent biases that enter into observations and some methodological and training solutions to these problems. It is assumed that biases will vary in their salience as different settings, records, and behaviors are utilized. It is also assumed that accuracy will increase if the observer is made aware of errors he will be tempted to make. Throughout the chapter, perceptual biases and methodological solutions have been noted in discussions of such topics as observer interference, observer editing, reliability, and the coding of intent. The present discussion attempts to pull together some of these scattered references.

INVENTORY OF BIASES

One of the more important papers on the topic of biases in observation is Campbell's (1958) discussion of systematic errors that humans make when they are links in a communication system. The present inventory draws heavily on this source. Campbell distinguished between errors in *duplicatory assignments* (relaying a message without an intended change in form) and in *reductive assignments* (complex input translated into a simple output language). Although the fit is not as clean as one might wish, duplicatory assignments resemble assignments to secure nonselective records and reductive assignments resemble the categorization of records. The resemblances, however, are only approximate because there is some overlap between the two assignments.

One of the most prominent biases in duplication is *abbreviation*. The "output, if imperfect, will on the average be shorter, simpler, and less detailed than input" (Campbell, 1958, p. 342). Purcell and Brady (1965, pp. 52–58) recorded the same event on tape and in a specimen record, and it is clear that the specimen records contained less detail than was present in the original events. But it is also clear that the structure of the event was retained and that mostly minor details dropped out. Campbell thus described a person in the process of abbreviation: "through an anticipatory monitoring of his own intended output, he makes an active effort to produce a coherent output, by suppressing remembered detail that does not now seem to fit and by confabulating detail where gaps are conspicuous" (1958, p. 342). Thus abbreviation involves reconstruction, and the reconstruction involves materials with which the observer is familiar. Thus, specimen records made of actions in Kansas (observational site for Barker and Wright, 1955) might look quite different if they were made by someone who was familiar with this way of life and someone who was not (see Yarrow and Raush, 1962, pp. 8–9 for discussion of this point).

A second error involves *middle-message loss*. It is presumed that the middle portion of a message is forgotten more readily than either the initial or final portion. This argues that the nonselective records should be most accurate concerning how events start and end, and least accurate concerning the content of what actually occurs. This bias is of interest because earlier it was noted that Riesman and Watson (1964, p. 253) found it easier to record the *middle* portion of events, not the ends. This apparent discrepancy is probably explained by the fact that Riesman and Watson were especially interested in the fate of conversational resources and their attention was directed to what occurred *during* the interaction.

Closure (or directional distortion) and *symmetry* (or balanced distortion) are common, especially when the input is unclear. The presence of this bias is significant because it suggests that unique or slightly irregular acts will probably be given a commonplace explanation. The observer's puzzlement is apt to get lost in a sensible explanation. The only reason for pausing on this point is that it suggests that observational methods may not have quite the sensitivity for hypothesis generation that is often ascribed to them.

Enhancement of contrast often occurs when an observer tries to duplicate an input. Essentially what he does is distort the message in the direction of dividing the content into "clear cut 'entities,' reducing gradations both by exaggerating some differences and losing others" (Campbell, 1958, p. 344). This bias is of especial relevance to the argument as to whether there are such things as natural units of behavior. The preceding principle implies that if there is a bias in nonselective records, it should be in the direction of portraying the stream of behavior in terms of several discrete entities that have integrity and that appear more *unlike* adjacent entities than may actually be the case. The tendency to fragment behavior into discrete, coherent units is crucial in observational methodology, because one of the most prominent units of analysis, the episode (for example, Barker and Wright, 1955; Flanders, 1960; Harris, 1964; Soskin and John, 1963; Watson and Potter, 1962) may be vulnerable to this error. The episode is regarded as a set of actions in which there is a single focus of attention, coherence, and a beginning and an ending. Examples of episodes would be such actions as writing spelling lesson at blackboard, getting new chalk from teacher, and doodling with chalk (Barker, 1963, pp. 291–293). Perceptual errors due to enhancement of contrast are relevant to this unit of analysis, because there is the suggestion that when records are obtained, the record may be biased toward the appearance of episodes.

A bias toward *central tendency* occurs when extreme events are "distorted toward the mean of the series" (Campbell, 1958, p. 345). Emotional outbursts should be underestimated in a nonselective record just as flatness of affect should appear more variable when recorded. Even though observers may be biased toward central tendencies, it is one of the assets of narratives that intense affect can usually be preserved, especially if bodily movements and the setting are also recorded.

Before proceeding, it should be noted that, even though nonselective records are vulnerable to each of these errors, in actuality many of these errors have little effect. The reason is that events are recorded as they occur; this means that little time elapses between the observation and the record. Each of the preceding errors becomes more prominent if recording is delayed or if long units are observed before a record is made. This means that studies in which observers must wait a considerable time before they record what they have seen (for example, Festinger, Riecken, and Schachter, 1956; Raush, Dittmann, and Taylor, 1959; Riesman, Potter, and Watson, 1960; Sherif and Sherif, 1964) should be interpreted with caution. However, even immediate output does not completely immunize the observer against these effects.

Several biases are found in both duplicatory and reductive assignments. The most prominent of these is the "tendency to distort messages in the direction of identity with previous inputs" (Campbell, 1958, p. 346). This tendency toward *assimilation to prior inputs* is affected by the frequency of previous messages and by similarities between present and prior inputs. One implication is that records should be biased toward ordinary, typical events since these events are most prominent in the observer's memory. This error would also bias records in the direction of regularity and orderliness. If current events assume the appearance of earlier events, investigators may conclude that events are patterned when in fact they are not.

Assimilation occurs to other objects than prior inputs. These additional objects include *expected message, own attitude,* and messages that were previously *rewarded and punished.* Assimilation to expected input is crucial where the observer is also the person who proposed the hypothesis. Even though observers can modify data to conform to expectations in the laboratory (Rosenthal, 1963, 1964), these biases are apt to be even more pronounced *in situ* where a larger portion of the event must be recorded by the observer. The other two forms of assimilation deal mostly with dispositions of the observer, a variable of obvious importance (for example, Back, 1956; Richardson, 1965; Shrauger and Altrocchi, 1964), but also one that is beyond the scope of this discussion.

In reductive coding the output is less complex than the input; this produces several additional sources of bias. One of the most common errors is *coding relativism*. According to this notion, which closely parallels the concept of adaptation level, "the coding thresholds employed tend to be relative to recent inputs rather than constant for physical attributes of the stimulus" (Campbell, 1958, p. 353). Thus, the standards which are used to place events in one category or another fluctuate as a function of what occurs while coding is taking place. If an interaction is prosaic and most of the acts are categorized as information exchange, a slight affective departure from these run-of-the-mill comments may be scored as an intense outburst because coding standards have altered.

Prior coding assignments also exert a systematic effect on coding—an individual may revert to prior coding assignments as the present task becomes difficult or boring. Thus, if the observer has several tasks to do, and the most prominent one is to make periodic ratings, he may revert to this task when he has to shift to the assignment of tallying the frequency of responses. It is likely that he will be tempted to make "summary" tallies rather than an entry for each event.

Contamination from associated cues can be a subtle source of bias in observation. The principle is described as follows (Campbell, 1958, p. 356):

If in the past, two dimensions have varied together, so that certain values of one have become associated with certain values of another, both dimensions will come to contribute to coding decisions.

Thus, if an observer is categorizing affiliative behavior on the basis of movement toward another person, and if in the past he has associated smiling with movements toward, then either smiles or movement or both may contribute to a categorization of "seeks affiliation." The reason this error is so subtle is that most category systems supposedly focus on only one aspect of behavior. However, since the observer is looking at a complex event, and since he commonly interprets complex events along several dimensions, these additional dimensions can readily contribute to his coding.

Assimilation to evaluative coding means that coding assignments often are vulnerable to affective bias. This should be especially true when lay language is involved. "The most natural coding of any input by the human operator seems to be of the general nature of 'like' versus 'dislike,' 'approach' versus 'avoid,' 'good' versus 'bad,' 'beautiful' versus 'ugly,' etc." (p. 357). Thus, even though the intent of coding is to represent the positive *and* negative components of an action, person, or event, the initial impressions tend to color subsequent coding.

The preceding list of biases is by no means exhaustive. But it is representative of biases that intrude on the recording process and it does exemplify the relevance of general psychology for the development of observational methods. While the naive observer is largely at the mercy of many of these errors, the scientific observer is not, even though he goes through many of the same motions. The following section explores some methodological solutions to these biases.

METHODOLOGICAL SOLUTIONS TO BIAS

One set of methodological solutions can be derived from laws of psychophysics, as Heyns and Lippitt (1954, pp. 400–402) have demonstrated. For example, "ordinal judgments are more accurate than absolute judgments" (p. 401). As valuable as these rules are they also have limitations, the most prominent one being that there are fewer judgmental "prompts in the field than the subject has in the laboratory" (Lambert, 1960, p. 885). The methodological solutions sampled here are not organized in a single model, as in the case of the analogy to psychophysics. Instead, they are largely methodological twists that seem to reduce errors. Frequently, as one type of error is reduced, the chances for other kinds of errors increase.

Most of the biases noted earlier involve memory. Almost all records are based on memory traces, the main differences being in the vividness of the trace. Memory distortions can be handled in several ways. Raush, Dittmann, and Taylor (1959) had each observer gauge the length of his observation to the amount of the specific activity that he could remember (p. 11). Observers could set their own limits on how much they saw before dictating; the mean length of observation was eight minutes. While such a rule takes account of individual differences, it leads to choppy records of intense episodes. As more events occur, observers are forced to watch for shorter periods of time. Sherif and Sherif (1964, p. 118) and Haeberle (1959) reduced the memory loss by having observers focus on one small portion of the problem at a time. Memory loss is often less critical because of a property of events themselves—recurrence (Pittenger, Hockett, and Danehy, 1960, p. 225). Significant themes tend to be repeated; if they are forgotten the first time they are observed, they may be remembered the second time.

Several of the errors associated with duplicatory assignments suggested that satiation or boredom contributed to the assimilation of unique events into commonplace labels. Satiation or habituation is a common problem in vigilance (for example, Frankmann and Adams, 1962). When stimuli show little variability, reports become increasingly inaccurate. This phenomenon suggests that variability may be a requirement for alertness and accuracy. Variability can be introduced by such means as "rest periods, high signal rate, knowledge of results, interpolated messages, use of tasks with multiple stimulus sources" (Campbell, 1958, p. 265). Most observational studies use sufficiently short exposures to events that habituation is unlikely. Furthermore, observers are usually given varied tasks, varied settings, or different persons to watch. Each of these changes introduces a new contingency that requires closer attention. But a frequent change of observers is not without problems. If observers shift frequently, actors notice them for much longer than if only one observer is used. Thus multiple observers may increase the accuracy of records, but they may also be much more reactive.

Many of the errors noted above thrive on ambiguity. Prior inputs have their greatest impact when present inputs are puzzling. Ambiguity is not just a function of the present situation, it also occurs because categories are imprecise, because the observer must make unrealistic judgments, or because he is overburdened. This suggests that simplicity and familiarization are crucial principles. The necessity for simplicity is best conveyed by Medley and Mitzel (1963, p. 263):

In any given study, between the record and the behavior it is supposed to represent should be interposed only the most primitive act of judgment or discrimination possible—the one needed to perceive whether the behavior has occurred or not. . . . An inaccurate record cannot be corrected once it is made.

From this point of view, it is less critical for the observer to score or quantify the behavior than to secure a record of it. This is one reason why we have emphasized simple, unequivocal behavioral indices. These usually require only a judgment of present-absent, they are concrete and easy to grasp, and do not impose excessive demands on the observer.

The merits of familiarity are implied by Miller's (1962, p. 151) assertion that "the unexpected is always hard to perceive clearly." Guest (1955) reported that the day before he was to observe and record the interaction of a foreman, he would spend about three hours becoming familiar with the personnel, problems, and the departmental layout. This undoubtedly lessened the novelty of the situation and, therefore, reduced the chances that it would be described in terms of prior inputs. Familiarization, however, has sizable disadvantages, as several persons have noted (Goode and Hatt, 1952, p. 124; Selltiz *et al.,* 1959, p. 215). The danger is that distinctive features become obscured as the observer learns more about them. The longer an observer waits, the fewer things he may have left to categorize.

Simplification is often accomplished by the use of multiple observers. Although each observer is prone to perceptual errors, his reports may be more accurate because he has less to watch. Multiple observers can be deployed in many ways. One can watch for instigations, the other for outcomes; each can watch for different instigations or for different outcomes; one can watch the person, the other the object; they can each operate at the same level of inference or at different levels; they can each watch one person and record what he does, or record everything that happens in a particular zone. Multiple observers are unusually effective in reducing the dangers of selective perception, a major problem in observation.

Selectivity can also be lessened by forcing the observer to attend to several different portions of an event, as Medley and Smith (1964) and Ekman (1957) have done. Formats promote scanning and their value may lie more in the increase of accuracy regarding the description of the central events than in the recording of incidental information about the setting.

TRAINING SOLUTIONS TO BIAS

The points considered in this discussion of calibration, if they are to be used at all, must be conveyed to the observer; this typically happens during training. The conduct of training is often crucial in the determination of the impact that errors will have. It is during training that events become more familiar and definitions of categories become more precise. Attention span may increase, with the result that errors of abbreviation, closure, and symmetry decline. As the observer gains more experience with a given system, former associations among dimensions may have less effect, with the result that evaluative coding gives way to neutral coding. Familiarity with codes and coding norms may decrease the effects of coding relativism. But these several accomplishments are not attained easily.

Heyns and Zander (1953, pp. 404–407) suggested several training procedures that help to offset observer errors. For example, they had observers watch and record action *before* they learned the system. Not only did this experience show the observer just how many behavioral cues are available, it also suggested the necessity of using categories with precise definitions. Similar orientation activities were used in the project in which sociable interaction was studied (Riesman and Watson, 1964). The observers were exposed to the motion picture *Marty,* they attended the same party and wrote individual accounts of it, and they attended different parties which they also described. These several written accounts not only produced an appreciation of the need for categories, but also suggested relevant content for the categories.

When the trainees first start to learn the definitions of categories and the rationale for the system, their initial reaction is typically one of awe at the apparent complexity of the system. This is one of the reasons it is especially important to provide information about how the categories were built, so that the observer literally can derive a similar set of categories and definitions. As training progresses the definitions may be applied to written protocols (Bales, 1950, p. 86), role playing (Heyns and Zander, 1953, p. 406), or training films (Medley and Smith, 1964). Bales noted that written protocols are valuable at first because they permit trainees to ponder an interpretation or look up a definition without the pressure of an immediate decision. But every effort is made to keep training with protocols short-lived because they can make an observer ineffectual in coding live action. The transition from protocols to live action can often be eased if the trainees next encode tape recordings. Greater demands are imposed to use additional cues, but only one modality rather than two is added.

The final stage, role playing, permits training in the coding of live action, yet trainees have the opportunity to stop the interaction if they have difficulties. Role playing permits the trainer to introduce systematically events which may be especially troublesome to the observers. Laughter, for example, is often difficult to encode and role playing enables trainees to gain experience coding it.

Heyns and Zander (1953, p. 406) added a final step to their training procedure that is crucial but often neglected. Trainees were given instruction and practice in etiquette and *entrée* with real groups. Earlier in the discussion of observer interference it was noted that the basis on which a person joins and stays in a group can have a marked effect on subsequent behavior. While most persons readily admit this, few make the effort to solve the problem via training.

Bales (1950) cited two additional subtle issues that pervade training. One concerns the frustration that occurs when an act is missed or placed in the wrong category. A good observer must develop tolerance for these errors. One means to promote this tolerance is to acquire "an ability to inhibit all but the present context of acts and to avoid jamming incoming stimuli with internal reflections" (p. 86).

A second, and potentially more important issue, concerns criteria for the correctness of categorization. Many observers see categorization as largely a commonsense activity, and they may be reluctant to admit that they make mistakes and that "someone else has more common sense." Persons in training often defend strongly their own interpretations. The best means to head off these confrontations is to maintain permissive training sessions and also to use an impersonal criterion of correctness such as "the manual."

As a final illustration of training as a means to reduce biases, the procedure used by Bunney and Hamburg (1963, p. 285) to instruct nurses in rating mental patients is exemplary. After initial discussions of group dynamics and the rating items, the nurses saw motion pictures of patients who represented certain positions on the rating scales. "Consensus sessions" were then held with the experimenter for two weeks. At these sessions, individual impressions of selected patients were pooled in order to arrive at a group rating. This gave each nurse familiarity with rating notions, and also some idea of judgmental processes used by other nurses. Following consensus sessions, the nurses made individual ratings for several weeks. It was not until all these steps had been completed that the actual raters for the study were chosen. Once the final team had been chosen, they met for an hour, two or three days a week, to discuss items, definitions, reliability, problem patients, etc. These review sessions were recorded so that nurses on the evening shift would have equivalent information. As a final refinement, at the end of one month each nurse wrote about the five items with which she had the most difficulty and why. Revisions were made and/or observers were calibrated on the basis of these reports.

Methods can affect some observer errors; training can affect others. Judicious choices of method and training techniques can help the investigator to retain the advantage of the human instrument without all the attendant errors. But such an outcome is hard to come by because the observer's task is often not very different from that of a person in everyday life.

CONCLUSION

The stature of systematic observational methods among the techniques available to the scientist has traditionally been quite equivocal because of the mystique surrounding this methodology, its use to study a surprisingly narrow range of problems, and the difficulty in delimiting this methodology; and also because those methodological limitations that have been imposed are often self-defeating. It is somewhat sobering to read older reviews of this methodology and see that they are surprisingly current. While this attests to the thoroughness of the earlier reviews, it also attests to the relatively slow pace at which observational methodology has developed.

Among the impediments to the improvement of this methodology have been imprecise specification of what constitutes a "natural" event, the assumption that naturalness and control are mutually exclusive, lack of systematizing of the inevitable editing that occurs when records are made, the designation of passivity and docility as the crucial role for the observer, excessive reliance on heavily judgmental measures which are vulnerable to several intractable errors, and over-estimation of the costs involved in an observational study. A sizable number of these impediments might be subsumed under a more general label, the *existential temptation*. When persons confront reality in natural settings, they may become gratified simply at seeing new things occur, and once these observations have been made, observers may be reluctant to do anything else. While gratification at un-covering secrets is understandable, it is not especially helpful. The observations must be abstracted, quantified, and summarized if they are to be useful. These processes invariably result in a loss of information, but there is no reason to assume that everything that is lost is of equal importance.

Several themes have been developed throughout this chapter, perhaps the most prominent being that demands on judgment and inference can be reduced if the observer selects and makes subtle interventions in settings, if he adopts behavioral measures that impose few demands for inference, if he makes accurate records of complex events, and if he calibrates observers in such a way as to offset perceptual biases. In essence, we are trying to unburden the often overburdened observer. If steps are taken to implement unburdening, then observational methods can be used more extensively and at less cost. If the observer intervenes in a setting, mindful of the cautions inherent in the phrase *tempered naturalness,* he can produce the desired events more quickly, with fewer distractions and with fewer demands on inference, *without* necessarily destroying the very phenomenon he wishes to study. It should be clear that interference by the observer is not so much a stumbling block to observation as many have presumed, and the pre-ceding discussion suggests ways in which interference can be assessed and reduced.

Observers have often resorted to judgmental measures because they assumed that this was the only way in which relatively complex events could be encoded. The extensive survey of molecular behaviors suggests that discrete, visible, subtle responses can often be just as valid indicators of complex events as are the more demanding judgmental indicators. It is not proposed that these behavioral measures necessarily be substituted for ratings, only that they be considered care-fully when a study is designed and that they be used to supplement more ambigu-ous measures.

Observers have often had misgivings about what role psychometric considera-tions such as reliability should play when a study is designed. Oversimplified views concerning reliability have often led observers either toward a wholesale rejection of the idea and toward imprecise descriptions of unstable phenomena, or toward an obsession with reliability and insignificant findings. The present chapter argues in favor of a multidimensional view of reliability, a view which suggests that some types of reliability can be sacrificed, and that different types of reliability are important at different stages of inquiry, but also that reliability cannot be ignored. It should be clear, however, that the approach developed in this chapter also tends to place the issue of reliability in perspective, because many of the strategies that are advocated reduce judgmental demands and thereby also reduce demands for reliability.

While the present enthusiasm for observational methods should not be construed as an argument that investigators should use this methodology alone, it seems clear that observational methods can be adapted to more problems with greater precision than investigators have realized. Perhaps this portrait of observational methods will help dissuade some scientists from the temptation to relegate this methodology to a position of secondary importance among their techniques.

REFERENCES

Alger, C. F. (1966). Interaction in a committee of the United Nations General Assembly. *Midwest J. polit. Sci., 10,* 411–447.

Allport, G. W. (1961). *Pattern and growth in personality.* New York: Holt, Rinehart, and Winston.

Allport, G. W., and P. E. Vernon (1933). *Studies in expressive movement.* New York: Macmillan.

Amrine, M., and F. Sanford (1956). In the matter of juries, democracy, science, truth, senators, and bugs. *Amer. Psychologist, 11,* 54–60.

Anderson, N. M. (1965). Primacy effects in personality impression formation using a generalized order effect paradigm. *J. Pers. soc. Psychol., 2,* 1–9.

Argyris, C. (1958). Some problems in conceptualizing organizational climate: a case study of a bank. *Admin. Sci. Quart., 2,* 501–520.

——— (1965). *Organization and innovation.* Homewood, Ill.: Dorsey.

Arrington, R. (1943). Time sampling in studies of social behavior: a critical review of techniques and results with research suggestions. *Psychol. Bull., 40,* 81–124.

Bachrach, A. J. (1962). *Psychological research: an introduction.* New York: Random House.

Back, K. W. (1956). The 'Einstellung' test and performance in factual interviewing. *J. abnorm. soc. Psychol., 52,* 28–32.

——— (1962). Social research as a communications system. *Soc. Forces, 41,* 61–68.

Back, K., L. Festinger, B. Hymovitch, H. Kelley, S. Schachter, and J. Thibaut (1950). The methodology of studying rumor transmission. *Hum. Relat., 3,* 307–312.

Baerends, G. P. (1954). Egg recognition in the herring gull. In *Proceedings of the Fourteenth International Congress of Psychology, Montreal.* Pp. 93–94.

Bales, R. F. (1950). *Interaction process analysis.* Cambridge, Mass.: Addison-Wesley.

——— (in press). Interaction process analysis. In D. L. Sills (Ed.), *International encyclopedia of the social sciences.* New York: Crowell-Collier and Macmillan.

Barch, A. M., D. Trumbo, and F. Nangle (1957). Social setting and conformity to a legal requirement. *J. abnorm. soc. Psychol., 55*, 396–398.

Barker, R. G. (1960). Ecology and motivation. In M. R. Jones (Ed.), *Nebraska symposium on motivation, 1960.* Lincoln: Univ. of Nebraska Press. Pp. 1–49.

———, Ed. (1963). *The stream of behavior.* New York: Appleton-Century.

——— (1964). Observation of behavior: ecological approaches. *J. Mount Sinai Hospital, 31*, 268–284.

——— (1965). Explorations in ecological psychology. *Amer. Psychologist, 20*, 1–14.

Barker, R. G.. and Louise S. Barker (1963). Social actions in the behavior streams of American and English children. In R. G. Barker (Ed.), *The stream of behavior.* New York: Appleton-Century. Pp. 127–159.

Barker, R. G., and P. V. Gump (1964). *Big school, small school.* Stanford: Stanford Univ. Press.

Barker, R. G., and H. F. Wright (1955). *Midwest and its children.* Evanston, Ill.: Row, Peterson.

Barker, R. G., H. F. Wright, Louise S. Barker, and Maxine Schoggen (1961). *Specimen records of American and English children.* Lawrence: Univ. of Kansas Publications, Social Science Studies.

Baumrind, Diana (1964). Naturalistic assessment of parent-child interaction. Paper presented at Conference on Research Methodology of Parent-Child Interaction, Syracuse, N.Y.

——— (1967). Child care practices anteceding three patterns of preschool behavior. *Genet. Psychol. Monogr., 75*, 43–88.

Bellak, L., and M. B. Smith (1956). An experimental exploration of the psychoanalytic process: exemplification of a method. *Psychoanal. Quart., 25*, 385–414.

Beller, E. K. (1959). Direct and inferential observations in the study of children. *Amer. J. Orthopsychiat., 29*, 560–573.

Berger, M. M. (1958). Nonverbal communication in group psychotherapy. *Int. J. Group Psychother., 8*, 161–178.

Bing, Elizabeth (1963). Effect of child-rearing practices on development of differential cognitive abilities. *Child Develpmt., 34*, 631–648.

Birdwhistell, R. L. (1952). *Introduction to kinesics.* Louisville, Ky.: Univ. of Louisville.

——— (1959). Contributions of linguistic-kinesic studies to the understanding of schizophrenia. In A. Auerbach (Ed.), *Schizophrenia.* New York: Ronald. Pp. 99–123.

——— (1961). Paralanguage: 25 years after Sapir. In H. W. Brosnin (Ed.), *Lectures on experimental psychiatry.* Pittsburgh: Univ. of Pittsburgh.

—— (1962a). An approach to communication. *Family Process, 1,* 194–201.

—— (1962b). Critical moments in the psychiatric interview. In T. T. Tourlentex (Ed.), *Research approaches to a psychiatric problem.* Chicago: Grune and Stratton. Pp. 179–188.

—— (in press). Body behavior and communication. In D. L. Sills (Ed.), *International encyclopedia of the social sciences.* New York: Crowell-Collier and Macmillan.

—— (in press). Communication as a multi-channel system. In D. L. Sills (Ed.), *International encyclopedia of the social sciences.* New York: Crowell-Collier and Macmillan.

Bishop, Barbara M. (1951). Mother-child interaction and the social behavior of children. *Psychol. Monogr., 65,* No. 11 (whole No. 328).

Blau, P. M. (1964). The research process in the study of "The Dynamics of Bureaucracy." In P. E. Hammond (Ed.), *Sociologists at work.* New York: Basic Books. Pp. 16–49.

Blood, R. O. (1958). The use of observational methods in family research. *Marriage and Family Living, 20,* 47–52.

Borgatta, E. F. (1961). Role-playing specification, personality, and performance. *Sociometry, 24,* 218–233.

—— (1962). A systematic study of interaction process scores, peer and self-assessments, personality and other variables. *Genet. Psychol. Monogr., 65,* 219–291.

—— (1963a). A new systematic interaction observation system: behavior scores system (BSs system). *J. psychol. Stud., 14,* 24–44.

—— (1963b). Some task factors in social interaction. *Sociol. and soc. Res., 48,* 5–12.

Borgatta, E. F., and Betty Crowther (1965). *A workbook for the study of social interaction processes.* Chicago: Rand McNally.

Bott, Helen M. (1933). Method in social studies of young children. *Toronto Univ. Stud. Child Develpmt. Ser.,* No. 1. Toronto: Univ. of Toronto Press.

Brock, T. C. (1965). Communicator-recipient similarity and decision change. *J. Pers. soc. Psychol., 1,* 650–654.

Bunney, W. E., and D. A. Hamburg (1963). Methods for reliable longitudinal observation of behavior. *Arch. gen. Psychiat., 9,* 280–294.

Burchard, W. W. (1957). A study of attitudes towards the use of concealed devices in social science research. *Soc. Forces, 36,* 111.

Butler, J. M., Laura N. Rice, and Alice K. Wagstaff (1963). *Quantitative naturalistic research.* Englewood Cliffs, N.J.: Prentice-Hall.

Byrne, D. (1964). Assessing personality variables and their alteration. In P. Worchel and D. Byrne (Eds.), *Personality change.* New York: Wiley. Pp. 38–68.

Calhoun, J. B. (1950). The study of wild animals under controlled conditions. *Ann. N. Y. Acad. Sci., 51,* 113–122.

Campbell, D. T. (1957). Factors relevant to the validity of experiments in social settings. *Psychol. Bull., 55,* 297–312.

—— (1958). Systematic error on the part of human links in communication systems. *Information and Control, 1,* 334–369.

—— (1961). The mutual methodological relevance of anthropology and psychology. In F. L. K. Hsu (Ed.), *Psychological anthropology*. Homewood, Ill.: Dorsey. Pp. 333–352.

Campbell, D. T., and D. W. Fiske (1959). Convergent and discriminant validation by the multitrait-multimethod matrix. *Psychol. Bull., 56,* 81–105.

Carlson, J., S. W. Cook, and E. L. Stomberg (1936). Sex differences in conversation. *J. appl. Psychol., 20,* 727–735.

Carmichael, H. T. (1956). Sound film recording of psychoanalytic therapy: a therapist's experiences and reactions. *J. Iowa State Med. Soc.,* November, 1956, pp. 590–595.

Carpenter, C. R. (1958). Territoriality: a review of concepts and problems. In A. Roe and G. G. Simpson (Eds.), *Behavior and evolution*. New Haven: Yale Univ. Press.

Cassotta, L., J. Jaffe, S. Feldstein, and R. Moses (1964). Operating manual: automatic vocal transaction analyzer. New York: William Alanson White Institute. Research Bulletin No. 1.

Chapple, E. D. (1939). Quantitative analysis of the interaction of individuals. *Proc. Nat. Acad. Sci., 25,* 58–67.

—— (1949). The Interaction Chronograph: its evolution and present application. *Personnel, 25,* 295–307.

—— (1953). The standard experimental (stress) interview as used in Interaction Chronograph investigations. *Hum. Organizat., 12,* 23–32.

—— (1962). Quantitative analysis of complex organizational systems. *Hum. Organizat., 21,* 67–87.

Chapple, E. D., Martha F. Chapple, Lucie A. Wood, Amy Miklowitz, N. S. Kline, and J. C. Saunders (1960). Interaction Chronograph method for analysis of differences between schizophrenics and controls. *Arch. gen. Psychiat., 3,* 160–167.

Christian, J. J., V. Flyger, and D. E. Davis (1960). Factors in mass mortality of a herd of Silka deer (Cervus nippon). *Chesapeake Sci., 1* (2), 79–95.

Cline, V. S. (1964). Interpersonal perception. In B. Maher (Ed.), *Progress in experimental personality research*. Vol. 1. New York: Academic Press. Pp. 221–284.

Coleman, J. C. (1949). Facial expressions of emotions. *Psychol. Monogr., 63,* No. 1 (whole No. 296).

Cook, S. W., and Claire Selltiz (1964). A multiple-indicator approach to attitude measurement. *Psychol. Bull., 62,* 36–55.

Cronbach, L. J. (1960). *Essentials of psychological testing* (2nd ed.). New York: Harper.

Dawe, Helen C. (1934). An analysis of two hundred quarrels of preschool children. *Child Develpmt., 5,* 139–157.

Deutsch, F. (1963). Analytic posturology and synesthesiology. *Psychoanal. Rev., 50,* 40–67.

Dickman, H. R. (1963). The perception of behavioral units. In R. G. Barker (Ed.), *The stream of behavior*. New York: Appleton-Century. Pp. 23–41.

Diersen, G., M. Lorenc, and R. M. Spitaleri (1961). A new method for graphic study of human movements. *Neurology, 11,* 610–618.

Dilger, W. C. (1962). The behavior of lovebirds. *Scientific American, 206* (1), 88–98.

Dittman, A. T. (1962). The relationship between body movements and moods in interviews. *J. consult. Psychol., 26,* 480.

Dittman, A. T., and L. C. Wynne (1961). Linguistic techniques and the analysis of emotionality in interviews. *J. abnorm. soc. Psychol., 63,* 201–204.

Drechsler, R. J., and M. I. Shapiro (1961). A procedure for direct observation of family interaction in a child guidance clinic. *Psychiatry, 24,* 163–170.

Dunnette, M. D. (1966). *Personnel selection and placement.* Belmont, Calif.: Wadsworth.

Dyck, A. J. (1963). The social contacts of some Midwest children with their parents and teachers. In R. G. Barker (Ed.), *The stream of behavior.* New York: Appleton-Century. Pp. 78–98.

Ekman, P. (1957). A methodological discussion of nonverbal behavior. *J. Psychol., 43,* 141–149.

———— (1965a). Communication through nonverbal behavior. Progress report, Langley Porter Inst.

———— (1965b). Communication through nonverbal behavior: a source of information about an interpersonal relationship. In S. S. Tomkins and C. E. Izard (Eds.), *Affect, cognition, and personality.* New York: Springer. Pp. 390–442.

———— (1965c). Differential communication of affect by head and body cues. *J. Pers. soc. Psychol., 2,* 726–735.

———— (1965d). Personality, pathology, affect, and nonverbal behavior. Paper presented at Western Psychol. Assoc.

Ekman, P., and W. V. Friesen (1965). System for the classification and analysis of nonverbal behavior. Unpublished manuscript, Langley Porter Inst.

Ellis, N. R., and R. S. Pryer (1959). Quantification of gross bodily activity in children with severe neuropathology. *Amer. J. ment. Defic., 63,* 1034–1037.

Errington, P. (1961). *Muskrats and marsh management.* Harrisburg, Pa.: Stackpole.

Esser, A. H., R. N. Chamberlain, E. D. Chapple, and N. S. Kline (1965). Territoriality of patients on a research ward. In J. Wortis (Ed.), *Recent advances in biological psychology.* Vol. 7. New York: Plenum. Pp. 37–44.

Exline, R. V. (1963). Explorations in the process of person perception: visual interaction in relation to competition, sex, and need for affiliation. *J. Pers., 31,* 1–20.

Exline, R. V., D. Gray, and Dorothy Schuette (1965). The incidence of mutual glances in dyads as a form of communication: avoidance as a function of interview content and sex of interviewee. *J. Pers. soc. Psychol., 1,* 201–209.

Exline, R., J. Thibaut, C. Brannon, and P. Gumpert (1961). Visual interaction in relation to Machiavellianism and an unethical act. *Amer. Psychologist, 16,* 396. (Abstract)

Exline, R. V., and L. C. Winters (1965). Affective relations and mutual glances in dyads. In S. Tomkins and C. Izard (Eds.), *Affect, cognition, and personality.* New York: Springer. Pp. 319–350.

Feldstein, S. (1964). Vocal patterning of emotional expression. In E. H. Masserman (Ed.), *Science and psychoanalysis.* Vol. 7. New York: Grune and Stratton. Pp. 193–208.

Feldstein, S., Marcia Brenner, and J. Jaffe (1963). The effect of subject sex, verbal inter-action, and topical focus on speech disruption. *Language and Speech, 6,* 229–239.

Festinger, L., H. W. Riecken, and S. Schachter (1956). *When prophecy fails.* Minneapolis: Univ. of Minnesota Press.

Flanders, N. A. (1960). *Teacher influence, pupil attitudes and achievement.* Minneapolis: Univ. of Minnesota. (Mimeo)

Frankmann, Judith P., and J. A. Adams (1962). Theories of vigilance. *Psychol. Bull., 59,* 257–272.

Friedman, N. (1964). The psychological experiment as a social interaction. Unpub-lished doctoral dissertation, Harvard University.

Friedman, N., D. Kurland, and R. Rosenthal (1965). Experimenter behavior as an unintended determinant of experimental results. *J. proj. Tech. Pers. Assess., 29,* 479–490.

Gamson, W. A. (1964). Experimental studies of coalition formation. In L. Berkowitz (Ed.), *Advances in experimental social psychology.* Vol. 1. New York: Academic Press. Pp. 81–110.

Garfinkel, H. (1963). A conception of, and experiments with, 'trust' as a condition of stable concerted actions. In O. J. Harvey (Ed.), *Motivation and social interaction.* New York: Ronald. Pp. 187–238.

Gellert, Elizabeth (1955). Systematic observation: a method in child study. *Harv. educ. Rev., 25,* 179–195.

————— (1961). Stability and fluctuation in the power relationships of young children. *J. abnorm. soc. Psychol., 62,* 8–15.

Glad, D. D., and Virginia B. Glad (1963). *Interpersonality synopsis.* New York: Libra.

Goldman-Eisler, Frieda (1958). Speech analysis and mental processes. *Language and Speech, 1,* 59–75.

————— (1961). The significance of changes in the rate of articulation. *Language and Speech, 4,* 171–174.

Goode, W. J., and P. K. Hatt (1952). *Methods in social research.* New York: McGraw-Hill.

Goodrich, D. W. (1959). The choice of situation for observational studies of children. *Amer. J. Orthopsychiat., 29,* 227–234.

Guest, R. M. (1955). Foremen at work: an interim report on method. *Hum. Organizat., 14*(2), 21–24.

Gump, P. V., and J. S. Kounin (1959). Issues raised by ecological and 'classical' research efforts. *Merrill-Palmer Quart., 6,* 145–152.

Gump, P. V., P. Schoggen, and F. Redl (1957). The camp milieu and its immediate effects. *J. soc. Issues, 13,* 40–46.

Gump, P. V., and B. Sutton-Smith (1955). The 'it' role in children's games. *Amer. Assoc. Group Workers, 17* (3), 3–8.

Gurman, E. B., and B. M. Bass (1961). Objective compared with subjective measures of the same behavior in groups. *J. abnorm. soc. Psychol., 63,* 368–374.

Haeberle, Ann W. (1959). Quantification of observational data in various stages of research. *Amer. J. Orthopsychiat., 29,* 583–589.

Haggard, E. A., Julia R. Hiken, and K. S. Isaacs (1965). Some effects of recording and filming on the psychotherapeutic process. *Psychiatry, 28,* 169–191.

Haggard, E. A., and K. S. Isaacs (1966). Micromomentary facial expressions as indicators of ego mechanisms in psychotherapy. In L. A. Gottschalk and A. H. Auerbach (Eds.), *Methods of research in psychotherapy.* New York: Appleton-Century. Pp. 154–165.

Hall, E. T. (1963a). Proxemics: the study of man's spatial relations. In I. Galdston (Ed.), *Man's image in medicine and anthropology.* New York: International Univ. Press. Pp. 422–445.

——— (1963b). A system for the notation of proxemic behavior. *Amer. Anthropologist, 65,* 1003–1026.

——— (1964). Silent assumptions in social communication. *Disorders of Communication, 42,* 41–55.

——— (1966). *The hidden dimension.* Garden City, N.Y.: Doubleday.

Hanawalt, N. G. (1944). The role of the upper and the lower parts of the face as the basis for judging facial expressions: II. In posed expressions and 'candid camera' pictures. *J. gen. Psychol., 31,* 23–36.

Hare, A. P., and R. F. Bales (1963). Seating position and small group interaction. *Sociometry, 26,* 480–486.

Hargreaves, W. A. (1960). A model for speech unit duration. *Language and Speech, 3,* 164–173.

——— (1965). Nursing rating of psychiatric patients. Unpublished manuscript. Langley Porter Inst.

Hargreaves, W. A., and J. A. Starkweather (1963). Recognition of speaker identity. *Language and Speech, 6,* 63–67.

——— (1965). Vocal and verbal indicators of depression. Unpublished manuscript. Langley Porter Inst.

Hargreaves, W. A., J. A. Starkweather, and K. H. Blacker (1965). Voice quality in depression. *J. abnorm. soc. Psychol., 70,* 218–220.

Harper, R. A., and J. W. Hudson (1952). The use of recordings in marriage counseling: a preliminary empirical investigation. *Marriage and Family Living, 14,* 332–334.

Harris, Marvin (1964). *The nature of cultural things.* New York: Random House.

Harvey, O. J. (1953). An experimental approach to the study of status relations in informal groups. *Amer. sociol. Rev., 18,* 357–367.

Haworth, Mary R. (1956). An exploratory study to determine the effectiveness of a filmed puppet show as a group projective technique for use with children. Unpublished doctoral dissertation, Pennsylvania State University.

Hayes, F. (1957). Gestures: a working bibliography. *South. Folklore Quart., 21,* 218–317.

Hazard, J. (1962). Furniture arrangement and judicial roles. *ETC., 19,* 181–188.

Heider, F. (1944). Social perception and phenomenal causality. *Psychol. Rev., 51,* 358–374.

Henle, Mary, and Marian B. Hubbell (1938). 'Egocentricity' in adult conversation. *J. soc. Psychol., 9,* 227–234.

Heyns, R. W., and R. Lippitt (1954). Systematic observational techniques. In G. Lindzey (Ed.), *Handbook of social psychology.* Vol. 1. Cambridge, Mass.: Addison-Wesley. Pp. 370–404.

Heyns, R. W., and A. F. Zander (1953). Observation of group behavior. In L. Festinger and D. Katz (Eds.), *Research methods in the behavioral sciences.* New York: Dryden. Pp. 381–417.

Hoffman, L. R., and N. R. F. Maier (1964). Valence in the adoption of solutions by problem-solving groups: concept, method, and results. *J. abnorm. soc. Psychol., 69,* 264–271.

Holmberg, A. R. (1954). Adventures in culture change. In R. F. Spencer (Ed.), *Method and perspective in anthropology.* Minneapolis: Univ. of Minnesota Press. Pp. 103–113.

Hyman, R. (1964). *The nature of psychological inquiry.* Englewood Cliffs, N.J.: Prentice-Hall.

Jecker, J. O., N. Maccoby, and H. S. Breitrose (1965). Improving accuracy in interpreting non-verbal cues of comprehension. *Psychology in the Schools, 2,* 239–244.

Jecker, J., N. Maccoby, H. S. Breitrose, and E. O. Rose (1964). Teacher accuracy in assessing cognitive visual feedback from students. *J. appl. Psychol., 48,* 393–397.

Jones, F. P., and J. A. Hanson (1961). Time-space pattern in a gross body movement. *Percept. mot. Skills, 12,* 35–41.

Jones, F. P., and M. Narva (1955). Interrupted light photography to record the effect of changes in the poise of the head upon patterns of movement and posture in man. *J. Psychol., 40,* 125–131.

Jones, F. P., D. N. O'Connell, and J. A. Hanson (1958). Color coated multiple image photography for studying related rates of movement. *J. Psychol., 45,* 247–251.

Jung, A. F. (1959). Price variations among automobile dealers in Chicago, Illinois. *J. Business, 32,* 315–326.

Kanfer, F. H. (1959). Verbal rate, content, and adjustment ratings in experimentally structured interviews. *J. abnorm. soc. Psychol., 58,* 305–311.

———— (1960). Verbal rate, eyeblink, and content in structured psychiatric interviews. *J. abnorm. soc. Psychol., 61,* 341–347.

Kaplan, A. (1964). *The conduct of inquiry.* San Francisco: Chandler.

Kasl, S. V., and G. F. Mahl (1956). A simple device for obtaining certain verbal activity measures during interviews. *J. abnorm. soc. Psychol., 53,* 388–390.

———— (1965). The relationship of disturbance and hesitations in spontaneous speech to anxiety. *J. Pers. soc. Psychol., 1,* 425–433.

Katz, Evelyn W. (1964). A content-analytic method for studying interpersonal behavior. Unpublished technical report No. 19, University of Illinois.

Katz, R. (1964). Body language: a study in unintentional communication. Unpublished doctoral dissertation, Harvard University.

Kogan, L. S. (1950). The electrical recording of social casework interviews. *Soc. Casework, 31,* 371–378.

Kounin, J. S., W. V. Friesen, and A. Evangeline Norton (1966). Managing emotionally disturbed children in regular classrooms. *J. educ. Psychol., 57,* 1–13.

Krause, M. S. (1961). The measurement of transitory anxiety. *Psychol. Rev., 68,* 178–189.

Krout, M. H. (1935). Autistic gestures: an experimental study in symbolic movement. *Psychol. Monogr., 46,* No. 4 (whole No. 208).

——— (1954a). An experimental attempt to determine the significance of unconscious manual symbolic movements. *J. gen. Psychol., 51,* 121–152.

———(1954b). An experimental attempt to produce unconscious manual symbolic movements. *J. gen. Psychol., 51,* 93–120.

Lambert, W. W. (1960). Interpersonal behavior. In P. H. Mussen (Ed.), *Handbook of research methods in child development.* New York: Wiley. Pp. 854–917.

——— (1963). Social psychology in relation to general psychology and other behavioral sciences. In S. Koch (Ed.), *Psychology: a study of a science.* Vol. 6: Investigations of man as socius. New York: McGraw-Hill. Pp. 173–244.

Landis, C., and W. A. Hunt (1937). Magnification of time as a research technique in the study of behavior. *Science, 85,* 384.

Leary, T. (1957). *Interpersonal diagnosis of personality.* New York: Ronald.

Lefkowitz, M., R. R. Blake, and J. S. Mouton (1955). Status factors in pedestrian violation of traffic signals. *J. abnorm. soc. Psychol., 51,* 704–706.

Leventhal, H., and Patricia Niles (1964). A field experiment on fear arousal with data on the validity of questionnaire measure. *J. Pers., 32,* 459–479.

Leventhal, H., and Elizabeth Sharp (1965). Facial expressions as indicators of distress. In S. S. Tomkins and C. E. Izard (Eds.), *Affect, cognition, and personality.* New York: Springer. Pp. 296–318.

Levin, H., A. L. Baldwin, M. Gallwey, and A. Paivio (1960). Audience stress, personality, and speech. *J. abnorm. soc. Psychol., 61,* 469–473.

Levitt, E. A. (1964). The relationship between abilities to express emotional meanings vocally and facially. In J. Davitz (Ed.), *The communication of emotional meaning.* New York: McGraw-Hill. Pp. 87–100.

Lewin, K. (1951). *Field theory in social science.* New York: Harper and Row.

Lewis, R. E. F. (1951). The objective measurement of driver behaviour: a preliminary report on "Test-retest consistency without traffic." A. P. U. 149/51. Cambridge, Eng.: Medical Research Council, Psychological Laboratory.

Little, K. B. (1965). Personal space. *J. exp. soc. Psychol., 1,* 237–247.

Longabaugh, R. (1963). A category system for coding interpersonal behavior as social exchange. *Sociometry, 26,* 319–344.

Loomis, E. A., and Lucille R. Meyer (1959). Observation and recording—a simultaneous process. *Amer. J. Orthopsychiat., 29,* 574–582.

Lyle, H. M. (1953). An experimental study of certain aspects of the electromagnetic movement meter as a criterion to audience attention. *Speech Monogr., 20,* 126.

Lyman, S. M., and M. B. Scott (1967). Territoriality: a neglected sociological dimension. *Soc. Problems, 15,* 236–249.

Maccoby, N., J. Jecker, H. Breitrose, and E. Rose (1964). Sound film recordings in improving classroom communications: experimental studies in non-verbal communication. Institute for Communication Research, Stanford University.

Maclay, H., and C. E. Osgood (1959). Hesitation phenomena in spontaneous English speech. *Word, 15,* 19–44.

Mahl, G. F. (1956). Disturbances and silences in the patient's speech in psychotherapy. *J. abnorm. soc. Psychol., 53,* 1–15.

——— (1957). Speech disturbances and emotional verbal content in initial interviews. Paper presented at Eastern Psychol. Assoc.

——— (1958). On the use of 'Ah' in spontaneous speech: quantitative, developmental, characterological, situational, and linguistic aspects. Digest of paper read at Amer. Psychol. Assoc.

——— (1959). Exploring emotional states by content analyses. In I. Pool (Ed.), *Trends in content analysis.* Urbana: Univ. of Illinois Press. Pp. 89–130.

——— (1961). Measures of two expressive aspects of a patient's speech in two psychotherapeutic interviews. In L. A. Gottschalk (Ed.), *Comparative psycholinguistic analysis of two psychotherapeutic interviews.* New York: International Univ. Press. Pp. 91–114.

——— (1964). Some observations about research on vocal behavior. *Disorders of Communication, 42,* 466–483.

Mahl, G. F., B. Danet, and N. Norton (1959). Reflection of major personality characteristics in gestures and body movement. Paper presented at Amer. Psychol. Assoc.

Mahl, G. F., and G. Schulze (1964). Psychological research in the extralinguistic area. In T. A. Sebeok, A. S. Hayes, and Mary C. Bateson (Eds.), *Approaches to semiotics.* London: Mouton and Co. Pp. 51–124.

Mann, R. D. (1967). *Interpersonal styles and group development.* New York: Wiley.

Matarazzo, J. D., H. F. Hess, and G. Saslow (1962). Frequency and duration characteristics of speech and silence behavior during interviews. *J. clin. Psychol., 18,* 416–426.

Matarazzo, J. D., and G. Saslow (1961). Differences in interview interaction behavior among normal and deviant groups. In I. A. Berg and B. M. Bass (Eds.), *Conformity and deviation.* New York: Harper and Row. Pp. 286–327.

Matarazzo, J. D., G. Saslow, and A. P. Hare (1958). Factor analysis of interview interaction behavior. *J. consult. Psychol., 22,* 419–429.

Matarazzo, J. D., G. Saslow, and Ruth G. Matarazzo (1956). The Interaction Chronograph as an instrument for objective measurement of interaction patterns during interviews. *J. Psychol., 41,* 347–367.

Matarazzo, J. D., M. Weitman, and G. Saslow (1963). Interview content and interviewee speech durations. *J. clin. Psychol., 19,* 463–472.

Matarazzo, J. D., M. Weitman, G. Saslow, and A. N. Wiens (1963). Interviewer influence on durations of interviewee speech. *J. verb. Learn. verb. Behav., 1,* 451–458.

Matarazzo, J. D., A. N. Wiens, and G. Saslow (1965). Studies in interview speech behavior. In L. Krasner and L. P. Ullmann (Eds.), *Research in behavior modification.* New York: Holt, Rinehart, and Winston. Pp. 181–210.

Matarazzo, J. D., A. N. Wiens, G. Saslow, R. M. Dunham, and R. B. Voas (1964). Speech durations of astronaut and ground communicators. *Science, 143,* 148–150.

Medley, D. M., and H. E. Mitzel (1963). Measuring classroom behavior by systematic observation. In N. L. Gage (Ed.), *Handbook of research on teaching.* Chicago: Rand McNally. Pp. 247–328.

Medley, D. M., and L. H. Smith (1964). Instructions for recording behavior with OScAR-R. Unpublished manuscript, City University of New York.

Melbin, M. (1954). An interaction recording device for participant observers. *Hum. Organizat., 13* (2), 29–33.

Michaelis, A. R. (1955). *Research films in biology, anthropology, psychology, and medicine.* New York: Academic Press.

Miller, G. A. (1956). The magical number seven, plus or minus two: some limits on our capacity for processing information. *Psychol. Rev., 63,* 81–97.

—— (1962). *Psychology: the science of mental life.* New York: Harper and Row.

Miller, N., and B. H. Levy (1967). Defaming and agreeing with the communicator as a function of communication extremity, emotional arousal, and evaluative set. *Sociometry, 30,* 158–175.

Mills, T. M. (1964). *Group transformation: an analysis of a learning group.* Englewood Cliffs, N.J.: Prentice-Hall.

Mishler, E. G., and Nancy Waxler (1966). Power structure and power strategies in schizophrenic and normal families. Unpublished manuscript.

Moustakas, C. E., I. E. Siegel, and H. D. Schalock (1956). An objective method for the measurement and analysis of child-adult interaction. *Child Develpmt., 27,* 109–134.

Murray, H. A. (1963). Studies of stressful interpersonal disputations. *Amer. Psychologist, 18,* 28–36.

Orne, M. T. (1962). On the social psychology of the psychological experiment, with particular reference to demand characteristics and their implications. *Amer. Psychologist, 17,* 776–783.

Osgood, C. E. (1963). Psycholinguistics. In S. Koch (Ed.), *Psychology: a study of a science.* Vol. 6. New York: McGraw-Hill. Pp. 244–316.

Peak, Helen (1953). Problems of objective observation. In L. Festinger and D. Katz (Eds.), *Research methods in the behavioral sciences.* New York: Holt, Rinehart, and Winston. Pp. 243–299.

Perkins, H. V. (1964). A procedure for assessing the classroom behavior of students and teachers. *Amer. educ. Res. J., 1,* 249–260.

Phillips, Jeanne S., Ruth G. Matarazzo, J. D. Matarazzo, G. Saslow, and F. H. Kanfer (1961). Relationships between descriptive content and interaction behavior in interviews. *J. consult. Psychol., 25*, 260–266.

Piaget, J. (1952). *The origins of intelligence in children.* New York: International Univ. Press.

Pittenger, R. E., C. F. Hockett, and J. J. Danehy (1960). *The first five minutes: a sample of microscopic interview analysis.* Ithaca, N.Y.: Paul Martineau.

Ponder, E., and W. P. Kennedy (1927). On the act of blinking. *Quart. J. exp. Physiol., 18*, 89–110.

Purcell, K., and K. Brady (1965). *Assessment of interpersonal behavior in natural settings: a research technique and manual.* Denver, Colo.: Children's Asthma Research Inst.

Raush, H. L. (1959). On the locus of behavior-observations in multiple settings within residential treatment. *Amer. J. Orthopsychiat., 29*, 235–242.

Raush, H. L., A. T. Dittmann, and T. J. Taylor (1959). The interpersonal behavior of children in residential treatment. *J. abnorm. soc. Psychol., 58*, 9–27.

Richardson, S. A. (1965). A study of selected personality characteristics of social science field workers. In S. A. Richardson, Barbara S. Dohrenwend, and D. Klein, *Interviewing: its form and functions.* New York: Basic Books. Pp. 328–358.

Richardson, S. A., Barbara S. Dohrenwend, and D. Klein (1965). *Interviewing: its forms and functions.* New York: Basic Books.

Riecken, H. W. (1962). A program for research on experiments in social psychology. In N. F. Washburne (Ed.), *Decisions, values, and groups.* Vol. 2. New York: Macmillan. Pp. 25–41.

Riesman, D., R. J. Potter, and Jeanne Watson (1960). The vanishing host. *Hum. Organizat., 19*, 17–27.

Riesman, D., and Jeanne Watson (1964). The sociability project: a chronicle of frustration and achievement. In P. E. Hammond (Ed.), *Sociologists at work.* New York: Basic Books. Pp. 235–321.

Riley, Matilda W. (1963). *Sociological research: a case approach.* New York: Harcourt, Brace, and World.

Roberts, R. R., and G. A. Renzaglia (1965). The influence of tape recording on counseling. *J. counsel. Psychol., 12*, 10–16.

Rokeach, M. (1964). *The three Christs of Ypsilanti.* New York: Knopf.

Rosenberg, M. J. (1965). When dissonance fails: on eliminating evaluation apprehension from attitude measurement. *J. Pers. soc. Psychol., 1*, 28–42.

Rosenfeld, H. M. (1965). Gestural and verbal communication of interpersonal affect. Paper presented at Midwestern Psychol. Assoc.

Rosenthal, R. (1963). On the social psychology of the psychological experiment: the experimenter's hypothesis as unintended determinant of experimental results. *Amer. Scientist, 51*, 268–283.

————— (1964). The effect of the experimenter on the results of psychological research. In B. H. Maher (Ed.), *Experimental personality research*. Vol. 1. New York: Academic Press. Pp. 79–114.

Sainsbury, P. (1954). A method of recording spontaneous movements by time-sampling motion pictures. *J. ment. Sci., 100,* 742–748.

————— (1955). Gestural movement during psychiatric interview. *Psychosom. Med., 17,* 458–469.

Saslow, G., and J. D. Matarazzo (1959). A technique for studying changes in interview behavior. In E. A. Rubinstein and M. S. Parloff (Eds.), *Research in psychotherapy.* Washington, D.C.: Amer. Psychol. Assoc. Pp. 125–159, 211–234.

Scheflen, A. E. (1963). Communication and regulation in psychotherapy. *Psychiatry, 26,* 126–136.

————— (1964). The significance of posture in communication systems. *Psychiatry, 27,* 316–331.

————— (1965). Communication systems such as psychotherapy. In J. H. Masserman (Ed.), *Current psychiatric therapies.* Vol. 5. New York: Grune and Stratton. Pp. 33–41.

————— (1966). Natural history method in psychotherapy: communicational research. In L. Gottschalk and A. H. Auerbach (Eds.), *Methods of research in psychotherapy.* New York: Appleton-Century. Pp. 263–289.

Schoggen, P. (1963). Environmental forces in the everyday lives of children. In R. G. Barker (Ed.), *The stream of behavior.* New York: Appleton-Century-Crofts. Pp. 42–69.

————— (1964a). Environmental forces in the everyday lives of children with physical disabilities. Unpublished manuscript.

————— (1964b). Mechanical aids for making specimen records of behavior. *Child Develpmt., 35,* 985–988.

Schulze, G., G. F. Mahl, and E. J. Murray (1960). Speech disturbances and content analysis categories as indices of underlying emotional states of patients in psychotherapy. *Amer. Psychologist, 15,* 405.

Scott, Frances G. (1962). Family group structure and patterns of social interaction. *Amer. J. Sociol., 68,* 214–228.

Sears, R. R. (1965). Comparison of interviews with questionnaires for measuring mothers' attitudes toward sex and aggression. *J. Pers. soc. Psychol., 2,* 37–44.

Selltiz, Claire, Marie Jahoda, M. Deutsch, and S. W. Cook (1959). *Research methods in social relations.* New York: Holt, Rinehart, and Winston.

Sherif, M., and Carolyn W. Sherif (1956). *An outline of social psychology* (rev. ed.). New York: Harper.

————— (1964). *Reference groups.* New York: Harper.

Shor, R. E. (1957). Effect of preinformation upon human characteristics attributed to animated geometric figures. *J. abnorm. soc. Psychol., 54,* 124–126.

Shrauger, S., and J. Altrocchi (1964). The personality of the perceiver as a factor in person perception. *Psychol. Bull., 62,* 289–308.

Smith, E. E. (1957). The effects of clear and unclear role expectations on group productivity and defensiveness. *J. abnorm. soc. Psychol., 55*, 213–217.

Sommer, R. (1959). Studies in personal space. *Sociometry, 22,* 247–260.

—— (1961). Leadership and group geography. *Sociometry, 24,* 99–110.

—— (1962). The distance for comfortable conversation: a further study. *Sociometry, 25,* 111–116.

Sommer, R., and H. Ross (1958). Social interaction on a geriatric ward. *Int. J. soc. Psychol., 4,* 128–133.

Soskin, W. F. (1953). Some aspects of communication and interpretation in psychotherapy. Paper presented at Amer. Psychol. Assoc., Cleveland, Ohio.

Soskin, W. F., and Vera P. John (1963). The study of spontaneous talk. In R. G. Barker (Ed.), *The stream of behavior.* New York: Appleton-Century-Crofts. Pp. 228–281.

Soskin, W. F., and P. E. Kauffman (1954). Intelligibility of varying samples of spontaneous utterances filtered to suppress frequencies above 550 cps. Unpublished manuscript, University of Chicago.

—— (1961). Judgment of emotion in word-free voice-samples. *J. Communic., 11,* 73–80.

Soskin, W. F., P. E. Kauffman, and E. Katz (1955). Judgment of affect in unintelligible spontaneous utterances. Unpublished manuscript, University of Chicago.

Spiegel, J. P., and P. Machotka (1965). A program for somatotactical testing. Unpublished manuscript, Harvard University.

Spiro, M. E. (1958). *Children of the Kibbutz.* Cambridge: Harvard Univ. Press.

Starkweather, J. A. (1960). A speech rate meter for vocal behavioral analysis. *J. exp. Anal. Behav., 3,* 111–114.

Sternberg, R. S., Jean Chapman, and D. Shakow (1958). Psychotherapy research and the problem of intrusions on privacy. *Psychiatry, 21,* 195–203.

Stoller, N., and G. S. Lesser (1963). A comparison of methods of observation in preservice teacher training. New York: Hunter College.

Straus, M. A. (1964). Measuring families. In H. T. Christensen (Ed.), *Handbook of marriage and the family.* Chicago: Rand McNally. Pp. 335–400.

Strauss, G. (1952). Direct observation as a source of quasi-sociometric information. *Sociometry, 15,* 141–145.

Strodtbeck, F. L. (1951). Husband-wife interaction over revealed differences. *Amer. sociol. Rev., 16,* 468–473.

Taft, R. (1955). The ability to judge people. *Psychol. Bull., 52,* 1–23.

Thomas, Dorothy S. (1929). *Some new techniques for studying social behavior.* New York: Columbia Univ. Press.

Tomkins, S. S. (1962). *Affect, imagery, and consciousness: the positive affects.* Vol. 1. New York: Springer.

Trager, G. L. (1958). Paralanguage: a first approximation. *Stud. Linguist., 13,* 1–12.

Verzeano, M., and J. E. Finesinger (1949). An automatic analyzer for the study of speech in interaction and in free association. *Science, 110,* 45–46.

Vidich, A. J. (1956). Methodological problems in the observation of husband-wife interaction. *Marriage and Family Living, 18,* 234–239.

Watson, Jeanne, W. Breed, and H. Posman (1948). A study in urban conversation: sample of 1001 remarks overheard in Manhattan. *J. soc. Psychol., 28,* 121–123.

Watson, Jeanne, and R. J. Potter (1962). An analytic unit for the study of interaction. *Hum. Relat., 15,* 245–263.

Watson, P. D., and S. S. Kanter (1956). Some influences of an experimental situation on the psychotherapeutic process: a report based on 44 treatment interviews, of the reactions of a patient and therapist to observation, recording, and physiological measurement. *Psychosom. Med., 18,* 457–470.

Webb, E. J., D. T. Campbell, R. D. Schwartz, and L. Sechrest (1966). *Unobtrusive measures: a survey of non-reactive research in social science.* Chicago: Rand McNally.

Weick, K. E. (1965). Laboratory experimentation with organizations. In J. G. March (Ed.), *Handbook of organizations.* Chicago: Rand McNally. Pp. 194–260.

Werner, H., and S. Wapner (1953). Changes in psychological distance under conditions of danger. *J. Pers., 24,* 153–167.

Whyte, W. F. (1955). *Streetcorner society.* Chicago: Univ. of Chicago Press.

—— (1959). *Man and organization.* Homewood, Ill.: Irwin.

Wiens, A. N., J. D. Matarazzo, and G. Saslow (1965). The Interaction Recorder: an electronic punched paper tape unit for recording speech behavior during interviews. *J. clin. Psychol., 21,* 142–145.

Winick, C., and H. Holt (1961). Seating positions as a non-verbal communication in group analysis. *Psychiatry, 24,* 171–182.

Worth, S. (1964). Filmmaking as an aid to action research. Paper presented at the 23rd annual meeting, Society for Applied Anthropology, San Juan, Puerto Rico, March 25, 1964.

—— (1965). Film communication: a study of reactions to some student films. *J. Screen Educ.,* July/August, 1965, pp. 3–19.

—— (1966). Film as a non-art: an approach to the study of film. *Amer. Scholar, 35,* 322–344.

Wright, E., J. Muriel, and Virginia H. Proctor (1961). *Systematic observation of verbal interaction as a method of comparing mathematics lessons.* St. Louis: Washington Univ. Press.

Wright, H. F. (1960). Observational child study. In P. H. Mussen (Ed.), *Handbook of research methods in child development.* New York: Wiley. Pp. 71–139.

Yarrow, Marian R., and H. L. Raush, Eds. (1962). Observational methods in research on socialization processes: a report of a conference. Unpublished manuscript, sponsored by Committee on Socialization and Social Structure of the Social Science Research Council.

Zimbardo, P. G., G. F. Mahl, and J. W. Barnard (1963). The measurement of speech disturbance in anxious children. *J. Speech and Hearing Disorder, 28,* 362–370.

14

Measurement of Social Choice
and Interpersonal Attractiveness

GARDNER LINDZEY, *University of Texas*
DONN BYRNE, *University of Texas*

The web of interpersonal relations, the attractions, repulsions, and indifferences that characterize individuals in interaction, the informal organization of groups, the social status of individuals—all these are of interest to the social psychologist, and aspects of all may be measured effectively through the use of sociometric techniques and related devices. These instruments are designed specifically to provide a sensitive and objective picture of the interpersonal relations existing within a group and between pairs of individuals. Consequently, they are of singular importance to the empirically oriented social psychologist.

The focus of our interest here is on a small number of closely related techniques that may be used to elicit responses from individuals concerning positive, neutral, and negative relations with other individuals. In the following sections we shall consider the conditions under which such responses are secured, the primary ways in which the resultant data may be analyzed, some common properties found in the analyzed data, and the areas of investigation in which such data may be expected to be of significance.

THE NATURE OF SOCIAL-CHOICE MEASURES

What qualities do measures of social choice possess that make them of special interest or significance to the social psychologist? While the detailed answer to this question is contained in the body of this chapter, there are a number of general points that may be suggested at this juncture. First, it is evident that the variables these measures represent are about as purely "social" as is possible. The

This chapter is a revision of an earlier paper by Lindzey and Edgar F. Borgatta. Although Professor Borgatta did not participate directly in this revision, many of his valuable contributions have been retained.

fact that these variables describe the quality of interpersonal relations makes clear that they deal with the basic data with which the social psychologist has been most interested, both conceptually and empirically. Second, the interdisciplinary popularity and appropriateness of these devices makes them of particular relevance to a subdiscipline that has developed largely in the void existing between two parent disciplines. In this connection, it is interesting that from the very beginning sociometric techniques have been widely employed by both sociologists and social psychologists, and to a lesser extent by social anthropologists and psychiatrists. Consequently, sociometric devices seem ideally equipped to function in a field where there is much interest in cross-disciplinary integration. Third, and this is related to the interdisciplinary popularity of these techniques, is their capacity to represent individuals in interaction within a miniature social system. Current theoretical formulations, in addition to the demands imposed by many empirical problems, make it necessary for the investigator to study the individual and his social environment simultaneously. Fourth, because of ease and speed of administration and a related lack of expense, the independent investigator can use these devices effectively without large-scale resources. Fifth, increasing emphasis on action research—investigations where the findings have direct implications for the concrete events under study—gives further merit to these techniques, since they lend themselves to the introduction of social change in an efficient and plausible fashion without seriously adding to the labor of the investigator. Sixth, these measures can be used in such a way as to provide a much higher degree of interest and motivation on the part of participant subjects than is typical of most psychological measuring instruments. The possibility that his environment may be manipulated so as to comply with his wishes encourages a high degree of interest and cooperativeness on the part of the respondent. Seventh, as we shall attempt to document later, these techniques provide relatively acceptable indices for a large number of empirical concepts that the social psychologist conventionally employs: prejudice, morale, social status, attraction, rejection, etc.

What other instruments in the psychologists' measurement battery show similarities to sociometric measures? Although there are some correspondences between these measures and attitude scales as well as questionnaires or inventories, the most important similarity seems to be to rating scales (Jennings, 1950; P. N. Pepinsky, 1949; Gardner and Thompson, 1956). It is easy to conceive of the sociometric test as a variety of rating scale—the members of the group are asked to rate or order other members of the group in terms of their attractiveness or desirability for sharing certain activities. Indeed, in our treatment we will freely refer to studies involving ratings of interpersonal attractiveness.

Sociometric measures are more limited in the variables they can be used to assess, and more restricted in the settings where they can be employed, than rating scales. On the other hand, there is no need to train raters to engage in sociometric ratings. The difficult and time-consuming task of attempting to produce common frames of reference and homogeneous criteria in terms of which ratings shall be assigned is avoided. The rater is asked to apply exactly those particular, unique, and sometimes irrational criteria he has spent a lifetime developing.

Everyone is an experienced or expert rater when it comes to social judgments. Each of us has a vast body of experience in deciding with whom we wish to interact and whom we wish to avoid. Liking and disliking, accepting and rejecting are part of the process of daily living. Given the past experience of these raters and the meaningfulness of the activity they are engaged in, it is small wonder sociometric devices have proven a powerful measurement tool in the hands of the social scientist. One might say that the individual who uses these techniques is taking advantage of the largest pool of sensitive and experienced raters that is anywhere available.

THE ORIGINS OF SOCIOMETRY

The origins and development of sociometry are intimately linked with the contributions of J. L. Moreno. There are few instances where a single individual has exerted so pervasive an influence on the evolution of a social-science area. Although it is clear that similar devices were used before, the important first step in the development of sociometry was the publication of *Who Shall Survive?* (1934). This volume reports a series of group studies carried out in public school and institutional settings using a variety of data-gathering techniques, including sociometric measures. The book is not a simple report of research, for it contains a mixture of speculative theory and applications of methods and their results to problems of broad social significance. This fusion of procedural sensitivity, speculative theorizing, and heavy concern with evaluative issues has remained typical of much sociometric writing.

Following this initial presentation of the method was the publication of the short-lived *Sociometric Review* (1936). This was superseded by *Sociometry: A Journal of Interpersonal Relations,* the first volume of which appeared in 1937–1938. This periodical played a crucial role in subsequent developments. Although the journal has been generous in publishing a large number of studies that bear no intimate relationship to Moreno's work, the overall impression certainly was one of an official or home organ. This led to more of an air of sectarianism than might otherwise have appeared. In spite of the fact that the first two editors of the journal were, respectively, a distinguished psychologist, Gardner Murphy, and a distinguished sociologist, George Lundberg, the expansive influence of Moreno was so great that most psychologists and sociologists tended to look upon individuals concerned with sociometry as having some of the cultish qualities that were characteristic of Rorschachers and psychoanalysts. This set of conditions may have served to slow down the interpenetration of conception and method in the various areas, but at the same time it performed the important function of preventing sociometric techniques from being seen as tools that were the primary property of either sociology or psychology. In the more recent past (1956) *Sociometry* has become an official publication of the American Sociological Association, and since then the journal has been much less explicitly linked to sociometric measures. At the same time the distinction between sociometric ratings and other means of estimating interpersonal attraction or choice has become much less clear. One might say that the success of sociometric measures in becoming an integral part of social psychology has been accompanied by a blurring of the boundaries between these measures and alternative approaches.

WHAT IS A SOCIOMETRIC MEASURE?

In simplest terms, a sociometric measure is a means of assessing the attractions, or attractions and repulsions, within a given group. It usually involves each member of the group privately specifying a number of other persons in the group with whom he would like to engage in some particular activity and, further, a number of persons with whom he would not like to participate in the activity.

The most important requirements of the sociometric test generally advocated by Moreno are as follows: (1) the limits of the group should be indicated to the subjects; (2) the subjects should be permitted an unlimited number of choices or rejections; (3) the subjects should be asked to indicate the individuals they choose or reject in terms of specific criteria; (4) results of the sociometric questions should be used to restructure the group; (5) the subjects should be permitted to make their choices and rejections privately, without other members of the group being able to identify the responses; (6) the questions used should be gauged to the level of understanding of the members of the group.

The requirements outlined above identify the sociometric measure in a more or less pure form, and are generally in agreement with Moreno's definition. However, relatively few studies in this area meet all these requirements. For example, the technique as used today seldom involves the promise of restructuring the group. In many cases, because of the nature of the group or the nature of the criterion, it is impossible to introduce such changes. The precondition that the groups be small enough to permit face-to-face interaction is often altered to the needs of the study. Moreno's (1934) original study was of a large closed community, but current research more frequently involves smaller closed groups, temporary experimental groups, two-person interactions, and even artificial groups. It is obvious that the precondition that the groups have existed over a period of time is often set aside. Barker's (1942) investigation of "first impressions" is an early example of a study where it was necessary to administer the sociometric technique *before* any prolonged interaction. There are also applications of the techniques in large groups and open communities (Lundberg and Steele, 1938; F. A. Stewart, 1946, 1947a, 1947b; I. A. Stewart, 1948). In these, the problems of statistical analysis are greatly increased (Bassett, 1948; F. A. Stewart, 1948), but the fundamental application remains the same.

One of the more frequent modifications involves specifying the number of choices the individual is required to make. Some investigators have limited their data to one or two or three choices—such as most and/or least preferred group members (for example, Fishbein, 1965; Haythorn, 1953; Izard, 1960b; Lott and Lott, 1960; Venable, 1954). More often, each subject is asked to respond to each of the group members by ranking them with respect to one or more variables (for example, Backman and Secord, 1962; Borgatta, 1960; Cohn, Yee, and Brown,

1961; Davitz, 1955; Horowitz, 1962; Horrocks and Wear, 1953; McCandless, Castaneda, and Palermo, 1956; Mann, 1958; Schachter, 1951; Smith, 1963; Tagiuri and Kogan, 1960; Wright and Evitts, 1963).

The comparability of these different approaches constitutes something of a problem. Eng and French (1948) found that, when they used a ranking derived from a paired comparison of each member in the group as a criterion, unlimited choices showed a closer correlation to this criterion than either three or five choices. In certain circumstances it is of considerable interest to examine the individual variability in number of choices the subjects make when there is no limit provided. Furthermore, if we wish to distinguish between the unchosen person and the isolate, the isolate being the person who neither chooses nor is chosen, we need an unspecified number of choices. In spite of these advantages adhering to the use of unlimited choices, there are sufficient disadvantages in terms of subjects' time required, rapport, statistical analysis of the data, and demands of a specific research design, that under many circumstances it is preferable to specify the number of choices to be made.

With children, verbal inquiries concerning choices are often supplemented or replaced by one of several alternative pictorial techniques in which photographs of all group members are utilized. McCandless and Marshall (1957) described the "picture sociometric technique" in which each child is asked to point to photographs of playmates preferred for specific activities. With minor variations, a similar approach has been employed in a number of studies (for example, Moore and Updegraff, 1964). Biehler (1954) made use of a "picture completion technique" in which a child was given a line drawing of five figures in a play situation, with instructions to place a photograph of his own face on one of the drawings. Then he was asked to select the faces of his four favorite playmates to add to the other drawings. This was followed by a three-figure and then a two-figure drawing. In determining the effect of sex and race variables on the sociometric choices of children, Abel and Sahinkaya (1962) presented subjects with pairs of photographs in which the relevant characteristics were systematically varied. With each pair, the subject was asked to indicate the one preferred as a playmate.

There is an appreciable number of techniques that fail to meet the general definition proposed above but still remain sufficiently similar to the sociometric measure to deserve consideration.

Sociometric self-rating or relational analysis

This technique is an extension of the sociometric test and is used in conjunction with it. It involves the use of the sociometric self-rating or prediction of one's sociometric choice, for example, "Who do you think will choose you?" This method was first mentioned by Moreno (1942) in connection with the training of subjects' perception of others through repeated sociometric trials. Among those using this technique have been Maucorps (1949) with French Army officers, Lundberg and Dickson (1952) and Ausubel (1953) with high school populations, Williams and Leavitt (1947) with Marine Corps officer candidates, Davitz (1955) with children at a summer camp, Borgatta (1954) with Air Force enlisted personnel, and Broxton (1963) with female college students.

Tagiuri (1952) has elaborated and developed this approach under the title of "relational analysis," and has indicated its usefulness in the study of social perception. A further step has been to ask subjects to guess *all* the sociometric choices of *all* members of the group (for example, Kogan and Tagiuri, 1958; Mann, 1958; Newcomb, 1961, 1963). The accuracy with which the individual perceives the choices and rejections of his associates and the conditions under which systematic distortions of these perceptions take place appear to be important additional variables in the sociometric situation.

Scaling methods

An extensive study by Gardner and Thompson (1956) attempted to incorporate traditional psychometric considerations into the framework of sociometric measurement. Initially they used Murray's need system to conceive of groups in terms of the kinds of satisfaction that could be provided by the group for the individual member. They then constructed a set of scales designed to elicit the individual's ratings of members of the group in terms of their capacity to satisfy the following needs: affiliation, playmirth, succorance, and achievement-recognition. The scales involved a series of forced-choice comparisons of group members and resulted in a rating on each variable, from each subject, for each other member of the group. The authors presented evidence indicating that the scales produced approximately equal interval scores and that the ratings were satisfactorily reliable. Although the method is somewhat cumbersome, it possesses clear measurement superiorities over most or all similar instruments.

Pepinsky, Siegel, and Vanatta (1952) used an approximation of the Thurstone Method of Equal Intervals in an attempt to develop a sociometric index that would measure "effectiveness of participation in group activity." One hundred seventy sociometric items were submitted to an undergraduate population for judging, and subsequently a reduced list of 40 items was submitted to a group of professionally trained psychologists. At the end of this process it was possible to select a group of 24 items that represented each of eight scale positions with three items all of which showed a reasonably small amount of variation among judges. In summarizing the results of their study, the authors state (pp. 418–419):

The Group Participation Scale, used as a sociometric test in four fraternity groups, yielded (1) almost the entire range of scores as defined operationally by our scale, (2) a more normalized distribution of scores than seems to be provided by most sociometric tests, and (3) a relatively high agreement . . . of group members in choosing given individuals.

Group preference record

This variation of the sociometric technique requires that members of the group respond in terms of like, dislike, or indifference to every member of the group

(Newstetter, Feldstein, and Newcomb, 1938; Zeleny, 1939, 1940). Thus it differs from the conventional sociometric test primarily in that it forces an explicit evaluation of all group members by the subject. It has frequently been used in combination with some system of weighting choices.

Multirelational sociometric survey

An extension of the customary sociometric test by systematically combining it with the collection of additional data has been suggested in several publications (Massarik *et al.*, 1953; Weschler, Tannenbaum, and Talbot, 1952). In this adaptation two classes of questions (criteria) are utilized, that is, organizational "goal-directed" and "non-goal-directed." For each goal-directed activity five relations are investigated: (1) the prescribed, defined by leaders of the organization or the table of organization; (2) the perceived, defined by the subjects' reports of the prescribed relations; (3) the actual relations which the subjects report; (4) the desired, the relations normally ascertained by a positive sociometric test; (5) the rejected, the relations normally ascertained by a negative sociometric test. With these five sets of data, expandable by the number of criteria used, it is possible to establish a large number of meaningful indices for the classification of relational patterns in an organization.

Estimates of time

An alternative procedure to the sociometric test was suggested by Moreno, Jennings, and Sargent (1940) in the use of estimates of time as a means of measuring the intensity of choice. In this procedure the investigator asks the members of the group to estimate the proportion of time, given a finite limit, that they would like to spend interacting with the other members of the group in a given activity. This technique has been further adapted by other researchers (Kanungo, 1966; Stogdill, 1949; Stogdill and Shartle, 1948) to require that the subjects estimate the actual amount of time spent in contact with various group members. A further modification involves securing information about actual visiting patterns in a community setting (Loomis and Davidson, 1939a, 1939b).

The Moreno and Jennings modification remains closely related to the conventional technique, since the subjects are still requested to make a choice at the level of wish or desire. The use of time is primarily to permit the weighting of choices made. The other modifications, however, take the response out of the level of wish and ask for a factual report of interaction. These are perhaps closer to customary observational techniques than to a sociometric test.

Guess-who technique

Another technique related to the sociometric test is the use of identification or "guess who" questions. Actually the origins of this method are as early as those of the sociometric technique, since they go back at least to the character studies of Hartshorne, May, and Maller (1929). This technique involves presenting the subjects with various behavior descriptions and asking them to "guess who" among the members of their group this description best fits. By varying the descriptions along various kinds of positive and negative continua it is possible to obtain, in terms of the frequency with which they are selected for the various descriptions, an ordering of the subjects that bears rough correspondence to sociometric data. In many cases these data have been used to supplement conventional sociometric techniques and provide a picture of the reputations or impressions created by the subjects on other members of the group (that is, the manifest personality). This technique may possess some advantage over the sociometric test in that it is slightly more indirect and the intent of the investigator is less apparent to the subjects. This would be an advantage only if there was reason to expect that subjects would attempt to interfere with or disrupt the sociometrists' intent. Moreover, the "guess who" device is largely limited to "choice" or "reputation" scores and does not provide much information about patterns of interaction or communication.

Ratings of interpersonal attractiveness

If the dependent variable in sociometric investigations is conceptualized in terms of degree of attraction or intensity of liking, it is obvious that measurement need not be limited to naming, choosing, or ranking friendship choices. Increasingly, other types of measuring devices are employed in an attempt to refine and simplify measurement of the attraction response.

Simple ordinal rating scales of various lengths have been employed as measures of interpersonal attraction. Examples include a two-point scale (Keislar, 1961), a five-point scale (Bonney, 1954; McCandless, Castaneda, and Palermo, 1956; Reese, 1961), a six-point scale (Pepitone and Sherberg, 1957), two seven-point scales the responses to which are summed to yield a single score (Byrne and Nelson, 1965), an eight-point scale (Kleiner, 1960), several nine-point scales (Deutsch and Solomon, 1959), a 21-point scale (Aronson and Linder, 1965), and a scale utilizing 100 points which may well represent the upper limits of this approach (Newcomb, 1961). A social-distance measure has been employed by Triandis (1964) in which subjects respond on a nine-point scale concerning various types of interaction. Factor analysis was used to explore the way in which subjects structure social relations.

A version of the semantic differential has been employed in several sociometric studies. The sum of the ratings on the evaluative (for example, good-bad) scales are summed to yield a subject's attitude toward any object, including another individual (Deutsch and Solomon, 1959; Fishbein, 1963, 1965).

A number of investigations have employed an adjective checklist consisting of positive and negative descriptive terms of adjective pairs of polar opposites or ratings on a series of traits. Attraction toward another individual is indicated in terms of positive or negative descriptions (for example, Davis and Warnath, 1957; Jones and Daugherty, 1959; Jones *et al.*, 1959; Lerner, 1965; Newcomb, 1961).

Still another type of measuring technique was utilized by Petersen, Komorita, and Quay (1964). A Q-sort was employed in which a series of sociometric statements were placed in a seven-point forced normal distribution in terms of appropriateness for describing each individual.

Finally, an open-ended question has been used. Subjects are simply asked, "How much do you like or dislike . . . ?" Their responses are then rated in terms of direction and intensity (Pepitone and Sherberg, 1957).

As we have said, sociometric techniques merge into general methods of systematic observation. No attempt will be made to discuss observational techniques here; the reader may refer to Chapter 13 for a complete account of such methods.

ANALYSIS AND REPRESENTATION OF SOCIAL-CHOICE DATA

The general increase in quantitative sophistication of social-science investigators is nowhere better reflected than in the use of sociometric measures and their derivatives. During the past twenty years there has been a steady transition from descriptive, nonstatistical procedures of analysis to a state where virtually all investigators concern themselves with quantification and statistical analysis. Our discussion will consider techniques for the analysis and representation of data under the following headings: graphical methods, simple quantitative methods, statistical methods, matrix methods, and fractionation of groups.

GRAPHICAL METHODS

In addition to introducing and popularizing the sociometric technique, Moreno presented a method for summarizing the results of this technique. This method, the *sociogram,* was first described in *Who Shall Survive?* (1934) and during the following decade or more served as the primary method of presenting sociometric data.

The sociogram is a diagrammatic device for summarizing the choices and rejections among members of a group. It employs geometric figures to represent members of the group, and various kinds of lines joining the figures to represent choices and rejections. There is no single convention for the drawing of diagrams but, rather, there are many alternatives available to the investigator.

The sociogram has received criticism from a number of quarters because there have been many examples of "unreadable" sociograms. In many cases the fault lies in poor drawings, but more often the trouble has been that the persons drawing the sociograms have not had as their purpose the analysis of data, but rather the presentation of a persuasive visual device. Several investigators have made attempts to standardize the drawing of sociograms in order to remove their subjectivity and unreliability, as well as to make the diagrams more readable. Some of these investigators have attempted to introduce elements of quantification.

Borgatta (1951) suggested that the primary principle in sociogramming should be that of minimizing the number of crossed lines. Proctor and Loomis (1951) have recommended a set of conventions to be applied in determining the distance separating individuals in sociogram positions. Essentially, they developed an index of social distance based on the reciprocal relation between each pair of individuals in the group. They then proposed that each point along this continuum of social distance be equated to some arbitrarily designated distance on the sociogram. These investigators assumed that if x chooses y he is closer to y than he is to other individuals whom he did not choose. Further, if x rejects y he is further away from y than from other individuals whom he did not reject. Finally, the combination of mutual choice or mutual rejection is viewed as respectively closer and further away than the single choice or rejection. If we overlook the symmetrical duplications that are possible, for example, x choosing y and y rejecting x, as opposed to x rejecting y and y choosing x, there are only six different kinds of interpersonal relationships. It is possible to overlook the symmetrical variations, since each variation implies the same distance or closeness. The types of interpersonal relations are as follows:

> Type A: i chooses j, and j chooses i
> Type B: i chooses j, and j ignores i
> Type C: i chooses j, and j rejects i
> Type D: i ignores j, and j ignores i
> Type E: i ignores j, and j rejects i
> Type F: i rejects j, and j rejects i

Making the further assumption that types C and D are equidistant, Proctor and Loomis proposed that it is now possible to array individual pairs on a close-distant or choice-rejection continuum, with type A representing the closest relationship and type F the most distant or aversive. Actually, if one objects to the assumption that a choice and a rejection are equivalent to two "ignores," there is no reason why these two types could not be made separate points on the distance continuum, perhaps with the choice and rejection being placed closer than the mutual "ignorers." The major intent of a sociogram drawn in this way is to cluster closely related persons and thus identify cliques. There is some danger, however, that this forced concentration may actually mask networks of communication, especially if the group is large and there is a high incidence of choices.

This procedure provides the investigator with a definite goal toward which he may aim, even though it will not always be attainable. At the same time it introduces a certain standardization into the practices of different individuals constructing sociograms. It is important to note that the larger the group, the less likely it is that the conventions of this system can be satisfied. When a subject is placed in relation to a large number of individuals who are simultaneously in relation to other individuals, and independent demands are made as to distance separating all these positions (persons), these demands will frequently not be satisfiable on a single plane surface.

Another attempt at standardization was made by Northway (1940) when she introduced the "target sociogram." In this diagram a series of concentric circles is used to designate areas in which individuals are to be placed according to their choice status. Usually, the field is divided by quartiles, and the center of the target is the location of the individuals in the quarter receiving most choices, the three bands around the center receiving the persons in the respective quarters. Thus the target sociogram identifies the relations among the group members in the usual sense, and further identifies the choice status of the individual at the same time. Northway and Quarrington (1946) suggested the use of sectors to separate members of the group in the target sociogram by characteristics such as sex or ethnic background, in order to facilitate examination of the data for cleavages. Bronfenbrenner (1944b) proposed the possibility of using the target sociogram with the concentric areas designated according to the probability with which the number of choices received exceed or are less than the expected number.

The Northway target diagram may be useful in indicating highly chosen and relatively unchosen persons, and quantification is relatively explicit, but this presentation is not intrinsically superior to other varieties of the sociogram, for example, one which uses identification symbols of different sizes to designate the relative number of choices received by the person. An example of the latter is seen in the sociograms used by Powell (1951). Furthermore, the use of sectors in a target diagram to designate sex or ethnic background distinction can be duplicated in ordinary sociograms (for example, Loomis, Beegle, and Longmore, 1947).

The kind of sociogram used is limited only by the investigator's needs and imagination. There are many alternative methods of presentation of sociometric data, and these may even include three-dimensional sociograms (Chapin, 1950; Weschler, Tannenbaum, and Talbot, 1952). The sociogram does not restrict the investigator to one variable; multiple-variable sociograms may be handled by using lines of different colors, overlays, or other devices.

An appraisal of the *utility of the sociogram* must begin by noting its dramatic and compelling qualities. The possibility of summarizing group relations in terms of a series of graphic conventions that appear directly understandable and interesting to most audiences is an important asset. Particularly in circumstances where the information is being presented in an "action" context, the possibility of easily engaging an audience without the necessity of presenting technical information or complex explanations may be of crucial importance. In many industrial and military applications, as well as in some educational settings, the "glamour" of the sociogram makes it almost a prerequisite, no matter what additional techniques may be used in analyzing and presenting sociometric results.

In spite of these desirable qualities, the sociogram, as customarily used, does have negative aspects. The representativeness of the sociogram has depended almost entirely on the vigilance and sensitivity of the investigator, with few or no external checks on the adequacy of the diagram he presents. Thus, depending on the particular spatial conventions or groupings the investigator uses, he can create different impressions of the group being examined. This absence of external or formal checks on the procedure has led generally to relatively low interjudge agreement.

The suggestions of Northway, of Proctor and Loomis, and of Borgatta may be viewed as attempts to minimize this particular shortcoming of the sociogram. A more recent approach to this problem has been described by Wright and Evitts (1961) who recommend the application of direct factor analysis to a matrix of sociometric choices. Once the factors are determined, the data are plotted on two-dimensional sociograms. We shall discuss this method further in a subsequent section.

SIMPLE QUANTITATIVE METHODS

Simultaneous with the development of graphical techniques, there have been important developments in the use of quantitative techniques for analyzing and summarizing sociometric data. We shall begin our discussion of these developments by considering tabular methods and scores or indices. In later sections we shall consider statistical and matrix methods.

Tabular methods

Sociometric data are summarized completely in the sociogram, but an equally complete method of summarization is the $N \times N$ table or matrix, in which N refers to the number of subjects. The subjects are placed along the left margin of the table in some arbitrary order, and then the order is reproduced along the top margin of the table. The responses of a given subject to the remaining $(N - 1)$ subjects may then be placed in the proper cells. Ordinarily the main diagonal of the table or matrix is empty, since subjects are not asked to respond to themselves. This technique makes the summarization of the number of choices and rejections made and received by each subject simply the task of adding across a column or down a row.

Scores and derived indices

Quite early in the use of sociometric measures, some investigators (for example, Moreno, 1934) chose to summarize what appeared to be important aspects of the choices and rejections within a group in terms of simple scores or ratios. Although individuals who hold to an organismic or holistic view of the world may mourn the loss of the complex interrelations that are to some extent present in the sociogram or the $N \times N$ table, the use of indices and their derivatives has become increasingly popular. Some of these indices represent the individual, while others represent the group as a whole. Still others represent the individual in interaction with other members of the group. Our intention here is not to present a systematic summarization of indices, but rather to illustrate the breadth and variety of indices that have been used by different investigators.

Moreno's *Who Shall Survive?* includes the explicit formulation of a number of indices and implicitly assumes a larger number. The identification of the "star," the "isolate," and the "rejected" provided the basis for a large number of the individual indices later developed. Moreno also proposed a number of group indices: *emotional expansiveness* refers to the amount of utilization of available choices. This index can be used only where the number of choices is not specified, that is, where the subjects are permitted to make unlimited choices or as many as they wish up to a certain limit. The *ratio of attraction* is equal to the number of attractions divided by the total number of attractions and rejections converted to a percentage. The *ratio of repulsions* is similarly computed. Moreno set the ground work for an index of "cleavage" in a group in his discussion of restriction of spheres of choice, and more directly in the use of the *ratio of interest* for home group and for outside groups, which is computed on the basis of available choices utilized. The index of relative popularity (of a group) is the proportion actually received of the possible choices the group could receive from the external groups.

The number of choices received serves as the basis for a number of indices. Individuals may be classified arbitrarily; for example, they may be stratified by quartiles, deciles, or other dividing points. An example of this is Jennings' (1950) stratification of persons in terms of dividing points established on the base of the mean number of choices received. She identified subjects one standard deviation above the mean number of choices received as overchosen, and those one standard deviation below the mean as underchosen. Still another classification is presented by Proctor and Loomis (1951) in their definition of choice status as the number of choices received divided by one less than the number of persons in the group, with a similar definition for rejection status. An important social-status index has been reported by Katz (1953). This measure employs vector concepts in order to take into consideration not only the number of choices but also the social position of those who choose.

Other investigators have employed various arbitrary definitions. For example, Venable (1954) investigated friendship patterns in a group of college girls and defined a "star" as an individual chosen as a best friend by at least five others and an "isolate" as one chosen by no others. Similarly, Marks (1954), in a study of 730 eighth- to twelfth-grade students, selected the relative extremes of the choice distribution as unacceptable (chosen by few or no peers) and acceptable (chosen by many peers). Croft and Grygier (1956) had sociometric data from 13 classes. To combine the data from these different-sized groups, they assigned a score of 1 to the six subjects in each group with the highest sociometric status, 2 to the next six, 5 to the worst six, 4 to the next worst six, and all the remaining individuals in any class received a score of 3. Arbitrary classification (or fractionization) of the types just described extends the utility of the data by allowing the possibility of comparison to or combination with data from additional groups, since the size of the group is considered in the classification. However, it should be noted that being one standard deviation above the mean in one group may have a different meaning from being one standard deviation above the mean in another group.

The number of mutual choices in a group serves as the basis of several indices. McKinney (1948) identified a *compatibility index* as the number of mutual choices divided by one less than the group size. Proctor and Loomis (1951) identified *group cohesion* as the number of mutual pairs divided by the possible number of mutual pairs in the group (as restricted by instructions for choosing). The same authors (1951) identified *group integration* as 1 divided by the number of persons receiving no choices. Proctor and Loomis (1951) presented an outline of indices that may serve as a beginning point for persons who wish to examine a range of the defined indices in sociometry. In addition to those we have already mentioned, they consider such indices as ingroup preference, ingroup cleavage, ingroup cohesion, and ingroup climate.

The specialized social-relations scales developed by Gardner and Thompson (1956) provide the basis for eight different indices of individual social status and nine indices of group structure. In general, these indices are only moderately intercorrelated and they show reasonable reliability. Moreover, the investigators have provided data bearing upon the relation between their indices and a variety of independent measures that support the utility of the indices.

In some respects, it seems reasonable to utilize more data than merely the number of positive choices an individual receives or his popularity ranking as defined by his peers. Seemingly, a more meaningful measure might be derived by combining *both* positive and negative sociometric responses in some way (for example, Norman, 1953). Many such indices have been employed. For example, the sum of acceptances plus the sum of rejections, divided by one less than the group size, is an index which McKinney (1948) identified as *social-status index*. Smucker (1949) identified this index as *social intensity*. *Choice-rejection status* is identified by Proctor and Loomis (1951) as the number of choices less the number of rejections received. In a group of preschool children, Dunnington (1957a) asked for first, second, and third choices for playmates and for those with whom the child would not like to play. Then, with respect to the remaining members of the group, the child was asked to give a yes or no in a forced-choice question. As an index of sociometric status, each subject received 14 points if named as a first choice, −14 if rejected first, 7 if named as a second choice, −7 if rejected second, 5 if named as a third choice, −5 if rejected third, and in the forced-choice question 1 for yes and −1 for no. Each subject's points were then summed algebraically to yield the sociometric status score.

With any of these combined acceptance-rejection indices, a difficulty arises in the relationship between the two scores. If acceptance and rejection are independent variables, combining the two in an index would provide a different sort of measure than either taken singly. If acceptance and rejection have a perfect inverse relationship, nothing is gained by utilizing both variables. If acceptance and rejection are positively related, the meaning of a combined index becomes somewhat ambiguous. An example of the latter instance is provided by Trent (1957), who investigated sociometric status among institutionalized delinquent boys. He decided to study popularity and rejection as separate entities, reasoning that the most popular boy with one clique might be the most unpopular with another. He found, in fact, that the number of positive choices and the number of rejections received by each individual correlated .75.

Finally, it is possible to consider choices and rejections simultaneously, and other data besides, by means of *profiles*. In this case, some unit of standardization is necessary among the scores. Jennings (1943, 1950) has dealt with profiles of individuals based on (1) choices made, (2) choices received, (3) positive reciprocations, (4) rejections made, (5) rejections received, and (6) negative reciprocations. The first three are given as the *choice pattern* of the individual, the last three as the *rejection pattern*, and the six together as the *choice-and-rejection pattern*. The pattern is identified by the ordered series of six pluses or minuses, a plus signifying that the person is above the mean in the particular item and a minus signifying that he is below the mean. Such presentation allows the researcher to examine the distribution of patterns and the relationship between performances on the individual items, by examining the distribution of types. Profiles have been reported elsewhere (McKinney, 1948; Smucker, 1949) in various contexts, but Jennings' contribution is standardization on the same criterion to facilitate examination of types. Bjerstedt (1952) extended this work and provided a systematic method of classification which is easily extended to at least two forms of sociographing. Bjerstedt's innovation is especially interesting because of the amount of information which is made available for immediate reading, as well as the fact that the sociogram, according to his specifications, is reproducible by independent investigators.

Certain problems are posed by the intensity of responses, that is, the differential meaning of first, second, third, . . . choices. Some investigators (for example, Zeleny, 1939, 1947) have made extensive use of ranked choices in their analyses and have incorporated them into their indices. This requires a simple adjustment in the computation of the index. However, very little work has been done at a theoretical level on the meaning of intensity in sociometric choices (Foa, 1950) or the value of assigning arbitrary weights. An exception is the Gronlund (1955) study in which weighted and unweighted sociometric choices were compared with respect to stability over time; weighting had no effect on stability. The investigator should, consequently, be cautious in weighting choices, especially if the choices are required. We shall discuss later Moreno's (1934) report on the greater stability of first as against second choices, which might lend support to the weighting of choices; but since weighting is ordinarily arbitrary, there is no evidence that equal weights (ignoring choice order) would not be as good as assigning weights by any other arbitrary technique.

Most often, investigators of sociometric status are interested, not in identifying a few typical individuals, but in relating differences in this variable to other variables. Thus, subjects may simply be ranked within a group on the basis of the raw number of choices received (for example, Marshall, 1958). Any such ordinal data are of immediate use where the sociometric status of individuals in a given group is to be examined in relation to other criteria. The problem of comparability of persons selected from two or more groups is no different from the problems involved in any psychological measurement involving ranking or rating techniques. Until it is possible to measure interpersonal attraction as precisely as we measure time or temperature, the general problem will persist. In the meantime, provided that choices and rejections in different groups have been made under the same experimental conditions, persons can be ordered by their relative positions in the group, as with Northway's quartiles or Jennings' standard-deviation classifications. In such cases the investigator should be aware that groups vary in the distribution (and range) of choices made, and that even the responses of the same individuals in very different groups may have different meanings as a consequence of adaptation-level effects. Nevertheless, in actual fact, unless a given group or sample is a very unusual one, the combination of data from different groups or the comparison of results from divergent samples probably does not involve an appreciable distortion of reality. Essentially, the problem of what type of measure is proper in a given situation is defined by the comparability of the situation to other situations, the use to which the measure is to be put, and the types of assumptions the investigator is willing to make.

STATISTICAL METHODS

Statistical techniques are widely used in analyses of sociometric data both to test the significance of observed findings and to provide derived scores or indices. Several investigators who have used quantitative methods have developed scores for the purpose of distinguishing between differences or deviations that should properly be assigned to chance factors, as opposed to those that represent actual, replicable deviations from the group norms.

Bronfenbrenner (1943, 1944a) developed the notion of a *chance model,* introducing the Pearson Type III Curve as the most adequate approximation to the binomial expansion for sociometric data, and elaborated on the concept of statistical significance as applied to sociometric data. Distribution of indices on a chance basis, given a level of significance, provides the upper and lower limits of variation beyond which phenomena may be judged to be statistically different from chance. Thus, for example, given any distribution of choices received in actual data, it is possible, by using the limits established by the chance model, to identify persons who receive significantly more or fewer choices than would be expected by chance. Bronfenbrenner's approach is intended to have the advantage of providing a constant frame of reference for comparison or pooling of data; that is (for example), persons who receive significantly more choices than would be expected by chance may be recruited from several different groups and pooled for comparison with a similarly selected group of underchosen persons; or persons who receive significantly more choices than would be expected by chance in one type of group may be compared with similarly selected persons in another type of group.

The usefulness of a probability model is unquestioned, although there are many discussions in sociometric literature of misapplications or the adoption of incorrect (or incomplete) assumptions (see Criswell, 1947; Proctor and Loomis, 1951). One example of an inappropriate assumption is Bronfenbrenner's (1943, 1944a) suggestion that the distribution of mutual choices will be in accordance with the binomial expansion. Criswell (1946, 1950), Edwards (1948), and Loomis and Pepinsky (1948) have all indicated the theoretical inadequacy of this formulation. Criswell's (1939) assumption that chi-square values may be ordered rather than treated as significant or not significant has been objected to by Loomis and Pepinsky (1948).

One special consideration in the use of Bronfenbrenner's method should be noted. Separating persons as significantly overchosen and significantly underchosen provides an aura of respectability in the handling of the data, but such a procedure may be unrealistic. Such classes are frequently very small and require a large number of samples, or large samples, to permit further statistical comparisons. On the other hand, there is good evidence that the stability of a person's choice status is high, so that ordering of persons on choice status will have a reasonably constant meaning. In using only classes of persons who are significantly above or below chance expectation, the researcher appears to assume that those who do not satisfy this condition of statistical significance receive other choice positions on a basis of chance. This assumption does not seem necessary and results in the loss of large amounts of data. Thus, unless the investigator is genuinely interested in the extremes of the distribution, there seems good reason for him to use in comparisons subjects who are selected arbitrarily or in terms of some rational criterion, rather than only those who deviate from the mean at some particular level of significance. Criswell (1950) has posed this criticism in a slightly different form in her detailed analysis of the constant-frame-of-reference problem.

An interesting application of Bronfenbrenner's method was executed by Lemann and Solomon (1952). They considered the possibility of making their high-status group consist of those individuals whose choice frequency exceeded the expected at the one-percent level of significance and whose rejections fell below the expected at the one-percent level of significance. The low-status group would be the converse, falling below the expected in choices and exceeding it in rejections. The subjects who did not fall into either of these two groups would be placed in the middle-status group. Partly as a consequence of the fact that the choice and rejection distributions did not coincide when one was inverted, Lemann and Solomon found that their logically defensible principle of fractionation was not workable. The vast majority of the subjects fell in the middle-status group and there were few cases in either the high- or low-status group. In the face of this experience they reasoned (p. 31):

> . . . let the high status group consist of all those who received significantly more choices than would be expected, and who at the same time did not receive more than the mean number of rejections; and let the low status group consist of those who received more rejections than would be expected, and who at the same time did not receive more than the mean number of choices; and let all others not included in these two extreme groups make up the middle status group.

This method seems defensible, since it places in the high group all those who secure significantly more choices than would be expected by chance, unless they also receive a large number of rejections. The low-status group is conversely defined, and the middle group is determined residually. Most important is the pragmatic outcome of reasonable numerical divisions of subjects into the three groups, and this was an important factor in the decision to employ this classification.

In contrast to Bronfenbrenner's method, which uses probability values as scores, Criswell's scoring procedures attempt to eliminate the influence of chance distributions. The first scoring method suggested by her (1939) was for the measurement of race preference expressed by a group as a whole. She devised a ratio in which a given racial group's preference for itself over another racial group was expressed as follows:

$$\text{group self-preference} = \frac{SO^1}{OS^1},$$

where S is the number of choices given by a group of itself, S^1 is the number of choices it would give itself by chance, O is the number of choices the group gives to the other racial group in the experimental population, and O^1 is the number of choices it would give by chance to the other racial group. Another method of probability scoring devised by Criswell (1946, 1947) defines group coherence as the ratio of reciprocated to unreciprocated choice divided by the corresponding chance distribution. The formula is then

$$\text{group coherence} = \frac{\text{number of reciprocated choices} \times q}{\text{number of unreciprocated choices} \times p},$$

where p/q is the chance ratio of reciprocated to unreciprocated choices.

Statistical methods have also been used to examine the likelihood that a given finding is the result of chance factors. The first use of the chance model with sociometric data was made by Moreno and Jennings (1938) when they set up an empirical random-selection procedure and generated sociometric groups. They then compared these groups, in terms of the distribution of choices, with a probability model (provided by Lazarsfeld) based on the binomial expansion and found no apparent differences. The chance model was then compared with actual data by means of the chi-square test, and significant differences between the obtained and chance distributions were immediately apparent. In the actual data, unchosen and highly chosen persons occurred more frequently, and mutual pairs also occurred more frequently than in the chance distribution.

Several attempts have been made to apply statistical methods in testing differential choice patterns within a group. The first of these was suggested by Criswell (1939), who used a chi-square test in which

$$\text{chi-square} = \frac{(\text{self-preference expressed} - \text{theoretical self-preference})^2}{\text{theoretical self-preference}}.$$

A critical discussion and extension of this approach is provided by Loomis and Pepinsky (1948). Seeman (1946) presents an alternate procedure in his study of intragroup Negro attitudes, in which he uses an analysis-of-variance design. It should be noted that Bronfenbrenner's (1943, 1944a) approach, using the Pearson Type III curve, may also be employed here.

MATRIX APPROACHES

For some time there has been interest in the analysis of sociometric data through methods of manipulating the $N \times N$ table on which sociometric responses are summarized. These methods are explicit and repeatable, and lend themselves to statistical analysis; some of them deal with large amounts of data relatively efficiently, and certain graphical features are retained.

The first of the matrix approaches to sociometric data was developed by Forsyth and Katz (1946). In their method, the $N \times N$ table is taken as the raw matrix. The original $N \times N$ matrix is then changed by moving pairs of rows and columns (the order of columns must always remain identical to that of the rows) to reveal subgroups within the structure, stars, isolates, and other characteristic forms. The ordering is one of trial and error, in large part, with the main goal of forcing mutual choices to gravitate toward each other or, more specifically, to concentrate choices along the main diagonal. Presumably, if rejections are included in the data they will gravitate away from the main diagonal as the choices gravitate toward it. The recommended procedure is to pick two persons with mutual choices and place them adjacent to each other in the matrix. Then select another person who has mutual choices with both, if such a person exists, or who is related by choice with one or both of the original two. Rearrange rows and columns as is necessary to maximize the concentration. When no persons can be added to this nucleus of individuals, consider this a subgroup and begin the rearrangement of the remaining individuals. Continue the procedure until all persons are related to a subgroup, or until only isolated or rejected individuals remain. Subgroups should be rearranged so that the maximum concentration of rejections (if any) is located in the corners of the matrix away from the main diagonal. Individuals who choose into a subgroup but are rejected or ignored are placed on the upper right boundary of the relevant subgroup, and persons who are relatively underchosen but apparently related to the subgroup may be placed at the lower left boundary of the subgroup; where both conditions are apparent, the second takes precedence in the arbitrary placement. Genuine isolates should appear near the center of the matrix. At this point the matrix may be reexamined to emphasize the concentration of subgroups; and so on.

Katz (1947) indicated as a special advantage of the matrix procedure that not only could positive and negative choices be included in the matrix but that, essentially, indifference is accounted for, and there is no necessary restriction that excludes the utilization of weighted choices. Moreover, choices may be unrestricted, limited, or required. The major contribution of this second paper, however, is in describing a canonical form for the matrix which would serve as the preferred ordering, namely, the maximization of concentration of positive choice about the main diagonal. Essentially, the form may be stated as follows:

Given N row vectors and N column vectors, and the interval from one row (or column) to the adjacent one taken as one, the square of the distance of the element in the ith row and jth column from the main diagonal is $\frac{1}{2}(i-j)^2$. Thus, if the constant is ignored, the least-square solution of this form is defined by the minimum value of $\Sigma_i\,\Sigma_j e_{ij}\,(i-j)^2$, where e_{ij} is the element of the ith row and jth column. Once in canonical form, the matrix is subject to various statistical operations. However, because of the difficulty of bringing a matrix to canonical form, these statistical suggestions of Katz are primarily of academic interest at present.

The utility of the matrix approach suggested by Forsyth and Katz is quite obvious, but its limitations should not be underestimated. Moreno (1946) commented on the presentation of Forsyth and Katz and suggested that he viewed the matrix approach as supplementing the sociographic approach rather than replacing it. He indicated that certain types of relationships, such as chains of communication, are quite difficult to locate in the matrix, though they are quite simple to trace on the sociogram. The "cumbersome" aspect of the matrix manipulation should not be underestimated. The fact that a canonical form has been described does not make the task of manipulating the matrix any easier; it still remains a matter of sophisticated trial and error to get as close to the canonical form as possible. In some cases this may be as time consuming as drawing and redrawing a number of sociograms. On the other hand, the Forsyth and Katz approach may have an advantage when the number of choices and rejections made by the subjects is very large. One objection to this method is that it forces the assumption of linearity upon the data examined, even where this assumption may not be warranted.

A matrix approach related to that of Forsyth and Katz is presented by Beum and Brundage (1950). Their method is designed to maximize choices about the main diagonal. The method makes no restrictions on the data to be entered in the cells. The procedure is based on the following demonstrable condition (p. 142):

If weights are assigned to the rows of a sociomatrix (from 1 to N beginning with the bottom row) . . . and the average product of the elements in each column and the corresponding weights is maximized for each column, the sum of the squares of the elements about the principal diagonal is minimized.

This would produce a canonical form defined in a way similar to that of Katz (1947). The procedure for achieving the canonical form is not one of trial and error, as in the Forsyth and Katz approach, but one of a systematic iterative process. When iteration of the procedure no longer produces changes in the structure (arrangement of rows and columns), the canonical form is reached. When iteration produces recurrence of arrangements of rows and columns, alternate and equally "good" arrangements are displayed. The procedure has the advantage over the Forsyth and Katz method that it is more systematic (different investigators get the same results). However, the authors point out that the iterative procedure converges slowly, and that consequently the labor involved may be excessive. Fortunately, a computer program (coded in FORTRAN II) for the rearrangement of matrices has recently been made available (Borgatta and Stolz, 1963). Coleman and MacRae (1960) have also presented a method for electronically processing a sociomatrix.

Bock and Husain (1950) considered the Forsyth and Katz (1946) matrix approach similar to identifying "clusters" of psychological tests. They introduced the notion of ranking choices in terms of "relatedness," that is, the degree of reciprocation (this assumes that the subjects ranked their choices). One generates a new matrix by replacing the original values by the rankings in this dimension. Having made this conversion, the matrix may be analyzed using Holzinger's *B*-coefficient. The procedure is not unlike that of Forsyth and Katz, beginning with two persons who are mutually related, and then picking additional persons who are highly related to the initial nucleus. If the Bock and Husain technique offers any single advantage, it is that a reasonable but quite arbitrary decision point can often be established to determine whether the last person added to the subgroup actually belongs to the subgroup, but it is not certain that this is actually better than what could be accomplished by inspection.

Luce and Perry (1949) with Festinger (1949) have developed a second method for matrix analysis of sociometric data which is based on matrix multiplication. This method is immediately differentiated from the Forsyth and Katz approach in that it places severe restrictions on the type of data that can be handled. Only choices or rejections on a single criterion can be treated and there can be no weighting of responses.

The $N \times N$ table or matrix is also the beginning point of this method. The basic operation involved is raising the raw matrix to various powers. The simplest problem for which the method may be used is to identify chains of communication, and the easiest of these to find is that of the two-step chain, where individual i chooses individual j, who in turn chooses someone else. Given an $N \times N$ matrix, the two-step chains can be identified by squaring the matrix. The operations involved in raising the matrix to various powers are described by Luce and Perry (1949), Festinger (1949), and Festinger, Schachter, and Back (1950). Given the squared matrix, the entry in the ijth cell indicates the number of two-step paths from i to j. The cells on the main diagonal contain the number of mutual choices in which each individual is involved. The total number of mutual choices in the group is obtained by summing the cells of the main diagonal and dividing by two (because each mutual choice appears twice). By raising the matrix to higher powers, cubing, and so on, it is possible to identify cliques by this method. Ordinarily, this method has defined cliques in a highly restrictive fashion, requiring that each member of the subgroup select all other members of the subgroup. Luce (1950), however, extended the generality of this approach by indicating how it is possible to alter the definition of the clique to include looser structures, that is, cliques in which there are indirect or incomplete patterns of choice among the members.

Harary and Ross (1957) presented an extension of Festinger's (1949) method of determining whether or not a group contains a clique. They indicated that it is possible to determine all the cliques in a group having three or fewer cliques by use of the concept of a unicliqual person. A *noncliqual* person is one who does not belong to any clique. A *unicliqual* person belongs to just one clique within a larger group. A *multicliqual* person belongs to more than one. The Harary and Ross procedure is to construct a matrix, S, of only reciprocated sociometric choices. Then, construct matrix $S^2 \times S$. All group members whose row in $S^2 \times S$ consists entirely of zeros are noncliqual. They are then deleted from the $S^2 \times S$ matrix to yield matrix M. At this point, the authors present a series of theorems: (1) If a group has just one clique, all persons in matrix M are unicliqual. (2) If a group has two cliques, then each clique has at least one unicliqual person. (3) If a group has three cliques, then at least two of those cliques have unicliqual persons. (4) There exist groups with exactly four cliques in which any number of these cliques may have unicliqual persons. Proofs are presented for each theorem, along with examples.

It is important to realize that, having identified particular kinds of patterns or structures, it is virtually always necessary to return to the original matrix in order to identify the persons who make up the pattern. One should also be aware of the fact that as the matrix is raised to higher powers redundancies will occur; that is, the same pattern may be counted more than once. A method for determining redundancies in five- and six-step chains has been proposed by Ross and Harary (1952).

The use of matrix multiplication in the analysis of sociometric data has the greatest potential for the development of standardized techniques for the identification of structures and channels of communication. However, the nonmathematically inclined may find some difficulty in understanding the procedure. At present the techniques are not sufficiently well developed for proper assessment. Nevertheless, the following difficulties are evident: (1) The limitation to unweighted choices or rejections may be found restrictive. (2) The matrix operations are laborious unless computers are utilized, and programming for this matrix procedure may be more effort than it is worth. (3) Even as extended by Luce, the definitions of structures which may be isolated are restrictive. Identification of patterns of a given definition will still leave many other patterns unidentified, requiring either retreatment or neglect of the data. (4) The holistic view possible with the Forsyth and Katz method and the sociogram approaches is not possible. In favor of the method is the fact that it is the only approach available which is relatively unrestricted as to the size of group that may be examined, and this alone may be sufficient reason for giving it attention. In addition, treatment of the data is readily repeatable in the hands of different investigators. Persons interested in reading relatively nonmathematical expositions of this approach should refer to Festinger (1949), Chabot (1950), and Rapoport (1963).

FACTOR ANALYSIS

The possible application of factor analysis to sociometric data has been suggested many times, although only a few such extensions have been reported. Cervinka

(1948) explicitly suggested the application of factor analysis to sociometric and similar structures by isolating factors related to the manifest data; Katz (1950) made similar suggestions. Bock and Husain (1950) carried out a factor analysis of a particular sociometric group and were able to identify two factors, "sex" and "reputation for science ability." Their presentation was primarily an exercise in which they demonstrated the possible utility of such an approach, especially in terms of factor scores computed for the group members. Proctor (1953) applied factor analysis to the classification of multiple sociometric questions.

MacRae (1960) presented a method for identifying clear-cut subgroups within a larger group by a computer method of factor analysis. This approach involves a factorial examination of the similarity of the choices given or received by group members. Thus, subgroups are identified on the basis of similarity of inter-personal preferences. Hubbell (1965) has presented an input-output model for identification of cliques which permits links to have fractional strength and negative direction as well as positive direction. With MacRae's (1960) data, Hubbell's method produced a somewhat different clique structure than did the factor-analytic approach.

A principal-component direct factor analysis has been suggested by Wright and Evitts (1961) as the most useful and objective means to summarize and describe sociometric data. A Q-technique system is utilized as the basic measure of interpersonal preferences. The data analysis differs from that of Bock and Husain (1950) in that the sociomatrix is factored directly and also in that a principal-component factoring method rather than the centroid method is used. Both the pattern of choosing and the pattern of being chosen are taken into account by the Wright and Evitts approach. As an illustration of this procedure, a study of 27 faculty members at a school of nursing was undertaken. The factor-analytic data were presented graphically in the form of sociograms. The authors pointed out (Wright and Evitts, 1961, p. 97): "Not only do the sociograms make accessible objective yet comprehensive maps of social structure, but the analysis of congruence provides an orderly basis for the inference of fundamental socio-metric laws."

A comparison of alternative methods of identifying subgroups was made by Nosanchuk (1963). He compared four sociometric partitioning techniques—the all-choice sociogram (Borgatta, 1951), the mutual-choice sociogram (Borgatta, 1951), matrix manipulation (Katz, 1947), and direct factor analysis (MacRae, 1960). These methods were applied to five 15-man pseudo-sociomatrices which were generated from a table of random numbers. Each of the five groups was built in such a way as to have different underlying choice structures, clique struc-tures, and differential probabilities of a choice being directed within or between cliques. The subgroups identified by the four different methods were compared to the known *a priori* structure, and the methods were contrasted with respect to objectivity, meaningfulness, and cost in time. The results indicated that direct factor analysis exceeds the others in cost but results in the most objective and meaningful partitioning of groups into subgroups.

RELIABILITY

The reliability of a measuring device is the consistency with which it measures or orders the variable in question. There are several possible sources of inconsistency or error of measurement and hence several different types of reliability coefficients (French and Michael, 1966). We shall discuss four types of reliability: interjudge consistency, consistency over time, consistency between equivalent test forms, and internal consistency.

It should be noted that we are not considering a single standardized measuring instrument. Therefore, we should not expect to find a single answer with respect to the reliability of sociometric measures. In addition, it should be noted that measurement in this area is still at a fairly primitive stage of development and does not yet involve the more complex problems of measurement consistency characteristic of multiresponse assessment devices such as intelligence tests or interest inventories, or the various scoring systems applied to projective techniques. As noted previously, most approaches to sociometric measurement involve relatively simple questions about friendship choices, simple rating scales, or checklists. Given the present status of attraction measurement, what can be said about its reliability?

INTERJUDGE CONSISTENCY: A NECESSARY PREREQUISITE

In order to obtain adequate reliability of measurement, it is necessary that independent investigators presented with the same response data arrive at essentially the same score or interpret the data in essentially the same way. Though such interjudge consistency is generally assumed in sociometric investigations, it seems very likely that the actual agreement between independent observers will vary with the particular technique chosen. Thus, if the data consist of a list of three friendship choices or a check mark on a nine-point scale, interjudge consistency should depart from unity only as a function of gross human error in perceiving or recording the response. The various combined scores, indices, matrix analyses, etc., represent only an extension of the same situation, and there are no subjective decisions intervening which could lead to possible differences among judges.

With respect to purely graphical representations of the sociometric responses of a group, a great deal of subjectivity and individual decision making is involved unless one of the detailed conventions is employed, such as that recommended by Wright and Evitts (1961). Otherwise, it is clear that different investigators confronted with the same list of the friendship choices of group members may produce quite different sociogrammatic representations of the group (Loomis, 1948).

A third and somewhat unusual aspect of interjudge consistency discussed in sociometric literature concerns the consistency among group members in ranking or rating each subject. Frequently, there is an arbitrary division of the group into halves (odd and even subjects), so that for any index each individual is given two scores, one from each half of the group. As P. N. Pepinsky (1949) has pointed out, reliability here becomes a measure of how consistently the individual is reacted to by the various members of the group, and no one has ever claimed that all members of a group ordinarily react to an individual in the same way. Thus, differences between the two halves are to be expected and are *not* evidence of what is normally meant by interjudge inconsistency. Nevertheless, it is reported with surprising frequency that such correlations of popularity scores between random halves of a group are statistically significant, and often in the .80's and .90's (for example, Ausubel, 1953; Clampitt and Charles, 1956; Hill, 1963; Hollander and Webb, 1955). Such coefficients are often labeled "split-half reliability" and are sometimes even corrected by the Spearman-Brown formula. Unless each group member is conceptualized as a test item which may be discarded if unreliable or reused with successive future subjects, these coefficients seem much closer to what is meant by interjudge consistency than to the split-half concept. Actually, such coefficients would seem to be most reasonably conceptualized as indicating the generalized versus specific quality of each person's popularity within a group.

One slightly different approach to the consistency of sociometric status involves ranking or ratings of an individual by different subjects in different situations. For example, if sociometric data are available for two different groups in which there is some overlapping membership, it is possible to determine the comparative sociometric standing of the joint members in the two settings. Again, it would seem to be the generality of sociometric status which is investigated, rather than reliability. One could even consider the two groups of respondents as representing equivalent test forms. Borgatta (1960) created five-person experimental groups of strangers and later these individuals were placed in completely new three-person groups. Thus, each subject served in two groups but those who judged him were two independent sets of strangers. Across situations, peer rankings correlated .38 to .44. In similarly recomposed six-person groups of college freshmen, Horrocks and Wear (1953) reported correlations of only .14 to .21 across groups. In a study of sociometric status in adolescent home economics and agricultural clubs, Marshall (1958) reported that 33 subjects were members of both types of organizations. Sociometric status in the two groups correlated .62. It has also been found that sociometric preference among peers is significantly related to teachers' personal preferences for sixth-grade children (Gronlund, 1953), but that sociometric status among student-teachers is unrelated to acceptance by their pupils (Smith, 1953).

CONSISTENCY OVER TIME

By far the greatest amount of work on the reliability of sociometric measures has been concentrated on the question of their temporal consistency. The meaning of test-retest coefficients in this instance is clouded with the same difficulties that beset discussion of all instruments purporting to measure variables that change with the passage of time. Just as the user of most personality measures would protest that he would be dissatisfied with his test if it showed no changes in the individual over time, so the sociometric investigator claims that his test must vary over time with concomitant changes in interpersonal relationships.

The issue is primarily one of the imputed effect of environmental variables on the response being measured. The psychologist's conception of test-retest reliability has been heavily influenced by the definitions and procedures developed by "ability testers" who are usually willing to assume that the variables of primary interest to them are not readily susceptible to environmental change. Such an assumption greatly simplifies the problem of examining instrument consistency, since it assigns all variability over time to test unreliability. For most response measures, however, a somewhat different conception is necessary. Given relevant changes in the situation, in the individual being rated, or in the person doing the rating, changes in the sociometric measure would not only be expected but would be required as evidence of its adequacy. On the other hand, if no changes have occurred, or if a very short time period is involved, a suitably reliable sociometric measure should be as stable as a reliable ability measure.

Mouton, Blake, and Fruchter (1955a) reviewed 53 studies which reported data relevant to the problem of the reliability of sociometric measures. On the basis of the data then available, they concluded that group members can make consistent judgments and that the reliability of these judgments is related to a number of specifiable factors. They went on to suggest nine hypotheses concerning the variables affecting sociometric reliability. Similarly, Lindzey and Borgatta (1954) advanced several generalizations with respect to the reliability of such measures. Here, we include both sets of conclusions together with certain more recent data.

1. Most investigators report a relatively high degree of *consistency over time,* especially if the time period is a fairly short one (Criswell, 1939; Jennings, 1950). The longer the time between the test and the retest, the less the consistency. For example, if the time period is relatively short (up to one week), test-retest coefficients over .90 are generally reported (for example, Gardner, 1956; Horowitz, 1962; McCandless *et al.,* 1956; Witryol and Thompson, 1953). With a longer time period (one week to two months), stability of responses tends to be somewhat lower and ranges from about .45 to .90 (for example, Davis and Warnath, 1957; Dunnington, 1957a; McCandless and Marshall, 1957; Moore and Updegraff, 1964). It should be noted that even with relatively long time periods, test-retest reliability coefficients remain statistically significant: .57 for a three-month period (Croft and Grygier, 1956) and .56 for a three-year period (Davis and Warnath, 1957).

2. There is some evidence that test-retest reliability increases as the *age* of the subjects increases, up to adulthood. With preschool children, for example, wide variations in stability coefficients have been reported but all fall below .90 (for example, Dunnington, 1957a; McCandless and Marshall, 1957; Moore and Updegraff, 1964). Once the child is in school, it is possible to obtain coefficients in the .80's and .90's (for example, Bonney, 1954; Davis and Warnath, 1957; Gardner, 1956; Horowitz, 1962; McCandless, Castaneda, and Palermo, 1956). It is

not clear whether the higher reliability in older children and adults is a function of greater stability in interpersonal relations or superior memory in comparison with very young children. Either view seems consistent with available evidence.

3. There is evidence that the greater the strength or *saliency of the choice,* the greater the stability over time. Thus, Moreno (1934) reported that following a three-month interval there was a shift in 8% of first choices and 18% of second choices, and this finding was in general replicated by Criswell (1939). When Venable (1954) asked 42 college girls to name their best friend within the group on three occasions with 30-day intervals between each, there were only four changes among the 126 choices. Obtaining first, second, and third friendship choices among Swedish school children, Bjerstedt (1958) found that stability over time was greatest for first choices and least for third choices. Gronlund (1955), over a four-month period, reported a median stability of 72% for first choice, 59% for second choice, 52% for third choice, 45% for fourth choice, and 38% for fifth choice. One investigator (Fjeld, 1965) has reported less stability in socio-metric response among pairs of individuals displaying mixed choice and rejection than among pairs displaying mutual choice or mutual indifference.

4. The stability of sociometric choices appears to increase with the passage of *time during which the group has been in existence* (Hunt and Solomon, 1942). There is a much higher incidence of change in sociometric choices during the early stages of group formation than during later stages. Newcomb (1963) studied two different sets of 17 college students living together in a housing unit, each over a 16-week period. Every week, subjects were given several measures, including the task of ranking the other group members in terms of attraction. Rankings of the other individuals became more and more stable with higher and higher correlations between adjacent weeks. For example, the test-retest coefficient for the first week was .51 in one sample and .65 in the other. In the last week, the comparable coefficients were .88 and .90.

5. There are *individual differences* in the stability of sociometric choices. For example, Davids and Parenti (1958a) compared the stability of friendship patterns for three groups of eleven-year-old boys in a residential psychiatric treatment center, a summer camp, and a public school. Over a three-week period, the emotionally disturbed group showed significantly more fluctuation in friendship patterns than the two normal groups. Even within a normal population, personality differences are found to influence choice consistency. Kipnis (1961) obtained self descriptions, descriptions of others, and sociometric data in a sample of 87 college freshmen. Over a six-week period friendship choices were most likely to vary for those subjects who described their best friends more negatively than themselves, and least likely to vary for those who ascribed better traits to best friends than to self.

6. *Differences among measuring devices* in stability are also reported. For example, Witryol and Thompson (1953) found that a paired-comparisons technique over one to five weeks yielded a median test-retest coefficient of .96; a partial-rank-order technique with the same subjects yielded a median coefficient of .75.

CONSISTENCY IN EQUIVALENT FORMS OF MEASUREMENT

Where multiple criteria are used in obtaining sociometric choices or where alternate measuring devices are used, one may inquire into the consistency of responses on these alternate forms. Often subjects are asked more than one question concerning their attraction toward other individuals. In general, there are substantial correlations among the responses to such questions if they deal with relatively similar activities or interactions. With bomber crews, Kipnis (1957) asked preferences with respect to other group members at a party, loading cargo, going to town for the evening, returning from behind enemy lines, and serving together at a lonely outpost. She found that these different sociometric items were highly correlated with one another. Similarly, Berkun and Meeland (1958) asked infantrymen for choices in a series of different situations and obtained highly comparable results with each. When Bonney, Hoblit, and Dreyer (1953) asked college students for roommate choices and also for leisure-time choices, the two were substantially correlated (.50 to .73). Among third-graders, Hill (1963) found that sociometric choices for work companion and play companion correlated .83.

Whenever such alternate sociometric questions yield variable results, it is easily explainable on the basis of the different demands of particular activities or specific criteria. Thus, any evidence of "unreliability" here may be a function not of the test's fallibility but rather an empirical demonstration that personal choice patterns vary to some extent with the activities in terms of which the choice is made.

It should be noted that, with few exceptions (for example, Witryol and Thompson, 1953), there has been little investigation of the equivalence of the different approaches to sociometric measurement (that is, friendship choices, ratings, rankings, etc.). Consequently, the relevance of findings based on one type of instrument for generalizations concerning other types of instruments remains a matter for conjecture.

INTERNAL CONSISTENCY

The one circumstance where it is clearly appropriate to use the relation between separate sociometric questions as a measure of the internal consistency of the test is that in which the investigator is using a cumulative sociometric score made up of the combined total of responses to two or more separate items. If it is assumed that the scores or choices on the various questions are functionally equivalent, it is necessary to show that they are significantly intercorrelated.

The use of such "multi-item" measures of attraction is relatively rare in sociometric research. For example, Kipnis (1957) combined choice responses for five situations into a single total score. With the rating approach, two seven-point scales dealing with liking for another person and his desirability as a work partner were summed by Byrne and Nelson (1965), who obtained a corrected split-half reliability of .85 for this two-item instrument.

VALIDITY

The degree to which a test is capable of achieving specified aims is defined as its validity. Three different kinds of validity coefficients are often distinguished (French and Michael, 1966) and we shall discuss the relevance of each to sociometric measurement. Initially, we shall consider whether it is even appropriate to apply the notion of validity to sociometric tests.

It seems possible to conceptualize sociometric measures in such a way that one purports to measure nothing more than verbal choice behavior, which is manifestly true, and therefore requires no further demonstration of validity. Measures of interpersonal attraction assess a response or series of responses that are ordinarily conceptualized as dependent variables. Thus, it is as meaningful to discuss the validity of sociometric choices or attraction ratings as it is to discuss the validity of running speed in an alley runway, the validity of lever pressing in a Skinner box, or the validity of a series of paired-associate words on a memory drum. All such techniques permit the quantification of some aspect of a class of responses. They are useful to the extent that lawful relationships can be established between such response variables and other variables. If such relationships are established, the response measures are of obvious interest in their own right and the question of their validity is a minor one.

The only relevant validity question here is a nonquantitative, subjective judgment as to the face validity of the assessment device. An experimenter's operational definition of response acquisition, extinction, emotionality, or such, should be reasonably congruent with the generally accepted definitions of the meaning of such terms. If the sociometric investigator limits his interest to a measure of interpersonal choice, it is clear that the somewhat inelegant concept of face validity is equally relevant here. The sociometric measure is made up of interpersonal choices or rankings or ratings, and to talk of external measures or criteria to demonstrate that this is the case is to misunderstand the operational base of sociometric scores. The assessment of attraction responses is not analogous to the construction of a test to measure some general disposition or underlying attribute. The difference between sociometric measures and many other psychological tests has been pointed out by both Pepinsky (1949) and Jennings (1950).

CONTENT VALIDITY

The content validity of a test is its adequacy in sampling the universe of situations that the test situation is supposed to represent. The clearest examples of tests for which this type of validity is relevant are academic achievement measures, in which the test constitutes a sample of a given field or body of knowledge, and industrial performance measures, in which the test is a sample of the specific skills and activities required for a given job.

Though this aspect of validity seems relatively inappropriate in the sociometric situation, it would be possible to utilize this general concept in building sociometric measures. For example, if one were interested in assessing the attraction of individual *A* toward individual *B*, it should be possible to define the universe of situations to which such a response refers. That is, the research interest should be focused on *A*'s liking for *B*, not on his evaluation of *B*'s leadership potential or his estimate of *B*'s physical strength. Therefore, as in many of the investigations cited earlier in this chapter, the relevant information would encompass *A*'s relative attraction toward *B* or choice of *B* as a companion in social interaction, as a friend, as a roommate, as a dining companion, as a work partner, as a guest at a party, as a confidant, etc. If such a universe of social interaction were defined arbitrarily or otherwise identified in some way, obviously the content validity of any given sociometric measure could be ascertained. The closest approximation to this approach is Gardner and Thompson's (1956) attempt to secure sociometric ratings in connection with all the dimensions that seemed to represent means by which the individual could secure gratification from a group of which he was a member.

CRITERION-RELATED VALIDITY

Whenever there is an identifiable criterion variable for what a test purports to measure, the test may be used to estimate an individual's present standing on that variable or to predict his future standing. For example, an adjustment test might be used to estimate an individual's ability to distinguish reality from fantasy or an intelligence test might be used to predict his college grades. Is this concept appropriate to sociometric measurement?

In one sense, the answer is "no." If the investigator's major interest is determination of the behavioral laws involving friendship choices or attraction ratings, the relationship between such responses and other responses such as overt behavioral interaction is a question of only peripheral interest. Failure to observe substantial relations between verbal behavior on the sociometric measure and physical behavior in another situation (for example, Sherif *et al.*, 1961) is not necessarily an indictment of the validity of the assessment device (or of the validity of the behavioral measure). For example, if one defines prejudice toward minority groups in terms of the extent to which an individual selectively chooses or avoids members of various minority groups, it would not necessarily be an indication of the invalidity of this measure of prejudice to show that it did not correspond closely to prejudice as measured by one of the paper-and-pencil attitude scales. Both sets of responses are undoubtedly determined by a series of antecedents, and not necessarily the same antecedents. A lack of relationship between such responses represents an interesting question for theoretical speculation and subsequent research, but it would scarcely suggest that investigators should cease defining prejudice in terms of sociometric responses (or in terms of attitude-scale responses).

The same consideration applies to differences between choice behavior as revealed in sociometric measures and overt choice behavior as revealed in an observational study. There are many determinants or conditions which influence overt behavior (for example, physical constraints, social obligations, perceived likelihood of reciprocation, estimation of the social acceptability of a given choice) that do not have the same effect on verbal choice behavior, and vice versa. Nevertheless, the relationship between the two types of behavior is of interest. Furthermore, if one actually uses sociometric responses to estimate or predict overt behavior, then the magnitude of the relationship is crucial and may even be conceptualized as a validity coefficient.

In a number of investigations concerned with sociometric choice and overt behavior, moderately high correlations have been reported between the two variables (for example, Byrd, 1951; Danielsson, 1949; Jennings, 1950). Sociometric choices are found to be significantly correlated with overt behavioral choices among preschool children (Marshall and McCandless, 1957), kindergarten children (Biehler, 1954), and eleven-year-olds (Bjerstedt, 1958). In a university class, sociometric choices were significantly related to the distance between seats chosen by the subjects in a laboratory section (King, 1964). When teachers were asked to guess the sociometric choices of preschool children, their estimates were relatively accurate (McCandless and Marshall, 1957). Another sort of validational evidence was provided in a study of adolescent boys. Feinberg (1953) reported that those individuals most accepted by their peers on a sociometric test also had a history of election as team captains, class presidents, and committee chairmen, while the rejected individuals had never been so chosen. It should also be noted that, on occasion, investigators have reported finding little or no relationship between sociometric responses and overt behavior (for example, Marshall, 1957; Polansky, Lippitt, and Redl, 1950).

CONSTRUCT VALIDITY

When a test is designed to measure some hypothetical trait or quality, construct validity is determined by the network of relationships between test performance and a variety of relevant measures. Ordinarily, a sociometric response is conceptualized as a dependent variable, a response to a particular stimulus person, and not as a general trait or quality of the subject.

Whenever the sociometric responses directed toward a particular individual are combined as a measure of his sociometric status, a generalized trait or quality is involved and construct validity is an appropriate concept. We shall discuss the research dealing with the correlates of sociometric status, and thus bearing on construct validity, in the following section. A focused discussion of such investigations in terms of validity is provided by Mouton, Blake, and Fruchter (1955b).

It should be emphasized that a far more useful question than whether a test actually measures what it purports to measure is the more general question of the extent to which it relates to significant independent measures that are of interest to the theorist and investigator. Whatever label is placed on the responses, if they relate successfully to a large number of pertinent variables, it is clear such findings will be of value and interest to students of behavior. In the following section we plan to deal at some length with this question, for it is in the area of research utility, and not in investigations specifically labeled validity studies, that one should look for a meaningful estimate of the usefulness of sociometric measures.

RESEARCH UTILITY

If one views the main purpose of scientific endeavor as the building of stable, significant relationships that are explicitly interrelated, the empirical value or usefulness of a response measure can be roughly equated to its capacity to relate significantly to independently measured variables. To the extent that empirical relationships are established and theoretical formulations are generated in connection with a response variable, one's measure is worthwhile. Here, the utility of measures of social choice will be evaluated in terms of the question: *What significant independent behavioral variables or stimulus variables have been shown to relate to sociometric variables?*

In our discussion we shall consider research findings relevant to two major variables: sociometric status and interpersonal attraction. Our consideration of studies will be schematic, since the number of relevant investigations is extremely large. We shall be content here to give a general impression of the ways in which these variables have been investigated and the outcomes of such studies.

SOCIOMETRIC STATUS

As has been noted earlier, sociometric status refers to the generalized tendency to evoke positive or negative interpersonal choices from one's peers. A great many studies have been directed at establishing the antecedents and correlates of individual differences in this tendency.

Leadership

Measures of leadership are legion in the psychological literature, and virtually all of them have dealt with interaction between and among individuals, usually in a group setting. It is consequently understandable that investigations of interpersonal choice often involve the study of leadership.

Perhaps the first sociometric study to address itself specifically to the problem of leadership was Jennings' (1937) longitudinal study of a single cottage in a school for delinquent girls. Further reports (Jennings, 1947, 1950) described how as part of her extensive investigation Jennings selected a group of overchosen and a group of underchosen subjects, the overchosen representing persons who were one standard deviation above the mean in the number of social choices they received, while the underchosen were one standard deviation below the mean. Approximately three months before the sociometric data were collected, the girls in the institution had elected a House Council. Examination of the two sets of data revealed that 90 percent, or 18 of the 20 council members, were in the overchosen group. Furthermore, the two persons who were not in this group fell only slightly below the necessary standard. The author concluded (p. 38):

When allowance is made for the difference between being chosen from a community-wide base and being elected from the limited house population, it is evident that there is practically a one-to-one relationship between being elected to represent the house body in matters concerning the group and being chosen by community members on the sociometric criteria of living and/or working with them.

A number of investigations have been concerned with leadership in the military and its relation to sociometric status. Wherry and Fryer (1949) examined the utility of sociometric ratings as criteria of leadership and concluded that they serve this purpose satisfactorily. Gibb (1950) proposed a comprehensive definition of leadership and then set out to examine the relation between observer ratings of this dimension and three kinds of sociometric response. The three sociometric questions employed the criteria of spending leisure time with, working with, and the person whose removal from the group would bring about the largest group change. Two sets of ten-man leaderless groups (college students and Army officer candidates) were studied. Observer ratings of leadership correlated in the neighborhood of .40 with sociometric choice for the criteria of spending leisure time and working together. Sociometric choice for the third criterion, however, correlated about .80 with the leadership ratings. Gibb's findings indicate both the imperfect association between sociometric choice and some aspects of leadership, and also the importance of the particular criterion that is used as the basis for the sociometric choice.

The hierarchical characteristics of military organizations make it possible to identify degrees of leadership and to investigate the relationship between this variable and sociometric status. For example, Masling, Greer, and Gilmore (1955) obtained interpersonal choices for social situations and for leaders from 900 infantrymen and 1000 Naval recruits. In each instance, the higher the status of the recruit (which was *not* determined by his peers), the more sociometric choices he received from his peers. The authors concluded that either the leaders were more capable individuals and were perceived that way by both officers and peers *or* that the nature of the military situation is such that leaders are simply perceived differently from nonleaders. Obtaining similar findings among enlisted men in rifle platoons, Petersen, Komorita, and Quay (1964) concluded that such factors as popularity are either bases for leadership choice or are highly correlated with leadership ability. In still other military studies of leadership, the relationship between leadership choices and friendship choices is found to be of moderate magnitude (Berkowitz, 1956; Borgatta, 1954). Observing a correlation of .47 between friendship nominations and leadership nominations among Naval Aviation Cadets, Hollander and Webb (1955) concluded (p. 166):

This finding tends to substantiate the fact that peer nominations are not mere "popularity contests," but represent, at least for the variables of this study, evaluations of the individual's potential for performance largely independent of the dimension of friendship.

In nonmilitary settings there has been somewhat greater research emphasis on the differentiation of leadership choices and friendship choices (for example, Gardner, 1956; Horrocks and Wear, 1953; Hunt and Solomon, 1942; Keislar, 1953). Moreno (1934) described the individual who secured a few key choices and consequently occupied an influential position in spite of the fact that his choice status was quite low. Gibb (1950) has pointed to the distinction between the individual who is the social center of the group and the person who is the functional leader of the group. In some cases the leader and the person who has the highest choice status are the same, but this is by no means always the case. In addition to situational differences (for example, military versus nonmilitary), there are apparently individual differences in the tendency to equate leadership and friendship choices. Smith (1963) had members of various groups rank their fellow members as to quality of ideas, leadership, and liking. For each subject, the three rankings were correlated, and the subjects were then divided into four types on the basis of the magnitude of the coefficients. The four types are:

Correlations between:

Type	Leadership and quality of ideas	Leadership and liking
1	High	High
2	High	Low
3	Low	High
4	Low	Low

A number of behavioral differences across the four types were identified. For example, attraction to the group was greatest for type 1 individuals and least for type 3 individuals; also types 1 and 3 were more active in group interaction than types 2 and 4. If it becomes possible to classify subjects in this way independently of their sociometric responses, it will help to clarify why it is sometimes reported that leadership is highly correlated with sociometric status and sometimes not.

It appears that the nature of the relationship between sociometric status and leadership is dependent on the demands of the situation and the characteristics of the individuals composing the group. It is clear, however, that sociometric measures can provide important data in the study of leadership and under some conditions can be used directly to measure this variable.

Adjustment

The relationship between adequacy of social adjustment (as indicated by sociometric status) and adequacy of personal adjustment has been investigated in a large number of studies. The use of sociometric methods to measure social adjustment is implicit in Moreno's original formulations. He implied that low choice status or high rejection status is evidence that the adjustment of the subject is not good. Concepts such as *isolate, neglectee,* and *rejectee* clearly connote adjustment.

Jennings (1943, 1950) pointed out that description of the individual as an "isolate" refers to the choice behavior of the group and provides no evidence of whether the isolated individual is isolated of his own accord or involuntarily. Similarly, being overchosen does not necessarily imply he is "happy" because of this status. Jennings suggested, reasonably, that the desirable sociometric pattern should be decided through consideration of the particular setting in which the choices are being made. Northway (1944) has suggested distinguishing between social "acceptability" and "acceptance." She suggests that sociometric data provide evidence of the *acceptance* of the person within a specific social setting. The social *acceptability* of the person can be measured only with a much wider range of information concerning reactions of people to this person in a variety of social settings. While this is a legitimate caution, it is important to realize that the problem of generalizing findings is always present and is in no way unique to sociometric data.

A group of 80 children in an elementary school were studied by Bonney (1944), using the California Test of Personality and a multiple-criterion sociometric questionnaire. He found that the total adjustment score of the inventory correlated .49 with sociometric status. Consistently, when the subjects were divided into quartiles in terms of social choice, the quartiles were arranged in a regular order with the high in social choice also the highest in mean adjustment scores. In a similar study, Grossman and Wrighter (1948) found that sixth-grade students who were very high in sociometric status secured much higher total adjustment scores on the California Test of Personality than did a similar group of students who were very low in sociometric status. The upper and lower quartiles in sociometric status of 692 ninth-grade students were compared by Kuhlen and Bretsch (1947) in their responses to the Mooney Problem Check List. The findings indicated that those low in status tended to check a significantly larger number of problems as "often" present, but the two groups were not differentiated in the frequency with which they checked problems as "sometimes" present. A large number of fifth- and sixth-grade students were divided into three sociometric status groups by Baron (1951) and compared in their responses to a mental health inventory. In general, the inventory appeared to differentiate among the three status groups, with the low in social status making more "unfavorable" responses than either of the other groups. In a large-scale study of fifth-grade children, Semler (1960) found substantial positive correlations between sociometric status and personal adjustment as measured by teacher ratings and the California Test of Personality. A number of other investigations have similarly indicated a significant relationship between sociometric status and various aspects of adjustment, including neuroticism (Thorpe, 1955a), psychopathy (Bonney, Hoblit, and Dreyer, 1953), incidence of psychosomatic ailments (Izard, 1959), and general adjustment as indicated by case-history material (Feinberg, 1953).

The MMPI, Rorschach, and TAT were utilized by Mills (1953) in comparing the 21 male college students who were the least popular individuals in their dormitory with the 21 who were the most popular. Among the findings were a number of indications of differential level of adjustment in the two groups. On the MMPI, the popular, as compared to the unpopular, students were significantly less deviant or eccentric in responding (*F*), more defensive (*K*), less psychopathic (*Pd*), less psychasthenic (*Pt*), less schizophrenic (*Sc*), less manic (*Ma*), and less anxious (*Welsh A*). On the Rorschach, the only difference was in *F*+ percent: the fact that the unpopular students had significantly poorer form level than the popular ones suggests less adequate functioning. On the TAT, those who were popular ". . . presented themes using the more tender emotions of congeniality, tranquility, offering aid to the parent, and showing contentment with a partner of the opposite sex. When hostility was aroused, they tended to give it direct expression . . ." (p. 165). Thus, across all three measuring instruments there is a consistent picture of contrasting adequacy of adjustment between the sociometrically popular and unpopular students.

As a specific component of adjustment, anxiety might be expected to be inversely related to sociometric status. In several sociometric studies of children, scores on the Children's Manifest Anxiety Scale have been found to correlate approximately $-.30$ with choice status (Horowitz, 1962; McCandless, Castaneda, and Palermo, 1956; Trent, 1957). In explanation, Trent (1957) suggested that anxiety tends to distort a child's perception of others and hence leads to inappropriate interpersonal behavior.

Several studies have attempted to relate sociometric status to adjustment through the use of differentiated groups. In a study by French (1951) of a large group of Navy enlisted men, adjustment was measured through psychiatric referrals, sick-bay attendance, and disciplinary offenses. These indices were then considered in relation to sociometric status. Sociometric choice was negatively related to sick-bay attendance and disciplinary offenses. The number of psychiatric cases was not large enough to provide an adequate test, although the evidence observed was in the expected direction, suggesting that those individuals who had undergone psychiatric examination were relatively lower in social status. Tagiuri (1952) compared three groups of preparatory-school students: those who were successful (good athletes, high grades, officeholders), average students, and maladjusted students (seeing a psychiatrist). He found that the maladjusted students were characterized by low social choice, while the successful students tended to be higher than the average students on this variable. Croft and Grygier (1956) gave a sociometric test to 13 classes of eleven- to fifteen-year-olds in a secondary school in a poor neighborhood. It was found that the truant and delinquent boys had lower sociometric status than the other students. Furthermore, sociometric status was negatively related to teacher ratings of "bad classroom behavior." Davids and Parenti (1958b) compared three groups of children: 48 emotionally disturbed in treatment, 80 normals at a summer camp, and 57 normals in public school. In both the disturbed and normal groups, social popularity was significantly associated with good emotional adjustment. Even within the emotionally disturbed group, the disliked children were more emotionally disturbed than the ignored or liked children. Similarly, among the adult patients in a psychiatric ward, sociometric rank was found to be inversely related to degree of illness (Brown, 1965).

The positive relationship between sociometric status and adequacy of personal adjustment seems well established. One implication of this relationship is the possibility of utilizing sociometric data as an index of changes in adjustment. For example, if psychotherapy is an effective behavior-change agent, sociometric status should improve following successful therapy. Cox (1953) obtained sociometric choices for 52 children (aged 5 to 13) in an Australian orphanage. Sociometric status was found to correlate .76 with composite adjustment ratings based on TAT stories, a social-adjustment questionnaire, and interviews with those caring for the children. The children were divided into two groups, matched for age, sex, residential placement ratings, and the sociometric measure. One of the groups received several weeks of play therapy while the other served as a control group. The sociometric procedure was repeated after 10 weeks of therapy and then again after an additional 14 weeks. At each testing, the experimental group showed a significant increase in sociometric status, while the control group showed no change. Further analysis revealed that it was the oldest children who were changing. Cox concluded that ". . . sociometric status is a sensitive and valid index of behavioral change" (p. 356). Thus, again we observe that sociometric status is well established as a correlate of adjustment and, somewhat more tentatively, sociometric measures may be used as an index of adjustment.

Other personality variables

In addition to personal adjustment, a number of other personality characteristics have been investigated as possible correlates of sociometric status. It might be noted that such studies often involve a reliance upon measures that are easy and inexpensive to administer as part of an exploratory study. Thus, the relationship between sociometric data and "random" personality attributes is sought with little or no attempt to engage in conceptual analysis in advance which could indicate the kinds of variables that might be expected to be associated with sociometric status.

In a study of three small women's dormitories in an urban college, Lemann and Solomon (1952) studied six personality variables. All the variables were bipolar, and the investigators divided them into two categories: *alpha*, those ratings that ran from good to bad (generous-stingy, affectionate-cold, enthusiastic-apathetic); and *beta*, those that ran from bad to good to bad (dominating-submissive, shy-bold, stubborn-yielding). Their findings indicated that sociometric status was related to ratings on the alpha scales but not on the beta scales. Those high in sociometric status, as measured by a combined choice and rejection score, were characterized as generous, enthusiastic, and affectionate. When the subjects were grouped in terms of the noticeability of their indifference score (the number of combined choices and rejections subtracted from the total number of responses possible), a relationship was found between this division and ratings received on the beta scales. Individuals low in noticeability were rated as dominating, bold, and stubborn. It is apparent that having the same individuals perform the personality ratings and the sociometric ratings poses certain problems in the interpretation of any association between these variables. Lemann and Solomon suggested: "It may be that a general 'halo effect' surrounding girls with high status causes them to be rated favorably on most traits" (p. 35).

In a similar investigation, French and Mensh (1948) studied 34 college students who were members of the same sorority. The subjects were asked to make three choices and three rejections for roommates and also were asked to rate each other on punctuality, sociability, fair-mindedness, intelligence, self-confidence, and sense of humor. Sociometric status was measured by dividing the group by inspection into the majority ingroup and nine isolates. The majority group was then further subdivided into those who received rejections and those who did not. This resulted in three groups of varying sociometric status. A comparison of these three groups in the personality ratings they received indicated that, in general, the individuals high in choice status were rated highest on those personality variables that are normatively most valued. In considering the association they found, French and Mensh (1948) suggested a number of possible explanations (p. 344):

Do individuals attain high status because they manifest these traits? Or do they develop these traits in consequence of having attained high status? Or are they merely thought by raters to stand high in these respects because they have high status or are admired as individuals? Or does high status permit the conspicuous display of these traits without there necessarily being any fundamental personality differences?

Consistently, with fourth-, fifth-, and sixth-grade boys, Winder and Rau (1962) reported that likability among peers is negatively related to peer ratings of aggression, dependency, withdrawal, and depression.

Kidd (1953) asked 639 male students in a residence hall to name those individuals they would find least acceptable as friends and to give reasons why. The most frequently stated reasons for rejection involved those who assumed a role of superiority (for example, egotistical, overconfident, sarcastic, domineering) or a role of inferiority (for example, timid, quiet, retiring). Beginning with Seagoe's (1933) investigation, there have been a number of studies which have shown that sociometric choice is related to behavior ratings secured through "guess who" techniques. Although these studies measure personality somewhat more indirectly than ordinary rating methods, they nevertheless seem open to the same criticisms as the studies which correlate sociometric ratings with personality ratings. The findings of such studies are both interesting and consistent with what we would expect if personality factors were closely related to social choice. However, the interaction between sociometric ratings and personality ratings makes such findings of little significance as evidence of the relation between interpersonal attraction and personality variables. To secure pertinent data it is necessary that the personality ratings be provided by someone other than the individuals making the social choice.

Several studies have met this criticism through the use of interviews, observational data, or some combination of the two methods. Perhaps the first of these was reported by Richmond (1936). In her paper she indicated simply that when student nurses were interviewed after sociometric data had been collected, the impressions they created in the interviewer were consistent with the interpersonal data. Another study in this area, carried out by Northway (1944), focused on children who were very low in choice status. She collected personality data through interviews and observation of children in the fifth and sixth grades who were in the lowest quartile in social choice. These data suggested to Northway that there were really three distinct types of "outsiders" or individuals low in sociometric status. The first group was made up of the "recessive children" who were low in energy, possessed little or no drive, and in general created a picture of listlessness and general lack of motivation. Second, there were the "socially disinterested children" who were less defective in general energy and motivation but did not seem interested in gaining social approval. Finally, there were the "socially ineffective children" who were characterized by aggression, boastfulness, and other social responses but who appeared strongly motivated to secure social acceptance. In a study of over 400 adolescent delinquent girls, Jennings (1947) compared the overchosen (one standard deviation above the mean in frequency of choices received) and the underchosen (one standard deviation below the mean). She concluded from observational and interview evidence that the over-chosen showed a large number of distinctive qualities, among which were ability to establish rapport quickly and effectively, fairness, tendency to exhibit anger primarily toward those they consider "should know better," and tendency to secure more and more responsibilities for members of their group. The under-chosen more frequently interfered with the group activities, showed little initiative in starting projects or promoting understanding among group members, and in general seemed to impede rather than facilitate interpersonal relations.

Dunnington (1957b) compared preschool children of high and low sociometric status by means of observer ratings of behavior in two 20-minute sessions a week apart. It was found that, compared to low-status children, those high in socio-metric status showed a higher proportion of positive affect to negative or aggressive affect, more aggression specific as to origin and object, less verbalization seeking interaction with adults, and more spontaneous verbalization. In a recent study of nursery-school children, Moore and Updegraff (1964) found that observer ratings of nurturance-giving and dependence on children were both positively related to sociometric status. In the same investigation, dependence on adults was found to be related to sociometric status ($r = -.55$) only in the youngest group of children. Two other investigations of preschool children have reported significant negative relationships between observer ratings of dependency on adults and sociometric status (McCandless, Bilous, and Bennett, 1961; Marshall and McCandless, 1957).

Probably the majority of studies of the relationship between sociometric choice and personality variables have utilized measures in which subjects are asked to describe themselves, to answer questionnaire items, or to respond to projective measures. A rather diverse array of personality characteristics has been investigated by such methods.

Lindzey and Urdan (1954) related measures of security, dominance, happiness, and achievement derived from self-ratings, questionnaires, and a sentence-completion test to various sociometric measures, including sociometric status and clique structure. They concluded that the questionnaire measures showed much stronger relations to the sociometric indices than either of the other two types of measure, although there was some reason for questioning the adequacy of the projective measure of these variables. They also found evidence for a curvilinear relation between sociometric status and the variables of dominance and security; that is, high social status was associated with medium security and dominance.

If we consider accident proneness a personality variable, there are several studies that relate this characteristic to sociometric indices. A study by Fuller and Baune (1951) of third-grade students found that when the subjects were divided into upper, middle, and lower thirds in terms of social choice there appeared to be a descending ordering of accident proneness; that is, the most popular children tended to have the smallest number of accidents. Not only did the children high in sociometric choice tend to have fewer accidents in general, but those accidents they did have were primarily nonsocial; that is, they did not occur during interaction or play with other children. On the other hand, the children low in social choice tended to have a relatively high incidence of social accidents. A related study was carried out by Speroff and Kerr (1952) with a group of 90 steel-mill workers. They found that a sociometric status score based on sociometric choice and rejection showed a highly significant relation with the frequency of industrial accidents, those low in status having accidents more frequently.

Northway and Wigdor (1947) have compared Rorschach responses of three groups of eighth-grade boys and girls who were high, low, and middle in sociometric status. The authors indicated that those high in status were characterized by "greater sensitivity in sensing the feelings of others, and a conscious striving for the approval of others" (p. 196). The middle group ". . . seems a more shallow, less introspective group with few anxiety or emotional disturbances" (p. 194). The low group "seems to be the most seriously disturbed. They show less ability to control their emotions, and seem to be a more egocentric, moody, and impulsive group" (p. 194).

A study by Lindzey and Goldwyn (1954) examined the relation between sociometric status, measured by choice and rejection, and certain P–F Study scores and TAT variables. When the 10 individuals highest in social status were compared with the 10 individuals lowest in social status, significant differences were observed on several of the P–F Study variables. The findings indicated that those high in sociometric status were less extrapunitive, more intrapunitive, and showed lower group conformity ratings than those low in social status. Krieger and Schwartz (1965) also found intrapunitiveness to be related to sociometric status. In a study of student nurses Holzberg and Posner (1951) used a sociometric technique with criteria designed to secure information about the assertiveness of group members. They found a significant positive relationship between sociometric status in this situation and scores on the A–S Reaction Study, as well as with ratings of assertiveness carried out by supervisors. Miller and Stine (1951) used a story-completion test in an effort to relate pregenital fixations to social choice as measured by a sociometric questionnaire. The expectation that individuals who were most characterized by pregenitality, as inferred from the story-completion test, would be most rejected was, in general, verified. The investigators divided their primary-school subjects into five status groups in terms of the incidence of choice and rejection and found a general increase in rated pregenitality as the degree of rejection increased. When the mean pregenital scores of the two high-status groups were combined and compared with the means of the low-status groups for each of 11 pregenital variables (orality, anality, passivity, direct aggression, etc.), the low-status group was higher on 10 of 11 variables, five of these differences reaching the five percent level of significance.

Marks (1954) administered an interest test and a sociometric questionnaire to 730 students in grades 8 to 12. He then compared the 302 students who were at the unacceptable and acceptable ends of the sociometric dimension. A number of differences were found between these two groups in terms of interest patterns: "In general the acceptable adolescent is seen as sociable, involved with people, and relatively impulsive" (p. 348). It appeared that mechanical interests for boys and intellectual interests for girls may act both to isolate and to compensate for isolation. In a study of third-grade children, Hill (1963) found that the relationship of sociometric status to test anxiety and defensiveness depended on whether same-sex or cross-sex sociometric status was involved. Popularity with members of the same sex was unrelated to either anxiety or defensiveness, while defensiveness was negatively related to cross-sex status. Girls were *less* popular with boys, the higher their test anxiety; boys, on the other hand, were *more* popular with girls as their test anxiety increased. Goldstone *et al.* (1963) required three groups of medical students to estimate the duration of sounds and also collected sociometric data. It was found that accuracy in time judgments was positively related to sociometric status. The authors suggested (pp. 308–309):

Interpersonal relations depend upon an individual's ability to deal with private experience in terms of socially agreed-upon units, standards and concepts that define reality for a group. . . . If prestige and friendship status are related to one's ability to calibrate private experience with social standards, more accurate people should be rated higher on these sociometric characteristics.

Several studies have dealt with various aspects of the self concept in relation to sociometric status. Turner and Vanderlippe (1958) used Q-sort items to measure self concept and ideal self in a group of 175 undergraduates. From this sample, the 25 with the greatest and the 25 with the smallest self-ideal discrepancy were selected for comparison on a number of variables, including sociometric status in their living groups. Those with the highest discrepancy (mean self-ideal correlation of .11) were less well liked than those with the least discrepancy (mean self-ideal correlation of .79). Somewhat different results were reported by Reese (1961) in a study of 507 children from the fourth, sixth, and eighth grades. Subjects with the most negative self concept (high self-ideal discrepancy) were again the least liked by their peers. However, the highest social acceptance was for those with moderate self-ideal discrepancy. Thus, sociometric status was curvilinearly related to self-concept measures. As part of a large study on the selection of clinical psychologists, Norman (1953) reported a significant positive correlation between sociometric status and self-insight. Insight was defined in terms of correspondence between self-ratings ànd ratings by peers and also correspondence between self-ratings and ratings by experienced clinicians. In a study of 50 high school students and their parents, Helper (1955) obtained self-concept measures for each member of the family and sociometric data were collected for the children. It was found that for boys, sociometric status was positively related to similarity to father. For girls, however, similarity to mother was unrelated to number of sociometric choices received.

Demographic variables

There have been numerous studies in which sociometric status has been correlated with age, sex, family size, socioeconomic status, and educational level. Depending on various characteristics of the group, *age* seems to be positively related to sociometric status. F. A. Stewart (1947a) found in his community study that individuals selected as influential tended to be older than individuals not so selected. Among elementary-school children and adolescents, the correlation between age and sociometric status is small ($r = .15$ to $.22$) but statistically significant in the samples studied (for example, Marshall, 1958; Thorpe, 1955a). With nursery-school children, Moore and Updegraff (1964) reported no relationship between sociometric status and age, but the restricted range of ages (three to five) acted against the possibility of finding such a relationship.

There is some evidence that sociometric status, depending on the ages of the subjects and the type of group, is related to the *sex* of the individual. F. A. Stewart (1947b) reported that in a Southern town women selected slightly more men than women as influential, while men selected almost 30 percent more men than women. This difference was observed in spite of the fact that subjects were asked to name both men and women. Several studies by Bonney (1942, 1943, 1944) have suggested differences between the sexes in elementary-school children, generally showing girls to have higher choice status. Among nursery-school children, sex was found to be unrelated to popularity (Moore and Updegraff, 1964).

Sociometric status has often been found to be negatively related to *family size*. A series of studies carried out by Bonney (1942, 1943, 1944, 1949) has indicated that the number of siblings appears to influence social choice, particularly at the extremes. Thus, individuals who are "only" children appear to secure more than their share of positive choices, while at the college level individuals who have six or more siblings tend to receive less than their share of positive choices. Among school children, family size has also been found to correlate negatively with choice status (Thorpe, 1955a). Nonsignificant relationships between the two variables have also been reported (Loomis, Baker, and Proctor, 1949).

Somewhat surprisingly, McDavid and Harari (1965) reported that independent ratings of the social desirability of first names show significant positive correlations with sociometric status.

There is a great deal of evidence that sociometric status is positively related to *socioeconomic status*. Various measures of social status in the community, such as occupation (Loomis, 1946) and observers' judgments (Powell, 1951), have been found to be related to sociometric status. A study of personal relationships in a small New England village by Lundberg (1937), Lundberg and Lawsing (1937), and Lundberg and Steele (1938) indicated that socioeconomic status was positively related to the frequency of sociometric choice. Among fifth-grade students, the same relationship was found (Bonney, 1944). Similarly, Grossman and Wrighter (1948) found that in a sixth-grade classroom socioeconomic status was related to sociometric status. An investigation of agricultural county agents and librarians who were participating in a university workshop indicated that sociometric status was positively related to annual income (Loomis and Proctor, 1950).

Level of *education* seems to be another sociometric correlate. F. A. Stewart (1947a) concluded that in "Southtown" education was "virtually a prerequisite" for occupying an influential position. Vreeland (1942) had fraternity members rank the other members of their group in terms of how friendly they felt toward them. Results indicated that upper classmen were given higher sociometric ranks than lower classmen.

Intelligence and performance

Most studies that have related sociometric variables to intelligence have found a positive association (for example, Izard, 1959; Thorpe, 1955a). Thus, Bonney (1944) found that sociometric choice in a group of elementary-school children was positively related to intelligence as measured by group intelligence tests, and he concluded that the upper quartile in social choice was distinctly superior intellectually to the lower quartile. This same finding held for third, fourth, and fifth grades. Hill (1963) found a positive relationship between IQ and sociometric status among third graders only with respect to girls' status among boys. The girls did not choose boys with respect to IQ nor was same-sex sociometric status related to intelligence. An investigation of a group of sixth-grade students carried out by Grossman and Wrighter (1948) related intelligence as measured by the Stanford-Binet Test to choice and rejection. The authors reported that the group that was high in sociometric status was significantly higher than the remainder of the group in intelligence. A somewhat more unusual finding was that among 164 mentally defective children Stanford-Binet mental age correlated significantly ($r = .35$ to $.39$) with sociometric status (Clampitt and Charles, 1956). Among 42 college girls, Venable (1954) found that ACE scores and popularity were unrelated ($r = .02$). Nevertheless, the mean ACE score of the stars in this group was significantly higher than the mean ACE score of the isolates.

Heber (1956) found that a high-IQ group of schoolchildren was significantly higher in social status than an average-IQ group, while a low-IQ group was significantly lower in social status. The deviation from the average group was much greater in the case of the low-IQ group; this led Heber to conclude: ". . . the decremental effect on social status of a low IQ . . . [is] greater than the incremental effect of a high IQ" (p. 162).

In a study of junior executives Kanungo (1966) found a significant positive association between peer ratings of leadership and a measure of intelligence, but observed no relationship between ratings of social choice or companionship and intelligence.

A study of sixth-grade students conducted by Grossman and Wrighter (1948) revealed a significant association between choice status and reading ability, at least to the extent that individuals in the lowest quarter of their group in choice status were significantly lower in measured reading ability than those in the upper quartile of social choice. Interested in a different kind of performance, Hunt and Solomon (1942) found that counselor ratings of athletic ability correlated .60 with a sociometric measure of status in the first week of a summer camp, but dropped to only .25 by the eighth week of the camp. In an investigation of 317 girls and 87 boys (aged 10 to 20) in a total of 31 clubs, Marshall (1958) found a positive relationship between choice status and possession of the particular knowledge or skills relevant to the group.

The purpose of this section has been to sample briefly some of the studies that have shown sociometric status to be associated with variables of psychological interest. There appears to be evidence for substantial relations between aspects of behavior measured by sociometric techniques and a great many other variables. On the basis of the data now available, it would be possible to construct a relatively complex description contrasting the individuals at the high and low extremes of sociometric status. One might reason that any behavioral variable associated with a large number of other variables is by definition a useful and meaningful one. However, two criticisms of the work on sociometric status must be noted. First, work in this area is almost totally devoid of theory. After three decades of research on sociometric status, it is disappointing to find that the typical investigation still is one in which readily available measures are correlated with some index of choice status. Without a coherent theoretical structure to integrate the numerous findings or to guide subsequent research toward critical questions, work on sociometric status remains a clear example of the limited return from a theoretic empiricism. A second, and possibly related, criticism is the lack of experimental, as opposed to correlational, research. One need not differentially value these two research approaches in order to recognize the special contributions associated with their joint use. For example, there is abundant correlational evidence of a positive association between socioeconomic status and sociometric status. Why? Do individuals of different socioeconomic levels behave differently and is it this behavior that influences choice? Is it merely the knowledge of another's socioeconomic standing that influences sociometric choice and would fictitious socioeconomic information have the same effect on choice? Does it simply enhance one's own prestige to name wealthier, more prestigeful individuals as friends, and is this the reason for choosing rather than any personal attraction toward them as individuals? It would not be difficult to devise simple experimental situations in which behavior, information about socioeconomic level, and anonymity of choices could be manipulated to begin to answer such questions. Further collection of correlational data showing that choice status is positively related to economic status would seem to serve little purpose; experimental data, however, should provide useful insights.

INTERPERSONAL ATTRACTION

In addition to generalized popularity within a group, research on interpersonal choice has increasingly dealt with the question: Why is a particular individual attracted or repelled by specified other persons? Even the most popular individuals are often disliked by some of those who know them and the most rejected individuals may find some friends.

Research aimed at determining the basis of attraction between individuals is, in one sense, more basic than research dealing with correlates of sociometric status. Once the laws governing attraction are known, it should be possible to derive predictions concerning an individual's status in a given group. It does not seem likely, however, that a knowledge of the correlates of sociometric status will lead to the derivation of the laws of attraction. It should also be noted that work on attraction, in contrast to work on status, has involved *both* correlational and experimental approaches and has led to a variety of theoretical formulations. We shall examine samples of research concerned with a range of determinants or antecedents of interpersonal attractiveness.

Propinquity

A number of investigations (for example, Byrne and Buehler, 1955; Caplow and Forman, 1950; Evans and Wilson, 1949; Festinger, Schachter, and Back, 1950; Lundberg and Beazley, 1948; Lundberg, Hertzler, and Dickson, 1949; Maisonneuve, Palmade, and Fourment, 1952; Whyte, 1956) have shown that friendship choice varies with propinquity or physical proximity. Individuals who are physically near to one another in terms of classroom seats, dormitory rooms, apartment units, or suburban housing are more likely to choose each other as friends than persons who are more remote. In a study of 355 children in the second through fifth grades, Gallagher (1958) found attraction to vary as a function of nearness of residence and concluded that elementary-school children choose their friends in part on the basis of how close they live to one another. In a cross-cultural approach to sociometric research, Danielsson (1949) reported that in a nonliterate society rejection is positively related to physical distance; the most distant groups within the prescribed area had the highest percentage of rejection. The effect of propinquity on attraction has also been investigated experimentally (Byrne, 1961b). With three college classes, seating patterns were differentially manipulated during the semester. A significantly higher proportion of seat neighbors than of nonneighbors indicated attraction to one another if the seating pattern was maintained 7 or 14 weeks, but 3.5 weeks was found to be an insufficient length of time for propinquity to influence attraction.

Several propinquity studies have involved military personnel. Blake *et al.* (1956) studied sociometric patterns among 353 air force recruits in three open and three closed cubicle barracks. Each was asked to name those in his barracks he knew, how much time he spent with them, and his three best buddies. It was found that interaction was significantly more intense in the closed cubicle barracks and that buddies were more likely to be drawn from within the cubicle. Blake *et al.* (1956, p. 138) concluded: "The interpretation is that walls, though constituting no legal or geographical boundary limiting interaction, do serve as psychological barriers." Kipnis (1957) pointed out that the amount of interaction possible or necessary between any two members of a B-29 bomber crew is dictated by their physical position within the plane. She studied both physical and functional propinquity. Physical propinquity is represented by the navigator and radio operator, who share the same compartment in isolation from the rest of the crew. Navigators were found to be preferred by radio operators more than by other airmen, and radio operators were preferred by navigators more than by other officers. Functionally, though not physically, the fire-control gunner and bombardier must interact repeatedly; as with the navigator and radio operator, these two crew members were found to be positively attracted. Kipnis (1957, p. 269) felt that the data suggest ". . . a process such that as two men interact with each other more and more, they begin to seem more likeable to each other." This process apparently is not limited to attraction between human beings; Cairns and Johnson (1965) were able to establish interspecies social attachments by confining young lambs with mature dogs for 105 days.

Hammer and Ikle (1957) have extended the propinquity findings to interactions between individuals in different cities as determined by telephone calls and airline traffic. The frequency of interactions between two persons can be expressed as a power function of distance with a negative exponent, $-b$, where b assumes various values between confidence limits of 1.3 and 1.8 in the case of telephone calls and airline traffic. The investigators also pointed out that the relationship cannot be explained by cost of interaction because it also holds for communication by letter and because the cities with the "greatest propensity to interact" have the lowest median family income.

Demographic variables

Not only is sociometric status found to be related to demographic variables such as socioeconomic status, religion, sex, and age, but similarity in these characteristics apparently leads to interpersonal attraction.

A number of investigations (Bonney, 1946; Byrne, Clore, and Worchel, 1966; Dahlke, 1953; Lundberg and Beazley, 1948) suggest that attraction is a function of similarity in *socioeconomic status*. At least, there is a tendency for individuals choosing one another to be of similar socioeconomic status. Using family visits to permit sociometric representation of a German village, Loomis (1946) was able to show that occupational role was an important determinant of sociometric cleavages. Loomis, Beegle, and Longmore (1947) have presented a detailed critique of the concept of social class or social stratification and proposed a procedure for testing empirically for the existence of social classes. They suggested using a modified sociometric technique (family visiting patterns) to provide a means of finding out whether, within the particular group studied, individuals tended to cluster or form interpersonal cleavages corresponding to the classes that were used in describing the group. A study by Longmore (1948) illustrates the application of this method in a concrete setting.

There is relatively clear evidence that congruence in *religion* is an important determinant of mutual attraction. Goodnow and Tagiuri (1952) found that cleavages tend to form around religious-ethnic groupings. Lundberg and Steele (1938) found membership in the same church to be one of the most important determinants of clique structure in a small New England village. In a large college sample, Bonney (1949) found more friendship choices within each subject's own religious group than would be expected by chance.

Beginning with Moreno's early investigations, there has been an abundance of evidence that friendships are more likely to form between members of the *same sex* than between males and females. One of the earliest and most enduring of the group cleavages that appear in our society is the one based on sex (Moreno, 1934; Criswell, 1939). The tendency for within-sex attraction significantly to exceed across-sex attraction has been found among nursery-school children (Abel and Sahinkaya, 1962; Moore and Updegraff, 1964), among elementary-school children (Bonney, 1954; Gronlund, 1953; Koch, 1957), and among teenagers (Faunce and Beegle, 1948; Bjerstedt, 1958). A note of caution in interpreting such findings is raised by the work of Kanous, Daugherty, and Cohn (1962), who suggested that sex cleavages are confined to middle-class subjects. With 375 children in the second through the eighth grades, they divided the subjects into "upper" and "lower" socioeconomic levels. The upper socioeconomic group showed sex cleavages comparable to those reported by Moreno and others. The lower socioeconomic group, however, was significantly less likely to confine attraction to members of the same sex. Situational factors also seem to influence choice patterns. Brehm and Behar (1966) presented subjects with bogus information concerning their degree of physiological sex arousal and obtained their preferences as to partners during a waiting period. Subjects in the low-arousal condition wanted to wait with members of the opposite sex while those in the high-arousal condition preferred their own sex, presumably as a function of anxiety and defensiveness.

A number of studies have dealt with *age* similarity and attraction. For example, Faunce and Beegle (1948), studying adolescent summer campers, found that age was a significant determiner of cleavages. With elementary-school children, Koch (1957) also found that a child's preferred playmate or best friend tended to be about his own age.

Minority-group prejudice

From the very outset of sociometric measurement there has been interest in applying this technique to the study of group cleavages and prejudice. Attraction is clearly influenced by such factors as race or, more precisely, by the interaction between an individual's racial membership and the amount of prejudice another individual feels toward that group.

In *Who Shall Survive?* Moreno (1934) reported a study of public-school children in which minority-group cleavages were observed only beyond the fourth grade. He also introduced the notion of a *saturation point,* a point beyond which introduction of further minority-group members will produce cleavages and other group changes.

The first study to focus primarily on minority-group cleavages was Criswell's (1937, 1939) investigation of Negro-white relations in a large number of urban classrooms ranging from kindergarten to the eighth grade. She measured cleavage by comparing the choices directed within the "own" ethnic group to the frequency of choices that would be expected by chance. Initially, she found that sex appeared to be a much more important determinant of cleavage than ethnic-group membership, and consequently she limited her group comparisons to individuals of the same sex. Her findings, in general, supported Moreno's, since there appeared to be little cleavage between the Negro and white children prior to grade three, and by grade five the cleavage had reached its height. Using a somewhat more controlled technique, Abel and Sahinkaya (1962) examined the emergence of race friendship preferences in a group of Caucasian preschool children. With a series of photograph pairs, each subject indicated which member of the pair he would like to play with or have as a friend. Among the choices were Negro-boy and white-boy pairs and Negro-girl and white-girl pairs. With respect to the four-year-olds, race did not affect the friendship choices. Among the five-year-olds, the girls again did not choose on the basis of race, but the boys expressed a preference for their own race. A study by Loomis (1943) employed a modified sociometric technique to study cleavages in two Southwestern high schools. He found that Spanish-American and Anglo-American students reported much greater association with members of their own group. The minority group, whether Spanish-American or Anglo-American, showed a stronger tendency toward ingroup selection and exclusion of the outgroup than was shown by the majority group.

Mann (1958) studied 78 Negro and white students in a graduate course in which leaderless discussion groups met four times a week for three weeks. After the groups had met for a week, friendship choices were obtained, and it was found that individuals preferred members of their own race as friends. It should be noted, however, that when sociometric choices during the first and third weeks were compared, there was a reduction in the effect of race on sociometric choice (Mann, 1959). Berkun and Meeland (1958) studied 300 infantrymen immediately after combat in Korea. The subjects were divided into 20 groups of 15 to 18 strangers who lived together for a week of psychological testing. At the end of the week, sociometric data were obtained. Each man was asked to name the two in his group most suitable and the two least suitable as a companion for rest and recreation, combat, sharing a bunker, and as a leader in combat. In each situation, the whites, at a level significantly greater than chance, selected other whites as most suitable and Negroes as least suitable. Also, Negroes selected other Negroes as most suitable in each situation except combat leadership.

Thus, where the sociometric technique is administered to groups containing appreciable numbers of one or more minority groups, a relatively direct and satisfactory measure of prejudice can be obtained. Various ratios or indices representing the relative choice by each individual of minority- and majority-group members can be obtained. Such a measure possesses obvious advantages because it gets away from an abstract notion of the minority-group members. Instead of asking the respondent to verbalize his attitudes toward the Protestant, Jew, Catholic, Oriental, or Negro, he is asked to select those individuals with whom he would like to associate in various activities, and perhaps those with whom he would not like to associate. A measure based on this kind of evidence represents not the subject's generalizations concerning his relations with minority-group members, but rather an indication of whether this person actually uses minority labels as criteria in the process of determining with whom he will interact.

If prejudice is reflected in sociometric choices and if there are individual differences in prejudice, it should be possible to predict attraction toward minority-group members on the basis of independent measures of minority-group prejudice. Wong (1961) measured prejudice toward Negroes in a group of 73 college students by means of the Desegregation Scale (Kelly, Ferson, and Holtzman, 1958). The subjects were later seen in small groups and told that they were to attempt to make various judgments about another student on the basis of minimal background information which he had written on a card. Actually, the only relevant variable on the card was race (white or Negro). Wong found that subjects high in prejudice were less attracted to the Negro stranger than to a white stranger and that they were more negative to a Negro stranger than were subjects low in prejudice.

It may be seen, then, that sociometric measures provide a convenient means of estimating the extent to which groups are divided or disrupted by negative attitudes toward minority-group members, and that they provide a sensitive measure of the extent to which prejudice determines an individual's personal choices and rejections. In addition, it is possible to predict specific attraction responses on the basis of measures of generalized attitudes toward a minority group.

Intelligence and ability

Festinger (1950, 1954) has presented a theory of social-comparison processes in which it is hypothesized that there exists in man "a drive to evaluate his opinions and his abilities" (p. 117). To a great extent, such evaluation must be achieved by means of comparison with others. On a number of bases, Festinger reasons that "A person will be less attracted to situations where others are very divergent from him than to situations where others are close to him for both abilities and opinions" (p. 123). It also follows that interpersonal attraction will be greatest toward others who are similar to oneself and least toward those who are dissimilar.

There is some evidence that individuals may choose as friends other individuals who are similar to themselves in intelligence. Bonney (1946) found that a group of elementary-school children who mutually chose each other were more similar in intelligence, as measured by group tests, than a corresponding group of subjects who did not choose each other. There was, however, very little relation between friends in their academic achievement as measured by a reading test. Similarly, Venable (1954) found, in a group of 42 college girls, that subgroups or clusters of friends were significantly different in mean scores on the ACE Psychological Examination. He concluded that the make-up of friendship groups is in part a function of similarity in intellectual ability as measured by the ACE. It should also be noted that some investigators have reported *no* relationship between intellectual similarity and attraction (for example, Gallagher, 1958; Lundberg and Beazley, 1948; Thorpe, 1955b).

A more direct test of social-comparison theory was provided by Zander and Havelin (1960). Using 32 groups composed of nine strangers of equal military rank in the Royal Norwegian Navy, the experimenters provided different degrees of success on a task for three-man subgroups. Attraction toward all group members was subsequently assessed. It was found that the subjects were most attracted to others whose competence, as observed on the experimental tasks, was closest to their own.

Personality variables

The relationship between individual differences and interpersonal attraction has been approached in two quite different ways. On the one hand, there has been considerable interest in the *need for affiliation,* both in terms of characteristic differences in this motive and in situational determinants of motive arousal. Second, there has been a good deal of research directed toward the possible effects, in determining attraction, of similarity or complementarity with respect to various personality variables. We shall examine examples of both lines of research interest.

The need for affiliation was defined by Murray (1938) as the need to be near others and to cooperate with them, to please and win the affection of friends, and the tendency to be friendly, sociable, genial, affectionate, trusting, and goodnatured. Somewhat later, a scoring system for thematic-apperception material was devised to measure this motive (Atkinson, Heyns, and Veroff, 1954; Shipley and Veroff, 1952). Individual differences in *n* Aff have been found to be related to such behavior as frequency of making telephone calls and writing letters (Lansing and Heyns, 1959) and expressed liking for people, parties, and clubs (Byrne, McDonald, and Mikawa, 1963). French (1956) hypothesized that attraction to another individual in a specific situation is a joint function of situational demands and motivational factors. She obtained friendship ratings and measures of affiliation and need for achievement for 137 airmen. In groups of four, the subjects worked on a concept-formation task. They were arranged so that three subjects liked one another and disliked the fourth. Furthermore, the three subjects were made to fail on the task, while the disliked individual succeeded. Then, each subject was asked to choose a work partner for further tasks. As hypothesized, those high in achievement need and low in affiliation need made significantly more choices of the success person; those with the reverse pattern tended to choose a partner who had failed. Affiliation need has been investigated in a somewhat different way by Schachter (1959). He proposed that individuals who are only children or the oldest child in the family would respond to anxiety-arousing situations by seeking interpersonal contact, while later-born individuals would not. In a series of studies, it was found that when they are subjected to anxiety-arousing conditions, college students who were firstborn or only children in their families were considerably more likely to be attracted to other people than were those who were later-born in their families. A recent study by Alexander (1966) suggests that the firstborn are also chosen by others more often than are the later-born. Among other subsequent findings is evidence that interpersonal contact is actually effective in reducing anxiety among firstborn or only children, whereas this effect does not hold for later-born individuals (Wrightsman, 1960). The role of need for affiliation in various types of sociometric situations is just beginning to be explored.

There is a somewhat longer history of research dealing with the effect of similarity or complementarity of personality variables on attraction. Such formulations as Festinger's social-comparison theory imply that similarity of personality characteristics should accompany interpersonal attraction. On the basis of need-reduction formulations, the most harmonious relationships should be those involving different though complementary characteristics such as dominance and submission. Among the early studies was that of Flemming (1935), who required a group of students to nominate their best friends and in addition fill out questionnaires designed to measure such variables as pleasingness of personality, steadiness of emotional response, social adjustment, introversion-extraversion, and social intelligence. The reported findings indicated that friends were similar to each other in most of these characteristics, especially pleasingness of personality and social adjustment. Van Dyne (1940) investigated the relation between personality factors and friendship in a group of 42 female summer-camp members. The campers were asked to indicate the five persons they would most like to have as friends, and they also filled out the Bernreuter Personality Inventory. Correlational findings indicated that girls tended to choose as friends other girls who were similar to them in dominance and stability. Although the correlations for these two variables were significant, they were very low in absolute magnitude. There was no evidence of any similarity between friends for the variables of self-sufficiency, emotional stability, introversion, and self-confidence. A study by Bonney (1946) showed little association between friends in their scores on the California Test of Personality in either elementary-school or college groups. There was, however, a moderate positive correlation between friends in the scores they received on the social and emotional dimensions of the Bell Adjustment Inventory.

A number of studies have utilized measures of needs. Winch, Ktsanes, and Ktsanes (1955) gave 25 married couples an interview, obtained case-history material, and administered an eight-card TAT. Each subject was then rated with respect to Murray's (1938) list of needs, several of which were categorized into receptive and assertive clusters. It was found that, regardless of sex, assertive persons tended to marry receptive persons. Furthermore, it was suggested that complementarity of needs may involve primarily this assertive-receptive dimension. Much of the research on needs has utilized the Edwards Personal Preference Schedule. Murstein (1961) gave the EPPS to pairs of newlyweds and to couples who had been married for some time. The average correlation on the need scales for newlywed pairs was .24, for older married couples .30, and for random pairs .04. The only need which was substantially correlated in both married samples was need for heterosexuality. In a college population, Mehlman (1962) obtained 32 pairs of best friends, 124 pairs of friends, and 28 pairs of enemies. Again, significant need similarity was found in both types of friends only for heterosexuality. Interestingly enough, enemies were significantly similar in aggression and in intraception. Izard (1960a) approached the EPPS by means of the overall profile similarity of pairs of friends rather than correlations between individual scales. Among both high school and college students, the need profiles of friends were significantly more similar than the profiles of random pairs of subjects. "Personality similarity was interpreted as essentially a facilitator of interpersonal positive affect, the latter being postulated as a key determinant of attraction as well as other aspects of interpersonal behavior" (p. 51).

If similarity does in fact lead to friendship, rather than *vice versa,* it should be possible to predict attraction on the basis of need similarity ascertained *prior* to acquaintance. Izard (1960b) tested this proposition by administering the EPPS to an entire freshman class when they entered college, and then obtained friendship choices six months later. It was found that prior-to-acquaintance personality profiles were similar among pairs of friends but not among pairs who mutually disliked one another. Banta and Hetherington (1963) gave the EPPS to 29 clusters of six subjects each. A cluster consisted of an engaged couple and a male and female friend of each. The engaged couples were similar to a significant degree on eight of the 15 needs, with heterosexuality again yielding the largest relationship. The other comparisons resulted in such findings as the tendency for females but not males to select same-sex friends similar to themselves, for the male fiancé to select a girl for a friend similar to the girl selected for a spouse, and for the female fiancée to select a boy for a friend dissimilar from the boy selected for a spouse. In spite of the rather consistent body of evidence indicating the role of needs in influencing attraction, there are also some negative findings with the EPPS and attraction (for example, Izard, 1963; Reilly, Commins, and Stefic, 1960).

The effect of similarity of *interests* on attraction has been studied in several ways. For example, Smith (1944) found a slight tendency for individuals engaging in similar athletic activities to select each other more often than would be expected by chance. Davitz (1955) asked 39 children at a summer camp to rank the others in his or her cabin in terms of desirability as a cabin-mate and as a guest at a party. In addition, each subject was given a list of pairs of activities (for example, dodge ball versus ping pong) and asked to indicate his preference and his guesses about the preferences of the persons he liked best and least. Perceived similarity of interests was greater for the liked person than for the disliked person. Also, perceived similarity of the positive-choice person to self was greater than actual similarity. Similar interests as the basis of clique formation have also been investigated. Marks (1959) studied cliques drawn from 730 eighth- to twelfth-graders. All subjects were given a 200-item interest test as well as a sociometric test. Analysis of variance of the interest scores of clique members (with grade level and neighborhood level held constant) indicated greater variability of interests between cliques than within cliques. In other words, interest homogeneity appears to be characteristic of cliques. King (1964) determined clique structure in a class by means of factor analysis. Two dimensions were found to account for 90 percent of the variance of the interpersonal attraction within the group. Among the variables falling in the two clusters were such things as membership in a religious society, membership in a student psychological association, smoking, and drinking. Finally, similarity of interests as measured by the Kuder test have been found to be related to attraction (Bonney, 1946), although other investigators have reported no relationship (Venable, 1954). In all these studies, it is unclear whether attraction is influenced by knowledge of common interests, the propinquity which results from common interests, or some other variable.

Self description as measured by such devices as the Q-sort technique and the adjective checklist appears to be related to attraction. Corsini (1956) obtained data on 20 married couples, administered a measure of marital happiness, and asked each subject to complete a Q-sort. Husbands and wives were no more similar in self-sorts than were random couples. There was, however, a positive relationship ($r = .64$ to $.73$) between similarity of Q-sorts and marital happiness for married couples. Most of the self studies have dealt with *perceived* similarity to self. With 87 male college freshmen, Kipnis (1961) found that subjects perceived themselves as significantly more similar to their best friends than to their least-liked roommates. McKenna, Hofstaetter, and O'Connor (1956) had 90 female college students do Q-sorts of self, ideal self, and two friends. Friends were perceived as being more like ideal self than like self. Among those subjects with very high self-ideal congruence, however, friends were perceived as more similar to self than to ideal self. Similar findings were reported by Lundy *et al.* (1955). Lundy (1956) dealt with perceived similarity in opposite-sex sociometric choices among undergraduates. Self descriptions were more like the descriptions of a positive opposite-sex sociometric choice than like a negative opposite-sex choice. In an experimental investigation, Griffitt (1966) found that both subjects with high and subjects with low self-ideal discrepancy were more attracted to strangers who were like themselves in self description than to strangers who were unlike themselves.

A number of other personality areas have also been investigated. For example, Maisonneuve (1954) obtained sociometric data plus personality-trait ratings by individuals who knew the subjects. He observed that subjects with similar personality profiles tend to mutually choose each other. Altrocchi (1959) investigated the relationship between dominance in a subject and the degree of dominance in those to whom he is attracted in a ten-minute sound movie depicting the interaction of four males, and found no relationship. Husbands and wives were found to be similar to a significant degree on Rokeach's measures of dogmatism and opinionation, but their perceived similarity was significantly greater than their actual similarity (Byrne and Blaylock, 1963). In a follow-up of that study, Levinger and Breedlove (1966) corroborated these findings with respect to actual and assumed similarity concerning a variety of marriage-relevant traits, goals, and values. Furthermore, it was found that assumed similarity is positively associated with marital satisfaction. The masculinity-femininity scale of the MMPI was utilized by Lundy (1958). The scale was filled out for self and also for positive and negative, same- and opposite-sex sociometric choices. It was found that liking of a person, either of the same or opposite sex, is directly related to degree of perceived similarity on the Mf. "The striking feature of the present results is that . . . the liked opposite-sex positive choice is idealized in terms of same-sex qualities" (p. 244). Beier, Rossi, and Garfield (1961) utilized the entire MMPI and had college students answer the items as they themselves would and as would their most- and least-liked acquaintances. The subjects saw their friends as similar to themselves and the disliked acquaintance as dissimilar on all scales except L and Pt. In a number of investigations it has been found that, when experimental groups are formed on the basis of similarity or dissimilarity of scores on a particular personality scale (the Guilford-Zimmerman Temperament Survey), attraction is unaffected (for example, Hoffman, 1958; Hoffman and Maier, 1966).

It may be seen, then, that similarity of personality characteristics, and, to a greater degree, *perceived* similarity of personality characteristics, tends to be associated with attraction. The relationship between personality similarity and attraction has been obscured in many investigations by methodological weaknesses as has been pointed out by Byrne, Griffitt, and Stefaniak (1967). Evidence for complementarity as an influence on attraction is rather minimal. There is evidence, moreover, that situational demands can alter such relationships (for example, Walster and Walster, 1963) and that the relationship between similarity and attraction decreases as the length of acquaintanceship increases (Rosenfeld and Jackson, 1965). Support for this contention is provided by Lerner and Becker (1962), who have reported that subjects preferred similar partners in a game at which both could win but dissimilar partners in a game where there was a winner and a loser. It may be, as Secord and Backman (1964) have suggested, that with such variables as needs, attraction should be determined not by simple similarity or dissimilarity but by *interpersonal congruency*. That is, when a person perceives another as behaving in a way that confirms his self concept, attraction is elicited. Such behavior may involve *either* similarity or dissimilarity, depending on the need in question and on the situation. Secord and Backman have presented evidence that *both* perceived similarity and interpersonal congruency are associated with attraction.

Attitudes, beliefs, and values

Perhaps the best documented and most widely studied relationship in the sociometric literature is that between attraction and congruity of attitudes, beliefs, and
values.

One of the earliest studies concerned with the similarity of attitudes among
friends was Winslow's (1937). He administered a long questionnaire to a group
of 86 students and asked each of them to have a friend fill out the questionnaire.
When the scores of friends were correlated on measures of attitudes toward
Negroes, American foreign policy, current economic policy, religion, and domestic
political policy, they were found to be significantly related in a positive direction
for all but attitudes toward foreign policy, and even that relationship approached
significance. A study by Richardson (1940) used observational data to determine
patterns of friendship and found that friends, both female college students and
adult women, tended to resemble one another in values as measured by the
Allport-Vernon Study of Values; Reilly, Commins, and Stefic (1960), however,
found no relationship between pairs of friends on this instrument. Friends have
been found to agree in their attitudes about other people (Newcomb, 1961).
Married couples have been found to be similar in values and in attitudes about
communism and birth control (Schooley, 1936), and about church, war, and
communism (Newcomb and Svehla, 1937).

A somewhat different research approach to the same problem was involved in
Newcomb's (1943) attempt to assess the role of personal and community factors
as determinants of attitudinal shifts in a small college for women. He found that
liberal political and economic views were positively associated with sociometric
choice, including choices of an individual to serve as an enduring friend. An
unpublished study by Smelser (1952) related attitude measures to sociometric
dimensions in a sample of six female college dormitories. When the results for
the six dormitories were combined there was no evidence of any association between choice status and the eight attitude dimensions measured. Within individual dormitories, however, all the attitudes were related to interpersonal
choice, although the direction and magnitude of the correlations varied considerably among the different dormitories. Smelser also divided his groups into
cliques, using the method of Forsyth and Katz (1946), and found the cliques to be
generally homogeneous in their attitude structure. In a study of a German village,
Loomis (1946) has provided evidence that sociometric cleavages may be at least
partly determined by political attitudes, as inferred from membership in various
political parties.

As with all correlational investigations, these various reports of attitude
homogeneity of pairs of friends, within cliques, and between husband and wife
leave the question of sequence unanswered. That is, close contact and behavioral
interaction could lead to the development of attitude and belief congruence, or
similarity in the latter attributes could lead to interpersonal attraction. A number of experimental investigations provide seemingly unequivocal evidence that
it is variation in the similarity-dissimilarity of attitudes which influences attrac-

tion, rather than the reverse. The general research strategy here has been to manipulate experimentally the relative similarity-dissimilarity of a stranger's attitudes, beliefs, or values with respect to those of the subject and then to assess the subject's attraction toward that stranger. The stranger may be physically present, depicted in a movie, recorded on tape, or represented by his written responses. Since the "stranger" in most of these investigations is either a confederate of the experimenter or an entirely fictitious person, it is possible to control for other possible influences on attraction (for example, propinquity, physical appearance, and social status), and then to vary only the degree of attitude similarity. Such investigations not only confirm the general correlational findings but suggest a relatively strong and highly predictable functional relationship between similarity-dissimilarity and attraction. For example, experimental investigations have shown attraction to be a function of similarity of values on the Allport-Vernon-Lindzey scale (Jones and Daugherty, 1959; Smith, 1958), of opinions about a labor board's decision in a small group setting (Berkowitz and Howard, 1959), of responses to miscellaneous attitude items (Byrne, 1961a, 1962), and of decisions concerning the solution of an interpersonal problem (Schachter, 1951; Worchel and McCormick, 1963). In addition, the relationship between attitude similarity-dissimilarity (varying from complete similarity to complete dissimilarity) and attraction has been found to be a linear one (Byrne and Nelson, 1965). The formula describing the relationship is

$$Y = mX + k,$$

where Y is the measure of attraction, X is the proportion of attitudes expressed by a stranger which are similar to those of the subject, and m and k are empirically determined constants.

A number of theories have been proposed to account for the affective relationship between individuals and their respective attitudes toward any object about which they communicate. At least three major theories (Festinger, 1957; Heider, 1958; Newcomb, 1953, 1961) are based on a model of cognitive homeostasis in which there is a normal state and a specified set of circumstances which can disrupt the normal state and hence activate a variety of mechanisms which serve to restore the normal state. With respect to interpersonal relationships, balanced or symmetrical or consonant states are represented by several possible combinations of positive and negative affective relationships; other combinations constitute imbalanced or asymmetrical or dissonant states, as depicted in Fig. 1. When asymmetrical states occur, there are a number of alternative behavioral possibilities which serve to restore symmetrical relationships, including an alteration in attraction toward the other person (for example, Byrne and Wong, 1962), an alteration in attitudes or beliefs (for example, Burdick and Burnes, 1958; Cohn, Yee, and Brown, 1961; Sampson and Insko, 1964), an effort to alter the attitude or beliefs of the other person (for example, Berkowitz and Howard, 1959; Festinger *et al.*, 1952), or a misperception of the other person's attitudes and beliefs so as to perceive oneself as more similar to a liked other and more dissimilar from

Symmetrical states

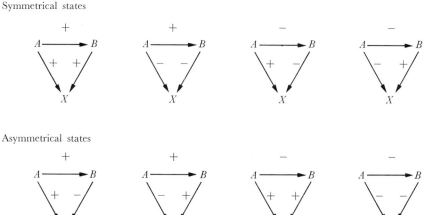

Asymmetrical states

Fig. 1. A depiction of various types of symmetrical and asymmetrical relationships between two individuals (A and B) and an object about which they are communicating (X).
The + and − signs refer to positive and negative attitudes.

a disliked other (for example, Backman and Secord, 1962; Berkowitz and Goranson, 1964; Broxton, 1963; Fiedler, Warrington, and Blaisdell, 1952; Kogan and
Tagiuri, 1958; Newcomb, 1963; Precker, 1953; Smith, 1958; Vroom, 1959).

Another theoretical approach has been taken by Fishbein (1965), who proposed that an individual's attitudes toward any object (including another individual) is a function of his beliefs about that object and the evaluative aspects
of those beliefs. In one investigation, 20 leaders each served with three different
four-person groups in a total of 60 groups. The groups were given negotiation
problems concerning religion. Afterward, the leaders' beliefs about the behavior
of each member, their evaluation of each behavior on a good-bad dimension, and
a sociometric measure of attraction were obtained. Attraction was predicted on
the basis of the formula

$$A_o = \sum_{i=1}^{N} B_i a_i,$$

where A_o is the attitude toward member o, B_i is the belief about o's behavior, a_i
is the evaluation of that behavior, and N is the number of such beliefs. The attraction responses predicted on the basis of this formula correlated .75 with the
actual attraction responses obtained on the sociometric test. Using the same
approach, Fishbein (1963) found that subject's predicted attitudes concerning
Negroes correlated .80 with obtained attitude scores.

Still another type of formulation, *reinforcement theory,* has been proposed
to account not only for attitude-similarity data but for all attraction data (for
example, Pepitone, 1964). Congruently with both hedonist philosophy and

modern behavior theory, it is proposed that man behaves in such a way as to maximize pleasure and minimize pain. Attraction toward or repulsion from others is a function of the relative number and relative magnitude of positive and negative reinforcements received (Byrne, in press). Attitude statements are conceptualized as simply a special case of reward and punishment (Clore, 1966; Golightly and Byrne, 1964; Nelson, 1965; Newcomb, 1956). In a number of investigations, various other types of reinforcements have been manipulated, with some measure of attraction serving as the dependent variable. For example, attraction toward an individual has been found to be influenced by his administering verbal punishment to another person and his apparent intentions in giving the punishment (Pepitone and Sherberg, 1957), by his giving positive or negative evaluations of the subject's performance (Deutsch and Solomon, 1959), by the magnitude of threat reduction for which that person is responsible (Kleiner, 1960), by the rewards and punishments administered during a group interaction (Lott and Lott, 1960; Phillips and D'Amico, 1956), by the relative number of high or low creativity ratings he assigns to stories produced by the subject (McDonald, 1962), and by his being responsible for the subject's failure at an experimental task (Lerner, 1965). If positive and negative evaluations of oneself may be interpreted in reinforcement terms, further support is provided by the finding that individuals are attracted to those who seem to like them and respond negatively to those who seem to dislike them (for example, Backman and Secord, 1959; Keislar, 1961). The latter relationship may be further influenced by such variables as the alleged psychological adjustment of the other person (Jones *et al.*, 1959), whether the other person is simply seen as utilizing ingratiation tactics (Jones, 1964), and whether the evaluations are uniformly positive, uniformly negative, or whether there is a shift from positive to negative or from negative to positive evaluations (Aronson and Linder, 1965; Berkowitz, 1960a, 1960b).

CONCLUDING REMARKS

We have just presented a discussion of studies concerned with social status and determinants of interpersonal attraction which makes clear the extensiveness and variety of research in this general area. There seems little doubt that sociometric measures and related devices have a high degree of demonstrated utility for the social psychologist dealing with these topics. In addition to the varieties of research sampled in this chapter, there are numerous other areas of active investigation within social psychology where these techniques have played an essential role. The interested reader will find considerable discussion of research employing these techniques in other portions of this *Handbook*, especially in chapters dealing with leadership (Chapter 31), small group behavior (Chapters 29 and 30), and such applied topics as prejudice (Chapter 37) and research on the educational process (Chapter 42). Given all this evidence, it seems a reasonable generalization that sociometric measures and related devices concerned with assessing interpersonal attraction constitute an important part of the measurement array available to modern social psychologists.

We have already commented on one of the principal developments of recent years in this area—the gradual loss of distinctiveness of the sociometric test or measure. It seems evident that there has been a progressive merging of the various methods of assessing social choice, with the end result that most investigators treat various types of rating scales and sociometric measures more or less interchangeably. The process whereby *Sociometry* has changed from a journal centered on the sociometric technique to a journal that is concerned primarily with reporting experimental social-psychological research, regardless of the particular measures employed, is probably an accurate gauge of general trends within the field.

While it is easy to approve of the general trend away from treating sociometric measures as distinctive from other means of assessing social choice, the trend has not been without some unfortunate features. Perhaps the most significant of these concerns a diminished frequency of methodological or measurement studies which are primarily oriented toward providing a better quantitative and theoretical understanding of the properties of the various measures being employed. The use of sociometric measures has been accompanied by a reasonable incidence of studies that are intended to contribute to better understanding of the measurement properties of these instruments. On the other hand, the ratings of interpersonal attraction that have been employed have typically been *ad hoc* in nature, and there has been little systematic attempt to explore the consequences of the many variations in procedure that are unsystematically or casually introduced by different investigators, or even by the same investigator on different occasions. In general, aside from findings and formulations bearing upon attitude scaling that occasionally may be generalized to the rating of social choice, there is little in the way of firm guidelines for the person who wishes to initiate investigation in this area. It is worth comment that in two successive editions of this *Handbook* a serious effort was made to include systematic coverage of rating scales as one approach to measuring social behavior and on neither occasion was this effort successful. The reluctance of authors to cover this topic is undoubtedly a valid reflector of the general lack of interest in it, in spite of the fact that reliance on rating scales is freely exhibited by many or most persons studying social behavior.

On the positive side, it may be noted that the general level of quantitative sophistication in this area has shown a marked improvement during the past decade and a half. While in the early days of sociometric measurement the typical investigator relied primarily on graphical or descriptive presentation of findings, it is now distinctly unusual to find a study in which quantitative indices are not employed in conjunction with some form of statistical analysis.

A final salutary trend is the increased tendency to embrace measures of social choice within the confines of some theoretical position. While many studies remain isolated attempts to investigate some casual or incidental empirical question, there is an undeniable increase in systematic and theoretically derived investigation. In particular, the influence of balance theories, the theory of social comparison, and reinforcement theory have created a marked increase in the theoretical relevance and coherence of much of the research in this area.

REFERENCES

Abel, H., and R. Sahinkaya (1962). Emergence of sex and race friendship preferences. *Child Develpmt., 33,* 939–943.

Alexander, C. N. (1966). Ordinal position and sociometric status. *Sociometry, 29,* 41–51.

Altrocchi, J. (1959). Dominance as a factor in interpersonal choice and perception. *J. abnorm. soc. Psychol., 59,* 303–308.

Aronson, E., and D. Linder (1965). Gain and loss of esteem as determinants of interpersonal attractiveness. *J. exp. soc. Psychol., 1,* 156–171.

Atkinson, J. W., R. W. Heyns, and J. Veroff (1954). The effect of experimental arousal of the affiliation motive on thematic apperception. *J. abnorm. soc. Psychol., 49,* 405–410.

Ausubel, D. P. (1953). Reciprocity and assumed reciprocity of acceptance among adolescents: a sociometric study. *Sociometry, 16,* 339–348.

Backman, C. W., and P. F. Secord (1959). The effect of perceived liking on interpersonal attraction. *Hum. Relat., 12,* 379–384.

———— (1962). Liking, selective interaction, and misperception in congruent interpersonal relations. *Sociometry, 25,* 321–335.

Banta, T. J., and Mavis Hetherington (1963). Relations between needs of friends and fiancés. *J. abnorm. soc. Psychol., 66,* 401–404.

Barker, R. G. (1942). The social interrelations of strangers and acquaintances. *Sociometry, 5,* 169–179.

Baron, D. (1951). Personal-social characteristics and classroom social status: a sociometric study of fifth- and sixth-grade girls. *Sociometry, 14,* 32–42.

Bassett, R. E. (1948). Sampling problems in influence studies. *Sociometry, 11,* 320–328.

Beier, E. G., A. M. Rossi, and R. L. Garfield (1961). Similarity plus dissimilarity of personality: basis for friendship? *Psychol. Reports, 8,* 3–8.

Berkowitz, L. (1956). Social desirability and frequency of influence attempts as factors in leadership choice. *J. Pers., 24,* 424–435.

———— (1960a). Some factors affecting the reduction of overt hostility. *J. abnorm. soc. Psychol., 60,* 14–21.

———— (1960b). Repeated frustrations and expectations in hostility arousal. *J. abnorm. soc. Psychol., 60,* 422–429.

Berkowitz, L., and R. E. Goranson (1964). Motivational and judgmental determinants of social perception. *J. abnorm. soc. Psychol., 69,* 296–302.

Berkowitz, L., and R. C. Howard (1959). Reactions to opinion deviates as affected by affiliation need (*n*) and group member interdependence. *Sociometry, 22,* 81–91.

Berkun, M., and T. Meeland (1958). Sociometric effects of race and of combat performance. *Sociometry, 21,* 145–149.

Beum, C. O., and E. G. Brundage (1950). A method for analyzing the sociomatrix. *Sociometry, 13,* 141–145.

Biehler, R. F. (1954). Companion choice behavior in the kindergarten. *Child Develpmt.,* 25, 45–50.

Bjerstedt, A. (1952). A 'chess-board sociogram' for sociographic representation of choice directions and for the analysis of 'sociometric locomotions.' *Sociometry, 15,* 244–262.

———— (1958). A field-force model as a basis for predictions of social behavior. *Hum. Relat., 11,* 331–340.

Blake, R. R., C. C. Rhead, B. Wedge, and Jane S. Mouton (1956). Housing architecture and social interaction. *Sociometry, 19,* 133–139.

Bock, R. D., and Suraya Z. Husain (1950). An adaptation of Holzinger's B-coefficients for the analysis of sociometric data. *Sociometry, 13,* 146–153.

Bonney, M. E. (1942). A study of social status on the second-grade level. *J. genet. Psychol., 60,* 271–305.

———— (1943). The constancy of sociometric scores and their relationship to teacher judgments of social success, and to personality self-ratings. *Sociometry, 6,* 409–424.

———— (1944). Relationships between social success, family size, socio-economic home background, and intelligence among school children in grades III to V. *Sociometry, 7,* 26–39.

———— (1946). A sociometric study of the relationship of some factors to mutual friendships on the elementary, secondary, and college levels. *Sociometry, 9,* 21–47.

———— (1949). A study of friendship choices in college in relation to church affiliation, in-church preferences, family size, and length of enrollment in college. *J. soc. Psychol., 29,* 153–166.

———— (1954). Choosing between the sexes on a sociometric measurement. *J. soc. Psychol., 39,* 99–114.

Bonney, M. E., R. E. Hoblit, and A. H. Dreyer (1953). A study of some factors related to sociometric status in a men's dormitory. *Sociometry, 16,* 287–301.

Borgatta, E. F. (1951). A diagnostic note on the construction of sociograms and action diagrams. *Group Psychother., 3,* 300–308.

———— (1954). Analysis of social interaction and sociometric perception. *Sociometry, 17,* 7–32.

———— (1960). The stability of interpersonal judgments in independent situations. *J. abnorm. soc. Psychol., 60,* 188–194.

Borgatta, E. F., and W. Stolz (1963). A note on a computer program for rearrangement of matrices. *Sociometry, 26,* 391–392.

Brehm, J. W., and Lenore B. Behar (1966). Sexual arousal, defensiveness, and sex preferences in affiliation. *J. exp. Res. Pers., 1,* 195–200.

Bronfenbrenner, U. (1943). A constant frame of reference for sociometric research. *Sociometry, 6,* 363–397.

———— (1944a). A constant frame of reference for sociometric research: II. Experiment and inference. *Sociometry, 7,* 40–75.

———— (1944b). The graphic presentation of sociometric data. *Sociometry, 7,* 283–289.

Brown, Julia S. (1965). Sociometric choices of patients in a therapeutic community. *Hum. Relat., 18,* 241–251.

Broxton, June A. (1963). A test of interpersonal attraction predictions derived from balance theory. *J. abnorm. soc. Psychol., 66,* 394–397.

Burdick, H. A., and A. J. Burnes (1958). A test of 'strain toward symmetry' theories. *J. abnorm. soc. Psychol., 57,* 367–370.

Byrd, E. (1951). A study of validity and constancy of scores in a sociometric test. *Sociometry, 14,* 175–181.

Byrne, D. (1961a). Interpersonal attraction and attitude similarity. *J. abnorm. soc. Psychol., 62,* 713–715.

——— (1961b). The influence of propinquity and opportunities for interaction on classroom relationships. *Hum. Relat., 14,* 63–69.

——— (1962). Response to attitude similarity-dissimilarity as a function of affiliation need. *J. Pers., 30,* 164–177.

——— (in press). Attitudes and attraction. In L. Berkowitz (Ed.), *Advances in experimental social psychology.* Vol. 4. New York: Academic Press.

Byrne, D., and Barbara Blaylock (1963). Similarity and assumed similarity of attitudes between husbands and wives. *J. abnorm. soc. Psychol., 67,* 636–640.

Byrne, D., and J. A. Buehler (1955). A note on the influence of propinquity upon acquaintanceships. *J. abnorm. soc. Psychol., 51,* 147–148.

Byrne, D., G. L. Clore, Jr., and P. Worchel (1966). The effect of economic similarity-dissimilarity on interpersonal attraction. *J. Pers. soc. Psychol., 4,* 220–224.

Byrne, D., W. Griffitt, and D. Stefaniak (1967). Attraction and similarity of personality characteristics. *J. Pers. soc. Psychol., 5,* 82–90.

Byrne, D., R. D. McDonald, and J. Mikawa (1963). Approach and avoidance affiliation motives. *J. Pers. 31,* 21–37.

Byrne, D., and T. J. Wong (1962). Racial prejudice, interpersonal attraction, and assumed dissimilarity of attitudes. *J. abnorm. soc. Psychol., 65,* 246–253.

Cairns, R. B., and D. L. Johnson (1965). The development of interspecies social attachments. *Psychon. Sci., 2,* 337–338.

Caplow, T., and R. Forman (1950). Neighborhood interaction in a homogeneous community. *Amer. sociol. Rev., 15,* 357–366.

Cervinka, V. (1948). A dimensional theory of groups. *Sociometry, 11,* 100–107.

Chabot, J. (1950). A simplified example of the use of matrix multiplication for the analysis of sociometric data. *Sociometry, 13,* 131–140.

Chapin, F. S. (1950). Sociometric stars as isolates. *Amer. J. Sociol., 56,* 263–267.

Clampitt, R. R., and D. C. Charles (1956). Sociometric status and supervisory evaluation of institutionalized mentally deficient children. *J. soc. Psychol., 44,* 223–231.

Clore, G. L., Jr. (1966). Discrimination learning as a function of awareness and magnitude of attitudinal reinforcement. Unpublished doctoral dissertation, University of Texas.

Cohn, T. S., W. Yee, and V. Brown (1961). Attitude change and interpersonal attraction. *J. soc. Psychol., 55,* 207–211.

Coleman, J. S., and D. MacRae, Jr. (1960). Electronic processing of sociometric data for groups up to 1,000 in size. *Amer. sociol. Rev., 25,* 722–727.

Corsini, R. J. (1956). Understanding and similarity in marriage. *J. abnorm. soc. Psychol., 52,* 327–332.

Cox, F. N. (1953). Sociometric status and individual adjustment before and after play therapy. *J. abnorm. soc. Psychol., 48,* 354–356.

Criswell, Joan H. (1937). Racial cleavage in Negro-white groups. *Sociometry, 1,* 81–89.

———— (1939). A sociometric study of race cleavage in the classroom. *Arch. Psychol.,* N.Y., No. 235.

———— (1946). Foundations of sociometric measurement. *Sociometry, 9,* 7–13.

———— (1947). The measurement of group integration. *Sociometry, 10,* 259–267.

———— (1950). Notes on the constant frame of reference problem. *Sociometry, 13,* 93–107.

Croft, I. J., and T. G. Grygier (1956). Social relationships of truants and juvenile delinquents. *Hum. Relat., 9,* 439–466.

Dahlke, H. O. (1953). Determinants of sociometric relations among children in the elementary school. *Sociometry, 16,* 327–338.

Danielsson, B. (1949). Some attraction and repulsion patterns among Jibaro Indians. *Sociometry, 12,* 83–105.

Davids, A., and Anita N. Parenti (1958a). Time orientation and interpersonal relations of emotionally disturbed and normal children. *J. abnorm. soc. Psychol., 57,* 299–305.

———— (1958b). Personality, social choice, and adults' perception of these factors in groups of disturbed and normal children. *Sociometry, 21,* 212–224.

Davis, J. A., and C. F. Warnath (1957). Reliability, validity, and stability of a sociometric rating scale. *J. soc. Psychol., 45,* 111–121.

Davitz, J. R. (1955). Social perception and sociometric choice of children. *J. abnorm. soc. Psychol., 50,* 173–176.

Deutsch, M., and L. Solomon (1959). Reactions to evaluations by others as influenced by self-evaluations. *Sociometry, 22,* 93–112.

Dunnington, Margaret J. (1957a). Investigation of areas of disagreement in sociometric measurement of preschool children. *Child Develpmt., 28,* 93–102.

———— (1957b). Behavioral differences of sociometric status groups in a nursery school. *Child Develpmt., 28,* 103–111.

Edwards, Daisy S. (1948). The constant frame of reference problem in sociometry. *Sociometry, 11,* 372–379.

Eng, E., and R. L. French (1948). The determination of sociometric status. *Sociometry, 11,* 368–371.

Evans, M. Catherine, and Margaret Wilson (1949). Friendship choices of university women students. *Educ. psychol. Measmt., 9,* 307–312.

Faunce, D., and J. A. Beegle (1948). Cleavages in a relatively homogeneous group of rural youth: an experiment in the use of sociometry in attaining and measuring integration. *Sociometry, 11,* 207–216.

Feinberg, M. R. (1953). Relation of background experience to social acceptance. *J. abnorm. soc. Psychol., 48,* 206–214.

Festinger, L. (1949). The analysis of sociograms using matrix algebra. *Hum. Relat., 2,* 153–158.

――― (1950). Informal social communication. *Psychol. Rev., 57,* 271–282.

――― (1954). A theory of social comparison processes. *Hum. Relat., 7,* 117–140.

――― (1957). *A theory of cognitive dissonance.* Stanford: Stanford Univ. Press.

Festinger, L., H. B. Gerard, H. Hymovitch, H. Kelley, and B. Rosen (1952). The influence process in the presence of extreme deviates. *Hum. Relat., 5,* 327–346.

Festinger, L., S. Schachter, and K. Back (1950). *Social pressures in informal groups: a study of human factors in housing.* New York: Harper.

Fiedler, F. E., W. G. Warrington, and F. J. Blaisdell (1952). Unconscious attitudes and the dynamics of sociometric choice in a social group. *J. abnorm. soc. Psychol., 47,* 790–796.

Fishbein, M. (1963). An investigation of the relationships between beliefs about an object and the attitude toward that object. *Hum. Relat., 16,* 233–239.

――― (1965). Prediction of interpersonal preferences and group member satisfaction from estimated attitudes. *J. Pers. soc. Psychol., 1,* 663–667.

Fjeld, S. (1965). A longitudinal study of sociometric choice and the communication of values. *J. soc. Psychol., 66,* 297–306.

Flemming, G. (1935). A factor analysis of the personality of high school leaders. *J. appl. Psychol., 19,* 597–605.

Foa, U. G. (1950). Scale and intensity analysis in sociometric research. *Sociometry, 13,* 358–362.

Forsyth, Elaine, and L. Katz (1946). A matrix approach to the analysis of sociometric data: preliminary report. *Sociometry, 9,* 340–347.

French, Elizabeth G. (1956). Motivation as a variable in work-partner selection. *J. abnorm. soc. Psychol., 53,* 96–99.

French, J. W., and W. B. Michael (1966). *Standards for educational and psychological tests and manuals.* Washington, D.C.: American Psychological Association.

French, R. L. (1951). Sociometric status and individual adjustment among naval recruits. *J. abnorm. soc. Psychol., 46,* 64–72.

French, R. L., and I. N. Mensh (1948). Some relationships between interpersonal judgments and sociometric status in a college group. *Sociometry, 11,* 335–345.

Fuller, Elizabeth M., and Helen B. Baune (1951). Injury-proneness and adjustment in a second grade: a sociometric study. *Sociometry, 14,* 210–225.

Gallagher, J. J. (1958). Social status of children related to intelligence, propinquity, and social perception. *Elementary School J., 59,* 225–231.

Gardner, E. F., and G. G. Thompson (1956). *Social relations and morale in small groups.* New York: Appleton-Century-Crofts.

Gardner, G. (1956). Functional leadership and popularity in small groups. *Hum. Relat., 9,* 491–509.

Gibb, C. A. (1950). The sociometry of leadership in temporary groups. *Sociometry, 13,* 226–243.

Goldstone, S., W. K. Boardman, W. T. Lhamon, F. L. Fason, and C. Jernigan (1963). Sociometric status and apparent duration. *J. soc. Psychol., 61,* 303–310.

Golightly, Carole, and D. Byrne (1964). Attitude statements as positive and negative reinforcements. *Science, 146,* 798–799.

Goodnow, R. E., and R. Tagiuri (1952). Religious ethnocentrism and its recognition among adolescent boys. *J. abnorm. soc. Psychol., 47,* 316–320.

Griffitt, W. B. (1966). Interpersonal attraction as a function of self-concept and personality similarity-dissimilarity. *J. Pers. soc. Psychol., 4,* 581–584.

Gronlund, N. E. (1953). Relationship between the sociometric status of pupils and teachers' preferences for or against having them in class. *Sociometry, 16,* 142–150.

——— (1955). The relative stability of classroom social status with unweighted and weighted sociometric choices. *J. educ. Psychol., 46,* 345–354.

Grossman, Beverly, and Joyce Wrighter (1948). The relationship between selection-rejection and intelligence, social status, and personality amongst sixth-grade children. *Sociometry, 11,* 346–355.

Hammer, C., and F. C. Ikle (1957). Intercity telephone and airline traffic related to distance and the 'propensity to interact.' *Sociometry, 20,* 306–316.

Harary, F., and I. C. Ross (1957). A procedure for clique detection using the group matrix. *Sociometry, 20,* 205–215.

Hartshorne, H. M., A. May, and J. B. Maller (1929). *Studies in the nature of character.* Vol. 2: Studies in service and self-control. New York: Macmillan.

Haythorn, W. (1953). The influence of individual members on the characteristics of small groups. *J. abnorm. soc. Psychol., 48,* 276–284.

Heber, R. F. (1956). The relation of intelligence and physical maturity to social status of children. *J. educ. Psychol., 47,* 158–162.

Heider, F. (1958). *The psychology of interpersonal relations.* New York: Wiley.

Helper, M. M. (1955). Learning theory and the self concept. *J. abnorm. soc. Psychol., 51,* 184–194.

Hill, K. T. (1963). Relation of test anxiety, defensiveness, and intelligence to sociometric status. *Child Develpmt., 34,* 767–776.

Hoffman, L. R. (1958). Similarity of personality: a basis for interpersonal attraction? *Sociometry, 21,* 300–308.

Hoffman, L. R., and N. R. F. Maier (1966). An experimental reexamination of the similarity-attraction hypothesis. *J. Pers. soc. Psychol., 3,* 145–152.

Hollander, E. P., and W. B. Webb (1955). Leadership, followership, and friendship: an analysis of peer nominations. *J. abnorm. soc. Psychol., 50*, 163–167.

Holzberg, J. D., and Rita Posner (1951). The relationship of extrapunitiveness on the Rosenzweig Picture-Frustration Study to aggression in overt behavior and fantasy. *Amer. J. Orthopsychiat., 21*, 767–779.

Horowitz, Frances D. (1962). The relationship of anxiety, self-concept, and sociometric status among fourth, fifth, and sixth grade children. *J. abnorm. soc. Psychol., 65*, 212–214.

Horrocks, J. E., and Betty A. Wear (1953). An analysis of interpersonal choice relationships of college students. *J. soc. Psychol., 38*, 87–98.

Hubbell, C. H. (1965). An input-output approach to clique identification. *Sociometry, 28*, 377–399.

Hunt, J. M., and R. L. Solomon (1942). The stability and some correlates of group-status in a summer-camp group of young boys. *Amer. J. Psychol., 55*, 33–45.

Izard, C. E. (1959). Personality correlates of sociometric status. *J. appl. Psychol., 43*, 89–93.

——— (1960a). Personality similarity and friendship. *J. abnorm. soc. Psychol., 61*, 47–51.

——— (1960b). Personality similarity, positive affect, and interpersonal attraction. *J. abnorm. soc. Psychol., 61*, 484–485.

——— (1963). Personality similarity and friendship: a follow-up study. *J. abnorm. soc. Psychol., 66*, 598–600.

Jennings, Helen H. (1937). Structure of leadership—development and sphere of influence. *Sociometry, 1*, 99–143.

——— (1943). *Leadership and isolation.* New York: Longmans, Green.

——— (1947). Leadership and sociometric choice. *Sociometry, 10*, 32–49.

——— (1950). *Leadership and isolation* (2nd ed.). New York: Longmans, Green.

Jones, E. E. (1964). *Ingratiation.* New York: Appleton-Century-Crofts.

Jones, E. E., and B. N. Daugherty (1959). Political orientation and the perceptual effects of an anticipated interaction. *J. abnorm. soc. Psychol., 59*, 340–349.

Jones, E. E., S. L. Hester, A. Farina, and K. E. Davis (1959). Reactions to unfavorable personal evaluations as a function of the evaluator's perceived adjustment. *J. abnorm. soc. Psychol., 59*, 363–370.

Kanous, E., R. A. Daugherty, and T. S. Cohn (1962). Relation between heterosexual friendship choices and socioeconomic level. *Child Develpmt., 33*, 251–255.

Kanungo, R. (1966). Sociometric ratings and perceived interpersonal behavior. *J. soc. Psychol., 68*, 253–268.

Katz, L. (1947). On the matrix analysis of sociometric data. *Sociometry, 10*, 233–241.

——— (1950). Punched card technique for the analysis of multiple level sociometric data. *Sociometry, 13*, 108–122.

——— (1953). A new status index derived from sociometric analysis. *Psychometrika, 18*, 39–43.

Keislar, E. R. (1953). A distinction between social acceptance and prestige among adolescents. *Child Develpmt., 24,* 275–283.

———— (1961). Experimental development of 'like' and 'dislike' of others among adolescent girls. *Child Develpmt., 32,* 59–66.

Kelly, J. G., Jean E. Ferson, and W. H. Holtzman (1958). The measurement of attitudes toward the Negro in the South. *J. soc. Psychol., 48,* 305–317.

Kidd, J. W. (1953). Personality traits as barriers to acceptability in a college men's residence hall. *J. soc. Psychol., 38,* 127–130.

King, M. G. (1964). Structural balance, tension, and segregation in a university group. *Hum. Relat., 17,* 221–225.

Kipnis, Dorothy M. (1957). Interaction between members of bomber crews as a determinant of sociometric choice. *Hum. Relat., 10,* 263–270.

———— (1961). Changes in self concepts in relation to perceptions of others. *J. Pers., 29,* 449–465.

Kleiner, R. J. (1960). The effects of threat reduction upon interpersonal attractiveness. *J. Pers., 28,* 145–155.

Koch, Helen L. (1957). The relation in young children between characteristics of their playmates and certain attributes of their siblings. *Child Develpmt., 28,* 175–202.

Kogan, N., and R. Tagiuri (1958). Interpersonal preference and cognitive organization. *J. abnorm. soc. Psychol., 56,* 113–116.

Krieger, L., and M. Schwartz (1965). The relationship between sociometric measures of popularity among children and their reactions to frustration. *J. soc. Psychol., 66,* 291–296.

Kuhlen, R. G., and H. S. Bretsch (1947). Sociometric status and personal problems of adolescents. *Sociometry, 10,* 122–132.

Lansing, J. B., and R. W. Heyns (1959). Need affiliation and frequency of four types of communication. *J. abnorm. soc. Psychol., 58,* 365–372.

Lemann, T. B., and R. L. Solomon (1952). Group characteristics as revealed in sociometric patterns and personality ratings. *Sociometry, 15,* 7–90.

Lerner, M. J. (1965). The effect of responsibility and choice on a partner's attractiveness following failure. *J. Pers., 33,* 178–187.

Lerner, M. J., and S. Becker (1962). Interpersonal choice as a function of ascribed similarity and definition of the situation. *Hum. Relat., 15,* 27–34.

Levinger, G., and J. Breedlove (1966). Interpersonal attraction and agreement: a study of marriage partners. *J. Pers. soc. Psychol., 3,* 367–372.

Lindzey, G., and E. F. Borgatta (1954). Sociometric measurement. In G. Lindzey (Ed.), *Handbook of social psychology.* Vol. 1. Cambridge, Mass.: Addison-Wesley. Pp. 405–448.

Lindzey, G., and R. Goldwyn (1954). Validity of the Rosenzweig Picture-Frustration Study. *J. Pers., 22,* 519–547.

Lindzey, G., and J. A. Urdan (1954). Personality and social choice. *Sociometry, 17,* 47–63.

Longmore, T. W. (1948). A matrix approach to the analysis of rank and status in a community in Peru. *Sociometry, 11,* 192–206.

Loomis, C. P. (1943). Ethnic cleavages in the southwest as reflected in two high schools. *Sociometry, 6,* 7–26.

———— (1946). Political and occupational cleavages in a Hanoverian village, Germany. *Sociometry, 9,* 316–333.

———— (1948). The most frequently chosen sociogram: or the seduction of rural sociologists by the neighborhood theory. *Sociometry, 11,* 230–234.

Loomis, C. P., W. B. Baker, and C. Proctor (1949). The size of the family as related to social success of children. *Sociometry, 12,* 313–320.

Loomis, C. P., J. A. Beegle, and T. W. Longmore (1947). Critique of class as related to social stratification. *Sociometry, 10,* 319–337.

Loomis, C. P., and D. M. Davidson, Jr. (1939a). Measurement of the dissolution of in-groups in the integration of a rural resettlement project. *Sociometry, 2,* 84–94.

———— (1939b). Sociometrics and the study of new rural communities. *Sociometry, 2,* 56–76.

Loomis, C. P., and H. B. Pepinsky (1948). Sociometry, 1937–1947: theory and methods. *Sociometry, 11,* 262–286.

Loomis, C. P., and C. Proctor (1950). The relationship between choice status and economic status in social systems. *Sociometry, 13,* 307–313.

Lott, Bernice E., and A. J. Lott (1960). The formation of positive attitudes toward group members. *J. abnorm. soc. Psychol., 61,* 297–300.

Luce, D. R. (1950). Connectivity and generalized cliques in sociometric group structure. *Psychometrika, 15,* 169–190.

Luce, D. R., and A. D. Perry (1949). A method of matrix analysis of group structure. *Psychometrika, 14,* 95–116.

Lundberg, G. A. (1937). Social attraction patterns in a rural village: a preliminary report. *Sociometry, 1,* 77–80.

Lundberg, G. A., and Virginia Beazley (1948). 'Consciousness of kind' in a college population. *Sociometry, 11,* 59–74.

Lundberg, G. A., and Lenore Dickson (1952). Inter-ethnic relations in a high-school population. *Amer. J. Sociol., 58,* 1–10.

Lundberg, G. A., Virginia B. Hertzler, and Lenore Dickson (1949). Attraction patterns in a university. *Sociometry, 12,* 158–169.

Lundberg, G. A., and Margaret Lawsing (1937). The sociography of some community relations. *Amer. sociol. Rev., 2,* 318–335.

Lundberg, G. A., and Mary Steele (1938). Social attraction-patterns in a village. *Sociometry, 1,* 375–419.

Lundy, R. M. (1956). Self-perceptions and descriptions of opposite sex sociometric choices. *Sociometry, 19,* 272–277.

———— (1958). Self-perceptions regarding masculinity-femininity and descriptions of same and opposite sex sociometric choices. *Sociometry, 21,* 238–246.

Lundy, R. M., W. Katkovsky, R. L. Cromwell, and D. J. Shoemaker (1955). Self acceptability and descriptions of sociometric choices. *J. abnorm. soc. Psychol., 51,* 260–262.

McCandless, B. R., Carolyn B. Bilous, and Hannah L. Bennett (1961). Peer popularity and dependence on adults in preschool-age socialization. *Child Develpmt., 32,* 511–518.

McCandless, B. R., A. Castaneda, and D. S. Palermo (1956). Anxiety in children and social status. *Child Develpmt., 27,* 385–391.

McCandless, B. R., and Helen R. Marshall (1957). A picture sociometric technique for preschool children and its relation to teacher judgments of friendship. *Child Develpmt., 28,* 139–147.

McDavid, J., and H. Harari (1965). Stereotyping of names and popularity in grade school children. *Child Develpmt., 37,* 453–459.

McDonald, R. D. (1962). The effect of reward-punishment and affiliation need on interpersonal attraction. Unpublished doctoral dissertation, University of Texas.

McKenna, Helen V., P. R. Hofstaetter, and J. P. O'Connor (1956). The concepts of the ideal self and of the friend. *J. Pers., 24,* 262–271.

McKinney, J. C. (1948). An educational application of a two-dimensional sociometric test. *Sociometry, 11,* 356–367.

MacRae, D., Jr. (1960). Direct factor analysis of sociometric data. *Sociometry, 23,* 360–371.

Maisonneuve, J. (1954). A contribution to the sociometry of mutual choices. *Sociometry, 17,* 33–46.

Maisonneuve, J., G. Palmade, and C. Fourment (1952). Selective choices and propinquity. *Sociometry, 15,* 135–140.

Mann, J. H. (1958). The influence of racial prejudice on sociometric choices and perceptions. *Sociometry, 21,* 150–158.

———— (1959). The effect of interracial contact on sociometric choices and perceptions. *J. soc. Psychol., 50,* 143–152.

Marks, J. B. (1954). Interests, leadership and sociometric status among adolescents. *Sociometry, 17,* 340–349.

———— (1959). Interests and group formation. *Hum. Relat., 12,* 385–390.

Marshall, Helen R. (1957). An evaluation of sociometric-social behavior research with preschool children. *Child Develpmt., 28,* 131–137.

———— (1958). Prediction of social acceptance in community youth groups. *Child Develpmt., 29,* 173–184.

Marshall, Helen R., and B. R. McCandless (1957). Relationships between dependence on adults and social acceptance by peers. *Child Develpmt., 28,* 413–419.

Masling, J., F. L. Greer, and R. Gilmore (1955). Status, authoritarianism, and sociometric choice. *J. soc. Psychol., 41,* 297–310.

Massarik, F., R. Tannenbaum, M. Kahane, and I. R. Weschler (1953). Sociometric choice and organizational effectiveness. *Sociometry, 16,* 211–238.

Maucorps, P. H. (1949). A sociometric inquiry in the French army. *Sociometry, 12,* 46–80.

Mehlman, B. (1962). Similarity in friendships. *J. soc. Psychol., 57,* 195–202.

Miller, D. R., and Margaret E. Stine (1951). The prediction of social acceptance by means of psychoanalytic concepts. *J. Pers., 20,* 162–174.

Mills, C. R. (1953). Personality patterns of sociometrically selected and sociometrically rejected male college students. *Sociometry, 16,* 151–167.

Moore, Shirley, and Ruth Updegraff (1964). Sociometric status of preschool children related to age, sex, nurturance-giving, and dependency. *Child Develpmt., 35,* 519–524.

Moreno, J. L. (1934). *Who shall survive?* Washington, D.C.: Nervous and Mental Disease Monograph, No. 58.

——— (1942). Sociometry in action. *Sociometry, 5,* 298–315.

——— (1946). Sociogram and sociomatrix. *Sociometry, 9,* 348–349.

Moreno, J. L., and Helen H. Jennings (1938). Statistics of social configurations. *Sociometry, 1,* 342–374.

Moreno, J. L., Helen H. Jennings, and J. Sargent (1940). Time as a quantitative index of interpersonal relations. *Sociometry, 3,* 62–80.

Mouton, Jane S., R. R. Blake, and B. Fruchter (1955a). The reliability of sociometric measures. *Sociometry, 18,* 7–48.

——— (1955b). The validity of sociometric responses. *Sociometry, 18,* 181–206.

Murray, H. A. (1938). *Explorations in personality.* New York: Oxford Univ. Press.

Murstein, B. I. (1961). The complementary need hypothesis in newlyweds and middle-aged married couples. *J. abnorm. soc. Psychol., 63,* 194–197.

Nelson, D. (1965). The effect of differential magnitude of reinforcement on interpersonal attraction. Unpublished doctoral dissertation, University of Texas.

Newcomb, T. M. (1943). *Personality and social change.* New York: Dryden.

——— (1953). An approach to the study of communicative acts. *Psychol. Rev., 60,* 393–404.

——— (1956). The prediction of interpersonal attraction. *Amer. Psychologist, 11,* 575–586.

——— (1961). *The acquaintance process.* New York: Holt, Rinehart, and Winston.

——— (1963). Stabilities underlying changes in interpersonal attraction. *J. abnorm. soc. Psychol., 66,* 376–386.

Newcomb, T. M., and G. Svehla (1937). Intrafamily relationships in attitude. *Sociometry, 1,* 180–205.

Newstetter, W. I., M. J. Feldstein, and T. M. Newcomb (1938). *Group adjustment: a study in experimental sociology.* Cleveland: School of Applied Social Sciences, Western Reserve University.

Norman, R. D. (1953). The interrelationships among acceptance-rejection, self-other identity, insight into self, and realistic perception of others. *J. soc. Psychol., 37,* 205–235.

Northway, Mary L. (1940). A method for depicting social relationships obtained by sociometric testing. *Sociometry, 3,* 144–150.

——— (1944). Outsiders: a study of the personality patterns of children least acceptable to their age mates. *Sociometry, 7,* 10–25.

Northway, Mary L., and B. Quarrington (1946). Depicting inter-cultural relations. *Sociometry, 9,* 334–339.

Northway, Mary L., and Blossom T. Wigdor (1947). Rorschach patterns related to the sociometric status of school children. *Sociometry, 10,* 186–199.

Nosanchuk, T. A. (1963). A comparison of several sociometric partitioning techniques. *Sociometry, 26,* 112–124.

Pepinsky, H. B., R. J. Clyde, Barbara A. Olesen, and E. L. Vanatta (1952). The criterion in counseling: I. Individual personality and behavior in a social group. *Educ. psychol. Measmt., 12,* 178–193.

Pepinsky, H. B., L. Siegel, and E. L. Vanatta (1952). The criterion in counseling: a group participation scale. *J. abnorm. soc. Psychol., 47,* 415–419.

Pepinsky, Pauline N. (1949). The meaning of 'validity' and 'reliability' as applied to sociometric tests. *Educ. psychol. Measmt., 9,* 39–49.

Pepitone, A. (1964). *Attraction and hostility.* New York: Atherton.

Pepitone, A., and Janet Sherberg (1957). Intentionality, responsibility, and interpersonal attraction. *J. Pers., 25,* 757–766.

Petersen, R. J., S. S. Komorita, and H. C. Quay (1964). Determinants of sociometric choices. *J. soc. Psychol., 62,* 65–75.

Phillips, B. N., and L. A. D'Amico (1956). Effects of cooperation and competition on the cohesiveness of small face-to-face groups. *J. educ. Psychol., 47,* 65–70.

Pintner, R., G. Forlano, and H. Freedman (1937). Personality and attitudinal similarity among classroom friends. *J. appl. Psychol., 21,* 48–65.

Polansky, N., R. Lippitt, and F. Redl (1950). The use of near-sociometric data in research on group treatment processes. *Sociometry, 13,* 39–62.

Powell, R. M. (1951). A comparative social class analysis of San Juan Sur, and Attiro, Costa Rica. *Sociometry, 14,* 182–202.

Precker, J. A. (1953). The automorphic process in the attribution of values. *J. Pers., 21,* 356–363.

Proctor, C. H. (1953). *Turrialba, Costa Rica: comparison of social system and change in small farm and hacienda villages.* East Lansing: Michigan State College Press.

Proctor, C. H., and C. P. Loomis (1951). Analysis of sociometric data. In Marie Jahoda, M. Deutsch, and S. W. Cook (Eds.), *Research methods in social relations: with especial reference to prejudice.* Part 2. New York: Dryden. Pp. 561–585.

Rapoport, A. (1963). Mathematical models of social interaction. In R. D. Luce, R. R. Bush, and E. Galanter (Eds.), *Handbook of mathematical psychology.* Vol. 2. New York: Wiley. Pp. 493–579.

Reese, H. W. (1961). Relationships between self-acceptance and sociometric choices. *J. abnorm. soc. Psychol., 62,* 472–474.

Reilly, Mary S. A., W. D. Commins, and E. C. Stefic (1960). The complementarity of personality needs in friendship choice. *J. abnorm. soc. Psychol., 61,* 292–294.

Richardson, Helen M. (1940). Community of values as a factor in friendships of college and adult women. *J. soc. Psychol., 11,* 303–312.

Richmond, Winifred (1950). Sociometric tests in a training school for nurses. *Sociometry, 13,* 29–38.

Rosenfeld, H. M., and J. Jackson (1965). Temporal mediation of the similarity-attraction hypothesis. *J. Pers., 33,* 649–656.

Ross, I. C., and F. Harary (1952). On the determination of redundancies in sociometric chains. *Psychometrika, 17,* 195–208.

Sampson, E. E., and C. A. Insko (1964). Cognitive consistency and performance in the autokinetic situation. *J. abnorm. soc. Psychol., 68,* 184–192.

Schachter, S. (1951). Deviation, rejection, and communication. *J. abnorm. soc. Psychol., 46,* 190–207.

———— (1959). *The psychology of affiliation.* Stanford: Stanford Univ. Press.

Schooley, Mary (1936). Personality resemblances among married couples. *J. abnorm. soc. Psychol., 31,* 340–347.

Seagoe, Mary V. (1933). Factors influencing the selection of associates. *J. educ. Res., 27,* 32–40.

Secord, P. F., and C. W. Backman (1964). Interpersonal congruency, perceived similarity, and friendship. *Sociometry, 27,* 115–127.

Seeman, M. (1946). A situational approach to intra-group Negro attitudes. *Sociometry, 9,* 199–206.

Semler, I. J. (1960). Relationship among several measures of pupil adjustment. *J. educ. Psychol., 51,* 60–68.

Sherif, M., O. J. Harvey, B. J. White, W. R. Hood, and Carolyn W. Sherif (1961). *Intergroup conflict and cooperation: the Robbers Cave experiment.* Norman, Okla.: Institute of Group Relations.

Shipley, T. W., and J. Veroff (1952). A projective measure of need for affiliation. *J. exp. Psychol., 43,* 349–356.

Smelser, N. (1952). Sociometric structure and its correlates: social class background and courtship-marriage attitudes. Unpublished honors thesis, Harvard University.

Smith, A. J. (1958). Perceived similarity and the projection of similarity: the influence of values. *J. abnorm. soc. Psychol., 57,* 376–378.

Smith, M. (1944). Some factors in friendship selections of high school students. *Sociometry, 7,* 303–310.

Smith, P. B. (1963). Differentiation between sociometric rankings: a test of four theories. *Hum. Relat., 16,* 335–350.

Smith, W. D. (1953). Social attraction patterns between elementary-school children and student-teachers: sociometric analysis. *J. educ. Psychol., 44,* 113–125.

Smucker, O. (1949). Near-sociometric analysis as a basis for guidance. *Sociometry, 12,* 326–340.

Speroff, B., and W. Kerr (1952). Steel mill 'hot strip' accidents and interpersonal desirability values. *J. clin. Psychol., 8,* 89–91.

Stewart, F. A. (1946). Sociometric testing at the adult level. *Sociometry, 9,* 147–148.

———— (1947a). A sociometric study of influence in Southtown. *Sociometry, 10,* 11–31.

———— (1947b). A study of influence in Southtown: II. *Sociometry, 10,* 273–286.

—— (1948). Some sampling problems in sociometric surveys. *Sociometry, 11,* 301–307.

Stewart, Isabel A. (1948). An interviewer's report on adult sociometric study. *Sociometry, 11,* 308–319.

Stogdill, R. M. (1949). The sociometry of working relationships in formal organizations. *Sociometry, 12,* 276–286.

Stogdill, R. M., and C. L. Shartle (1948). Methods for determining patterns of leadership behavior in relation to organization structure and objectives. *J. appl. Psychol., 32,* 286–291.

Tagiuri, R. (1952). Relational analysis: an extension of sociometric method with emphasis upon social perception. *Sociometry, 15,* 91–104.

Tagiuri, R., and N. Kogan (1960). Personal preference and the attribution of influence in small groups. *J. Pers., 28,* 257–265.

Thorpe, J. G. (1955a). An investigation into some correlates of sociometric status within school classes. *Sociometry, 18,* 49–61.

—— (1955b). A study of some factors in friendship formation. *Sociometry, 18,* 207–214.

Trent, R. D. (1957). The relationship of anxiety to popularity and rejection among institutionalized delinquent boys. *Child Develpmt., 28,* 379–384.

Triandis, H. C. (1964). Exploratory factor analyses of the behavioral component of social attitudes. *J. abnorm. soc. Psychol., 68,* 420–430.

Turner, R. H., and R. H. Vanderlippe (1958). Self-ideal congruence as an index of adjustment. *J. abnorm. soc. Psychol., 57,* 202–206.

Van Dyne, Virginia E. (1940). Personality traits and friendship formation in adolescent girls. *J. soc. Psychol., 12,* 291–303.

Venable, T. C. (1954). The relationship of selected factors to the social structure of a stable group. *Sociometry, 17,* 355–357.

Vreeland, F. M. (1942). Social relations in the college fraternity. *Sociometry, 5,* 151–162.

Vroom, V. H. (1959). Projection, negation, and the self concept. *Hum. Relat., 12,* 335–344.

Walster, Elaine, and B. Walster (1963). Effect of expecting to be liked on choice of associates. *J. abnorm. soc. Psychol., 67,* 402–404.

Weschler, I. R., R. Tannenbaum, and E. Talbot (1952). A new management tool: the multi-relational sociometric survey. *Personnel, 29,* 85–94.

Wherry, R. J., and D. Fryer (1949). Buddy ratings: popularity contest or leadership criteria? *Sociometry, 12,* 179–190.

Whyte, W. H., Jr. (1956). *The organization man.* New York: Simon and Schuster.

Williams, S. B., and H. J. Leavitt (1947). Group opinion as a predictor of military leadership. *J. consult. Psychol., 11,* 283–291.

Winch, R. F., T. Ktsanes, and Virginia Ktsanes (1955). Empirical elaboration of the theory of complementary needs in mate-selection. *J. abnorm. soc. Psychol., 51,* 508–513.

Winder, C. L., and Lucy Rau (1962). Parental attitudes associated with social deviance in preadolescent boys. *J. abnorm. soc. Psychol., 64,* 418–424.

Winslow, C. N. (1937). A study of the extent of agreement between friends' opinions and their ability to estimate the opinions of each other. *J. soc. Psychol., 8,* 433–442.

Witryol, S. L., and G. G. Thompson (1953). An experimental comparison of the stability of social acceptability scores obtained with the partial-rank-order and the paired-comparison scales. *J. educ. Psychol., 44,* 20–30.

Wong, T. J. (1961). The effect of attitude similarity and prejudice on interpersonal evaluation and attraction. Unpublished Master's thesis, University of Texas.

Worchel, P., and Betty L. McCormick (1963). Self-concept and dissonance reduction. *J. Pers., 31,* 588–599.

Wright, B., and Mary S. Evitts (1961). Direct factor analysis in sociometry. *Sociometry, 24,* 82–98.

Wright, B., and Sue Evitts (1963). Multiple regression in the explanation of social structure. *J. soc. Psychol., 61,* 87–98.

Wrightsman, L. S., Jr. (1960). Effects of waiting with others on changes in level of felt anxiety. *J. abnorm. soc. Psychol., 61,* 216–222.

Zander, A., and A. Havelin (1960). Social comparison and interpersonal attraction. *Hum. Relat., 13,* 21–32.

Zeleny, L. D. (1939). Sociometry of morale. *Amer. sociol. Rev., 4,* 799–808.

—— (1940). Measurement of social status. *Amer. J. Sociol., 45,* 576–582.

—— (1947). Selection of compatible flying partners. *Amer. J. Sociol., 52,* 424–431.

15

Interviewing

CHARLES F. CANNELL, *University of Michigan*
ROBERT L. KAHN, *University of Michigan*

In one of the first systematic discussions of interviewing methods, Bingham and Moore (1924) described the interview as "a conversation with a purpose." The description is still relevant, but it is extremely broad; the purposes for which interviews are conducted are many and various. They include the purpose of therapeutic change, as in the psychiatric interview; the purpose of instruction and appraisal, as in interviews initiated by a supervisor with a subordinate; purposes of selection and assessment, as in interviews conducted with applicants for jobs or with students applying for admission to universities. In all these situations, there is the transaction of information giving and getting, and the understanding of this transaction as the immediate task of interviewer and respondent. This immediate task, however, is embedded in a larger cycle of purposive activities which define more exactly the role of interviewer and respondent, reflect the motives of both for undertaking the interview, and stipulate the consequences of the interview for other aspects of their lives.

THE NATURE OF THE RESEARCH INTERVIEW

To label an interview psychiatric or therapeutic implies that it has probably been initiated by the respondent (or patient), and that his motivation in doing so is to obtain relief from certain symptoms or strains. Moreover, the interviewer is seen not only as an information-getter but as a direct and powerful source of help; the interview is seen not only as an information transaction but as part of the therapeutic experience. Its purpose is to change the behavior and the inner life of the person, and its success is defined in terms of such changes. Therapeutic interviewing is thus a highly specialized form of informational and interpersonal transaction, and it has become the subject of an equally specialized literature (Sullivan, 1954; Rogers, 1942, 1951).

By contrast, the research interview, with which we are here concerned, can be defined as a two-person conversation, initiated by the interviewer for the specific purpose of obtaining research-relevant information, and focused by him on content specified by research objectives of systematic description, prediction, or explanation. Other characteristics of the research interview are more variable. Typically, however, the differentiation of role between interviewer and respondent is pronounced. The interviewer not only initiates the conversation; he presents each topic by means of specific questions, and he decides when the conversation on a topic has satisfied the research objectives (or the specific criteria which represent them) and another topic shall be introduced. The respondent in the research interview is led to restrict his discussion to the specific questions posed by the interviewer.

In contrast to therapeutic or assessment interviews, the consequences of the research interview for the individual respondent are often minimal and almost always removed in time, space, and person from the interview experience itself. The respondent is asked to provide information about himself, his experiences, his perceptions, or his attitudes to an interviewer who has no direct power or intention to provide therapy, instruction, a job, or any other major tangible reward. If the research interview does contribute to such respondent outcomes, it does so through a sequence of events which involves the aggregation of responses from numerous interviews, some process of data reduction and inference, and some additions to the description or explanation of social facts. From this enlarged base of knowledge may come applications or decisions of policy which have great importance for the respondent, but the sequence is complex and often uncertain. Nevertheless, the prospect of ultimate benefit, public or personal, from the accumulation of knowledge is one major reason for the agreement of the respondent to participate in a research interview.

Perhaps the prototypical example of research interviews is provided by the national census. Most countries of the world conduct some kind of population count, and in many countries the census has been expanded to provide with regularity an inventory of social resources and problems. Census interviews usually make only modest demands on interviewer and respondent. They are brief; they ask for demographic data well within the respondent's knowledge and not of a kind which he is likely to regard as confidential. Moreover, the information is requested under circumstances familiar to or expected by most respondents, and the request is backed by the legitimate power of the national government.

Similar to the census in most of these respects is a whole class of brief, officially sponsored, information-getting interview surveys. In the United States alone, hundreds of thousands of such interviews are conducted by agencies of government each year in randomly selected homes to provide continuous flow of data on family income, employment and unemployment, health and illness, and other aspects of economic and social welfare.

Almost as widely known as census taking and the descriptive research interviewing of government are the activities of private agencies and academic groups which conduct recurrent interview studies of public opinion on national and international affairs, family life, and other subjects of public interest. It is possible to do very intensive, theoretically oriented research on such problems, and this type of work is being done with increasing frequency. To the general public, however, the visible sources of research information on public affairs are the various opinion polls, which concentrate on the production of quantitative data regarding issues of current social interest, approached and described in colloquial terms.

The interviews conducted by such polls resemble those of the census in brevity and simplicity, and in the avoidance of very private material. Public-opinion interviewing differs from most government-sponsored surveys in dealing with matters of attitude rather than fact, and in depending on interviewer persuasiveness rather than legal authority and prestige to obtain respondent cooperation. Market research and studies of readership are usually of like simplicity and brevity, although more elaborate and indirect techniques of interviewing have sometimes been used in such studies.

It is likely, however, that the most ambitious and demanding use of the interview as a research technique has been made by social scientists in the course of psychological, sociological, political, and economic investigations. Such studies often involve interviews of an hour or more, on subjects which may raise difficult problems of recall, potential embarrassment, and self-awareness. Consider as examples the recurring studies of consumer behavior and family income (Katona, 1960), of fertility and family planning (Freedman, Whelpton, and Campbell, 1959), of sexual behavior (Kinsey, Pomeroy, and Martin, 1948), of mental health and illness (Gurin, Veroff, and Feld, 1960), of political behavior (Campbell *et al.*, 1960), and the many studies of supervisor-subordinate relations and worker attitudes (Argyris, 1965; Herzberg, Mausner, and Snyderman, 1959; Kahn *et al.*, 1964; Likert, 1961).

Moreover, the use of the interview in these disciplines is not limited to surveys and other studies done in the field; interviewing is a necessary element in laboratory research as well. Laboratory experiments in social psychology and other social sciences typically involve a situation contrived by the experimenter in order to introduce some factor into the experience of the people who are his experimental subjects, and to do so under conditions in which their reactions can be closely studied. This type of study often requires interviewing as well as observation, physiological measures, and the like. The experimenter depends on the subject to report anxiety or elation, increased confidence or reduced self-esteem, feelings of acceptance or rejection (see, for example, Asch, 1952; Milgram, 1965). The interview helps the experimenter to learn whether the intended manipulation of a variable really "took," and if so, whether it had the predicted effects.

It seems likely that this form of interview is widespread among social psychologists, but that they do not typically recognize it as interviewing. Experimental research has its special vocabulary, as does survey research. The experimenter speaks of subjects, while the survey researcher speaks of respondents. The implication is that respondents are interviewed without any other form of intervention by the field researcher, and that laboratory subjects react to some situation of the experimenter's making but are not interviewed. The facts are to the contrary. The collection of *Basic Studies in Social Psychology* (Proshansky and Seidenberg, 1965) includes 61 studies, of which 37 involve verbal responses of subjects in answer to some series of questions or demands by the researcher. Moreover, of the studies which do not involve interview data, all but four use written responses of subjects to questionnaire items or similar stimuli. The companion volume, *Current Studies in Social Psychology* (Steiner and Fishbein, 1965), shows a somewhat similar pattern. Fifty-two studies are reported, of which 19 utilize interview data and 17 involve written responses. The remaining 16 studies include indeterminate cases as well as designs involving neither interview nor questionnaire.

These examples suggest a conclusion which can hardly be questioned: much of the data of social psychology is generated by means of the interview, and the quality of social-psychological research is therefore dependent in part on the competence with which interview questions are phrased and interviews are conducted. Sociologist and psychologist, anthropologist, political scientist, and economist depend on interviews to obtain data for describing the phenomena of interest to them and for testing their theories and hypotheses about those phenomena. Some agreement with this view is perhaps implied by the several serious attempts in recent years to state the rationale and technique for constructing interview schedules and conducting interviews in the context of social research. These include Merton, Fiske, and Kendall (1956), Hyman *et al.* (1954), Maccoby and Maccoby (1954), Kahn and Cannell (1957), and Richardson, Dohrenwend, and Klein (1965).

To find the importance of interviewing emphasized in a chapter on the same subject is hardly surprising. Our purpose in pointing to the wide use of the technique is not single-minded advocacy, however. On the contrary, we feel strongly that social psychology already suffers from some symptoms of parochialism in research methods, and we have no wish to contribute to a full-blown case of methodological addiction. Individual social psychologists tend to remain with their individual methodological specialties. Some seldom venture out of the laboratory; others do only field studies, regardless of the problem under investigation or the phase of investigation which has been attained. Campbell and Fiske (1959) several years ago demonstrated the inferential risks as well as the empirical limitations of such misplaced methodological loyalty, and others have offered similar judgments. We concur; we advocate methodological breadth, choice of method on the basis of the substantive problem under investigation and the specific aims of the research, and the use of multiple methods in order to avoid mistaking artifacts for substantive research findings.

We urge competence in interviewing and in questionnaire design not as the sole criterion for methodological success, but as research qualifications of great importance. They are not sufficient conditions, but they are necessary for the social psychologist.

A final qualification remains, of a very different sort. This chapter contains much negative information about the interview—its biases, its risks, and its costs.

We take seriously the inherent limitations of verbal reporting, as well as many avoidable but common errors and biases. But this no more argues abolition or avoidance of the technique than the previous points urge unvarying preference for it. Interviewing is often the instrument of choice for collecting social-psychological data, and it is not infrequently the only choice available. To emphasize its limitations is, we hope, to promote the improvement of the technique and its wise use.

In short, the social scientist, from the first nineteenth-century British surveys of poverty (Booth, 1892–1897) and the early psychophysical experiments in the laboratory (see Boring, 1950), has been willy-nilly an interviewer, and the prospects are that he will remain so. Whether he has been too much an interviewer (Webb *et al.,* 1966) is a question of prime importance for the strategy of social science and one to which we shall return. Like other scientists the social psychologist attempts to measure, not merely to describe in qualitative terms. For him the interview has been the key instrument in the measurement process, and it must be judged as an instrument of measurement.

INTERVIEW AS MEASUREMENT

We have defined the interview as *a conversation with a purpose,* and further specified that the purpose with which we are concerned is *information getting.* Some of the kinds of information sought in interviewing for social research are illustrated by the examples in the foregoing section of this chapter. The research interview, however, is not after mere information; it has to do with that particular quantitative form of information getting called *measurement.* The interview is one part, and a crucial one, in the measurement process as it is conducted in much of social research. As such, the use of the interview is subject to the laws of measurement; it can be properly judged by the standards of measurement, and it suffers from the limitations of all measurement processes in degrees peculiar to itself.

By measurement we mean the process of *assigning numbers* to some population of objects or events, in accordance with some set of rules. This process is usually described as *mapping* objects or events into an abstract space of some particular structure, defined by rules and represented or described in terms of numbers or other symbols.

For example, we might decide to measure the height of students in a classroom. The end product of the measurement process would be the assignment of a number to each student—62 inches, 66 inches, etc. The rules would include the requirement that the student be standing straight against the wall, that the measurer sight across the top of the student's head and make a mark on the wall corresponding to his height, and that the distance from this mark to the floor be ascertained with a steel tape measure. Less obvious as part of the measurement process, but even more important, would be those "rules" which defined the inch as the unit of measurement and the decimal system of numbering as the means of counting those units.

In social research, as this definition and example of measurement imply, the actual conduct of an interview is only a part of the measurement process. The total process would include at least the following five discrete steps:

1. *Creating or selecting an interview schedule (set of questions, statements, pictures, or other stimuli to evoke responses) and a set of rules or procedures for using the schedule.*

2. *Conducting the interview (that is, evoking the responses or events that are to be classified).*

3. *Recording these responses (by means of paper-and-pencil notes, electronic equipment, or other devices).*

4. *Creating a numerical code (that is, a scale or other system of numbers into which the recorded responses are to be translated, and a set of rules for making the translation).*

5. *Coding the interview responses.*

At this point we would have evoked a set of events and assigned numbers to them, in accordance with some specific rules both for the evocation of response and for the translation of verbal responses into numbers; we would thus have met the definition of measurement.

The example would be no less measurement if our aim were to determine the liking or disliking of students for school, instead of their height. True, there would be no tape measure and no widely accepted unit of measurement. We might, however, ask each student to answer the question: "All in all, how do you feel about going to school?" And we might record the answers verbatim and subsequently sort them into three categories labeled "like," "neutral," and "dislike," and numbered 1, 2, and 3. This we feel intuitively is crude measurement but measurement nonetheless, and so it is. Some of its crudities are immediately apparent. For one thing, we are attempting to measure degrees of liking without any defined unit of measurement; we do not know that the difference in liking represented by the gap between 1 and 2 is equal to the difference between 2 and 3. Moreover, we are attempting measurement without any zero point; we do not know what response and code number represent the complete absence of the thing we are attempting to measure. In addition to these limitations of measurement, we have asked only a single question to determine liking for school, one out of the infinite number of questions which might be chosen or invented to measure the attitude in question.

More than such miscellaneous observations is needed, however, to assess and improve the quality of measurement by means of interviewing. We need systematic answers to the following three questions:

1. *How can the adequacy of measurement be conceptualized?*

2. *How can the actual adequacy of any given measurement be determined, in terms of the chosen conceptualization?*

3. *What can be done to remedy such inadequacies as the preceding steps define and bring to light?*

CONCEPTUALIZATION OF MEASUREMENT ADEQUACY

The key concept for thinking about the adequacy of measurement is *validity,* defined as the extent to which an instrument and the rules for its use in fact measure what they purport to measure (Kaplan, 1965; Selltiz *et al.,* 1959). Validity can also be thought of in terms of average deviation of a given measure from the "true value" of the attribute being measured. This is a common form of expression, but involves a serious oversimplification. There is no such thing as "true value" in the prevailing metatheory of science; the value of an object in measurement terms is defined by the act of measurement.

Particularly in interviewing, inferences about validity are made too often on the basis of *face validity,* that is, whether the questions asked look as if they are measuring what they purport to measure. A preferable way of thinking about validity, and a basis for developing tests of validity, is the question of what a given measurement will do. Does the measure do the things which theory and experiment have convinced us it should do (Campbell, 1957; Cronbach, 1946; Coombs, 1964)? For example, does an attitude scale which purports to measure intensity of religious feeling produce somewhat similar values for Jesuits and orthodox rabbinical students, and drastically lesser scores for nonchurchgoers? Does a test which purports to measure intelligence enable us to predict scholastic achievement to some significant degree?

An approach to the validation of interview measures, which is similar in its logic to that just described, involves comparison of the interview measure with some other measure which has already met the test of validity. This kind of comparison has been called *convergent validity,* in part to distinguish it from other approaches to construct validation. If the two measures in fact agree, then one may presume that the validity of the measure being tested is at least as great as that of the measure taken as standard. Thus hospitalization data obtained from interviews might be validated against admissions records.

When the standard is already validated, the method of convergent validity is powerful. When the results of political surveys correspond to election statistics, or when the results of consumer surveys agree with the volume of actual purchases, we feel confidence in the survey measures. The problem of validation becomes more difficult, however, in the case of interview measures of attitudes, for which there are no independent and objective measures existing on quite the same level of simplicity.

Questions of validity and invalidity are only part of the problem of measurement adequacy, however. A measure is invalid to the extent that it measures something more than or less than it purports to measure. Put another way, the mark of invalidity is *bias,* which is a systematic or persistent tendency to make errors in the same direction, that is, to overstate or understate the "true value" of an attribute. Scarcely less important than validity is *reliability,* which has to do with the stability and equivalence of a measure (Cronbach, 1960). The reliability of an interview measure is defined by such questions as these: If the measure is used repeatedly in the same circumstances, will it yield the same results? If it is used by different interviewers to measure the same attribute, will it produce the same results?

The methods of determining the reliability of a measure are to arrange for repetitions of it in identical circumstances (*test-retest* reliability) or, if the measure involves numerous items, to compare the results obtained on the basis of one-half of the items, randomly selected, with the results obtained by using the other half of the items. This is called *split-half* reliability.

The relationship between validity and reliability is complex. For the interview method, however, it is important to remind ourselves that a measure may be valid without being reliable; such an interview procedure measures what it purports to, but does so badly. On the average, it obtains the "true value," but its variance is large. Repeated use of the measure in the same circumstances produces values which are random about the mean, but vary from it by large amounts.

Still a third aspect of measurement adequacy is *sensitivity* or *precision*. Any measuring device has limits in its power of discrimination, beyond which are differences too small for it to measure. Beyond these limits the measuring device calls differing things the same. For example, an interview which attempts only to distinguish between people who favor and people who oppose a given action, even if it makes this distinction with validity and reliability, is most imprecise in that it calls all degrees of favoring the same, and all degrees of opposition the same.

These three aspects of measurement adequacy—validity, reliability, and precision—are neither wholly independent nor simply interrelated. Rather, the relationships among them are complex. For example, one way of increasing one's reliability with a given procedure is to decrease the attempted sensitivity; we can collapse a nine-point scale to a three-point scale and often gain reliability by so doing. Similar problems of trade-off in measurement adequacy are sometimes encountered between reliability and validity; for example, a carefully constructed intelligence test of the paper-and-pencil variety may show superior reliability to one requiring individual administration and inferences made from responses regarding forms, number groupings, and other object relations. But the paper-and-pencil test is by definition culture-bound and language-bound (that is, biased) to a degree which the other procedure need not be.

Detailed procedures for the determination of measurement adequacy for interview data are beyond the scope of the present discussion. The logic of such procedures, however, is straightforward. For the determination of validity, this logic requires the comparison of the obtained measurement to some other measure which serves as a "standard" in any of several ways: as some value which the measure ought to predict (for example, an intelligence test ought to predict academic achievement); as some value the measure ought to agree with (interview reports of voting behavior ought to agree with election records); or as some value the measure ought to be different from (an interview measure of intrinsic job satisfaction ought not to yield identical values with an interview measure of satisfaction with salary). The most widely used quantitative techniques for the determination of reliability of interview data, as we have pointed out, can be applied only after the interview responses have been coded or mapped into some system of numbers. At that point it becomes possible to compute test-retest or split-half coefficients of reliability. Prior to such content analysis or coding, only qualitative comparisons are possible, and such comparisons are sometimes made between the results obtained by different interviewers in identical or randomly assigned circumstances.

The question of how to ensure or achieve measurement adequacy by means of interview procedures is more complicated. One solution, of course, is to restrict oneself to measures already developed, for which the coefficients of reliability and validity are available. Many paper-and-pencil tests and some interview scales have been developed with enough attention to methodological considerations that such data are available. Examples include numerous personality scales, tests of intelligence and reading ability, the census procedure for ascertaining labor-force status and occupation, measures of political party identification, and others. The availability of adequate measures and rules for using them is a major characteristic of a mature science, and a commonplace in physics, chemistry, and biology. In these fields it is only at the frontiers that the investigator is devising new concepts and new means for measuring them.

In social psychology, however, there is as yet no agreed-upon conceptual vocabulary; still less is there a standard set of measures for concepts in common use. As a result, the investigator is commonly also an inventor of measures, concepts, or both, although this tendency may perhaps be diminishing.

Three recent books offer some basis for optimism in this respect. *Social Indicators* (Bauer, 1966) provides a broad survey of the major measures of social description in continuing use, and discusses the most pressing needs for additional measures of this kind. Shaw and Wright (1967) have compiled some 200 attitudinal measures in eight substantive areas: social practices, social problems, international issues, abstract concepts, political and religious systems, ethnic and national groups, significant others (including the self), and social institutions. For each of these measures, they provide a description of the measure itself, a statement of the subjects on which it was developed and tested, procedures for scoring the results, and data on reliability and validity. The scarcity of such data is conspicuous, especially for validity. Nevertheless, the compilation at least clarifies an unsatisfactory state of affairs, and by so doing contributes to its improvement.

Robinson, Athanasiou, and Head (1967) have published a substantial monograph that provides similar information for a large number of measures of occupational characteristics and attitudes, scales of job satisfaction, and other work-relevant attitudes. Moreover, they propose a series of such compilations on measures of authoritarianism and alienation, political orientations, values, marriage and the family, and religion. It seems reasonable to propose that the handicraft stage of questionnaire construction is slowly passing, and that carefully validated measures will be available for an increasing number of major concepts and interest areas.

For the investigator who must create his own interview measures, there is a considerable accumulation of general principles and specific procedures for the preparation of questions, scales or sets of questions, and questionnaires (Payne, 1951; Kahn and Cannell, 1957; Richardson, Dohrenwend, and Klein, 1965). These will help in achieving validity in measurement. It is also possible to improve validity by including in the data collection measures of potential sources of bias, so that there can be an after-the-fact assessment of the extent of their intrusion and a correction in the raw data. The "lie scale" of the Minnesota Multiphasic Personality Inventory, the Edwards Social Acceptability Scale, and the Mandler-Sarason Test Anxiety Scale are examples of measures which are used for such *post facto* statistical corrections with some success.

The achievement of high reliability depends on the same basic principles, but is particularly enhanced by specifying the exact wording of the questions to be asked in the interview, specifying the forms and range of behavior which may be used in the interview to evoke response, and by using multiple questions rather than single questions for the measurement of each concept or variable.

In short, adequacy of measurement by means of interview requires knowledge of the conditions for a successful interview, and the skill to meet those conditions both in the construction of questionnaires or interview schedules and in the conduct of the interview itself. These issues are the subjects of the following sections of this chapter.

CONDITIONS FOR SUCCESSFUL INTERVIEW

Interviews are not uniformly successful in attaining validity, reliability, and precision of measurement. Interviewers differ in skill; respondents differ in ability and motivation; interview content differs in feasibility. The problems associated with these differences have been described in many terms, and many approaches have been taken to their solution. Three broad concepts seem to comprise much of the available research and advice, and to summarize well the conditions required for successful interviewing. These are *accessibility* of the required data to the respondent, *cognition* or understanding by the respondent of his role and the informational transaction required of him, and *motivation* of the respondent to take the role and fulfill its requirements.

These are not independent factors; they can be thought of as a set of interrelated conditions for attaining adequate measurement by means of interviewing, provided the task of conceptualization has been successfully completed and the researcher has defined the object of his measurement attempt. We will use accessibility, cognition, and motivation as the organizing ideas for reviewing studies of reliability and validity in interviewing, for discussing the formulation of interview questions, and for describing interviewing techniques.

Accessibility

The simplest condition for interviewing occurs when the datum which the interviewer requires is completely accessible to the respondent; that is, he has the information in conscious form, clearly conceptualized in the terms used by the interviewer. This condition is typically met for simple demographic data—age, family size, and the like. To the extent that the required data are accessible to the respondent, the interviewer can turn his attention to problems of cognition and motivation, making sure that the respondent understands what is asked of him and that he is willing to provide the information he possesses. To the extent that the data are inaccessible to the respondent, this inaccessibility constitutes the first problem in interviewing.

Three major reasons for inaccessibility can be distinguished, each with its own implications for the formulation of questions and the conduct of the interview:

1. The material may simply have been forgotten (Bartlett, 1932). The respondent may once have been in conscious possession of the required information, but it has receded from conscious recollection. For example, he once knew the month as well as the year in which he bought his automobile, or the day of the week on which he saw a particular movie, but he no longer remembers. No major processes of repression or suppression seem to be involved, merely the gradual loss of unimportant material.

2. A second kind of inaccessibility has to do with repression; an event is important or recent enough to be remembered, but it involves sufficient emotional stress that it has been pushed from conscious memory. The embarrassing incident in the classroom, the painful argument with a sick parent are not forgotten in the same sense as trivial events; they have vanished from conscious recollection precisely because of their psychological importance and stressfulness for the respondent. As a result, it requires special effort to retrieve them and special motivation to report them.

3. The third category of inaccessibility has to do, not with the intrinsic content of the material sought, but with the terms or categories in which the interview requires recollection and communication. Problems of language, vocabulary, and sophistication are involved; differences in social class, subculture, and region are also implicated. This aspect of inaccessibility is related to the cognitive condition for successful interviewing. For example, an interviewer might be so ill-advised as to ask workers to recount recent experiences on the job which were ego-threatening and ego-enhancing. A respondent might be quite insightful and observant, quite able to describe in some detail his experience on the job, and yet be unable to respond meaningfully to this question. The categories or terms of reference which it assumes are not those in which he codes his experience, and the data are therefore inaccessible, at least until he is helped to get clearly in mind the meaning of the terms ego-enhancing and ego-threatening and to recapitulate his recent work experience in these terms.

Cognitive conditions for the interview

A second requirement for successful interviewing has to do with respondent cognition or understanding. The respondent role is by definition an active, self-conscious one; in most circumstances the respondent can meet its expectations best when he understands them fully. Specifically, he needs to know what constitutes successful completion of the role requirements; he needs to know the concepts or terms of reference by means of which he is being asked to provide data. Without this understanding, data accessible to the respondent are likely nevertheless to remain unreported because interviewer and respondent lack a common frame of reference, a common conceptual language, or common standards of response adequacy and excellence.

How much respondent understanding of the research enterprise is appropriate will vary with the demands being made in the interview, and how much interviewer effort must go into the development of such understanding will depend on the extent of the interview demand and the sophistication of the respondent. Typically, the respondent need not understand the nature of the measurement being attempted, the construction of scales, or the plans for computer analysis. He should understand the requirements of his own role in the interview—the demands to be made on him and the criteria for relevance and completeness. To understand these things, and to be motivated to accept the role, may in turn require acquaintance with the overall aims of the research enterprise, information about its compatibility with the respondent's own goals, and reassurance about its risks. These latter issues bring us to the third condition for successful interviewing.

Motivation as a condition for the interview

There is general agreement among students and practitioners of interviewing that respondent motivation or willingness to report is a prime condition for successful data collection; it could hardly be otherwise. There is agreement, however, neither about the theory or model of motivation which is most appropriate to the interview, nor about the major sources of respondent motivation. Kahn and Cannell (1957) have proposed a dual emphasis—intrinsic motivation, because the experience and relationship with the interviewer is valued by the respondent; and instrumental motivation, because the respondent sees that the enterprise of which the interview is a part is congruent with his own goals and values. Kinsey and his colleagues (1948) stressed altruism as the initial source of respondent motivation, although many of their interview descriptions seem to rely more on the assumption of legitimate authority and the use of medical-scientific prestige. Richardson, Dohrenwend, and Klein (1965), have explained respondent motivation in terms of altruism, emotional satisfaction, and intellectual satisfaction. Such partial agreements and discontinuities are hardly surprising; they reflect the more general diversity of motivational theories. The interview is one form of complex molar behavior; attempts to understand it will share inevitably the contemporary strengths and weaknesses of motivational theory as a whole.

Despite the lack of agreement on any one motivational model, the research evidence on the interviewing process (Hyman *et al.*, 1954; Riesman, 1958; Kahn and Cannell, 1957; Richardson, Dohrenwend, and Klein, 1965) strongly urges that respondent motivation be conceptualized in terms that take account of the social situation of interviewer and respondent, of the nature of the transaction between them, of their mutual perceptions of each other and their joint task, and of the

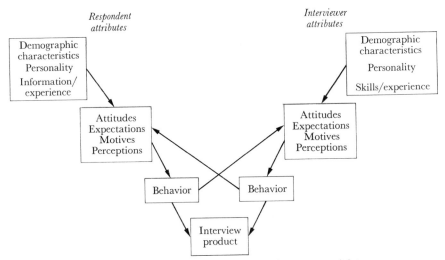

Fig. 1. A motivational model of the interview as a social process.

effects of such perceptions. In short, the evidence argues in favor of a motivational model which treats the interview as a social process and regards the interview product as a social outcome. One such model is presented in Fig. 1.

This model is compatible with the role-oriented view of the interview. It stipulates that the interview product or outcome is the immediate and joint result of interviewer and respondent behavior; that the behavior of both interviewer and respondent stems from their attitudes, motives, expectations, and perceptions; and that these in turn can be understood as reflecting more enduring attributes of demography and personality. The model also emphasizes the interaction of respondent and interviewer. The behavior of the interviewer is perceived by the respondent, and the perception generates or modifies his attitudes and his motivation to continue the interaction. However, the respondent is reacting not only to the interviewer behavior as such; he is reacting to it as a cue which evokes role behavior already familiar in other contexts, attitudes already formed. Thus the respondent may behave toward the interviewer as polite stranger, as hospitable host, as dutiful citizen, as fellow research worker and scientist, or even as obedient servant or intimidated inferior. The interviewer's expectations and behavior in turn are a mixed product of his own personality and experience, and his immediate reaction to what the respondent is doing.

Such a general model of the interview requires additional specification. It requires, among other things, some means for representing the moment-by-moment representation of the respondent's motivation to provide complete and accurate data. The various forces tending at any point in the interview to increase or decrease respondent motivation to work in this sense can be well represented by the Lewinian model of the quasi-stationary equilibrium (Lewin, 1947), in which each factor urging compliance or resistance is depicted as an arrow (force),

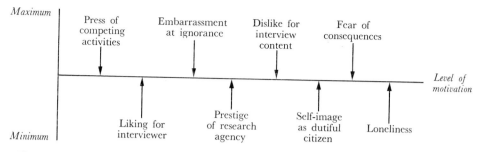

Fig. 2. *Factors affecting the respondent's motivation to provide complete and accurate information to the interviewer.*

and the level of motivation is depicted as a horizontal line which is the resultant of the opposing forces. In Fig. 2, the factors identified as opposing forces have been taken from current research on the interview process (Fowler, 1966; Cannell and Fowler, 1965).

To represent the field of motivational forces which characterizes an interview during each moment of its brief history is thus conceptually feasible, but it involves methodological problems which have yet to be solved. For most purposes it may be sufficient to distinguish successive stages or patterns of respondent motivation. The first is the motivational pattern at the outset of the encounter, when the individual decides whether to accept or reject the respondent role. (We can omit that still earlier motive pattern, when he decides whether he will even listen to the interviewer's introductory remarks and request for cooperation.) On the basis of his first personal impressions of the interviewer and the introductory information about the demands, duration, difficulty, and threatening or positive outcomes of the interview, the respondent decides whether indeed to become a respondent. The motive pattern at this moment of decision is of particular importance. The decision having been made in the affirmative, the respondent is now "in role." A psychological contract has been executed; both interviewer and respondent know it, and from that point on the fact of their role agreement constitutes a major motivational force to continue the interview.

It does not guarantee maintenance of motivation sufficient to complete the interview, of course. The respondent's net motivation to continue may drop because of the introduction of unexpected or unacceptable content, because of interviewer demands or style deemed inappropriate or in violation of the introductory commitment, or for other such reasons. New problems of accessibility, cognition, or threat may always make insufficient a motivational equilibrium which had previously been enough to ensure continuation of the interview. The respondent again considers the decision to allow the transaction and to remain in role, and the interviewer provides new information about the research, or attempts in other ways to make the new demands relevant, legitimate, and consistent with the original agreement. It becomes relevant again to attempt a detailed analysis of the respondent's motive pattern at such moments of decision.

The research that has been done over the years on interviewing, and on problems of reliability and validity of interview data, has not been done in the theoretical terms just proposed, nor has it utilized the concepts of accessibility, cognition, and motivation in this fashion. These concepts seem nevertheless appropriate as a basis for organizing a review of the relevant research on interviewing.

STUDIES IN RELIABILITY AND VALIDITY

Most published studies on interviewing report significant invalidity in the data. One cannot say with certainty whether these studies are representative of all data collected by means of interviewing. They may overstate the problem of invalidity, since positive research findings (in this case, findings of *invalid* data) tend to be published, while negative findings (that is, findings of validity) are seen less often. On the other hand, methodological research may be carried out more often on good data than on bad. The careless or unsophisticated researcher is not likely to offer his data for methodological research and is still less likely to do such research himself.

The problem of representativeness restricts seriously our ability to generalize from currently available studies of reliability and validity, but some generalizations may nevertheless be attempted. One can define patterns with respect to the kind of material sought in the interview, with respect to the manner or technique by which it is sought, and with respect to the characteristics of the actors (interviewer and respondent) in the situation.

Such patterns as we find, however, are subject to several qualifications in addition to the problem of representativeness mentioned above. One such qualification has to do with lack of consistency in the methodological data; almost any substantive datum can be shown to have been reported in biased fashion in some studies, but accurately in one or more others. Such conflicting results are characteristically accompanied by unspecified differences in the process of data collection and reduction, so that it becomes most difficult to isolate the effects of interviewing technique from those of question formulation, coding, or even selection of respondents.

Given these limitations and taking full account of the numerous encouraging exceptions, we believe that the generalization to be made with greatest confidence is that significant problems of invalidity and unreliability are common in interview data, even for apparently simple questions asked under conditions of obvious legitimacy. For example, Myers (1940) found, when he plotted an age curve for the population of the United States as reported in the decennial census, a marked "heaping" of ages ending in zero (10, 20, 30, etc.) and smaller peaks at years ending in five. Lansing, Ginsberg, and Braaten (1961) and Ferber (1959) have both shown poor reporting of bank accounts; fewer were reported than actually existed and the amounts reported differed from bank records, often in the direction of understating assets. Conversely, Lansing and Blood (1964) found an over-reporting of the number of airplane trips taken during the course of a year.

Goddard, Broder, and Wenar (1961) showed that mothers are accurate reporters of some items about the delivery and very early life of their children, but that other information about pediatric history is far from accurate. Weiss *et al.* (1961) reported similar erratic discrepancies when persons were questioned about their work history; some information corresponded closely to plant and office records, but much was in error. Cannell, Fisher, and Bakker (1961), Cannell and Fowler (1965), and Madow (1967) have shown that, in comparison with medical records, respondents underreport illness persistently but at differing rates—from 10 percent underreporting of hospitalization episodes to almost 50 percent underreporting of chronic conditions.

These studies seem to indicate that invalidity is a persistent problem in interviews and that the problem is not limited to a narrow range of data but is widespread. An intensive examination of bias studies, however, indicates that inaccuracy is not so random and unsystematic as may appear from the studies listed above.

CONTENT, TECHNIQUE, AND INVALIDITY

Let us look for order first in terms of the characteristics of the events to be reported: their accessibility to the respondent, the cognitive problems which they pose for him, and the motivational issues which they raise.

Accessibility

If the researcher were content with asking respondents how old they were, the size of their families, their education, occupation, and the like, there would be few problems of accessibility of information to respondents and, from that standpoint, few problems of validity. As soon as one asks questions about information which is not current or is not particularly relevant to the respondent's current life, problems of accuracy of report arise. In fact, when one examines the methodological studies, it is a surprise to discover how rapidly such problems arise and how serious they become in spite of apparent effort on the part of the respondent to recall and provide information. Such inaccessibility constitutes the first problem in question wording and interviewing. In a logical sense, problems of motivation do not arise at all unless data are accessible to the respondent.

Several separate issues of accessibility can be distinguished, each implying particular problems of data collection.

One aspect of accessibility has to do with memory decay or forgetting. The respondent may once have had the requested information readily available, but it has now receded from easy recollection or may be completely unavailable (Bartlett, 1932). Such decay of information is a function of elapsed time between the moment of attempted recall and the time at which the event occurred. Jaeger and Pennock (1961) reported a study in which housewives were asked the purchase date of their washing machines. The accuracy of the dating decreased sharply with the length of time the respondent had owned the machine. Weiss *et al.* (1961) demonstrated that information about jobs and job histories becomes less accurate as time increases. The proportion of known visits to doctors actually reported decreases by about one-third within a period of two weeks. Similarly, underreports of hospitalizations range from about 7 percent underreporting for the first 20 weeks to about 30 percent for the hospitalizations that occurred 41 to 53 weeks prior to the interview (Cannell, Fisher, and Bakker, 1961). Neter and Waksberg (1965) found that the date of household repairs could be reported correctly for recent occurrences, but that those occurring earlier were grossly underreported or misplaced in time.

A second aspect of accessibility which shows a strong relationship to reporting accuracy has to do with the importance or salience of the event for the person reporting. The present importance of an event can be thought of as the amount of space in one's psychic life which the event occupies at the present time. In this sense, the importance of all events is reduced by time. Nevertheless, events having great original significance for one's life are usually recalled better than minor ones, and this is true even for events that occurred some long time in the past.

Mooney (1962) showed that reported incidence of illnesses decreased as the elapsed time since illness increased from one to four weeks preceding the interview. The drop was not nearly so pronounced, however, for illness serious enough to restrict activity or require medical attention. Hospitalizations involving surgery and those of longer duration are reported significantly better than short-term, nonsurgical hospital experiences (Cannell, Fisher, and Bakker, 1961). All these data show the interaction of both factors in memory; recency and importance of events affect reporting separately and in combination.

A third characteristic of memory which is at times important to accuracy of reporting is the tendency to repress especially threatening experiences. It is not easy to determine which events are "forgotten" or are inaccessible because of repression, since the mechanisms of repression are well hidden. The explanation of repression seems most plausible, however, in situations where the usual effects of recency and importance are contravened. Janis (1958) found that hospitalized patients could not report fully their preoperative anxieties a few days after their surgery. Mothers whose infants had difficulties immediately following delivery greatly underreported this fact, although they were able to report other events surrounding the delivery with substantial accuracy (Goddard *et al.,* 1961). It is impossible to know whether this pattern of underreporting is due to repression, but it is the pattern one would predict for especially threatening events, given the hypothesis of repression as a mechanism of ego defense.

The fourth type of inaccessibility results neither from problems of memory nor repression, but rather reflects limitations in the respondent's original possession of the information sought. The interviewer who asks the respondent about the behavior or opinions of other persons typically encounters this form of the inaccessibility problem. Reporting accuracy has been shown to drop when "proxy respondents" are used (Cannell, Fisher, and Bakker, 1961; Cannell and Fowler, 1965), but the economy of such procedures in survey research makes them a continuing temptation. Under some circumstances, particularly when data are sought about families or households as units, the identification of the most appropriate respondent may be a problem in itself. The common assumption is that the "head of the household" is a better reporter than other members. Politz (1958) found, however, that it made little difference in the accuracy of data about household expenditures whether the husband or the wife served as respondent. In any event, the researcher should assure himself that his prospective respondents were at one time in possession of the information he hopes they will now reproduce. Such possession is a necessary but by no means sufficient condition for accuracy of report.

A borderline inaccessibility occurs when the respondent was exposed to the information but did not understand or comprehend it. The responses of mothers regarding the use of instruments in the delivery of their children do not agree with hospital records, and mothers' reports of the duration of labor also are substantially in error (Macfarlane, 1938; Chess *et al.*, 1960). Belloc (1954) found that while many kinds of hospital experiences were reported accurately, patients' descriptions of surgical procedures were quite inaccurate. Physical presence does not assure acquisition of information, especially if the respondent lacks relevant expertise, is handicapped by pain or illness, or is made a poor observer for reasons of emotionality.

"Remembered," "forgotten," and "never known" should not be regarded as absolute categories. "Forgotten" material can often be recalled with sufficient effort, and personal records are often available if respondents wish to consult them. There is a powerful interaction between memory and motivation. It is a common experience to be asked, for example, the date of an event and to be unable to recall it accurately. If it is important to us, we will think about the event, search out clues, look up a record, or ask another family member, and thus perhaps arrive at the correct date. This process requires time, thought, and effort. If respondents are not stimulated to devote such energy to the task of recollection, the data are more likely to be in error.

Cognition

Several cognitive factors help to determine the level of reporting accuracy. Of most importance are the respondent's understanding of his role, his comprehension of the meaning of the questions asked him, and the depth and level of specificity of the responses desired. The respondent needs to know what constitutes successful completion of his task; he needs to know the concepts and frames of reference implied by the questions, because they define the criteria of response adequacy. Without this understanding, data accessible to the respondent may go unreported. Respondent and interviewer must develop a common frame of reference, a common conceptual language, and a common understanding of what constitutes an adequate response.

Little research has been done on these cognitive problems in relation to the accuracy of interview data. What studies do exist emphasize the importance of question wording, the use of multiple questions for the measurement of each major variable, the number or adequacy of the interviewer's spontaneous probe questions, and the interviewer's direct explication of the respondent's role. All these are significant factors in the respondent's understanding of what is required of him.

In an investigation of the accuracy with which medical data are reported, the following question was asked: "Last week or the week before, did anyone in the family talk to a doctor or go to a doctor's office or clinic?" The question was intended not only to include routine office visits, but also telephone calls for medical advice and visits for inoculations or other treatments given by a nurse or technician in a doctor's office. It was intended to include calls and visits by any member of the family, whether on his own behalf or for another. The mother's call to ask the doctor about her child was to be included, whether or not the child was present. From the researcher's viewpoint this single question included all these situations, and an analysis of the words supports the claim in a literal sense. The respondents' frame of reference, however, often produced very different interpretations. Many respondents understood the question to include only personal visits, and then only when the physician himself was seen. The subsequent inclusion of probe questions asking specifically about these other events resulted in a sizable increase in the number of calls and visits reported (Cannell and Fowler, 1965). Mooney (1962) found similar improvement when supplementary questions were introduced in his studies of health and illness.

Several studies show similar problems in other content areas, when the researcher fails to take account of the respondent's frame of reference. Mauldin and Marks (1950) described efforts to obtain accurate data on education level. For many years the Bureau of the Census interviewers asked the education question in this form: "What is the highest grade of school you have completed?" Interpreted literally, this question should offer no difficulty for the vast majority of people. However, many people heard the phrase "highest grade of school" and immediately thought in terms of the highest grade of school they "went to." Some people did not even hear the final word in the question, that is, the word "completed." When interviewers obtained answers to the above question and then said, "Did you complete that grade?" a substantial number of respondents answered "No."

In the same study the authors told of asking farmers whether they had any fruit or nut trees or grapevines. Those who answered that they did not were asked whether they had even one or two trees or vines, or whether they had any not now producing fruit. To these probe questions over half the farmers who originally said they had no trees or vines now said they did. Mauldin and Marks concluded that the farmers were trying to be helpful rather than deceptive. They took it for granted that the Census enumerators would not be interested in one or two trees, especially if they were not producing.

Bancroft and Welch (1946) showed that respondents answer questions about their labor force status in terms of what they consider to be their major activity, rather than in terms of the actual wording of the question. Even if they were working part time, people who considered themselves primarily students or housewives answered "No" to the question, "Did you do any work last week for pay or profit?" A very substantial improvement in the validity of employment estimates was attained by accepting the respondents' frame of reference and building a sequence of questions which first asked for their major activity and then asked students and housewives whether they were also doing any paid work.

However, all such problems of misunderstanding do not stem from the tenacity of respondents for their preferred frames of reference. Guest (1947) and Flowerman and his colleagues (1950) reported research on the fidelity with which interviewers followed the prescribed wording of primary questions. They agreed that interviewers often changed the wording of questions, sometimes embellishing and sometimes omitting, so that the original content was distorted. The changes were seemingly made to fit the interviewer's sense of the respondent's needs or level of sophistication, but they are more plausibly interpreted as reflecting the needs of interviewers than of respondents.

Motivation

There is general agreement among students and practitioners of interviewing that the respondents' motivation or willingness to report is the most important issue in the accuracy of interview data, and that the content of the material sought has a major effect on respondent motivation. The data from methodological research are best interpreted, we believe, in terms of a postulated need on the respondent's part to maintain self-esteem, to be perceived by the interviewer as a person who does not violate important social norms in thought or act, and to present an image of consistency and worthiness.

For example, Lamale (1959), analyzing the accuracy of data on consumer expenditures, concluded that respondents' reports are quite accurate for the annual expenditures on gas and electricity, rent, automobile purchase, and medical care, but are substantially inaccurate for purchases of alcoholic beverages. Respondents consistently underreport liquor consumption. Lamale cited other studies with similar patterns of bias. We have already noted that reports of work history become less accurate over time. The pattern of inaccuracies involves an upgrading of the work history—higher level of job and higher pay reported than shown in the records.

Lansing and Blood (1964) interpreted the overreporting of plane trips in the same terms; plane travel is, according to them, still prestigeful. Conversely, they found that automobile loans are underreported and that the rate of underreporting is greatest among high-income respondents, for whom such loans might seem inappropriate and embarrassing. In general, respondents in upper-income groups reported savings accounts more accurately than others, and cash loans less accurately.

Wenar (1963) reported that mothers distort facts of their children's developmental history, and that they do so in ways that make the children appear precocious. Similarly, the reports of mothers regarding their own child-training practices tend to conform more closely to the advice of pediatricians than is justified by data from other sources.

Clark and Wallin (1964) describe an example of response bias stemming from a different respondent need. They compared the individual reporting of husbands and wives on the frequency of sexual intercourse and found that the agreement was close for partners who expressed satisfaction with their sexual relations. Those who expressed dissatisfaction showed a greater discrepancy in report. Those who wanted more frequent sexual contacts tended also to report a lower frequency of marital coitus.

Earlier research showed the same pattern of ego-enhancing distortion with respect to issues then relevant. Twila Neely (1937) found, for example, that one out of every nine families receiving city relief failed to report this fact when asked the specific question in the course of an interview. In another study she found that victims of auto accidents tended to exaggerate the amount of work time they had lost, and to report inaccurately the amount of pay lost.

Hyman *et al.* (1954) reported several such studies. In one study, made during World War II, he found that in the upper-income groups nearly half the respondents who had cashed government bonds during the previous week failed to report having done so, on being asked directly.

Parry and Crossley (1950) reported a study in which five sets of experienced interviewers took more than 900 interviews in a single community. These interviews included data on a number of the respondents' characteristics that could be checked from objective sources. On almost every topic, significant differences were found between the data obtained by interview and those obtained from the records of appropriate agencies, with both magnitude and direction of difference suggesting the factor of social acceptability, among others. The differences are summarized in Table 1.

TABLE 1

INACCURACY OF REPORT IN RELATION TO SUBJECT MATTER

Subject	Respondents giving inaccurate reports
Contributions to Community Chest	40%
Voting and registration	25
Age	17
Ownership of library card	10
Ownership of driver's license	10
Home ownership	4
Auto ownership	3
Possession of telephone	2

Cobb and Cannell (1966) reported a comparison of two more recent studies, one in which college students were asked how willing they would be to have their friends know if they had a particular disease (column 1 of Table 2), and the second showing the proportion of known medical conditions reported in a household interview (column 2).

The respondent populations which generated these two sets of data are grossly different, of course—a sample of 79 college students from the University of Michigan and a sample of 1388 households drawn from the membership records of the Health Insurance Plan of Greater New York. Nevertheless, the rank-order correlation between column 1 and column 2 is perfect for serious conditions and very substantial for less serious conditions. The latter are less well reported than some of the serious diseases, and are also less affected by willingness to report.

TABLE 2

HYPOTHETICAL WILLINGNESS TO REPORT MEDICAL CONDITIONS IN RELATION TO PERCENTAGE OF CASES ACTUALLY REPORTED

Conditions	Percent willing to report (79 students)	Percent reported* (1388 households)
More serious conditions		
1. Asthma	84%	71%
2. Heart disease	58	60
3. Hernia	55	54
4. Malignant neoplasm	31	33
5. Mental disease	19	25
6. Genito-urinary disease	14	22
Less serious conditions		
1. Sinusitis	89	48
2. Indigestion	88	41
3. Hypertension	83	46
4. Varicose veins	65	42
5. Hemorrhoids	21	38

* Conditions with a frequency of less than 30 percent were excluded as providing unstable estimates of percentage reported.

Studies of the interaction of cognitive and motivational factors in relation to interview validity are rare, but one such is reported by Cannell and his colleagues (1961). Their study was focused primarily on problems of underreporting of hospital episodes, and the sample consisted of 1491 persons who had been hospitalized at some time during the year preceding the interview, in one of 21 hospitals throughout the country. The records of the hospital were treated as final evidence of hospitalization in each case; thus a comparison of interview data with the hospital record for the same individual provided the basis for estimating underreport (or overreport, but this was so rare as to be unimportant).

Table 3 presents the main findings of the research and makes clear the separate and combined effects of recency (number of weeks since discharge), importance (duration of hospitalization), and diagnostic rating (degree of threat judged to be associated with the disease and treatment). The latter is interpreted as affecting respondent motivation, although other interpretations (for example, repression) are certainly plausible.

TABLE 3

PERCENTAGE OF UNDERREPORTING OF HOSPITAL EPISODES IN RELATION TO LENGTH OF STAY, RECENCY, AND DIAGNOSTIC RATING

Length of stay and number of weeks between discharge and interview	Number of episodes recorded	*Diagnostic rating,* %		
		Most threat-ening	Somewhat threat-ening	Least threat-ening
Stay of 1–4 days				
Discharge 1–20 weeks before interview	223	7	9	7
Discharge 21–40 weeks before interview	355	26	16	9
Discharge 41–53 weeks before interview	219	56	27	27
Stay of 5+ days				
Discharge 1–20 weeks before interview	308	0	7	3
Discharge 21–40 weeks before interview	442	15	5	5
Discharge 41–53 weeks before interview	273	33	22	17

The data are a sharp reminder of the validity problems of the interview. Recency makes a substantial difference, with the percentage of underreporting rising from relatively low levels (0–9) to relatively high ones (17–56) as the time since hospitalization increases. The degree of threat of the illness is almost as potent a factor, with the percentage of underreport increasing as threat increases. Length of stay, interpreted as reflecting memory and accessibility uncomplicated by phenomena of repression, operates in a direction opposite to the threat factor; the longer the hospitalization, the less the percentage of underreporting. In short, elapsed time since the event being reported, the threat associated with the event, and the brevity or unimportance of the event all act significantly against validity, and there are additional interaction effects when they act in combination. The underreport for recent, nonthreatening hospitalizations of long duration was only 3 percent; for less recent, threatening hospitalizations of short duration, underreport was 56 percent.

INTERVIEWER AND RESPONDENT CHARACTERISTICS AS SOURCES OF BIAS

The foregoing studies imply that much of the bias in interview data can be explained in terms of the content sought and its demands on the respondent. Other studies have examined problems of invalidity in interview data in terms of certain characteristics of interviewers or respondents. These studies first demonstrated the fragile nature of the interview and its susceptibility to unintended influence.

One of the earliest of such researches showed a correlation between interviewers' attitudes and the data they reported obtaining from respondents (Rice, 1929). In working with some survey data, Rice was struck by the fact that the interviews from one interviewer seemed similar to each other in certain respects and consistently different from the results obtained by another interviewer. The purpose of the study was to determine causes of destitution, and the respondents were transients in flophouses and cheap hotels. The men interviewed by one interviewer consistently cited overindulgence in liquor as a cause of their destitution, whereas the respondents of a second interviewer tended to blame social and industrial conditions. Rice's suspicions were confirmed and a motif for methodological research was set when he discovered that the first interviewer was a prohibitionist and the second a socialist!

Cahalan, Tamulonis, and Verner (1947) reported a study in which interviews taken by more than 100 different interviewers were tabulated separately. About three-fourths of the 51 interview questions showed significant differences in the responses obtained by different interviewers. Many of these differences were in the direction of the interviewers' own opinions. Apparently, the interviewers tended to see respondents in their own image.

A study by Ferber and Wales (1952) on opinions toward prefabricated houses showed that the respondents of interviewers who favored such housing themselves were more favorable to prefabricated houses than were respondents of interviewers who were unfavorable. Blankenship (1940) reported similar results in 300 interviews dealing with political attitudes. Of the 31 questions on the questionnaire, seven showed significant interviewer differences and three were in the direction of the interviewer's own attitudes.

The model of interaction in the interview proposed earlier (Fig. 1) presents our interpretation of the ways in which respondent and interviewer characteristics may interact to generate biased data. Each person comes to the interview with many fixed attitudes, personality characteristics, and stereotypes of other groups. Both respondent and interviewer also possess characteristics visible to the other and suggestive of group memberships and group identifications—age, sex, race, religious background, income, and educational status. Such background characteristics enter into the interaction of the interview in two ways (Kahn and Cannell, 1957).

1. Background characteristics can be regarded as the source of many attitudes, perceptions, expectations, and motives. For example, individuals of high socio-economic status tend to be somewhat more favorable toward management and more critical of labor unions than people at the other end of the socioeconomic scale. The extent to which an individual's age determines his attitudes toward many topics is so much a part of day-to-day observation that little documentation is needed. In the same way, the other background factors—education, race, sex, religion, etc.—play their part in determining the psychological characteristics of interviewer and respondent, including those perceptions, attitudes, and motives that have particular relevance for the interview process. If the interviewer and respondent are widely divergent in their background characteristics, we would anticipate widely differing attitudes and motives. Such divergence makes mutual understanding more difficult, and may limit seriously the interaction that can take place between the two.

2. Background characteristics also affect interviewer-respondent interaction through the cues that such characteristics provide to each participant about the other. If, for example, the respondent perceives the interviewer to be of a different race, this perception may have profound effects on his attitude toward the interviewer, on his behavior toward the interviewer, and therefore on the results of the interview itself.

These kinds of cues are as important for the interviewer as for the respondent. They provide the interviewer with some of the earliest cues to which he may react. The respondent's skin color or facial cast, his apparent economic status, and other observable characteristics may lead the interviewer to certain expectations regarding the respondent's probable attitudes on certain topics, his level of information in various fields, and the like.

In summary, then, background factors are important in the interview because they constitute a kind of subsoil in which many of an individual's attitudes, motives, and perceptions have direct roots. But the background characteristics of each participant in the interview have additional importance because they provide cues for the other participant. Certain attitudes, motives, and stereotypes are triggered in the respondent's mind by his perception that the interviewer possesses certain background characteristics. The interviewer may be influenced in the same fashion by his initial perceptions of the respondent. Such reactions may in turn influence the behavior of both participants.

Many studies demonstrate the effects of background factors on response validity. For example, Hyman *et al.* (1954) reported a study in which Negro and white interviewers each interviewed a random sample of Negroes on problems of discrimination. Negro interviewers obtained significantly more information on resentment over discrimination than did the white interviewers.

Robinson and Rohde (1946) conducted an experiment in which several groups of selected interviewers were assigned to interview samples of New York City householders on the subject of attitudes toward Jews. One group of interviewers included persons who were judged to be non-Semitic in appearance and in name.

A second group included interviewers who were judged to be Semitic in appearance but non-Semitic in name; a third group of interviewers consisted of persons who were judged to be Semitic in both appearance and name. The responses obtained by these interviewers showed significant differences among the three groups with respect to the number of expressed anti-Semitic attitudes or stereotyped anti-Jewish statements obtained in the course of discussing attitudes toward Jews with their respondents. Robinson and Rohde concluded that the more likely respondents were to identify the interviewers as Jewish, the less likely they were to make anti-Semitic statements in the course of the interview. Respondents apparently were motivated to avoid making statements which they anticipated would be painful to the interviewer or of which the interviewer would disapprove.

Katz (1942) found that interviewers from working-class backgrounds consistently obtained more radical social and political opinions from respondents than did interviewers from the middle class. The differences were marked on labor issues, particularly among respondents who were members of trade unions. For example, working-class interviewers found that 44 percent of their respondents favored a law against sit-down strikes; the middle-class interviewers found that 59 percent favored such a law.

Erlich and Riesman (1961) found that the age of the interviewer had an effect on information reported by adolescent girls. Older interviewers obtained fewer reports of behavior undesirable by middle-class adult standards. Adolescent respondents interviewed by older interviewers also reported greater adherence to parental instructions than respondents reporting to younger interviewers.

Williams (1964), in a study of Negro respondents, concluded that racial difference between interviewers and respondents is a potentially biasing factor, but that the bias becomes actual and significant only as the perceived social distance becomes great and the interview content threatening.

AVOIDANCE OF BIAS

The avoidance of bias and the attainment of valid measurement is the underlying subject of this entire chapter. A few generalizations can be derived, however, from the preceding examples of methodological research. To the extent that bias is associated with certain kinds of substantive questions, one can avoid the risk of bias by eliminating such content from the interview, in favor of other material or other methods of data collection. Such a strategy of renunciation is not likely to appeal to research workers, but it has its place.

To the extent that bias is associated with certain interviewer characteristics and behaviors, it can be avoided or reduced by devising procedures that reduce the amount of interviewer improvisation, by selecting and assigning interviewers in ways that minimize undesirable interaction with respondents, and by developing and training interviewers in techniques that maximize respondent motivation and minimize cues with respect to differential acceptability of relevant responses.

In survey research the outstanding example of building bias-free procedures that circumvent the interviewer and his demonstrably biased judgment is the development of procedures for probability sampling of respondents (Kish, 1965). The earlier and more inexpensive procedure of having interviewers select survey respondents to fit quotas defined in terms of demographic characteristics is conspicuously bias-prone.

There is also ample evidence for the feasibility of reducing interviewer biases by means of training. In one of the early researches on the subject, Stanton and Baker (1942) presented a number of geometric designs to an experimental population of 200 students. Several days later, in an interview situation, the students were shown the designs they had seen in combination with an equal number which they had not seen, and were asked to select from the total array those they had previously studied. The interviewers utilized for this task had some polling experience but no specific training. Before they began interviewing, however, the interviewers were told that certain designs had been seen by the respondents. In fact the interviewers were given false information, which identified some of the new designs as having been previously seen. In general the interviewers obtained results significantly biased toward what they thought to be correct responses, although the bias did not affect all interviewers. A replication of the Stanton and Baker research was conducted by Friedman (1942), using interviewers who were explicitly trained to avoid the intrusion of their own expectations into the process of data collection. The results showed no significant tendency toward the incorporation of the misleading information in the interviews.

Neither probability sampling, the careful formulation of questions in advance of the interview, the use of "nonleading" or "nondirective" interview techniques, the careful selection and training of interviewers—nor all of these together—can guarantee validity of interview data. They can, however, increase significantly the range and quality of the interview as a source of data. The remainder of the chapter is given over to a more detailed consideration of these procedures.

THE FORMULATION OF QUESTIONS

The research worker judges interview questions in terms of their adequacy as instruments of measurement, that is, in terms of their validity, reliability, and precision. The actual assessment of these properties may be difficult, as the preceding section of this chapter suggests, but the logic for determining measurement adequacy is straightforward (see pp. 533–535).

To discuss the formulation of questions (developing an instrument of measurement) as distinct from interviewing itself (using the instrument) is already to engage in controversy with those who consider question formulation and question asking as aspects of a single process. Certainly the two are closely related, and the relationship is particularly apparent when the same person is performing the functions of question formulation and question asking in rapid succession, as anthropologists do habitually and social psychologists do at least in the early phases of investigation. Even when question formulation and data collection are conspicuously separated in time and space and by the division of labor, the connection remains. The instrument both limits and assists the interviewer, and the interviewer necessarily modifies the instrument and the accompanying rules in the very act of using them.

We shall assume that such separation is characteristic of social-psychological research, that the interviewer approaches the respondent equipped with questions that he will ask verbatim and with procedures for clarification and enlargement on those questions. The use of such predetermined questions does not ensure the presentation of an equivalent stimulus to each respondent, but this is a minor problem compared to the uncontrolled and almost unknowable variance of interviewing *ad lib*. The burden is thus on the researcher to provide questions that can be used verbatim, and that contribute to the conditions of cognition, accessibility, and motivation described earlier. Question wording is relevant to all of these, but it is crucial for respondent cognition.

COGNITIVE FACTORS IN QUESTION FORMULATION

The formulation of questions involves complicated cognitive processes. We want to obtain comparable information about the experience of many respondents, and yet this experience is uniquely organized for each individual. Events are not merely absorbed into human experience; rather, each individual perceives and organizes the events of his life into meaningful patterns in characteristic ways and at levels of conceptualization which reflect his education and background as well as more idiosyncratic factors. The cognitive task in question formulation is to find ways of evoking that diverse experience by the presentation of uniform questions. Cognitive factors in question formulation thus include problems of communication, frame of reference, language, and the conceptual level of questions.

Language

In the construction of questions the primary criterion for the choice of language is that the vocabulary and syntax offer the maximum opportunity for complete and accurate communication of ideas between the researcher (or interviewer) and the respondent. The language of the question must conform to the vocabulary level of the respondent. Interview questions need not imitate the colloquialisms and linguistic informalities of the respondent, but they must be understandable to him even though he himself might have expressed their content in different words. Ultimately, the choice of language should be made from the shared vocabulary of respondent and researcher. The shared vocabulary may be large or small, depending on the characteristics of the individuals involved and the subject matter of the investigation.

The social scientist sampling the national population finds himself severely restricted with respect to language. Linguists estimate that the average American adult knows fewer than ten percent of the words in the English language, and the vocabulary held in common by heterogeneous population samples would be still smaller. Other language problems between researchers and respondents have to do not with vocabulary level but with differences in the use of words, usually reflecting factors of geography, age, education, or socioeconomic background. In some sections of the United States evening begins at sunset, for others at one or two in the afternoon. Dinner refers to a meal, but of what elaborateness and at what time of day varies from region to region. The slang of the parents' era is a source of amusement to the teenager, and the language of adolescence is a mystery for the parents. Communication can occur across the boundaries of age and background, but the form and content of questions is limited by the shared vocabulary between researcher and respondent. How large that shared vocabulary must be will depend on the subject matter, complexity, and conceptual level of the topics under investigation. The issue is not the size of the shared vocabulary, but its adequacy for communicating material required by the research objectives.

The process of formulating questions for cross-sectional studies usually means simplification of words and ideas to the level of the least sophisticated respondent. One of the researcher's biggest problems is to express abstract concepts in terms that unsophisticated respondents can understand. The frequency of this situation is reflected in the bulk of the literature on question formulation, which emphasizes the need to simplify language. The most frequent error of the inexperienced researcher in formulating questions continues to be the confusion of respondents with linguistic and conceptual complexities.

Nevertheless, the goal of simplification is to approximate the language level of the respondent, not merely to simplify. Suppose that we were to conduct a study among physicians to discover the ways in which they keep themselves informed about new medical techniques. The interview schedule for such a study would bear little resemblance in language level and degree of simplicity to the interview schedules required for broad, heterogeneous respondent populations. To begin with, the general vocabulary of the physician is more extensive than that of the population as a whole because of the breadth of his education and experience. In addition, physicians share among themselves a highly specialized vocabulary for the description of medical content and procedures. Moreover, this vocabulary is considerably more precise, as well as more comprehensive, than the language a layman might employ for the description of medical phenomena. The obvious course of action on the part of the researcher is to make the most of this specialized and precise language. Indeed, it would appear to the physician respondents both inefficient and irritating if the researcher failed to show some appropriate knowledge of their scientific vocabulary.

The problem of oversimplification is serious even in less specialized circumstances. The sophisticated respondent can understand an oversimplified question but may well resent it as an insulting underestimate of his intellectual capacity. As Payne (1951) suggests, one person in 100 may not understand the term "income tax." For him we might ask "How do you feel about your income tax, that is, the amount you have to pay the government on the money you take in during the year?" For the remaining 99 percent such a wording would be redundant if not insulting.

Thus the researcher is typically searching for compromises that take into account the content of the interview and the characteristics of the people to be interviewed. His problem is complicated further by the fact that, without previous experience with the groups to be sampled, he may be ignorant of their vocabulary and level of conceptual sophistication. If he uses words beyond the understanding of the respondent, his information will suffer for cognitive reasons. Furthermore, the respondent may react to the language difficulty as implying a gap between himself and the interviewer that cannot easily be bridged. He may conclude that it is useless to attempt to communicate with someone who cannot really understand him. Like oversimplified questions, the overdifficult tend to lower respondent motivation to communicate.

But how does the researcher know whether his language is on target, understandable, and appropriate? Such knowledge comes mainly from experience with groups to which communication will be attempted. One of the principal reasons for pretesting questions is to discover whether or not they are understood and communicate the research objectives to respondents. Such trial and revision should be routine.

Frame of reference

Whitehead (1929) once wrote that "language is always ambiguous as to the exact proposition which it indicates." The basic reason for the ambiguity of language is that each individual necessarily interprets spoken or written communication from his own experience and personal viewpoint. As a result, in some degree the meaning which an individual attaches to a communication must be uniquely his own and not shared by others.

Communications differ in the extent to which they demand interpretation by their recipients, and in the extent to which they invite idiosyncratic interpretation. On the whole, the more fragmentary and ambiguous the stimulus, the more the individual has to draw on his own experience and point of view in order to give the stimulus meaning. Suppose, for example, we meet an acquaintance on the street and greet him with the standard American colloquialism, "How are things going?" Our question provides him with almost no frame of reference except an invitation to respond in general terms of satisfaction or dissatisfaction. Moreover, we have no way of knowing from his reply of "Fine," or "So-so," or "Not so good," whether he is answering our question in terms of his job, the state of his wife's health, or the fact that his favorite ball team just lost a game. He has provided his own frame of reference in order to answer our question, but the chances are that we have few clues to the context from which he replied.

In some cases the frame of reference is implied by the role relationship of the people involved in the communication, so that a verbal stimulus no more specific than that given in the previous example may acquire a more precise frame of reference. Suppose that the same question—"How are things going?"—is put to a man by his supervisor on the job. The ambiguity of the verbal stimulus is considerably reduced by the role relationship of the two persons involved and the content of their joint work. A specific frame of reference is provided, not by the words used, but by the shared knowledge that when the supervisor in the shop asks how things are going he is thinking about the job, not about the worker's family affairs or financial situation.

Sometimes the respondent is so dominated by his own immediate needs that all communications tend to be interpreted in relation to these needs. Such strong needs then determine his frame of reference. The father whose son is fighting in a war may be so concerned about the son's welfare that he is unable to discuss current affairs in any other context. The worker who has an acute grievance with his foreman may be quite unable to discuss any aspect of the work situation without getting into the nature of his grievance, or at least permitting the emotion generated by that grievance to condition his discussion of other aspects of the work situation. For many topics, however, the respondent's frame of reference is less idiosyncratic; it may reflect national or regional characteristics, membership in other subcultures, occupational groups, social classes, or the like. The New Yorker and the rural Arkansan are likely to disagree on whether Little Rock is a big city; the Alaskan and the Texan will have different ideas of what constitutes a hot summer; the airline pilot and the timid passenger will have different answers when asked whether a trip was pleasant and uneventful.

In formulating questions the research worker has only three possibilities with respect to the frame-of-reference problem. He can ignore it, he can attempt to ascertain it, or he can attempt to control it. The first is risky and often leads to difficult problems of interpretation. The second and third deserve more consideration.

Our reason for wanting to ascertain the frame of reference within which a respondent answers a question is straightforward; we will be able to interpret his response more fully and accurately in the light of this information. The most common means for ascertaining frame of reference are no less straightforward; we follow a primary question about attitudes or intentions or behavior with a secondary one: "Why?"

For example, an interview study of fertility and family size might include questions on the plans and attitudes of husband and wife toward having more children, and the answers to such questions might provide some basis for improved population projections. But interpretation of the responses would be restricted. Are people who want no further increases in family thinking of economic problems or the threat of war? Are they concerned with overpopulation, health, or the prospect of leisure? Any of these is plausible and all are reasonably accessible to the "why" question. No other single probe can give us so much of the respondent's frame of reference or add so much to the accurate interpretation of his answers.

Nevertheless, the task of ascertaining frame of reference can be cumbersome, and the researcher probably is more often interested in controlling it. Without taking much interviewing time to make a particular frame of reference explicit to the respondent and without attempting to ascertain the frame of reference each respondent is using, the researcher wants nevertheless to be reasonably confident that the respondent answers the question within the terms of reference the researcher had in mind when he formulated it. Moreover, if many respondents are to be interviewed, the researcher wants to be sure that each of them is answering the question from the same frame of reference, so that their responses are comparable.

One way of exerting such control is to incorporate some specific frame of reference as part of the question. In effect the respondent is instructed, as part of the question, with respect to the frame of reference which he is to employ. A phrase is sometimes sufficient for this purpose. For example, we might say to a respondent in a survey, "How have you people been getting along this year? Financially, I mean." The parenthetical "Financially, I mean" is simply an instruction to the respondent to use the economic frame of reference rather than answering in terms of health, family arrangements, job situation, or any other terms that might be paramount in his own mind. A common type of question in industrial studies is, "Compared to other plants in this area, how satisfied are you with this one?" The first phrase sets the frame of reference for the respondent.

As an alternative to requiring such adaptation by the respondent, the researcher may formulate questions which accept a frame of reference common to his respondent population—provided, of course, that he knows what it is or can infer it from the responses themselves. Indeed, it is sometimes necessary to allow the respondent to answer a question in his own terms before it becomes feasible to propose a different frame of reference.

Bancroft and Welch (1946) provided a classic illustration of this point, in a study cited in our summary of research on reliability and validity (pp. 540–549). They found that the series of questions used by the Bureau of the Census to ascertain the number of people in the labor market consistently underestimated the number of employed persons. When asked the question, "Did you do any work for pay or profit last week?" respondents reported in terms of what they considered their major activity, in spite of the explicit defining phrase "for pay or profit." Young people attending college considered themselves to be students even if they were also employed on a part-time basis. Women who cooked, cleaned house, and raised children spoke of themselves as housewives, even if they also did some work for pay outside the home. The effect of the respondents' frame of reference was to classify as nonworkers many thousands of people who met the census definition of workers. The solution involved revising the questions, beginning with the acceptance of the respondent's classification of himself. People were asked first what their major activity was; those who gave nonworker responses were asked whether in addition to their major activity they did any work for pay. The effect of this change was to raise the official estimate of employment by more than a million persons.

It is instructive for the question writer to keep in mind the issues involved in the distortion which Bancroft and Welch reported. The respondents' frames of reference with respect to what constituted work were different from that of the researchers who formulated the questions. Respondents tended to consider as work only those jobs which made up their major activity during the week. The research people had defined as work any service performed for pay during the week, even if the proportion of the respondent's time devoted to this activity was extremely small. The result of this difference in frame of reference meant that the simple word "work" failed to communicate to the respondent the meaning which the researchers intended. As a result the respondent's answer, accurate enough in terms of his own frame of reference, was in error with respect to the frame of reference of the researchers.

Conceptual level

Closely related to language and frame of reference is the problem of conceptual level. A respondent may have information to provide and may understand the language of a question, yet he may find it difficult to respond if the question asks for a conceptual organization of material which he has not attempted. As a result, he is likely to be reluctant to try and inept if he does so. Consider such questions as the following: "Is your closest friend an introvert or an extrovert?" Even if the respondent has the necessary words in his vocabulary to make sense of this question, a great deal of work might be necessary for him in order to organize his own experience and feelings in response to it. The respondent may have some notion of the extreme introvert as a person who tries to avoid interacting with others, and he may have a great deal of information about the behavior of his closest friend. Nevertheless, he has not organized his observations and feelings about his friend around the concept of introversion. He has only a very limited understanding of the term, and less skill in using it to order his own experience.

Such problems of conceptual level can also be considered as failures of the researcher to operationalize his concepts adequately. Consider, for example, the question, "How is morale in the office where you work?" Morale may be the concept which the researcher has chosen to measure but his operation for measuring it, if it is to be successful, must go beyond simply presenting the concept in the form of a question to a respondent. The researcher may find that, in order to tap the respondent's relevant knowledge in this area, he must ask such questions as: "When the workload is unusually high in your office, do people tend to help each other out or is it every man for himself?" Or, "If you had the opportunity to do the same kind of work for the same pay in a different office, how would you feel about moving?" The research interviewer is not limited, of course, to questions for which the respondent has already done the work of cognitive organization. Such work can be undertaken during the interview, but doing so increases substantially the effort and motivation required of the respondent.

The single idea

One of the traditional advices to the researcher has been to avoid "double-barreled questions" and use only questions with a single idea. The advice is still relevant and the error still common. It is in a sense a variation on the frame-of-reference theme already discussed. The double-barreled question is ambiguous with respect to its referent, and the response is correspondingly difficult to interpret.

The importance of the single idea in question writing can be readily illustrated by the following question taken from a hypothetical survey of urban and suburban trends: "How do you feel about the development of a rapid transit system between the central city and the suburbs, and the redevelopment of central city residential areas?" The respondent who is confronted with this question has several possibilities, all of them complex. Suppose that he feels very differently about the two solutions to metropolitan living proposed in the question; he is much in favor of improved transportation, but he feels that the attempt to bring the suburbanites permanently back to city residence is impractical and ridiculous. He can, if he chooses to do so, undertake the task of instructing the interviewer about his views on these two aspects of the question; in so doing the respondent in effect rewrites the questionnaire by breaking the original "double-barreled" question into two single-idea questions. If all respondents could be depended on to undertake such tasks, no damage would be done. A more likely outcome, however, is that the respondent will focus on the aspect of the question which is most important to him, and give an overall response to the question without informing the interviewer as to the structure of his opinions. Such a respondent, if he were strongly in favor of improved suburban transportation, might simply answer, "I think that's a good idea," neglecting to inform the interviewer of his opposition to the urban redevelopment scheme. When the time came to code and analyze such a response, there would be no basis for distinguishing it from the response of a person who was genuinely in favor of both aspects of the proposal.

The emphasis on the single idea rests primarily on cognitive grounds; it avoids unintended ambiguity in the stimulus and consequent uncertainty about the respondent's frame of reference. But there are motivational implications as well. We must assume that, whenever a respondent is confronted in the process of data collection with a task which strikes him as unreasonable, poorly formulated, or inappropriate to his skills and situation, there will be some negative motivational consequence. Even if the respondent undertakes to compensate for the ambiguities in question formulation by explaining the structure of his opinions, he is likely to reach some negative conclusions regarding the skills and competence of the researchers and to experience some consequent reduction in motivation. In short, the respondent who is confronted with "double-barreled" questions becomes less certain of his role requirements; his task is unclear, and his mood is likely to be one of annoyance and minor frustration.

ACCESSIBILITY AND QUESTION FORMULATION

Accessibility and inaccessibility have to do with the respondent's possession of information, and include problems of several different kinds. A respondent may never have known the facts, had the experiences, or developed the attitudes in which the researcher is interested. In such cases problems of question wording are secondary, although it is worth noting that many people find nay-saying un-pleasant and attempt to avoid it. If the interview questions are of the short-answer, "closed" form, it is relatively easy for respondents to offer inaccurate but ego-maintaining answers. Open questions are less vulnerable to this particular kind of bias.

However, the researcher confronted with persistent problems of inaccessibility should consider other remedies than reformulation of questions. One such remedy is to select a more appropriate person to be interviewed, provided, of course, that doing so does not compromise some other aspect of the research. (This is not to be construed, for example, as a justification for quota sampling.) Household interviewing has too often been done without designation of a respondent other than "responsible adult." In general, respondents are more accurate in reporting their own behaviors than in reporting behaviors of other family members. Data on family expenditures and buying intentions indicate that in many families some one individual has the responsibility for financial matters. The implication for the researcher is that he should select the respondent most qualified to provide the information he requires. An alternative is to devise some procedure, such as consulting of records by the respondent during the interview, which makes addi-tional information available to the respondent.

Problems of memory

But let us assume that we have selected appropriate respondents and are pre-paring to formulate questions by means of which to get information from them. Each respondent once possessed the information or had the experience which is to be the subject of our questions. Our problem now, so far as accessibility is con-cerned, is to bring the relevant events to the consciousness of the respondent. If the event is both recent and from the respondent's point of view significant, it may require no more than the communication of our intention to bring the episode fully into his memory. If the elapsed time since the event is greater or the event unimportant, our problem will be correspondingly more difficult. In part, this is a problem of the gradual decay which studies of memory have long since made apparent (Bartlett, 1932; Boring, 1950). Events of trivial significance for the respondent may be forgotten almost as quickly as they occur. Even experi-ences which were prominent for him, however, are likely to be forgotten if they have little relevance to his current life. The adult is unlikely to remember the age at which he developed chicken pox, even though the event may have had dramatic importance for him at the time in his childhood when it occurred. He may have forgotten the exact income which he earned on his first job, although at the time it was one of the more important things in his life. For such routine matters as one's breakfast menu or the content of the previous evening's television programs, recollection may be gone within a matter of hours. In short, the material which a respondent is likely to find accessible to him will be a complex function of elapsed time since the event, current cues or relevance for his present affairs, and the significance of the event in his life.

The major effect of these processes is reduction in the amount of information available to the researcher. In the extreme case, the reduction is complete; the respondent is completely unable to recall the event, and it remains forever inaccessible. Unfortunately for the accuracy of descriptive research data and the progress of social science, however, the process of memory decay is not uniform and orderly. The events of the past do not fade gradually from view while retaining their original proportions and major outline. On the contrary, the process of remembering and forgetting involves considerable distortion from the original event and experience. Certain aspects are dropped from view, others are elevated to prominence, and the entire past is recalled in a way which makes it more plausible and consistent in terms of the present experience of the respondent. To some extent, distortions of this kind seem to represent a tendency toward consistency and organization which are not in the service of any particular respondent motive. For example, Withey (1952) has found that the statements of people regarding income earned in previous years tend to distort in the direction of making previous income closer to current income.

Related to, and perhaps inseparable from, this selective process of memory decay is the distortion of previous experience in the general service of ego enhancement and maintenance of self-esteem. Janis (1958) has found that among patients who have undergone surgery there is a substantial postoperative failure to recall the amount and the manifestations of preoperative anxiety. The interpretation he makes is that such recollection is not only painful for the respondent but presents him as displaying a lack of fortitude that is inconsistent with his self-image, and that he wishes and needs to forget. A similar pattern is apparent when we ask people the reasons which led them to leave the first job they ever held. The aggregate responses to this question show a pattern of blamelessness and voluntarism which is plausible for any individual case but impossible in totality. People apparently forget, repress, or at least refrain from reporting leaving jobs because of inadequate performance, unsuccessful competition with peers, petty theft, and the like. We suspect that such distortions do not so much represent conscious reporting of false information as unconscious repression of facts intolerable to the self. Whichever is the case, the process occurs even for events much less ego-relevant than job loss. Studies of political behavior have provided outstanding examples of such distortion. National samples of voters have been asked in many such studies to name the candidate for whom they voted in previous Presidential elections. The longer the elapsed time since an election, the greater is the overreport of votes for the successful candidate. Again, the surrounding qualitative material makes this appear to be less a question of deliberate falsification than of unconscious distortion of previous events into a more reassuring and ego-supportive form. In short, a number of complex processes are going on simultaneously, and in combination determine and affect the accessibility of information to the researcher. These processes have to do with the initial importance of an event, and its pleasure or pain for the respondent; they have to do also with the characteristic strain toward congruence and plausibility in previous experience; finally, they have to do with the defensive capacities of the self and with the familiar processes of repression, rationalization, and the other ego defenses.

Several ways of formulating questions are useful in dealing with problems of forgotten events, repressed experiences, and other such material. The researcher's first aim is to increase the accessibility of such content to the respondent in undistorted form. He can do this by asking the respondent to consult records (when this is appropriate), by providing a context and sequence of questions that helps the respondent to reconstruct the past, by alerting the respondent to the problem of bias in recall, by wording questions that require recognition rather than recall, and by utilizing indirect rather than direct questions.

The consultation of records is feasible only for certain inquiries, of course. It it worth mention, however, because it is utilized so seldom, even for material which is a matter of record. Bank deposits, family income, mortgage debt and payments, and many other forms of consumer expenditure are typically recorded, and the records kept in many households. Dates of birth, of moving, of acquiring a new residence or job are also commonly documented. It is possible for an interview question to include a request for such verification, and the contribution to reliability and validity of report is very substantial. Researchers have often avoided such questions for fear of refusals, but they have been used routinely in some national samples with good results.

The providing of context can sometimes be done in a phrase or two that helps a respondent to locate an event in time or space, and thus bring it into recollection. For example, a question about voting behavior in the 1948 Presidential election might begin by reminding the respondent that it was the election in which Truman defeated Dewey. An inquiry about job history might ask the respondent to recall the time and place of his leaving school, and move from that to the first job.

Another possibility that seems psychologically plausible, but for which no evidence is available, is to alert the respondent to the problem of distortion. For example, consider the following: "Most men tend to exaggerate their athletic accomplishments as boys, but we would like to know . . . "; "As you may know, more people remember voting for winning candidates than the records bear out, but we are trying to find out . . . "; "Many childhood fears are forgotten, but try to remember whether you ever . . . ."

Probably the most common and perhaps the most effective way of formulating questions to assist memory is to ask for recognition rather than recall. The physician who takes a medical history does not merely ask the patient to mention present or early diseases. He presents the patient with a list, one item at a time, in order to stimulate memory. Social research, in this respect at least, can learn from the technique of the medical interview. Recollection of books read, people met, places visited, events witnessed, and the like is greatly assisted by the presentation of a list, verbally or in writing, from which the respondent can make choices. Other sources of bias may be risked in the process—the yea-saying or nay-saying respondent is particularly dangerous when presented with such temptations—but memory is unquestionably stimulated. The main advantages of the closed form of questioning in comparison to the open form is that the task of response is often reduced thereby from recall and composition of reply to recognition and simple choice. The old controversy of open versus closed questions is discussed in a later section. Its present relevance is that the closed form tends to facilitate the accessibility of "forgotten" material.

Finally, the problems of memory and repression can be dealt with by means of indirect questions. One strength of the indirect approach is that it permits inferences about inaccessible material, based on more accessible data. When a respondent tells a story based on the verbal or pictorial presentation of a TAT theme, he is providing accessible reactions which are of interest only insofar as they provide bases for inference about less accessible characteristics—his needs for power, affiliation, or achievement, for example. To ask directly about the strength of these needs would be to present him with severe difficulties of data accessibility, as well as problems of cognition and motivation. Since the issue of direct versus indirect question formulation involves all these considerations, it will be discussed separately. Here we need remind ourselves only that the indirect approach avoids problems of inaccessibility at some cost in inferential risk and invalidity.

MOTIVATION AND QUESTION FORMULATION

Respondent motivation has long been proposed as the most important single factor in determining the quality of the responses, although it is usually considered only in terms of the interviewer's technique. The questionnaire, however, is the basis of the interview and it should be designed to assist, or at least not to hamper, the interviewer in motivating respondent performance. Probably the most frequent damage to positive respondent motivation is done by questions that make the respondent appear poorly informed on important issues, or make his opinions and behavior appear socially unacceptable. The long-educated and widely-read researcher considers too seldom the reluctance of respondents to find themselves persistently on the negatively valued end of the scale. And the societal values are explicit and widely held: it is better to go to college, hold a skilled job, earn substantially, be informed on issues of the day, participate in civic affairs, know the answer, vote in the election, love one's parents, support one's children, and so on. Respondents tend to become defensive when questions imply that they are deficient in such matters, especially if the offending questions seem unnecessary or irrelevant to the main content of the interview.

Such problems of defensiveness can be dealt with in many ways, primarily in the technique of interviewing rather than in the formulation of questions. Nevertheless, the wording of questions can facilitate or inhibit the respondent's admission to facts or opinions that are potentially ego-threatening. The most effective means of handling such topics in direct questioning is to include in the questions material that makes them relevant and reduces threat. For example, the mere inclusion of a wide range of alternatives increases the likelihood that respondents will admit to extreme statements and to negatively valued opinions or behaviors (Kahn, 1952). Similar effects are produced by including in the question some phrase of reassurance, some reminder of the purpose of the inquiry and its relevance to the immediate question, or some factual indication that the "unacceptable" is common and—at least in the context of the interview—acceptable. A question on whether the respondent voted in the last election might be introduced by the statement that for various reasons almost half the people found themselves unable to get to the polls. Income and other demographic data may be made relevant to matters of opinion by the simple statement that people's opinions differ and that such factors sometimes help us understand the differences. The essential process is one of sanctioning, building into the question the implication that one answer is as acceptable as another throughout a range which easily includes the respondent.

The problem of social acceptability and sanctioning can be thought of as a special case of a traditional problem in question formulation, the intentional or inadvertent use of leading questions. Avoiding "biased" or "leading" questions is a standard and oversimplified piece of advice urged on research workers. A leading question is any item so formulated that respondents find it easier or more acceptable to answer one way than another, or to choose one alternative over another. When such questions are used inadvertently and the responses interpreted without regard to the asymmetrical tendency of the questions, the results are biased. One of the most common examples in survey research is the yes-no type of question, in which "yes" respondents are subjected to a long series of additional questions about time, place, reason, and reaction, while "no" respondents are asked no further questions on the topic. People learn quickly that under such circumstances there are advantages to saying no.

Still more crude is the use of question wording that assumes a particular answer, and forces the respondent to contradict the interviewer in order to formulate a response of his own. Even questions that begin "Are you in favor of . . . " or "Do you agree that . . . " create a respondent tendency to say yes; it seems to be expected. Where possible, the question should explicitly offer the alternatives of agreement or disagreement, and do so in balanced form. Where this is not possible (for example, in a questionnaire of the true-false or agree-disagree format), the form and order of the statements should be randomized. This cannot ensure the validity of responses to individual items, but it will randomize the tendency of some respondents to be chronic yea-sayers or nay-sayers (Couch and Keniston, 1960).

The use of emotionally laden words and phrases in questions produces similar response biases. For example, a question about higher taxes will be answered more favorably if the purpose of national defense is invoked. The principle is not that such wording is necessarily inappropriate, but that it should be employed only for the purpose of imposing some additional stress or task on the respondent —to identify people whose feelings are strong enough to contradict the interviewer or overcome the built-in bias of the question (Smith, Bruner, and White, 1956; Litwak, 1956; Kahn and Cannell, 1957; Kinsey, Pomeroy, and Martin, 1948). The rule of thumb justly favors balanced and neutral wording, questions designed to equalize the amount of work and the degree of social acceptability regardless of the direction of response, and avoidance of emotionally laden words and phrases.

OPEN AND CLOSED QUESTIONS

Of the many decisions which the research worker must make about the form of question, none has been more debated than the issue of "open" versus "closed" questions. Openness has to do with the form of the response which a question requires; open questions (also called free-response or unrestricted questions) invite the respondent to reply in his own words. Closed questions (also called restricted or forced-choice questions) ask him to select from a series of alternatives the answer that best approximates his situation. The closed question thus controls the form, length, and content of the possible response. The classic example is the trial lawyer's instruction to the witness that he "answer yes or no."

The following questions illustrate more fully the contrast between the open and closed form:

(open) What happens in your work group when things go wrong?
(closed) When things go wrong in your work group, do the people blame each other or don't they?

(open) How do people in this union feel about attending meetings?
(closed) Do most people in this local feel they should attend meetings, or do some, or don't any feel they should?

(open) How would you say you and your family are getting along financially now compared to a year ago?
(closed) Would you say you and your family are better off or worse off financially than you were a year ago?

The intolerant advocacy of the open or closed question form has been largely abandoned, as Lazarsfeld (1944) proposed years ago it should be; the persistent problem is to recognize the indicia for one question form or the other, and to choose wisely. Five considerations at least are relevant to the choice between open and closed questions: interview objectives, respondent information level, structure of respondent opinions, respondent motivation to communicate, and initial interviewer knowledge of the preceding respondent characteristics.

The objectives of the interview

The open question is more appropriate when the research objective is not only to discover some respondent attitude or attribute, but also to learn something about his level of information, the structure or basis on which he has formed his opinion, the frame of reference within which he answers the question, and the intensity of his feelings on the topic.

The closed question is appropriate when the objective is limited to the classification of the respondent with respect to some attitude, perception, or other clearly understood dimension. Even this decision needs to be made with caution, since other factors may make the closed question inappropriate even for such classification purposes. It is possible, of course, to substitute an array of closed questions for an open question or two. We can, for example, attempt to measure intensity by asking an additional closed question to get at this dimension. Similarly, we can ask other closed questions to illuminate the respondent's frame of reference and the structuredness of his views. If research objectives are ambitious, however, and if the relevant structure of perceptions and attitudes is complex, formulating batteries of closed questions often becomes more difficult and less satisfactory than the use of open questions to meet the same objectives.

The respondent's level of information

The respondent's level of information poses a minor paradox in the choice between open and closed questions. The ill-informed respondent may prefer the closed question; it demands less of him, and he can choose among alternative answers without feeling that his ignorance is becoming embarrassingly obvious. This may contribute to respondent comfort and motivation to continue the interview, but it usually leaves the interviewer unable to distinguish between responses based on extensive knowledge and those chosen blindly. The open question provides an opportunity to ascertain lack of information or uncertainty of feeling on the part of the respondent. It is possible, of course, to determine level of information by means of a battery of closed questions, but these pose additional problems of validation, and may be embarrassing to respondents who must reveal their ignorance by a string of negative answers. The open questions seem more appropriate, therefore, if there is reason to believe that the topic will be outside the experience of many respondents, or if there are other reasons for wanting to assess level of information. It is indicated also for inquiries directed to a population in which level of information is extremely variable or unknown to the interviewer.

Structuring of respondent thought

The choice between open and closed questions should also be guided by the probable degree of structuring of respondent opinion or experience. In other words, does the respondent have a clear-cut attitude on the question? Has he enough information, and has he given the topic enough thought, to define a position for himself? To the extent that the respondent has done his cognitive work in advance, so to speak, and has formulated his ideas in terms close to those of the question, the closed form is appropriate and, as always, economical of interviewer time and respondent effort. To the extent that the respondent's thoughts are less structured on the topic in question, the interviewer must assist the respondent to recall, order, and perhaps evaluate his experience. A closed question asks him to express a preference for one of several alternative responses, but provides little incentive and less assistance for him to go through the complicated process of "making up his mind" about something that he has not already thought through. The use of a closed question in such circumstances involves the serious risk that the respondent's quick choice of an offered alternative may be quite different from the conclusion he would reach if he went through the process of recall, organization, and evaluation of his own experience. The open question, calling for a full response, gives reason and opportunity for pulling together experience; supplemented by the permissible probing and encouragement of the interviewer, it may also provide assistance for this cognitive work.

Motivation to communicate

Definitive research on the motivational advantages of open versus closed questions is yet to be done. The closed question demands less respondent effort, demands less revelation, and probably is less threatening under some circumstances. To the extent that the closed question incorporates extreme alternative responses, it also makes these extremes more admissible. On the other hand, the closed question may be restrictive, and may also invite an easy invalid response instead of the more difficult "don't know." The closed form is most appropriate when the interviewer knows in advance the likely range of responses and has reason to minimize the demand on the respondent. This argument, however, does not generalize readily to an entire interview. An interview in which the respondent is never invited or allowed to express himself in his own words had best demand little motivation, for it is likely to generate little.

Insight into respondent's situation

Finally, the choice between the closed and open question form should take into account the research worker's advance knowledge of the situation. Investigating a topic successfully by means of closed questions requires possession of substantial information about respondents' knowledge or expertness in the area, a realistic assessment of the extent to which they have thought through or structured their views on the topic, and equally good assumptions about respondents' motivation to communicate. The importance of such knowledge as a basis for formulating closed questions was well illustrated in a study that examined the frames of reference from which respondents answered a single closed question on social change (Crutchfield and Gordon, 1947). Respondents answered the closed question from seven different frames of reference, where the researcher had assumed but one. The closed question appears to be best adapted to situations where (1) there are a limited number of known frames of reference from which the respondent can answer the question, (2) within these few possible frames of reference there is a known range of possible responses, and (3) within this range there are clearly defined choice points that approximate well the positions of respondents.

If the researcher knows relatively little about the range or terms of response he will encounter, he is obviously in a poor position to formulate closed questions, which are meaningful and successful only when their limited alternatives fit respondent experience, vocabulary, and frame of reference. If these conditions are not met, the open question is likely to be preferable, in spite of its characteristically higher demand of time, money, interviewing skill, and respondent effort. It is for these reasons that it has become almost standard in social research to begin with open questions during the early phases of sizable research projects, and to move through successively less open versions of the interview in preparation for large-scale interviewing and quantitative analysis.

We believe that, for many interviewing situations, the open question involves fewer risks and produces a greater volume of useful information. The closed question represents a kind of efficient small-bore ammunition. If the objective is clearly in sight and if the researcher is confident of his marksmanship, all is well. For more ambitious games or in less well-defined situations, the greater range, spread, and firepower of the open question are distinct advantages.

DIRECT AND INDIRECT QUESTIONS

Directness and indirectness have to do not with the relationship between question and response, but rather with the relationship between question and objective, that is, the interviewer's purpose in asking the question, or the concept he wishes to measure. For example, when a respondent is shown an ambiguous picture and asked to tell a story about its meaning for him, so that the story can be subsequently used to infer the level of the respondent's need for achievement (Atkinson, 1958), we consider the question to be indirect. A direct (but probably ill-advised) question to meet the same objective would have asked the respondent how achievement-oriented he considered himself to be.

The use of the term *indirect* is a relative matter; all questions are really indirect, in that they are not concepts but rather operationalizations of concepts. The act of asking a person how old he is or when he was born, and evoking a response, is not identical with the concept *age;* it is, however, as close to the concept as language can make it. We expect interviewer and respondent to have the same understanding of the term *age* and to measure it in the same units (years). There is an isomorphism between operation and concept by virtue of the language shared by interviewer and respondent, and the isomorphism is obvious on inspection by anyone who knows the language.

An indirect question is not isomorphic with a concept in the same sense; it is linked to it by some theory or sequence of inferences. To use an earlier example, there is no isomorphism or formal identity between a respondent's story about a TAT picture and his level of need achievement. The connectedness depends on and is defined by a theory of personality and behavior, and by the psychoanalytic mechanism of projection. Degrees of indirectness vary with the complexity of the inferential linkage between operation and concept (question and answer). We can define as indirect, however, all measures for which the language of the question is different from the language of conceptual definition.

The advantages of the direct question are obvious; it avoids the risks and complexities of inference just described. On the other hand, the direct question requires by definition that the respondent share the conceptual language of the researcher, that his experience be accessible to him in these terms, and that he be motivated to report it. It is the failure to realize these conditions that leads the researcher to indirect approaches. More specifically, the circumstances in which indirect questions are appropriate include the following:

1. *The respondent and interviewer do not share an understanding of the concept under investigation or a common language for speaking about it. The index of any text or collection of readings in social psychology provides abundant examples of concepts which for these reasons may require indirect measures: dissonance, identification, regression, role conflict, status congruence, etc.*

2. *The research involves respondent characteristics or experience that cannot be reported in answer to direct questions because of strong emotional barriers or repressive mechanisms. A person is typically unable to describe some of his strong fears, self-doubts, aggressive impulses, etc.*

3. *The research seeks to discover material about the individual which he perceives to be socially undesirable or as unacceptable to the interviewer. Cowardice, malice, ignorance, negligence, laziness, and other vices and faults are implied by the negative end of many social-psychological dimensions. They may be all too accessible to the respondent, but by no means likely to be discussed by him in direct terms.*

4. *The use of indirect questions is also appropriate when we want the respondent to react to a stimulus too complex to be presented easily in verbal form. The TAT pictures are useful in part because they present at a glance a combination of stimuli that might not be easily translated. The Rorschach plates provide more vivid examples of the same point.*

Several indirect approaches are available to the researcher, differing both in the degree of indirectness and the complexity of the measures. Some of the major classes of indirect measures are described below:

Use of the third person. A question may be phrased with reference to an anonymous third person, on the assumption that the respondent will impute his own views to that person. For example, a recent investigation of attitudes toward foreign travel discovered that many persons suppress some of their real concerns about visits to foreign countries for fear of appearing provincial, or incompetent to cope with new and strange situations (Lansing and Blood, 1964). In addition to direct questions, two types of indirect questions in the third-person question form were used. One merely asked why the respondent thought some people did not want to visit foreign countries. The second involved a series of questions about a hypothetical Mrs. Jones who had won a free trip to Europe in a contest. Questions asked whether she would or would not accept the trip, the reasons for her choice, and what some of her concerns about such travel might be. Responses to the questions in the third person included more expressions of doubt, fear, and hostility.

Manifest and latent content. Meaningful questions may be asked directly, and answered directly by the respondent about himself. The interpretation, however, is indirect and is based on assumptions or hypotheses which have meaning for the researcher but of which the respondent is unaware. A good example of this is the F-Scale of authoritarianism. The respondent ostensibly gives information on current norms of morality, the state of the world, and various subgroups. The analyst infers from these responses his degree of authoritarianism. In studies of race prejudice in children, researchers have asked children to choose among dolls or indicate after looking at pictures of groups which group they would prefer to play with. The responses are coded for indications of prejudice, according to the child's preference for white or nonwhite dolls, and for white or racially mixed groups.

The ambiguous stimulus. A third approach, still more indirect, involves presentation of a stimulus that is purposely ambiguous. Such stimuli include pictures, stories (often uncompleted), incomplete sentences, and the like. The TAT pictures and Rorschach ink blots already described are familiar examples. These techniques are used mainly for measuring needs and other personality attributes.

The strength of the indirect approach is clear; it makes accessible to the interviewer data that would otherwise be withheld or that the respondent himself is unaware of. The disadvantages of indirection are no less clear; they have to do mainly with validity. Face validity is always risky, but with indirect measures it is meaningless. Empirical studies of validation, which are done much too infrequently, become particularly urgent necessities when indirect measures are used. Without them the researcher has little or no basis for distinguishing between disconfirmation of a hypothesis and a failure of measurement.

This is not to say, of course, that the burden of validation rests only on the user of indirect measures. Face validity is a poor basis for research, regardless of the measurement technique. The use of intensive pretest interviewing is helpful in generating supporting evidence for validity, but quantitative studies of prediction, convergence, and discrimination are badly needed.

ORGANIZATION AND SEQUENCE OF QUESTIONS

Issues of organization and sequence of questions, like so much else in interviewing, cannot be settled by easy generalization, but must be resolved in relation to the interview objectives and the characteristics of the population from whom information is sought. With that qualification, the following are some of the more dependable regularities suggested in part by experience and in part by studies of reliability and validity already cited:

1. *In general, a battery of questions is preferable to a single question, both for reasons of reliability and validity. The more complex the issue and the less tested the approach, the more important it becomes to use multiple questions.*

2. *When multiple closed questions are used, and the respondent is asked to indicate agreement or disagreement with a stated proposition, it is important to randomize the form of the statements. The purpose of doing so, as we have*

already suggested, is to randomize the tendency of some respondents to be chronic "yea-sayers" or "nay-sayers" (Couch and Keniston, 1960).

3. *Similarly, if lists of items are being presented to respondents, the order should be varied, since some respondents show a tendency to select the alternatives first presented or create other kinds of position bias.*

4. *Within a topic area, the sequence of questions should be such as to lead the respondent meaningfully through the process of exploration. Often this can be done by means of the "funnel sequence," which proceeds from the broadest and most open of questions to the most specific.*

5. *The sequence of topics themselves should be planned to make the total interview experience as meaningful as possible, to give it a beginning, a middle, and an end. More specifically, the early questions should serve to engage the respondent's interest without threatening or taxing him before he is really committed to the transaction, and to exemplify and teach him the kind of task the interview represents. The most demanding of questions might well be placed later in the interview, when respondent commitment can be presumed to have peaked—and fatigue has not yet set in. Sometimes the riskiest of questions may be put very late in the interview, so that if they trigger a refusal to continue, relatively little information is lost. This procedure seems prudent, but it risks also the possibility of an unpleasant leave-taking.*

6. *Transitions from area to area are usually facilitated by some material written into the interview schedule or interpolated by the interviewer, to make the new topic plausible and to relate it to things already discussed. Only Kinsey (1948), consistent with his convictions of the advantages of stressfulness, has advocated abruptness of transition.*

INTERVIEWING TECHNIQUE

We earlier stipulated five discrete steps in the process of measurement by means of interviewing: (1) the creation or selection of a schedule of questions and a set of rules for its use; (2) the actual use of these questions and rules as the interview is conducted; (3) the recording of responses in some form; (4) the creation of a numerical code or number system of some kind into which the verbal responses can be translated; (5) the actual coding of responses into this number system. These steps are consistent with the more general definition of measurement as the assignment of numbers to objects or events, in accordance with some set of rules. The creation and use of a code, however, are beyond the scope of this chapter.

The actual process of interviewing, the speaking of questions and answers, can be thought of as the act of evoking the verbal representations of events—or, more exactly, evoking the verbal events which are really the stuff of measurement. The interviewer attempts to so manage the conversation that all material relevant to the content objectives of the interview is evoked and most irrelevant material is withheld. To the extent that he fails to evoke relevant material, measurement becomes invalid or unreliable; to the extent that he fails to discourage the communication of irrelevant material, measurement becomes inefficient and costly.

It is tempting to think of the interview process as one in which the interviewer uses his native skill and acquired technique to extract from the respondent a statement which was in a sense "already there." The respondent already knew how old he was, whether he was a Republican or a Democrat, and perhaps whether or not he was satisfied with his job, and whether he thought the younger generation promising or hopeless. To the extent that the interview is thought of in these terms, the task of the interviewer is merely to get a good verbal "print" of the respondent's information or attitude, and to do it without getting his own interviewing thumbprints all over it.

This view of the interviewing process is limited, however, and inconsistent with the interaction model proposed earlier (Fig. 1). Consider the interviewer-respondent exchange on topics which the respondent has not previously considered or thought through. The interviewer may supply information and ask for a reaction, or show a picture and ask for a narrative response. It is clear in these instances (but no less true in the former examples) that the data generated are the product of interaction, and that the notion of interviewer as catalyst is less than appropriate. The test of validity for interview data is not whether the interviewer has been active or inactive in the process of data generation, but whether the data explain the unexplained, predict to appropriate criteria, and correspond to measures already proven satisfactory in these respects.

If we consider the interview as a process of interaction, and read the verbatim transcription as the record of that interaction, we find ourselves in need of a conceptual unit for understanding and analyzing the record. This may seem to be a matter too simple for consideration; the self-evident unit is the question and the respondent's answer to it. But this is not quite the case. For purposes of substantive social research the usual unit for coding or content analysis consists of the respondent's answers to a primary question (usually formulated in advance of the interview as part of a written schedule of such questions) and to one or more secondary or "probe" questions (usually formulated by the interviewer in the course of spontaneous interaction with the respondent in order to encourage answers that meet more fully the objectives of the primary question).

A more useful unit of analysis for understanding the process of interviewing as mutual interaction consists of three interdependent verbal acts—a question by the interviewer, an answer by the respondent, and a sanctioning statement or sign by the interviewer. The third element in this sequence is typically improvised by the interviewer and serves to tell the respondent whether or not he has met the requirements of the initial question; if he has not, it should also tell him what additional response on his part is required. Thus the interview can be thought of as a series of interaction cycles which typically take the form I_1, R_1, I_2. In this unit I_1 represents a primary question by the interviewer, in which he introduces a new topic or variable, or asks for new content; R_1 is the answer which the primary question elicits from the respondent, and I_2 is the indication of acceptance or nonacceptance which the interviewer gives to this answer. If the answer is acceptable, I_2 is followed (usually as part of the same statement) by a new primary question. If the answer is unacceptable, I_2 usually includes some indication of that fact, and a probe question or some other indication of the respondent behavior necessary to make the answer acceptable. In this case, I_2 is followed by R_2, which the interviewer must now assess as acceptable or still unacceptable. Theoretically, there is no limit to the number of such molar units of interaction which the interviewer may initiate to supplement a single primary question. In practice, limits are set by the endurance of interviewer and respondent, and by reasonable approximation to the objectives of the primary question. Thus the I_2 terms in a successful interview include requests for additional information, clarifications of meaning, and direct feedback to the respondent about his performance. Such feedback serves to increase the respondent's understanding of his role and to motivate him to perform it more adequately.

In structured interviewing, all primary questions (I_1's) are typically preformulated and used by the interviewer verbatim. Few if any of the supplementary questions (I_2's) are preformulated, but the rules by which the interviewer is to formulate them and the indications for doing so are usually stipulated in writing, and may be the subject of substantial theorizing and training. When we speak of an interviewer as particularly skilled or unskilled, successful or unsuccessful, we are speaking of differences which have to do largely with his judgment of response adequacy, his spontaneous formulation of supplementary questions, and his ability to teach the respondent role and to attain the necessary motivation by the respondent to fulfill the requirements of that role.

These interviewer functions are characteristically underestimated in discussions of interviewing technique and in the training of interviewers. Moreover, even when the importance of interviewing technique is acknowledged and the contribution of the interviewer to maintaining respondent motivation and attaining valid responses is emphasized, the criteria for interviewer judgments of response adequacy and interviewer formulation of supplementary questions and instructions to the respondent are left unexplicit. One major reason for these omissions and for the neglect of the interviewer's teaching function vis-à-vis the respondent is that these behaviors are typically unrecorded by interviewers and therefore undiscovered by research investigators. (The people who write instructions and books for interviewers are not themselves given much to interviewing.)

Interviewers, in the haste of conversation or the selectiveness of recollection, usually record those of the respondent's statements which seem most relevant, omitting the irrelevant and omitting also much of their own probing, explaining, persuading, and teaching. Yet these are the behaviors which distinguish the skilled from the unskilled interviewer. They are the core of *interviewing* technique, as distinguished from the technique of constructing an interview schedule, and they are the subject of this section.

The technique of interviewing, then, as distinct from the construction of interview questions, comprises all spontaneous, unprogrammed behavior of the interviewer relevant to attaining the three basic conditions for successful measurement by interviewing—cognition, accessibility, and motivation. The cognitive condition is fulfilled when the respondent understands the content of the specific questions being asked and the role-task which has been defined for him in answering them. The condition of accessibility has been met when the respondent is able to recall or construct the required information. The condition of motivation is met when the respondent is willing to invest the energy and time necessary to do these things and verbalize the information—in short, to fulfill his role as respondent.

Many interviewer behaviors have implications for the attainment or failure to attain all three of these conditions. To some extent it therefore becomes artificial to identify separate components of interviewer behavior as relevant for cognition, accessibility, or motivation. It is often more relevant to ask how the interviewer actually behaves, and what the consequences of his behavior are for the quality and completeness of the data. For example, explaining the content and purpose of a study to a prospective respondent begins the task of teaching the respondent his role, and is to this extent cognitive in function. But it also initiates the task of recall; the respondent who is informed that the interview will have to do with his reactions to the job is almost certainly led to begin thinking about that topic and to bring relevant material to consciousness. Moreover, his motivation to participate in the interview is also affected by the initial statement of content and purpose. Thus all three of the conditions for interviewing are affected by the interviewer's introductory words.

Nevertheless, we can make some differentiation among the acts of the interviewer in terms of these three conditions, and we can improve our analysis and understanding of the interview process by so doing. Let us consider them one at a time, in order of their relevance to interviewing technique.

MOTIVATION

Interviewing technique, as distinct from the formulation of primary questions, is important first of all for respondent motivation. The advance formulation of questions is of lesser significance in generating positive respondent motivation to accept the role of information giver and to work at it, although the wording of questions can certainly have drastic effects of a negative sort. A clumsily worded question on a topic of surprising and intimate content may produce an abrupt termination of an interview, but it does not follow that a properly worded question on a neutral or even an interesting topic will generate a strong wish to continue the interview.

It is the interviewer who must make the interviewing experience and task sufficiently meaningful, sufficiently rewarding, and sufficiently enjoyable to attain and maintain the necessary respondent motivation. The alternative is either collapse of the transaction and absence of data, or a grudging compliance which tends to produce meager and biased material. Attempts are often made to write introductory and transitional material which can be read or recited by the interviewer in order to establish a meaningful relationship with the respondent and generate adequate respondent motivation. The effectiveness of such devices has yet to be researched, but we would assess it as low, especially after the introduction has been made. The canned heartiness of programmed explanations, delivered irrespective of the respondent's mood or need for explanation, are poor substitutes for spontaneous interaction in which a skilled and sensitive interviewer provides explanations when the respondent is puzzled or hesitant, and does so in terms that fit the respondent's level of sophistication. A highly educated and sophisticated respondent may bear with an oversimple question in an interview, but he will not be satisfied with an oversimple explanation. Kinsey's classic phrase of assurance that the requested information "will help the doctors" constitutes neither explanation nor assurance for educated and analytical respondents.

COGNITION

Next in importance, in terms of sensitivity to spontaneous interviewer behavior, is the condition of respondent cognition. The introductory remarks of the interviewer are typically the respondent's first encounter with the demands to be made on him and the rationale for making them. The explanations given him do much to determine his motivation to take the role at all, but they also determine to a considerable extent the adequacy with which he is *able* to take it. The property of role readiness, which is so important for the graceful and skillful assumption of many of life's roles, is not often realized for the role of respondent. In other words, few of us are familiar with the role; still fewer of us have had much experience in it, and virtually none of us has been trained for it. The result is that the interviewer must define the role for the respondent, teach it to him, let him practice it, so to speak, and then instruct him as to his weak and strong points in performing it. There must be a continuous checking and communicating from interviewer to respondent, a kind of quality control which is undertaken to bring the respondent to a level of understanding which will produce valid data. For the same reasons, the interviewer must be alert to signs of puzzlement, prepared to meet such problems in the terms and at the moment in which they arise —restating questions, explaining seeming irrelevancies, making clear the unclear.

ACCESSIBILITY

This condition of the interview is least affected by interviewer skills and most determined by the predetermined content of the inquiry. The interviewer's skills affect the accessibility of data to respondents only indirectly, for the most part. Thus the interviewer may, by means of explanation and improved respondent cognition, render accessible data that the respondent would otherwise have been unable to report. Or the interviewer may so increase the respondent's motivation to perform ably that he will bring into consciousness by main effort data which are ordinarily inaccessible to him. And on the negative side, a clumsy and insensitive interviewer might so intimidate a respondent that material accessible under usual circumstances would be literally repressed and inaccessible during the interview. But these are extreme examples, and accessibility *per se* remains primarily a function of the substantive demands made by the interview rather than a function of the skills of the interviewer.

In practice, as we have said, the interviewer behaviors conducive to attaining one of these conditions for data generation tend to have implications for the others as well. The analysis of the interview in terms of the conditions of cognition, accessibility, and motivation is a compartmental convenience; reality as usual is not compartmentalized. When we look at interviewer behaviors, therefore, it is useful to consider them in their totality, preferably in the sequence in which they commonly occur, and to interpret them as appropriate in terms of their contribution to cognition, accessibility, and motivation.

Three further qualifications must be made before we proceed to more specific problems and examples of interviewing technique. First, the field of interviewing research has shown signs of resurgence and new departures in very recent years, with the result that views on interviewing techniques are in flux. With a notable exception or two, social-research workers for the past twenty years have approached the interviewing task relying on various adaptations of clinical styles, particularly that of nondirective, nonjudgmental, nonevaluative behavior on the part of the interviewer. Warmth and permissiveness have been key words. The results of current research urge the importance of respondent-interviewer interaction, of direct (and in a sense, directive) behavior by the interviewer. The respondent's learning of his role and the ability of the interviewer to teach it may be no less important than the respondent's affective acceptance of that role and the interviewer's ability to motivate that acceptance. Such a process of learning and teaching is almost certainly more important in determining the quality of data than is the linking of the interview to distant rewarding outcomes, and it may be more important also than the intrinsic satisfaction which the respondent experiences from the interview process. The collection of data by interview will not stop, however, pending the development of more adequate theoretical models; we must describe what currently seems most workable in interviewing techniques, in spite of unsolved problems of motivation and measurement.

The second qualification to the present discussion stems from a problem of explication. Describing what the interviewer actually does and what he should do to extend and make workable the primary questions which he has in hand as he approaches the interview creates a false dichotomy in the telling. The technique of the interviewer is not really so separable from the formulation of primary questions. In almost all situations, the interviewer is in some degree a formulator of such questions. In much case study and anthropological work the interviewer formulates and asks questions almost simultaneously; he interacts spontaneously with the respondent with little in the way of programmed phrases. At the other extreme is the Census enumerator, who is enjoined to ask each question precisely as worded, to do no improvising of additional questions, and to respond to requests for explanation by repeating the question as originally worded. Even under such constrained circumstances, methodological research has shown the effects of variations in interviewer technique (Hansen *et al.,* 1951; Kish and

Slater, 1960). Moreover, we suspect that the universal tendency of interviewers to introduce flexibility into rigid procedures probably has the effect of saving some distant question writers from the fate they prescribe for themselves. Most human enterprises would collapse if subordinates did no more nor less than their superiors specified, and the collection of data by interviewing is no exception.

The third qualification to our advice on interviewing technique is that the most appropriate advice must differ with the situation—as defined by respondent characteristics, interviewer characteristics, and above all by the task requirements of the interview itself. To invest much time and energy in developing a close and trusting relationship as a preliminary to asking a few questions for a school census is ludicrous; to neglect the early development of such a relationship in psychiatric diagnosis and therapy is equally inappropriate and more damaging.

It follows that recommendations about technique, if they are to be both specific and appropriate, must be stated in relation to situational factors. Such factors include the magnitude of the demand to be made on the respondent in terms of time, effort at recall, and endurance of threat or embarrassment. They include also the magnitude and basis of the power on which the interviewer must rely in attaining respondent compliance. The Census enumerator stands before the householder with the power of law and a very limited number of conventional questions about matters either directly observable or generally treated as public information. The Kinsey interviewer greeted the same respondent with a long, complicated, surprisingly intimate array of queries, and without a shred of legitimate authority to bolster his request.

Our present advice to interviewers is based on the situational factors which we believe to be most common in social research, including but by no means limited to survey research. In such research the respondent is free to give information or refuse it; being interviewed is an act of voluntarism on his part. Moreover, the power of the interviewer over the respondent is limited; he can impose no formal penalties for nonresponse nor offer any prize for rich and complete answers. The demands on respondent time and effort are significant but not overwhelming, perhaps as little as one-half hour or as much as two hours. The interviewer approaches the respondent as a stranger; the interviewer is identified with some sponsoring agency (university, research institute, or the like) which has at least modest prestige value without possessing legitimate authority or coercive power to demand information. For the rest, the interviewer must generate a sufficient basis of personal liking, respect, or appreciation of the value of the research to carry the respondent through the task of the interview. In other words, the interviewer must generate and maintain sufficient respondent motivation to meet the interview objectives, and he must direct and control the communication process in the service of these objectives. He does these things by describing the purpose of the interview in terms likely to be meaningful to the respondent, by treating the respondent with a reasonable amount of warmth and interest, by indicating directly and approvingly those responses which are relevant and complete, and by letting the respondent know when he is being irrelevant or fragmentary in his answers. These things the interviewer does by building on the specific questions which have been prepared in advance of the interview. He adds supplementary or "probe" questions; he comments on the completeness or inadequacy of responses; he nods, murmurs, and in other ways exerts control over the communication process. Let us consider these behaviors sequentially and specifically, as they occur in the context of social research described above.

INTRODUCING THE INTERVIEW TO THE RESPONDENT

The primary purpose of the interviewer's introductory remarks is to get the prospective respondent "in role." Unless there is some minimum level of respondent understanding of the nature of the encounter, and at least that tentative acceptance that permits the process of data collection to begin, there can be no interview at all. The introduction must achieve that minimum of compliance, and often it neither can nor should attempt more. Many respondents comply initially out of a slightly favorable balance of small motivational forces: they may be a little annoyed at an unexpected interruption of some other activity and even a little apprehensive at the appearance of a stranger, but they are also mildly curious about his mission and they share the usual norms about showing reasonable politeness toward a person who addresses you courteously, perhaps especially if he calls at your home or office.

The interviewer begins by identifying himself, the research agency or university from which he comes, and the general topic of the research in which he is engaged. He explains something of the method by which people have been selected for interview and makes some reference to the amount of time required of the respondent. All this may often be done very briefly indeed; the following introduction, for example, has been used by interviewers from the Survey Research Center in connection with surveys of consumer finances:

Interviewer: "I'm from the Survey Research Center of The University of Michigan. We're doing a survey at this time, as we have for a number of years now, on how people feel things are going financially these days. The study is done throughout the country, and the results are used by government and industry.

"The addresses at which we interview were chosen entirely by chance, and the interview will take only about a half hour. All information is entirely confidential, of course."

In many cases, this is introduction enough. If the respondent seems content, the interviewer should proceed with the task itself. Compliance may be only tentative initially, and the respondent's understanding of the interview may be modest. But the tentative compliance can be built upon during the early minutes of the interview itself, and the experience of answering the early questions (which have been chosen to be relatively easy, interesting, and nonthreatening) both teaches the respondent role and deepens the commitment to go ahead with the interview. Most respondents are not researchers; they do not have the researcher's interest in the purposes and design subtleties of the study. The interviewer has in mind many more things he could say about the research and its value, but unless the respondent gives some sign of question, reluctance, or special interest, it is better to resist the intellectualizing and get on with the interviewing.

How the introduction should be elaborated will depend upon the expressed needs of the respondent or the interviewer's hunches about them, and upon the interviewer's knowledge of the nature and demandingness of the interview which is to come. He must provide enough in the introduction and in his early enlargements on it to make the rest of the interview plausible. To begin a long interview on a sensitive topic with an introduction which promises only a few casual questions is not only deceitful and unethical; it is likely to precipitate a crisis of nonresponse later in the interview process.

Among the issues on which respondents often require early reassurance are the following: the interviewer's identity, the legitimacy of the research, the process by which they were chosen for interview, the protection which they may expect as respondents, the extent of the demands which are to be made upon them, and their own adequacy to meet these demands. What the interviewer may say on these several topics must depend, of course, on the facts of the case. He should be prepared, however, to identify himself, preferably by means of some card or letter which documents his connection with the university or research agency which he claims to represent. If he is calling at the respondent's home or place of business, he should also be able to refer the respondent to a telephone number at which confirming information can be obtained. The practice of sending advance letters to respondents or of using the mass media to announce large-scale data collection is helpful and is increasingly common.

The legitimacy of the research is established in part by the same means—official documents, letters on appropriate stationery, use of the university name and address, and the like. The interviewer should also be prepared to become very explicit with respect to the uses of the data, the sponsoring agencies, and the kinds of reports to be issued. If reports of similar studies, journal articles, or books are available and can be shown, these can be useful and reassuring evidence of good faith and legitimate research activity. Establishing the interview as a legitimate research process may also require dissociating it from any of the various non-research contexts in which some respondents have encountered interviewers and the respondent role. Bill collectors and credit investigators ask questions; so do welfare officers, policemen, truant officers, and a whole array of civil servants and private employees who appear very differently to people of different socioeconomic classes and experiences.

The interviewer should be informed about the means by which respondents were chosen, and he should be able to offer an accurate and nontechnical account of the process if this is wanted. Usually the respondent wants only the assurance that he is not being sought for some special and personal reason; the brief description of random and anonymous selection is enough. If selection has been made for some special reason of education, occupation, or other demographic or experiential characteristic, this can usually be stated in broad terms without compromising the content of the study.

The protection which the respondent usually wants, and which the usual ethics of research require, is that he shall be submitted to no serious unpleasantness or embarrassment in the course of the interview, and that the information he gives shall reach the possession of no person or agency which might use it against his interests. An important basis for such assurance is the statistical anonymity of quantitative research, and the interviewer should be prepared to show by means of research reports, IBM cards, or any other relevant illustrative material, just how the protection of respondent identity is assured. In addition to handling such negative factors, he must be prepared to present the positive, respondent-relevant uses of the interview; depending on the curiosity and sophistication of the respondent, these may vary from Kinsey's classic assertion that "it will help the doctors" to detailed descriptions of the linkage between research and social policy, and presentation of samples of publications. In deciding on the amount of detail appropriate, the interviewer will be guided by the demandingness of the respondent task, and by his initial impression of the respondent's sophistication and interest. These signs can be overused, however, and it is wise for the interviewer to ask the respondent directly whether there are other things he would like to know or ask about the process before he proceeds.

A remaining problem which arises in the introductory moments of an interview has to do with the ethics of persuasion, particularly in describing the purpose of the interview and the uses to which it will be put. To counsel absolute and complete truthfulness is easy and irreproachable, but there are circumstances in which the effect of such completeness would negate the purpose of the interview. The purpose of a study may be to ascertain the prevalence of mental illness, and the inquiry of symptoms may be undertaken to classify respondents accordingly. To state these facts so bluntly in the introduction would almost certainly create serious inadequacies in the data. It seems consistent with the ethics of the social sciences in general to resolve such problems by telling the respondent as much as possible without risking such damage, by then withholding or generalizing rather than fabricating explanations, and by being uncompromising in letting the respondent know what the interview will require of him. The principle by which the researcher should be guided is that of informed consent by the respondent, but information need not be complete in every detail. The respondent should be told unequivocally the demands to be made in terms of time and subject matter, the risks of exposure (if any), and the authority by which the request for his cooperation is made. He then has a reasonable basis for accepting or rejecting the request. The present concern over invasions of privacy is not likely to be shortlived, and the obligations of researchers to respondents are likely to be elaborated.

The development of intrinsic motivation in the interview—emotional and intellectual satisfaction in the process itself—may begin with the introduction, but matures only as the task and relationship acquire meaning for the respondent. The opportunity to talk to a good listener, to find one's opinions of serious interest to another person, to see that person making a real and successful effort to understand rather than to evaluate or criticize, to encounter the stimulation of moving sequentially and logically through a series of related issues—these are experiences which are rare for many people and which are intrinsically satisfying. To provide such experiences and to generate the additional motivation to respond which they provide, the interviewer should create and maintain an atmosphere in which the respondent feels that he is fully understood and in which it is safe to communicate fully without fear of being judged, criticized, or subsequently identified and disadvantaged. The interviewer at the same time focuses attention on the content of the communication, encouraging the respondent to consider each topic as deeply, fully, and frankly as the interview objectives require.

The interviewer's means for doing these things are not mysterious; they are his elaborations on the primary (prepared) interview questions and in some respects resemble the processes of mutual influence familiar in informal conversation. Richardson and his colleagues (1965) refer to them as "encouragements, silences, guggles, and interruptions": Kahn and Cannell (1957) called them collectively "controlled nondirective probing," and other authors have used still other terms. The specific behaviors proposed for the interviewer by these various authors are more alike than their terminology. In the following list of such behaviors, each category is accompanied, where appropriate, by examples of its use and by research references bearing on its effectiveness:

Brief expressions of understanding and interest

Examples: I see; um-hm; yes, I understand.

Research: Krasner (1958), Quay (1959), Richardson, Hastorf, and Dornbusch (1964), Salzinger (1956), Salzinger and Pisoni (1960), on the ineffectiveness of infrequent encouragement; Mandler and Kaplan (1956), on occasional respondent misinterpretation of "um-hm" encouragements; Hildum and Brown (1956), on the biasing effect of "Good" as an encouragement.

Brief expectant pauses

Research: Gorden (1954) and Saslow *et al.* (1957), on the positive effects of short pauses (2–3 seconds) as compared to the negative effects of long pauses (in excess of 10–15 seconds).

Neutral requests for additional information

Examples: How do you mean? I'd like to know more of your thinking on that. What do you have in mind there? Is there anything else? Can you tell me more about that?

Research: Guest (1947), Shapiro and Eberhart (1947).

Echo or near repetition of the respondent's words

Example: *Respondent*—I've taken these treatments for almost six months, and I'm not getting any better. *Interviewer*—You're not getting better?

Research: No direct evidence, but agreement that sensitive use of the echo conveys close attention, sympathy, and encouragement to continue (Kahn and Cannell, 1957; Richardson, Dohrenwend, and Klein, 1965; Rogers, 1951).

Summarizing or reflecting respondent expressions

Examples would follow respondent statements, stating the interviewer's understanding of a key feeling or meaning. Such summaries often begin with phrases like, "You feel that . . ." or "You mean that. . . ."

Research: Rogers (1942, 1951), on effectiveness in counseling and psychotherapy; Campbell *et al.* (1960), Couch and Keniston (1960), Lenski and Leggett (1960), on dangers of acquiescence bias; Beezer (1956), on limitation to acquiescence bias.

Requests for specific kinds of additional information

Examples: *Why* do you think that is so? *How* did that become clear to you? *When* was that?

Requests for clarification

Examples: I'm not clear on that. Could you explain what you meant?

Repetition of a primary question

Examples: *Interviewer*—What kind of work do you do? *Respondent*—Work at the paper mill. *Interviewer*—I see. What kind of work do you do there?

To these specific forms of supplementing the primary questions in an interview must be added explanations, reassurances, and further information about any aspect of the interview—its general purpose, the manner by which respondents were selected, its sponsorship, the intended uses of results, and the rationale for specific questions.

Which of these various techniques will be used at any given moment depends on the interviewer's assessment of response adequacy. If responses are relevant and at the depth and detail sought, and if the respondent seems interested and willing, the interviewer will do no such elaborating on the primary questions. He turns to supplementary procedures at signs of respondent discomfort, of disinterest, or at symptoms of response inadequacy. These include sudden silence and nonresponse, partial but relevant response, irrelevant response, apparent inaccuracy or inconsistency in response, and direct statements of response problems (reluctance, disagreement, misunderstanding, and the like) by the respondent himself.

The separation of such interviewing techniques and the questions they involve from the formulation of the major questions which present the topics of inquiry is in some degree arbitrary, as we have said. This distinction between primary and supplementary or "probe" questions is perhaps least useful in the two extreme forms of the interview, that is, when the interviewer is formulating all questions on the spur of the moment in a completely unstructured situation, and when the interviewer is absolutely restricted to reading prepared questions from a script or schedule. But most interviews are well within these extremes, and involve some mixture of predetermined questions and spontaneous interactive elaborations on them. In most social research of scale, this functional distinction is emphasized by a division of labor; the people who conduct the interviews have usually not developed the basic questions to be asked. In such circumstances, it becomes essential to develop an understanding of the complementary functions of question formulation and elaboration or probing, so that they may in fact complement each other instead of producing a validity-destroying and unintended competition.

SELECTION, TRAINING, AND SUPERVISION

It is perhaps appropriate to conclude a discussion of research interviewing with a consideration of some very practical issues. Every researcher who depends upon interviewers to collect research data in the field becomes concerned with such questions as the following: Who can interview? How can potentially competent interviewers be selected? What methods of training will develop that potential competence? How can interviewers best be supervised, particularly when substantial distances separate the interviewers from the research office? How can the rate of production of interviews be estimated? How can the costs of interviewing be estimated?

These issues are so mundane that they are seldom discussed in the research literature; yet they are so important that they are never left undiscussed when interviewing for social research is being attempted on any substantial scale. Gross underestimation of time and costs involved in data collection and in preparation for data collection is all too common in social research. These matters are no less amenable to empirical study than other aspects of research methodology, but unfortunately few relevant studies have been done and fewer published. In attempting to deal with such problems here, we are therefore presenting the results of accumulated experience in data gathering by interview rather than the results of experimentation and measurement.

SELECTION OF INTERVIEWERS

Little empirical work has been done on criteria for selecting interviewers, although there has been some speculation on characteristics to look for in choosing people to interview (Hyman *et al.*, 1954; Richardson, Dohrenwend, and Klein, 1965; Riesman, 1958). Attempts to use standardized selection tests have not been particularly successful. It seems likely that there is no "interviewing personality," no characteristics which dramatically differentiate "born interviewers" from the rest of the population. Moreover, the skill demands of interviewing depend on subject matter, length, legitimacy, and many other factors. The tasks are too variable to make plausible a single successful interviewer type. Rogers (1942), in talking about the qualifications for counseling, offers some observations that seem relevant to much research interviewing (p. 254):

The person who is quite obtuse to the reactions of others, who does not realize that his remarks have caused another pleasure or distress, who does not sense the hostility or friendliness which exists between himself and others or between two of his acquaintances, is not likely to become a satisfactory counselor. There is no doubt that this quality can be developed. But unless an individual has a considerable degree of this social sensitivity, it is doubtful that counseling is his most promising field of effort.

The few studies of characteristics of successful interviewers that have been conducted are merely suggestive of significant relationships. Richardson (1954), in an experiment involving the measurement of experienced field workers and student interviewers (after training) on eleven TAT variables, found only three significant and one near significant correlation with overall performance ratings for both groups. Human relations, introspection, and receptivity were positively related to performance; intragression (contrary to hypothesis) was related negatively to the same criterion. The results are interesting but are based on only eleven student interviewers and fourteen experienced field workers; moreover, the research involved what the authors describe as "non-schedule interviewing," and may be less applicable to interviewing based on a fixed schedule of questions. Axelrod and Cannell (1959) found that interviewers rated by supervisors as successful showed somewhat higher scores for interpersonal types of jobs, according to the Strong interest inventory. Hauck and Steinkamp (1964), using the Edwards Personal Preference Schedule, found interviewers to be above the general population norm in "intraception," a dimension described as measuring empathic and interpersonal sensitivity. Thus the scattered evidence shows positive but modest relationships between a number of measures of interpersonal sensitivity and success as an interviewer.

It is also clear that other interviewer characteristics—demographic and attitudinal—can affect the interview product. It is less clear under what circumstances and through what chain of events these effects occur. Race and religion have been shown to inhibit responses, particularly when the respondent holds critical views of a minority group to which the interviewer apparently belongs (Hyman *et al.*, 1954; Robinson and Rohde, 1946). Differences in age and sex between interviewer and respondent have been shown to reduce the communication of some kinds of data (Benney, Riesman, and Star, 1956). In a study of mental health these investigators found that communication was maximized when both interviewer and respondent were young and were of the same sex; communication was least complete when interviewer and respondent were of the same age and opposite sex. Social class of interviewers was found by Katz (1942) to be reflected in the data they obtained on political issues, but this appears to be a relationship that can be eliminated by means of training. Unwanted relationships between interviewer attitudes and interview data have been cited earlier in connection with our discussion of reliability and validity. The irregularity of such findings in methodological research suggests also that the relationships are not necessary and that interviewers can be trained to keep their own attitudes from becoming manifest in the course of the interview.

Interviewers cannot be trained, of course, to modify their demographic characteristics, and to some extent such characteristics (age, race, socioeconomic status, and the like) should be taken into account in interviewer selection. This implies that interviewers should be selected or assigned to a particular project with selective attention to the characteristics of the respondents to be interviewed and the subject matter of the interview itself. The principle is that the interviewers will have easier access to respondents and will be more successful in the collection of valid data to the extent that they are seen as "within range of communication" by the respondents. If a sample of college professors is to be asked about problems of research support and university administration, it is unlikely that college undergraduates would be appropriate interviewers. If Negro respondents are to be interviewed on problems of living in previously white neighborhoods, it is likely that the race of the interviewer will be an important consideration in his ability to collect data.

To summarize, not enough research on the interviewing process has yet been done to permit very certain inferences about interviewer selection. What has been done suggests that in the selection of interviewers experience is a desirable criterion, provided that the experience was obtained in interviewing tasks similar to that for which selection is being made. Intelligence and empathic ability (not mere gregariousness or inquisitiveness in a particularistic sense) are relevant. Education is important, but interviewers overeducated for simple tasks may not be the best choices. Characteristics such as age, sex, race, and religion are relevant to the selection of interviewers in complex ways, depending on the content of the interview and the characteristics of respondents. The selection or assignment of interviewers should be made with the interviewer-respondent dyad in mind, rather than according to some more general or abstract criteria of excellence.

The problem of interviewing elite groups successfully is merely a special case of the goodness-of-fit issues just described among interviewer characteristics, respondent characteristics, and characteristics of the task itself. In addition to intelligence, relevant experience, empathic ability, and other such desiderata, the interviewer must be seen by the respondent as within range of communication on the required topic. This does not imply a matching of interviewer and respondent; one can hardly require that bankers be interviewed by fellow bankers, or statesmen by other statesmen. The interviewer must be seen, however, as sufficiently knowledgeable and specifically educated so that he can understand and appreciate the role and experience of the elite person. Dress, manner, speech, and apparent background offer initial clues to the elite respondent, but they will not suffice. Special training, as well as special criteria of selection, is likely to be necessary.

TRAINING

There is general agreement that an interviewer should be thoroughly trained in principles and procedures, but there is little research to suggest what methods of training are most effective or how much training is required. Evidence for the effects of interviewer training under varying circumstances is sketchy; opinions are strong—and variable. They range from a hopeful reliance on brief written instructions (characteristic of much commercial opinion polling and market research) to the proposals of Nadel (1951) and Kluckhohn (1945) that interviewers in anthropological research should have been psychoanalyzed as well as trained intensively in more specific ways. There is evidence that training makes a difference, some of it indirect and some direct. Cannell (1953) found that carefully trained interviewers produced results relatively free of class and attitudinal biases other investigators had reported; his research, however, did not include experimental comparisons among interviewers differing in training. Richardson (1954) found that intensive training in field methods produced significant increases in measures of interviewing performance, and no significant changes in personality measures (TAT). Individual differences in training effects were large so that the performance of individual interviewers before training was a poor predictor of post-training performance.

We believe that a training program for interviewers should do the following things:

1. *Provide the new interviewers with the principles of measurement, give them an intellectual grasp of the data-collecting function and a basis for evaluating interviewing behavior.*

2. *Teach the techniques of interviewing.*

3. *Provide opportunity for practice and evaluation by actually conducting interviews under controlled conditions.*

4. *Offer careful evaluation of interviews, especially at the beginning of actual data collection. Such evaluation should include review of interview protocols.*

The greatest emphasis and by far the most time in training should be spent on the third of these steps—practice in interviewing. In every type of skill training people rediscover the old dictum of John Dewey (1916) that training is not so much a matter of telling someone how to do something as of providing him with opportunities to do it—to participate actively in practicing the skill he wishes to attain. Steps 1 and 2 provide information on what good procedures are; steps 3 and 4 are crucial in making that information usable by the interviewer, making the insights and the skills really his.

Canter and his colleagues (1953) elaborated the principles of skill learning as follows:

People must have an opportunity to practice new ways of behaving if these are to become part of themselves. This fact lies behind the frequently stated principle that we learn to do by doing. The principle is true as far as it goes. But doing will lead to desirable learning only if certain conditions are present in the practice situation. What are these conditions?

First, the learner must be free to try something new. This means that he must be free to make mistakes as well as to achieve success. . . .

Second, the learner must be able to see and know the effects which his behavior achieves if he is to weed out behavior which gets effects he doesn't want and establish those behaviors which lead to the effects he desires. Otherwise he doesn't acquire the *meaning* of his acts as he practices them. . . . This process of getting feedback on the effects of what we do, in order to improve what we do in terms of better achieving some desired effect is a part of all intelligent practice.

The application of these principles to training interviewers is obvious. It means giving each trainee an opportunity to discuss interviewing principles, to practice interviews, to describe his own successes and failures and discuss those of others, in an environment in which he feels secure. He must know that his clumsiest efforts will not excite ridicule, that the worst of his early mistakes will bring help rather than blame, that the others in the situation share and understand his problems. He must be confident that he is accepted and valued by his colleagues, trainees and veterans, that they also want to learn from his experiences and help him acquire proficiency. The trainee learns not only from practice and interaction, but also from relating his practical experiences to principles and theory. He sees how poor interview techniques lead to inaccurate information or poor human relationships with respondents. He learns to eliminate poor techniques by seeing why they are poor. He is motivated to use good techniques by seeing that they obtain more satisfactory results.

*Use of role playing**

A number of specific training methods are available which can provide opportunity to practice and to analyze the results of practice under favorable conditions. One of these, role playing, is so well adapted to interviewer training that it deserves special consideration. Role playing or "reality practice" was pioneered by J. L. Moreno as a technique of psychological therapy, and has long since moved into the public domain as a technique for training in various behavioral skills, especially those involving interpersonal relationships.

In the application of role playing to interviewer training, one member of the group plays the part of a respondent, perhaps identifying himself with some actual person whom he knows, and responds to the interviewer in terms of the role which he is playing. One of the other members of the group plays the interviewer. The rest of the group act as observers. When the role playing session ends, there is a general discussion of the techniques which the interviewer used, the problems posed by the respondent, and the strengths and weaknesses which were demonstrated.

The trainee who plays the interviewer role gets the benefit of practicing directly the words and techniques he must use in the interview situation. He also gets the experience of facing real problems without real penalties; the game has reality, but he is not playing "for keeps." As a result, he is freer in his approach and more able to observe himself than in an actual interview situation.

The trainee usually gets as much out of playing the role of the respondent, however, as he does out of playing the interviewer role. As a respondent, he can

---

* Adapted from R. L. Kahn and C. F. Cannell, *The Dynamics of Interviewing.* New York: Wiley, 1957.

perceive where the interviewer failed to get information that was potentially available, and when the interviewer used techniques that were irritating. By analyzing his own reactions to being interviewed, and experiencing directly the effects of different interviewing techniques, the trainee becomes sensitized to reactions of respondents. Meanwhile, the trainees who are observers have a chance to see the performance in a more detached way and to plan the elimination of errors in their own interview techniques.

Recording interviews

Another technique, especially useful after the interviewer has completed original training, is the use of tape recordings of his interviews. These may be role-played interviews but, where circumstances permit, they should be actual interviews. Recording, of course, provides an excellent feedback opportunity. Usually the interviewer is readily able to evaluate his own performance and to correct his errors in technique.

Respondents should always be informed if recordings are to be made, and an opportunity provided for all or part of the interview to be "off the record" if the respondent so desires. Very seldom will the respondent make such a request. Experience has shown that respondents are not nervous about recording; they do not get stage fright at the sight of microphone or moving tape. The one who needs reassurance and support is the interviewer!

Additional training

For a major program of interviewer training the researcher should expect to spend a week or more before "real" interviews are to be taken. Even thereafter, supervision, feedback, and additional training are necessary for proficient interviewing. Recordings or actual observation of sampled interviews should be continued throughout the interviewing period. As with recordings, the presence of an observer appears to have little effect on the respondent's performance, although it may make the interviewer uneasy. Unfortunately, there is no substitute for some direct observation of real life behavior.

Supervision of interviewers

In most work situations it is a truism that employees, especially new employees, require supervision. Researchers have a tendency, however, to hire interviewers, train them, and leave them alone, often to discover later that the absence of supervision and performance review is costly. In large-scale field studies a supervisor should not be expected to supervise more than ten interviewers, and a more favorable ratio may improve costs and quality, especially when the task is complex.

COSTS OF INTERVIEWERS

Most researchers have a good deal of information about questionnaire development and interviewing techniques. They are not so well informed on what production goals to expect from interviewers. Most estimates are too high, and many are wildly optimistic. Generalizations are difficult, but we can attempt to offer a few administrative illustrations.

Consider, first, research on a probability sample with clusters of three or four dwellings scattered over a city, county, or some other relatively large geographic area. We will assume that the interview is an hour long, has some open and some closed questions, that the respondent is not known prior to the first visit to the dwelling, and is randomly selected by listing all household members. We will assume also that no other member of the household is to be interviewed, that a minimum response rate of 80 percent is required, and that all field work required to select the sample of dwellings has already been completed. Supervisory costs and cost of initial training of the interviewers are also excluded.

A study by Sudman (1967) shows an analysis of surveys by three organizations under approximately these conditions. Sudman found considerable stability in the proportion of time spent by interviewers in different activities. About 35 percent of the interviewer's total time on a study is actually spent in interviewing. About 40 percent is spent in travel, and in locating and identifying eligible respondents. Editing interviews and doing other required clerical work takes about 15 percent of the time, and the remainder goes to the study of materials and to administrative matters.

The time estimates for interviewing include not only the actual time spent in asking questions and recording responses, but time spent in getting into the house, in social communication and introductory statements to the interview, and in brief social interaction after the interview.

The total time spent per interview under these conditions averaged from six to seven hours. Costs for such time will vary according to travel and salary. In the cases analyzed in 1965 and 1966, the actual cost of such interviews averaged between $17 and $21.

By contrast, we offer a recent experience in a very different setting. Interviews were conducted in a single industrial plant, and appointments were made for each interview. The average length of interview was one to one-and-a-half hours but the range was from three-quarters of an hour to nearly two-and-a-half hours. Most questions were open; full notes were taken during the interview and dictated after each interview. Experienced interviewers were able to average one-and-a-half to two interviews per day. Time required to reconstruct and dictate each interview exceeded the original "take time." Costs were less than those for the population surveys described above, but only modestly so.

CONCLUSION

Any present-day discussion of interviewing for social research should be tentative in tone; the field is in flux. For one thing, some new ideas have been proposed after a long and relatively static period. Webb and his colleagues (1966) have argued persuasively for less addiction to interviewing among social-research workers and more attention to "unobtrusive measures." Richardson and his coauthors (1965) have presented the opposing notions of "stressed" versus "unstressed" interviews in terms that invite research on the appropriate use of differing techniques. Cannell and Fowler (1965), Fowler (1966), and others have questioned the earlier emphasis on avoidance of interviewer influence and have begun research on the interviewer's functions as teacher and reinforcer of appropriate respondent behavior, as well as permissive encourager of conversation.

A second factor which makes for change in interviewing theory and practice is cultural and historical; the violation of privacy for trivial or questionable purposes, usually having nothing to do with research, has brought the rights and roles of interviewers and respondents under intensive consideration. This is a poor time for predicting the outcome of a trend so new, and one which may take many different forms. Nevertheless, it seems likely that sophistication about the reasons for interviewing and the consequences of the interview will increase. Whether such increasing respondent sophistication will make the collection of data by interviewing easier, more difficult, or virtually impossible depends on the visible uses and abuses of the interview. In all but its most extreme and indirect forms, the interviewing technique is ultimately dependent upon a societal record of individual protection, respect for the confidentiality of personal data, and relevant and benign use of information. Each research necessarily contributes, positively or negatively, to that record.

REFERENCES

American Psychological Association (1954). *Ethical standards for psychologists.* Washington, D.C.: American Psychological Association.

Argyris, C. (1965). *Integrating the individual and the organization.* New York: Wiley.

Asch, S. (1952). *Social psychology.* Englewood Cliffs, N.J.: Prentice-Hall.

Atkinson, J. W., Ed. (1958). *Motives in fantasy, action, and society.* Princeton, N.J.: Van Nostrand.

Axelrod, M., and C. F. Cannell (1959). A research note on an attempt to predict interviewer effectiveness. *Publ. Opin. Quart., 23,* 571–574.

Bancroft, Gertrude, and E. H. Welch (1946). Recent experience with problems of labor force measurement. *J. Amer. Statist. Assoc., 41,* 303–312.

Bartlett, F. C. (1932). *Remembering.* London: Cambridge Univ. Press.

Bauer, R. A. (1966). *Social indicators.* Cambridge: M.I.T. Press.

Beezer, R. H. (1956). *Research on methods of interviewing foreign informants.* George Washington University Human Technology Reports, No. 30.

Belloc, Nedra B. (1954). Validation of morbidity survey data by comparison with hospital records. *J. Amer. Statist. Assoc., 49,* 832–847.

Benney, M., D. Riesman, and Shirley A. Star (1956). Age and sex in the interview. *Amer. J. Sociol., 62,* 143–152.

Bingham, W. V. D., and B. V. Moore (1924). *How to interview.* New York: Harper and Row.

Blankenship, A. B. (1940). The effect of the interviewer upon the response in a public opinion poll. *J. consult. Psychol., 4,* 134–136.

Booth, C. (1892–1897). *Life and labour of the people of London* (17 vols.). London: Macmillan.

Boring, E. G. (1950). *A history of experimental psychology* (2nd ed.). New York: Appleton.

Cahalan, D., V. Tamulonis, and H. W. Verner (1947). Interviewer bias involved in certain types of opinion survey questions. *Int. J. Opin. Attitude Res., 1* (1), 63–77.

Campbell, A., P. E. Converse, W. Miller, and D. E. Stokes (1960). *The American voter.* New York: Wiley.

Campbell, D. T. (1957). Factors relevant to the validity of experiments in social settings. *Psychol. Bull., 54,* 297–312.

Campbell, D. T., and D. W. Fiske (1959). Convergent and discriminant validation by the multitrait multimethod matrix. *Psychol. Bull., 56,* 81–105.

Cannell, C. F. (1953). A study of the effects of interviewers' expectations upon interviewing results. Doctoral dissertation, Ohio State University.

Cannell, C. F., G. Fisher, and T. Bakker (1961). Reporting of hospitalization in the health interview survey. *Health Statistics,* Series D, No. 4. (Reprinted in *Vital and Health Statistics,* 1965, Series 2, No. 6.) U.S. Department of Health, Education, and Welfare. Public Health Service.

Cannell, C. F., and F. Fowler (1965). Comparison of hospitalization reporting in three survey procedures. *Vital and Health Statistics,* Series 2, No. 8. U.S. Department of Health, Education, and Welfare. Public Health Service.

Canter, R., *et al.* (1953). The crucial conditions of training. *Adult Leadership, 2* (2), 5–8, 31.

Chess, S., *et al.* (1960). Implications of a longitudinal study of child development for child psychiatry. *Amer. J. Psychiat., 117,* 434.

Clark, A. L., and P. Wallin (1964). The accuracy of husbands' and wives' reports of the frequency of marital coitus. *Population Studies, 18* (2), 165–173.

Cobb, S., and C. F. Cannell (1966). Some thoughts about interview data. *Int. Epidemiol. Bull., 13,* 43–54.

Coombs, C. H. (1964). *A theory of data.* New York: Wiley.

Couch, A., and K. Keniston (1960). Yeasayers and naysayers: agreeing response set as a personality variable. *J. abnorm. soc. Psychol., 60,* 150–174.

Cronbach, L. J. (1946). Response sets and test validity. *Educ. psychol. Measmt., 6,* 475–494.

———— (1960). *Essentials of psychological testing* (2nd ed.). New York: Harper and Row.

Crutchfield, R. S., and D. A. Gordon (1947). Variations in respondents' interpretations of an opinion poll question. *Int. J. Opin. Attitude Res., 1* (3), 1–12.

Dewey, J. (1916). *Democracy in education.* New York: Macmillan.

Erlich, June, and D. Riesman (1961). Age and authority in the interview. *Publ. Opin. Quart., 25,* 39–56.

Ferber, R. (1959). *Collecting financial data by consumer panel techniques.* Urbana, Ill.: Bureau of Economic and Business Research, Univ. of Illinois.

Ferber, R., and H. Wales (1952). Detection and correction of interviewer bias. *Publ. Opin. Quart., 16,* 107–127.

Flowerman, S. H., *et al.* (1950). Unpublished report. American Jewish Committee.

Fowler, F. J., Jr. (1966). Education, interaction, and interview performance. Doctoral dissertation, University of Michigan.

Freedman, R., P. K. Whelpton, and A. A. Campbell (1959). *Family planning, sterility, and population growth.* New York: McGraw-Hill.

Friedman, P. A. (1942). A second experiment of interviewer bias. *Sociometry, 15,* 378–381.

Goddard, Katherine E., G. Broder, and C. Wenar (1961). Reliability of pediatric histories, a preliminary study. *Pediatrics, 28,* 1011–1018.

Gorden, R. L. (1954). An interaction analysis of the depth interview. Doctoral dissertation, University of Chicago.

Guest, L. L. (1947). A study of interviewer competence. *Int. J. Opin. Attitude Res., 1* (4), 17–30.

Guest, L. L., and R. Nuckols (1950). A laboratory experiment in recording in public opinion interviewing. *Int. J. Opin. Attitude Res., 4,* 336–352.

Gurin, G., J. Veroff, and S. Feld (1960). *Americans view their mental health.* New York: Basic Books.

Hansen, M. H., W. N. Hurwitz, E. S. Marks, and W. P. Mauldin (1951). Response errors in surveys. *J. Amer. Statist. Assoc., 46,* 147–190.

Hauck, M., and S. Steinkamp (1964). *Survey reliability and interviewer competence.* Urbana, Ill.: Bureau of Economic and Business Research, Univ. of Illinois.

Herzberg, F., B. Mausner, and B. Snyderman (1959). *The motivation to work.* New York: Wiley.

Hildum, D., and R. W. Brown (1956). Verbal reinforcement and interviewer bias. *J. abnorm. soc. Psychol., 53,* 108–111.

Hyman, H., *et al.* (1954). *Interviewing in social research.* Chicago: Univ. of Chicago Press.

Jaeger, Carol, and Jean L. Pennock (1961). An analysis of consistency of response in household surveys. *J. Amer. Statist. Assoc., 56,* 320–327.

Janis, I. L. (1958). *Psychological stress.* New York: Wiley.

Kahn, R. L. (1952). A comparison of two methods of collecting data for social research. Doctoral dissertation, University of Michigan.

Kahn, R. L., and C. F. Cannell (1957). *The dynamics of interviewing.* New York: Wiley.

Kahn, R. L., D. M. Wolfe, R. P. Quinn, and J. D. Snoek (1964). *Organizational stress.* New York: Wiley.

Kaplan, A. (1965). *The conduct of inquiry.* San Francisco: Chandler.

Katona, G. (1960). *The powerful consumer.* New York: McGraw-Hill.

Katz, D. (1942). Do interviewers bias poll results? *Publ. Opin. Quart., 6,* 248–268.

Kinsey, A. C., W. B. Pomeroy, and C. E. Martin (1948). *Sexual behavior in the human male*. Philadelphia: W. B. Saunders.

Kish, L. (1965). *Survey sampling*. New York: Wiley.

Kish, L., and Carol W. Slater (1960). Two studies of interviewer variance of socio-psychological variables. In *American Statistical Association, Social Statistics Section Proceedings, 1960*. Pp. 66–70.

Kluckhohn, C. (1945). The personal document in anthropological science. In L. Gottschalk, C. Kluckhohn, and R. Angell, *The use of personal documents in history, anthropology and sociology*. New York: Social Science Research Council.

Krasner, L. (1958). Studies of the conditioning of verbal behavior. *Psychol. Bull., 55*, 148–170.

Lamale, Helen H. (1959). Methodology of the survey of consumer expenditures in 1950. Philadelphia: Univ. of Pennsylvania.

Lansing, J. B., and D. M. Blood (1964). *The changing travel market*. Ann Arbor, Mich.: Survey Research Center. Monograph No. 38.

Lansing, J. B., G. P. Ginsberg, and Kaisa Braaten (1961). *An investigation of response error*. Bureau of Economic and Business Research, Univ. of Illinois.

Lazarsfeld, P. F. (1944). The controversy over detailed interviews—an offer for negotiation. *Publ. Opin. Quart., 8*, 38–60.

Lenski, G. E., and J. C. Leggett (1960). Caste, class, and deference in the research interview. *Amer. J. Sociol., 65*, 463–467.

Lewin, K. (1947). Frontiers in group dynamics. *Hum. Relat., 1*, 5–41.

Likert, R. (1961). *New patterns of management*. New York: McGraw-Hill.

Litwak, E. (1956). A classification of biased questions. *Amer. J. Sociol., 62*, 182–186.

Maccoby, Eleanor, and N. Maccoby (1954). The interview: a tool of social science. In G. Lindzey (Ed.), *Handbook of social psychology*. Vol. 1. Cambridge, Mass.: Addison-Wesley. Pp. 449–487.

Macfarlane, J. W. (1938). Studies in child guidance: I. Methodology of data collection and organization. *Monogr. Soc. Res. Child Develpmt., 3*, No. 6.

Madow, W. G. (1967). Interview data on chronic conditions compared with information derived from medical records. *Vital and Health Statistics*, Series 2, No. 23. U.S. Department of Health, Education, and Welfare. Public Health Service.

Mandler, G., and W. K. Kaplan (1956). Subjective evaluation and reinforcing effect of a verbal stimulus. *Science, 124*, 582–583.

Mauldin, W. P., and E. S. Marks (1950). Problems of response in enumerative surveys. *Amer. Sociol. Rev., 15*, 5.

Merton, R. K., Marjorie Fiske, and Patricia L. Kendall (1956). *The focused interview*. Glencoe, Ill.: Free Press.

Milgram, S. (1965). Some conditions of obedience and disobedience to authority. In J. D. Steiner and M. Fishbein (Eds.), *Current studies in social psychology*. New York: Holt.

Mooney, H. W. (1962). Methodology in two California health surveys. Public Health Monograph No. 70, U.S. Government Printing Office.

Myers, R. J. (1940). Errors and bias in the reporting of ages in census data. *Trans. Actuarial Soc. Amer., 41,* 395–415.

Nadel, S. F. (1951). *Foundations of social anthropology.* London: Cohen and West.

Neely, Twila (1937). *A study of error in the interview.* (Privately printed)

Neter, J., and J. Waksberg (1965). Response errors in collection of expenditures data by household interviews: an experimental study. Technical Paper No. 11, U.S. Bureau of the Census, U.S. Government Printing Office.

Parry, H., and Helen Crossley (1950). Validity of responses to survey questions. *Publ. Opin. Quart., 14,* 61–80.

Payne, S. L. (1951). *The art of asking questions.* Princeton, N.J.: Princeton Univ. Press.

Politz, A. (1958). Description of operational design and procedures. *Life,* Study of Consumer Expenditures, Vol. 4.

Proshansky, H., and B. Seidenberg, Eds. (1965). *Basic studies in social psychology.* New York: Holt.

Quay, H. (1959). The effect of verbal reinforcement on the recall of early memories. *J. abnorm. soc. Psychol., 59,* 254–257.

Rice, S. A. (1929). Contagious bias in the interview: a methodological note. *Amer. J. Sociol., 35,* 420–423.

Richardson, S. A. (1954). A study of selected personality characteristics of social science field workers. Doctoral dissertation, Cornell University.

Richardson, S. A., Barbara S. Dohrenwend, and D. Klein (1965). *Interviewing.* New York: Basic Books.

Richardson, S. A., A. H. Hastorf, and S. M. Dornbusch (1964). Effects of physical disability on a child's description of himself. *Child Develpmt., 35,* 893–907.

Riesman, D. (1958). Some observations on interviewing in the teacher apprehension study. In P. F. Lazarsfeld and W. Thielens (Eds.), *The academic mind.* Glencoe, Ill.: Free Press.

Robinson, D., and S. Rohde (1946). Two experiments with an anti-Semitism poll. *J. abnorm. soc. Psychol., 41,* 136–144.

Robinson, J. P., R. Athanasiou, and Kendra Head (1967). *Measures of occupational attitudes and occupational characteristics.* Ann Arbor, Mich.: Survey Research Center.

Rogers, C. R. (1942). *Counseling and psychotherapy.* Boston: Houghton Mifflin.

——— (1951). *Client-centered therapy.* Boston: Houghton Mifflin.

Salzinger, K., and Stephanie Pisoni (1960). Reinforcement of verbal affect responses of normal subjects during an interview. *J. abnorm. soc. Psychol., 60,* 127–130.

Salzinger, Suzanne (1956). Rate of affect response in schizophrenics as a function of three types of interviewer verbal behavior. Paper read at Eastern Psychol. Assoc. meeting. Atlantic City, March 1956.

Saslow, G., *et al.* (1957). Test-retest stability of interaction patterns during interviews conducted one week apart. *J. abnorm. soc. Psychol., 54,* 295–302.

Selltiz, C., M. Jahoda, M. Deutsch, and S. W. Cook (1959). *Research methods in social relations.* New York: Holt.

Shapiro, S., and J. C. Eberhart (1947). Interviewer differences in an intensive interview survey. *Int. J. Opin. Attitude Res., 1* (2), 1–17.

Shaw, M. E., and J. M. Wright (1967). *Scales for the measurement of attitudes.* New York: McGraw-Hill.

Smith, M. B., J. S. Bruner, and R. W. White (1956). *Opinions and personality.* New York: Wiley.

Stanton, F., and K. H. Baker (1942). Interview bias and the recall of incompletely learned materials. *Sociometry, 5,* 123–134.

Steiner, I., and M. Fishbein, Eds. (1965). *Current studies in social psychology.* New York: Holt.

Sudman, S. (1967). *Reducing the cost of surveys.* Chicago: Aldine.

Sullivan, H. S. (1954). *The psychiatric interview.* New York: Norton.

Webb, E. J., D. T. Campbell, R. D. Schwartz, and L. Sechrest (1966). *Unobtrusive measures.* Chicago: Rand McNally.

Weiss, D. J., R. V. Davis, G. W. England, and L. H. Lotquist (1961). Validity of work histories obtained by interview. *Minn. Stud. Vocational Rehabilitation, 12,* No. 41.

Wenar, C. (1963). The reliability of development histories—summary and evaluation of evidence. Univ. of Pennsylvania School of Medicine. (Mimeo)

Whitehead, A. N. (1929). *Process and reality.* New York: Macmillan.

Williams, J. Allen, Jr. (1964). Interviewer-respondent interaction: a study of bias in the information interview. *Sociometry, 27,* 338–352.

Withey, S. (1952). Consistency of immediate and delayed report of financial data. Doctoral dissertation, University of Michigan, Ann Arbor.

16

Content Analysis

OLE R. HOLSTI, *University of British Columbia*
With the collaboration of Joanne K. Loomba and Robert C. North

The communication process is an intrinsic part of all social interaction from the interpersonal to the international level. Groups, institutions, and organizations, from the family to the nation, exist by virtue of communication and cease to exist once it becomes totally disrupted. It is thus axiomatic that the study of the processes and content of communication is basic to all social sciences, "for most social facts worth studying are embedded in a process of communication" (Pool, 1954, p. 352).

The interest of the social psychologist in the content of communication has been described by Cartwright (1953, p. 422):

When one stops to think of it, it is really surprising how much of the subject matter of social psychology is in the form of verbal behavior. The formation and transmission of group standards, values, attitudes, and skills are accomplished largely by means of verbal communication. Education in the schools, in the home, in business, in the neighborhood, and through the mass media is brought about by the transmission of information and by the exercise of controls which are largely mediated through written or spoken words. If one is concerned with problems of social organization, the situation is similar. Supervision, management, coordination, and the exertion of influence are principally matters of verbal interaction. Social and political conflicts, although often stemming from divergent economic interests and power, cannot be fully understood without studying the words employed in the interaction of conflicting groups, and the process of mediation consists largely in talking things out. The work of the world, and its entertainment, too, is in no small measure mediated by verbal and other symbolic behavior.

Useful comments and suggestions on an earlier draft of this chapter were offered by Richard R. Fagen, Bo Ohlström, Kenneth C. Prewitt, Philip J. Stone, Lois Swirsky, and Robert G. Weinland. Their assistance is gratefully acknowledged, as is that of Mrs. Arlee Ellis and Mrs. Violet Lofgren, whose contributions are too numerous to list exhaustively.

These comments are equally appropriate for other social sciences. As a consequence, the study of communication content has been approached from a variety of different starting points and undertaken with the tools and conceptual frameworks of several disciplines.

Content analysis is a multipurpose research method developed specifically for investigating a broad spectrum of problems in which the content of communication serves as the basis of inference. In the introductory section of this chapter we discuss specific definitions of content analysis, types of content-analysis research designs, and major trends in the development of content analysis. Within the framework developed in the introduction, the second section surveys research in which content analysis has been employed. This is followed by an examination of some problems of research design: units and categories of analysis, and types of measurement. The fourth section is concerned with the problems of sampling, reliability, and validity. The chapter concludes with a discussion of content analysis by means of electronic computers, a recent development with important implications for many types of research problems.

DEFINITION OF CONTENT ANALYSIS

Nearly all research in the social sciences and humanities depends in one way or another on careful reading of written materials. Given the ubiquity of this process in research, what characteristics distinguish content analysis from any careful reading of documents? Definitions of content analysis have tended to change over time with developments in technique and with the application of the tool itself to new problems and types of materials. Among the definitions which have been proposed are the following:

Content analysis is the statistical semantics of political discourse. (Kaplan, 1943, p. 230)

"Content analysis" may be defined as referring to any technique (a) for the *classification* of the *sign-vehicles*, (b) which relies solely upon the *judgments* (which theoretically, may range from perceptual discriminations to sheer guesses) of an analyst or group of analysts as to which sign-vehicles fall into which categories, (c) on the basis of *explicitly formulated rules*, (d) provided that the analyst's judgments are regarded as the reports of a *scientific observer*. (Janis, 1949, p. 55)

Content analysis is a research technique for the objective, systematic, and quantitative description of the manifest content of communication. (Berelson, 1952, p. 18)

We propose to use the terms "content analysis" and "coding" interchangeably to refer to the objective, systematic, and quantitative description of any symbolic behavior. (Cartwright, 1953, p. 424)

The term "content analysis" is used here to mean the scientific analysis of communications messages. . . . The method is broadly speaking the "scientific method," and while being catholic in nature, it requires that the analysis be rigorous and systematic. (Barcus, 1959, p. 8)

Content analysis refers to any procedure for assessing the relative extent to which specified references, attitudes, or themes permeate a given message or document. (Stone, 1964)

This selective sampling of definitions indicates that, along with a persisting consensus about some characteristics, there has been a marked tendency to broaden the boundaries of content analysis by means of less restrictive definitions.

Among the characteristics of content analysis on which there is wide agreement are those of *objectivity, system,* and *generality.* To have *objectivity,* the analysis must be carried out on the basis of explicitly formulated rules which will enable two or more persons to obtain the same results from the same documents. In a *systematic* analysis the inclusion and exclusion of content or categories is done according to consistently applied criteria of selection; this requirement eliminates analyses in which only materials supporting the investigator's hypotheses are examined. By *generality* we mean that the findings must have theoretical relevance; purely descriptive information about content, unrelated to other attributes of content or to the characteristics of the sender or recipient of the message, is of little scientific value. These three requirements are not unique to content analysis, but are necessary conditions for all scientific inquiry. They serve to indicate that, in general terms, content analysis can be regarded as the application of the principles of scientific research to the analysis of communication content.

Alongside general consensus on the defining characteristics of content analysis —objectivity, system, and generality—considerable debate on two other requirements has been generated in recent literature. First, must content analysis be *quantitative?* And second, must it be limited to the *manifest* content, or may it be used also to probe for the more latent aspects of communication?

Quantification has usually been accepted as one of the most important characteristics of content analysis. According to one standard source, "There is clearly no reason for content analysis unless the question one wants answered is quantitative" (Lasswell, Lerner, and Pool, 1952, p. 45). However, there is considerable disagreement about the meaning of the term "quantitative." Some definitions equate it with *numerical:* "Content analysis aims at a classification of content in more precise, *numerical terms* than is provided by impressionistic 'more or less' judgments of 'either-or' " (Kaplan and Goldsen, 1949, p. 83). Other definitions are less restrictive and include studies in which findings are reported in such terms as "more," "less," or "increasing" (Berelson, 1952, p. 17). However, qualitativeness and quantitativeness are not dichotomous attributes, but fall along a continuum (Lazarsfeld and Barton, 1951). To state that attribute *A* became more important in *X*'s messages with the passing of time is a qualitative assertion, but it is not without a quantitative aspect; nor is such a statement as "In document *Y*, *A* asserts *X*" purely qualitative. Data reported in this form imply ordinal and nominal scaling. Moreover, statistical methods can be used with such data.

Definitions of content analysis requiring that inferences be derived strictly from counts of *frequency* (for example, Leites and Pool, 1942, pp. 1–2; Janis, 1943, p. 429) place a number of standard methods on the borderline of acceptability. A pioneering application of content analysis, the RADIR studies, combined frequency and nonfrequency techniques; each editorial in the sample taken from a series of "prestige newspapers" during a sixty-year period was coded according to the appearance or nonappearance of certain key symbols (Lasswell, Lerner, and Pool, 1952). Thus a strict frequency count, including multiple use of any symbol within an editorial, was not employed. A similarly "mixed" characteristic is found in the technique of *contingency analysis,* in which the coding of material depends on the absence or presence of the attribute within some content unit, rather than on the frequency of its presence (Osgood, 1959, p. 63).

The case for content analysis based on exact counts of frequency is a powerful one. Foremost among the arguments is the degree of precision with which one's conclusions may be stated. Descriptions such as "45 percent" or "27 times out of a possible 30" convey information more precisely than statements such as "less than half" or "almost always." In response to the question "Why quantify?" Lasswell, Lerner, and Pool (1952, pp. 31–32) have pointed to a number of other questions which often remain unanswered in qualitative symbol studies:

Can we assume that a scholar read his sources with the same degree of care throughout his research? Did he allow his eye to travel over the thousands of pages of parliamentary debates, newspapers, magazines and other source lists in his bibliography or notes? Or did he use a sampling system scanning some pages superficially, though concentrating upon certain periods? Was the sampling system for the *Frankfurter Zeitung,* if one was employed, comparable with the one for the *Manchester Guardian?* Were the leaflets chosen simply because they were conveniently available to the scholar, or were they genuinely representative of the most widely circulated propaganda leaflets?

Finally, statistical methods, which permit a more accurate description of the degree of covariation of two or more attributes, require some degree of quantification. They also permit a more precise answer to a recurring question raised by case studies: with what degree of confidence can one generalize from the results obtained in the sample under study? But the use of statistics is not dependent solely on frequency counts or any other single system of enumeration.

Despite the widely recognized advantages of quantitative methods, the tendency to equate content analysis with tabulation of frequencies has been criticized on a number of grounds. The most general of these is the charge that such a restriction leads to bias in the selection of problems to be investigated, undue emphasis being placed on precision at the cost of problem significance (Barcus, 1959; Smythe, 1952).

Related to this general criticism is the view that one can draw more meaningful inferences by nonquantitative methods (Kracauer, 1952). Qualitative content analysis, which has sometimes been defined as the drawing of inferences on the basis of appearance or nonappearance of attributes in messages, has been defended largely, though not solely, for its superior performance in problems of applied social science (George, 1959b, pp. 9–10). When content from propaganda sources is used to predict enemy behavior, the pressure of time, the inability to control variables, and the possibility that nonrecurring phenomena may provide major clues to policy often render exhaustive quantitative analyses uneconomical and difficult, if not impossible, to design and carry out. Citing instances in which qualitative analysts were able to draw more accurate inferences from studies of Nazi propaganda during World War II than could those using quantitative techniques, George concluded: "Qualitative analysis of a limited number of crucial communications may often yield better clues to the particular intentions of a particular speaker at one moment in time than more standardized techniques" (1959b, p. 7).

In line with this reasoning, proponents of qualitative techniques also question the assumption that, for purposes of inference, frequency of assertion is necessarily related to the importance of the assertion; these critics suggest that the single appearance or omission of an attribute in a document may be of more significance than the relative frequency of other characteristics (George, 1959b). An example of this point is found in a study of Chinese documents prior to China's active entry into the Korean war in October 1950. The change from the passive term *fan tui* to the word *k'ang yi*, previously used as an exhortation to action against Japan and against the Chinese Nationalists, provided the first clue that Chinese leaders had decided to intervene in the war (Whiting, 1960, p. 99). But even studies which emphasize the unique aspects of each document are not simply qualitative; rather than counting frequencies, the analysts have chosen to formulate nominal categories into which one of two scores is recorded —present or absent.

Finally, whether stated explicitly or not, even the most rigorously quantitative study uses qualitative techniques at some stage in the research, either as a preliminary step in determining which variables are most likely to prove useful when measured, or as a final check on the face validity of the findings. Pool (1959, p. 192) summarizes this point: "It should not be assumed that qualitative methods are insightful, and quantitative ones merely mechanical methods for checking hypotheses. The relationship is a circular one; each provides new insights on which the other can feed."

It is worth noting in conclusion that for most scientific research the advantages to be gained by some type of quantification continue to be important. Nevertheless, for purposes of definition there are few compelling reasons for excluding studies which fail to conform to any single system of enumeration from the proper jurisdiction of content analysis.

A second major source of disagreement among those defining content analysis is whether it must be limited to manifest content, that is, the surface meaning of the content. Or may content analysis be used to analyze the deeper layers of meaning embedded in the content? The manifest-latent controversy can be considered at two levels. The requirement of objectivity stipulates that only those symbols and combinations of symbols actually appearing in the message be recorded. In other words, the *coding* process cannot be one of "reading between the lines." In this sense, content analysis is limited to manifest attributes of text.

The second aspect of the manifest-latent issue concerns the *interpretation* of results. This debate is essentially one concerning the dimensions of communication which may properly be analyzed (Morris, 1946). Earlier definitions tended to limit content analysis to questions of semantics, the relationship of signs to referents, and to questions of syntactics, the relationship of signs to signs (Kaplan, 1943; Janis, 1949; Berelson, 1952). The restriction against analysis of the pragmatical dimension of language, the relationship of signs to those that produce or receive them, was usually based on the difficulty of drawing valid inferences about the causes or effects of communication directly from content data.

As has been the case in the quantitative-qualitative debate, the recent trend has been in the direction of a broader definition (Cartwright, 1953, p. 424; Barcus, 1959, p. 19; Dunphy, 1964). Nearly the entire volume of papers from the Work Conference on Content Analysis of the Social Science Research Council was addressed to using messages for purposes of answering questions about the causes or effects of communication (Pool, 1959). This trend toward a broader view of content analysis is evident in Osgood's definition (1959, p. 36):

. . . we define content analysis as a procedure whereby one makes inferences about sources and receivers from evidence in the messages they exchange. . . . [W]hen the interest of the content analyst lies in making inferences about the source of a message, he must rely upon encoding dependencies, that is, the dependencies of message events upon psychological processes in speakers and writers. When his interest lies in making inferences about the effects of a message upon its receivers, on the other hand, he relies upon decoding dependencies, that is, the dependencies of events in listeners and readers (their meanings, emotions, attitudes, and the like) upon the content and structure of messages.

In this view, content analysis is considered an integral part of the field of psycholinguistics (Osgood and Sebeok, 1954; Jaffe, 1966).

Actually, the differences between the broader and more restrictive views are not so great as suggested at first glance. Both Kaplan (1943, p. 223) and Janis (1943, p. 437) exclude pragmatical content analysis because inferences as to the causes or effects of content can rarely be validated solely by analysis of the messages themselves. On the other hand, proponents of a broader definition usually assume that content data will be used, directly or indirectly, in conjunction with independent behavioral indices.

For present purposes, a broad definition of the field will be adopted: *Content analysis is any technique for making inferences by systematically and objectively identifying specified characteristics of messages.* While any definition adopted is open to criticism, one which errs on the side of inclusiveness permits a broader consideration of the literature, and thus has an advantage over one which is overly restrictive.

WHEN TO USE CONTENT ANALYSIS

When should one use content analysis? The wide range of possibilities is suggested by reference to a few of the diverse problems which have been subjected to content-analysis techniques in recent years:

1. What differences among cultures are reflected in the songs and literature of various nations (Sebald, 1962; Lewin, 1947)?

2. *To what extent have the political symbols of the New Deal been adopted by American conservatives (Prothro, 1956)?*

3. *What differences characterize the language behavior of schizophrenic and normal persons (Mann, 1944; Fairbanks, 1944)?*

4. *Is editorial support of a political candidate also reflected in biased news sections (Kobre, 1953; Klein and Maccoby, 1954)?*

5. *What has been the Soviet reaction to Voice of America broadcasts (Inkeles, 1952)?*

6. *Is the Riesman hypothesis about the increasing other-directedness of American society supported by changing content of consumer goods advertising (Dornbusch and Hickman, 1959)?*

7. *How is sentence length related to the comprehensibility of literature (Coleman, 1962)?*

8. *How are expressions of the "need for achievement" related to stages in the development of a civilization (McClelland, 1961; deCharms and Moeller, 1962)?*

9. *Who was the author of the Federalist Papers, Nos. 49–58, 62, and 63 (Mosteller and Wallace, 1964)?*

Content analysis is not relevant to all documentary research, however. It can rarely be used to determine the truth of an assertion, or to evaluate the esthetic qualities of poetry. Moreover, if the social scientist uses documents to settle limited issues of fact, such as to determine which newspapers supported Kennedy and Nixon in 1960, methods other than content analysis could be used more efficiently. But the investigator's questions and the content of documents are rarely coterminous (Dibble, 1963, p. 216). One approach to documentary research is exemplified by a recent manual, which suggests dependence on "a sort of sixth sense that will alert you to tell-tale signs" (quoted in Dibble, 1963, p. 204). Content analysis may be considered as a supplement to, not a substitute for, subjective examination of documents. On the other hand, the limitation of depending solely on ordinary reading of documents for purposes of scientific research are illustrated in a study of Richard Wright's autobiography, *Black Boy* (White, 1947). Although the investigator was a trained psychologist, his preliminary appraisal of the book failed to uncover a number of major themes. Systematic content analysis, however, revealed Wright's emphasis on personal safety (18 percent of all value judgments), failure to identify with other Negroes, and lack of interest in social goals. In general, then, content analysis is useful whenever the problem requires precise and replicable methods for analyzing those aspects of symbolic behavior which may escape casual scrutiny.

More specifically, content analysis is likely to prove especially useful for at least three general classes of research problems. Content analysis may be helpful when there are technical advantages because the volume of material to be examined is such that the investigator must either (1) confine his study to some sample of the total universe of communication, (2) use a team of assistants, each with his own subjective predispositions, or (3) both. For example, an analysis of key symbols appearing in "elite" newspapers over a sixty-year period (Lasswell, Lerner, and Pool, 1952), could not be undertaken on a nonsystematic basis; nor could every issue of each newspaper for the entire period be examined. Such a study clearly required the use of both sampling and many research assistants. Unless rigorous and explicitly formulated rules for systematic sampling and reliable coding were used, inferences drawn from these data would be of questionable value. Content analysis is a technique for meeting these requirements.

Content analysis may also prove useful when data accessibility is a problem and the investigator's data are limited to the messages produced by individuals. Restrictions of time or space often do not permit the social scientist to gain direct access to his subject. In such cases the subject must be studied "at a distance," with the consequence that other social-science research techniques (interview, questionnaire, observation) are not applicable. If the subject is no longer alive, he can be studied only through the record of his activities, through what his contemporaries set down about him, or through whatever writings he has left. In some instances the third category constitutes the most revealing, and occasionally the only surviving, source. Thus content analysis can serve as a "last resort" approach to social research when more direct techniques of analysis are ruled out by circumstances. Identification of unknown authors (Yule, 1944; Paisley, 1964), inferences from enemy propaganda (George, 1959a; Lasswell, Leites *et al.*, 1949; Whiting, 1960), or analysis of decision makers' attitudes during international crisis (Holsti, Brody, and North, 1965) illustrate this use of content analysis.

Finally, some form of content analysis is often necessary when, given certain theoretical components of the data themselves, the subject's own language is crucial to the research problem. To analyze psychiatric interviews, projective tests, or open-ended questionnaires, the social scientist often requires information of a subtlety or complexity which renders casual scrutiny inadequate, even if undertaken by a skilled and sensitive reader. One would have little confidence in rough estimates of the degree of "need achievement" in Indian folklore (McClelland and Friedman, 1952), or of the type/token ratio—the number of different words in text of a given length—in the language of schizophrenics (Fairbanks, 1944; Page, 1953), regardless of the investigator's skill or training.

CONTENT-ANALYSIS RESEARCH DESIGNS

All communication is composed of six basic elements: a *source* or sender; an *encoding process* which results in a *message;* a *channel* of transmission; a *detector* or recipient of the message; and a *decoding process*. Although content analysis is always performed on the message, it may be used to answer questions about each of the other elements of communication. The classical formulation of these questions is, "Who says what, to whom, how, and with what effect?" (Lasswell, Lerner, and Pool, 1952, p. 12), to which one more questions—"Why?"—may be added.

Each of these questions may be subsumed under research designed for three different purposes. The investigator may analyze messages to test hypotheses and make inferences about (1) characteristics of the text, (2) causes or antecedents of the message, or (3) effects of the communication. These three categories differ with respect to the questions asked of the data, the dimension of communication analyzed, and the research design. These differences are summarized in Table 1. Here it will be useful to consider problems and implications inherent in each of the three categories.

The first and most frequent application of content analysis has been for the purpose of *describing the attributes of the message,* without reference to either the intentions (encoding process) of the sender or the effect of the message on those to whom it is directed (decoding process). Much of the research has addressed itself to some variety of the "what" question, testing hypotheses about such matters as focus of attention, trends in communication, or cross-media differences. The investigator may also want to answer the question "to whom," as when testing hypotheses about the way in which the content of messages will differ according to audience (Berkman, 1963), or to answer questions about "how,"

TABLE 1

CONTENT-ANALYSIS RESEARCH DESIGNS

Purpose	*Branch of semiotics*	*Types of comparisons*	*Questions*	*Research problem*
To describe characteristics of communication	Semantics (sign/referent) Syntactics (sign/sign)	Messages source type *A* 1. Variable *X* across time 2. Variable *X* across situations 3. Variable *X* across audience 4. Variables *X* and *Y* within same universe of document	What?	To describe trends in communication content To relate known characteristics of sources to the messages they produce To audit communication content against standards
		Messages source type *A* / messages source type *B*	How?	To analyze techniques of persuasion To analyze style
		Messages/standard 1. *A priori* 2. Content 3. Noncontent	To whom?	To relate known characteristics of the audience to messages produced for them To describe patterns of communication
To make inferences as to the antecedents of communication (the encoding process)	Pragmatics (sender/sign)	Messages/nonsymbolic behavioral data 1. Direct 2. Indirect	Why?	To secure political and military intelligence To analyze psychological traits of individuals To infer aspects of culture and cultural change To provide legal evidence
			Who?	To answer questions of disputed authorship
To make inferences as to the effects of communication (the decoding process)	Pragmatics (sign/receiver)	Sender messages/recipient messages Sender messages/recipient behavioral data	With what effect?	To measure readability To analyze the flow of information To assess responses to communication

for example, studies of style (Skinner, 1939) or of techniques of persuasion (Lee, 1952).

The type of research design will depend on the questions the investigator seeks to answer and on his data. In order to state meaningful conclusions, however, *all* content data must be compared to some other data. To determine that an editorial used the term "freedom" X number of times is a meaningless finding by itself. When content analysis is used to describe text, there are three basic types of comparison to be made.

The analyst may compare documents derived from *a single source.* One application of this method is the comparison of the messages over *time.* Such studies have been undertaken to analyze trends in the development of a discipline (Allport and Bruner, 1940; Tannenbaum and Greenberg, 1961b), and changes in the content of a rural newspaper (Taeuber, 1932) or Negro attitudes toward discrimination (Rosen, 1964). The investigator may also compare messages from a single source in differing *situations,* as in a study of international communication under conditions of low and high stress (Holsti, 1965b). Another, less widely used, approach using content data from a single source involves comparisons across *audience.* Comparisons of communication attributes across time, situation, or audience are intermessage analyses. Inferences may also be based on the *covariation of two or more variables,* such as self concepts and feeling toward others (Sheerer, 1949; Stock, 1949), within a single document or set of documents.

Hypotheses may be tested by comparing the messages of *two or more different sources.* Usually the purpose is to relate theoretically significant attributes of communication sources to differences in the messages they produce. For example, this design has been used to determine whether competitive newspapers provide significantly better news coverage than noncompetitive ones (Willoughby, 1955; Nixon and Jones, 1956), to examine linguistic differences in messages produced by "normal" persons and those on the point of committing suicide (Osgood and Walker, 1959), or to identify differences in propaganda appeals of two or more orators (Shneidman, 1963), political parties (Almond, 1954), or nations (Lasswell, 1927).

Finally, content data may be compared to some *standard* of adequacy or performance. Many studies have employed *a priori* standards defined, often implicitly, by the investigator's preferences. Even when *a priori* standards are made explicit, the problems of defining operationally such deviations as "bias" have rarely been dealt with in a satisfactory manner. An alternative to the deductive approach is to derive standards inductively from *content data.* A representative sample of messages produced by a class of communicators may provide norms against which the products of any single communicator may be compared. This technique has often been used in mass media research: the content of a given newspaper, magazine, or network is compared to the performance of the medium as a whole. A third type of standard against which content data may be compared is one defined by *noncontent indices,* such as aggregate data or expert opinion. A classic study of this type compared the incidence of minority group characters in popular magazine fiction with census data (Berelson and Salter, 1946).

Many research designs use two or more types of comparison together. For example, hypotheses about the relative potency of role and personal variables in decision making were tested by analyzing the statements of Democratic and Republican Senators (comparisons across sources) during the Truman and Eisenhower Administrations (comparisons across situations) (Rosenau, 1968).

The second major classification of studies is that in which the text is analyzed in order to make *inferences about the causes or antecedents of the message,* and more specifically, about the sender. Thus content analysis is employed to discover "lawful relations *between* events in messages and processes transpiring in the individuals who produce . . . them" (Osgood, 1959, p. 36). Within the communication paradigm, messages are examined for the purpose of answering the questions "who" and "why." Who was the author of a given document? What are the meanings, associations, values, motives, or intentions of the communicator which can be inferred from his messages? Whereas the description of text can be classified under semantics or syntactics, this use of content analysis is a problem in pragmatics, the relationship of signs to those who produce them.

In order to draw valid inferences about sources from the messages they send, the content data must be compared, *directly* or *indirectly,* with independent behavioral indices. Because of possible differences in encoding habits—words may have different semantical meanings for different sources—inferences as to the antecedent causes of messages drawn solely from content data cannot be considered self-validating.

The relationship of symbolic behavior and its causes may be established by comparing content-analysis data *directly* with some other indices of behavior, as in a study of the 1914 crisis in which the degree of hostility in documents written by European decision makers was compared to the level of violence in their military actions (Holsti, North, and Brody, 1968).

Inferences based on an *indirect* relationship between symbolic and other forms of behavior are much more frequent in the content-analysis literature. The logic of such inferences can be stated as a syllogism: In a given situation, individuals whose behavior patterns are known to be A, B, and C produce messages with characteristics r-s-t, u-v-w, and x-y-z, respectively. If in similar circumstances a source produces messages with attributes x-y-z, the inference is that it was related to behavior pattern C. A classic example of this research design is the comparison between Nazi propaganda themes with the books, periodicals, and transoceanic cables of certain domestic organizations suspected of sedition, in which content analysis revealed significant similarities on a number of dimensions (Lasswell, 1949). The data obtained by content analysis were admitted by the court as legal evidence supporting the charge of sedition. In this case the likenesses in the messages of *two separate sources* served as the basis for inferences about the similarity of motives—support for the German war effort.

The research design may also focus on the relationship of events to symbols for a *single source.* The intelligence analyst may examine enemy documents for attributes that have in the past provided a clue to some aspect of the enemy's behavior. In general, the investigator bases his inferences on some demonstrated relationship between events and symbols for the same or for comparable communicators. One weakness of many content-analysis studies is that such a relationship between symbolic behavior and other forms of behavior has not been established.

The third major classification of content-analysis studies is that in which *inferences are made about the effects of messages* (the decoding process) on the recipient. The question "with what effect" is a crucial aspect of the communication paradigm; it includes such a traditional concern of social psychology as attitude change. Nevertheless, relatively few studies have attempted to answer this question by content analysis. Probably the most systematic research on the decoding process has focused on research to measure the readability of text.

As in the other types of research design, the sender's message serves as the data. Two types of comparison may be used to measure the impact of the message. First, the investigator may determine the effects of *A*'s messages to *B* by content-analyzing *B*'s messages. For example, reviews of a book have been analyzed to investigate the responses it elicits (Lerner, 1950). An alternative approach to studying the effects of communication is to examine other aspects of the recipient's behavior. In studies of readability, for example, various independent tests have been used to measure the extent of the reader's comprehension.

TRENDS IN CONTENT-ANALYSIS RESEARCH

The history of content analysis as a research technique dates from the beginning of the twentieth century, although scattered studies going as far back as the 1740's have been cited (Dovring, 1954). During this time the method has gone through a number of phases. The description that follows relies in part on the findings presented in a study of content analysis from 1900 through 1958 (Barcus, 1959).

The most evident trend in content analysis is an almost geometric increase in the frequency of such research. During the first two decades of the century, an average of approximately 2.5 content-analysis studies appeared each year. During the next three decades, the annual average frequencies rose to 13.8, 22.8, and 43.3 respectively, and by 1950–1958, this figure had more than doubled again to 96.3. Or, to state this somewhat differently, there were more studies employing content analysis in the nine years after 1950 than during the previous half-century. Even a casual survey of the literature suggests that the trend toward increased content-analysis research has not abated.

A more revealing view of the history of content analysis can be presented when the studies are classified according to purpose, discipline or approach, and sources examined. Empirical studies account for an overwhelming proportion of the content-analysis literature. Barcus, in surveying 1719 titles, found that nearly four out of five could be so classified, the remainder being divided between methodological research (for example, studies of sampling or reliability in content analysis) (14.2%) and studies of form or style (6.9%). This three-fold classification underestimates the concern of content analysts with methodological problems; unquestionably many works listed as empirical studies of content have explicitly come to grips with such issues. Nevertheless, concern with methodological issues has been notably more evident recently than in earlier content-analysis research. During the first two decades of the twentieth century, more than 98 percent of the studies dealt primarily with the content of text. By the 1950's, this figure had dropped to 75 percent, whereas one study in six was concerned with methodological problems. The recent development of various techniques of computer content analysis has served as an added impetus to the consideration of theoretical and methodological issues. This trend has not been without its critics, however. On the one hand, content analysts have been accused of being overly concerned with developing techniques, to the neglect of testing significant communication hypotheses (Stephenson, 1963). On the other hand, they have been charged with a lack of serious attention to theoretical and methodological defects (Krippendorff, 1966).

Another way to describe trends in content-analysis research is by approach or discipline. Three disciplines have accounted for approximately three-quarters of all empirical studies: sociological-anthropological (27.7%), general communications (25.9%), and political (21.5%). Using more specific categories, Barcus found that over three-fifths of all empirical content-analysis research has been focused in five mutually exclusive areas of inquiry, each of which accounts for at least 10 percent of the total: the study of social values, propaganda analyses, journalistic studies, media inventories, and psychological-psychoanalytic research.

Various phases have characterized the history of content analysis. Early investigations were confined largely to media inventories and journalistic studies, most of them devoted to studies of general American dailies. On the other hand, relatively little attention was paid to the foreign press. During the 1930's newspaper research continued to account for the largest number of studies. At the same time content analysis was increasingly being adapted for sociological, historical, and political research. The latter category included studies of propaganda—many of them stimulated by the seminal work of Harold Lasswell and his associates— foreshadowing a trend which gained added impetus during World War II. In the course of the 1940's, political research using propaganda materials accounted for nearly a quarter of all empirical content-analysis investigations. The dominating influence of political studies during the period of World War II is reflected in one of the definitions cited earlier, in which content analysis was characterized as "the statistical semantics of political discourse" (Kaplan, 1943, p. 230). Newspapers continue to be the source most frequently examined; but whereas such research accounted for over 60 percent of the studies prior to 1920, the figure had dropped to less than 30 percent by the 1950's. The development of new mass media (movies, radio, television) has also stimulated considerable content-analysis research.

Although journalistic and political studies continue to appear with increasing frequency, the most discernible trend has been toward wider application within a variety of disciplines. One of the milestone publications in the history of content analysis, appearing at the end of the 1950's, reveals something of the diversity which has come to characterize the applications of the technique within such disciplines and spheres of specialized inquiry as folkloristics, biography, history, psychoanalysis, linguistics, propaganda, cognitive organization, and psychotherapy (Pool, 1959). These studies also clearly indicate a shift of interest away from descriptive studies toward research for testing hypotheses, especially regarding the antecedents and effects of communication. In recent years there have also been some successful attempts to use content analysis in areas beyond the traditional boundaries of communication by written or spoken word—for example, the analysis of pictorial communication (Gordon, 1952; Wayne, 1956; McClelland, 1958; Badri and Dennis, 1964), studies of bodily gesture and facial expression (Ekman, 1965), vocal tone (Starkweather, 1956), and even dreams (Hall and Van de Castle, 1966).

Finally, earlier uses of content analysis were largely confined to analyses of "natural" or "available" data—that is, data which exist without any active participation by the social scientist, such as newspapers, books, government documents, and personal documents.

Increasingly, however, content analysis has also been applied to messages generated in the course of the research process. This class of data may be of two somewhat different types. There is, in the first place, the research method generating only verbal data, which may then be subjected to content analysis. The psychiatric interview and various projective instruments, such as the Thematic Apperception Test, are representative examples. A second type of data is the by-product of other standard techniques of social research, which the investigator may then wish to content-analyze. Among the latter we may include responses to open-ended questions generated in survey research (Scheuch and Stone, 1964), written messages derived from a simulation study (Brody, 1963), or verbal communication produced during group interaction (Bales, 1950; Mills, 1964).

One inevitable result of this trend toward analysis of more diverse data has been a weakening of rigid boundaries between content analysis and other techniques of social research. The coding of open-ended questionnaires, for example, can often be considered to fall under the rubric of both content analysis and survey research.

In summary, the history of content analysis reveals a series of interrelated trends toward:

1. *Increased use of content analysis.*

2. *Heightened concern for theoretical and methodological issues.*

3. *Application to a broader spectrum of problems, especially those focusing on the antecedents and effects of communication.*

4. *Increased use for testing hypotheses, as opposed to purely descriptive research.*

5. *Greater diversity in the materials studied.*

6. *Use in conjunction with other techniques of social research.*

7. *Content analysis by means of computers.*

THE USES OF CONTENT ANALYSIS

Content analysis encompasses a widely varying set of techniques which have been employed to analyze symbolic materials ranging from propaganda tracts to Greek vases. Its scope and method can be described in greater detail through examination of problems to which it has been applied, either alone or in conjunction with other methods of social research.

One disclaimer must be made explicit at the outset: limitations of space restrict our review to a small sample of the total content-analysis literature. Only a few studies of each type can be described, and then only in summary fashion. Citations keyed to other studies listed in the reference section will be used to supplement the review, but even this bibliography can encompass only a fraction of the entire literature. Even though the scope of content analysis has been defined broadly, its application to some of the less frequently studied aspects of communication—handwriting, nonverbal communication, and content-free communication—will be excluded. The reader interested in these might turn to articles by Wolfson (1951), Ekman (1965), and Starkweather (1956).

This summary review is organized according to the categories depicted in Table 1. Research is initially divided according to major purpose: (1) to describe the characteristics of content; (2) to make inferences about the causes of content; and (3) to make inferences about the effect of content. Within this trichotomy studies are classified by type of question in the communication paradigm (what, how, to whom, why, who, with what effect), and are further subdivided according to the subgroups in the right-hand column of Table 1.

CHARACTERISTICS OF CONTENT: WHAT

Content analysis has been used most frequently for research problems in which the question can be answered *directly* from a description of the attributes of content. In such studies the investigator is in large part freed from problems of validity, except to the extent that validity is related to sampling and reliability; the content data serve as a direct answer to the research question, rather than as an indicator from which other characteristics are to be inferred.

To describe trends in communication content

Interest in measuring trends in national attitudes relevant to international politics has stimulated considerable analysis of the printed media. An early study applied scaling techniques developed by Thurstone to Chinese and Japanese materials during the Far Eastern crisis of 1930–1932 (Russell and Wright, 1933). The same techniques were used to examine trends in American attitudes toward Japan and China along a favorable-hostile continuum (Wright and Nelson, 1939).

After the outbreak of World War II, Lasswell (1941) suggested that a "world attention survey" be conducted by ongoing analyses of the world's press. This idea subsequently led to an extensive survey of political symbols as one aspect of research on Revolution and Development of International Relations (RADIR).

The studies were designed to test hypotheses relating to a "world revolution" by identifying and mapping trends in the usage of those symbols expressing major goal values of modern politics. Editorials from one "prestige" newspaper representing each of five countries—the United States, Great Britain, France, Germany, and the Soviet Union—were analyzed for the period 1890–1949 (Pool, 1952a). The choice of newspapers rather than other sources of political symbols was based on both theoretical and practical considerations (Lasswell, Lerner, and Pool, 1952, p. 17):

In many countries the head of state makes few public statements, and these may be almost purely ceremonial. Party platforms often go unrevised year after year. So far as pressure groups are concerned, there are great differences in importance from state to state, and the task of gathering such fugitive material is a vast research project. The published proceedings of legislative bodies are often scanty, or altogether lacking. All states are modern enough to publish newspapers, however, so that comparable channels can be used for comparative purposes. Further, we can be relatively sure of who controls and who reads the news. In nearly all states some papers are understood to be leading organs of the party in office and of the government. Where the party system is competitive, the principal organ of parties and factions can be identified. Even with the coming of radio and television, the daily paper continues to occupy an important position in the media (and newspaper content is more accessible to study than are broadcasts).

Editorials appearing on the first and fifteenth day of each month were coded for the presence of 416 key symbols. These included 206 geographical terms, such as names of countries, international organizations, and minority groups, and 210 major ideological and doctrinal symbols—democracy, equality, proletariat, communism, nazism, nationalism, fatherland, and the like—relating to world politics in the first half of the twentieth century. Each time a symbol appeared it was scored as present, and furthermore, expressed attitudes toward the symbol— approval, disapproval, or neutrality—were recorded. Frequency counts were based on the *number of editorials* in which symbols appeared, not the frequency with which the symbol itself appeared.

Data from 19,553 editorials were used to trace changing foci of attention and attitude, as indexed by key symbols, for the sixty-year period. Among many findings were the following:

Symbols of representative government are used where the practice is under dispute, not where it is an accepted part of the traditions. (Pool, 1952b, p. 72)

Hostility to the outside world . . . seems to be very much of a function of insecurity. Those nations which have at any given moment dominated the world scene have generally said little that was adverse to "prestige papers" in the other power. The insecure or unsatisfied powers, on the other hand, have generally had editorials full of hostile judgments of foreign states. (Pool, 1951, p. 62)

Two main trends in the modern world are: (1) a shift in the center of attention, in which traditional liberalism is being replaced by proletarian doctrines, and (2) a growing threat of war and a corresponding increase of nationalism and militarism. (Pool, 1952a, p. 84)

One important area of inquiry left relatively untouched by the RADIR studies is that of differences and trends in meaning, beyond approval or disapproval, of such symbols as "democracy" or "peace" (Stedman, 1951; Rainey, 1966). This is an area in which a variety of content-analysis methods might usefully be applied to supplement more traditional approaches to textual exegesis.

Other somewhat similar studies of political symbols have examined trends in Soviet May Day slogans (Yakobson and Lasswell, 1949), symbols used by the Communist International (Leites, 1949), and response of Communist propaganda to defeat in elections and strikes (Leites and Pool, 1949).

Various types of literature have been examined to reveal trends in religious values. Hamilton's (1942) examination of themes relating to faith, the nature of man, science, education, and social problems in published Protestant sermons demonstrated a significant change from social optimism to social pessimism during the decade prior to World War II. Forty-six inspirational best sellers published between 1875 and 1955 were analyzed in order to identify themes and trends in American popular religion (Schneider and Dornbusch, 1958). Constant themes during the period included the views that religion promotes success; that the individual can make changes beneficial to himself by religious means; and that man is inherently good. A number of other themes increased substantially in the more recent literature: religion is linked to national political aspirations, and religion promotes mental and physical health. On the assumption that individuals are motivated to purchase books which coincide with their own values (a premise well supported by independent evidence), and in view of the best seller status of this literature, inferences regarding trends in popular religious values can also be drawn from these findings.

These studies illustrate trend analyses in which a sample of relevant material is compared continuously over a period of time. In other cases the investigator may simply base his comparisons on two points in time. The validity of assertions identifying anti-intellectualism as an important American characteristic was tested by Hage (1959). Media analyzed were newspapers published during the 1828 Jackson-Adams and 1952 Eisenhower-Stevenson campaigns, in each of which an "intellectual" ran unsuccessfully against a military hero. Issues, candidates' traits, and their positions on the issues were recorded for two newspapers during each campaign. In 1952, the press was more prone to discuss the campaign in terms of issues, rather than personalities. Comments about Stevenson's intellectualism were predominantly favorable, although significant differences appeared between the "quality press" (favorable) and the "mass press" (unfavorable). The press of 1828 dealt with Adams' intellectualism and Jackson's unreflective traits strictly along partisan lines. In 1952, on the other hand, all segments of the press—mass and quality, pro-Stevenson and pro-Eisenhower—commented favorably on the latter's nonintellectual attributes. The results suggested considerable anti-intellectualism in the press during both campaigns. Whether these findings depict two isolated instances of anti-intellectualism or a persisting aspect of American culture cannot, of course, be determined solely from a study of this type.

Other trend analyses have examined various aspects of newspaper development, with heavy emphasis on American newspapers. Trends in general dailies, country weeklies, comics, and Presidential news have been described by Mott (1942), Taeuber (1932), Barcus (1961), and Cornwell (1959), respectively. Considerable research has also been devoted to surveys of other sources, including movies (Dale, 1935), radio (Albig, 1956), television (Smythe, 1953), propaganda (Kris and Leites, 1953), popular heroes in magazines (Lowenthal, 1944; Winick, 1963), and child-development materials (Ojemann *et al.*, 1948).

Trend inventories have varied widely in purpose and quality. Such studies can be useful for identifying major changes across long periods of time, and are relatively easy to undertake; on the other hand, surveys depending on gross categories often conceal more information of interest than they reveal. According to one source, "The most valuable use of studies of content . . . is in noting trends and changes in content. Systems of classification may be inadequate and unstandardized; nevertheless, if a system is used consistently over a time period valuable facts may appear" (quoted in Berelson, 1952, p. 29). This seems a dubious premise upon which to stake very much research effort. Certainly, little is to be gained by precise measurement if the system of categories employed is inadequate.

A special application of the trend study is the analysis of professional publications to index changing foci of scholarly interest. Articles in the *American Journal of Sociology* were classified by central topic to describe trends in the discipline (Becker, 1930, 1932; Shanas, 1945). As Berelson has pointed out, studies based solely on a few professional journals may distort the actual focus of research interest (1952, p. 34). Changes in classification of articles on the borderline of two disciplines might affect the results of studies covering a long time span. An additional problem is that of editorial policy. For example, articles on social reform accounted for 13 percent of all space in the *American Journal of Sociology* at the turn of the century, but no such article was published after 1935 (Shanas, 1945). Does this finding indicate changing professional interests, a shift in editorial taste, or perhaps establishment of a separate new journal for the specific purpose of presenting policy-oriented research?

Owing to a broader research design, a study of changing interests in American psychology over the half-century prior to 1938 is less vulnerable to this criticism. Articles appearing every tenth year, in 14 journals rated most "significant" by members of the profession, were coded for 32 categories reflecting the type of subjects used, topics, techniques of investigation, and modes of conceptualization. Each article was thus listed under a number of categories, usually ranging from five to 15 (Allport and Bruner, 1940). Use of more than a single journal and coding into multiple categories minimized potential distortion.

Other studies have examined trends in fields as general as physics (Rainoff, 1929), journalism (Tannenbaum and Greenberg, 1961b; Webb and Salancik, 1965), and botany (Stevens, 1932), and as specific as content analysis (Barcus, 1959) and Freud's dream theory (Herma, Kris, and Shor, 1943).

To relate known characteristics of sources to the messages they produce

An important aspect of social research is the testing of hypotheses of the form, "sources with characteristic *A* are likely to produce messages with attributes *w* and *x,* whereas those with characteristics *B* are likely to produce messages of types *y* and *z.*" This formulation covers a broad spectrum of studies. Sources may be two individual authors or newspapers; or different media, such as radio and magazines; or communication sources in two or more different countries.

The relationship between ideological orientation of media and the nature of their news reporting has been an area of considerable research interest in Europe and the United States. As early as 1910 Max Weber urged (quoted in Krippendorff, 1966, p. 5):

. . . we will have to start measuring, plainly speaking, in a pedestrian way, with the scissors and the compass, how the contents of the newspapers has quantitatively shifted in the course of the last generation . . . between feuilleton and editorial, between editorial and news, between what is presented as news and what is no longer offered . . . and from the quantitative results we have to move toward qualitative ones. We have to pursue the style of presentation of the paper, the way in which similar problems are treated inside and outside the papers, the apparent expression of emotions in the papers.

More recently Gerbner has been among the most articulate proponents of the position that all analysis of the mass media must proceed with a sensitivity to the ideological framework of the media: "all editorial choice patterns in what and what not to make public (and in what proportion, with what emphasis, etc.) have an ideological basis and a political dimension rooted in the structural characteristics of the medium" (1964, p. 495). The general proposition that "all news are views" was tested by an examination of nine French newspapers of the political left, the right, and the commercial press. Reporting of a nonpolitical incident, the shooting of a schoolboy by a teacher, was subjected to a propositional analysis. On the basis of significant differences among newspaper types, the author concluded: "There is no fundamentally non-ideological, apolitical, non-partisan news gathering and reporting system" (Gerbner, 1964, p. 508).

Interest in the role of the press in electoral campaigns has been strong, especially since the Presidential elections of 1936 and 1940, in which the vast majority of the press supported Landon and Willkie in their campaigns against Roosevelt. Several studies have sought to determine whether editorial support is systematically related to other aspects of campaign coverage, such as the amount of space devoted to stories of each candidate. Evidence from such investigations is mixed, depending largely on the selection of newspapers and elections. Blumberg (1954) examined 35 American dailies during the 1952 campaign and found little evidence of bias in news coverage. This finding was supported by Markham and Stempel (1957). Studies of 15 "prestige" dailies during the 1960 and 1964 campaigns indicated that "as a group they gave the Democratic and Republican campaigns virtually equal amount of space in their news columns" (Stempel, 1961, p. 157; Stempel, 1965). But analyses of dailies in Florida and California revealed that endorsed political candidates received better coverage (Kobre, 1953; Batlin, 1954).

A serious limitation of investigations based on space measures is that they tap only a single dimension of bias. Some rough equality of space allocation may be a necessary condition of unbiased coverage, but probably it is not sufficient. During the 1940 campaign the press and radio *focused* on Roosevelt by a margin of 3–2, but *favored* Willkie by better than 2–1 (Lazarsfeld, Berelson, and Gaudet, 1944, p. 117). The more subtle, and probably more important, methods of slanting news have received less attention than measures of space. One exception is an analysis of eight major daily newspapers during the 1952 campaign. Newspapers were rated on eighteen indices, including size and tone of headline, placement of stories, number of biased remarks, number of pictures, and total column inches of stories on various pages. These measurements gave strong indications of systematic bias in favor of the endorsed candidate (Klein and Maccoby, 1954).

A similar finding emerged from a study of the British press, which concluded that, with the exception of *The Times,* "There could be no doubt in the reader's mind as to which side the different newspapers supported. News and comment were inextricably mixed in the 'news' reports and special articles" (Royal Commission on the Press, 1949, p. 359).

Differential coverage of "civil rights" stories has also been related to various characteristics of newspapers, including geographical location, ownership (Negro, white), and political orientation. In general, the findings have supported hypotheses of systematic quantitative and qualitative differences in news coverage (Broom and Reece, 1955; Carter, 1957; Breed, 1958).

The hypothesis that local newspaper competition is related to more adequate news coverage has received some attention. A comparison of 97 newspapers revealed no significant difference in allocation of nonadvertising space related to the presence or absence of competition. A second test of 260 newspapers matched for circulation and other characteristics replicated the analysis, and the data again rejected the hypotheses that competitive status has any significant bearing on allocation of news space (Nixon and Jones, 1956). Similar conclusions were reached by Willoughby (1955, p. 204). Adequacy of news coverage during the 1960 Presidential campaign was related to various characteristics of newspapers in a survey of 90 dailies (Danielson and Adams, 1961). From this research a "news potential index" was developed which, on the basis of five newspaper attributes, predicts the adequacy of news coverage.

Studies comparing the content of two or more mass media have been relatively infrequent. In this respect development of new modes of communication has had less impact on content-analysis research than might be expected. This can be attributed in part to the problem of devising coding units, other than simple time and space measures, which can be compared. A strong bias toward research on the more easily accessible printed materials has also restricted cross-media comparisons and limited the kinds of statements that can be made about the media.

The question of what happens to a book when it is adapted into a movie was examined by Asheim (1950). An "index of deviation," based on the proportion of space devoted to main story lines and subplots in 24 books and movies, revealed that fidelity in adaptation ranged from 89 percent (*Pride and Prejudice*) to 38 percent (*The House of Seven Gables*). Book and film endings were classified as "happy" or "unhappy"; in 21 cases the type of ending was accurately portrayed in the film, although details of the action were altered in three of them. The study also revealed that chronological sequence was followed more closely in the film than in the book, and that the incidence of violence, brutality, and sadism was reduced in the film.

Mental health content of the mass media has been the subject of a number of cross-media studies (Taylor, 1957; Nunnally, 1957; Gerbner and Tannenbaum, 1960). Space allocations differed considerably, broadcasting media (radio and television) carrying more relevant material than printed media (magazines and newspapers). However, the content of assertions about mental health was almost identical across all media. The three most frequently appearing themes were: the mentally ill look and act differently; mental health problems originate in environmental stresses; and the problem is a serious one (Taylor, 1957).

Content analysis has frequently been used on documents produced by political action groups. Comparative analysis of Communist publications was used to develop a model against which perceptions and experiences of former party members (determined by interviews) could be compared (see Table 2). Categories incorporating qualities of the "ideal communist" were used to code a Communist classic, publications of a party in power (Soviet Union), and of a weak party (United States) (Almond, 1954, p. 77).

TABLE 2

QUALITIES ATTRIBUTED TO THE SELF IN STALIN'S "HISTORY," THE COMINFORM PERIODICAL, AND THE "DAILY WORKER"

Qualities	History		Cominform		Daily Worker	
Goal Qualities	6 %		8 %		26 %	
Esoteric		4		0.5		
Exoteric		2		7.5		26
Tactical Qualities	94		92		74	
Militance		28		25		35
Rationality		23		10		2
Organization		16		9		3
Leadership		13		19		11
Activism		3		7		6
Uniqueness		3		6		1
Dedication		3		7		13
Confidence		5		9		3
Total percent	100		100		100	

The American business community (Lane, 1951; Bernstein, 1953), right-wing organizations (Wilcox, 1962; Abcarian and Stanage, 1965), and various groups of lobbyists (McPherson, 1964) are among other groups whose publications have been analyzed.

Content analysis has also been used on a variety of materials to discover international differences in the content of communication. A comparative study of newspapers in 17 countries during a seven-day period in March 1951 was conducted under auspices of UNESCO (Kayser, 1953). The morning newspaper with the largest circulation in each country was analyzed for a period of time selected in advance of actual publication. Comparisons were made of both format and content: the front page, space allocation, origin of news, and coverage of specific events during the week. A supplementary analysis compared four "prestige" papers published in Moscow, Paris, London, and New York. Other cross-national studies have compared aspects of the press in the Middle East (Abu-Lughod, 1962), Australia-New Zealand (Budd, 1964), and the United States-Great Britain (Hart, 1965, 1966).

An examination of fifteen "prestige" newspapers published on November 2, 1956, during the dual crises in Hungary and Suez, revealed differences in coverage of these events which were ascribed to the degree of involvement in one event or the other, or to instrumental handling of the news. News of the Suez invasion crowded Hungary out of these newspapers; even in the West, "attention was so overwhelmingly on Suez that the full significance of what was happening in Hungary was never made clear" (Schramm, 1959, p. 138). A less comprehensive study compared Indian and German coverage of the concurrent crises on the Sino-Indian border and in Cuba during October 1962 (Roat, 1963).

Cross-national content analysis has not been confined to printed media. Wolfenstein and Leites (1950), in a study of plot configurations of British, French, and American movies, found that British movies emphasized that danger lies in the nature of man himself, especially in his impulses of destructiveness; many of the themes of Shakespearean drama were preserved, although cloaked in a modern idiom. French movie plots revealed human wishes opposed by the nature of life itself which, in the end, defeats all, including the virtuous, and both old and young suffered inevitable disappointments in love. In American movies, hazards of life were found in the situation, rather than in the nature of the individual or life itself. Winning was stressed, although not always achieved easily, and disappointment in love was denied.

Two studies compared the literature and songs of youth groups in Nazi Germany and the United States. Youth literature in the two countries yielded nearly 1000 expressions of various organizational goals (Lewin, 1947). By frequency count, the German literature placed significantly greater stress on national loyalty, national identification, and determination, whereas American Boy Scout materials emphasized altruism, religion, and creativity. A parallel study of children's songbooks yielded similar results (Sebald, 1962). German sources stressed national loyalty, obedience, and heroic death, and paid less attention to the beauty of nature, play, and Christianity. Content analysis of such materials can reveal

important international differences at a specified point in time, but further inferences, unsupported by independent data, are often open to question. A case in
point is Sebald's generalization, based solely on Nazi songbooks issued in 1940,
that the modal character of Germans is basically authoritarian.

Content analysis has also been used to examine cross-national or cross-cultural
differences in the content of television programming (Gardiner, 1962), magazines
(Ginglinger, 1955), textbooks (Walworth, 1938), folktales (Colby, Collier, and
Postal, 1963), sermons (Parker, Barry, and Smythe, 1955), and magazine photographs (Wayne, 1956).

To audit communication content against standards

Content data have often been compared to *a priori* standards. Early content-
analysis research in the United States was stimulated by concern over the spread
of yellow journalism; studies of New York newspapers by Speed (1893) and
Matthews (1910) are examples. This research was almost wholly devoted to measuring space allocation for various subject-matter categories, and much of it has
been justly criticized for subjective and arbitrary procedures; Matthews, for
instance, aggregated his categories into four major classes: "demoralizing," "un-
wholesome," "trivial," and "worthwhile." Interest in standards of the mass
media has been sustained, however, and many serious technical problems of the
early studies have been resolved.

The standard of "social norms" was used in a study of goals and goal achievement as portrayed in television programs for children, adult, and mixed children-
adult audiences (Larson, Gray, and Fortis, 1963). Each act by a character which
was identifiably connected with a specific goal was coded. Goals were classified
into categories such as power and prestige, property, self-preservation, affection,
sentiments, and psychological goals. Means to achieve the goals were coded as
socially approved (legal) or socially disapproved (nonlegal, violent, or escape).
Results revealed that means with the *least* likelihood of success were those classified as socially approved. There was no essential difference in this respect between
those programs which were viewed primarily by adults and those designed for
younger audiences.

A study of three major American news magazines—*Time, Newsweek,* and
U.S. News & World Report—against the standard of "responsibility in mass communication" indicated that the "neatly reconstructed picture of the world" they
present is often biased, distorted, or factually false (Bagdikian, 1959). While
apparently strong evidence of systematic bias was presented, the absence of explicit
coding categories or sampling methods raises some questions about the findings.
A rigorous study of the same news magazines during the period of the 1960 conventions revealed that Republican candidates as a group received only slightly
more favorable treatment than their Democratic counterparts (Westley *et al.,*
1963). But when the data were reexamined according to individual candidates,
each magazine was found to have treated the conservative candidates (Nixon and
Johnson) more favorably than the liberal ones (Rockefeller and Kennedy).

An analysis of six types of bias (attribution bias, adjective bias, adverbial bias, contextual bias, outright opinion, and photographic bias) revealed that *Time* used each technique extensively to describe recent American Presidents. *Time's* presentation of Truman was totally negative, Eisenhower was depicted in an unambiguously favorable light, and only Kennedy was described in somewhat balanced terms (Merrill, 1965). "Repeated distortion and misinformation" were also discovered in public affairs articles in *Reader's Digest* (Christenson, 1964).

Ash (1948) examined 50 periodicals over a period of 10 months to determine whether the public was given a fair opportunity to learn both sides of the controversial Taft-Hartley Labor act. The analysis uncovered almost unanimous support for the act; moreover, those few anti-Taft-Hartley items which did appear were largely confined to low-circulation periodicals. High-circulation news magazines failed to print any items opposing the act, and the general magazines were similarly one-sided. When item counts were adjusted for circulation, 55.7 percent of the material favored the act and 1.8 percent opposed it, the remainder being neutral. However, no attempt was made to test the relevance or justice of the arguments, pro and con.

Another aspect of distortion was studied by Cony, who tested the hypothesis that "Newspapers emphasize conflict to the extent that reality is twisted out of shape and a false picture of society as a jungle is presented to the reader" (1953, p. 15). The data revealed conspicuous differences among a sample of five newspapers; but, although 1952 was a time of considerable conflict, a substantial amount of space (31 to 46 percent) was devoted to reporting cooperative behavior.

The most common weakness of studies using an *a priori* standard stems from the absence of a clearly defined basis for judgment, rather than from technical problems of applying content analysis to the data. What constitutes "adequacy" in the coverage of local news? Or, how close to "equal time/space" must the media come to be considered "fair"? It is doubtful whether unbiased reporting of every controversial situation calls for equal presentation or evaluation, as is sometimes assumed by indices of bias. Often the investigator's own values serve as the standard of comparison, but failure to define such terms explicitly makes it difficult to interpret findings. In his study of country weeklies, for example, Willey concluded that "The Connecticut weekly newspapers are deficient in the amount of local news material they print" (1926, p. 111). Yet his data revealed that space allocation to local news ranged from four percent to 92 percent, and more than half the newspapers devoted over 50 percent to local news.

One answer to the difficult problem of defining standards against which to audit sources is to make comparisons against other sources; that is, general norms for classes of communicators are developed inductively. The investigator may then rank sources along one or more dimensions. This technique has been used to rate radio commentators (Budlong, 1952) and reporting of specific events by magazines, newspapers, radio, television, and wire services (Rosi, 1964; Klapper and Glock, 1949; Sussman, 1945; Lang and Lang, 1955; Rucker, 1960). A more precise method, the technique of "successive approximations," was used to construct a "socialization-sensationalism" index. Six rough indicators were first applied to a large number of newspapers to identify those with highest scores on socialization (*Christian Science Monitor, Wall Street Journal*) and sensationalism (*New York Daily News, New York Daily Mirror*). Detailed analysis of these newspapers yielded a more precise scoring system of 23 categories which, when applied to front-page headlines, can be used to rate any newspaper (Kingsbury, Hart *et al.,* 1937).

Finally, content data may be evaluated against *noncontent indices.* Census data have been used as a standard of "reality" against which to assess the portrayal of characters in the mass media (Berelson and Salter, 1946). De Fleur (1964) investigated the portrayal of occupations to children on television. The incidence of characters appearing in 250 half-hour segments revealed considerable overrepresentation of professional occupations, and a concomitant underrepresentation of skilled labor, craftsmen, and related workers. Background settings, interactive patterns, and characteristics of various occupations were compared with preferences stated by children on questionnaires. Little distortion was discovered in the television portrayal of dominant-submissive interaction among occupations. But, when television portrayals were compared with census data for the viewing area, the authors concluded that "television presents *least often* and as *least desirable* (from the child's standpoint) those occupations in which its youngest viewers are most likely to find themselves later" (De Fleur, 1964, p. 70). Findings from similar studies of radio serials, magazine fiction, movies, and television are summarized in Table 3.

Expert opinion has served as a second type of noncontent standard against which to audit communication content. Questionnaire responses of professional psychiatrists and psychologists provided criteria against which conception of mental health problems of laymen and the mass media were compared (Nunnally, 1957). The study revealed that, rather than providing a bridge between professional and public views, the printed and broadcasting media presented ideas about mental health which were further removed from the experts than were those of the average person.

A set of Lasswellian symbols was divided by a panel of experts on American culture into those consistent with, and those opposed to, the American creed. The content of five Negro newspapers was assessed against this standard. Over 5000 occurrences of relevant symbols were coded; only three percent of anti-American symbols were approved by the Negro press, and a similarly small proportion of symbols integral to the American creed were disapproved (Brooks, 1959).

A different approach was used to assess the adequacy of coverage of the National Coal Board press conference on December 22, 1947 by British newspapers. Background notes to the press included 33 major points of information about production, marketing, education, and the like. Nine newspapers were then analyzed to determine how many of these items were reported or commented upon editorially (Royal Commission on the Press, 1949, pp. 268–271). This method yielded precise results, but its use is probably limited to those events about which there can be little ambiguity as to "what happened."

TABLE 3

INCIDENCE OF OCCUPATIONS IN VARIOUS MASS MEDIA

Occupations	Jones (1942): movies	Arnheim (1944): radio serials	Berelson and Salter (1946): magazine fiction — Type of character			Johns-Heine and Gerth (1949): magazine fiction — Published in the:		Spiegelman, Terwilliger, and Fearing (1953a): comics — Type of character		Head (1954): television — Type of character		De Fleur (1964): television
			Americans	Anglo-Saxon and Nordics	Others	1920's	1930's	Sympathetic	Unsympathetic	Protagonist	Antagonist	
Upper status:												
Business-managerial	—	33%	—	—	—	31%	29%	—	—	10%	5%	4%
Professional	—	73	—	—	—	24	25	—	—	10	4	16
Others and unclassified	46%	40	59%	29%	20%	—	—	8%	8%	—	—	1
Middle status:												
Upper middle class	—	—	—	—	—	—	—	29	13	—	—	—
Small business	—	31	—	—	—	—	—	—	—	—	—	7
Clerical	—	—	—	—	—	—	—	—	—	—	—	7
Skilled labor	—	19	—	—	—	—	—	—	—	24	1	3
Law enforcement	—	—	—	—	—	—	—	—	—	7	2	29
Military	—	—	10	19	9	—	—	—	—	—	—	5
Lower middle class	—	—	—	—	—	—	—	—	—	—	—	—
Others and unclassified	32	—	19	23	20	19	17	31	46	—	—	1
Lower status:												
Unskilled labor	—	—	—	—	—	—	—	—	—	—	—	—
Servants	—	—	—	—	—	—	—	—	—	—	—	8
Criminals	—	—	1	2	15	—	—	—	—	7	70	6
Others and unclassified	17	6	11	27	36	—	—	32	33	—	—	2
Unclassified (housewives, etc.)	5	65	—	—	—	26	29	—	—	42	18	11
Total	100	*	100	100	100	100	100	100	100	100	100	100

* More than 100%—serials coded for number of settings in which different occupations appear.

CHARACTERISTICS OF CONTENT: HOW

To analyze techniques of persuasion

Content analysis usually focuses on the substance (the "what" question) of messages. It has also been used to analyze form or style (the "how" question). For the past three decades, and particularly during World War II, considerable research has focused on propaganda, "the manipulation of symbols as a means of influencing attitudes on controversial matters" (Lasswell, 1942, p. 106). Often the purpose has been to infer intentions of communicators from propaganda content, a type of analysis to be discussed later. The remaining research has aimed at developing a theory of form, style, and structure of persuasive communication.

A pioneering study in this area was Lasswell's analysis of propaganda techniques during World War I, in which four major objectives of propaganda and appropriate techniques of appeal for each goal were identified: (1) to mobilize hatred against the enemy; (2) to preserve the friendship of allies; (3) to preserve the friendship and, if possible, to procure the cooperation of neutrals; (4) to demoralize the enemy (1927, p. 195). Lasswell concluded that, although all four themes were present in the propaganda of every nation, they were applied with varying degrees of success; much German propaganda turned out to "boomerang," partly because of the lasting impression that Germany was the aggressor, partly because of the ineptness of the appeals. On the other hand, British propagandists were successful in picturing humanitarian war aims, and the French were able to portray the Germans in satanic terms, such as "Hun," and "Boche" (1927, pp. 196–199). More quantitative methods were used to examine the organization, media, techniques, and symbols of Communist propaganda in Chicago during the depression of the 1930's (Lasswell and Blumenstock, 1939). The Lasswellian influence in propaganda studies continues to the present, as is evident in two recent books (Dovring, 1959; Barghoorn, 1964).

A different conception of propaganda, stressing omissions and selectivity in presentation of factual materials rather than use of demagogical tricks or misuse of logic, was tested by examining arguments relating to the acquisition of nuclear weapons in Swedish newspaper editorials (Ohlström, 1966).

Several sets of categories for describing and analyzing various aspects of propaganda have been proposed. One scheme, developed at the Institute of Propaganda Analysis, enumerates content (name calling, testimonial, bandwagon, etc.) and strategic (stalling, scapegoating, etc.) techniques which have been identified in propaganda (Lee, 1952, pp. 42–79, 210–234).

A somewhat different set of categories emerged from a comparative study of British and German radio broadcasts to the United States during 1940 (Bruner, 1941). A tentative list identified nine dimensions for describing propaganda: dissolvent-unifying, negative-positive, temporal, personal-impersonal, stratified-homogeneous, authoritative-casual, colloquiality, immediate-remote, and repetitiousness.

"Value analysis," a set of categories for studying personality from written materials, was used to examine the propaganda style of Hitler and Roosevelt (White, 1949; for a detailed explanation of value analysis, see White, 1951). A number of similarities were found: both Hitler and Roosevelt stressed traditional grandeur, and both often used black-white dichotomies. Hitler also appears to have used an indirect approach to the preparation of the German people for war, by emphasizing the theme of persecution by outsiders. The same method and categories were found useful for distinguishing writings by political figures of various ideological persuasions: Khrushchev, Stalin, Hitler, Mussolini, Goldwater, Hoover, Churchill, Kennedy, and Franklin D. Roosevelt (Eckhardt, 1965). Other propagandists whose techniques have been examined by means of content analysis include Father Coughlin (Lee and Lee, 1939) and Gerald L. K. Smith (Janowitz, 1944).

A study of the picture magazines *USSR* and *American Illustrated,* which are produced by the Soviet Union and the United States for readers of the other country, revealed how persuasive literature is often framed in the value context of the audience. Both the American and Soviet magazines put greater emphasis on values often attributed to the other nation; that is, *USSR* emphasized such aspects of Soviet life as industrial growth and a high standard of living, whereas *American Illustrated* stressed the cultural and esthetic interests of its citizens (Garver, 1961).

Although the most pervasive form of persuasive communication—advertising —has received comparatively little attention from content analysists, research has not been limited to official governmental propaganda. For example, campaign biographies, a form of persuasive literature which appears on the American political scene quadrennially, have been analyzed. The basic theme, to fashion an image of the ideal citizen of the Republic, has remained the same since 1824. Moreover, "rival candidates appear in campaign biographies to be as alike as Tweedledum and Tweedledee" (Brown, 1960). Considerable content-analysis research has also focused on public letters, such as those written to congressmen (Wyant and Herzog, 1941), to various newspapers in the United States (Foster and Friedrich, 1937; Toch, Deutsch, and Wilkins, 1960), the Soviet Union (Inkeles and Geiger, 1952, 1953), and Communist China (Wang, 1955), and to a magazine by radical right-wingers (McEvoy, 1966).

The most evident weakness of propaganda analysis has been the absence of systematic research to relate categories of appeal, techniques, and dimensions (and combinations of these) to effects. What types of appeals are most effective? Under what circumstances? For which subject matter categories? One exception is a detailed investigation of Kate Smith's war bond drive. Content analysis was used to identify characteristics of her appeals which might be expected to elicit particular responses from the audience. The validity of inferences based on the content data was then checked by interviewing the audience (Merton, 1946). But in the main, questions about how technique and content of appeals are related to effects have remained unanswered.

To analyze style

Studies of style have differed widely in method and have ranged from investigations of a single author to analyses of an entire language. Word counts have yielded concordances of individual authors, including Yeats (Parrish and Painter, 1963) and Matthew Arnold (Parrish, 1959), and have been used to describe continuities and discontinuities in the Russian language (Josselson, 1953). Characteristics of style which distinguish good paintings from mediocre ones and best-selling novels from those less successful financially have been investigated (Gordon, 1952; Harvey, 1953). And relative frequencies of various parts of speech—for example, verb-noun-adjective ratios—were used to describe constant and varying characteristics of poetic style across five centuries (Miles, 1951).

Generalizations about qualitative features of literature have been tested by content analysis. The metaphorical qualities of Jane Austen's *Persuasion,* Emily Brontë's *Wuthering Heights,* and George Eliot's *Middlemarch* were examined to illustrate the thesis that "metaphorical language reveals to us the character of any imaginative work . . . more tellingly perhaps than any other element" (Schorer, 1949, p. 560). Skinner analyzed the pattern of alliteration—the appearance of two or more syllables beginning with the same consonant near each other—in Shakespeare's sonnets. After adjustment for the number of occurrences deriving from repetition of the same words, the frequency of alliteration did not differ significantly from chance; "so far as this aspect of poetry is concerned, Shakespeare might as well have drawn his words out of a hat" (Skinner, 1939, p. 191). A related aspect of style, in which the character rather than the word or phrase serves as the recording unit, is letter redundancy. Paisley (1966) content-analyzed 39 samples from English translations of Greek texts covering three time periods, 18 authors, and nine topics. Letter redundancy was shown to vary systematically with authorship, topic, structure, and time of composition.

Political rhetoric, especially that of American Presidents or Presidential candidates, has been a favorite subject for study. One approach is illustrated by a study of Woodrow Wilson's speeches (Runion, 1936). Categories were developed around grammatical aspects of discourse—sentence length, sentence structures, and figures of speech. A more revealing examination of political rhetoric, a study of broadcast addresses by Eisenhower and Stevenson during the 1956 campaign, related substantive and stylistic categories (Knepprath, 1962). Styles of the two candidates were compared for subject matter, form of reasoned discourse, use of "loaded terms," and types of motive appeals.

CHARACTERISTICS OF CONTENT: TO WHOM

To relate known characteristics of the audience to messages produced for them

The proposition that communicators tend to cast their messages in the idiom of the intended audience has been tested occasionally. Such studies have tended to center on messages produced to change attitudes. An examination of two mass circulation magazines, *Life* and *Ebony,* supported the hypothesis that differences in advertising are based on the socioeconomic levels of the two audiences (Berkman, 1963). When the offered product or service was predicated on the Negro's present lower status, the advertising was in a form appropriate to that status. On the other hand, when the advertised items reflected the status to which the Negro was thought to aspire, there was little essential difference in the two magazines; except for the substitution of Negro models in *Ebony*, two-thirds of the advertisers selling to middle-class markets used identical ads in the two magazines.

Albrecht (1956) analyzed short stories in large-circulation magazines with lower (*True Story, True Confessions*), middle (*American, Saturday Evening Post*), and upper (*Atlantic, New Yorker*) level readers, recording the distribution and evaluation of 10 "family values." Stories produced for each level strongly supported American family norms as a group, the least deviation being found in magazines for middle level readers. The degree of approval of some specific values, however, differed significantly from level to level.

Such data may lend themselves to three different interpretations: that authors *write differently* for dissimilar audiences, that the literature *reflects* basic value differences of the audiences, or that such materials *shape* the values and predispositions of the audience. These are not mutually exclusive aspects of the communication process, but rather, represent three types of inferences which have been drawn from content data. The first interpretation presents the fewest problems of validity and can be made directly from attributes of the content. The second explanation is a variation of the theme, often debated with respect to the mass media, that producers of communication are only giving audiences "what they want." This may or may not be true, and generally can be confirmed only by means other than content analysis. The third inference is the most tenuous unless supported by data other than the description of the content.

To describe patterns of communication

How are patterns of communication affected by situational or systemic changes? Analysis of documents written by leaders of the Dual Alliance and Triple Entente nations during the summer of 1914 indicated that as war approached, there was a significant increase in messages exchanged within alliances, with a concomitant decrease in intercoalition communication (Holsti, 1965b). Messages produced in 17 "Inter-Nation Simulations" revealed that after all members of an alliance had obtained nuclear weapons, the modal pattern of communication changed from a "wheel" configuration to an "all channels" pattern (Brody, 1963).

THE ANTECEDENTS OF CONTENT: WHY

Many definitions of content analysis explicitly exclude its use for purposes of inferring the antecedents or causes of content. Nevertheless, such inferences have often been drawn from content data. One major goal of propaganda analysis, for example, has been to make inferences about values, intentions, and strategy of communicators. And, as indicated earlier, research on the pragmatic dimension of communication has become a major aspect of content-analysis studies. The problem, then, is no longer whether content analysts *should* make inferences concerning the cause of communication, but rather, given the trend of research, what steps the investigator can take to enhance confidence in the validity of his inferences. Studies selected for review in this section were chosen in part to illustrate a variety of research applications and in part to examine alternative approaches to the problem of validation.

To secure political and military intelligence

An important impetus to the development of content analysis was the large-scale propaganda research during World War II. Social scientists, many of whom later made significant theoretical and methodological contributions to content analysis, were engaged by the Federal Communications Commission, the Library of Congress, and the Justice Department to study these materials.

The most difficult problem, because of the constraints within which the propaganda analyst operates, is that of establishing criteria for inference. The FCC used both *direct* and *indirect* techniques. The first method operates from a "representational" model of communication; that is, the investigator assumes that words in the message are valid indicators, irrespective of circumstance. Inferences regarding intentions, expectations, and situational factors are drawn *directly* from attributes of propaganda, based on a past correlation of conditions or events and content characteristics. The direct method is illustrated by a study to determine the degree of collaboration between German and Italian propaganda agencies. From consistent differences in broadcasts originating in Rome and Berlin, analysts concluded that there was no collaboration. Evidence gathered after the war validated the inference (Berelson and De Grazia, 1947).

The single-step approach has been criticized for two deficiencies: past regularities are often based on a very few cases, and the method is insensitive to changes in propaganda strategy, which may render past correlations invalid.

An "instrumental" model of communication, in which it is assumed that the important aspect of the message consists in what it conveys, given context and circumstances, underlies the indirect method of inference (the representational and instrumental models are further discussed in Pool, 1959). The initial step in the indirect method is to establish the propaganda goal or strategy underlying the characteristics of content. A series of interconnected causal imputations is derived from this point (George, 1959a, p. 41):

| *Situational factor* | ← | *Elite estimate* | ← | *Elite expectation* | ← | *Elite intention or policy* | ← | *Propaganda strategy* | ← | *Content* |

In the indirect method, then, the process of inference is broken up into a number of smaller steps. The relationship of the two methods of inference to one another is summarized by George (1959a, p. 43):

It is [recommended], first, that the direct approach be utilized in *hypothesis formation* for whatever it is worth (which depends upon the number and quality of the tentative, incompletely confirmed one-to-one correlations that are available) and that the indirect method be utilized in the *assessment,* or testing, of the inferential hunches derived from the direct approach. Second, it is recommended that such transitions from the direct to the indirect approach be made quite deliberately, in full awareness that the indirect method requires logic-of-the-situation reasoning and the use of generalizations other than the one-to-one type of correlation between a content indicator and an aspect of the elite's political behavior or situational milieu.

Despite many difficulties facing analysts, documentary material on the Nazi conduct of the war indicated that FCC inferences were accurate in an impressive number of cases. For a two-month period (March–April 1943), 101 out of 119 inferences made by the German section were scored as correct. Of methodological interest is the finding that frequency and nonfrequency indicators were about equally successful (George, 1959a, pp. 264–266).

To analyze psychological traits of individuals

It is a widely held belief among social scientists that symbolic behavior of the individual can provide important psychological data about personality, values, intentions, and other characteristics of the communicator. Personal documents—defined as "any self-revealing record that intentionally or unintentionally yields information regarding the structure, dynamics, and functioning of the author's mental life"—may take many forms, ranging from a diary or intimate letters to autobiographies and speeches addressed to a wide audience (Allport, 1942, p. xii). The motives for producing personal documents may vary from psychotherapy to hopes of literary fame. Finally, investigators' purposes in analyzing personal documents have differed, despite the common goal of making inference about the communicator.

Written materials have been content-analyzed to infer personality traits of their authors. A study of Richard Wright's autobiography (White, 1947) was discussed earlier. The letters of an Irishwoman, Jenny Gove Masterson, were subjected to "personal structure analysis," a system developed to aid the clinician "as a supplement to his more or less brilliant insight, a technique offering evaluation and analysis which will have the virtue of objectivity and will also reveal aspects of the material that may have eluded his scrutiny" (Baldwin, 1942, p. 163). The procedure was grounded on the assumptions that frequency of an item in the case material is a measure of its importance in the personality. From a table of frequencies and correspondences, three well-integrated but independent ideational clusters were isolated. These revolved around Jenny's attitudes toward self and son, jobs, and death (the text of the letters can be found in Allport, 1946). Baldwin's study has been replicated using computer analysis (Paige, 1966).

Although critical of Baldwin's statistical analysis, Andrews and Muhlhan employed a modified version of personal structure analysis to study congruent idea patterns in the personal diary of a young girl (1943). As in Baldwin's study, independent checks were used to test the validity of content-analysis data, with satisfactory results. The method of "contingency analysis" employed in both of these studies has been further developed by Osgood (1959).

A number of categories have been used to analyze themes, plots, and characters of novels to infer psychological traits of their authors. As in other studies of this type, the analyst assumes that key psychological traits of the writer must manifest themselves in his writing. Novels by D. H. Lawrence (McCurdy, 1939), the Brontë sisters (McCurdy, 1947), Charles Kingsley (Deutsch, 1947), Dostoevsky (Kanzer, 1948), and Knut Hamsun (Lowenthal, 1949) have been analyzed, as have Shakespeare's plays (McCurdy, 1953). Studies of this nature have not been limited to fictional materials. The content of Justice Robert Jackson's legal opinions, for example, were analyzed and related to other aspects of his behavior in an effort to reconstruct continuities and changes in his legal philosophy (Schubert, 1965).

Unlike descriptive studies of literary style, such as those discussed earlier, problems arising in the analysis of literature for the purpose of inferring psychological traits are not confined to those of developing adequate analytic categories. A number of methods have been used to validate content data. Investigation of the author's biography may provide at least a partial check on the validity of inferences drawn from the data; that is, are events and experiences in the writer's life consistent with psychological inferences drawn from content data? This method was applied in the studies of the Brontës, Dostoevsky, Lawrence, Shakespeare, and Jackson.

An interesting variation of the validity problem, validation by prediction, is illustrated in Lowenthal's 1937 study of Knut Hamsun. Hamsun's novels revealed themes consistent with fascism: stress on race and natural community, pantheism, and reduction of women to reproductive functions. From these data Lowenthal concluded that Hamsun was intrinsically a fascist, a conclusion borne out a few years later by Hamsun's collaboration with the Nazis during World War II (1949).

A very different kind of personal document, political rhetoric, has been analyzed to infer personality traits of the speaker from logical and cognitive characteristics of his verbal production (Shneidman, 1963). The text is first coded into two category sets. *Idiosyncrasies of reasoning* include 32 categories consisting of idiosyncrasies of relevance, idiosyncrasies of meaning, arguments containing suppressed premises or conclusions, idiosyncrasies of logical structure, and idiosyncrasies of logical interrelations. *Cognitive maneuvers* consist of 65 styles of thought development; for example, to switch from normative to descriptive mode, or to render another's argument weaker or stronger by paraphrase.

To illustrate the method, Shneidman (1961, 1963) examined the logical styles of Kennedy and Nixon on their first two television debates, and that of Khrushchev in speeches delivered after the collapse of the Paris "Summit" Conference and at the United Nations. A partial comparison of "idiosyncrasies of reasoning" and "cognitive maneuvers" in the rhetoric of Kennedy, Nixon, and Khrushchev appears in Table 4.

The second step in the analysis is to construct, for each idiosyncrasy of reasoning, the logical conditions under which idiosyncrasy is controverted or canceled or, to use the author's term, *contralogic*. Inferences regarding psychological characteristics of the communicator are then drawn from the contralogic as illustrated in Table 5 (Shneidman, 1961, p. 22).

TABLE 4

IDIOSYNCRASIES OF REASONING AND COGNITIVE MANEUVERS IN THE
RHETORIC OF JOHN F. KENNEDY, RICHARD M. NIXON, AND NIKITA
KHRUSHCHEV

Stylistic features	Kennedy	Nixon	Khrushchev
Idiosyncrasies of reasoning:			
Irrelevant premise	8.7%	4.9%	2.2%
Argumentum ad populum	3.4	12.0	22.6
Complex question	0.0	1.9	21.5
Derogation	0.9	4.9	11.8
Stranded predicate	6.6	7.1	5.4
Truth-type confusion	2.2	6.4	0.0
Cognitive maneuvers:			
To enlarge or elaborate the proceeding	7.9%	6.0%	0.6%
To smuggle debatable point into alien context	5.8	8.4	0.0
To be irrelevant	7.3	9.6	16.8
To allege but not substantiate	4.4	6.3	4.6
To introduce new notion	0.0	0.0	2.3

Shneidman's inference regarding the personalities of Kennedy, Nixon, and Khrushchev appears to have considerable face validity. For example, Khrushchev is characterized in these terms (1961, pp. 61–62):

He feels that others are prone to misunderstand his position and yet he desires acceptance and will even sacrifice other needs or ends to achieve it. He is moody and needful of approval. But with his pessimism about resolving differences, he enjoys conflict and struggle, as much for its own sake as a means to an end. . . . He trusts his own instinct, his "natural feel" for things. He is painstaking in certain areas, but in general is impatient and suspicious of detail or subtlety.

Pending considerable further research, the psychological correlates of logical styles are only working hypotheses. Nevertheless, as a method of studying style, this technique represents a substantially more sophisticated approach than earlier attempts to analyze political discourse through content analysis (Hayworth, 1930; McDiarmid, 1937; Runion, 1936).

The utility of content analysis in psychiatry stems from the view that "psychiatric disorders, regardless of their etiology, are ultimately manifest as disorders of social communication" (Jaffe, 1966, p. 689). Sound recording of psychotherapeutic interviews has opened an entirely new field and a vast source of personal documents for analysis.

TABLE 5   ILLUSTRATIONS OF METHOD OF ANNULLING (OR CONTROVERTING) LOGICAL IDIOSYNCRASIES

Column I: Idiologic	*Column II: Contralogic*	*Column III: Psycho-logic*
Samples of specific ways of thinking, in terms of idiosyncrasies of logic	Logical conditions under which the logical idiosyncrasy (column I) is controverted or annulled	Psychological state consistent with the logical condition (II) which would annul the idiosyncrasy (I)
Example (from Bleuler, von Domarus, and Ariety): "Switzerland loves freedom; I love freedom; therefore I am Switzerland." *Fallacy:* identification in terms of attributes of the predicate (or undistributed middle).	If one supplies the implicit premise that Switzerland is the only member of the class of freedom lovers (and if I loved freedom), then it would follow, without logical error, that I would have to be Switzerland.	The reasoning reflects a psychological state in which the range of attention is constricted and narrowed (to one member of a class). *Psychological symptoms:* intense concentration, oblivion to ordinary stimuli, hypesthesia, acute withdrawal, and, at its extreme, catatonia.
Example (from Binswanger's "The Case of Ellen West"): At 16 her motto is *Aut Caesar aut nihil* ("Either the greatest or nothing"). Before her death she says, "If I cannot remain young, beautiful, and thin, then rather—nothingness." *Fallacy:* dichotomization.	If one supplies the implicit assumption that the aspects of the universe under discussion are organized in a binary manner, then it follows logically that the alternative to leading a perfect *life* is death.	The reasoning reflects a psychological state in which the basic identifications are confused, the basic attitudes toward self-control are ambivalent, and there is a general polarized approach to concepts and people, with unhappy vacillations between the extremes of the dichotomized polarities. *Psychological symptoms:* obsessions, abulia, fixed ideas, anxiety, general impotence, rumination, suicide.
Example (from Wertheimer): Question to the young Gauss—"What is the sum of $1 + 2 + 3 + 4 + 5 + 6 + 7 + 8 + 9 + 10$?" *Response:* correct answer (55) in amazingly short time. *Fallacy:* none.	One can do the task correctly and quickly if one sees (makes the assumption) that (a) there are pairs of numbers ($1 + 10$, $2 + 9$, etc.) each of which totals 11; (b) there are 5 such pairs; (c) 5 times 11 equals 55. The principle is represented by the formula $(n + 1)$ $(n/2)$.	The reasoning reflects a psychological state in which there is a high intelligence, active curiosity, open mind, freedom to explore intellectually, inquiring mind that is original but not destructive, freedom from fear of teacher (or authority generally? or father?) The psychological label for this state is "genius."

Much research has been directed toward developing and validating measures for diagnosis and for evaluation of psychotherapy. A partial listing of such indices follows.

The *type-token ratio* (TTR) measures variability in the communicator's working vocabulary. A score is based on the number of different words found in samples of standard length: 100, 200, 500, or 1000 words (Johnson, 1944). The hypothesis that speech variability increases with successful therapy has generally been supported. A test of 12 schizophrenics and 12 college freshmen revealed that the mean TTR for schizophrenic patients was significantly lower; also, the stability of their TTR scores in successive samples was significantly lower than that of freshmen (Mann, 1944; Fairbanks, 1944). In addition, the language of the patients was characterized by a more negative tone, preoccupation with the past, and more frequent self-references. Roshal (1953) tested the hypothesis that language variability, as measured by TTR scores for both 100 and 200-word samples, is related to adjustment. Difference in TTR's between the first and final interview were significantly higher for the group in which therapy was judged to be "more successful using both measures." Further clinical applications of the TTR are described in Gottschalk (1961).

The *adjective-verb* ratio scores the number of adjectives per 100 verbs (Boder, 1940). This measure has been found to differentiate the language structure of "normal" subjects from that of schizophrenics. Normal subjects have more adjectives per verb, as well as more adjectives per noun (Mann, 1944).

The *discomfort-relief quotient* (DRQ), derived from learning theory, measures the amount of drive borne by the client (Dollard and Mowrer, 1947). The DRQ is computed by dividing the number of discomfort (drive) words by the total number of discomfort and comfort (relief) words. Tests with the DRQ have produced rather mixed results. In some cases it has been significantly correlated with measures such as palmar sweating, but in others no relationship with success in therapy was noted.

The *positive-negative-ambivalent quotient* (PNAvQ) resembles the DRQ except that, unlike the DRQ, only the patient's self-evaluations are scored (Raimy, 1948). DRQ and PNAvQ scores were computed for 17 interviews, with strong evidence that the two scores are highly correlated (Kauffman and Raimy, 1949). However, this finding was not confirmed by a second study.

The hypothesis that there is a positive correlation between the extent to which an individual expresses acceptance of and respect for himself and the degree to which he expresses these feelings toward others has been investigated (although not with the PNAvQ). Although the samples studied were small (10 subjects), in both cases the data supported the hypothesis (Sheerer, 1949; Stock, 1949).

A measure of *defensiveness* was developed on the premise that defensiveness follows perceptions of threat, an experience perceived to be inconsistent with a value or concept of self or the environment (Haigh, 1949, p. 181). A defensive reaction is one in which perceptions are distorted to reduce awareness of perceived incongruence, and is inferred from such client responses as denials, rationalizations, and projections.

Scales for thematic analysis of *hostility* and *anxiety* found in verbal samples have been developed. One is a weighted scale for measuring three types of hostility classified on the basis of direction—outward, ambivalent, and inward (Gottschalk, Gleser, and Springer, 1963). A second scale is based on a system of weighted scoring for six categories of anxiety—death, mutilation, separation, guilt, shame, and nonspecific anxiety (Gleser, Gottschalk, and Springer, 1961).

Lasswell's general-purpose system classifies responses according to communicator (self, interviewer, other), direction (pro or anti), and object of statement (self, interviewer, other) (Lasswell, 1938).

A measure of *speech disturbance* has been found to correlate significantly with anxiety and conflict in therapeutic interviews. The ratio is calculated by dividing the number of speech disturbances by the number of words in the sample (Mahl, 1959).

On the theory that "motivation and psychological conflict play significant roles in shaping and distorting language responses," a general approach to the study of normal and pathological speech by word associations has been developed (Laffal, 1965, p. x). The subject's entire vocabulary (rather than only certain types of words, as in the DQR, PNAvQ, and adjective-verb ratio), is coded into 114 categories for which extensive definitions and scoring rules are presented.

Content-analysis systems have also been developed for systematic examination of Rorschach (Elizur, 1949; Lindner, 1950) and Thematic Apperception Tests (Shneidman, 1951; Hafner and Kaplan, 1960). Research relating other language categories to psychotherapy is reviewed in Mowrer (1953), Snyder (1953), Auld and Murray (1955), and Mardsen (1965).

Content-analysis research in psychotherapy has yielded somewhat mixed results. In some cases, contradictory findings have been obtained using the same measure with different samples of subjects. In others, the small samples of subjects have tended to raise questions about the generality of the findings. The primary difficulty has often rested not with the analytical scheme for scoring responses, but with the absence of clearly defined criteria of "success" (Auld and Murray, 1955, p. 389). This is a restatement of the recurring problem in using content data to make inferences about communicators and audiences: content data are not self-validating, and clear measures of the dependent variables that they are intended to index are often lacking. Nevertheless, the psycholinguistic approach to therapeutic materials appears to offer a fertile area for research. Rarely has the richness of communication been so dramatically illustrated as in an extensive linguistic and paralinguistic content analysis limited to the first five minutes of a psychiatric interview (Pittenger, Hockett, and Danehy, 1960). Some of the possibilities in this area are also suggested in an extensive, multimeasure psycholinguistic analysis of two interviews. Minute-by-minute readings on heart rate and skin temperature were related to a number of verbal measures, including the TTR, Speech Disturbance Ratio, and rating scales for anxiety and hostility (Gottschalk, 1961).

Use of language measures for purposes other than psychotherapy can be illustrated by a study comparing genuine suicide notes with ordinary letters and simulated suicide notes (Osgood and Walker, 1959). Among many content-analysis methods used were the TTR, DRQ, and adjective-adverb/noun-verb measures, all of which differentiated real suicide notes from the letters. Only the latter measure, however, was successful in distinguishing real from simulated notes. Content analyses of real and simulated suicide notes are also reported in Gottschalk and Gleser (1960) and Stone and Hunt (1963).

Several techniques for scoring verbal interaction among group members have been developed. Interaction Process Analysis uses 12 content categories for classifying responses in six problem areas: communication, evaluation, control, decision, tension reduction, and reintegration (Bales, 1950). Sign Process Analysis is another technique for recording systematically what is said in the course of group interaction. The scoring scheme abstracts and records the distribution of positive, negative, and neutral assertions about objects, which are grouped into subsets according to locus (internal or external), sex, and status (Mills, 1964, p. 103). The Leary content-analysis approach (1957, p. 65) identifies eight interpersonal processes: managerial-autocratic, competitive-narcissistic, aggressive-sadistic, rebellious-distrustful, self-effacing–masochistic, docile-dependent, cooperative-overconventional, and responsible-hypernormal. Although developed for the diagnosis of personality, the Leary System has been adapted for use in simulation studies (Brody, 1963).

Content analysis is increasingly being used to assess psychological variables in the context of political decision making, particularly in the area of foreign policy. One approach, a continuation of the Lasswellian tradition, has emphasized elite values and ideology. In the absence of direct measures, Soviet and American publications representing political, economic, labor, military, scientific, and cultural elites were examined to identify major values. Themes regarding the economy, social and internal political affairs, and external relations were coded into more than 40 category sets. An investigation of elite foreign-policy attitudes for the same period focused on perceptions of the international system, power relationships, and operational codes. Although Soviet and American value preferences were found to be symmetrical in some respects, and incompatible in others, the data also revealed that elites in both nations displayed "a powerful tendency to act and speak in such a way as to exacerbate differences" (Angell, Dunham, and Singer, 1964, p. 473).

A second approach to foreign-policy studies has focused on analysis of documents written by officials holding key decision-making roles. The basic assumption is that foreign-policy decisions, like all decisions, are in part a product of the policy maker's perceptions; that if men define situations as real, they are real in their consequences. Again, the choice of content analysis is based largely on the inability to use more direct methods by which to assess the perceptions, attitudes, and values of foreign-policy leaders at the time of decision; systematic analysis of diplomatic documents provides an indirect method to bridge gaps in time and space. Themes, which have been classified into categories such as friendship, hostility, frustration, and satisfaction, have served as the unit of analysis (North *et al.,* 1963).

An initial study tested two basic hypotheses about the relationship between perceptions of threat and perceptions of capability during an international crisis

(Zinnes, North, and Koch, 1961). During the weeks prior to war in 1914, perceptions of capability appeared much less frequently in decision makers' documents as perceptions of threat increased. This study also revealed the limitations, for many purposes, of using frequency as the sole basis of inference. After the 1914 data were recoded to permit analysis on the basis of intensity as well as frequency, hypotheses relating to perceptions of capability and injury were reexamined. Decision makers of each nation most strongly felt themselves to be victims of persecution and rejection precisely at the time when they were making policy decisions of the most crucial nature (Holsti and North, 1965).

Other analyses of the 1914 data, within the framework of a model linking actions and perceptions, have consistently shown that the more intense the interaction between parties, the more important it is to incorporate perceptual variables, as indexed by content data, into the analysis (Holsti, North, and Brody, 1968). This strong relationship between perceptions of hostility, feelings of involvement, and policy decisions has also been found in a study of Soviet and Chinese leaders during three crisis situations (Zaninovich, 1964).

A number of prominent hypotheses in the decision-making literature were tested using documents from the 1914 crisis. The data revealed that as stress increased, decision makers perceived time as an increasingly salient factor in formulating policy and they became preoccupied with the short-term, rather than long-range, implications of their actions. Leaders in various capitals of Europe also perceived the alternatives open to themselves to decrease, and those of their adversaries to increase, as they came under more intense stress (Holsti, 1965b).

In a study comparing events during the Cuban missile crisis of 1962 with those in the summer of 1914, some important differences emerged. During the Cuban crisis both sides tended to perceive rather accurately the nature of the adversary's actions, and then proceeded to respond at an "appropriate" level. Thus, unlike the situation in 1914, efforts by either party to delay or reverse the escalation were generally perceived as such, and responded to in a like manner (Holsti, Brody, and North, 1965).

To infer aspects of culture and cultural change

Anthropologists, sociologists, and others have traditionally examined societal artifacts to describe constant and changing characteristics of cultures. Content analysis for this purpose can be illustrated by a series of studies centering on hypotheses relating "need of achievement" and "inner/other direction" to major states in cultural development.

A person with high *n* Achievement is someone who wants to succeed, who is energetic and nonconforming, and who enjoys tasks which involve elements of risk; *n* Achievement has been defined operationally as "a sum of the number of instances of achievement 'ideas' or images" (McClelland, 1958, p. 520). The hypothesis that "a society with a relatively high percentage of individuals with high *n* Achievement should contain a strong entrepreneurial class which will tend to be active and successful particularly in business enterprises so that *the society*

TABLE 6

NUMBER OF *n* ACHIEVEMENT IMAGES PER 100 LINES BY TYPE OF SAMPLE BY TIME PERIOD

Period	Man and his gods	Estate manage-ment	Funeral celebra-tions	Poetry	Epi-grams	War speeches	Average
Growth 900–475 B.C.	2.01	3.54	7.93	2.87	4.72	7.38	4.74
Climax 475–362 B.C.	1.21	0.82	5.94	0.38	2.36	5.55	2.71
Decline 362–100 B.C.	0.81	0.00	2.54	0.16	1.57	3.00	1.35

will grow in power and influence" was tested by scoring samples of literature from the periods of growth (900–475 B.C.), climax (475–362 B.C.), and decline (362–100 B.C.) of Greek civilization (McClelland, 1958). As an index of economic power and influence, the location of vase remains was used to construct maps of the area within which Greece traded in the sixth, fifth, and fourth centuries B.C.; these figures were 1.2, 3.4, and 1.9 million square miles, respectively. The amount of *n* Achievement imagery found in various kinds of literature is revealed in Table 6. When compared to trade area, the findings supported the hypothesis that expressions of *n* Achievement index stages in the development of a civilization.

An independent check on these results was made by analyzing inscriptions on vases produced in various eras of Greek civilization. Aronson (1958) found that "doodling" styles can be used to discriminate persons with high *n* Achievement from those with low *n* Achievement. An objective scoring system for lines, shapes, and spaces of spontaneous "doodles" has been cross-validated against several groups of subjects. Without serious modification, the same scoring system was applied to inscriptions on Greek vases. The results substantiated the other findings; signs of high *n* Achievement were significantly more frequent in the period of growth and less frequent in the period of climax. The same system of content analysis has also been used in a cross-cultural study relating child-training practices to *n* Achievement in Indian folktales (McClelland and Friedman, 1952; for other examples, see McClelland, 1961).

According to some students of American culture, there has been a notable trend from the "Protestant ethic" or inner-direction to a "social ethic" or other-direction (Riesman, Glazer, and Reuel, 1950). On the assumption that inner- and other-direction could be measured by achievement motive and affiliation motive (as defined by McClelland, 1958), respectively, children's readers for the period 1800–1950 were content-analyzed to determine whether these psychological variables index observed cultural change in the United States. Three hypotheses were tested: (1) that there has been a decrease in the incidence of achievement motivation and moral teachings; (2) that there has been an increase in occurrence of the affiliation motive; and (3) that incidence of the achievement motive has been positively correlated to an independent measure of achievement—the number of patents issued. Achievement motivation in the readers increased steadily throughout the nineteenth century and began to decline only around the turn of the century; the same trend was found in the number of patents issued. The hypotheses relating to moral teachings and affiliation motivation were also supported (deCharms and Moeller, 1962).

A somewhat different test of the hypothesis of increasing other-direction was provided by a content analysis of advertising in a mass circulation women's magazine for the period 1890–1956 (Dornbusch and Hickman, 1959). The null hypothesis, that there was no difference in the proportion of other-directed advertisement before and after the midpoint of 1921, was rejected at the 0.001 level in eight tests.

These studies illustrate some of the many possible ways in which content analysis of social and historical documents can be used to test hypotheses. At the same time it should be pointed out that there are many pitfalls, aside from such technical problems as coding reliability, to be avoided. A most important problem, one rarely resolved beyond doubt, is the selection of materials which do in fact represent the culture, or at least some significant segment of it. Do newspapers, drama, or literature of a period, taken collectively, represent merely a manifestation of the authors' personalities, or do they reflect the more general milieu?

A partial solution to the problem is to rely on materials which meet the criterion of popularity, as was done in the study of achievement motivation in Greek literature. The rationale for this approach has been spelled out in a cross-cultural study of themes in popular drama (McGranahan and Wayne, 1948, p. 430):

Our first assumpton in this study is that popular drama can be regarded as a case of "social fantasy"—that the psychological constellations in a dramatic work indicate sensitive areas in the personalities of those for whom the work has appeal; their needs, assumptions and values are expressed ("projected") in the drama. The successful play must be attuned to the audience.

A second approach involves examining materials which explicitly perform the function of transmitting and instilling social norms. Such materials, which may take very different forms across culture and time, have been widely used in content-analysis research; examples include folktales (McClelland and Friedman, 1952; Colby, 1966b), children's readers (deCharms and Moeller, 1962), youth manuals (Lewin, 1947), songs (Sebald, 1962), and textbooks (Walworth, 1938).

A third method is to use one or more independent indices against which to correlate content data. In their comparative study of German and American drama during the 1927 season, McGranahan and Wayne used six separate sets of data, both content and noncontent, to support their conclusion that there were real and persistent differences in the psychology of Germans and Americans (1948). A sample of plays from the 1909–1910 season was analyzed to determine whether differences could be attributed to Germany's defeat in World War I. Another test compared German audience reactions to movies which had been successful or unsuccessful in the United States. Each supplementary test supported findings based on content analysis, thereby increasing confidence in them.

To provide legal evidence

During World War II the United States government asked Harold Lasswell to analyze certain materials and to testify about their content in four cases of suspected criminal sedition. The purpose was to demonstrate that statements by the accused publishers conformed to enemy propaganda themes. Materials ranged from over two hundred books in English and Russian in the *Bookniga* case to eleven issues of the periodical *The Galilean,* published by William Dudley Pelley. Eight tests were developed to analyze the materials, the results of which were accepted in evidence by the court (Lasswell, 1949, pp. 177–178):

1. *Avowal: Explicit identification with one side of a controversy.*

2. *Parallel: The content of a given channel is compared with the content of a known propaganda channel. Content is classified according to themes.*

3. *Consistency: The consistency of a stream of communication with the declared propaganda aims of a party to a controversy. The aims may be official declarations or propaganda instructions.*

4. *Presentation: The balance of favorable and unfavorable treatment given to each symbol (and statement) in controversy.*

5. *Source: Relatively heavy reliance on one party to a controversy for material.*

6. *Concealed source: The use of one party to a controversy as a source, without disclosure.*

7. *Distinctiveness: The use of vocabulary peculiar to one side of a controversy.*

8. *Distortion: Persistent modification of statements on a common topic in a direction favorable to one side of a controversy. Statements may be omitted, added, or over- or under-emphasized.*

The most outspoken critics (St. George and Dennis, 1946; Hughes, 1950) of the content-analysis data presented in the sedition trials hardly qualify as dispassionate observers. Yet some of their specific objections are not wholly without merit. It has been pointed out that "There is almost no theory of language which predicts the specific words one will emit in the course of expressing the content of his thoughts" (Lasswell, Lerner, and Pool, 1952, p. 49). In the absence of such a theory, a posture of great skepticism is warranted toward use of content-analysis data for other than descriptive purposes in legal proceedings.

A form of content analysis, intended to yield only descriptive information, has been used by the Federal Communications Commission to determine whether radio-station owners conform to prescribed standards (Content Analysis . . . , 1948, p. 910). In its annual survey, the FCC compares station logs with ideal ratios between commercial and local live, sustaining, and public-issue programs. In one case the American Jewish Congress sought to deny an application by the *New York Daily News* for an FM broadcasting license on grounds of unfavorable bias against minority groups. In a split opinion the Commission ruled that both qualitative and quantitative data contained "technical deficiencies . . . so serious as to vitiate any real value the analysis might otherwise have had." At the same time, the Commission ruled in unambiguous terms that content analysis is an acceptable evidentiary technique if the data are deemed to be of adequate quality (Content Analysis . . . , 1948, p. 914).

On the whole, content analysis has been used sparingly as a source of legal evidence. Literary infringement cases are perhaps the legal area in which it might be used most suitably. Existing tests suffer from precisely those deficiencies which can be remedied through careful content analysis (Sorenson and Sorenson, 1955, p. 264):

> To distinguish the ideas, plots, title, phraseology, characters and locale, all of which are not infringible from the "original form of expression, language or thought sequence and literary style" is simply too difficult a job for the ordinary observer making a superficial comparison.
>
> Meanwhile, copyright counsel have no way of knowing whether the judge read all of the works, scanned part of each, used his own sampling system, or how much weight, if any, he may give to the exhibits submitted.

The tests developed in the sedition cases, as well as those developed by "literary detectives," might well provide data better than impressionistic scanning.

THE ANTECEDENTS OF CONTENT: WHO

Who wrote *The Imitation of Christ?* Was James Madison or Alexander Hamilton the author of *The Federalist Papers* Nos. 49–58, 62, and 63? These are two of many problems of literary detection which have been investigated by content analysis. The belief that each person's style contains certain unique characteristics is an old one, and methods of inference from statistical description of content attributes go back at least to the nineteenth century (Mendenhall, 1887). But because there are so many possible characteristics of style which might be used to discriminate between authors, the major task is that of selecting proper indicators. The problem must often be tackled in a "fishing expedition" manner, as reliable discriminators in one case may fail in another. For example, sentence length, often a useful index, proved useless in the case of the *Federalist Papers*—the undisputed writings of Madison and Hamilton averaged 34.59 and 34.55 words per sentence, respectively.

Frequencies of various classes of nouns were used to determine whether Thomas à Kempis or Jean Gerson wrote *The Imitation of Christ*. Five independent tests, based on the incidence of approximately 8200 nouns each, yielded the results in Table 7 (Yule, 1944, p. 274). On this basis Yule concluded that Gerson was not the author. Although it is impossible to "prove" that *The Imitation of Christ* was written by Thomas à Kempis, these data are clearly consistent with the hypothesis of his authorship.

The frequency of 265 words in known writings of Madison and Hamilton served as the test for 12 *Federalist Papers* whose authorship was disputed (Mosteller and Wallace, 1964). The data strongly supported the claim of Madison's authorship. The weakest odds in Madison's case were 80 to 1 on *Paper* No. 55;

TABLE 7

INCIDENCE OF SPECIAL NOUNS IN "THE IMITATION OF CHRIST"
AND KNOWN WRITINGS OF THOMAS À KEMPIS AND JEAN
GERSON

	The Imitation of Christ	Thomas à Kempis	Gerson
Test 1	671	709	912
Test 2	376	365	823
Test 3	59	58	162
Test 4	6	7	21
Test 5	0	1	24

No. 56 was next weakest, at odds of 800 to 1 for Madison. Politically important words turned out to be far less effective discriminators than the high-frequency "function words." This finding is consistent with one generalization which has emerged from other studies of the "unknown communicator" in painting, literature, and music; it is the "minor encoding habits," the apparently trivial details of style, which vary systematically within and between communicators' works (Paisley, 1964).

Other statistical methods for identifying authors from content characteristics have emerged from studies of the "Quintus Curtius Snodgrass Letters" (Brinegar, 1963) and the "Junius Letters," a series of political pamphlets written in 1769–1772 (Ellegård, 1962).

The pitfalls of authorship studies can be illustrated by the controversy over the assertion that Paul wrote only five of the Epistles (Morton, 1963). The claim was based on an analysis of seven indicators assumed to be reliable as "fingerprints of the mind" for discriminating style: *sentence length,* and the frequency of the *definite article, third-person pronouns,* the aggregate of all parts of the verb *to be,* and the words *and, but,* and *in.* Using these tests, Morton concluded that six authors wrote the 14 Pauline Epistles. However, subsequent tests have at least disproved the generality of the seven indicators; the same tests indicated that James Joyce's *Ulysses* was written by six authors, none of whom wrote *Portrait of the Artist as a Young Man* (Ellison, 1965). While not resolving the question of who wrote the Epistles, such results clearly raise doubts about Morton's findings.

THE RESULTS OF COMMUNICATION: WITH WHAT EFFECT

The basic format of content-analysis research designed to study the effects of communication is: If messages have attributes *A, B,* and *C,* then the prediction is that the effect on the recipient will be *x, y,* and *z.* Content analysis serves to describe the relevant attributes of the independent variables (*A, B,* and *C*). But, as indicated earlier, any direct inference as to effects from content is at best tenuous. When a government-controlled newspaper such as the Chinese *People's*

Daily is analyzed to measure elite attitudes (Eto and Okabe, 1965), problems of inference are somewhat limited. The assumption that this source does reflect leadership views is plausible and can be verified by independent analyses of content or noncontent indices. But it would not necessarily follow that the same source could be used to measure mass opinion.

Evidence demonstrating that effects of communication are related not only to attributes of content but also to predispositions of the audience is too voluminous to review here (*cf.* Klapper, 1960; Bauer, 1964). A single example will suffice. Major themes of political appeals during the 1940 Presidential campaign were identified by content analysis of both public and private media. Reactions of the public to the content of the arguments were then measured by interview. The interaction between content and other factors is summarized by Berelson (1942, p. 63):

Why do people come across arguments and why do they accept them? Briefly, our answers are these. Mainly, people come across the arguments which the mediums of communication emphasize; they also tend to see the arguments they want to see and other arguments whose statement is appealing. Mainly (within a given time), people accept the arguments which support their own general position; they also tend to accept the arguments which they see in the public communications and those whose statement is persuasive.

Berelson's conclusion can be restated within the framework of content-analysis research: because of the variety of audience predispositions and decoding habits, the effects of communication cannot be inferred directly from the attributes of content ("what") or style ("how") without independent validation.

This problem was anticipated in an early proposal to measure public opinion by quantitative newspaper analysis. Woodward's (1934) research design incorporated systematic efforts to test the relationship between public attitudes and newspaper content. Often, however, this relationship is simply assumed to be a positive one. For example, frequencies of British and American place-names in colonial American newspapers were tabulated to index sentiments of national identity (Merritt, 1966). But the absence of evidence demonstrating that the appearance of these symbols either reflected or shaped public views calls into serious question inferences drawn from the content data. In short, the burden of proof is on the investigator to present evidence that audience attitudes can indeed be inferred directly from communications produced for that audience. As indicated in Table 1, measures of effects may be derived by analyses of (a) subsequent messages produced by the recipient to determine whether they are consistent with predicted effect, or (b) noncontent indices of the recipient's behavior.

To measure readability

Perhaps the most systematic content-analysis research measuring effects of communication has centered on correlating attributes of style with ease of comprehension. Characteristics of text which have often been tested include various aspects of vocabulary (diversity, hard words, long words, abstract words), sentence structure (length, type, number of prepositional phrases or indeterminate clauses), and human-interest elements (personal pronouns, colorful words).

There have generally been two approaches to identifying and validating elements of readability. The first has been to identify the distinguishing attributes of materials prejudged to have a certain level of difficulty—for example, adventure stories and philosophical writings. This approach assumes that the investigator can judge *a priori* the level of difficulty of such materials—often a dubious premise. The more reliable technique has been to use independent tests to determine reading comprehension of subjects.

One of the earliest systematic studies on readability was undertaken by Gray and Leary (1935). They found that 24 of 44 language variables were significantly correlated with comprehension scores. After eliminating some variables which were highly correlated with others, five were selected to index readability: the number of different words, uncommon words, personal pronouns, prepositional phrases, and the average length of sentences.

Flesch (1943) and Lorge (1944) developed formulas based on three factors— sentence length, and two measures of vocabulary. The Flesch system was later revised, with formulas to measure both "reading ease" and "human interest" characteristics of text.

Subsequent research has focused in large part on developing easier methods of scoring the vocabulary factor in Flesch's formula. One method is to count only those words falling outside a standard 3000-word list (Dale and Chall, 1948). Another study demonstrated that incidence of one-syllable words is so highly correlated with the Flesch vocabulary factor that it may be used in its place, with a considerable saving of scoring time (Farr, Jenkins, and Patterson, 1951).

While readability research has consistently pointed to the importance of vocabulary load and sentence length (Brinton and Danielson, 1958), the limitations of these measures must be recognized. These formulas measure only *style,* not other important elements of readability: content, organization, and format (Kearl, 1948). Second, readability measures cannot be applied mechanically; for example, it is true only to a point that the shorter the sentence, the more readable the text. Finally, these formulas are geared to the effect of style on the "general" audience; little allowance is made for the reader's experience and expectations, each of which can have an important bearing on the extent to which the text is understood (Waples, Berelson, and Bradshaw, 1940, pp. 135–145).

The "Cloze Procedure," which represents a radical departure from traditional approaches to readability, overcomes the first two of these limitations. The text is initially mutilated by removal of every fifth, seventh, tenth, or *n*th word, after which the reader is asked to supply the missing words (Taylor, 1953). The index of readability is based on the percentage of blanks correctly filled in. The advantage of the method is that it is effective in cases where other methods break down; that is, when idiosyncratic use of language (for example, the writings of James Joyce or Gertrude Stein) produces invalid readability scores. Although originally developed to measure readability, because the Cloze system is sensitive to semantic, associational, grammatical, and syntactical determinants of verbal behavior, it has subsequently proved useful in personality (Honigfeld, Platz, and Gillis, 1964) and psychiatric research (Fillenbaum and Jones, 1962; Salzinger, Portnoy, and Feldman, 1964).

Other attributes of style whose effects have been studied, and for which measures have been developed, include "sensationalism" (Tannenbaum and Lynch, 1960) and "abstraction" (Gillie, 1957; Haskins, 1960).

To analyze the flow of information

The flow of news to the United States from the outbreak of World War I to America's entry in April 1917 was analyzed by Foster (1935, 1937). Over 11,000 items appearing on the front page of the *New York Times* and in the Chicago press were coded according to origin of the news, and to type of appeal contained within it which might make the reader favor American participation. The data revealed that American readers were almost wholly dependent on news directly from, or dispatched through, the Entente powers. Thus, events such as the German invasion of Belgium were reported almost exclusively by news received from Germany's enemies. As war approached, the proportion of news from American sources increased sharply, as did news containing some appeal favoring American participation.

Content analysis was used to determine whether the Associated Press and United Press International, each of which had full-time bureaus in Havana, were responsible for charges of inadequate public information about the Cuban revolution. All stories about events in Cuba filed during December 1958 were analyzed. Tables summarizing AP and UPI reports were compared to coverage of the Castro revolution by major newspapers published in Washington, Cleveland, and Louisville. Scores were computed for percentage of available AP and UPI information used, and the prominence (headlines, placement) with which it was displayed. On the basis of the comparison, the author absolved the news services from charges of inadequate coverage: "The newspapers received enough wire copy to tell the long, continuing story of the Cuban revolution. They made little use of this material, however, until the last six days" (Lewis, 1960, p. 646).

A form of content analysis was used to study the transmission of rumors through six removes from an original source (De Fleur, 1962). Subjects in a community were informed that prizes would be offered to those who could repeat a short advertising slogan to a team of investigators. The slogan was given to a sample of subjects, and interview responses three days later were analyzed to determine the degree of distortion in the original message. By asking subjects to identify their source of information, it was possible to determine how many steps removed each respondent was from the original source.

Studies employing some form of content analysis to chart flow of news include Carter (1957), Schramm (1959), Hart (1961), and Galtung and Ruge (1965).

To assess responses to communication

One aspect of the effects of a communication is the degree to which its symbols become assimilated by the audience. Prothro tested the hypothesis that political symbols of the New Deal have become a "permanent increment to the main body of the American tradition," and that not even successful spokesmen for conservatism reject them (1956, p. 727). The first Acceptance, Inaugural, and State of the Union addresses of Presidents Hoover, Roosevelt, Truman, and Eisenhower were coded for relative frequencies of "political appeals" (government aid, government regulation, national power, etc.) and "demand symbols" (peace, freedom, faith, controls, initiative, etc.). While demand symbols distinguished Hoover and Eisenhower from Roosevelt and Truman, Eisenhower's political appeals were free from any repudiation of the New Deal, thereby supporting the hypothesis.

Soviet newspapers and domestic and foreign broadcasts were analyzed to assess the effects of Voice of America broadcasts. For a four-year period beginning in 1947, mass communication materials were examined for all references to the Voice of America. A number of content-analysis techniques were used to answer different questions. Frequency counts were used to measure focus of attention and distribution of Soviet references to VOA. Most foreign attacks on VOA were directed to Eastern and Western Europe, with little attention to Latin American audiences. During the four-year period there was a relative increase in attention directed to domestic audiences, especially in those publications read predominantly by the Soviet intelligentsia. Thematic analysis was used to code more than 2500 references to VOA. These data revealed that the Soviets, rather than posing a counterimage of Soviet virtues, responded by counteracting the image they assumed VOA had created of the United States (Inkeles, 1952; see also Massing, 1963).

Does the content of communication have a greater effect on the audience when it is attributed to a high-prestige source? Attitudes before and after exposure to three messages attributed to Thomas Gates, Walter Lippmann, and James Conant indicated that messages with a by-line do produce greater change in the direction of the message, but only when the by-line is located at or near the top of the message (Tannenbaum and Greenberg, 1961a; see also Hovland, Janis, and Kelley, 1953).

Two studies have examined the effects of scholarship by analyzing published reactions to research. Lerner undertook a thematic content analysis of the published reviews of *The American Soldier,* a study of Army morale during World War II by a large team of social scientists. Responses were related to professional affiliation and other attributes of the reviewer. In his conclusion, Lerner suggested how content and predispositions combined to shape the nature and tone of reviews (1950, pp. 241–242):

By the test of response, *The Soldier* surely is an important book. The challenge it presents to the stock attitudes of readers is clear from the depth of the affects exhibited by its reviewers: the responsive postures range from piety to diabolism. . . . The lack of time, skill, or inclination to refigure one's position in *The Soldier's* universe of discourse meant that most reviewers had to draw upon their already available stock of attitudes. This leads to "spontaneous" self-positioning, which accounts for both the regularity of alignment by occupation (i.e., prior commitment as to scientific research in human affairs) and the readiness to displace affective responses from the concrete object *The Soldier* to the general symbol Social Science.

A somewhat similar study examined the treatment of Freud's theory of dreams in general psychology, abnormal psychology, and psychiatry textbooks (Herma, Kris, and Shor, 1943). The investigators initially developed a list of 30 propositions basic to the theory of dreams. All available textbooks published between 1901 and 1940 were coded according to: mention of the theory of dreams; frequency of basic propositions cited; attitude toward the theory as a whole and toward specific propositions comprising the theory; and, if the theory was rejected, the basis of rejection (ridicule, moral grounds, scientific grounds, etc.). The data revealed that the theory of dreams had become a predominant interest only in texts on abnormal behavior, and that those who rejected the theory did so on grounds other than scientific.

CODING CONTENT DATA

Coding is the process whereby raw data are systematically transformed and aggregated into units which permit precise description of relevant content characteristics. Coding rules serve as the operational link between the investigator's data and his theory and hypotheses. Coding rules are thus an integral part of the research design, and in preparing them the analyst makes a number of decisions. Specifically:

> *How is the research problem defined in terms of categories?*
> *What unit of content is to be classified?*
> *What system of enumeration will be used?*

Although coding is discussed under these three headings, the division is solely for purposes of exposition. It does not imply that selection of categories, units, and system of enumeration are independent decisions. These represent a series of interrelated choices, each of which carries with it certain assumptions.

CATEGORIES OF ANALYSIS

A central problem in any research design is selection and definition of categories, the "pigeonholes" into which content units are to be classified: "Content analysis stands or falls by its categories. Particular studies have been productive to the extent that the categories were clearly formulated and well adapted to the problem and to the content" (Berelson, 1952, p. 147). There are as many possible schemes for classifying content data as there are questions which may be asked of the data. Among the types of categories used frequently in content-analysis research are the following (some of which are described in greater detail in Berelson, 1952, pp. 147–168):

"What is said" categories:

Subject matter. What is the communication about?

Direction. How is the subject matter treated (for example, favorable-unfavorable; strong-weak)?

Standard. What is the basis on which the classification by direction is made?

Values. What values, goals, or wants are revealed?

Methods. What means are used to achieve goals?

Traits. What are the characteristics used in description of people?

Actor. Who is represented as undertaking certain acts?

Authority. In whose name are statements made?

Origin. Where does the communication originate?

Target. To what persons or groups is the communication directed?

Location. Where does the action take place?

Conflict. What are the sources and levels of conflict?

Endings. Are conflicts resolved happily, ambiguously, or tragically?

Time. When does the action take place?

"How it is said" categories:

Form or type of communication. What is the medium of communication (newspaper, radio, television, speech, etc.)?

Form of statement. What is the grammatical or syntactical form of the communication?

Device. What is the rhetorical or propagandistic method used?

This list is neither exhaustive nor does it define the limits of content analysis. It is merely an enumeration of categories which have been employed more or less frequently. Nor are the categories at the same conceptual level. Subject matter categories can be used independently, as is done when newspaper content is classified into various types of news. But one cannot code items for direction (for example, approval-disapproval) independently of a referent. The same is true of the "standard" category. The coder may first be asked to isolate a subject matter unit (for example, Freud's dream theory), then classify it for direction of attitude (favorable or unfavorable), after which some judgment is made as to the standard used for acceptance or rejection (Herma, Kris, and Shor, 1943).

One of the questions frequently raised in the literature is that of standard categories. The advantages of standardization are the same as in any area of scholarship: results may be compared across studies and findings will tend to become cumulative. On the other hand, the disparity of purpose which characterizes content-analysis research makes standardization difficult to achieve. Some categories have been rather widely employed in descriptive studies of newspaper content (Bush, 1961; Willey, 1926; Woodward, 1930), values (Lasswell, 1935; White, 1951), political symbols (Pool, 1952a), attitudes (Osgood, Suci, and Tannenbaum, 1957), and a few other areas. There have also been recent attempts to develop standard categories for general psycholinguistic analysis (Laffal, 1965) and dream analysis (Hall and Van de Castle, 1966). But in general, Pool's observation (1959, p. 213) accurately reflects the current state of the field:

It is questionable, however, how ready we are to establish standard measures . . . in content analysis. Such a measure is convenient when a considerable number of researchers are working on the same variable, and when someone succeeds in working out good categories for that variable. It is doubtful that either of those criteria can be met in most areas of content analysis.

This state of affairs, understandable as it may be, has effectively prevented development of content norms for most classes of communicators. The absence of norms, in turn, often presents the investigator with knotty problems of inference. Do his findings regarding the communication content of a single source represent a significant deviation from those of the general class of communicators (for example, metropolitan dailies, mass circulation magazines, politicians, schizophrenics, etc.)? In view of the importance of such questions, formulation of standard categories and content norms would appear to be a high-priority area for future investigations.

In the absence of standard schemes of classification the analyst often is faced with the task of constructing appropriate categories by trial-and-error methods. This process usually consists of moving back and forth from theory to data, testing the usefulness of tentative categories, and then modifying them in light of the data. It is important to bear in mind, however, that the choice of categories can significantly affect one's findings. In a content analysis of American colonial newspapers a frequency count revealed an increase in American place-names after 1763, with a concomitant decline in the appearance of British symbols. But when references were classified as favorable, unfavorable, or neutral, changes were virtually nonexistent, even during a thirty-year period (Merritt, 1966, p. 49).

Definition of categories requires that they actually represent the elements of the investigator's theory; that they be exhaustive, to ensure that every item relevant to the study can be classified; and that they be mutually exclusive, so that no item can be scored more than once within a category set. To ensure results which are replicable, the investigator must specify explicitly the *indicators* that determine which units fall into each category. How, for example, is the coder to recognize a statement of "need achievement" (McClelland, 1958) or indications of anti-intellectualism in political reporting (Hage, 1959)? Rarely are categories so self-evident that coders will not require clear and specific instructions to guide their judgment.

A category can be defined exhaustively by enumerating each content unit to be placed in the category. In the RADIR studies the coders were supplied with a list of 416 key symbols which defined the limits of the required information (Pool, 1952a). The coding process was thus reduced from a judgmental task to a clerical one. Most categories, however, do not lend themselves to exhaustive definition, especially if units more inclusive than the word are used. Each category must then be defined more or less precisely by characterizing its major properties. These are the rules which the coder uses to determine whether units fall within the boundaries of the category.

UNITS OF ANALYSIS

Recording units

In addition to defining the categories into which content data may be classified, the analyst must designate the size of the units to be coded. The initial decision is the choice of *recording unit,* the specific segment of content that is characterized by placing it in a given category.

A number of recording units have been used frequently in content-analysis research.

The single word or symbol. In the past this unit has often been avoided in mass media research involving a great volume of data, a notable exception being the RADIR studies, in which nearly 20,000 editorials were analyzed. More recently, computer content-analysis programs have materially reduced the costs and increased the reliability of analyses based on word frequencies. The word has most frequently been used in research on readability (Gray and Leary, 1935; Flesch, 1948; Taylor, 1953), style (Skinner, 1939; Miles, 1951; Parrish, 1959), psychotherapy (Dollard and Mowrer, 1947), and literary detection (Yule, 1944; Mosteller and Wallace, 1964).

The theme. For many purposes the theme, a single assertion about some subject, is the most useful unit of content analysis. It is almost indispensable in the study of propaganda, values, attitudes, and the like. A major drawback to coding themes is that it is usually time-consuming. Another difficulty is that it is not an easily identified "natural" unit like the word, paragraph, or item; thus the coder must make an intermediate judgment to identify the boundaries of the theme. The sentence, "These clandestine Soviet actions on the imprisoned island of Cuba will not be tolerated by the American people," contains assertions about three nations. The coder must be able to reduce this sentence into its component themes before they may be placed in the proper categories.

The character. Studies of entertainment materials in the mass media have often employed the character as the recording unit. In this case the coder tallies the number of persons, rather than the number of words or themes, into the appropriate categories. Such research has focused on ethnic, socioeconomic, marital, psychological, and other traits of characters as portrayed in magazines (Berelson and Salter, 1946), movies (Jones, 1942), television (De Fleur, 1964), comics (Spiegelman, Terwilliger, and Fearing, 1953a), and other products of the mass media. Similar units have been used to examine traits of characters appearing in novels or drama for the purpose of drawing inferences about the personalities of authors (Kanzer, 1948; McCurdy, 1939, 1947, 1953).

The paragraph, the sentence, or other grammatical units. In part because these units often do not lend themselves to classification in a single category, they have rarely been used. The sentence about Soviet actions in Cuba, cited above, illustrates a problem that is even more severe when the paragraph is the recording unit.

The item. In this case the entire article, film, book, or radio program is characterized. This unit is too gross for most research, and may present problems when items fall between two categories; for example, is a war film with a comic theme classified under "war" or "comedy?" Item analysis is most useful for coding great amounts of materials when gross categories will suffice.

Context units

It may not be possible to classify a recording unit without some further reference to the context in which it appears. Attitudes toward democracy cannot be inferred solely on the basis of how frequently the word itself—and others defining the category "democracy"—appears in the communication; the *context unit* is the largest body of content that may be searched to characterize a recording unit. The coder may be instructed to refer to the sentence, the paragraph, or the entire document, in order to determine the attitude toward the symbol democracy.

Selection of recording and context units should rest upon two considerations. First, which units will best meet the requirements of the research problem? This question can only be answered in light of the hypotheses and the nature of the data. The important point is that *the units chosen may affect the results of the analysis.* Geller, Kaplan, and Lasswell (1942b) performed an experiment comparing four different recording and context units on the same sample of editorial matter.

Method	*Recording unit*	*Context unit*
I	Symbol	Sentence
II	Paragraph	Paragraph
III	3 sentences	3 sentences
IV	Article	Article

The four methods were in agreement in indicating *direction* of bias (favorable, unfavorable, neutral), but differed considerably in revealing its *extent*. In general, the larger the recording unit, the more the degree of bias in editorials was emphasized, and as the size of context unit was increased, the number of neutral entries diminished.

The effect on one's findings which may result from the choice of context units can be further illustrated in *contingency analysis.* In this method of content analysis, inferences are based on co-occurrence of attributes within the same unit. If the context unit is very small, few co-occurrences will be found; on the other hand, if the entire message is the context unit, everything which appears will be contingent with everything else. Osgood very tentatively suggested that stable results can be achieved with units of 120 to 210 words (Osgood, 1959, p. 62).

A second factor which few investigators can afford to overlook is efficiency; that is, which units give satisfactory results with the least expenditure of resources?

In an analysis of best-selling inspirational literature, themes appearing in each paragraph were initially coded, a task which proved disappointingly time-consuming and difficult (Schneider and Dornbusch, 1958, Appendix C). A second coding method was also used: the entire book was read and assigned a single summary score for each category. A comparison of results derived by the two methods revealed that little substantive information was lost with the latter approach. Questions of efficiency can often be answered only by comparing two or more methods on the same set of data. Unfortunately, relatively few studies have reported experiments of this kind.

SYSTEMS OF ENUMERATION

The analyst must also choose the unit of enumeration, that is, the unit in terms of which quantification is to be performed. The recording unit and the unit of enumeration may be identical, as was the case in a study of occupations portrayed on television; the occupation of each character was recorded and tallied (De Fleur, 1964). In a similar study of soap operas, recording and enumeration units were different. The occupation of each character was recorded, but the results were reported according to the number of scenes in which any occupational type appeared; thus a scene involving three housewives was tallied only once (Arnheim, 1944).

Systems of enumeration vary considerably in precision and in time required to code a given sample of data. The investigator must determine how fine are the discriminations he needs in order to satisfy the requirements of his problem; generally, the greater the need for precision, the higher will be the costs of the analysis. Often the nature of the categories and data are such that the search for maximum precision will not only entail considerably higher costs, but also may sacrifice reliability. The choice may also affect the results of the analysis. For example, editorials may be coded according to the frequency of favorable or unfavorable assertions about a specific issue. If the unit of enumeration is the single assertion, results will indicate whether the editorial was only slightly (50+%) or predominantly on one side or the other. If the entire editorial serves as the unit of enumeration, that is, if the whole editorial is scored pro or con, this distinction will be lost.

The most important aspect of the investigator's choice, however, is that each system of measurement carries with it a certain set of assumptions regarding the nature of the data and inferences which may be drawn therefrom.

Time/space

Most early studies employed measures of space (for example, column inches) to describe relative emphases in the content of newspapers. The analogous unit for film, radio, and television is time. The popularity of space/time measures can be attributed largely to the relative ease and reliability with which they may be used. For some purposes space/time measures may serve as an adequate substitute for other more time-consuming methods. Markham and Stempel (1957) compared newspaper political coverage as measured by the amount of space in column inches, frequency of issues mentioned, and size of headlines. The three methods yielded similar results, but coding for space was done considerably more rapidly than coding of issues. The limitations of space/time units derive mostly from a lack of sensitivity to other than the grossest attributes of content. In general, such measures are most appropriate for descriptions of mass media, but are too imprecise to index attitudes, values, style, and the like. For example, the use of space/time measures to answer questions about the degree of political bias in newspapers is at best questionable, inasmuch as a one-to-one relationship between focus of attention and bias cannot be assumed.

Appearance

One alternative to space/time units is that of searching the document, or some subunit of the text, for appearance of the attribute. The size of the context unit determines the frequency with which repeated items occurring in close proximity to each other are counted separately. Depending on the context unit, repetition of a given attribute within a sentence (White, 1947), paragraph (Schneider and Dornbusch, 1958), or item (Lasswell, Lerner, and Pool, 1952) does not change the tally. This method of enumeration has two important advantages. It can usually be done with relative ease and with high reliability because the coder is faced with a dichotomous decision (appearance-nonappearance). Moreover, this method is useful if one cannot assume a linear relationship between frequency and importance of content attributes. Some investigators have labeled this type of nominal measurement as "qualitative" content analysis, although the term is somewhat misleading because data coded in this manner may be presented numerically (for example, the percentage of items in which a given theme appears), as well as subjected to certain statistical tests.

Frequency

The most commonly used method of measuring characteristics of content is that of frequency, in which *every* occurrence of a given attribute is tallied. For example, how frequently do the folktales of various Indian tribes express need to achieve (McClelland and Friedman, 1952), or, how frequently did Madison and Hamilton use the words "whilst" or "upon" (Mosteller and Wallace, 1964)?

Again, the important point is that the analyst using a measure of frequency to test his hypotheses incorporates two related assumptions into his research design. First, he assumes that the frequency with which an attribute appears in messages is a valid indicator of some variable such as focus of attention, intensity, value, importance, and so on. Second, he assumes that each unit of content—word, theme, character, or item—should be given equal weight with every other unit, permitting aggregation or direct comparison.

George (1959b) and others have contended that, for purposes of drawing inferences about causes and effects of communication, the first premise is often untenable. Other questions have been raised regarding frequency measures.

For example, what is the relationship between distribution, or permeability, of attributes in the text and their importance (Dunphy, 1964)? Is there a difference between two variables appearing equally often if their distribution in the documents under analysis is different?

The dubious validity, for many research problems, of the assumption that each unit should be assigned equal weight has more often received recognition from content analysts (*cf.* Stewart, 1943). Descriptions of newspaper content, for example, routinely differentiate items appearing on the front page from those printed elsewhere, either by coding them separately, or by using a system of "weighting" to reflect the factor of prominence. Similar devices have been used to reflect the position of items within the page and size of headlines. Ash's (1948) study of the Taft-Hartley Act illustrates a method of adjusting scores to reflect circulation. An evaluation of the act received a score proportional to the circulation of the magazine in which it appeared.

Intensity

For research dealing with values and attitudes, a serious problem engendered by the use of pure frequency counts is that of intensity. In other words, the assumption that valid inferences regarding attitudes can be drawn from frequency scores, unadjusted for intensity of expression, is often untenable. Some of the problems can be illustrated by examining four Soviet statements:

> *The Chinese may be preparing to denounce Khrushchev's policies.*
> *The Chinese sometimes disagree with Khrushchev's policies.*
> *The Chinese will soon begin denouncing Khrushchev's policies.*
> *The Chinese are bitterly denouncing Khrushchev's policies.*

An analyst wanting to map trends in Sino-Soviet relations would require some method of differentiating the intensity of the four themes.

Categorization of content units for intensity normally presents more problems than other coding processes. Construction of scales is usually a difficult process. Moreover, the broad range of linguistic elements which indicate intensity makes it difficult to list all criteria the coder may have to consider in making his decisions. In the themes cited above, there are at least four elements to be considered in judging intensity: (1) the relative intensities of the verbs "disagree" and "denounce"; (2) the function of the adverbial modifiers "sometimes" and "bitterly"; (3) the element of tense—past, present, and future actions; (4) the probabilistic character of the first theme. This list by no means exhausts the intricacies of language which may denote intensity.

One method of coding for intensity is the "paired comparison" technique developed by Thurstone. Judges decide which of each possible pair of indicators is rated higher on a linear scale of attitudes. The judgments are used to construct categories into which content units are placed. A simplified version of this procedure was used to study national attitudes, as revealed in newspapers and journals, during two crisis periods in the Far East (Russell and Wright, 1933;

TABLE 8

EVALUATIVE ASSERTION ANALYSIS: AN ILLUSTRATIVE EXAMPLE

Soviet rulers are ruthless, atheistic despots. These men have in the past pursued evil goals. Yet there now appears some possibility that they will agree to some measures designed to relax world tensions. Perhaps they will be more willing to forgo aggressive designs.

Attitude object	Verbal connector	Value	Common-meaning term	Value	Product
1. Soviet rulers	are	+3	ruthless	−3	−9
2. Soviet rulers	are	+3	atheistic	−3	−9
3. Soviet rulers	are	+3	despots	−3	−9
4. Soviet rulers	have in the past pursued	+2	evil goals	−3	−6
5. Soviet rulers	may now possibly agree to	+1	some measures designed to relax world tensions	+2	+2
6. Soviet rulers	perhaps will be more willing to forego	−1	aggressive designs	−3	+3

Wright and Nelson, 1939). One study has demonstrated that scales derived empirically, as by the Thurstone technique, sometimes yield more satisfactory results than logical scales when relatively untrained coders are used. Differences between the two methods of scale construction were not significant when experienced and trained personnel did the coding (Exline and Long, 1965).

The Q-sort scaling technique has also been applied to content data. Judges are instructed to place content units into a fixed-distribution nine-point scale (North *et al.,* 1963). This is essentially a rank-order method, the rank of any unit relative to all other items determining its intensity score. Both paired-comparison and rank-order methods depend on the assumption that content units are sufficiently homogeneous on a single continuum that they may usefully be compared.

An "atomic" approach to coding for intensity, "Evaluative Assertion Analysis," has been developed by Osgood and his associates (Osgood, Saporta, and Nunnally, 1956; Osgood, 1959). The initial step is to translate all sentences into one of two common sentence structures:

> *Attitude object / Verbal connector / Common-meaning term*
> *Attitude object₁ / Verbal connector / Attitude object₂*

For example, the sentence, "An aggressive Soviet Union threatens the United States," is translated to read:

> *The Soviet Union / is / aggressive*
> *The Soviet Union / threatens / United States*

Attitudes are computed on the basis of values assigned to verbal connectors and common-meaning terms. These range from +3 to −3 depending on their direction and intensity. The method is illustrated more fully in Table 8.

The final step is the computation of values for each attitude object, in this case, a single one—Soviet rulers. Extensive rules for coding and scoring have been formulated (Osgood, Saporta, and Nunnally, 1956).

Because this method first reduces the theme to its parts and specifies which elements of the theme are to be scored, it can be used with a high degree of reliability. Coders can be trained rapidly, but the method is too laborious to be used for large volumes of data, and it is uneconomical if only gross measures of attitude (for example, pro or con) are required. It is probably most useful when the analyst requires precise data on only a limited number of attitude objects; it has been used, for example, to assess the treatment of Presidential candidates by three major news magazines during the 1960 campaign (Westley *et al.*, 1963), to examine John Foster Dulles' attitude toward the Soviet Union (Holsti, 1967), and to analyze editorial treatment of India in the *New York Times* (Lynch and Effendi, 1964).

Other methods of accounting for intensity in content data are described in Jacob (1942) and Kaplan and Goldsen (1949).

SAMPLING, RELIABILITY, AND VALIDITY

The purpose of content-analysis research is to present a systematic and objective description of the attributes of communication. These data may be used to make inferences about communicators or audiences. But whatever the specific purpose of the study, there are certain problems which the content analyst shares with all social scientists. What is the universe of communication to be described, and what sample is to be drawn therefrom? Do independent measures of the same data yield results capable of verification within stated confidence limits? Do the categories actually index the variable they are intended to measure? Careful attention to these questions must be an integral part of every research design if it is to meet meaningful standards of systematic investigation. A comprehensive discussion of sampling, reliability, and validity is beyond the scope of this chapter; the present review considers only some general issues of particular relevance to content analysis.

SAMPLING

Because communication pervades society, the investigator is always faced with a problem of selecting some portion of it for his research. Content-analysis findings are usually discussed, implicitly or explicitly, as being relevant for some universe beyond the specific documents under study. Hence, both practical requirements of narrowing data to manageable proportions and problems of generalization present the analyst with sampling decisions.

Choices at any one step in the research design are not independent of those made at earlier stages. Thus, once the research problem has been defined, the sampling design has been partly determined. The investigator comparing coverage of a Presidential election in the prestige and mass press has already limited his data according to time period and class of communicators.

Ideally, the next step should be to list all members of the universe of communication from which a sample is to be drawn, in order to minimize the probability of systematic sampling error. But this is not possible in every case. The analyst of American daily newspapers has a relatively simple task; he may, for example, define his universe as those newspapers catalogued in *Editor and Publisher Yearbook*. The psychologist working with personal documents is faced with a considerably more difficult problem. In a small-group experiment the investigator has access to the entire universe of the subjects' communication in that situation, from which a true probability sample can be drawn. On the other hand, in studies of political communication during an international crisis one rarely has access to more than the written messages; oral communication represents an inaccessible, and generally unknown, proportion of the whole. Moreover, misfiling or destruction of documents, and bias or carelessness by those commissioned to collect and publish the documents, may further complicate matters.

Once the universe of relevant communication has been defined, a single-stage sampling design may suffice. More often, a multistage sample is required. This may involve as many as three decisions: selecting *sources* of communication, sampling *documents,* and sampling *within documents.*

Selecting communication sources

The first sampling decision is that of sources. Which newspapers, magazines, books, authors, speeches, broadcasts, movies, etc., will be selected as representative of the universe? The analyst may draw a random sample by one of several standard methods. This procedure is applicable when every source can be considered equally important for purposes of the study. If this assumption is not warranted, a purposive sample may be used to reflect qualitative or quantitative aspects of the sources which are deemed important. Studies of newspaper content have focused on prestige papers and journals because they were felt to represent most adequately the views of political elites (Lasswell, Lerner, and Pool, 1952; Angell, Dunham, and Singer, 1964). In studies of decision makers' attitudes during international crises, communicators were selected on the basis of role; thus heads of state, heads of government, and foreign ministers were selected, but ambassadors were excluded (Holsti, North, and Brody, 1968; Holsti, Brody, and North, 1965). Purposive samples have also been selected by relying on expert opinion. In studies of psychological research (Allport and Bruner, 1940) and of newspaper coverage of the 1960 election (Stempel, 1961), sources rated most important by professional psychologists and journalists, respectively, were analyzed.

However, for other purposes quantitative criteria are more important than qualitative ones. Kayser (1953) analyzed the largest-circulation newspaper in each of 15 countries; Schneider and Dornbusch (1958) examined only that sample of inspirational literature on best-seller lists; and McGranahan and Wayne (1948) confined their study of German drama to the most widely attended plays. Other criteria which have been used to select a sample of communication sources include editorial position (Hage, 1959), geographical location (Willey, 1926; Taeuber, 1932), and time of issue (Danielson and Adams, 1961).

Stratified sampling is often used in studies of the mass media to permit weighting of units according to certain criteria. A technique which permits stratification on the basis of circulation and geographical location has been developed (Maccoby, Sabghir, and Cushing, 1950). All dailies in the United States were originally listed in descending order of circulation within each of the nine census districts. The sampling rate was obtained by dividing the number of newspapers desired for the study into the total newspaper circulation, providing "circulation units." Each newspaper in which the *n*th circulation unit appeared was chosen—with the first paper selected from a table of random numbers—to yield a true probability sample of circulation units in the universe. Another successful stratified sampling design for newspapers is described in Coats and Mulkey (1950).

Sampling documents

After communication sources have been selected, the investigator may have reduced his data to manageable proportions. If the universe of communication is still too large, the next step is the selection of documents. Here "document" refers to every item comprising the universe of items produced by the communication source. For example, if every Nazi broadcast to England during World War II is the universe, the investigator may decide to examine only a subset consisting of every third broadcast. In preparing a sampling design the analyst must weigh a number of factors. First, how large should the sample be to permit generalization within specified confidence limits? The necessary sample size varies depending on the kinds of questions that are being asked of the data and on the nature of the data. Though there is no answer to the question of sample size which can be applied to every problem, some guidelines are available from experiments. Four methods of sampling newspaper headlines in *Pravda* were compared with data for the entire month (Mintz, 1949). The results revealed that every-fifth-day samples (5th, 10th, 15th, 20th, 25th, and 30th day of each month) and odd-day samples did not differ significantly from the figures for the entire month. On the other hand, weekly samples and every-tenth-day samples (5th, 15th, and 25th day of each month) were inferior. These findings were supported by another study, in which every-sixth-day samples provided sufficiently accurate results for research purposes (Davis and Turner, 1951). Stempel (1952) drew samples of 6, 12, 18, 24, and 48 issues of a newspaper and compared the average content for a single subject matter category against the average for the entire year. The data indicated that each of the five sample sizes was adequate, and that increasing the sample size beyond 12 did not produce significantly more accurate results.

The analyst must also ensure that his sample, whatever its size, is free of any regular cycles within the universe which may bias results. Some types of content may be subject to seasonal variations; news about Congress will be heavier during the first half of the year than during the second, but the reverse is usually true about news of the United Nations General Assembly. Unless taken into account in the sampling design, such variations can render invalid an otherwise well-designed and executed project. A study of marriage announcements in the *New York Times,* based on Sunday issues of the newspaper appearing in June during the years 1932–1942, revealed no announcement of a marriage in a Jewish synagogue (Hatch and Hatch, 1947). A critic later pointed out that June almost invariably falls within a period during which tradition prohibits Jewish marriages (Cahnman, 1948). There are also regular variations within the week which may affect the content of mass media; for example, a study of Monday newspapers for financial news or news regarding governmental agencies would result in serious underestimation of coverage.

Several methods of accounting for variations within the week can be used. Every-*n*th-day samples will ensure an equal distribution of days within the week if two conditions are met: *n* must not equal seven; and the number of weeks studied must be divisible by *n*. Jones and Carter (1959) have developed a "constructed week" procedure in which the period under study is divided into seven subpopulations; all Mondays are grouped together, as are all Tuesdays, and so on. A random sample of *n* newspapers is then taken from each.

A final consideration is that of efficiency. Which method of sampling will yield satisfactory results at least cost? Again, no definite answer covering every situation is possible. A case in point is the "cluster" design, in which the analyst selects units containing more than one item: the unit identifies a cluster consisting of all items appearing in it. For example, rather than listing all *articles* and drawing a sample from them, the investigator may sample *issues* of the magazine, and then analyze all articles which appear within the selected issues. Economy results from the reduced cost of listing. However, lower costs must be weighed against other factors. An experiment with content data revealed that, depending on the data, cluster sampling frequently results in overestimating levels of significance (Backman, 1956).

Sampling within documents

Even after selecting documents, the investigator may wish to reduce his data further by some sort of sampling *within* the document; for example, he may restrict his study to 30 pages drawn at random from a book (Harvey, 1953), to only the front page of a newspaper (Kingsbury, Hart *et al.*, 1937), or to every other story in a magazine (Berelson and Salter, 1946). The problem is the same as for other sampling decisions: does the selected sample accurately represent the attributes of content relevant to the study? The front page of newspapers may be a valid sample for some purposes, but it would not accurately reflect the volume of advertising or sports news.

In conclusion, it is worth repeating that sampling procedures applicable to all projects cannot be specified; nearly every content-analysis study presents a different problem. Furthermore, the choice between sampling designs—each of which carries with it certain assumptions—may significantly affect the results (Kaplan, 1964, p. 244):

What is important is the recognition that each sampling plan calls for its own standardization, and its own way of computing stability. As with measurement where there are many different scales that might be used, each having its own properties, sampling is not a simple uniform procedure but one which varies from problem to problem in a way that permits and even demands correspondingly different mathematical treatment.

RELIABILITY

If content analysis is to meet the requirement of objectivity, results must be reliable; that is, the research must yield results capable of verification by independent observers. The degree to which a given study will prove reliable is a function of the judges' skill, insight, and experience, and the categories into which content data are to be classified. The content analyst is thus concerned with the reliability of both coders and categories, each of which is important to the overall results of the research.

Individual reliability

Individual reliability reflects the extent of agreement between any coder and the rest of the judges. Before the actual coding begins, the investigator may want to run experiments to identify and eliminate judges deviating consistently from the group. This can be done by tabulating the correlation or percentage of agreement between every pair of judges. Even assuming that judges possess the skills necessary to make the discriminations required in the coding process, training is usually necessary to enable all coders to rely upon the same aspects of their experience in their decisions. Experimental studies have demonstrated that training prior to coding can significantly increase the level of intercoder agreement (Kaplan and Goldsen, 1949; Woodward and Franzen, 1948). In another study, however, nondirected discussion of categories and rules failed to result in significantly higher agreement (Spiegelman, Terwilliger, and Fearing, 1953b).

Category reliability

One goal of a content-analysis research design is to formulate categories "for which the empirical evidence is clear enough so that competent judges will agree to a sufficiently high degree on which items of a certain population belong in the category and which do not" (Schutz, 1958, p. 512). In coding content data, the judges must first be able to agree with respect to the boundaries of units coded—sometimes called the process of *unitizing*. If the unit is a symbol, a paragraph, or an item, unitizing presents relatively few difficulties because the data provide coders with certain physical guides. For example, the symbol is bounded by spaces, the paragraph is set off by indentation, and so on. Thematic analysis presents the most serious problem because the theme is not a "natural unit" for which physical guides exist. Many sentences contain more than one theme, and the proper boundaries between them are often ambiguous.

In addition to identifying boundaries of the content unit, the judge must decide the category into which the unit is to be placed. Reliability of classification is largely a function of category definition and the types and numbers of discriminations to be made. Pretesting of categories on a sample of the material to be coded will enable the investigator to determine which categories require further clarification. Guetzkow (1950) has derived reliability estimates for both unitizing and categorizing operations which permit the investigator to determine how much of the body of data needs to be cross-checked to ensure any desired level of accuracy.

The investigator faced with low agreement levels at the pretesting stage may attempt to solve his problem in one of several ways. Training coders has already been discussed. One might suspect, however, that a major source of error lies in the categories themselves; that untrained coders are more likely to agree if categories are defined clearly than are well-trained coders working with ambiguous categories. This reasoning was supported by at least one content-analysis experiment; for both theme analysis and symbol coding, significant error variance was found between categories, but not between coders (Stempel, 1955).

The content-analysis literature contains a number of approaches which may be used to resolve problems of reliability attributable to categories. First, the analyst may define his categories exhaustively, attempting to reduce coding from a judgmental task to a clerical one. An extensive experiment has demonstrated that flexible coding of symbols yields significantly less reliable results than methods in which every member of a category is specified (Geller, Kaplan, and Lasswell, 1942b). However, inasmuch as few categories lend themselves to exhaustive defition, this solution is appropriate only for a limited number of research problems.

Second, fine discriminations between categories often result in a high incidence of disagreement. After pretesting, the investigator may aggregate such categories, but this approach is applicable only if the fine distinctions are not of major theoretical significance.

A third approach to the problem of low reliability is the introduction of additional judges. While this expedient may be necessary for the most difficult judgmental tasks—for example, scaling the intensity of the themes (North *et al.,* 1963)—it adds considerably to research costs and is a poor substitute for precise coding rules.

A solution more generally applicable to decisions of categorization—but not unitizing or scaling for intensity—consists of reducing each judgment to a dichotomous decision; that is, one in which only a single operation is required of the judge (Schutz, 1958). Consider an example from the study of comic strips. Judges were instructed to code the location of action into six categories: United States, rural, historical, interstellar, urban, or foreign. One source of difficulty in this classification scheme is that the categories are at different levels of generality; for example, the distinction between "United States" and "foreign" actually depends on a prior decision of a more general nature, the choice between "interstellar" and "earth." Arrangement of these categories into a series of dichotomous decisions can be illustrated schematically:

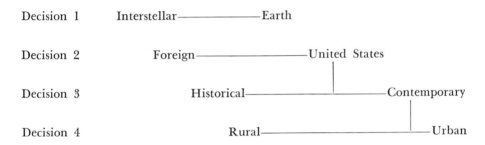

Decision 1   Interstellar——————Earth

Decision 2   Foreign——————————United States

Decision 3   Historical————————————Contemporary

Decision 4   Rural——————————————Urban

Note that for purposes of this study, not all logically possible categories were used; for example, once an item was classified as "foreign," no further discrimination as to "historical-contemporary" or "rural-urban" was required. Schutz (1958, p. 507) found that interjudge agreement was raised from 61 percent with traditional methods of judgment to not less than 90 percent with the dichotomous-decision method. Tables of confidence limits have been developed, from which one can determine, knowing the number of judges and the number of judgments they are required to make, the percentage of agreement necessary for acceptance at the 0.01 and 0.05 levels (Schutz, 1952).

There are several advantages associated with the dichotomous-decision technique. First, it permits coders to focus on a single decision at a time, and to review the criteria for choice at each step. It has been demonstrated that, with traditional methods, increasing the number of categories within the category set decreases reliability (Janis, Fadner, and Janowitz, 1943). Thus the dichotomous-decision method should be particularly useful when many categories are necessary. Second, difficulties arise when the process of categorization consists of several judgments, but one decision is logically prior to another because it is relevant to a larger class, as in the example cited above from the study of comic strips. The dichotomous-decision method ensures that the choices given to judges are logical. Third, the method permits the analyst to determine precisely where agreement between judges is breaking down, information which is useful in redefining categories.

Intercoder agreement may be computed by a variety of methods, of which correlation and percentage of agreement are most frequently used. Simple percentage of agreement is not an adequate measure of reliability because it does not take into account the extent of intercoder agreement which may result from chance (Bennett, Alpert, and Goldstein, 1954). By chance alone agreement should increase as the number of categories decreases. Scott (1955) subsequently developed an index of reliability (pi) which corrects not only for the number of categories in the category set, but also for the probable frequency with which each is used. Originally developed for coding data into nominal categories, Scott's formula may also be used for ordinal and interval data. (For an extensive illustration of this method, see Angell, Dunham, and Singer, 1964). Other methods of computing agreement applicable to content analysis are described in Kaplan and Goldsen (1949), Robinson (1957), and Stempel (1955), but Scott's formula, which produces a conservative estimate of reliability, appears to be the most useful.

A method of computing and reporting the overall reliability of any category set with a single figure has been developed (Spiegelman, Terwilliger, and Fearing, 1953b). The technique involves ranking the patterns of agreement among judges on each item. For example, with four judges, five patterns are possible: 4 (complete agreement), 3-1, 2-2, 2-1-1, and 1-1-1-1 (complete disagreement). The reliability of the category set is then reported as the mean rank order of all items. With four judges, scores would range from 1.0 (complete agreement on all items) to 5.0 (complete disagreement on all items).

Although individual and category reliability have been discussed separately, this distinction is a somewhat artificial one. Indeed, the investigator may find that it is not always readily apparent to which factor low reliability should be attributed. The "Random-Systematic-Error Coefficient" is a measure which can be used to determine the nature and source of disagreement in coding. Interpretation of the RSE Coefficient is based on the finding that "errors resulting from a defective code (for example, an ambiguous code) seem generally to be scattered about the range of possible disagreements, while errors originating in the coders tend to fall into systematic patterns" (Funkhouser and Parker, 1966, p. 3). Calculation of the RSE Coefficients can be programmed into the same computer routines that calculate Scott's pi for the overall test of reliability.

An *acceptable level of reliability* is one of many issues for which there is no ready definition. The question can only be answered in the context of a given research problem. That high reliability can be achieved for simple forms of content analysis, in which coding is essentially a mechanical task, is amply documented in the literature. Conversely, as categories and units of analysis become more complex, they are likely to become both more useful and less reliable. In formulating and testing a content-analysis research design, the analyst may thus be forced to strike some appropriate balance between reliability and problem significance.

VALIDITY

Validity is often defined as the extent to which an instrument is measuring what it is intended to measure. The validity of any study is inextricably interrelated with its sampling design and reliability. If the analyst studying the proportion of international news in the American daily newspaper samples only issues of the *New York Times,* well-constructed categories or precise measurement will not ensure the validity of his findings. Even if the universe from which the sample was drawn were expanded to make it more representative, low reliability on categorizing international news would render the results suspect. Thus, adequate sampling and reliability are necessary, but not sufficient, conditions for validity.

The meaning of validity may differ from study to study, depending on the investigator's purposes. The American Psychological Association Committee on Psychological Tests has distinguished between *content validity, predictive validity, concurrent validity,* and *construct validity.* The distinction between them can be illustrated by an example. Documents may be analyzed by means of a measure such as the type-token ratio, the number of different words in message samples of a given length. Results may be used as a direct measure of the author's vocabulary; in this case the analyst is concerned with content validity. The same measure might also be used to predict subjects' success in college; to distinguish schizophrenics from normal persons; or to make inferences about the writer's general intellectual capacity. For these purposes, the investigator would be interested in the predictive validity, concurrent validity, and construct validity, respectively, of his measure (Technical Recommendations ... , 1954, p. 13).

Content validity, also sometimes referred to as face validity, has been most frequently relied upon by content analysts. If the purpose of the research is a purely descriptive one, content validity is normally sufficient. Content validity is usually established through the informed judgment of the investigator—that is, "Are the results plausible?"

Predictive validity is concerned with the ability of an instrument to predict events for which evidence is not currently available. On the basis of his data, the analyst may predict the occurrence of future events, or of events for which data are at present inaccessible. An example of predictive validity has been cited in a study of Knut Hamsun's novels; the inference that Hamsun was a latent fascist was later validated by his collaboration with the Nazis (Lowenthal, 1949). Extensive use of predictive validity in the content-analysis literature exists in the area of propaganda analysis. Access to Nazi documents following World War II permitted those engaged in predicting aspects of Axis behavior to assess the accuracy of their inferences (George, 1959a, pp. 253–284; Berelson and De Grazia, 1947).

Concurrent validity is also established by prediction to an outside criterion; it differs from predictive validity only with respect to the time element. If a measure is able to distinguish sources with known differences, as the type-token ratio has done with schizophrenic and normal patients, the validity of the measure for that purpose is confirmed. Documents written by designated decision makers during the crisis leading to World War I were content-analyzed to determine day-to-day changes in international "tensions." In order to test the validity of the content measures, a number of independent indices assumed to be sensitive to international tensions—stock market prices, gold flow, commodity futures, and exchange rates—were charted on a daily basis. A high correlation between financial indices and content data enhanced confidence in the latter measure (Holsti and North, 1966).

The important aspect of both predictive and concurrent validity is the criterion; it may be difficult to ensure that the criterion itself is valid. The authors of a simplified readability formula demonstrated that their test correlated significantly with those derived by the Flesch method (Farr, Jenkins, and Patterson, 1951). To the extent that the latter is a true measure of readability, the validity of the Farr formula was established. But it has been demonstrated that the applicability of the Flesch method is limited to certain types of writing (Taylor, 1953); thus, unless established by other methods, the validity of the Farr formula is similarly limited.

Construct validity is concerned not only with validating the measure, but also the theory underlying the measure. It may be established by several methods; that most frequently discussed in the literature involves interrelating the measure within a "nomological network" of external variables from many different sources (Cronbach and Meehl, 1955, p. 290; see also Janis, 1949, pp. 78–79, and Technical Recommendations . . . , 1954).

Corroborating construct validity in content analysis can be illustrated with the concept of "need achievement." A number of studies have established an impressive network of evidence supporting the validity of both the measure and its underlying theory. That need achievement can successfully differentiate between groups known to differ in regard to relevant characteristics, as predicted by the theory, has been demonstrated in a study of various Indian tribes (McClelland and Friedman, 1952) and nations (McClelland, 1961). Need achievement, as measured by content analysis of diverse literary products, has also been shown to correlate with broad patterns of culture change in settings as different as ancient Greece and the United States. Finally, the concept has been found to correlate significantly with such external measures of entrepreneurial achievement as trade and issuance of patents (McClelland, 1958; deCharms and Moeller, 1962).

These, then, are some of the problems which content analysts share with all scientists. On the whole they have been somewhat lax in this respect; for example, in regard to reliability, Berelson noted in 1952 (p. 172):

Whatever the actual state of reliability in content analysis, the published record is less than satisfactory. Only about 15–20% of the studies report the reliability of the analysis contained in them. In addition, about five reliability experiments are reported in the literature.

The recent literature reveals that content analysts are sharing the widespread concern within the social sciences with the issues of sampling, reliability, and validity. At the same time, it is clear both that these problems have by no means been resolved, and that progress has been far from even. For example, one has little difficulty finding either experimental studies or imaginative examples of sampling the printed mass media. On the other hand, given the tendency of analysts to draw inferences as to the causes of communication from their data, considerably less than a commensurate share of attention has been paid to problems of validity.

COMPUTERS IN CONTENT ANALYSIS

The most significant recent development in content analysis is the programming of electronic computers to handle a variety of operations involved in textual analysis.

Manual methods of content analysis suffer in varying degrees from a number of limitations. Even elementary forms of the method are expensive and time-consuming. Moreover, most techniques lack flexibility and have a limited ability to deal with complex units. Finally, content analysis usually requires skilled and sensitive coders, the very type of persons who soon become bored and frustrated by the tedious and repetitive nature of the task. These difficulties lend considerable support for Berelson's warning (1952, p. 198):

Unless there is a sensible, or clever, or sound, or revealing, or unusual, or important notion underlying the analysis, it is not worth going through the rigor of the procedure, especially when it is so arduous and so costly of effort.

Many of these problems can be minimized or overcome by use of computers, but computers are not currently able to undertake all the repetitive and routine chores associated with content analysis. Nor is use of computers warranted for every type of research. For example, the analyst wishing to determine the space allocated in newspapers to various types of news may find computers of little use; the research could be completed more efficiently using simpler instruments of measurement such as a ruler. In general, content-analysis problems which are most appropriately analyzed by space/time or item measures will profit little from computers, except perhaps in the final stages of research for purely numerical operations (cross tabulations, correlational analyses, and the like). On the other hand, computers can be of significant help in research for which the symbol or the theme is a suitable unit of analysis.

At present, most computer content-analysis programs fall into one of two categories. Those of the first type are essentially word-count programs, the output consisting of the frequency with which each word in the text appears. The second type of computer program is characterized by a dictionary system in which text words are looked up in the dictionary and automatically coded with information representing the investigator's frame of reference and assumptions. The coded text may then be manipulated, categorized, tallied, and retrieved according to the analyst's data requirements.

WORD-COUNT PROGRAMS

Word or symbol counting is one of the most widely used forms of content analysis. Although considerably less complex than some other methods, notably theme analysis, symbol counting can nevertheless present serious problems of reliability. In the RADIR studies, for example, although categories were defined exhaustively, reliability tests on inclusion and exclusion indicated only 66, 68, and 70 percent agreement (Lasswell, Lerner, and Pool, 1952, p. 62). This is one of the operations for which computers are ideally suited. Computers will perform frequency counts at high speeds with perfect reliability, provided there are no errors in the punched IBM cards. Moreover, computers can pick up all symbols, not only those believed *a priori* to be of interest or significance. Thus examination of the output may well reveal the appearance of theoretically important symbols which might not have been considered in the original research design.

There are currently several word-counting programs being used across a broad spectrum of research problems. Content analysis based on word counting has been used extensively in psychotherapy. A program for building specialized dictionaries within the vocabulary usage of individual patients has been developed. The computer prints out, in rank order of frequency, the patient's entire vocabulary, as well as tabulating a type-token ratio (Starkweather and Decker, 1964). A somewhat similar set of programs also being used for content analysis of psychotherapeutic interviews, orders and lists all words with exact frequencies. The incidence of each different word within a segment of text is correlated with every other word across all segments, and the resulting matrix can be factor-analyzed (Harway and Iker, 1964; Iker and Harway, 1965; see also Jaffe, 1964).

One of the standard readability formulas has been adapted for computer analysis. Despite difficulties in programming—for example, in defining rules of identification of monosyllables—the program operates at better than 99 percent reliability. At the same time, desire for greater efficiency led the investigators to develop a new readability formula more suitable to the capabilities of the machine (Danielson and Bryan, 1963). A method of computing various scores from the "Cloze" readability formula has also been developed. Scores are tabulated for relative entropy, type-token ratios, and noun/verb ratios (Carstenson and Stolz, 1964).

A combination word-count and information-retrieval system produces concordances of poetry (Painter, 1960; Sebeok and Zeps, 1961). Such programs have been used to analyze the complete works of Matthew Arnold and Yeats (Parrish, 1959; Parrish and Painter, 1963). The program first produces an index of all words appearing in the text in the order of frequency. On the concordance pages, the line in which each word appears is followed by the page number in the standard edition of the poet's collected works, the abbreviated title of the poem, and the line number within the poem:

YOUTHFUL

DEAD HER PRINCELY YOUTHFUL HUSBAND .   14 CHURCH BROU I   49
LAY BEFORE HIS YOUTHFUL WIFE . . . .   14 CHURCH BROU I   50

PASSING ALL HER YOUTHFUL HOUR . . . 131 TRISTAM 1   39

BUT THE BRILLIANT YOUTHFUL KNIGHT . . 134 TRISTAM 1   127

CHATTING WITH HER YOUTHFUL KNIGHT . . 134 TRISTAM 1   214

OF HIS TIMID YOUTHFUL BRIDE . . . . . 137 TRISTAM 1   269

One limitation of word-count analyses is the problem of context, which may lend a given word a considerably different meaning. This problem is partially solved in a program which searches the text for concepts of importance to the investigator and prints them out together with up to 120 words appearing before and after each key concept. The program may be operated with two search options: exact matching of key and content words, or the matching of initial letters in the key and content words (Danielson and Jackson, 1963).

THE "GENERAL INQUIRER" PROGRAMS

Probably the computer content-analysis programs currently in widest use are those which have been developed as part of the "General Inquirer" system, "a set of computer procedures for processing 'natural text' . . . that locates, counts, and tabulates text characteristics" (Stone, 1964). Originally developed at the Laboratory for Social Relations at Harvard University for studying psychological and sociological materials (Stone *et al.*, 1962; Dunphy, Stone, and Smith, 1965), this system now encompasses a family of dictionaries, data-preparation systems, and data-analysis programs being used in nearly all social sciences.

Dictionaries

The core of each General Inquirer system of content analysis is a dictionary in which each entry word is defined with one or more "tags" representing categories in the investigator's theory. The dictionary provides the vital link between the theoretical formulation of the research problem and the mechanics of analysis. The necessity for developing rigorous rules concerning "tagging" of words, by forcing unstated assumptions into the open for critical scrutiny, is an important check on many theoretical aspects of the project—unambiguous definition of categories, precise delineation of the boundaries between concepts, and internal logic of the research design.

Entry words may be listed in the dictionary in root form, without frequently appearing suffix endings such as *-e, -s, -es, -ed, -ing, -ion,* and *-ly.* If a word in the text with such a suffix is not found in the dictionary, the computer will automatically remove the suffix and look up the word root. A single dictionary form (*attack*) can pick up all forms (*attack, attacks, attacked, attacking*) appearing in the text. Thus dictionaries of moderate size, in the range of 4000 words, have a much larger effective capacity. Users of various General Inquirer dictionaries report analysis of 92 to 98 percent of the text, excluding proper nouns. Words appearing in the text but not in the dictionary are printed out separately on a "leftover" list, and may later be added to the dictionary if deemed important. A dictionary entry may also specify that the computer check whether certain neighboring words are present in the text; the tags assigned then depend on the idiom found.

More than a dozen General Inquirer dictionaries are currently in operation. The Harvard psychosociological dictionary of some 3500 entries uses 83 tag categories, all but three of which consist of at least 20 words. Two sets of tags are incorporated into the dictionary. Each word is assigned a single "first-order" tag which represents the common or manifest meaning of the word. These are discrete, independent variables and can be treated as such statistically. Fifty-five first-order tags are grouped under eleven major headings: persons, groups, physical objects, physical qualifiers, environments, culture, emotion, thought, evaluation, social-emotional actions, and impersonal actions.

Entry words may also be assigned "second-order" tags which represent their connotative meanings. The second-order tags are not independent variables. The meaning of an entry word may be defined by using as many of the 28 second-order tags—which refer to institutional contexts, status connotations, and psychological themes—as appear necessary to give a satisfactory definition. For example, *teacher* is tagged with three meanings: job-role, higher-status, and academic—one first-order tag followed by two second-order tags.

The Harvard dictionary has been used in a number of different applications, including an examination of self-analytic small groups (Dunphy, 1966), a case study of the "Letters from Jenny" (Paige, 1966), and comparative analyses of Presidential nomination acceptance speeches (Smith, with Stone and Glenn, 1966), writings of popular and unpopular students (Goldberg, 1966), projected autobiographies by Radcliffe and Egyptian students (Dahlberg and Stone, 1966), reports written by successful and unsuccessful volunteers for field work in Africa (Ramallo, 1966), and real and simulated suicide notes (Ogilvie, Stone, and Shneidman, 1966).

The Stanford political dictionary incorporates considerable theoretical work on semantic differentiation (Osgood, 1962; Osgood, Suci, and Tannenbaum, 1957). Nearly 4000 words are tagged along three dimensions—positive-negative, strong-weak, and active-passive. These dimensions correspond to the *evaluative, potency,* and *activity* dimensions which have been found to be primary in human cognition in a variety of cultures. Each tag is further defined for three levels of intensity. Sample entries in the dictionary include the following:

> ABANDON = NEGATIVE 2 WEAK 3 PASSIVE 3
> ABET = POSITIVE 2 ACTIVE 3
> ABSURD = NEGATIVE 2

In addition to the main dictionary, a dictionary of proper names has been written. Names of persons and places serve as entry words which are tagged with as much information as desired for identification. The following are some examples of current entries:

> GROMYKO = SOVIET-UNION   FOREIGN-MINISTER   EXECUTIVE   COMMUNIST
> WASHINGTON = UNITED-STATES   CAPITAL
> SOVIET-UNION = NATION   EUROPE   COMMUNIST
> RUSSIA = NATION   EUROPE   COMMUNIST   SOVIET-UNION

The proper-name dictionary ensures uniformity of identification, and serves to cross-reference proper names, as with Gromyko, Soviet Union, and Russia in the above example. In addition, this dictionary is useful for analyses which depend on discriminating between units and subunits, or for aggregating subunits. This version of the General Inquirer is being used to develop and test hypotheses relating to decision making in crisis (Holsti, Brody, and North, 1965), cohesion within the Soviet bloc (Holsti, 1965b; Hopmann, 1967), and attitudinal components of neutralism (Choucri, 1967).

The New Mexico anthropological dictionary written by Colby (1966c) for cross-cultural comparison of folktales and projective test materials, incorporates 99 tag categories, including a number of value categories developed by Clyde Kluckhohn. Initial studies with the dictionary have included analyses of folktales from five cultures (Kwakiutl, Egyptian, Eskimo, Indian, and Chinese), and TAT, protocols of Navajos and Zuñis (Colby, 1966a; Colby, Collier, and Postal, 1963; Colby and Menchik, 1964).

A number of special-purpose dictionaries have also been prepared. An "alcohol" dictionary of 95 separate tags has been constructed for testing hypotheses relating themes to cultural uses of alcohol. This dictionary of about 3600 entry words and 99 tags has been used to analyze a worldwide sample of folktale collections (Kalin, Davis, and McClelland, 1966). A set of dictionaries has been developed to analyze themes, images, and evaluations associated with both products and corporate images. Some 2500 entries are classified into 70 tag categories, such as product properties, institutional references, and product areas (Stone *et al.,* 1966). The "need achievement" dictionary (D. M. Ogilvie and Louise Woodhead, Harvard) follows the rules developed by McClelland for manual scoring of achievement imagery in projective test materials. The dictionary classifies about 1200 entries into 25 tag categories. Thirty-eight tag concepts suggested by the theoretical work of Talcott Parsons are used to classify about 2400 entries in a political dictionary developed for analyzing lobbying behavior (McPherson, 1964). In the WAI dictionary, developed for analyzing multiple open-ended responses to the question "Who am I," 3000 entry words are used to define 30 tag categories (McLaughlin, 1966). A dictionary for studying survey responses, based on the Harvard dictionary but incorporating adjustments for language used by middle and lower-class subjects has been written by B. Frisbie (University of Chicago). Eight value categories developed in Lasswell's and Kaplan's *Power and Society* (1950) define the tag categories in a political dictionary written at Yale (Peterson and Brewer, n.d.). Finally, dictionaries have been prepared to score "need affiliation" (J. Williamson, Harvard), modes of reaction to psilocybin (Tara Dinkel, Chicago), and Icarian imagery (D. M. Ogilvie and D. C. Dunphy, Harvard).

One of the many advantages of the General Inquirer system is that the dictionaries are basically interchangeable; thus the investigator may run his data on another dictionary tagged for different variables. For example, Presidential nomination acceptance speeches were analyzed on several different dictionaries (Smith, Stone, and Glenn, 1966). In interpreting the results it is, of course, important to be cognizant of the theoretical assumptions underlying the dictionary, including the premise that it will be used with populations similar to those for which it was constructed.

Data Preparation

The text to be analyzed is punched on IBM cards with as little or as much pre-editing as required by the analyst's problem. Most investigations use text directly transcribed onto IBM cards without any coding. Minimal coding normally involves the separation of complex sentences into one or more themes or "thought sequences," and identification of indefinite terms such as pronouns.

To answer some research questions on the basis of communications content, it may not be enough to know that *X, Y,* or both *X* and *Y* occur in a sentence; it may be more important to know the perceived relationship between *X* and *Y.* Consider the following three sentences:

> *This Soviet decision is a deliberately provocative and unjustified threat to American security.*
>
> *This American decision is a deliberately provocative and unjustified threat to Soviet security.*
>
> *This deliberately provocative unjustified decision is a threat to Soviet and American security.*

Each theme contains exactly the same words but their meaning is clearly different. Neither word frequency nor contingency analysis can distinguish among these three sentences. To do so requires some form of theme analysis which, in turn, necessitates some prior coding of data. More elaborate coding systems include the identification of syntactical position of key *words* in the text, and the addition of certain other codes for the *theme* as a whole (Holsti, 1964; Stone *et al.,* 1962). For example, a sentence might be coded as follows:

> CV   *A free/3 American/3 people/3 must/4 reject/4 all fatalistic/7 philosophies/7 of history/7.*

These codes identify the subject-verb-object (3-4-7) relationship, links between modifiers and referents, time (C = current), and mode of expression (V = imperative). While such operations add to the time and effort required for data preparation, they also permit use of more elaborate analysis programs which may yield data important to the investigator's research design. As automated language-processing routines and syntax-identification programs become available, it will be possible to forgo most if not all precoding. A realistic appraisal of present achievements and future prospects along these lines has been prepared by Simmons (1966).

Data-analysis programs

The General Inquirer system includes a broad spectrum of programs for analyzing text. A *text and tag list* program prints out the text and tags assigned by sentence in the form of a bilingual book. A *tag tally* program counts words in the text which have been tagged in the dictionary. In addition to raw scores, an index based on the ratio of occurrence of tag words to total words in the document is computed. For rapid visual interpretation of results, tag tallies can be printed in graph form. A separate list of all text words not found in the dictionary is also printed out.

A *question and search* program retrieves, tallies, and prints out all sentences meeting any desired specifications. The analyst may wish to search the text for all sentences containing a certain *text word* or *cluster of words*—for example, all sentences in which "Soviet Union" occurs as the subject and which also contain the words "nuclear" and "weapons." Questions may also retrieve themes in terms of *tags,* with or without specification of intensity or syntax position. The *theme codes* may also be used for retrieval. Any of the question specifications may be used singly or in any desired combination, and up to 100 retrieval questions can be processed at once.

Parsons, Shils, and Olds (1952, p. 57) have pointed out that social objects may be significant as *complexes of qualities* or *complexes of performance.* In the former case the object is considered in terms of its attributes, of *what he is,* whereas in the latter case the object is viewed in terms of *what he does.* A *direct table* program provides answers to both types of questions for any specified attitude objects —nations, institutions, groups, persons, concepts, programs, ideologies, and the like—which appear within the data (Armour, 1964; Holsti, 1966). The program operates only on text with syntax codes. Row headings are defined by the dictionary variables and column headings represent attitude objects specified by the investigator.

If the analysts wished to determine Chinese attitudes, as expressed in any given document or set of documents, toward China, the Test-Ban Treaty, and the original signators of that treaty, the information would be printed out, using the Stanford dictionary, in the following format:

0331   KUO MO JO   CHINA   7-26-63   PEKING DOMESTIC SERVICE
BROADCAST NUMBER OF WORDS IN TEXT - 3834

	U.S.	SOV. UN.	GT. BRIT.	CHINA	TEST BAN
POSITIVE AFFECT	10.00	18.00	4.00	54.20	26.00
NEGATIVE AFFECT	260.40	26.00	28.00	33.00	57.00
STRONG	163.40	55.00	12.00	117.00	77.00
WEAK	2.00	10.00	6.00	5.40	26.00
ACTIVE	129.50	26.00	6.00	71.40	57.00
PASSIVE	8.00	6.00	7.00	21.00	31.00

Information at the top of the table identifies the document number (0331), author (Kuo Mo Jo of China), date (July 26, 1963), and source. Cell scores in the table indicate a summary score (frequency × intensity) of expressed attitudes toward each nation and toward the treaty for tag categories in the dictionary. Immediately following is a table which indicates the precise frequency count for each intensity level (for example, strong 1, strong 2, strong 3, etc.). Separate pairs of tables are produced to score assertions about qualities and performance.

Scores for up to a dozen attitude objects (that is, the column headings) may be analyzed in each pass through the data. Column headings can be changed simply by inserting different control cards; hence, the data may be rerun as often as is necessary to satisfy the requirements of the research problem. A special feature of this program is that the intensity level of words in the dictionary may be adjusted according to the mode of expression; for example, the score of the word "aid" in the sentence "The United States may aid India" can be reduced by a constant to reflect the probabilistic nature of the assertion. Tables are also punched out in card form for direct statistical analysis by computer. This program may be used with any dictionary punched in a standard format.

Users of content analysis often require psychological indexes that will discriminate between two sources. The General Inquirer program has been combined with the Hunt-Hovland "Concept Learner" to produce a program for identifying discriminant functions. The strategy on which the program is based is to search the text for a single concept (or combination of concepts) which discriminates sentences in document *A* from those in document *B*. Failing this, the program will continue the process of subdivision until a subgroup is found where a test does apply, or one of the document sources runs out of sentences (Hunt, Kreuter, and Stone, 1965; Stone and Hunt, 1963).

Another variation of the General Inquirer approach to content analysis involves efforts to duplicate manual scoring methods by constructing rules that enable *the computer* to analyze its own tag applications and to make decisions about the nature of a document on the basis of tag profiles. The following document was scored by the Woodhead-Ogilvie Need-Achievement scoring system:

SENTENCE 1	(TAGS APPLIED)
THE STUDENT IS DREAMING ABOUT BECOMING A GREAT INVENTOR.	NEED TO-BE ADJECTIVE-POSITIVE ROLE-POSITIVE SENTENCE SUMMARY = ACHIEVEMENT IMAGERY

SENTENCE 2	
AFTER YEARS OF LABOR THE CRUCIAL MOMENT ARRIVES.	TIME VERB-POSITIVE SENTENCE SUMMARY = UNRELATED IMAGERY

SENTENCE 3	
HE HOPES EVERYTHING WILL PAN OUT PROPERLY.	NEED VERB-POSITIVE ADVERB-POSITIVE SENTENCE SUMMARY = ACHIEVEMENT IMAGERY

SENTENCE 4

BUT THE <u>INVENTION</u> WILL BE A <u>FAILURE.</u>

VALUES-POSITIVE <u>FAILURE</u> SENTENCE SUMMARY = UNRELATED IMAGERY

SENTENCE 5

HE WILL DIE <u>DISCOURAGED.</u>

AFFECT-NEGATIVE SENTENCE SUMMARY = ACHIEVEMENT IMAGERY

*****SUMMARY*****

THIS DOCUMENT CONTAINS ACHIEVEMENT IMAGERY

Tags correspond to the underlined sentence words. Underlined tag words indicate that a prespecified achievement-related sequence has been matched. For a document to be scored "Achievement Imagery" it must contain at least one sentence that meets the criteria of one or more of the prespecified rules within the program. For example, Sentence 1 contains the sequence: NEED TO-BE ROLE-POSITIVE. This matches an Achievement Imagery rule. A more complex rule is matched in Sentence 5: this rule states that when AFFECT is evident, check the preceding sentence for mention of SUCCESS or FAILURE. If either of these tags is located, the sentence containing reference to AFFECT is scored Achievement Imagery. The computer scoring method correlates well with manual coding.

OTHER COMPUTER CONTENT-ANALYSIS PROGRAMS

One by-product of recent interest in machine translation of text has been computer programs for syntactical, as distinct from semantic, discriminations. These may be used for a variety of content-analysis problems concerning the question "how it is said"; for example, analysis of literary style (Sedelow, Sedelow, and Ruggles, 1964). One difficulty of these programs is that there may be more than one possible translation from a given sentence. This defect for the purpose of translation can be turned into an advantage for the content analyst. Two studies have shown how the ability of the computer, unencumbered by any preconceptions or "cognitive set," may be used to produce all possible interpretations of legal literature. Allen (1963) and Langevin and Owens (1963) both analyzed sections of the Nuclear Test Ban Treaty to determine the degree of structural ambiguity in its text. While not all solutions were meaningful, several sentences yielded more than one reasonable, and substantively significant, interpretation. Such programs appear to have wide potential application, not only for legal analysis but also in many other aspects of communication research.

Content analysis by computer is in its infancy and it appears certain that the various programs described here will be modified, if not superseded, in the near future. Five periodical publications may be consulted by the reader wishing to inform himself of the rapid developments which are likely to take place: *Behavioral Science* (quarterly, Mental Health Research Institute, University of Michigan), *Current Research and Development in Scientific Documentation* (semiannual, National Science Foundation), *Computer Newsletter* (occasional, Michigan State University), *Computers and the Humanities* (quarterly, Queens College), and *Computer Studies in the Humanities and Verbal Behavior* (quarterly, Universities of Colorado, Kansas, and North Carolina).

GENERAL IMPLICATIONS OF USING COMPUTERS IN CONTENT ANALYSIS

The most apparent characteristic of computers, the ability to analyze text reliably at almost unbelievable speed, requires no further elaboration. Less obvious, but perhaps of greater importance, are the following points.

First, computers impose rigor and discipline on the formulation of research. The investigator using computers for content analysis is forced to make every step of his research design explicit. For example, the dictionary requires an explicit and unambiguous definition of each variable. Similarly, each step in data analysis by computer must be specified with precision. Every analyst approaches his data with a set of assumptions and a theory, however crude or implicit. At minimum, making premises and rules of inference explicit permits informed communication and evaluation of results. Thus, it is not wholly facetious to suggest that all content-analysis research should be designed *as if* it were to be done by computer.

Second, when data are punched on IBM cards they are amenable to reanalysis as often and for as many different purposes as desired. Traditional methods of content analysis rarely permit the degree of flexibility necessary to exhaust the potential information in one's data. Even the most meticulously coded data can rarely be used later for answering research questions that were not incorporated in the original design. In conventional content-analysis research the analyst almost of necessity instructs coders to prepare the data to yield answers only for the initial theoretical problems. When content analysis is done manually, if a new hypothesis suggests itself after the data have been coded, the investigator often must choose between recoding the data and dropping the new idea because he is "locked in" by his research design. Data on IBM cards, on the other hand, may be rerun to test hypotheses that had not even been considered at the time of data preparation. The investigator's theory and assumptions are built into the dictionary, not into the data, and the dictionary can be expanded in response to new questions. For example, a set of documents was originally prepared to analyze Sino-Soviet-American interaction during a number of recent crisis periods. Later the same materials were rerun for the purpose of testing a quite different hypothesis about the effects of East-West conflict on relations between Moscow and Peking.

Third, use of computers enables the analyst to undertake very complex data manipulations, such as contingency analyses involving numerous variables, which often cannot be done reliably or economically by hand. When computers are used, the problem of scoring reliability is completely resolved; this does not mean, of course, that the investigator can assume the validity of his results.

Fourth, documents punched on IBM cards can readily be reproduced and exchanged between scholars. At the time of this writing, General Inquirer users have prepared over 50 different studies, comprising over six million words on IBM cards. These have been shared informally and will be formally stored and available at the Survey Research Center Archive, University of Michigan.

Fifth, computers can free the scholar from many of the most laborious chores associated with content-analysis research. The computer, like any tool properly used, can enhance the creativity of the scholar by freeing more of his time for those indispensable ingredients of significant research—the original idea, the creative hunch, the insight which is necessary to make "facts" meaningful.

Despite this optimistic appraisal of the implications of computers, it may be well to conclude on a more cautious note. Just as all research does not lend itself to content analysis, not all content analysis should be done by computer. It is important to remain aware of the dangers in what Kaplan (1964, p. 28) called the "law of the instrument," exemplified by the child who, when given a hammer, suddenly discovers that everything needs pounding. Nor should the limitations of computers be overlooked. Bad data are no better for having been analyzed by a computer. Perhaps the single greatest danger in the use of computers is that the investigator may be lulled into accepting the validity of findings without a critical consideration of the steps preceding and following machine processing. Computers cannot save a sloppy research design, nor will they transform a trivial research problem into an important one. The machine output only reflects the skill and insight—or lack thereof—with which the investigator constructed his dictionary and formulated his research design. Some years ago Bernard Berelson (1954, p. 518) wrote, "Content analysis, as a method, has no magical qualities—you rarely get out of it more than you put in, and sometimes you get less. In the last analysis, there is no substitute for a good idea." Development of computer content-analysis programs detracts nothing from the wisdom of that assertion.

REFERENCES

Abcarian, G., and S. M. Stanage (1965). Alienation and the radical right. *J. Politics, 27,* 776–796.

Abu-Lughod, I. (1962). International news in the Arabic press: a comparative content analysis. *Publ. Opin. Quart., 26,* 600–612.

Albig, W. (1956). The content of radio programs, 1925–1935. In *Modern public opinion.* New York: McGraw-Hill. Pp. 446–450.

Albrecht, M. C. (1956). Does literature reflect common values? *Amer. sociol. Rev., 21,* 272–279.

*Allen, L. E. (1963). Automation: substitute and supplement in legal practice. *Amer. behav. Scientist, 7,* 39–44.

*Allport, G. W. (1942). *The use of personal documents in psychological science.* Social Science Research Council. Bulletin No. 49.

——— (1946). Letters from Jenny. *J. abnorm. soc. Psychol., 41,* 315–350, 449–480.

Allport, G. W., and J. Bruner (1940). Fifty years of change in American psychology. *Psychol. Bull., 37,* 757–776.

Almond, G. A. (1954). *The appeals of communism.* Princeton: Princeton Univ. Press.

Andrews, T. G., and Gertrude Muhlhan (1943). Analysis of congruent idea patterns as a study in personality. *Char. and Pers., 12,* 101–110.

Angell, R. C., Vera S. Dunham, and J. D. Singer (1964). Social values and foreign policy attitudes of Soviet and American elites. *J. Confl. Resol., 8,* 330–491.

Armour, Anne (1964). A Balgol program for quantitative format in automated content analysis. Stanford University. (Mimeo)

Arnheim, R. (1944). The world of the daytime serial. In P. F. Lazarsfeld and F. N. Stanton (Eds.), *Radio research: 1942–1943.* New York: Duell, Sloan, and Pearce. Pp. 34–85.

Aronson, E. (1958). The need for achievement as measured by graphic expression. In J. W. Atkinson (Ed.), *Motives in fantasy, action and society.* Princeton: Van Nostrand. Pp. 249–265.

Ash, P. (1948). The periodical press and the Taft-Hartley Act. *Publ. Opin. Quart., 12,* 266–271.

Asheim, L. (1950). From book to film. In B. Berelson and M. Janowitz (Eds.), *Reader in public opinion and communication.* Glencoe, Ill.: Free Press. Pp. 299–306.

*Auld, P., Jr., and E. J. Murray (1955). Content analysis studies of psychotherapy. *Psychol. Bull. 52,* 377–395.

Backman, C. W. (1956). Sampling mass media content: the use of the cluster design. *Amer. sociol. Rev., 21,* 729–733.

Badri, M. B., and W. Dennis (1964). Human-figure drawings in relation to moderniza-tion in Sudan. *J. Psychol., 58,* 421–425.

Bagdikian, B. H. (1959). The newsmagazines. *The New Republic, 16,* Feb. 2, p. 23.

Baldwin, A. L. (1942). Personality structure analysis: a statistical method for investigating the single personality. *J. abnorm. soc. Psychol., 37,* 163–183.

Bales, R. F. (1950). *Interaction process analysis.* Cambridge, Mass: Addison-Wesley.

†Barcus, F. E. (1959). Communications content: analysis of the research, 1900–1958. Un-published doctor's dissertation, University of Illinois.

---

* Includes useful special bibliography.
† Includes useful general bibliography.

—— (1961). A content analysis of trends in Sunday comics, 1900–1959. *Journalism Quart., 38,* 171–180.

Barghoorn, F. C. (1964). *Soviet foreign propaganda.* Princeton: Princeton Univ. Press.

Batlin, R. (1954). San Francisco newspapers' campaign coverage: 1896, 1952. *Journalism Quart., 31,* 297–303.

Bauer, R. A. (1964). The obstinate audience: the influence process from the point of view of social communication. *Amer. Psychologist, 19,* 319–328.

Becker, H. P. (1930). Distribution of space in the American Journal of Sociology, 1895–1927. *Amer. J. Sociol., 36,* 461–466.

—— (1932). Space apportioned forty-eight topics in the American Journal of Sociology, 1895–1930. *Amer. J. Sociol., 38,* 71–78.

Bennett, E. M., R. Alpert, and A. C. Goldstein (1954). Communications through limited response questioning. *Publ. Opin. Quart., 18,* 303–308.

Berelson, B. (1942). The effects of print upon public opinion. In D. Waples (Ed.), *Print, radio, and film in a democracy.* Chicago: Univ. of Chicago Press. Pp. 41–65.

†—— (1952). *Content analysis in communication research.* Glencoe, Ill.: Free Press.

†—— (1954). Content analysis. In G. Lindzey (Ed.), *Handbook of social psychology.* Cambridge, Mass.: Addison-Wesley. Pp. 488–518.

Berelson, B., and S. De Grazia (1947). Detecting collaboration in propaganda. *Publ. Opin. Quart., 9,* 244–253.

Berelson, B., and Patricia J. Salter (1946). Majority and minority Americans: an analysis of magazine fiction. *Publ. Opin. Quart., 10,* 168–190.

Berkman, D. (1963). Advertising in Ebony and Life: Negro aspirations vs. reality. *Journalism Quart., 40,* 53–64.

Bernstein, M. H. (1953). Political ideas of selected American business journals. *Publ. Opin. Quart., 17,* 258–267.

Blumberg, N. B. (1954). *One party press? Coverage of the 1952 presidential campaign in 35 daily newspapers.* Lincoln: Univ. of Nebraska Press.

Boder, D. P. (1940). The adjective-verb quotient: a contribution to the psychology of language. *Psychol. Record, 3,* 310–343.

Breed, W. (1958). Comparative newspaper handling of the Emmett Till case. *Journalism Quart., 35,* 291–298.

Brinegar, C. (1963). Mark Twain and the Quintus Curtius Snodgrass letters: a statistical test of authorship. *J. Amer. Statist. Assoc., 58,* 85–96.

Brinton, J., and W. A. Danielson (1958). A factor analysis of language elements affecting readability. *Journalism Quart., 35,* 420–426.

Brody, R. A. (1963). Some systemic effects of the spread of nuclear weapons technology: a study through simulation of a multi-nuclear future. *J. Confl. Resol., 7,* 663–753.

Brooks, M. R. (1959). *The Negro press re-examined.* Houston: Christopher.

Broom, L., and Shirley Reece (1955). Political and racial interest: a study in content analysis. *Publ. Opin. Quart., 19,* 5–19.

Brown, W. B. (1960). *The people's choice*. Baton Rouge: Louisiana State Univ. Press.

Bruner, J. S. (1941). The dimensions of propaganda: German shortwave broadcasts to America. *J. abnorm. soc. Psychol., 41*, 311–337.

Budd, R. W. (1964). U.S. news in the press down under. *Publ. Opin. Quart., 28*, 39–56.

Budlong, D. H. (1952). Analysis of radio programs by four commentators. *Journalism Quart., 29*, 458–459.

Bush, C. R. (1961). A system of categories for general news content. *Journalism Quart., 38*, 312–322.

Cahnman, W. J. (1948). A note on marriage announcements in the New York Times. *Amer. sociol. Rev., 13*, 96–97.

Carstenson, F. W., and W. S. Stolz (1964). Cloze procedure analysis programs. *Computer Newsletter, 3*, 5–6.

Carter, R. E., Jr. (1957). Segregation and the news: a regional content study. *Journalism Quart., 34*, 3–18.

†Cartwright, D. P. (1953). Analysis of qualitative material. In L. Festinger and D. Katz (Eds.), *Research methods in the behavioral sciences*. New York: Holt, Rinehart, and Winston. Pp. 421–470.

Choucri, Nazli (1967). Nonalignment in international politics: an analysis of attitudes and behavior. Doctoral dissertation, Stanford University.

Christenson, R. M. (1964). Report on the Reader's Digest. *Columbia Journalism Rev., 3*, 30–36.

Coats, W. J., and S. W. Mulkey (1950). A study in newspaper sampling. *Publ. Opin. Quart., 14*, 533–546.

Colby, B. N. (1966a). The analysis of culture content and the patterning of narrative concern in texts. *Amer. Anthropologist, 68*, 374–388.

——— (1966b). Cultural patterns in narrative. *Science, 151*, 793–798.

——— (1966c). Development and application of an anthropological dictionary. In P. J. Stone, D. C. Dunphy, M. S. Smith, and D. M. Ogilvie, *The General Inquirer: a computer approach to content analysis in the behavioral sciences*. Cambridge: M.I.T. Press.

Colby, B. N., G. A. Collier, and Susan K. Postal (1963). Comparison of themes in folktales by the General Inquirer system. *J. Amer. Folklore, 76*, 318–323.

Colby, B. N., and M. D. Menchik (1964). A study of Thematic Apperception Tests with the General Inquirer system. *El Palacio, 71*, 29–36.

Coleman, E. B. (1962). Improving comprehensibility by shortening sentences. *J. appl. Psychol., 44*, 131–134.

Content analysis—a new evidentiary technique (1948). *Univ. Chicago Law Rev., 15*, 910–925.

Cony, E. R. (1953). Conflict-cooperation of five American dailies. *Journalism Quart., 30*, 15–22.

Cornwell, E. E., Jr. (1959). Presidential news: the expanding public image. *Journalism Quart., 36*, 275–283.

*Cronbach, L., and P. Meehl (1955). Construct validity of psychological tests. *Psychol. Bull., 52,* 281–302.

Dahlberg, Frances M., and P. J. Stone (1966). Cross-cultural contrasts in interpersonal structuring. In P. J. Stone, D. C. Dunphy, M. S. Smith, and D. M. Ogilvie, *The General Inquirer: a computer approach to content analysis in the behavioral sciences.* Cambridge: M.I.T. Press. Pp. 589–602.

Dale, E. (1935). *The content of motion pictures.* New York: Macmillan.

Dale, E., and Jeanne S. Chall (1948). A formula for predicting readability. *Educ. Res. Bull., 27,* 11–20, 37–54.

Danielson, W. A., and J. B. Adams (1961). Completeness of press coverage of the 1960 campaign. *Journalism Quart., 38,* 441–452.

Danielson, W. A., and S. D. Bryan (1963). Computer automation of two readability formulas. *Journalism Quart., 40,* 201–206.

Danielson, W. A., and H. Jackson (1963). A computer program for scanning tapes for key concepts and their immediate contexts. *Computer Newsletter, 1,* 1–2.

Davis, F. J., and L. W. Turner (1951). Sampling efficiency in quantitative newspaper content analysis. *Publ. Opin. Quart., 15,* 762–763.

deCharms, R., and G. H. Moeller (1962). Values expressed in American children's readers: 1900–1950. *J. abnorm. soc. Psychol., 64,* 136–142.

De Fleur, M. L. (1962). Mass communication and the study of rumor. *Sociol. Inquiry, 32,* 51–70.

——— (1964). Occupational roles as portrayed on television. *Publ. Opin. Quart., 28,* 57–74.

Deutsch, F. (1947). Artistic expression and neurotic illness. *Amer. Imago, 4,* 64–102.

Dibble, V. K. (1963). Four types of inference from documents to events. *History and Theory, 3,* 203–221.

Dollard, J., and O. H. Mowrer (1947). A method of measuring tension in written documents. *J. abnorm. soc. Psychol., 42,* 3–32.

Dornbusch, S. M., and Lauren C. Hickman (1959). Other-directedness in consumer-goods advertising: a test of Riesman's historical theory. *Soc. Forces, 38,* 99–102.

Dovring, Karin (1954). Quantitative semantics in 18th century Sweden. *Publ. Opin. Quart., 18,* 389–394.

——— (1959). *Road of propaganda: the semantics of biased communication.* New York: Philosophical Library.

Dunphy, D. C. (1964). Content analysis—development and critical issues. Cambridge: Harvard University. (Mimeo)

——— (1966). Social change in self-analytic groups. In P. J. Stone, D. C. Dunphy, M. S. Smith, and D. M. Ogilvie, *The General Inquirer: a computer approach to content analysis in the behavioral sciences.* Cambridge: M.I.T. Press. Pp. 287–340.

Dunphy, D. C., P. J. Stone, and M. S. Smith (1965). The general inquirer: further developments in a computer system for content analysis of verbal data in the social sciences. *Behav. Sci., 10,* 468–480.

Eckhardt, W. (1965). War propaganda, welfare values and political ideologies. *J. Confl. Resol., 9,* 345–358.

*Ekman, P. (1965). Communication through nonverbal behavior: a source of information about an interpersonal relationship. In S. S. Tomkins and C. E. Izard (Eds.), *Affect, cognition and personality.* New York: Springer.

Elizur, A. (1949). A content analysis of the Rorschach with regard to anxiety and hostility. *Rorschach Res. Exch., 13,* 247–284.

Ellegård, A. (1962). *A statistical method for determining authorship.* Göteborg, Sweden: Acta Universitatis Gothoburgensis.

Ellison, J. W. (1965). Computers and the Testaments. In *Computers for the humanities.* New Haven: Yale Univ. Press. Pp. 64–74.

Eto, S., and T. Okabe (1965). Content analysis of statements in regard to Japan made by the People's Republic of China. *Developing Economies, 3,* 49–72.

Exline, R. V., and Barbara H. Long (1965). An application of psychological scaling methods to content analysis: the use of empirically derived criterion weights to improve intercoder reliability. *J. appl. Psychol., 49,* 142–149.

Fairbanks, H. (1944). Studies in language behavior: II. The quantitative differentiation of samples of spoken language. *Psychol. Monogr., 56,* 13–38.

Farr, J. N., J. J. Jenkins, and D. G. Patterson (1951). Simplification of the Flesch reading ease formula. *J. appl. Psychol., 35,* 333–337.

Fillenbaum, S., and L. V. Jones (1962). An application of 'Cloze' technique to the study of aphasic speech. *J. abnorm. soc. Psychol., 65,* 183–189.

Flesch, R. (1943). *Marks of readable style.* New York: Teachers College, Columbia Univ.

——— (1948). A new readability yardstick. *J. appl. Psychol., 32,* 221–233.

Foster, H. S. (1935). How America became belligerent: a quantitative study of war news. *Amer. J. Sociol., 40,* 464–475.

——— (1937). Charting America's news of the world war. *Foreign Affairs, 15,* 311–319.

Foster, H. S., and C. J. Friedrich (1937). Letters to the editor as a means of measuring the effectiveness of propaganda. *Amer. polit. Sci. Rev., 31,* 71–79.

Funkhouser, G. R., and E. B. Parker (1966). A method of analyzing coding reliability. In E. B. Parker *et al., Patterns of adult information seeking.* Stanford University: Institute for Communication Research.

Galtung, J., and Mari Holmboe Ruge (1965). The structure of foreign news: the presentation of the Congo, Cuba and Cyprus crises in four Norwegian newspapers. *J. Peace Res., 1,* 64–91.

Gardiner, L. W. (1962). A content analysis of Japanese and American television. *J. Broadcasting, 6,* 45–52.

Garver, R. A. (1961). Polite propaganda: "USSR" and "American Illustrated." *Journalism Quart., 38,* 480–484.

Geller, A., D. Kaplan, and H. D. Lasswell (1942a). The differential use of flexible and rigid procedures of content analysis. Washington, D.C.: Library of Congress, Experimental Division for Study of War-Time Communications, Document No. 12.

———— (1942b). An experimental comparison of four ways of coding editorial content. *Journalism Quart., 19,* 362–370.

George, A. L. (1959a). *Propaganda analysis.* White Plains, N. Y.: Row, Peterson.

———— (1959b). Quantitative and qualitative approaches to content analysis. In I. de S. Pool (Ed.), *Trends in content analysis.* Urbana: Univ. of Illinois Press. Pp. 7–32.

Gerbner, G. (1964). Ideological perspectives and political tendencies in news reporting. *Journalism Quart., 41,* 495–508.

Gerbner, G., and P. H. Tannenbaum (1960). Regulation of mental illness content in motion pictures and television. *Gazette, 6,* 365–385.

Gillie, P. A. (1957). A simplified formula for measuring abstraction in writing. *J. appl. Psychol., 41,* 214–217.

Ginglinger, Genevieve (1955). Basic values in Reader's Digest, Selection and Constellation. *Journalism Quart., 32,* 56–61.

Gleser, Goldine C., L. A. Gottschalk, and Kayla J. Springer (1961). An anxiety scale applicable to verbal samples. *Arch. gen. Psychiat., 5,* 593–605.

Goldberg, Janice B. (1966). Computer analysis of sentence completions. *J. proj. Tech. Pers. Assess., 30,* 37–45.

Gordon, D. A. (1952). Methodology in the study of art evaluation. *J. Aesthet., 10,* 338–352.

*Gottschalk, L. A., Ed. (1961). *Comparative psycholinguistic analysis of two psychotherapeutic interviews.* New York: International Univ. Press.

Gottschalk, L. A., and Goldine C. Gleser (1960). An analysis of the verbal content of suicide notes. *Brit. J. Med. Psychol., 33,* 195–204.

Gottschalk, L. A., Goldine C. Gleser, E. B. Magliocco, and T. D'Zmura (1961). Further studies on the speech patterns of schizophrenic patients: measuring inter-individual differences in relative degree of personal disorganization and social alienation. *J. nerv. ment. Dis., 132,* 101–113.

Gottschalk, L. A., Goldine C. Gleser, and Kayla J. Springer (1963). Three hostility scales applicable to verbal samples. *Arch. gen. Psychiat., 9,* 254–279.

Gray, W. S., and Bernice E. Leary (1935). *What makes a book readable.* Chicago: Univ. of Chicago Press.

Guetzkow, H. (1950). Unitizing and categorizing problems in coding qualitative data. *J. clin. Psychol., 6,* 47–58.

Hafner, A. J., and A. M. Kaplan (1960). Hostility content analysis of the Rorschach and TAT. *J. proj. Tech., 24,* 137–143.

Hage, G. S. (1959). Anti-intellectualism in press comment, 1828 and 1952. *Journalism Quart., 36,* 439–446.

Haigh, G. (1949). Defensive behavior in client-centered therapy. *J. consult. Psychol., 13,* 181–189.

Hall, C. S., and R. L. Van de Castle (1966). *The content analysis of dreams.* New York: Appleton-Century-Crofts.

Hamilton, T. (1942). Social optimism and pessimism in American Protestantism. *Publ. Opin. Quart., 6,* 280–283.

Hart, J. A. (1961). The flow of international news into Ohio. *Journalism Quart., 38,* 541–543.

——— (1965). Election campaign coverage in English and U.S. daily newspapers. *Journalism Quart., 42,* 213–218.

——— (1966). Foreign news in U.S. and English daily newspapers: a comparison. *Journalism Quart., 43,* 443–448.

Harvey, J. (1953). The content characteristics of best-selling novels. *Publ. Opin. Quart., 17,* 91–114.

Harway, N. I., and H. P. Iker (1964). Computer analysis of content in psychotherapy. *Psychol. Reports, 14,* 720–722.

Haskins, J. B. (1960). Validation of the abstraction index as a tool for counter-effects analysis and content analysis. *J. appl. Psychol., 44,* 102–106.

Hatch, D. L., and Mary Hatch (1947). Criteria of social status as derived from marriage announcements in the New York Times. *Amer. sociol. Rev., 12,* 396–403.

Hayworth, D. (1930). An analysis of speeches in the presidential campaigns from 1884–1920. *Quart. J. Speech, 16,* 35–42.

Head, S. W. (1954). Content analysis of television drama programs. *Quart. of Film, Radio and Television, 9,* 175–194.

Herma, H., H. Kris, and J. Shor (1943). Freud's theory of the dream in American textbooks. *J. abnorm. soc. Psychol., 38,* 319–334.

Holsti, O. R. (1964). An adaptation of the 'General Inquirer' for the systematic analysis of political documents. *Behav. Sci., 9,* 382–388.

——— (1965a). East-West conflict and Sino-Soviet relations. *J. appl. behav. Sci., 1,* 115–130.

——— (1965b). The 1914 case. *Amer. polit. Sci. Rev., 59,* 365–378.

——— (1966). Content analysis research in the social sciences. Paper read at IBM-Texas A and M Conference on Computers in Humanistic Research.

——— (1967). Cognitive dynamics and images of the enemy. In D. J. Finlay, O. R. Holsti, and R. R. Fagen, *Enemies in politics.* Chicago: Rand McNally. Pp. 25–96.

Holsti, O. R., R. A. Brody, and R. C. North (1965). Measuring affect and action in international reaction models: empirical materials from the 1962 Cuban crisis. *Peace Res. Soc. Papers, 2,* 170–190.

Holsti, O. R., and R. C. North (1965). History of human conflict. In E. B. McNeil (Ed.), *Social science and human conflict.* Englewood Cliffs, N.J.: Prentice-Hall. Pp. 155–171.

——— (1966). Perceptions of hostility and economic variables. In R. Merritt and S. Rokkan (Eds.), *Comparing nations.* New Haven: Yale Univ. Press. Pp. 169–190.

Holsti, O. R., R. C. North, and R. A. Brody (1968). Perception and action in the 1914 crisis. In J. D. Singer (Ed.), *Quantitative international politics: insights and evidence.* New York: Free Press. Pp. 123–158.

Honigfeld, G., A. Platz, and R. D. Gillis (1964). Verbal style and personality authoritarianism. *J. Communic., 14,* 215–218.

Hopmann, P. T. (1967). International conflict and cohesion in the communist system. *Int. Stud. Quart., 11,* 212–236.

Hovland, C. I., I. L. Janis, and H. H. Kelley (1953). *Communication and persuasion.* New Haven: Yale Univ. Press.

Hughes, F. (1950). *Prejudice and the press.* New York: Devin-Adair.

Hunt, E. B., J. Kreuter, and P. J. Stone (1965). *Experiments in induction.* New York: Academic Press.

Iker, H. P., and N. I. Harway (1965). A computer approach toward the analysis of content. *Behav. Sci., 10,* 173–182.

Inkeles, A. (1952). Soviet reactions to the Voice of America. *Publ. Opin. Quart., 16,* 612–617.

Inkeles, A., and H. Geiger (1952). Critical letters to the editors of the Soviet press: I. Areas and modes of complaint. *Amer. sociol. Rev., 17,* 694–703.

———— (1953). Critical letters to the editors of the Soviet press: II. Social characteristics and interrelations of critics and the criticized. *Amer. sociol. Rev., 18,* 12–22.

Jacob, P. E. (1942). Atrocity propaganda. In H. L. Childs and J. B. Whiton (Eds.), *Propaganda by short wave.* Princeton: Princeton Univ. Press. Pp. 211–259.

*Jaffe, J. (1964). Computer analysis of verbal behavior in psychiatric interviews. In D. M. Rioch and E. A. Weinstein (Eds.), *Disorders of communication.* Research Publications of the Association for Research on Nervous and Mental Disorders, No. 42. Pp. 389–399.

*———— (1966). The study of language in psychiatry: psycholinguistics and computational linguistics. In S. Arieti (Ed.), *American handbook of psychiatry.* Vol. 3. New York: Basic Books. Pp. 689–704.

Janis, I. L. (1943). Meaning and the study of symbolic behavior. *Psychiatry, 6,* 425–439.

———— (1949). The problem of validating content analysis. In H. D. Lasswell, N. Leites *et al.* (Eds.), *The language of politics: studies in quantitative semantics.* New York: George Stewart. Pp. 55–82.

Janis, I. L., and R. Fadner (1949). The coefficient of imbalance. In H. D. Lasswell, N. Leites *et al.* (Eds.), *The language of politics: studies in quantitative semantics.* New York: George Stewart. Pp. 155–169.

Janis, I., R. H. Fadner, and M. Janowitz (1943). The reliability of a content analysis technique. *Publ. Opin. Quart., 7,* 293–296.

Janowitz, M. (1944). The technique of propaganda for reaction: Gerald L. Smith's radio speeches. *Publ. Opin. Quart., 8,* 84–93.

Johns-Heine, P., and H. H. Gerth (1949). Values in mass periodical fiction, 1921–1940. *Publ. Opin. Quart., 13,* 105–113.

Johnson, W. (1944). Studies in language behavior: I. A program of research. *Psychol. Monogr., 56,* No. 2 (whole No. 255).

Jones, Dorothy B. (1942). Quantitative analysis of motion picture content. *Publ. Opin. Quart., 6,* 411–428.

Jones, R., and R. Carter (1959). Some procedures for estimating 'news hole' in content analysis. *Publ. Opin. Quart., 23,* 399–403.

Josselson, H. H. (1953). *The Russian word count.* Detroit: Wayne State Univ. Press.

Kalin, R., W. N. Davis, and D. C. McClelland (1966). The relationship between use of alcohol and thematic content of folktales in primitive societies. In P. J. Stone, D. C. Dunphy, M. S. Smith, and D. M. Ogilvie, *The General Inquirer: a computer approach to content analysis in the behavioral sciences.* Cambridge: M.I.T. Press. Pp. 569–588.

Kanzer, M. (1948). Dostoevsky's matricidal impulses. *Psychoanal. Rev., 35,* 115–125.

Kaplan, A. (1943). Content analysis and the theory of signs. *Philos. Sci., 10,* 230–247.

—— (1964). *The conduct of inquiry.* San Francisco: Chandler.

Kaplan, A., and J. M. Goldsen (1949). The reliability of content analysis categories. In H. D. Lasswell, N. Leites *et al.* (Eds.), *The language of politics: studies in quantitative semantics.* New York: George Stewart. Pp. 83–112.

Kauffman, P. E., and V. C. Raimy (1949). Two methods of assessing therapeutic progress. *J. abnorm. soc. Psychol., 44,* 379–385.

Kayser, J. (1953). *One week's news: comparative study of seventeen major dailies for a seven-day period.* Paris: Paul Dupont, for UNESCO.

Kearl, B. (1948). A closer look at readability formulas. *Journalism Quart., 25,* 344–348.

Kingsbury, Susan M., H. Hart, *et al.* (1937). *Newspapers and the news.* New York: Putnam.

Klapper, J. (1960). *The effects of mass communication.* Glencoe, Ill.: Free Press.

Klapper, J., and C. Glock (1949). Trial by newspaper. *Sci. Amer., 180* (February, 1949), 16–21.

Klein, M. W., and N. Maccoby (1954). Newspaper objectivity in the 1952 campaign. *Journalism Quart., 31,* 285–296.

Knepprath, H. E. (1962). The elements of persuasion in the nationally broadcast speeches of Eisenhower and Stevenson during the 1956 presidential campaign. Unpublished doctor's dissertation, University of Wisconsin.

Kobre, S. (1953). How Florida dailies handled the 1952 presidential campaign. *Journalism Quart., 30,* 163–169.

Kracauer, S. (1952). The challenge of qualitative content analysis. *Publ. Opin. Quart., 16,* 631–642.

Krippendorff, K. (1966). Content analysis: history and critical issues. Unpublished doctor's dissertation, University of Pennsylvania.

Kris, E., and N. Leites (1953). Trends in twentieth century propaganda. In B. Berelson and M. Janowitz (Eds.), *Public opinion and communication.* Glencoe, Ill.: Free Press. Pp. 278–288.

Kuhn, A. (1963). *The study of society: a unified approach.* Homewood, Ill.: Dorsey.

Laffal, J. (1965). *Pathological and normal language.* New York: Atherton.

Lane, R. E. (1951). Government regulation and the business mind. *Amer. sociol. Rev., 16,* 163–173.

Lang, Gladys E., and K. Lang (1955). The inferential structure of political communications: a study in unwitting bias. *Publ. Opin. Quart., 19,* 168–183.

Langevin, R. A., and M. Owens (1963). Application of automatic syntactic analysis to the Nuclear Test Ban Treaty. Burlington, Mass.: Technical Operations Research. (Mimeo)

Larson, O. N., L. N. Gray, and J. G. Fortis (1963). Goals and goal-achievement methods in television content: models for anomie? *Sociol. Inquiry, 33,* 180–196.

Lasswell, H. D. (1927). *Propaganda technique in the world war.* New York: Knopf.

────── (1935). *World politics and personal insecurity.* New York: McGraw-Hill.

────── (1938). A provisional classification of symbol data. *Psychiatry, 1,* 197–204.

────── (1941). The world attention survey. *Publ. Opin. Quart., 5,* 456–462.

────── (1942). Communications research and politics. In D. Waples (Ed.), *Print, radio, and film in a democracy.* Chicago: Univ. of Chicago Press. Pp. 101–117.

†────── (1946). Describing the content of communication. In B. L. Smith, H. D. Lasswell, and R. D. Casey (Eds.), *Propaganda, communication and public opinion.* Princeton: Princeton Univ. Press. Pp. 74–94.

────── (1949). Detection: propaganda detection and the courts. In H. D. Lasswell, N. Leites *et al.* (Eds.), *The language of politics: studies in quantitative semantics.* New York: George Stewart. Pp. 173–232.

Lasswell, H. D., and Dorothy Blumenstock (1939). *World revolutionary propaganda: a Chicago study.* New York: Knopf.

Lasswell, H. D., and A. Kaplan (1950). *Power and society.* New Haven: Yale Univ. Press.

Lasswell, H. D., N. Leites *et al.* (1949). *The language of politics: studies in quantitative semantics.* New York: George Stewart.

Lasswell, H. D., D. Lerner, and I. de S. Pool (1952). *The comparative study of symbols.* Stanford: Stanford Univ. Press.

Lazarsfeld, P. F., and A. H. Barton (1951). Qualitative measurement in the social sciences, classification, typologies, and indices. In D. Lerner and H. D. Lasswell (Eds.), *The policy sciences: recent developments in scope and method.* Stanford: Stanford Univ. Press. Pp. 180–188.

Lazarsfeld, P. F., B. Berelson, and Hazel Gaudet (1944). *The people's choice: how the voter makes up his mind in a presidential campaign.* New York: Duel, Sloan, and Pearce.

Leary, T. (1957). *Interpersonal diagnosis of personality.* New York: Ronald.

Lee, A. M. (1952). *How to understand propaganda.* New York: Rinehart.

Lee, A. M., and Elizabeth B. Lee, Eds. (1939). *The fine art of propaganda.* New York: Harcourt, Brace.

Leites, N. C. (1949). Interaction: the Third International on its change of policy. In H. D. Lasswell, N. Leites *et al.* (Eds.), *The language of politics: studies in quantitative semantics.* New York: George Stewart. Pp. 298–333.

Leites, N. C., and I. de S. Pool (1942). On content analysis. Washington, D.C.: Library of Congress, Experimental Division for Study of War-Time Communications, Document No. 26.

———— (1949). Interaction: the response of communist propaganda to frustration. In H. D. Lasswell, N. Leites *et al.* (Eds.), *The language of politics: studies in quantitative semantics.* New York: George Stewart. Pp. 334–381.

Lerner, D. (1950). "The American Soldier" and the public. In R. Merton and P. Lazarsfeld (Eds.), *Continuities in social research.* Glencoe, Ill.: Free Press. Pp. 212–251.

Lewin, H. S. (1947). Hitler youth and the Boy Scouts of America: a comparison of aims. *Hum. Relat., 1,* 206–227.

Lewis, H. L. (1960). The Cuban revolt story: AP, UPI and 3 papers. *Journalism Quart., 37,* 573–578, 646.

Lindner, R. M. (1950). The content analysis of the Rorschach protocol. In L. Abt and L. Bellak (Eds.), *Projective psychology.* New York: Knopf. Pp. 75–90.

Lorge, I. (1944). Predicting readability. *Teachers College Record, 45,* 404–419.

Lowenthal, L. (1944). Biographies in popular magazines. In P. F. Lazarsfeld and F. N. Stanton (Eds.), *Radio research 1942–1943.* New York: Duell, Sloan, and Pearce. Pp. 507–548.

———— (1949). The sociology of literature. In W. Schramm (Ed.), *Communications in modern society.* Urbana: Univ. of Illinois Press. Pp. 82–100.

Lynch, M. D., and A. Effendi (1964). Editorial treatment of India in the New York Times. *Journalism Quart., 41,* 430–432.

*McClelland, D. C. (1958). The use of measures of human motivation in the study of society. In J. W. Atkinson (Ed.), *Motives in fantasy, action and society.* Princeton: Van Nostrand. Pp. 518–552.

*———— (1961). *The achieving society.* Princeton: Van Nostrand.

McClelland, D. C., and G. A. Friedman (1952). A cross-cultural study of the relationship between child-rearing practices and achievement motivation appearing in folk tales. In G. E. Swanson, T. M. Newcomb, and E. L. Hartley (Eds.), *Readings in social psychology* (2nd ed.). New York: Henry Holt. Pp. 243–249.

Maccoby, N., F. O. Sabghir, and B. Cushing (1950). A method for the analysis of the news coverage of industry. *Publ. Opin. Quart., 14,* 753–758.

McCurdy, H. G. (1939). Literature and personality: analysis of the novels of D. H. Lawrence. *Char. and Pers., 8,* 181–203, 311–322.

———— (1947). A study of the novels of Charlotte and Emily Brontë as an expression of their personalities. *J. Pers., 16,* 109–152.

———— (1953). *The personality of Shakespeare: a venture in psychological method.* New Haven: Yale Univ. Press.

McDiarmid, M. (1937). Presidential inaugural addresses: a study of verbal symbols. *Publ. Opin. Quart., 1,* 79–82.

McEvoy, J., with the collaboration of R. Schmuck and M. Chesler (1966). Letters from the right: content-analysis of a letter writing campaign. Institute for Social Research, University of Michigan. (Mimeo)

McGranahan, D. V., and I. Wayne (1948). German and American traits reflected in popular drama. *Hum. Relat., 1,* 429–455.

McLaughlin, B. (1966). The WAI dictionary and self-perceived identity in college students. In P. J. Stone, D. C. Dunphy, M. S. Smith, and D. M. Ogilvie, *The General Inquirer: a computer approach to content analysis in the behavioral sciences.* Cambridge: M.I.T. Press.

McPherson, W. (1964). Lobbying and communication processes. Paper read at American Political Science Association Meeting, Chicago.

Mahl, G. F. (1959). Exploring emotional states by content analysis. In I. de S. Pool (Ed.), *Trends in content analysis.* Urbana: Univ. of Illinois Press. Pp. 89–130.

Mann, Mary B. (1944). Studies in language behavior: III. The qualitative differentiation of samples of written language. *Psychol. Monogr., 56,* No. 2 (whole No. 255).

Mardsen, G. (1965). Content analysis studies of therapeutic interviews: 1954 to 1964. *Psychol. Bull., 63,* 298–321.

Markham, J. W., and G. H. Stempel III (1957). Analysis of techniques in measuring press performance. *Journalism Quart., 34,* 187–190.

Massing, P. W. (1963). The image of the Voice of America as drawn in Soviet media. In Matilda W. Riley (Ed.), *Sociological research: a case approach.* New York: Harcourt, Brace, and World. Pp. 308–314.

Matthews, B. C. (1910). A study of a New York daily. *Independent, 68,* 82–86.

Merrill, J. C. (1962). The image of the United States in ten Mexican dailies. *Journalism Quart., 39,* 203–209.

———— (1965). How Time stereotyped three U.S. Presidents. *Journalism Quart., 42,* 563–570.

Merritt, R. L. (1966). *Symbols of American community, 1735–1775.* New Haven: Yale Univ. Press.

Mendenhall, T. C. (1887). The characteristic curves of composition. *Science, 9,* 237–246.

Merton, R. K. (1946). *Mass persuasion: the social psychology of a war bond drive.* New York and London: Harper.

———— (1957). Science and economy of 17th century England. In R. K. Merton, *Social theory and social structure.* Glencoe, Ill.: Free Press. Pp. 607–627.

Miles, Josephine (1951). The continuity of English poetic language. Univ. of California Publications in English. Berkeley: Univ. of California Press. Pp. 517–535.

Mills, T. M. (1964). *Group transformation.* Englewood Cliffs, N.J.: Prentice-Hall.

Mintz, A. (1949). The feasibility of the use of samples in content analysis. In H. D. Lasswell, N. Leites *et al.* (Eds.), *The language of politics: studies in quantitative semantics.* New York: George Stewart. Pp. 127–152.

Morris, C. W. (1946). *Signs, language, and behavior.* New York: Prentice-Hall.

Morton, A. Q. (1963). A computer challenges the church. *The Observer,* Nov. 3, 1963.

Mosteller, F., and D. L. Wallace (1964). *Inference and disputed authorship: the Federalist.* Reading, Mass.: Addison-Wesley.

Mott, F. L. (1942). Trends in newspaper content. *Annals, 219,* 60–65.

Mowrer, O. H. (1953). Changes in verbal behavior during psychotherapy. In O. H. Mowrer (Ed.), *Psychotherapy theory and research.* New York: Ronald. Pp. 463–545.

Nixon, R. B., and R. R. Jones (1956). The content of non-competitive newspapers. *Journalism Quart., 33,* 299–314.

†North, R. C., O. R. Holsti, M. G. Zaninovich, and Dina A. Zinnes (1963). *Content analysis: a handbook with applications for the study of international crisis.* Evanston, Ill.: Northwestern Univ. Press.

Nunnally, J. (1957). The communication of mental health information: a comparison of the opinions of experts and the public with mass media presentations. *Behav. Sci., 2,* 222–230.

Ogilvie, D. M., P. J. Stone, and E. S. Shneidman (1966). Some characteristics of genuine versus simulated suicide notes. In P. J. Stone, D. C. Dunphy, M. S. Smith, and D. M. Ogilvie, *The General Inquirer: a computer approach to content analysis in the behavioral sciences.* Cambridge: M.I.T. Press. Pp. 527–535.

Ohlström, B. (1966). Information and propaganda. *J. Peace Res., 1,* 75–88.

Ojemann, R. H., *et al.* (1948). A functional analysis of child development material in current newspapers and magazines. *Child Develpmt., 19,* 76–92.

Osgood, C. E. (1959). The representational model and relevant research methods. In I. de S. Pool (Ed.), *Trends in content analysis.* Urbana: Univ. of Illinois Press. Pp. 33–88.

——— (1962). Studies on the generality of affective meaning systems. *Amer. Psychologist, 17,* 10–28.

Osgood, C. E., S. Saporta, and J. C. Nunnally (1956). Evaluative assertion analysis. *Litera, 3,* 47–102.

Osgood, C. E., and T. A. Sebeok, Eds. (1954). Psycholinguistics: a survey of theory and research problems. *J. abnorm. soc. Psychol. (Suppl.), 49,* No. 4, part 2.

Osgood, C. E., G. J. Suci, and P. H. Tannenbaum (1957). *The measurement of meaning.* Urbana: Univ. of Illinois Press.

Osgood, C. E., and Evelyn G. Walker (1959). Motivation and language behavior: content analysis of suicide notes. *J. abnorm. soc. Psychol., 59,* 58–67.

Page, H. W. (1953). An assessment of the predictive value of certain language measures in psychotherapeutic counseling. In W. U. Snyder (Ed.), *Group report of a program of research in psychotherapy.* University Park, Pa.: Pennsylvania State College. Pp. 88–93.

Paige, J. M. (1966). Letters from Jenny: an approach to the clinical analysis of personality structure by computer. In P. J. Stone, D. C. Dunphy, M. S. Smith, and D. M. Ogilvie, *The General Inquirer: a computer approach to content analysis in the behavioral sciences.* Cambridge: M.I.T. Press. Pp. 431–451.

Painter, J. A. (1960). Computer preparation of a poetry concordance. *Communic. Assoc. for Computing Machinery, 3,* 91–95.

*Paisley, W. J. (1964). Identifying the unknown communicator in painting, literature and music: the significance of minor encoding habits. *J. Communic., 14,* 219–237.

——— (1966). The effects of authorship, topic, structure, and time of composition on letter redundancy in English texts. *J. verb. Learn. verb. Behav., 5,* 28–34.

Parker, E. C., D. W. Barry, and D. W. Smythe, Eds. (1955). *The television-radio audience and religion.* New York: Harper.

Parrish, S. M., Ed. (1959). *A concordance to the poems of Matthew Arnold.* Ithaca, N.Y.: Cornell Univ. Press.

Parrish, S. M., and J. A. Painter (1963). *A concordance to the poems of W. B. Yeats.* Ithaca, N.Y.: Cornell Univ. Press.

Parsons, T., E. A. Shils, and J. Olds (1952). Values, motives, and systems of action. In T. Parsons and E. A. Shils, *Toward a general theory of action.* Cambridge: Harvard Univ. Press. Pp. 47–243.

Peterson, R. L., and T. L. Brewer (n.d.). The Lasswell value dictionary. New Haven: Yale University. (Mimeo)

Pittenger, R. E., C. F. Hockett, and J. J. Danehy (1960). *The first five minutes: a sample of microscopic interview analysis.* Ithaca, N.Y.: Paul Martineau.

Pool, I. de S. (1951). *Symbols of internationalism.* Stanford: Stanford Univ. Press.

————— (1952a). *The 'prestige papers': a survey of their editorials.* Stanford: Stanford Univ. Press.

————— (1952b). *Symbols of democracy.* Stanford: Stanford Univ. Press.

————— (1954). Symbols, meaning, and social sciences. In L. Bryson (Ed.), *Symbols and values: an initial study.* New York: Harper.

†—————, Ed. (1959). *Trends in content analysis.* Urbana: Univ. of Illinois Press.

Prothro, J. W. (1956). Verbal shifts in the American presidency: a content analysis. *Amer. polit. Sci. Rev., 50,* 726–739.

Raimy, V. C. (1948). Self reference in counseling interviews. *J. consult. Psychol., 12,* 153–163.

Rainey, G. E. (1966). The American image of peace. Doctoral dissertation, American University.

Rainoff, T. J. (1929). Wave-like fluctuations of creative productivity in the development of west-European physics in the eighteenth and nineteenth centuries. *Isis, 12,* 287–307.

Ramallo, L. I. (1966). The integration of subject and object in the context of action: a study of reports written by successful and unsuccessful volunteers for field work in Africa. In P. J. Stone, D. C. Dunphy, M. S. Smith, and D. M. Ogilvie, *The General Inquirer: a computer approach to content analysis in the behavioral sciences.* Cambridge: M.I.T. Press. Pp. 536–547.

Riesman, D., N. Glazer, and D. Reuel (1950). *The lonely crowd.* New Haven: Yale Univ. Press.

Roat, R. (1963). Crisis news in the press abroad. *Quill,* June, 1963, pp. 20–21.

Robinson, W. S. (1957). The statistical measure of agreement. *Amer. sociol. Rev., 22,* 17–25.

Role of content analysis in opinion and communications research, The (1951). *Publ. Opin. Quart., 15,* 782–786.

Rosen, B. (1964). Attitude change within the Negro press toward segregation and discrimination. *J. soc. Psychol., 62,* 77–83.

Rosenau, J. N. (1968). Private preferences and public responsibility: the relative potency of individual and role variables in the behavior of U.S. senators. In J. D. Singer (Ed.), *Quantitative international politics: insights and evidence.* New York: Free Press. Pp. 17–50.

Roshal, Jean J. G. (1953). The type-token ratio as a measure of changes in behavior variability during psychotherapy. In W. U. Snyder (Ed.), *Group report of a program of research in psychotherapy.* University Park, Pa.: Pennsylvania State College. Pp. 94–104.

Rosi, E. J. (1964). How 50 periodicals and the Times interpreted the Test Ban controversy. *Journalism Quart., 41,* 545–556.

Royal Commission on the Press, 1947–1949 (1949). Report, Appendix VII. London: His Majesty's Stationery Office.

Rucker, B. W. (1960). News services' crowd reporting in the 1956 presidential campaign. *Journalism Quart., 37,* 195–198.

Runion, H. L. (1936). An objective study of the speech style of Woodrow Wilson. *Speech Monogr., 3,* 75–94.

Russell, J. T., and Q. Wright (1933). National attitudes on the Far Eastern controversy. *Amer. polit. Sci. Rev., 27,* 555–576.

St. George, M., and L. Dennis (1946). *A trial on trial: the great sedition trial of 1944.* National Civil Rights Committee.

*Salzinger, K., Stephanie Portnoy, and R. S. Feldman (1964). Verbal behavior of schizophrenic and normal subjects. *Ann. N.Y. Acad. Sci., 105,* 845–860.

Scheuch, E. K., and P. J. Stone (1964). The General Inquirer approach to an international retrieval system for survey archives. *Amer. behav. Scientist, 7,* 23–28.

Schneider, L., and S. M. Dornbusch (1958). *Popular religion: inspirational books in America.* Chicago: Univ. of Chicago Press.

Schorer, M. (1949). Fiction and the 'matrix of analogy.' *Kenyon Rev., 11,* 539–560.

Schramm, W., Ed. (1959). *One day in the world's press.* Stanford: Stanford Univ. Press.

Schubert, G. (1965). Jackson's judicial philosophy: an exploration in value analysis. *Amer. polit. Sci. Rev., 59,* 940–963.

Schutz, W. C. (1952). Reliability, ambiguity and content analysis. *Psychol. Rev., 59,* 119–129.

———— (1958). On categorizing qualitative data in content analysis. *Publ. Opin. Quart., 22,* 503–515.

Scott, W. A. (1955). Reliability of content analysis: the case of nominal scale coding. *Publ. Opin. Quart., 19,* 321–325.

Sebald, H. (1962). Studying national character through comparative content analysis. *Soc. Forces, 40,* 318–322.

Sebeok, T. A., and V. J. Zeps (1961). Computer research in psycholinguistics: toward an analysis of poetic language. *Behav. Sci., 6,* 365–369.

Sedelow, Sally Y., W. A. Sedelow, Jr., and T. Ruggles (1964). Some parameters for computational stylistics: computer aids to the use of traditional categories in stylistic analysis. In *Proceedings of the IBM literary data processing conference.* Yorktown Heights, N.Y.: IBM. Pp. 211–229.

Shanas, Ethel (1945). The American Journal of Sociology through fifty years. *Amer. J. Sociol., 50,* 522–533.

Sheerer, Elizabeth T. (1949). An analysis of the relationship between acceptance of and respect for self and acceptance of and respect for others in ten counseling cases. *J. consult. Psychol., 13,* 169–175.

Shneidman, E. S. (1951). *Thematic test analysis.* New York: Grune and Stratton.

——— (1961). A psycho-logical analysis of political thinking: the Kennedy-Nixon 'Great Debates' and the Kennedy-Khrushchev 'Grim Debates.' Cambridge: Harvard University. (Mimeo)

*——— (1963). Plan 11. The logic of politics. In L. Arons and M. A. May (Eds.), *Television and human behavior.* New York: Appleton-Century-Crofts. Pp. 177–199.

Simmons, R. F. (1966). Automated language processing. In C. A. Cuadra (Ed.), *Annual review of information science and technology.* Vol. 1. New York: Interscience. Pp. 137–169.

Skinner, B. F. (1939). The alliteration in Shakespeare's sonnets: a study in literary behavior. *Psychol. Record, 3,* 186–192.

Smith, M. S., with P. J. Stone and E. N. Glenn (1966). A content analysis of twenty presidential nominating speeches. In P. J. Stone, D. C. Dunphy, M. S. Smith, and D. M. Ogilvie, *The General Inquirer: a computer approach to content analysis in the behavioral sciences.* Cambridge: M.I.T. Press. Pp. 359–400.

Smythe, D. W. (1952). Some observations of communications theory. *Audio-visual Communic. Rev., 2,* 24–37.

——— (1953). *Three years of New York television, 1951–1953.* Urbana: National Association of Educational Broadcasters, Univ. of Illinois.

Snyder, W. E., Ed. (1953). *Group report of a program of research in psychotherapy.* University Park, Pa.: Pennsylvania State College.

Sorenson, R. C., and T. C. Sorenson (1955). Proposal for the use of content analysis in literary infringement cases. *Soc. Forces, 33,* 262–267.

Speed, J. G. (1893). Do newspapers now give the news? *The Forum, 15,* 705–711.

Spiegelman, M., C. Terwilliger, and F. Fearing (1953a). The content of comics: goals and means to goals of comic strip characters. *J. soc. Psychol., 37,* 189–203.

——— (1953b). The reliability of agreement in content analysis. *J. soc. Psychol., 37,* 175–187.

Starkweather, J. A. (1956). Content-free speech as a source of information about the speakers. *J. abnorm. soc. Psychol., 52,* 394–402.

Starkweather, J. A., and J. B. Decker (1964). Computer analysis of interview content. *Psychol. Reports, 15,* 875–882.

Stedman, M. S. (1951). Democracy in American communal and socialist literature. *J. History of Ideas, 12,* 147–154.

Stempel, G. H., III (1952). Research in brief: sample size for classifying subject matter in dailies. *Journalism Quart., 29,* 333–334.

——— (1955). Increasing reliability in content analysis. *Journalism Quart., 32,* 449–455.

—— (1961). The prestige press covers the 1960 presidential campaign. *Journalism Quart., 38,* 157–163.

—— (1965). The prestige press in two presidential elections. *Journalism Quart., 42,* 15–21.

Stephenson, W. (1963). Critique of content analysis. *Psychol. Record, 13,* 155–162.

Stevens, N. E. (1932). The fad as a factor in botanical publication. *Science, 75,* 286–293.

Stewart, M. (1943). Importance in content analysis: a validity problem. *Journalism Quart., 20,* 286–293.

Stock, Dorothy (1949). The self concept and feelings toward others. *J. consult. Psychol., 13,* 176–180.

Stone, P. J. (1964). An introduction to the General Inquirer: a computer system for the study of spoken or written material. Harvard Univ. and Simulmatics Corp. (Mimeo)

Stone, P. J., R. F. Bales, J. Z. Namenwirth, and D. M. Ogilvie (1962). The General Inquirer: a computer system for content analysis and retrieval based on the sentence as a unit of information. *Behav. Sci., 7,* 484–494.

Stone, P. J., D. C. Dunphy, and A. Bernstein (1965). Content analysis applications at simulmatics. *Amer. behav. Scientist, 8,* 23–28.

†Stone, P. J., D. C. Dunphy, M. S. Smith, and D. M. Ogilvie (1966). *The General Inquirer: a computer approach to content analysis in the behavioral sciences.* Cambridge: M.I.T. Press.

Stone, P. J., and E. B. Hunt (1963). A computer approach to content analysis. In *Proceedings of the spring joint computer conference, 1963.* Pp. 241–256.

Stone, P. J., D. M. Ogilvie, and D. C. Dunphy (1963). Distinguishing real from simulated suicide notes using General Inquirer procedures. Paper read at the Joint Annual Meeting of the American College of Neuropsychopharmacology.

Sussman, Leila (1945). Labor in the radio news: an analysis of content. *Journalism Quart., 22,* 207–214.

Taeuber, Irene B. (1932). Changes in the content and presentation of reading material in Minnesota weekly newspapers, 1860–1929. *Journalism Quart., 9,* 281–289.

Tannenbaum, P. H., and B. S. Greenberg (1961a). The effects of bylines on attitude change. *Journalism Quart., 38,* 535–537.

—— (1961b). 'J.Q.' references: a study of professional change. *Journalism Quart., 38,* 203–207.

Tannenbaum, P. H., and M. D. Lynch (1960). Sensationalism: the concept and its measurement. *Journalism Quart., 37,* 381–392.

Taylor, W. L. (1953). 'Cloze Procedure'; a new tool for measuring readability. *Journalism Quart., 30,* 415–433.

—— (1956). Recent developments in the use of 'Cloze Procedure.' *Journalism Quart., 33,* 42–48, 99.

—— (1957). Gauging the mental health content of the mass media. *Journalism Quart., 34,* 191–201.

Technical recommendations for psychological tests and diagnostic techniques (1954). *Psychol. Bull., 51,* Suppl., 201–238.

Toch, H. H., S. E. Deutsch, and D. M. Wilkins (1960). The wrath of the bigot: an analysis of protest mail. *Journalism Quart., 37,* 173–185, 266.

Walworth, A. (1938). *School histories at war: a study of the treatment of our wars in the secondary school history books of the United States and in those of its former enemies.* Cambridge: Harvard Univ. Press.

Wang, C. K. A. (1955). Reactions in Communist China: an analysis of letters to newspaper editors. USAF Personnel Training Research Center, Technical Report No. 33. HHRI Project: "Chinese Documents Project." January 1955.

Waples, D., B. Berelson, and F. R. Bradshaw (1940). *What reading does to people.* Chicago: Univ. of Chicago Press.

Wayne, I. (1956). American and Soviet themes and values: a content analysis of pictures in popular magazines. *Publ. Opin. Quart., 20,* 314–320.

Webb, E. J., and J. R. Salancik (1965). Notes on the sociology of knowledge. *Journalism Quart., 42,* 591–595.

Westley, B. H., C. E. Higbie, T. Burke, D. J. Lippert, L. Maurer, and V. A. Stone (1963). The news magazines and the 1960 conventions. *Journalism Quart., 40,* 525–531, 647.

White, R. K. (1947). "Black Boy": a value-analysis. *J. abnorm. soc. Psychol., 42,* 440–461.

———— (1949). Hitler, Roosevelt and the nature of war propaganda. *J. abnorm. soc. Psychol., 44,* 157–174.

———— (1951). *Value-analysis: the nature and use of the method.* Glen Gardiner, N.J.: Libertarian Press.

Whiting, A. S. (1960). *China crosses the Yalu.* New York: Macmillan.

Wilcox, W. (1962). The press of the radical right: an exploratory analysis. *Journalism Quart., 39,* 152–160.

Willey, M. (1926). *The country newspaper.* Chapel Hill: Univ. of North Carolina Press.

Willoughby, W. F. (1955). Are two competing dailies necessarily better than one? *Journalism Quart., 32,* 197–204.

Winick, C. (1963). Trends in the occupation of celebrities—a study of news magazine profiles and television interviews. *J. soc. Psychol., 60,* 301–310.

Wolfenstein, Martha, and N. Leites (1950). *Movies: a psychological study.* Glencoe, Ill.: Free Press.

*Wolfson, Rose (1951). Graphology. In H. H. Anderson and G. M. L. Anderson (Eds.), *An introduction to projective techniques.* New York: Prentice-Hall. Pp. 416–456.

Woodward, J. L. (1930). *Foreign news in American morning newspapers.* New York: Columbia Univ. Press.

———— (1934). Quantitative newspaper analysis as a technique of opinion research. *Soc. Forces, 12,* 526–537.

Woodward, J. L., and R. Franzen (1948). A study of coding reliability. *Publ. Opin. Quart., 12,* 253–257.

Wright, Q., and C. J. Nelson (1939). American attitudes toward Japan and China. *Publ. Opin. Quart., 3,* 46–62.

Wyant, Rowena, and Herta Herzog (1941). Voting via the Senate mailbag. *Publ. Opin. Quart., 5,* 359–382, 590–624.

Yakobson, S., and H. D. Lasswell (1949). Trend: May Day slogans in Soviet Russia. In H. D. Lasswell, N. Leites *et al.* (Eds.), *The language of politics: studies in quantitative semantics.* New York: George Stewart. Pp. 232–297.

Yule, G. U. (1944). *The statistical study of literary vocabulary.* London: Cambridge Univ. Press.

Zaninovich, M. G. (1964). An empirical theory of state response: the Sino-Soviet case. Unpublished doctor's dissertation, Stanford University.

Zinnes, Dina A., R. C. North, and H. E. Koch, Jr. (1961). Capability, threat and the outbreak of war. In J. N. Rosenau (Ed.), *International politics and foreign policy.* New York: Free Press. Pp. 469–482.

17

Methods and Problems in Cross-Cultural Research

JOHN W. M. WHITING, Harvard University

The cross-cultural method utilizes data collected by anthropologists concerning the customs and characteristics of various peoples throughout the world to test hypotheses concerning human behavior. Some of the hypotheses tested have been derived from theories of cultural evolution, others from theories concerned with the integration of culture, and still others, particularly in recent years, from theories of individual, developmental, physiological, and social psychology.

Although the comparison of the ways of different peoples is ancient, E. B. Tylor (1889), who presented at a meeting of the Royal Anthropological Institute of Great Britain a paper entitled "On a Method of Investigating the Development of Institutions; Applied to Laws of Marriage and Descent," was the first to use statistical methods for this purpose. It is interesting that Sir Francis Galton, one of the fathers of modern statistics, presided at this meeting. Although the intent of the study was to support Tylor's particular view of cultural evolution, its importance was that in the paper and the discussion which followed, most of the basic assumptions and problems of cross-cultural research were touched upon.

For the next fifty years the method was almost completely neglected, Nieboer's study (1910) of slavery, and Hobhouse, Wheeler, and Ginsberg's (1915) essay on the correlations between material culture and social institutions being notable exceptions. The method was revived by G. P. Murdock (1937) in a test of the evolutionary priority of matrilineal and patrilineal institutions. Since that time, studies using the cross-cultural method have appeared at an ever increasing rate. For a listing of some of these studies see the attached bibliography.

Recently the cross-cultural method has been used more and more by psychologists. In fact, the names of more psychologists appear as authors of the cross-cultural articles listed in the bibliography than of any other discipline. Furthermore, most anthropologists currently using the method consider themselves psychological anthropologists. This essay will be addressed, therefore, primarily to psychologists.

ADVANTAGES OF THE CROSS-CULTURAL METHOD

It might be asked at this point why ethnographic material should be drawn upon to test psychological principles. Why not stick to materials gathered in one's own society, where the language and culture are familiar and where more adequate control of the process of data collection is possible?

The advantages of the cross-cultural method are twofold. First, it ensures that one's findings relate to human behavior in general rather than being bound to a single culture; and second, it increases the range of variation of many variables.

With respect to the first point, that of generality, one might ask questions such as the following: Is the Oedipus complex a universal phenomenon or is it peculiar to middle-class western Europeans? Does the relation between the age of independence training and need achievement hold in societies other than our own? Since most social-psychological studies are done within the framework of western European culture, one can never be certain whether the discovered relationships are valid for all mankind or whether they are an artifact of some limitation or special circumstance of the culture in which they have been discovered. An example will serve to illustrate this point. Sears and Wise (1950) found as a result of a study of a sample of 80 children living in Kansas City that there was a positive relationship between the age of weaning and the degree to which the infant gave indications of emotional disturbance. That is, the later a child was weaned the more disturbance he showed. This relationship reached the one-percent level of significance.

One might ask whether this relation between age of weaning and emotional disturbance is a general human trait or whether it is peculiar to the culture of Kansas City. Anthropologists are only too eager to find exceptions to any rule. Thus, Beatrice Blackwood (1935) reported that the Kurtatchi of the Solomon Islands do not wean their children until they are over three years old and that Kurtatchi children show no signs of emotional disturbance. Does this single case disprove the rule? More than two cases, Kansas City and Kurtatchi, are needed to answer this question.

Fortunately the data are available. Whiting and Child (1953) in a cross-cultural study of child training and personality collected material, on the same variables used by Sears and Wise, from a sample of 75 societies distributed throughout the world (Fig. 1). Evidence was available so that judgments could be made for age of weaning and emotional disturbance for 37 societies. The mean score for emotional disturbance on a seven-point scale for the 17 societies in which the onset of weaning was at two years or less was 3.5, whereas the mean score for the 20 societies in which weaning took place later than two years was 2.8.

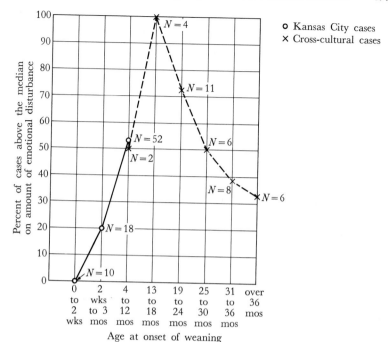

Fig. 1. *Relation between age at onset of weaning and amount of emotional disturbance shown by child. Comparable data from 80 individual children from Kansas City (Sears and Wise, 1950) and from 37 societies (Whiting and Child, 1953) are presented.*

It will be seen from this that in this instance the Kurtatchi are not a single exception but are typical of a tendency for late weaning to result in low rather than high emotional disturbance and thus there really seems to be a contradiction between the Sears and Wise findings and the cross-cultural evidence. If the methods of measuring these two variables are accepted as reliable and comparable in the two sets of data, one might conclude that different psychological principles were operating in Kansas City than in the rest of the world. Closer examination of the data, however, reveals a much more plausible explanation and illustrates the second advantage of the cross-cultural method, namely, that of increased range.

The effective range of age of weaning for the Kansas City sample was zero to seven months (only five of the 80 cases were later than seven months), whereas for the cross-cultural sample, with the exception of two cases, it was from 12 months to six years. Thus, there is practically no overlap between the two distributions and, as shown in Fig. 1, the two findings complement each other to indicate a curvilinear rather than a linear relation between the two variables. Because of lack of range, neither study tells the whole story.

The preceding case illustrates that, with respect to age of weaning at least, psychologists may be hampered by lack of range in developing a theory that would be applicable the world over. There is considerable evidence that this lack of range is not restricted to age of weaning. Thus, although much of the accuracy of measurement and experimental control generally found in psychological research on individuals in our society is lacking in cross-cultural studies, this spread in the variables provides a useful check upon and supplement to psychological research. Studies of individual differences carried out in a series of contrasting cultures has the advantages of both methods. Although costly, such a strategy is being carried out to an ever increasing extent. Prothro (1961) and Landy (1959) have repeated the Sears, Maccoby, and Levin (1957) study in Lebanon and the Caribbean, respectively. Within-culture replication was also the design of the comparative study of child rearing in *Six Cultures* (Whiting *et al.*, 1966a).

Even though extreme cases on some variables may be found in our society, these are deviant from the cultural norms. In cross-cultural research the norm for a whole society is taken as a score. Thus, no matter how extreme a case may be from our point of view, the individuals who manifest this customary behavior do not perceive themselves to be deviant. To return to the age of weaning, a Kurtatchi mother who postpones weaning her child until he is between three and four years old is doing just what other Kurtatchi mothers do. If an American mother nursed her three-year-old child, however, she could not help but be aware that she was deviating from the usual practice—a factor which might have considerable effect on both her and the child and might therefore contaminate one's findings if one were interested in the consequences of late weaning rather than of deviant behavior.

Furthermore, the cross-cultural method, by studying cultural norms, holds individual variation constant. Psychological studies of individuals in a single society do just the opposite, in that cultural norms are held constant and individual variations are studied. These two methods in combination should supplement and correct each other in the development of a general theory of human behavior.

THE DEFINITION OF A CASE

There are a number of technical problems that confront anyone who undertakes a cross-cultural study. Perhaps the most difficult is the selection of cases. This involves not only problems of sampling and the independence of cases, but more fundamentally an appropriate definition of a case. Is it a tribe, a society, a dialect group, a community, or a culture? This problem has long been a concern of those engaged in cross-cultural research (see Hobhouse, Wheeler, and Ginsberg, 1915). Recently an issue of *Current Anthropology* was devoted to a major article on the subject by Naroll (1964b) together with comments on his paper by over twenty anthropologists from North and South America, Europe, and Asia.

Naroll (1964b), after reviewing the various explicit and implicit ways in which cross-cultural researchers have defined their units, proposed a new term—the *cultunit*—with the following definition (p. 286): "a group of territorially contiguous people who not only are domestic speakers of mutually intelligible dialects but also belong to the same state or contact group." He then proceeded to specify four subtypes of this unit: (1) the stateless, (2) the linguistically homogeneous state, (3) the ruling group of a linguistically diverse state, and (4) the subject group of the linguistically diverse state.

Most commentators, while agreeing with Naroll's general definition, took exception to his subtypes. Thus Murdock (1964b, p. 301):

The concept of "cultunit" is valid and important, but the term itself is an ambiguous barbarism. . . . I emphatically reject the fourfold classification . . . into types. To inject cultural content, such as the presence or absence of "state" or a "lingua franca" into the overall definition of a culture bearing unit seems to me quite indefensible. Cross-cultural studies have demonstrated strong correlations between the occurrence of states and other such cultural phenomena as complexity of social stratification and the degree of urbanization. If Naroll were to be taken literally, however, any such study would be invalid because of the noncomparability of units. For cross-cultural comparisons to be possible, any culture must be comparable with any other and this means that there can be only a single kind of "cultunit"—not four or any other number of non-comparable types.

Leach (1964) in his comments on Naroll's paper took a similar view with respect to the need for comparability of units, but despaired of finding them and was skeptical of the validity of the cross-cultural method. He wrote (p. 299):

I have previously argued that any system of cross-cultural comparison which can be so used as to make "the Tikopia" and "the Chinese" units of comparable type is self-evidently absurd, and I do not see that the absurdity is reduced by calling the units 'cultunits' instead of 'tribes'.

Unit comparability is indeed a serious problem for cross-cultural research. As I argued in my comments on Naroll's paper (Whiting 1964a, p. 305),

[I believe it can be met by making the unit definition appropriate to the problem.] I do not, however, agree that there is any one "ideal type" of unit, but rather feel that its definition should depend upon the problem being investigated. Thus, a comparative investigation of a problem in human biology or genetics should consider a set of breeding populations or endogamous groups as the appropriate universe; while for problems in linguistics, speech communities comprise the appropriate universe. For problems of environmental adaptation, the inhabitants of ecological regions—for example desert peoples, tropical rainforest peoples—might provide the best sample.

Even if the problem is cultural, I do not feel that a single definition such as that offered for the cultunit is appropriate for all problems. As will be discussed below, nations or states might be more appropriate for the study of problems involving political variables, whereas local communities may be the more appropriate unit for the study of kinship or of child rearing.

Naroll (1964b) objected to the local community as a unit for cross-cultural research on the presumption that descriptions of such groups are not available in sufficient numbers. He wrote (p. 286):

Restricting the unit of study to certain local communities is clearly impossible in certain other kinds. In a cross-cultural survey which seeks a random or stratified random sample (Ember, 1963; Naroll, 1961), such a unit definition is operationally worthless. It is hard enough to get something resembling a complete list of societies, but impossible to get anything resembling a complete inventory of local communities.

Naroll's criticism of the local community as a unit is not as devastating as it seems (Whiting, 1964a, p. 305):

It does not take account of the fact that the unit most intensively studied by standard ethnographic techniques is, in fact, a community rather than a larger unit. The anthropologist in the field typically pitches his tent in a hamlet or village or wanders with a band. Although he will ordinarily get some material from other communities of the tribe by visiting them during the course of his investigation, the detailed workings of the social life are documented from observations on the community in which he lives. Here, after taking a census, drawing a map, and constructing the genealogies of the families, he participates in the intimate details of daily life in a manner vividly described by Malinowski in the introduction to *Argonauts of the Western Pacific* (1922). The method is also described in Whiting and Whiting (1960).

The local community, then, is in fact the unit described in greatest detail in the bulk of the extant ethnographic literature. Thus, the local community, rather than being "operationally worthless" as Naroll suggested, is more appropriate for testing many hypotheses simply on the grounds of the amount of detailed information available.

Young (1965) and Murdock (1966) have also decided that the local community is the most appropriate unit for cross-cultural research. Both authors agree that such is the reference group for most ethnographic studies. As Young wrote (pp. 43–44):

For large countries, such as the United States or Japan there was no question; the ethnography is explicitly concerned with a particular community. But close examination indicates that this is also true of tribal studies. . . . Thus, in terms of what ethnographers actually do, one usually has no choice but to study locality groups.

He was able to specify the community in 54 of a sample of 56 societies. Similarly, the local community was chosen as the primary sampling unit (PSU) in a comparative field study of child-rearing practices (Whiting *et al.,* 1966a).

In studies involving child-rearing variables, there is a theoretical as well as a practical reason for choosing the local community as a unit. When, in cross-cultural research, a score represents an estimate of some individual psychological process such as "emotional disturbance at weaning," it is presumed to refer to an average or typical person occupying a culturally defined status. In large complex societies the cultural diversity with respect to such variables is often so great that even if such a typical individual could be found, he would be representative of but a small minority of the population. In small homogeneous communities, however, where statuses are more clearly defined and appropriate rules more explicit, the typical or average individual is much more likely to represent a substantial majority of his fellow villagers. Furthermore, since the individual sampling universe is small in a local community as compared to a larger society, ethnographic statements are much more likely to be valid.

To ensure that the local community units are reasonably equivalent with respect to homogeneity, they should ideally have features which serve to reduce the variability of both individual behavior and the cultural beliefs, values, and techniques held by the community members. Although this has not been put to a systematic cross-cultural test—and it would be desirable to do so—most local communities the world over, whether they be nomadic bands, hamlets, village segments, or urban neighborhoods, have the following features: (1) members have frequent face-to-face contact with one another; (2) they speak the same dialect; (3) they have some degree of sovereignty; (4) they have a group name.

Each of the above criteria is relevant for maximizing cultural homogeneity. People who interact with one another on a face-to-face basis must, despite differences in personality, share culturally prescribed role expectancies. Deviation from the prescribed rules leads to negative sanctions and ultimate ostracism or execution if they are persisted in. A common dialect ensures that metaphors and idioms are shared, and thus intercommunication is maximized.

The criterion of sovereignty needs some discussion. Murdock (1962), following Swanson (1960), has defined the term as follows (p. 269):

Sovereignty is characterized by original and definitive jurisdiction over some sphere of social life in which the organization has the legitimate right to make decisions having a significant effect on its members, for example distribution of food, allocation of productive resources, punishment of delicts, assignment or conscription of labor, levying of taxes, initiation of war and peace.

Except for a few small tribes in out-of-the-way places, no community in the world today has anything approaching complete sovereignty. The right to initiate war and peace has been assumed by the great nations of the world and thus taken out of the hands of local face-to-face groups. On the other hand, in every viable society there are communities that have original and definitive jurisdiction over *some* sphere of social life. The criterion of sovereignty for a community then implies some degree of organization in which meetings are called and decisions made affecting its members. The word sovereignty may imply a greater degree of autonomy than is intended. A meeting to allocate responsibilities for some ceremony such as a harvest festival, a church fair, or a wedding, a group decision to move camp, or to maintain communal facilities such as a path or a men's house, or a P.T.A. meeting, would constitute an adequate degree of sovereignty for the purposes of this definition. This criterion, then, is intended to exclude the members of some block or neighborhood who have face-to-face contact, speak the same dialect, and belong to the same endogamous group, but are not organized in this way. Such anomic communities are often found in modern industrial cities.

The last criterion, that of a common name, is perhaps the least important and I am not sure that it is necessary. It is included because it is an index of group identity. These group names may be totemic but more commonly are place-names referring to water holes, crossroads, fords, harbors, and the like. Some communities that meet all the above criteria are nevertheless heterogeneous, particularly with respect to matters relevant to psychological anthropology, such as child-rearing practices. The community chosen in India for the "Six-Culture Study" mentioned above provides an example. This community, a neighborhood in the town of Khalapur in Uttar Pradesh, consisted primarily of members of the

Rajput caste. Dwelling among them were, however, several families of the lower "Sweeper" caste who performed menial tasks for the dominant Rajput caste. Minturn and Hitchcock (1966), in drawing their sample of families for an intensive study of child rearing, decided to omit the "Sweepers" and draw only upon Rajputs. Although members of these two castes met frequently in face-to-face contact and spoke the same dialect, they subscribed mutually to strict rules against intermarriage. Thus they did not have the opportunity to share the values and intimate practices that is possible and indeed required of parents deciding upon child-rearing policy. Most of the Rajput families, on the other hand, consisted of fathers who were born and brought up in the community and wives that were drawn from the Rajput caste in a limited number of villages to the north of Khalapur. Thus, both members of the family were part of an endogamous group or connubium whose members had intermarried for generations. The grandparents, great-grand-parents, and great-great-grandparents of this group have thus shared the same tradition; they hold sacred the same myths and rituals and obey the same cultural rules.

The "Sweepers" are also members of an endogamous group, but a different one, and although they share a tradition with one another, it has had ample opportunity to diverge from that of the Rajputs. Studies of child rearing in our own society have shown over and over again that there are striking differences between the child-rearing practices and basic attitude of members of different social classes, ethnic groups, and religious persuasion living in the same community, even when the rules against intermarriage are not nearly so strict as those in India. Endogamous rules thus create not only a gene pool, but what may be called a "culture pool" that maximizes homogeneity.

It may, therefore, be well to consider the addition of an endogamous criterion to be added to the definition of an appropriate unit for our purposes. In simpler societies most communities are homogeneous in this regard. Although members are often prevented by incest rules from marrying within the community itself, nevertheless, like the Rajputs described above, all seek mates from the same set of neighboring communities and thus belong to the same endogamous group. Such communities would, of course, constitute appropriate units.

In more complex societies it is often the case that communities are heterogeneous with respect to marriage rules. Catholics and Protestants, Muslims and Pagans may live in face-to-face contact, speak the same dialect, and be members of a group with both a degree of sovereignty and a name, but have rules or preferences against intermarriage. Similarly, as suggested above, members of different castes and classes may live in the same community and not intermarry. In such cases it is suggested that one homogeneous segment of the community be chosen on the basis of common endogamous rules as the appropriate unit.

It would be desirable if a list of all the communities studied were available. Such is not the case. In fact, the standard practice of ethnographers to refer in the titles of their reports to the larger society of which the community most intensively studied is a part makes the compilation of such a list more difficult than it might otherwise be. My own experience with the Kwoma (1941) is not atypical of ethnographic practice. The Kwoma are a tribe situated in central New Guinea. The total population of some 900 people is divided into four subtribes. Each subtribe is in turn divided into sibs and each sib into hamlets. Except for a brief trip to the other subtribes and a few visits to other hamlets, virtually all my observations were made on Rumbima hamlet of the Hayamekwo sib of the Hongwam subtribe of Kwoma. The choice of "Becoming a Kwoma" as the title of the ethnography has resulted in *Kwoma* being listed in most cross-cultural studies in which it has been a case. It should be listed as Young (1965) did, by referring both to the tribe or society, Kwoma, and to the community, Rumbima. Fortunately, anthropologists usually identify the group on which they actually gathered their material. This is generally done in the introductory chapter. If the community is adopted as the unit of comparison, care should be taken to identify it properly.

A special problem arises when several communities in a given society have been studied intensively by either the same or different ethnographers. Murdock (1953) proposed adoption of a policy suggested by biological taxonomy. He equated a tribe with a species and suggested that communities of the same tribe could be considered as equivalent if there were no geographic or dialectic barriers to communication or diffusion. He stated: "We therefore propose to define a culture as including all local cultural variants exhibited by communities within a particular geographical area which speak mutually intelligible languages and have essentially similar forms of economic adjustment."

An example is provided by Okinawa. Villages were studied by two different ethnographers. Maretski and Maretski (1966) did their work in Taira, a village in the forest region on the east coast of the northern part of the island. Glacken (1953) worked in three different communities. One of them, Matsuda, was also on the northeast coast of the island; the other two villages were located in the southern part of the island in open grasslands. Taira and Matsuda are in adjoining townships. Both have a central village with satellite hamlets and both are situated between the forested mountains and the sea. Wet rice is the main crop for both. In both instances, fishing is carried on by a small outcaste group from Itoman. There are, no doubt, differences between these groups; Matsuda, for example, has a population of approximately 1400, whereas Taira's population is slightly over 700. Since the authors differed in their interest, the Maretskis being psychological anthropologists and Glacken a geographer, there are details in the description of each community that are lacking in the other.

If it should be found that unless both studies were used, no community could be drawn from Northern Okinawa, the following procedure is suggested: One of the communities should be chosen as a case, but data from the other can be used on an inferential basis and so indicated. Common sense should dictate when such inferences can appropriately be made.

A similar problem arises when the same community has been studied at different time periods. In this case the most appropriate date should be chosen as the *ethnographic present* and this should be indicated. Common sense should again dictate when inferences can properly be made from studies made at a different time. If there is evidence of rapid cultural change, great caution should be exercised in making such inferences.

It is often advantageous in cross-cultural research to use scores made in previous studies by other researchers. If this is done, special care should be taken that the groups and the ethnographic present correspond for the two sets of ratings. It should be noted that in the Ethnographic Atlas (Murdock, 1962), which provides the best source of coded material, the unit is defined as a society rather than a community. As indicated above, because of the nature of most ethnographic reports, the appropriate community can be identified only by reference to the bibliography. It should be noted also that the date chosen as the ethnographic present in *Ethnology* is often taken from the earliest standard work, in order to minimize the effects of acculturation and modernization. The best reports on child rearing and other more psychologically relevant variables may, however, be in a more recent report. If the latter are to be used, the Atlas variables should be rescored if the time difference is great or there is evidence of rapid change.

It is proposed, then, that for cross-cultural research involving assumptions concerning the relations between psychological process and culture, the homogeneous community is the most appropriate organized culture-bearing unit and that a sufficient number of these have been described to provide an adequate sample. If the homogeneous community is accepted as the unit, Leach's structure becomes an empirical question rather than the absurdity he suggests. A Tikopian community may legitimately be compared with a Chinese community. If it turns out that, with respect to the relationship between the variables being investigated, communities drawn from small tribes differ systematically from those drawn from large states or nations, this is an important fact. If this is suspected to be the case, an analysis of variance using some estimate of complexity of the parent culture as one of the independent variables is suggested.

SAMPLING

If one is to undertake a cross-cultural study, how is the sample to be chosen? If the homogeneous community is to be taken as a unit, there is no appropriate list available from which to draw a sample. One is forced either to compile such a list from published ethnographies or to use the strategy of first drawing a sample at some higher level of organization such as the tribe or the culture, where lists are available, and then searching for some community that has been described within such a unit. Care must be taken, however, if such a strategy is to be used, that the original list contains units at the same taxonomic level. It would obviously be inappropriate to use the *Outline of World Cultures* (Murdock *et al.,* 1963), which purports to list all the known cultures of the world at the time it was compiled, since it contains units which vary in level from the major regions such as Asia and Africa, and nations such as Korea and Uganda, to tribes and subtribes. Even "the world" is listed as a case. The Ethnographic Atlas, which now lists over 1000 societies, keeps to the societal level with reasonable consistency and thus provides a much more appropriate sampling list.

The sampling list in the Ethnographic Atlas, however, does not solve what has been called "Galton's problem." Naroll (1961, 1964a) and Naroll and D'Andrade (1963), who have concerned themselves with the problem, put it as follows (p. 1053):

Galton's problem is widely considered to be a crucial weakness in the cross-cultural survey method. Galton raised his problem at the meeting of the Royal Anthropological Institute in 1889 when Tylor read his pioneer paper introducing the cross-cultural survey method (Tylor, 1889). Tylor showed correlations ("adhesions" he called them) between certain traits often spread by diffusion—by borrowing or migration. Since this is often so, how many independent trials of his correlations did Tylor have? Boas, for decades the immensely influential dean of American anthropologists, once told his student Lowie (1946) that when he first read Tylor's paper, he became greatly enthusiastic. This seemed to him an ideal research technique. On reflecting further, however, Galton's objection seemed to him a devastating one; unless there was a solution to Galton's problem, Boas considered the cross-cultural survey method valueless.

We believe that the concept of independence of cases is an unfruitful approach to the difficulty. The difficulty is to distinguish the effect of functional associations, of "adhesions" in Tylor's graphic term, from the effect of mere common historical association through diffusion, whether through genetic relationship of common cultural ancestry or through borrowing from a common cultural center. The problem here is to control a correlation between factors considered related functionally to see whether this relationship is an artifact of common historical circumstances.

Naroll's analysis is quite correct. True nonindependence of cases, statistically speaking, would apply only if the unit defined were larger than a community and two communities were each counted as representing that larger unit. Since for the purposes of this essay, the community has been chosen as the unit, such a criticism does not apply.

It is important to distinguish historical from functional explanations for a discovered relation between variables. Many anthropologists are concerned with establishing historical connections and for them Galton's problem consists of ruling out the possibility of functional interpretations of similarities between groups (*cf.* Driver, 1966). For most psychologists the opposite is generally the case. To minimize or in some way estimate the effects of history in order to get a true estimate of functional relationships is more likely to fit their requirements.

Naroll and D'Andrade have presented five different methods for separately estimating historical and functional effects. There are elegant and rather complex solutions to the problem that are especially appropriate for those who are interested in both historical and functional effects. Since it is assumed that most readers will be more interested in ruling out or minimizing the effects of history rather than directly estimating them, procedures for accomplishing this will be discussed here. It is suggested that those interested read the original articles by these authors.

To choose a sample that minimizes rather than directly estimates the effects of history is a less elegant but a more practical solution to Galton's problem. Since the historical relatedness of sets of neighboring cultures varies widely over the world, a random sample of all known cultures would leave the effects of history completely uncontrolled. For example, there are over 50 cultures listed in the Atlas that are all located in or adjacent to the Great Basin area of the United States, all of whom speak a dialect of the Shoshonean subfamily of the Uto-Aztecan linguistic phylum. Rather than being independent instances of a cultural adjustment, they should more properly be considered local variants of a common culture. If two or more of these cases should fall by chance in a sample, this would unduly weight any relationship between variables that was the result of historical accident. A sample stratified so that only one from such sets of closely related cultures could be chosen would minimize such an error.

There are several ways to stratify a sample to prevent the type of historically determined duplication described above. The one that has been most commonly used takes advantage of the taxonomy of the Ethnographic Atlas, which divides the world into six major regions: Africa, the Circum-Mediterranean, East Eurasia, the Insular Pacific, North America, and South America. The cultures in each of these regions have been grouped into ten culture areas, thus yielding 60 sets of cultures that are reasonably independent of one another. Most of the Shoshonean-speaking cases mentioned above, for example, fall in the Great Basin culture area of the North American region.

This culture-area method has several disadvantages. In the first place, it limits the sample size to 60 cases, which is usually too small if one wishes to get a stable estimate of the interaction of several variables. More seriously, the Atlas list was never intended as a basis for sampling. The decision to set the number of culture areas in each region at ten was done for convenience of listing, and does not assume the correspondence from one region to another in the effects of diffusion and fission required for sampling purposes.

Another, and perhaps better, technique for minimizing historical effects has been proposed by Murdock (1963, 1966). Aiming to solve Galton's problem, Murdock is preparing a roster of what he has called the *culture types* of the world. A culture type is defined as follows (Murdock, 1963, p. 249):

... a single unquestionably distinctive culture or group of cultures which differ from one another to a degree not significantly greater than the local variations to be expected in the culture of any homogeneous society of substantial geographic extent.

It is doubtful whether anyone with less than Murdock's vast knowledge of the ethnographic literature of the world could apply such a definition with any degree of reliability. The roster that he has prepared for the Africa–Circum-Mediterranean macroregion provides some examples that help to operationalize the formal definition given above. *British,* one of his culture types, is defined as follows: "modern Great Britain or Eire or any of their regional sub-cultures, for example, Cornish, Northern Irish, Manx; the English, Irish, Scots, or Welsh of any historical period, including those when Celtic languages were spoken; any people of English language and British culture outside of the British Isles or any regional sub-division thereof, during the colonial or modern period, for example, Americans, Anglo-Canadians, Australians, British South Africans, New Zealanders" (1966, p. 109). The Americans of modern New England, the modern Irish of County Clare, and the inhabitants of Tristan de Cunha are three cases in this culture type that have been coded in the Ethnographic Atlas. Some of the other culture types listed for Europe are the Greeks, the Italians, Iberians, Basques, Germans, Scandinavians, Lapps, Finns, etc. The subcultures belonging to each of these are listed in a manner comparable to that for the British culture type.

It would seem from the above list that linguistic criteria play a major role in determining a culture type. The Dutch are classed with the Germans, the Spanish with the Portuguese, and the French-Canadians with the French. Similarly, in Africa, for example, groups speaking different dialects of the Yoruba language—the Oyo, Egba, Ekiti, and Ife—are grouped in a single culture type. Language is clearly not the only criterion, however. If this were so, a Celtic-language community in Wales should not be considered part of the British culture type when a Dutch-speaking community in Holland is not, since the English and Dutch languages are much more closely related historically than English and Celtic. Even more striking is the case of the Luo in East Africa, who speak a language belonging to the Eastern subfamily of the macro-Sudanic linguistic phylum but are classed with the Gusii who speak a language belonging to the Bantu subfamily of the Niger-Congo phylum. It is true that the Luo and Gusii have contiguous boundaries and have presumably had ample opportunity to borrow from one another. It is also true, however, that the Luo have contiguous boundaries with the Kipsigis, who also speak a macro-Sudanic language. The Kipsigis, however, are assigned to another culture type. It is not likely that these are isolated cases and it is probable that Murdock is using some implicit criteria other than either language or contiguity as a basis for defining a culture type. It might be hoped that he could be more explicit in his definition so that a community report on some society that does not appear in the Murdock roster could be assigned to a proper culture type.

Although the Murdock culture-type roster, when it is completed, will greatly improve the sampling base for cross-cultural research, a roster based strictly on linguistic affiliation and geographic location would, in my opinion, be preferable. In preliterate societies where recorded evidence of cultural fission is lacking, the best estimate of the number of years any two cultures speaking related languages have been separated is one based on glotto-chronology or lexico-statistics, which estimates the historical connection between two languages on the basis of the number of cognates in a standard list of 200 common terms (Swadesh, 1959). If this method is accepted as valid, linguistic affiliation is the most appropriate method for controlling for common origins. The appropriate control for diffusion is more difficult but the simple expedient of permitting no two cultures in a sample if they have contiguous boundaries is suggested.

Such a method has been used by Whiting and Ayres (n.d) to draw what they have called a "world linguistic sample." The lexico-statistical criterion used for this sample required that no two societies be chosen from the same subfamily, which would imply that no two cases could have been a part of the same culture for at least 1000 years. The linguistic affiliation of each culture was taken from column 64 of the Ethnographic Atlas, except for the Insular Pacific, where Murdock's (1964c) summary of Dyen's lexico-statistical analysis of the languages of the Pacific was used.

As we pointed out above, one could have both a German and a British community in a sample based on Murdock's culture-type approach. This would be ruled out in the language-and-location approach, since both German and English are members of the Germanic subfamily of Indo-European and hence judged to be too closely related historically. On the other hand, both a Celtic-speaking community in Ireland and an English-speaking community in the United States could be drawn by the language-and-location method but not by the culture-type method. The two methods are most strikingly in contrast in Africa. Murdock's culture-type roster lists 125 culture types for this continent, whereas only 14 appear in the world linguistic sample. This difference is largely accounted for by the great proliferation (177 cases) of tribes speaking a language classified as belonging to the Bantu subfamily of the Niger-Congo phylum. Both on the basis of the recent common origin of Bantu-speaking peoples—their dispersal is estimated to have taken place in the first millennium of the Christian era (Murdock, 1959)—and the similarity of many features of their culture, a linguistic-affiliation criterion is preferable to the culture-type criterion.

The greater conservatism of the language-and-location approach has its drawbacks, however. The world linguistic sample drawn on this basis was limited to 136 cases. Murdock estimates that his culture-type approach when completed will probably approximate 400 types. A larger sample, however, could be drawn by the language-and-location method if a less strict linguistic criterion were used. To prepare such a roster that pretended to include a reasonable proportion of the cultures of the world would be a substantial research task, but one that would be worth doing. A comparison between a sample drawn from such a roster and one drawn from the culture-type roster when it is completed would be informative.

If a sample of less than one case from each of the sets of historically related cultures listed in any one of the above described rosters is desired, it should be chosen by some random procedure. When the sets have been selected, one should proceed to choose randomly a culture from each set. The sources for each set should then be scanned to see whether (1) an identifiable homogeneous community is described and (2) the variables under consideration are adequately covered. If either of these requirements cannot be met, the case should be dropped and another from the same set substituted. Murdock, in the culture-type roster, has distinguished between those cultures that are generally well covered and those that are not. It is suggested that the random selection of cultures from a set be only from those listed as well covered. Before finally settling upon a sample, no matter which roster is used, it is suggested that no two cases should be parts of societies with contiguous borders. As suggested before, this procedure should minimize the effect of informal contacts that may have led to mutual borrowing.

It should be stressed that these three methods of sampling are intended only to minimize the effects of common origin and diffusion. A simple procedure may be used to check the success of the sampling strategy chosen. The world sample may be divided into the six major regions and the hypothesis retested within each region. If the magnitude and direction of the functional relationship being investigated is reasonably comparable for each of these subtests, it is unlikely that it can be attributed to some single accident of history.

In two instances (Whiting and Child, 1953; Landauer and Whiting, 1964) when the above test was applied, the magnitude of the correlations was substantially the same for each regional subtest and thus the functional rather than a historical interpretation was supported.

Sometimes such a subtest cannot be performed because of the geographic distribution of the variables involved. A study by Barry, Child, and Bacon (1959) will serve to illustrate this point. They presented evidence on the basis of a world sample in support of the hypothesis that, in societies where the subsistence economy emphasizes the accumulation of food supplies, compliance rather than assertiveness is emphasized in child rearing. As indicated in Table 1, the absence of cases makes a test impossible for the effect of differences in extremes in accumulation in Africa, Circum-Mediterranean, and East Eurasia. Likewise, such a test is impossible for cases contrasting intermediate accumulation in Africa, Circum-Mediterranean, East Eurasia, and South America. Furthermore, only for the intermediate contrast in the Insular Pacific does the number of cases approach adequacy. It is evident that, for variables unequally distributed over the world in the original sample, this strategy cannot be used in such a way as to provide an adequate contrast in the values for the independent variable.

Whenever either the regional continental subtests or a retest maximizing historical effects fails to reject a historical interpretation, it is suggested that one

TABLE 1

THE DISTRIBUTION OF CASES BY REGIONS
IN THE BARRY, CHILD, AND BACON (1959) SAMPLE

	Extremes in accumulation		*Intermediate in accumulation*	
Regions	High (animal husbandry)	Low (hunting, fishing)	High (agriculture only)	Low (agriculture, hunting, fishing)
Africa	15	0	3	0
Circum-Mediterranean	0	0	0	0
East Eurasia	2	0	0	0
Insular Pacific	3	3	7	11
North America	1	16	5	4
South America	2	3	0	3

of the methods described by Naroll or D'Andrade (see above) be used, since these enable a direct estimate of the effects of diffusion and common origins.

Eggan's (1954) method of "controlled comparison," although based on a strategy of replication on sets of cases known to be historically related, differs from the method described above in that no test on a world sample is suggested. Eggan wrote (pp. 747–748):

My own preference is for the utilization of the comparative method on a smaller scale and with as much control over the frame of comparison as it is possible to secure. It has seemed natural to utilize regions of relatively homogeneous culture or to work within social or cultural types, and to further control the ecology and the historical factors so far as it is possible to do so. Radcliffe-Brown has done this with great skill in *The Social Organization of Australian Tribes* (1931). After comparing Australian moiety structures and finding their common denominators, I would prefer to make a comparison with the results of a similar study of moiety structures and associated practices of the Indians of Southern California, who approximate rather closely the Australian sociocultural situation. The results of this comparison could then be matched against comparable studies of Northwest Coast and other similar moiety systems and the similarities and differences systematically examined by the method of concomitant variation.

Although Eggan's suggestion has been commended in principle, no one to my knowledge has carried out such a series of controlled comparisons. It is hoped that this might soon be remedied, since the method has considerable merit, particularly when cultural change or historical process is one of the variables under consideration.

There are some drawbacks to the method of controlled comparison. First, there are not enough cases in many of the sets of cultures known to be historically related to adequately jeopardize a hypothesis. It is impossible to reject a null hypothesis by statistical procedures with fewer than six cases, and it is difficult with fewer than 30. If, then, the method of controlled comparison were used only in those culture areas where 30 cases are available, the results would be biased in favor of highly fissionable cultures. Second, the sequential strategy suggested by Eggan might lead to a definition of variables appropriate to the first area studied but not to the second. If this were the case, true replication would be impossible. Only if the variables are defined transculturally can results from two culture areas be compared.

A powerful strategy is to test a hypothesis both on a world sample that is intended to minimize historical effects and on a series of controlled comparison samples in which historical effects are both known and maximized. Such a strategy tends to cancel the error inherent in each method if used alone. The validity of any hypothesis that can stand such double jeopardy is greatly enhanced.

TRANSCULTURAL DEFINITION OF VARIABLES

Having decided upon the nature of the unit that will constitute the cases in his study, and having decided upon his sample, the cross-cultural researcher must decide upon the nature of the variables and the type of codes that he is to use.

They must be such that material will be available to make reliable judgments on the basis of available ethnographic reports and they must relate to transcultural dimensions.

The physical environment in which people live can, of course, be directly compared by objective measures such as mean annual temperature, rainfall, soil type, and types and distribution of flora and fauna. Demographic facts such as birth and death rates, the incidence of diseases of various kinds, as well as facts of descriptive somatology—height, weight, skin color, hair form, cephalic index, and blood type—may be objectively described, and societies can easily be compared on such variables. When the physical environment has been modified and shaped into tools, utensils, and other items of material culture, these items can also be described in transcultural dimensions such as shape, size, color, and the type of materials used. Thus the coding of the environment or of material things presents no problems, provided the data are available.

The coding of customary behavior is somewhat more difficult. Ford (1937), on the basis of an analysis of the possible methods for coding technology, suggested that there are a limited number of motor habits such as cutting, hammering, lashing, plaiting, etc., involved in the production of artifacts. He pointed out that the *uses* that artifacts are put to are limited in number and can be objectively coded. Examples are hooks for fishing, sheds for sheltering animals, pots for cooking, etc. As he said (1966, p. 90), "To make a cup that will hold water out of a coconut is the same problem everywhere, and the ways to solve it are limited by the laws of physics and chemistry and the particular nature of coconuts and water."

It is in the realm of culture defined as shared meanings, beliefs, and values that the problem of defining and measuring transcultural variables becomes more difficult. Clocks and yardsticks no longer suffice. Long ago anthropologists noted that cultures differed in the way kinsmen were classified (Morgan, 1871) and such differences were often used as an illustration of the relativity of culture. Anthropologists were warned not to take it for granted that if an informant introduced him to his "brother" this meant that he was a son of the same father. In fact, the genealogical method (Rivers, 1910) was developed for the purpose of eliciting an accurate native code for kinsmen. More recently, a group of anthropologists who call themselves "ethnoscientists" have been engaged in developing techniques for discovering and accurately describing native codes in other domains. (For a summary of this work, see Sturtevant, 1964.)

Were these native codes unique to each culture, cross-cultural comparison would be impossible. Happily this is not the case. Again it was in the realm of kinship that the problem was first solved. Kroeber (1909) noted that, although there were many different ways in which peoples classified their kinsmen, a limited number of attributes were used to do so. These attributes were biological, such as sex and age, or genealogical, such as lineal, collateral, and affinal; and thus, no matter how they were combined in a given structure, they provided a transcultural bridge for comparison. (Ethnoscientists refer to such attributes as *etic*, from "phonetic," in contrast to a category in a native code which they refer to as *emic*, from "phonemic.")

Once this fact was established, it was discovered that although these attributes could yield a huge number of systems there were in fact a very limited number actually reported. Thus it became evident that a second basis for comparison was possible, that of structural types.

A recent cross-cultural study of kin terms for siblings (Nerlove and Romney, in press) illustrates the above two bases of comparison very clearly. From an analysis of a sample of 250 societies, Nerlove and Romney discovered that but three attributes were used; the sex of the sibling, the sex of the sibling relative to that of the speaker, and the age of the sibling relative to that of the speaker. Thus cultures can be compared on the basis of whether or not any one of these attributes is used as a basis of classification. Our two-term system, for example, used only the first, the sex of the sibling, as a criterion for classification.

The three attributes of sex, relative sex, and relative age yield eight distinct relationships: male to younger male sibling; male to older male sibling; male to younger female sibling, etc. It was pointed out by the authors that, logically, these eight relationships could be combined in 4140 distinct structures. If all of these had an equal probability of occurring, it would take a much larger sample than the number of reported cultures to make any comparison among them. General principles of cognitive coherence, however, rule out most of the theoretically possible structures and, in fact, over 90 percent of the structures for coding siblings reported in their sample fell into but twelve types, most of which occurred in a sufficient number of instances that comparison at the structural level was possible.

Kinship is by no means the only domain in which peoples all over the world have hit upon the same attributes for building a taxonomy and in which the resulting structures are limited in number. Succession, inheritance, and descent, patterns of residence, political and economic structures, and even myth and ritual have these characteristics, and cultures may be compared in these domains either on the basis of a single relevant attribute or on the basis of identical structures.

CODING PROCEDURES

For the most part, the coding procedures used in cross-cultural research are the same as those used in social psychology. There are some peculiarities of ethnographic data that lead to special problems.

When one is using a presence-absence code, it is often difficult to decide between "absent" and "nonascertainable." Ethnographies seldom state explicitly that a given trait or custom is absent or never occurs. If they included a listing of all the potential beliefs and practices which did *not* occur, as well as those which did, the bulk of the monograph would consist of negative evidence, since any one society has but a small fraction of the total number of customs that may be found throughout the world.

How should societies for which there is no mention of a particular trait be treated? Can it be assumed that the trait is absent if it is not mentioned, or should these societies be omitted on the basis of inadequate information? The latter solution is the more conservative and, as a rule of thumb, should generally be followed. Otherwise one may obtain a spurious positive correlation which reflects only differences in the adequacy of ethnographic coverage. That is, both traits would tend not to be reported more frequently in the poorly covered tribes than in the well-covered tribes.

The practice of always omitting cases with no information, however, often reduces the number of cases so that an adequate test cannot be made. To overcome these difficulties it is suggested, in instances where a presence-absence or a frequency scale is used, that a distinction be made between (1) those societies in which no mention is made of a particular custom, but the context in which such a custom normally occurs is described in detail, and (2) those societies in which the appropriate context is not described. The former can be scored as *inferred absence,* whereas the latter can be scored as not ascertainable and the case omitted. Thus, for example, if one is interested in "bloodletting" and finds no mention of this practice in an ethnography which has a complete and detailed description of medical theory and therapeutic techniques, it could be fairly safely assumed that the practice was either absent or quite unimportant. If, however, there was no discussion of medical practices at all, it would be much safer and more appropriate to omit the case.

When one is coding a domain in which structure types such as those described above can be isolated, the problem of judging absence does not pertain. Every case must be classed as using one or another of the structures isolated. Thus, if it were determined that descent systems were either patrilineal, matrilineal, or ambilineal, and if the features of these three structures were properly specified, each case would have to be coded as having one or another of these structures or omitted—this assumes, of course, that the three structural types defined are indeed exhaustive.

Two standard methods have been found useful for the coding of cultural rules. One of them, developed by Murdock (Ethnographic Atlas, Vol. 1, No. 1), is designed to distinguish between *prescriptive rules* (those with no alternative) and *preferred rules* (where there is an explicit and common alternative permitted under the rules of the culture). For example, in coding the rules for postmarital residence (Ethnographic Atlas, Vol. 1, No. 1), a "V" designates a prescriptive rule for virilocal residence; that is, a newly married couple is expected to establish their household in or near that of the groom's parents. A coding of "Vu" indicates that although virilocal residence is preferred, uxorilocal residence, the establishment of a household near the bride's parents, is a permitted, though less preferred, alternative. This system does not permit scoring a society where virilocal and uxorilocal residence are both equally important.

A somewhat more fine-grained scoring system is sometimes more appropriate for estimating the rigidity of cultural rules. This has been used with reasonably high reliability to measure the rules regarding premarital sex (Goethals and Whiting, n.d.). The code is based on the fact that a given type of behavior, such as residence or premarital sex, may in any given community be either proscribed or prohibited; disapproved of, preferred, or prescribed; or that there are no rules governing such behavior. Such a scale for cultural rules may be generalized in the following form:

0. *X (the behavior in question) is prohibited, proscribed, or taboo. Strong negative sanctions are brought to bear on those who deviate.*

1. *X is disapproved. Weak negative sanctions against deviation.*

2. *X is permitted but neither approved nor disapproved. Members of the community react with indifference with regard to its occurrence.*

3. *X is preferred or approved. Alternatives are disapproved.*

4. *X is prescribed. Failure to perform X leads to strong negative sanction.*

There are several advantages to such a scale. In the first place, it permits the use of parametric tests whenever the scores for the sample are appropriately distributed. It also permits a median division of the scores for nonparametric tests.

Behavioral frequency scales, rather than rule-rigidity scales, have also been used in cross-cultural research. Such scales take the general form of *always, usually, half the time, sometimes, never.* As stated above, because of limitation in the size of the population of local communities, such scales are inappropriate for any behavior that occurs infrequently. When a frequency scale is used in such instances, it is usually based on the statements of informants rather than the direct observations of the ethnographer. Sometimes such data can be taken as reasonably reliable; more often, little confidence can be placed in frequency statements based on informant reports. It should be noted that the *never* rating on a frequency scale runs into the problem of distinguishing between such a rating and *nonascertainable.*

It is particularly dangerous to code private behavior on a frequency scale. The statement that parents never punish their children, often found in early ethnographies, should be treated with considerable skepticism. It is often more probable that the ethnographer never saw a parent punish a child because of a cultural rule that children should not be punished in public, and especially not before strangers.

On the other hand, for public events, a frequency code may be both reliable and appropriate. Suicide and homicide rates (Naroll, 1962), the frequency of theft and personal crime (Bacon, Child, and Barry, 1963), and divorce rates (Ackerman, 1963) are appropriate when adequate records over a sufficient time span are available.

For some variables, especially those for which ethnographic evidence is scanty, it is tempting to construct a code combining a rules scale and a frequency scale. The low point on such a scale might be "X is prohibited and/or never occurs." Such a scale presumes a greater isomorphism between rules and behavior than is warranted, and is not recommended.

For coding beliefs, values, and techniques, a system by which alternatives can be ranked or rated is most appropriate. In such a code the alternatives are listed and an estimate of the proportion of times each alternative occurs in a given context is required. The Atlas (Ethnographic Atlas, Vol. 1, No. 1) code for subsistence economy is a good example. The alternative subsistence techniques of hunting, gathering, fishing, animal husbandry, and agriculture are listed, and an estimate of the proportion of food produced by each technique is made for each culture on a ten-point scale.

To estimate the importance of sorcery, B. Whiting (1950) coded beliefs in this manner. She listed the various beliefs about the cause of death, such as gods, ghosts, witches, and natural causes. The proportion of death attributed to witchcraft provided an index of the salience of this belief in each culture. Whiting and Child (1953) used a similar method for coding the explanations for illness.

For judging emotions, intensity scales are usually most appropriate. Here some description which specifies appropriate indices of intensity of fear, anger, joy, etc., should be made. The degree of emotional disturbance at weaning in the example cited at the beginning of the chapter specified prolonged crying and the occurrence of temper tantrums as indices of a high degree of this emotional state. Ratings of socialization anxiety made by Whiting and Child (1953) are another example of this type of rating.

Often a composite or overall scale formed by combining subscales in some manner is desirable. There are several acceptable techniques for doing this. In cases where there are theoretically meaningful alternative indices of some variable, each of which is of rare occurrence, these may be combined into a complex index which estimates that the variable is present if any one of the indices is present, and absent if none of them is judged to be present. This assumes, of course, that the indices are alternative rather than cumulative. The Landauer and Whiting (1964) index of infant stress exemplifies this procedure. Infant stress was judged to be present in any culture if it was reported that the skins of children under the age of two were customarily pierced, either by inoculation, circumcision, ear piercing, nose piercing, lip piercing, cutting or burning of tribal marks and the like, or if the practice of moulding the head or limbs by daily manipulation were present.

A cumulative composite index may be constructed simply by adding the raw or weighted scores of subscales. It is desirable in constructing such an index to present a matrix of intercorrelations showing the relation between the variables to be combined. Naroll's (1962) composite index of cultural stress consisted of the following four frequency scales: drunken brawling, defiant homicide, protest suicide, and witchcraft attribution. As an empirical justification for combining these items, he showed that they are all positively related to one another to a reasonable degree.

Factor analysis is, of course, another method of arriving at a composite index. Sawyer and LeVine (1966) have nicely illustrated the value of this method in cross-cultural research. They used 30 scales of 565 societies published in the World Ethnographic Sample (Murdock, 1957) that estimate the basic economic and social structure of each society. Their factor analysis indicated that these 30 scores could be reasonably reduced to ten factor scores. Prothro (1960) has reduced the child-rearing scores of the Whiting and Child study (1953) by factor-analytic procedures.

Guttman scales have been used effectively in a number of cross-cultural studies. Stephens (1962) was the first to use such a method in cross-cultural research. He demonstrated that the following items relating to the extensiveness of menstrual taboos were scalable: menstrual huts, menstrual cooking taboo, many other menstrual taboos, both menstrual sex taboo and belief that menstrual blood is dangerous. Thus, if it was reported for any culture that women were isolated in special huts during menstruation, one could with high confidence predict that each of the other practices was present in that culture. Young and Backayan (1965) have constructed a revised menstruation scale that has higher reproducibility than Stephens' original one. Young (1965) has also shown that "dramatic sex-role recognition" as a feature of male initiation rites and "community-nation articulation" as a feature of social rigidity can be successfully scaled. The scaling of cultural features such as these provides one of the most elegant methods of measuring variables in cross-cultural research.

Sometimes, when two or more independent variables are found to be related to some dependent variable, it is theoretically desirable to measure the distinctive effects of each rather than to combine them into a composite index or scale. When nonparametric scores are used, a simple method consists of dichotomizing the sample on the first independent variable and testing the relation between the second independent variable and the third. The data may be presented in a table taking the following form:

Independent variables		*Dependent variable*		
I	II	III		
		Absent	Present	
Present	Present			A
	Absent			B
Absent	Present			C
	Absent			D
		X	Y	

$P(AB \cdot XY = \quad)$; $P(CD \cdot XY = \quad)$; $P(AC \cdot XY = \quad)$; $P(BD \cdot XY = \quad)$

When such an analysis is made it is sometimes the case, for example, that variable II is related to variable III if and only if variable I is present. Thus, the fear of ghosts at funerals (Whiting, 1959) was found to be related both to low parental indulgence in infancy and to the punishment for aggression in later childhood. When an interaction analysis of the above type was made, however, the relation between punishment for aggression and the fear of ghosts was indicated only in societies low in infant indulgence. Some form of analysis of variance or covariance provides a more elegant statistical analysis of three or more variables. This is particularly recommended when the variables are continuous and normally distributed rather than nonparametric.

To present only the first-order effects of a set of variables on a dependent variable is misleading and incomplete. Unless some interaction analysis such as those described above is carried out, there is no way of determining how many independent relationships have been discovered. Murdock (1964a), for example, showed significant relationships between attitudes toward premarital sex and the level of subsistence economy, technological development, demography, level of political organization, system of descent, and religion. Although his interpretation that all these independent variables are an index of cultural development or complexity is probably correct, it would have been more convincing had he shown the interaction between them.

The requirement of establishing the reliability of the coded judgments to be used is familiar to psychologists and need not be detailed here. There are, however, some special problems in cross-cultural research involving coder bias. Although in many of the early cross-cultural studies the coding of both the independent and the dependent variables was done by the investigator himself, this is clearly not a good practice. Bias can hardly be avoided, despite honest and objective efforts by the investigator. To lean over backwards by coding all doubtful cases against your theory produces as great an error as unconsciously coding to favor the hypothesis. If one's budget does not permit hiring different judges to code the independent and dependent variables, it is expedient to search the cross-cultural literature to discover whether there are ratings already available that might provide a reasonable index of one or another of the variables in the hypothesis to be tested. As an aid to this procedure, studies with published ratings are starred in the bibliography. If an appropriate code is discovered, the sample may be drawn in such a way as to make use of such ratings, thus avoiding bias if the judge rating the other variable remains ignorant of the published judgments.

Even if care is taken to prevent bias by making use of already coded material, because of the limited number of cases that have been adequately described for problems involving psychological anthropology, these cases will be drawn in sample after sample. Anyone familiar with the subject then soon becomes familiar with many of the characteristics of the Navaho and the Zuni, the Ashanti and the Arapesh, the Samoans, and the Copper Eskimo. With this familiarity, he can hardly make a completely unbiased judgment on any feature of these cultures. The use of completely naive judges is one way out of this dilemma if the judgments do not necessitate a technical knowledge of the vocabulary of anthropology. To abstract relevant materials on cards with references on the back and occurrences of the tribal name in the text deleted is another precaution that may be followed.

If it is necessary for an investigator who has a wide ethnographic knowledge to do the coding himself on certain variables, it is suggested that, as a minimal check for bias, a naive judge code at least a part of the total sample. Then, as a technique of quality control, the cases in which there is disagreement between the investigator and the naive judge should be examined. If the investigator's judgments either favor or disfavor his theory to a significant extent, he will be warned of his bias and can take appropriate steps to remedy it.

Problems of reliability and bias are not restricted to coding. As Naroll (1962) pointed out in his excellent monograph on quality control in cross-cultural research, informants may be ignorant or deceiving and ethnographers may use inappropriate or inadequate techniques. This had long been suspected, but no systematic way of correcting for it had been developed before Naroll presented his ingenious method. He listed the possible sources of bias in the collecting and reporting of ethnographic data. The consideration of the following may produce questionable evidence (1962, pp. 14–15):

1. *Documentation of statements by case reports.*
2. *Use of participant observation.*
3. *Length of stay in the community.*
4. *Familiarity with the native language.*
5. *Professional status of ethnographer.*
6. *Explicitness and generality of reports.*

Having judged each ethnographic report on these six items, Naroll proceeded to correlate them with the scores on his four substantive variables: drunken brawling, defiant homicide, protest suicide, and witchcraft attribution. A high and statistically significant correlation between any substantive variable and a quality-control variable suggested a dangerous degree of contamination. For example, there was a correlation of 0.86 between the length of time the ethnographer stayed in the field and the rating his report yielded on the degree of witchcraft attribution. This error may even be malignant (that is, produce spuriously biased results) if the ethnographer's length of stay is also related to the other variables under investigation. At least it introduces an uncomfortable degree of error variance.

Naroll's quality-control procedures enable one to solve the often difficult problem of whether or not a case should be omitted because of inadequate reporting. If too high standards are set, sample size shrinks rapidly. On the other hand, if questionably reported cases are included, one runs the danger of unreliability and possible bias. Quality-control procedures suggest that one start with questionable cases included in the sample and, for each substantive variable, set a standard for adequacy of report high enough that the correlation between the substantive variable and the control variable disappears.

A quality-control variable in addition to the six suggested by Naroll turned out to be important in a cross-cultural study by George Goethals and myself on the frequency of premarital sex (Goethals and Whiting, n.d.). We were surprised by the high incidence of tribes in North America that had strict rules against sexual behavior before marriage. This was not predicted by hypotheses which were confirmed in the other regions of the world. In searching for an explanation, it occurred to us that, more than elsewhere in the world, reports on the Indians of North America were carried out by historically oriented anthropologists who used informants to tell them about the customs of the past. To test this notion we constructed a quality-control scale which consisted of the number of years between the ethnographic present, as coded in the Ethnographic Atlas, and the date of field work. This scale produced a high and statistically significant positive correlation with the strictness of rules against premarital sex. Thus old informants agreed that rules were restrictive when they were young. Apparently the feeling that youths are seen as enjoying greater sexual freedom than the previous generation has some cross-cultural generality. In any case, this quality control enabled us to treat retrospective reports by old informants differently from contemporary accounts.

Even after the cross-cultural investigator has decided upon his unit, drawn his sample, constructed his codes and established their reliability, performed adequate quality controls, and made appropriate statistical tests of his hypothesis, he still has to interpret his results. Since cross-cultural studies are of necessity based on correlational methods, the comparativist, as he is often told, cannot be sure that the discovered relationship between variables is not an artifact of the association of one or both of them with some other variable. If Goethals and I had concluded that the apparently strict rules against premarital sexual behavior among the Indians of North America were the outcome of the sex attitudes of the Indians rather than of retrospective interviewing, we would probably have been in error. It should be noted, however, that statistical analysis alone did not tell us this. We accepted the latter interpretation because it seemed more plausible to us. Plausibility is, in fact, the most common basis for accepting or rejecting an interpretation of a cross-cultural finding.

Sometimes plausibility seems fairly satisfactory. In a recent study it was shown (Whiting, 1964b) that husbands and wives generally sleep in the same bed if the temperature drops below 30 degrees Fahrenheit in the winter, but in separate beds in warmer climates. The interpretation that temperature influences sleeping arrangements is more plausible than the reverse. It is rather unlikely that sleeping arrangements cause it to be cold outside.

The relative plausibility of two alternative interpretations may not be so intuitively evident as in the above case. For example, Cohen (1966) suggested an alternative to an explanation offered by Landauer and Whiting (1964) for one of the factors related to human growth. In a cross-cultural study these latter authors discovered a statistically significant positive association between the occurrence of physical stress in infancy and the adult stature of males. They interpreted these findings as supporting the hypothesis that early stress enhances growth. Cohen's alternative is as follows (pp. 355–356):

The range in stature in any given population is due primarily to dietary factors: taller stature in adults and emotional stress during infancy tend to covary with each other because, I hypothesize, infants and children who are subject to considerable stress will eat more, as one means of coping with their anxiety.

To the layman, Cohen's hypothesis would in all probability seem more plausible since there is a widely accepted belief that, as Cohen states, "the range in stature in any given population is due primarily to dietary factors." It is difficult to account for the prevalence and wide acceptance of this belief. The scientifically verified evidence for the belief indicates that diet has a permanent effect on stature only under conditions of extreme malnutrition. Tanner (1962), summarizing the research on this problem, wrote (pp. 121–123):

... malnutrition during childhood delays growth, and malnutrition in the years preceding adolescence delays the appearance of the adolescent spurt. ... Both animals and man, however, have great recuperative powers provided the adverse conditions are not carried too far or continued too long. ... Severe malnutrition prolonged throughout a large part of the growth period may cause some permanent stunting but even in these circumstances the powers of recuperation, at least of rats, are remarkable.

Perhaps belief that nutrition is a primary determinant of normal growth derives from cases of severe malnutrition, or perhaps it is generalized from a knowledge of the importance of fertilizer for the growth of plants.

On the other hand, a large number of recent animal studies have repeatedly shown that (Levine, 1960, p. 80)

... In all respects, in fact, the manipulated infants exhibit a more rapid rate of development. They open their eyes earlier and achieve motor coordination sooner. Their body hair grows faster, and they tend to be significantly heavier at weaning. They continue to gain weight more rapidly than the nonstimulated animals even after the course of stimulation has been completed at three weeks of age. Their more vigorous growth does not seem to be related to food intake but to better utilization of the food consumed and probably to a higher output of the somatotrophic (growth) hormone from the pituitary.

In the light of the supporting evidence, the Landauer-Whiting interpretation gains in relative plausibility over the Cohen interpretation. This is not to say that the former explanation is right and the latter wrong, but it does suggest that, in cross-cultural research, supporting evidence for an interpretation is especially important—much more so than when experimental control is possible.

The plausibility of an interpretation may also be increased by putting it in further jeopardy. Roberts, Sutton-Smith, and Kendon (1963) have used such a method, which they aptly label *subsystem validation,* in a series of studies of the function of games. Following up two previous cross-cultural studies (Roberts *et al.,* 1959; Roberts and Sutton-Smith, 1962), they found a relationship between the number of games of strategy reported for a culture and a judgment as to the degree to which parents of that culture required obedience in their children. They also found an association between games of chance and reward for responsibility, and between games of physical skill and regard for achievement. The subsystem validation consisted of a questionnaire given to 1900 American schoolchildren asking their preference for each item in a list of common games. Girls, who were reported (Sears, Maccoby, and Levin, 1957) in American culture to be more strongly rewarded than boys for both obedience and responsibility, preferred both games of chance and strategy. Boys, with greater rewards for achievement, preferred games of physical skill. This replication lends considerable support to the authors' interpretation of their cross-cultural findings.

Where the effects of child rearing on adult personality are being investigated, subsystem validation is sometimes difficult. If one is lucky, longitudinal data are both appropriate and available, but the possibility of this being the case is limited to a few problems. Retrospective estimates of child rearing derived from adults are notoriously unreliable, but sometimes a sufficiently objective one may be found. Carlsmith (1964), in a subsystem validation of the Burton and Whiting (1961) interpretation of the cross-cultural finding of a relation between male initiation rites and the salience of the father in infancy, was able to obtain from college students a presumably reliable report as to whether their fathers were overseas in World War II during their infancy. When methods such as these are impossible, the immediate effect of the independent variable on the child rather than on the adult can often reasonably be assumed. Stress in infancy, if it is to predict differences in adult stature, can be measured in growth rate during childhood. Gunders and Whiting (1964) used this strategy in a subsystem validation of the Landauer-Whiting (1964) cross-cultural findings. D'Andrade (1962) used a battery of psychological tests of children brought up in father-absent and father-present homes as a subsystem validation of the Burton-Whiting (1961) interpretation of male initiation rites.

An intensive psychological investigation of adults who vary in the degree to which they practice some custom used as a cross-cultural index variable provides another possible technique of subsystem validation. Munroe (1964) was able to find a sample of Black Carib males who varied in the degree to which they practiced the couvade. By appropriate tests and interviews he was able to show that the high couvaders had feminine characteristics and thus support his interpretation of the couvade in a cross-cultural study that he had previously carried out.

Sometimes it is expedient to reverse the order of cross validation by undertaking a cross-cultural investigation to test an interpretation of a within-culture study. B. Whiting (1950) made a detailed analysis of the function of sorcery among the Paiute, a hunting and gathering tribe in the Great Basin. She showed that sorcery was used as a means of social control and made the interpretation that this was necessitated by the lack of chiefs or judges with the authority to deal with crime. She was able to support this interpretation by a cross-cultural study which showed sorcery to be more important in cultures without a system of delegated authority. LeVine (1962) and Whiting *et al.* (1966b) have used a similar strategy. This procedure of making a cross-cultural test of a hypothesis clearly formulated and explicitly derived from an intensive within-culture study has a great advantage in plausibility over *post hoc* interpretations of a cross-cultural finding.

A warning should be issued, especially to anyone undertaking cross-cultural research who plans to use scores from the Ethnographic Atlas or other published sources. Unless he is very familiar with ethnographic literature, the code descriptions are seldom explicit enough to enable a sufficient operational understanding of the variables being measured. It is strongly recommended that, before interpreting their meaning, he consult the ethnographic sources and score at least a subsample on the basis of the published code description.

Most of the above suggestions apply to any research involving the use of correlational methods. They spring from the general caveats and rules governing proper scientific inquiry. That they may be appropriately applied to the comparative study of human societies and cultures is a basic assumption made in this essay. I do not share the pessimism expressed by Professor Evans-Pritchard (1963) in his essay on the comparative method, that little of value has been discovered in the past by this method or indeed can be in the near future. Even though he implies that anthropology has been and probably should be more humanistic than scientific, he agrees that we should not cease "to look for such regularities as can be established by various forms of the comparative method. It would be a great convenience if we were to succeed in finding them. If we do not, we shall at least in the search have achieved a deeper understanding of human society." It is the purport of this chapter that the pursuit of comparative methods such as the one discussed here will yield something more than "convenient regularities and a deeper understanding of human society," and that it is one of the methods by which the scientific laws governing humans and their behavior can be established. It provides one more way in which our presumptions and prejudices may be put in jeopardy.

BIBLIOGRAPHICAL INFORMATION

There are two exceedingly valuable sources for anyone undertaking a cross-cultural investigation. First is the Human Relations Area Files. This consists of the materials from the major sources on a world sample of some 200 societies distributed paragraph by paragraph in appropriate categories as defined in the *Outline of Cultural Materials* (Murdock *et al.*, 1965). These materials are not coded or abstracted but are copies of the original text. In addition, foreign-language texts have been translated and both the original and the translation made available. A reasonably complete annotated bibliography is also provided for each society. Although the processing of this material is carried out by the Human Relations Area Files, P. O. Box 2054, 755 Prospect Street, New Haven, Connecticut, under the direction of C. S. Ford, this is an interuniversity cooperative venture and complete copies of the files are available for research use at each of the member institutions, which at present are:

> University of Chicago
> University of Colorado
> Cornell University
> Harvard University
> University of Hawaii
> University of Illinois
> Indiana University
> State University of Iowa
> Kyoto University
> Maison des Sciences de l'Homme, Paris
> University of Michigan
> State University of New York at Buffalo

University of North Carolina
University of Oklahoma
University of Pennsylvania
University of Pittsburgh
Princeton University
Smithsonian Institution
University of Southern California
Southern Illinois University
University of Utah
University of Washington
Yale University

Microfilm copies of the files on 112 societies are more widely available. Microfilm subscribers as of March 1966 are as follows:

University of Alaska; College, Alaska
University of Alberta, Calgary; Calgary, Alberta, Canada
Antioch College; Yellow Springs, Ohio
Brandeis University; Waltham, Massachusetts
Brigham Young University; Provo, Utah
University of British Columbia; Vancouver, British Columbia, Canada
University of California; Davis, California
University of California, Los Angeles; Los Angeles, California
University of California; Santa Barbara, California
Carleton College; Northfield, Minnesota
Catholic University of Nijmegen; Nijmegen, Holland
Columbia University; New York, New York
University of Connecticut; Storrs, Connecticut
Dalhousie University; Halifax, Nova Scotia, Canada
Dartmouth College; Hanover, New Hampshire
Dickinson College; Carlisle, Pennsylvania
University of Florida; Gainesville, Florida
Florida Atlantic University; Boca Raton, Florida
Florida State University; Tallahassee, Florida
Franklin and Marshall College; Lancaster, Pennsylvania
University of Goteborg; Goteborg, Sweden
University of Guelph; Guelph, Ontario, Canada
University of Heidelberg; Heidelberg, Germany
Hunter College; New York, New York
Indian School of International Studies; New Delhi, India
Institute of Asian Economic Affairs; Tokyo, Japan
University of Kansas; Lawrence, Kansas
University of Kentucky; Lexington, Kentucky
Korea University; Seoul, Korea
Louisiana State University; Baton Rouge, Louisiana
University of Louisville; Louisville, Kentucky
McMaster University; Hamilton, Ontario, Canada
University of Maryland; College Park, Maryland
University of Massachusetts; Amherst, Massachusetts
Memorial University of Newfoundland; St. John's, Newfoundland, Canada
Michigan State University; East Lansing, Michigan

University of Minnesota; Minneapolis, Minnesota
University of Missouri; Columbia, Missouri
Missouri State Library; Jefferson City, Missouri
University of Montreal; Montreal, Canada
National Library of Nigeria; Lagos, Nigeria
National Museum of Canada; Ottawa, Ontario, Canada
University of New Hampshire; Durham, New Hampshire
New York Public Library; New York, New York
New York University; New York, New York
State University of New York at Albany; Albany, New York
State University of New York at Stony Brook; Stony Brook, New York
Ohio State University; Columbus, Ohio
University of Oregon; Eugene, Oregon
Pennsylvania State University; University Park, Pennsylvania
Portland State College; Portland, Oregon
Purdue University; Lafayette, Indiana
University of Queensland; Brisbane, Queensland, Australia
Rice University; Houston, Texas
University of Saarlandes; Saarbrucken, Germany
Saint Louis University; Saint Louis, Missouri
San Diego State College; San Diego, California
Stanford University; Palo Alto, California
Syracuse University; Syracuse, New York
Temple University; Philadelphia, Pennsylvania
Tohoku University; Sendai City, Japan
University of Tokyo; Tokyo, Japan
University of Toronto; Toronto, Ontario, Canada
U.S. Army Human Engineering Laboratories; Aberdeen Proving Ground, Maryland
Washington State University; Pullman, Washington
Washington University; Saint Louis, Missouri
University of Western Ontario; London, Ontario, Canada
University of Wisconsin, Milwaukee; Milwaukee, Wisconsin

By far the most extensive source of coded materials is to be found in the Ethnographic Atlas. Prepared and published by G. P. Murdock and the associate editors of *Ethnology: an International Journal of Cultural and Social Anthropology,* put out by the University of Pittsburgh Press under Murdock's editorship, it appears cumulatively in each issue of the journal from Vol. I, No. 1 (which appeared in January 1962) to the present. By April, 1966 (Vol. V, No. 2) over 900 societies had been listed and over 100 codes defined. These codes define, as well as the regional and culture-area identification for each tribe, many of the essential features of the economic, social, and political structure of a culture. The scores for these codes, when sufficient data are available, are listed for each society on most of these codes. In addition, the major bibliographical reference is presented for each case.

There are in addition a number of published sources for codes and scores which, although they are on considerably smaller samples, are also useful to consult if they are topically relevant. Studies which contain original scores for a world-wide sample of at least 25 societies have therefore been indicated by an asterisk preceding the author's name in the References.

REFERENCES

*Ackerman, C. (1963). Affiliations: structural determinants of differential divorce rates. *Amer. J. Sociol., 69,* 13–20.

*Bacon, M. K., H. Barry, I. L. Child, and L. Snyder (1965). A cross-cultural study of drinking: detailed definitions and data. *Quart. J. Stud. Alcohol, 5* (3), 78–111.

*Bacon, M. K., I. L. Child, and H. Barry (1963). A cross-cultural study of correlates of crime. *J. abnorm. soc. Psychol., 66,* 291–300.

*Barry, H., I. L. Child, and M. K. Bacon (1959). Relation of child training to subsistence economy. *Amer. Anthropologist, 61,* 51–63.

Blackwood, B. (1935). *Both sides of Buka Passage.* Oxford: Clarendon Press.

*Brown, Judith K. (1963). A cross-cultural study of female initiation rites. *Amer. Anthropologist, 65,* 837–853.

Burton, R. V., and J. W. M. Whiting (1961). The absent father and cross-sex identity. *Merrill-Palmer Quart., 7* (20), 85–95.

Carlsmith, L. K. (1964). Effect of early father absence on scholastic aptitude. *Harv. educ. Rev., 34* (1), 4–21.

Child, I. L., T. Storm, and J. Veroff (1958). Achievement themes in folktales related to socialization practices. In J. W. Atkinson (Ed.), *Motives in fantasy, action and society.* New York: Van Nostrand.

Cohen, Yehudi A. (1961). Food and its vicissitudes. In Y. A. Cohen (Ed.), *Social structure and personality.* New York: Holt, Rinehart, and Winston.

——— (1964). *The transition from childhood to adolescence.* Chicago: Aldine.

——— (1966). On alternative views of the individual in culture-and-personality studies. *Amer. Anthropologist, 68,* 355–361.

Conklin, H. C. (1964). Ethnogenealogical method. In W. H. Goodenough, *Explorations in cultural anthropology.* New York: McGraw-Hill.

*D'Andrade, R. G. (1961). Anthropological studies of dreams. In F. L. K. Hsu (Ed.), *Psychological anthropology: approaches to culture and personality.* Homewood, Ill.: Dorsey.

——— (1962). Father absence and cross-sex identification. Ph.D. Thesis, Department of Social Relations, Harvard University.

Driver, H. E. (1966). Geographical-historical versus psycho-functional explanations of kin avoidances. *Current Anthropol., 7* (2), 131–182.

Eggan, F. (1954). Social anthropology and the method of controlled comparison. *Amer. Anthropologist, 56,* 743–763.

*Ember, M. (1963). The relationships between economic and political development in non-industrialized societies. *Ethnology, 2,* 228–248.

*Ethnographic atlas. See Murdock (1962, 1963).

Evans-Pritchard, E. E. (1963). *The comparative method in social anthropology.* L. T. Hobhouse Memorial Trust Lecture, No. 33. London: Athlone.

*Fischer, J. L. (1961). Art styles as cognitive maps. *Amer. Anthropologist, 63,* 79–93.

Ford, C. S. (1937). A sample comparative analysis of material culture. In G. P. Murdock (Ed.), *Studies in the science of society.* New Haven: Yale Univ. Press.

*——— (1945). *A comparative study of human reproduction.* New Haven: Yale Univ. Publications in Anthropology, No. 32.

——— (1966). On the analysis of behavior for cross-cultural comparisons. *Behav. Sci. Notes, 1* (2), 79–97.

*Ford, C. S., and F. A. Beach (1957). *Patterns of sexual behavior.* New York: Harper and Row.

Frake, C. O. (1962). The ethnographic study of cognitive systems. In T. Gladwin and W. C. Sturtevant (Eds.), *Anthropology and human behavior.* Washington, D.C.: Anthropological Society of Washington. Pp. 72–85, 91–93.

*Freeman, L. C., and R. F. Winch (1957). Societal complexity: an empirical test of a typology of societies. *Amer. J. Sociol., 57,* 641–666.

Glacken, C. J. (1953). Studies of Okinawan life. Report No. 4, Pacific Science Board, National Research Council. (Mimeo)

Goethals, G., and J. W. M. Whiting (n.d.). A cross-cultural study of premarital sex. Research in progress, Harvard University.

Goodenough, W. H. (1957). Cultural anthropology and linguistics. In Paul L. Garvin (Ed.), *Report of the seventh annual round-table meeting on linguistics and language study* (Monograph Series in Languages and Linguistics, No. 9). Washington, D.C.: Georgetown Univ. Press.

Gunders, J. N., and J. W. M. Whiting (1964). The effects of periodic separation from the mother during infancy upon growth and development. Paper presented at International Congress of Anthropological and Ethnological Sciences, Moscow.

*Hobhouse, L. T., G. C. Wheeler, and M. Ginsberg (1915). *The material culture and social institutions of the simpler peoples: an essay in correlation.* London: Chapman and Hall.

*Horton, D. (1943). The functions of alcohol in primitive societies: a cross-cultural study. *Quart. J. Stud. Alcohol, 4* (2), 199–320.

Kroeber, A. H. (1909). Classificatory systems of relationship. *J. Roy. Anthropol. Inst., 39,* 77–84.

*Lambert, W. W., L. Triandis, and M. Wolf (1959). Some correlates of beliefs in the malevolence and benevolence of supernatural beings: a cross-cultural study. *J. abnorm. soc. Psychol., 58,* 162–168.

*Landauer, T. K., and J. W. M. Whiting (1964). Infantile stimulation and adult stature of human males. *Amer. Anthropologist, 66,* 1007–1027.

Landy, D. (1959). *Tropical childhood.* Chapel Hill: Univ. of North Carolina Press.

Leach, E. (1964). Comment on Naroll's "On ethnic unit classification." *Current Anthropol., 5* (4), 299.

LeVine, R. A. (1962). Witchcraft and co-wife proximity in southwestern Kenya. *Ethnology, 1* (1), 39–45.

Levine, S. S. (1960). Stimulation in infancy. *Sci. Amer., 202,* 80–86.

Lévi-Strauss, C. (1963). *Totemism.* Boston: Beacon Press.

Lounsbury, F. G. (1956). A semantic analysis of Pawnee kinship usage. *Language, 34,* 482–491.

Lowie, R. H. (1946). Evolution in cultural anthropology: a reply to Leslie White. *Amer. Anthropologist, 48,* 227–230.

*McClelland, D. C. (1961). *The achieving society.* Princeton, N.J.: Van Nostrand.

*McClelland, D. C., and G. A. Friedman (1952). A cross-cultural study of the relationship between child-training practices and achievement motivation appearing in folktales. In G. E. Swanson, T. M. Newcomb, and E. H. Hartley (Eds.), *Readings in social psychology* (rev. ed.). New York: Henry Holt.

Malinowski, B. (1922). *Argonauts of the western Pacific.* New York: Dutton.

Maretzki, T. W., and H. Maretzki (1966). *Taira: an Okinawan village.* Six Culture Series, Vol. 7. New York: Wiley.

Metzger, D. (1963). Some ethnographic procedures. Paper read at annual meeting of Southwestern Anthropological Association, Riverside, California, April 11–13.

Minturn, L., and J. T. Hitchcock (1966). *The Rājpūts of Khalapur, India.* Six Culture Series, Vol. 3. New York: Wiley.

Morgan, L. H. (1871). *Systems of consanguinity and affinity of the human family.* Smithsonian Contributions to Knowledge, No. 218. Washington, D.C.: Smithsonian Institution. Pp. 10–15.

Munroe, R. L. (1964). Couvade practices of the Black Carib: a psychological study. Ph.D. Thesis, Department of Social Relations, Harvard University.

*Murdock, G. P. (1937). Correlations of matrilineal and patrilineal institutions. In G. P. Murdock, (Ed.), *Studies in the science of society.* New Haven: Yale Univ. Press. Pp. 445–470.

*———— (1949). *Social structure.* New York: Macmillan.

*———— (1953). The processing of anthropological materials. In A. L. Kroeber (Ed.), *Anthropology today.* Chicago: Univ. of Chicago Press.

*———— (1957). World ethnographic sample. *Amer. Anthropologist, 59,* 664–687.

———— (1959). *Africa: its peoples and their culture history.* New York: McGraw-Hill.

*———— (1962). Ethnographic atlas. *Ethnology, 1.*

*———— (1963). Ethnographic atlas. *Ethnology, 5* (1), 249–268.

———— (1964a). Cultural correlates of the regulation of premarital sex behavior. In R. A. Manners (Ed.), *Process and pattern in culture.* Chicago: Aldine.

———— (1964b). Comment on Naroll's "On ethnic unit classification." *Current Anthropol., 5* (4), 301–302.

———— (1964c). Genetic classification of the Austronesian languages: a key to Oceanic culture history. *Ethnology, 3* (2), 117–126.

———— (1966). Cross-cultural sampling. *Ethnology, 5* (1), 97–115.

Murdock, G. P., *et al.* (1963). *Outline of world cultures* (3rd ed.). New Haven: Human Relations Area Files.

Murdock, G. P., *et al.* (1965). *Outline of cultural materials* (4th rev. ed.). New Haven: Human Relations Area Files.

*Nag, M. (1962). *Factors affecting human fertility in non-industrial societies.* New Haven: Yale Univ. Publications in Anthropology, No. 36.

Naroll, R. (1956). A preliminary index of social development. *Amer. Anthropologist, 58,* 687–716.

——— (1961). Two solutions to Galton's Problem. *Philos. Sci., 28,* 15–39.

——— (1962). *Data quality control.* Glencoe, Ill.: Free Press.

——— (1964a). A fifth solution to Galton's Problem. *Amer. Anthropologist, 66,* 863–867.

——— (1964b). On ethnic unit classification. *Current Anthropol., 5* (4), 283–313.

Naroll, R., and R. G. D'Andrade (1963). Two further solutions to Galton's problem. *Amer. Anthropologist, 65,* 1053–1067.

Nerlove, S., and A. K. Romney (in press). Sibling terminology and cross-sex behavior. *Amer. Anthropologist.*

*Nieboer, H. J. (1910). *Slavery as an industrial system* (2nd ed.). The Hague: M. Nijhoff.

Prothro, E. T. (1960). Patterns of permissiveness among preliterate peoples. *J. abnorm. soc. Psychol., 61,* 151–154.

——— (1961). *Child rearing in Lebanon.* Cambridge: Harvard Middle Eastern Monographs, No. 7.

Radcliffe-Brown, A. R. (1931). *The social organization of Australian tribes.* Oceania Monographs, No. 1.

Rivers, W. H. R. (1910). The genealogical method of anthropological inquiry. *Sociol. Rev., 3,* 1–12.

*Roberts, J. M. (1965). Oaths, autonomic ordeals, and power. *Amer. Anthropologist, 67,* 187–212.

*Roberts, J. M., and B. Sutton-Smith (1962). Child training and game involvement. *Ethnology, 1* (2), 166–185.

Roberts, J. M., B. Sutton-Smith, and A. Kendon (1963). Strategy in games and folktales. *J. soc. Psychol., 61,* 185–199.

*Roberts, J. M., *et al.* (1959). Games in culture. *Amer. Anthropologist, 61,* 597–605.

Romney, A. K., and R. G. D'Andrade (1964). Cognitive aspects of English kin terms. *Amer. Anthropologist, 66,* 146–170.

Sapir, E. (1921). *Language: an introduction to the study of speech.* New York: Harcourt, Brace.

Sawyer, J., and R. A. LeVine (1966). Cultural dimensions: a factor analysis of the world ethnographic sample. *Amer. Anthropologist, 68,* 708–731.

Sears, R. R., E. E. Maccoby, and H. Levin (1957). *Patterns of child rearing.* Evanston, Ill.: Row, Peterson.

Sears, R. R., and G. W. Wise (1950). Relation of cup feeding in infancy to thumb-sucking and the oral drive. *Amer. J. Orthopsychiat., 20,* 123–138.

*Shirley, R. W., and A. K. Romney (1962). Love magic and socialization anxiety. *Amer. Anthropologist, 64,* 1028–1032.

*Simmons, L. W. (1937). Statistical correlations in the science of society. In G. P. Murdock (Ed.), *Studies in the science of society.* New Haven: Yale Univ. Press. Pp. 495–517.

Spiro, M. E. (1965). A typology of social structure and the patterning of social institutions. *Amer. Anthropologist, 67,* 1097–1120.

*Stephens, W. E. (1962). *The Oedipus complex: cross-cultural evidence.* Glencoe, Ill.: Free Press.

*——— (1963). *The family in cross-cultural perspective.* New York: Holt, Rinehart, and Winston.

Sturtevant, W. C. (1964). Studies in ethnoscience. *Amer. Anthropologist, 66,* 99–131.

Swadesh, M. (1959). Linguistics as an instrument of prehistory. *Southwest. J. Anthropol., 15,* 20–35.

*Swanson, G. E. (1960). *The birth of the gods.* Ann Arbor: Univ. of Michigan Press.

Tanner, J. M. (1962). *Growth at adolescence.* Springfield, Ill.: Charles C. Thomas.

Tylor, E. B. (1889). On a method of investigating the development of institutions, applied to laws of marriage and descent. *J. Anthropol. Inst. Gr. Brit. Irel., 18,* 245–269.

*Udy, S. H. (1959). *Organization of work: a comparative analysis of production among non-industrial peoples.* New Haven: Human Relations Area Files.

Vogt, E. Z. (n.d.). Zinacantan: a Maya community in the highlands of Chiapas. Unpublished manuscript.

*Whiting, B. B. (1950). *Paiute sorcery.* New York: Viking Fund Publications in Anthropology, No. 15.

———, Ed. (1963). *Six cultures: studies of child rearing.* New York: Wiley.

Whiting, J. W. M. (1941). *Becoming a Kwoma.* New Haven: Yale Univ. Press.

*——— (1959). Sorcery, sin, and the superego. In M. R. Jones (Ed.), *Nebraska symposium on motivation, 1959.* Lincoln: Univ. of Nebraska Press.

——— (1964a). Comments on Naroll's "On ethnic unit classification." *Current Anthropol., 5* (4), 305–306.

*——— (1964b). Effects of climate on certain cultural practices. In W. H. Goodenough (Ed.), *Explorations in cultural anthropology.* New York: McGraw-Hill.

*——— (1965). Menarcheal age and infant stress in humans. In F. A. Beach (Ed.), *Sex and behavior.* New York: Wiley.

Whiting, J. W. M., and B. Ayres (n.d.). Inferences from the shape of dwellings. Unpublished manuscript.

*Whiting, J. W. M., and I. L. Child (1953). *Child training and personality.* New Haven: Yale Univ. Press.

*Whiting, J. W. M., R. Kluckhohn, and A. A. Anthony (1960). The function of male initiation ceremonies at puberty. In E. E. Maccoby, T. M. Newcomb, and E. L. Hartley (Eds.), *Readings in social psychology* (3rd ed.). New York: Wiley.

Whiting, J. W. M., and B. B. Whiting (1960). Contributions of anthropology to the methods of studying child rearing. In *Handbook of research methods in child development*. New York: Wiley.

Whiting, J. W. M., *et al.* (1966a). *Field guide for a study of socialization.* Six Culture Series, Vol. 1. New York: Wiley.

—————— (1966b). The learning of values. In E. Z. Vogt and E. M. Albert (Eds.), *The people of Rimrock.* Cambridge: Harvard Univ. Press.

Wright, G. O. (1954). Projection and displacement: a cross-cultural study of folktale aggression. *J. abnorm. soc. Psychol., 49,* 523–528.

*Young, F. W. (1965). *Initiation ceremonies: a cross-cultural study of status dramatization.* New York: Bobbs-Merrill.

*Young, F., and A. Backayan (1965). Menstrual taboos and social rigidity. *Ethnology, 4* (2), 225–241.

18

The Social Significance of Animal Studies

D. O. HEBB, McGill University

W. R. THOMPSON, Queen's University

We do not restrict ourselves in the present chapter to making a review of studies of social behavior in subhuman animals; in fact, not even a thorough review of this kind can be attempted. Our aim instead is to deal with the animal work that may help in understanding human society. In doing so, we must emphasize intellectual processes, and we shall give a large proportion of our space to emotion and motivation in the individual animal. Thus we neglect some important studies of social organization, especially in the ant and the bee (but also in birds and mammals when it does not seem that anything in particular is added to the understanding of man). Our treatment is largely determined by the look of open astonishment that we have often seen at the idea that the study of animals has any interest for social psychologists. We cannot do justice in one chapter to the literature of comparative social psychology, but we do hope to convince the reader that he should read further, and that he need not think it a social error to be found with a copy of the *Journal of Comparative and Physiological Psychology* in hand.

The study of animal behavior is significant in social problems for the same reason as in the problem of learning; we shall, in fact, try to show that social psychology must be dangerously myopic if it restricts itself to the human literature. Our aim is thus to treat here the subhuman-animal data which relate to the problems, methods, and theories of human social psychology. After looking briefly at the logic of this relation, our discussion will concern itself first with intellectual factors in communication and cooperation and will then go on to motivational factors, although we recognize fully that this is an artificial separation. Finally, we shall try to add all this up in a theoretical approach to human society from the comparative point of view.

We gratefully acknowledge the critical advice received from graduate students at McGill University and from Drs. D. Bindra, D. Krech, A. S. Luchins, H. W. Nissen, T. C. Schneirla, D. C. Williams, and J. P. Zubek.

VALIDITY OF ANIMAL STUDIES

There is a common opinion that understanding human behavior will result from the study of human behavior only, on the ground that proving something true of an animal does not prove it for man. The latter part of this statement is both correct and irrelevant. It implies that an empirical science proceeds by proof and disproof, which is a most misleading idea.

No scientific theory can ever be proved true; nor indeed can we ever be finally sure of having proved one wrong. Too often in the history of science the demolished hypothesis has turned up again full of new life, following some slight modification of its assumptions. Lavoisier's oxygen theory of combustion was early disproved (Conant, 1947); Newton's corpuscular theory of light, once discarded on the assumption that light must be either corpuscular or undulatory, but not both, is now in good standing again in somewhat modified form. As for proving that a hypothesis is true, it is notorious that ten thousand confirmations cannot prevent some spoilsport from thinking tomorrow of a new experiment that upsets it at one blow.

Thus the statement that animal experiment proves nothing for man does not go far enough: finding that something is true *of man* up till now, and for the limited sample of men that one has actually been able to test, cannot logically establish that it will be true of other men in the future, as Hume noted long ago. Finding that a psychotic behaves in a certain way does not prove anything about normal persons, but no one would argue from this that clinical studies have not helped in our understanding of the normal. In principle, study of animals has exactly the same status.

All very fine, says the social psychologist, but when in fact has animal psychology lived up to this billing, and helped in the way that abnormal psychology certainly has? As a first answer we choose an example that may seem to have little bearing on social psychology—partly because it does have a bearing, and partly because it clears up the logic of the way in which animal experiment contributes to a knowledge of man.

STUDIES OF ANIMAL INTELLIGENCE

The example is from the study of individual problem solving in the rat. There is a confused and extensive literature on the relation of environment and heredity to the development of human intelligence. One group of studies has seemed to show that environment can have little to do with intelligence; another that it must have a great deal. In either case the argument is somewhat indirect and not clearly decisive, and the literature itself has not led to a resolution of the apparent contradiction. Indeed, both Goodenough (1946), and Jones (1946), in reviewing the literature, express dissatisfaction with the ambiguities of human experiments on the subject. Studies on the effects of nursery-school training on IQ, for example, do not agree whether there is any increase in measurable intelligence. And the few case studies available on single individuals who have been severely restricted in infancy (Davis, 1940, 1947; Hill and Robinson, 1929; Mason, 1942) usually involve so many uncontrolled variables that interpretation is exceedingly difficult. The situation obviously calls for a systematic human breeding experiment together with a radical variation of the environment during growth. Of course no such experiment can be done. And of course if it were done with animals it would prove nothing for man. However, the animal experiments have been done, and the significance they do have, *vis-à-vis* the human problem, is to show that the entire contradiction may stem from implicit assumptions about man for which there is no factual support. The animal experiments, furthermore, suggest that they are wrong.

Experimental studies have shown clearly that when the postnatal environment is held constant the level of learning capacity and problem solving in the rat is innately determined (Heron, 1935; Thompson and Bindra, 1952; Tryon, 1940); that is, one can breed rats that will be brighter, or duller, when brought up in the same environment. But they show equally clearly that when heredity is held constant between experimental groups, by the split-litter method, infant experience determines the level of adult problem solving (Bingham and Griffiths, 1952; Forgays and Forgays, 1952; Hymovitch, 1952). The rat brought up in a "free environment," or even with almost no freedom of bodily movement but with wide and extensive perceptual experience, is the better problem solver at maturity. For the rat, then, adult intelligence depends both on heredity and on the stimulating action of the postnatal environment.

Now the implicit assumption has been made in interpreting the human data that the effect of learning on intelligence can be estimated at any time during growth; if special experiences at the age of ten or twelve have little effect on the IQ, if a radical change of environment at age six has only a slight effect on the IQ by age seven, it is concluded that the kind of experience the child has, at any time during his growth, is not an important factor in his intellectual development. This is, in effect, the assumption that the learning process is the same at all stages of growth, as is also the generality of transfer effects.

But we have no evidence to show that this is so. The animal evidence, furthermore, indicates that the assumption is wrong. If instead we assume for man, as for the rat, that experiences early in development may have a widely generalized and lasting effect which they do not have at a later age, the contradictions of the human data disappear. It is still necessary to see how the principle is to be applied to man in detail. We still must discover at what ages the various aspects of his experience have their lasting effects, and what these experiences are. But finding that the adult IQ is unmodifiable, or that putting the underprivileged six-year-old into a good school does not greatly raise his IQ in the next year or so, is no longer inconsistent with the idea that the man reared from birth in an impoverished environment has a lower IQ than he would otherwise.

Thus the first point we make in citing this work is that animal experiment may clarify a human problem without "proving" anything. It may draw attention to facets of human behavior one has not noticed; it may point to a trouble-making but implicit assumption; it may suggest a new principle of human behavior. Furthermore, animal experiment in the past has repeatedly shown that the treatment of some human problem or other has been oversimplified. But in all these cases, the relevance of the animal work is strictly dependent on whether, when applied to man, it does clarify the human problem.

The closer one stays to man's behavior the less one can hope to see its broader outlines. One takes for granted too easily the things that all men have in common without seeing how extraordinary some of them are. We concede that animal psychology has had its own myopic errors, but these have usually arisen when study is concentrated on some one laboratory animal, rat or cat, regarded simply as a convenient substitute for man and not as the object of comparative study. For effective recent discussions of the distinction between animal psychology and comparative psychology see Beach (1950) and Schneirla (1952).

THE EARLY ENVIRONMENT

The second point we wish to make, in connection with the experiments cited in the preceding section, has to do with the role of the early environment in the development of social intelligence and social attitudes. The problem is on all fours with the "mental hygiene" problem of emotional development. What childhood experiences make for an ability to "understand people," to be sensitive to another's mood, to know how a contemplated action will affect someone else? We can no longer assume that the insensitive person simply fails to inherit the necessary social intelligence. He may or may not. The social problem of education is not limited to the guidance of emotional development and the establishment of desirable attitudes toward others.

Mental hygiene in this sense is not enough. It would be silly to think that a young woman would have much chance of being emotionally stable if she continually blundered in her human relationships, frustrating herself socially; or that a politician could put "democratic" principles into effect, no matter how good his intentions, without being able to recognize ability and honesty and enthusiasm, or without knowing how to lead except by giving orders. There is no proof whatever that man's social intelligence, his social skills, must be fostered in childhood to reach full development, but everything we know suggests that this is so. For a true mental hygiene, therefore, as well as for a better social order, we must find out in what circumstances the child's social intelligence reaches its full development.

As to social attitudes, again, there is no reason to think that all the recently emphasized work on the role of the early environment in lower animals can be applied directly to man, but there is little doubt that it applies in principle, when we can homologize properly. Hoarding in the adult rat (Hunt, 1941; Hunt *et al.*, 1947), increased by hunger in infancy, may or may not be homologous with miserliness in man. It is even harder to draw a human moral directly from the very important experiments of Lorenz (1935a, 1935b, 1952) on "imprinting" in young ducks and geese. But taken more broadly, with other studies showing a general importance of early experience on social attitudes and emotionality, such as those of Hall and Whiteman (1951), Bernstein (1952), Levy (1934), Ross, Smith, and Denenberg (1950), and Thompson and Heron (1954), the observations in question assume greater significance—presenting as it were undiluted examples of a kind of lasting fixation that may be fundamental in mammalian behavior but obscured or overlaid by the greater complexities of learning in higher forms. This possibility is brought closer to man by Nissen's (1951) estimate of the relation between sexual deviations in the chimpanzee and extensive early exposure to man.

Failing the possibility of radical rearing experiments with human children, it seems that comparative study offers a solid line of advance in this field. Studies of emotionality and social attitude in a number of species will provide some basis for tentative extrapolation of the curves of phylogenetic development through chimpanzee to man, where the ideas thus arrived at can be tested for their value in clarifying clinical and naturalistic observations. The striking parallel in the implications of von Senden's (1932) data on human congenital blindness and Riesen's (1947, 1950) on chimpanzees reared in darkness, and the equally significant study by Nissen, Chow, and Semmes (1951) on the role of early experience in somesthesis, show that in one area at least, that of perceptual function, some of the effects of the early environment on human behavior could have been predicted from animal experiment. The problem with respect to social attitudes should not be intrinsically more difficult, and the more the points that are determined in the phylogenetic curve the more certain the extrapolations can be.

SOCIAL PHENOMENA AMONG INSECTS

President Lowell of Harvard is said to have introduced W. M. Wheeler for an honorary degree as a distinguished scientist who had shown that ants, too, can build a complex society without recourse to reason. We would not argue against Lowell that human society is the product of dispassionate deliberation. We do urge that even its primitive forms would be impossible if its members did not have their capacity for thought and speech. Whether he uses his reason in a reasonable way or not, it is quite clear from phyletic comparison that the first key to man's social structure lies in his distinctive intellectual qualities.

The point can be put briefly: the ant's social mechanisms are sensory, man's ideational. This is a distinction that is fundamental to our whole treatment. Accordingly, we shall first clarify this use of terms, and go on in the present section to describe some of the social behavior of insects. It contains striking parallels with human society. But these parallels are superficial, as most of the rest of this chapter will try to show.

On the use of terms: first, though our definition may not be rigorous, we shall consider a social act to be one that is determined by past or present stimulation, or expectancy of stimulation, from another member of the species; or done with the expectancy (intention) of evoking a response from him. This does not wholly exclude interaction between members of different species, if the behavior of the two is at all similar and produces relationships similar to those within a species; a pet dog is sometimes considered, and considers himself to be, a member of the family. But we do exclude pet goldfish; together with cattle-herding, fly-swatting, lion-taming, salmon-fishing, and other forms of predation. It is important also to exclude pseudosocial behavior, in which grouping occurs only because of some stimulus external to the group: examples are animals running from a forest fire, moths attracted to a light, and (a slightly closer approach to social phenomena) situations in which a by-product of one animal's existence attracts another, as in the association of a worm-seeking robin with a ploughman, or the huddling of cattle for warmth.

Next, for an adequate description of what happens in phylogenesis, there is no escape from distinguishing between behavior that is more and less stimulus-bound (Goldstein, 1940) or, more broadly, situation-bound. This is Schneirla's (1946) "biosocial" versus "psychosocial" distinction. The biosocial act is one which is dominated by the present environment (including humoral factors which are part of the environment of the nervous system) as distinct from the psychosocial act, in which "ideation" and "purpose" appear to be crucial.

The empirical criteria of sense-dominated or biosocial behavior are immediacy of response and the possibility of eliciting the same response repeatedly by presentation of the same stimulating situation. The predictability may be for the individual animal only, but the picture is clearest when the same stimulus-response relationship holds for the whole species (which does not necessarily mean that it is entirely "unlearned"). Examples: the response of bird or fish to one of the "releasers" of Lorenz and Tinbergen (Tinbergen, 1951), or the dog's aggressive response to the growl of another dog.

The psychosocial act, under ideational control, is harder to define—there may in fact be several categories here if we know how to distinguish them—but in general it falls under the heading of behavior which has led in the past to use of the term expectancy, or some other reference to a nonsensory determinant of response. The behavior is well adapted to the environment and hence partly under sensory control, but is not predictable from the present stimulation alone and makes it necessary to postulate expectancy, set, attitude, or selective attention as codeterminant of the response.

The reader is likely to have difficulty with this distinction if he regards it as absolute, or primarily due to some theory or other. It is primarily empirical. It is not a distinction between learned and unlearned, and our emphasis is not on supposed differences in the complexity of the response mechanism. One can hardly be certain that all "ideational" responses, about which we know little, are more complex or "higher" than all reflex responses, some of which are known to be complex indeed. Our emphasis instead is on differences in the directness of control of response by sensory and humoral influences.

The most elaborate social structures occur far apart in the phyletic scale: man's at the top, the social insects' near the bottom. In between, organization is loose and sporadic. Apart from the division of labor involved in sex behavior and in parental care, there are few cases in which subhuman vertebrates are essentially dependent on other members of the species for specialized functions that they do not have themselves. Individual animals may act in a way that serves the whole group, but the service could be performed about as well by other members and there seems to be nothing in the behavior of the gregarious birds and mammals that parallels the specialization of function in the castes of social insects, or the specialization of the human officeworker who might die if he were suddenly left without food and clothing produced by others, before he learned how to produce the tools or weapons he would need to support life.

The figures of speech, *caste, queen, soldier,* and *worker,* point up this analogy between social insects and man. But as Schneirla (1946) in particular has insisted, it is an analogy, not to be pushed too far. Despite having only a rudimentary social structure, the chimpanzee has more to tell us concerning the nature of human society than all the social insects taken together. However, the phenomena of the insect's social organization are fascinating in themselves, and (as we have said) they do clarify the human problem by setting it in perspective.

THE PHENOMENA OF INSECT SOCIETIES

The founding of a colony varies only slightly with the family. In most wasps, ants, and termites, the fertilized female leaves with or without a small company of swarming workers to found a new home. In the bumblebee, a queen, alone, selects some cavity in the ground or in a log and at first behaves like a solitary bee. Later, the social behavior characteristic of a worker appears in the care of her young. Still later, when there are workers, she takes the role of the queen only. The progression of the colony from a rather primitive to a more complex social organization is also characteristic of ants. In a new colony the first brood is composed of workers only. These take care of the second brood, in which soldiers appear.

The division of labor in human societies is approximate and flexible. In the social insects it is much more exact and rigid, based on the needs of reproduction, nutrition, and protection which underlie colony life. Each insect caste is dedicated to a certain function, the queens to reproduction, the workers to nutrition, and, in wasps, to protection also, although in ants and termites this latter function is served by soldier castes. Each caste is highly specialized structurally to perform its appropriate task. In a manner, though there seems little to be gained by it (*cf.* Schneirla, 1946), they may be considered as analogous to parts of a "supraorganism" (Allee *et al.,* 1949).

The determination of castes is probably genetic as well as nutritional. In the cases of the two sexes (and thus of the two reproductive castes) it appears to derive from genetic differences in the egg (Light, 1942, 1943). But in bees and wasps, determination of queen and worker castes depends largely on nutritive factors. The larvae that are to become queens are fed entirely on "royal jelly," the worker larvae on "royal jelly" only for the first three days and then on "bee nectar." (The workers are a sterile caste which may be said to have been "nutritionally castrated," to use Wheeler's phrase.) The queen reaches maturity in about sixteen days, as compared with twenty-one for workers and twenty-four for drones. Similarly, in ants, caste differentiations between queen, workers, and soldiers of the same sex appears to be determined more by environmental than by hereditary factors. It is known, for example, that ant colonies with a small supply of food will produce only workers (Light, 1942), and again that soldier ants in a colony over a given threshold number will inhibit the development of more soldiers (Gregg, 1942), this possibly being accomplished by the soldiers' exuding an exo-hormone that passes on to developing individuals or sometimes to the unlaid eggs (Allee *et al.*, 1949). In general, caste determination appears to be fairly flexible in the first stages of growth in the social insects but, once determined, an individual's caste seems to remain rigidly fixed.

The structural differences of the castes, underlying the functional ones, are often striking, involving gross differences in size as well as in specific characters. In one genus of ant (*Carebara*) the queen is several thousand times as large as the worker (Wheeler, 1922). The wasp workers which double as soldiers are equipped with a sting, unlike the drones; but in some ants and termites, the soldier may guard the colony merely by blocking the entrance with his head. In other species, the soldiers are equipped with large, powerful jaws. Many mandibulate termite soldiers and all the nasute have a large frontal gland which excretes a sticky liquid or "latex" capable of disabling enemies.

In addition to the different castes, there are often "guests" and "slaves," more often in ant colonies, but also in those of bees, wasps, and termites. Wasmann (1905), Wheeler (1928), Plath (1935), and others have discussed these phenomena fully. Treatment of guests ranges from bare tolerance to definite encouragement. An interesting example of an ant guest (*Leptothorax emersoni*) is described by Wheeler. It is associated with a larger host (*Myrmica canadensis*) and lives in small chambers near the surface of the latter's nest. The smaller ants have the habit of climbing on the backs of passing host workers and licking their bodies, especially the heads and mouthparts. The hosts permit this and occasionally regurgitate droplets of food which the guests eat. The guests, on the other hand, do not allow *Myrmica* into their own colony, except under special conditions. Many species are able to induce *Phytophthora* (plant lice, scale insects, mealy bugs, etc.), by stroking them with their antennae, to regurgitate honeydew the latter have sucked up from plants. These guests are often housed in specially constructed caverns ("barns") in the nest, and thus were called by Linnaeus "the dairy cattle of the ants."

The extraordinary social phenomena of the insect world include slaves also. Ant slavemakers have been classified into two types, "obligatory" and "facultative," depending upon whether slaves are necessary for existence or not. Four known genera of ants are slavemakers (*Formica, Polyergus, Strongylognathus,* and *Harpagoxenus*). One commonly has slaves but can get along without them; three are of the obligatory class and must have slaves to survive. The slaves are generally taken as larvae in raids on other colonies, hatched and raised in the slavemakers' nest, and put to work excavating the nest, feeding and caring for the young, and doing other chores normally carried out by the workers of that colony. *Polyergus* ants are completely dependent on their slaves and often deplete a whole nest of its larvae and pupae, although the attendant workers are not harmed unless they resist (Plath, 1935). A similar phenomenon, but this time analogous to child labor instead of slavemaking, is found in another species (*Oecophylla smaragdina*): the worker ants use silk produced by their larvae to bind leaves together for the nest. The head of a larva is applied to each leaf in turn by the worker's holding it in the appropriate position. During the process the larva "cooperates" by bending its head whenever it is lowered to a leaf (Plath, 1935). Many other similar examples could be cited.

COMMUNICATION IN INSECT SOCIETIES

One essential key to social organization is the means of communication, in the broad sense of the way in which the behavior of one animal induces cooperative behavior in another. As a prelude to examining the development of communication, let us see what the cues are upon which the complex social organization of insects depends.

For the ant, the "signals" are mainly tactual, chemical, and auditory (Allee *et al.*, 1949). Of these, the chemical may be dominant. An ant with a strange odor is attacked, even if a member of the colony; a foreigner, experimentally provided with the colony odor, can be introduced safely (Dropkin, 1941). But this is by no means representative of all insect interaction. Wheeler (1928) reported that the hungry larvae of a wasp colony protrude their heads from their cells and may actually scratch on the walls of the cell, thereby attracting the attention of wasp nurses which, in feeding the larvae, are rewarded by drops of sweet saliva excreted from the mouths of their charges. A most interesting type of communication occurs in those species of ants and termites whose soldiers block the exits to the nest with their heads. When a worker wishes to leave or enter the nest, she strokes the soldier's head or abdomen with her antennae, whereupon the living "door" moves back to let her pass. After she has gone, he moves back into position (Wheeler, 1928). The ability of the soldier to discriminate a friend from a stranger is, in itself, a remarkable feat. How it is done is not known, nor whether it is learned (that is, whether the discrimination requires practice or improves with repetition).

The most remarkable communication occurs in bees, brilliantly demonstrated in systematic experiments by von Frisch (1950). As he remarks (p. 85), the results at first glance seem fantastic, but they have been attested by Thorpe (1950) and others. The worker who has found a food source is able without leaving the hive to give her fellows not only the direction but also the distance of the food, by the "wagging dance." The farther the food, the fewer the number of turns in the dance. The angle of the dance on the vertical comb, relative to gravity, gives the direction relative to that of the sun. If the sun is hidden, polarized light from an area of blue sky still provides orientation, and it appears that the polarization is the essential cue whether the sun is out or not; no communication is possible if the sky is completely overcast. Through this extraordinary behavior other workers are enabled to find the food source.

LEVELS OF COMMUNICATION AND COOPERATION

Such phenomena raise at once the question of their similarity to human communication. Does von Frisch's evidence mean that the bee has the equivalent of a human sign language, though with a small vocabulary? The question might be phrased, "Is the bee's behavior symbolic?", but the term symbolic has been used in so many ways that we find it confusing. A main purpose of this section is to find out how to ask the question better, to find better ways of defining the essential differences of communication at various phyletic levels.

Most insect communication is clearly in the class of the sense-dominated social act. The typical stimulus is a scent, touch, or sound that evokes a typical response, not varying much at different times. The invariability of insect behavior has often been exaggerated, but certainly the relation between stimulus and response is much closer than with mammals.

The behavior described by von Frisch does not appear to be essentially different, although it does appear unusually complex. The wagging dance or "message" involves a delayed response but is directly controlled otherwise by the special effects of polarized light on the complex eye of the bee. The number of turns in the dance may be determined by fatigue or in some other equally elementary way, since it actually corresponds to amount of effort or elapsed time rather than distance; it decreases with distance, and also with a head wind, but increases with a tail wind. No one, of course, would suggest that the bee performs some kind of trigonometric computation which is then expressed in the dance, and remarkable as the whole behavior is, it may still lie in the reflexive class.

Similarly, the problem of the way in which other bees receive the message is unsolved. It has not been shown that the behavior has the characteristic of intentionality (Bierens de Haan, 1929) or purposiveness (Maier and Schneirla, 1935), which is essential before one can conclude that the bee has a language. This point is spelled out in the following section, but we can anticipate here to the extent of suggesting the sort of evidence that might be looked for. Evidence of intentionality might be provided, for example, if only the first of several returning bees made the wagging dance—if the message is already being conveyed to the colony by ten other bees there is little sign of purpose in the behavior that conveys it once more. Or again, if one could remove the returning bee's audience experimentally, would she still make the wagging dance, as if the audience were there? We have no intention of making light of this extraordinary behavior, but understanding it requires that we see its limits as well as its extent. The evolutionary origins of so-called instinctive behavior in general are as difficult to understand, as miraculous, as those of the so-called intelligent behavior of higher mammals; but let us avoid mixing up our miracles.

PURPOSIVE COMMUNICATION AND LANGUAGE

Bierens de Haan and Maier and Schneirla have reserved the term *communication* for purposive communication, the act that is done "with regard to the effect it has on other individuals." We propose here to use the term more broadly but not to lose their essential distinction. By including a class of "reflexive" (non-purposive) communication, we are able to recognize von Frisch's phenomenon as communication and still not confuse it with phenomena of a psychologically higher level.

The conception of purposive behavior is not, of course, a vitalistic one. The difficulty in identifying behavior as such is that it may have to be seen repeatedly in order to be sure that its objective is achieved neither accidentally nor mechanically: that it shows "means-end-readiness" (Tolman, 1932), or a variation with circumstances that tends toward the same end effect. A bird's "warning" cry would be purposive, for example, if made only when the young were exposed and stopped when they got under cover, or if the warner approached the warned and called quietly, without drawing the marauder's attention also. The essence of the purposive communication is that the sender remains sensitive to the receiver's responses, during sending, and by modification of his sending shows that his behavior is, in fact, guided by the intention (expectancy) of achieving a particular behavioral effect in the receiver. The "broken wing" behavior of the grouse, for example, is purposive, since it is modified according to the marauder's behavior in such a way as to draw him away from the hiding chicks; but the warning cry of the gull, although it tends to produce a protective immobility in the chicks, seems quite reflexive. Carpenter (1942) points out that the alarm calls of a group of primates, startled by an observer, continue long after they have got away out of danger. The calls are therefore more emotional expression than purposive.

Birds and animals do show purposive communication. It seems likely that the crow, for example, or the parrot, may on occasion call or "speak" with intent to influence another. A dog's bark, or a chimpanzee's begging gestures, may be unmistakably purposeful. This does not mean, however, that the bird or sub-human mammal has language. It is important to recognize that purposeful communication occurs in animals, and just as important to recognize that language is something more.

The criterion of language is not only that it is representational, for representational acts occur in animals. Man has what neither chimpanzee nor parrot has: the capacity to combine *and readily recombine* representative or symbolic noises (words), movements (gestures), or modifications of inert things (writing, carving). We propose therefore that the minimal criterion of language, as distinct from other purposive communication, is twofold. First, language combines *two or more* representative gestures or noises purposefully, for a single effect; and second, it uses the *same* gestures in different combinations for different effects, changing readily with circumstances. As Morris (1946) and Schneirla (1946) have noted, language has other distinctive characteristics, but we believe that these criteria are enough to set it off fully from animal communication. Too much attention, we believe, has been given to man's special vocal behavior. In sign language and gesture man's distinctiveness is equally clear (Révész, 1944), and we avoid the confusing issue of whether the subhuman primate has the vocal equipment for producing human sounds.

From this point of view, the outstanding fact is man's capacity for a varied combination of symbolic acts, and we therefore propose to call language *syntactic behavior*. We thus have three classes of communication: (1) reflexive (not true communication); (2) purposive but nonsyntactic; and (3) syntactic (and usually purposive), or true language.

There are evidently differences of level within each of these classes, and though it seems clear that true language is unique to man, we can trace an increasing complexity of purposive behavior in subhuman animals which suggests that the discontinuity between ape and man, in communication, is less than it appears. The chimpanzee may well be close to a liminal level that would make language possible (Hayes and Hayes, 1951a).

Underlying syntactic behavior there must be a certain independence or autonomy of conceptual processes. Two or more concepts must be capable of being aroused simultaneously, instead of one crowding the other out; and, as the term *concept* itself implies, they must be arousable by associative mechanisms in the absence of the sensory events that originally gave rise to them. That is, they are independent of any particular external environment, and of each other. Conceptual process *A* may be linked momentarily with conceptual process *B* at one time, with *C* or *D* at another. We are not talking now of the processes underlying the elaborate sentences of adults, but simply of what is needed to account for the performance of the child who can use a vocabulary of four words to form the propositions "Daddy go," "Mommy go," "Mommy come," and "Daddy come." This is beyond the level of any animal except man; but putting the problem in these terms allows us to relate it to other phenomena that do occur in the animal world.

Let us propose as hypothesis the more general proposition, that the intellectual development in phylogenesis that eventually makes speech possible is an increasing independence of the conceptual activity from the present sensory environment, and an increasing capacity for entertaining diverse conceptual processes at the same time. This is the capacity to respond to the present environment in one way and think of responding in another; for perceiving the present situation as it now is, and conceptually adding something else to it; for planning a series of actions of which only the first is immediately feasible. At the lowest level, it is the capacity for delayed response or a simple expectancy; at the highest level, for "holding" not only a series of words but also of sentences, whose meaning only becomes clear with later words or sentences (Hebb and Bindra, 1952).

There is clear evidence of phylogenetic development in such capacities. The chimpanzee moving a box to stand on, to get fruit that is otherwise out of reach, manifests a "first this, then that" planning which is beyond the dog, and Köhler's (1927) evidence leaves little doubt that the sequence of acts is, in fact, planned in advance. Entirely unmistakable evidence of such ability is found in the deceitful attack that almost any adult chimpanzee is capable of. We shall return to this behavior in a later section, but here we may cite the chimpanzees of the Yerkes colony who, seeing a visitor being escorted through the Laboratories, (1) slip over quietly to the faucet and get loaded, (2) return to the front of the cage nearest to where the procession will pass and sit quietly, with no sign of hostility, until (3) the visitor is within range, at which point he is suddenly drenched with a pint or so of water. This makes two points. It is evident, first, that a series of actions is planned in advance; and second, that the chimpanzee has the ability to act in one way while thinking about acting in the opposite way.

Closely related is the empathy described by Köhler (1927, p. 168 and Plate VII). One chimpanzee watches another precariously reaching for food. The watcher stays at a distance, does not try for the fruit himself, and still identifies with the other to the extent of making identical reaching movements. That such spontaneous imitation can occur in chimpanzees is confirmed by the socially significant paper of Hayes and Hayes (1951b), and Köhler's empathy should be collated with Mead's idea (Morris, 1946, p. 45) that communication involves "taking the role of the other" and "the ability to be the other *at the same time* that he is himself" (italics ours). Such a proposal becomes intelligible if two or more phase sequences (Hebb, 1949b), or trains of thought, can exist side by side in the brain of the higher mammal.

But this, of course, is not the place to elaborate a whole theory of communication. We can sum up the present discussion by saying first that the criterion of syntactic behavior clearly separates man from ape, in communication; but second, that the appearance of some other aspects of behavior in the chimpanzee shows that the ape may be closer to man in this respect than he seems.

ANIMAL COOPERATION

Much the same conclusions must be drawn concerning cooperation. Phyletically, cooperation parallels communication to such a degree that there is a *prima facie* case for concluding that both depend on the same intellectual characteristics. The cooperation of insects, as we have seen, is complex indeed but shows little sign of purpose. Short of man, the highest level that has been demonstrated experimentally is in the chimpanzee (Crawford, 1937, 1941) but it seems true of his cooperation, as of his communication, that the ape is not decisively superior to other mammals and definitely lacks a kind of teamwork that is common in man (Nissen, 1951). Crawford's experiments have been summarized by Nissen (1951, p. 444) as follows:

In a laboratory experiment, Crawford first trained young chimpanzees individually to pull in a weighted box, by means of an attached rope, in order to obtain the food reward on the box. Then the weight of the box was increased (so that one animal could not move it); next, two ropes were attached, the box was baited with two portions of reward, and two animals were put in the cage. At first each chimpanzee pulled without any reference to his partner's actions; only by chance did the two pull at the same time and so move the box. It was necessary for the experimenter to give a signal, which the partners had individually associated with initiating the pull, to get them to pull together. Once the temporal coordination of effort had been established in this way, the extraneous signal could be omitted. One of the partners, *A*, usually watched the other one, *B*, and was ready to add her pull as soon as *B* started heaving on the rope. Sometimes it was arranged that *B* was satiated when the experiment began; *A* would then urge and direct *B* to pull. Eventually *B* would pull, although she had no desire for the food reward. In these circumstances *A* often reaped the entire material benefits of the teamwork.

In a later experiment by Crawford one animal was trained to push against four colored plaques, arranged around the sides of a cage, in a certain order. The cage was then divided into two sections by a partition of bars; the colors to be pushed first and third were on one side, the colors to be pushed second and fourth were in the other part of the cage. The trained animal was then put on one side, and her partner, who knew the mechanics of pushing the plaques but not the correct order, was put on the other side of the partition. The trained animal X watched her partner's actions and pushed the color available to her after Y had pushed the color preceding it in the sequence; X sometimes solicited her partner, using begging gestures . . . that were spatially directed toward the particular color on her partner's side that was the next one in order.

We know of no reliable report of cooperation by other animals that quite comes up to this, with its evidence of purposiveness. Yet it must be pointed out that there was hardly more than the barest beginning of teamwork as we know it in man, and that even this was achieved only in an artificial experimental setting which needed the planning of the human experimenter. The experiment may be thought of as parallel to that of Hayes and Hayes (1951a) in communication, who managed by careful training to get a chimpanzee to produce recognizable English words, but still without achieving real language.

What may be described as a "one-sided cooperation" certainly occurs in the chimpanzee. An adult animal rescues an infant heading for trouble (Nissen, 1931, p. 87): A helps B, but B does not simultaneously help A. Teamwork at the human level is another matter. It involves a kind of prior understanding between cooperators that is impossible, perhaps, without a human capacity for communication. When X and Y cooperate fully, very complex mental processes are required. At each stage of action, X must anticipate not only his own next act and its effect, but also those of Y. Further, X may have to keep a number of possible eventualities in mind, and in each case have the expectancy of Y's acting in an appropriate way. This is the relationship that Sears (1951) has defined as *dyadic*. It is clear that the expectancies involved become very complex when the situation is not under the complete control of the cooperating partners. Teamwork thus makes intellectual demands of the same order as those made by language. Psychologically, it may, in fact, be hard to distinguish the two.

Let us then define three levels of cooperation, corresponding very well on the whole to the three levels of communication already proposed: (1) reflexive, or nonpurposive; (2) purposive, but "one-sided"; and (3) "two-sided", or teamwork. The second of these is seen in higher vertebrates; the last seems to occur only in man, as far as one can tell from the available evidence.

The difficulty in reviewing the literature on cooperation in its various forms is that those reporting have usually not known or have not understood the significance of Tolman's (1932) clarification of purpose as a behavioral and non-teleological conception. They have tended therefore to see purpose in all behavior, since almost any act is bound to have *some* biological significance; or at the other extreme have tended to make all infrahuman social behavior reflexive and without any insight whatever. In either case the details of the behavior are often not reported in a way that allows one to judge whether its end effect is achieved with insight and intention or not. There is a great deal of anecdotal material to suggest the existence of altruism and cooperation in primate societies, for example, but the evidence in general has been so poor that Zuckerman (1932) had to conclude that no altruism exists, that the behavior is always "immediate responses to specific stimuli," without comprehension. We shall try to show that this is not so, and that one-sided purposive cooperation and even the beginnings of altruism can be found in lower animals, but it certainly seems that much which at first sight is a planned cooperation is no more so than a litter of kittens is planned parenthood on the part of a tomcat.

Lorenz (1934) has reported a good example of behavior that only looks altruistic. He found that jackdaws would always come to the aid of another daw that had fallen into the hands of a common enemy, like Lorenz himself. When he had a captive bird in his hand, the others would attack him vigorously. But they would also attack him, with equal enthusiasm, when carrying a wet black bathing suit. Assuming that the jackdaws' visual acuity is equal to the discrimination involved, as it must be, there is no reason to suppose that either attack was a purposeful attempt to help a fellow.

A further difficulty, in reviewing the literature on cooperation, is that some of the most interesting and significant observations are made in the field, and are naturalistic instead of experimental. The behavior cannot be repeated at will, varying the circumstances for analysis. The phenomenon of leadership is an outstanding example: leadership can be quite independent of dominance and has much greater social significance, as an integrating instead of disintegrating influence (Carpenter, 1942; Darling, 1937). But leadership cannot easily be studied in a cage, and dominance can. As a result, dominance has been greatly overrated as a social phenomenon (Schneirla, 1952), and despite such excellent reports as Carpenter's or Darling's we know little about the psychological conditions of leadership or the closely related role of the sentinel.

Dominance often determines leadership, but often not. Greenberg (1947), for example, found that dominant sunfish also tend to be the leaders in group maze-running. Fischel (1927), on the other hand, did not find such a relationship in hens. The leaders in foraging expeditions in an orchard were not always the dominant birds. Katz (1949) with Barbary sheep as subjects, Scott (1945) with domestic sheep, and Stewart and Scott (1947) with goats, report that dominance does not play a major role in group organization. Leadership, however, is of great importance and usually rests with a female. Such "matriarchal" societies are very different from the "patriarchal" societies of roe deer (Darling, 1937) or baboons (Carpenter, 1942), in which the most aggressive and dominant male occupies the central position of control, and Darling has stressed the value of matriarchy as making for true group cohesion. The leadership of the hind is more "selfless," whereas in a patriarchal society the dominance relation between leader and followers is directly at odds with the leadership relation. Thus the hind group among the red deer is much more closely knit than the stag group.

As we have said, not much is known about the way in which leadership is acquired, or the level of insight that is involved on the part of leader and follower. That is, we do not know whether the follower is less alert than the leader *because* the leader is already acting as sentinel, or whether the follower is simply a less alert animal. Is the leader more alert, as leader, than he would be as a solitary animal? Even in Darling's (1937) report of the greater selflessness of the leader, who did not go to food until satisfied that the coast was clear and who as a result got less food, it is not clear that concern for others was in question, or anything more than a special wariness.

FRIENDSHIP AND ALTRUISM

But we do not regard Darling's opinion as fantastic, or even as intrinsically improbable, although it must be hard to establish in the conditions of his study. There is definite evidence in other animals of a phylogenetic development of something we shall call altruism, defined as an intrinsically motivated concern for others. Without attempting to make the definition exact, we use "altruistic" as a convenient designation for certain behavior that is not reflexive or immediately rewarding biologically: not necessarily "generosity," nor acting against inclination, but due to a capacity—or weakness—for developing a nondestructive interest in others. The weakness is very marked in man, and it does not matter for our present purposes whether it is a "learned drive" (Miller, 1951) or not. If the concern for others must be learned, the comparative evidence still indicates that we are dealing with something fundamental to man's nature, for we can trace phyletically some signs of an increasing readiness for such learning and an increasing frequency of the behavior in question without special conditions of reinforcement.

The biologically primitive form of a concern for others is, first, in parental care, at a purposive level. Second, it is clearly seen when an attachment to a sexual partner extends beyond the actual period of copulation, a phenomenon which is said to occur in some birds and mammals.

A further step in development appears in selective friendships which do not depend directly on primary reinforcement in Hull's (1943) sense. Such friendships are occasionally seen between dogs, and we may cite also the pet dog's protective behavior toward younger members of the family, when they are not the ones who feed or pet him. The clearest evidence that this behavior can be independent of primary reinforcement is from the dog that makes a nuisance of himself by persistent "rescue" of children in swimming, despite repeated punishment.

With the chimpanzee one cannot fail to see a step closer to man. Most chimpanzees, most of the time, seem entirely selfish; but so often are people. Friendships are marked (Köhler, 1927), and as Nissen (1951) has shown, the chimpanzee may be upset and unhappy when the long-time friend is taken away, even though other animals are still present.

Nissen's description of the effect of begging is particularly interesting here. It seems to be "both unpleasant and a very compelling stimulus. . . . Often it appears that the [chimpanzee with food] cannot tolerate this; reluctantly or even with some show of irritation or anger, he hands over some of the food, or throws it violently at the beggar" (Nissen, 1951, p. 445). From one point of view this is not generosity at all, but from another the very reluctance to give makes the gift all the more significant, by showing the strength of the compulsion behind it.

Here we can also give an example of what seems a purely altruistic concern for another chimpanzee, in an attempt to get the other out of danger. In the "bold and timid man" experiment described in the following section, Lia was afraid of the experimenter (outside the cage) playing the part of the bold man, and usually preferred to stay away from him. But Mimi, with whom she was caged, had other ideas. She stayed close to the cagewire and attacked repeatedly. The role of the bold man demanded that aggression be met with aggression, and the following note was made on the data sheet:

Feb. 14, 1944. Mimi tried to get my hand into reach, obviously to repeat her earlier attacks. I caught one of her fingers with my gloved hand and bent it back slightly, enough to hurt, whereupon she screamed with rage, beat on the wire, and then returned to putting her hands out through the wire, trying to catch hold of me. Lia, in the meantime, was also angry at first, when I hurt Mimi, and attacked me until I struck at her hand with my fist. Thereafter she was alternately aggressive in my direction (but not getting within reach) and protective of Mimi, five or six times *pulling Mimi's hands back from the wire*, first one, then the other, to get her out of danger.

A week later when the next bold-man test was made, Lia showed no anger or aggression but, when the foolhardy Mimi persisted in trying to get the bold man into position for an attack, strenuously tried to pull her away for the whole observation period of one or two minutes.

Finally, we may conclude with a remarkable observation of friendship between porpoises which is reported by McBride (1940, p. 26)—remarkable especially because the female referred to was sexually receptive, and before and after the incident described the two males were each bent only on preventing the other's access to her:

The smaller of the two large males was removed from the tank and transported by means of our tank truck to Tampa. It was exhibited there under the auspices of the State Conservation Department in a concrete tank for three weeks. When the animal was released into the tank, the greatest amount of excitement on the part of the larger male was exhibited. No doubt could exist that the two recognized each other, and for several hours they swam side by side rushing frenziedly through the water, and on several occasions they leaped completely out of water. For several days, the two males were inseparable and neither paid any attention to the female.

Socially, the porpoise is an interesting animal indeed, and it is most unfortunate that naturalistic observation outside captivity is impossible. On the one hand, dominance is clearly marked, and vicious attacks with no apparent reason have been repeatedly seen. On the other, very elaborate and apparently unmalicious teasing and social play are prominent in the animal's behavior, as well as clearly marked cooperation. At sea in their own habitat the female presumably gives birth in isolation; at any rate, the female giving birth in captivity in the Marine Studios was very exciting to the males, one of which became aggressive. The other females gathered round the one in labor and helped ward off the attacking male. When the newborn infant began its first gradual ascent to the surface to breathe, another female accompanied the mother in swimming just below the infant in readiness to support it if it had failed to make the grade (McBride and Hebb, 1948). From other behavior in these animals it is reasonably certain that the behavior described was purposive, to assist the infant if necessary to get to the surface (as it must, of course, to breathe), for another mother whose infant died during the night was found in the morning steadily supporting the dead body at the surface. If such a level of behavior at first seems surprising, it may be remembered that the porpoise is a mammal with a brain fifty percent bigger, and with more cortex and a more convoluted cortex, than man's. The brain lacks a frontal lobe, but in other respects it has striking similarity to that of the higher primate (Grünthal, 1948). It is not anomalous, accordingly, to class the porpoise (*Tursiops truncatus*) as a higher animal (McBride and Hebb, 1948).

The evidence indicates, therefore, that a disinterested concern for others can be found in mammalian development. Although it reaches its greatest potential only in man, it is not foreign to any higher mammal, and is not something that is imposed only by reward and punishment on the growing human child. It can, of course, be stultified or fostered during growth, but by his intellectual and emotional characteristics man has a greater *aptitude* for altruistic attitudes than any other animal, and it is of great importance to gain a more precise knowledge of the conditions of its development. It is not likely that such knowledge will be obtained by human study alone (who would attempt such an experiment?), but here again there is hope that real advances will be made in pooling the methods of animal experiment and naturalistic human observation.

THE ANALYSIS OF SOCIAL ATTITUDES

We have argued that there is a definite gap between man and his nearest relatives in their effective levels of cooperation and communication. No chimpanzee has language, or takes part in teamwork as we know it in man. But it was suggested also that the chimpanzee may not really be as far from man as he seems in these matters, and we turn now, in this and the following section, to behavior in which he seems human indeed. The evidence with which we deal here concerns, in general, the chimpanzee's social motivations; and the social situations considered will be those particularly which comprise two individuals, the dyadic unit of Sears (1951): chimpanzee-chimpanzee or chimpanzee-caretaker.

We also come now to things that have more obvious meaning for human social psychology. In this chapter, one of our objects, of course, is to persuade the reader that there is such meaning in animal work. Since it is most evident and direct with chimpanzees, it is here that most of our emphasis must lie; and this in turn implies giving most of our attention to observations made at the Yerkes Laboratories of Primate Biology, the chimpanzee breeding and research station in Orange Park, Florida. The work at the Yerkes colony is of unique importance for psychology, especially in the general area of personality or temperament. Not only does it constitute the only really extensive body of work on the great apes (Köhler's was a single-handed attack, now nearly forty years ago), it also constitutes the only thorough longitudinal study, from birth onward, of a higher mammal, the same animals being studied by a number of persons from a variety of points of view (Yerkes, 1943).

It has been noted elsewhere (Hebb, 1946a) that exposure to a group of adult chimpanzees gives one the overwhelming conviction that one is dealing with an essentially human set of attitudes and motivations. The feeling is not less strong in the psychologically trained than in the untrained (and its strength can be embarrassing to the purist who thinks that naming an animal's attitude or emotion is "subjective" and commits the deadly sin of anthropomorphism). It is probably a common experience to all who have worked at the Yerkes Laboratories to feel that the bare bones of human personality, the raw essentials, are being laid open before his eyes. At the same time, it is hard to convey this to others, and to support it with behavioral evidence.

Merely describing what the chimpanzee did that gave one this feeling is not enough. One would also have to take the space to put the act into its setting: a life history of the animal, plus a detailed description of his usual habits. As the reader will see, interpretation of the act depends on such a background. The interpreter usually does not realize how he arrives at the interpretation, and so is embarrassed to find himself holding what seem to be unscientific convictions; but it is possible to show that the answers, though highly inferential, are based on objective evidence of the same kind that is used in identifying human attitudes and emotions (Hebb, 1946a). Even though such studies have not gone far, they have significance for understanding human social interaction.

Some of the chimpanzee behavior with which we are concerned takes the form of rather dramatic episodes that are infrequent and cannot be repeated at will for study. These verge on the anecdotal, perhaps, but cannot be left entirely without mention when one wishes to show at what social level the chimpanzee operates, at least on occasion. For example, May more than once convinced competent observers that she was skillfully and intentionally transforming the hostile pursuit of a male, bigger than she, into a friendly game of chase. Another example is Lia's attempt to keep Mimi from a foolhardy attack on the "bold man," cited in the preceding section. Perhaps the most striking of these isolated observations is Vera's deliberately picking a fight with Jack in the next cage in order to distract Shorty's attention from the food being brought for them both—Shorty and she being caged together, Shorty dominant and sometimes taking her food. The interpretation in this last case rests partly on the fact that Vera's hair was not erect (as an excited chimpanzee's would be). Also, she left the fight as soon as Shorty entered it on her side and came without evident excitement to get and eat her food. Finally, she screamed loudly again, without leaving her food, when the fight between Jack and Shorty began to peter out without her help. The scream renewed it for the better part of a minute.

Such reports, being reports of interpretation as well as of fact, do not, of course, make very satisfactory evidence. The objection may apply less strongly to some of the repeatedly recorded aspects of the chimpanzee's sexual behavior. Examples are Pan's preferential interest in a young female with whom he had never copulated, so that he masturbated while she was led by out of his reach and disregarded the fully receptive female within his own cage; and Fifi's repeated refusal to copulate with Bokar over a three-month period (three periods of oestrus) though she had mated satisfactorily with him on earlier occasions and though the two were on friendly terms in other respects. Placed with Frank, Fifi then mated at once, quite normally. Such a selectivity has been observed repeatedly, with a number of animals. A refusal to copulate may or may not show social intelligence, but it does show how far the chimpanzee's sex motivation is from the more reflexive (hormone- and sense-dominated) behavior of dog or cat. It shows, in short, the dominant role that attitude may have in the chimpanzee's social behavior, and as such a closeness to man.

Yerkes and Elder (1936) have given a detailed description of the chimpanzee's mating behavior, and the reader will also find accounts of a fascinating interplay between sex and dominance in the chimpanzee in papers by Yerkes (1939, 1940, 1941), Crawford (1940), and Clark and Birch (Clark and Birch, 1945; Birch and Clark, 1946, 1950). In general, there is a clear relationship between phylogenetic level and a developing complexity in sexual behavior which Beach (1947, 1948) has worked out in detail, and which is applied by Ford and Beach (1951) to a clarification of human sex behavior. Their last chapter in particular, "Human Sexual Behavior in Perspective," is an excellent example of the contribution that a comparative study can make to an understanding of man.

RECOGNITION OF SOCIAL ATTITUDES

The conditions in which social attitudes are identified in the chimpanzee allow one to undertake a kind of analysis that is rather rare in comparative psychology. That is, while pretending to study the chimpanzee, one can really be analyzing the reactions of the caretaking staff (including one's own reactions) and ask, "Just what cues in the chimpanzee's behavior determine the human judgment that he is interested, or friendly, or malicious?" With the animal safely behind cagewire, unable to bring suit for damage to his self-esteem, one can experiment with emotion better than if the subject were man, but one can also study better the human recognition of emotions, with fewer confusing variables and more complete access to the data affecting the observer's judgment.

If the judgments were made at random, the analysis would have little significance. But it will be found that the experienced man refuses more often than not to say what the motivation is behind a given act. The behavior is often very puzzling to the caretaker, but when he names an attitude or motivation with confidence it is generally a dependable guide to the animal's future behavior. The naming is not made from superficial similarities with man, which are often very misleading, and the worker may want to know an animal for years before venturing an opinion as to what lies behind some particular act (Hebb, 1946a).

This provides an exceptional opportunity for study of the complex social stimulus. What are the actual cues that determine a social response? What parts of the response determine the further responses of others? When a child acquires some attitude from his parents we neither know what stimuli entered into the learning, nor how the learning occurs. We know little about the effective cues by which an emotion or attitude spreads infectiously through a crowd. As Allport (1940) and Jones (1944) have pointed out, it is urgent for psychology to find out what happens in the common-sense intuitive social judgment. Until that is done, there remains a fundamental defect in the data of social psychology. One could almost wish that the various rating and ranking methods had not been devised, for their success in quantifying social judgments has allowed us to forget that we do not know what is being quantified and has led us to neglect the essential task of analyzing these implicit predictions of human behavior so that we can learn to improve on them.

The first key fact is that recognition of a "mental state" in the chimpanzee usually does not depend on the present behavior alone. It is a perception of the relation of the present behavior to what the animal does in other circumstances. "Interest" describes a heightened level of responsiveness, not a particular level: the behavior that is a sign of interest in one animal is apathy in another. "Anger" implies a sharp deviation of behavior from an accustomed base line.

Accordingly, such identifications usually require a thorough, long-time knowledge of the individual, in addition to background knowledge of the species. Experienced caretakers refused, for example, to make any statement about the attitudes of two chimpanzees, Shorty and Vera, with whom they had worked for some months, on the ground that they did not know them well enough yet. The animal's history seems crucial always. A single observation of aggressive behavior on the part of Frank, in rather unusual circumstances, caused a serious revision of the generally held view that he was friendly to man, and these doubts persisted despite Frank's exemplary behavior afterward. At one time Dita had not attacked a member of the staff of the Laboratories for several years at least, but a knowledge of some of her earlier behavior still made her distrusted.

On the other hand, animals like Bimba and Fifi were frequently aggressive, but their aggressions were put down to brief bouts of anger, again to a great extent on the basis of their histories. The judgment that an animal is basically friendly, therefore, is an especially complex inference; this view is supported by the fact that there may be some disagreement among the staff as to the friendliness of a particular animal, and that the judgment is often made very tentatively. Although it is definitely based on behavior, and thus "objective," it is hard to find the crucial factors that determine it.

But other judgments are more amenable to analysis. Let us present next a method of recording used in a study of individual differences, or of temperament, in the chimpanzee (Hebb, 1949a).

A METHOD OF RECORDING SOCIAL ACTIONS

Systematic samples of the behavior of thirty adult chimpanzees were taken during the course of the ordinary routine of the Yerkes Laboratories, and records taken also of behavior in the "bold and timid man" experiment, to be described shortly.

Describing the behavior was the essential problem. It would have begged the question completely to record that the chimpanzee was friendly or frightened or bluffing: such judgments were the ones to be analyzed. It was also very difficult to avoid contamination of the data by such judgments made implicitly. Eventually some thirty-six specific acts ("first-order categories" of behavior) were defined in which interpretation was at a minimum, such that all observers could agree in their use. All records were made in terms of these acts, and thus seemed fully "objective."

At this level, however, the raw data were an indigestible mass in which no order or meaning could be found. The next step was to group together acts that had roughly the same behavioral significance. These "second-order categories" were *friendly behavior, aggression, quasi-aggression* and *avoidance* (together with a class of *no response*). Interpretation is definitely involved in making the classification, but it remains under control, and the data are recorded in first-order categories only. *Friendly behavior* does *not* mean "friendliness" but is defined as the occurrence of one of the following actions: putting the head, shoulder, back, belly, or arm against the cagewire at the observer's approach, or (if it was there already) keeping it there while the observer scratches or rubs the skin; thrusting fingers or mobile lips through the two-inch wire mesh (a common invitation to contact); grooming the observer's skin; and making a sputtering noise with the lips (Bronx cheer) while approaching the observer. *Aggression* and *avoidance* are self-explanatory; *quasi-aggression* is a combined category of intimidating and nuisance behavior: walking erect with the threatening swagger of the chimpanzee about to attack (or trying to bluff), beating the ground or some noise-making surface, throwing sand or feces, and spitting.

Order could now be found in the data, but it was still clear that something was missing: two animals that were known to be quite different might show quite similar totals in these higher categories. With the next step, however, light began to break through. The "third-order category" of behavior was defined as (1) the occurrence of behavior from two second-order categories in definite sequence (for example, avoidance followed by aggression is one category, aggression followed by avoidance another) or (2) the occurrence of an act in one second-order category in the absence of any act from another specified second-order category (for example, aggression not preceded by quasi-aggression). When the data were arranged in this way new meaning began to appear.

The change in analysis made by the third-order category is most clearly shown in the data for males versus females, in their relationships to the staff. First consider the second-order categories of friendly behavior, quasi-aggression, and aggression, as in Table 1. These data say that male and female show friendly behavior about equally often, but that the male is significantly more aggressive. The implied conclusion, "Look out for the male," is markedly out of line with the caretakers' experience; nineteen out of twenty cuts or scratches they receive come from the female. Now consider the third-order categories of *aggression preceded by quasi-aggression* (the openly prepared attack), and *aggression preceded by friendly behavior* (deceitful attack), as in Table 2.

TABLE 1

INCIDENCE OF THREE FORMS OF BEHAVIOR
BY MALES AND FEMALES: SECOND-ORDER CATEGORIES

Form of behavior		8 males	22 females
Friendly behavior	Total	205	531
	Mean	25.6	24.1
Quasi-aggression	Total	73	25
	Mean	9.1	1.1
Aggression	Total	41	38
	Mean	5.1	1.7

TABLE 2

INCIDENCE OF TWO FORMS OF BEHAVIOR
BY MALES AND FEMALES: THIRD-ORDER CATEGORIES

Form of behavior	8 males	22 females
Quasi-aggression, then aggression	37	0
Friendly behavior, then aggression	0	15

Since Table 2 may seem to have an antifeminist bias, we hasten to add several things. The male does not appear from the data to be less often desirous of doing injury than the female, but may be less astute about it. The deceptive attack on the staff by males does occur, although rarely enough that it was not found in the behavior sample; and seven deceptive attacks were made by males in the timid-man experiment (mean, 0.9; for females, 1.4). Some females, also, tend to show a male directness of attack, and individual differences in this respect seem to be greater than among males.

The method of analysis also clarifies certain judgments about individual animals which would puzzle an outside observer, or perhaps confirm his suspicion that the one making the judgment is going far beyond the facts, when a caretaker says that exactly the same behavior in one animal is the expression of anger and in another attention-getting. The judgments are complex, but one can now show that they are based on observable behavior.

Take the simple case in which the same act, spitting, is called evidence of *desire for attention* in one animal, *malice* in another. At the lowest level, we are dealing with two sequences of behavior, spitting followed by friendly behavior and spitting followed by aggression. From past observation of each animal the observer can predict the second part of the sequence and as soon as the spitting is seen, without further observation, can say, "That is (or is not) malicious." The diagnosis is a prediction, and the prediction does not arise from some esoteric penetration into the consciousness of the chimpanzee but from a knowledge (1) of what chimpanzees in general are capable of and (2) of what this chimpanzee in particular has done in the past. Again, *bluff* is the sequence of intimidating behavior followed by retreat if the opponent does not retreat but moves forward. As soon as he sees the intimidating behavior in certain circumstances the observer may call it "bluff" without having to see what follows. But he can do this only from prior observation, so his diagnosis once more is a prediction.

The reader may think all this too simple to need to be spelled out. In practice it is not. One's *present* perception of behavior is deeply colored by past experience. Experimentally, one may waste months in a futile effort to identify subtle distinguishing marks that are not there.

For example, it usually seems to the observer that there is something in the manner of the bluffing chimpanzee that is different from the manner of one that is really going to attack. Perhaps there is, but the experienced handler of chimpanzees still declines to make the judgment with confidence until he has seen a good deal of the animal, which indicates that he does not really identify the bluff by present behavior alone. One of us (Hebb) had worked on this whole problem of analysis for three years before he discovered that he was still recording intimidating behavior in two ways, according to what he thought it meant: he recorded "bluff" when aggression did not follow immediately, but "aggression" when it did. In the latter case the prior intimidating behavior did not seem something separate—it was a natural part of the whole picture of *one* aggressive act. The record of behavior became clear only when the two patterns were put down as (1) quasi-aggression followed by aggression, and (2) quasi-aggression not followed by aggression. Bluffing is a third-order category, that is, not first-order. Bluffing, as such, should not be entered in the record of behavior.

The same keen observer took two years to discover that his observations of Bimba's attacks were colored by his belief that the behavior was caused by anger, not cunning malevolence, so that he failed to see that the attacks were sometimes preceded by friendly behavior to get the victim within reach. Only when a satisfactory method of recording was used did the truth appear.

THE "BOLD AND TIMID MAN" EXPERIMENT

Any sensible person working with adult chimpanzees is constantly on guard, even with animals that in general are well disposed. But this very caution may be an incitement to attack, and it seemed possible that further light on individual differences might be had if one could test the animals' reactions to a person with no fear, on the one hand, and to an exceptionally fearful one, on the other.

Accordingly, the two roles were set up, played by the same person in two disguises. In the one, with hands protected by heavy gloves, the experimenter strode confidently up to the outside of the cage, making rough but friendly contact when the animal stayed within reach without aggression; but any attempt to scratch or bite was answered by striking back. The timid man acted the part of an excessively nervous person, very hesitant in approach, starting back at any sudden move of the animal, and making no near approach to the animal as long as he was aggressive in manner.

Some of the results are given in Table 3. The outstanding one was fear of the bold man, although he did nothing to start trouble but only answered in kind.

TABLE 3

PERCENT OF TRIALS (2700 WITH STAFF, 450 WITH TIMID, 450 WITH
BOLD MAN) SHOWING CERTAIN RESPONSES: *Fr*, FRIENDLY BEHAVIOR;
Ag, AGGRESSION; *QAg*, QUASI-AGGRESSION; *Av*, AVOIDANCE (DATA
FROM HEBB, 1949a)

Response	Staff	Timid	Bold
Apparently friendly (*Fr* alone)	26	29	23
Fear (*Av* alone)	0.2	7.1	37
Aggression (*Ag* in any combination: second-order category)	5.0	13	13
Annoying or teasing (*QAg* without *Av* or *Ag*)	3.7	24	3.8
Bluffing (*QAg-Av*)	0.0	2.2	5.6
Deceit (*Fr-Ag* or *Fr-QAg*)	0.9	17	2.7
deceitful attack (*Fr-Ag*)	0.6	8.7	2.2
deceitfully startling or annoying (*Fr-QAg*)	0.3	8.4	0.4
Afraid but friendly (*Av-Fr, Fr-Av*)	0.0	2.7	2.7
Afraid, antagonistic (*Av* plus *Ag* or *QAg*)	0.0	2.7	10

Avoidance alone occurred on 37 percent of trials with the bold man, as in the table, but if the trials in which avoidance was combined with some other behavior were included, the total would be 49 percent. Some of the fear of the bold man presumably was due to the strange costume worn, since the rather similar appearance of the timid man also aroused some fear (bold and timid man each wore false faces); but the two costumes were similar, so it may be concluded that the difference between 37 percent avoidance of the bold man and 7 percent of the timid man was due to the difference in behavior. It will be recalled that both roles were played by the same person.

A more significant result for our present purposes is the high frequency of aggression and quasi-aggression to the timid man, and especially the frequency of behavior which, to state the matter as clearly as we can, enticed an innocent close just to scare the hell out of him. The role, of course, demanded that the timid man fall into this trap as often as it was laid, and that he should show a maximum of startle every time. Many animals found the temptation irresistible; only nine out of thirty failed to show such behavior on one or more trials.

The individual differences revealed by the test method are at least as interesting as the group results, although they cannot be gone into thoroughly here. Pan, often aggressive to the staff but considered a gentleman because he always gave clear warning, began by attacking the bold man; being outbluffed (thanks to a strong cagewire), he appeared to lose all interest and moved off to a far corner of the cage whenever the bold man appeared. Two much more vicious animals, Pati and Beta, were equally impressed by their failure to cow the bold man, but in a different way. Like Pan, they first attacked; when the bold man did not retreat but struck back, they became markedly friendly. To the observer this transition was little short of astonishing. Instead of their usual lack of interest in man, alternating with vicious attack, they now vigorously solicited friendly contact. The behavior was not fawning by any means (both tried occasional further attacks, for example), but they appeared to be strongly impressed by the bold man, and on the whole very favorably.

Another pattern of response was shown by Mimi. She was markedly friendly to the timid man, and was tempted into only one attack on him, midway through the experiment; but she attacked the bold man with persistence and determination. Still other responses were shown by Jack and Frank, who were highly interested but unaggressive, and unafraid, with both bold and timid man.

THE CONDITIONS OF FEAR AND HOSTILITY

The results of the experiment just described serve very well to introduce our next main point, which is that the social determinants of fear and hostility are very complex. If the reader does not find this conclusion new and startling we can say it another way. The problem of social motivation is apt to be taken too lightly, with too much of the reversed-panacea approach—the idea that all our social troubles stem from economic pressure, *or* Oedipus difficulties, *or* frustration, or some other single source. Fix whichever one it is that makes the trouble, and all will be well. A main object here is to show that the infrahuman animal has a more complicated set of motivations than is allowed to man by these one-shot prescriptions.

Some of our conclusions in this chapter will be quite obvious ones: frustration is not a sufficient statement of the causes of aggression; the unknown, as such, may cause fear; man, who so often avoids pain and effort, also goes to some trouble to expose himself to threat of pain and to situations demanding effort. These things are common knowledge. But they are not common knowledge in psychology, and we must remind the reader that everyone knows a lot of things that are not true. One necessary task for scientific psychology is to sort out, among the obvious facts of human nature, the true from the untrue, the useful ideas from the useless. The reason for preferring simpler theories of human action is not that anyone thinks that the facts are really simple, but that it is too easy to postulate explanatory entities whenever the going gets hard. Which are the fertile postulates? Which are really needed to account for the facts? It is especially necessary to be careful when a discrepancy between fact and theory is found only at the human level, in the adult subject, because of the multifarious and uncontrolled experiences that occur during the long period of human growth, together with the special effects of verbal learning. So it will not be new if we conclude from the animal data that man is hostile to strangers; this is "known" already, but the need for taking theoretical account of it is clearer if its phylogenetic development can be traced, and when related behavior can be demonstrated in lower animals, in more controlled conditions and without the contaminating influence of language.

CHIMPANZEE FEARS AND AGGRESSIONS

Fear of innocuous objects is very common in the chimpanzee, even though these objects are not associated with some more primitive cause of avoidance. The diary records of the Yerkes Laboratories contain a great many references to unexplained fears of a particular person, some piece of apparatus or part of it, rope of a particular size, color, and texture but not other ropes, a biscuit in which a worm is found, a vegetable of a peculiar shape, and so on. There are great individual differences, of course, but as a group the adult chimpanzees are markedly subject to such fears. Köhler's (1927) observation of panic at sight of small animal models such as a toy donkey is well known. A chance observation, made with a clay model of a chimpanzee head (Hebb, 1946b), extended the range of objects known to have such effects. The clay model, reasonably lifelike in proportions but about half life size, produced extreme panic in nearly half the thirty-two adults to whom it was shown, and very marked signs of fear in most of the rest. An actual head preserved in formalin had the same effects, and so had a very lifelike colored model of a human head from a display dummy.

An attempt to deal with such facts theoretically (Hebb, 1949b) is not too satisfactory in certain respects, but the line of reasoning suggested a relationship to human emotional disturbance at sight of a mutilated body and fear of the dead, and so the following observations were also made. These are cited in full because of the socially significant aggressions that were elicited along with the fear. A dead chimpanzee was not available for experiment, but anesthetized ones were available:

Aug. 15, 1943. Mars, a young animal who had been anesthetized by nembutal, in order to make physical measurements, was carried out and shown to four of the adults, Jack, Dick, Don, and Dita. The first three of these were markedly excited (Dita less so) and Don attempted to attack. *Aug. 17.* Mars, anesthetized again, was laid on the ground in the infants' enclosure, with his fellow youngsters. One of them, Art, was persistently aggressive, biting and hitting the inert animal, who had to be rescued. Mars was then carried to the cages of some of the adults. Nana and Helene showed interest but no emotional excitement; Don was excited, with hair erect, and somewhat aggressive in manner; Dina and Bula manifested a nonspecific excitation, with hair erect; Wendy's hair was erect, she did not seem as excited, but she came close and remained; and Josie (as it happened Mars' mother, from whom he had been separated early) manifested an apparent mixture of aggression and fear—she was very excited, ran inside when Mars was first brought near, then attacked him through the cagewire. Her hair was erect throughout.

Since the sight of an anesthetized infant being carried by one of the staff was common, the observations above were later repeated with an anesthetized adult. *Feb. 11, 1945.* Don, under nembutal, was wheeled on a handcart up to the cages of nine other adults. Ami, Nira, and Vera showed fear, and Dina and Bokar did also but then followed this by a show of aggression at a distance; Kambi showed generalized excitation and screaming only; Frank, with hair erect, spat at the anesthetized Don; Pan first avoided, then attacked through the cagewire; and Lia, with general excitation but not avoidance, also attacked. (The youngsters in the infants' enclosure were afraid, one very much so, and all showed signs of marked excitation.)

Now let us look at the chimpanzee's aggressions as they occur in more ordinary circumstances, in the form of teasing, jealousy, anger, or chronic malice.

The motivation for teasing is often strong. It seems certain that the chimpanzee gets satisfaction simply from the discomfiture of the human being who is startled and frightened, or angered, by a sudden screaming attack on the cagewire nearest him or on being squirted with water. Certainly the animal goes to considerable trouble to achieve such results, in spite of being often punished for it and getting no other reward than seeing the effects of the act. Other chimpanzees are teased as well as human beings, as Köhler (1927, pp. 83ff) noted. Deliberate planning is involved, with an evident expectancy of the end effects of the behavior. "Teasing" is too mild a word for some attacks that seemed to be made only for the sake of others' discomfiture (as when Alpha would occasionally yank a handful of hair out of a thoroughly dominated cagemate, with no provocation), but it is important to note that these minor aggressions are not always indications of a desire to do more serious damage if only the victim were within reach. Quite often he *is* within reach, or becomes so later without receiving more damage. In the timid-man observations, some of the animals seemed genuinely malicious, but others, after once getting a rise out of the experimenter, became gentle and made no attempt to injure him when he came within reach.

Look next at the causes of anger, and their relation to frustration. The usual stimulus to anger is the behavior of a person or another chimpanzee acting in a way that is not desired, or failing to act in a desired way. "Desire" is one of the terms proscribed in Watson's revolution along with images and ideas, not because of its vagueness or trouble in defining it (after all, "learning," "intelligence," and "emotion" were retained), but because such terms were thought to be entirely subjective and anthropomorphic in their reference. We can now see that they are much better treated as referring to intervening variables, postulated processes, either with man or animal. As such they are more or less suitable for use in an objective psychology. They are still vague, but the fault is not in the way the terms are defined but in our theoretical conceptions, which will not be made any better just by using new terms. If one is really serious about stating the conditions in which anger occurs, a reference to desire or some equivalent is necessary.

To speak of "frustration" instead does not avoid the necessity, for it is clear that it is a *desire* or an *expectancy* that is frustrated. By some writers, of course, the term "frustration" has been used to emphasize the complexity and importance of internal representative processes in a Freudian or near-Freudian way (see, for example, Rosenzweig, 1944). With this we have no quarrel. But some writers have seemed to feel that the reference to frustration is a means of simplifying the problem, and that it avoids the need of postulating conceptual processes. Others have pointed out that this will not work for man (for example, McKellar, 1950; Sargent, 1948). The evidence seems even clearer for the chimpanzee.

When a female chimpanzee in heat is introduced into the next cage, the male seeing her gets up and comes as close as he can, until he is stopped by intervening cagewire. At this time he shows no anger, although a goal-directed response, strongly motivated, has been interrupted. But anger becomes highly predictable if the male is first led to expect, by the caretaker's actions, that he will be admitted to the female's cage, and then is not. It is the expectancy that gives the physical barrier its effect. In other situations, one can only say that the chimpanzee is angry because he does not *like* what another is doing. No goal-directed response is interrupted, and a physical barrier has nothing to do with the cause of anger (although it may prevent the effects of the anger from being visited on its object).

Thus Pan had a temper tantrum at the sight of two experimenters taking a vaginal smear from a female in heat in another cage. Mimi was driven to paroxysms of rage by the two inmates of the next cage, who would wait till her back was turned and then spring screaming at the intervening cagewire, repeatedly startling her. Bokar was almost as much infuriated by Dick's spitting water at him, even when he was not hit. Köhler (1927, p. 293) has noted that noise-making, and social disturbance as such, may be a cause of anger for a chimpanzee just as for man. The diaries of the Yerkes Laboratories likewise record a number of instances in which a noisy temper tantrum by one animal has led another to attack him. We have already commented (in discussing "altruism") on the anger of the chimpanzee at another's begging, even as he yields and hands over food. Defining the frustration in such cases of anger will present difficulty, unless it is frankly incorporated in a theory of thought so that frustration can be treated as some sort of conflict with the thought process. With anger, as with fear, the phenomena of emotion point to the intimate relationship of motivation to intellectual processes, and the impossibility of treating these things in separate compartments of theory.

THE PRACTICAL PROBLEMS OF SOCIAL MOTIVATION

It is reasonable, even desirable, to oversimplify theory in its preliminary stages, so long as one is concerned only with theoretical problems. The idea is that later stages of theory will do justice to the facts if early ones cannot. But it is quite another thing to forget that theory is still in these early stages when one is advising on a practical problem. What is virtue in one endeavor is vice in the other, and the more difficult the problem the truer this becomes. No other scientist deals with issues of such practical urgency as the social psychologist, and even though he has recognized the complexity of his problem the social psychologist may still find it worthwhile to consider some of the practical implications of the emotional behavior of higher animals, and perhaps also to be reminded, by the animal data, of the practical dangers of tacitly accepting too simple a view of motivation.

This last remark, be it noted, is not a covert attack on the theory of biological rewards (plus conditioning). Although we have probably betrayed our preference for another sort of approach, such as that of Harlow (1951) or Maslow (1954), we must point out that biological-reward theory is being greatly elaborated by such recent treatments of secondary reward as those of Meehl and MacCorquodale (1948, 1951), Mowrer (1950, 1952), and Miller (1951). These discussions imply no simple approach to the problem of social motivation.

In the year 1950 the main explanations of social hostility, as outlined by Katz (1951) in a review of the literature, make the hostility learned, *or* in some way a product of frustration. Although the difficulties in the way of one or the other of such simplifications have been recognized (for example, Katz, p. 155, concludes in favor of multiple causation), the comparative psychologist may point out that the literature reviewed by Katz predicates a view of motivation that on our present knowledge is doubtfully adequate for the laboratory rat and quite inadequate for the dog or chimpanzee, let alone man.

From the practical point of view in this matter, the animal evidence offers good news as well as bad. It complicates the issues theoretically, but some of the complications mean that there may be hope for man as a social animal. On the plus side there is, as we have seen, evidence of a fundamental aptitude in higher animals for friendship and helping others. We do not know just what conditions of rearing foster this altruism, but it should be possible to find out experimentally.

A further plus item is that frustration does not always increase hostility, and may even decrease it without evidence of undesirable side effects ("displacement"). Punishing an adult chimpanzee for a misdemeanor like spitting or scratching the caretaker does not usually produce signs of resentment. On one occasion at least, punishment of a young animal for repeated biting led to a strong friendship (diary of Gamma, Yerkes Laboratories, 1935). The reader may be reminded also of the sudden friendliness of Beta and Pati to the bold man, when he promptly answered attack with attack. In animals, as in man, the effect of aggression in some circumstances is *respect* and *liking*. Nissen (personal communication) points out that forcing a chimpanzee to do something, or forcibly depriving him of something, is as often followed by an increase of friendliness as by a decrease. The friendliness cannot be an effect of the frustration alone; it must depend also on the fact that the frustrater is a rewarder at other times. But with a background of beneficence, the important thing is that deprivation need not decrease goodwill. Social living and education inevitably mean an unending series of frustrations but these, it seems, should not be thought of as always making for hostility.

But the bad news must be reckoned with, too. On the minus side is the evidence that timidity, as such, may incite aggression. Fortunately, this is not always so, and the consistently friendly behavior of some chimpanzees to the timid man justifies some hope concerning primate behavior in this respect. Also in the debit column are the mammal's fear and hostility with strangers, even when no injury has ever been received from a stranger (Hebb and Riesen, 1943). This has an evident meaning for social problems, and so has the combined fear and hostility toward a fellow chimpanzee under anesthesia (if, as it seems, this means that the cause of aggression was the failure of the anesthetized animal to behave in the normal way).

There is also another kind of evidence, which has both good and bad implications. It shows, in brief, that mammals seek excitement, and this search has desirable possibilities in society as well as extremely undesirable ones. The animal that is so vulnerable to emotional disturbance nevertheless seeks the situations that produce emotional disturbance in mild degree. There may be difficulty about dealing with this theoretically (Hebb, 1949b, pp. 232ff), but it appears empirically that for any one animal there is an optimal level of fear or frustration. First, the evidence concerning fear: strange surroundings tend to produce emotional disturbance in the rat, but Montgomery (1951, 1952) and Thompson (1953) have shown experimentally that the rat which has the choice of familiar and unfamiliar territory will tend to move toward the unfamiliar—the well-known exploratory drive. Whiting and Mowrer (1943) and Berlyne (1950) have suggested a connection between fear and investigative tendencies, and the dog that is frightened by a strange object is nevertheless apt to return to look at it again, balanced between closer approach and flight (Melzack, 1952). The same thing can be observed in chimpanzees, and Woodworth (1921) and Valentine (1930) have described the behavior of young children who ask to be shown again—at a safe distance—the object that has frightened them. Secondly, concerning frustration: Harlow, Harlow, and Meyer (1950) have demonstrated the monkey's willingness to expose itself repeatedly to the frustrations inherent in problem solving, without extrinsic reward. Mahut, working in the McGill laboratory, has shown that the rat which is offered two routes to food, one short and direct, the other via a maze problem, will choose the problem on twenty to forty percent of the runs. *Some* of the time even a rat prefers to work for his living.

Such phenomena are, of course, well known in man: in the liking for dangerous sports or roller coasters, where fear is deliberately courted, and in the addiction to bridge or golf or solitaire, vices whose very existence depends on the difficulty of the problems presented and an optimal level of frustration. Once more, when we find such attitudes toward fear and frustration in animals, we have a better basis for supposing that we are dealing with something fundamental if a man prefers skis to the less dangerous snowshoes, or when we observe an unashamed love of work (problem solving and frustration included) in the scientist, or in the businessman who cannot retire. Such behavior in man is usually accounted for as a search for prestige, but the animal data make this untenable. It seems much more likely that solving problems and running mild risks are inherently rewarding or, in more general terms, that the animal will always act so as to produce an optimal level of excitation. One explanation has been attempted by Hebb (1949b); another, into which the facts on the whole would fit very well, is the treatment by Mowrer (1950, 1952) of anxiety reduction as a reward (though here one needs to assume that problem solving is also a cause of anxiety).

The potential social benefits of a liking for work and (in some essential occupations) for taking risks are sufficiently obvious. This is the plus side of the mammal's liking for excitement. But, as the chimpanzee's behavior shows, excitement may be sought in other less desirable ways. The plain fact is that the primate is only too ready to become a troublemaker when things are dull, and we had better stop comforting ourselves with the accurate but insufficient statement that man has no instinct to make war. He also needs no special coaching to discover a taste for "adventure," and some of his adventures may be socially disastrous. Fear or dislike of the strange is not innate, since it depends on certain prior experiences, yet it still does not have to be taught (Hebb, 1946b). If, therefore, man is not born with a dislike for those who differ from him in habits or appearance, he can still pick up the dislike with no help or encouragement. Making war is not instinctive; neither, unfortunately, is an aversion to certain forms of excitement that may lead to war.

It appears, therefore, that we stand on very slippery ground when we suppose that social harmony is to be had on a negative basis, by minimizing frustration for the growing child and not teaching him bad ideas about others. Suppose we do give the child as much freedom as we can; suppose the adult does see that he is not being injured or threatened by other groups—is there not still a strong presumption that more will be necessary? That the child must be taught somehow to *like* others different from himself, to get *pleasure* from knowing more about them and learning about their unusual ways? In addition to correcting economic injustice, may it not be necessary also to develop, systematically, socially harmless sources of excitation? Poker and bridge and pennant races, and bowling alleys and detective stories, may have more to do with our social stability than we think. Even today, an economically successful society may require circuses, in some form, as well as bread.

Economic factors obviously play a large part in social conflict; it is only too evident that children can learn hostile attitudes from their elders. We must recognize and control these factors for a sound society. But it is equally essential to recognize that there is no scientific basis for asserting that these are the only factors underlying war and race prejudice. We may even doubt that they are ever effective by themselves, without the deep-seated tendency to be disturbed emotionally by what is different from ourselves.

A THEORETICAL APPROACH TO HUMAN NATURE AND SOCIETY

We have made some effort in the preceding pages to be economical of theory, using no more than was needed to make a connected story. If we have nevertheless been speculative, we must now become more so. Our purpose in this final section is to offer a theoretical view concerning human emotions which, we believe, casts light on the evolution and structure of society.

Doing so is not outside the scope of the present chapter. The views we set forth derive from the study of animal emotions; and we may remind the reader, if need be, that comparative psychology includes man, regarding him simply as the highest in the animal series. Human culture is unique, but this only makes it the more interesting as a comparative phenomenon. From the comparative point of view it constitutes a special problem.

Man is the most intelligent animal; and the most striking feature of his behavior, comparatively, is an increasing control of the physical environment and the accumulation of "wealth" and wealth-producing skills. But almost equally striking is the progressive modification that has gone on in other aspects of human behavior: broadly speaking, a moral and political development. The economic growth can be treated as the result of a search for comfort by an exceptionally intelligent animal; a unique power of communication, particularly, allows for progressive problem solving. But can the cumulative change in other respects be ascribed to the same source?

Can we derive man's social evolution from his exceptional intellectual characteristics? Perhaps we would also allow him some altruism, on occasion, and we must certainly recognize that his powers of learning and communication will perpetuate some mistakes, so that if we see man as intellectually distinctive only we need not imply that all his social arrangements are intelligent ones. Even after making these allowances, however, we may ask whether such a simple model of the origins of society would not be significantly improved by recognizing that man also has exceptional emotional characteristics.

We have already proposed that the mammal seeks excitement when things are dull. This by itself makes an important change in the theory of "economic man." That theory can hold only in an impoverished society (in which the level of frustration is already above the optimum) and *not* in an economically successful one. With a general increase in wealth and security, the risky venture may be preferred to the sure thing, the interesting occupation to one that pays well.

But let us now go further. Evidence from species comparison suggests that emotional susceptibility increases with intellectual capacity. Man is the most emotional as well as the most rational animal. But this susceptibility is partly self-concealing: its possessor tends to seek the environment in which a too strong emotion is least likely to occur, the one in which disturbance is nearer the optimal level. In man, this makes for the establishment of "civilized" societies, the chief characteristic of which (at least until recently) is not that they improve the economic lot of the average member, but that they provide an environment in which the frequency of acute fear, disgust, anger, and jealousy is decreased. The further a society has advanced along this path, the less subject to strong emotion its members must appear. Violent emotional outbursts vanish, the wellbred man becomes the norm, and psychologists who seldom see the strong, acute disturbance (except in young children) begin to think of adult man as typically unemotional. But the susceptibility to disturbance may still be there and, although concealed, have a major influence on social organization.

EMOTIONALITY AND INTELLECT

Such views and their comparative origin will be more intelligible if we see how they were arrived at, in the course of constructing a theory presented elsewhere (Hebb, 1949b):

The first aim was relatively modest: to find some way of bringing together the facts of learning, perception, and set or attitude. This, it seemed, might be feasible if one could treat the thought process as a "phase sequence," as a series of events in the brain each of which might be aroused sensorily or centrally, or both.

The principal question was as to the nature of these events in the brain. Existing anatomical evidence, and some of the psychological evidence, led to the conception that each of the series of activities would be the activity of an "assembly" of neural cells. These assemblies would have to be established before overt learning could occur, which seemed to deny the truth of the theory, until von Senden's (1932) evidence was recalled. The second main difficulty entailed by such ideas, however, is the one that concerns us more. The assembly as postulated would be rather fragile in its function, easily disturbed or disrupted by unusual sensory conditions. The theory thus arrived at the improbable conclusion that a strange environment would interfere with thinking, or might disorganize it completely.

Then came a freeing hypothesis: suppose the interference with thought to be what we already know as *emotion,* and that it is usually mild. The neurophysiological speculations would permit the disturbance to occur in varying degrees, so let us assume that in mild degree it would not disrupt the phase sequence but only slow it. Slowing the phase sequence would mean that thought would continue, with the same general content, for a longer time. The thing thought about (or perceived) would be by definition more "interesting," more capable of arresting and holding attention. A mild disturbance might thus be positively motivating; and a strong disturbance, even though of the same kind, have opposite effects. Since (as we have seen) the behavioral evidence shows that there are such paradoxical effects of emotional stimulation, these neurophysiological notions seemed to have theoretical possibilities even though they still left much to be accounted for.

If such ideas were to be taken seriously, however, they had a further implication which led, rather deviously, to the present problem. If emotion is in some sense a breakdown of the thought process, it seemed that emotionality would become more marked when thought is more complex. The more elaborate the machinery, the more ways its operation can be disturbed. It seemed therefore that development of a higher level of intelligence would mean an increased vulnerability to emotional disturbance.

When the evidence was examined, some support for this idea appeared. The chimpanzee seems to be more subject to emotional disturbance than the dog, and the dog more so than the rat. There were also hints of an ontogenetic correlation, of increased emotionality with intellectual development from infancy to maturity. Now we come to our problem: adult man should be still more emotional than the very emotional chimpanzee and more emotional than the three-year-old child, and he does not seem to be.

But certain aspects of man's social behavior were very suggestive when they were examined from this point of view, and led us to the conclusion that the predicted susceptibility exists, that it is a major influence on social evolution, and that it tends to produce societies such as ours in which it can hardly be detected.

This view depends in part on the phylogenetic correlation. Let us therefore consider it first. There are certain primitive causes of avoidance and aggression that seem to work equally well at all levels of mammalian development: pain stimuli, sudden loud noise, sudden loss of support, restriction of movement by the animal that is used to freedom—all have immediate effects that are comparable in laboratory rat and man. But as we go from rat to man there is a progressive increase in the range of effective stimuli to avoidance and aggression, and in the duration and complexity of the response.

In the rat, for example, there is little need of such a term as "anger" for describing the animal's behavior. A rat is aggressive or he is not, and the aggression has about the same pattern in different circumstances. The same seems true of the dog, although occasionally he shows something that may be homologous with the primate's sulking. But with the chimpanzee, it is essential to distinguish anger from chronic malice if the animal is to be handled safely. The peculiarly human patterns of temper tantrum and sulking occur frequently. The causes of aggression are more varied in the dog than in the rat, and far more varied in the chimpanzee than in the dog. Finally, the period of emotional disturbance following a brief stimulation also increases from rat to dog to chimpanzee (the chimpanzee Fifi, for example, sulked for three weeks over not getting a cup of milk, first showing outright anger, then refusing to accept milk from anyone for a day or so, and continuing for three weeks to refuse it from the one who had denied it to her).

The phylogenetic development of fear susceptibilities is even clearer. In higher mammals' irrational fears, the motionless object may be nearly as much avoided as the moving one. For a lower form like the rat, avoidance of a strange motionless object may occur (Hudson, 1950) but it certainly is not a prominent part of the behavior. The dog falls part way between rat and chimpanzee. Melzack (1952) has described fears in the dog which are obviously like those of the chimpanzee, although the disturbance seems less intense. As for man's nearest relatives, the apes, it would take a page or more to list the specific objects and situations that are known to have caused *persistent* fear in the chimpanzee, as reported in the Yerkes Laboratories diaries and in systematic experiments (Hebb, 1946b; Köhler, 1927; McCulloch and Haslerud, 1939; Yerkes and Yerkes, 1936).

When one considers also his manifold angers and hostilities, the chimpanzee at first sight is a bundle of emotional disturbances. This is not really so, of course. Most of the time the chimpanzee is no more angry or afraid than his human caretaker, and frequently less. The thing that one fears another does not. Some animals are "nervous" or short-tempered, but others are placid. Our point here, however, is that as one goes from rat to dog to chimpanzee one finds an increasing variety in the causes of emotional disturbance, an increasing variety of manifestation, and an increasing duration following brief stimulation, all of which is consistent with the idea that susceptibility to emotional disturbance increases with intellectual development.

To this phylogenetic correlation may be added an ontogenetic one. In the observations with anesthetized animals as test objects (described in the preceding section) the frequency and degree of excitation aroused in the half-grown chimpanzees was markedly less than in the full-grown. The clay model of a head hardly got a second glance from the one- and two-year-olds; it absorbed the attention of the five- and six-year-olds but produced no avoidance; in most of the adults it produced strong fear, with some avoidance in all of them. Jacobsen, Jacobsen, and Yoshioka (1932) and McCulloch and Haslerud (1939) have described the increasing emotional responses of the chimpanzee in the first years of life. For man, Jersild and Holmes (1935) have shown a similar increase up to the age of five; they conclude that the trend is thereafter reversed, but we shall try to show that this may indicate, not a reduction of emotional susceptibility after five years, but the success of our society in protecting us from most of the situations that would produce fear in older children and adults.

Jones and Jones (1928) demonstrated that fear of snakes, at least, is much stronger and more frequent in young adults than in children, none of their subjects having had prior exposure to snakes. This was a cross-sectional study, and a longitudinal observation may be added. Two young children, two years apart in age, were encouraged by a parent to handle snakes and liked to do so whenever they saw and could capture one. But the older at the age of eight, the younger at seven, began to show not a fear but a dislike of touching a snake, and this repugnance subsequently became strong in both, still definitely without fear and definitely without any associated injury, in a part of the country where poisonous snakes are never found.

Even without the special theoretical views from which the discussion took off, such phylogenetic and ontogenetic correlations between increasing intellect and increasing emotionality would suggest that thought and emotion are intimately, essentially related. There must be doubt concerning any treatment of emotion as a state or process independent of intellectual processes, and having a separate seat in the nervous system. Brainstem theories of emotion, as developed originally by Head and by Cannon and Bard or more recently by Lindsley (1951), do not seem to give enough weight to the evident cortical elements in the fears and angers of the higher animal. These appear in the kind of perception that can cause emotion in the higher animal (including the role of fantasy reported by the human subject), as well as in the correlation with intellectual level that has just been discussed.

EMOTION AND SOCIETY

Such theoretical considerations lead one to expect that adult man will be more subject to emotional disturbance than the young child or subhuman animal. But such an expectation, surely, is nonsensical. At the age of three to four years the child is apt to be plagued by imaginative fears (Jersild and Holmes, 1935), and to plague his parents with his strong dislikes and outbursts of temper. The adult chimpanzee must be treated, in effect, as a wild animal, and as yet no one has been able to domesticate him. Surely it is adult man who is *least* subject to emotional disturbance. The chimpanzee, it seems, is explosive, unreliable, fearful, dangerous; man (normal man, normally reared) is ordinarily quiet, not given to sudden violent attack on others without warning, not forever in fear of this or that harmless object.

Perhaps so, but let us look more closely.

First, in most primitive societies it is clear that man has generally found himself ringed around by malignant ghosts and devils, with beneficent spirits in the minority, and has found it constantly necessary to spend time, effort, and wealth to propitiate even the friendly ones. Fellow members of the tribe commonly possess evil powers; and the one who has the evil eye is feared and hated, or killed, according to circumstances. For any one of the members to be greatly different from the others in appearance, habits, skills, or tastes would be more than apt to cost him his life. As for an outsider, even of the same race, language, and culture —*any* foreigner is distrusted and feared. He may be a convenient source of trophies (a scalp or an embalmed head to show that one is a self-respecting human adult), or alternatively may be captured and brought back whole for torture or ceremonial sacrifice for the edification of the whole tribe.

These are well-established facts of human behavior, and not rare exceptions either. However, if they are cited, and if one cites also the concentration and slave-labor camps of our own generation, to show that man *is* to be thought of as a wild animal, emotionally unstable and often vicious, the answer one will receive is that these things may happen if people are taught as children to behave in these ways, but that fear, hatred, and cruelty are not inherent in man's nature.

If so, one might wonder at the coincidences that allowed the same teaching to originate in so many parts of the globe.

However, we should make it clear at once that we do not argue that these attitudes are inborn. We do argue that man by birth and maturation has a tremendous emotional susceptibility on the one hand and some need for excitement on the other; that if these are handled carefully in the growing child, with a highly specialized environment, the results may be most admirable; but that these qualities by themselves, with no teaching from others or in spite of ineffective teaching, may by reaction to other environments produce socially disastrous results.

So far as we have gone, therefore, and thinking of our own suburban milieux as providing exceptional rather than typical examples of human social behavior, we might be justified in considering man not a tame animal but inherently dangerous, to be domesticated only with great pains. Picking a human society at random from all those that have existed, one might say that the risk taken by a stranger entering it—a member of another society, also chosen at random—would not be less than that taken by a chimpanzee or a wolf encountering a group of his fellows. It is not wholly fantastic, consequently, to suggest that man is more emotionally excited by what is strange than lower animals are, except after special training.

Perhaps we can go further. Even in ourselves, the civilized, amiable, and admirable part of mankind, well brought up and not constantly in a state of fear, there are signs that this urbanity depends as much on our successfully avoiding disturbing stimulation as on a lowered sensitivity. As already suggested, the capacity for emotional breakdown may be self-concealing, leading the animal to find or create an environment in which the stimuli to excessive emotional response are at a minimum. So effective is our society in this respect that its members—*especially* the well-to-do and educated ones—may not even guess at some of their own potentialities. One usually thinks of education, in the broad sense, as producing a resourceful, emotionally stable adult, without respect to the environment in which these traits are to appear. To some extent this may be true. But education can be seen as being also the means of establishing a protective social environment in which emotional stability is possible. Perhaps it strengthens the individual against unreasonable fears and rages, but it certainly produces a uniformity of appearance and behavior which reduces the frequency with which the individual member of the society encounters the causes of such emotion. On *this* view, the susceptibility to emotional disturbance may not be decreased. It may in fact be increased. The protective cocoon of uniformity, in personal appearance, manners, and social activity generally, will make small deviations from custom appear increasingly strange and thus (if the general thesis is sound) increasingly intolerable. The inevitable small deviations from custom will bulk increasingly large, and the members of the society, finding themselves tolerating trivial deviations well, will continue to think of themselves as socially adaptable.

The educated man usually prides himself on his broad-mindedness, his judgment of persons by their essential qualities, and his disregard of the superficial. The college student is, if anything, even more confident of his own contempt for appearances. Now suppose that someone whose appearance, only, departed significantly from the usual pattern applied for a job as a university instructor. Suppose it is a male who takes the highly reasonable view that women's clothing is more comfortable in the North American summer, or a female who decides that long hair is a nuisance and shaves her head bare. Or suppose it is a war casualty whose face is really disfigured by scar tissue, without ears, nose, eyebrows, or orbital ridges, but whose senses, intellect, and speech are unimpaired: what chance would any of these have to get a job? If he got the job, what chance would there be that students would sit in a classroom and listen to him, no matter how wise he were? None of these are major deviations from the usual human appearance. Merely asking these questions of an undergraduate class allows one to observe a curious mixture of uneasiness and incredulity. The degree of uniformity in the social environment is such that one has difficulty even thinking of a really different one. The trivial changes of fashion from one year to the next look big to us, and we flatter ourselves that a man's appearance does not fundamentally affect our behavior toward him.

Similarly, the adult may think that he is not disturbed by strange places, darkness, or solitude, although young children are. As our lives are usually arranged, this belief is easy to maintain. It is more difficult if one has tried being separated from one's companions in the deep woods at night; reportedly, it is also difficult for those who have suffered solitary confinement.

All this, it seems, casts grave doubt on the idea that man has intrinsically a greater emotional stability than the chimpanzee or other animals. The real difference may be in the protective environment man has created for himself, which he so takes for granted that he becomes unable to see how his stability is achieved, and how his behavior would look to someone not used to it.

More clearly than anywhere else, this is seen in taboo phenomena. The travelers of the eighteenth and nineteenth centuries were completely astonished by taboo—something new, quite foreign to their own lives. Scholars now recognize that taboo has always existed in civilized cultures, but even today it seems not to be recognized how complete and typical its manifestations are, nor how far-reaching in social effect.

Taboo is relevant to the present discussion in several respects. It was drawn to our attention, in the first place, by observing the chimpanzee's response to a chimpanzee or human head (described earlier). This reminded us of the equally puzzling response to the sight of a major operation or autopsy, so the further observations were made with an apparently dead (that is, anesthetized) chimpanzee as test object. The ambivalence of the behavior this aroused then recalled Freud's (1919) emphasis on the puzzling ambivalence of some primitive taboos: the object may be simultaneously regarded with reverence, and as dangerous or contaminating. It seems to be thought that in more enlightened societies such anomalies have disappeared. Any remnants of taboo in our own society are thought of simply as "moral prohibitions." Our taboos are thus regarded as purely negative, and more or less based on rational attitudes. But with the chimpanzee's behavior as a starting point, and with the question in mind whether man is really as free of susceptibility to irrational emotion as he seems, we found something different.

Consider first a relatively mild taboo, on the word "God." Although the taboo has become much less strong in recent years, its ambivalence is still beautifully clear. The word (1) has a reverent use, and (2) is also on occasion described literally as a "dirty word," for using which one of the writers some time ago (about 1910) had his mouth washed out with soap. The lexicographer need not be puzzled to find modern examples to illustrate the double meaning of the Latin *sacer*.

A much more powerful taboo on the dead human body is equally ambivalent. Be reverent to the dead, speak in whispers and make no jokes at the funeral service, and, if you are male, remove your hat. There are still remnants of the Middle Ages and Renaissance prohibition against cutting up the human body, shown in the difficulty of getting bodies for medical-school teaching or permission for autopsy. Dissection violates the sanctity of the dead. But in opposition to such reverence, the corpse is also contaminating, unpleasant, disgusting; disgust may be expressed, for example, at a report that relatives have kissed the dead man after preparation for burial. In general, members of this society are rarely exposed to dead bodies, except in war or disaster, and they tend to be ashamed of their emotional sensitivity thereto, so it is hard to produce formal evidence of the repugnance. An undergraduate class of 198 persons, including some nurses and some veterans, was polled to find out how many had encountered a dead body. Thirty-seven had never seen a corpse in any circumstances; 91 had seen one only after it was prepared for burial—a total of 65 percent who had either not seen a corpse or who had seen one only in the ritualized procedure that rigidly limits exposure to it. These statistics show clearly that society, for some reason, protects its members from something about the dead body, and if there should still be some doubt that this is the emotional disturbance that the body arouses, the reader can get the evidence for himself if he will obtain a human head from the dissecting room and try to carry it home openly in the subway.

Sex taboos are multifarious, but some of them clearly show the ambivalence we are discussing. On the one hand, marriage is holy; on the other, unsanctified sexual activity is—once more—"dirty," contaminating, filthy. We read with amusement and incredulity of the behavior of the primitive people who put to death those who violate a taboo; but the death sentence for rape and the prison sentence for the bigamist or seller of pictures of sexual congress is exactly in the same class, for it does not have to be shown that physical or psychological harm has been done to anyone, only that the taboo is violated.

That there is a double standard of morals is the old way of saying that as a sex object the human female has a stronger taboo than the male. For the ambivalence of taboos, it is significant that the swing from one extreme to the other is greater with the female than the male: her virginity is more sacred than the male's (which is apt to be a source of derision, except when the male in question is under another taboo, of the clergy), and she is more degraded *and dangerous or contaminating to others* when the taboo has been flagrantly broken. Observe also that young men have been known to say, and even on credible report to feel, that they are "not worthy" of some young woman or other; the converse point of view is notably rare.

The only apparent way of accounting for these ambivalences is to suppose that the taboo object is, in the first place, simply a very exciting one; and that this emotional arousal in some circumstances tends to be channeled into one motor outlet (for example, aggression), in other circumstances another outlet (for example, fawning or abasement). This implies that there might be individual differences in response to the same object, just as there must be differences in what is exciting to different individuals. It is, of course, evident socially that the growing child left to himself would develop his own set of taboos. "Moral education" has as one of its main objectives to establish uniformity: uniformity of taboo, but more broadly a uniformity of emotional sensitivity.

If all persons could be given the same emotional attitudes, including a fear of acting in a way that arouses emotion too strongly in others, internal social conflict would disappear, if at the same time the society is economically successful and provides its members with comfort and safety. This is the direction, it seems, in which society tends to move, up to the point at which the moral prohibition reduces provocative behavior below the optimal level. This level itself varies, of course, with individuals according to past experience, which means that society will never reach complete uniformity. There will always be a tendency to "test the limits" of the social code; the result in some cases will anger or horrify too many members of society, and the testing will be suppressed. In other cases, however, the tester will elicit a degree of response that is acceptable, and the innovation will be socially perpetuated.

We may see human society, therefore, as conditioned primarily by the avoidance of the too strong emotional disturbance. In the first place, this may be the action of "economic man": the search for wealth in the form of shelter and safety. Primitive man is likely to have more than enough emotional disturbance imposed on him by insufficient control of his physical environment. But an equally important determinant of early society is a means of controlling man's own behavior, as a source of emotional disturbance. This influence may have definitely uneconomic results, even at an early stage in the development.

If thus we consider man as distinctive not only intellectually but also emotionally, a more adequate picture of human society emerges. Although we have oversimplified, even our account does not make it a simple picture of enforced conformity and avoidance of fear- and rage-provoking stimulation. There are, also, the search for the optimal level of arousal, and individual differences of emotional susceptibility. Our society, as well, has a long way to go before it can be supposed to have reached the maximal degree of conformity. But it does not seem to have been recognized how consistently our society has moved in the direction of arranging that its members act so as not to excite their fellows beyond a certain point. When the strong excitation is not avoided, it is aroused under carefully specified conditions only (marriage, law court, and prizefighting are examples) in which the sexual arousal, fear, or anger aroused in one does not spread uncontrolled to others. Producing a low-level chronic excitation in others, such as fear of losing a job or not passing an examination, is not frowned on; but the hypothetical civilized man, the goal at which approved social education aims, does not, except in the special circumstances referred to, act so as to produce acute, strong sexual arousal, jealousy, anger, or fear. He does not display disgusting objects openly; he is equally careful not to get into situations in which his own emotions make a display of him.

Our social arrangements fall short of this admirable goal, but they have, on the whole, achieved in some segments of this society a remarkable success in avoiding the causes of strong emotional arousal in ordinary life. This result seems quite unpredictable from the assumption that man is in himself a relatively unemotional animal, distinctive mainly by his intellect. It does become intelligible if man has a manifold susceptibility to emotional disturbance; if he tends to avoid actions that lead to strong emotion, and if one of the causes of emotion is the sight of it in others; and if the gradual establishment of conformity makes things become exciting which would otherwise not be so, because of their strangeness.

Man is a rational, unemotional animal so long as there is nothing to disturb his emotions. Also, the causes of strong emotion are few, as we usually consider them; for all we take account of are the causes that *do* operate in a society the main function of which may be to control and limit strong emotion, and we are almost incapable of thinking of an environment that differs from the social and physical one in which we live and which we have so carefully tailored to our needs. The animal evidence shows that the altruism and friendship so prominent in *Homo sapiens* are fundamental to his nature: if we are to learn how to foster such attitudes, we must recognize and provide the kind of protective social environment in which it is possible for them to develop.

REFERENCES

Allee, W. C., A. E. Emerson, O. Park, T. Park, and K. P. Schmidt (1949). *Principles of animal ecology*. Philadelphia: W. B. Saunders.

Allport, G. W. (1940). The psychologist's frame of reference. *Psychol. Bull., 37,* 1–28.

Beach, F. A. (1947). Evolutionary changes in the physiological control of mating behavior in mammals. *Psychol. Rev., 54,* 297–315.

—— (1948). *Hormones and behavior.* New York: Hoeber.

—— (1950). The snark was a boojum. *Amer. Psychologist, 5,* 115–124.

Berlyne, D. E. (1950). Novelty and curiosity as determinants of exploratory behavior. *Brit. J. Psychol., 41,* 68–80.

Bernstein, L. (1952). A note on Christie's "Experimental naïveté and experiential naïveté." *Psychol. Bull., 49,* 38–40.

Bierens de Haan, J. A. (1929). Animal language in relation to that of man. *Biol. Rev., 4,* 249–268.

Bingham, W. E., and W. J. Griffiths (1952). The effect of different environments during infancy on adult behavior in the rat. *J. comp. physiol. Psychol., 45,* 307–312.

Birch, H. G., and G. Clark (1946). Hormonal modification of social behavior: II. The effects of sex-hormone administration on the social dominance status of the female-castrate chimpanzee. *Psychosom. Med., 8,* 320–331.

—— (1950). Hormonal modification of social behavior: IV. The mechanism of estrogen-induced dominance in chimpanzees. *J. comp. physiol. Psychol., 43,* 181–193.

Carpenter, C. R. (1942). Societies of monkeys and apes. *Biol. Sympos., 8,* 177–204.

Clark, G., and H. G. Birch (1945). Hormonal modifications of social behavior: I. The effect of sex-hormone administration on the social status of a male-castrate chimpanzee. *Psychosom. Med., 7,* 321–331.

Conant, J. B. (1947). *On understanding science: an historical approach.* New Haven: Yale Univ. Press.

Crawford, M. P. (1937). The cooperative solving of problems by young chimpanzees. *Comp. Psychol. Monogr., 14,* 1–88 (whole No. 68).

—— (1940). The relation between social dominance and the menstrual cycle in female chimpanzees. *J. comp. Psychol., 30,* 483–513.

—— (1941). The cooperative solving by chimpanzees of problems requiring serial responses to color cues. *J. soc. Psychol., 13,* 259–280.

Darling, F. F. (1937). *A herd of red deer.* Oxford: Oxford Univ. Press.

Davis, K. (1940). Extreme social isolation of a child. *Amer. J. Sociol., 45,* 554–565.

—— (1947). Final note on a case of extreme isolation. *Amer. J. Sociol., 52,* 432–437.

Dropkin, V. H. (1941). Host specificity relations of termite protozoa. *Ecology, 22,* 200–202.

Fischel, W. (1927). Beiträge zur Soziologie des Haushuhns. *Biol. Zbl., 47,* 678–696.

Ford, C. S., and F. A. Beach (1951). *Patterns of sexual behavior.* New York: Harper (Hoeber).

Forgays, D. G., and J. W. Forgays (1952). The nature of the effect of free-environmental experience in the rat. *J. comp. physiol. Psychol., 45,* 322–328.

Freud, S. (1919). *Totem and taboo* (transl. A. A. Brill). London: Routledge.

Frisch, K. von (1950). *Bees: their vision, chemical senses, and language.* Ithaca: Cornell Univ. Press.

Goldstein, K. (1940). *Human nature in the light of psychopathology.* Cambridge: Harvard Univ. Press.

Goodenough, Florence L. (1946). The measurement of mental growth in childhood. In L. Carmichael (Ed.), *Manual of child psychology.* New York: Wiley. Pp. 450–475.

Greenberg, B. (1947). Some relations between territory, social hierarchy, and leadership in the green sunfish (*Lepomis cyanellus*). *Physiol. Zoöl., 20,* 267–299.

Gregg, R. E. (1942). The origin of castes in ants with special reference to *Pheidole morrisi* Forel. *Ecology, 23,* 295–308.

Grünthal, E. (1948). Zur Frage der Entstehung des Menschenhirns. *Mschr. Psychiat. Neurol., 115,* 129–160.

Hall, C. S., and P. H. Whiteman (1951). The effects of infantile stimulation upon later emotional stability in the mouse. *J. comp. physiol. Psychol., 44,* 61–66.

Harlow, H. F. (1951). Levels of integration along the phylogenetic scale: learning aspect. In J. H. Rohrer and M. Sherif (Eds.), *Social psychology at the crossroads.* New York: Harper. Pp. 121–144.

Harlow, H. F., Margaret K. Harlow, and D. R. Meyer (1950). Learning motivated by a manipulation drive. *J. exp. Psychol., 40,* 228–234.

Hayes, K. J., and Catherine Hayes (1951a). The intellectual development of a home-raised chimpanzee. *Proc. Amer. Phil. Soc., 95,* 105–109.

—— (1951b). Imitation in a home-raised chimpanzee. *J. comp. physiol. Psychol., 45,* 450–459.

Hebb, D. O. (1946a). Emotion in man and animal: an analysis of the intuitive processes of recognition. *Psychol. Rev., 53,* 88–106.

—— (1946b). On the nature of fear. *Psychol. Rev., 53,* 259–276.

—— (1949a). Temperament in chimpanzees: I. Method of analysis. *J. comp. physiol. Psychol., 42,* 192–206.

—— (1949b). *The organization of behavior.* New York: Wiley.

Hebb, D. O., and D. Bindra (1952). Scientific writing and the general problem of communication. *Amer. Psychologist, 7,* 569–573.

Hebb, D. O., and A. H. Riesen (1943). The genesis of irrational fears. *Bull. Canad. Psychol. Assoc., 3,* 49–50.

Heron, W. T. (1935). The inheritance of maze learning ability in rats. *J. comp. Psychol., 19,* 77–89.

Hill, J. C., and B. Robinson (1929). A case of retarded mental development associated with restricted movement in infancy. *Brit. J. med. Psychol., 9,* 268–277.

Hudson, B. B. (1950). One-trial learning in the domestic rat. *Genet. Psychol. Monogr., 41,* 99–145.

Hull, C. L. (1943). *Principles of behavior.* New York: Appleton-Century.

Hunt, J. M. (1941). The effects of infant feeding-frustration upon adult hoarding in the albino rat. *J. abnorm. soc. Psychol., 36,* 338–360.

Hunt, J. M., H. Schlosberg, R. L. Solomon, and E. Stellar (1947). Studies of the effects of infantile experience on adult behavior in rats: I. Effects of infantile feeding-frustration on adult hoarding. *J. comp. physiol. Psychol., 40,* 291–304.

Hymovitch, B. (1952). The effects of experiential variations on problem-solving in the rat. *J. comp. physiol. Psychol., 45,* 313–321.

Jacobsen, C. F., M. M. Jacobsen, and J. G. Yoshioka (1932). Development of an infant chimpanzee during her first year. *Comp. Psychol. Monogr., 9,* 1–94 (whole No. 41).

Jersild, A. T., and F. B. Holmes (1935). *Children's fears.* New York: Teach. Coll. Bur. Publ.

Jones, E. S. (1944). Subjective evaluations of personality. In J. M. Hunt (Ed.), *Personality and the behavior disorders.* Vol. 1. New York: Ronald. Pp. 139–169.

Jones, H. E. (1946). Environmental influences on mental development. In L. Carmichael (Ed.), *Manual of child psychology.* New York: Wiley. Pp. 582–632.

Jones, H. E., and M. C. Jones (1928). A study of fear. *Childhood Educ., 5,* 136–143.

Katz, D. (1951). Social psychology and group processes. *Annu. Rev. Psychol., 2,* 137–172.

Katz, I. (1949). Behavioral interaction in a herd of Barbary sheep (*Ammotragus Lervia*). *Zoologica (N.Y.), 34,* 9–18.

Köhler, W. (1927). *The mentality of apes* (2nd ed.). New York: Harcourt, Brace.

Levy, D. M. (1934). Experiments on the sucking reflex and social behavior in dogs. *Amer. J. Orthopsychiat., 4,* 203–224.

Light, S. F. (1942). The determination of the castes of social insects. *Quart. Rev. Biol., 17,* 312–326.

——— (1943). The determination of the castes of social insects. *Quart. Rev. Biol., 18,* 46–63.

Lindsley, D. B. (1951). Emotion. In S. S. Stevens (Ed.), *Handbook of experimental psychology.* New York: Wiley. Pp. 473–516.

Lorenz, K. (1934). A contribution to the comparative sociology of colonial-nesting birds. *Proc. Int. Ornithol. Congr. (Amsterdam), 8,* 207–218.

——— (1935a). Der Kumpan in der Umwelt des Vogels. *J. Ornithol. (Leipzig), 83,* 137–213.

——— (1935b). Der Kumpan in der Umwelt des Vogels. *J. Ornithol. (Leipzig), 83,* 289–413.

——— (1952). *King Solomon's ring.* London: Methuen.

McBride, A. F. (1940). Meet Mister Porpoise. *Nat. Hist. Mag., 45,* 16–29.

McBride, A. F., and D. O. Hebb (1948). Behavior of the captive bottle-nose dolphin, *Tursiops truncatus. J. comp. physiol. Psychol., 41,* 111–123.

McCulloch, T. L., and G. M. Haslerud (1939). Affective responses of an infant chimpanzee reared in isolation from its kind. *J. comp. Psychol., 28,* 437–445.

McKellar, P. (1950). Provocation to anger and the development of attitudes of hostility. *Brit. J. Psychol., 40,* 104–114.

Maier, N. R. F., and T. C. Schneirla (1935). *Principles of animal psychology.* New York: McGraw-Hill.

Maslow, A. H. (1954). The instinctoid nature of basic needs. *J. Pers., 22,* 320–347.

Mason, Marie K. (1942). Learning to speak after six and one-half years of silence. *J. Speech Disorders, 7,* 295–304.

Meehl, P. E., and K. MacCorquodale (1948). A further study of latent learning in the T-maze. *J. comp. physiol. Psychol., 41,* 372–396.

—— (1951). Some methodological comments concerning expectancy theory. *Psychol. Rev., 58,* 230–233.

Melzack, R. (1952). Irrational fears in the dog. *Canad. J. Psychol., 6,* 141–147.

Miller, N. E. (1951). Learnable drives and rewards. In S. S. Stevens (Ed.), *Handbook of experimental psychology.* New York: Wiley. Pp. 435–472.

Montgomery, K. C. (1951). The relation between exploratory behavior and spontaneous alternation in the white rat. *J. comp. physiol. Psychol., 44,* 582–589.

—— (1952). Exploratory behavior and its relation to spontaneous alternation in a series of maze exposures. *J. comp. physiol. Psychol., 45,* 50–57.

Morris, C. (1946). *Signs, language and behavior.* New York: Prentice-Hall.

Mowrer, O. H. (1950). *Learning theory and personality dynamics.* New York: Ronald.

—— (1952). Motivation. *Annu. Rev. Psychol., 3,* 419–438.

Nissen, H. W. (1931). A field study of the chimpanzee. *Comp. Psychol. Monogr., 8,* 1–122 (whole No. 36).

—— (1951). Social behavior in primates. In C. P. Stone (Ed.), *Comparative psychology* (3rd ed.). New York: Prentice-Hall. Pp. 423–457.

Nissen, H. W., K. L. Chow, and Josephine Semmes (1951). Effects of restricted opportunity for tactual, kinesthetic, and manipulative experience on the behavior of a chimpanzee. *Amer. J. Psychol., 64,* 485–507.

Plath, O. E. (1935). Insect societies. In C. Murchison (Ed.), *A handbook of social psychology.* Worcester, Mass.: Clark Univ. Press. Pp. 83–141.

Révész, G. (1944). The language of animals. *J. gen. Psychol., 30,* 117–147.

Riesen, A. H. (1947). The development of visual perception in man and chimpanzee. *Science, 106,* 107–108.

—— (1950). Arrested vision. *Sci. Amer., 183,* 16–19.

Rosenzweig, S. (1944). An outline of frustration theory. In J. M. Hunt (Ed.), *Personality and the behavior disorders.* Vol. 1. New York: Ronald. Pp. 379–388.

Ross, S., W. I. Smith, and V. Denenberg (1950). A preliminary study of individual and group hoarding in the white rat. *J. genet. Psychol., 77,* 123–127.

Sargent, S. S. (1948). Reaction to frustration—a critique and hypothesis. *Psychol. Rev., 55,* 108–114.

Schneirla, T. C. (1946). Problems in the biopsychology of social organization. *J. abnorm. soc. Psychol., 41,* 385–402.

—— (1952). A consideration of some conceptual trends in comparative psychology. *Psychol. Bull., 49,* 559–597.

Scott, J. P. (1945). Social behavior, organization and leadership in a small flock of domestic sheep. *Comp. Psychol. Monogr., 18,* 1–29 (whole No. 96).

Sears, R. R. (1951). A theoretical framework for personality and social behavior. *Amer. Psychologist, 6,* 476–483.

Senden, M. von (1932). *Raum- und Gestaltauffassung bei operierten Blindgeborenen vor und nach der Operation.* Leipzig: Barth.

Stewart, Jeannie C., and J. P. Scott (1947). Lack of correlation between leadership and dominance relationships in a herd of goats. *J. comp. physiol. Psychol., 40,* 255–264.

Thompson, W. R. (1953). Exploratory behavior as a function of hunger in 'bright' and 'dull' rats. *J. comp. physiol. Psychol., 46,* 323–326.

Thompson, W. R., and D. Bindra (1952). Motivational and emotional characteristics of 'bright' and 'dull' rats. *Canad. J. Psychol., 6,* 116–122.

Thompson, W. R., and W. Heron (1954). The effects of early restriction on activity in dogs. *J. comp. physiol. Psychol., 47,* 77–82.

Thorpe, W. H. (1950). The concepts of learning and their relation to those of instinct. *Sympos. soc. exp. Biol., 4,* 387–408.

Tinbergen, N. (1951). *The study of instinct.* Oxford: Oxford Univ. Press.

Tolman, E. C. (1932). *Purposive behavior in animals and men.* New York: Century.

Tryon, R. C. (1940). Genetic differences in maze learning ability in rats. *Yearb. Nat. Soc. Stud. Educ., 39* (1), 111–119.

Valentine, C. W. (1930). The innate bases of fear. *J. genet. Psychol., 37,* 394–419.

Wasmann, E. (1905). *Psychology of ants and of higher animals.* St. Louis: B. Herder.

Wheeler, W. M. (1922). Social life among insects: IV. *Sci. Mon., 25,* 385–404.

———— (1928). *The social insects, their origin and evolution.* New York: Harcourt, Brace.

Whiting, J. W. M., and O. H. Mowrer (1943). Habit progression and regression—a laboratory study of some factors relevant to human socialization. *J. comp. Psychol., 36,* 229–253.

Woodworth, R. S. (1921). *Psychology.* New York: Holt.

Yerkes, R. M. (1939). Dominance and sexual status in the chimpanzee. *Quart. Rev. Biol., 14,* 115–136.

———— (1940). Social behavior of chimpanzees: dominance between mates, in relation to sexual status. *J. comp. Psychol., 30,* 147–185.

———— (1941). Conjugal contrasts among chimpanzees. *J. abnorm. soc. Psychol., 36,* 175–199.

———— (1943). *Chimpanzees: a laboratory colony.* New Haven: Yale Univ. Press.

Yerkes, R. M., and J. H. Elder (1936). Oestrus, receptivity, and mating in chimpanzee. *Comp. Psychol. Monogr., 13,* 1–39 (whole No. 65).

Yerkes, R. M., and A. W. Yerkes (1936). Nature and conditions of avoidance (fear) response in chimpanzee. *J. comp. Psychol., 21,* 53–66.

Zuckerman, S. (1932). *The social life of monkeys and apes.* London: Kegan Paul.

Author Index

Abcarian, G., 617, 673
Abel H., 456, 498, 499, 511
Abelson, R. P., 24, 26, 46, 65, 75, 78, 278, 290, 292, 293, 299, 304, 307, 308, 311, 320, 322, 326, 327, 332–334, 336, 337, 340, 344
Abrahams, D., 37, 79
Abt, C., 279, 347
Abt, L., 684
Abu-Lughod, I., 617, 673
Ackerman, C., 712, 723
Adams, J. A., 428, 432, 442
Adams, J. B., 615, 677
Ager, J., 241, 272
Albert, E. M., 728
Albig, W., 613, 673
Albrecht, M. C., 625, 674
Alexander, C. N., 502, 511
Alger, C. F., 390, 437
Alger, R., 350
Allee, W. C., 735–737, 769
Allen, L. E., 671, 674
Allport, G. W., 377, 387, 392, 437, 506, 507, 605, 613, 627, 655, 674, 749, 769
Almond, G. A., 605, 616, 674
Alpert, R., 660, 675
Altrocchi, J., 431, 449, 504, 511
Amosov, N. M., 309, 347
Amrine, M., 373, 437
Anderson, B., 354
Anderson, C. A., 351
Anderson, G. M. L., 691
Anderson, H. H., 691
Anderson, N. M., 428, 437
Andrews, T. G., 627, 674

Angell, R. C., 593, 633, 654, 660, 674
Anscombe, F. J., 121, 200
Anthony, A. A., 728
Arden, B. W., 297, 347
Argyris, C., 366, 396, 407, 437, 528, 590
Arieti, S., 681
Armer, P., 281, 347
Armour, A., 669, 674
Arnheim, R., 621, 649, 674
Arnold, M., 664, 687
Arons, L., 689
Aronson, E., 4, 7, 11, 14–20, 23, 24, 27, 37–40, 42–45, 50, 51, 54–57, 59, 60, 64, 65, 69, 75, 77, 79, 360, 459, 509, 511, 635, 674
Asch, S., 18, 19, 22, 24, 27, 28, 30, 32, 38, 75, 528, 590
Ash, P., 619, 651, 674
Asheim, L., 615, 649, 674
Athanasiou, R., 534, 594
Atkinson, J. W., 501, 511, 568, 590, 674, 684, 723
Attneave, F., 258, 266
Auerbach, A. H., 438, 443, 449
Auld, P., Jr., 632, 674
Austen, J., 624
Ausubel, D. P., 456, 476, 511
Ax, A. F., 44, 45, 75
Axelrod, M., 584, 590
Ayres, B., 705, 727

Bachrach, A. J., 369, 437
Back, K. W., 43, 75, 364, 376, 408, 431, 437, 472, 496, 515

775

Backayan, A., 714, 728
Backman, C. W., 455, 505, 508, 509, 511, 523, 656, 674
Bacon, M. K., 707, 712, 723
Badri, M. B., 609, 674
Baerends, G. P., 362, 438
Bagdikian, A. L., 618, 674
Baker, K. H., 552, 595
Baker, W. B., 493, 519
Bakker, T., 541, 542, 591
Balderston, F. E., 322, 347
Baldwin, A. L., 445, 627, 674
Bales, R. F., 324, 325, 355, 389, 396–398, 423, 425, 434, 435, 438, 443, 609, 633, 674, 690
Balintfy, J. L., 353
Ballachey, E. L., 207, 270
Bancroft, G., 544, 557, 590
Banta, T. J., 503, 511
Barber, J. D., 280, 347
Barch, A. M., 377, 438
Barcus, F. E., 597, 599, 601, 607, 613, 674
Bard, P., 764
Barghoorn, F. C., 675, 622
Barker, L. S., 407, 438
Barker, R. G., 364, 367, 368, 370, 372, 374, 375, 379, 407, 408, 416, 425–427, 429, 430, 438, 440, 441, 449, 450, 455, 511
Barnard, G. A., 161
Barnard, J. W., 396, 451
Baron, D., 486, 511
Barry, D. W., 618, 687
Barry, H., 707, 712, 723
Bartlett, C. J., 241, 266
Bartlett, F. C., 536, 541, 560, 590
Bartlett, M. S., 161, 198, 200
Barton, A. H., 598, 683
Barzun, J., 276, 347
Bass, B. M., 266, 271, 403, 442, 446
Bassett, R. E., 455, 511
Bateson, M. C., 446
Batlin, R., 614, 675
Bauer, R. A., 534, 590, 640, 675
Baumrind, D., 75, 77, 365, 379, 396, 407, 408, 411, 422, 426, 427, 438
Baune, H. B., 491, 515
Bayes, T., 160, 162, 163, 167, 168, 172, 179, 180, 200
Baylor, G. W., 314, 347
Beach, F. A., 724, 727, 732, 748, 769, 770
Beazley, L., 496, 497, 501, 519
Becker, H. P., 613, 675
Becker, S., 505, 518
Beegle, J. A., 462, 497, 498, 515, 519
Beezer, R. H., 582, 590

Behar, L. B., 498, 512
Behrens, W. V., 183
Beier, E. G., 505, 511
Bell, H. M., 502
Bellak, L., 371, 438, 684
Beller, E. K., 422, 438
Belloc, N. B., 543, 590
Bennett, E., 59, 75
Bennett, E. M., 660, 675
Bennett, H. L., 490, 520
Benney, M., 584, 590
Benson, O., 279, 347
Berelson, B., 597, 598, 601, 605, 613, 615, 620, 621, 626, 640, 641, 644, 645, 657, 661, 662, 663, 673, 674, 675, 682, 683, 691
Berg, I. A., 243, 266, 271, 446
Berger, J., 354
Berger, M. M., 381, 438
Bergs, L. P., 241, 266
Berkman, D., 604, 625, 675
Berkowitz, L., 347, 442, 484, 507–509, 511, 513
Berkun, M., 479, 499, 511
Berlyne, D. E., 759, 770
Bernreuter, R. G., 502
Bernstein, A., 290, 293, 322, 332, 337, 344, 347, 690
Bernstein, L., 733, 770
Bernstein, M. H., 617, 675
Berry, P. C., 26, 79
Beshers, J. M., 334, 347
Beum, C. O., 471, 511
Beveridge, W. I. B., 2, 76
Biehler, R. F., 456, 482, 512
Biel, W. C., 348
Bierens de Haan, J. A., 738, 770
Bilous, C. B., 490, 520
Bindra, D., 731, 740, 771, 774
Binet, A., 253
Bing, E., 379, 438
Bingham, W. E., 731, 770
Bingham, W. V. D., 526, 591
Binswanger, 630
Birch, H. G., 748, 770
Birdwhistell, R. L., 381, 387, 438, 439
Bishop, B. M., 370, 374, 439
Bitzer, D. L., 314, 347
Bjerstedt, A., 466, 478, 482, 498, 512
Blacker, K. H., 392, 443
Blackwood, B., 694, 723
Blaisdell, F. J., 508, 515
Blake, R. R., 59, 77, 378, 445, 477, 482, 497, 512, 521
Blankenship, A. B., 549, 591
Blau, P. M., 375, 439

Blaylock, B., 505, 513
Block, C. H., 26, 79
Blood, D. M., 540, 569, 593
Blood, R. O., 379, 439
Blumberg, N. B., 614, 675
Blumenstock, D., 622, 682
Boardman, W. K., 516
Boas, F., 703
Bobrow, D. G., 300, 314, 347
Bock, R. D., 472, 474, 512
Boder, D. P., 631, 675
Bonini, C. P., 322, 347
Bonney, M. E., 459, 477, 479, 486, 493, 494, 497, 498, 500, 502, 504, 512
Booth, C., 531, 591
Borgatta, E. F., 223, 266, 272, 397–401, 423, 427, 439, 455, 457, 460, 463, 472, 474, 476, 477, 484, 512, 518
Boring, E. G., 274, 531, 560, 591
Borko, H., 279, 347, 349, 354
Bott, H. M., 405, 439
Boudon, R., 332, 347
Bowman, M. J., 351
Boyd, D. F., 278, 347
Braaten, K., 540, 593
Bradshaw, F. R., 641, 691
Brady, K., 365, 372, 396, 410, 423, 424, 429, 448
Breed, W., 373, 451, 615, 675
Breedlove, J., 505, 518
Brehm, J. W., 45, 76, 78, 498, 512
Breitrose, H. S., 382, 383, 385, 444, 446
Brenner, M., 394, 442
Bretsch, H. S., 486, 518
Brewer, T. L., 667, 687
Brillinger, D. R., 160, 200
Brinegar, C., 639, 675
Brinton, J., 641, 675
Broadbent, D. E., 309, 348
Brock, T. C., 378, 439
Broder, G., 541, 592
Brody, R. A., 279, 348, 350, 603, 606, 609, 625, 633, 634, 655, 667, 675, 680
Bronfenbrenner, U., 462, 467–470, 512
Brontë, C., 627, 684
Brontë, E., 624, 627, 684
Brooks, M. R., 620, 675
Broom, L., 615, 675
Brosnin, H. W., 438
Brown, J. K., 723
Brown, J. S., 487, 513
Brown, R., 27, 76
Brown, R. W., 581, 592
Brown, V., 455, 507, 514
Brown, W., 476

Brown, W. B., 623, 676
Brown, Z., 37, 79
Browning, R., 322
Broxton, J. A., 457, 508, 513
Brundage, E. G., 471, 511
Bruner, J. S., 564, 595, 605, 613, 622, 655, 674, 676
Brunswik, E., 16, 76
Bryan, S. D., 664, 677
Bryson, L., 687
Budd, R. W., 617, 676
Budlong, D. H., 619, 676
Budrose, C. R., 330, 354
Buehler, J. A., 496, 513
Bunge, M., 276, 348
Bunney, W. E., 376, 403, 420, 435, 439
Burchard, W. W., 373, 439
Burdick, H. A., 18, 76, 507, 513
Burke, T., 691
Burnes, A. J., 18, 76, 507, 513
Burrau, Ø., 86, 200
Burton, R. V., 719, 723
Bush, C. R., 645, 676
Bush, R. R., 80, 83, 202, 353, 354, 522
Butler, J. M., 363, 439
Byrd, E., 482, 513
Byrne, D., 401, 403, 406, 439, 459, 479, 496, 497, 501, 505, 507, 509, 513, 516

Cahalan, D., 549, 591
Cahnman, W. J., 656, 676
Cairns, R. B., 497, 513
Calhoun, J. B., 362, 439
Callis, R., 243, 268
Campbell, A., 252, 266, 528, 582, 591
Campbell, A. A., 528, 592
Campbell, D., 232, 266
Campbell, D. P., 238, 243, 266, 267
Campbell, D. T., 7, 16, 24, 25, 60, 76, 79, 205, 215, 216, 241, 242, 253, 260, 267, 272, 367, 403, 409, 422, 428, 429, 430, 431, 432, 439, 440, 451, 529, 532, 591, 595
Campbell, J., 26, 76
Cannell, C. F., 534, 537, 541, 542, 544, 546, 547, 549, 564, 581, 584, 586, 587, 590, 591, 592
Cannon, W. B., 764
Canter, R., 586, 591
Cantril, H., 206, 267
Caplow, T., 496, 513
Carlsmith, J. M., 18, 19, 20, 38, 40, 42, 44, 45, 47, 49, 50, 56, 57, 58, 59, 60, 64, 69, 75, 76, 360
Carlsmith, L. K., 719, 723
Carlson, J., 373, 440

Carmichael, H. T., 371, 412, 440
Carmichael, L., 771, 772
Carpenter, C. R., 390, 440, 739, 743, 770
Carroll, J. D., 299, 307, 311, 320, 347
Carstenson, F. W., 664, 676
Carter, R., 656, 682
Carter, R. E., Jr., 615, 642, 676
Cartwright, D. P., 596, 597, 601, 676
Cartwright, D. S., 209, 242, 267
Casey, R. D., 683
Cassotta, L., 393, 440
Castaneda, A., 456, 459, 477, 487, 520
Cattell, R. B., 209, 236, 242, 267
Cervinka, V., 473, 513
Chabot, J., 473, 513
Chall, J. S., 641, 677
Chamberlain, R. N., 441
Chammah, A., 280, 354
Chapanis, A., 287, 348
Chapin, F. S., 462, 513
Chapman, J., 371, 412, 450
Chapman, R. L., 278, 348
Chapple, E. D., 378, 392, 393, 395, 440, 441
Chapple, M. F., 440
Charles, D. C., 476, 494, 513
Chatterjee, B. B., 259, 268
Chave, E. J., 224, 225, 273
Chesler, M., 684
Chess, S., 543, 591
Child, I. L., 694, 695, 707, 712–714, 723, 727
Childs, H. L., 681
Chomsky, C., 350
Choucri, N., 667, 676
Christensen, H. T., 450
Christenson, R. M., 619, 676
Christian, J. J., 362, 440
Christie, R., 280, 348, 770
Chow, K. L., 732, 773
Chu, K., 353
Clampitt, R. R., 476, 494, 513
Clark, A. L., 546, 591
Clark, G., 770
Clark, K. E., 238, 243, 267
Clarkson, G. P., 303, 308, 312, 348
Cline, V. S., 428, 440
Clore, G. L., Jr., 497, 513
Clyde, R. J., 522
Coats, W. J., 655, 676
Cobb, S., 546, 591
Cochran, W. G., 144, 145, 200
Coe, R. M., 322, 348
Cohen, A. R., 43, 76, 79
Cohen, B. C., 280, 348
Cohen, E. R., 132, 200

Cohen, K. J., 276, 279, 322, 348
Cohen, Y. A., 717, 723
Colby, B. N., 618, 636, 667, 676
Colby, K. M., 278, 292, 294, 295, 309, 310, 313, 314, 348
Cole, A. H., 45, 76
Coleman, E. B., 602, 676
Coleman, J. C., 383, 440
Coleman, J. S., 280, 284, 287, 298, 322, 324, 326, 329, 348, 349, 472, 514
Collier, G. A., 618, 667, 676
Collins, B. E., 58, 64, 76
Commins, W. D., 503, 506, 522
Conant, J., 643
Conant, J. B., 730, 770
Condon, E. U., 200
Condry, J. C., Jr., 351
Conklin, H. C., 723
Converse, P. E., 204, 266, 271, 591
Cony, E. R., 619, 676
Cook, S. W., 79, 215, 216, 217, 235, 238, 241, 242, 254, 267, 273, 373, 409, 440, 449, 522, 595
Coombs, C. H., 267, 209, 211, 219, 231, 233, 532, 591
Cope, V. M., 54, 55, 69, 75
Cornwell, E. E., Jr., 613, 676
Corsini, R. J., 504, 514
Cottrell, N. B., 69, 76
Couch, A., 237, 259, 267, 564, 571, 582, 591
Cox, D. R., 161
Cox, F. N., 488, 514
Cozan, L. W., 241, 267
Crawford, M. P., 741, 742, 748, 770
Criswell, J. H., 467, 468, 469, 477, 478, 498, 499, 514
Croft, I. J., 464, 477, 487, 514
Cromwell, R. L., 518
Cronbach, L. J., 237, 253, 257, 260, 267, 405, 440, 532, 591, 662, 677
Crossley, H., 546, 594
Crosson, F. J., 352
Crowne, D. P., 243, 263, 267
Crowther, B., 401, 439
Crutchfield, R. S., 28, 76, 204, 207, 270, 564, 591
Cushing, B., 655, 684
Cyert, R. M., 276, 322, 348, 349

Dahlberg, F. M., 666, 676
Dahlke, A. E., 351
Dahlke, H. O., 497, 514
Dale, E., 613, 641, 677
Damarin, F. T., 216, 267

D'Amico, L. A., 509, 522
D'Andrade, R. G., 703, 708, 719, 723, 726
Danehy, J. J., 391, 406, 408, 432, 448, 632, 687
Danet, B., 387, 446
Danielson, W. A., 615, 641, 655, 664, 665, 675, 677
Danielsson, B., 482, 496, 514
Darley, J. M., 18, 77
Darling, F. F., 743, 744, 770
Daugherty, B. N., 459, 507, 517
Daugherty, R. A., 498, 517
Davids, A., 478, 487, 514
Davidson, D. M., Jr., 458, 519
Davis, D. E., 362, 440
Davis, F. J., 656, 677
Davis, J. A., 459, 477, 514
Davis, K., 731, 770
Davis, K. E., 517
Davis, R. V., 595
Davis, W. N., 667, 682
Davitz, J. R., 445, 456, 503, 514
Dawe, H. C., 357, 440
Dawes, R. M., 253, 268
Dawson, R. E., 276, 349
deCharms, R., 602, 636, 662, 677
Decker, J. B., 664, 689
DeFleur, M. L., 216, 217, 268, 273, 620, 621, 642, 647, 649, 677
De Grazia, S., 626, 661, 675
DeGroot, A. D., 308, 315, 349
Denenberg, V., 733, 773
Dennis, L., 637, 688
Dennis, W., 609, 674
Deutsch, F., 381, 440, 628, 677
Deutsch, M., 28, 76, 79, 280, 349, 449, 459, 509, 514, 522, 595
Deutsch, S. E., 623, 691
Dewey, J., 586, 591
Dewey, T., 562
Dibble, V. K., 602, 677
Dickman, H. R., 426, 440
Dickson, L., 456, 496, 519
Dickson, W. J., 65, 78
Diersen, G., 381, 440
Dilger, W. C., 362, 440
Dill, W. R., 280, 348, 349
Dinkel, J., 667
Dittman, A. T., 381, 423, 430, 432, 441, 448
Dixon, W. J., 192, 200
Dohrenwend, B. S., 363, 448, 529, 534, 537, 581, 583, 594
Dollard, J., 631, 647, 677
Doob, L. W., 205, 268

Doppelt, N., 280, 349
Dornbush, S. M., 581, 594, 602, 612, 636, 649, 650, 655, 677, 688
Dostoyevsky, F., 628, 682
Dovring, K., 607, 622, 677
Drechsler, R. J., 377, 441
Dreyer, A. H., 479, 486, 512
Driver, H. E., 703, 723
Dropkin, V. H., 737, 770
DuBois, P. H., 220, 271
Dulles, J. F., 653
DuMond, J. W. M., 132, 200
Dunham, R. M., 447
Dunham, V. S., 633, 654, 660, 674
Dunnette, M. D., 26, 76, 208, 231, 268, 404, 405, 441
Dunnington, M. J., 465, 477, 490, 514
Dunphy, D. C., 314, 349, 355, 601, 651, 665–667, 676, 677, 682, 685–687, 689, 690
Durbin, J., 160, 201
Dworkin, L., 79
Dyck, A. J., 396, 406, 407, 441
D'Zmura, T., 679

Eberhart, J. C., 581, 595
Eckhardt, W., 623, 678
Edwards, A. L., 208, 224, 225, 228, 230, 237, 241, 243, 260, 268, 503, 584
Edwards, D. S., 467, 514
Edwards, W., 161, 201
Effendi, A., 653, 684
Eggan, F., 708, 723
Eisenhower, D. D., 606, 612, 619, 624, 643
Ekman, G., 233, 268
Ekman, P., 381–383, 387, 410, 412, 415, 424, 433, 441, 609, 610, 678
Elam, S., 347, 349, 351
Elder, J. H., 748, 774
Eliot, G., 624
Eliot, T. S., 44
Elizur, A., 632, 678
Ellegård, A., 639, 678
Ellis, N. R., 381, 441
Ellison, J. W., 639, 678
Ember, M., 697, 723
Emerson, A. E., 769
Enea, H., 314, 348
Eng, E., 456, 514
England, G. W., 595
Erlich, J., 551, 591
Errington, P., 362, 441
Esser, A. H., 389, 390, 441
Eto, S., 640, 678
Etzioni, A., 279

Evan, W. M., 279, 356
Evans, M. C., 496, 514
Evans-Pritchard, E. E., 720, 723
Evitts, M. S., 463, 474, 475, 525
Evitts, S., 456, 525
Exline, R. V., 385, 386, 441, 652, 678

Fadner, R. H., 659, 681
Fagen, R. R., 680
Fairbanks, H., 602, 603, 631, 678
Farber, D. J., 299, 349
Farina, A., 517
Faris, R. E. L., 348
Farr, J. N., 641, 662, 678
Fason, F. L., 516
Fattu, N. A., 276, 312, 347, 349, 351
Faunce, D., 498, 515
Fearing, F., 621, 647, 657, 660, 689
Feigenbaum, E. A., 276, 278, 299, 308, 309,
    312, 314, 315, 317, 320, 322, 347, 349,
    352, 353, 355
Feinberg, M. R., 482, 486, 515
Feld, S., 528, 592
Feldman, J., 278, 308, 309, 312, 316, 317,
    347, 349, 352, 353, 355
Feldman, R. S., 642, 688
Feldstein, M. J., 458, 521
Feldstein, S., 393, 394, 396, 440, 441, 442
Ferber, R., 540, 549, 592
Ferguson, J., 278, 322, 332, 352
Fernbach, S., 294, 349
Ferson, J. E., 500, 518
Festinger, L., 2, 38, 43, 45, 49, 57, 59, 76,
    267, 373, 430, 437, 442, 444, 447, 472, 473,
    496, 500, 502, 507, 515, 676
Fetter, R., 322, 350
Feurzeig, W., 314, 355
Fey, W. R., 350
Fiedler, F. E., 508, 515
Filbeck, R. W., 243, 268
Fillenbaum, S., 642, 678
Finesinger, J. E., 393, 451
Finlay, D. J., 680
Firestone, I., 79
Fischel, W., 743, 770
Fishbein, M., 455, 459, 508, 515, 529, 593,
    595
Fisher, G., 541, 542, 591
Fisher, J. L., 724
Fisher, R. A., 83, 183, 187, 191, 201
Fiske, D. W., 242, 260, 267, 409, 440, 591
Fiske, M., 529, 593
Fjeld, S., 478, 515
Flanders, N. A., 396, 424, 430, 442
Flemming, G., 502, 515

Flesch, R., 641, 647, 678
Flink, J. J., 205, 270
Flowerman, S. H., 545, 592
Floyd, J., 37, 51, 57, 75
Flyger, V., 362, 440
Foa, U. G., 466, 515
Fode, K. L., 67, 68, 78
Ford, C. S., 709, 720, 724, 748, 770
Ford, R. N., 224, 268
Forehand, G. A., 237, 268
Forgays, D. G., 731, 770
Forgays, J. W., 731, 770
Forlano, G., 522
Forman, R., 496, 513
Forrester, J., 279, 350
Forsyth, E., 470, 471, 472, 506, 515
Fortis, J. G., 618, 662, 683
Foster, H. S., 623, 642, 678
Foster, R. J., 237, 245, 272
Fourment, C., 496, 520
Fowler, F., 539, 541, 542, 544, 590, 591
Fowler, F. J., Jr., 539, 590, 592
Frager, R., 55, 58, 77 .
Frake, C. O., 724
Frankmann, J. P., 428, 432, 442
Fransworth, P. R., 270
Franzen, R., 657, 691
Frederiksen, N., 346
Freedman, H., 522
Freedman, J. L., 20, 56, 76
Freedman, R., 528, 592
Freeman, L. C., 724
Freeman, M. F., 199, 201, 202
French, E. G., 501, 515
French, J. W., 475, 480, 515
French, R. L., 456, 487, 489, 514, 515
French, V., 207, 208, 268
Freud, S., 613, 644, 645, 767, 770
Friedman, G. A., 603, 635, 650, 662, 684,
    725
Friedman, N., 386, 412, 413, 442
Friedman, P. A., 552, 592
Friedrich, C. J., 623, 678
Friesen, W. V., 412, 413, 415, 424, 441, 445
Frijda, N. H., 316, 350
Frisbie, B., 667
Frisch, K. von, 737–739, 770
Fruchter, B., 477, 482, 521
Fryer, D., 484, 524
Fuller, E. M., 491, 515
Funkhouser, G. R., 660, 678

Gage, N. L., 76, 259, 268, 447
Galanter, E., 76, 308, 352–354, 522
Gallagher, J. J., 496, 501, 515

Galler, B. F., 297, 350
Gallwey, M., 445
Galton, F., 693, 703, 726
Galtung, J., 642, 678
Gamson, W. A., 370, 442
Gardiner, L. W., 618, 678
Gardner, E. F., 453, 457, 465, 481, 516
Gardner, G., 477, 485, 516
Garfield, R. L., 505, 511
Garfinkel, H., 378, 442
Garner, W. R., 76
Garrison, W. L., 351
Garver, R. A., 623, 678
Garvin, P. L., 724
Gates, T., 643
Gaudet, H., 615, 683
Gauss, K. F., 121, 630
Geiger, H., 623, 681
Geis, F. L., 280, 348
Gelernter, H., 299, 350
Geller, A., 648, 658, 678, 679
Gellert, E., 363, 396, 403, 405, 421, 422, 424, 442
George, A. L., 599, 600, 603, 626, 627, 650, 661, 679
Gerard, H. B., 17, 28, 43, 60, 76, 77, 515
Gerberich, C. L., 299, 350
Gerbner, G., 614, 616, 679
Gerson, J., 638, 639
Gerth, H. H., 621, 681
Ghiselli, E. E., 208, 209, 231, 268
Ghurye, S. G., 202
Gibb, C. A., 484, 485, 516
Gibson, C. T., 292, 320, 350
Giffin, S. F., 280, 350
Gilbert, J. P., 278, 292, 311, 313, 322, 335, 348, 350
Gillespie, R. W., 322, 351
Gillie, P. A., 642, 679
Gillis, R. D., 642, 680
Gilmore, R., 484, 520
Gilson, C., 350
Ginglinger, G., 618, 679
Ginsberg, G. P., 540, 593
Ginsberg, M., 693, 696, 724
Glacken, C. J., 701, 724
Glad, D. D., 425, 442
Glad, V. B., 425, 442
Gladstone, I., 443
Gladwin, T., 724
Glaser, W. A., 352
Glazer, N., 635, 687
Glenn, E. N., 666, 667, 689
Gleser, G. C., 220, 271, 632, 633, 679
Glock, C., 619, 682

Goddard, K. E., 541, 542, 592
Goethals, G., 712, 716, 717, 724
Goldberg, J. B., 666, 679
Golden, J. T., 297, 350
Goldman-Eisler, F., 392, 393, 442
Goldsen, J. M., 598, 653, 657, 660, 682
Goldstein, A. C., 660, 675
Goldstein, G. D., 353
Goldstein, K., 734, 770
Goldstone, S., 492, 516
Goldwater, B., 623
Goldwyn, R., 491, 518
Golightly, C., 509, 516
Golovan, E. T., 347
Goode, W. J., 370, 433, 442
Goodenough, F. L., 730, 771
Goodenough, W. H., 723, 724, 727
Goodnow, R. E., 498, 516
Goodrich, D. W., 370, 442
Goranson, R. E., 508, 511
Gorden, R. L., 235, 268, 581, 592
Gordon, C., 223, 268
Gordon, D. A., 564, 591, 609, 624, 679
Gordon, L. V., 241, 269
Goring, C., 197
Gosset, W. S. ("Student"), 80–88, 93, 98, 127, 128, 135, 201, 202
Gottschalk, L. A., 443, 446, 449, 593, 631, 632, 633, 679
Gough, H. G., 243, 269
Gray, D., 385, 386, 441
Gray, L. N., 618, 683
Gray, W. S., 641, 647, 679
Green, B. F., 223, 224, 227–229, 269, 282, 299, 301, 309, 314, 350, 353
Greenberg, B., 743, 771
Greenberg, B. S., 605, 613, 643, 690
Greenberger, M., 292, 350, 353
Greer, F. L., 484, 520
Gregg, L. W., 326, 350
Gregg, R. E., 736, 771
Griffiths, W. J., 731, 770
Griffitt, W. B., 504, 505, 513, 516
Griswold, R. E., 299, 349
Gronlund, N. E., 466, 476, 478, 498, 516
Gross, A., 45, 47, 60, 76
Grossman, B., 486, 494, 495, 516
Grove, R. B., 309, 354
Gromyko, A. A., 667
Grünthal, E., 746, 771
Grygier, T. G., 464, 477, 487, 514
Guest, L. L., 545, 581, 592
Guest, R. M., 418, 433, 442
Guetzkow, H., 75, 279, 349, 350, 354, 356, 658, 679

Guilford, J. P., 208, 225, 228, 233, 269
Gullahorn, J., 292, 299, 306, 309, 312, 332–326, 335, 350
Gullahorn, Jeanne E., 292, 299, 306, 309, 312, 322–326, 335, 350
Gulliksen, H., 208, 218, 248, 269, 270, 346
Gump, P. V., 366, 376, 377, 379, 438, 442
Gunders, J. N., 719, 724
Gurin, G., 528, 592
Gurman, E. B., 403, 442
Guttman, L., 209, 221, 250, 266, 268, 269, 273, 714

Hadworth, M. R., 443
Haeberle, A. W., 410, 432, 443
Hafner, A. J., 632, 679
Hage, G. S., 612, 646, 655, 679
Hägerstrand, T., 322, 331, 332, 336, 350
Haggard, E. A., 371, 381, 383, 385, 412, 415, 443
Haigh, G., 631, 679
Hall, C. S., 609, 646, 679, 733, 771
Hall, E. T., 389, 418, 419, 420, 443
Hamburg, D. A., 376, 403, 420, 435, 439
Hamilton, A., 147, 148, 149, 150, 151, 153, 155, 158, 159, 165, 166, 167, 638, 650
Hamilton, T., 612, 679
Hammel, E. A., 322, 335, 350
Hammer, C., 497, 516
Hammond, K. R., 216, 269
Hammond, P. E., 439, 448
Hamsun, K., 628, 661
Hanawalt, N. G., 383, 443
Hansen, J. R., 299, 350
Hansen, M. H., 576, 592
Hansford, E. A., 280, 355
Hanson, J. A., 381, 444
Harari, H., 493, 520
Harary, F., 472, 473, 516, 523
Hare, A. P., 335, 351, 389, 394, 443, 446
Hargreaves, W. A., 376, 392, 394, 409, 443
Harlow, H. F., 757, 759, 771
Harlow, M. K., 759, 771
Harman, H. H., 220, 269
Harper, R. A., 371, 443
Harris, C. W., 76
Harris, M., 427, 430, 443
Hart, J. A., 617, 620, 642, 657, 680
Hartley, E. H., 725
Hartley, E. L., 206, 269, 684, 728
Hartley, R. E., 206, 269
Hartshorne, H. M., 458, 516
Harvey, J., 624, 657, 680
Harvey, O. J., 376, 442, 443, 523

Harway, N. I., 664, 680, 681
Haskins, J. B., 642, 680
Haslerud, G. M., 763, 772
Hastorf, A. H., 581, 594
Hatch, D. L., 656, 680
Hatch, M., 656, 680
Hathaway, S. R., 243, 244, 269, 271
Hatt, P. K., 370, 433, 442
Hauck, M., 584, 592
Havelin, A., 501, 525
Havell, F. W., 141, 201
Haworth, M. R., 412, 414, 443
Hawthorne, G. B., Jr., 279, 351
Hax, H., 259, 270
Hayes, A. S., 446
Hayes, C., 740–742, 771
Hayes, F., 381, 443
Hayes, K. J., 740, 741, 742, 771
Hays, D. G., 272, 279, 351
Haythorn, W., 455, 516
Haythorn, W. W., 279, 355
Hayworth, D., 629, 680
Hazard, J., 389, 443
Head, H., 764
Head, K., 534, 594
Head, S. W., 621, 680
Hebb, D. O., 76, 740, 741, 746–749, 752, 753, 755, 758–761, 763, 771, 772
Heber, R. F., 494, 516
Heider, F., 426, 444, 507, 516
Heilbrun, A. B., Jr., 244, 259, 269
Helmreich, R. L., 58, 64, 76
Helmstadter, G. C., 245, 269
Helper, M. M., 493, 516
Henle, M., 373, 444
Henry, A. F., 272
Herma, H., 613, 644, 645, 680
Hermann, C. F., 279, 351
Heron, W., 733, 774
Heron, W. T., 731, 771
Hertzler, V. B., 496, 519
Herzberg, F., 528, 592
Herzog, H., 623, 692
Hess, E. H., 18, 60, 76, 77, 216, 269
Hess, H. F., 392, 394, 446
Hester, S. L., 517
Hetherington, M., 503, 511
Heyns, R. W., 358, 405, 416, 421, 422, 425, 426, 432, 434, 444, 501, 511, 518
Hickman, L. C., 602, 636, 677
Higbie, C. E., 691
Hiken, J. R., 371, 443
Hildum, D., 581, 592
Hilferty, M. M., 80, 89, 90, 124, 203

Hill, A. H., 351
Hill, J. C., 731, 771
Hill, K. T., 476, 479, 492, 494, 516
Himelstein, P., 237, 273
Hitchcock, J. T., 700, 725
Hitler, A., 623
Hobhouse, L. T., 693, 696, 723, 724
Hoblit, R. E., 479, 486, 512
Hockett, C. F., 391, 406, 408, 432, 448, 632, 687
Hoeffding, W., 202
Hoffman, L. R., 396, 444, 505, 516
Hofstaetter, P. R., 504, 520
Hoggatt, A. C., 322, 347
Holland, E., 322, 351
Hollander, E. P., 476, 484, 517
Holmberg, A. R., 377, 444
Holmes, F. B., 763, 764, 772
Holsti, O. R., 603, 605, 606, 625, 634, 653, 655, 662, 667, 668, 669, 680, 686
Holt H., 389, 451
Holtzman, W. H., 500, 518
Holzberg, J. D., 491, 517
Holzinger, K. J., 472, 512
Homans, G. C., 323
Honigfeld, G., 642, 680
Hood, W. R., 523
Hoover, H., 623, 643
Hopmann, P. T., 667, 680
Horowitz, E. L., 215, 269
Horowitz, F. D., 456, 477, 487, 517
Horrocks, J. E., 456, 476, 485, 517
Horton, D., 724
Hotelling, H., 203
Hovland, C. I., 12, 30, 63, 77, 78, 205, 208, 229, 269, 308, 320, 351, 643, 670, 681
Howard, C., 507, 511
Hsu, F. L. K., 440, 723
Hubbell, C. H., 474, 517
Hubbell, M. B., 373, 444
Hudson, B. B., 763, 771
Hudson, J. W., 371, 443
Hughes, F., 637, 681
Hull, C. L., 744, 771
Hume, D., 730
Humphrey, H. H., 333
Humphreys, L. G., 258, 269
Hunt, E. B., 299, 306, 308, 316, 320, 351, 633, 670, 681, 690
Hunt, H. F., 76
Hunt, J. M., 478, 485, 495, 517, 732, 771–773
Hunt, W. A., 412, 445
Hurwitz, W. N., 592

Husain, S. Z., 472, 474, 512
Hyman, H., 529, 537, 546, 550, 583, 584, 592
Hyman, R., 428, 444
Hymes, D., 350, 351
Hymovitch, B., 437, 515, 731, 772

Iker, H. P., 664, 680, 681
Ikle, F. C., 497, 516
Inkeles, A., 602, 623, 643, 681
Insko, C. A., 507, 523
Isaacs, K. S., 371, 381, 383, 385, 412, 415, 443
Izard, C. E., 441, 445, 455, 486, 494, 503, 517, 678

Jaastad, K., 26, 76
Jackson, D. N., 237, 270
Jackson, H., 665, 677
Jackson, J., 505, 523
Jackson, R., 628, 688
Jacob, P. E., 205, 270, 653, 681
Jacobi, G. T., 353
Jacobsen, C. F., 763, 772
Jacobsen, M. M., 763, 772
Jaeger, C., 541, 592
Jaffe, J., 393, 394, 440, 442, 601, 629, 664
Jahoda, M., 79, 449, 522, 595
Janis, I. L., 205, 208, 269, 542, 561, 592, 597, 598, 601, 643, 659, 662, 681
Janowitz, M., 623, 659, 674, 682
Jaynes, E. T., 276, 351
Jecker, J. O., 382, 383, 385, 412, 444, 446
Jefferson, G., 274, 351
Jenkins, J. J., 641, 662, 678
Jennings, H. H., 453, 458, 464, 466, 467, 469, 477, 480, 482, 483, 486, 490, 517, 521
Jernigan, C., 516
Jersild, A. T., 763, 764, 772
John, V. P., 372, 393, 394, 410, 430, 450
Johns-Heine, P., 621, 681
Johnson, D. L., 497, 513
Johnson, E. S., 318, 351
Johnson, P. O., 128, 129, 130, 201
Johnson, W., 631, 681
Jones, D. B., 621, 647, 681
Jones, E. E., 459, 507, 509, 517
Jones, E. S., 749, 772
Jones, F. P., 381, 444
Jones, H. E., 730, 764, 772
Jones, H. L., 160, 201
Jones, L. V., 312, 351, 642, 678
Jones, M. C., 764, 772
Jones, M. R., 355, 438, 727

Jones, R. R., 605, 615, 656, 682, 686
Jordan, N., 26, 77
Josselson, H. H., 624, 682
Joyce, J., 639, 641
Jung, A. F., 378, 444

Kahane, M., 520
Kahn, R. L., 528, 529, 534, 537, 549, 563, 564, 581, 587, 592
Kalin, R., 667, 682
Kanfer, F. H., 394, 444, 448
Kanous, E., 498, 517
Kanter, S. S., 371, 451
Kanungo, R., 458, 495, 517
Kanzer, M., 628, 647, 682
Kaplan, A., 403, 408, 425, 444, 532, 592, 597, 598, 601, 653, 657, 660, 667, 673, 682, 683
Kaplan, A. M., 632, 679
Kaplan, D., 608, 648, 658, 678, 679
Kaplan, W. K., 581, 593
Kappauf, W. E., 198, 199
Kasl, S. V., 393, 395, 396, 444
Katkovsky, W., 519
Katona, G., 528, 592
Katz, D., 267, 444, 447, 551, 584, 592, 676, 743, 758, 772
Katz, E. W., 392, 396, 426, 427, 444, 450
Katz, I., 772
Katz, L., 464, 470–474, 506, 515, 517
Katz, R., 387, 412, 445
Kauffman, P. E., 392, 450, 631, 682
Kayser, J., 617, 655, 682
Kearl, B., 641, 682
Keislar, E. R., 459, 485, 509, 518
Kelley, H. H., 205, 208, 269, 280, 345, 351, 437, 515, 643, 681
Kelly, J. G., 500, 518
Kelly, R., 263, 267
Kelman, H. C., 28, 77
Kendall, M. G., 91, 160, 197, 201
Kendall, P. L., 529, 593
Kendall, S. F. H., 91, 201
Kendon, A., 718, 726
Keniston, K., 237, 259, 267, 564, 571, 582, 591
Kennedy, J. F., 37, 333, 334, 602, 618, 619, 623, 628, 629, 689
Kennedy, J. L., 348
Kennedy, W. P., 383, 448
Kenney, K. C., 230, 268
Kerr, W., 491, 523
Kessler, A., 292, 322, 354
Khrushchev, N., 623, 628, 629, 651, 689

Kidd, J. W., 489, 518
King, M. G., 482, 504, 518
Kingsbury, S. M., 620, 657, 682
Kingsley, C., 628
Kinsey, A. C., 528, 537, 564, 571, 575, 577, 580, 593
Kipnis, D. M., 478, 479, 497, 504, 518
Kish, L., 552, 576, 593
Klapper, J., 619, 640, 682
Klein, D., 363, 448, 529, 535, 537, 581, 583, 594
Klein, M. W., 602, 615, 682
Kleiner, R. J., 459, 509, 518
Kleinmuntz, B., 308, 309, 350, 351, 353
Kline, N. S., 440, 441
Kluckhohn, C., 205, 270, 586, 593, 667
Kluckhohn, F. R., 119, 201
Kluckhohn, R., 728
Knepprath, H. E., 624, 682
Kobre, S., 602, 614, 682
Koch, H. E., Jr., 634, 692
Koch, H. L., 498, 518
Koch, S., 267, 445, 447
Kogan, L. S., 371, 445
Kogan, N., 231, 270, 456, 457, 508, 518, 524
Köhler, W., 740, 741, 744, 747, 755–757, 763, 772
Komorita, S. S., 460, 484, 522
Korbel, J., 353
Kotovsky, K., 276, 320, 355
Kounin, J. S., 366, 412, 413, 424, 442, 445
Kracauer, S., 599, 682
Krasner, L., 447, 581, 593
Krasnow, H. S., 278, 299, 347, 351
Krause, M. S., 392, 445
Krauss, R. M., 280, 349
Krech, D., 204, 207, 270
Kreuter, J., 670, 681
Krieger, L., 491, 518
Krippendorff, K., 608, 614, 682
Kris, H., 613, 644, 645, 680, 682
Kroeber, A. H., 709, 724
Kroeber, A. L., 725
Krout, M. H., 381, 387, 445
Ktsanes, T., 502, 524
Ktsanes, V., 502, 524
Kuder, G. F., 243, 257, 270, 504
Kuehn, A. A., 348
Kuhlen, R. G., 486, 518
Kuhn, A., 682
Kurland, D., 386, 412, 413, 442

Lackner, M. R., 279, 351
Laffal, J., 632, 646, 682

Lamale, H. H., 545, 593
Lambert, W. W., 358, 365, 405, 425, 426, 427, 432, 445, 724
Landauer, T. K., 707, 713, 717, 718, 719, 724
Landis, C., 412, 445
Landy, D., 43, 77, 696, 724
Lane, R. E., 617, 682
Lang, G. E., 619, 683
Lang, K., 619, 683
Langevin, R. A., 671, 683
Lansing, J. B., 501, 518, 540, 545, 569, 593
LaPiere, R. T., 252, 270
Larson, O. N., 618, 683
Lasswell, H. D., 598, 599, 603, 605, 606, 608, 610, 611, 612, 622, 632, 637, 645, 648, 650, 658, 664, 667, 678, 679, 681–685, 692
Latané, B., 18, 77
Laughery, K., 350
Lavoisier, A. L., 730
Lawrence, D. H., 628, 684
Lawrence, Douglas H., 76
Lawsing, M., 494, 519
Lawson, R., 67, 78
Lazarsfeld, P. F., 209, 270, 469, 565, 593, 594, 598, 615, 674, 683, 684
Leach, E., 697, 702, 724
Leary, B. E., 641, 647, 679
Leary, T., 424, 427, 445, 633, 683
Leavitt, G. S., 268
Leavitt, H. J., 259, 270, 456, 524
Lee, A. M., 605, 622, 623, 683
Lee, E. B., 623, 683
Lee, M. C., 231, 270
Lefkowitz, M., 59, 77, 378, 448
Leggett, J. C., 582, 593
Leiderman, P., 77
Leites, N., 598, 603, 612, 613, 617, 681–685, 691, 692
Lemann, T. B., 116, 117, 118, 201, 468, 488, 489, 518
Lenski, G. E., 582, 593
Lerner, D., 79, 598, 599, 603, 607, 611, 637, 643, 650, 664, 683, 684
Lerner, M. J., 459, 505, 509, 518
Lesser, G. S., 412, 450
Lev, J., 202
Leventhal, H., 367, 383, 384, 385, 445
Levin, H., 394, 445, 696, 718, 726
Levin, M. L., 322, 351
LeVine, R. A., 713, 719, 724, 726
Levine, S. S., 718, 725
Levinger, G., 505, 518

Lévi-Strauss, C., 725
Levitt, E. A., 383, 445
Levy, B. H., 367, 373, 447
Levy, D. M., 733, 772
Lewin, H. S., 601, 617, 636, 684
Lewin, K., 207, 270, 368, 445, 538, 593
Lewis, H. L., 642, 684
Lewis, R. E. F., 412, 445
Lhamon, W. T., 516
Light, S. F., 735, 736, 772
Likert, R., 218, 219, 230, 266, 268, 270, 593
Linder, D., 45, 55, 57, 64, 65, 75, 459, 509, 511
Lindley, D. V., 161, 201
Lindman, H., 161, 201
Lindner, R. M., 632, 684
Lindsay, R., 299, 314, 352
Lindsley, D. B., 764, 772
Lindzey, G., 202, 269, 444, 447, 490, 491, 507, 518, 593, 675
Linnaeus, C., 736
Lippert, D. J., 691
Lippitt, R., 358, 363, 405, 416, 421, 422, 426, 432, 444, 482, 522
Lippmann, W., 643
Little, K. B., 389, 445
Litwak, E., 564, 593
Loehlin, J. C., 322, 325, 352
Loevinger, J., 208, 220, 221, 223, 231, 232, 241, 253, 254, 270, 271
Loewenfeld, I. E., 216, 271
Long, B. H., 652, 678
Longabaugh, R., 396, 398, 425, 445
Longmore, T. W., 462, 497, 498, 518, 519
Loomis, C. P., 458, 460–465, 467–469, 475, 493, 494, 497, 499, 506, 519, 522
Loomis, E. A., 410, 420, 446
Lord, F. M., 253, 258, 271
Lorenc, M., 381, 440
Lorenz, K., 732, 734, 743, 772
Lorge, I., 641, 684
Lotquist, L. H., 595
Lott, A. J., 455, 509, 519
Lott, B. E., 455, 509, 519
Lounsbury, F. G., 725
Lowenthal, L., 613, 628, 661, 684
Lowie, R. H., 725
Lucas, J., 343, 352
Luce, D. R., 472, 473, 519
Luce, R. D., 353, 354, 522
Lundberg, G. A., 454, 455, 456, 494, 496, 497, 498, 501, 519
Lundy, R. M., 504, 505, 519
Lyle, H. M., 381, 446

Lyman, S. M., 390, 446
Lynch, M. D., 642, 653, 684, 690

McBride, A. F., 745, 746, 772
McCandless, B. R., 456, 459, 477, 482, 487, 490, 520
McCarthy, J., 299, 352
McClelland, D. C., 602, 603, 609, 634, 635, 646, 650, 662, 667, 682, 684, 725
Maccoby, E. E., 529, 593, 696, 718, 726, 728
Maccoby, N., 382, 383, 385, 412, 413, 444, 446, 529, 593, 602, 615, 655, 682, 684
McCormick, B. L., 507, 525
MacCorquodale, K., 757, 773
McCracken, D. F., 297, 352
McCulloch, T. L., 763, 772
McCurdy, H. G., 627, 628, 647, 684
McDavid, J., 493, 520
McDavid, J. M., 61, 77
McDiarmid, M., 629, 684
Macdonald, N. J., 110, 201
McDonald, R. D., 501, 509, 513, 520
McEvoy, J., 623, 684
Macfarlane, J. W., 543, 593
McGovern, P. J., 314, 352
McGranahan, D. V., 636, 655, 685
McGuigan, F. J., 77
McGuire, W. J., 78
Machotka, P., 386, 387, 450
McKellar, P., 756, 772
McKenna, H. V., 504, 520
McKinley, J. C., 243, 244, 269, 271, 464, 465, 466, 520
McLaughlin, B., 667, 685
McLaughlin, D. H., 94, 203
Maclay, H., 392, 446
McNeil, E. B., 680
McNemar, Q., 74, 77
McPhee, W. N., 278, 284, 289, 298, 322, 332, 333, 336, 352
McPherson, W., 667, 685
McQuitty, L., 231, 271
MacRae, D., Jr., 472, 474, 514, 520
McWhinney, W. H., 278, 330, 352
Madison, J., 147–151, 153, 155, 158, 159, 165–167, 638, 639, 650
Madow, W. G., 202, 541, 542, 593
Maher, B. H., 449
Magliocco, E. B., 679
Mahl, G. F., 375, 387, 391, 392, 393, 395, 396, 444, 446, 449, 451, 632, 685
Mahut, H., 759
Maier, N. R. F., 396, 444, 505, 516, 738, 772
Maisonneuve, J., 496, 504, 520

Malcolm, D. G., 279, 352
Malinowski, B., 698, 725
Maller, J. B., 458, 516
Mandler, G., 76, 581, 593
Mann, H. B., 202
Mann, J. H., 456, 457, 499, 520
Mann, M. B., 602, 631, 685
Mann, R. D., 397, 398, 422, 424, 426, 446
Manners, R. A., 725
March, J. G., 322, 348, 349, 451
Mardsen, G., 632, 685
Maretzki, H., 701, 725
Maretzki, T. W., 701, 725
Marin, J., 299, 308, 316, 320, 351
Markham, J. W., 614, 649, 685
Marks, E. S., 544, 592, 593
Marks, J. B., 464, 492, 504, 520
Marlowe, D., 55, 58, 77, 243, 267
Marshall, H. R., 456, 466, 476, 477, 482, 490, 493, 495, 520
Martin, B., 241, 266
Martin, C. E., 528, 564, 593
Marx, M., 355
Masling, J., 62, 77, 484, 520
Maslow, A. H., 757, 772
Mason, M. K., 731, 772
Massarik, F., 458, 520
Masserman, E. H., 441
Masserman, J. H., 449
Massing, P. W., 643, 685
Masuyama, M., 198, 201
Matarazzo, J. D., 379, 392–394, 446–449, 451
Matarazzo, R. G., 393, 446, 448
Mather, K., 191, 201
Mathewson, G. C., 17, 43, 77
Matilda, W. R., 685
Matthews, B. C., 618, 685
Maucorps, P. H., 456, 520
Mauldin, W. P., 544, 592, 593
Maurer, L., 691
Mausner, B., 528, 592
May, A., 458, 516
May, M. A., 689
Mead, G. H., 741
Mealy, G., 353
Medley, D. M., 358, 396, 403, 404, 407, 417, 418, 421, 422, 424, 427, 433, 434, 447
Meehl, P. E., 244, 253, 267, 271, 662, 677, 757, 773
Meeker, R. J., 280, 355
Meeland, T., 479, 499, 511
Mehlman, B., 503, 520
Melbin, M., 418, 447
Melzack, R., 759, 763, 773

Menchik, M. D., 667, 676
Mendenhall, T. C., 638, 685
Mensh, I. N., 489, 515
Menzel, H., 271
Merikallio, R. A., 299, 351
Merrill, J. C., 619, 685
Merritt, R. L., 640, 646, 680, 685
Merton, R. K., 529, 593, 623, 684, 685
Messick, S., 237, 245, 259, 270, 271, 346, 348, 352, 354, 356
Metzger, D., 725
Meyer, D. R., 759, 771
Meyer, L. R., 410, 420, 446
Michael, W. B., 475, 480, 515
Michaelis, A. R., 412, 413, 448
Mickey, M. R., 160, 201
Mikawa, J., 501, 513
Miklich, D. R., 237, 245, 271
Miklowitz, A., 440
Miles, J., 624, 647, 685
Milgram, S., 22–25, 27, 34, 38, 44, 46, 62, 75, 77, 528, 593
Milholland, J. E., 253, 271
Miller, D. R., 491, 520
Miller, G. A., 308, 309, 352, 428, 433, 447
Miller, J. C., 24, 46, 65, 75
Miller, N., 367, 373, 447
Miller, N. E., 15, 16, 77, 744, 757, 773
Miller, Robert G., 110, 201
Miller, Rupert G., Jr., 160, 201
Miller, W. E., 266, 591
Mills, C. R., 486, 521
Mills, J., 4, 7, 11, 14–17, 19, 24, 27, 38, 39, 43, 69, 75
Mills, T. M., 396, 422, 447, 609, 633, 685
Minsky, M., 276, 313, 352
Minturn, L., 700, 725
Mintz, A., 656, 685
Mishler, E. G., 394, 395, 447
Mitzel, H. E., 358, 403, 404, 417, 418, 421, 422, 425, 427, 433, 447
Moeller, G. H., 602, 636, 662, 677
Montgomery, K. C., 759, 773
Mood, A. M., 192, 200
Mooney, H. W., 542, 544, 594
Mooney, R. L., 486
Moore, B. V., 526, 591
Moore, S., 456, 477, 490, 493, 498, 499, 521
Moreno, J. L., 217, 271, 454–456, 458, 460, 463, 464, 466, 469, 471, 478, 485, 498, 499, 521, 587
Morgan, L. H., 709, 725
Morgan, T. B., 334, 352
Morrill, R. L., 331, 352

Morris, C. W., 600, 685, 739, 741, 773
Morton, A. Q., 639, 685
Moses, L., 194, 202
Moses, R., 393, 440
Mosteller, F., 80, 83, 148, 150, 161, 166, 180, 184, 185, 186, 190, 198, 199, 202, 343, 602, 638, 647, 650, 685
Mott, F. L., 613, 685
Moustakas, C. E., 424, 447
Mouton, J. S., 59, 77, 378, 445, 477, 482, 512, 521
Mowrer, O. H., 631, 632, 647, 677, 686, 773, 774, 757, 759
Muhlhan, G., 627, 674
Mulkey, S. W., 655, 676
Mullins, C. J., 238, 271
Mulry, R. C., 67, 68, 78
Munroe, R. L., 719, 725
Murchison, C., 773
Murdock, G. P., 693, 697–699, 701, 702, 704–706, 711, 713, 715, 718, 722–727
Muriel, J., 451
Murphy, G., 454
Murray, E. J., 396, 449, 632, 674
Murray, H. A., 12, 13, 23, 77, 410, 447, 457, 501, 502, 521
Murstein, B. I., 503, 521
Mussen, P. H., 445, 451
Mussolini, B., 623
Myers, R. J., 540, 594

Nadel, S. F., 586, 594
Nag, M., 726
Namenwirth, J. Z., 355, 690
Nangle, F., 377, 438
Naroll, R., 696–698, 703, 708, 712, 713, 716, 724–727
Naylor, T. H., 279, 353
Neely, T., 546, 594
Neisser, U., 315, 353
Nelson, C. J., 610, 652, 692
Nelson, D., 459, 479, 507, 509, 521
Nerlove, S., 710, 726
Neter, J., 542, 594
Neumann, J. von, 276, 305, 308, 356
Newcomb, T. M., 204, 271, 458, 459, 478, 506–509, 521, 684, 725, 728
Newell, A., 276, 281, 284, 299, 303, 306, 308, 310, 312, 313, 315, 316, 344, 348, 353, 355
Newstetter, W. I., 458, 521
Newton, I., 730
Nieboer, H. J., 693, 726
Niles, P., 367, 445

Nissen, H. W., 733, 741, 742, 744, 758, 773
Nixon, R., 333, 602, 618, 628, 629, 689
Nixon, R. B., 605, 615, 686
Noel, R., 350
Norman, R. D., 465, 493, 521
Norman, W. T., 243, 244, 271
North, R. C., 603, 606, 633, 634, 652, 655, 659, 662, 667, 680, 686, 692
Northway, M. L., 461–463, 467, 486, 490, 491, 521, 522
Norton, A. E., 412, 413, 424, 445
Norton, N., 387, 446
Nosanchuk, T. A., 474, 522
Nuckols, R., 592
Nunnally, J. C., 616, 620, 652, 653, 686
Nuttall, R. L., 55, 58, 77

O'Connell, D. N., 381, 444
O'Connor, J. P., 504, 520
Odishaw, H., 200
Ogilvie, D. M., 355, 666, 667, 670, 676, 677, 682, 685–687, 689, 690
Ohlström, B., 622, 686
Ojemann, R. H., 613, 686
Okabe, T., 640, 678
Olesen, B. A., 522
Olkins, I., 202
Olds, J., 669, 687
Oppenheimer, J. R., 11, 15, 63, 64
Orcutt, G. H., 322, 334, 353
Organick, E. I., 297, 353
Orne, M., 28, 61, 62, 72, 78, 369, 447
Osgood, C. E., 76, 391, 392, 446, 447, 599, 601, 605, 606, 627, 632, 645, 648, 652, 653, 666, 686
Owens, M., 671, 683

Page, H. W., 603, 686
Paige, J. M., 314, 353, 627, 666, 686
Painter, J. A., 687, 664, 686, 687
Paisley, W. J., 603, 624, 639, 686
Paivo, A., 445
Palermo, D. S., 456, 459, 477, 487, 520
Palmade, G., 496, 520
Parenti, A. N., 478, 487, 514
Park, O., 769
Park, T., 769
Parker, E. B., 660, 678
Parker, E. C., 618, 687
Parloff, M. S., 449
Parrish, S. M., 624, 647, 664, 687
Parry, H., 546, 594
Parsons, T., 270, 667, 669, 687
Patterson, D. G., 641, 662, 678

Payne, S. L., 534, 554, 594
Peabody, D., 237, 271
Peak, H., 421, 447
Pearson, E. S., 161, 167, 197, 202, 467, 470
Peirson, G. W., 347, 350, 356
Pelley, W. D., 637
Pennock, J. L., 541, 592
Pepinsky, H. B., 457, 468, 469, 519, 522
Pepinsky, P. N., 453, 475, 480, 522
Pepitone, A., 62, 78, 459, 460, 508, 509, 522
Perkins, H. V., 396, 447
Perry, A. D., 472, 519
Persinger, G. W., 67, 68, 78
Peters, C. C., 219, 271
Petersen, R. J., 460, 484, 522
Peterson, R. L., 667, 687
Petrullo, L., 78
Phillips, B. N., 509, 522
Phillips, J. S., 410, 448
Piaget, J., 357, 448
Pierce, C. S., 80, 89–91, 123, 124, 128, 202, 203
Pilisuk, M., 280, 353
Pintner, R., 522
Pisoni, S., 581, 594
Pittenger, R. E., 391, 406, 408, 432, 448, 632, 687
Pitts, F. R., 322, 331, 353
Plath, O. E., 736, 737, 773
Platz, A., 642, 680
Poisson, S. D., 165, 166, 178, 179, 184, 190, 202
Polansky, N., 482, 522
Politz, A., 543, 594
Polonsky, I. P., 299, 349
Pomeroy, W. B., 528, 564, 593
Ponder, E., 383, 448
Pool, I. de S., 278, 292, 322, 333, 334, 336, 340, 353, 354, 446, 596, 598–601, 603, 609, 611, 612, 626, 637, 645, 646, 650, 664, 679, 683, 685–687
Popkin, S., 278, 322, 333, 334, 336, 340, 353
Portnoy, S., 642, 688
Posman, H., 373, 451
Posner, R., 491, 517
Postal, S. K., 618, 667, 676
Potter, J., 430, 448
Potter, P., 353
Potter, R. J., 396, 407, 451
Powell, R. M., 462, 494, 522
Precker, J. A., 508, 522
Pribram, K. H., 308, 352
Proctor, C. H., 460, 461, 463, 464, 465, 467, 474, 493, 494, 519, 522

Proctor, V. H., 423, 451
Proshansky, H., 216, 272, 529, 594
Prothro, E. T., 696, 714, 726
Prothro, J. W., 602, 643, 687
Pryer, R. S., 381, 441
Purcell, K., 365, 372, 396, 410, 423, 424, 429, 448
Pythagoras, 188

Quarrington, B., 462, 521
Quay, H. C., 460, 484, 522, 581, 594
Quay, L. C., 241, 266
Quenouille, M. H., 160, 201, 202
Quillian, M. R., 314, 354
Quinn, R. P., 592

Radcliffe-Brown, A. R., 708, 726
Raiffa, H., 161, 202
Raimy, V. C., 631, 682, 687
Rainey, G. E., 612, 687
Rainio, K., 278, 292, 322, 327–330, 336, 337, 354
Rainoff, T. J., 613, 687
Ramallo, L. I., 666, 687
Rankin, R. E., 216, 272
Raphael, B., 299, 300, 314, 347, 354
Rapoport, A., 280, 326, 353, 354, 473, 522
Rau, L., 489, 524
Raush, H. L., 408, 422, 429, 430, 432, 448, 451
Redl, F., 377, 442, 482, 522
Reece, M., 241, 272
Reece, S., 615, 675
Reese, H. W., 459, 492, 522
Reilly, M. S. A., 503, 506, 522
Reitman, W. R., 306, 309, 312, 314, 315, 317, 321, 354
Renzaglia, G. A., 371, 448
Reuel, D., 635, 687
Révész, G., 739, 773
Rhead, C. C., 512
Rice, L. N., 363, 439
Rice, S. A., 549, 594
Richardson, H. M., 506, 522
Richardson, M. W., 257, 270
Richardson, S. A., 363, 431, 448, 529, 534, 537, 581, 583, 584, 586, 590, 594
Richmond, W., 489, 522
Riecken, H. W., 28, 61, 78, 369, 373, 430, 442, 448
Riesen, A. H., 733, 758, 771, 773
Riesman, D., 363, 374, 422, 429, 430, 434, 448, 537, 551, 583, 584, 590, 591, 594, 602, 635, 687

Riley, M. W., 363, 365, 448
Rioch, D. M., 681
Rivers, W. H. R., 709, 726
Rivlin, A. H., 353
Roat, R., 617, 687
Roberts, J. M., 718, 726
Roberts, R. R., 371, 448
Robinson, B., 731, 771
Robinson, D., 550, 551, 584, 594
Robinson, J. P., 534, 594
Robinson, W. S., 660, 687
Robson, D. S., 141, 160, 201, 202
Roby, T., 330, 354
Roche, J. A., 259, 270
Rochester, N., 299, 350
Roe, A., 440
Roethlisberger, F. J., 65, 78
Rogers, C. R., 526, 581–583, 594
Rohde, S., 550, 551, 584, 594
Rohrer, J. H., 771
Rokeach, M., 259, 272, 371, 448, 505
Rokkan, S., 680
Rome, B., 279, 354
Rome, S., 279, 354
Romney, A. K., 710, 726, 727
Roosevelt, F. D., 614, 615, 623, 643, 691
Rorer, L. G., 235, 237, 272
Rose, E. O., 444, 446
Rosen, A., 253, 271
Rosen, B., 515, 605, 687
Rosenau, J. N., 279, 354, 606, 688, 692
Rosenberg, M. H., 26, 28, 78
Rosenberg, M. J., 28, 61, 64, 78, 369, 448,
Rosenfeld, H. M., 381, 389, 488, 505, 523
Rosenthal, H., 334, 354
Rosenthal, R., 61, 67, 68, 78, 369, 386, 408, 412, 413, 431, 442, 448, 449
Rosenzweig, S., 517, 518, 756, 773
Roshal, J. J. G., 631, 688
Rosi, E. J., 619, 688
Ross, H., 389, 450
Ross, I. C., 472, 473, 516, 523
Ross, S., 773
Rossi, A. M., 505, 511
Rourke, R. E. K., 186, 202
Rubinstein, E. A., 449
Rucker, B. W., 619, 688
Ruge, M. H., 642, 678
Ruggles, T., 671, 688
Runion, H. L., 624, 629, 688
Russell, J. T., 610, 651, 688

Sabghir, O., 655, 684
Sadalla, E., 41, 45, 79

Sahinkaya, R., 456, 498, 499, 511
Sainsbury, P., 381, 449
St. George, M., 637, 688
Sakoda, J. M., 299, 354
Salancik, J. R., 613, 691
Salter, P. J., 605, 620, 621, 647, 657, 675
Saltz, E., 241, 272
Salzinger, K., 581, 594, 642, 688
Salzinger, S., 581, 594
Samuel, A. L., 281, 355
Sampson, E. E., 507, 523
Sanford, F., 373, 437
Sapir, E., 438, 726
Saporta, S., 652, 653, 686
Sargent, J., 458, 521
Sargent, S. S., 732, 756, 773
Saslow, G., 379, 392–394, 446–449, 451, 581, 594
Sass, M., 313, 355
Saunders, D. R., 204, 209, 231, 272
Saunders, J. C., 440
Savage, L. J., 161, 201, 202
Sawyer, J., 713, 726
Sayre, K. M., 352
Schachter, S., 31, 38, 41, 43, 45, 63, 78, 373, 430, 437, 442, 456, 472, 496, 502, 507, 515, 523
Schade, J. P., 353
Schalock, H. D., 424, 447
Schanck, R. L., 235, 272
Scheflen, A. E., 381, 382, 388, 410, 412, 449
Scheuch, E. K., 609, 688
Schlaifer, R., 161, 202
Schlosberg, H., 771
Schmidt, K. P., 769
Schmuck, R., 684
Schneider, L., 612, 649, 650, 655, 688
Schneirla, T. C., 732, 734, 735, 738, 739, 743, 772, 773
Schoggen, M., 438
Schoggen, P., 369, 375, 377, 396, 417, 421, 425, 442, 449
Schooley, M., 506, 523
Schorer, M., 624, 688
Schramm, W., 617, 642, 684, 688
Schubert, G., 628, 688
Schuette, D., 385, 386, 441
Schulze, G., 391, 396, 446, 449
Schutz, R. E., 237, 245, 272
Schutz, W. C., 658, 659, 688
Schwartz, D., 79
Schwartz, M., 491, 518
Schwartz, R. D., 451, 595
Scott, F. G., 377, 449

Scott, J. P., 743, 773, 774
Scott, M. B., 390, 446
Scott, W. A., 205–208, 216, 229, 241, 254, 258, 260, 261, 272, 660, 688
Seagoe, M. V., 489, 523
Sears, R. R., 379, 449, 694–696, 718, 726, 727, 742, 746, 774
Sebald, T. A., 601, 617, 618, 636, 688
Sebeok, T. A., 446, 601, 664, 686, 688
Sechrest, L., 79, 451, 595
Secord, P. F., 455, 505, 508, 509, 511, 523
Sedelow, S. Y., 671, 688
Sedelow, W. A., Jr., 671, 688
Seeman, M., 469, 523
Seidenberg, B., 529, 594
Selltiz, C., 7, 79, 215–217, 236, 238, 241, 242, 254, 267, 408, 409, 433, 440, 449, 532, 595
Selz, O., 308
Semler, I. J., 486, 523
Semmes, J., 733, 773
Senden, M. von, 733, 762, 774
Shakespeare, W., 624, 628, 684, 689
Shakow, D., 371, 412, 450
Shanas, E., 613, 689
Shapiro, D., 77
Shapiro, M. I., 377, 441
Shapiro, S., 581, 595
Sharp, E., 383–385, 445
Shartle, C. L., 458, 524
Shaw, J. C., 276, 299, 303, 308, 310, 315, 344, 353
Shaw, M. E., 534, 595
Sheerer, E. T., 605, 631, 689
Shepard, R. N., 281, 355
Sherberg, J., 459, 460, 509, 522
Sherif, C. W., 365, 369, 373, 375, 376, 425, 430, 432, 449, 523
Sherif, M., 229, 269, 365, 369, 373, 375, 376, 425, 430, 432, 449, 481, 523, 771
Shewhart, W., 114, 124, 125
Shils, E. A., 30, 79, 270, 669, 687
Shipley, T. W., 501, 523
Shirley, R. W., 727
Shneidman, E. S., 605, 628, 629, 632, 666, 689
Shoemaker, D. J., 519
Shor, J., 613, 644, 645, 680
Shor, R. E., 426, 449
Shrauger, S., 431, 449
Shoup, R. G., 309, 354
Shubik, M., 279, 322, 355
Shure, G. H., 280, 355
Siegal, I. E., 424, 447

Siegel, L., 457, 522
Sigall, H., 69, 79
Sills, D. L., 76, 438, 439
Silverman, I., 61, 79
Simmons, L. W., 727
Simmons, P. L., 313, 355
Simmons, R. F., 313, 314, 355, 668, 689
Simon, H. A., 276, 278, 281, 284, 299, 303, 308, 309, 312–316, 320, 326, 344, 347–350, 353, 355
Simon, P. A., 303, 355
Simpson, G. G., 440
Singer, J. D., 437, 633, 654, 660, 674, 680, 688
Singer, J. E., 45, 78
Sjöberg, L., 233, 268
Skinner, B. F., 76, 480, 605, 624, 647, 689
Slater, C. W., 577, 593
Smelser, N., 506, 523
Smith, A. J., 507, 508, 523
Smith, B. B., 91, 201
Smith, B. L., 683
Smith, C. A. B., 161
Smith, E. E., 370, 450
Smith, L. H., 396, 407, 417, 424, 433, 434, 447
Smith, M., 503, 523
Smith, M. B., 371, 438, 564, 595
Smith, M. S., 314, 349, 355, 665, 666, 667, 676, 677, 682, 685–687, 689, 690
Smith, P. B., 456, 485, 523
Smith, R. B., 298, 322, 332, 352
Smith, W. D., 476, 523
Smith, W. I., 733, 773
Smith, W. N., 198, 199
Smythe, D. W., 599, 613, 618, 687, 689
Smucker, O., 465, 466, 523
Snodgrass, Q. C., 675
Snoek, J. D., 592
Snyder, L., 723
Snyder, R., 350
Snyder, W. E., 632, 689
Snyder, W. U., 686, 688
Snyderman, B., 528, 592
Solomon, L., 459, 509, 514
Solomon, R. L., 116–118, 201, 468, 478, 485, 488, 489, 495, 517, 518, 771
Sommer, R., 389, 450
Sorenson, R. C., 638, 689
Sorenson, T. C., 638, 689
Sorenson, W. W., 238, 266
Soskin, W. F., 372, 392–394, 410, 430, 450
Spearman, C. E., 201, 476
Speed, J. G., 618, 689

Spencer, R. F., 444
Speroff, B., 491, 523
Spiegel, M. E., 386, 387, 450
Spiegelman, M. C., 621, 647, 657, 660, 689
Spiro, M. E., 371, 450, 727
Spitaleri, R. M., 381, 440
Springer, K. J., 632, 679
Sprowls, R. C., 322, 355
Stacy, R. W., 348
Stanley, J. C., 7, 16, 60, 76
Stanton, F., 552, 595
Star, S. A., 584, 590
Starinets, V. S., 347
Steele, M., 455, 494, 498, 519
Stefaniak, P., 505, 513
Stefic, E. C., 503, 506, 522
Steiner, I., 528, 595
Steiner, J. D., 593
Steinkamp, S., 584, 592
Stellar, E., 771
Stephens, M. W., 263, 267
Stephens, W. E., 714, 727
Stern, W., 206, 272
Sternberg, R. S., 371, 412, 450
Stevens, S. S., 772, 773
Stewart, F. A., 455, 493, 494, 523, 524
Stewart, I. A., 455, 524
Stewart, J. C., 743, 774
Stine, M. E., 491, 520
Stogdill, R. M., 458, 524
Stokes, D. E., 266, 591
Stoller, N., 412, 450
Stolz, W., 472, 512
Stomberg, E. L., 373, 440
Stone, C. P., 773
Stone, G. C., 259, 268
Storm, T., 723
Stouffer, S. A., 223, 269, 270, 272, 273
Straus, G., 389, 450
Straus, M. A., 375, 401, 402, 405, 411, 450
Stricker, L. J., 237, 272
Strodtbeck, F. L., 119, 201, 377, 450
Student (W. S. Gosset), 80–88, 93, 98, 127, 128, 135, 201, 202
Stuart, A., 160, 201
Sturtevant, W. C., 709, 724, 727
Suchman, E. A., 206, 223, 273
Sudman, S., 589, 595
Sullivan, H. S., 526, 595
Sutton-Smith, B., 376, 442, 718, 726
Svehla, G., 506, 521
Swadesh, M., 705, 727
Swanson, G. E., 699, 725, 727

Sweetland, A., 279, 355
Swets, J. A., 314, 355

Taeuber, I. B., 605, 613, 655, 690
Taft, R., 382, 450
Tagiuri, R., 78, 456, 457, 487, 498, 508, 516, 518, 524
Talbot, E., 458, 462, 524
Tamulonis, V., 549, 591
Tannenbaum, P. H., 605, 613, 616, 642, 643, 645, 666, 679, 686, 690
Tannenbaum, R., 458, 462, 520, 524
Tanner, J. M., 718, 727
Taylor, D. W., 26, 76, 79, 309, 355
Taylor, T. J., 430, 432, 448
Taylor, W. L., 616, 641, 647, 662, 690
Terwilliger, C., 621, 647, 657, 660, 689
Thibaut, J., 43, 76, 437
Thielens, W., 594
Thomas, D. S., 389, 450
Thomas, G. B., Jr., 186, 202
Thomas à Kempis, 638, 639
Thompson, G. G., 453, 457, 465, 477–479, 481, 516, 524
Thompson, W. R., 731, 733, 759, 774
Thorpe, J. G., 486, 493, 494, 501, 524
Thorpe, W. H., 737, 774
Thurstone, L. L., 208, 224, 225, 228, 265, 266, 268, 269, 273, 457, 610, 651, 652
Till, E., 675
Tinbergen, N., 734, 774
Toch, H. H., 623, 691
Tocher, K. D., 337, 355
Tolman, E. C., 739, 742, 774
Tomkins, S., 346, 348, 352, 354, 356, 382, 441, 445, 450, 678
Tonge, F., 353
Torgerson, W. S., 208, 233, 273
Tourlentex, T. T., 439
Trager, G. L., 391, 450
Trent, R. D., 465, 487, 524
Triandis, H. C., 459, 524
Triandis, L., 724
Trockman, R. W., 243, 267
Trumbo, D., 377, 438
Tryon, R. C., 731, 774
Tsao, F., 128–130, 201
Tsujioka, B., 242, 267
Tucker, L. R., 122, 202
Tuggle, F., 303, 348
Tukey, J. W., 94, 95, 113, 121, 135, 141, 160, 184, 185, 190, 198, 199, 200–203, 343
Turing, A. M., 246, 276, 316–319, 335, 336, 355

Turner, J., 44, 69, 75
Turner, L. W., 656, 677
Turner, R. H., 204, 271, 492, 524
Tylor, E. B., 693, 703, 727

Udy, S. H., 727
Uhr, L., 306, 356
Ullmann, L. P., 447
Updegraff, R., 456, 477, 490, 492, 498, 521
Urdan, J. A., 490, 518
Uttal, W. R., 282, 356

Valentine, C. W., 759, 774
Vanatta, E. L., 457, 522
Van de Castle, R. L., 609, 646, 679
Vanderlippe, R. H., 492, 524
Van Dyne, V. E., 502, 524
Van Voorhis, W. R., 219, 271
van Zandt, B. R., 237, 273
Venable, T. C., 455, 464, 478, 494, 501, 504, 524
Verba, S., 279, 356
Verner, H. W., 549, 591
Vernon, P. E., 377, 437, 506, 507
Veroff, J., 501, 511, 523, 528, 592, 723
Verzeano, M., 393, 451
Vidich, A. J., 370, 377, 451
Vikan-Kline, L., 67, 68, 78
Voas, R. B., 447
Vogt, E. Z., 727, 728
von Frisch, K., 737–739, 770
von Neumann, J., 276, 305, 308, 356
von Senden, M., 733, 762, 774
Vreeland, F. M., 494, 524
Vroom, V. H., 508, 524

Wagstaff, A. K., 363, 439
Waksberg, J., 542, 594
Wales, H., 549, 592
Walker, E. G., 605, 632, 686
Walker, H. M., 202
Wallace, D. L., 148, 150, 161, 166, 180, 202, 602, 638, 647, 650, 685
Wallace, J., 41, 45, 79
Wallach, M. A., 231, 270
Wallin, P., 546, 591
Walster, B., 37, 79, 505, 524
Walster, E., 23, 37, 79, 505, 524
Walworth, A., 618, 636, 691
Waly, P., 216, 273
Wang, C. K. A., 623, 691
Waples, D., 641, 675, 691
Wapner, S., 387, 389, 451
Ward, F., 110, 201

Warnath, C. F., 459, 477, 514
Warrington, W. G., 508, 515
Washburne, N. F., 78, 448
Wasmann, E., 736, 774
Watson, J., 363, 373, 374, 396, 407, 422, 429, 430, 434, 448, 451
Watson, J. B., 756
Watson, P. D., 371, 451
Watt, J., 313, 348
Waxler, N., 394, 395, 447
Waxman, B. D., 348
Wayne, I., 609, 618, 636, 655, 685, 691
Wear, B. A., 456, 476, 485, 517
Webb, E. J., 61, 79, 364, 367, 375, 377, 409, 451, 530, 589, 595, 613, 691
Webb, W. B., 476, 484, 517
Weber, M., 614
Wedge, B., 512
Weick, K. E., 360, 451
Weinstein, E. A., 681
Weisenberg, M., 79
Weiss, D. J., 541, 595
Weiss, W., 12, 30, 63, 77
Weitman, M., 394, 447
Weizenbaum, J., 295, 299, 313, 314, 356
Welch, E. H., 544, 557, 590
Wenar, C., 541, 545, 592, 595
Werner, H., 387, 389, 451
Werner, R. A., 223, 273
Wertheimer, M., 76, 258, 272, 630
Weschler, I. R., 216, 273, 458, 462, 520, 524
Westie, F. R., 216, 217, 268, 273
Westley, B. H., 618, 653, 691
Wheeler, G. C., 693, 696, 724
Wheeler, W. M., 733, 735, 736, 737, 774
Whelpton, P. K., 528, 592
Wherry, R. J., 484, 524
White, B. J., 523
White, L., 725
White, R. K., 602, 623, 627, 645, 650, 691
White, R. W., 564, 595
Whitehead, A. N., 555, 595
Whiteman, P. H., 733, 771
Whiting, A. S., 600, 603, 691
Whiting, B. B., 713, 719, 727, 728
Whiting, J. W. M., 694–698, 705, 707, 712–714, 716–719, 723, 724, 727, 728, 759, 774
Whitlock, J. H., 160, 202
Whiton, J. B., 681
Whyte, W. F., 376, 389, 451
Whyte, W. H., Jr., 496, 524
Wiener, N., 353
Wiens, A. N., 393, 394, 447, 451
Wigdor, B. T., 491, 522

Wilcox, W., 617, 691
Wilkins, D. M., 623, 691
Willey, M., 619, 645, 655, 691
Williams, J. A., Jr., 551, 595
Williams, S. B., 456, 524
Williamson, J., 667
Willerman, B., 37, 51, 57, 75
Willis, R. H., 219, 273
Wilkinson, W. D., 313, 355
Willoughby, W. F., 605, 615, 691
Wilson, E. B., 67, 79, 80, 89, 90, 124, 203
Wilson, M., 497, 514
Wilson, W., 624, 688
Winch, R. F., 502, 524, 724
Winder, C. L., 489, 524
Winick, C., 389, 451, 613, 691
Winslow, C. N., 506, 524
Winter, J. A., 353
Winters, L. C., 385, 386, 441
Winters, P. R., 348
Wise, G. W., 694, 695, 727
Wishart, J., 202
Withey, S. B., 205, 272, 561, 595
Witryol, S. L., 477, 478, 479, 524
Wolf, A., 350
Wolf, M., 724
Wolfe, D. M., 592
Wolfenstein, M., 617, 691
Wolfson, R., 610, 691
Wong, T. J., 500, 507, 513, 525
Wood, L. A., 440
Woodhead, L., 667, 670
Woodmansee, J. J., 216, 238, 273
Woodward, J. L., 640, 645, 657, 691
Woodworth, R. S., 759, 774
Worchel, P., 439, 497, 507, 513, 525
Worth, S., 412, 415, 451
Wortis, J., 441
Wright, B., 456, 463, 474, 475, 525
Wright, E., 423, 451
Wright, G. O., 728
Wright, H. F., 357, 358, 366, 368, 370, 372, 374, 375, 405, 407, 409, 416, 422, 425–427, 429, 430, 438, 451
Wright, J. M., 534, 595
Wright, Q., 610, 651, 652, 688, 692
Wright, R., 602, 610, 627
Wrighter, J., 486, 494, 495, 516
Wrightsman, L. S., Jr., 241, 266, 502, 525
Wyant, R., 623, 692
Wynne, L. C., 423, 441

Yakobson, S., 612, 692
Yarrow, M. R., 408, 422, 429, 451

Yates, F., 103, 203
Yeats, W. B., 624, 664, 687
Yee, W., 455, 507, 514
Yerkes, A. W., 740, 746, 749, 755, 757, 758, 763, 774
Yerkes, R. M., 740, 746–749, 755, 757, 758, 763, 774
Yngve, V. H., 299, 356
Yoshioka, J. G., 763, 772
Young, F. W., 698, 701, 714, 728
Youtz, C., 202
Yovits, M. C., 353
Yule, G. U., 603, 638, 647, 692

Zajac, E. E., 119, 120, 203
Zajonc, R. B., 207, 273
Zander, A. F., 358, 425, 434, 444, 501, 525
Zaninovich, M. G., 634, 686, 692
Zaslavsky, S. Y., 347
Zavala, A., 241, 273
Zelditch, M., Jr., 279, 354, 356
Zeleny, L. D., 458, 466, 525
Zeps, V. J., 664, 688
Zimbardo, P. G., 43, 50, 79, 396, 451
Zinnes, D. A., 634, 686, 692
Zuckerman, S., 743, 774

Subject Index

Abbreviation, as a duplicatory error, 429, 434

"Absorbing situation" strategy, in observation, 375

Acceptance-rejection indices, 465

Accessibility, of information in interviewing, 535–536, 539–543, 548, 559–563, 573–578

memory problems, 541–543, 548, 560–563

in question formulation, 559–563

"Accident" manipulations, 45, 59–60

Accident proneness, and sociometric status, 491

Accomplices, use of, 378

Accuracy, of interview data, 542–549

Acquiescence, 24, 66, 235, 237–240, 242, 245, 255, 257, 263

"Acting out," 365

Action

modes, 426

tendency, 207

Activity sequence, 324

Additive response model, of attitude assessment, 248–250, 255

Address, numerical and symbolic, 296, 298

"Adhesions," 703

Adjacency effects, 229

Adjective-adverb/noun-verb ratio, 633

Adjective-verb ratio, 631, 632

Adjustment, and sociometric status, 485–488

anxiety, 487

social "acceptability" *vs.* "acceptance," 486

social and personal, 485

sociometric status as an index of successful therapy, 488

Affect

facial expressions and, 382–383, 385

speech disturbances and, 396

Affection dimension, 397, 399

Affective bias, 431

Affective salience, 207

Affiliation

motive, and content analysis, 635–636

motive, and interpersonal attraction, 501–502

observational, 385, 431

research and ethics, 31

After-only designs, 66

Age

interpersonal attraction and, 498

sociometric status and, 493

Aggregative approach to social simulation, 321–322

Aggression, 750–754, 758, 762–763

Agreement, 327–329, 333

"Aldous," 325

ALGOL, 294, 297, 313

Algorithm, 310

Altruism

animal studies and, 743–746, 757–758, 761, 769

respondent motivation and, 537

Ambiguous stimuli, and interviewing, 570
Ambivalence, 206
  of taboos, 767–768
Amplification of incipient responses, 378–380
Anchor
  dimension, 318–319, 336
  effects, 218
Anger, 756–757
Animal studies, social significance of, 729–769
  analysis of social attitudes, 732–733, 746–754
    recognition of social attitudes, 748–749
    recording social actions, 749–752
  animal cooperation, 729, 741–744, 746
  biosocial *vs.* psychosocial behavior, 734–735
  "bold and timid man" experiments, 749, 751–754, 756
  chimpanzee fears and aggressions, 755–757
  emotion and society, 764–769
  emotionality and intellect, 761–764
  expectancy, 734, 739–740, 742, 756–757
  fear and hostility, 754–769
  friendship and altruism, 744–746
  heredity *vs.* environment, 730–731, 736
  human nature and society, 760–769
  phylogenetic development, 733–734, 738, 740–741, 744, 748, 754, 762–764
  problem solving, 730–731, 759, 761
  problems of social motivation, 729, 746–748, 754, 757–760
  purposive communication and language, 738–741
  purposiveness, 738–746
  sensory *vs.* ideational mechanisms, 733–734, 738–741
  social phenomena among insects, 733–737
    communication in insect societies, 737
    insect societies, 735–737
  validity of, 730–733
    animal intelligence studies, 730–732
    early environment, 732–733
Anxiety
  categorization of, 400
  experimentation and bias, 63
  interpersonal attraction, 502
  reduction, 759

  scales, 632
  sociometric status, 487
  speech disruptions and, 394–396
Archival data, 375–376
Arousal level, and body position, 383
Arrays, 297–299, 301–302, 313
Artifact, 21, 73
  in cross-cultural research, 703, 717
  the observer as, 369–376
    assessment of, 371–373
    instances of interference, 370–371
    solutions to, 373–376
"As-if" experiments, 26–28
Assembler, 296
Assertion, input, 312
Assertiveness, 400–401, 503
Assimilation, and coding, 430–431
Associationism, 309
Attention getting, 751
Attention span and observational bias, 434
Attenuation, 262
Attitude change
  content analysis and, 624–625
  experimentation in, 4, 12, 59, 63, 69
Attitude measurement, 204–266
  adequacy of attitude measures, 245–265
    additive response model, 248–250
    correlation between instruments, 253–254
    correlation with external variables, 263–264
    dimensionality, 250–251
    distribution of scores, 258–259
    homogeneity, 254–255
    insensitivity to extraneous variables, 259–263
    measurement models, 246–251
    measures of adequacy, 251–265
    relations among criteria, 265
    reliability, 256–257
    scaling models, 246–248
    validity, 251–253, 532
    verbal responses, 210–216
  administration and types of instrument, 210–217
    forced choice between pairs, 212, 219, 225, 241, 260
    indirect measures, 214–216
    method of controlled marginals, 219
    method of paired comparisons, 225, 227–229

method of single stimuli, 212, 225, 241, 260
method of successive intervals, 225, 228
multiple choice, 213–214
open *vs.* closed questions, 210–211
overt behavior, 217
physiological measures of attitude, 216–217
realistic decision situations, 217
role playing, 217
single *vs.* multiple items, 211
sociometric method, 217
extraneous determinants, 233–238
instrument-specific determinants, 236–238
subject characteristics, 234–236
minimizing extraneous determinants, 238–245
conditions of administration, 239
correction for contamination, 244–245
detection of contaminated scores, 242–244
instrument construction, 239–242
scoring responses, 217–233
configural scoring, 231–232
consensual location scaling, 224–230, 232, 246–248
criterion-oriented scales, 230–231
cumulative scaling, 221–225, 232, 246–248, 254
factor scoring, 220–221
group and individual scales, 232–233
judgmental scoring, 218
summative scales, 218–221, 224, 230, 232, 247
Attitudes
emotional, 768
interpersonal attraction, 506–509
properties of, 206–208
simulation and, 311–315, 346
social and animal studies, 732–733, 746–754
Attraction
and competence, methodology, 51
and initiation, methodology, 4–10
interpersonal, and bias in experimentation, 65
ratio, 464
Authority relations, categorization of, 399
Authorship studies, 638–639
Automatic vocal transaction analyzer, 393

Autonomic arousal, 216
Avoidance, 750–751, 753, 755, 762, 769
Axis, 407

Background characteristics, and interviewing, 549, 557
Bales category system, 324–325
Barycentric coordinates, 114–119, 184
barycenter, 114–115
isometric paper, 116, 118
three-category problems, 115–119
two-category problems, 114–115, 118
Base percentage *vs.* test percentage, 318–319
Bayesian statistics, 160–183
Bayes theorem, 162–163, 167–168, 172
beta priors and binomial data distributions, 173–178
confidence statements, 180–183
empirical priors, 163–167, 179
evidence as odds-changing, 165–167
gentle priors, 162, 169–171, 179, 182
likelihood ratio, 166–167, 173–174, 180
Poisson data and gamma prior distributions, 178–180
posterior probabilities and distributions, 162–163, 170–174, 178–179, 182–183
precisions, 172–173, 183
priors and normal distributions, 171–173
reporting error, 164
Before-after design, 66
Begging, and altruism, 744–745, 757
Behavior
Behavior Scores System, 397, 400–401, 427
categories for, 396–401
coping, 387
effect *vs.* intent, 425-427
equivalence of, 423
evoking, 377–378
expressive, 387
extralinguistic, 391–396
continuity, 394–396
interaction dimension, 391
temporal dimension, 391–394
verbal-stylistic dimension, 391
vocal dimension, 391–392
generality of, 694–695
linguistic, 396–401
molar *vs.* molecular, and observational methods, 358–360

nonverbal, observation of, 381–388
  body movements, 381, 383, 386–388, 415, 430
  conversational clustering, 390
  exchanged glances, 385–386
  facial expressions, 382–385
  interpersonal distance, 388–390
  private *vs.* public interaction, 390–391
  territoriality, 390
 provocation of, 360–361, 376–380
 range of behavioral variation, 367
 recording, 401–427, 436
 spatial, 388–391, 415
 stream, 367, 369
Behavioral measures, 359, 362, 380, 436
Beliefs, and interpersonal attraction, 506–509
Belief systems and simulation, 311, 313–314
Beta functions, 88
Bias; *see also* Interference
 abbreviation, 429, 434
 adjustment, 140–145
 affective, 431
 assimilation to prior inputs, 430
 "blind" technique, 68–70
 central tendency bias, 430
 closure and symmetry, 429, 434
 coder, in cross-cultural methods, 715–716
 coding relativism, 431, 434
 commitment, 65
 contamination by associated cues, 431
 in content analysis, 599, 656
 in cross-cultural methods, 715–717
 demand characteristics, 61–66
 enhancement of contrast, 429–430
 errors in duplicatory *vs.* reductive assignments, 428–432
 in estimates of variability, 134, 140
 evaluative coding assimilation, 431, 434
 in experimentation, 21–22, 29, 48, 52–53, 57, 61–70
 interviewing and, 532, 535, 540–552, 560, 582
 methodological solutions to, in observation, 432–434
 middle-message loss, 429
 observational training solutions to, 434–435
 prior coding experience, 431
 response, 235–236, 546
 subject as experimenter, 64

types of journalistic bias, 619
 adjective, 619
 adverbial, 619
 attribution, 619
 contextual, 619
 outright opinion, 619
 photographic, 619
 unintentional influence of the experimenter, 66–70
Binomial expansion, in sociometry, 467–469
Binomial probability paper, 114, 183–199
 angular transformations of paired counts, 198–199
 chi square, 188–189, 195–197
 crab addition, 188–189, 195–197
 double square-root transformation, 184, 187
 homogeneity, 195–198
 individual counts, 191
 plotting, 184–186, 189–190
 sign test, 192–195
 split *vs.* paired count, 184–187, 189–199
Binomial theory, 117
Biodocumentary technique, 415–416
Biological rewards theory, 757
Biosocial behavior, 734–735
Birth order, 502
"Bit," 292–293, 298
"Blind" techniques, 68–70
Blinking, and observation of behavior, 383
Bluffing, 751–752
Body movements, and observation of behavior, 381, 383, 386–388, 415, 430
"Bold and timid man" experiments, 749, 751–754, 756
"Bookending," 388
Bounded events, 376
Branches, 290

Campaign simulator, 332–333
Capitalizing on chance factors, 74, 110
Carelessness, 237, 239, 243–244
Cases, in cross-cultural research, 696–702
 independence of, 696, 703
Castes, among insects, 735–736
Categorization
 content analysis and, 644–647
 observational data and, 358–360, 385, 387, 396–401, 403–404, 407, 409–411, 417, 421–427, 429, 433–435

Behavior Scores System, 397, 400–401, 427
  category construction, 422–425
  category content, 425–427
  exhaustiveness, 424–425
  first, second, and third order, 750–752
  interaction, 397
  Interaction Process Analysis (IPA), 396–398
  Interaction Process Scores (IPS), 397–399, 423
  Member-Leader Analysis, 397, 399–400
  postcategorization, 422
Causality, in experimentation, 7–10
Cell assembly, 761–762
Centrality, 207
Central tendency bias, 430
Chance model, and sociometry, 467–470
Child training, and cross-cultural methods, 694–696, 698–700, 707, 714, 719
Chi square, 92, 175, 179, 188–189, 195–197, 469
Choice
  manipulation of perception of, 42
  rejection status, 465
  social; *see* Sociometric techniques
"Cleavages," 464, 497–499, 506
Clinical styles, 576
Cliques, 389, 461, 472–474, 498, 504, 506
Closed-circuit television, 69
Closed systems, 285
Closure, as an observational error, 429, 434
Cloze procedure, 641–642, 664
Coalition formation, 324
Coding of behavior, 401
  assimilation to evaluative, 431, 434
  of beliefs, values, and techniques, 713
  in content analysis, 597, 600–601, 603, 615, 618, 644–653, 657–660, 668–669
  in cross-cultural research, 708–720
  inferred absence, 711
  of interview data, 531, 533, 571, 572
  native code, 709–710
  precoding, 422
  presence-absence, 710–711
  relativism, 431, 434
  structural types, 710–711
Coefficient alpha, 257, 260
Coefficient of observer agreement, 403
Coefficient of reproducibility, 222
Coefficient of scalability, 223

Cognitions, 205
Cognitive complexity, 207
Cognitive factors, in interviewing, 535–537, 539–540, 543–545, 547, 552–559, 573, 575
  conceptual level, 558
  frame of reference, 539, 543–545, 555–559, 567
  language, 553–555
  in question formulation, 552–559
Cognitive romeostasis, and interdersonal attraction, 507–508
Cognitive maneuvers, 628–630
Cognitive processes, simulation of, 276–277, 284–285, 288, 292, 299, 308–321, 343–344
Cognitive structures, 314
Cohesiveness, manipulation of, 43
COMIT, 299–300
Commitment, 55, 65
Common methods variance, 264
Communication, 729, 742, 746, 761; *see also* Content analysis
  "cell," 300
  channel of, 603
  decoding, 601, 603–604, 607, 640
  detector, 603
  encoding, 601, 603–604, 606, 639
  frequency *vs.* nonfrequency techniques, 598–600
  instrumental *vs.* representational models of, 626
  manifest *vs.* latent aspects of, 598, 600–601
  mass, 332, 338
  message, 603–604, 605
  motivation and interviewing, 567
  networks, 286–287, 461
  patterns of, 625
  purposive, and language, 738–741
  quantification, 598–601
  reflexive *vs.* purposive, 739–740
  source of, 603, 605–606, 654–655
  three classes of, 740
Compatibility index, 464
Competition of forces, 286–287
Compiler, 296–298, 301
Complementarity of needs and interests, 502–505
Compliance, methodology and, 46–47
Comprehension, 314

Computers
  in content analysis, 663–673
  in data analysis, 111–113, 119–122
Computer simulation of behavior, 274–346;
    see also Simulation of social behavior
Concealment, in observational methods,
    373–375
  ethics of, 373–374
  nonconcealment, 374–375
  partial, 374
Conceptual definition, 401–402, 568
Conceptual variable, 13–21, 25–26, 53
Confederates, 45
Confidence statements, 83–87, 93–94, 97,
    101, 114, 128, 132, 134–135, 138–141,
    147, 155, 180–183, 192–194
  frequency *vs.* degree-of-belief meaning,
    180–183
  for percentages, 192
  for population median, 194
  for population proportions, 193–194
  shortcut to inference, 81–86
  typicality and absence of selection, 180–
    181
Configural scoring, 231–232
Conformity; *see also* Uniformity
  dimension, 397
  embedded measurement of, 377
  evocation of, 378
Congruence *vs.* noncongruence (postural),
    388
Consensual location scaling, 224–230, 232,
    246–248
Consensus sessions, in observer training,
    435
Consequences or outcomes of simulations,
    285–286, 340–341
  outcome variables, 344
  panel *vs.* symbolic outcomes, 341
Constant-frame-of-reference problem, in
    sociometry, 468
"Constructed week," in sampling, 656
Contamination, 233–245
Content analysis, 596–673
  antecedents of content, 604, 606, 609,
    625–639
    authorship studies, 638–639
    for cultural change, 634–636
    for legal evidence, 637–638
    for political and military intelligence,
      626–627
    for psychological traits, 627–634

bias, 599, 656
characteristics of the message content,
    610–621
  comparison of content against stan-
    dards, 618–621
  plot configurations in movies, 617
  trend description, 610–613
coding of content, 597, 600–601, 603, 615,
    618, 644–653, 657–660, 668–669
  categories, 644–647
  enumeration systems, 649–653
  recording and context units, 647–648
computers in, 663–673
  dictionary systems, 663–673
  "General Inquirer" programs, 665–671
  syntactical *vs.* semantic discriminations,
    671
  word-count programs, 663–665
continuity measures and, 396
defined, 597–601
effects of audience on content, 624–625
effects of communication, 604, 607, 609,
    639–644
frequency *vs.* nonfrequency techniques,
    598–600, 627
  appearance-nonappearance, 650
  contingency analysis, 599, 627, 648,
    668, 673
  frequency counts, 598–600, 611, 634,
    647, 650–651, 663–664, 668
"how" content characteristics, 622–624
  style analysis, 624
  techniques of persuasion, 622–623
  value analysis, 623
intensity, 651–653, 659
"intentional," 426
manifest *vs.* latent content, 598, 600–601
methodological research, 607–609
qualitative *vs.* quantitative, 598–601
readability of text, 607, 640–642, 664
reliability, 649, 653, 657–662, 664, 673
  category, 658–660
  dichotomous-decision technique, 659
  index of, 660
  individual, 657
  intercoder, 657, 660
research design, 603–607
sampling, 599, 603, 618, 653–657, 661–663
  cluster design, 656
  documents, 655–657
  quantitative *vs.* qualitative criteria, 655
  random *vs.* purposive, 654–655

single *vs.* multistage, 654
stratified, 655
standards of adequacy, 605, 618–621
   a priori, content, and noncontent indices, 604, 618–620
   social norms, 618
studies
   of advertising, 623, 625, 636
   of cross-media material, 615–616
   of form and style, 607, 624, 640–642
   of journalism, 608, 618–619
   of logical styles, 628–630
   of mass media, 605, 608, 612–620, 624–625, 636, 642–643, 647, 650, 654–656, 663
   of mental health, 616, 620
   of occupations, 620–621
   in political research, 608, 610–612, 614–616, 624, 626, 628–629, 633–634
   of propaganda, 608, 622–623, 626, 661
   in psychiatry and psychotherapy, 629–632, 664
   of psychological traits, 627–634
   of religious values, 612
   of space allocation in mass media, 614–619
   in survey research, 609, 613
   of youth literature, 617–618
  uses, 601–603, 610–644
  validity, 610, 623, 625–628, 653, 661–663, 673
Content-free measures, 245
Content norms, 646
Contextual information, 423
Contiguity, in cross-cultural research, 705
Contingency analysis, 599, 627, 648, 668, 673
Contralogic, 628–630
Contrast enhancement, 429–430
Control
  charts, Shewhart and Cusum, 114
  in cross-cultural research, 694, 696, 703, 708
  experimental, 7–10, 23, 40, 42, 52, 54, 57, 69
  impact *vs.,* 11–20, 43
  in interviewing, 556–557
  in observation, 358–359, 365–366, 436
  over the stimulus situation, 11–20, 52
  over subjects, 10
"Controlled comparison" method in cross-cultural research, 708

Controlled marginals method of assessment, 219
Controversy, 332
Conversation, 314, 318
"Conversation tree," 314, 324
Conversational clustering, 390
Cooperation
  animal studies and, 729, 741–744, 746
  "one-sided," 742
  teamwork, 741–742
  three levels of, 742
Cooperativeness in subjects, 29, 42, 56, 62, 64–65, 72–73
Correlation
  between instruments, 253–254
  functional *vs.* historical, 703, 707
Correlational methods, 7–10, 40–41, 495–496, 506, 717, 720
Counseling qualifications, 583–584
Counterbalancing, 240–242, 257
Coupled models, 340–343
Couvade, 719
"Cover" story, 2, 26, 30, 32, 37–39, 49, 52–53, 63
Crab addition, 188–189, 195–197
Credibility
  bias and, 63–64
  of communicator, manipulation of, 12–13, 15
  of experiments, 25, 49; *see also* Impact "test," 307, 312
Criterion-oriented scales, 230–231
Cross-cultural research, 6, 693–722
  case, definition of, 696–702
  coding, 710–720
  content analysis, 617, 618, 667
  contiguity, 705
  cultunits, 696–697
  cultural rules, 711–712
  culture-area method, 704
  culture types, 704–706
  diffusion and fission, 703–708
  functional *vs.* historical association, 703, 707
  generality of behavior, 694–695
  group name, 699–700
  homogeneity of units, 698–702, 706
  independence of cases, 696, 703
  kinship studies, 709–710
  language-and-location approach, 705–706
  linguistic criteria, 705–706
  local community as a unit, 697–703, 706

method of "controlled comparison," 708
noncomparability of units, 697
range of variation, 694–696
reliability, 704, 712, 715–716
sampling, 696–697, 702–708
  sampling list, 702–703
and sociometry, 496
sovereignty, 699–700
transcultural definition of variables, 708–710
validation, 718–719
validity, 697–708
Cross-validation, 100, 103, 109–112, 147, 153–160, 719
  simple *vs.* double, 110–112
Cues
  for social organization of insects, 737
  of social responses, 748–749
Cultunit, 696–697
Cutural change, 702, 708
Cultural evolution, 693
Culture, content analysis and, 634–636
Culture-area method, 704
Culture in observational editing, 408
"Culture pool," 700
Culture types, 704–706
Cumulative scaling, 221–225, 232, 246–248, 254
Cycles, 290, 407
  in content analysis, 656
  "cycle time," 294
  interaction, 572–573

Data
  "packing," 293, 300–301
  reduction of, 361, 401; *see also* Categorization
  retrospective, 364
  T-data *vs.* O-data, 408–409
  utilization of, in simulations, 307–308
Data analysis, 80–200
  approach to, 80–99
    distributions, 81, 86–91
    indication, determination, and inference, 81, 98–99
    nonnormality and robustness, 80, 91–95
    role of vague concepts, 95–98
    "the staircase," 81–83
    Student's contribution, 84–86
  Bayesian approach, 81, 160–183
    Bayes theorem, 167–168

binomial data and beta prior distributions, 173–178
confidence statements, 180–183
empirical priors, 163–165
evidence as odds-changing, 165–167
gentle priors, 169–171
Poisson data and gamma prior distributions, 178–179
prior information and normal distributions, 171–173
  binomial probability paper, 81, 183–200
    crab addition and chi square, 188–189
    individual counts, 191
    measurements of deviations, 187–188
    paired counts, 195–199
    plotting, 184–186, 189–190
    sign test, 192–195
  computers and graphs, 112–122
    barycentric coordinates, 114–119
    computers, 113, 119–120
    graphs as indicators, 113–114
    graphs in determination and inference, 114
    residuals, 121–122
  indication and indicators, 99–112
    choice of indicators, 105–109
    concealed inference, 104–105
    indications of quality: cross-validation, 109–112
    value of, 100–104
  jackknifing, 107–108, 133–160
    cross-validation, 153–154
    individuals, 138–144
    "leave-out-one," 154–158
    using groups, 144–153
  uncertainty, 122–133
    choice of error term, 125–128
    direct assessment of variability, 124–125, 128–131, 133–160
    internal and supplementary uncertainty, 122–133
Debriefing, 31–32, 34, 70–72, 365
"Debugging," 295, 304–305
Decay of information, and interviewing, 541, 560–563
Deception in experimentation, 2, 18–19, 26–37, 52–53, 62, 70, 365, 368
  ethical considerations, 29–36
  interviews as, 30
  projective techniques as deceptive, 30
Decisions
  group, 397

motive patterns and, 539
realistic decision situations in attitude assessment, 217
Decoding, in communication, 601, 603–604, 607, 640
Defense, ego and reporting accuracy, 542, 546, 560–563
Defensiveness
  content analysis and, 631
  sociometric status and, 492
Degree of belief, 161, 166, 169–171
Degrees of freedom, 85, 89, 92, 116, 127, 135–136, 179, 327
Demand characteristics, 61–66, 369
Demographic variables, 535, 552, 584
  and interpersonal attraction, 497–498
  sociometric status and, 493–494
Demonstration models, 323–326
Denial, 311–312
Dependency, categorization of, 399
Dependent variable, 19, 41, 49, 54–61; *see also* Questionnaires
  behavioral *vs.* pencil-and-paper measures, 54–58, 66
  "behavioroid" measures, 54–58
  "different context" technique, 59
  impact *vs.* concealment, 55–61
  open-ended *vs.* constrained measures, 58
  reactivity, 60–61
  setting and, 38–39
Depression, categorization of, 400
Desegregation scale, 500
Detection scales, 243–245
Determination, 98–99; *see also* Uncertainty
Deutero-problem, 369
Deviation index, in content analysis, 615
Dialect, 696, 699–701, 705
Dichotomous-decision technique, in content analysis, 659
Dictionaries, in computer content analysis, 663–673
  "alcohol," 667
  Harvard psychosociological, 666
  "need achievement," 667
  New Mexico anthropological, 667
  proper names, 666–667
  Stanford political, 666, 669–670
Differential exposure, 332–333
Differentiation, 207
 intersubject, 258
Diffusion and fission, cultural, 703–708
Dimensionality, 250–251

Dimension of appraisal, 210–211
Direction, of attitudes, 206, 209–210, 217–218, 225, 265
Discernment, manipulation of, 43–44
Discomfort-relief quotient (DRQ), 631–633
Disconfirmed expectations, observation of, 378
Discriminant functions, 148–160
Discrimination net, 314
"Disguised" measures, 241–242
Displacement, of hostility, 758
Dissonance, and dependent measures, 57–58
Distortion, ego-enhancing, 546, 561–562
Distribution-free procedures, 83
Distributions, 86–95
  bell-shaped curves, 86, 98, 175
  beta functions, 88, 173–178
  binomial, 124, 173–178, 184, 186
  chi-square, 92, 175, 179
  contaminated, 94–95
  cumulative, 161
  of derived statistics *vs.* of individual values, 87, 93
  discreteness, 90–91, 135
  of the estimate, 106–107
  exponential, 140–141
  gamma, 174–175, 178–180
  histogram, 88
  irregularity, 91
  linear transformation, 88
  location, 88, 107–108
  logarithmic transformation, 90
  nonnormality and robustness, 91–95, 144–182
  normal or Gaussian, 87–89, 91, 94–95, 105, 107–108, 125, 141, 159
    and priors, 171–173
    unit normal, 187
  normality, 83, 89–90, 94
  Poisson, 165–167, 178–180, 184, 190
  prior and posterior, 161–183
  rectangular, 92–93, 135
  scale, 88, 94–95
  shape, 88–90, 92–96, 105, 144, 155, 175, 182
  skewness and kurtosis, 89
  spread, 95–98, 153
  tails of, 88–89, 91, 93–96, 98, 107–109, 135, 138, 140
  triangular, 92–93
  Winsor's "principle," 91

Diversion of natural events in observation, 373
Division of labor, 734–735
Dominance, 502–503, 505
    animal studies and, 743, 745
    and territoriality, 390
"Doodling" styles, 635
"Double blind," 68, 112
Drive, exploratory, 759
Dummy variable, 286
Duplicatory errors in observation, 428–432
Dyadic relationship, and expectancies, 742, 746
DYSTAL, 299

"Echo," in interviewing, 581
Ecology, psychological, 368–369
"Economic man," 761, 768
Editing of observational data, 408–409, 412, 430
Efficiency, 197
    in content analysis, 648–649, 656, 664
    of distributions, 94–95, 108
    relative, 94–95
Effort, manipulation of, 14–16, 43, 59
Ego defenses, and reporting accuracy, 542, 546, 560–563
Ego state, categorization of, 399–400
Elementary Perception and Memory (EPAM), 278, 314–315, 320
Embeddedness, 207
Embedding of measures, 376–377
Emic attributes, 710
Emotion, 401, 729, 733
    brainstem theories of, 764
    and intellect, 761–764
    and society, 764–769
    stability of, 765–766
    susceptibility to, 761, 765, 768–769
Emotional disturbance, 758–769
    and age of weaning, 694–696, 698, 713
Emotional expansiveness, 464
Empathy
    in animal behavior, 741
    in interviewing, 584–585
Empirical realization of variables, 16–20, 24–25
Encoding
    in communication, 601, 603–606, 639
    of observational data, 360–361
Environment
    changes in, and observational error, 404

effects of early, 732–733
effects and observation, 427
vs. heredity, 730–731, 736
influence of, 734, 740, 765–766
Equilibrium
    motivational, 538–539
    quasi-stationary, 538
Erosion measures, 375–376
Error
    chance response tendencies, 404
    changes in the environment, 404
    changes in the person, 404
    component of a score, 248–249
    constant, 342
    in duplicative *vs.* reductive assignments, 428–432
    inadequate sampling of content, 404
    of measurement, 123, 249
    messages, 304
    "noncorrespondence," 342
    in observation, 404
    principle of minimal, 223–224, 248
    random, 248
    ratio, 223
    "response," 234
    systematic, 239
    term, choice of, 125–128, 130–131, 147
    variable, 342
Error-choice technique, 216
Estimates, estimator, and estimands, 99, 105–109, 137–138, 178
    ratio estimate, 144-147
Ethics
    of concealed observation, 373–374
    in experimentation, 11, 23, 26, 29–36, 70
    of interview research, 579–580
    stress interviews, 378–379
    undermanning, 379–380
Ethnographic Atlas, 702–706, 711, 713, 717, 719
Ethnographic present, 701–702
Ethnography; *see* Cross-cultural research
Etic attributes, 709
Euphoria, manipulation of, 45
Evaluation apprehension, 24, 66, 369
Evaluations, in simulation of belief systems, 312
Evaluative assertion analysis, 652–653
Evocation of behavior, 377–378
    scarcity of props, 377
    use of accomplices, 378
Excitation, optimal level of, 759, 765

Executive control, 322
Exit, 290
Expectancy
    disconfirmed, observation of, 378
    psychosocial behavior and, 734, 739–740, 742, 756–757
Expectant pauses, in interviewing, 581
Experimental demands, 24, 58–61
    bias and, 61–66
Experimental *vs.* correlational research, 7–10, 495–496, 506
Experimental *vs.* observational methods, 743
Experimentation, 1–75
    advantages, 3–10
        causation, 7–10
        control, 7–10
        random assignment, 7–10
        random assignment *vs.* correlational methods, 7–10
    ethical problems, 29–36
    goals of, 13
    in situ, 360–362, 380, 431
    planning and conducting, 36–75
        the "accident," 45, 59–60
        behavioral *vs.* pencil-and-paper measures, 54–58, 66
        "behavioroid" measures, 54–58
        bias, 61–70
        "blind" technique, 68–70
        checks on the independent variable, 49–51
        demand characteristics, 61–66
        dependent variable, 54–61
        disguising the measure, 58–60
        event *vs.* instruction manipulation, 42–44
        the experiment as the independent variable, 45–46
        experimenter role, 53–54
        impact *vs.* concealment, 55–61
        independent variable, 39–54
        live experimenter *vs.* "canned" operations, 52–53
        pilot testing and pretesting, 42
        postexperimental interview, 70–73
        reactivity, 60–61
        setting, 37–39
        subject as experimenter, 64
        subject awareness, 44–46
        unintentional influence, 66–70
        use of a confederate, 45

problems, 10–28
    deception and experimental realism, 26–28
    experimental *vs.* mundane realism, 22–28
    impact *vs.* control, 11–20, 43
    individual differences, 10–12
    internal *vs.* external validity, 24–25
    multiple meaning, 13–20
    multiplicity of response measures, 25
    purification, 15–20, 24–25, 43
    replications, 15–22, 25
Experimenter bias, 61–70, 369
Experimenter effects, and eye contact, 386
Experimenter role, 53–54
Experimenter-subject relationship, 30–31, 35–36, 61, 368
Expressiveness, and observation of facial expressions, 385
Extremity, as an instrument contaminant, 237–238, 240, 257
Eye contact, 385–386

Facial expressions, in observation, 382–385
Factor analysis, 122, 125
    in cross-cultural research, 713–714
    in sociometry, 473–474
Factor scoring, 220–221
Family size, and sociometric status, 493
Family values, 625
Fear, 754–769
    chimpanzee fears and aggressions, 755–757
    of the dead, 755, 767
    manipulation of, 37–38
    phylogenetic development of fear susceptibilities, 763
    of the unknown, 759–760
Field formats, in observation, 418–420, 433
Fixation, 733
Flamboyance, 237
Flesch system, in content analysis, 64, 662
Flexibility, of attitudes, 207
Flow charts, 288–292
FLPL, 299
Forced-choice method of attitude measurement, 212, 219, 225, 241, 260
Force field, motivational, and interviewing, 539
"Form," 109–110
Formula 20, 257
FORTRAN, 297, 301

Fractionation, in sociometry, 464, 468
Frame of reference, 468, 537, 543–545, 555–559, 567
Frequency counts, in content analysis, 598–600, 611, 634, 647, 650–651, 663–664, 668
Friendly behavior, 750–751, 753
Friendship and animal studies, 744–746, 769
Frustration, 754, 756–759, 761
Funnel sequence, 571

"Galton's problem," 703
Galvanic skin response (GSR), 17
Games, 277, 280–281
    function of, in cross-cultural research, 718
    mixed-motive games, 280
    normative *vs.* descriptive approach, 280–281
"General Inquirer" programs, 314, 665–671
    direct table program, 669
    question and search program, 669
    tag tally program, 669
    "text and tag list" program, 668–669
General Problem Solver (GPS), 276, 309–311, 316
"Generation interval," 331
Glotto-chronology, 705
Genotypes (psychological), 220–221
Goal-directed response, 756–757
Goals and subgoals in simulation, 310
Graphs, 100, 112
    barycentric coordinates, 114–119
    computers as a source of, 119–122
    in determination and inference, 114
    graphical methods in sociometry, 460–463
    graphical summary, 98
    as indicators, 113–114
Group
    coherence, 469
    cohesion, 465, 743
    decision, 397
    development, 400
    direction of movement of, 397–398
    endogamous, 697, 699–700
    group-oriented action, 400–401
    identity, 699
    initiation and attraction, methodology of, 4–17
    integration, 465
    interaction, manipulation of, 5

measurement of attraction in, 452–510; *see also* Sociometric techniques
    name, 699–700
    participation scale, 457
    preference record, 457–458
    processes, recording of, 396–401
    roles and status in, 397
    scales, 232–233
    self-preference, 469
    social process simulation, 292, 321–346
    structure indices, 465
Guess-who technique, in sociometry, 458–459, 489
Guilt, categorization of, 399

Habit, 205, 208
Habitat, 369
Halo effect, 123, 488–489
Heredity *vs.* environment, 730–731, 736
Heterotrait correlations, 260, 262–263
Heuristics, 310
Histograms, 88
Holzinger's *B*-coefficient, 472
Homogeneity
    of paired counts, 196–198
    of proportions, 195
    ratio, 254–255
    of a test, 254–255, 257, 265
    of units in cross-cultural research, 698–702
Homunculus model, 323–326
Hostility, 754–769
    scales, 632
    social, 758
Hunger, manipulation of, 15
Hypothesis testing
    content analysis and, 608–609, 611, 614, 627
    in cross-cultural research, 698
    observational methods and, 358–359, 362, 368–369, 376

Ideational *vs.* sensory behavior, 733–734, 738–741
Ideology machine, 311–313
Idiologic, 630
Idiosyncrasies of reasoning, 628–630
Imitation game, 317–318
Impact, 11–14, 22–28, 37–38, 42, 44, 46, 52–55, 69
Impressionistic analysis, 420–421

Imprinting, 732–733
Impulse category, 399
Incest rules, 700
Inclusion *vs.* noninclusion, and observation of behavior, 388
Independent variable
  construction of, 39–54
  control over, 12–13
  dependent measure and, 58
  empirical realization of, 16–20, 25
  number of, 51–52
  setting and, 38–39
Index numbers, 297–298
Indication, 98–122, 138, 145, 154, 159-160, 184, 190
  vs. anecdote, 98
  choice of indicators, 105–109
  concealed inference, 104–105
  defined, 98, 100–101
  estimates, estimators, and estimands, 99, 105–109, 137–138, 178
  indications of quality: cross-validation, 109–112, 154
  numerical and graphical summaries, 98
  problems of multiplicity, 102–103
  quantitative *vs.* qualitative, 99
Indices, 463–467
  acceptance-rejection, 465
  of attraction, 464
  behavioral, of intent, 427
  choice-rejection pattern, 466
  choice-rejection status, 465
  of "cleavage," 463
  compatibility, 464
  of consistency, 223
  deviation, 615
  emotional expansiveness, 464
  of emotional states, 392
  of group cohesion, 465
  of group integration, 465
  individual *vs.* group, 464
  of infant stress, 713
  of interest, 464
  profiles, 466
  of repulsions, 464
  social intensity, 465
  "socialization-sensationalism," 619–620
  social-relations, 465
  social-status, 464–465
Indirect measures of attitudes, 214–216
Individual; *see* Simulation of social behavior: cognitive processes

Individual differences
  analysis of, 124–125
  in arousal level, 768–769
  in chimpanzees, 749–753, 755
  in interpersonal attraction, 501
  interviewer training and, 586
  in observation, 432
  in sociometric choices, 485
  in sociometric stability, 478
  vs. standardization, 46–49
  unmeasured, 10–12
Individual scales, 233
Induction *vs.* deduction, 401–402
Inference, 98–99, 101–105, 111, 138, 161–162, 167
  Bayesian, 160–183
  classical *vs.* Bayesian, 161–162
  concealed (or informal), 104–105
  formal, 98–99
  Student's shortcut to, 81–83
Inferred absence, of a custom, 711
Infrared filming, 414
"Initialization," 311, 313–314
Initiation, manipulation of, 4–17, 38–39
Innovation diffusion, 330, 332
Instructions, use of for independent-variable manipulation, 42–44
Inputs, 285
  input assertion, 312
  list or "script," 314
Instrument-specific contaminants, 236–238, 259
Intelligence
  artificial, 277, 281
  and emotionality, 761–764
  and interpersonal attraction, 500–501
  social, 732, 748
  sociometric status and, 494–496
Intensity
  of attitudes, 206, 216–217
  discrimination of, in observation of groups, 398
  embedded measurement of, 377
Intent *vs.* effect, 425–427
Intentional Content Analysis, 426
Intentionality, 738–746
Interaction analysis, in cross-cultural methods, 715
Interaction chronograph, 392
Interaction effects, 51, 53, 70
Interaction Process Analysis (IPA), 396–398, 633

Interaction Process Scores (IPS), 397–399, 423

Interaction Recorder, 393

Interacts, 407

Interchange unit, 407

Interest ratio, in sociometry, 464

Interference, observer, 368–376, 435
  assessment of, 371–373
  instances of, 370–371
  solutions to, 373–376

Internal analysis, 41

Interobserver agreement, 404

Interpersonal attraction, measurement of, 452–510; *see also* Sociometric techniques

Interpersonal congruency, 505

Interpersonal distance, 388–390

Interquartile range, 96–97

Interruptions, and observation of behavior, 394–395

Intervention, in observational methods, 358–359, 361, 366–369, 401, 403, 408, 436

Interviewing, 364, 378–379, 386, 526–590
  accessibility, 535-536, 539–543, 548, 559–563, 573–578
    memory problems, 541–543, 548, 560–563
    in question formulation, 559–563
  bias, 532, 535, 540–552, 560, 582
  as a check on independent variable, 49
  cognitive factors, 535–537, 539, 540, 543–545, 547, 552–559, 563, 573, 575
    conceptual level, 558
    frame of reference, 537, 543–545, 555–559, 567
    language, 553–555
    in question formulation, 552–559
    single idea, 558–559
  conditions for, 535–540
  costs, 588–589
  as deceptive, 30
  as a dependent measure, 55
  direct and indirect questions, 563, 568–570
    ambiguous stimuli, 570
    manifest *vs.* latent content, 569–570
    use of third person, 569
  interview as measurement, 530–535
  interviewer and respondent roles, 527, 536–539, 544, 555–556, 573–576, 578–579

interviewer's teaching function, 573, 576, 578

interviewer training, 583–590
  recording, 588
  use of role playing, 587–588

interviewing techniques, 571–583

introducing the interview, 578–583

laboratory use of, 528

market research, 528, 585–586

measurement-item adequacy, 531–535

methodological research, 540–552, 576, 584

motivation, 535–540, 543, 545–549, 551, 558–559, 563–564, 566–567, 573–575, 577
  intrinsic *vs.* instrumental, 537
  in question formulation, 563–564

open and closed questions, 560, 562–563, 565–568, 570
  interview objectives, 565–566
  respondent factors, 566–568

organization and sequence of questions, 570–571

"personality" for, 583

postexperimental, 31, 70–73

public-opinion polls, 528, 585

question formulation, 552–571

reliability, 532–535, 540–552, 562

research *vs.* psychiatric and therapeutic interviews, 526–530

respondent-interviewer interaction, 550, 572, 576, 585

schedules, 529, 531, 535, 573, 584

stress, 378–379, 392, 590

structured, 57

survey research, 527–528, 551

validity, 532–535, 540–552, 562, 572
  content and technique, 541–549
  interviewer and respondent characteristics, 549–551

Introspection, 421

Invasion of privacy, 35–36, 374, 580

IPL-V, 299–302, 310, 323, 344

Item
  clusters, 220
  magnitude, 224, 248
  monotone, 219, 224–225, 230, 247–248, 254
  operating characteristic, 247
  selection, 219
  single *vs.* multiple, 211
  subject-item interaction, 231

Jackknifing, 107-108, 133–160, 343
  adjusting degrees of freedom, 135–136
  combinations and reexpressions, 136–138
  discrimination, 147–160
  dispersion of μ's, 158–159
  with individuals, 138–144
  jackknifed discriminant, 152, 156–157
  "leave-one-out" assessment of stability, 147–160
  pseudo-discriminant, 152, 155–157
  pseudo-values, 134–136, 139, 143–144, 155
  ratio estimate, 144–147
  using groups, 144–160
Journalistic studies, content analysis of, 608, 618–619
Judgmental scoring, 218

Kinesic movements, and interpersonal relationships, 388
Kinship research, 709–710
Kurtosis, 89

Laboratory research; *see* Experimentation
Laboratory research *vs.* observational methods, 357–362, 365–367, 369, 376, 379, 386, 402, 414, 431–432
Laboratory sociology, 279
Language, 742, 746, 754
  criterion of, 739
  in interviewing, 553–555
  and purposive communication, 738–741
  shared vocabulary, 553–554
  syntactic behavior, 739–740
"Language of action," 427
Language-and-location approach, 705–706
Latency, as an observational method, 392–393
Laws of Comparative Judgment, 225–226, 228
Leadership
  and animal studies, 743–744
  among delinquents, 483
  and friendship choices, 484–485
  in military settings, 484
  and sociometric status, 483–485, 495
Leading question, 210, 564
Learning, 314
  concept, 320
  "constant," 327
  languages, 309
  operators, 327

skill, 586–587
social, and reinforcement, 323–325
Least squares, theory of, 121
Lexico-statistics, 705–706
Likelihood ratio, 166–167, 173–174, 180
Liking; *see also* Sociometric techniques
  animal behavior and, 758
  measurement of, 54–55
Linguistic affiliation, 705–706
Linguistic criteria, in cross-cultural research, 705–706
LISP, 299–300
Lists; *see* Programming languages: list-processing
Location, of behaviors, 415
Logical styles, 628–630
Loops, 296
"Lovers' quarrel" phenomenon, 325

"Machine code," 295–296
MAD, 297, 301
"Mad Doctor," 313–314, 318
Magnitude of attitudes, 206, 208–210, 214, 218–233, 246–250, 265
  item *vs.* attribute, 248, 251
  probabilistic *vs.* ideal model of magnitude measurement, 247–248
Manifest *vs.* latent content, 569–570, 598, 600–601
Manifest personality, 459
Manipulation
  checks on, 41, 74
  of dependent variables, 54–61
  of independent variables, 39–54
Market research, 528, 585–586
Marriage rules, 700
Masculinity-femininity, 505
Mass media, research and content analysis of, 605, 612–621, 624–625, 636, 642–643, 647, 650, 654–656, 663
Mathematical models, 81, 99
  vs. simulation, 322, 326, 340, 344
Matrices, in simulation, 297–298
Matrix approaches to sociometry, 470–473
Mean
  deviation, 95
  simple arithmetic *vs.* trimmed, 107–109
"Means-ends analysis," 310
"Means-end-readiness," 739
Measurement
  of attitudes; *see* Attitude measurement
  by interview, 530-535. 552, 571

accuracy of, 542–549
  adequacy of, 531–535
  models, 246–251, 265
    additive response model, 248–250
    dimensionality, 250–251
    scaling models, 246–248
Median, 107–108, 136
Member-Leader Analysis, 397, 399–400
Memo-motion, 414–415
Memory
  "auxiliary," 293
  capacity of computers, 292–293, 298, 300, 313
  core, 293
  "dumps," 305
  and observational bias, 432
  problems in interviewing, 541–543, 548, 560–563
Mental hygiene, 732
Mental tests, theory of, 208
Meta-simulations, 319
Methodological research
  in content analysis, 607–609
  in interviewing, 540–552, 576, 584
Methods factors, 238, 245, 254
Micromomentary expressions (MME), 383, 385
Middle-message loss, 429
Mixed-motive games, 280
Moderator variable, 231–232
Modular construction of simulation models, 290, 300
Monotone, 219, 224–225, 230, 247–248, 254
Monotrait correlations, 260, 262–264
"Monte Carlo" features, 338
Mother-child interaction, observation of, 374, 379
Motivation
  factors in interviewing, 535–540, 543, 545–549, 551, 558–559, 563–564, 566–567, 573–575, 577
  in question formulation, 563–564
  social, 729, 746–748, 754, 757–760
  systematic differences in, and correlational methods, 9
Motive, 205, 208
Movies, as observational records, 412–418
Multidimensionality, 250–251
Multi-item measures in sociometry, 479
Multimethod approach, 409–411
Multiple-choice questions, 213–214
Multiple-control methods, 102

Multiple meaning, 13–20
Multiple regression, 109–110, 134, 149
Multiple response (ordered) categories, 240–241
Multiplexity, 207
Multiplicity, 102–103
  application of many tests to the same data, 86
  of response measures, 25
Multitrait-multimethod analysis, 254, 260–264
Murray's need system, 457

Need for achievement, 634–636, 662, 667, 670
Need system, Murray's, 457
Neurotic belief systems simulation, 311, 313–314
Newman-Pearson lemma, 167
News potential index, 615
Nominal-scale dispersion, 258
Nomological network, 662
"Non-ah Ratio," 395–396
Nonnormality, 91–95
  gross *vs.* at the tails, 94
"Nonobvious" predictions, 66
Nonparametric methods, 83, 114
  and cross-cultural methods, 714–715
Normality, 83, 89–90, 94
Normalization, 184
Normal theory, 82, 141
Noticeability, 488
Null hypothesis, 100, 102, 132, 183
Numerical summary, 97–98

Obedience, and methodology, 22–23
Observational methods, 357–437
  behaviors for observation, 380–401
  bias, 428–435
  category systems as selective records, 385–387, 403–404, 407, 409–411, 417, 421–427, 429, 433–435
    category construction, 422–425
    category content, 425–427
  defining, 358–362
  directed settings, 376–380
    amplifying an incipient response, 378–380
    embedding of measures, 376–377
    evoking a behavior, 377–378
  editing, 403, 408–409, 412, 436
  extralinguistic behavior, 391–396

continuity, 394–396
temporal, 392–394
vocal, 392
vs. laboratory research, 357–362, 365–367, 369, 376, 379, 386, 402, 414, 431–432
linguistic behavior, 396–401
Behavior System Scores, 400–401
Interaction Process Analysis, 396–398
Interaction Process Scores, 398–399
Member-Leader Analysis, 399–400
multiple measures, 403, 409–411
composite or summated scores, 410–411
nonparticipant, 370
nonverbal behavior, 381
body movements, 386–388
exchanged (mutual) glances, 385–386
facial expressions, 382–385
observational records, 360–361, 401–427
inductive *vs.* deductive approach, 401–402
rational *vs.* empirical approach, 401–402
observer as artifact, 369–376
interference, 370–376
observers, 428–435
multiple, 433
lay, 376
occasions for, 363–366
passive observer, 359, 366, 436
records, 411–421, 436
field formats, 418–420
impressionistic analysis, 420–421
movies, 412–416
sign analysis, 417–418
specimen records, 368, 416–417
reliability, 380, 403–406, 412, 422–424, 436–437
settings, 359–362, 365–382, 387, 390, 401, 403, 430, 432–433, 436
equivalence of, 366
obligations and opportunities of, 379
social interaction, 406–407
spatial behavior, 388–391
studies of children, 363
studies of delinquent groups, 365
training, 358, 360, 434–435
unstructured, 363
validity, 360, 362, 365–366, 402, 405, 409, 412, 416, 423
Observational Schedule and Record-Reading (OScAR-R), 417
Odds, 165–167

"On-line" access, 295
Ontogenetic development, and emotionality, 762–764
Operating characteristics, 83, 192, 195
Opinion; *see* Attitudes
Opinion expression and social contact, 327–329, 346
Optimization, 110–112
Overreporting, 561
Overt behavioral measures of attitude, 217
Overtness, of attitudes, 207

Paired comparisons method, 225, 227–229
in content analysis, 651
in sociometry, 456, 478
Panel, 337–343
Panic, 345–346
Parameter, 105–106, 108–109
"free," 327, 330
punishment, 328
reward, 328
stochastic learning, 327–328
Paranoia, caused by observation, 370–371
Parsimony, 344–345
Pearson Type III curve, 467, 470
Peer ratings, 397, 399–400, 427
Pencil-and-paper measures, 54–58, 66, 534
Percentages, 186, 191–193
Personality variables
content analysis and, 623
manipulation of, 40–41
observational methods and, 387
sociometry and, 488–493, 501–505
Personal Preference Schedule (EPPS), 260
Personal structure analysis, 627
Person-stimulus transactionalism, 246
Persuasion, 291
embedded measurement of, 377
techniques of, by content analysis, 622, 623
"Phase sequence," 761
Phasing of processes in simulation, 285, 290, 292, 310, 322
Phylogenetic development, 733–734, 738, 740–741, 744, 748, 754, 762–764
Physiological indicators, 17, 60
of attitude, 216–217
in observation, 410
Picture completion technique, 456
Picture sociometric technique, 456
Pilot testing, 42, 53, 58
Plausibility of interpretations, 717–718

PL/I, 297
Plotting, 184–186, 189–190
  percentages, 186, 191–193
  split *vs.* paired count, 184–187, 189–199
"Pointer," 298, 301
Political research, content analysis of, 608, 610–612, 614–616, 624, 626, 628–629, 633–634
Pooling, 249–250
Popularity, 248, 258–259
Positive-negative-ambivalent quotient (PNAQ), 631–632
Posterior distributions, 162–163, 170–174, 178–179, 182–183
Postexperimental interview, 31, 70–73
Posture changes, and observation of behavior, 383, 387–388
Power
  dimension, 397, 399
  legitimate, and interviewing, 527, 537, 577
  of tests, 83, 192
Pragmatics, 604–606
Precision, 285
  in content analysis, 599
  in interviewing, 533, 535, 552
  in observation, 404
Precisions, 172–173, 183
Pregenital fixations, and sociometric status, 491–492
Prejudice, 498–500
Premarital sex, cross-cultural study of, 712, 715-717
Presence-absence coding, 710–711
Pretesting, 555, 570
  of categories for content analysis, 658
  in experimentation, 42, 49–50, 74
Primary sampling units (PSU), 698
Prior distributions, 161–183
  belief, 169–171
  beta, 173–178
  degree of belief *vs.* frequency-based, 161
  empirical, 163–167, 169, 179
  flat, 170, 178
  gamma, 178–180
  gentle, 162, 169–171, 179, 182
  normal, 170–171, 173
Probabilistic effects in simulation, 338–343
Probabilities, 165–166
  conditional posterior *vs.* unconditional prior, 163, 168

density function, 87, 92, 107–108, 161, 168
Poisson, 165–167
posterior, 161, 163, 168
Probability model, in sociometry, 467–469
Probability scoring, in sociometry, 469
Problem solving, 308–311, 330, 730–731, 759, 761
"Procedure," 109–110
Processes
  in computer simulation, 285, 288
  macroprocesses, 288–290, 300, 307
  microprocesses, 288, 290–292, 300, 306, 320
  parallel processing *vs.* serial processing, 290
  process simulation, 334
  stochastic, 334
Profiles, in sociometry, 466
Program listing, 304
Programming languages, 292–302
  algebraic compiler, 295–298, 302
  list-processing, 298–302, 344
  "simulation," 299
Programs
  computer, 288
  "systems," 293
Program trace, 305
"Progressive deepening," 315
Projective techniques
  as deceptive, 30
  interpersonal attraction and, 501
  sociometric status and, 491
Propaganda, content analysis of, 608, 622–623, 626, 661
Propinquity, 330
  interpersonal attraction, 496–497
  physical *vs.* functional, 497
Proportions, 191–196
Provocation of behavior, 360–361, 376–380
Proxemics, 389, 419
"Proxy respondents," 542
Pseudosocial behavior, 734
Pseudo-values, 134–136, 139, 143–144, 155
"Psychic cost," 323
Psycholinguistics, and content analysis, 601
Psycho-logic, 630
Psychological models for computer simulation, 284–286
  as a closed system, 285
  features of, 284–285

narrowness *vs.* precision, 285
specification, 284–285
Psychometric theory, 208–209, 218. 242,
248–249, 254, 265–266
Psychophysical laws, and bias solutions, 432
Psychosocial behavior, 734–735
Psychotherapy and assessment of interfer-
ence, 371–372
Public-opinion polls, 528, 585
Pupillary dilation and constriction, 18
Purification, 15–20, 24–25, 43
discriminant, 262
Purposiveness, 738–746
Pythagorean theorem, 186, 188

Q-sort technique, 460, 504, 652
Q-technique system, 474
Qualitative products, 287
Quality control, in cross-cultural research,
715–717
Quantitative continuum model, 246
Quantitative precision, 287
Quasi-aggression, 750–753
Quasi-experimental designs, 7
Quasi-stationary equilibrium, 539
Question formulation, 552–571
accessibility, 559–563
cognitive factors, 553–559
direct and indirect, 563, 568–570
double-barreled, 558–559
funnel sequence, 571
leading, 564
motivation, 563–564
multiple, 535, 543, 570
multiple-choice, 213–214
open *vs.* closed, 210–211, 237, 460, 560,
562–563, 565–568, 570
organization and sequence, 570–571
pretesting, 555, 570
primary, 572–574, 576, 581–582
probe, 543–544, 556, 572–573, 578, 582–
583
single *vs.* battery, 570
wording, 541, 543, 553, 559, 563–564
yes-no, 564
Questionnaires, 55–56, 377

Race, in interpersonal attraction, 499–500
Racial differences, and interviewing ac-
curacy, 551
Random assignment, 7–10, 40–42

Random-Systematic-Error (RSE) Coefficient,
660
Rapport, 35, 53, 61, 215, 239, 242, 371, 490
Reactance, manipulation of, 45
Reactivity of measures, 376, 433
Readability of text, 607, 640–642, 664
Realism, 7, 12
experimental, and deception, 26–28
experimental *vs.* mundane, 22–28, 360
Realistic decision situations in attitude
assessment, 217
Reality practice, 587
Recency effects, in interviewing, 542, 548–
549
Recognition *vs.* recall, 562–563
Records, 401–427, 436
of events, 411–421
field formats, 418–420, 433
impressionistic analysis, 420–421
movies, 412–418
sign analysis, 417–418
six components of, 418–419
static *vs.* dynamic events, 417
videotapes, 413
interview, 531, 588
Recursive systems, 310
Reductive errors in observation, 428–432
Refraction factors, 236
Reinforcement
altruism and, 744
and interpersonal attraction, 508–509
simulation models and, 292, 323–325
Relational analysis, in sociometry, 456–457
multirelational sociometric survey, 458
"Releasers," 734
Reliability, 103, 105, 343
in attitude measurement, 255–257, 260,
265
category, 658–660
consistency in equivalent forms, 479
consistency over time, 476–478
in content analysis, 649, 653, 657–662,
664, 673
in cross-cultural research, 704, 712, 715–
716
dichotomous-decision technique, 659
index of, 660
individual, 657
instrument, 262
intercoder, 657, 660
interjudge consistency, 475–476

internal consistency, 479
in interviewing, 532–535, 540–552, 562
in observational methods, 380, 403–406, 412, 422–424, 436–437
in sociometry, 465, 475–479
split-half, 476, 479, 533–534
test-retest coefficients, 476–477, 533–534
Religion, and interpersonal attraction, 498
Religious values, content analysis of, 612
Replication, 340–343
conceptual, 17–22
successful and unsuccessful, 20–22
systematic, 15–20, 25
Repression, and inaccessibility of interview data, 536, 542, 548, 561–563, 569, 575
Repulsion ratio, 464
Research designs, for content analysis, 603–607
Residuals, 121–122
Response set, 238–239, 376
Response tendencies, 404
chance and observational error, 404
Resultant, of opposing forces, and interviewing, 539
Revolution and Development of International Relations (RADIR) studies, in content analysis, 598, 610, 612, 646–647, 664
Reward, 323, 328
anxiety reduction as, 759
secondary, 757
theory of biosocial rewards, 757
"Ripple effect," 366
Robustness, 91–95, 144, 182
of efficiency, 94
of validity, 93
Role
expectancies, culturally prescribed, 699
interviewer and respondent, 527, 536–539, 544, 555–556, 559, 573–576, 578–579
readiness, 575
relationships, and observation of behavior, 426
taking the role of the other, 741
Role playing, 217, 243, 399
in experimentation, 26–28
in interviewer training, 587–588
and observer training, 434
Routines
J-routines, 300
subroutines, 300–301, 307, 309–312

Rules
premarital sex, 712
prescriptive *vs.* preferred, 711–712
rigidity of cultural, 711–712
Rumor transmission, and content analysis, 642

Salience, 206
and reporting accuracy in interviewing, 542–544
Sampling, 126–127
cluster, 194, 656
in content analysis, 599, 603, 618, 653–657, 661–663
in cross-cultural research, 696, 697, 702–708
design, 655–656
documents, 655–657
inadequate sampling of content, 404
interpenetrating, 128, 130
plurality, 124
primary sampling unit (PSU), 698
quantitative *vs.* qualitative criteria, 655
quota, 552, 560
random, 126, 194, 654–655, 697
random *vs.* purposive, 654–655
of respondents, 551–552, 560
sampling list, 702–703
single- *vs.* multistage, 654
size, 85, 104, 106–107, 191, 655–656, 704
stratified, 128, 194, 655, 697, 704
theory, 104, 123
time, 409, 412, 414, 423
world linguistic, 705–708
Satiation, and observational bias, 432
Scales
alpha and beta, 488
behavioral frequency, and cross-cultural data, 711–712
composite, 713–714
consensual location, 224–230, 232, 246–248
criterion-oriented, 230–231
cumulative, 221–225, 232, 246–248, 254
detection, 243–245
distance, 226–227
group and individual, 232–233
group participation scale, 457
Guttman, 714
intensity, for judging emotion, 713
interview, 534

methods in sociometry, 453, 457, 459, 510
normal-scale dispersion, 258
ordinal rating, 459
Q-sort, 460, 652
quality-control, 717
scale types, 222–223, 253
scaling models, 246–248
semantic differential, 459
social desirability, 243
social distance, 459
social-relations, 465
summative, 218–221, 224, 230, 232, 247
suppressor, 244
theory, 208, 221, 265
Scalogram board, 223–224
Scenario, 5, 26, 37
Scores
    composite or summated, 410–411
    configural, 231–232
    multiple scoring, 424
Script, 314
Selective avoidance, 291–292
Self concept
    interpersonal attraction and, 505
    manipulation of, 40, 41
    sociometric status and, 492–493
Self-description, and interpersonal attraction, 504
Self-esteem, and respondent motivation, 545, 561–563
Self-evaluations, in content analysis, 631
Self-ideal discrepancy, and sociometric status, 492, 504
Self-insight, and sociometric status, 492–493
Self-presentation, 236
Self-rating, in sociometry, 456–457
Self-satisfaction, 263–264
Semantic differential, in sociometry, 459
Semantics, 601, 604, 606
Semiotics, 604
Sensory *vs.* ideational behavior, 733–734, 738–741
"Sentences," 312
Sequences, in observation, 407
Sequential Time Interval Measurement System (STIMS), 393
Serial position effect, 315
Setting of an experiment, 37–39
Settings for observational research, 359–362, 365–382, 387, 390, 401, 403, 430, 432–433, 436

directed settings, 376–380
    amplification of incipient responses, 378–380
    embedded measures, 376–377
    evoking a behavior, 377–378
    equivalence of, 366
    obligations and opportunities of, 379
    observer interference, 368–376
Severity of initiation, as methodology, 4–17, 38–39
Sex
    and interpersonal attraction, 498–499
    sociometric status and, 493
Sexual arousal, manipulation of, 48
Shared meanings, 709
Shared symbols, 215
Shrinkage, 153
Sign analysis, in observation, 417–418
Significance testing, 83–87, 93, 97, 100–101, 114, 132, 167, 183, 193
    binomial, 187, 190
Sign Process Analysis, 633
Sign test, 93, 192–195
Sign-Vehicles, 597
Similarity
    of attitudes, 506–507
    of interests, 503–505
    of needs, 502–505
Simulation of social behavior, 274–346
    cognitive processes, simulation of, 276–277, 284–285, 288, 292, 299, 308–321, 343–344
    communication problem, 320–321
    Elementary Perception and Memory (EPAM), 278, 314–315, 320
    General Problem Solver (GPS), 276, 309–311, 316
    Ideology Machine, 311–313
    the "mad doctor," 313–314, 318
    Thought-is-a-Program theory, 308, 321
    validation problem, 310, 315–320
    methodology of, 281–308
    choice of problem, 283
    "debugging" and revision, 304–307
    flow charts, 288–292
    formulation of a psychological model, 284–286
    "hand simulation," 303–304
    programming languages, 295–302
    suitability of simulation, 286–288
    use of computers, 292–295
    utilization of data, 307–308

simulation gap, 276, 279, 321
social processes, simulation of, 292, 321–346
  aggregative *vs.* "systemic" approach, 321–322
  elementary behavior models, 326–330
  Homunculus, 323–326
  large-scale social and political processes, 330–335
  statistical analysis, 336–343
  validation, 335–336
  types of, 275–281
    "all-computer," 277
    "all-man," 277, 280
    anthropological, 335
    artificial intelligence, 277, 281
    beliefs and attitude change, 311–315
    computer, 277–278, 281–346
    gaming, 277, 280–281
    "hand simulation," 303–304
    individual *vs.* group, 278
    internation, 277, 279
    in the laboratory, 279
    "man-machine," 277–278
    meta-simulation, 319
    "null," 330
    panel, 337–343
    population, 334–335
    problem solving, 308–311
    process, 334
    prognostic, 334
    system, 277–279, 299
Single-stimuli method of attitude assessment, 212, 225, 241, 260
"Situation," 325
Situation tree, 324, 335
Skewness, 89
"Snapshot," 305
SNOBOL, 299, 302
Sociability, 400
Social acceptability, 486, 546, 564, 569
Social "acceptance" *vs.* acceptability, 486
Social act, 733
Social actions, recording of, 749–752
Social choice, measurement of, 452–510; *see also* Sociometric techniques
Social-comparison processes, and interpersonal attraction, 500–502
Social contacts, 327–328, 331, 407
  stochastic theory of, 327–329
Social couplings, 340

Social desirability, 235, 239, 241, 243, 257, 263–264
  and bias, 62; *see also* Experimental demands
Social distance, 331, 459, 461, 551
Social evolution, 761–762
Social influence, 332–333; *see also* Simulation of social behavior: social processes
  simulation model, 291
Social intensity, 465
Social interaction, observation of, 396–401, 406–407
Social mechanisms, 733
  biosocial *vs.* psychosocial, 734
  pseudosocial behavior, 734
  sensory *vs.* ideational, 733–734, 738–741
Social and political simulations, 330–335
Social processes, simulation of, 292, 321–346
Social-psychological evaluative space, 397–398
Social sensitivity, and interviewing, 584
"Socialization-sensationalism" index, 619–620
Society
  and emotion, 764–769
  and human nature, 760–769
Socioeconomic status
  and interpersonal attraction, 497–498
  sociometric status and, 494–495
Sociogram, 328–329, 460–461, 471, 474
Sociomatrix, 471–472, 474
Sociometric techniques, 217, 452–510
  with children, 456
    picture completion technique, 456
    picture sociometric technique, 456
  cliques, 461, 472–474, 498, 504, 506
  estimates of time, 458
  factor analysis, 473–474
    Q-technique system, 474
  graphical methods, 460–463, 475
    quartiles and sectors, 462
    sociogram, 460–463, 471, 474–475
    target sociogram, 461–462
  group preference record, 457–458
  guess-who technique, 458–459
  intensity of choice, 458, 466, 478
  interpersonal attraction ratings, 459–460
  interpersonal attraction research, 496–509
    attitudes, beliefs, and values, 506–509

demographic variables, 497–498
intelligence and ability, 500–501
minority-group prejudice, 498–500
personality variables, 501–505
propinquity, 496–497
matrix approaches, 470–473
canonical form, 470–471
Holzinger's *B*-coefficient, 472
matrix multiplication, 471–474
sociomatrix, 471–472, 474
network, 297
origins of, 454–455
reliability, 475–479
consistency in equivalent forms, 479
consistency over time, 476–478
interjudge consistency, 475–476
internal consistency, 479
requirements of, 455–456
scaling methods, 457
group participation scale, 457
self-rating or relational analysis, 456–457
goal- *vs.* nongoal-directed, 458
multirelational survey, 458
simple quantitative methods, 463–467
scores and derived indices, 463–467
tabular methods, 463
social distance index and measures, 459, 461
sociometric status research, 483–496
adjustment, 485–488
demographic variables, 493–494
intelligence and performance, 494–496
leadership, 483–485, 495
personality variables, 488–493
statistical methods, 467–470
chance model, 467–470
validity, 480–483
construct, 482–483
content, 480–481
criterion-related, 481–482
Sovereignty, as a cross-cultural criterion, 699–700
Space allocation measures, in content analysis, 614–619
Spearman-Brown formula, 476
Specialization of function, 735
Specifications, 306–307
Specimen record, 368, 407, 416–417, 426, 429
Speech disturbance
content analysis and, 631–632

disruptions and observational methods, 394–396
ratio, 395
Split-frame technique, 414
Split-litter method, 731
Spread, measures of, 98, 153
interquartile range, 96–97
standard deviation, 96–98, 123–124, 138–139, 141
standard deviation *vs.* mean deviation, 95
variance, 96, 127–128, 134–135, 141, 172–173, 187
analysis of, 123–124, 126, 130–131, 198–199, 714–715
stabilization, 199
Stability; *see also* Uncertainty
indicators and assessment of, 82, 105, 107, 111, 122, 126, 134, 136, 147, 153–155, 159–160
"leave-one-out" assessment of, 147–160
in observation, 403–406, 411
in sociometric measures, 466, 477–478
"Staircase," 82–83
Standard deviation, 95–98, 123–124, 138–139, 141
Standardization
in content analysis, 645–646, 657
in experimental procedures, 69, 73
vs. individual differences, 46–49
in sociometry, 460–461, 466, 473
Statistics, 80–200
classical descriptive, 100
primary, secondary, tertiary, quarternary, 81–83, 98–99
of social simulations, 336–343
and sociometric measures, 467–470
Status; *see also* Sociometric techniques
culturally defined, 698
distinctions and posture, 388
Stochastic theory of social contacts, 327–329
Stop rule, 290
Stress
facial expressions and, 385
infant, 713, 717, 719
interviews, 378–379, 392
speech disruptions and, 394–396
Structural types, in cross-cultural research, 710–711
Student's *t*, 82–89, 93, 127–128, 135
advantages, 85

Burrau's modification, 86
  distribution of, 82–86, 96
  problems, 85–86
Subject characteristics, in attitude measurement, 234–236, 254
Subject-item interaction, 231
Subjective reports, 18–19, 27, 49–50
Subjective sensory scales, 208
Subscripting, 297
Subsystem validation, 718–719
Successive-intervals method, 225, 228
Summative scales, 218–221, 224, 230, 232, 247
Supportive action, 401
Survey, 337
  multirelational sociometric, 458
  research, 527–528, 551
    in content analysis, 609, 613
Symbolic populations, 338–339
Symmetric List Processor (SLIP), 299–302
Symmetry, as an observational error, 429, 434
Syntactic behavior, language as, 739–740
Syntactics, 601, 604, 606
System for the Classification and Analysis of Nonverbal Behavior (SCAN), 415
System design, 278
"Systemic" approach to social simulation, 322

Taboo phenomena, 766–768
  of the dead, 767
  sex, 767–768
Tagging, of behaviors, 415
"Tagging" of words, 665–671
  first- and second-order, 666
  tag profiles, 670
  tag programs, 668–669
Teamwork, 741–742, 746
Teasing, motivation for, 756
Telemetry, 410
Tempered naturalness, in observational methods, 367, 369, 376, 436
Territoriality, 390
Test anxiety, and sociometric status, 492
"Text and tag list" program, 668–669
Themes, in content analysis, 647, 658–659, 663–664, 668–669
Thinking, information-processing theory of, 308–309, 321, 323

Threat
  and interviewing accuracy, 548–549, 551, 563
  manipulation of, 18, 42, 50
Time
  duration, 392–394
  estimates, as measures of intensity of choice, 458
  "filled time," 393
  initiative, 394
  in interaction, 392, 394
  intervals specified for scoring, 424
  judgments, and sociometric status, 492
  latency, 392–394
  patterns, and extralinguistic behavior, 392
  reaction, 394
  sampling, 409, 412, 414, 423
  sharing, 292
Time-lapse photography, 414
Time/space measures in content analysis, 649–650
Timidity, and aggression, 749, 751–754, 756, 758
Trace measures, 375–376
Training
  interviewer, 583–590
  observational bias and, 434–435
Transcultural definitions, 708–710
Trend description by content analysis, 610–613
Turing's Test, 316–319
Turn-around time, 295
Type-token ratio (TTR), 631, 633, 661, 664
Typical values, 98, 107

Uncertainty, 97–101, 104, 122–160, 163
  choice of error term, 125–128, 130–131
  "cookie cutter" type, 132
  direct assessment of variability, 124–133
    jackknifing, 133–160
  "distributional" type, 132
  supplementary, 122–124, 130–133
    halo effect, 123
    internal, 122–133
  systematic errors of measurement, 123
Uncoupled panels, 341
Undermanning, in amplification of responses, 379–380
Underreporting, in interviewing, 540–542, 545, 547–549

Unidimensionality, 250
Uniformity, and emotionality, 765–766, 768–769
Unitizing, 658–659
Unobtrusive measures, 590

Validation, 310, 315–320, 323, 335–336, 342
    comparability of internal contingencies (sequential dependency tests), 316–317, 335
    construct, 253–254, 263–264, 482–483, 532, 661–662
    convergent, 254, 263, 532
    cross-sectional distribution over individuals, 336
    cross-validation, 100, 103, 109–112, 147, 153–160, 316, 719
    discriminant, 260, 262–264
    experimental tests, 320, 335
    "known-groups" method, 253
    response-match, 316, 335, 343
    subsystem, 718–719
    Turing's test, 316–319, 335–336
Validity
    of animal studies, 730–733
    of attitude measures, 233–238, 241–244, 251–253, 256, 265
    bias and, 61
    concurrent, 661–662
    content, 480–481, 661–662
    of content analysis, 610, 623, 625–628, 653, 661–663, 673
    criterion-related, 481–482
    of cross-cultural methods, 697, 708
    of distributions, 93–94
    face, 416, 480, 532, 570, 600, 661
    internal *vs.* external, 24, 25, 367
    in interviewing, 532–535, 540–552, 562, 572
    in observational methods, 360, 362, 365–366, 402, 405, 409, 412, 416, 423
    predictive, 628, 661–662
    single- *vs.* multiple-criterion approach, 252–254, 263

in sociometry, 480–483
Value analysis, 623
Values, and interpersonal attraction, 506–509
Variance, 96, 127–128, 134–135, 141, 172–173, 187
    analysis of, 123–124, 126, 130–131, 198–199
    common methods, 264
    realization, 340–342
    sampling, 340–342
    stabilization, 199
Variation and variability, 101–103, 105, 108, 122–123, 126–128, 135, 141, 148, 153, 158, 194; *see also* Uncertainty
    binomial, 124
    choice of error term, 125–128, 130, 131
    cluster-to-cluster, 147
    direct assessment of, 124–133
        jackknifing, 133–160
    range of, and cross-cultural research, 694–696
    stratum-to-stratum, 147
Vector, 297
Verbal responses, in attitude assessment, 210–216
Verbosity, 237, 245
Videotapes, in observation, 413
Visual avoidance, 385–386
Voice spectrometer, 392
Voter types, 334

"Wagging dance," 737–738
Weaning age, and cross-cultural methods, 694–696, 698, 713
Weighting
    in content analysis, 651, 655
    of sociometric choices, 458, 466, 470, 472
Winsor's principle, 91
Withdrawal, 400–401
"Word," 292–293, 296
Word counts, in content analysis, 624, 663–665, 668
World linguistic sample, 705–708

58391